The Court and the Charter

LEADING CASES

Thomas M.J. Bateman
St. Thomas University

Janet L. Hiebert
Queen's University

Rainer Knopff
University of Calgary

Peter H. Russell
University of Toronto

em 2008
Emond Montgomery Publications Limited
Toronto, Canada

Emond Montgomery Publications Limited
60 Shaftesbury Avenue
Toronto ON M4T 1A3
http://www.emp.ca

Printed in Canada on 100 percent recycled paper.

We acknowledge the financial support of the Government of Canada through the Book Publishing Industry Development Program (BPIDP) for our publishing activities.

Acquisitions and developmental editor: Mike Thompson
Marketing manager: Christine Davidson
Copy editor: Nancy Ennis, WordsWorth Communications
Proofreader: David Handelsman, WordsWorth Communications
Production editor: Jim Lyons, WordsWorth Communications
Text designer: Tara Wells, WordsWorth Communications
Cover designers: Stephen Cribbin & Simon Evers
Back cover photo: Mike Thompson

Library and Archives Canada Cataloguing in Publication

The Court and the Charter : leading cases / Thomas Bateman ... [et al.].

Includes the text of The Charter of Rights and Freedoms.
ISBN 978-1-55239-276-8

   1. Canada. Canadian Charter of Rights and Freedoms—Cases.   2. Civil rights—Canada—Cases.   3. Canada. Supreme Court.   4. Judgments—Canada.   I. Bateman, Thomas Michael Joseph, 1962-

KE4381.5.A7C69 2008   342.7108'5   C2008-901855-9
KF4483.C5C69 2008

Contents

PART FOUR
Democratic Rights

PART FIVE
Legal Rights

PART SIX
Social and Economic Rights

PART SEVEN
Remedies

PART EIGHT
Equality Rights

PART NINE

Language Rights

APPENDIX

Preface

This collection of leading Supreme Court of Canada *Charter of Rights* decisions stems from successful collections of edited Supreme Court decisions first published in 1965. Peter Russell's *Leading Constitutional Decisions* became the standard reference for undergraduate political science students of Supreme Court decision making. Not a few law students used it to prepare for their exams as well. It underwent several successful editions and culminated in *Federalism and the Charter: Leading Constitutional Decisions*, published in 1989 with the collaboration of F.L. Morton and Rainer Knopff.

In that year, the Court had five years' experience with the *Charter* and was only beginning to settle some fundamental interpretive issues raised by the *Charter* and by the expectations set for it by litigants, interest groups, governments, and other commentators. But it was clear by then that the Supreme Court would apply the *Charter* with enthusiasm and vigor, boldly going where the pre-*Charter* Court had feared to tread. By 1989, several major pieces of legislation had been struck down. Perhaps the most spectacular exercise of judicial review was the Court's January 28, 1988 decision to declare null and void Canada's *Criminal Code* provisions restricting access to abortion. Newspapers headlines the next day blared that the Court advanced a women's right to abortion. The decision was praised and pilloried. If the *Charter* made little impression on Canadians before then, the *Morgentaler* decision would henceforth change popular opinion about the *Charter* and the power of courts.

Now that the *Charter* is well past its 25th anniversary, the time is ripe for a new collection of Supreme Court *Charter* decisions. Since 1989, the Court has rendered a great many *Charter* decisions in myriad areas of federal and provincial law and government conduct. In some respects, we have a clear idea of how the *Charter* is to be understood and can readily identify some basic interpretive doctrines developed by the Court. In other respects, we are as uncertain as ever about the meaning of the *Charter*. Many *Charter* decisions reveal deep divisions among justices. The Canadian Court experiences a rather high rate of turnover (particularly in comparison to the United States Supreme Court, whose justices are appointed for life rather than until 75 years of age as in Canada) and this contributes to doctrinal uncertainty. The Court has also shown that it is willing to reconsider and reverse its earlier *Charter* decisions. As new issues come up, the Court is often faced with situations that neither it nor the drafters of the *Charter* had anticipated.

The *Charter* enjoys the affection of Canadians, especially young Canadians. So keen are they about their rights that they often think the *Charter is* the Constitution. They are wrong on this point, of course, and they are often unclear about the purposes of the *Charter* or how *Charter* decisions are made. Undergraduate students, for example, generally associate the *Charter* with all things good and just. They commonly know that the courts have enforced the *Charter*'s legal rights protections vigorously in favour of those charged with crimes and those subject to national security policies. They are likely to know that the Supreme Court upheld Canada's anti-hate speech law and may applaud the Court for doing so.

They are often surprised, however, to learn that the Supreme Court has struck down legislation limiting tobacco companies' right to advertise their products; that it has allowed some forms of child pornography to be produced in Canada; that it forbade the Minister of Justice from surrendering a murder suspect (who was later convicted) to the United States in the absence of assurances that the death penalty will not be administered upon conviction; that it has denied a claim for public payment for autism treatments; and that extreme drunkenness, according to a 1994 decision, can diminish one's guilt in sexual assault cases. Students are often distressed to learn that justices are divided on the merits of controversial *Charter* decisions and that judicial opinions both for and against a result are highly persuasive. They are surprised to learn that Supreme Court decisions are difficult to understand and much more complex than media reports suggest. They are often perplexed by the Court's (sometimes selective) use of non-legal evidence in its decision making. More broadly, they are unsettled by the fact that rights cannot be enjoyed absolutely and that rights often conflict with one another.

We hope that this collection of *Charter* decisions continues to unsettle students, because only in this way can they confront and correct received opinion on the nature and consequences of *Charter* review in Canada. While the secondary literature on the *Charter* is massive and rich, there is no substitute for reading the primary data of the Supreme Court— its decisions. Wrestling with the decisions stimulates an appreciation for the complexity of the issues, the indeterminacy of *Charter* provisions, the different views of justices, the strategic calculations of litigants and interveners, and the way in which decisions are translated by the media for public consumption.

This collection contains a small but, we hope, representative sample of the hundreds of Supreme Court *Charter* decisions that have been rendered since 1984. We have selected cases for inclusion on the basis of three criteria: (1) Does the decision break new and enduring doctrinal ground? For example, *R. v. Oakes* (1986) was included because it set the template for applying the section 1 reasonable limits clause to legislative violations of *Charter* rights. (2) Does the case reveal a particularly difficult issue that divides justices and also requires the Court to weigh evidence that stretches its institutional capacity? On this basis, *R. v. Keegstra* (1990) and *Sauvé v. Canada* (2002) are obvious candidates for inclusion. (3) Does the case either stimulate or proceed from political controversy? On this criterion, *R. v. Seaboyer* (1991) and *Reference Re: Same-Sex Marriage* (2004) are instructive examples.

This book is a companion to another volume of cases, *The Court and the Constitution*, also published by Emond Montgomery. While *The Court and the Constitution* covers both federalism and the *Charter* (and thus a broader sweep of history), this volume zeroes in on the *Charter*. We follow a similar format in both volumes, editing the decisions to manageable length and providing introductory editors' notes to set each decision in political and legal context. In this volume, each decision is followed by discussion questions to test understanding and probe issues further.

Constitutional jurisprudence is a moving target and any decision has the potential to alter the course of constitutional law. For this reason we accompany both books with a website containing edited Supreme Court decisions and introductory editors' notes (see below).

Our project is made possible by the enthusiastic support of Emond Montgomery Publications, and particularly Mike Thompson. Many thanks to him and the staff.

The authors and the publisher wish to thank the following people for providing their comments and suggestions during the development of this book: Marek Debicki, University of Manitoba; Jay Haaland, Kwantlen University College; Peter McCormick, University of Lethbridge; and Nadia Verrelli, Carleton University.

Website

This book is supplemented by an extensive password-protected website containing introductions and edited decisions for many additional Supreme Court of Canada cases not included in this book. Instructors who have selected this book for course use can contact an Emond Montgomery sales representative for more information at 1-888-837-0815, or visit www.emp.ca/university.

About the Authors

Thomas M.J. Bateman is Associate Professor of Political Science at St. Thomas University. Janet L. Hiebert is Professor of Political Studies at Queen's University. Rainer Knopff is Professor of Political Science at the University of Calgary. Peter H. Russell is Professor of Political Science at the University of Toronto.

Introduction

The entrenchment of the *Canadian Charter of Rights and Freedoms* into the Canadian Constitution on April 17, 1982 is among the most significant developments in Canadian constitutional history. While the *Charter* is only part of the Canadian Constitution, which has both written and unwritten components, and was merely a part of the package of changes entrenched when the Constitution was patriated from Britain in 1982, in the popular mind the *Charter* towers over other pillars of Canadian constitutionalism. While federalism and parliamentary government continue to pervade our constitutional self-understanding and the actual workings of the country, the *Charter* routinely makes the headlines. *Charter* rights claimants become celebrities or media villains. Canadians increasingly articulate their values and their political demands as rights. Supreme Court justices travel the lecture circuit. Supreme Court nominees now appear before Parliament prior to appointment. Canadian life is very different in the post-*Charter* era. This introduction explores the changes that the *Charter* has produced.

Is the *Charter* the cause of change in Canada or the effect of change? Alan Cairns, one of Canada's most insightful students of constitutional politics, has argued that the *Charter* has not only produced institutional changes that elevate the status of courts and litigation in Canada; it has also activated a variety of groups and identities whose interests and rights can now be advanced through the rhetoric of rights the *Charter* has spawned. The *Charter*, in his view, has produced *Charter* Canadians.[1] Others argue that the *Charter* is an institutional consequence of deep cultural changes taking shape in the post-war era. The shift from materialist values, stressing economic growth and physical security, to post-materialist orientations, emphasizing egalitarianism, environmentalism, gender, sexual and ethnic identities, and the general ideal of self-fulfillment, generated political conditions favourable to entrenched citizen rights.[2] While debates about the causal influence of the *Charter* on Canadian political life will continue for a long time, it is a fact that the Canadian *Charter* was entrenched in the swirl of larger forces, and itself has led to important changes in Canadian politics and government. To understand the *Charter*, one must understand Canada and the political and cultural changes that it has experienced over the last century. To understand Canada, one must now understand the *Charter*, how it is interpreted, and what consequences *Charter* decisions have for litigants and the broader community.

---

1 Alan C. Cairns, *Reconfigurations: Canadian Citizenship and Constitutional Change*, Douglas E. Williams, ed. (Toronto: McClelland & Stewart, 1995).

2 Neil Nevitte and Ian Brodie, "Evaluating the Citizens' Constitution Theory" (1993) 26 *Canadian Journal of Political Science* 235.

ROOTS OF THE CHARTER

The inclusion of a bill of rights in Canada's Constitution was not even considered at the time the country was founded. The Fathers of Confederation were mid-Victorian British colonials. The Constitution they revered was not the American, but the British. The British Constitution most certainly did not contain a bill of rights. Its first and highest principle was parliamentary sovereignty.[3]

This did not mean that Canada's founders were hostile to rights. Indeed, as Janet Ajzenstat has shown, the founding debates were full of claims about rights and rights protection.[4] Although it may sound strange to modern ears, Canada's founders believed that rights were better protected by the British parliamentary system than by the U.S. institutional system, including the latter's constitutionally entrenched bill of rights. During the Confederation debates in the Canadian legislature, for example, David Christie, quoting the American *Declaration of Independence* virtually word for word, maintained that both the British and American Constitutions rest "on the same great principle"—"that life, liberty and the pursuit of happiness are the unalienable rights of man, and that to secure these rights, governments are instituted among men, deriving their just powers from the consent of the governed."[5] Christie simply preferred the British constitutional route to these ends. In a similar vein, Richard Cartwright saw as many rights-protecting "checks and balances" in parliamentary government as in the U.S. Constitution.[6]

Although Canada's founding Constitution, the *British North America Act* (in 1982, renamed the *Constitution Act, 1867*), did not explicitly entrench civil liberties based on philosophical theories of human rights, it did secure some practical, historical rights aimed at protecting the interests of the English Protestant minority in Quebec and the French-Catholic minority outside Quebec. Section 93 guaranteed Quebec Protestants the right to denominational schools that Roman Catholics at that time enjoyed in Ontario. Section 133 ensured that English could be used in the Quebec legislature and French in the Canadian Parliament, that both languages could be used in the courts of Canada and Quebec, and that the laws of Canada and Quebec would be published in both languages. Inclusion of these minority rights in the Constitution was a crucial part of the Confederation bargain.

At the time of Confederation, and for a long time thereafter, Canada did not have a well-established practice of citizens using courts to challenge violations of their rights by governments. Section 93 invited minorities to appeal to the federal government for remedial action against deprivations of their school rights by provincial governments. In the 1890s Manitoba school crisis, Charles Tupper's Conservative government proposed to use its remedial power under section 93 to protect the rights of Manitoba's French-Catholic minority. The Tupper

---

3   Donald Creighton, *The Road to Confederation: The Emergence of Canada, 1863-1867* (Toronto: Macmillan, 1964), and Peter H. Russell, *Constitutional Odyssey: Can Canadians Become a Sovereign People?*, 3d ed. (Toronto: University of Toronto Press, 2004) c. 2.

4   Janet Ajzenstat, *The Canadian Founding: John Locke and Parliament* (Montreal and Kingston: McGill-Queen's University Press, 2007) c. 3.

5   Janet Ajzenstat, Paul Romney, Ian Gentles, and William D. Gairdner, *Canada's Founding Debates* (Toronto: Stoddart, 1999) 191.

6   *Ibid.* at 19.

Conservatives were defeated in the 1896 general election by Wilfrid Laurier's Liberals, who favoured provincial rights over minority rights. This was the last time any federal government considered using its section 93 remedial power. French-Catholic minorities outside Quebec fared no better when they tried to secure their rights through the courts. Canada's highest court, the Judicial Committee of the Privy Council, was anything but activist in interpreting the ambit of section 93 rights. When lower courts ruled that legislation in 1890 making English Manitoba's official language violated the constitutional rights of francophones, Manitoba's governments simply ignored the decisions—and got away with it until the late 1970s.[7]

World War II marked the turning point in Canadian attitudes toward civil liberties and human rights. Canada's participation in the war and the post-war settlement heightened awareness of the need to protect fundamental rights and liberties against all governments, including democratically elected governments. Canada took a leading role in the founding of the United Nations and the adoption of the Universal Declaration of Human Rights. These developments created significant public interest in Canada's adoption of its own charter of fundamental rights and freedoms. Between 1947 and 1950, two joint parliamentary committees and a Senate committee considered proposals for a constitutional bill of rights.[8] At this point, leaders of the Liberals, Canada's so-called government party, opposed a constitutional charter on the grounds that it would undermine parliamentary sovereignty and provincial rights. Nonetheless there was now a growing body of opinion in Canada, across the political spectrum, seeking stronger protection of rights and freedoms.

The removal and dispossession of west-coast Japanese Canadians during the war, followed after the war by the Gouzenko espionage inquiry's gross violation of basic civil rights, broadened support for a charter among Canadian civil liberties organizations. A series of court cases in the 1950s focused attention on the use of the courts to thwart the repressive policies of the Duplessis regime in Quebec. In seven cases between 1953 and 1959 the Supreme Court of Canada, now Canada's highest court, upheld challenges by religious and political minorities to Quebec laws and policies.[9] These Supreme Court decisions were based on a variety of grounds, including common law, the constitutional division of powers, and a doctrine first put forward in 1938 by Chief Justice Duff that the *British North America (B.N.A.) Act* contained an implied constitutional bill of rights that at least protected the right of free public discussion essential for the proper working of the parliamentary system of government.[10]

The implied bill of rights was invoked by a number of Supreme Court justices in the Quebec civil liberties cases decided by the Court in the 1950s, but never gained the support of a majority of the judges. While civil libertarians were pleased with the immediate results

---

7   For a discussion of these developments, see the introduction to *Mahe v. Alberta*, case 31.

8   For an account, see Christopher MacLennan, *Toward the Charter: Canadians and the Demand for a National Bill of Rights, 1929-1960* (Montreal and Kingston: McGill-Queen's University Press, 2003).

9   For a discussion of these cases, see the introduction to *Saumur v. Quebec and Attorney General of Quebec*, case 20 in Peter H. Russell, Rainer Knopff, Thomas M.J. Bateman, and Janet L. Hiebert, *The Court and the Constitution: Leading Cases* (Toronto: Emond Montgomery, 2008).

10   *Reference re Alberta Statutes*, case 1.

of the Quebec cases, the decisions strengthened their determination to secure legal protection for civil liberties in a stronger form than that afforded by the vague and uncertain implied bill of rights doctrine.

It took the election in 1957 of a Conservative government under the leadership of John Diefenbaker to put a Canadian bill of rights proposal back on the political agenda. Diefenbaker had been an ardent advocate of a bill of rights for many years and his support for such a measure was an important factor in his rise to political prominence. Diefenbaker's advocacy focused on traditional "blue" or classical-liberal rights, which lawyers cherish to protect individual rights from an intrusive state, rather than second-generation, economic or social "red" rights, which advance social equality. This was evident in the contents of the bill of rights that his government put forward in 1959. The *Canadian Bill of Rights* was not an addition to the Constitution of Canada. It was passed as an ordinary Act of Parliament.[11] As such, it is not entrenched and can be set aside by future parliaments, and it has no application to the provinces. The Act has two main clauses. Section 1 declares that in Canada certain fundamental rights and freedoms "have existed and shall continue to exist without discrimination by reason of race, national origin, colour, religion or sex." It identifies as fundamental rights the right to life, liberty, security of the person and property, and the right not to be deprived thereof except by due process of law; the right to equality before the law and the protection of the law; and freedom of religion, speech, assembly, association, and the press. Section 2 provides that unless the *Bill of Rights* is explicitly set aside, every federal law shall "be so construed and applied as not to abrogate, abridge or infringe" the rights and freedoms set out in the *Bill*.

The *Canadian Bill of Rights* remains part of Canadian law to this day, but it has been almost totally eclipsed by the *Canadian Charter of Rights and Freedoms*, which became part of the Constitution in 1982. This is not only because of its limited contents and non-constitutional status, but also because the Supreme Court of Canada gave it little force. In a handful of cases, the Court used the *Bill of Rights* as a basis for interpreting a federal law in a liberal way, but on only one occasion did the Court rule a federal law inoperative because it conflicted with the Bill. This was in the 1970 *Drybones* case,[12] where the Court, in a 6-to-3 decision, ruled inoperative a section of the *Indian Act* restricting Indians' access to alcohol, on the ground that it violated Indians' right to equality before the law. Four years later, in *Lavell and Bédard*,[13] the Court drew back from *Drybones*, when a majority reduced equality before the law to a procedural right and upheld the section of the *Indian Act* that denied an Indian woman who married a non-Indian her Indian status, while allowing Indian men who marry non-Indians to retain their status.

The very ineffectiveness of the *Canadian Bill of Rights* added momentum to the drive for a constitutional bill of rights. The jurisprudence the Supreme Court developed in interpreting the *Bill of Rights* did not carry over into the Court's interpretation of the *Charter of Rights and Freedoms*. The one part of the *Bill of Rights* that has enduring importance is its recognition of a right to the enjoyment of property. There is no right to property in the *Charter*.

---

11   R.S.C. 1970, c. S-19.

12   *The Queen v. Drybones*, [1970] S.C.R. 282.

13   *Attorney General of Canada v. Lavell and Bédard*, case 2.

By the time the Diefenbaker bill of rights was adopted, the Liberal Party had totally reversed its position on protecting rights and freedoms. The Liberals now contended that nothing but an entrenched constitutional bill of rights would do. In the 1960s, they found a strong champion of that cause in Pierre Elliott Trudeau. When Trudeau became Justice Minister in the Pearson Liberal government in 1967, he made a Canadian charter of human rights the centrepiece of a federal constitutional counterattack against constitutional changes Quebec was proposing that aimed at strengthening provincial powers so that the Québécois could be "*maitres chez nous.*"[14] The core of what became known as the Trudeau vision was a constitutional charter of rights expressing the values shared by all Canadians that would serve as a common bond of Canadian citizenship. It was its potential as an instrument of national unity, more than its civil libertarian values, that made the *Charter* Trudeau's "magnificent obsession."[15] In his final parliamentary speech on the *Charter*, Trudeau emphasized its nation-building aspect:[16]

> Lest the forces of self-interest tear us apart, we must now define the common thread that binds us together.

Trudeau became Prime Minister in 1968; from then until the end of the 1970s he was engaged in a continuing struggle with Quebec and the other provinces over patriating and reforming the Canadian Constitution. Throughout this struggle, a constitutional charter of rights was the first priority of Trudeau and his government. At Victoria in 1971, Trudeau and the provincial first ministers seemed to have reached a resolution of their differences when they signed the Victoria Charter.[17] Taking pride of place at the top of the proposed amendment package was a mini-charter of rights. It included the fundamental rights of conscience, expression, association, and assembly and such basic rights of parliamentary democracy as universal suffrage, annual sessions of Parliament, and elections every five years. English and French language rights, so crucial to the Trudeau government's national unity objective, were included but applied to the provinces on a checkerboard basis according to each premier's willingness to opt in. The Victoria Charter died when Quebec's Liberal Premier, Robert Bourassa, under attack for getting so little for Quebec, withdrew his support.

The Quebec election of 1976 brought to power the Parti Québécois, headed by René Lévesque, whose constitutional objective was a sovereign Quebec loosely associated with Canada. The constitutional battle heated up. The Trudeau government was now convinced that renewal of the federation required nothing less than an entirely new Constitution. In 1977, it appointed the Pepin-Robarts Task Force on National Unity to tour the country and bring forward ideas and initiatives on the question of Canadian unity. Trudeau did not wait for the National Unity Task Force to complete its work. In 1978, he published a booklet entitled *A Time for Action*, setting out a two-stage process of constitutional renewal, the first

---

14 Pierre Elliott Trudeau, *A Canadian Charter of Human Rights* (Ottawa: Queen's Printer, 1968).

15 Stephen Clarkson and Christina McCall, *Trudeau and Our Times, Volume 1: The Magnificent Obsession* (Toronto: McClelland & Stewart, 1990).

16 Quoted in Peter H. Russell, "The Political Purposes of the Canadian Charter of Rights and Freedoms" (1983) 61 *Canadian Bar Review* 30 at 36.

17 Peter H. Russell, *Constitutional Odyssey: Can Canadians Become a Sovereign People?*, 3d ed. (Toronto: University of Toronto Press, 2004) at 85-91.

stage to be completed unilaterally by the federal government and Parliament, the second stage with the provinces.[18] A charter of rights would be included in the first stage, but it would apply only at the federal level. Details of the first phase were set out in a *Constitutional Amendment Act* (Bill C-60).

By this time, the constitutional landscape was littered with proposals from provincial governments, Aboriginal organizations, political parties, and private groups, pushing for everything from Senate reform to replacing the monarchical head of state. A charter of rights did not figure prominently in these proposals or in the final report of the Task Force on National Unity. The Task Force emphasized recognition of Canada's regional divisions and its linguistic and cultural diversity as the most effective recipe for national unity.[19] In the fall of 1978, amid this frenzy of new constitutionalism, Trudeau and the provincial first ministers returned to constitutional negotiations. To no one's surprise, with so many cross-cutting proposals on the table, those talks ended in failure in February 1979.[20]

Three months later, Trudeau and his government were defeated by Joe Clark's Conservatives in the May 1979 federal election. Constitutional renewal was not a priority of the Clark government. In November 1979, Trudeau announced his retirement from politics. This might have marked the end of the road for a charter of rights, at least for quite a long time, had it not been for a remarkable reversal in the political fortunes of the federal Liberal Party and Pierre Trudeau. In December, the Clark minority government was defeated on a vote of no confidence. In the ensuing election, Pierre Trudeau, who had come back from the political dead, led his party to victory. He immediately girded for battle in the Quebec referendum organized by the Lévesque government to secure a popular mandate for negotiating Quebec sovereignty and association with Canada. In the May 1980 referendum, Trudeau's leadership was crucial in defeating the sovereignty-association proposal by a margin of 60 to 40 percent. In the referendum campaign, Trudeau promised that, if his side won, he would lead a process of constitutional renewal.

Trudeau's promise of constitutional renewal was vague and did not highlight a charter of rights. Soon after the referendum, his government resumed negotiations with the provincial governments on a broad range of proposals, including a constitutional charter of rights. Once again, these efforts to reach agreement among federal and provincial leaders failed. Following this failure, Trudeau broke dramatically with the traditional, elite-accommodation approach to constitutional reform. On the evening of October 2, 1980, in a televised address to the country, he announced that his government intended to proceed unilaterally with patriation and a few constitutional changes, dubbed "the people's package." The people's package contained an all-Canadian Constitution-amending formula, a charter of rights and freedoms, and constitutional recognition of the principle of fiscal equalization. Trudeau said he would put this package of constitutional proposals forward for consideration in the federal Parliament, and, once the proposals passed there, the federal government

18   Prime Minister's Office, *A Time for Action: Toward the Renewal of the Canadian Federation* (Ottawa: Government of Canada, 1978).

19   Task Force on National Unity, *A Future Together: Observations and Recommendations* (Ottawa: Supply and Services Canada, 1979).

20   Roy Romanow, John Whyte, and Howard Leeson, *Canada . . . Notwithstanding: The Making of the Constitution, 1976-1982* (Toronto: Carswell/Methuen, 1984).

would proceed, with or without the provinces' consent, to request that the British Parliament give them legal effect.[21] A new path was now open to a charter of rights and freedoms. It would take a year and a half to move along that path. In the process, the proposed charter would be significantly changed before it became part of Canada's Constitution in 1982.

MAKING THE CHARTER

Four stages were involved in the making of the *Canadian Charter of Rights and Freedoms*: first was the draft developed by the federal government and submitted to Parliament in October 1980; second was the submission of the people's package for consideration by a joint parliamentary committee on the Constitution that sat through the fall and winter of 1980-81 and produced important changes in the government's draft Charter; third was the addition of two significant clauses to the Charter after the joint parliamentary committee had completed its work—one in the parliamentary debate on the Charter in the spring of 1981 and the other following the First Ministers meeting in November 1981; fourth, and finally, was the Charter's enactment into law by the British Parliament.

The draft Charter that the Trudeau government submitted to Parliament in October 1980 was considerably bolder and more comprehensive than either the mini-charter it had proposed at Victoria in 1971 or the charter that was part of its 1978 time-for-action plan. Added to the political and democratic rights from earlier proposals was a more comprehensive set of rights: an equality-rights section aimed at overcoming the inadequacies of the *Canadian Bill of Rights* and adding age to the prohibited categories of discrimination, language-of-government rights that were no longer on a provincial opt-in basis, and new minority-language education rights and mobility rights aimed at strengthening the unity of the country.

But the federal government's draft was still fundamentally a blue rights charter, limiting what government can do. Absent were the red rights that require action by the state to enhance citizens' opportunities and well-being—rights that Trudeau in his 1967 booklet on a charter of human rights said "are desirable and should be an ultimate objective for Canada."[22] The political left could take some solace from the absence of any protection of property rights, as well as from a clause in the equality-rights section permitting affirmative action programs to ameliorate the conditions of disadvantaged groups. The general limiting clause that emerged through the exchange of draft charters in the intergovernmental meetings held in the summer of 1980 no longer focused on national security and emergencies as the justification for encroachments on rights. But the limiting clause designed to secure provincial support made compatibility with parliamentary government the test of acceptable limits on rights and freedoms. The new wording seemed to expose constitutional rights to easy override by legislatures. The 1980 meetings with the provinces similarly led to language in the legal-rights sections that would restrict rights to what is available under existing law—a qualification of legal rights strongly advocated by Ontario.

The second stage in the making of the Charter began on November 7, 1980, when Jean Chrétien, Minister of Justice in the Trudeau government, opened the proceedings of the

---

21 See David Milne, *The New Canadian Constitution* (Toronto: James Lorimer, 1982).

22 Trudeau, *supra* note 14 at 27.

Joint Parliamentary Committee on the Constitution. The committee was made up of 15 members of Parliament (MPs) and 10 senators—15 Liberals, 8 Conservatives, and 2 New Democratic Party (NDP) members. The joint committee held 106 meetings in 56 hearing days. It heard from 6 governments, 93 groups, and 5 individuals and received over 1,200 submissions and letters.[23] All committee hearings were televised. The parliamentary committee was an unprecedented opening up of the constitutional process in Canada and an integral part of Trudeau's effort to go over the heads of provincial leaders and engage the public directly in the constitutional reform process. While, in principle, the joint committee dealt with all the components of the people's package, the focus was very much on the Charter, especially for the many interest groups who made submissions. Most of these groups were intent on strengthening the Charter. There was little interest in what a strong, judicially enforced Charter might mean for the policy-making role of courts or for parliamentary democracy more generally.

The changes in the Charter that resulted from the joint committee's hearings and deliberations came about through governmental interaction with the committee. The real framers of the Charter were, in effect, Jean Chrétien, the Minister of Justice, his senior advisers, and the members of the joint committee. Supported by officials from his department, Chrétien attended committee meetings to explain the thinking behind the government's draft and participated in discussions of proposed changes. On January 12, 1981, Chrétien put an amended version of the Charter before the committee. The amendments responded to criticisms of the government's draft and incorporated a number of suggested amendments. On February 13, 1981, the government submitted a slightly amended version of its January 12th draft to the committee. This is the version of the Charter that the committee approved and that, save for two later additions, is the basis of the *Charter* we now have.

The most important change made by the joint committee, in terms of how the Charter would be applied by the courts, was to the general limiting clause at the beginning of the Charter. The revised section 1, instead of requiring that acceptable limits on rights be compatible with the parliamentary system of government, requires that they be "demonstrably justified in a free and democratic society." Another important change is that limitations on rights must be prescribed by law, and cannot simply occur through the course of police conduct or the actions of other public authorities working on behalf of the state. These changes put the burden of proof on government to justify laws that encroach on *Charter* rights and freedoms. As is evident in many of the cases included in this volume, the wording of section 1 opens the door wide to judicial appraisal of government policy. Almost as important as the revision of section 1 was the strengthening of legal rights and the addition of a remedial provision to strengthen the enforcement of these rights. Section 24(2) of the *Charter* requires the exclusion of evidence obtained in a manner that violates *Charter* rights if a court determines that its inclusion "would bring the administration of justice into disrepute." This provision of the *Charter* has made judicial scrutiny of police conduct an important phase of criminal trials. Other important changes made in response to submissions to the parliamentary committee were the addition of mental or physical disability to the explicitly prohibited grounds of discrimination listed in section 15; section 27, requiring

---

23   Romanow et al., *supra* note 20 at 247-48.

that the *Charter* be interpreted "in a manner consistent with the preservation and enhancement of the multicultural heritage of Canadians"; and section 16(2), making English and French the official languages of New Brunswick.

Though generally supportive of proposals to strengthen and broaden the Charter, the parliamentary committee stage by no means led to the adoption of all such proposals. For instance, an environmental group failed to have the rights of trees written into the Charter. More significantly, an amendment put forward by Conservative committee members to include a right to property was first accepted by the government. But when NDP leader Ed Broadbent said his party would withdraw its support for the Trudeau government's constitutional proposals if constitutional protection of private property were included, the government dropped the property right proposal. At this point in the constitutional political struggle, the Liberals, knowing the Conservatives were opposed to Trudeau's unilateralism, needed NDP support to broaden the political base for their constitutional plan. Advocacy groups for gays and lesbians were also unsuccessful in having sexual orientation added to the list of unconstitutional grounds of discrimination in section 15. However, members of the committee suggested that judicial interpretation of section 15 might evolve to protect gays and lesbians from state discrimination.

A major addition to the rights provisions of the people's package that occurred through the committee hearings was a new section of the package, outside the Charter, giving constitutional recognition to "the aboriginal and treaty rights of the aboriginal peoples of Canada." With one change, this became section 35 of the *Constitution Act, 1982.* The Aboriginal rights addition to the people's package was dropped entirely when Trudeau met with the provincial premiers in November 1981 to secure their support for his patriation package. However, in response to public demonstrations across the country, it was quickly restored, with one change—the addition of the word "existing" before "aboriginal and treaty rights."[24] This word was added to gain the support of Alberta's Premier Peter Lougheed for the section. As it turns out, the qualification of Aboriginal and treaty rights by the word "existing" has not prevented the courts from rendering a generous and liberal interpretation of these rights.[25] Although Aboriginal rights were not themselves included in the *Charter*, section 25 of the *Charter* was inserted to ensure that *Charter* rights and freedoms are not construed so as to derogate from Aboriginal or treaty rights or other rights of Aboriginal peoples recognized through the *Royal Proclamation of 1763* or that may be secured through modern land-claims agreements.

The *Canadian Charter of Rights and Freedoms* was basically complete when it emerged from the joint parliamentary committee in February 1981. Only a few changes would be made after this. The first occurred when the Charter came before the House of Commons for approval as part of the revised package of proposed constitutional amendments in the early spring of 1981. In the final days of the House debate, as a result of intense lobbying

---

24   For an account, see Douglas E. Sanders, "The Indian Lobby" in Keith Banting and Richard Simeon, *And No One Cheered: Federalism, Democracy, and the Constitution Act* (Toronto: Methuen, 1983) at 301-32.

25   Judicial decisions on Aboriginal and treaty rights are not included in this book. Five of the leading cases on Aboriginal rights are discussed in Russell et al., *supra* note 9.

by women's organizations, section 28 was added to the Charter stating that "[n]otwithstanding anything in this Charter, the rights and freedoms referred to in it are guaranteed equally to male and female persons."[26] Though the battle to obtain this addition to the Charter was waged with great fury and passion, it has not played a significant role in *Charter* interpretation. This is also true of another change accepted at this time—a reference to the "supremacy of God" in the Charter's preamble.

The final changes to the Charter occurred in November 1981 when Canada's Constitution makers returned to the traditional process of elite accommodation—a First Ministers meeting. This meeting was a direct consequence of the Supreme Court of Canada's ruling in September 1981 on the constitutional validity of the Trudeau government's unilateral approach to constitutional reform and patriation. Two provinces, New Brunswick and Ontario, supported Trudeau's approach, but the other eight did not. Three of the dissenting provinces, Manitoba, Newfoundland, and Quebec, referred the question of the constitutionality of Trudeau's unilateral approach to their provincial courts of appeal. The decisions of these courts (Manitoba's and Quebec's courts deciding federal unilateralism was constitutional, Newfoundland's that it was not) were appealed to the Supreme Court of Canada. In the *Patriation Reference* decision, the Court found that a new constitutional amending formula and a charter of rights would affect the powers and role of the provinces, but nonetheless ruled 7 to 2 that there was no legal requirement that the federal government secure the consent of the provinces before requesting the U.K. Parliament to enact these amendments to Canada's Constitution. However, the Court balanced this finding with another that held 6 to 3 that the federal government would be violating an unwritten convention of the Constitution if it requested such constitutional changes without "a substantial degree of provincial consent."[27]

Prime Minister Trudeau decided to respect the Supreme Court's opinion on constitutional convention and invited the provincial premiers to the Ottawa Conference Centre in the first week of November 1981 to see if he could secure their support for his package of constitutional proposals. At this meeting, with the country watching every move on television, Trudeau and the premiers of nine provinces agreed on the basis for proceeding with the revised package of constitutional reforms. Only Quebec's premier, René Lévesque, refused to commit his province to the agreement.

To obtain provincial support, Trudeau had to make two major concessions. One was to accept the amending formula favoured by the provinces and scrap his own formula, which included a referendum as a deadlock-breaking device. The other was to add a legislative override clause, section 33, to the *Charter of Rights and Freedoms*. This section empowers the federal Parliament and provincial legislatures to declare that a law shall operate "notwithstanding" certain sections of the *Charter*. This section applies to the more universal rights in the *Charter*—the political freedoms in section 2, the legal rights in sections 7 to 14, and the equality rights in section 15. It does not apply to the parliamentary democracy rights or the language and mobility rights that were central to Trudeau's national unity aims. Legislation using the notwithstanding clause, or "override," is, in effect, insulated from

---

26   See Penny Kome, *The Taking of Twenty of Twenty-Eight: Women Challenge the Constitution* (Toronto: Women's Educational Press, 1983).

27   Russell et al., *supra* note 9, case 46.

Charter review. The provision can also be invoked to set aside the effects of a judicial ruling. Either use of the notwithstanding clause can be in force for five years and can be renewed.

The notwithstanding clause was placed in the Charter to meet the concerns of several premiers, notably Allan Blakeney, the NDP premier of Saskatchewan, and Sterling Lyon, the Conservative premier of Manitoba, to balance the judicial protection of rights with parliamentary democracy. Advocates of the clause thought the override should be available for those rare occasions when *Charter*-based judicial review goes against the strongly held views of an elected legislature. In essence, it was designed to be a democratic safety valve. The legislative override has been used infrequently[28] and remains highly controversial.[29] Its most dramatic use was by Quebec, in 1988, in response to a Supreme Court decision overturning its French-only sign law.[30]

The First Ministers meeting produced one other modification of the Charter—an affirmative action rider to the mobility rights allowing provinces with below-average employment rates to protect jobs from out-of-province job seekers. This change was made primarily to meet the concerns of Newfoundland.

The Charter was now almost complete. When the amended draft emerged from the First Ministers meeting, and it appeared that the guarantee of gender equality in section 28 was not protected from the legislative override, all hell broke loose. The government and Parliament quickly agreed to restore the words "[n]otwithstanding anything in this Charter" at the beginning of section 28. Thus the *Charter* has two notwithstanding clauses and provides no guidance as to what should happen if they ever collide with each other. The text of the Charter was now in its final form.

It still remained for the Charter to become part of Canada's constitutional law. This fourth and final stage of making the Charter occurred in two steps. In early December 1981, a resolution supporting the revised package of constitutional amendments passed in both Houses of the Canadian Parliament. In the House of Commons, 247 members supported the motion and only 24 members—17 Conservatives, 5 Liberals, and 2 NDP—opposed it. The next step was to ask the U.K. Parliament, for the last time, to enact an amendment to Canada's Constitution. This it did by passing the *Canada Act 1982*, which enacted the *Constitution Act, 1982* and stated that the U.K. Parliament would never again legislate with respect to Canada. The *Constitution Act, 1982* was attached to the *Canada Act 1982* as a schedule. It contains all the constitutional amendments that make up the revised people's package, including a made-in-Canada Constitution-amending formula and the *Canadian Charter of Rights and Freedoms*. In March 1981, the *Canada Act 1982* was passed by both Houses of the U.K. Parliament. On April 17, 1982, in a signing ceremony on Parliament Hill, Queen Elizabeth proclaimed the *Canada Act 1982* in force. The *Charter* was now Canadian law.

---

28 See Howard Leeson, "Section 33, the Notwithstanding Clause: A Paper Tiger?" in Paul Howe and Peter H. Russell, eds., *Judicial Power and Canadian Democracy* (Montreal and Kingston: McGill-Queen's University Press, 2001) 297.

29 For contrasting views on section 33, see John D. Whyte, "On Not Standing for Notwithstanding" (1990) *Alberta Law Review* 347, and Peter H. Russell, "Standing Up for Notwithstanding" (1991) *Alberta Law Review* 293.

30 See *Quebec v. Ford et al.*, case 4.

THE CHARTER GOES TO COURT

While this book features interpretations of the *Charter* by the Supreme Court of Canada, *Charter* decisions are only a part of this Court's workload. The Supreme Court is not only Canada's "supreme" or final judicial authority, it is also a general court of appeal, meaning that it acts as final arbiter of legal disputes concerning all federal and provincial legislation and official conduct. It sets a national interpretive standard even for laws passed by individual provinces. And, of course, the Supreme Court has the ultimate judicial say on disputes about how to interpret the Constitution, including not just the *Charter*, but also the *Constitution Act, 1867*, formerly the *B.N.A. Act*, which establishes Canada's parliamentary and federal democracy. The nine judges of the Supreme Court supervise this extensive legal terrain by rendering approximately 100 judgments per year, though this number has dipped to as low as 58 since Beverley McLachlin became Chief Justice in 2000.[31] Obviously, this means that the vast majority of legal disputes will never get our top court's attention and will be settled by courts lower in the judicial hierarchy.

Cases get to the Supreme Court in one of two ways, either by appeal or by reference. In almost all cases, the Court decides issues coming to it on appeal from provincial courts of appeal or from the appeal division of the Federal Court of Canada. But the *Supreme Court Act*, which defines the Court's jurisdiction, also allows the federal government to submit "reference questions" directly to the Court. These are questions raising legal issues that are not part of live legal disputes brought by real-life parties or litigants. A reference may ask the Court for its opinion on the constitutionality of a proposed law. An example is the reference on the constitutionality of the bill to legalize same-sex marriage on which the Court rendered its opinion in 2004 (see case 30). The reference procedure allows for expeditious consideration of legal issues before they become the subjects of protracted and expensive lawsuits. It also provides governments the opportunity either to avoid deciding a contentious political issue themselves or to use the authority of the Court to support a policy position they already hold. It may be too much to say that the reference procedure facilitates an abuse of judicial authority, but certainly the procedure often inserts the Supreme Court into salient political issues of the day.

Because references do not concern live legal disputes, the Court's answers to reference questions do not technically have the force of law, but its opinions nonetheless are considered to be legal precedents. The Court has the discretion to refuse to answer questions that are non-legal in character or too hypothetical, and it sometimes exercises that discretion.[32]

The provinces have similarly given themselves the legislative authority to pose reference questions to their highest courts (the provincial courts of appeal) and decisions on these cases may be appealed to the Supreme Court. A prominent example is the 1981 *Patriation Reference*, in which the Supreme Court heard the consolidated appeal of three provincial reference-case decisions on the constitutional validity of the Trudeau government's proposal to significantly reform the Constitution in the face of substantial provincial opposition.

Unlike provincial references, most cases that arrive at the Supreme Court on appeal begin not in provincial courts of appeal but in trial courts at the bottom of the judicial hierarchy.

---

31   Supreme Court of Canada, *Statistics: 1996-2007*, online at <http://www.scc-csc.gc.ca/information/statistics/download/ecourt.pdf>.

32   See *Reference re Same Sex Marriage*, case 30.

Trial judges face both factual and legal issues. In a criminal trial, for example, part of the judicial task (sometimes assisted by a jury) is to determine the "facts" of the case, or what actually happened. Did the accused commit the alleged acts, for example, or was it someone else? If the relevant law is clear, a trial court's work may be limited to such factual determinations. However, the law is often ambiguous, and an accused may argue that what he or she has been charged with is not actually illegal. For example, in 1987, when Donald Victor Butler (see case 6) was charged under the *Criminal Code* prohibition of obscenity, the "fact" that he was selling sexually explicit materials was beyond doubt, but were all of these materials "obscene"? The answer to that question required the trial judge to choose between competing interpretations of the obscenity law, and thus to engage in a kind of legal policy making. But the legal issues, and hence opportunity for legal policy making, did not stop there. Even if Butler's materials were deemed to be obscene under the censorship law, he could not be found guilty if that law itself was an unconstitutional violation of the *Charter*'s guarantee of freedom of expression. In order to dispose of Butler's case, the trial judge thus also had to engage in constitutional interpretation. It is mostly the legal interpretations, not the factual determinations, of trial courts that are appealed up the judicial hierarchy, sometimes all the way to the Supreme Court.

When cases reach the top court, the particular factual situation of the parties tends no longer to be an important focus of the judicial task. True, the disputing parties are the occasion for the Supreme Court's work, and the Court's decision will ultimately decide their legal fate, but they have already had their day(s) in court (a trial and an appeal) and generally have no right to the Supreme Court's attention. The Court has considerable control over its own docket, and it chooses to hear most cases not because of their importance to the parties but in order to settle important issues of legal policy for the country as a whole. Indeed, the Court was given almost complete control over its own docket in 1975 precisely in recognition of its primary role as a legal policy-maker and not just another appeal opportunity for litigants. Prior to 1975, most cases came to the Court "as of right"—that is, because the litigants had a right to this additional appeal. Since 1975, some cases—including provincial references and serious criminal cases where a provincial Court of Appeal has divided on a point of law—still come "as of right," but these amount to only about 15 percent of the Court's workload. In the other 85 percent of its cases, the Court grants "leave to appeal." The Court receives 500 to 600 applications for leave to appeal per year and grants approximately 11 percent of them.

Granting leave to appeal is an important exercise of the Court's discretionary power. While most Supreme Court operations are shrouded in secrecy, we have some sense of how leave decisions are made. Applications for leave are first considered by Supreme Court staff and submitted to panels of three justices with a recommendation to grant or deny leave. The votes of two justices are needed to grant leave, but the vast majority of applications are decided unanimously. Panels can vote to delay a decision as well. All recommendations of the panels are finally considered by all nine justices. No reasons are published for decisions to grant or deny leave.[33]

---

33 See Roy Flemming, *Tournament of Appeals: Granting Judicial Review on Canada* (Vancouver: University of British Columbia Press, 2004) c. 1.

Section 40(1) of the *Supreme Court Act* contains the criteria applied to applications for leave. The Court may grant leave to appeal where the Supreme Court "is of the opinion that any question involved therein is, by reason of its public importance or the importance of any issue of law or any issue of mixed law and fact involved in that question, one that ought to be decided by the Supreme Court or is, for any other reason, of such a nature or significance as to warrant decision by it, and leave to appeal from that judgment is accordingly granted by the Supreme Court." This public-importance test gives the Court a lot of room to decide what appeals it wants to hear. But we have some indication of what the test concretely means. Leave to appeal is granted, for example, when a novel constitutional issue is raised, when provincial courts of appeal have arrived at different resolutions to the problem, when a novel point of law is at issue, when the case concerns an important statute, when a dispute concerns a provincial law that is similar to laws in other provinces, when Aboriginal rights are in play, and/or when the Court wants to set a national standard relating to a decision of a provincial court of appeal.[34]

It is important to understand all the conditions that make *Charter* litigation possible. Certainly the existence of an entrenched charter of rights is a necessary condition. But it is not a sufficient condition. A receptive political culture of rights-consciousness also contributes to rights-based litigation, but this too is insufficient. Political scientist Charles Epp argues that a supportive resource infrastructure is also necessary for the *Charter* to go to court:[35]

> [C]ases do not arrive in supreme courts as if by magic. . . . [T]he process of legal mobilization—the process by which individuals make claims about their rights and pursue lawsuits to defend or develop those rights—is not in any simple way a direct response to opportunities by constitutional promises or judicial decisions, or to expectations arising from political culture. Legal mobilization also depends on resources, and resources for rights litigation depend on a support structure of rights-advocacy lawyers, rights-advocacy organizations, and sources of financing.

In Canada, such an infrastructure was in the making even before the *Charter* was entrenched and is now a highly developed part of post-*Charter* Canada. Some litigation support organizations have enjoyed public support, but different governments have taken different views on the merits of public funding of organizations dedicated to the use of the *Charter* to promote legal change.[36]

Since the *Charter*'s entrenchment in 1982, cases involving its interpretation have taken up 22 percent of the Court's caseload. Two-thirds of *Charter* cases concern legal rights set out in sections 7 to 14 of the *Charter*. Approximately half of *Charter* challenges concern actions of administrative and law enforcement officials; the other half concern challenges to legislation and regulations made pursuant to legislation.[37]

---

34 *Ibid.* at 63-64.

35 Charles R. Epp, *The Rights Revolution: Lawyers, Activists, and Supreme Courts in Comparative Perspective* (Chicago: University of Chicago Press, 1998) at 18.

36 For a critical account of legal resource mobilization structures in Canada, see F.L. Morton and Rainer Knopff, *The Charter Revolution and the Court Party* (Peterborough, ON: Broadview Press, 2000).

37 See James B. Kelly, "The Supreme Court of Canada's Charter of Rights Decisions, 1982-1999: A Statistical Analysis" in F.L. Morton, ed., *Law, Politics, and the Judicial Process in Canada*, 3d ed. (Calgary: University of Calgary Press, 2002) 496.

The Court's nine members do not generally sit as a whole bench to hear appeals, although Beverley McLachlin seems to have encouraged this since her elevation to Chief Justice in 2000. More commonly, seven justices will sit on appeals to allow the Court's workload to be handled more efficiently. Parties and interveners submit written briefs (whose length is strictly limited by a rule of the Court) in advance of the hearing.[38] At the hearing, each party is allowed one hour for its oral submission. Justices can interrupt at any time with questions. Interveners do not make oral submissions. After the hearing, the justices convene in private conference, speaking in reverse order of seniority about the case and how they would propose to settle it. Justices volunteer to write opinions. As the drafting process unfolds, justices decide whether to join opinions or write opinions of their own. Their clerks play a role in research and writing but former clerks at the Canadian Supreme Court insist that the justices themselves make the decisions, marshal the arguments, and do much of the writing.

A DISTINCTIVE CANADIAN JURISPRUDENCE

As noted above, after a period of civil-liberties activism in the 1950s, based on federalism and common-law principles, the Supreme Court took a decidedly restrained approach to the 1960 statutory *Bill of Rights*. Of 34 Supreme Court cases engaging the *Bill of Rights*, in only 4 did the rights claimant win, and in only 1 decision did the Court strike down a provision of a federal law.[39] The Supreme Court was unsure of its ability to use an Act of Parliament to strike down other Acts of Parliament and it remained stolidly under the influence of the constitutional doctrine of parliamentary sovereignty.

When the Supreme Court was first faced with a case involving a *Charter* challenge, it dispelled doubts that it would interpret the new *Charter* vigorously. *Law Society of Upper Canada v. Skapinker*[40] was not the most propitious of cases in which to break new ground. It involved a lawyer seeking to practise law, but who was prohibited from doing so because he was not a Canadian citizen. Of greatest use to him was the section 15 equality rights provision, but that section would not come into force until April 1985.[41] Instead, he argued that the citizenship requirement was contrary to his mobility rights protected by section 6. Mobility rights do not exactly stir the passions of civil libertarians. Skapinker lost the case based on the Court's highly legalistic reading of section 6. But the Court's *obiter* was telling. "We are here engaged in a new task, the interpretation and application of the *Canadian Charter of Rights and Freedoms*," wrote Justice Estey. With the *Constitution Act, 1982*, of which the *Charter* is a central part, comes "a new dimension, a new yardstick of reconciliation

---

38 Interveners must apply for leave to submit a brief. The Court has been more generous in granting access to interest groups as interveners since it was criticized for its restrictive approach in the late 1980s. See Ian Brodie, *Friends of the Court: The Privileging of Interest Group Litigants in Canada* (Albany, NY: SUNY Press, 2002).

39 Christpher P. Manfredi and James B. Kelly, "Misrepresenting the Supreme Court's Record? A Comment on Sujit Choudhry and Claire E. Hunter, 'Measuring Judicial Activism on the Supreme Court of Canada'" (2004) 49 *McGill Law Journal* 741.

40 [1984] 1 S.C.R. 357.

41 We know that section 15 was the most useful provision in a challenge like this because a similar challenge to the citizenship requirement, made years later and based on section 15, succeeded. See *Andrews*, case 25.

between the individual and the community and their respective rights." Estey invoked nothing less than *Marbury v. Madison*,[42] the historic U.S. Supreme Court decision in which Chief Justice John Marshall claimed for the Court the power of judicial review—the power to strike down laws passed by the legislative branch of government. Estey's liberal attitude toward rights and the role of the Court pervaded many early decisions of the Court, consigning the deferential record of the pre-*Charter* Court to fading memory.[43]

As part of its new activism, the Court was at pains to disavow the "frozen concepts" approach to constitutional interpretation that had characterized much of its jurisprudence under the 1960 *Bill of Rights*. According to this view, the *Bill of Rights* protected rights and freedoms as they existed at the time of its passage. This meant, for example, that the *Bill's* protection of religious freedom must be read in the light of the longstanding federal *Lord's Day Act*—that is, that this *Act* was compatible with the kind of religious freedom protected by the *Bill*.[44] Very early in its *Charter* jurisprudence, the Court rejected this approach and made it clear that it would treat the *Charter* as a "living tree" instead. Thus, while the Court had upheld the *Lord's Day Act* under the *Bill of Rights*, it struck the Act down under the *Charter* (*The Queen v. Big M Drug Mart Ltd.*, case 3).

If the meaning of the *Charter* was not to be frozen by existing law and practice at the time of its passing, neither would it be constrained by the framers' intent. In another early *Charter* case (*Re B.C. Motor Vehicle Act*, case 13), the Court, speaking through Justice Lamer, warned that judicial fidelity to original intent or understanding would "freeze" the meaning of the *Charter*, making it incapable of "growth, development, and adjustment to changing social needs."

While the Court minimized the intent or purposes of the *Charter*'s framers as a guide to its interpretation, it did not reject the relevance of "purpose" altogether. Indeed, in a number of early *Charter* decisions, Chief Justice Dickson emphasized a "purposive" approach that would read *Charter* provisions in the light of the interests or purposes they were meant to protect. These purposes were to be discovered not in the intentions of the framers, however, but in our evolving liberal democratic tradition. That tradition, of course, contained laws, such as the federal *Lord's Day Act*, that the Court wanted to strike down. The essence of the purposive approach was thus to discover the principled direction in which the tradition was evolving in order to identify the anachronistic policies that had to be left behind.

As it turned out, the Court's purposive approach often led to a broad (or "large and liberal") reading of *Charter* rights and freedoms. Ironically, it was aided in this expansive interpretation by the fact that the *Charter*'s first section explicitly recognizes that its rights can be subject to limits where these are demonstrably justified, prescribed by law, and consistent with a free and democratic society. Virtually everyone agrees that rights and freedoms cannot be absolute, that they must be subject to sensible limitations. Where, as in the United States, there is no explicit clause recognizing limits on constitutional rights, courts have often achieved the necessary limits by defining rights restrictively. Thus, the U.S. Supreme

---

42   5 U.S. (1 Cranch) 137 (1803).

43   Perhaps the most brazen example of judicial activism in this period is *R. v. Therens*, [1985] 1 S.C.R. 613.

44   *Robertson and Rosetanni v. R.*, [1963] S.C.R. 651.

Court has excluded obscenity from the ambit of the First Amendment's guarantee of freedom of speech and press. In Canada, by contrast, the explicit recognition of rights limitations in section 1 has allowed our Supreme Court to establish a two-stage process of *Charter* interpretation that separates the question whether a right has been infringed from the question whether that infringement can be justified as a "reasonable limit in a free and democratic society." This *Charter* "two-step" enables the Supreme Court of Canada to interpret rights broadly, thus making it relatively easy to establish a *prima facie* violation, leaving to a second stage of analysis the question whether the challenged law can be justified under section 1. Thus, the Canadian Supreme Court, unlike its American counterpart, has found that "obscenity" enjoys the *Charter*'s freedom-of-expression guarantee in principle, but has nevertheless upheld censorship of obscenity as a "reasonable limit" on constitutional freedom.

Once the Court rules that legislation violates a right, the government has the responsibility and burden of persuasion to satisfy the Court that the impugned legislation is both reasonable and constitutionally valid. The test for this was first outlined in *The Queen v. Oakes*[45] (case 14), which remains, with modifications, the general standard that governments must meet. The test asks two main questions. The first is whether the legislative objective is sufficiently "pressing and substantial" to warrant restricting a right. The second is whether the legislative means are "proportional" to the objective. The proportionality test has three components: (1) there must be a "rational connection" between the legislative means and their objective—that is, the means must be non-arbitrary and actually achieve the objective; (2) the legislative means must impair the right as little as possible (known as the "minimal impairment" requirement); and (3) the deleterious nature of the rights infringement must be proportionate to the beneficial purposes of the legislation.[46]

Rarely does the Supreme Court rule that the *Charter* prevents Parliament or a provincial legislature from pursuing outright a specific legislative goal. The Court has become extremely deferential to Parliament and the provincial legislatures on the first element of its section 1 test—that is, whether legislation is important enough to restrict rights. Only rarely do governments fail at this stage. However, this has meant that the Court must depend on the second aspect of this section 1 test, the proportionality criteria, to determine whether the impugned legislation is valid even though it restricts rights.

The *Charter* two-step has generated considerable controversy. In the early days of the *Charter*, some scholars argued against the idea of an explicit two-stage approach to interpreting *Charter* rights, suggesting that the limitation clause simply acknowledges the obvious fact that rights are not absolute and that judicial review should define their scope restrictively as in the American example.[47] One argument in favour of imposing such definitional limits on rights is that it reduces the frequency of judicial oversight of legislation, particularly in circumstances where legislation does not implicate a fundamental right. In this view, to

---

45   [1986] 1 S.C.R. 103.

46   This last component was mentioned in *Oakes*, but elaborated in *Dagenais v. Canadian Broadcasting Corporation*, [1994] 3 S.C.R. 835.

47   Paul Bender, "Justification for Limiting Constitutionally Guaranteed Rights and Freedoms: Some Remarks About the Proper Role of Section One of the Canadian Charter" (1983) 13 *Manitoba Law Journal* 674.

interpret rights so broadly or abstractly that their judicial meaning is divorced from a theory or understanding of the function and role of rights in a liberal democracy would result in judicial review of legislation even in circumstances where the rights claim is peripheral to why a democratic community would accept constraints on duly enacted legislation.

A broad interpretation of rights in the first stage of judicial review encourages protracted and costly litigation, in the hope, often vain, that a judicial finding of a rights violation will result in the invalidation of the disputed legislation. The *Charter* two-step also puts governments in the unattractive position of appearing to be against rights, since they are defending legislation that the Court has ruled to be a restriction on *Charter* rights. Sometimes the government argues that it is necessary to restrict one *Charter* right to protect another right. However, more often, the crux of the government's argument is not that it is necessary to restrict a specific *Charter* right to protect another right, but that it is necessary to restrict a *Charter* right to promote a justifiable and compelling public interest. What makes the latter argument difficult to defend, politically, is that most people reflexively believe that rights should trump interests.

This raises an interesting quandary for the Court. How strict should the Court be when determining if the government has discharged its burden for demonstrating the justification of its legislation? The danger of an onerous justificatory burden is that governments may not be able to prove that society would be harmed if the legislation were not allowed. This is because it is often difficult to predict or measure what effects legislation (or the absence of legislation) will have on society. But there is also a danger if the Court does not demand strong justification for legislation that restricts rights. If it is too easy for governments to restrict rights, the *Charter* will cease to represent an effective constraint on rights-offending legislation, and governments will no longer worry about ensuring that legislation is sensitive to *Charter* rights.

The Supreme Court's post-*Charter* turn to judicial activism is evident in the fact that it upheld the *Charter* claim in nine of the first 15 *Charter* cases it decided, striking down five pieces of legislation (two provincial, three federal) in the process.[48] In addition, all but two of the Court's first 15 *Charter* decisions were unanimous. This early enthusiasm did not last, however. Greater caution and disagreement soon emerged. Three trends, in particular, succeeded the early activist period.

First, the Court became somewhat more restrained in its application of *Charter* rights as time went on. One early indication was how the Court relaxed the minimal-impairment component of the *Oakes* test. As originally formulated, the test implied that legislatures must choose the very least restrictive legislative way of achieving their objective. In a federal system, this might mean that provinces addressing similar issues within their jurisdictions would have to converge on the legislative approach of the least rights-restrictive province. This is precisely the kind of federal homogenization feared by many of the provinces during the Charter-making period. Instead of confirming these fears, the Court, soon after *Oakes*, in *Edwards Books,*[49] tweaked its minimal-impairment test, suggesting that a law need impair a right "as little as reasonably possible" in order to pass the section 1 test. Another indication

---

48   One of the federal laws that was overturned was the *Lord's Day Act;* see case 3.

49   *R. v. Edwards Books and Art Ltd.*, [1986] 2 S.C.R. 713.

of judicial caution occurred in *Morgentaler v. The Queen.*[50] Here, the Court struck down Canada's *Criminal Code* provision regulating access to abortion, but a majority of justices did so on the narrowest procedural terms possible, while only Justice Wilson asserted an expansive interpretation of *Charter* rights to invalidate the law.

The Court has undergone waves of activism and restraint, but the general trend that has emerged in *Charter* cases is that claimants win about one-third of the time. What explains this relative moderation? One possibility is offered by James Kelly, who attributes this trend to legal learning on the part of post-*Charter* governments. Not only are they aware of what is likely not to pass *Charter* muster; they also engage in rights activism of their own, drafting laws that avoid conflicting with *Charter* rights.[51]

Second, the court was more inclined to strike down laws that were passed in the pre-*Charter* environment than to strike down laws passed after the *Charter* was enacted. The most striking example of an old law ripe for invalidation was Parliament's *Lord's Day Act* of 1906. What had helped this law withstand challenge under the 1960 *Bill of Rights*—its age—now made it vulnerable to *Charter* attack.[52] Moreover, the Court struck down this old law precisely because it had an unconstitutionally religious purpose, as reflected in its name. By contrast, when the Court invalidated more recently passed legislation, it rarely took issue with legislative objectives, but instead quarrelled with the means the legislature used to achieve them. An example is the Court's invalidation of most of Canada's 1988 tobacco-advertising-control law.[53]

The third important trend is that early unanimity gave way to disagreement on the Court. The Supreme Court has nine members. Each justice enjoys individual judicial independence, not simply from the parties to a dispute and government officials more generally, but also from other justices on the Court. Justices, accordingly, may disagree with one another about the result in a case and/or about the reasons for a result. Many commentators consider disagreement a healthy sign of intellectual vigour on the Court and also a hint at future directions in which the law may develop. These benefits compete, however, with the institutional imperative that the Court's decision-making resolve disagreement about the meaning of the law for the benefit of present and future litigants as well as all others bound by the law. A basic function of the Court is to state what the law is and give guidance to those bound by it. Thus, there is pressure for consensus among the justices as to the result and the reasons for the result.[54]

It can be said with certainty that the *Charter* has divided the Court. Peter McCormick has found that either dissenting or concurring votes were cast in *Charter* cases much more frequently than in other types of legal actions. When Brian Dickson was Chief Justice from 1984 to 1990, *Charter* cases were two-and-a-half times more likely to be non-unanimous

---

50 See case 15.

51 James B. Kelly, *Governing with the Charter: Legislative and Judicial Activism and Framers' Intent* (Vancouver: University of British Columbia Press, 2005).

52 See *Her Majesty The Queen v. Big M Drug Mart Ltd.*, case 3.

53 See *RJR-MacDonald Inc. v. The Attorney General of Canada*, case 7.

54 For a recent discussion of the need for consensus on high courts, see Jeffrey Rosen, "Roberts' Rules" (2007) 299 *Atlantic Monthly* 104.

than other cases. This disparity has slowly declined over time, but in the early McLachlin Court, 2000-2002, the *Charter* was only somewhat less exceptional in its ability to generate disagreement. The nature of *Charter*-based disagreement has changed. Early in the *Charter* era, disagreement was fragmented and consistent blocs of disagreement were hard to discern. This began to change in the 1990s and justices' decision-making patterns became easier to identify. Court watchers noticed the formation of blocs of opinion among justices with regard to section 15, section 1, and legal rights interpretation. In the recent period, however, McCormick detects a "marvelous democratization of disagreement, with everyone taking a turn and no one taking too many."[55]

The degree of disagreement among justices is itself an interesting object of institutional analysis. But it leads to questions about the basis of disagreement. Why do learned judges disagree with one another when they are exposed to the same facts, the same law, and the same arguments? The traditional legal or "formalist" model of judicial decision-making suggests that legal problems are amenable to legal solutions; legal criteria yield a single correct answer to legal disputes. However important this model is for supporting the principle of an independent, impartial judiciary charged with declaring what the law is, it cannot explain what actually happens. Judges do disagree with one another frequently and, more interesting, their disagreements follow patterns. For example, Justice L'Heureux-Dubé, who dissented often, was not merely a contrarian on the Court. Her votes and reasons indicate a consistently activist approach to section 15 equality rights claims, particularly in cases involving women's rights claims.[56] And, when she dissented in cases like these, she would frequently cite as precedent her own previous dissenting reasons. She also consistently voted for the government brief in cases involving criminal legal rights. By contrast, Justice Sopinka and Chief Justice Lamer generally sided with *Charter* claimants (accused persons) in criminal legal rights cases, even when granting that the *Charter* claim would run contrary to the interests of female victims of crime.[57] Justices La Forest and Gonthier tended to be more sensitive to the limitations of courts in settling disputes involving evidence on which courts are not expert.[58]

Decision-making patterns like these indicate that the legal model is simplistic. Other explanations include the personal-attribute model, according to which certain traits or attributes of judges—for example, their religion, professional experience, place of birth, and upbringing—influence their decision making.[59] Scholars have also developed the powerful attitudinal model, according to which judges are understood to possess public policy preferences. They advance those preferences by picking from particular cases those precedents and interpretive principles that support their preferred results in a persuasive, legally accept-

---

55 Peter McCormick, "Blocs, Swarms, and Outliers: Conceptualizing Disagreement on the Modern Supreme Court of Canada" (2004) 42 *Osgoode Hall Law Journal* 99.

56 See *Symes v. Canada*, [1993] 4 S.C.R 695, and *Thibaudeau v. Canada*, [1995] 2 S.C.R. 627.

57 See *R. v. Seaboyer*, case 16.

58 See *RJR-MacDonald*, *supra* note 53.

59 See Donald R. Songer and Susan W. Johnson, "Judicial Decision Making in the Supreme Court of Canada: Updating the Personal Attribute Model" (2007) 40 *Canadian Journal of Political Science* 911.

able manner.[60] Related to the attitudinal model is the strategic model of judicial decision making, according to which judges will vote strategically, sometimes against their deeply felt preferences, in order to maximize the chances that those preferences will be reflected in the policies of other institutional actors in other branches of government.[61] Strategic behaviour may operate in the manner in which justices decide to grant or deny leave to appeal to the Court. For example, a judge who favours the lower court result in a case being appealed to the Supreme Court may vote to deny leave if she thinks that her colleagues would vote to reverse on the merits. It also undoubtedly operates in the negotiations among justices and in the drafting of opinions to attract votes to convert either dissenting or plurality judgments into a majority ruling. Canadian scholarship has a long way to go to catch up with American writing on this dimension of law and politics, but Canadians are increasingly aware that *Charter* decision making is not a simple matter of appointing persons of the right technical qualifications to the Supreme Court. Growing interest in Supreme Court appointment reform is ample testimony to this.[62]

THE CHARTER AND CANADIAN DEMOCRACY

The foregoing discussion makes clear that *Charter* review entangles the courts, particularly the Supreme Court, in policy making. The Court frequently insists that it refrains from pronouncing on the merits or wisdom of particular policies or laws and that it merely measures laws and policies against a constitutional standard, but its assurances do not entirely succeed. The constitutional standards are vague and the evidence of actual judicial decision making indicates that there is more discretion available to judges, especially high court judges, than a superficial impression suggests. As Christopher Manfredi has argued, judicial review highlights a paradox of liberal democratic constitutionalism. Liberal democracy is constitutional democracy—democracy subject to certain principled limits contained in the Constitution and applied by courts. Courts should be independent of the political departments of government so that law can be applied, and seen to be applied, impartially. But if judicial review is inescapably "political"—that is, entangling courts in public policy decisions made by the representative chambers of government—then such

---

60 The classic text on the attitudinal model is Jeffrey A. Segal and Harold J. Spaeth, *The Supreme Court and the Attitudinal Model Revisited* (New York: Cambridge University Press, 2002). For a review of early Canadian work on this topic, see Thaddeus Hwong, "A Review of Quantitative Studies of Decision Making in the Supreme Court of Canada" (2004) 30 *Manitoba Law Journal* 353. For more recent work, see C.L. Ostberg and Matthew E. Wetstein, *Attitudinal Decision Making in the Supreme Court of Canada* (Vancouver: University of British Columbia Press, 2007).

61 The classic works here are Walter F. Murphy, *Elements of Judicial Strategy* (Chicago: University of Chicago Press, 1964), and Lee Epstein and Jack Knight, *The Choices Judges Make* (Washington: Congressional Quarterly Press, 1998). For Canadian work in this field, see Manfredi and Kelly, *supra* note 39.

62 See Christopher P. Manfredi, "Strategic Behaviour and the Canadian Charter of Rights and Freedoms" in Patrick James et al., eds., *The Myth of the Sacred: The Charter, the Courts, and the Politics of the Constitution in Canada* (Montreal and Kingston: McGill-Queen's University Press, 2002) 147.

independence becomes as problematic as it is salutary. Liberal constitutionalism requires that independent courts impartially enforce the law. Democratic principles require that courts be accountable for the policy-laden decisions they render. *Charter* review puts courts in an awkward relation to the representative institutions of democratic government.[63]

Three issues flow from the paradox of liberal constitutionalism. First, civil society actors routinely and systematically attempt to use *Charter* review to achieve policy objectives they cannot or will not obtain in the representative chambers of government. Second, observers have inquired whether the *Charter* has produced a "juristocracy"[64] in Canada, in which the judges are the philosopher-kings. Third, the paradox has stimulated some political actors to reform the judicial appointment process in Canada, making more transparent and democratically accountable a process that has until recently escaped most Canadians' attention.

The *Charter* provides strong incentives for interest groups to pursue their policy objectives through the courts rather than through lobbying elected politicians and public servants. The classic argument for this is that majoritarian institutions are inherently insensitive to minoritarian rights claims and that courts, as "forums of principle," act on arguments of principle regardless of how many legislators support them. But this argument assumes that there is a bright line distinguishing claims of right and claims of policy interest. Such bright lines rarely exist. More common is the pursuit of policy objectives articulated as *Charter* rights claims by means of litigation strategies.[65] Is this an abuse of the judicial process? Individuals or groups that can make a plausible rights-based claim and have standing before a court are limited only by their available resources and of their prospects of success. If courts are receptive to rights-based arguments with significant policy implications, why should groups or individuals not be permitted to litigate? The entrenchment of the *Charter* was widely understood from the beginning to judicialize politics and politicize the judiciary. Further, as Gregory Hein has suggested, the *Charter* is available to all parties of all partisan and ideological persuasions, and *Charter* review can be considered a healthy, dynamic, and ultimately democratic means of securing rights in Canada.[66] On the other hand, to the extent that interest groups ask courts to advance policy objectives, they ask judges to do what judges disavow and what courts are institutionally unfit to do. The long-term public reputation of courts as independent and impartial tribunals may suffer.

The second issue concerns what role legislatures have with respect to *Charter* review. Are they now impotent observers of the politics of rights, increasingly passed over in favour of policy making by the courts, and without recourse themselves? The *Charter*, of course, does

---

63   Christopher P. Manfredi, *Judicial Power and the Charter: Canada and the Paradox of Liberal Constitutionalism*, 2d ed. (Toronto: Oxford University Press, 2001).

64   Ran Hirschl, *Towards Juristocracy: The Origins and Consequences of the New Constitutionalism* (Cambridge, MA: Harvard University Press, 2004).

65   The classic work on the litigation strategy of the American National Association for the Advancement of Coloured People is Richard Kluger, *Simple Justice: The History of Brown v. Board of Education and Black America's Struggle for Equality* (New York: Knopf, 1975). In the Canadian context, see M. Elizabeth Atcheson et al., *Women and Legal Action: Precedents, Resources, and Strategies for the Future* (Ottawa: Canadian Advisory Council on the Status of Women, 1984).

66   Gregory Hein, "Interest Group Litigation and Canadian Democracy" (2000) 6 *Choices* 3 (retrieved from <http://www.irpp.org/fasttrak/index.htm>).

contain the section 33 notwithstanding clause, but politicians have become extremely wary of invoking it. The popularity of the *Charter* and citizens' greater confidence in judges' versus legislators' judgments about the meaning of the *Charter*[67] all militate against its use. Although the notwithstanding clause has been used 16 times, many uses of this power occurred in the early years of the *Charter*.[68] Moreover, most uses of the clause did not set aside judicial decisions but pre-empted judicial review and protected policy distinctions before it was clear how the Court would rule.[69] But in the past 20 years, the notwithstanding clause has become so politically contentious that it has been rendered, in one commentator's eyes, a "paper tiger."[70] Prime Minister Paul Martin damaged Conservative leader Stephen Harper's electoral prospects in the 2004 federal election campaign by accusing him of willingness to use section 33 to protect the traditional definition of marriage from the *Charter*. Harper learned his lesson and has since disavowed any resort to the clause on the same-sex marriage issue.

What else can governments do? In an influential study, Peter Hogg and Allison Thornton have argued that, in fact, there is an active and fruitful dialogue between the courts and legislatures on *Charter* issues even when section 33 is not invoked.[71] Especially when, as is usually the case, the Court merely quarrels with the means a law uses to achieve an objective, legislatures can respond by fine-tuning the law. The dialogue theory quickly achieved Supreme Court support when it was cited approvingly in *Vriend v. Alberta*.[72] And there are many other instances, some of them described in this collection of Supreme Court decisions, in which dialogue theory has played a prominent role.

Not everyone accepts dialogue theory, however. Critics argue that a more accurate metaphor to describe the institutional relationship between courts and legislatures under the *Charter* is monologue[73] or ventriloquism[74] because courts generally dominate the conversation, leaving Parliament only the option of replicating judicial suggestions, rather than making independent choices.

Noting that courts normally strike down laws based on the proportionality criteria outlined in *Oakes* is not a complete answer to concerns about the political power of courts. One concern with this emphasis on proportionality criteria is that it stresses the particular aspect of judicial review—the evaluation of the quality of how a legislative goal is being pursued— that challenges the skills and expertise that judges reasonably possess. Scrutinizing how policy is developed is inherently value-laden and subjective, as is the development of policy

---

67 Nik Nanos, "The Charter Values Don't Equal Canadian Values: Strong Support for Same-Sex and Property Rights" (2007) 28 *Policy Options* 50.

68 Tsvi Kahana, "The Notwithstanding Mechanism and Public Discussion: Lessons from the Ignored Practice of Section 33 of the Charter" (2001) 44 *Canadian Public Administration* 255.

69 This interpretation is drawn from a review of all uses of this power, as compiled by Kahana, *ibid.*

70 Leeson, *supra* note 28.

71 See Peter Hogg and Allison Thornton, "The Charter Dialogue Between Courts and Legislatures (Or Perhaps the Charter Isn't Such a Bad Thing After All)" (1997) 35 *Osgoode Hall Law Journal* 7.

72 [1998] 1 S.C.R. 493.

73 F.L. Morton, "Dialogue or Monologue?" in Howe and Russell, *supra* note 28 at 111.

74 Christopher P. Manfredi and James B. Kelly, "Six Degrees of Dialogue: A Response to Hogg and Bushell" (1999) 37 *Osgoode Hall Law Journal* 513.

itself. It is rarely possible to identify precisely how best to achieve a particular legislative goal because those developing legislation do so in a policy environment of competing data about whether identified policy means will be effective when addressing the policy objective and uncertainty about whether and how the policy goals will affect the behaviour, attitudes, and expectations of those who are affected. Nevertheless, the Court's approach ensures that it will regularly have to don the hat of the policy analyst in assessing whether the way Parliament or a provincial legislature pursues its intended goals compares favourably with some other hypothetical policy scheme.[75]

But there is another important implication for the dialogue thesis of the Court's approach to section 1 of the *Charter*. The Court's reliance on predictable and regularly cited criteria for evaluating impugned legislation, when combined with the frequency with which legislation is found to have *Charter* implications, has encouraged public officials to develop legislation that anticipates and tries to satisfy judicial concerns. This is happening throughout the country, but has become particularly entrenched at the federal level. James Kelly argues that a significant transformation has occurred in how proposed legislation is evaluated. This is the result of the introduction of a *Charter* screening process that has increased the role and influence of government lawyers in the policy process. Kelly interprets the use of *Charter* norms in pre-legislative evaluations, and their influence on Cabinet decisions, as evidence that a new bureaucratic rights culture has emerged that allows government to implement its legislative agenda in a manner consistent with the *Charter*.[76]

One manifestation of this *Charter*-oriented focus on policy is a new requirement that *Charter* issues be anticipated and certain associated risks identified as part of the process for securing approval before an initiative can go to Cabinet for consideration. Consequently, the policy governing the Memorandum to Cabinet was changed in 1991 to include *Charter* analysis in terms of "an assessment of the risk of successful challenge in the courts, the impact of adverse decisions, and possible litigation costs."[77] A second way this objective of protecting legislation from *Charter* vulnerability has been pursued is by placing more emphasis in policy evaluation on determining ways to lower the risk of litigation and invalidation, in particular, by replicating and applying the Court's proportionality criteria.[78] This emphasis on *Charter* compatibility, which is equated with consistency with judicial section 1 considerations, has enhanced significantly the influence of governmental lawyers in the policy process, whose role has changed from being the provider of "a technical review of legislation to a substantive role in the development of new policy," so much so that other departments now regularly rely on its advice in the course of developing legislation.[79] Many

---

75   Janet L. Hiebert, *Charter Conflicts: What Is Parliament's Role?* (Montreal and Kingston: McGill-Queen's University Press, 2002) at 58.

76   Kelly, *supra* note 51.

77   Mary Dawson, "The Impact of the Charter on the Public Policy Process and the Department of Justice" in Patrick Monahan and Marie Finkelstein, eds., *The Impact of the Charter on the Public Policy Process* (Toronto: York University Centre for Public Law and Public Policy, 1993) 53.

78   Hiebert, *supra* note 75 at 9-10.

79   James B. Kelly, "Bureaucratic Activism and the Charter of Rights and Freedoms: The Department of Justice and Its Entry into the Centre of Government" (1999) 42 *Canadian Public Administration* 494.

provincial governments have also adopted procedures to identify and redress *Charter* concerns before legislation is introduced to the legislature.[80]

Yet not all political actors believe this emphasis on *Charter* compatibility necessary leads to better policy. As one former provincial attorney general states:[81]

> In my experience, *Charter* compliance in the legislative process is inherently reactive, rather than proactive, as it requires government to approach policy-making from the perspective of risk analysis rather than from the perspective of broader social and economic priorities or the balancing of differing societal interests. In other words, although the question "is this legislation *Charter*-compliant?" often leads to a different answer than the question "is this legislation good public policy?," the former question often takes precedence in public policy analysis. As a result, risk management becomes the driver of the analysis.

Arguably, the most significant way judicial rulings affect legislation is indirect—through the incorporation of judicial criteria in the policy process. This form of judicial influence is substantial because it has the potential to affect the entire range of a government's policy agenda. Only a fraction of the legislation Parliament or a provincial legislature passes is ever subject to *Charter* litigation, and only a small portion of that is successfully litigated. But adopting judicial criteria to modify legislative objectives and their means ensures judicial influence on a day-to-day level, even when legislation is never subject to *Charter* litigation.

The final issue stemming from the paradox of liberal constitutionalism concerns judicial appointment. High Court judges have historically been appointed by means of quiet consultations between senior Justice Department officials and members of the legal community, leading to formal appointment by the Cabinet. The Prime Minister himself would make the decision regarding appointments to the Supreme Court of Canada. This constantly raises the ire of provincial politicians who argue that, in division-of-powers disputes, one of the players of the game was able to bring his own referee.

More recently, elected politicians have declared that some form of public, parliamentary process is needed to vet nominees to the Supreme Court. Paul Martin broached the matter in 2003 and, as Prime Minister, oversaw an interim process according to which the names, curriculum vitae, and decisional output of two nominees, Justices Charron and Abella, were considered. This was a breakthrough for Canadian judicial appointment, but far short of what reformers had hoped. However, it was already much more than what others thought was advisable in a liberal democracy. Judicial independence would be compromised, they argued, if nominees were subjected to questioning by elected politicians before their appointment. The judiciary would be "politicized." Advocates of a more open process, of course, replied that the judiciary is already politicized, which is why the need for a more open process exists.

In the fall of 2005, the Martin Liberal government established an Advisory Committee to assist it in filling the vacancy created on the Court when Justice Major reached the mandatory retirement age of 75. The nine-person Advisory Committee consisted of four MPs (one from each party), a retired judge chosen by the Canadian Judicial Council, a lawyer chosen by the Law Societies of the Prairie provinces (Justice Major was from Alberta), a

---

80 Kelly, *supra* note 51 at 214.

81 Geoffrey Plant, "Governing in the Shadow of the Charter" (2007) paper presented at the Canadian Bar Association Conference, Calgary, June 1, 2007 (unpublished).

representative of the three Prairie provinces, and two lay persons of "integrity and distinction" from the region chosen by Justice Minister Irving Cotler. The committee was given the limited role of assessing the merits of five to eight persons selected by the Justice Minister and passing on their assessments to the government.

By the time the Advisory Committee process was completed, an election had been called resulting in a change of government. The leader of the newly elected Conservative government, Stephen Harper, completed the final stage of the process introduced by the Liberals and added an important new step of his own. From the Advisory Committee's list of three names, Prime Minister Harper chose Mr. Justice Rothstein of the Federal Court of Appeal. He then invited Justice Rothstein to be interviewed by an ad hoc committee of parliamentarians. On February 27, 2006, Canadians had an opportunity to witness this extraordinary development in public law on national television. The committee did not vote on his "nomination" and had no other names to consider. Members were unfailingly polite and discreet in their questioning. After the hearing the government appointed Justice Rothstein in the usual manner.

The process stitched together by the Martin and Liberal governments left the impression that reforming the method of appointing Supreme Court justices is still very much a work in progress. Regardless, Canada has undoubtedly entered a new era in judicial appointment politics. The tentative movement toward a more open process for appointments to its highest court is in step with developments elsewhere in the world. And the rationale for the reforms comports with the salient policy role of courts in post-*Charter* Canada.[82] Further refinements of the appointment reform process will undoubtedly be sought as the government seeks a replacement for Justice Michel Bastarache, who retired in 2008.

CONCLUSION

Studying the life and times of Canada's *Charter of Rights and Freedoms* shows how difficult it is to separate the realms of law and politics. Eliminating the political context in which the *Charter* came into being and the political forces with which it interacts would make it impossible to understand its unfolding meaning in Canadian life. And yet, although we readily acknowledge this, we also insist that the *Charter* and its interpretation by the courts are not simply an undifferentiated part of the political process. Citizens in a constitutional democracy have expectations of non-partisan rationality and—dare we say it?—justice in the decisions of the judicial arbiters of their constitutional rights, expectations that they do not apply to the avowedly political branches of government. The challenge for the judges and for those who assess their work is to ascertain how such expectations are best satisfied.

---

82   On recent reforms to the federal judicial appointment process, see Lorne B. Neudorf, "Independence and the Public Process: Evolution or Erosion?" (2007) 70 *Saskatchewan Law Review* 93; Kate Malleson, "Parliamentary Scrutiny of Supreme Court Nominees: A View from the United Kingdom" (2006) 44 *Osgoode Hall Law Journal* 557; and Jacob Ziegel, "A New Era in the Selection of Supreme Court Judges?" (2006) 44 *Osgoode Hall Law Journal* 547. For a general comparative examination of judicial appointment, see Kate Malleson and Peter H. Russell, eds., *Appointing Judges in an Age of Judicial Power: Critical Perspectives from Around the World* (Toronto: University of Toronto Press, 2006).

PART ONE
The Pre-Charter Era

Reference re Alberta Statutes (Alberta Press Case), 1938

Until 1982, the Canadian Constitution, unlike that of the United States, did not contain a comprehensive bill of rights protecting a list of fundamental civil liberties from legislative encroachment. The enactment of the *Canadian Bill of Rights* in 1960 did not change that situation. The *Canadian Bill of Rights* was simply a federal statute, not an amendment to the *B.N.A. Act*. As such, it did not apply to the provinces and, even at the federal level, could be set aside by ordinary federal legislation. Besides, as the *Lavell and Bédard*[1] case shows, the Supreme Court was reluctant to give much weight to its provisions.

The absence of a comprehensive charter of rights in the *B.N.A. Act*, however, did not mean that no entrenched constitutional rights could be found there. The mistake was often made of stating that the powers of self-government had been exhaustively distributed between the two levels of government provided for in the *B.N.A. Act*. According to this "exhaustion theory," the only constitutional limitation on legislative supremacy in Canada prior to 1982 was the division of legislative powers. But this theory was a slight exaggeration. Sections 93 and 133 of the *B.N.A. Act* enshrine minority education and language rights[2] that it would appear cannot be diminished by either federal or provincial legislation without a constitutional amendment. In addition, constitutional safeguards of more fundamental rights may be implied by some of the institutional provisions of the *B.N.A. Act*. For instance, section 99, providing security of tenure for the judges of Superior Courts (Canada's trial courts for the most serious civil and criminal cases), restricts the legislative powers not only of the provinces but of the federal Parliament as well.[3]

In the *Alberta Press* case, constitutional protection of another cluster of rights of fundamental importance to the practice of liberal democracy was first suggested in the reasons given by Chief Justice Duff and Justice Cannon for declaring Alberta's *Accurate News and Information Act* unconstitutional. The federal government had asked the Supreme Court to examine the constitutional validity of this *Act* along with two other Social Credit Bills enacted by the Alberta Legislature in 1937. The other two *Acts* concerned some of the regulations and institutions required for a Social Credit system of credit and exchange. The *Accurate News and Information Act* was designed to ensure that newspaper presentation of Social Credit policy satisfied the government's criterion of accuracy. The Supreme Court unanimously found all three *Acts ultra vires*. Only its decision on the *Bank Taxation Act* was appealed to the Privy Council.

Chief Justice Duff's opinion, with which Justice Davis concurred, characterized the *Accurate News and Information Act* as legislation affecting the "right of free public discussion of public affairs." This right, he maintained, is essential for the proper working of the parliamentary system of government called for by those sections of the *B.N.A. Act* vesting legislative

---

1 See case 2.

2 See the introduction to case 31.

3 See *McEvoy v. Attorney General for New Brunswick*, [1983] 1 S.C.R. 704.

power at the national level in a federal parliament and by the reference in the *B.N.A. Act*'s preamble to "a constitution similar in Principle to that of the United Kingdom." He considered provincial legislation abrogating this right to be unconstitutional. While he stated that the federal Parliament was empowered to protect this right, he did not suggest that it was beyond Ottawa's power to restrict it. While Justice Cannon also held that the Alberta legislation should be struck down because it interfered with the freedom of discussion essential to a democratic state, he based his opinion on a more conventional division-of-powers ground. Legislation curtailing freedom of the press was traditionally part of the criminal law and therefore could be enacted only by the federal Parliament under its exclusive criminal law power.

If one looks only at the Court's prior decisions, the invocation of an implied bill of rights by three of its members is somewhat surprising, especially since it was unnecessary to invalidating the legislation. As Carl Baar notes, "[t]he Court had no record of support for civil liberties," and Justice Duff himself, a British Columbian, "had written opinions in previous years that reflected the anti-oriental sentiments of the Canadian west coast."[4] The answer to this riddle appears to lie in the political context in which the decision was made. The federal government had already disallowed earlier Social Credit legislation in Alberta and disallowance was seriously considered in this case. One argument in favour of disallowance was that it could be justified on the broad ground of protecting freedom of speech and press, while judicial invalidation was likely to focus on narrow jurisdictional considerations. On the other hand, too frequent resort to disallowance could be seen as an attack on the province by a heavy-handed central government. Ottawa chose a legal reference, but its own factum clearly invited an implied-bill-of-rights interpretation. In addition, most of the public criticism of the Press Bill was based on civil libertarian considerations. Given the widespread consensus on the importance of a free press, "it was both politically safe and politically heroic for the Supreme Court to defend civil liberties."[5] It was an inviting context for a new departure. ～

Discussion Questions

1. On what parts of the Constitution did Chief Justice Duff base his finding of an implied right to free public discussion?
2. What is the "exhaustion theory" of the Canadian Constitution? How does Chief Justice Duff's opinion depart from it, and how is Justice Cannon's opinion consistent with it?
3. To what extent was Chief Justice Duff's doctrine of implied rights followed by the Supreme Court in subsequent cases?
4. What are the limitations of an implied rights doctrine?

---

4   Carl Baar, "Using Process Theory to Explain Judicial Decision Making" (1986) 1 *Canadian Journal of Law and Society* 73.

5   *Ibid.* at 74.

REFERENCE RE ALBERTA STATUTES
[1938] 2 S.C.R. 100

Hearing: January 11, 12, 13, 14, 17, 1938; Judgment: March 4, 1938.

Present: Duff C.J. and Cannon, Crocket, Davis, Kerwin, and Hudson JJ.

DUFF C.J.:

[The Chief Justice first examined the constitutional validity of the *Bank Taxation Act* and the *Credit of Alberta Regulation Act* and concluded that both of these bills were *ultra vires*.]

We now turn to Bill No. 9.

This Bill contains two substantive provisions. Both of them impose duties upon newspapers published in Alberta which they are required to perform on the demand of "the Chairman," who is, by the interpretation clause, the Chairman of "the Board constituted by section 3 of [t]he *Alberta Social Credit Act.*"

The Board, upon the acts of whose Chairman the operation of this statute depends, is, in point of law, a non-existent body (there is, in a word, no "board" in existence "constituted by section 3 of [t]he *Alberta Social Credit Act*") and both of the substantive sections, sections 3 and 4, are, therefore, inoperative. The same, indeed, may be said of sections 6 and 7 which are the enactments creating sanctions. It appears to us, furthermore, that this Bill is a part of the general scheme of Social Credit legislation, the basis of which is [t]he *Alberta Social Credit Act*; the Bill presupposes, as a condition of its operation, that [t]he *Alberta Social Credit Act* is validly enacted; and since that Act is *ultra vires*, the ancillary and dependent legislation must fall with it.

This is sufficient for disposing of the question referred to us but, we think, there are some further observations upon the Bill which may properly be made.

Under the constitution established by [t]he *British North America Act*, legislative power for Canada is vested in one Parliament consisting of the Sovereign, an upper house styled the Senate, and the House of Commons. Without entering in detail upon an examination of the enactments of the *Act* relating to the House of Commons, it can be said that these provisions manifestly contemplate a House of Commons which is to be, as the name itself implies, a representative body; constituted, that is to say, by members elected by such of the population of the united provinces as may be qualified to vote. The preamble of the statute, moreover, shows plainly enough that the constitution of the Dominion is to be similar in principle to that of the United Kingdom. The statute contemplates a parliament working under the influence of public opinion and public discussion. There can be no controversy that such institutions derive their efficacy from the free public discussion of affairs, from criticism and answer and counter-criticism, from attack upon policy and administration and defence and counter-attack; from the freest and fullest analysis and examination from every point of view of political proposals. This is signally true in respect of the discharge by Ministers of the Crown of their responsibility to Parliament, by members of Parliament of their duty to the electors, and by the electors themselves of their responsibilities in the election of their representatives.

The right of public discussion is, of course, subject to legal restrictions; those based upon considerations of decency and public order, and others conceived for the protection of various private and public interests with which, for example, the laws of defamation and sedition are concerned. In a word, freedom of discussion means, to quote the words of Lord Wright in *James v. Commonwealth* [[1936] A.C. 578, at 627], "freedom governed by law."

Even within its legal limits, it is liable to abuse and grave abuse, and such abuse is constantly exemplified before our eyes; but it is axiomatic that the practice of this right of free public discussion of public affairs, notwithstanding its incidental mischiefs, is the breath of life for parliamentary institutions.

We do not doubt that (in addition to the power of disallowance vested in the Governor General) the Parliament of Canada possesses authority to legislate for the protection of this right. That authority rests upon the principle that the powers requisite for the protection of the constitution itself arise by necessary implication from [t]he *British North America Act* as a whole (*Fort Frances Pulp & Power Co. Ltd. v. Manitoba Free Press Co. Ltd.* [[1923] A.C. 695]); and since the subject-matter in relation to which the power is exercised is not exclusively a provincial matter, it is necessarily vested in Parliament.

But this by no means exhausts the matter. Any attempt to abrogate this right of public debate or to suppress the traditional forms of the exercise of the right (in public meeting and through the press) would, in our opinion, be incompetent to the legislatures of the provinces, or to the legislature of any one of the provinces, as repugnant to the provisions of [t]he *British North America Act*, by which the Parliament of Canada is established as the legislative organ of the people of Canada under the Crown, and Dominion legislation enacted pursuant to the legislative authority given by those provisions. The subject matter of such legislation could not be described as a provincial matter purely; as in substance exclusively a matter of property and civil rights within the province, or a matter private or local within the province. It would not be, to quote the words of the judgment of the Judicial Committee in *Great West Saddlery Co. v. The King* [[1921] 2 A.C. 91, at 122], "legislation directed solely to the purposes specified in section 92"; and it would be invalid on the principles enunciated in that judgment and adopted in *Caron v. The King* [[1924] A.C. 999 at 1005-6].

The question, discussed in argument, of the validity of the legislation before us, considered as a wholly independent enactment having no relation to the *Alberta Social Credit Act*, presents no little difficulty. Some degree of regulation of newspapers everybody would concede to the provinces. Indeed, there is a very wide field in which the provinces undoubtedly are invested with legislative authority over newspapers; but the limit, in our opinion, is reached when the legislation effects such a curtailment of the exercise of the right of public discussion as substantially to interfere with the working of the parliamentary institutions of Canada as contemplated by the provisions of [t]he *British North America Act* and the statutes of the Dominion of Canada. Such a limitation is necessary, in our opinion, "in order," to adapt the words quoted above from the judgment in *Bank of Toronto v. Lambe* [(1887), 12 A.C. 575] "to afford scope" for the working of such parliamentary institutions. In this region of constitutional practice, it is not permitted to a provincial legislature to do indirectly what cannot be done directly (*Great West Saddlery Co. v. The King* [[1921] 2 A.C. 91 at 100]).

Section 129 of [t]he *British North America Act* is in these words:

> 129. Except as otherwise provided by this *Act*, all Laws in force in Canada, Nova Scotia or New Brunswick, at the Union, and all Courts of Civil and Criminal Jurisdiction, and all legal Commissions, Powers, and Authorities, and all Officers, Judicial, Administrative, and Ministerial, existing therein at the Union, shall continue in Ontario, Quebec, Nova Scotia, and New Brunswick respectively, as if the Union had not been made; subject nevertheless (except with respect to such as are enacted by or exist under *Acts* of the Parliament of Great Britain or of the Parliament of the United Kingdom of Great Britain and Ireland), to be repealed, abolished, or altered by the Parliament of Canada, or by the Legislature of the respective Province, according to the Authority of the Parliament or of that Legislature under this *Act*.

The law by which the right of public discussion is protected existed at the time of the enactment of [t]he *British North America Act* and, as far as Alberta is concerned, at the date on which the *Alberta Act* came into force, the 1st of September, 1905. In our opinion (on the broad principle of the cases mentioned which has been recognized as limiting the scope of general words defining the legislative authority of the Dominion) the Legislature of Alberta has not the capacity

under section 129 to alter that law by legislation obnoxious to the principle stated.

The legislation now under consideration manifestly places in the hands of the Chairman of the Social Credit Commission autocratic powers which, it may well be thought, could, if arbitrarily wielded, be employed to frustrate in Alberta these rights of the Crown and the people of Canada as a whole. We do not, however, find it necessary to express an opinion upon the concrete question whether or not this particular measure is invalid as exceeding the limits indicated above.

The answer to the question concerning this Bill is that it is *ultra vires.*

CANNON J.:

[Justice Cannon first examined the *Bank Taxation Act* and the *Credit of Alberta Regulation Act* and concluded that both were *ultra vires.*]

The third question put to us is the following:

> Is Bill No. 9, entitled *An Act to ensure the Publication of Accurate News and Information,* or any of the provisions thereof and in what particular or particulars or to what extent *intra vires* of the legislature of the province of Alberta?

. . . The preamble of the bill, which I will hereafter call the "Press bill" recites that it is

> expedient and in the public interest that the newspapers published in the Province should furnish to the people of the Province statements made by the authority of the Government of the Province as to the true and exact objects of the policy of the Government and as to the hindrances to or difficulties in achieving such objects to the end that the people may be informed with respect thereto.

Section 3 provides that any proprietor, editor, publisher or manager of any newspaper published in the province shall, when required to do so by the Chairman of the Board constituted by section 3 of the *Alberta Social Credit Act,* publish in that newspaper any statement furnished by the Chairman which has for its object the correction or amplification of any statement relating to any policy or activity of the government of the province published by that newspaper within the next preceding thirty-one days.

And section 4 provides that the proprietor, etc., of any newspaper upon being required by the Chairman in writing shall within twenty-four hours after the delivery of the requirement

> make a return in writing setting out every source from which any information emanated, as to any statement

contained in any issue of the newspaper published within sixty days of the making of the requirement and the names, addresses and occupations of all persons by whom such information was furnished to the newspaper and the name and address of the writer of any editorial, article or news item contained in any such issue of the newspaper.

Section 5 denies any action for libel on account of the publication of any statement pursuant to the *Act*.

Section 6 enacts that in the event of a proprietor, etc., of any newspaper being guilty of any contravention of any of the provisions of the *Act*, the Lieutenant-Governor-in-Council, upon a recommendation of the Chairman, may by order prohibit,

> (a) the publication of such newspaper either for a definite time or until further order;
> (b) the publication in any newspaper of anything written by any person specified in the order;
> (c) the publication of any information emanating from any person or source specified in the order.

Section 7 provides for penalties for contraventions or defaults in complying with any requirement of the *Act*.

The policy referred to in the preamble of the Press bill regarding which the people of the province are to be informed from the government standpoint is undoubtedly the Social Credit policy of the government. The administration of the bill is in the hands of the Chairman of the Social Credit Board who is given complete and discretionary power by the bill. "Social Credit," according to sec. 2(b) of ch. 3, 1937, second session, of [t]he *Alberta Social Credit Amendment Act* is

> the power resulting from the belief inherent within society that its individual members in association can gain the objectives they desire;

and the objectives in which the people of Alberta must have a firm and unshaken belief are the monetization of credit and the creation of a provincial medium of exchange instead of money to be used for the purpose of distributing to Albertans loans without interest, per capita dividends and discount rates to purchase goods from retailers. This free distribution would be based on the unused capacity of the industries and people of the province of Alberta to produce goods and services, which capacity remains unused on account of the lack or absence of purchasing power in the consumers in the province. The purchasing power would equal or absorb this hitherto unused capacity to produce goods and services by the issue of Treasury Credit certificates against a Credit Fund or Provincial credit account established by the Commission each year representing the monetary value of this "unused capacity"— which is also called "Alberta credit."

It seems obvious that this kind of credit cannot succeed unless every one should be induced to believe in it and help it along. The word "credit" comes from the latin: *credere*, to believe. It is, therefore, essential to control the sources of information of the people of Alberta, in order to keep them immune from any vacillation in their absolute faith in the plan of the government. The Social Credit doctrine must become, for the people of Alberta, a sort of religious dogma of which a free and uncontrolled discussion is not permissible. The bill aims to control any statement relating to any policy or activity of the government of the province and declares this object to be a matter of public interest. The bill does not regulate the relations of the newspapers' owners with private individual members of the public, but deals exclusively with expressions of opinion by the newspapers concerning government policies and activities. The pith and substance of the bill is to regulate the press of Alberta from the viewpoint of public policy by preventing the public from being misled or deceived as to any policy or activity of the Social Credit Government and by reducing any opposition to silence or bring upon it ridicule and public contempt.

I agree with the submission of the Attorney-General for Canada that this bill deals with the regulation of the press of Alberta, not from the viewpoint of private wrongs or civil injuries resulting from any alleged infringement or privation of civil rights which belong to individuals, considered as individuals, but from the viewpoint of public wrongs or crimes, i.e., involving a violation of the public rights and duties to the whole community, considered as a community, in its social aggregate capacity.

Do the provisions of this bill, as alleged by the Attorney-General for Canada, invade the domain of criminal law and trench upon the exclusive legislative jurisdiction of the Dominion of this regard?

The object of an amendment of the criminal law, as a rule, is to deprive the citizen of the right to do that [which], apart from the amendment, he could lawfully do. Sections 130 to 136 of the *Criminal Code* deal with seditious words and seditious publications; and sect. 133(a) reads as follows:—

> No one shall be deemed to have a seditious intention only because he intends in good faith,—
> (a) to show that His Majesty has been misled or mistaken in his measures; or
> (b) to point out errors or defect in the government or constitution of the United Kingdom, or of any part of it, or of Canada or any province thereof, or in either House of Parliament of the United Kingdom or of Canada, or in any legislature, or in the administration of justice; or to excite His Majesty's subjects to attempt to procure, by lawful means, the alteration of any matter of state; or

(c) to point out, in order to their removal, matters which are producing or have a tendency to produce feelings of hatred and ill-will between different classes of His Majesty's subjects.

It appears that in England, at first, criticism of any government policy was regarded as a crime involving severe penalties and punishable as such; but since the passing of *Fox's Libel Act* in 1792, the considerations now found in the above article of our criminal code that it is not criminal to point out errors in the Government of the country and to urge their removal by lawful means have been admitted as a valid defence in a trial for libel.

Now, it seems to me that the Alberta legislature by this retrograde Bill is attempting to revive the old theory of the crime of seditious libel by enacting penalties, confiscation of space in newspapers and prohibitions for actions which, after due consideration by the Dominion Parliament, have been declared innocuous and which, therefore, every citizen of Canada can do lawfully and without hindrance or fear of punishment. It is an attempt by the legislature to amend the *Criminal Code* in this respect and to deny the advantage of sect. 133(a) to the Alberta newspaper publishers.

Under the British system, which is ours, no political party can erect a prohibitory barrier to prevent the electors from getting information concerning the policy of the government. Freedom of discussion is essential to enlighten public opinion in a democratic State; it cannot be curtailed without affecting the right of the people to be informed through sources independent of the government concerning matters of public interest. There must be an untrammelled publication of the news and political opinions of the political parties contending for ascendancy. As stated in the preamble of [t]he *British North America Act*, our constitution is and will remain, unless radically changed, "similar in principle to that of the United Kingdom." At the time of Confederation, the United Kingdom was a democracy. Democracy cannot be maintained without its foundation: free public opinion and free discussion throughout the nation of all matters affecting the State within the limits set by the criminal code and the common law. Every

inhabitant in Alberta is also a citizen of the Dominion. The province may deal with his property and civil rights of a local and private nature within the province; but the province cannot interfere with his status as a Canadian citizen and his fundamental right to express freely his untrammelled opinion about government policies and discuss matters of public concern. The mandatory and prohibitory provisions of the Press Bill are, in my opinion, *ultra vires* of the provincial legislature. They interfere with the free working of the political organization of the Dominion. They have a tendency to nullify the political rights of the inhabitants of Alberta, as citizens of Canada, and cannot be considered as dealing with matters purely private and local in that province. The federal parliament is the sole authority to curtail, if deemed expedient and in the public interest, the freedom of the press in discussing public affairs and the equal rights in that respect of all citizens throughout the Dominion. These subjects were matters of criminal law before Confederation, have been recognized by Parliament as criminal matters and have been expressly dealt with by the criminal code. No province has the power to reduce in that province the political rights of its citizens as compared with those enjoyed by the citizens of other provinces of Canada. Moreover, citizens outside the province of Alberta have a vital interest in having full information and comment, favourable and unfavourable, regarding the policy of the Alberta government and concerning events in that province which would, in the ordinary course, be the subject of Alberta newspapers' news items and articles.

I would, therefore, answer the question as to Bill No. 9 in the negative.

[Justice Davis concurred with Chief Justice Duff. Justices Kerwin, Crocket, and Hudson all concluded that the three bills were *ultra vires*. However, their conclusion that the Press Bill was *ultra vires* was based not on the considerations regarding freedom of the press advanced by Chief Justice Duff and Justice Cannon, but on the much narrower ground that the *Act* was ancillary to and dependent on the *Alberta Social Credit Act*, which was itself *ultra vires*.]

Attorney General of Canada v. Lavell and Bédard, 1974

A new chapter in Canadian civil liberties was inaugurated in 1960 with the enactment of the *Canadian Bill of Rights*. Technically, the new *Bill of Rights* was not an addition to Canada's formal Constitution. It was passed as an ordinary *Act* of the federal Parliament. As such it did not apply to the provinces and could be set aside by subsequent federal legislation. The *Act* had two main clauses. Section 1 declared that in Canada certain fundamental rights and freedoms "have existed and shall continue to exist without discrimination by reason of race, national origin, colour, religion or sex." It listed such fundamental rights as the right to life, liberty, security of the person, and enjoyment of property and the right not to be deprived thereof except by due process of law; the individual's right to equality before the law and protection of the law; and freedom of religion, speech, assembly, association, and the press. Section 2 provided that unless the *Bill of Rights* was explicitly set aside, every federal law shall "be so construed and applied as not to abrogate, abridge or infringe" the rights and freedoms set out in the Bill. It added to the rights listed in section 1 a list of procedural rights, including the right of arrested persons to legal counsel, *habeas corpus*, the presumption of innocence, the right to an interpreter, and the right to a fair hearing when a person's rights or duties are being determined. The final section of the Bill provided that the *Bill of Rights* would not apply to anything done under the *War Measures Act*.

The first real test of the Supreme Court's treatment of the *Bill of Rights* came in 1963 in the *Robertson and Rosetanni* case.[1] Robertson and Rosetanni had been charged with an offence under the federal *Lord's Day Act*, namely, operating a bowling alley on Sunday. On appeal their main defence was that the *Lord's Day Act* conflicted with the *Canadian Bill of Rights* and was therefore inoperative. Justice Ritchie (supported by the three Quebec justices, Taschereau, Fauteux, and Abbott) wrote the majority's opinion, dismissing the appeal. His approach to the *Bill of Rights* was basically conservative. He interpreted it not as a charter designed to enlarge the fundamental rights and freedoms of Canadians, but as a means of conserving these rights in their 1960 form. The *Canadian Bill of Rights*, he argued, "is not concerned with 'human rights and fundamental freedoms' in any abstract sense, but rather with such 'rights and freedoms' as they existed in Canada immediately before the statute was enacted." His review of Canadian history and jurisprudence revealed that the concept of religious freedom was well enshrined in Canadian law as was Lord's Day observance legislation long before 1960. Thus he concluded that the freedom of religion guaranteed by the *Bill of Rights* was not infringed by the *Lord's Day Act*. Justice Cartwright, the sole dissenter, rejected the implication in the majority's position that the *Bill of Rights* could have no effect on laws enacted before the *Bill of Rights*. In his view, section 5 made it clear that the Bill was "to apply to all laws of Canada already in existence at the time it came into force as well as those thereafter enacted."

If Canadian civil libertarians were dismayed by the Court's decision in *Robertson and Rosetanni*, they found new ground for hope in the Court's next major decision on the *Bill*

---

1 [1963] S.C.R. 651.

of Rights. This did not occur until 1970 in the *Drybones* decision, which concerned the compatibility of provisions in the *Indian Act* restricting the drinking rights of Indians with the egalitarian provisions of the *Bill of Rights.* Ironically, on this occasion, the positions of Cartwright and Ritchie were completely reversed. Justice Ritchie still spoke for the majority, but this time it was an "activist" majority willing to use the *Bill of Rights* to invalidate a long-established piece of federal legislation. Cartwright, now Chief Justice, along with Justices Abbott and Pigeon, refused to give the Bill such a wide-reaching effect.

The Supreme Court's decision in the *Lavell and Bédard* case indicated that a majority of the judges felt the Court had gone too far in an "activist" direction in *Drybones.* The majority opinion did not retreat from the position established in *Drybones* that the *Bill of Rights* can render inoperative legislation that clearly violates rights enshrined in the Bill, but it did considerably water down the significance of the right to equality before the law.

The decision dealt with appeals in two cases involving Indian women who claimed that section 12(1)(*b*) of the *Indian Act* infringed their right to equality before the law under the *Bill of Rights.* Section 12(1)(*b*) denied an Indian woman who married a non-Indian her Indian status, including her right to hold property and live on an Indian reserve. A male Indian who married a non-Indian could retain his Indian status. Thus, Mrs. Lavell and Mrs. Bédard argued that section 12(1)(*b*) constituted discrimination by reason of sex. While they were supported by the Native Council of Canada representing non-status Indians and by several non-Indian women's organizations, most of the organizations representing status Indians, including eight provincial and two territorial organizations and the National Indian Brotherhood, intervened to oppose Mrs. Lavell and Mrs. Bédard.

The Supreme Court decided, 5 to 4, that section 12(1)(*b*) did not constitute a violation of equality before the law. Again, Justice Ritchie wrote the majority opinion. Just as it is difficult to reconcile his opinion in *Drybones* with the position he had taken earlier in *Robertson and Rosetanni,* it is a daunting task to trace a thread of consistency between his approach to equality before the law in *Lavell and Bédard* and his treatment of that concept in *Drybones.* Citing A.V. Dicey, the 19th-century English constitutional writer, as his authority, Justice Ritchie now defined equality before the law not as a substantive requirement of the law itself, but as a requirement of the way in which laws are administered. The *Indian Act* might well discriminate against women, but so long as it was applied equally to all whom it affected there would be no violation of equality before the law. To this argument Justice Ritchie added the concern expressed by Justice Pigeon in his dissenting opinion in *Drybones:* it would be unreasonable to extend the *Bill of Rights* so far as to make it impossible for Parliament to enact special legislation concerning the property and civil rights of Indians.

Justice Laskin, as was so often the case in civil liberties cases, wrote a vigorous dissent. He could not reconcile the majority's interpretation of equality before the law with the Court's decision in *Drybones.* The opening paragraph of section 1 of the *Canadian Bill of Rights,* in his view, amounted to a prohibition of legal classifications based on race, national origin, colour, religion, or sex. In this sense, the *Canadian Bill of Rights* was more specific and categorical than the equal protection of laws clause in the American Constitution, which did not prohibit any specific form of discrimination, leaving it to the judiciary to distinguish reasonable and unreasonable forms of discrimination. Laskin could not see why laws based on Parliament's power under section 91(24) of the *B.N.A. Act* to legislate in relation to Indians should enjoy any special immunity from the *Bill of Rights.* To decide otherwise in this case would, in his view, compound racial inequality with sexual inequality. Justice

Laskin's dissent was supported by Justices Spence, Hall, and Abbott. Justice Abbott had dissented in *Drybones*, but regarded that decision as now requiring him to support Justice Laskin's dissent. Justice Pigeon, on the other hand, who also dissented in *Drybones*, this time joined the majority and appeared to regard the results of this case as supportive of the position that he had taken in *Drybones*.

The most promising explanation for the logical difficulties posed by the majority opinion is political, not jurisprudential. The judges had been made aware that ruling section 12(1)(*b*) inoperative would cause political and policy difficulties not posed by the *Drybones* decision, and they drew back in an attempt to avoid the political thicket Justice Cartwright had warned them about in *Drybones*.

The central question was whether a broad interpretation of the *Bill of Rights* equality guarantee would undermine the entire *Indian Act*. This concern had been expressed by Justice Pigeon in his dissenting opinion in *Drybones*. By the time of the *Lavell and Bédard* case, the Indian community had become alerted to the threat posed to the *Indian Act* by this jurisprudence and had mobilized to oppose it. Although Indians were not happy with all aspects of the *Act* and its administration, they were not prepared to abandon the idea of special status as such. Not long before, they had successfully resisted the Trudeau government's 1969 proposal to dismantle the *Indian Act* in favour of an individualized concept of equal Canadian citizenship, and they worried that their political victory might now be judicially undone.

In addition to the implicit challenge to the idea of special status, serious political problems were raised by the possible invalidation of section 12(1)(*b*) itself. The liquor provisions of the *Indian Act* struck down in *Drybones* were relatively unimportant parts of the *Act*, with few implications for the system of special status established there. Their invalidation did not really change anything. To the contrary, in most of the country they had already been repealed under local option provisions of the *Indian Act* and they were nowhere actively supported. Thus, in *Drybones*, the "Supreme Court was invited to strike down the feeble remnants of 19th century Indian liquor laws."[2] To do so, moreover, would create no legal gap and pose no policy dilemmas; the relevant laws for the rest of the population would now simply apply to Indians as well.

The same could not be said of the status-defining provisions of section 12(1)(*b*). Some way of determining status was required, and if these rules were invalidated what would replace them? The Court, which could invalidate them, could not itself fill the legal gap that would ensue. Furthermore, what would be the practical, particularly the financial, implications of returning status to women who had lost it? Through the Minister of Indian Affairs, the National Indian Brotherhood expressed strong opposition "to the principles contained in the *Lavell* decision [in the Federal Court] and, in particular, to the effects which they fear it will have on their already overcrowded reserves and their already overcrowded schools." For example, the Minister estimated that it would cost $1 million to reimburse women like Lavell for the share of band funds they did not receive following their marriages to non-

---

2   Douglas Sanders, "The Bill of Rights and the Indian Act" in Anne Bayefsky and Mary Eberts, eds., *Equality Rights and the Charter* (Toronto: Carswell, 1985) 539.

Indians, "even if the principle of the *Lavell* case only applies to marriages which have taken place since the *Canadian Bill of Rights* was enacted."[3]

The existence of major political problems and the extent of the opposition to the invalidation of section 12(1)(*b*) was underlined for the Supreme Court by the number of aspiring interveners clamouring at its door. Whereas in *Drybones* the judges were faced with an antiquated and insignificant section of the *Act* that nobody was willing to defend, in *Lavell and Bédard* they saw the federal government and all the status Indian organizations lining up in vigorous support of the status quo. Indeed, "the provincial Indian Associations, along with the National Indian Brotherhood, joined together in support of a single submission to the Court in support of section 12(1)(*b*), a rare show of unity and organization."[4] In this context, the concerns Justice Cartwright expressed in *Drybones* about the dangers of the political thicket must have loomed much larger for the Court as a whole.

After *Lavell and Bédard* the Supreme Court rejected a series of attacks on discriminatory provisions in federal legislation. In *Burnshine,*[5] the Court dismissed an attack on provisions of the *Prisons and Reformatories Act* under which young offenders in British Columbia and Ontario may serve longer periods of detention than adults or youths in other provinces. In the *Canard* case,[6] the Court held that provisions of the *Indian Act* giving a federal minister the power to administer the estates of Indians did not infringe the right of Indians to equality before the law. Justice Laskin (who between these two cases had been elevated to the Chief Justiceship) wrote dissents in both cases.

The *Bliss* case[7] concerned amendments to the *Unemployment Insurance Act* that created a special pregnancy benefit, but made it conditional on serving a much longer employment period than required for other benefits and denied a woman who left the workforce because of pregnancy access to the ordinary benefits. The Court unanimously (Chief Justice Laskin did not participate in this decision) held that these provisions involved no denial of equality before the law. Justice Ritchie, who authored the Court's opinion, contended that they were "an integral part of a legislative scheme enacted for valid federal objectives and they are concerned with conditions from which men are excluded. Any inequality between the sexes in this area is not created by legislation but by nature." The idea that so long as legislation serves "a valid federal objective" it is a justifiable discrimination was enunciated three years earlier in the *Prata* case,[8] in which the Court unanimously rejected the contention that provisions of the *Immigration Act* restricting the rights of persons deemed to be security risks constituted a denial of equality before the law.

However, there was still no clear consensus among the members of the Supreme Court as to whether the test of "serving a valid federal objective" means more than that legislation should be in relation to a matter constitutionally within the federal Parliament's jurisdiction.

---

3   *Ibid.* at 543.

4   Carl Baar, "Using Process Theory to Explain Judicial Decision Making" (1986) 1 *Canadian Journal of Law and Society* 86.

5   *The Queen v. Burnshine,* [1975] 1 S.C.R. 693.

6   *A.G. of Canada v. Canard,* [1976] 1 S.C.R. 170.

7   *Bliss v. Canada (Attorney General),* [1979] 1 S.C.R. 183.

8   *Prata v. Minister of Manpower and Immigration,* [1976] 1 S.C.R. 376.

The *MacKay* case, decided in 1980, provided a good test of the justices' position on this question. The case concerned provisions of the *National Defence Act*, under which a member of the armed forces had been convicted by a court martial for a number of drug offences committed at a military base. While the Court decided, 7 to 2, that in these circumstances there was no denial of equality before the law, two of the judges who supported the majority (Justices McIntyre and Dickson) took the position that equality before the law would be violated by the broad provisions of the *Act* that subjected members of the armed forces to military trials for *all* criminal offences, even those having no relationship to a military context. In reaching this conclusion, Justice McIntyre held that, in determining whether a discriminatory classification in federal legislation served a valid federal objective and therefore did not violate equality before the law, the Court must decide whether the inequality "has been created rationally in the sense that it is not arbitrary or capricious and not based upon any ulterior motive . . . and whether it is a necessary departure from the general principle of universal application of the law for the attainment of some necessary and desirable social objective."[9] The two dissenting judges, Chief Justice Laskin and Justice Estey, also appeared to accept the view that discriminatory laws must be based on reasonable classifications. Still, this test of the rationality of legislative classifications, borrowed from American constitutional law, was endorsed by a majority of Supreme Court judges.

The equality clause of the *Charter of Rights*, section 15, was certainly meant to have a more significant effect than the equality provisions in the *Canadian Bill of Rights*. Indeed, the section contains wording explicitly intended to counteract the *Lavell and Bédard* and *Bliss* cases. In addition to equality before the law and the equal protection of the law, section 15 protects equality under the law (to overrule *Lavell and Bédard*) and equal benefit of the law (to overrule *Bliss*). The section stipulates that these rights are to be enjoyed "without discrimination and, in particular, without discrimination based on race, national or ethnic origin, colour, religion, sex, age or mental or physical disability." An interpretation imposed on the equal protection of laws by the U.S. Supreme Court is explicitly overcome by providing that affirmative action laws that discriminate in order to improve the condition of disadvantaged individuals or groups shall not be regarded as violating the equality rights.

Indian women did not have to wait for the *Charter* to overcome the *Indian Act*'s discrimination against them. In 1977, Sandra Lovelace took her case to a hearing before the United Nation's Human Rights Committee. The committee ruled that the section of Canada's *Indian Act* that had been upheld in *Lavell and Bédard* violated the United Nations Convention on Civil and Political Rights.[10] Although this decision was not legally binding on Canada, it was a key factor in putting political pressure on the federal government to amend the *Act*. In 1985, section 12(1)(*b*) was removed from the *Act*, restoring the status of an estimated 22,000 Indian women who had lost it under that provision. The status of the children of these women was left to be determined by Indian bands, which were given power to determine their own membership systems.

The *Charter of Rights and Freedoms* has clear constitutional status and is much more comprehensive in its rights coverage than the *Canadian Bill of Rights*. It has eclipsed the Bill

---

9   *MacKay v. The Queen*, [1980] 2 S.C.R. 370 at 407.

10   *Lovelace v. Canada*, No. 24/1977. Selected Decisions of the Human Rights Committee Under the Optional Protocol, U.N. Doc. CCPR/OP/1 (1988), 86-90.

as an instrument for litigating civil rights in Canada. The Supreme Court's sterile and inconsistent jurisprudence interpreting the *Bill of Rights* stands as a marker of where *Charter* jurisprudence will not go. However, the *Canadian Bill of Rights* remains on the statute book. The one point where it might have practical significance is its recognition of a right to property and the right not to be deprived thereof except by due process of law. The *Charter* contains no right of property. ∼

Discussion Questions

1. Can *Drybones* be distinguished from *Lavell and Bédard*?
2. How appropriate was it for Justice Pigeon to side with the majority in *Lavell and Bédard* if, as he concedes for the sake of argument, *Drybones* cannot be distinguished?
3. Justice Ritchie concludes that the principle of "equality in the administration and application of the law" was not infringed. How could it have been infringed in the application of section 12(1)(*b*) of the *Indian Act*? Assess the pros and cons of this equality principle.

ATTORNEY GENERAL OF CANADA
v. LAVELL AND BÉDARD
[1974] S.C.R. 1349

Judgment: August 27, 1973.

Present: Fauteux C.J. and Abbott, Martland, Judson, Ritchie, Hall, Spence, Pigeon, and Laskin JJ.

Interveners: Six Nations Band of Indians of the County of Brant; Native Council of Canada; Rose Wilhelm, Alberta Committee on Indian Rights for Indian Women Inc., Viola Shannacaffo, University Women's Club of Toronto, University Women Graduates Ltd., North Toronto Business and Professional Women's Club Inc., and Monica Agnes Turner; Treaty Voice of Alberta, Anishnarvbekwek of Ontario Inc.; Indian Association of Alberta, the Union of British Columbia Indian Chiefs, the Manitoba Indian Brotherhood Inc., the Union of New Brunswick Indians, the Indian Brotherhood of the Northwest Territories, the Union of Nova Scotia Indians, the Union of Ontario Indians, the Federation of Saskatchewan Indians, the Indian Association of Quebec, the Yukon Native Brotherhood, and the National Indian Brotherhood.

The judgment of Fauteux C.J. and Martland, Judson, and Ritchie JJ. was delivered by

RICHIE J.: ... These appeals, which were heard together, are from two judgments holding that the provisions of s. 12(1)(*b*) of the *Indian Act*, R.S.C. 1970, c. I-6, are rendered inoperative by s. 1(*b*) of the *Canadian Bill of Rights*, 1960 (Can.), c. 44, as denying equality before the law to the two respondents.

Both respondents were registered Indians and "Band" members within the meaning of s. 11(*b*) of the *Indian Act* when they elected to marry non-Indians and thereby relinquished their status as Indians in conformity with the said s. 12(1)(*b*) which reads as follows:

> 12.(1) The following persons are not entitled to be registered, namely,
> (*b*) a woman who married a person who is not an Indian, unless that woman is subsequently the wife or widow of a person described in section 11.

It is contended on behalf of both respondents that s. 12(1)(*b*) of the *Act* should be held to be inoperative as discriminating between Indian men and women and as being in conflict with the provisions of the *Canadian Bill of Rights* and particularly s. 1 thereof which provides:

> 1. It is hereby recognized and declared that in Canada there have existed and shall continue to exist without discrimination by reason of race, national origin, colour, religion or sex, the following human rights and fundamental freedoms, namely, ...

> (*b*) the right of the individual to equality before the law and the protection of the law; ...

... The contention which formed the basis of the argument submitted by both respondents was that they had been denied equality before the law by reason of sex, and I propose to deal with the matter on this basis. ...

In my opinion the exclusive legislative authority vested in Parliament under s. 91(24) could not have been effectively exercised without enacting laws establishing the qualifications required to entitle persons to status as Indians and to the use and benefit of Crown "lands reserved for Indians." The legislation enacted to this end was, in my view, necessary for the implementation of the authority so vested in Parliament under the constitution.

To suggest that the provisions of the *Bill of Rights* have the effect of making the whole *Indian Act* inoperative as discriminatory is to assert that the Bill has rendered Parliament powerless to exercise the authority entrusted to it under the constitution of enacting legislation which treats Indians living on Reserves differently from other Canadians in relation to their property and civil rights. The proposition that such a wide effect is to be given to the *Bill of Rights* was expressly reserved by the majority of this Court in the case of *The Queen v. Drybones* [[1970] S.C.R. 282], at 298, to which reference will hereafter be made, and I do not think that it can be sustained.

What is at issue here is whether the *Bill of Rights* is to be construed as rendering inoperative one of the conditions imposed by Parliament for the use and occupation of Crown lands reserved for Indians. These conditions were imposed as a necessary part of the structure created by Parliament for the internal administration of the life of Indians on reserves and their entitlement to the use and benefit of Crown lands situate thereon, they were thus imposed, in discharge of Parliament's constitutional function under s. 91(24) and in my view can only be changed by plain statutory language expressly enacted for the purpose. It does not appear to me that Parliament can be taken to have made or intended to make such a change by the use of broad general language directed at the statutory proclamation of the fundamental rights and freedoms enjoyed by all Canadians, and I am therefore of opinion that the *Bill of Rights* had no such effect. ...

The contention that the *Bill of Rights* is to be construed as overriding all of the special legislation imposed by Parliament under the *Indian Act* is, in my view, fully answered by Pigeon J. in his dissenting opinion in the *Drybones* case where he said, at p. 304:

> If one of the effects of the *Canadian Bill of Rights* is to render inoperative all legal provisions whereby Indians as such are not dealt with in the same way as the general public, the conclusion is inescapable that Parliament, by

the enactment of the Bill, has not only fundamentally altered the status of the Indians in that indirect fashion but has also made any future use of federal legislative authority over them subject to the requirement of expressly declaring every time "that the law shall operate notwithstanding the *Canadian Bill of Rights.*" I find it very difficult to believe that Parliament so intended when enacting the Bill. If a virtual suppression of federal legislation over Indians as such was meant, one would have expected this important change to be made explicitly not surreptitiously so to speak. . . .

In considering the meaning to be given to section 1(*b*) of the *Bill of Rights,* regard must of course be had to what was said by Mr. Justice Laskin, speaking in this regard for the whole of the Court in *Curr v. The Queen* [[1972] S.C.R. 889, at pp. 896 and 897], where he interpreted sections 1(*a*) and 1(*b*) of the Bill in the following passage:

In considering the reach of s. 1(*a*) and s. 1(*b*), and, indeed, of s. 1 as a whole, I would observe, first, that the section is given its controlling force over federal law by its referential incorporation into s. 2; and, second, that I do not read it as making the existence of any of the forms of prohibited discrimination, a *sine qua non* of its operation. Rather, the prohibited discrimination is an additional lever to which federal legislation must respond. Putting the matter another way, federal legislation which does not offend s. 1 in respect of any of the prohibited kinds of discrimination may nonetheless be offensive to s. 1 if it is violative of what is specified in any of the clauses (*a*) to (*f*) of s. 1. It is, *a fortiori,* offensive if there is discrimination by reason of race so as to deny equality before the law. That is what this Court decided in *Regina v. Drybones* and I need say no more on this point.

It is, therefore, not an answer to reliance by the appellant on s. 1(*a*) and s. 1(*b*) of the *Canadian Bill of Rights* that s. 223 does not discriminate against any person by reason of race, national origin, colour, religion or sex. The absence of such discrimination still leaves open the question whether s. 223 can be construed and applied without abrogating, abridging or infringing the rights of the individual listed in s. 1(*a*) and s. 1(*b*).

My understanding of this passage is that the effect of s. 1 of the *Bill of Rights* is to guarantee to all Canadians the rights specified in paragraphs (*a*) to (*f*) of that section, irrespective of race, national origin, colour or sex. This interpretation appears to me to be borne out by the French version which reads:

1. *Il est par les présentes reconnu et déclaré que les droits de l'homme et les libertés fondamentales ci-après énoncés ont existé et continueront à exister pour tout individu au*

Canada quels que soient sa race, son origine nationale, sa couleur, sa religion ou son sexe:

It was stressed on behalf of the respondents that the provisions of s. 12(1)(*b*) of the *Indian Act* constituted "discrimination by reason of sex" and that the section could be declared inoperative on this ground alone even if such discrimination did not result in the infringement of any of the rights and freedoms specifically guaranteed by s. 1 of the Bill.

I can find no support for such a contention in the *Curr* case in which, in any event, no question of any kind of discrimination was either directly or indirectly involved. My own understanding of the passage which I have quoted from that case was that it recognized the fact that the primary concern evidenced by the first two sections of the *Bill of Rights* is to ensure that the rights and freedoms thereby recognized and declared shall continue to exist for all Canadians, and it follows, in my view, that those sections cannot be invoked unless one of the enumerated rights and freedoms has been denied to an individual Canadian or group of Canadians. Section 2 of the *Bill of Rights* provides for the manner in which the rights and freedoms which are recognized and declared by s. 1 are to be enforced and the effect of this section is that every law of Canada shall "be so construed and applied as not to abrogate, abridge or infringe or authorize the abrogation, abridgment or infringement of any of the rights and freedoms herein recognized and declared . . . ," (*i.e.* by s. 1). There is no language anywhere in the *Bill of Rights* stipulating that the laws of Canada are to be construed without discrimination unless that discrimination involves the denial of one of the guaranteed rights and freedoms, but when, as in the case of *The Queen v. Drybones, supra,* denial of one of the enumerated rights is occasioned by reason of discrimination, then, as Mr. Justice Laskin has said, the discrimination affords an "additional lever to which federal legislation must respond."

The opening words of s. 2 of the *Bill of Rights* are, in my view, determinative of the test to be applied in deciding whether the section here impugned is to be declared inoperative. The words to which I refer are:

2. Every law of Canada shall, unless it is expressly declared by an act of the Parliament of Canada that it shall operate notwithstanding the *Canadian Bill of Rights,* be so construed and applied as not to abrogate, abridge or infringe or authorize the abrogation, abridgement or infringement of the freedoms herein recognized and declared . . .

In the course of the reasons for judgment rendered on behalf of the majority of this Court in *The Queen v. Drybones, supra,* this language was interpreted in the following passage at p. 294:

It seems to me that a more realistic meaning must be given to the words in question and they afford, in my view, the clearest indication that s. 2 is intended to mean and does mean that if a law of Canada cannot be "sensibly construed and applied" so that it does not abrogate, abridge or infringe one of the rights and freedoms, recognized and declared by the *Bill*, then such law is inoperative "unless it is expressly declared by an Act of the Parliament of Canada that it shall operate notwithstanding the *Canadian Bill of Rights.*"

Accordingly, in my opinion, the question to be determined in these appeals is confined to deciding whether the Parliament of Canada in defining the prerequisites of Indian status so as not to include women of Indian birth who have chosen to marry non-Indians, enacted a law which cannot be sensibly construed and applied without abrogating, abridging or infringing the rights of such women to equality before the law.

In my view the meaning to be given to the language employed in the *Bill of Rights* is the meaning which it bore in Canada at the time when the *Bill* was enacted, and it follows that the phrase "equality before the law" is to be construed in light of the law existing in Canada at that time.

In considering the meaning to be attached to "equality before the law" as those words occur in section 1(*b*) of the *Bill*, I think it important to point out that in my opinion this phrase is not effective to invoke the egalitarian concept exemplified by the 14th Amendment of the U.S. Constitution as interpreted by the courts of that country. (See *Smythe v. The Queen* [[1971] S.C.R. 680 *per* Fauteux C.J. at pp. 683 and 686]). I think rather that, having regard to the language employed in the second paragraph of the preamble to the *Bill of Rights*, the phrase "equality before the law" as used in s. 1 is to be read in its context as a part of "the rule of law" to which overriding authority is accorded by the terms of that paragraph.

In this connection I refer to Stephens *Commentaries on the Laws of England*, 21st Ed. 1950, where it is said in Vol. III at p. 337:

Now the great constitutional lawyer Dicey writing in 1885 was so deeply impressed by the absence of arbitrary governments present and past, that he coined the phrase "the rule of law" to express the regime under which Englishmen lived; and he tried to give precision to it in the following words which have exercised a profound influence on all subsequent thought and conduct.

That the "rule of law" which forms a fundamental principle of the constitution has three meanings or may be regarded from three different points of view....

The second meaning proposed by Dicey is the one with which we are here concerned and it was stated in the following terms:

It means again equality before the law or the equal subjection of all classes to the ordinary law of the land administered by the ordinary courts; the "rule of law" in this sense excludes the idea of any exemption of officials or others from the duty of obedience to the law which governs other citizens or from the jurisdiction of the ordinary courts.

"Equality before the law" in this sense is frequently invoked to demonstrate that the same law applies to the highest official of government as to any other ordinary citizen, and in this regard Professor F.R. Scott, in delivering the Plaunt Memorial Lectures on Civil Liberties and Canadian Federalism in 1959, speaking of the case of *Roncarelli v. Duplessis* [[1959] S.C.R. 121], had occasion to say:

It is always a triumph for the law to show that it is applied equally to all without fear or favour. This is what we mean when we say that all are equal before the law.

The relevance of these quotations to the present circumstances is that "equality before the law" as recognized by Dicey as a segment of the rule of law, carries the meaning of equal subjection of all classes to the ordinary law of the land *as administered by the ordinary courts*, and in my opinion the phrase "equality before the law" as employed in section 1(*b*) of the *Bill of Rights* is to be treated as meaning equality in the administration or application of the law by the law enforcement authorities and the ordinary courts of the land. This construction is, in my view, supported by the provisions of subsections (*a*) to (*g*) of s. 2 of the *Bill* which clearly indicate to me that it was equality in the administration and enforcement of the law with which Parliament was concerned when it guaranteed the continued existence of "equality before the law."

Turning to the *Indian Act* itself, it should first be observed that by far the greater part of that *Act* is concerned with the internal regulation of the lives of Indians on Reserves and that the exceptional provisions dealing with the conduct of Indians off Reserves and their contacts with other Canadian citizens fall into an entirely different category. ...

A careful reading of the *Act* discloses that section 95 (formerly 94) is the only provision therein made which creates an offence for any behaviour of an Indian *off* a Reserve and it will be plain that there is a wide difference between legislation such as s. 12(1)(*b*) governing the civil rights of designated persons living on Indian Reserves to the use and benefit of Crown lands, and criminal legislation such as s. 95 which creates an offence punishable at law for Indians to act in a certain fashion when *off* a Reserve. The former legislation is enacted as a part of the plan devised by Parliament, under s. 91(24) for the regulation of the internal domestic life of Indians on Reserves. The latter is criminal legislation exclusively concerned with behaviour of Indians off a Reserve. ...

The *Drybones* case can, in my opinion, have no application to the present appeals as it was in no way concerned with the internal regulation of the lives of Indians *on* Reserves or their right to the use and benefit of Crown lands thereon, but rather deals exclusively with the effect of the *Bill of Rights* on a section of the *Indian Act* creating a crime with attendant penalties for the conduct by Indians *off* a Reserve in an area where non-Indians, who were also governed by federal law, were not subject to any such restriction.

The fundamental distinction between the present case and that of *Drybones*, however, appears to me to be that the impugned section in the latter case could not be enforced without denying equality of treatment in the administration and enforcement of the law before the ordinary courts of the land to a racial group, whereas no such inequality of treatment between Indian men and women flows as a necessary result of the application of s. 12(1)(*b*) of the *Indian Act*.

To summarize the above, I am of opinion:

1. That the *Bill of Rights* is not effective to render inoperative legislation, such as s. 12(1)(*b*) of the *Indian Act*, passed by the Parliament of Canada in discharge of its constitutional function under s. 91(24) of the *B.N.A. Act*, to specify how and by whom Crown lands reserved for Indians are to be used;

2. that the *Bill of Rights* does not require federal legislation to be declared inoperative unless it offends against one of the rights specifically guaranteed by section 1, but where legislation is found to be discriminatory, this affords an added reason for rendering it ineffective;

3. that equality before the law under the *Bill of Rights* means equality of treatment in the enforcement and application of the laws of Canada before the law enforcement authorities and the ordinary courts of the land, and no such inequality is necessarily entailed in the construction and application of s. 12(1)(*b*)....

ABBOTT J. (dissenting): The facts which are not in dispute are set out in the reasons of Ritchie and Laskin JJ. which I have had the advantage of reading. I am in agreement with the reasons of Laskin J. and wish to add only a few observations.

I share his view that the decision of this Court in *The Queen v. Drybones* [[1970] S.C.R. 282] cannot be distinguished from the two cases under appeal although in these two appeals the consequences of the discrimination by reason of sex under s. 12(1)(*b*) of the *Indian Act* are more serious than the relatively minor penalty for the drinking offence under s. 94 of the *Act* which was in issue in *Drybones*.

In that case, this Court rejected the contention that s. 1 of the *Canadian Bill of Rights* provided merely a canon of construction for the interpretation of legislation existing when the *Bill* was passed. With respect I cannot interpret "equality before the law" as used in s. 1(*b*) of the *Bill* as meaning simply "the equal subjection of all classes to the ordinary law of the land as administered by the ordinary courts" to use the language of Dicey which is quoted in the reasons of Ritchie J.

Unless the words "without discrimination by reason of race, national origin, colour, religion or sex" used in s. 1 are to be treated as mere rhetorical window dressing, effect must be given to them in interpreting the section. I agree with Laskin J. that s. 1(*b*) must be read as if those words were recited therein.

In my view the *Canadian Bill of Rights* has substantially affected the doctrine of the supremacy of Parliament. Like any other statute it can of course be repealed or amended, or a particular law declared to be applicable notwithstanding the provisions of the *Bill*. In form the supremacy of Parliament is maintained but in practice I think that it has been substantially curtailed. In my opinion that result is undesirable, but that is a matter for consideration by Parliament not the courts.

Ritchie J. said in his reasons for judgment in *Drybones* that the implementation of the *Bill of Rights* by the courts can give rise to great difficulties and that statement has been borne out in subsequent litigation. Of one thing I am certain, the *Bill* will continue to supply ample grist to the judicial mills for some time to come....

The judgment of Hall, Spence, and Laskin JJ. was delivered by

LASKIN J. (dissenting): ... In my opinion, unless we are to depart from what was said in *Drybones*, both appeals now before us must be dismissed. I have no disposition to reject what was decided in *Drybones*; and on the central issue of prohibited discrimination as catalogued in s. 1 of the *Canadian Bill of Rights*, it is, in my opinion, impossible to distinguish *Drybones* from the two cases in appeal. If, as in *Drybones*, discrimination by reason of race makes certain statutory provisions inoperative, the same result must follow as to statutory provisions which exhibit discrimination by reason of sex....

In both cases, which were argued together, leave was given to various bodies and organizations and to a number of individuals to intervene by representation and by submissions to this Court. The position of the Attorney General of Canada in the *Lavell* case was supported by counsel appearing on behalf of The Indian Association of Alberta, The Union of British Columbia Indian Chiefs, The Manitoba Indian Brotherhood Inc., The Union of New Brunswick Indians, The Indian Brotherhood of the Northwest Territories, The Union of Nova Scotia Indians, The Union of Ontario Indians, The Federation of Saskatchewan Indians, The Indian Association of Quebec,

The Yukon Native Brotherhood and The National Indian Brotherhood, by counsel appearing on behalf of the Six Nations Band and by counsel appearing on behalf of the Treaty Voice of Alberta Association. The position of the respondent was supported by counsel appearing for the Native Council of Canada, by counsel appearing for Rose Wilhelm, Alberta Committee on Indian Rights for Indian Women Inc., Viola Shannacappo, University Women's Club of Toronto and University Women Graduates Limited, The North Toronto Business and Professional Women's Club Inc. and Monica Agnes Turner, and by counsel for Anishnawbekwek of Ontario Incorporated. There was the same division of support for the appellants and the respondent in the *Bédard* case, in which the Attorney General of Canada also intervened to support the position of the appellants. . . .

The contentions of the appellants in both cases in appeal, stripped of their detail, amount to a submission that the *Canadian Bill of Rights* does not apply to Indians on a Reserve, nor to Indians in their relations to one another whether or not on a Reserve. This submission does not deny that the effect of s. 12(1)(*b*) of the *Indian Act* is to prescribe substantive discrimination by reason of sex, a differentiation in the treatment of Indian men and Indian women when they marry non-Indians, this differentiation being exhibited in the loss by the women of their status as Indians under the *Act*. It does, however, involve the assertion that the particular discrimination upon which the two appeals are focused is not offensive to the relevant provisions of the *Canadian Bill of Rights*; and it also involves the assertion that the *Drybones* case is distinguishable or, if not, that it has been overcome by the re-enactment of the *Indian Act* in the Revised Statutes of Canada, 1970, including the then s. 94 (now s. 95) which was in issue in that case. I regard this last-mentioned assertion, which is posited on the fact that the *Canadian Bill of Rights* was not so re-enacted, as simply an oblique appeal for the overruling of the *Drybones* case.

The *Drybones* case decided two things. It decided first— and this decision was a necessary basis for the second point in it—that the *Canadian Bill of Rights* was more than a mere interpretation statute whose terms would yield to a contrary intention; it had paramount force when a federal enactment conflicted with its terms, and it was the incompatible federal enactment which had to give way. This was the issue upon which the then Chief Justice of this Court, Chief Justice Cartwright, and Justices Abbott and Pigeon, dissented. Pigeon J. fortified his view on this main point by additional observations, bringing into consideration, *inter alia*, s. 91(24) of the *British North America Act*. The second thing decided by *Drybones* was that the accused in that case, an Indian under the *Indian Act*, was denied equality before the law, under s. 1(*b*) of the *Canadian Bill of Rights*, when it was made a punishable

offence for him, on account of his race, to do something which his fellow Canadians were free to do without being liable to punishment for an offence. Ritchie J., who delivered the majority opinion of the Court, reiterated this basis of decision by concluding his reasons as follows:

> It appears to me to be desirable to make it plain that these reasons for judgment are limited to a situation in which, under the laws of Canada, it is made an offence punishable at law on account of race, for a person to do something which all Canadians who are not members of that race may do with impunity.

It would be unsupportable in principle to view the *Drybones* case as turning on the fact that the challenged s. 94 of the *Indian Act* created an offence visited by punishment. The gist of the judgment lay in the legal disability imposed upon a person by reason of his race when other persons were under no similar restraint. If for the words "on account of race" there are substituted the words "on account of sex" the result must surely be the same where a federal enactment imposes disabilities or prescribes disqualifications for members of the female sex which are not imposed upon members of the male sex in the same circumstances.

It is said, however, that although this may be so as between males and females in general, it does not follow where the distinction on the basis of sex is limited as here to members of the Indian race. This, it is said further, does not offend the guarantee of "equality before the law" upon which the *Drybones* case proceeded. I wish to deal with these two points in turn and to review, in connection with the first point, the legal consequences for an Indian woman under the *Indian Act* when she marries a non-Indian.

It appears to me that the contention that a differentiation on the basis of sex is not offensive to the *Canadian Bill of Rights* where that differentiation operates only among Indians under the *Indian Act* is one that compounds racial inequality even beyond the point that the *Drybones* case found unacceptable. In any event, taking the *Indian Act* as it stands, as a law of Canada whose various provisions fall to be assessed under the *Canadian Bill of Rights*, I am unable to appreciate upon what basis the command of the *Canadian Bill of Rights*, that laws of Canada shall operate without discrimination by reason of sex, can be ignored in the operation of the *Indian Act*.

The *Indian Act* defines an Indian as a person who is registered as an Indian pursuant to the *Act* or is entitled to be so registered. It is registration or registrability upon a Band list or upon a general list that is the key to the scheme and application of the *Act*. The Registrar, charged with keeping the membership records, is the person to whom protests may be made by a Band Council or by an affected person respecting the inclusion or deletion of a name from the Indian Register. By s. 9(2) his decision on a protest is final subject to a reference to a judge under s. 9(3). The *Lavell* case arose in this way. Section 11 of the *Act* enumerates the persons entitled to be registered, and it is common ground that both Mrs. Lavell and Mrs. Bédard were so entitled prior to their respective marriages. Section 12 lists the classes of persons not entitled to be registered, and the only clause thereof relevant here is subsection 1(*b*) which I have already quoted. Section 14 has a peripheral relevance to the present case in its provision that a woman member of a Band who marries a person outside that Band ceases to be a member thereof but becomes a member of the Band of which her husband is a member. There is no absolute disqualification of an Indian woman from registrability on the Indian Register (that is, as a member on the general list) by marrying outside a Band unless the marriage is to a non-Indian.

Registration or registrability entitles an Indian as a member of a Band (and that was the status of both Mrs. Lavell and Mrs. Bédard prior to their respective marriages) to the use and benefit of the Reserve set aside for the Band. This may take the form of possession or occupation of particular land in the Reserve under an allotment by the Council of the Band with the approval of the responsible Minister, and it may be evidenced by a certificate of possession or a certificate of occupation, the latter representing possession for a limited period only. Indians may make wills disposing of their property, and it may also pass on intestacy, in either case subject to approval or control of the Minister or of a competent court; and in the case of a devise or descent of land in a Reserve the claimant's possession must be approved by the Minister under s. 49. Section 50 has only a remote bearing on the *Bédard* case in providing that a person who is not entitled to reside on a Reserve does not by devise or descent acquire a right to possession or occupation of land in that Reserve. It begs the question in that the issue here is whether or not Mrs. Bédard became disentitled to reside on the land in the Reserve which was left to her by her mother upon the latter's death in 1969. The fact that the respondent's brother now holds a certificate of possession of all the land formerly possessed by the mother, that certificate having been issued after the respondent transferred her interest to her brother in February, 1971, does not affect the overriding question of the respondent's right to reside on the land, having her brother's consent to residence thereon.

Indians entitled to be registered and to live on a Reserve are members of a society in which, through Band Councils, they share in the administration of the Reserve subject to overriding governmental authority. There is provision for election of councillors by Band members residing on a Reserve, and I note that there is no statutory discrimination between Indian men and women either as qualified electors or as qualified candidates for election as councillors. Other advantages that come from membership in the social unit relate to farm operations and to eligibility for governmental loans for various enumerated purposes.

Section 12(1)(*b*) effects a statutory excommunication of Indian women from this society but not of Indian men. Indeed, as was pointed out by counsel for the Native Council of Canada, the effect of ss. 11 and 12(1)(*b*) is to excommunicate the children of a union of an Indian woman with a non-Indian. There is also the invidious distinction, invidious at least in the light of the *Canadian Bill of Rights*, that the *Indian Act* creates between brothers and sisters who are Indians and who respectively marry non-Indians. The statutory banishment directed by s. 12(1)(*b*) is not qualified by the provision in s. 109(2) for a governmental order declaring an Indian woman who has married a non-Indian to be enfranchised. Such an order is not automatic and no such order was made in relation to Mrs. Bédard; but when made the woman affected is, by s. 110, deemed not to be an Indian within the *Indian Act* or any other statute or law. It is, if anything, an additional legal instrument of separation of an Indian woman from her native society and from her kin, a separation to which no Indian man who marries a non-Indian is exposed.

It was urged, in reliance in part on history, that the discrimination embodied in the *Indian Act* under s. 12(1)(*b*) is based upon a reasonable classification of Indians as a race, that the *Indian Act* reflects this classification and that the paramount purpose of the *Act* to preserve and protect the members of the race is promoted by the statutory preference for Indian men. Reference was made in this connection to various judgments of the Supreme Court of the United States to illustrate the adoption by that Court of reasonable classifications to square with the due process clause of the Fifth Amendment and with due process and equal protection under the Fourteenth Amendment. Those cases have at best a marginal relevance because the *Canadian Bill of Rights* itself enumerates prohibited classifications which the judiciary is bound to respect; and, moreover, I doubt whether discrimination on account of sex, where as here it has no biological or physiological rationale, could be sustained as a reasonable classification even if the direction against it was not as explicit as it is in the *Canadian Bill of Rights*.

I do not think it is possible to leap over the telling words of s. 1, "without discrimination by reason of race, national origin, colour, religion or sex," in order to explain away any such discrimination by invoking the words "equality before the law" in clause (*b*) and attempting to make them alone the touchstone of reasonable classification. That was not done in the *Drybones* case; and this Court made it clear in *Curr v. The Queen*, that federal legislation, which might be compatible with the command of "equality before the law" taken alone, may nonetheless be inoperative if it manifests any of the prohibited forms of discrimination. In short, the proscribed discriminations in s. 1 have a force either independent of the subsequently enumerated clauses (*a*) to (*f*) or, if they are found in any federal legislation, they offend those clauses because each must be read as if the prohibited forms of discrimination were recited therein as a part thereof.

This seems to me an obvious construction of s. 1 of the *Canadian Bill of Rights*. When that provision states that the enumerated human rights and fundamental freedoms shall continue to exist "without discrimination by reason of race, national origin, colour, religion or sex," it is expressly adding these words to clauses (*a*) to (*f*). Section 1(*b*) must read therefore as "the right of the individual to equality before the law and the protection of the law without discrimination by reason of race, national origin, colour, religion or sex." It is worth repeating that this is what emerges from the *Drybones* case and what is found in the *Curr* case.

There is no clear historical basis for the position taken by the appellants, certainly not in relation to Indians in Canada as a whole, and this was in effect conceded during the hearing in this Court. In any event, history cannot avail against the clear words of ss. 1 and 2 of the *Canadian Bill of Rights*. It is s. 2 that gives this enactment its effective voice, because without it s. 1 would remain a purely declaratory provision. Section 2 brings the terms of s. 1 into its orbit, and its reference to "every law of Canada" is a reference, as set out in s. 5(2), to any Act of the Parliament of Canada enacted before or after the effective date of the *Canadian Bill of Rights*. Pre-existing Canadian legislation as well as subsequent Canadian legislation is expressly made subject to the commands of the *Canadian Bill of Rights*, and those commands, where they are as clear as the one which is relevant here, cannot be diluted by appeals to history. Ritchie J. in his reasons in the *Drybones* case touched on this very point when he rejected the contention that the terms of s. 1 of the *Canadian Bill of Rights* must be circumscribed by the provisions of Canadian statutes in force at the date of the enactment of the *Canadian Bill of Rights*: see [1970] S.C.R. 282, at pp. 295-296. I subscribe fully to the rejection of that contention. Clarity here is emphasized by looking at the French version of the *Canadian Bill of Rights* which speaks in s. 1 of the enumerated human rights and fundamental freedoms "*pour tout individu au Canada quels que soient sa race, son origine nationale, sa couleur, sa religion ou son sexe.*"

In my opinion, the appellants' contentions gain no additional force because the *Indian Act*, including the challenged s. 12(1)(*b*) thereof, is a fruit of the exercise of Parliament's exclusive legislative power in relation to "Indians, and Lands reserved for the Indians" under s. 91(24) of the *British North America Act*. Discriminatory treatment on the basis of race or colour or sex does not inhere in that grant of legislative power. The fact that its exercise may be attended by forms of discrimination prohibited by the *Canadian Bill of Rights* is no more a justification for a breach of the *Canadian Bill of Rights* than there would be in the case of the exercise of any other head of federal legislative power involving provisions offensive to the *Canadian Bill of Rights*. The majority opinion in the *Drybones* case dispels any attempt to rely on the grant of legislative power as a ground for escaping from the force of the *Canadian Bill of Rights*. The latter does not differentiate among the various heads of legislative power; it embraces all exercises under whatever head or heads they arise. Section 3 which directs the Minister of Justice to scrutinize every Bill to ascertain whether any of its provisions are inconsistent with ss. 1 and 2 is simply an affirmation of this fact which is evident enough from ss. 1 and 2.

There was an intimation during the argument of these appeals that the *Canadian Bill of Rights* is properly invoked only to resolve a clash under its terms between two federal statutes, and the *Drybones* case was relied on in that connection. It is a spurious contention, if seriously advanced, because the *Canadian Bill of Rights* is itself the indicator to which any Canadian statute or any provision thereof must yield unless Parliament has declared that the statute or the particular provision is to operate notwithstanding the *Canadian Bill of Rights*. A statute may in itself be offensive to the *Canadian Bill of Rights*, or it may be by relation to another statute that it is so offensive.

I would dismiss both appeals with costs.

PIGEON J.: I agree in the result with Ritchie J. I certainly cannot disagree with the view I did express in *The Queen v. Drybones* [at p. 304] that the enactment of the *Canadian Bill of Rights* was not intended to effect a virtual suppression of federal legislation over Indians. My difficulty is Laskin J.'s strongly reasoned opinion that, unless we are to depart from what was said by the majority in *Drybones*, these appeals should be dismissed because, if discrimination by reason of race makes certain statutory provisions inoperative, the same result must follow as to statutory provisions which exhibit discrimination by reason of sex. In the end, it appears to me, that, in the circumstances, I need not reach a firm conclusion on that point. Assuming the situation is such as Laskin J. says, it cannot be improper for me to adhere to what was my dissenting view, when a majority of those who did not agree with it in respect of a particular section of the *Indian Act*, now adopt it for the main body of this important statute.

I would observe that this result does not conflict with any of our decisions subsequent to *Drybones*. In no case was the *Canadian Bill of Rights* given an invalidating effect over prior legislation.

In *Lowry and Lepper v. The Queen* [(1972), 26 D.L.R. (3d) 224] and in *Brownridge v. The Queen* [[1972] S.C.R. 926], the application of criminal legislation, past and subsequent, was held to be subject to provisions respecting a "fair hearing" and "the right to retain and instruct counsel." These decisions are important illustrations of the effectiveness of the *Bill* without any invalidating effect.

In *Smythe v. The Queen* [[1971] S.C.R. 680] it was held that provisions for stiffer penalties depending on the method of prosecution were not rendered inoperative by the *Canadian Bill of Rights* as infringing equality before the law, although the choice of the method of prosecution always depends on executive discretion.

In *Curr v. The Queen* [[1972] S.C.R. 889] recent *Criminal Code* provisions for compulsory breath analysis were held not to infringe the right to the "protection of the law" any more than the right to the "protection against self-crimination."

Finally, in *Duke v. The Queen* [[1972] S.C.R. 917] these same provisions were said not to deprive the accused of a "fair trial" although proclaimed without some paragraphs contemplating a specimen being offered and given on request to the suspect.

PART TWO

Fundamental Freedoms

The Queen v. Big M Drug Mart Ltd., 1985

Big M Drug Mart was among the first *Charter* cases to be decided by the Supreme Court. It clearly demonstrates the contrast between the Supreme Court's treatment of the *Charter of Rights and Freedoms* and its treatment two decades earlier of the *Canadian Bill of Rights*. In 1963 in *Robertson and Rosetanni*[1] the Court, with only one dissent, found that the federal *Lord's Day Act* did not contravene the right to freedom of religion in the *Canadian Bill of Rights*. Twenty-two years later, in *Big M*, the Court struck down the federal *Lord's Day Act* on the ground that it violated the right to freedom of conscience and religion in section 2 of the Charter.

In its initial approach to the *Bill of Rights*, the Court had adopted the view that the rights and freedoms in that document must be no wider than what was provided for under Canadian law at the time the Bill was adopted. There was no trace of that "frozen rights" thesis in the Court's early treatment of the *Charter*. The fact that the *Lord's Day Act* had been on the statute book since 1906 had no bearing on whether it violated the *Charter*'s guarantee of religious freedom. In *Robertson and Rosetanni*, the majority considered the effect, not the purpose, of the legislation, and held that because compulsory Sunday closing did not actually force anyone to worship in a Christian manner it did not affect freedom of religion. In *Big M*, for all of the justices except Justice Wilson, analysis of the challenged legislation began with the purpose behind the legislation at the time of its enactment. In the Court's view, that purpose in 1906 was clearly religious—to secure the observance by all of the Christian Sabbath. Legislation passed for such a purpose, in the Court's view, clearly violated the right to freedom of religion.

The majority and Justice Wilson differed on whether the assessment of challenged legislation should begin with its purpose or effect, while agreeing that if either the purpose or effect of legislation violates the *Charter* the legislation must be considered unconstitutional. Perhaps the majority's preference for beginning with the purpose of legislation was to avoid, if possible, the extensive examination of the practical consequences of legislation. Justice Wilson was less diffident about the judiciary's capacity for this kind of policy analysis.

Central to the Court's "purposive" approach to *Charter* interpretation was Chief Justice Dickson's inquiry into the meaning of "freedom of religion." The purpose he looks for here is not the stated intent of the *Charter*'s drafters, but the broad historical reasons for this freedom becoming a cherished ideal in western civilization. While this "purposive" approach may yield a fairly generous interpretation of *Charter* rights and freedoms, the Chief Justice was careful to point out that it must not be pushed so far as to "overshoot the actual purpose of the right or freedom in question." The Chief Justice was laying the groundwork for a moderate activism.

The Court's decision in *Big M* by no means settled the Sunday-closing issue in Canada. By ruling out a religious or moral rationale for Sunday-closing legislation, it eliminated the criminal law power, the only basis for federal legislation, thereby leaving this controversial policy issue to the provinces. All the provinces had developed more contemporary and

---

1   [1963] S.C.R. 651. For a discussion of this case, see case 2.

secular legislation regulating commercial activities on Sundays. The following year, in *Edwards Books*,[2] the Court upheld Ontario's *Retail Business Holiday Act*, which prohibited most retailing on Sundays, but exempted the owners of small businesses whose religion required them to close their stores on Saturdays.

The Supreme Court's decision in *Big M Drug Mart* recognizes that a major transformation has taken place in Canadian society. Canada was no longer to be considered, in any official or legal sense, a Christian society. Chief Justice Dickson's opinion brought into play, for the first time, section 27 of the *Charter*, directing the courts to interpret the *Charter* "in a manner consistent with the preservation and enhancement of the multicultural heritage of Canadians." The Chief Justice cited this section as a further reason for interpreting the right to freedom of religion as excluding laws enacted for the purpose of enforcing the precepts of the Christian religion. Religious pluralism is to be an essential ingredient of the cultural pluralism of the modern Canadian state. ⌁

Discussion Questions

1. Justice Wilson differs with Chief Justice Dickson on the "appropriate analytic approach to a *Charter* case." What is the disagreement? Does it matter?
2. For Chief Justice Dickson, what is the difference between characterizing the purpose of a statute and the purpose of a *Charter* provision?
3. In the light of *Big M*, what is the constitutional status of Christmas and Easter holidays?

---

2 *R. v. Edwards Books and Art Ltd.*, [1986] 2 S.C.R. 713.

HER MAJESTY THE QUEEN v.
BIG M DRUG MART LTD.
[1985] 1 S.C.R. 295

Hearing: March 6, 7, 1984; Judgment: April 24, 1985.

Present: Dickson C.J. and Ritchie,* Beetz, McIntyre, Chouinard, Lamer, and Wilson JJ.

Interveners: The Attorney General of Canada, the Attorney General of New Brunswick, and the Attorney General of Saskatchewan.

* Ritchie J. took no part in the judgment.

The judgment of Dickson C.J. and Beetz, McIntyre, Chouinard, and Lamer JJ. was delivered by

[1] **DICKSON C.J.:** Big M Drug Mart Ltd. was charged with unlawfully carrying on the sale of goods, on Sunday, May 30, 1982 in the City of Calgary, Alberta, contrary to the *Lord's Day Act*, R.S.C. 1970, c. L-13.

[2] Big M has challenged the constitutionality of the *Lord's Day Act*, both in terms of the division of powers and the *Canadian Charter of Rights and Freedoms*. Such challenge places in issue before this Court, for the first time, one of the fundamental freedoms protected by the *Charter*, the guarantee of "freedom of conscience and religion" entrenched in s. 2.

[3] The constitutional validity of Sunday observance legislation has in the past been tested largely through the division of powers provided in ss. 91 and 92 of the *Constitution Act, 1867*. Freedom of religion has been seen to be a matter falling within federal legislative competence. Today, following the advent of the *Constitution Act, 1982*, we must address squarely the fundamental issues raised by individual rights and freedoms enshrined in the *Charter*, as well as those concerned with legislative powers....

V. The Characterization of the Lord's Day Act

... [48] There are obviously two possible ways to characterize the purpose of Lord's Day legislation, the one religious, namely securing public observance of the Christian institution of the Sabbath and the other secular, namely providing a uniform day of rest from labour. It is undoubtedly true that both elements may be present in any given enactment, indeed it is almost inevitable that they will be, considering that such laws combine a prohibition of ordinary employment for one day out of seven with a specification that this day of rest shall be the Christian Sabbath—Sunday. In the Anglo-Canadian tradition this intertwining is to be seen as far back as early Saxon times in such laws as that promulgated by Ine, King of Wessex from 688–725....

[51] Historically, there seems little doubt that it was religious purpose which underlay the enactment of English Lord's Day legislation. From early times the moral exhortation found in the Fourth Commandment (Exodus 20: 8-11) "Remember the Sabbath day, to keep it holy" increasingly became a legislative imperative. The first major piece of legislation, *The Sunday Fairs Act*, 27 Hen. 6, c. 5, prefaced its prohibition of fairs and markets on Sunday with a recital of "abomenable injuries and offences done to Almighty God and to his Saints" because of bodily labour, deceitful bargaining, drunkenness and religious non-observance associated with fairs. Following the Reformation under Henry VIII, religious observance acquired an added political significance and a number of statutes aimed at securing religious conformity were promulgated....

[52] Under Charles I the first modern Sunday observance statutes were enacted and their religious purpose is reflected in their titles, *An Act for punishing divers Abuses committed on the Lord's Day, called Sunday*, 1 Car. 1, c. 1 and *An Act for the further Reformation of sundry Abuses committed on the Lord's Day, commonly called Sunday*, 3 Car. 1, c. 2. During the Commonwealth or Interregnum period, the Puritan Parliament passed strict laws prohibiting the profanation of the Lord's Day by any form of marketing, travel, worldly labour, sports or recourse to taverns, tobacco shops or restaurants. With the Restoration came *An Act for the better Observation of the Lord's Day commonly called Sunday*, 29 Car. 2, c. 7, also known as the *Sunday Observance Act*. As its full title indicates, the primary object of this legislation, like that of its predecessors, was clearly religious rather than secular....

[53] The *Sunday Observance Act* of 1677 served as a model for Canadian pre-Confederation legislation, especially *An Act to prevent the Profanation of the Lord's Day, commonly called Sunday, in Upper Canada*, 1845 (Can.), c. 45, which substantially re-enacted the English law with only minor alterations designed to suit it to the specific conditions and activities of Upper Canada. It was this statute, as re-enacted by the post-Confederation legislature of Ontario (R.S.O. 1897, c. 246), that the Privy Council found to be beyond the competence of the province to enact in *Attorney-General for Ontario v. Hamilton Street Railway Co.*, [1903] A.C. 524, a decision which lay behind the passage in 1906 of the federal *Lord's Day Act*. Like the Ontario *Act*, the federal *Act* embodied the basic framework and much of the language of the English *Sunday Observance Act* of 1677. After four consolidations, it still exhibits these same essential characteristics in its present form....

[54] From the time of Confederation until the Privy Council decision in 1903 in *Hamilton Street Railway*, *supra*, it was the widely-held view that Sunday observance legislation

fell within provincial purview under the *Constitution Act, 1867* as being a matter falling under either s. 92(13), property and civil rights within the province, or s. 92(16), a matter of merely local or private nature in the Province. Several of the provinces passed laws prohibiting Sunday activities. In the *Hamilton Street Railway* case the Ontario statute fell to be considered. Aylesworth K.C. argued before the Privy Council that the primary object of the *Act* under consideration was the promotion of public order, safety and morals, and not the regulation of civil rights as between subject and subject. That view would seem to have prevailed, as their Lordships held that the *Act* as a whole was beyond the competence of the Ontario Legislature to enact....

[55] ... The Parliament of Canada passed the federal *Lord's Day Act*, 1906 (Can.), c. 27, with what would appear to have been some degree of reluctance because, firstly, s. 14 provided that nothing in the *Act* should be construed to repeal or in any way affect "any provisions of any Act or law relating in any way to the observance of the Lord's Day in force in any province of Canada when this *Act* comes into force." Sunday observance legislation in force in a province at the time it entered Confederation was expressly preserved. Secondly, while the *Act* prohibited a very few activities unconditionally, such as shooting in such a manner as to disturb public worship or observance of the day, or selling foreign newspapers, the most important sections of the *Act* made other activities unlawful only to the extent that provincial legislation did not provide otherwise.

[56] Acting under the authority of the federal *Lord's Day Act*, the provinces have enacted legislation such as the *Lord's Day (Ontario) Act*, R.S.O. 1980, c. 253, and *The Lord's Day (Saskatchewan) Act*, R.S.S. 1978, c. L-34. Provincial legislation of this nature was upheld by the Judicial Committee of the Privy Council in *Lord's Day Alliance of Canada v. Attorney-General for Manitoba*, [1925] A.C. 384, and more recently by this Court in *Lord's Day Alliance of Canada v. Attorney General of British Columbia*, [1959] S.C.R. 497....

[65] We come now to the case of *Robertson and Rosetanni* [(1963) S.C.R. 651], *supra*, to which much attention was directed during argument. The appellants were convicted on a charge of operating a bowling alley on a Sunday, contrary to the *Lord's Day Act*. They contended that the *Canadian Bill of Rights*, R.S.C. 1970, App. III, had in effect repealed s. 4 of the *Lord's Day Act* or, in any event, rendered it inoperative. The Court, Cartwright J. dissenting, rejected the contention and dismissed the appeal....

[73] The United States Supreme Court has sustained the constitutionality of Sunday observance legislation against First Amendment challenges: *McGowan v. Maryland*, 366 U.S. 420 (1961); *Braunfeld v. Brown*, 366 U.S. 599 (1961), *Gallagher v. Crown Kosher Super Market of Massachusetts, Inc.*, 366 U.S. 617 (1961), and *Two Guys from Harrison-Allentown, Inc. v. McGinley*, 366 U.S. 582 (1961). Despite the undoubted religious motivation of the state laws in question at the time of their passage and their clear origin in the religiously coercive statutes of Stuart England, Chief Justice Warren, writing for the majority, found that those statutes had evolved to become purely secular labour regulation. In his view, none of the impugned state statutes violated the First Amendment guarantee of freedom of religion. Whatever religious terminology still appeared in the legislation (such as the use of the term "Lord's Day" in the Maryland statute) was to be seen simply as a historical curiosity....

[77] It is somewhat ironic that the United States courts upheld the validity of Sunday observance laws, characterizing them as secular in order not to run afoul of the religion clauses of the First Amendment, while in contrast, in *Robertson v. Rosetanni*, *supra*, the Court found in the same type of legislation, a religious purpose in order to sustain its *vires* as criminal law. At the same time it accorded to the legislation a secular effect in order not to bring it into conflict with the religious freedom recognized and declared in the *Canadian Bill of Rights*....

VI. Purpose and Effect of Legislation

[78] A finding that the *Lord's Day Act* has a secular purpose is, on the authorities, simply not possible. Its religious purpose, in compelling sabbatical observance, has been long-established and consistently maintained by the courts of this country.

[79] The Attorney General for Alberta concedes that the *Act* is characterized by this religious purpose. He contends, however, that it is not the purpose but the effects of the *Act* which are relevant. In his submission, *Robertson and Rosetanni*, *supra*, is support for the proposition that it is effects alone which must be assessed in determining whether legislation violates a constitutional guarantee of freedom of religion.

[80] I cannot agree. In my view, both purpose and effect are relevant in determining constitutionality; either an unconstitutional purpose or an unconstitutional effect can invalidate legislation. All legislation is animated by an object the legislature intends to achieve. This object is realized through the impact produced by the operation and application of the legislation. Purpose and effect respectively, in the sense of the legislation's object and its ultimate impact, are clearly linked, if not indivisible. Intended and actual effects have often been looked to for guidance in assessing the legislation's object and thus, its validity.

[81] Moreover, consideration of the object of legislation is vital if rights are to be fully protected. The assessment by the courts of legislative purpose focuses scrutiny upon the

aims and objectives of the legislature and ensures they are consonant with the guarantees enshrined in the *Charter*. The declaration that certain objects lie outside the legislature's power checks governmental action at the first stage of unconstitutional conduct. Further, it will provide more ready and more vigorous protection of constitutional rights by obviating the individual litigant's need to prove effects violative of *Charter* rights. It will also allow courts to dispose of cases where the object is clearly improper, without inquiring into the legislation's actual impact. . . .

[88] In short, I agree with the respondent that the legislation's purpose is the initial test of constitutional validity and its effects are to be considered when the law under review has passed or, at least, has purportedly passed the purpose test. If the legislation fails the purpose test, there is no need to consider further its effects, since it has already been demonstrated to be invalid. Thus, if a law with a valid purpose interferes by its impact, with rights or freedoms, a litigant could still argue the effects of the legislation as a means to defeat its applicability and possibly its validity. In short, the effects test will only be necessary to defeat legislation with a valid purpose; effects can never be relied upon to save legislation with an invalid purpose.

[89] A second related submission is made by the Attorney General of Saskatchewan with respect to the characterization of the *Lord's Day Act*. Both Stevenson, Prov. Ct. J., at trial, and the American Supreme Court, in its quartet on Sunday observance legislation, suggest that the purpose of legislation may shift, or be transformed over time by changing social conditions. . . . A number of objections can be advanced to this "shifting purpose" argument.

[90] First, there are the practical difficulties. No legislation would be safe from a revised judicial assessment of purpose. Laws assumed valid on the basis of persuasive and powerful authority could, at any time, be struck down as invalid. Not only would this create uncertainty in the law, but it would encourage re-litigation of the same issues and, it could be argued, provide the courts with a means by which to arrive at a result dictated by other than legal considerations. . . .

[91] Furthermore, the theory of a shifting purpose stands in stark contrast to fundamental notions developed in our law concerning the nature of "Parliamentary intention." Purpose is a function of the intent of those who drafted and enacted the legislation at the time, and not of any shifting variable. . . .

[93] While the effect of such legislation as the *Lord's Day Act* may be more secular today than it was in 1677 or in 1906, such a finding cannot justify a conclusion that its purpose has similarly changed. In result, therefore, the *Lord's Day Act* must be characterized as it has always been, a law the primary purpose of which is the compulsion of sabbatical observance.

VII. Freedom of Religion

[94] A truly free society is one which can accommodate a wide variety of beliefs, diversity of tastes and pursuits, customs and codes of conduct. A free society is one which aims at equality with respect to the enjoyment of fundamental freedoms and I say this without any reliance upon s. 15 of the *Charter*. Freedom must surely be founded in respect for the inherent dignity and the inviolable rights of the human person. The essence of the concept of freedom of religion is the right to entertain such religious beliefs as a person chooses, the right to declare religious beliefs openly and without fear of hindrance or reprisal, and the right to manifest religious belief by worship and practice or by teaching and dissemination. But the concept means more than that.

[95] Freedom can primarily be characterized by the absence of coercion or constraint. If a person is compelled by the state or the will of another to a course of action or inaction which he would not otherwise have chosen, he is not acting of his own volition and he cannot be said to be truly free. One of the major purposes of the *Charter* is to protect, within reason, from compulsion or restraint. Coercion includes not only such blatant forms of compulsion as direct commands to act or refrain from acting on pain of sanction, coercion includes indirect forms of control which determine or limit alternative courses of conduct available to others. Freedom in a broad sense embraces both the absence of coercion and constraint, and the right to manifest beliefs and practices. Freedom means that, subject to such limitations as are necessary to protect public safety, order, health, or morals or the fundamental rights and freedoms of others, no one is to be forced to act in a way contrary to his beliefs or his conscience.

[96] What may appear good and true to a majoritarian religious group, or to the state acting at their behest, may not, for religious reasons, be imposed upon citizens who take a contrary view. The *Charter* safeguards religious minorities from the threat of "the tyranny of the majority."

[97] To the extent that it binds all to a sectarian Christian ideal, the *Lord's Day Act* works a form of coercion inimical to the spirit of the *Charter* and the dignity of all non-Christians. In proclaiming the standards of the Christian faith, the *Act* creates a climate hostile to, and gives the appearance of discrimination against, non-Christian Canadians. It takes religious values rooted in Christian morality and, using the force of the state, translates them into a positive law binding on believers and non-believers alike. The theological content of the legislation remains as a subtle and constant reminder to religious minorities within the country of their differences with, and alienation from, the dominant religious culture.

[98] Non-Christians are prohibited for religious reasons from carrying out activities which are otherwise lawful, moral

and normal. The arm of the state requires all to remember the Lord's day of the Christians and to keep it holy. The protection of one religion and the concomitant non-protection of others imports disparate impact destructive of the religious freedom of the collectivity.

[99] I agree with the submission of the respondent that to accept that Parliament retains the right to compel universal observance of the day of rest preferred by one religion is not consistent with the preservation and enhancement of the multicultural heritage of Canadians. To do so is contrary to the expressed provisions of s. 27. . . .

[100] If I am a Jew or a Sabbatarian or a Muslim, the practice of my religion at least implies my right to work on a Sunday if I wish. It seems to me that any law purely religious in purpose, which denies me that right, must surely infringe my religious freedom. . . .

[103] Much of the argument before this Court on the issue of the meaning of freedom of conscience and religion was in terms of "free exercise" and "establishment." These categories derive from the guarantee of freedom of religion in the First Amendment to the Constitution of the United States. The relevant part of the First Amendment reads:

> Congress shall make no law respecting an establishment of religion, or prohibiting the free exercise thereof; . . .

[104] It is the appellant's argument that unlike the American *Bill of Rights*, the *Canadian Charter of Rights and Freedoms* does not include an "establishment clause." He urged therefore that the protection of freedom of conscience and religion extends only to the "free exercise" of religion. . . .

[105] In my view this recourse to categories from the American jurisprudence is not particulary helpful in defining the meaning of freedom of conscience and religion under the *Charter*. The adoption in the United States of the categories "establishment" and "free exercise" is perhaps an inevitable consequence of the wording of the First Amendment. The cases illustrate, however, that these are not two totally separate and distinct categories, but rather, as the Supreme Court of the United States has frequently recognized, in specific instances "the two clauses may overlap." . . .

[106] Thus while it is true that in its four Sunday closing cases the United States Supreme Court does categorize compulsory religious observance as a potential violation of the "anti-establishment" principle, more frequently and more typically these same words signify the very different principle of the prohibition of preferential treatment of, or state financial support to, particular religions or religious institutions.

[107] In further support for this line of argument the appellant cites s. 29 of the *Charter* quoted earlier, and s. 93 of the *Constitution Act, 1867*. These provisions were cited as proof of the non-existence of an anti-establishment principle because they guarantee existing rights to financial support from the state for denominational schools. The respondent replies that these express provisions constitute specific and limited exceptions to the general principle of religious freedom which would otherwise prohibit any support or preference to denominational schools. Subsequent cases will decide the extent to which the *Charter* allows for state financial support for, or preferential treatment of, particular religions or religious institutions. That issue is not before us in the present case. . . .

[115] It is not necessary to reopen the issue of the meaning of freedom of religion under the *Canadian Bill of Rights*, because whatever the situation under that document, it is certain that the *Canadian Charter of Rights and Freedoms* does not simply "recognize and declare" existing rights as they were circumscribed by legislation current at the time of the *Charter's* entrenchment. The language of the *Charter* is imperative. It avoids any reference to existing or continuing rights but rather proclaims in the ringing terms of s. 2 that:

> Everyone has the following fundamental freedoms:
>   (*a*) Freedom of conscience and religion.

I agree with the submission of the respondent that the *Charter* is intended to set a standard upon which *present as well as future* legislation is to be tested. . . .

[116] This Court has already, in some measure, set out the basic approach to be taken in interpreting the *Charter*. In *Hunter v. Southam Inc.*, [1984] 2 S.C.R. 145, this Court expressed the view that the proper approach to the definition of the rights and freedoms guaranteed by the *Charter* was a purposive one. The meaning of a right or freedom guaranteed by the *Charter* was to be ascertained by an analysis of the *purpose* of such a guarantee; it was to be understood, in other words, in the light of the interests it was meant to protect.

[117] In my view this analysis is to be undertaken, and the purpose of the right or freedom in question is to be sought by reference to the character and the larger objects of the *Charter* itself, to the language chosen to articulate the specific right or freedom, to the historical origins of the concepts enshrined, and where applicable, to the meaning and purpose of the other specific rights and freedoms with which it is associated within the text of the *Charter*. The interpretation should be, as the judgment in *Southam* emphasizes, a generous rather than a legalistic one, aimed at fulfilling the purpose of the guarantee and securing for individuals the full benefit of the *Charter's* protection. At the same time it is important not to overshoot the actual purpose of the right or freedom in question, but to recall that the *Charter* was not enacted in a vacuum, and must therefore, as this Court's decision in *Law*

Society of Upper Canada v. Skapinker, [1984] 1 S.C.R. 357, illustrates, be placed in its proper linguistic, philosophic and historical contexts.

[118] With regard to freedom of conscience and religion, the historical context is clear. As they are relevant to the *Charter*, the origins of the demand for such freedom are to be found in the religious struggles in post-Reformation Europe. The spread of new beliefs, the changing religious allegiance of kings and princes, the shifting military fortunes of their armies and the consequent repeated redrawing of national and imperial frontiers led to situations in which large numbers of people—sometimes even the majority in a given territory—found themselves living under rulers who professed faiths different from, and often hostile to, their own and subject to laws aimed at enforcing conformity to religious beliefs and practices they did not share.

[119] English examples of such laws, passed during the Tudor and Stuart periods have been alluded to in the discussion above of the criminal law character of Sunday observance legislation. Opposition to such laws was confined at first to those who upheld the prohibited faiths and practices, and was designed primarily to avoid the disabilities and penalties to which these specific adherents were subject. As a consequence, when history or geography put power into the hands of these erstwhile victims of religious oppression the persecuted all too often became the persecutors.

[120] Beginning, however, with the Independent faction within the Parliamentary party during the Commonwealth or Interregnum, many, even among those who shared the basic beliefs of the ascendent religion, came to voice opposition to the use of the State's coercive power to secure obedience to religious precepts and to extirpate non-conforming beliefs. The basis of this opposition was no longer simply a conviction that the State was enforcing the wrong set of beliefs and practices but rather the perception that belief itself was not amenable to compulsion. Attempts to compel belief or practice denied the reality of individual conscience and dishonoured the God that had planted it in His creatures. It is from these antecedents that the concepts of freedom of religion and freedom of conscience became associated, to form, as they do in s. 2(*a*) of our *Charter*, the single integrated concept of "freedom of conscience and religion."

[121] What unites enunciated freedoms in the American First Amendment, s. 2(*a*) of the *Charter* and in the provisions of other human rights documents in which they are associated is the notion of the centrality of individual conscience and the inappropriateness of governmental intervention to compel or to constrain its manifestation. In *Hunter v. Southam Inc.*, *supra*, the purpose of the *Charter* was identified, at p. 155, as "the unremitting protection of individual rights and liberties."

It is easy to see the relationship between respect for individual conscience and the valuation of human dignity that motivates such unremitting protection.

[122] It should also be noted, however, that an emphasis on individual conscience and individual judgment also lies at the heart of our democratic political tradition. The ability of each citizen to make free and informed decisions is the absolute prerequisite for the legitimacy, acceptability, and efficacy of our system of self-government. It is because of the centrality of the rights associated with freedom of individual conscience both to basic beliefs about human worth and dignity and to a free and democractic political system that American jurisprudence has emphasized the primacy or "firstness" of the First Amendment. It is this same centrality that in my view underlies their designation in the *Canadian Charter of Rights and Freedoms* as "fundamental." They are the *sine qua non* of the political tradition underlying the *Charter*.

[123] Viewed in this context, the purpose of freedom of conscience and religion becomes clear. The values that underlie our political and philosophic traditions demand that every individual be free to hold and to manifest whatever beliefs and opinions his or her conscience dictates, provided *inter alia* only that such manifestations do not injure his or her neighbours or their parallel rights to hold and manifest beliefs and opinions of their own. Religious belief and practice are historically prototypical and, in many ways, paradigmatic of conscientiously-held beliefs and manifestations and are therefore protected by the *Charter*. Equally protected, and for the same reasons, are expressions and manifestations of religious non-belief and refusals to participate in religious practice. It may perhaps be that freedom of conscience and religion extends beyond these principles to prohibit other sorts of governmental involvement in matters having to do with religion. For the present case it is sufficient in my opinion to say that whatever else freedom of conscience and religion may mean, it must at the very least mean this: government may not coerce individuals to affirm a specific religious belief or to manifest a specific religious practice for a sectarian purpose. . . .

[133] In my view, the guarantee of freedom of conscience and religion prevents the government from compelling individuals to perform or abstain from performing otherwise harmless acts because of the religious significance of those acts to others. The element of religious compulsion is perhaps somewhat more difficult to perceive (especially for those whose beliefs are being enforced) when, as here, it is non-action rather than action that is being decreed, but in my view compulsion is nevertheless what it amounts to.

[134] I would like to stress that nothing in these reasons should be read as suggesting any opposition to Sunday being spent as a religious day; quite the contrary. It is recognized

that for a great number of Canadians, Sunday is the day when their souls rest in God, when the spiritual takes priority over the material, a day which, to them, gives security and meaning because it is linked to Creation and the Creator. It is a day which brings a balanced perspective to life, an opportunity for man to be in communion with man and with God. In my view, however, as I read the *Charter*, it mandates that the legislative preservation of a Sunday day of rest should be secular, the diversity of belief and non-belief, the diverse socio-cultural backgrounds of Canadians make it constitutionally incompetent for the federal Parliament to provide legislative preference for any one religion at the expense of those of another religious persuasion.

[135] In an earlier time, when people believed in the collective responsibility of the community toward some deity, the enforcement of religious conformity may have been a legitimate object of government, but since the *Charter*, it is no longer legitimate. With the *Charter*, it has become the right of every Canadian to work out for himself or herself what his or her religious obligations, if any, should be and it is not for the state to dictate otherwise. The state shall not use the criminal sanctions at its disposal to achieve a religious purpose, namely, the uniform observance of the day chosen by the Christian religion as its day of rest.

[136] On the authorities and for the reasons outlined, the true purpose of the *Lord's Day Act* is to compel the observance of the Christian Sabbath and I find the *Act*, and especially s. 4 thereof, infringes upon the freedom conscience and religion guaranteed in s. 2(*a*) of the *Charter*. . . .

VIII. Section 1 of the Charter

. . . [138] The appellant submits that even if the *Lord's Day Act* does involve a violation of freedom of conscience and religion as guaranteed by s. 2(*a*) of the *Charter*, the provisions of the *Act* constitute a reasonable limit, demonstrably justifiable in a free and democratic society on that right and that therefore the *Act* can be saved pursuant to s. 1 of the *Charter*. . . .

[140] Two reasons have been advanced to justify the legislation here in issue as a reasonable limit. It can be urged that the choice of the day of rest adhered to by the Christian majority is the most practical. This submission is really no more than an argument of convenience and expediency and is fundamentally repugnant because it would justify the law upon the very basis upon which it is attacked for violating s. 2(*a*).

[141] The other more plausible argument is that everyone accepts the need and value of a universal day of rest from all work, business and labour and it may as well be the day traditionally observed in our society. I accept the secular justification for a day of rest in a Canadian context and the reasonableness of a day of rest has been clearly enunciated by the courts in

the United States of America. The first and fatal difficulty with this argument is, as I have said, that it asserts an objective which has never been found by this Court to be the motivation for the legislation. It seems disingenuous to say that the legislation is valid criminal law and offends s. 2(*a*) because it compels the observance of a Christian religious duty, yet is still a reasonable limit demonstrably justifiable because it achieves the secular objective the legislators did not primarily intend. The appellant can no more assert under s. 1 a secular objective to validate legislation which in pith and substance involves a religious matter than it could assert a secular objective as the basis for the argument that the legislation does not offend s. 2(*a*). While there is no authority on this point, it seems clear that Parliament cannot rely upon an *ultra vires* purpose under s. 1 of the *Charter*. This use of s. 1 would invite colourability, allowing Parliament to do indirectly what it could not do directly. . . .

IX. Classification

[144] The third question put in issue by this Court is this:

> Is the *Lord's Day Act*, R.S.C. 1970, c. L-13, and especially s. 4 thereof enacted pursuant to the criminal law power under s. 91(27) of the *Constitution Act, 1867*?

[145] All members of the Alberta Court of Appeal agreed that settled authority compelled the conclusion that the *Lord's Day Act* was competent to Parliament pursuant to its power to legislate in relation to criminal law under s. 91(27). The appellant and his supporting interveners submit that the Court of Appeal was correct in their conclusion and the respondent concedes the point. . . .

[149] It should be noted, however, that this conclusion as to the federal Parliament's legislative competence to enact the *Lord's Day Act* depends on the identification of the purpose of the *Act* as compelling observance of Sunday by virtue of its religious significance. Were its purpose not religious but rather the secular goal of enforcing a uniform day of rest from labour, the *Act* would come under s. 92(13), property and civil rights in the province and, hence, fall under provincial rather than federal competence. . . .

WILSON J.: . . .

[153] In his reasons for judgment Dickson J. (Chief Justice at the date of the judgment) has canvassed in a most thorough fashion all the substantive questions entailed in the analysis of constitutionality and has come to the conclusion that the *Lord's Day Act* is validly enacted pursuant to the federal criminal law power under s. 91(27) of the *Constitution Act, 1867*. He has concluded, however, that it infringes upon the right to freedom of religion in s. 2(*a*) of the *Charter* and

that such infringement cannot be justified under s. 1 of the *Charter*. I agree with those conclusions and the only issue I wish to address in these reasons is the appropriate analytic approach to a *Charter* case, in a word, the distinction between the analysis demanded by the *Charter* and the analysis traditionally pursued in resolving division of powers litigation under ss. 91 and 92 of the *Constitution Act, 1867*.

[154] It is, of course, trite law that the analytic starting point in a division of powers case is the determination of the "pith and substance" of the challenged enactment. In the words of Professor Bora Laskin (as he then was) the court endeavours to achieve a "distillation of the 'constitutional value' represented by the challenged legislation ... and its attribution to a head of power." ...

[156] The division of powers jurisprudence is repleat with instances where the analytic focal point in determining whether a given piece of legislation is *ultra vires* the enacting legislature is the purpose or primary function of the legislation. Only when the effects of the legislation so directly impinge on some other subject matter as to reflect some alternative or ulterior purpose do the effects themselves take on analytic significance. ...

[158] In my view, the constitutional entrenchment of civil liberties in the *Canadian Charter of Rights and Freedoms* necessarily changes the analytic approach the courts must adopt in such cases. As Chief Justice Burger indicated in the celebrated anti-discrimination case of *Griggs v. Duke Power Co.*, 401 U.S. 424 (1970), at p. 432, the starting point for any analysis of a civil rights violation is "the *consequences* of [discriminatory] employment practices, not simply the motivation." Speaking in the context of equality rights as they pertain to employment, Burger C.J. stated at p. 432:

> ... good intent or absence of discriminatory intent does not redeem employment procedures or testing mechanisms that operate as "built-in headwinds" for minority groups. ...

While it remains perfectly valid to evaluate the purpose underlying a particular enactment in order to determine whether the legislature has acted within its constitutional authority in division of powers terms, the *Charter* demands an evaluation of the impingement of even *intra vires* legislation on the fundamental rights and freedoms of the individual. It asks not whether the legislature has acted for a purpose that is within the scope of the authority of that tier of government, but rather whether in so acting it has had the effect of violating an entrenched individual right. It is, in other words, first and foremost an effects-oriented document. ...

[161] Applying such reasoning to the case at bar, one can agree with Dickson J. at p. 337, that in enacting the *Lord's Day Act* "[t]he arm of the state requires all to remember the Lord's day of the Christians and to keep it holy," and that "[t]he protection of one religion and the concomitant non-protection of others imports disparate impact destructive of the religious freedom of the collectivity." Accordingly, the *Act* infringes upon the freedom of conscience and religion guaranteed in s. 2(*a*) of the *Charter*. This is not, however, because the statute was enacted for this *purpose* but because it has this *effect*. In my view, so long as a statute has such an actual or potential effect on an entrenched right, it does not matter what the purpose behind the enactment was. ...

[164] Accordingly, I agree with Dickson J. that the appeal in this case must be dismissed. The *Lord's Day Act* is in pith and substance legislation with a criminal law purpose and is therefore enacted by Parliament pursuant to the federal criminal law power in s. 91(27) of the *Constitution Act, 1867*. In so far as the *Charter of Rights* is concerned, however, I believe that the appropriate analytic starting point is the effect rather than the purpose of the enactment. ...

Quebec v. Ford et al. (Quebec Sign Case), 1988

The decision that the Supreme Court of Canada rendered on December 15, 1988 striking down Quebec's French-only sign law is one of the Court's most important *Charter* decisions. The decision moved constitutional jurisprudence in two different directions simultaneously: while it embraced a wide interpretation of "freedom of expression" as a constitutional right, it also established a broad basis for legislatures to use the power they have under section 33 of the *Charter* to override constitutional rights and freedoms. In addition to these important developments in the interpretation of the *Charter*, the decision had a major impact on constitutional politics in Canada.

This was by no means the first Supreme Court decision overturning sections of Bill 101, the *Charter of the French Language*, introduced by the PQ government in 1977. In 1979, the Court struck down provisions of Bill 101 making French the official language of the province's legislature and courts. Another decision in 1984 forced Quebec to open its English schools to Canadians moving to Quebec from other provinces.[1] Both decisions were based on entrenched constitutional language rights to which the legislative override in the *Charter* did not apply. But the attack on sections of Bill 101 making French the exclusive language for commercial signs and firm names was based not on specific language rights but on the right to freedom of expression—a right found in section 2(*b*) of the *Canadian Charter* (a section to which the override does apply) as well as in Quebec's *Charter of Human Rights and Freedoms*.

In June 1982, just two months after the *Charter* was proclaimed, Quebec's National Assembly, in a defiant gesture against the constitutional settlement of 1982 to which Quebec had not consented, passed a law re-enacting all laws passed prior to the *Charter*, but adding to each a section invoking the override.[2] After five years, in 1987, this omnibus use of the override lapsed and was not renewed. However, Quebec had used the override a second time: in February 1984, a law came into force applying the override just to the French-only sign provision of Bill 101. This override, if valid, was still in force when the Supreme Court was deciding the sign case. But the section of Bill 101 requiring French-only firm names had not been protected from judicial review by the override clause. Also, the Quebec *Charter of Human Rights* contained a right to freedom of expression, and it had not been overridden. Thus, whether or not an override was still in force, the Supreme Court had to consider the compatibility of French-only commercial regulations with the right to freedom of expression.

In the 1985 election campaign in which the Liberals, led by Robert Bourassa, threw the Parti Québécois out of office, the Liberals indicated that they would lift restrictions on the use of bilingual commercial signs. This promise was important in attracting some outstanding representatives of Quebec's English-speaking minority to the Liberal team. On the other

---

1 These cases are discussed in the introduction to case 31.

2 For a discussion of the "notwithstanding clause," or "override," as it is often called, see the introduction to this book.

hand, it threatened to alienate many Quebec Francophones who regarded the French-only sign policy as essential for ensuring that the public face of Quebec would be French.

After the election, Premier Bourassa decided not to act on this controversial issue until the constitutional litigation under way had run its course. A number of firms had challenged provisions of Bill 101 requiring French-only commercial signs and firm names.[3] A challenge had also been brought by Alan Singer, the owner of a stationery shop in an English-speaking district of Montreal, against provisions of Bill 101 that, for some commercial activities—for instance, the publication of catalogues and the signs of firms employing less than four persons or specializing in foreign products—required the use of French, but also permitted the use of another language.[4] Like other politicians in Charterland, Bourassa hoped that the Court might take a deeply divisive issue off his hands.

The litigation may have given the Premier a temporary reprieve, but when the Court's decision finally came down it did not make his political burden any lighter. On the contrary, the Supreme Court's finding that laws prohibiting the use of any language other than French violated the right to freedom of expression in both the *Canadian Charter* and the Quebec *Charter* deepened the resentment of the English-speaking community. The right to advertise in the language of one's choice could now be referred to as "a fundamental right." On the other hand, the Court's argument that a French-only policy was not necessary to preserve the French face of Quebec failed to make much impression on the Francophone majority.

The Court took a remarkably liberal approach to the concept of "freedom of expression." It built into this freedom a new, universal language right—a right to communicate in one's own language, a right, it argued, that is essential to personal identity. The Court rejected arguments that commercial speech should be excluded from freedom of expression. It recognized that when consumer-protection regulations of advertising are under review consideration would have to be given to competing policy interests. But the Court took the position that this kind of balancing was to be done not by narrowly defining freedom of expression but by considering the justification for limits on the right under section 1 of the *Charter*. Applying section 1 to the cases at hand, the Court felt that the objective of maintaining the predominantly French character of Quebec could justify requiring the use of French on a joint-use basis and even a law requiring the "marked predominance" of the French language. However, it saw no evidence justifying the exclusive use of French. Hence it struck down the French-only provisions attacked in *Ford*, but upheld bilingual requirements attacked by Singer.

While the Court's expansive interpretation of freedom of expression expanded the basis for judicial review, the Court in this same decision made it easier for legislatures to use section 33 of the *Charter*, the override clause, to immunize their laws from judicial review. Quebec's Court of Appeal had found Quebec's broad-brush use of the override to be unconstitutional, insisting that to fulfill its democratic purpose the override must be used in an accountable way with the legislature indicating precisely which rights and freedoms it was overriding. But here in *Ford* the Supreme Court rejected this argument: it would come too

---

3 Only one of the five businesses raising the challenge—Valerie Ford's wool shop—was not incorporated. Her name appears to have been used for the citation in this case because equality rights arguments were also made in the case and the Supreme Court had not yet decided whether equality rights extend to corporations.

4 The citation for the Supreme Court decision in this case is *Devine v. Quebec*.

close to requiring "a *prima facie* justification of the decision to exercise the override." The Supreme Court made it clear that it wished to minimize judicial review of the use of the override.

And use the override is exactly what Premier Bourassa did in response to the Court's decision. After agonizing for 48 hours, Bourassa announced his decision to bring in legislation permitting bilingual signs indoors but requiring French-only signs outside. To fend off a court challenge, the override clause was applied to this legislation. The new law, Bill 178, cost Bourassa the services of three of his Anglophone ministers and aroused the ire of English-speaking Quebecers. From the other side it was attacked by the opposition PQ party and by many Quebec Francophones who resented compromising the French-only program of Bill 101.

In the arena of constitutional politics Bourassa's action was a bombshell. By December 1988, there remained only two provinces, Manitoba and New Brunswick, whose legislatures had not approved the Meech Lake package of constitutional amendments. On the day after the Supreme Court decision, the Premier of Manitoba, Gary Filmon, introduced the Meech Lake Accord in the Manitoba legislature. But a few days later, following Premier Bourassa's decision to use the override and restore a unilingual French policy for outdoor signs, Filmon announced that he was suspending legislative consideration of the Meech Lake Accord. Legislative hearings, he said, "may invite a very negative anti-Quebec backlash."[5]

So at this stage the Meech Lake Accord, with its controversial clause recognizing Quebec as a "distinct society," was stalled if not dead. Although this meant that the prospects of a constitutional reconciliation with Quebec were dimmed, the French majority in Quebec learned through these events that the 1982 constitutional changes had left them with considerable power to protect their distinctive culture. For all Canadians the really ominous implication of these events was that they pointed to a deep gulf between the French majority in Quebec and the non-French majority in Canada over what should be regarded as fundamental in Canadian constitutionalism. ⌒

Discussion Questions

1. In what way is the Court's treatment of section 1 in this case exceptional?
2. In what sense does the underlying issue in this case involve two conflicting visions of Canada?
3. What light does this case shed on the use of the override clause in the *Charter*?

---

5   *The Globe and Mail* (20 December 1988).

QUEBEC v. FORD, ET AL.
[1988] 2 S.C.R. 712

Hearing: November 16, 17, 18, 1987; Judgment: December 15, 1988.

Present: Dickson C.J. and Beetz, Estey,* McIntyre, Lamer, Wilson, and Le Dain* JJ.

Interveners: The Attorney General of Canada, the Attorney General for Ontario, and the Attorney General for New Brunswick. 1987: November 16, 17, 18; 1988: December 15.

* Estey and Le Dain JJ. took no part in the judgment.

[1] **THE COURT:**[1] The principal issue in this appeal is whether ss. 58 and 69 of the Quebec *Charter of the French Language*, R.S.Q., c. C-11, which require that public signs and posters and commercial advertising shall be in the French language only and that only the French version of a firm name may be used, infringe the freedom of expression guaranteed by s. 2(*b*) of the *Canadian Charter of Rights and Freedoms* and s. 3 of the Quebec *Charter of Human Rights and Freedoms*, R.S.Q., c. C-12. There is also an issue as to whether ss. 58 and 69 of the *Charter of the French Language* infringe the guarantee against discrimination based on language in s. 10 of the Quebec *Charter of Human Rights and Freedoms*. The application of the *Canadian Charter of Rights and Freedoms* turns initially on whether there is a valid and applicable override provision, enacted pursuant to s. 33 of the Canadian *Charter*, that ss. 58 and 69 of the *Charter of the French Language* shall operate notwithstanding s. 2(*b*) of the Canadian *Charter*.

[2] The appeal is by leave of this Court from the judgment of the Quebec Court of Appeal on December 22, 1986, [1987] R.J.Q. 80, 5 Q.A.C. 119, 36 D.L.R. (4th) 374, dismissing the appeal of the Attorney General of Quebec from the judgment of Boudreault J. in the Superior Court for the District of Montreal on December 28, 1984, [1985] C.S. 147, 18 D.L.R. (4th) 711, which, on an application for a declaratory judgment, declared s. 58 of the *Charter of the French Language* to be inoperative to the extent that it prescribes that public signs and posters and commercial advertising shall be solely in the French language. The appeal is also from the judgment of the Court of Appeal in so far as it allowed the incidental appeal

---

1 Chief Justice Dickson and Justices Beetz, Estey, McIntyre, Lamer, Wilson, and Le Dain heard the case when it was argued in November 1987. But Estey and Le Dain did not participate in the decision— Estey because he resigned soon after the hearing and Le Dain because he was too ill.

of the respondents from the judgment of Boudreault J. and declared s. 69 of the *Charter of the French Language* to be inoperative to the extent that it prescribes that only the French version of a firm name may be used. In allowing the incidental appeal the Court of Appeal also declared ss. 205 to 208 of the *Charter of the French Language* respecting offences, penalties and other sanctions for a contravention of any of its provisions to be inoperative in so far as they apply to ss. 58 and 69.

I. The Respondents' Application for a Declaratory Judgment

[3] On February 15, 1984 the respondents brought a motion for a declaratory judgment pursuant to art. 454 of the Quebec *Code of Civil Procedure* and s. 24(1) of the *Canadian Charter of Rights and Freedoms*. The commercial advertising and signs displayed by the five respondents are described in paragraphs 1 to 5 of their petition as follows:

1. La Chaussure Brown's Inc. ("Brown's") operates a business of retail shoe stores throughout the Province of Quebec, and since at least September 1, 1981, it has used and displayed within and on its premises of its store situated in the Fairview Shopping Centre, 6801 Trans-Canada Highway, Pointe-Claire, commercial advertising containing the following words:

BRAVO	BRAVO
"Brown's quality	"la qualité a tout prix."
Bravo's price"	

2. Valerie Ford, carrying on business under the firm name and style of Les Lainages du Petit Mouton Enr. ("Ford"), operates a retail store selling, *inter alia*, wool, and since at least September 1, 1981, she has used and displayed on her premises at 311 St. Johns Boulevard, Pointe-Claire, an exterior sign containing the following words:

"laine   wool"

3. Nettoyeur et Tailleur Masson Inc. ("Nettoyeur Masson") carries on the business of a tailor and dry cleaner, and since at least September 1, 1981, it has used and displayed on its premises at 3259 Masson Street, Montreal an exterior sign containing the following words:

NETTOYEURS	Masson inc.	CLEANERS
TAILLEUR	TAILOR	
SERVICE	ALTERATIONS	
	REPAIRS	
1 HEURE	1 HOUR	

4. McKenna Inc. ("McKenna") carries on business as a florist in the City of Montreal and since at least September 1, 1981, it has used and displayed on its premises at

4509 Côte Des Neiges Road, Montreal, an exterior sign containing the following words:

> "Fleurs   McKENNA   Flowers"

5. La Compagnie de Fromage Nationale Ltée ("Fromage Nationale") carries on the business of a cheese distributor and since at least September 1, 1981, it has used and displayed on its premises at 9001 Salley Street, Ville LaSalle, exterior signs containing the following words:

> "NATIONAL CHEESE Co Ltd.
> La Cie de FROMAGE NATIONALE Ltée"

[4] The petition further alleges that the respondents La Chaussure Brown's Inc., Valerie Ford and La Compagnie de Fromage Nationale Ltée received a *mise en demeure* from the Commission de surveillance de la langue française advising them that their signs were not in conformity with the provisions of the *Charter of the French Language* and calling on them to conform to such provisions and that the respondents McKenna Inc. and Nettoyeur et Tailleur Masson Inc. were charged with violation of the *Charter of the French Language*.

[5] The respondents conclude in their petition for a declaration that they have the right, notwithstanding ss. 58, 69 and 205 to 208 of the *Charter of the French Language*, to use the signs, posters and commercial advertising described in their petition and a declaration that ss. 58 and 69 and ss. 205 to 208, as they apply to ss. 58 and 69 of the *Charter of the French Language*, are inoperative and of no force or effect.

II. The Relevant Legislative and Constitutional Provisions

[6] To facilitate an understanding of the issues in the appeal, as they are reflected in the reasons for judgment of the Superior Court and the Court of Appeal and in the constitutional questions and submissions of the parties in this Court, it is desirable at this point to set out the relevant legislative and constitutional provisions.

A. The Charter of the French Language

[7] Sections 1, 58, 69, 89, 205, 206 . . . of the *Charter of the French Language*, R.S.Q., c. C-11, provide:

> 1. French is the official language of Québec.
> 58. Public signs and posters and commercial advertising shall be solely in the official language.
>
> Notwithstanding the foregoing, in the cases and under the conditions or circumstances prescribed by regulation of the Office de la langue française, public signs and posters and commercial advertising may be both in French and in another language or solely in another language.

> 69. Subject to section 68, only the French version of a firm name may be used in Québec.
> 89. Where this act does not require the use of the official language exclusively, the official language and another language may be used together.
> 205. Every person who contravenes a provision of this act other than section 136 or of a regulation made under this act by the Gouvernement or by the Office de la langue française is guilty of an offence and liable, in addition to costs,
>
> (a) for each offence, to a fine of $30 to $575 in the case of a natural person, and of $60 to $1150 in the case of an artificial person.
>
> (b) for any subsequent offence within two years of a first offence, to a fine of $60 to $1150 in the case of a natural person, and of $575 to $5750 in the case of an artificial person.
> 206. A business firm guilty of an offence contemplated in section 136 is liable, in addition to costs, to a fine of $125 to $2300 for each day during which it carries on its business without a certificate.

B. The Quebec Charter of Human Rights and Freedoms

[8] Sections 3, 9.1 and 10 of the *Quebec Charter of Human Rights and Freedoms*, R.S.Q., c. C-12, provide:

> 3. Every person is the possessor of the fundamental freedoms, including freedom of conscience, freedom of religion, freedom of opinion, freedom of expression, freedom of peaceful assembly and freedom of association.
> 9.1 In exercising his fundamental freedoms and rights, a person shall maintain a proper regard for democratic values, public order and the general well-being of the citizens of Québec.
>
> In this respect, the scope of the freedoms and rights, and limits to their exercise, may be fixed by law.
> 10. Every person has a right to full and equal recognition and exercise of his human rights and freedoms, without distinction, exclusion or preference based on race, colour, sex, pregnancy, sexual orientation, civil status, age except as provided by law, religion, political convictions, language, ethnic or national origin, social condition, a handicap or the use of any means to palliate a handicap.
>
> Discrimination exists where such a distinction, exclusion or preference has the effect of nullifying or impairing such right.

[9] Sections 51 and 52 of the *Quebec Charter of Human Rights and Freedoms*, R.S.Q., c. C-12, provide:

> 51. The Charter shall not be so interpreted as to extend, limit or amend the scope of a provision of law except to the extent provided in section 52.

52. No provision of any Act, even subsequent to the Charter, may derogate from sections 1 to 38, except so far as provided by those sections, unless such Act expressly states that it applies despite the Charter.

[10] Prior to its amendment by s. 16 of *An Act to amend the Charter of Human Rights and Freedoms,* S.Q. 1982, c. 61, s. 52 of the Quebec *Charter* read as follows:

52. Sections 9 to 38 prevail over any provision of any subsequent act which may be inconsistent therewith unless such act expressly states that it applies despite the Charter....

IV. The Constitutional Questions and the Issues in the Appeal

[20] On the appeal to this Court the following constitutional questions were stated by Lamer J. in his order of May 11, 1987:

1. Are section 214 of the *Charter of the French Language,* R.S.Q. 1977, c. C-11, as enacted by S.Q. 1982, c. 21, s. 1, and s. 52 of *An Act to amend the Charter of the French Language,* S.Q. 1983, c. 56, inconsistent with s. 33(1) of the *Constitution Act, 1982* and therefore inoperative and of no force or effect under s. 52(1) of the latter Act?
2. If the answer to question 1 is affirmative, to the extent that they require the exclusive use of the French language, are ss. 58 and 69, and ss. 205 to 208 to the extent they apply thereto, of the *Charter of the French Language,* R.S.Q. 1977, c. C-11, as amended by S.Q. 1983, c. 56, inconsistent with the guarantee of freedom of expression under s. 2(b) of the *Canadian Charter of Rights and Freedoms?*
3. If the answer to question 2 is affirmative in whole or in part, are ss. 58 and 69, and ss. 205 to 208 to the extent they apply thereto, of the *Charter of the French Language,* R.S.Q. 1977, c. C-11, as amended by S.Q. 1983, c. 56, justified by the application of s. 1 of the *Canadian Charter of Rights and Freedoms* and therefore not inconsistent with the *Constitution Act, 1982?*

[21] The issues in the appeal, as reflected in the above constitutional questions, the reasons for judgment of the Superior Court and the Court of Appeal and the submissions in this Court, may be summarized as follows:

1. Is section 58 or s. 69 of the *Charter of the French Language* protected from the application of s. 2(b) of the *Canadian Charter of Rights and Freedoms* by a

valid and applicable override provision enacted in conformity with s. 33 of the Canadian *Charter?*
2. What are the dates from which s. 3 of the Quebec *Charter of Human Rights and Freedoms* took precedence, in case of conflict, over ss. 58 and 69 of the *Charter of the French Language?*
3. Does the freedom of expression guaranteed by s. 2(b) of the Canadian *Charter* and by s. 3 of the Quebec *Charter* include the freedom to express oneself in the language of one's choice?
4. Does the freedom of expression guaranteed by s. 2(b) of the Canadian *Charter* and s. 3 of the Quebec *Charter* extend to commercial expression?
5. If the requirement of the exclusive use of French by ss. 58 and 69 of the *Charter of the French Language* infringes the freedom of expression guaranteed by s. 2(b) of the Canadian *Charter* and s. 3 of the Quebec *Charter,* is the limit on freedom of expression imposed by ss. 58 and 69 justified under s. 1 of the Canadian *Charter* and s. 9.1 of the Quebec *Charter?*
6. Do sections 58 and 69 of the *Charter of the French Language* infringe the guarantee against discrimination based on language in s. 10 of the Quebec *Charter of Human Rights and Freedoms?*

[22] Submissions with respect to the validity and application of the override provisions in issue, as well as the content of freedom of expression and the effect of s. 1 of the Canadian *Charter* and s. 9.1 of the Quebec *Charter,* were also made in the appeals in *Devine v. Quebec (Attorney General),* [1988] 2 S.C.R. 790, and *Irwin Toy Ltd. v. Quebec (Attorney General),* S.C.C., No. 20074, which were heard at the same time as this appeal. They will necessarily be taken into consideration in disposing of the issues in this appeal.

V. Is Section 58 or Section 69 of the Charter of the French Language Protected from the Application of Section 2(b) of the Canadian Charter of Rights and Freedoms by a Valid and Applicable Override Provision Enacted in Conformity with Section 33 of the Canadian Charter?

[23] ... [T]here are two override provisions in issue: (a) s. 214 of the *Charter of the French Language,* which was enacted by s. 1 of *An Act respecting the Constitution Act, 1982,* S.Q. 1982, c. 21; and (b) s. 52 of *An Act to amend the Charter of the French Language,* S.Q. 1983, c. 56. The two override provisions are in identical terms, reading as follows: "This Act shall operate notwithstanding the provisions of sections 2 and 7 to 15 of the *Constitution Act, 1982* (Schedule B of the *Canada Act,*

chapter 11 in the 1982 volume of *Acts of Parliament of the United Kingdom*)." The issue of validity that is common to both s. 214 and s. 52 is whether a declaration in this form is one that is made in conformity with the override authority conferred by s. 33 of the *Canadian Charter of Rights and Freedoms*. There are additional issues of validity applicable to s. 214 of the *Charter of the French Language* arising from the manner of its enactment, that is, the "omnibus" character of the Act which enacted it, and from the retrospective effect given to s. 214 by s. 7 of the Act, which has been quoted above.

[24] Section 214 of the *Charter of the French Language* ceased to have effect by operation of s. 33(3) of the *Canadian Charter of Rights and Freedoms* five years after it came into force, and it was not re-enacted pursuant to s. 33(4) of the *Charter*. If the retrospective effect to April 17, 1982 given to s. 214 by s. 7 of *An Act respecting the Constitution Act, 1982*, was valid, s. 214 ceased to have effect on April 17, 1987. If not, it ceased to have effect on June 23, 1987, which was five years after the enacting Act came into force on the day of its sanction. In either case the question of the validity of s. 214 is moot, on the assumption, which was the one on which the appeal was argued, that on an application for a declaratory judgment in a case of this kind the Court should declare the law as it exists at the time of its judgment. We were, nevertheless, invited by the parties in this appeal and the appeals that were heard at the same time to rule on the validity of the standard override provision as enacted by *An Act respecting the Constitution Act, 1982*, because of the possible significance of that issue in cases pending before other tribunals. Before considering how the Court should respond to that invitation we propose to consider the other override provision in issue which, as we have said, raises a common question of validity.

[25] Section 52 of *An Act to amend the Charter of the French Language*, which was proclaimed in force on February 1, 1984, will not cease to have effect by operation of s. 33(3) of the *Canadian Charter of Rights and Freedoms* until February 1, 1989. It is therefore necessary to consider its validity since the Attorney General of Quebec contends that it protects s. 58 of the *Charter of the French Language* from the application of s. 2(*b*) of the *Canadian Charter of Rights and Freedoms*. . . .

[27] Those who challenged the constitutionality of the override provisions in s. 214 of the *Charter of the French Language* and s. 52 of *An Act to amend the Charter of the French Language* placed particular reliance on the judgment of the Quebec Court of Appeal in *Alliance des professeurs de Montréal v. Procureur général du Québec, supra*, in which the Court of Appeal held that the standard override provision was *ultra vires* and null as not being in conformity with the authority conferred by s. 33 of the *Canadian Charter of Rights and Freedoms*. . . .

[28] In that case the petitioners, Alliance des professeurs de Montréal, sought declarations that s. 1 and other provisions of *An Act respecting the Constitution Act, 1982*, which purported to add the standard override provision to all provincial legislation enacted up to June 23, 1982, and the standard override provisions enacted in some forty-nine statutes after that date were *ultra vires* and null as not being in conformity with s. 33 of the *Canadian Charter of Rights and Freedoms*. Thus the petitioners put in issue not only the validity of the standard override provision as enacted by the "omnibus" *Act respecting the Constitution Act, 1982*, but also its validity as separately enacted in particular statutes. . . .

[29] The essential contention in *Alliance des professeurs*, as in the present appeals, against the validity of the standard override provision, which was rejected by the Superior Court but upheld by the Court of Appeal, was that the provision did not sufficiently specify the guaranteed rights or freedoms which the legislation intended to override. In support of this contention reliance was placed not only on the wording of s. 33(1) and (2) of the *Charter* but on general considerations concerning the effectiveness of the democratic process. For convenience the standard override provision that is in issue, as well as s. 33(1) and (2) of the *Charter*, are quoted again:

> This Act shall operate notwithstanding the provisions of sections 2 and 7 to 15 of the *Constitution Act, 1982* (Schedule B of the *Canada Act*, chapter 11 in the 1982 volume of the *Acts of the Parliament of the United Kingdom*).
>
> **33.**(1) Parliament or the legislature of a province may expressly declare in an Act of Parliament or of the legislature, as the case may be, that the Act or a provision thereof shall operate notwithstanding a provision included in section 2 or sections 7 to 15 of this *Charter*.
>
> (2) An Act or a provision of an Act in respect of which a declaration made under this section is in effect shall have such operation as it would have but for the provision of this *Charter* referred to in the declaration.

[30] It was contended that the words "a provision included in section 2 or sections 7 to 15 of this *Charter*" in s. 33(1) and the words "but for the provision of this *Charter* referred to in the declaration" in s. 33(2) indicate that in order to be valid, a declaration pursuant to s. 33 must specify the particular provision within a section of the *Charter* which Parliament or the legislature of a province intends to override. That is, the specific guaranteed right or freedom to be overridden must be referred to in the words of the *Charter* and not merely by the number of the section or paragraph in which it appears. The rationale underlying this contention is that the nature of the guaranteed right or freedom must be sufficiently drawn

to the attention of the members of the legislature and of the public so that the relative seriousness of what is proposed may be perceived and reacted to through the democratic process. As the Attorney General for Ontario, who argued against the constitutionality of the standard override provision, put it, there must be a "political cost" for overriding a guaranteed right or freedom. . . .

[33] In the course of argument different views were expressed as to the constitutional perspective from which the meaning and application of s. 33 of the *Canadian Charter of Rights and Freedoms* should be approached: the one suggesting that it reflects the continuing importance of legislative supremacy, the other suggesting the seriousness of a legislative decision to override guaranteed rights and freedoms and the importance that such a decision be taken only as a result of a fully informed democratic process. These two perspectives are not, however, particularly relevant or helpful in construing the requirements of s. 33. Section 33 lays down requirements of form only, and there is no warrant for importing into it grounds for substantive review of the legislative policy in exercising the override authority in a particular case. The requirement of an apparent link or relationship between the overriding Act and the guaranteed rights or freedoms to be overridden seems to be a substantive ground of review. It appears to require that the legislature identify the provisions of the Act in question which might otherwise infringe specified guaranteed rights or freedoms. That would seem to require a *prima facie* justification of the decision to exercise the override authority rather than merely a certain formal expression of it. There is, however, no warrant in the terms of s. 33 for such a requirement. A legislature may not be in a position to judge with any degree of certainty what provisions of the *Canadian Charter of Rights and Freedoms* might be successfully invoked against various aspects of the Act in question. For this reason it must be permitted in a particular case to override more than one provision of the *Charter* and indeed all of the provisions which it is permitted to override by the terms of s. 33. The standard override provision in issue in this appeal is, therefore, a valid exercise of the authority conferred by s. 33 in so far as it purports to override all of the provisions in s. 2 and ss. 7 to 15 of the *Charter*. The essential requirement of form laid down by s. 33 is that the override declaration must be an express declaration that an Act or a provision of an Act shall operate notwithstanding a provision included in s. 2 or ss. 7 to 15 of the *Charter*. With great respect for the contrary view, this Court is of the opinion that a s. 33 declaration is sufficiently express if it refers to the number of the section, subsection or paragraph of the *Charter* which contains the provision or provisions to be overridden. Of course, if it is intended to override only a part of the provision

or provisions contained in a section, subsection or paragraph then there would have to be a sufficient reference in words to the part to be overridden. . . .

[34] Therefore, s. 52 of *An Act to amend the Charter of the French Language* is a valid and subsisting exercise of the override authority conferred by s. 33 of the *Canadian Charter of Rights and Freedoms* that protects s. 58 of the *Charter of the French Language* from the application of s. 2(*b*) of the Canadian *Charter*. Section 69 of the *Charter of the French Language* is not so protected since it was not affected by *An Act to amend the Charter of the French Language*. In the result, as indicated in the following Part VI of these reasons, s. 58 is subject to s. 3 of the Quebec *Charter of Human Rights and Freedoms* while s. 69 is subject to both s. 2(*b*) of the Canadian *Charter* and s. 3 of the Quebec *Charter*.

[35] Before leaving Part V of these reasons, it remains to be considered whether the Court should exercise its discretion to rule on the other aspects of the validity of the standard override provision as enacted by *An Act respecting the Constitution Act, 1982*: the "omnibus" character of the enactment; and the retrospective effect given to the override provision. These issues affect both s. 214 of the *Charter of the French Language*, which is in issue in this appeal and in the *Devine* appeal and s. 364 of the *Consumer Protection Act*, R.S.Q., c. P-40.1, in the *Irwin Toy* appeal. The Court has concluded that although both of these provisions have ceased to have effect it is better that all questions concerning their validity should be settled in these appeals because of their possible continuing importance in other cases. Given the conclusion that the enactment of the standard override provision in the form indicated above is a valid exercise of the authority conferred by s. 33 of the *Canadian Charter of Rights and Freedoms*, this Court is of the opinion that the validity of its enactment is not affected by the fact that it was introduced into all Quebec statutes enacted prior to a certain date by a single enactment. That was an effective exercise of legislative authority that did not prevent the override declaration so enacted in each statute from being an express declaration within the meaning of s. 33 of the Canadian *Charter*. Counsel referred to this form of enactment as reflecting an impermissibly "routine" exercise of the override authority or even a "perversion" of it. It was even suggested that it amounted to an attempted amendment of the *Charter*. These are once again essentially submissions concerning permissible legislative policy in the exercise of the override authority rather than what constitutes a sufficiently express declaration of override. As has been stated, there is no warrant in s. 33 for such considerations as a basis of judicial review of a particular exercise of the authority conferred by s. 33. The Court is of a different view, however, concerning the retrospective effect given to the standard override provision by s. 7

of *An Act respecting the Constitution Act, 1982.* ... In providing that s. 1, which re-enacted all of the Quebec statutes adopted before April 17, 1982 with the addition in each of the standard override provision, should have effect from that date, s. 7 purported to give retrospective effect to the override provision. ...

[36] ... In *Gustavson Drilling (1964) Ltd. v. Minister of National Revenue*, [1977] 1 S.C.R. 271, Dickson J. (as he then was) wrote, for the majority (at p. 279):

> The general rule is that statutes are not to be construed as having retrospective operation unless such a construction is expressly or by necessary implication required by the language of the Act.

Where, as here, an enabling provision is ambiguous as to whether it allows for retroactive legislation, the same rule of construction applies. In this case, s. 33(1) admits of two interpretations; one that allows Parliament or a legislature to enact retroactive override provisions, the other that permits prospective derogation only. We conclude that the latter and narrower interpretation is the proper one, and that s. 7 cannot give retrospective effect to the override provision. Section 7 of *An Act respecting the Constitution Act, 1982*, is to the extent of this inconsistency with s. 33 of the Canadian *Charter*, of no force or effect, with the result that the standard override provisions enacted by s. 1 of that *Act* came into force on June 23, 1982 in accordance with the first paragraph of s. 7. ...

VII. Whether the Freedom of Expression Guaranteed by Section 2(b) of the Canadian Charter of Rights and Freedoms and by Section 3 of the Quebec Charter of Human Rights and Freedoms Includes the Freedom to Express Oneself in the Language of One's Choice

[39] In so far as this issue is concerned, the words "freedom of expression" in s. 2(*b*) of the Canadian *Charter* and s. 3 of the Quebec *Charter* should be given the same meaning. As indicated above, both the Superior Court and the Court of Appeal held that freedom of expression includes the freedom to express oneself in the language of one's choice. After indicating the essential relationship between expression and language by reference to dictionary definitions of both, Boudreault J. in the Superior Court said that in the ordinary or general form of expression there cannot be expression without language. Bisson J.A. in the Court of Appeal said that he agreed with the reasons of Boudreault J. on this issue and expressed his own view in the form of the following question: "Is there a purer form of freedom of expression than the spoken language and written language?" He supported his conclusion by quotation of the following statement of this Court in *Reference re Manitoba Language Rights*, [1985] 1 S.C.R. 721, at p. 744: "The

importance of language rights is grounded in the essential role that language plays in human existence, development and dignity. It is through language that we are able to form concepts; to structure and order the world around us. Language bridges the gap between isolation and community, allowing humans to delineate the rights and duties they hold in respect of one another, and thus to live in society."

[40] The conclusion of the Superior Court and the Court of Appeal on this issue is correct. Language is so intimately related to the form and content of expression that there cannot be true freedom of expression by means of language if one is prohibited from using the language of one's choice. Language is not merely a means or medium of expression; it colours the content and meaning of expression. It is, as the preamble of the *Charter of the French Language* itself indicates, a means by which a people may express its cultural identity. It is also the means by which the individual expresses his or her personal identity and sense of individuality. That the concept of "expression" in s. 2(*b*) of the Canadian *Charter* and s. 3 of the Quebec *Charter* goes beyond mere content is indicated by the specific protection accorded to "freedom of thought, belief [and] opinion" in s. 2 and to "freedom of conscience" and "freedom of opinion" in s. 3. That suggests that "freedom of expression" is intended to extend to more than the content of expression in its narrow sense.

[41] The Attorney General of Quebec made several submissions against the conclusion reached by the Superior Court and the Court of Appeal on this issue, the most important of which may be summarized as follows: (a) in determining the meaning of freedom of expression the Court should apply the distinction between the message and the medium which must have been known to the framers of the Canadian and Quebec *Charters*; (b) the express provision for the guarantee of language rights in ss. 16 to 23 of the Canadian *Charter* indicate that it was not intended that a language freedom should result incidentally from the guarantee of freedom of expression in s. 2(*b*); (c) the recognition of a freedom to express oneself in the language of one's choice under s. 2(*b*) of the Canadian *Charter* and s. 3 of the Quebec *Charter* would undermine the special and limited constitutional position of the specific guarantees of language rights in s. 133 of the *Constitution Act, 1867* and ss. 16 to 23 of the Canadian *Charter* that was emphasized by the Court in *MacDonald v. City of Montreal*, [1986] 1 S.C.R. 460, and *Société des Acadiens du Nouveau-Brunswick Inc. v. Association of Parents for Fairness in Education*, [1986] 1 S.C.R. 549; and (d) the recognition that freedom of expression includes the freedom to express oneself in the language of one's choice would be contrary to the views expressed on this issue by the European Commission of Human Rights and the European Court of Human Rights.

[42] The distinction between the message and the medium was applied by Dugas J. of the Superior Court in *Devine v. Procureur général du Québec, supra,* in holding that freedom of expression does not include freedom to express oneself in the language of one's choice. It has already been indicated why that distinction is inappropriate as applied to language as a means of expression because of the intimate relationship between language and meaning. As one of the authorities on language quoted by the appellant Singer in the *Devine* appeal, J. Fishman, *The Sociology of Language* (1972), at p. 4, puts it: ". . . language is not merely a *means* of interpersonal communication and influence. It is not merely a *carrier* of content, whether latent or manifest. Language itself *is* content, a reference for loyalties and animosities, an indicator of social statuses and personal relationships, a marker of situations and topics as well as of the societal goals and the large-scale value-laden arenas of interaction that typify every speech community." . . .

[43] The second and third of the submissions of the Attorney General of Quebec which have been summarized above, with reference to the implications for this issue of the express or specific guarantees of language rights in s. 133 of the *Constitution Act, 1867,* and ss. 16 to 23 of the *Canadian Charter of Rights and Freedoms,* are closely related and may be addressed together. These special guarantees of language rights do not, by implication, preclude a construction of freedom of expression that includes the freedom to express oneself in the language of one's choice. . . . The central unifying feature of all of the language rights given explicit recognition in the Constitution of Canada is that they pertain to governmental institutions and for the most part they oblige the government to provide for, or at least tolerate, the use of both official languages. In this sense they are more akin to rights, properly understood, than freedoms. They grant entitlement to a specific benefit from the government or in relation to one's dealing with the government. Correspondingly, the government is obliged to provide certain services or benefits in both languages or at least permit use of either language by persons conducting certain affairs with the government. . . . In contrast, what the respondents seek in this case is a freedom as that term was explained by Dickson J. (as he then was) in *R. v. Big M Drug Mart Ltd.,* [1985] 1 S.C.R. 295, at p. 336: "Freedom can primarily be characterized by the absence of coercion or constraint. If a person is compelled by the state or the will of another to a course of action or inaction which he would not otherwise have chosen, he is not acting of his own volition and he cannot be said to be truly free. One of the major purposes of the *Charter* is to protect, within reason, from compulsion or restraint." The respondents seek to be free of the state imposed requirement that their commercial signs and advertising be in French only, and seek the freedom, in the entirely private or non-governmental realm of commercial activity, to display signs and advertising in the language of their choice as well as that of French. Manifestly the respondents are not seeking to use the language of their choice in any form of direct relations with any branch of government and are not seeking to oblige government to provide them any services or other benefits in the language of their choice. In this sense the respondents are asserting a freedom, the freedom to express oneself in the language of one's choice in an area of non-governmental activity, as opposed to a language right of the kind guaranteed in the Constitution. The recognition that freedom of expression includes the freedom to express oneself in the language of one's choice does not undermine or run counter to the special guarantees of official language rights in areas of governmental jurisdiction or responsibility. . . .

[44] The decisions of the European Commission of Human Rights and the European Court of Human Rights on which the Attorney General of Quebec relied are all distinguishable on the same basis, apart from the fact that, as Bisson J.A. observed in the Court of Appeal, they arose in an entirely different constitutional context. They all involved claims to language rights in relations with government that would have imposed some obligation on government. . . .

VIII. Whether the Guarantee of Freedom of Expression Extends to Commercial Expression

[45] In argument there arose a question whether the above issue is an issue in this appeal. The Attorney General of Quebec contended that if the guarantee of freedom of expression included the freedom to express oneself in the language of one's choice the respondents must still show that the guarantee extends to commercial expression. The respondents disputed this on the ground that the challenged provisions are directed to the language used and not to regulation of the substantive content of the expression. At the same time they made alternative submissions that the guarantee extended to commercial expression. The Attorney General of Quebec is correct on this issue: there cannot be a guaranteed freedom to express oneself in the language of one's choice in respect of a form or kind of expression that is not covered by the guarantee of freedom of expression. The question whether the guarantee of freedom of expression in s. 2(*b*) of the Canadian *Charter* and s. 3 of the Quebec *Charter* extends to the kind of expression contemplated by ss. 58 and 69 of the *Charter of the French Language,* which for convenience is referred to as commercial expression, is therefore an issue in this appeal. The submissions that were made on the question of commercial expression in the *Devine* and *Irwin Toy* appeals will be considered in determining that issue in this appeal.

[46] It was not disputed that the public signs and posters, the commercial advertising, and the firm name referred to in ss. 58 and 69 of the *Charter of the French Language* are forms of expression, and it was also assumed or accepted in argument that the expression contemplated by these provisions may be conveniently characterized or referred to as commercial expression. Sections 58 and 69 appear in Chapter VII of the *Charter of the French Language,* entitled "The Language of Commerce and Business." It must be kept in mind, however, that while the words "commercial expression" are a convenient reference to the kind of expression contemplated by the provisions in issue, they do not have any particular meaning or significance in Canadian constitutional law, unlike the corresponding expression "commercial speech," which in the United States has been recognized as a particular category of speech entitled to First Amendment protection of a more limited character than that enjoyed by other kinds of speech. The issue in the appeal is not whether the guarantee of freedom of expression in s. 2(*b*) of the Canadian *Charter* and s. 3 of the Quebec *Charter* should be construed as extending to particular categories of expression, giving rise to difficult definitional problems, but whether there is any reason why the guarantee should not extend to a particular kind of expression, in this case the expression contemplated by ss. 58 and 69 of the *Charter of the French Language.* Because, however, the American experience with the First Amendment protection of "commercial speech" was invoked in argument, as it has been in other cases, both for and against the recognition in Canada that the guarantee of freedom of expression extends to the kinds of expression that may be described as commercial expression, it is convenient to make brief reference to it at this point.

[47] In *Valentine v. Chrestensen,* 316 U.S. 52 (1942), the Supreme Court of the United States declined to afford First Amendment protection to speech which did no more than propose a commercial transaction. Some thirty-four years later, in *Virginia State Board of Pharmacy v. Virginia Citizens Consumer Council Inc.,* 425 U.S. 748 (1976), the Supreme Court affirmed a repudiation of the notion that commercial speech constituted an unprotected exception to the First Amendment guarantee. *Virginia Pharmacy* concerned a Virginia statute which prohibited pharmacists from advertising prices for prescription drugs. The statute was challenged by customers who asserted a First Amendment right to receive drug price information that the pharmacist wished to communicate. The speech at issue was purely commercial in that it simply proposed a commercial transaction. By holding that price advertising was not outside the First Amendment, the Court rejected the central premise of the commercial speech doctrine—that is, that business advertising which merely

solicits a commercial transaction is susceptible to government regulation on the same terms as any other aspect of the market place. The reasons of Blackmun J., writing for the Court, focus on the informative function of the speech from the point of view of the listener whose interest, it was said, "may be as keen, if not keener by far, than his interest in the day's most urgent political debate" (p. 763). The rationale stated by the Court for a First Amendment protection of commercial speech was the interest of the individual consumer and the society generally in the free flow of commercial information as indispensable to informed economic choice. The reasons are careful to note, however, that although commercial speech is protected it is entitled to a lesser degree of protection than that afforded to other forms of speech. . . .

[48] By 1980, when the Court decided *Central Hudson Gas & Electric Corp. v. Public Service Commission of New York,* 447 U.S. 557 (1980), it was apparent that some control of truthful advertising was legitimate as long as the regulation directly advanced a substantial state interest. Powell J., writing for the Court, formulated a four-part analysis for determining whether a particular regulation of commercial speech is consistent with the First Amendment, which he summed up as follows at p. 566:

> In commercial speech cases, then, a four-part analysis has developed. At the outset, we must determine whether the expression is protected by the First Amendment. For commercial speech to come within that provision, it at least must concern lawful activity and not be misleading. Next, we ask whether the asserted governmental interest is substantial. If both inquiries yield positive answers, we must determine whether the regulation directly advances the governmental interest asserted, and whether it is not more extensive than is necessary to serve that interest.

. . . It has been observed that this test is very similar to the test that was adopted by this Court in *R. v. Oakes,* [1986] 1 S.C.R. 103, for justification under s. 1 of the *Charter.* The *Central Hudson* test has been described as "an uneasy compromise" between competing strains of commercial speech theory. It is an attempt to balance the legitimacy of government regulations intended to protect consumers from harmful commercial speech with the belief that a free market in ideas and information is necessary to an informed and autonomous consumer.

[49] In *Posadas de Puerto Rico Associates v. Tourism Co. of Puerto Rico,* 106 S.Ct. 2968 (1986), the Court applied the *Central Hudson* test in a manner that attracted much criticism as reflecting, in the opinion of some commentators, an excessively deferential attitude to government regulation in the face of little or no demonstration by the state that the legislative

means it had adopted either directly advanced the asserted substantial interest or minimally restricted first amendment interests. See, for example, Philip B. Kurland, "*Posadas de Puerto Rico v. Tourism Company*: 'Twas Strange, 'Twas Passing Strange; 'Twas Pitiful, 'Twas Wondrous Pitiful," [1986] *Sup. Ct. Rev.* 1; and "The Supreme Court—Leading Cases" (1986), 100 *Harv. L. Rev.* 100, at p. 172. *Posadas* reflects how differences of view or emphasis in the application of the *Central Hudson* test can determine the effective extent of the protection of commercial speech from legislative limitation or restriction. It reveals the tension between two values: the value of the free circulation of commercial information and the value of consumer protection against harmful commercial speech. The American experience with the constitutional protection of commercial speech further indicates the difficulties inherent in its application, in particular the degree to which the courts are involved in the evaluation of regulatory policy in the field of consumer protection. The American jurisprudence with respect to commercial speech has been the subject of much scholarly analysis and criticism. Among the leading articles are the following: Jackson and Jeffries, "Commercial Speech: Economic Due Process and the First Amendment" (1979), 65 *Va. L. Rev.* 1; Weinberg, "Constitutional Protection of Commercial Speech" (1982), 82 *Colum. L. Rev.* 720; and Lively, "The Supreme Court and Commercial Speech: New Words with an Old Message" (1987), 72 *Minn. L. Rev.* 289. There is also an analysis of the American jurisprudence in the very helpful article on commercial expression by Professor Robert J. Sharpe, "Commercial Expression and the Charter" (1987), 37 *U. of T.L.J.* 229.

[50] In the case at bar Boudreault J. in the Superior Court held that the guarantee of freedom of expression in s. 3 of the Quebec *Charter* extended to commercial expression. He relied particularly on the reasoning in the American decisions, quoting at length from the judgment of Blackmun J. in *Virginia Pharmacy* for the rationale underlying the protection of commercial speech in the United States. He emphasized, as does that case, that it is not only the speaker but the listener who has an interest in freedom of expression. In the Court of Appeal, Bisson J.A. applied the judgment of the majority of the Court on this issue in *Irwin Toy Ltd. v. Procureur général du Québec*, [1986] R.J.Q. 2441, and quoted from the opinions of Jacques J.A. and Vallerand J.A. in that case. In *Irwin Toy*, Jacques J.A. held that there was no basis on the face of s. 2(*b*) of the Canadian *Charter* for distinguishing, in respect of the guarantee of freedom of expression, between different kinds of expression, whether they be of a political, artistic, cultural or other nature. He held that commercial expression was as much entitled to protection as other kinds of expression because of the important role played by it in assisting persons

to make informed economic choices. He added, however, that commercial expression might be subject to reasonable limits under s. 1 of the Canadian *Charter* of a kind that would not be reasonable in the case of political expression. . . .

[51] In the course of argument reference was made to two other Canadian decisions which reflect the contrasting positions on the question whether freedom of expression should extend to commercial expression: the majority decision of the Ontario Divisional Court in *Re Klein and Law Society of Upper Canada* (1985), 16 D.L.R. (4th) 489, and the unanimous decision of the Alberta Court of Appeal in *Re Grier and Alberta Optometric Association* (1987), 42 D.L.R. (4th) 327. In *Klein*, on which the Attorney General of Quebec and those who supported his contention that freedom of expression should not extend to commercial expression placed particular reliance, the relevant issue was whether the Rules of Professional Conduct of the Law Society of Upper Canada prohibiting fee advertising by solicitors infringed the guarantee of freedom of expression in s. 2(*b*) of the *Charter*. After referring to the pre-*Charter* decisions on freedom of speech and the American jurisprudence on commercial speech, Callaghan J., with whom Eberle J. concurred, concluded that the guarantee of freedom of expression in s. 2(*b*) should not extend to commercial expression. He held that commercial expression was unrelated to political expression, which in his view was the principal if not exclusive object of the protection afforded by s. 2(*b*). He said at p. 532: "The *Charter* reflects a concern with the political rights of the individual and does not, in my view, reflect a similar concern with the economic sphere nor with its incidents such as commercial speech" and "*Prima facie* then, the freedom of expression guaranteed by s. 2(*b*) of the *Charter* would appear to apply to the expression of ideas relating to the political and governmental domains of the country. (I leave aside the question of whether or not artistic expression falls within s. 2(*b*))." After a very full discussion of American jurisprudence and experience with respect to the First Amendment protection of commercial speech Callaghan J. expressed the view that there were good reasons for not following it, among them the extent to which such protection involved the courts in a difficult case-by-case review of regulatory policy. He concluded as follows at p. 539: "I would conclude that there is no reason to expand the meaning of the word 'expression' in s. 2(*b*) of the *Charter* to cover pure commercial speech. Commercial speech contributes nothing to democratic government because it says nothing about how people are governed or how they should govern themselves. It does not relate to government policies or matters of public concern essential to a democratic process. It pertains to the economic realm and is a matter appropriate to regulation by the Legislature." . . .

[52] In *Grier*, the Alberta Court of Appeal (Lieberman, Kerans and Irving JJ.A.) held that a brochure mailed by a licensed optometrist to patients and others quoting prices for various services was protected expression within the meaning of s. 2(*b*) of the *Charter*. It declined to follow *Klein* on the question of commercial expression and expressed agreement with the decision of the Quebec Court of Appeal in *Irwin Toy* on that question....

[53] The submissions of the Attorney General of Quebec and those who supported him on this issue may be summarized as follows. The scope of a guaranteed freedom must be determined, as required by *R. v. Big M Drug Mart Ltd.*, *supra*, in the light of the character and larger objects of the Canadian *Charter* and the linguistic, philosophic and historical context of the particular freedom. There is no historical basis for a guarantee of freedom of commercial expression in pre-*Charter* jurisprudence, in which recognition was given, on the basis of the division of powers and the "implied bill of rights," to freedom of political expression. Freedom of expression appears in both the Canadian *Charter* and the Quebec *Charter* under the heading of "Fundamental Freedoms"; there is nothing fundamental about commercial expression. A guarantee of freedom of expression which embraces commercial advertising would be the protection of an economic right, when both the Canadian *Charter* and the Quebec *Charter* clearly indicate that they are not concerned with the protection of such rights. The American decisions recognizing a limited First Amendment protection for commercial speech must be seen in the context of a constitution that protects the right of property, whereas that right was deliberately omitted from the protection afforded by s. 7 of the Canadian *Charter*. This Court, in refusing to constitutionalize the right to strike, has recognized that the Canadian *Charter* does not extend to economic rights or freedoms. To extend freedom of expression beyond political expression, and possibly artistic and cultural expression, would trivialize that freedom and lead inevitably to the adoption of different justificatory standards under s. 1 according to the kind of expression involved. The terms of s. 1, as interpreted and applied by the courts, do not permit of such differential application. Freedom of commercial expression, and in particular commercial advertising, does not serve any of the values that would justify its constitutional protection. Commercial advertising is manipulative and seeks to condition or control economic choice rather than to provide the basis of a truly informed choice. As the American experience shows, the recognition of a limited protection for commercial expression involves an evaluation of regulatory policy that is better left to the legislature. Academic criticism of the American approach to commercial speech and judicial expression of misgivings concerning it provide sufficient reason for declining to follow it.

[54] It is apparent to this Court that the guarantee of freedom of expression in s. 2(*b*) of the Canadian *Charter* and s. 3 of the Quebec *Charter* cannot be confined to political expression, important as that form of expression is in a free and democratic society. The pre-*Charter* jurisprudence emphasized the importance of political expression because it was a challenge to that form of expression that most often arose under the division of powers and the "implied bill of rights," where freedom of political expression could be related to the maintenance and operation of the institutions of democratic government. But political expression is only one form of the great range of expression that is deserving of constitutional protection because it serves individual and societal values in a free and democratic society.

[55] The post-*Charter* jurisprudence of this Court has indicated that the guarantee of freedom of expression in s. 2(*b*) of the *Charter* is not to be confined to political expression. In holding, in *RWDSU v. Dolphin Delivery Ltd.*, [1986] 2 S.C.R. 573, that secondary picketing was a form of expression within the meaning of s. 2(*b*) the Court recognized that the constitutional guarantee of freedom of expression extended to expression that could not be characterized as political expression in the traditional sense but, if anything, was in the nature of expression having an economic purpose....

[56] Various attempts have been made to identify and formulate the values which justify the constitutional protection of freedom of expression. Probably the best known is that of Professor Thomas I. Emerson in his article, "Toward a General Theory of the First Amendment" (1963), 72 *Yale L.J.* 877, where he sums up these values as follows at p. 878:

> The values sought by society in protecting the right to freedom of expression may be grouped into four broad categories. Maintenance of a system of free expression is necessary (1) as assuring individual self-fulfillment, (2) as a means of attaining the truth, (3) as a method of securing participation by the members of the society in social, including political, decision-making, and (4) as maintaining the balance between stability and change in society.

The third and fourth of these values would appear to be closely related if not overlapping. Generally the values said to justify the constitutional protection of freedom of expression are stated as three-fold in nature, as appears from the article by Professor Sharpe referred to above on "Commercial Expression and the Charter," where he speaks of the three "rationales" for such protection as follows at p. 232:

> The first is that freedom of expression is essential to intelligent and democratic self-government.... The second theory is that freedom of expression protects an open exchange of views, thereby creating a competitive

market-place of ideas which will enhance the search for the truth. ...

The third theory values expression for its own sake. On this view, expression is seen as an aspect of individual autonomy. Expression is to be protected because it is essential to personal growth and self-realization.

[57] While these attempts to identify and define the values which justify the constitutional protection of freedom of expression are helpful in emphasizing the most important of them, they tend to be formulated in a philosophical context which fuses the separate questions of whether a particular form or act of expression is within the ambit of the interests protected by the value of freedom of expression and the question whether that form or act of expression, in the final analysis, deserves protection from interference under the structure of the Canadian *Charter* and the Quebec *Charter*. These are two distinct questions and call for two distinct analytical processes. The first, at least for the Canadian *Charter*, is to be determined by the purposive approach to interpretation set out by this Court in *Hunter v. Southam Inc.*, [1984] 2 S.C.R. 145, and *Big M Drug Mart Ltd.*, *supra*. The second, the question of the limitation on the protected values, is to be determined under s. 1 of the *Charter* as interpreted in *Oakes, supra,* and *R. v. Edwards Books and Art Ltd.*, [1986] 2 S.C.R. 713. The division between the two analytical processes has been established by this Court in the above decisions. First, consideration will be given to the interests and purposes that are meant to be protected by the particular right or freedom in order to determine whether the right or freedom has been infringed in the context presented to the court. If the particular right or freedom is found to have been infringed, the second step is to determine whether the infringement can be justified by the state within the constraints of s. 1. It is within the perimeters of s. 1 that courts will in most instances weigh competing values in order to determine which should prevail.

[58] In order to address the issues presented by this case it is not necessary for the Court to delineate the boundaries of the broad range of expression deserving of protection under s. 2(*b*) of the Canadian *Charter* or s. 3 of the Quebec *Charter*. It is necessary only to decide if the respondents have a constitutionally protected right to use the English language in the signs they display, or more precisely, whether the fact that such signs have a commercial purpose removes the expression contained therein from the scope of protected freedom.

[59] In our view, the commercial element does not have this effect. Given the earlier pronouncements of this Court to the effect that the rights and freedoms guaranteed in the Canadian *Charter* should be given a large and liberal interpretation, there is no sound basis on which commercial

expression can be excluded from the protection of s. 2(*b*) of the *Charter*. It is worth noting that the courts below applied a similar generous and broad interpretation to include commercial expression within the protection of freedom of expression contained in s. 3 of the Quebec *Charter*. Over and above its intrinsic value as expression, commercial expression which, as has been pointed out, protects listeners as well as speakers plays a significant role in enabling individuals to make informed economic choices, an important aspect of individual self-fulfillment and personal autonomy. The Court accordingly rejects the view that commercial expression serves no individual or societal value in a free and democratic society and for this reason is undeserving of any constitutional protection.

[60] Rather, the expression contemplated by ss. 58 and 69 of the *Charter of the French Language* is expression within the meaning of both s. 2(*b*) of the Canadian *Charter* and s. 3 of the Quebec *Charter*. This leads to the conclusion that s. 58 infringes the freedom of expression guaranteed by s. 3 of the Quebec *Charter* and s. 69 infringes the guaranteed freedom of expression under both s. 2(*b*) of the Canadian *Charter* and s. 3 of the Quebec *Charter*. Although the expression in this case has a commercial element, it should be noted that the focus here is on choice of language and on a law which prohibits the use of a language. We are not asked in this case to deal with the distinct issue of the permissible scope of regulation of advertising (for example to protect consumers) where different governmental interests come into play, particularly when assessing the reasonableness of limits on such commercial expression pursuant to s. 1 of the Canadian *Charter* or to s. 9.1 of the Quebec *Charter*. It remains to be considered whether the limit imposed on freedom of expression by ss. 58 and 69 is justified under either s. 1 of the Canadian *Charter* or s. 9.1 of the Quebec *Charter*, as the case may be.

IX. Whether the Limit Imposed on Freedom of Expression by Sections 58 and 69 of the Charter of the French Language Is Justified Under Section 9.1 of the Quebec Charter of Human Rights and Freedoms and Section 1 of the Canadian Charter of Rights and Freedoms

[61] The issues raised in this part are as follows: (a) the meaning of s. 9.1 of the Quebec *Charter* and whether its role and effect are essentially different from that of s. 1 of the Canadian *Charter*; (b) whether the requirement of the exclusive use of French by ss. 58 and 69 of the *Charter of the French Language* is a limit within the meaning of s. 9.1 and s. 1; (c) whether the material (hereinafter referred to as the s. 1 and s. 9.1 materials) relied on by the Attorney General of Quebec in justification

of the limit is properly before the Court; and (d) whether the material justifies the prohibition of the use of any language other than French.

A. The Meaning of Section 9.1 of the Quebec Charter of Human Rights and Freedoms

[62] The issue here is whether s. 9.1 is a justificatory provision similar in its purpose and effect to s. 1 of the Canadian *Charter* and if so what is the test to be applied under it. Section 9.1 is worded differently from s. 1, and it is convenient to set out the two provisions again for comparison, as well as the test under s. 1. Section 9.1 of the Quebec *Charter of Human Rights and Freedoms*, which was added to the *Charter* by *An Act to amend the Charter of Human Rights and Freedoms*, S.Q. 1982, c. 61, s. 2 and entered into force by proclamation on October 1, 1983, reads as follows:

> 9.1. In exercising his fundamental freedoms and rights, a person shall maintain a proper regard for democratic values, public order and the general well-being of the citizens of Québec.
>
> In this respect, the scope of the freedoms and rights, and limits to their exercise, may be fixed by law.

Section 1 of the Canadian *Charter* provides:

> 1. The *Canadian Charter of Rights and Freedoms* guarantees the rights and freedoms set out in it subject only to such reasonable limits prescribed by law as can be demonstrably justified in a free and democratic society.

The test under s. 1 of the Canadian *Charter* was laid down by this Court in *R. v. Oakes, supra*, and restated by the Chief Justice in *R. v. Edwards Books and Art Ltd., supra*, as follows at pp. 768-69:

> Two requirements must be satisfied to establish that a limit is reasonable and demonstrably justified in a free and democratic society. First, the legislative objective which the limitation is designed to promote must be of sufficient importance to warrant overriding a constitutional right. It must bear on a "pressing and substantial concern." Second, the means chosen to attain those objectives must be proportional or appropriate to the ends. The proportionality requirement, in turn, normally has three aspects: the limiting measures must be carefully designed, or rationally connected, to the objective; they must impair the right as little as possible; and their effects must not so severely trench on individual or group rights that the legislative objective, albeit important, is nevertheless outweighed by the abridgment of rights. The Court stated that the nature of the proportionality test would vary depending on the circumstances. Both in articulating the

standard of proof and in describing the criteria comprising the proportionality requirement the Court has been careful to avoid rigid and inflexible standards.

[63] It was suggested in argument that because of its quite different wording s. 9.1 was not a justificatory provision similar to s. 1 but merely a provision indicating that the fundamental freedoms and rights guaranteed by the Quebec *Charter* are not absolute but relative and must be construed and exercised in a manner consistent with the values, interests and considerations indicated in s. 9.1—"democratic values, public order and the general well-being of the citizens of Québec." In the case at bar the Superior Court and the Court of Appeal held that s. 9.1 was a justificatory provision corresponding to s. 1 of the Canadian *Charter* and that it was subject, in its application, to a similar test of rational connection and proportionality. This Court agrees with that conclusion. . . .

B. Whether the Prohibition of the Use of Any Language Other than French by Sections 58 and 69 of the Charter of the French Language Is a "Limit" on Freedom of Expression Within the Meaning of Section 1 of the Canadian Charter and Section 9.1 of the Quebec Charter

[64] The respondents contended that ss. 58 and 69 of the *Charter of the French Language* were not subject to justification under s. 1 of the *Canadian Charter of Rights and Freedoms* because they prescribe a denial or negation of freedom of expression rather than a limit on it within the meaning of that provision. In support of this contention they referred to the opinion to this effect of Deschênes C.J. in the Superior Court and of a majority of the Court of Appeal in *Quebec Association of Protestant School Boards v. Procureur général du Québec*, [1982] C.S. 673, at pp. 689-93; [1983] C.A. 77, at p. 78. They submitted that while this Court did not rule on the general question whether a denial or negation of a guaranteed right or freedom could be a limit within s. 1, it did not expressly or implicitly disavow the opinion expressed by the Superior Court and the Court of Appeal (*Attorney General of Quebec v. Quebec Association of Protestant School Boards*, [1984] 2 S.C.R. 66, at p. 78). . . .

[65] In the *Quebec Association of Protestant School Boards* case, the minority language educational rights created by s. 23 of the Canadian *Charter* were, as the Court observed, of a very specific, special and limited nature, unlike the fundamental rights and freedoms guaranteed by other provisions. They were well defined rights for specific classes of persons. In the opinion of the Court, the effect of ss. 72 and 73 of Bill 101 was to create an exception to s. 23 for Quebec, that is, to make it inapplicable as a whole in Quebec. There was thus what

amounted to a complete denial in Quebec of the rights created by s. 23. The extent of the denial was co-extensive with the potential exercise of the very specific and limited rights created by s. 23. Such an exception to s. 23, as the Court characterized it, was tantamount to an impermissible attempt to override or amend s. 23. An exception of such effect could not be a limit within the meaning of s. 1 of the *Charter*. Thus in so far as the distinction between a complete denial of a right or freedom and a limitation of it is concerned, the *Quebec Association of Protestant School Boards* is a rather unique example of a truly complete denial of guaranteed rights—a denial that is co-extensive with the complete scope of the potential exercise of the rights. The decision is thus not authority for the proposition that where the effect of a legislative provision is to deny or prohibit the exercise of a guaranteed right or freedom in a limited area of its potential exercise that provision cannot be a limit on the right or freedom subject to justification under s. 1.

[66] In the opinion of this Court, apart from the rare case of a truly complete denial of a guaranteed right or freedom in the sense indicated above, the distinction between the negation of a right or freedom and the limitation of it is not a sound basis for denying the application of s. 1 of the *Charter*. Many, if not most, legislative qualifications of a right or freedom in a particular area of its potential exercise will amount to a denial of the right or freedom to that limited extent. If this effect were to mean that s. 1 could have no application in such a case, the section could have little application in practice....

C. The Admissibility of the Section 1 and Section 9.1 Materials Submitted in Justification of the Limit Imposed on Freedom of Expression by Sections 58 and 69 of the Charter of the French Language

[68] In the Court of Appeal the Attorney General of Quebec attached to his factum certain material of a justificatory nature which Bisson J.A. referred to as linguistic and sociological studies from Quebec and elsewhere and which the respondents describe in their factum in this Court as "numerous sociological, demographic and linguistic studies." The respondents moved to have this material struck from the record as not being in conformity with art. 507 of the *Code of Civil Procedure* and art. 10 of the Rules of Practice of the Court of Appeal respecting the parts of the record that must be attached to or form part of a factum. The ground of attack was presumably that the material did not form part of the record before the trial judge....

[71] In view of the fact that the parties did not appear to be taken by surprise or placed at an unfair disadvantage by the submission of the s. 1 and s. 9.1 materials in this Court, but showed themselves fully prepared to argue the merits of the

material, which they did, this Court is of the opinion that the material should be considered as properly before the Court and should be considered by it. The material is of the kind that has been invited and considered by the Court in other cases involving the application of s. 1 of the *Charter*, without having been subjected to the evidentiary testing of the adversary process. It is material that is treated similarly to treatises and articles in other judicial contexts. Due regard should be given, however, to the submissions of the appellant Singer in *Devine* concerning some of the statistical material.

D. Whether the Section 1 and Section 9.1 Materials Justify the Prohibition of the Use of Any Language Other than French

[72] The section 1 and s. 9.1 materials consist of some fourteen items ranging in nature from the general theory of language policy and planning to statistical analysis of the position of the French language in Quebec and Canada. The material deals with two matters of particular relevance to the issue in the appeal: (a) the vulnerable position of the French language in Quebec and Canada, which is the reason for the language policy reflected in the *Charter of the French Language*; and (b) the importance attached by language planning theory to the role of language in the public domain, including the communication or expression by language contemplated by the challenged provisions of the *Charter of the French Language*. As to the first, the material amply establishes the importance of the legislative purpose reflected in the *Charter of the French Language* and that it is a response to a substantial and pressing need. Indeed, this was conceded by the respondents both in the Court of Appeal and in this Court. The vulnerable position of the French language in Quebec and Canada was described in a series of reports by commissions of inquiry beginning with the Report of the Royal Commission on Bilingualism and Biculturalism in 1969 and continuing with the Parent Commission and the Gendron Commission. It is reflected in statistics referred to in these reports and in later studies forming part of the materials, with due adjustment made in the light of the submissions of the appellant Singer in *Devine* with respect to some of the later statistical material. The causal factors for the threatened position of the French language that have generally been identified are: (a) the declining birth rate of Quebec francophones resulting in a decline in the Quebec francophone proportion of the Canadian population as a whole; (b) the decline of the francophone population outside Quebec as a result of assimilation; (c) the greater rate of assimilation of immigrants to Quebec by the anglophone community of Quebec; and (d) the continuing dominance of English at the higher levels of the economic sector. These factors have favoured the use of the English

language despite the predominance in Quebec of a franco-phone population. Thus, in the period prior to the enactment of the legislation at issue, the "*visage linguistique*" of Quebec often gave the impression that English had become as significant as French. This "*visage linguistique*" reinforced the concern among francophones that English was gaining in importance, that the French language was threatened and that it would ultimately disappear. It strongly suggested to young and ambitious francophones that the language of success was almost exclusively English. It confirmed to anglophones that there was no great need to learn the majority language. And it suggested to immigrants that the prudent course lay in joining the anglophone community. The aim of such provisions as ss. 58 and 69 of the *Charter of the French Language* was, in the words of its preamble, "to see the quality and influence of the French language assured." The threat to the French language demonstrated to the government that it should, in particular, take steps to assure that the "*visage linguistique*" of Quebec would reflect the predominance of the French language.

[73] The section 1 and s. 9.1 materials establish that the aim of the language policy underlying the *Charter of the French Language* was a serious and legitimate one. They indicate the concern about the survival of the French language and the perceived need for an adequate legislative response to the problem. Moreover, they indicate a rational connection between protecting the French language and assuring that the reality of Quebec society is communicated through the "*visage linguistique*." The section 1 and s. 9.1 materials do not, however, demonstrate that the requirement of the use of French only is either necessary for the achievement of the legislative objective or proportionate to it. That specific question is simply not addressed by the materials. Indeed, in his factum and oral argument the Attorney General of Quebec did not attempt to justify the requirement of the exclusive use of French. He concentrated on the reasons for the adoption of the *Charter of the French Language* and the earlier language legislation, which, as was noted above, were conceded by the respondents. The Attorney General of Quebec relied on what he referred to as the general democratic legitimacy of Quebec language policy without referring explicitly to the requirement of the exclusive use of French. In so far as proportionality is concerned, the Attorney General of Quebec referred to the American jurisprudence with respect to commercial speech, presumably as indicating the judicial deference that should be paid to the legislative choice of means to serve an admittedly legitimate legislative purpose, at least in the area of commercial expression. He did, however, refer in justification of the requirement of the exclusive use of French to the attenuation of this requirement reflected in ss. 59 to 62 of the *Charter of the French Language* and the regulations. He submitted that these

exceptions to the requirement of the exclusive use of French indicate the concern for carefully designed measures and for interfering as little as possible with commercial expression. The qualifications of the requirement of the exclusive use of French in other provisions of the *Charter of the French Language* and the regulations do not make ss. 58 and 69 any less prohibitions of the use of any language other than French as applied to the respondents. The issue is whether any such prohibition is justified. In the opinion of this Court it has not been demonstrated that the prohibition of the use of any language other than French in ss. 58 and 69 of the *Charter of the French Language* is necessary to the defence and enhancement of the status of the French language in Quebec or that it is proportionate to that legislative purpose. Since the evidence put to us by the government showed that the predominance of the French language was not reflected in the "*visage linguistique*" of Quebec, the governmental response could well have been tailored to meet that specific problem and to impair freedom of expression minimally. Thus, whereas requiring the predominant display of the French language, even its marked predominance, would be proportional to the goal of promoting and maintaining a French "*visage linguistique*" in Quebec and therefore justified under the Quebec *Charter* and the Canadian *Charter*, requiring the exclusive use of French has not been so justified. French could be required in addition to any other language or it could be required to have greater visibility than that accorded to other languages. Such measures would ensure that the "*visage linguistique*" reflected the demography of Quebec: the predominant language is French. This reality should be communicated to all citizens and non-citizens alike, irrespective of their mother tongue. But exclusivity for the French language has not survived the scrutiny of a proportionality test and does not reflect the reality of Quebec society. Accordingly, we are of the view that the limit imposed on freedom of expression by s. 58 of the *Charter of the French Language* respecting the exclusive use of French on public signs and posters and in commercial advertising is not justified under s. 9.1 of the Quebec *Charter*. In like measure, the limit imposed on freedom of expression by s. 69 of the *Charter of the French Language* respecting the exclusive use of the French version of a firm name is not justified under either s. 9.1 of the Quebec *Charter* or s. 1 of the Canadian *Charter*. . . .

X. Do Sections 58 and 69 of the Charter of the French Language Infringe the Guarantee Against Discrimination Based on Language in Section 10 of the Quebec Charter of Human Rights and Freedoms?

[74] In view of the above conclusion it is not necessary to the disposition of the appeal that the Court should pronounce

on the contention of the respondents that ss. 58 and 69 of the *Charter of the French Language* are inoperative as infringing the guarantee against discrimination based on language in s. 10 of the Quebec *Charter of Human Rights and Freedoms*. In view, however, of the fact that this issue is also raised in the *Devine* appeal and the Superior Court and the Court of Appeal addressed it in both cases it is probably desirable that this Court should do so as well because of the general importance of the question.

[75] For convenience s. 10 of the Quebec *Charter* is quoted again:

> 10. Every person has a right to full and equal recognition and exercise of his human rights and freedoms, without distinction, exclusion or preference based on race, colour, sex, pregnancy, sexual orientation, civil status, age except as provided by law, religion, political convictions, language, ethnic or national origin, social condition, a handicap or the use of any means to palliate a handicap.
>
> Discrimination exists where such a distinction, exclusion or preference has the effect of nullifying or impairing such right. . . .

[82] Thus in addressing the question whether s. 58 of the *Charter of the French Language* infringes the guarantee against discrimination based on language in s. 10 of the Quebec *Charter of Human Rights and Freedoms* we are obliged to consider the effect of s. 58, in so far as that may be ascertained. The second observation to be made here is that in order for a distinction based on a prohibited ground to constitute discrimination within the meaning of s. 10 it must have the effect of nullifying or impairing the right to full and equal recognition and exercise of a human right or freedom, which must mean a human right or freedom recognized by the Quebec *Charter of Human Rights and Freedoms*. With these observations in mind we turn to the question whether s. 58 infringes s. 10. It purports, as was said by the Superior Court and the Court of Appeal, to apply to everyone, regardless of their language of use, the requirement of the exclusive use of French. It has the effect, however, of impinging differentially on different classes of persons according to their language of use. Francophones are permitted to use their language of use while anglophones and other non-francophones are prohibited from doing so. Does this differential effect constitute a distinction based on language within the meaning of s. 10 of the Quebec *Charter*? In this Court's opinion it does. Section 58 of the *Charter of the French Language*, because of its differential effect or impact on persons according to their language of use, creates a distinction between such persons based on language of use. It is then necessary to consider whether this distinction has the effect of nullifying or impairing the right to full and equal

recognition and exercise of a human right or freedom recognized by the Quebec *Charter*. The human right or freedom in issue in this case is the freedom to express oneself in the language of one's choice, which has been held to be recognized by s. 3 of the Quebec *Charter*. In this case, the limit imposed on that right was not a justifiable one under s. 9.1 of the Quebec *Charter*. The distinction based on language of use created by s. 58 of the *Charter of the French Language* thus has the effect of nullifying the right to full and equal recognition and exercise of this freedom. Section 58 is therefore also of no force or effect as infringing s. 10 of the Quebec *Charter*. The same conclusion must apply to s. 69 of the *Charter of the French Language*. We note that since one of the respondents, Valerie Ford, is an individual and not a corporation, it is unnecessary in this case to decide whether corporations are entitled to claim the benefit of equality guarantees and we do not do so.

[83] For these reasons the appeal is dismissed with costs and the constitutional questions are answered as follows:

> 1. Are section 214 of the *Charter of the French Language*, R.S.Q. 1977, c. C-11, as enacted by S.Q. 1982, c. 21, s. 1, and s. 52 of *An Act to amend the Charter of the French Language*, S.Q. 1983, c. 56, inconsistent with s. 33(1) of the *Constitution Act, 1982* and therefore inoperative and of no force or effect under s. 52(1) of the latter *Act*?

Answer: No, except in so far as s. 214 is given retrospective effect by s. 7 of *An Act respecting the Constitution Act, 1982*, S.Q. 1982, c. 21.

> 2. If the answer to question 1 is affirmative, to the extent that they require the exclusive use of the French language, are ss. 58 and 69, and ss. 205 to 208 to the extent they apply thereto, of the *Charter of the French Language*, R.S.Q. 1977, c. C-11, as amended by S.Q. 1983, c. 56, inconsistent with the guarantee of freedom of expression under s. 2(b) of the *Canadian Charter of Rights and Freedoms*?

Answer: In so far as s. 214 of the *Charter of the French Language* has ceased to have effect but s. 52 of *An Act to amend the Charter of the French Language* remains in effect, s. 58 of the *Charter of the French Language* is protected from the application of the *Canadian Charter of Rights and Freedoms* but it is inoperative as infringing the guarantee of freedom of expression in s. 3 of the Quebec *Charter of Human Rights and Freedoms* and the guarantee against discrimination based on language in s. 10 of the Quebec *Charter*. In so far as s. 214 of the *Charter of the French Language* has ceased to have effect, s. 69 thereof is inconsistent with the guarantee of freedom of expression under s. 2(b) of the *Canadian Charter of Rights and*

Freedoms. Sections 205 to 208 of the *Charter of the French Language* to the extent they apply to s. 69 thereof are inconsistent with the guarantee of freedom of expression under s. 2(b) of the *Canadian Charter of Rights and Freedoms*. Section 69 of the *Charter of the French Language*, and ss. 205 to 208 thereof, to the extent they apply to ss. 58 and 69, are also inconsistent with the guarantee of freedom of expression under s. 3 of the Quebec *Charter of Human Rights and Freedoms*.

3. If the answer to question 2 is affirmative in whole or in part, are ss. 58 and 69, and ss. 205 to 208 to the extent they apply thereto, of the *Charter of the French Language*, R.S.Q. 1977, c. C-11, as amended by S.Q. 1983, c. 56, justified by the application of s. 1 of the

Canadian Charter of Rights and Freedoms and therefore not inconsistent with the *Constitution Act, 1982*?

Answer: Section 58 of the *Charter of the French Language* is not justified under s. 9.1 of the Quebec *Charter of Human Rights and Freedoms*. Section 69 of the *Charter of the French Language*, and ss. 205 to 208 thereof, to the extent they apply to s. 69, are not justified under s. 1 of the *Canadian Charter of Rights and Freedoms* and are therefore inconsistent with the *Constitution Act, 1982*. Nor is s. 69 of the *Charter of the French Language*, or ss. 205 to 208 thereof, to the extent they apply to ss. 58 and 69, justified under s. 9.1 of the Quebec *Charter of Human Rights and Freedoms*.

R. v. Keegstra, 1990

In 1984, James Keegstra was charged under the *Criminal Code* with "wilfully promot[ing] hatred" against a group "distinguished by colour, race, religion, ethnic origin, or [since 2004] sexual orientation." Keegstra, a high school teacher in Eckville, Alberta, had taught his students that Jews were "treacherous," "subversive," "sadistic," "money-loving," "power hungry," "child killers," who had "created the Holocaust to gain sympathy." Students who failed to parrot these teachings lost marks. Keegstra defended himself in court by challenging the constitutionality of the "hate speech" provision used to charge him. He maintained that the provision infringed both the *Charter*'s section 2(*b*) guarantee of freedom of expression and the presumption of innocence guaranteed by section 11(*d*). The Court upheld the law by a 4-to-3 margin on the section 2(*b*) issue and a 4-to-2 margin on the section 11(*d*) issue (which Justice La Forest did not find it necessary to address). We reproduce only the freedom-of-expression debate below.

Previous cases had established that, short of violence, any activity "convey[ing] or attempt[ing] to convey a meaning . . . has expressive content and *prima facie* falls within the scope" of the *Charter*'s freedom-of-expression guarantee. Because Keegstra's teaching was obviously covered by this broad interpretation of section 2(*b*), all seven participating judges agreed that the law could be applied to him only if it could be sustained as a section 1 "reasonable limit" on freedom of expression. The judges all agreed, moreover, that the law had the kind of "pressing and substantial" purpose needed under the *Oakes* test to establish a "reasonable limit." They parted company on whether the legislative means were proportional to that purpose.

Chief Justice Dickson, writing for the majority, underlined the fact that Keegstra's anti-Semitism contributed little to three fundamental values previously identified by the Court as underpinning freedom of expression in a liberal democracy: "the quest for truth, the promotion of individual self-development [and] the protection and fostering of a vibrant democracy." Indeed, Keegstra's hate speech was, for Dickson, generally contrary to these central freedom-of-expression principles. Quoting Justice McLachlin's opinion in *Rocket v. Royal College of Dental Surgeons of Ontario*, Dickson concluded that restrictions on expression so distant from the core of section 2(*b*) "might be easier to justify than other infringements of" that section.

Applying this perspective, Chief Justice Dickson found that the hate speech provision was proportional to its pressing and substantial purpose. Justice McLachlin, often on the more libertarian side of freedom-of-expression issues, disagreed. Thus, on the "rational connection" component of *Oakes*, Dickson emphasized the egalitarian educative message sent by the prosecution of racist expression while McLachlin thought such prosecution was more likely to backfire, giving people reason "to believe that there must be some truth in the racist expression because the government is trying to suppress it." Similarly, on the "minimal impairment" question, Dickson considered the wording of the law precise enough to prevent the unjustified prosecution of "merely unpopular or unconventional opinion," while McLachlin, believing such prosecutions to be possible, worried about the "chilling effect" this prospect would have on robust public expression.

Justice McLachlin's willingness to invalidate the hate-speech law on "rational connection" grounds is noteworthy. In the introduction to *Oakes* (case 14), we observed that laws rarely fail the "pressing and substantial purpose" part of the *Oakes* test, partly because judges are reluctant to accuse governments of harbouring completely illegitimate objectives. It is similarly uncommon for judges, under the rational-connection test, to accuse governments of being so obtuse as to choose completely irrational means to their legislative ends—that is, means that don't attain those ends at all or backfire so badly that they achieve the very opposite of what was intended. Accordingly, most invalidated laws pass the rational-connection test and fail on minimal impairment grounds. There are exceptions, however, and Justice McLachlin fell just one vote short of putting *Keegstra* in that category. She would later have more success in striking down legislation on rational-connection grounds (for example, *RJR-MacDonald*, case 7, and *Sauvé*, case 11). Indeed, two years after *Keegstra*, in the closely related case of *R. v. Zundel*, Justice McLachlin would strike down legislation for the even more unusual lack of a "pressing and substantial" purpose (for further discussion, see the introduction to *Butler*, case 6).

Among the groups sufficiently concerned with the hate-speech issues in *Keegstra* to intervene in the case was the Women's Legal Education and Action Fund (LEAF). *Keegstra* did not directly concern women's issues, but LEAF understood that it could be an important precedent for cases involving the censorship of obscenity and pornography. LEAF wished to defend such censorship, not on the traditional ground that public sexuality was immoral, but on the egalitarian theory that certain kinds of public sexuality constituted an inegalitarian assault on women—in effect, a kind of "hate expression" toward women. This interpretive goal would obviously have been jeopardized had the hate-speech provision of the *Criminal Code* been ruled unconstitutional in *Keegstra*. Instead, *Keegstra* helped set the stage for LEAF's successful arguments in *Butler*. ∼

Discussion Questions

1. What do you make of the debate between Justice Dickson and Justice McLachlin about the example of Nazi Germany?
2. Who gets the better of the debates about whether hate speech is dignified by its suppression and whether its suppression will have a "chilling effect" on legitimate expression?
3. Keegstra taught his anti-Semitic views to students in a classroom. Would (should) it have made any difference to either the judicial majority or minority if he had expressed the same opinions on a public soapbox?
4. The terms of section 319 of the *Criminal Code* are considered by its supporters to be a careful parliamentary attempt to limit harmful speech. What is the evidence for this opinion?

R. v. KEEGSTRA
[1990] 3 S.C.R. 697

Hearing: December 5, 6, 1989; Judgment: December 13, 1990.

Present: Dickson C.J.* and Wilson, La Forest, L'Heureux-Dubé, Sopinka, Gonthier, and McLachlin JJ.

Interveners: The Attorney General of Canada, the Attorney General for Ontario, the Attorney General of Quebec, the Attorney General for New Brunswick, the Attorney General of Manitoba, the Canadian Jewish Congress, the League for Human Rights of B'nai Brith Canada, Interamicus, the Women's Legal Education and Action Fund, and the Canadian Civil Liberties Association.

* Chief Justice at the time of hearing.

The judgment of Dickson C.J. and Wilson, L'Heureux-Dubé, and Gonthier JJ. was delivered by

DICKSON C.J.: This appeal . . . raises a delicate and highly controversial issue as to the constitutional validity of s. 319(2) of the *Criminal Code*, R.S.C., 1985, c. C-46, a legislative provision which prohibits the wilful promotion of hatred, other than in private conversation, towards any section of the public distinguished by colour, race, religion or ethnic origin. In particular, the Court must decide whether this section infringes the guarantee of freedom of expression found in s. 2(*b*) of the *Canadian Charter of Rights and Freedoms* in a manner that cannot be justified under s. 1 of the *Charter*. . . .

The first step in the . . . analysis involves asking whether the activity of the litigant who alleges an infringement of the freedom of expression falls within the protected s. 2(*b*) sphere. . . . Apart from rare cases where expression is communicated in a physically violent form, . . . "if the activity conveys or attempts to convey a meaning, it has expressive content and *prima facie* falls within the scope of the guarantee." In other words, the term "expression" as used in s. 2(*b*) of the *Charter* embraces all content of expression irrespective of the particular meaning or message sought to be conveyed (*Reference re ss. 193 and 195.1(1)(c) of the Criminal Code (Man.)*, [[1990] 1 S.C.R. 1123], at p. 1181, *per* Lamer J.).

. . . I thus find s. 319(2) to constitute an infringement of the freedom of expression guaranteed by s. 2(*b*) of the *Charter*. . . .

VII. Section 1 Analysis of Section 319(2)

. . . Under the approach in *Oakes*, it must first be established that impugned state action has an objective of pressing and substantial concern in a free and democratic society. Only such an objective is of sufficient stature to warrant overriding a constitutionally protected right or freedom. . . .

In my opinion, it would be impossible to deny that Parliament's objective in enacting s. 319(2) is of the utmost importance. Parliament has recognized the substantial harm that can flow from hate propaganda, and in trying to prevent the pain suffered by target group members and to reduce racial, ethnic and religious tension in Canada has decided to suppress the wilful promotion of hatred against identifiable groups. The nature of Parliament's objective is supported not only by the work of numerous study groups, but also by our collective historical knowledge of the potentially catastrophic effects of the promotion of hatred (*Jones*, [[1986] 2 S.C.R. 284], *per* La Forest J., at pp. 299-300). Additionally, the international commitment to eradicate hate propaganda and the stress placed upon equality and multiculturalism in the *Charter* strongly buttress the importance of this objective. I consequently find that the first part of the test under s. 1 of the *Charter* is easily satisfied and that a powerfully convincing legislative objective exists such as to justify some limit on freedom of expression.

The second branch of the *Oakes* test—proportionality—poses the most challenging questions with respect to the validity of s. 319(2) as a reasonable limit on freedom of expression in a free and democratic society. It is therefore not surprising to find most commentators, as well as the litigants in the case at bar, agreeing that the objective of the provision is of great importance, but to observe considerable disagreement when it comes to deciding whether the means chosen to further the objective are proportional to the ends. . . .

In my opinion . . . the s. 1 analysis of a limit upon s. 2(*b*) cannot ignore the nature of the expressive activity which the state seeks to restrict. While we must guard carefully against judging expression according to its popularity, it is equally destructive of free expression values, as well as the other values which underlie a free and democratic society, to treat all expression as equally crucial to those principles at the core of s. 2(*b*). . . .

At the core of freedom of expression lies the need to ensure that truth and the common good are attained, whether in scientific and artistic endeavors or in the process of determining the best course to take in our political affairs. Since truth and the ideal form of political and social organization can rarely, if at all, be identified with absolute certainty, it is difficult to prohibit expression without impeding the free exchange of potentially valuable information. Nevertheless, the argument from truth does not provide convincing support for the protection of hate propaganda. Taken to its extreme, this argument would require us to permit the communication of all expression, it being impossible to know with *absolute* certainty which factual statements are true, or which ideas obtain the greatest good. The problem with this extreme position, however, is that the greater the degree of certainty that a statement is erroneous or mendacious, the less its value in the quest for truth. Indeed, expression can be used to the detriment of our search for truth; the state should not be the sole arbiter of truth, but neither should we overplay the view that rationality will overcome all falsehoods in the unregulated marketplace of ideas. There is very little chance that statements intended to promote hatred against an identifiable group are true, or that their vision of society will lead to a better world. . . .

Another component central to the rationale underlying s. 2(*b*) concerns the vital role of free expression as a means of ensuring individuals the ability to gain self-fulfillment by developing and articulating thoughts and ideas as they see fit. It is true that s. 319(2) inhibits this process among those individuals whose expression it limits, and hence arguably works against freedom of expression values. On the other hand, such self-autonomy stems in large part from one's ability to articulate and nurture an identity derived from membership in a cultural or religious group. The message put forth by individuals who fall within the ambit of s. 319(2) represents a most extreme opposition to the idea that members of identifiable groups should enjoy this aspect of the s. 2(*b*) benefit. The extent to which the unhindered promotion of this message furthers free expression values must therefore be tempered insofar as it advocates with inordinate vitriol an intolerance and prejudice which view as execrable the process of individual self-development and human flourishing among all members of society.

Moving on to a third strain of thought said to justify the protection of free expression, one's attention is brought specifically to the political realm. The connection between freedom of expression and the political process is perhaps the linchpin of the s. 2(*b*) guarantee, and the nature of this connection is largely derived from the Canadian commitment to democracy. Freedom of expression is a crucial aspect of the democratic commitment, not merely because it permits the best policies to be chosen from among a wide array of proffered options, but additionally because it helps to ensure that participation in the political process is open to all persons. Such open participation must involve to a substantial degree the notion that all persons are equally deserving of respect and dignity. The state therefore cannot act to hinder or condemn a political view without to some extent harming the openness of Canadian democracy and its associated tenet of equality for all.

The suppression of hate propaganda undeniably muzzles the participation of a few individuals in the democratic process, and hence detracts somewhat from free expression values, but the degree of this limitation is not substantial. I am aware that the use of strong language in political and social debate— indeed, perhaps even language intended to promote hatred—

is an unavoidable part of the democratic process. Moreover, I recognize that hate propaganda is expression of a type which would generally be categorized as "political," thus putatively placing it at the very heart of the principle extolling freedom of expression as vital to the democratic process. Nonetheless, expression can work to undermine our commitment to democracy where employed to propagate ideas anathemic to democratic values. Hate propaganda works in just such a way, arguing as it does for a society in which the democratic process is subverted and individuals are denied respect and dignity simply because of racial or religious characteristics. This brand of expressive activity is thus wholly inimical to the democratic aspirations of the free expression guarantee.

Indeed, one may quite plausibly contend that it is through rejecting hate propaganda that the state can best encourage the protection of values central to freedom of expression, while simultaneously demonstrating dislike for the vision forwarded by hate-mongers. In this regard, the reaction to various types of expression by a democratic government may be perceived as meaningful expression on behalf of the vast majority of citizens. I do not wish to be construed as saying that an infringement of s. 2(*b*) can be justified under s. 1 merely because it is the product of a democratic process; the *Charter* will not permit even the democratically elected legislature to restrict the rights and freedoms crucial to a free and democratic society. What I do wish to emphasize, however, is that one must be careful not to accept blindly that the suppression of expression must always and unremittingly detract from values central to freedom of expression (L.C. Bollinger, *The Tolerant Society: Freedom of Speech and Extremist Speech in America* (1986), at pp. 87-93). . . .

. . . I am of the opinion that hate propaganda contributes little to the aspirations of Canadians or Canada in either the quest for truth, the promotion of individual self-development or the protection and fostering of a vibrant democracy where the participation of all individuals is accepted and encouraged. While I cannot conclude that hate propaganda deserves only marginal protection under the s. 1 analysis, I can take cognizance of the fact that limitations upon hate propaganda are directed at a special category of expression which strays some distance from the spirit of s. 2(*b*), and hence conclude that "restrictions on expression of this kind might be easier to justify than other infringements of s. 2(*b*)" (*Royal College*, [[1990] 2 S.C.R. 232], at p. 247). . . .

Having made some preliminary comments as to the nature of the expression at stake in this appeal, it is now possible to ask whether s. 319(2) is an acceptably proportional response to Parliament's valid objective. . . .

[T]he proportionality aspect of the *Oakes* test requires the Court to decide whether the impugned state action: i) is rationally connected to the objective; ii) minimally impairs the *Charter* right or freedom at issue; and iii) does not produce effects of such severity so as to make the impairment unjustifiable....

... Those who would uphold the provision argue that the criminal prohibition of hate propaganda obviously bears a rational connection to the legitimate Parliamentary objective of protecting target group members and fostering harmonious social relations in a community dedicated to equality and multiculturalism. I agree, for in my opinion it would be difficult to deny that the suppression of hate propaganda reduces the harm such expression does to individuals who belong to identifiable groups and to relations between various cultural and religious groups in Canadian society.

Doubts have been raised, however, as to whether the actual effect of s. 319(2) is to undermine any rational connection between it and Parliament's objective. As stated in the reasons of McLachlin J., there are three primary ways in which the effect of the impugned legislation might be seen as an irrational means of carrying out the Parliamentary purpose. First, it is argued that the provision may actually promote the cause of hate-mongers by earning them extensive media attention. In this vein, it is also suggested that persons accused of intentionally promoting hatred often see themselves as martyrs, and may actually generate sympathy from the community in the role of underdogs engaged in battle against the immense powers of the state. Second, the public may view the suppression of expression by the government with suspicion, making it possible that such expression—even if it be hate propaganda—is perceived as containing an element of truth. Finally, it is often noted, citing the writings of A. Neier, *Defending My Enemy: American Nazis, the Skokie Case, and the Risks of Freedom* (1979), that Germany of the 1920s and 1930s possessed and used hate propaganda laws similar to those existing in Canada, and yet these laws did nothing to stop the triumph of a racist philosophy under the Nazis....

It is undeniable that media attention has been extensive on those occasions when s. 319(2) has been used. Yet from my perspective, s. 319(2) serves to illustrate to the public the severe reprobation with which society holds messages of hate directed towards racial and religious groups. The existence of a particular criminal law, and the process of holding a trial when that law is used, is thus itself a form of expression, and the message sent out is that hate propaganda is harmful to target group members and threatening to a harmonious society (see Rauf, ["Freedom of Expression, the Presumption of Innocence, and Reasonable Limits: An Analysis of Keegstra and Andrews" (1988), 65 C.R. (3d) 356], at p. 359). As I stated in my reasons in *R. v. Morgentaler,* [1988] 1 S.C.R. 30, at p. 70:

The criminal law is a very special form of governmental regulation, for it seeks to express our society's collective disapprobation of certain acts and omissions.

The many, many Canadians who belong to identifiable groups surely gain a great deal of comfort from the knowledge that the hate-monger is criminally prosecuted and his or her ideas rejected. Equally, the community as a whole is reminded of the importance of diversity and multiculturalism in Canada, the value of equality and the worth and dignity of each human person being particularly emphasized.

In this context, it can also be said that government suppression of hate propaganda will not make the expression attractive and hence increase acceptance of its content. Similarly, it is very doubtful that Canadians will have sympathy for either propagators of hatred or their ideas. Governmental disapproval of hate propaganda does not invariably result in dignifying the suppressed ideology. Pornography is not dignified by its suppression, nor are defamatory statements against individuals seen as meritorious because the common law lends its support to their prohibition. Again, I stress my belief that hate propaganda legislation and trials are a means by which the values beneficial to a free and democratic society can be publicized. In this context, no dignity will be unwittingly foisted upon the convicted hate-monger or his or her philosophy, and that a hate-monger might see him or herself as a martyr is of no matter to the content of the state's message.

As for the use of hate propaganda laws in pre-World War Two Germany, I am skeptical as to the relevance of the observation that legislation similar to s. 319(2) proved ineffective in curbing the racism of the Nazis. No one is contending that hate propaganda laws can in themselves prevent the tragedy of a Holocaust; conditions particular to Germany made the rise of Nazi ideology possible despite the existence and use of these laws (see A. Doskow and S.B. Jacoby, "Anti-Semitism and the Law in Pre-Nazi Germany" (1940), 3 *Contemporary Jewish Record* 498, at p. 509). Rather, hate propaganda laws are one part of a free and democratic society's bid to prevent the spread of racism, and their rational connection to this objective must be seen in such a context. Certainly West Germany has not reacted to the failure of pre-war laws by seeking their removal, a new set of criminal offences having been implemented as recently as 1985 (see E. Stein, "History Against Free Speech: The New German Law Against the 'Auschwitz'—and other— 'Lies'" (1987), 85 *Mich. L. Rev.* 277). Nor, as has been discussed, has the international community regarded the promulgation of laws suppressing hate propaganda as futile or counter-productive. Indeed, this Court's attention has been drawn to the fact that a great many countries possess legislation similar to that found in Canada....

In sum, having found that the purpose of the challenged legislation is valid, I also find that the means chosen to further this purpose are rational in both theory and operation, and therefore conclude that the first branch of the proportionality test has been met....

The criminal nature of the impugned provision, involving the associated risks of prejudice through prosecution, conviction and the imposition of up to two years imprisonment, indicates that the means embodied in hate propaganda legislation should be carefully tailored so as to minimize impairment of the freedom of expression....

It is ... submitted that the legislation is overbroad, its terms so wide as to include expression which does not relate to Parliament's objective, and also unduly vague, in that a lack of clarity and precision in its words prevents individuals from discerning its meaning with any accuracy. In either instance, it is said that the effect of s. 319(2) is to limit the expression of merely unpopular or unconventional communications. Such communications may present no risk of causing the harm which Parliament seeks to prevent, and will perhaps be closely associated with the core values of s. 2(*b*). This overbreadth and vagueness could consequently allow the state to employ s. 319(2) to infringe excessively the freedom of expression or, what is more likely, could have a chilling effect whereby persons potentially within s. 319(2) would exercise self-censorship....

In assessing the constitutionality of s. 319(2), especially as concerns arguments of overbreadth and vagueness, an immediate observation is that statements made "in private conversation" are not included in the criminalized expression.... [A] conversation or communication intended to be private does not satisfy the requirements of the provision if through accident or negligence an individual's expression of hatred for an identifiable group is made public.

Is s. 319(2) nevertheless overbroad because it captures *all* public expression intended to promote hatred? It would appear not, for the harm which the government seeks to prevent is not restricted to certain mediums and/or locations. To attempt to distinguish between various forms and fora would therefore be incongruent with Parliament's legitimate objective.

A second important element of s. 319(2) is its requirement that the promotion of hatred be "wilful." [T]his mental element ... is satisfied only where an accused subjectively desires the promotion of hatred or foresees such a consequence as certain or substantially certain to result from an act done in order to achieve some other purpose.... This mental element, requiring more than merely negligence or recklessness as to result, significantly restricts the reach of the provision, and thereby reduces the scope of the targeted expression....

It has been argued, however, that even a demanding *mens rea* component fails to give s. 319(2) a constitutionally accept-

able breadth. The problem is said to lie in the failure of the offence to require proof of actual hatred resulting from a communication, the assumption being that only such proof can demonstrate a harm serious enough to justify limiting the freedom of expression under s. 1.... [However, to] predicate the limitation of free expression upon proof of actual hatred gives insufficient attention to the severe psychological trauma suffered by members of those identifiable groups targeted by hate propaganda. [Moreover], it is clearly difficult to prove a causative link between a specific statement and hatred of an identifiable group. In fact, to require direct proof of hatred in listeners would severely debilitate the effectiveness of s. 319(2) in achieving Parliament's aim. It is well accepted that Parliament can use the criminal law to prevent the risk of serious harms, a leading example being the drinking and driving provisions in the *Criminal Code*. ... I conclude that proof of actual hatred is not required in order to justify a limit under s. 1.

The next feature of the provision that must be explored is the phrase "promotes hatred against any identifiable group." ... In "promotes" we ... have a word that indicates more than simple encouragement or advancement. The hate-monger must intend or foresee as substantially certain a direct and active stimulation of hatred against an identifiable group. As for the term "identifiable group," s. 318(4) states that an " 'identifiable group' means any section of the public distinguished by colour, race, religion or ethnic origin." The act to be targeted is therefore the intentional fostering of hatred against particular members of our society, as opposed to any individual.

The meaning of "hatred" remains to be elucidated. Just as "wilfully" must be interpreted in the setting of s. 319(2), so must the word "hatred" be defined according to the context in which it is found. A dictionary definition may be of limited aid to such an exercise, for by its nature a dictionary seeks to offer a panoply of possible usages, rather than the correct meaning of a word as contemplated by Parliament. Noting the purpose of s. 319(2), in my opinion the term "hatred" connotes emotion of an intense and extreme nature that is clearly associated with vilification and detestation.... Hatred is predicated on destruction, and hatred against identifiable groups therefore thrives on insensitivity, bigotry and destruction of both the target group and of the values of our society. Hatred in this sense is a most extreme emotion that belies reason; an emotion that, if exercised against members of an identifiable group, implies that those individuals are to be despised, scorned, denied respect and made subject to ill-treatment on the basis of group affiliation....

... [T]he sense in which "hatred" is used in s. 319(2) does not denote a wide range of diverse emotions, but is circumscribed so as to cover only the most intense form of dislike....

The factors mentioned above suggest that s. 319(2) does not unduly restrict the s. 2(*b*) guarantee. The terms of the offence, as I have defined them, rather indicate that s. 319(2) possesses definitional limits which act as safeguards to ensure that it will capture only expressive activity which is openly hostile to Parliament's objective, and will thus attack only the harm at which the prohibition is targeted. The specific defences provided are further glosses on the purview of the offence. . . .

[Chief Justice Dickson then considers the defences to "wilful promotion of hatred" that are provided by section 319(3). That section reads as follows:

(3) No person shall be convicted of an offence under subsection (2)

(*a*) if he establishes that the statements communicated were true;

(*b*) if, in good faith, he expressed or attempted to establish by argument an opinion on a religious subject;

(*c*) if the statements were relevant to any subject of public interest, the discussion of which was for the public benefit, and if on reasonable grounds he believed them to be true; or

(*d*) if, in good faith, he intended to point out, for the purpose of removal, matters producing or tending to produce feelings of hatred towards an identifiable group in Canada.]

A careful reading of the s. 319(3) defences shows them to take in examples of expressive activity that generally would not fall within the "wilful promotion of hatred" as I have defined the phrase. . . . [O]nly rarely will one who intends to promote hatred be acting in good faith or upon honest belief. These defences are hence intended to aid in making the scope of the wilful promotion of hatred more explicit. . . .

. . . [I]f a situation arises where an individual uses statements of truth in order to promote hatred against identifiable groups, the accused is acquitted despite the existence of the harm which Parliament seeks to prevent. . . .

It has been forcefully argued before us that the defence of truth is insufficient protection against an overly broad hate propaganda law. In this vein, it is rightly pointed out that many (if not most) of the communications coming within s. 319(2) are not susceptible to a true/false categorization, existing instead as ideas or opinions in the mind of the communicator. The accused could therefore sincerely believe in the worth of his or her viewpoint and yet be unable to utilize the s. 319(3)(*a*) defence. Moreover, it is said that, even where a statement is capable of categorization as true or false, the individual honestly mistaken as to the validity of his or her position (even if innocently so) is left unprotected, a result

which dangerously restricts freedom of expression, causing a "chill" on communications as those who fear that their statements may be false exercise self-censorship. Finally, one might wonder if the courts are not on dangerous ground in attempting to distinguish between truthfulness and falsehood. The potential for bias in making such a determination, be it intentional or subconscious, is a danger frequently noted in freedom of expression theory (this potential is equally evident in s. 319(3)(*c*), insofar as ideas are assessed in light of "reasonableness" and the "public benefit").

The way in which I have defined the s. 319(2) offence, in the context of the objective sought by society and the value of the prohibited expression, gives me some doubt as to whether the *Charter* mandates that truthful statements communicated *with an intention to promote hatred* need be excepted from criminal condemnation. Truth may be used for widely disparate ends, and I find it difficult to accept that circumstances exist where factually accurate statements can be used for no other purpose than to stir up hatred against a racial or religious group. It would seem to follow that there is no reason why the individual who intentionally employs such statements to achieve harmful ends must *under the Charter* be protected from criminal censure.

Nevertheless, it is open to Parliament to make a concession to free expression values, whether or not such is required by the *Charter*. Deference to truth as a value central to free expression has thus led Parliament to include the defence in s. 319(3)(*a*), even though the accused has used truthful statements to cause harm of the type falling squarely within the objective of the legislation. When the statement contains no truth, however, this flicker of justification for the intentional promotion of hatred is extinguished, and the harmful malice of the disseminator stands alone. . . .

Because the presence of truth, though legally a defence to a charge under s. 319(2), does not change the fact that the accused has intended to promote the hatred of an identifiable group, I cannot find excessive impairment of the freedom of expression merely because s. 319(3)(*a*) does not cover negligent or innocent error. Whether or not a statement is susceptible to classification as true or false, my inclination is therefore to accept that such error should not excuse an accused who has wilfully used a statement in order to promote hatred against an identifiable group. That the legislative line is drawn so as to convict the accused who is negligent or even innocent regarding the accuracy of his or her statements is perfectly acceptable, for the mistake is not as to the use to which the information is put, namely, the promotion of hatred against an identifiable group. As for the argument that the courts and legislature should not involve themselves in the evaluation of "truth," "reasonable grounds for finding truth" or "public interest," the same response applies. Where the likelihood of truth or benefit from an idea diminishes to the point of vanishing, and the statement in question has harmful consequences inimical to the most central values of a free and democratic society, it is not excessively problematic to make a judgment that involves limiting expression.

... I should comment on a final argument marshalled in support of striking down s. 319(2) because of overbreadth or vagueness. It is said that the presence of the legislation has led authorities to interfere with a diverse range of political, educational and artistic expression, demonstrating only too well the way in which overbreadth and vagueness can result in undue intrusion and the threat of persecution. In this regard, a number of incidents are cited where authorities appear to have been overzealous in their interpretation of the law, including the arrest of individuals distributing pamphlets admonishing Americans to leave the country and the temporary holdup at the border of a film entitled *Nelson Mandela* and Salman Rushdie's novel *Satanic Verses*. . . .

... [O]ne can safely say that the incidents mentioned above illustrate not over-expansive breadth and vagueness in the law, but rather actions by the state which cannot be lawfully taken pursuant to s. 319(2). The possibility of *illegal* police harassment clearly has minimal bearing on the proportionality of hate propaganda legislation to legitimate Parliamentary objectives, and hence the argument based on such harassment can be rejected.

... [E]ven though the terms of s. 319(2) and the nature of the available defences expose an individual to conviction only in narrow and clearly defined circumstances, it is said that non-criminal responses can more effectively combat the harm caused by hate propaganda. Most generally, it is said that discriminatory ideas can best be met with information and education programmes extolling the merits of tolerance and cooperation between racial and religious groups. As for the prohibition of hate propaganda, human rights statutes are pointed to as being a less severe and more effective response than the criminal law. Such statutes not only subject the disseminator of hate propaganda to reduced stigma and punishment, but also take a less confrontational approach to the suppression of such expression. This conciliatory tack is said to be preferable to penal sanction because an incentive is offered the disseminator to cooperate with human rights tribunals and thus to amend his or her conduct. . . .

In assessing the proportionality of a legislative enactment to a valid governmental objective, however, s. 1 should not operate in every instance so as to force the government to rely upon only the mode of intervention least intrusive of a *Charter* right or freedom. It may be that a number of courses of action are available in the furtherance of a pressing and substantial objective, each imposing a varying degree of restriction upon a right or freedom. In such circumstances, the government may legitimately employ a more restrictive measure, either alone or as part of a larger programme of action, if that measure is not redundant, furthering the objective in ways that alternative responses could not, and is in all other respects proportionate to a valid s. 1 aim.

... At the moment, for example, the state has the option of responding to hate propaganda by acting under either the *Criminal Code* or human rights provisions. In my view, having both avenues of redress at the state's disposal is justified in a free and democratic society. I see no reason to assume that the state will always utilize the most severe tool at hand, namely, the criminal law, to prevent the dissemination of hate propaganda. Where use of the sanction provided by s. 319(2) is imprudent, employing human rights legislation may be the more attractive route to take, but there may equally be circumstances in which the more confrontational response of criminal prosecution is best suited to punish a recalcitrant hate-monger. To send out a strong message of condemnation, both reinforcing the values underlying s. 319(2) and deterring the few individuals who would harm target group members and the larger community by intentionally communicating hate propaganda, will occasionally require use of the criminal law.

To summarize ... I find that the terms of s. 319(2) create a narrowly confined offence which suffers from neither overbreadth nor vagueness. . . .

The third branch of the proportionality test entails a weighing of the importance of the state objective against the effect of limits imposed upon a *Charter* right or guarantee. Even if the purpose of the limiting measure is substantial and the first two components of the proportionality test are satisfied, the deleterious effects of a limit may be too great to permit the infringement of the right or guarantee in issue.

... It will by now be quite clear that I do not view the infringement of s. 2(*b*) by s. 319(2) as a restriction of the most serious kind. The expressive activity at which this provision aims is of a special category, a category only tenuously connected with the values underlying the guarantee of freedom of speech. Moreover, the narrowly drawn terms of s. 319(2) and its defences prevent the prohibition of expression lying outside of this narrow category. Consequently, the suppression of hate propaganda affected by s. 319(2) represents an impairment of the individual's freedom of expression which is not of a most serious nature.

It is also apposite to stress yet again the enormous importance of the objective fueling s. 319(2), an objective of such magnitude as to support even the severe response of criminal prohibition. Few concerns can be as central to the concept of a free and democratic society as the dissipation of racism, and the especially strong value which Canadian society attaches to this goal must never be forgotten in assessing the effects of an impugned legislative measure. When the purpose of s. 319(2) is thus recognized, I have little trouble in finding that its effects, involving as they do the restriction of expression largely removed from the heart of free expression values, are not of such a deleterious nature as to outweigh any advantage gleaned from the limitation of s. 2(*b*). . . .

LA FOREST J. (dissenting): I agree with Justice McLachlin on the issues respecting freedom of expression and I would accordingly dispose of the appeal and answer the first two constitutional questions as she does. I find it unnecessary to consider the issues respecting the right to be presumed innocent and, in consequence, to answer the other constitutional questions.

The reasons of Sopinka and McLachlin JJ. were delivered by

McLACHLIN J. (dissenting):

[Lengthy sections of Justice McLachlin's opinion, in which she essentially agrees with Dickson that the law in question infringes section 2(*b*) of the *Charter* and must be justified under section 1, are omitted. Justice McLachlin agrees, moreover, that the law meets the "pressing and substantial" purpose component of the *Oakes* test. She dissents on all three components of the "proportional means" dimension of the *Oakes* test.]

The first question [under the proportionality test] is whether s. 319(2) of the *Criminal Code* may be seen as carefully designed or rationally connected to the objectives which it is aimed at promoting. . . .

. . . [I]t is clear that the legislation does, at least at one level, further Parliament's objectives. Prosecutions of individuals for offensive material directed at a particular group may bolster its members' beliefs that they are valued and respected in their community, and that the views of a malicious few do not reflect those of the population as a whole. Such a use of the criminal law may well affirm certain values and priorities which are of a pressing and substantial nature.

It is necessary, however, to go further, and consider not only Parliament's intention, but whether, given the actual effect of the legislation, a rational connection exists between it and its objectives. Legislation designed to promote an objective may in fact impede that objective. In *R. v. Morgentaler*, [1988] 1 S.C.R. 30, this Court considered the actual effect of abortion legislation designed to preserve women's life and health and found that it had the opposite effect of the legislative goals by imposing unreasonable procedural requirements

and delays. This Court was particularly mindful of the effects that these requirements had in practice of substantially increasing the risks to the health of pregnant women, especially in certain locations. Dickson C.J. treated this in the context of rational connection, stating, "to the extent that s. 251(4) is designed to protect the life and health of women, the procedures it establishes may actually defeat that objective" (pp. 75-76).

This approach recognizes that s. 1 of the *Charter* could easily become diluted if an intention on the part of government to act on behalf of a disadvantaged group sufficed in all cases to establish the necessary rational connection between the legislation and its objective. In some cases the link between the intention of the legislators and the achievement of the goal may be self-evident. In others, there may be doubt about whether the legislation will in fact achieve its ends; in resolving that doubt deference must be paid to the Parliament and the legislatures. But in cases such as *Morgentaler*, where it appears that the legislation not only may fail to achieve its goal but may have a contrary effect, the Court is justified in finding that the rational connection between the measure and the objective is absent. . . .

In my view, s. 319(2) of the *Criminal Code* falls in this class of case. Section 319(2) may well have a chilling effect on defensible expression by law-abiding citizens. At the same time, it is far from clear that it provides an effective way of curbing hate-mongers. Indeed, many have suggested it may promote their cause. Prosecutions under the *Criminal Code* for racist expression have attracted extensive media coverage. Zundel, prosecuted not under s. 319(2) but for the crime of spreading false news (s. 181), claimed that his court battle had given him "a million dollars worth of publicity": *Globe and Mail*, March 1, 1985, p. P1. There is an unmistakable hint of the joy of martyrdom in some of the literature for which Andrews, in the companion appeal, was prosecuted: . . .

Not only does the criminal process confer on the accused publicity for his dubious causes—it may even bring him sympathy. The criminal process is cast as a conflict between the accused and the state, a conflict in which the accused may appear at his most sympathetic. Franz Kafka was not being entirely whimsical when he wrote, "If you have the right eye for these things, you can see that accused men are often attractive" (*The Trial* (1976), at p. 203).

The argument that criminal prosecutions for this kind of expression will reduce racism and foster multiculturalism depends on the assumption that some listeners are gullible enough to believe the expression if exposed to it. But if this assumption is valid, these listeners might be just as likely to believe that there must be some truth in the racist expression because the government is trying to suppress it. Theories of a grand conspiracy between government and elements of society wrongly perceived as malevolent can become all too appealing if government dignifies them by completely suppressing their utterance. It is therefore not surprising that the criminalization of hate propaganda and prosecutions under such legislation have been subject to so much controversy in this country.

Historical evidence also gives reason to be suspicious of the claim that hate propaganda laws contribute to the cause of multiculturalism and equality. This evidence is summarized by A.A. Borovoy, *When Freedoms Collide: The Case for our Civil Liberties* (1988), at p. 50:

> Remarkably, pre-Hitler Germany had laws very much like the Canadian anti-hate law. Moreover, those laws were enforced with some vigour. During the fifteen years before Hitler came to power, there were more than two hundred prosecutions based on anti-semitic speech. And, in the opinion of the leading Jewish organization of that era, no more than 10 per cent of the cases were mishandled by the authorities. As subsequent history so painfully testifies, this type of legislation proved ineffectual on the one occasion when there was a real argument for it. Indeed, there is some indication that the Nazis of pre-Hitler Germany shrewdly exploited their criminal trials in order to increase the size of their constituency. They used the trials as platforms to propagate their message.

Viewed from the point of view of actual effect, the rational connection between s. 319(2) and the goals it promotes may be argued to be tenuous. Certainly it cannot be said that there is a strong and evident connection between the criminalization of hate propaganda and its suppression.

The second matter which must be considered in determining whether the infringement represented by the legislation is proportionate to its ends is whether the legislation impairs the right to the minimum extent possible.

. . . Despite the limitations found in s. 319(2), a strong case can be made that it is overbroad in that its definition of offending speech may catch many expressions which should be protected.

The first difficulty lies in the different interpretations which may be placed on the word "hatred." The *Shorter Oxford English Dictionary* defines "hatred" as: "The condition or state of relations in which one person hates another; the emotion of hate; active dislike, detestation; enmity, ill-will, malevolence." The wide range of diverse emotions which the word "hatred" is capable of denoting is evident from this definition. Those who defend its use in s. 319(2) of the *Criminal Code* emphasize one end of this range—hatred, they say, indicates the most powerful of virulent emotions lying beyond

the bounds of human decency and limiting s. 319(2) to extreme materials. Those who object to its use point to the other end of the range, insisting that "active dislike" is not an emotion for the promotion of which a person should be convicted as a criminal. To state the arguments is to make the case; "hatred" is a broad term capable of catching a wide variety of emotion.

It is not only the breadth of the term "hatred" which presents dangers; it is its subjectivity. "Hatred" is proved by inference—the inference of the jury or the judge who sits as trier of fact—and inferences are more likely to be drawn when the speech is unpopular. The subjective and emotional nature of the concept of promoting hatred compounds the difficulty of ensuring that only cases meriting prosecution are pursued and that only those whose conduct is calculated to dissolve the social bonds of society are convicted. . . . It is argued that the requirement of "wilful promotion" eliminates from the ambit of s. 319(2) statements which are made for honest purposes such as telling a perceived truth or contributing to a political or social debate. The difficulty with this argument is that those purposes are compatible with the intention (or presumed intention by reason of foreseeability) of promoting hatred. A belief that what one says about a group is true and important to political and social debate is quite compatible with and indeed may inspire an intention to promote active dislike of that group. Such a belief is equally compatible with foreseeing that promotion of such dislike may stem from one's statements. The result is that people who make statements primarily for non-nefarious reasons may be convicted of wilfully promoting hatred.

The absence of any requirement that actual harm or incitement to hatred be shown further broadens the scope of s. 319(2) of the *Criminal Code*. This, in the view of the Court of Appeal, was the section's main defect. In effect, the provision makes a crime not only of actually inciting others to hatred, but also of attempting to do so. The Court of Appeal accepted the argument that this made the crime, at least potentially, a victimless one. . . .

Though I regard this breadth as a relevant factor, I would be hesitant to treat it as constitutionally determinative. To view hate propaganda as "victimless" in the absence of any proof that it moved its listeners to hatred is to discount the wrenching impact that it may have on members of the target group themselves. For Jews, many of whom have personally been touched by the terrible consequences of the degeneration of a seemingly civilized society into unparalleled barbarism, statements such as Keegstra's may raise very real fears of history repeating itself. Moreover, it is simply not possible to assess with any precision the effects that expression of a particular message will have on all those who are ultimately exposed to it. The process of "proving" that listeners were moved to hatred has a fictitious air about it. These considerations undermine the notion that we can draw a bright line between provisions which are justifiable because they require proof that hatred actually resulted, and provisions which are unjustifiable because they require only an intent to promote hatred.

The breadth of s. 319(2) is narrowed somewhat by the defences. Statements made in good faith on religious subjects and statements on matters of public interest which the accused reasonably believed to be true, as well as statements made for the purpose of removing hatred, are exempted.

Quite apart from the fact that the onus lies on the accused to prove these defences, it is far from clear that in practice they significantly narrow the ambit of s. 319(2) of the *Criminal Code*. The most important defence is truth—if the accused establishes that his statements are true, s. 319(2) is not violated. On the other hand, as already mentioned, conviction may result for true statements given that the onus of proof lies on the accused. Moreover, the concepts of "truth" and "reasonable belief in truth" may not always be applicable. Statements of opinion may be incapable of being classified as true or false, communicating not facts so much as sentiments and beliefs. Polemic statements frequently do not lend themselves to proof of truth or falsity. As for the defence of reasonable belief, how is a court to evaluate the reasonableness of diverse theories, political or otherwise? The defence of statements in the public interest poses similar problems. How is a court to determine what is in the public interest, given the wide range of views which may be held on matters potentially caught by s. 319(2)?

Not only is the category of speech caught by s. 319(2) defined broadly. The application of the definition of offending speech, i.e., the circumstances in which the offending statements are prohibited, is virtually unlimited. Only private conversations are exempt from state scrutiny. Section 319(2) is calculated to prevent absolutely expression of the offending ideas in any and all public forums through any and all mediums. Speeches are caught. The corner soap-box is no longer open. Books, films and works of art—all these fall under the censor's scrutiny because of s. 319(2) of the *Criminal Code*.

The real answer to the debate about whether s. 319(2) is overbroad is provided by the section's track record. Although the section is of relatively recent origin, it has provoked many questionable actions on the part of the authorities. There have been no reported convictions, other than the instant appeals. But the record amply demonstrates that intemperate statements about identifiable groups, particularly if they represent an unpopular viewpoint, may attract state involvement or calls for police action. Novels such as Leon Uris's pro-Zionist novel, *The Haj*, face calls for banning: *Toronto Star*, September 26, 1984, p. A6. Other works, such as Salman Rushdie's *Satanic Verses*, are stopped at the border on the ground that they violate s. 319(2). Films may be temporarily kept out, as happened to a film entitled *Nelson Mandela*, ordered as an educational film by Ryerson Polytechnic Institute in 1986: *Globe and Mail*, December 24, 1986, p. A14. Arrests are even made for distributing pamphlets containing the words "Yankee Go Home": *Globe and Mail*, July 4, 1975, p. 1. Experience shows that many cases are winnowed out due to prosecutorial discretion and other factors. It shows equally, however, that initially quite a lot of speech is caught by s. 319(2).

Even where investigations are not initiated or prosecutions pursued, the vagueness and subjectivity inherent in s. 319(2) of the *Criminal Code* give ground for concern that the chilling effect of the law may be substantial. . . . The danger here is not so much that the legislation will deter those bent on promoting hatred—in so far as it does so (and of this I remain skeptical) it is arguably not overbroad. The danger is rather that the legislation may have a chilling effect on legitimate activities important to our society by subjecting innocent persons to constraints born out of a fear of the criminal process. Given the vagueness of the prohibition of expression in s. 319(2), one may ask how speakers are to know when their speech may be seen as encroaching on the forbidden area. The reaction is predictable. The combination of overbreadth and criminalization may well lead people desirous of avoiding even the slightest brush with the criminal law to protect themselves in the best way they can—by confining their expression to non-controversial matters. Novelists may steer clear of controversial characterizations of ethnic characteristics, such as Shakespeare's portrayal of Shylock in *The Merchant of Venice*. Scientists may well think twice before researching and publishing results of research suggesting difference between ethnic or racial groups. Given the serious consequences of criminal prosecution, it is not entirely speculative to suppose that even political debate on crucial issues such as immigration, educational language rights, foreign ownership and trade may be tempered. These matters go to the heart of the traditional justifications for protecting freedom of expression.

This brings me to the second aspect of minimum impairment. The examples I have just given suggest that the very fact of criminalization itself may be argued to represent an excessive response to the problem of hate propagation. The procedures and sanctions associated with the criminal law are comparatively severe. Given the stigma that attaches and the freedom which is at stake, the contest between the individual and the state imposed by a criminal trial must be regarded as difficult and harrowing in the extreme. The seriousness of the imprisonment which may follow conviction requires no comment.

Moreover, the chilling effect of prohibitions on expression is at its most severe where they are effected by means of the criminal law. It is this branch of the law more than any other which the ordinary, law-abiding citizen seeks to avoid. The additional sanction of the criminal law may pose little deterrent to a convinced hate-monger who may welcome the publicity it brings; it may, however, deter the ordinary individual.

Moreover, it is arguable whether criminalization of expression calculated to promote racial hatred is necessary. Other remedies are perhaps more appropriate and more effective. Discrimination on grounds of race and religion is worthy of suppression. Human rights legislation, focusing on reparation rather than punishment, has had considerable success in discouraging such conduct. This is the conclusion of Borovoy, op. cit., at pp. 221-25. After noting the emphasis in human rights codes on amendment of conduct and their general success in effecting settlements before hearing, Borovoy addresses the suggestion that "racial discriminators be prosecuted or sued without having any opportunity to make amends" (p. 223). He concludes that criminal prosecution is not only unnecessary, but may be counterproductive. It is unnecessary because proceedings under the human rights codes show strong success in achieving their essential purpose, the curtailment of discrimination. It may be counterproductive in that: (1) racial discriminators threatened with prosecution may have little or no incentive to cooperate with human rights boards and voluntarily amend their conduct (p. 223); and (2) it leaves open the argument that "where a prosecutorial remedy exists, the state is obliged to adopt such a route first" (p. 225), thereby eliminating the possibility of voluntary amendment of conduct. For these reasons, Borovoy concludes that: "[a]part from collateral matters such as obstructing complaint investigations, the criminal process can safely be eliminated from human rights matters" (p. 225).

It is true that the focus of most human rights legislation is acts rather than words. But if it is inappropriate and ineffective to criminalize discriminatory conduct, it must necessarily be unjustifiable to criminalize discriminatory expression falling short of conduct.

Finally, it can be argued that greater precision is required in the criminal law than, for example, in human rights legislation because of the different character of the two types of proceedings. The consequences of alleging a violation of s. 319(2) of the *Criminal Code* are direct and serious in the extreme. Under the human rights process a tribunal has considerable discretion in determining what messages or conduct should be banned and by its order may indicate more precisely their exact nature, all of which occurs before any consequences inure to the alleged violator.

In summary, s. 319(2) of the *Criminal Code* catches a broad range of speech and prohibits it in a broad manner, allowing only private conversations to escape scrutiny. Moreover, the process by which the prohibition is effected—the criminal law—is the severest our society can impose and is arguably unnecessary given the availability of alternate remedies. I conclude that the criminalization of hate statements does not impair free speech to the minimum extent permitted by its objectives.

The third consideration in determining whether the infringement represented by the legislation is proportionate to the ends is the balance between the importance of the infringement of the right in question and the benefit conferred by the legislation. The analysis is essentially a cost-benefit analysis. . . .

I deal first with the significance of the infringement of the constitutionally guaranteed freedom at issue in this case. Viewed from the perspective of our society as a whole, the infringement of the guarantee of freedom of expression before this Court is a serious one. Section 319(2) of the *Criminal Code* does not merely regulate the form or tone of expression—it strikes directly at its content and at the viewpoints of individuals. It strikes, moreover, at viewpoints in widely diverse domains, whether artistic, social or political. It is capable of catching not only statements like those at issue in this case, but works of art and the intemperate statement made in the heat of social controversy. While few may actually be prosecuted to conviction under s. 319(2), many fall within the shadow of its broad prohibition. These dangers are exacerbated by the fact that s. 319(2) applies to all public expression. In short, the limitation on freedom of expression created by s. 319(2) of the *Criminal Code* invokes all of the values upon which s. 2(*b*) of the *Charter* rests—the value of fostering a vibrant and creative society through the marketplace of ideas; the value of the vigourous and open debate essential to democratic government and preservation of our rights and freedoms; and the value of a society which fosters the self-actualization and freedom of its members.

The consequences of the infringement of freedom of speech imposed by s. 319(2) of the *Criminal Code* considered from the viewpoint of the individual caught within its net are equally serious. The exercise of the right of free speech contrary to its provisions may result in a criminal record and imprisonment of up to two years. No warning, other than the description in s. 319(2) itself (which necessarily includes subjective elements), is given as to what speech is liable to result in prosecution. And those individuals not caught may find their expression restricted by the fear of running afoul of a vague and subjective law.

These considerations establish an infringement of the guarantee of freedom of expression of the most serious nature—much more serious, for example, than that which this Court upheld under s. 1 in *Irwin Toy*. There the only value which could be prayed in aid of free expression was the right to earn a profit. Section 319(2) of the *Criminal Code*, in contrast, touches on values vital to the preservation of democratic government and our fundamental rights and freedoms, as well as our right to individual self-actualization. And its broad sweep makes the infringement it effects not only serious in nature, but in extent. An infringement of this seriousness can only be justified by a countervailing state interest of the most compelling nature.

I turn then to the other side of the scale and the benefit to be gained by maintenance of the limitation on freedom of expression effected by s. 319(2) of the *Criminal Code*. As indi-cated earlier, there is no question but that the objectives which underlie this legislation are of a most worthy nature. Unfortunately, the claims of gains to be achieved at the cost of the infringement of free speech represented by s. 319(2) are tenuous. It is far from clear that the legislation does not promote the cause of hate-mongering extremists and hinder the possibility of voluntary amendment of conduct more than it discourages the spread of hate propaganda. Accepting the importance to our society of the goals of social harmony and individual dignity, of multiculturalism and equality, it remains difficult to see how s. 319(2) fosters them.

In my opinion, the result is clear. Any questionable benefit of the legislation is outweighed by the significant infringement on the constitutional guarantee of free expression effected by s. 319(2) of the *Criminal Code*. . . .

6 R. v. Butler, 1992

While a narrow 4-to-3 majority upheld the hate speech law in *Keegstra*, all nine Supreme Court judges (via two opinions) voted to uphold the censorship of obscenity in *Butler*. At issue was section 163(8) of the *Criminal Code*, which defined prohibited obscenity as "any publication a dominant characteristic of which is the undue exploitation of sex, or of sex and any one or more of the following subjects, namely, crime, horror, cruelty and violence." As in the case of hate speech, obscenity was expression protected by section 2(*b*) of the *Charter*, meaning that the censorship provision could be sustained only as a section 1 "reasonable limit" on freedom of expression. At the same time, and again like hate speech, obscenity was judged to fall some distance from the core freedom-of-expression values— "the search for truth, participation in the political process, and individual self-fulfilment"— making its restriction "easier to justify [under section 1] than other infringements."

Did the censorship law have the kind of "pressing and substantial" purpose required of a "reasonable limit" under the *Oakes* test? Not if the law's purpose was simply to protect moral sensibilities from the public display of any kind of explicit sexuality. That was indeed the purpose of censorship laws in the past, but "the prevention of 'dirt for dirt's sake,'" wrote Justice Sopinka, "is not a legitimate objective which would justify the violation of one of the most fundamental freedoms enshrined in the *Charter*." A valid objective must emphasize "not moral disapprobation but the avoidance of harm to society." Justice Sopinka was careful to reject a strict separation of law and morality. Indeed, he considered "moral corruption and harm to society [not as] distinct, but [as] inextricably linked [because it] is moral corruption of a certain kind which leads to the detrimental effect on society." His point was that while immorality may indeed cause the kind of harm needed for section 1 justification, not everything traditionally considered immoral causes such harm. Whether a depiction of sexuality was harmful was to be determined by "community standards," which had changed over time. No doubt, those who previously prohibited "dirt for dirt's sake" thought they were preventing "harm to society," but "our understanding of the harms caused by these materials has developed considerably."

For Justice Sopinka, this meant that in the *Charter* era a censorship law could not fully cover three common categories of pornography: (1) explicit sex with violence; (2) explicit sex without violence, but which subjects people to treatment that is degrading or dehumanizing; and (3) explicit sex without violence that is neither degrading nor dehumanizing. The first two categories were clearly harmful according to modern "community standards"; the third, with the crucial exception of child pornography, was not. As long as it depicts adults, the third kind of pornography is "good pornography" (or "erotica") that celebrates consensual sexuality based on equality between the participants. Bad pornography, the kind that could legitimately be censored, especially involved harm to women and children. Finding that section 163(8) was indeed targeted at the "harmful" categories of pornography and not at the legitimate "erotica," Justice Sopinka concluded that it met the "pressing and substantial purpose" part of the *Oakes* test.

Justice Sopinka had clearly responded to the request by the Women's Legal Education and Action Fund (LEAF) "to redefine the rationale for the *Criminal Code* obscenity provisions by focusing on its equality implications for women and children."[1] This feminist reading of section 163(8) attracted international attention as a pathbreaking innovation. *The New York Times* reported that the decision made "Canada the first place in the world that says what is obscene is what harms women."[2] The prominent American feminist Catherine MacKinnon, who had helped write LEAF's factum, devoted significant portions of her 1993 book *Only Words* to praising the innovation wrought by *Butler*.[3] Kathleen Mahoney, another co-author of LEAF's factum, called the ruling "world historic."[4]

Had this "world historic" innovation been in the minds of the legislators who enacted section 163 in 1959? It seems unlikely, and that posed a difficulty for Justice Sopinka. In *Big M Drug Mart* (case 3), the Court, rejecting the idea that a "shifting purpose" had transformed the obviously religious *Lord's Day Act* into secular day-of-rest legislation, insisted that the legislative purpose subjected to *Charter* scrutiny had to be what was in the minds of the legislature at the time of enactment. If he wished to respect the *Big M* precedent, as he clearly did, Justice Sopinka had to show that his innovative reading of section 163(8) did not amount to a "shifting purpose." He did so by distinguishing a "permissible shift in emphasis" from a complete shift in purpose. Preventing harm had always been the purpose of section 163; there had simply been a "shift in emphasis" in how we understand harm.[5] LEAF had considered asking the Court "to strike down the *Criminal Code* provisions and [invite] Parliament to introduce new legislation,"[6] but decided to press instead for a significant reinterpretation of the existing law. The former strategy would have required no "shifting purpose"; the latter required at least a "shift in emphasis."

Justice Gonthier (joined by Justice L'Heureux-Dubé) concurred in the result and supported much of the majority's reasoning, but thought that the modern understanding of harm might still reach adult "erotica" in some cases. Gonthier emphasized the distinction between private activity and its public representation in various media. A sexual activity that is good and meaningful in private can be stripped of its human significance when it is represented to the public in ways that do not "reflect the richness of human sexuality, but rather turn it into pure animality." Such misrepresentations of human sexuality can be more or less problematic depending on the kind of media and publicity involved. Thus, a portrayal of explicit "erotica" that would be of little concern in the pages of a book might, "[i]f found on a billboard sign, . . . be an undue exploitation of sex, because the community does not tolerate it, on the basis of its harmfulness." Gonthier worried that Justice Sopinka's liberation of "erotica" might extend too far.

---

1   Karen Busby, "LEAF and Pornography: Litigating on Equality and Sexual Representations" (1994) 9 *Canadian Journal of Law and Society* 169.

2   (28 February 1992).

3   Catherine MacKinnon, *Only Words* (Boston: Harvard University Press, 1993).

4   Stephen Bindman, "Top court upholds anti-pornography law" *Montreal Gazette* (28 February 1992) B1.

5   Not everyone finds the distinction persuasive. See Jonathon Daniels, "Valid Despite Vagueness: The Relationship Between Vagueness and Shifting Objective" (1994) *Saskatchewan Law Review* 58.

6   Busby, *supra* note 1.

In *Keegstra* (case 5), Justice Sopinka (along with Justice La Forest) had joined in Justice McLachlin's opinion that the hate-speech provision was not rationally connected to its objective because, instead of promoting egalitarian sentiments, censorship was more likely to strengthen racist expression. In *Butler*, Sopinka (with the support of McLachlin and La Forest) came to the opposite conclusion about the censorship of obscenity: "In contrast to the hate-monger who may succeed, by the sudden media attention, in gaining an audience, the prohibition of obscene materials does nothing to promote the pornographer's cause." Censorship of obscenity, in other words, does not irrationally produce the opposite of what it intends. But does it actually produce what it intends? What if obscenity is a reflection or symptom of bad attitudes rather than their cause? What if it actually provides a safety valve for the safe release of attitudes that might otherwise be acted out in truly harmful ways? Would censorship not then be irrational? Perhaps, but the social science evidence on whether obscenity is harmful is contradictory and inconclusive. Here, Sopinka reaffirmed the holding of earlier decisions that "in the face of inconclusive social science evidence" legislatures need only a "reasonable basis" for their ameliorative initiatives, a criterion fulfilled in the case of the obscenity provision. Similarly, on the basis of precedents holding that a law need not be perfectly tailored in order to satisfy the "minimal impairment" part of the *Oakes* test, Sopinka found that section 163 met that test and that its "restriction on freedom of expression [did] not outweigh the importance of the legislative objective."

The judicial agreement in *Butler* stands in stark contrast not only to the earlier disagreement in *Keegstra* but also to the subsequent disagreement in *R. v. Zundel*, which was heard and decided at roughly the same time as *Butler*.[7] Ernst Zundel, a Holocaust denier, had been charged under section 181 of the *Criminal Code*, which made it an indictable offence for anyone to "wilfully" publish "a statement, tale or news that he knows is false and that causes or is likely to cause injury or mischief to a public interest." As in *Keegstra*, a 7-judge panel split 4 to 3, but this time Justice McLachlin wrote the majority opinion invalidating the law. She was joined by Justices La Forest and Sopinka, who had supported her *Keegstra* dissent, and by Justice L'Heureux-Dubé, who had been part of the *Keegstra* majority. For McLachlin, the "false news" provision was an unreasonable limit on freedom of expression because its original purpose—dating back to 1275—was to protect the King and the nobles against slander that might undermine their legitimacy and destabilize the state. This could not be the kind of "pressing and substantial purpose" needed to override freedom of expression in the *Charter* era. The dissenting judgment, written by Justice Gonthier, argued that this original purpose had evolved in the same way that the purpose of the obscenity provision at stake in *Butler* had evolved. While the original purpose of the false-news provision may have been to protect the interest of the nobles, it was now targeted at "the dissemination of false information which strikes at important interests of *society as a whole*" (emphasis added). This, for Justice Gonthier, was a "permissible shift in emphasis" rather than the kind of "shifting purpose" rejected in *Big M*. Justice McLachlin's majority, all of whom had agreed in *Butler* to introduce the distinction Gonthier was using, vigorously disagreed. It is by no means uncommon to see a concept unanimously introduced to resolve one case fueling disagreement in others down the road.

---

7   *Butler* was heard on June 6, 1991 and decided on February 27, 1992; *Zundel* was heard on December 10, 1991 and decided on August 27, 1992.

While LEAF and pro-censorship feminists exulted in their victory in *Butler*, others, including libertarian feminists and gay and lesbian activists, opposed the decision. It was argued, for example, that *Butler's* criminalizing of violent, degrading, and dehumanizing sex would disproportionately affect gay and lesbian pornography, where sado-masochistic portrayals do not involve structured inequality between the sexes and may be strongly related to sexual identity. In this view, the *Butler* definition of illegal pornography was fundamentally "heterosexist" and did not leave enough room for sexual diversity. This issue arrived at the Supreme Court in 2000 in *Little Sisters Book and Art Emporium v. Canada*.[8] Little Sisters is a gay and lesbian bookstore whose imports had indeed been disproportionately targeted at the border by Canada Customs. The Supreme Court agreed that Customs had been applying the law in a discriminatory manner, but rejected the position, supported by LEAF, "that sado-masochism performs an emancipatory role in gay and lesbian culture and should therefore be judged by a different standard from that applicable to heterosexual culture." The *Butler* standard of harm, as determined by "community standards," would apply equally to heterosexual and homosexual pornography.

The Court revisited the issue of obscenity again in 2001 in *R. v. Sharpe*.[9] In the immediate aftermath of *Butler*, the federal government added a new, explicit child-pornography dimension to the *Criminal Code*. Among other things, the new section 163.1 criminalizes not just the "possession" of child pornography for purposes of distribution or sale but also purely private possession of such material. John Robin Sharpe was charged on both counts for possessing such material as "Sam Paloc's Boyabuse—Flogging, Fun and Fortitude: A Collection of Kiddiekink Classics." He did not constitutionally challenge the charge of possession for distribution and sale, but argued that prohibiting mere private possession could not be justified as a reasonable limit on freedom of expression. The trial court and a majority of the Court of Appeal agreed with him, striking down the simple possession provision and bringing its enforcement temporarily to a halt in British Columbia. As soon as the trial court handed down its decision in January 1999 there was an immense public outcry. All parties in the House of Commons severely criticized the decision, though they disagreed about the appropriate response, with the Reform Party opposition advocating the use of section 33 of the *Charter* to immediately restore the provision and the Liberal government expressing its confidence that higher courts, including ultimately the Supreme Court, would overrule the trial court.[10] The Liberals were wrong about the Court of Appeal, but right about the Supreme Court.

The Court heard *Sharpe* on January 18 and 19, 2000, but did not hand down its decision until January 26, 2001. This was two to three times the normal gestation period, leading to speculation that the Court dragged out its ruling until after the 2000 election.[11] In the event,

---

8   [2000] 2 S.C.R. 1120.

9   [2001] 1 S.C.R. 45.

10   See Rainer Knopff, "A Delicate Dance: The Courts and the Chrétien Government, 1993-2000" in Leslie A. Pal, ed., *How Ottawa Spends 2001-2002: Power in Transition* (Toronto: Oxford University Press, 2001).

11   "Analysts speculate judges may be holding back pornography ruling for political reasons" *The National Post* (15 November 2000).

the Court unanimously upheld the prohibition of simple possession of child pornography. Three of the judges—L'Heureux-Dubé, Gonthier, and Bastarache—would have upheld the law without reservation. Writing for the other six, Justice McLachlin read two exceptions into the provision. First, the prohibition of simple possession would not extend to "any written material or visual representation created by the accused alone, and held by the accused alone, exclusively for his or her own personal use." To illustrate, Justice McLachlin used the example of a teenager's confidential diary. Second, the provision would not reach "any visual recording, created by or depicting the accused, provided it does not depict unlawful sexual activity and is held by the accused exclusively for private use." Here the example was "a teenage couple [who created and kept] sexually explicit pictures featuring each other alone, or together engaged in lawful sexual activity, provided these pictures were created together and shared only with one another."

In *Sharpe*, as elsewhere, Justice McLachlin was on the more libertarian side of a freedom-of-expression issue, though this was much more moderate libertarianism than had been exhibited by the lower courts. McLachlin's *Sharpe* decision, in writing new meaning into the legislation, represented important legal innovation in the context of overall deference to a government policy. The same, of course, was true of Justice Sopinka's *Butler* opinion, which, while not activist in the sense of striking down a law, was widely recognized as a dramatic—even "world historic"—interpretive innovation. ⌒

Discussion Questions

1. Under the *Butler* ruling, is *Playboy Magazine* erotica or obscenity?
2. What would Justice Gonthier be prepared to censor that Justice Sopinka would not? How significant is this disagreement?
3. Justices Sopinka and McLachlin vote to strike down the censorship of hate speech in *Keegstra* and to uphold the censorship of obscenity in *Butler*. Are you persuaded by Justice Sopinka's explanation of this difference?

R. v. BUTLER
[1992] 1 S.C.R. 452

Hearing: June 6, 1991; Judgment: February 27, 1992.

Present: Lamer C.J. and La Forest, L'Heureux-Dubé, Sopinka, Gonthier, Cory, McLachlin, Stevenson, and Iacobucci JJ.

Interveners: The Attorney General of Canada, the Attorney General for Ontario, the Attorney General of Quebec, the Attorney General of British Columbia, the Attorney General for Alberta, Canadian Civil Liberties Association, Manitoba Association for Rights and Liberties, British Columbia Civil Liberties Association, Women's Legal Education and Action Fund, and G.A.P. (Group Against Pornography) Inc.

The judgment of Lamer C.J. and La Forest, Sopinka, Cory, McLachlin, Stevenson, and Iacobucci JJ. was delivered by

SOPINKA J.: This appeal calls into question the constitutionality of the obscenity provisions of the *Criminal Code*, R.S.C., 1985, c. C-46, s. 163. They are attacked on the ground that they contravene s. 2(*b*) of the *Canadian Charter of Rights and Freedoms.* . . .

. . .[T]his appeal should be confined to the examination of the constitutional validity of s. 163(8) only. . . .

(8) For the purposes of this Act, any publication a dominant characteristic of which is the undue exploitation of sex, or of sex and any one or more of the following subjects, namely, crime, horror, cruelty and violence, shall be deemed to be obscene.

. . . Pornography can be usefully divided into three categories: (1) explicit sex with violence, (2) explicit sex without violence but which subjects people to treatment that is degrading or dehumanizing, and (3) explicit sex without violence that is neither degrading nor dehumanizing. Violence in this context includes both actual physical violence and threats of physical violence. Relating these three categories to the terms of s. 163(8) of the *Code*, the first, explicit sex coupled with violence, is expressly mentioned. Sex coupled with crime, horror or cruelty will sometimes involve violence. Cruelty, for instance, will usually do so. But, even in the absence of violence, sex coupled with crime, horror or cruelty may fall within the second category. As for category (3), subject to the exception referred to below, it is not covered.

Some segments of society would consider that all three categories of pornography cause harm to society because they tend to undermine its moral fibre. Others would contend that none of the categories cause harm. Furthermore there is a range of opinion as to what is degrading or dehumanizing. See *Pornography and Prostitution in Canada: Report of the Special Committee on Pornography and Prostitution* (1985) (the Fraser Report), vol. 1, at p. 51. Because this is not a matter that is susceptible of proof in the traditional way and because we do not wish to leave it to the individual tastes of judges, we must have a norm that will serve as an arbiter in determining what amounts to an undue exploitation of sex. That arbiter is the community as a whole.

The courts must determine as best they can what the community would tolerate others being exposed to on the basis of the degree of harm that may flow from such exposure. Harm in this context means that it predisposes persons to act in an anti-social manner as, for example, the physical or mental mistreatment of women by men, or, what is perhaps debatable, the reverse. Anti-social conduct for this purpose is conduct which society formally recognizes as incompatible with its proper functioning. The stronger the inference of a risk of harm the lesser the likelihood of tolerance. The inference may be drawn from the material itself or from the material and other evidence. Similarly evidence as to the community standards is desirable but not essential.

In making this determination with respect to the three categories of pornography referred to above, the portrayal of sex coupled with violence will almost always constitute the undue exploitation of sex. Explicit sex which is degrading or dehumanizing may be undue if the risk of harm is substantial. Finally, explicit sex that is not violent and neither degrading nor dehumanizing is generally tolerated in our society and will not qualify as the undue exploitation of sex unless it employs children in its production.

If material is not obscene under this framework, it does not become so by reason of the person to whom it is or may be shown or exposed nor by reason of the place or manner in which it is shown. The availability of sexually explicit materials in theatres and other public places is subject to regulation by competent provincial legislation. Typically such legislation imposes restrictions on the material available to children. See *Nova Scotia Board of Censors v. McNeil*, [1978] 2 S.C.R. 662.

[It is also necessary to determine whether the] undue exploitation of sex [is] the main object of the work or [whether] this portrayal of sex [is] essential to a wider artistic, literary, or other similar purpose? Since the threshold determination must be made on the basis of community standards, that is, whether the sexually explicit aspect is undue, its impact when considered in context must be determined on the same basis. The court must determine whether the sexually explicit material when viewed in the context of the whole work would be tolerated by the community as a whole. Artistic expression rests at the heart of freedom of expression values and any doubt in this regard must be resolved in favour of freedom of expression. . . .

In light of our recent decision in *R. v. Keegstra*, [1990] 3 S.C.R. 697, the respondent, and most of the parties intervening in support of the respondent, do not take issue with the proposition that s. 163 of the *Criminal Code* violates s. 2(*b*) of the *Charter*. In *Keegstra*, we were unanimous in advocating a generous approach to the protection afforded by s. 2(*b*) of the *Charter*. Our Court confirmed the view expressed in *Reference re ss. 193 and 195.1(1)(c) of the Criminal Code (Man.)*, [1990] 1 S.C.R. 1123 (the *"Prostitution Reference"*), that activities cannot be excluded from the scope of the guaranteed freedom on the basis of the content or meaning being conveyed....

Meaning sought to be expressed need not be "redeeming" in the eyes of the court to merit the protection of s. 2(*b*), whose purpose is to ensure that thoughts and feelings may be conveyed freely in non-violent ways without fear of censure.

In this case, both the purpose and effect of s. 163 are specifically to restrict the communication of certain types of materials based on their content. In my view, there is no doubt that s. 163 seeks to prohibit certain types of expressive activity and thereby infringes s. 2(*b*) of the *Charter*.

Before turning to consider whether this infringement is justified under s. 1 of the *Charter*, I wish to address the argument advanced by the Attorney General of B.C. that in applying s. 2(*b*), a distinction should be made between films and written works. It is argued that by its very nature, the medium of the written word is such that it is, when used, inherently an attempt to convey meaning. In contrast, British Columbia argues that the medium of film can be used for a purpose "not significantly communicative." In its factum, British Columbia maintains that if the activity captured in hard core pornographic magazines and videotapes is itself not expression, the fact that they are reproduced by the technology of a camera does not magically transform them into "expression": the appellant cannot hide behind the label "film" to claim protection for the reproduction of activity the sole purpose of which is to arouse or shock.

In my view, this submission cannot be maintained. This position is not far from that taken by the majority of the Court of Appeal, that the depiction of purely physical activity does not convey meaning. First, I cannot agree with the premise that purely physical activity, such as sexual activity, cannot be expression. Second, in creating a film, regardless of its content, the maker of the film is consciously choosing the particular images which together constitute the film. In choosing his or her images, the creator of the film is attempting to convey some meaning. The meaning to be ascribed to the work cannot be measured by the reaction of the audience, which, in some cases, may amount to no more than physical arousal or shock. Rather, the meaning of the work derives from the fact that it has been intentionally created by its author. To use an example, it may very well be said that a blank wall in itself conveys no meaning. However, if one deliberately chooses to capture that image by the medium of film, the work necessarily has some meaning for its author and thereby constitutes expression. The same would apply to the depiction of persons engaged in purely sexual activity.

D. Is Section 163 Justified Under Section 1 of the Charter?

The appellant argues that the provision is so vague that ... it does not qualify as "a limit prescribed by law"; ... so imprecise that it is not a reasonable limit....

Standards which escape precise technical definition, such as "undue," are an inevitable part of the law.... It is within the role of the judiciary to attempt to interpret these terms. If such interpretation yields an intelligible standard, the threshold test for the application of s. 1 is met. In my opinion, the interpretation of s. 163(8) in prior judgments which I have reviewed, as supplemented by these reasons, provides an intelligible standard....

The respondent argues that there are several pressing and substantial objectives which justify overriding the freedom to distribute obscene materials. Essentially, these objectives are the avoidance of harm resulting from antisocial attitudinal changes that exposure to obscene material causes and the public interest in maintaining a "decent society." On the other hand, the appellant argues that the objective of s. 163 is to have the state act as "moral custodian" in sexual matters and to impose subjective standards of morality.

The obscenity legislation and jurisprudence prior to the enactment of s. 163 were evidently concerned with prohibiting the "immoral influences" of obscene publications and safeguarding the morals of individuals into whose hands such works could fall....

I agree with Twaddle J.A. of the Court of Appeal that this particular objective is no longer defensible in view of the *Charter*. To impose a certain standard of public and sexual morality, solely because it reflects the conventions of a given community, is inimical to the exercise and enjoyment of individual freedoms, which form the basis of our social contract.... The prevention of "dirt for dirt's sake" is not a legitimate objective which would justify the violation of one of the most fundamental freedoms enshrined in the *Charter*.

On the other hand, I cannot agree with the suggestion of the appellant that Parliament does not have the right to legislate on the basis of some fundamental conception of morality for the purposes of safeguarding the values which are integral to a free and democratic society. As Dyzenhaus ["Obscenity and the Charter: Autonomy and Equality" (1991), 1 C.R. (4th) 367], at p. 376, writes:

> Moral disapprobation is recognized as an appropriate response when it has its basis in *Charter* values.

As the respondent and many of the interveners have pointed out, much of the criminal law is based on moral conceptions of right and wrong and the mere fact that a law is grounded in morality does not automatically render it illegitimate. In this regard, criminalizing the proliferation of materials which undermine another basic *Charter* right may indeed be a legitimate objective.

In my view, however, the overriding objective of s. 163 is not moral disapprobation but the avoidance of harm to society....

The harm was described in the following way in the Report on Pornography by the Standing Committee on Justice and Legal Affairs (MacGuigan Report) (1978), at p. 18:4:

> The clear and unquestionable danger of this type of material is that it reinforces some unhealthy tendencies in Canadian society. The effect of this type of material is to reinforce male–female stereotypes to the detriment of both sexes. It attempts to make degradation, humiliation, victimization, and violence in human relationships appear normal and acceptable. A society which holds that egalitarianism, non-violence, consensualism, and mutuality are basic to any human interaction, whether sexual or other, is clearly justified in controlling and prohibiting any medium of depiction, description or advocacy which violates these principles.

The appellant argues that to accept the objective of the provision as being related to the harm associated with obscenity would be to adopt the "shifting purpose" doctrine explicitly rejected in *R. v. Big M Drug Mart Ltd.*, [1985] 1 S.C.R. 295. This Court concluded in that case that a finding that the *Lord's Day Act* has a secular purpose was not possible given that its religious purpose, in compelling sabbatical observance, has been long-established and consistently maintained by the courts....

I do not agree that to identify the objective of the impugned legislation as the prevention of harm to society, one must resort to the "shifting purpose" doctrine. First, the notions of moral corruption and harm to society are not distinct, as the appellant suggests, but are inextricably linked. It is moral corruption of a certain kind which leads to the detrimental effect on society. Second, and more importantly, I am of the view that with the enactment of s. 163, Parliament explicitly sought to address the harms which are linked to certain types of obscene materials. The prohibition of such materials was based on a belief that they had a detrimental impact on individuals exposed to them and consequently on society as a whole. Our understanding of the harms caused by these materials has developed considerably since that time; however this does not detract from the fact that the purpose of this legis-

lation remains, as it was in 1959, the protection of society from harms caused by the exposure to obscene materials....

A permissible shift in emphasis was built into the legislation when, as interpreted by the courts, it adopted the community standards test. Community standards as to what is harmful have changed since 1959.

This being the objective, is it pressing and substantial? Does the prevention of the harm associated with the dissemination of certain obscene materials constitute a sufficiently pressing and substantial concern to warrant a restriction on the freedom of expression? In this regard, it should be recalled that in *Keegstra*, *supra*, this Court unanimously accepted that the prevention of the influence of hate propaganda on society at large was a legitimate objective....

This Court has thus recognized that the harm caused by the proliferation of materials which seriously offend the values fundamental to our society is a substantial concern which justifies restricting the otherwise full exercise of the freedom of expression. In my view, the harm sought to be avoided in the case of the dissemination of obscene materials is similar....

In reaching the conclusion that legislation proscribing obscenity is a valid objective which justifies some encroachment on the right to freedom of expression, I am persuaded in part that such legislation may be found in most free and democratic societies. As Nemetz C.J.B.C. aptly pointed out in *R. v. Red Hot Video*, [(1985), 45 C.R. (3d) 36 (B.C.C.A.)], for centuries democratic societies have set certain limits to freedom of expression. He cited (at p. 40) the following passage of Dickson J.A. (as he then was) in *R. v. Great West News Ltd.*, *supra*, at p. 309:

> ... [A]ll organized societies have sought in one manner or another to suppress obscenity. The right of the state to legislate to protect its moral fibre and well-being has long been recognized, with roots deep in history. It is within this frame that the Courts and Judges must work.

The advent of the *Charter* did not have the effect of dramatically depriving Parliament of a power which it has historically enjoyed. It is also noteworthy that the criminalization of obscenity was considered to be compatible with the *Canadian Bill of Rights*....

The enactment of the impugned provision is also consistent with Canada's international obligations (Agreement for the Suppression of the Circulation of Obscene Publications and the Convention for the Suppression of the Circulation of and Traffic in Obscene Publications).

Finally, it should be noted that the burgeoning pornography industry renders the concern even more pressing and substantial than when the impugned provisions were first enacted. I would therefore conclude that the objective of avoiding the harm associated with the dissemination of pornography in this case is sufficiently pressing and substantial to warrant some restriction on full exercise of the right to freedom of expression. The analysis of whether the measure is proportional to the objective must, in my view, be undertaken in light of the conclusion that the objective of the impugned section is valid only in so far as it relates to the harm to society associated with obscene materials. Indeed, the section as interpreted in previous decisions and in these reasons is fully consistent with that objective. The objective of maintaining conventional standards of propriety, independently of any harm to society, is no longer justified in light of the values of individual liberty which underlie the *Charter*. . . .

In assessing whether the proportionality test is met, it is important to keep in mind the nature of expression which has been infringed. In the *Prostitution Reference, supra,* Dickson C.J. wrote, at p. 1136:

> When a *Charter* freedom has been infringed by state action that takes the form of criminalization, the Crown bears the heavy burden of justifying that infringement. Yet, the expressive activity, as with any infringed *Charter* right, should also be analysed in the particular context of the case. Here, the activity to which the impugned legislation is directed is expression with an economic purpose. It can hardly be said that communications regarding an economic transaction of sex for money lie at, or even near, the core of the guarantee of freedom of expression.

The values which underlie the protection of freedom of expression relate to the search for truth, participation in the political process, and individual self-fulfilment. The Attorney General for Ontario argues that of these, only "individual self-fulfilment," and only in its most base aspect, that of physical arousal, is engaged by pornography. On the other hand, the civil liberties groups argue that pornography forces us to question conventional notions of sexuality and thereby launches us into an inherently political discourse. In their factum, the B.C. Civil Liberties Association adopts a passage from R. West, "The Feminist-Conservative Anti-Pornography Alliance and the 1986 Attorney General's Commission on Pornography Report" (1987), 4 *Am. Bar Found. Res. Jo.* 681, at p. 696:

> Good pornography has value because it validates women's will to pleasure. It celebrates female nature. It validates a range of female sexuality that is wider and truer than that legitimated by the non-pornographic culture. Pornography (when it is good) celebrates both female pleasure and male rationality.

A proper application of the test should not suppress what West refers to as "good pornography." The objective of the impugned provision is not to inhibit the celebration of human sexuality. However, it cannot be ignored that the realities of the pornography industry are far from the picture which the B.C. Civil Liberties Association would have us paint. Shannon J., in *R. v. Wagner,* [(1985), 43 C.R. (3d) 318 (Alta. Q.B.)], described the materials more accurately when he observed, at p. 331:

> Women, particularly, are deprived of unique human character or identity and are depicted as sexual playthings, hysterically and instantly responsive to male sexual demands. They worship male genitals and their own value depends upon the quality of their genitals and breasts.

In my view, the kind of expression which is sought to be advanced does not stand on an equal footing with other kinds of expression which directly engage the "core" of the freedom of expression values.

This conclusion is further buttressed by the fact that the targeted material is expression which is motivated, in the overwhelming majority of cases, by economic profit. This Court held in *Rocket v. Royal College of Dental Surgeons of Ontario,* [1990] 2 S.C.R. 232, at p. 247, that an economic motive for expression means that restrictions on the expression might "be easier to justify than other infringements."

I will now turn to an examination of the three basic aspects of the proportionality test.

. . . [T]he rational link between s. 163 and the objective of Parliament relates to the actual causal relationship between obscenity and the risk of harm to society at large. On this point, it is clear that the literature of the social sciences remains subject to controversy. . . .

In the face of inconclusive social science evidence, the approach adopted by our Court in *Irwin Toy* is instructive. In that case, the basis for the legislation was that television advertising directed at young children is *per se* manipulative. The Court made it clear, at p. 994, that in choosing its mode of intervention, it is sufficient that Parliament had a *reasonable basis:*

> In the instant case, the Court is called upon to assess competing social science evidence respecting the appropriate means for addressing the problem of children's advertising. The question is whether the government had a reasonable basis, on the evidence tendered, for concluding that the ban on all advertising directed at children impaired freedom of expression as little as possible given the government's pressing and substantial objective.

And at p. 990:

> . . . [T]he Court also recognized that the government was afforded a margin of appreciation to form legitimate

objectives based on somewhat inconclusive social science evidence.

Similarly, in *Keegstra, supra*, the absence of proof of a causative link between hate propaganda and hatred of an identifiable group was discounted as a determinative factor in assessing the constitutionality of the hate literature provisions of the *Criminal Code*. Dickson C.J. stated, at p. 776:

> First, to predicate the limitation of free expression upon proof of actual hatred gives insufficient attention to the severe psychological trauma suffered by members of those identifiable groups targeted by hate propaganda. Second, it is clearly difficult to prove a causative link between a specific statement and hatred of an identifiable group.

McLachlin J. (dissenting) expressed it as follows, at p. 857:

> To view hate propaganda as "victimless" in the absence of any proof that it moved its listeners to hatred is to discount the wrenching impact that it may have on members of the target group themselves.... Moreover, it is simply not possible to assess with any precision the effects that expression of a particular message will have on all those who are ultimately exposed to it.

> ...Accordingly, I am of the view that there is a sufficiently rational link between the criminal sanction, which demonstrates our community's disapproval of the dissemination of materials which potentially victimize women and which restricts the negative influence which such materials have on changes in attitudes and behaviour, and the objective.

Finally, I wish to distinguish this case from *Keegstra*, in which the minority adopted the view that there was no rational connection between the criminalization of hate propaganda and its suppression. As McLachlin J. noted, prosecutions under the *Criminal Code* for racist expression have attracted extensive media coverage. The criminal process confers on the accused publicity for his or her causes and succeeds even in generating sympathy. The same cannot be said of the kinds of expression sought to be suppressed in the present case. The general availability of the subject materials and the rampant pornography industry are such that, in the words of Dickson C.J. in *Keegstra*, "pornography is not dignified by its suppression." In contrast to the hate-monger who may succeed, by the sudden media attention, in gaining an audience, the prohibition of obscene materials does nothing to promote the pornographer's cause....

In determining whether less intrusive legislation may be imagined, this Court stressed in the *Prostitution Reference, supra*, that it is not necessary that the legislative scheme be the "perfect" scheme, but that it be appropriately tailored *in the context of the infringed right* (at p. 1138). Furthermore, in

Irwin Toy, supra, Dickson C.J., Lamer and Wilson JJ. stated, at p. 999:

> While evidence exists that other less intrusive options reflecting more modest objectives were available to the government, there is evidence establishing the necessity of a ban to meet the objectives the government had reasonably set. This Court will not, in the name of minimal impairment, take a restrictive approach to social science evidence and require legislatures to choose the least ambitious means to protect vulnerable groups.

There are several factors which contribute to the finding that the provision minimally impairs the freedom which is infringed.

First, the impugned provision does not proscribe sexually explicit erotica without violence that is not degrading or dehumanizing. It is designed to catch material that creates a risk of harm to society....

Second, materials which have scientific, artistic or literary merit are not captured by the provision. As discussed above, the court must be generous in its application of the "artistic defence." For example, in certain cases, materials such as photographs, prints, books and films which may undoubtedly be produced with some motive for economic profit, may nonetheless claim the protection of the *Charter* in so far as their defining characteristic is that of aesthetic expression, and thus represent the artist's attempt at individual fulfilment. The existence of an accompanying economic motive does not, of itself, deprive a work of significance as an example of individual artistic or self-fulfilment.

Third, in considering whether the provision minimally impairs the freedom in question, it is legitimate for the court to take into account Parliament's past abortive attempts to replace the definition with one that is more explicit. In *Irwin Toy*, our Court recognized that it is legitimate to take into account the fact that earlier laws and proposed alternatives were thought to be less effective than the legislation that is presently being challenged. The attempt to provide exhaustive instances of obscenity has been shown to be destined to fail (Bill C-54, 2nd Sess., 33rd Parl.). It seems that the only practicable alternative is to strive towards a more abstract definition of obscenity which is contextually sensitive and responsive to progress in the knowledge and understanding of the phenomenon to which the legislation is directed. In my view, the standard of "undue exploitation" is therefore appropriate. The intractable nature of the problem and the impossibility of precisely defining a notion which is inherently elusive makes the possibility of a more explicit provision remote. In this light, it is appropriate to question whether, and at what cost, greater legislative precision can be demanded.

Fourth, while the discussion in this appeal has been limited to the definition portion of s. 163, I would note that the impugned section, with the possible exception of subs. 1, which is not in issue here, has been held by this Court not to extend its reach to the private use or viewing of obscene materials. . . .

Accordingly, it is only the public distribution and exhibition of obscene materials which is in issue here.

Finally, I wish to address the arguments of the interveners, the Canadian Civil Liberties Association and Manitoba Association for Rights and Liberties, that the objectives of this kind of legislation may be met by alternative, less intrusive measures. First, it is submitted that reasonable time, manner and place restrictions would be preferable to outright prohibition. I am of the view that this argument should be rejected. Once it has been established that the objective is the avoidance of harm caused by the degradation which many women feel as "victims" of the message of obscenity, and of the negative impact exposure to such material has on perceptions and attitudes towards women, it is untenable to argue that these harms could be avoided by placing restrictions on access to such material. Making the materials more difficult to obtain by increasing their cost and reducing their availability does not achieve the same objective. Once Parliament has reasonably concluded that certain acts are harmful to certain groups in society and to society in general, it would be inconsistent, if not hypocritical, to argue that such acts could be committed in more restrictive conditions. The harm sought to be avoided would remain the same in either case.

It is also submitted that there are more effective techniques to promote the objectives of Parliament. For example, if pornography is seen as encouraging violence against women, there are certain activities which discourage it—counselling rape victims to charge their assailants, provision of shelter and assistance for battered women, campaigns for laws against discrimination on the grounds of sex, education to increase the sensitivity of law enforcement agencies and other governmental authorities. In addition, it is submitted that education is an under-used response.

It is noteworthy that many of the above suggested alternatives are in the form of *responses* to the harm engendered by negative attitudes against women. The role of the impugned provision is to control the dissemination of the very images that contribute to such attitudes. Moreover, it is true that there are additional measures which could alleviate the problem of violence against women. However, given the gravity of the harm, and the threat to the values at stake, I do not believe that the measure chosen by Parliament is equalled by the alternatives which have been suggested. Education, too, may offer a means of combating negative attitudes to women, just as it is currently used as a means of addressing other problems dealt with in the *Code*. However, there is no reason to rely on education alone. It should be emphasized that this is in no way intended to deny the value of other educational and counselling measures to deal with the roots and effects of negative attitudes. Rather, it is only to stress the arbitrariness and unacceptability of the claim that such measures represent the sole legitimate means of addressing the phenomenon. Serious social problems such as violence against women require multi-pronged approaches by government. Education and legislation are not alternatives but complements in addressing such problems. There is nothing in the *Charter* which requires Parliament to choose between such complementary measures.

The final question to be answered in the proportionality test is whether the effects of the law so severely trench on a protected right that the legislative objective is outweighed by the infringement. The infringement on freedom of expression is confined to a measure designed to prohibit the distribution of sexually explicit materials accompanied by violence, and those without violence that are degrading or dehumanizing. As I have already concluded, this kind of expression lies far from the core of the guarantee of freedom of expression. It appeals only to the most base aspect of individual fulfilment, and it is primarily economically motivated.

The objective of the legislation, on the other hand, is of fundamental importance in a free and democratic society. It is aimed at avoiding harm, which Parliament has reasonably concluded will be caused directly or indirectly, to individuals, groups such as women and children, and consequently to society as a whole, by the distribution of these materials. It thus seeks to enhance respect for all members of society, and non-violence and equality in their relations with each other.

I therefore conclude that the restriction on freedom of expression does not outweigh the importance of the legislative objective.

I conclude that while s. 163(8) infringes s. 2(*b*) of the *Charter*, freedom of expression, it constitutes a reasonable limit and is saved by virtue of the provisions of s. 1. . . .

The reasons of L'Heureux-Dubé and Gonthier JJ. were delivered by

GONTHIER J.: I have had the benefit of the reasons of Justice Sopinka and, while I agree both with his disposition of the case and with his reasons generally, I wish to add to them with respect to the judicial interpretation of s. 163 of the *Criminal Code*, R.S.C., 1985, c. C-46, and to its constitutional validity.

Section 163 of the *Code* offers a peculiar structure. Its subject matter, obscene materials, comprises the dual elements of representation and content. Representation here is understood in the sense of public suggestion. A representation is a portrayal, a description meant to evoke something to the mind and senses. . . . By "content" I mean of course the content of the representation.

It is the combination of the two, the representation and its content, that attracts criminal liability. A representation as such is not enough, of course, to create the subject matter of s. 163, but neither is an act included in the content of s. 163 of the *Code*, without an element of representation. . . .

. . . The type of scenes vividly described in *R. v. Wagner* (1985), 43 C.R. (3d) 318 (Alta. Q.B.), *R. v. Doug Rankine Co.* (1983), 9 C.C.C. (3d) 53 (Ont. Co. Ct.) or *R. v. Ramsingh* (1984), 14 C.C.C. (3d) 230 (Man. Q.B.), might perhaps be legal if done between consenting adults, but they become obscene when they are represented.

Without launching into a lengthy debate on the reasons why Parliament may have enacted s. 163 of the *Code* . . . it can be seen that the combination of representation and content that constitutes obscenity leads to many ills. . . . Obscene materials . . . convey a distorted image of human sexuality, by making public and open elements of the human nature which are usually hidden behind a veil of modesty and privacy. D. A. Downs, *The New Politics of Pornography* (1989), aptly describes how these materials do not reflect the richness of human sexuality, but rather turn it into pure animality, at p. 183:

> . . . the deeper objection to sheer pornography or obscenity . . . is that it represents a retreat from the human dilemma and the responsibility of acknowledging the tensions in our nature. Sheer pornography also reduces us to the lower aspects of our natures by stripping away the modesty that arises from our encounter with our animality. . . .

To summarize . . . the particular combination of a representation and its content that forms the subject matter of s. 163 of the *Code* was seen by Parliament as putting forward a distorted image of human sexuality, which in turn can induce harmful behavioural changes. This must be kept in mind when interpreting s. 163 of the *Code*. . . .

. . . Sopinka J. essentially aligns the definition of obscenity in s. 163(8) of the *Code* with the definition of pornography nowadays. He introduces a three-part categorization that has surfaced in contemporary theory, and that had been adopted in some Canadian cases throughout the 80s:

(a) Explicit sex with violence, which generally constitutes "undue exploitation of sex" within the meaning of s. 163(8) of the *Code*, on the basis of demonstrable harm;

(b) Explicit sex that is degrading or dehumanizing, which will be "undue exploitation of sex" if it creates a substantial risk of harm; the risk of harm can be assessed with reference to the tolerance of the community, under the "community standard of tolerance" test; and

(c) Explicit sex that is neither violent nor degrading or dehumanizing, which will not generally fall under s. 163(8) of the *Code*, according to Sopinka J.

I must say at the outset that I differ only with respect to the third category of materials. I am not prepared to affirm as boldly as my colleague Sopinka J. does that it escapes the application of s. 163(8). . . .

The dual nature, as representation and content, of the subject matter of s. 163 comes into play here. Yet the classification proposed by my colleague Sopinka J. focuses only on content. The content of the first two categories of materials is so likely to harm that the characteristics of the representation do not really matter: if there is violence or degradation or dehumanization, as long as the element of representation is present, harm will probably ensue.

The content of the third category of materials is generally perceived as unlikely to cause harm, as Sopinka J. rightly points out. He mentions as an exception child pornography, i.e. materials in the production of which children were employed. This exception is important, since it obviously flows from the high likelihood of harm ensuing from the production and dissemination of child pornography.

In addition to this exception, it is quite conceivable that the representation may cause harm, even if its content as such may not be seen as harmful. . . .

. . . After all, it is the element of representation that gives this material its power of suggestion, and it seems quite conceivable that this power may cause harm despite the apparent neutrality of the content. A host of factors could intervene in the manner of representation to affect the characterization of the material, among which are the medium, the type or the use.

The medium provides a good example. Indeed the differences between the various media are not acknowledged often enough in opinions dealing with s. 163 of the *Code*. . . .

Nevertheless it seems natural to me that the likelihood of harm, and the tolerance of the community, may vary according to the medium of representation, even if the content stays the same. Let me take, as an example, an explicit portrayal of "plain" sexual intercourse, where two individuals are making love. This falls within the third category of Sopinka J. If found in words in a book, it is unlikely to be of much concern (if found in a children's book, though, this may be different). If found depicted in a magazine or in a movie, the likelihood of harm increases but remains low. If found on a poster, it is already more troublesome. If found on a billboard sign, then

I would venture that it may well be an undue exploitation of sex, because the community does not tolerate it, on the basis of its harmfulness.

The harmfulness, in the billboard sign example, would come from the immediacy of the representation, inasmuch as the sign stands all by itself (as opposed to a passage in a book, a film or a magazine). Its message is at once crude and inescapable. It distorts human sexuality by taking it out of any context whatsoever and projecting it to the public. This example goes to the extreme, of course, but it is meant to show that the element of representation may create a likelihood of harm that may lead to the application of s. 163 of the *Code*, even if the content of the representation as such is not objectionable.

As I mentioned, the medium of representation is but one variable pertaining to representation that may trigger the application of s. 163 to third-category materials. The overall type or use of the representation, be it education, art, advertising, sexual arousal or other, may also be relevant, among other factors. These factors tie in to the "internal necessities" test to some extent. This test, if it is to find a place within the interpretive framework of Sopinka J., must intervene at the representational level, to change the characterization that would ensue from a mere look at the content of the materials.

For these reasons, therefore, I would hold that materials falling within Sopinka J.'s third category (explicit sex with neither violence nor degradation or dehumanization), while generally less likely to cause harm than those of the first two categories, may nevertheless come within the definition of obscene at s. 163(8) of the *Code*, if their content (child pornography) or their representational element (the manner of representation) is found conducive of harm. . . .

The assessment of the risk of harm here depends on the tolerance of the community, as is the case with the second category of materials. This brings me to outline a certain shift in the meaning of "tolerance." In *Towne Cinema*, [[1985] 1 S.C.R. 494], Dickson C.J. formulated the community standard test as follows at p. 508:

> . . . it is a standard of *tolerance*, not taste, that is relevant. What matters is not what Canadians think is right for themselves to see. What matters is what Canadians would not abide other Canadians seeing because it would be beyond the contemporary Canadian standard of tolerance to allow them to see it. [Emphasis in original.]

It is unclear from this excerpt what the basis of tolerance is. It seems that tolerance is for taste the conceptual equivalent of the reasonable person to the actual plaintiff: an abstraction, an average perhaps. Tolerance would be some form of enlightened, altruistic taste, which would factor in and sum up the tastes of the whole population.

In the mind of Dickson C.J., there exists no necessary relationship between tolerance and harm, as he mentions at p. 505:

> However, as I have noted above, there is no *necessary* coincidence between the undueness of publications which degrade people by linking violence, cruelty or other forms of dehumanizing treatment with sex, and the community standard of tolerance. Even if certain sex related materials were found to be within the standard of tolerance of the community, it would still be necessary to ensure that they were not "undue" in some other sense, for example in the sense that they portray persons in a degrading manner as objects of violence, cruelty, or other forms of dehumanizing treatment. [Emphasis in original.]

Sopinka J. uses the community standard of tolerance to gauge the risk of harm. In this context, tolerance must be related to the harm. It must mean not only tolerance of the materials, but also tolerance of the harm which they may bring about. It is a more complicated and more reflective form of tolerance than what was considered by Dickson C.J. in *Towne Cinema, supra*. Such a development is fully in accordance with the emphasis put by this Court on harm as the central element in the interpretation of s. 163(8).

In the context of the third category, the harm sought to be avoided is the same as in the first two categories, that is attitudinal changes. While this type of harm was clear in the case of the first category and was probable in the case of the second, it is perhaps more remote here, and will likely occur only in a limited number of cases. The main difference between the second and third categories lies in the presumed likelihood of harm: while degrading or dehumanizing materials are likely to cause harm regardless of whether the community may be ready to tolerate such harm, materials which show no violence, no degradation or dehumanization are less likely to cause harm, and the evidence with respect to the lack of tolerance of the community will be central. Still the risk of harm flowing from the content or the representational element of third-category materials is not always so slight as my colleague Sopinka J. pictures it. If the community cannot tolerate this risk of harm, then in my opinion these materials, even though they may offer a non-violent, non-degrading, non-dehumanizing content, will constitute undue exploitation of sex and will fall under the definition of obscenity at s. 163(8) of the *Code*. . . .

With respect to the constitutional aspects of this case, I am in agreement with Sopinka J., and I wish only to complement his reasons on the objective of s. 163 of the *Code*.

In his reasons, Sopinka J. rules out the possibility that "public morality" can be a legitimate objective for s. 163 of the *Code* and, while admitting that Parliament may legislate to protect "fundamental conceptions of morality," he goes on to conclude that the true objective of s. 163 is the avoidance of harm to society.

In my opinion, the distinction between the two orders of morality advanced by my colleague is correct, and the avoidance of harm to society is but one instance of a fundamental conception of morality.

First of all, I cannot conceive that the State could not legitimately act on the basis of morality. Since its earliest *Charter* pronouncements, this Court has acknowledged this possibility. In *R. v. Big M Drug Mart Ltd.*, [1985] 1 S.C.R. 295, Dickson J. (as he then was) wrote for the Court at p. 337:

> Freedom means that, subject to such limitations as are necessary to protect public safety, order, health, or morals or the fundamental rights and freedoms of others, no one is to be forced to act in a way contrary to his beliefs or his conscience.

Morality is also listed as one of the grounds for which freedom of expression can be restricted in the *European Convention on Human Rights* at article 10:

> 1. Everyone has the right to freedom of expression. . . .
> 2. The exercise of these freedoms, since it carries with it duties and responsibilities, may be subject to such formalities, conditions, restrictions or penalties as are prescribed by law and are necessary in a democratic society, in the interests of national security, territorial integrity or public safety, for the prevention of disorder or crime, for the protection of health or morals, for the protection of the reputation or rights of others, for preventing the disclosure of information received in confidence, or for maintaining the authority and impartiality of the judiciary.

The European Court of Human Rights has recognized the validity of prohibitions of obscene materials in English and Swiss law, respectively, on the basis that they concern morals, in the *Handyside Case*, judgment of 7 December 1976, Series A No. 24 and in the *Case of Müller and Others*, judgment of 24 May 1988, Series A No. 133.

Indeed the problem is not so much to assess whether morality is a valid objective under the *Charter* as to determine under which conditions it is a pressing and substantial objective. Not all moral claims will be sufficient to warrant an override of *Charter* rights. As R. Dworkin wrote in the chapter of *Taking Rights Seriously* (1977) entitled "Liberty and Moralism" at p. 255:

> The claim that a moral consensus exists is not itself based on a poll. It is based on an appeal to the legislator's sense of how his community reacts to some disfavored practice.

But this same sense includes an awareness of the grounds on which that reaction is generally supported. If there has been a public debate involving the editorial columns, speeches of his colleagues, the testimony of interested groups, and his own correspondence, these will sharpen his awareness of what arguments and positions are in the field. He must sift these arguments and positions, suppose general principles or theories vast parts of the population could not be supposed to accept, and so on.

This task that Dworkin assigns to Parliament is also entrusted to this Court in *Charter* review. Two dimensions are important here, which allow one to distinguish between morality in the general sense and "fundamental conceptions of morality."

First of all, the moral claims must be grounded. They must involve concrete problems such as life, harm, well-being, to name a few, and not merely differences of opinion or of taste. Parliament cannot restrict *Charter* rights simply on the basis of dislike; this is what is meant by the expression "substantial and pressing" concern.

Secondly, a consensus must exist among the population on these claims. They must attract the support of more than a simple majority of people. In a pluralistic society like ours, many different conceptions of the good are held by various segments of the population. The guarantees of s. 2 of the *Charter* protect this pluralistic diversity. However, if the holders of these different conceptions agree that some conduct is not good, then the respect for pluralism that underlies s. 2 of the *Charter* becomes less insurmountable an objection to State action (this argument has recently been rejuvenated and reformulated in S. Gardbaum, "Why the Liberal State Can Promote Moral Ideals After All" (1991), 104 *Harv. L. Rev.* 1350). In this sense a wide consensus among holders of different conceptions of the good is necessary before the State can intervene in the name of morality. This is also comprised in the phrase "pressing and substantial."

The avoidance of harm caused to society through attitudinal changes certainly qualifies as a "fundamental conception of morality." After all, one of the chief aspirations of morality is the avoidance of harm. It is well grounded, since the harm takes the form of violations of the principles of human equality and dignity. Obscene materials debase sexuality. They lead to the humiliation of women, and sometimes to violence against them. This is more than just a matter of taste. Without entering into the examination of the rational connection, some empirical evidence even elucidates the link between these materials and actual violence. Even then, as was said by this Court in *Irwin Toy Ltd. v. Quebec (Attorney General)*, [1989] 1 S.C.R. 927, in *R. v. Keegstra*, [1990] 3 S.C.R. 697, and as is reiterated by my colleague in his reasons, scientific proof is not required, and reason and common experience will often suffice.

Furthermore, taking into account that people hold different conceptions about good taste and the acceptable level of sexual explicitness, most would agree that these attitudinal changes are serious and warrant State intervention (civil liberty groups who advocated that this Court strike down s. 163 of the *Code* concede that harm can justify State intervention, but they deny that any harm flows from obscene materials; that is a different question).

I agree with Sopinka J. that s. 163 of the *Code* aims at preventing harm to society and I fully endorse his analysis, and as I tried to demonstrate I would not hesitate to affirm that the prevention of harm is a moral objective that is valid under s. 1 of the *Charter*.

I also agree with Sopinka J.'s analysis of the proportionality between the restriction effected by s. 163 of the *Code* and its objectives. I would add a remark, however, on the first factor listed by Sopinka J. under the minimal impairment branch of the proportionality test, that is the exception for materials of the third category. Contrary to Sopinka J., I consider that the third category may sometimes attract criminal liability. The requirement that the impugned materials exceed the community standard of tolerance of harm provides sufficient precision and protection for those whose activities are at stake. This is so as, on the one hand, the field of sexual exploitation is one of first apprehension, directly related to one of the primary aspects of human personality, and well known to all, including particularly those engaged in it. On the other hand, the criterion of tolerance of harm by the community as a whole is one that, by definition, reflects the general level of tolerance throughout all sectors of the community, hence generally of all its members. It is therefore a very demanding criterion to meet as it must be by definition generally known or apprehended. It is indeed not far removed from the domain of public notoriety and, inasmuch as it falls within it, may be the subject of judicial notice not requiring specific proof.

Subject to the foregoing comments, I otherwise concur both with the reasons and the disposition of the case of my colleague Sopinka J.

RJR-MacDonald Inc. v. Canada (Attorney General), 1995

In this case, major tobacco companies claimed that a federal ban on tobacco advertising fell beyond Ottawa's criminal law power and constituted an unreasonable infringement of the *Charter*'s freedom-of-expression guarantee. Speaking through seven separate opinions (most of them short), a substantial majority (7 to 2) of the Court found that the ban was valid criminal law while a narrow majority (5 to 4) voted to strike it down on freedom-of-expression grounds. We reproduce below only the primary majority and dissenting opinions on the *Charter* issue.

The law at issue prohibited the advertising and promotion of tobacco products and required the packaging for those products to display non-attributed warnings about the toxic ingredients and negative health effects of tobacco. As in other freedom-of-expression cases, a *Charter* violation was (mostly) conceded, and the analysis turned mainly on determining whether the law could be justified as a "reasonable limit" under section 1.

The Court has established two ways of determining how much deference is owed to Parliament in the section 1 stage of analysis. First, as we have seen (for example, in *Keegstra*, case 5, and in *Butler*, case 6), the farther the infringed expression falls from the "core" freedom-of-expression values—"the search for political, artistic and scientific truth, the protection of individual autonomy and self-development, and the *promotion of public participation in the democratic process*"—the lower the standard justification. Second, because courts have well-established expertise in matters of criminal law, where the state acts as the "singular antagonist of the individual," they can apply higher levels of scrutiny than when legislation is aimed at "mediating between different groups" or social interests, which requires policy judgments that lie outside traditional judicial expertise.

While both the main opinions in the case—Justice McLachlin's for the majority and Justice La Forest's for the minority—agreed with these distinctions in principle, they applied them very differently. Thus, while La Forest saw the kind of expression at stake in this case—commercial advertising aimed at increasing profits—as falling far from the core of expression values, McLachlin rejected his reliance on the profit motive, pointing out that booksellers and newspaper owners—surely close to the core—were also profit-oriented enterprises. And while La Forest saw the legislation as compromising "among the competing interests of smokers, non-smokers and manufacturers, with an eye to protecting vulnerable groups in society," and thus as "the very type of legislation to which this Court has generally accorded a high degree of deference," McLachlin observed that it was also a criminal law that "pits the state against the offender." In any case, said McLachlin, "[t]o carry judicial deference to the point of accepting Parliament's view simply on the basis that the problem is serious and the solution difficult"—as she clearly thought La Forest had done—"would be to diminish the role of the courts in the constitutional process and to weaken the structure of rights upon which our constitution and our nation is founded."

One of the reasons La Forest considered the problem serious and the solution difficult is that the law was 20 years in the making and that similarly protracted policy processes had led at least 20 other liberal democracies to enact similar laws. Moreover, in countries such as

France and the United States, such laws had been upheld as constitutional. Justice McLachlin was unimpressed.

Given their different orientations to the question of deference, the contrasting conclusions of McLachlin and La Forest on the components of the *Oakes* test come as no surprise. While La Forest found the law to pass all parts of the test, McLachlin saw it as failing all parts of the critical proportionality component.

True, both sides conceded that the law had a "pressing and substantial purpose," but McLachlin defined that purpose more narrowly than did La Forest. For La Forest, the compelling purpose of the law was "protecting Canadians from the health risks associated with tobacco use, and informing them about these risks." For McLachlin, this overly broad purpose made it too easy to find the means proportional. Her narrower purpose was to "prevent people in Canada from being persuaded by advertising and promotion to use tobacco products [and] to discourage people who see the package from tobacco use."

Did a total advertising ban actually prevent people from being persuaded to use tobacco products? In addressing this question, McLachlin distinguished between "informational" and "lifestyle" advertising. Informational advertising simply identifies brands and may even provide useful information about different levels of toxins in various brands. Lifestyle advertising, by contrast, associates smoking with attractive people and activities. While McLachlin thought that "lifestyle advertising may, as a matter of common sense, be seen as having a tendency to discourage those who might otherwise cease tobacco use from doing so," she could find no solid connection, either in empirical scientific evidence or in "reason and logic," between a ban on informational advertising and its intended effect. It was "hard to imagine," she wrote, "how the presence of a tobacco logo on a cigarette lighter, for example, would increase consumption; yet, such use is banned." She concluded that a total ban—one that encompassed purely informational advertising—was not rationally connected to its purpose. Similarly, although a limited prohibition of only lifestyle advertising might pass the minimal impairment part of proportionality analysis, a total ban clearly infringed that criterion.

For Justice La Forest it was not nearly as clear that a ban of informational advertising was irrational, even in the light of Justice McLachlin's more narrowly defined purpose. As a "powerful common sense observation," he found it "difficult to believe that Canadian tobacco companies would spend over 75 million dollars every year on advertising if they did not know that advertising increases the consumption of their product." The government, he maintained, was entitled to come to a similar common-sense conclusion. For Justice McLachlin, such "common sense" did not satisfy the section 1 criterion for evidence or logic sufficient to "demonstrate" the need for a total ban. But note that when McLachlin justified her preferred option of a ban limited to "lifestyle" advertising, she did so "as a matter of [her own] common sense." The tension between the standard McLachlin applied to government policy preferences and the standard she applied to her own has not gone unremarked in the literature.[1]

---

1   Janet Hiebert, *Charter Conflicts* (Montreal and Kingston: McGill-Queen's University Press, 2002) at 77-78.

RJR-MacDonald attracted considerable attention and controversy. Perhaps most dramatically, it led Ed Broadbent, former national leader of the New Democratic Party, to change his mind about the *Charter*'s section 33 notwithstanding clause. When the *Charter* was being drafted and enacted, Broadbent had opposed section 33. At a 20th-anniversary *Charter* conference in Ottawa in 2002, he expressed his outrage that the *RJR* Court had given the economic freedom of corporations priority over public health. He now understood, he announced, why section 33 was a useful *Charter* provision. *RJR* was for him a prime example of a case that deserved a "notwithstanding" response.

In response to the *RJR* decision—subscribing to the then fashionable notion of inter-institutional "dialogue"—the government enacted a new advertising ban, one that carefully followed Justice McLachlin's recommended limitation to "lifestyle" advertising. That law, too, was challenged by tobacco companies in a subsequent case, *JTI-Macdonald*.[2] This time, a unanimous Court, speaking through now Chief Justice McLachlin, upheld the law as a "reasonable limit" on freedom of expression. ⌒

Discussion Questions

1. How and why did Justices McLachlin and La Forest disagree on the minimal impairment component of the *Oakes* test? Which of their arguments do you find most persuasive?
2. Justices McLachlin and La Forest disagree about whether an advertising ban limited to "lifestyle advertising" can be effective. What do you think about the evidence and arguments they use to support their contrary views?
3. Should Parliament have resorted to the section 33 notwithstanding clause to override the majority ruling in *RJR-MacDonald*?

---

2 *Canada (Attorney General) v. JTI-Macdonald Corp.*, 2007 SCC 30.

RJR-MACDONALD INC. v. THE
ATTORNEY GENERAL OF CANADA
[1995] 3 S.C.R. 199

Hearing: November 29, 30, 1994; Judgment: September 21, 1995.

Present: Lamer C.J. and La Forest, L'Heureux-Dubé, Sopinka, Gonthier, Cory, McLachlin, Iacobucci, and Major JJ.

Interveners: The Attorney General for Ontario, the Heart and Stroke Foundation of Canada, the Canadian Cancer Society, the Canadian Council on Smoking and Health, the Canadian Medical Association, and the Canadian Lung Association.

The reasons of La Forest, L'Heureux-Dubé, and Gonthier JJ. were delivered by

[2] **LA FOREST J.** (dissenting): The issues in these appeals are whether the *Tobacco Products Control Act*, S.C. 1988, c. 20 (the "Act"), falls within the legislative competence of the Parliament of Canada under s. 91 of the *Constitution Act, 1867*, either as criminal law or under the peace, order and good government clause, and if so whether it constitutes an infringement of freedom of expression under s. 2(*b*) of the *Canadian Charter of Rights and Freedoms* which is not justified under s. 1 of the *Charter*. In broad terms, the Act prohibits, subject to specified exceptions, all advertising and promotion of tobacco products, and prohibits the sale of a tobacco product unless the package containing it sets forth prescribed health warnings and a list of the toxic constituents of the product and of the smoke produced from its combustion....

[58] The Attorney General conceded that the prohibition on advertising and promotion under the Act constitutes an infringement of the appellants' right to freedom of expression under s. 2(*b*) of the *Charter*, and directed his submissions solely to justifying the infringement under s. 1 of the *Charter*. In my view, the Attorney General was correct in making this concession....

[59] [H]owever, it is appropriate to draw attention to the fact that the Attorney General did not concede that s. 9 of the Act, which requires tobacco manufacturers to place an unattributed health warning on packages of these products, constitutes an infringement of the appellants' right to freedom of expression. In my view, the Attorney General was correct in not making this concession. However, since there is considerable overlap between my discussion of this issue and my discussion of s. 1, I shall for convenience address this distinct issue separately at the conclusion of my general s. 1 analysis....

[61] The appellants have conceded that the objective of protecting Canadians from the health risks associated with tobacco use, and informing them about these risks, is pressing and substantial. Rather than focusing upon the objective, the appellants submit that the measures employed under the Act are not proportional to the objective....

[63] This Court has on many occasions affirmed that the *Oakes* requirements must be applied flexibly, having regard to the specific factual and social context of each case. The word "reasonable" in s. 1 necessarily imports flexibility.... This Court has on many occasions stated that the evidentiary requirements under s. 1 will vary substantially depending upon both the nature of the legislation and the nature of the right infringed....

[67] It appears ... that there is a significant gap between our understanding of the health *effects* of tobacco consumption and of the root *causes* of tobacco consumption. In my view, this gap raises a fundamental institutional problem that must be taken into account in undertaking the s. 1 balancing. Simply put, a strict application of the proportionality analysis in cases of this nature would place an impossible onus on Parliament by requiring it to produce definitive social scientific evidence respecting the root causes of a pressing area of social concern every time it wishes to address its effects. This could have the effect of virtually paralyzing the operation of government in the socio-economic sphere. As I noted in *McKinney* [*v. University of Guelph*, [1990] 3 S.C.R. 229], at pp. 304-5, predictions respecting the ramifications of legal rules upon the social and economic order are not matters capable of precise measurement, and are often "the product of a mix of conjecture, fragmentary knowledge, general experience and knowledge of the needs, aspirations and resources of society, and other components." To require Parliament to wait for definitive social science conclusions every time it wishes to make social policy would impose an unjustifiable limit on legislative power by attributing a degree of scientific accuracy to the art of government which, in my view, is simply not consonant with reality....

[68] In several recent cases, this Court has recognized the need to attenuate the *Oakes* standard of justification when institutional constraints analogous to those in the present cases arise.... [For example, i]n drawing a distinction between legislation aimed at "mediating between different groups," where a lower standard of s. 1 justification may be appropriate, and legislation where the state acts as the "singular antagonist of the individual," where a higher standard of justification is necessary, the Court in *Irwin Toy* was drawing upon the more fundamental institutional distinction between the legislative and judicial functions that lies at the very heart of our political and constitutional system. Courts are specialists in the protection of liberty and the interpretation of legislation and are, accordingly, well placed to subject criminal justice legislation to careful scrutiny. However, courts are not special-

ists in the realm of policy-making, nor should they be. This is a role properly assigned to the elected representatives of the people, who have at their disposal the necessary institutional resources to enable them to compile and assess social science evidence, to mediate between competing social interests and to reach out and protect vulnerable groups. In according a greater degree of deference to social legislation than to legislation in the criminal justice context, this Court has recognized these important institutional differences between legislatures and the judiciary.

[69] ... In enacting this legislation, Parliament was facing a difficult policy dilemma. On the one hand, Parliament is aware of the detrimental health effects of tobacco use, and has a legitimate interest in protecting Canadians from, and in informing them about, the dangers of tobacco use. Health underlies many of our most cherished rights and values, and the protection of public health is one of the fundamental responsibilities of Parliament. On the other hand, however, it is clear that a prohibition on the manufacture, sale or use of tobacco products is unrealistic. Nearly seven million Canadians use tobacco products, which are highly addictive. Undoubtedly, a prohibition of this nature would lead to an increase in illegal activity, smuggling and, quite possibly, civil disobedience. Well aware of these difficulties, Parliament chose a less drastic, and more incremental, response to the tobacco health problem. In prohibiting the advertising and promotion of tobacco products, as opposed to their manufacture or sale, Parliament has sought to achieve a compromise among the competing interests of smokers, non-smokers and manufacturers, with an eye to protecting vulnerable groups in society. Given the fact that advertising, by its very nature, is intended to influence consumers and create demand, this was a reasonable policy decision. Moreover, ... the Act is the product of a legislative process dating back to 1969, when the first report recommending a full prohibition on tobacco advertising was published; see *Report of the Standing Committee on Health, Welfare and Social Affairs on Tobacco and Cigarette Smoking* [(1969)], *supra*. In drafting this legislation, Parliament took into account the views of Canadians from many different sectors of society, representing many different interests. Indeed, the legislative committee responsible for drafting Bill C-51, which was subsequently adopted by Parliament as the Act, heard from 104 organizations during hearings in 1988 representing a variety of interests, including medicine, transport, advertising, smokers' rights, non-smokers' rights, and tobacco production.

[70] Seen in this way, it is clear that the Act is the very type of legislation to which this Court has generally accorded a high degree of deference. In drafting this legislation, which is directed toward a laudable social goal and is designed to

protect vulnerable groups, Parliament was required to compile and assess complex social science evidence and to mediate between competing social interests. Decisions such as these are properly assigned to our elected representatives, who have at their disposal the necessary resources to undertake them, and who are ultimately accountable to the electorate. ...

[71] Turning now to the nature of the right infringed under the Act, it is once again necessary to place the appellants' claim in context. This Court has recognized, in a line of freedom of expression cases dating back to *Edmonton Journal*, *supra*, that, depending on its nature, expression will be entitled to varying levels of constitutional protection. ...

[72] ... In *Keegstra* ..., Dickson C.J. identified these fundamental or "core" values as including the search for political, artistic and scientific truth, the protection of individual autonomy and self-development, and the promotion of public participation in the democratic process. When state action places such values in jeopardy, this Court has been careful to subject it to a searching degree of scrutiny. ...

[73] In cases where the expression in question is farther from the "core" of freedom of expression values, this Court has applied a lower standard of justification. For example, in *Keegstra*, where a majority of this Court ruled that a prohibition on hate speech under s. 319(2) of the *Criminal Code*, R.S.C., 1985, c. C-46, was a justifiable limitation on freedom of expression, Dickson C.J. found that this limited infringement was justified because hate propaganda was a form of expression that was only remotely related to "core" free expression values. ...

[74] This Court adopted a similar approach in *R. v. Butler*, [1992] 1 S.C.R. 452, where it found a prohibition upon publications whose dominant characteristic was the "undue exploitation of sex" under s. 163(8) of the *Criminal Code*, R.S.C., 1985, c. C-46, to be a justifiable infringement upon freedom of expression. In so ruling, this Court found it significant, at p. 500, that "the kind of expression which is sought to be advanced does not stand on an equal footing with other kinds of expression which directly engage the 'core' of the freedom of expression values." ... The Court has adopted a similar approach with respect to prostitution, which was also accorded a lower level of protection in the *Prostitution Reference*. ...

[75] In my view, the harm engendered by tobacco, and the profit motive underlying its promotion, place this form of expression as far from the "core" of freedom of expression values as prostitution, hate mongering, or pornography, and thus entitle it to a very low degree of protection under s. 1. It must be kept in mind that tobacco advertising serves no political, scientific or artistic ends; nor does it promote participation in the political process. Rather, its sole purpose is

to inform consumers about, and promote the use of, a product that is harmful, and often fatal, to the consumers who use it. The main, if not sole, motivation for this advertising is, of course, profit. . . .

[76] The appellants, both of whom are large multinational corporations, spend millions of dollars every year to promote their products (in 1987 alone, RJR and Imperial spent over $75 million dollars on advertising and promotion). . . . The sophistication of the advertising campaigns employed by these corporations, in my view, undermines their claim to freedom of expression protection because it creates an enormous power differential between these companies and tobacco consumers in the "marketplace of ideas." . . . The power differential between advertiser and consumer is even more pronounced with respect to children who, as this Court observed in *Irwin Toy*, at p. 987, are "particularly vulnerable to the techniques of seduction and manipulation abundant in advertising." . . . In this respect, it is critical to keep in mind Dickson C.J.'s reminder in *Edwards Books* [[1986] 2 S.C.R. 713], at p. 779:

> In interpreting and applying the *Charter* I believe that the courts must be cautious to ensure that it does not simply become an instrument of better situated individuals to roll back legislation which has as its object the improvement of the condition of less advantaged persons.

[77] I conclude, therefore, that an attenuated level of s. 1 justification is appropriate in these cases. . . . With these observations firmly in mind, I now proceed to an application of the proportionality test. . . .

[83] . . . The appellants . . . base their argument principally upon the claim that there is no rational connection between the prohibition on advertising and promotion of tobacco products under ss. 4, 5, 6, and 8 and the objective of reducing tobacco consumption. In my view, the appellants' argument fails. . . .

[84] I begin with what I consider to be a powerful common sense observation. Simply put, it is difficult to believe that Canadian tobacco companies would spend over 75 million dollars every year on advertising if they did not know that advertising increases the consumption of their product. In response to this observation, the appellants insist that their advertising is directed solely toward preserving and expanding brand loyalty among smokers, and not toward expanding the tobacco market by inducing non-smokers to start. In my view, the appellants' claim is untenable for two principal reasons. First, brand loyalty alone will not, and logically cannot, maintain the profit levels of these companies if the overall number of smokers declines. A proportionate piece of a smaller pie is still a smaller piece. . . . Second, even if this Court were to

accept the appellants' brand loyalty argument, the appellants have not adequately addressed the further problem that even commercials targeted solely at brand loyalty may also serve as inducements for smokers not to quit. . . .

[86] . . . [T]he power of the common-sense connection between advertising and consumption is sufficient to satisfy the rational connection requirement.

[87] However, it is not necessary to rely solely upon common sense to reach this conclusion. . . .

[92] [A] number of reports introduced at trial . . . attest to the causal connection between tobacco advertising and consumption. . . .

[93] The views expressed in these reports are not, of course, definitive or conclusive. Indeed, there is currently a lively debate in the social sciences respecting the connection between advertising and consumption, a debate that has been carried on for years and will no doubt persist well into the near future. However, these reports attest, at the very least, to the existence of what LeBel J.A. called a "body of opinion" supporting the existence of a causal connection between advertising and consumption. . . .

[94] . . . I conclude that there is a rational connection between the prohibition on advertising and consumption under ss. 4, 5, 6 and 8 of the Act and the reduction of tobacco consumption. . . .

[95] The next step in the proportionality analysis is to determine whether the legislative means chosen impair the right or freedom in question as little as possible. The appellants submit that Parliament has unjustifiably imposed a complete prohibition on tobacco advertising and promotion when it could have imposed a partial prohibition with equal effectiveness. They suggest that Parliament could have instituted a partial prohibition by forbidding "lifestyle" advertising (which seeks to promote an image by associating the consumption of the product with a particular lifestyle) or advertising directed at children, without at the same time prohibiting "brand preference" advertising (which seeks to promote one brand over another based on the colour and design of the package) or "informational" advertising (which seeks to inform the consumer about product content, taste and strength and the availability of different or new brands). According to the appellants, there is no need to prohibit brand preference or informational advertising because both are targeted solely at smokers, and serve a beneficial function by promoting consumer choice.

[96] In my view, the appellants' argument fails. . . . [T]he minimal impairment requirement does not impose an obligation on the government to employ the least intrusive measures available. Rather, it only requires it to demonstrate that the measures employed were the least intrusive, *in light of both the legislative objective and the infringed right*. . . .

[97] . . . It must be kept in mind that the infringed right at issue in these cases is the right of tobacco corporations to advertise the only legal product sold in Canada which, when used precisely as directed, harms and often kills those who use it. As I discussed above, I have no doubt that Parliament could validly have employed the criminal law power to prohibit the manufacture and sale of tobacco products, and that such a prohibition would have been fully justifiable under the *Charter*. There is no right to sell harmful products in Canada, nor should there be. Thus, in choosing to prohibit solely the advertisement of tobacco products, it is clear that Parliament in fact adopted a relatively *unintrusive* legislative approach to the control of tobacco products. . . . Under the Act, tobacco companies continue to enjoy the right to manufacture and sell their products, to engage in public or private debate concerning the health effects of their products, and to publish consumer information on their product packages pertaining to the content of the products. The prohibition under this Act serves only to prevent these companies from employing sophisticated marketing and social psychology techniques to induce consumers to purchase their products. This type of expression, which is directed solely toward the pursuit of profit, is neither political nor artistic in nature, and therefore falls very far from the "core" of freedom of expression values discussed by this Court in *Keegstra*. . . .

[98] Furthermore, . . . the measures adopted under the Act were the product of an intensive 20-year public policy process, which involved extensive consultation with an array of national and international health groups and numerous studies, and educational and legislative programs. Over the course of this 20-year period, the government adopted an incremental legislative approach by experimenting with a variety of less intrusive measures before determining that a full prohibition on advertising was necessary. . . .

[99] . . . It is of great significance, in my view, that over 20 democratic nations have, in recent years, adopted complete prohibitions on tobacco advertising similar to those adopted under the Act, including Australia, New Zealand, Norway, Finland and France. It is also of significance that the constitutionality of full advertising prohibitions have been upheld by the French Conseil constitutionnel (Décision No. 90-283 DC (Jan. 8, 1991) declaring the *Loi n° 91-32 relative à la lutte contre le tabagisme et l'alcoolisme*, which prohibits all direct and indirect tobacco advertising), to be constitutionally valid and by American courts (upholding full prohibitions on alcohol advertising and gambling advertising as a reasonable limitation on freedom of expression under the United States Constitution in *Central Hudson* [*Gas & Electric Corp. v. Public Service Commission of New York*, 447 U.S. 557 (1980)]; *Oklahoma Telecasters* [699 F.2d 490 (1983)]; *Metromedia* [453

U.S. 490 (1981)]; *Posadas* [*de Puerto Rico Associates v. Tourism Co. of Puerto Rico*, 478 U.S. 328 (1986)]; *Dunagin* [*v. City of Oxford, Mississippi*, 718 F.2d 738 (1983)]). The decisions of the American courts, which have traditionally been jealous guardians of the right to freedom of expression, are particularly instructive in this context because they demonstrate that the adoption of a full prohibition upon tobacco advertising is perceived as neither novel nor radical in other democratic nations. Given the background of the legislation and the overwhelming acceptance by other democratic countries of this type of prohibition as a reasonable means for combating the serious evils flowing from the sale and distribution of tobacco products, it seems difficult to argue that the impugned legislation is not a reasonable limit on the appellants' rights demonstrably justified in a free and democratic society under s. 1 of the *Charter*. . . .

[103] Moreover, in considering the comparative advantages of partial and full advertising prohibitions, it is also significant that, in countries where governments have instituted partial prohibitions upon tobacco advertising such as those suggested by the appellants, the tobacco companies have developed ingenious tactics to circumvent the restrictions. For example, when France attempted to institute a partial prohibition on tobacco advertising in the 1980s (by prohibiting "lifestyle" tobacco advertising but not informational or brand preference advertising), the tobacco companies devised techniques for associating their product with "lifestyle" images which included placing pictures on the brand name and reproducing those pictures when an advertisement showed the package, and taking out a full-page magazine advertisement and subcontracting three-quarters of the advertisement to Club Med, whose lifestyle advertisements contributed to a lifestyle association for the brand; see Luc Joossens, "Strategy of the Tobacco Industry Concerning Legislation on Tobacco Advertising in some Western European Countries" in *Proceedings of the 5th World Conference on Smoking and Health* (1983).

[104] Thus, it appears that Parliament had compelling reasons for rejecting a partial prohibition on advertising and instituting a full prohibition. In this light, it would be highly artificial for this Court to decide, on a purely abstract basis, that a partial prohibition on advertising would be as effective as a full prohibition. In my view, this is precisely the type of "line drawing" that this Court has identified as being within the institutional competence of legislatures and not courts. . . .

[107] In reaching the conclusion that the Act satisfies the *Oakes* minimal impairment criterion, I am well aware of the statements of this Court in *Ford* [*v. Quebec (Attorney General)*, [1988] 2 S.C.R. 712], and *Rocket* [*v. Royal College of Dental Surgeons of Ontario*, [1990] 2 S.C.R. 232], to the effect that a complete prohibition on a type of expression will be more

difficult to justify than a partial prohibition. In my view, however, these decisions are fully distinguishable from the present cases. Once again, I emphasize the importance of context in the minimal impairment analysis. In *Rocket*, this Court found that a prohibition on advertising by dentists under s. 37(39) and (40) of *Regulation 447 of the Health Disciplines Act*, R.R.O. 1980, was an infringement of s. 2(*b*) and could not be justified under s. 1....

[108] ... [T]he contrast with *Rocket* could not be more striking. Making an informed choice about dentists serves to promote health by allowing patients to seek out the best care; making an informed choice about tobacco simply permits consumers to choose between equally dangerous products....

[109] A similar contrast can be drawn between the present cases and *Ford, supra*.... While, in these cases, the Act prohibits only tobacco advertising, in *Ford*, the law prohibited all non-French commercial expression in Quebec. It was therefore much broader in scope than the prohibition under the Act. Moreover, while the Act prohibits expression that has little or no connection with "core" freedom of expression values, the commercial expression in *Ford* was intimately connected with such core values. The impugned law in that case represented an attempt by the government of Quebec to eradicate the commercial use in public of any language other than French. Given the close historical relationship between language, culture and politics in Canada, it cannot seriously be denied that the implications of this prohibition extended well beyond the commercial sphere and impacted upon the dignity of all minority language groups in Quebec....

[112] The third part of the proportionality analysis requires a proportionality between the deleterious and the salutary effects of the measures.... For the reasons I have given with respect to both the nature of the legislation and the nature of the right infringed in these cases, it is my view that the deleterious effects of this limitation, a restriction on the rights of tobacco companies to advertise products for profit that are inherently dangerous and harmful, do not outweigh the legislative objective of reducing the number of direct inducements for Canadians to consume these products.

[113] I now turn to the appellants' final argument, namely, that s. 9 of the Act constitutes an unjustifiable infringement of their freedom of expression by compelling them to place on tobacco packages an unattributed health message. I agree, to use Wilson J.'s phrase, that if the effect of this provision is "to put a particular message into the mouth of the plaintiff, as is metaphorically alleged to be the case here," the section runs afoul of s. 2(*b*) of the *Charter*; see *Lavigne* [*v. Ontario Public Service Employees Union*, [1991] 2 S.C.R. 211], at p. 267.... [However] it must be remembered that this statement is *unattributed* and I have some difficulty in seeing,

in the context in which it was made, that it can in any real sense be considered to be attributed to the appellants. Simply because tobacco manufacturers are required to place unattributed warnings on their products does not mean that they must endorse these messages, or that they are perceived by consumers to endorse them. In a modern state, labelling of products, and especially products for human consumption, are subject to state regulation as a matter of course. It is common knowledge amongst the public at large that such statements emanate from the government, not the tobacco manufacturers. In this respect, there is an important distinction between messages directly *attributed* to tobacco manufacturers, which would create the impression that the message emanates from the appellants and would violate their right to silence, and the *unattributed* messages at issue in these cases, which emanate from the government and create no such impression. Seen in this way, the mandatory health warnings under s. 9 are no different from unattributed labelling requirements under the *Hazardous Products Act*, under which manufacturers of hazardous products are required to place unattributed warnings, such as "DANGER" or "POISON," and hazard symbols, such as skull and crossbones on their products; see *Consumer Chemicals and Containers Regulations*, SOR/88-556. I should add that the issue has ramifications for many other spheres of activity where individuals may in certain prescribed circumstances be required to place danger signs on facilities used by the public or on construction sites, and so on. This is not really an expression of opinion by the person in control of the facility or the construction site. It is rather a requirement imposed by the government as a condition of participating in a regulated activity.

[116] Even if I were of the view that there was an infringement, I am firmly convinced that it is fully justifiable under s. 1. Once again, I stress the importance of context in the s. 1 analysis. The appellants are large corporations selling a product for profit which, on the basis of overwhelming evidence, is dangerous, yet maintain the right to engage in "counterspeech" against warnings which do nothing more than bring the dangerous nature of these products to the attention of consumers. Given that the objective of the unattributed health message requirement is simply to increase the likelihood that every literate consumer of tobacco products will be made aware of the risks entailed by the use of that product, and that these warnings have no political, social or religious content, it is clear that we are a long way in this context from cases where the state seeks to coerce a lone individual to make political, social or religious statements without a right to respond. I believe a lower level of constitutional scrutiny is justified in this context. These cases seem to me to be a far more compelling situation than *Slaight* [*Communications Inc. v. Davidson*,

[1989] 1 S.C.R. 1038], where a majority of the Court held the infringement there was justified under s. 1. The *Charter* was essentially enacted to protect individuals, not corporations. It may, at times it is true, be necessary to protect the rights of corporations so as to protect the rights of the individual. But I do not think this is such a case, and I again draw inspiration from the statement of Dickson C.J. in *Edwards Books, supra,* at p. 779, that the courts must ensure that the *Charter* not become simply an instrument "of better situated individuals to roll back legislation which has as its object the improvement of the condition of less advantaged persons."

[117] In my view, the requirement that health warnings must be unattributed is also proportional to the objective of informing consumers about the risks of tobacco use. Unattributed warnings are rationally connected to this objective because they increase the visual impact of the warning. It is not difficult to see that bold unattributed messages on a tobacco package (such as, for example, "SMOKING CAN KILL YOU") are more striking to the eye than messages cluttered by subtitles and attributions. Moreover, the attribution of the warnings also tends to dilute the factual impact of the messages. As Brossard J.A. observed, at p. 383:

> ... [I]t seems to me to leap to the eye that an "attributed" message can quickly become meaningless, or even ridiculous.
>
> As an example, the message that is supposed to come from the "Surgeon-General" remains a message imputed to an abstract entity or a political body which obviously cannot by simple decree make something hazardous that otherwise would not be. This, it seems to me, rationally weakens and attenuates the message.

These considerations are particularly relevant with respect to Parliament's goal of protecting children, who constitute the largest single group of new smokers every year in this country. In a report submitted at trial ("A Report on the Special Vulnerabilities of Children and Adolescents" [(1989)]), Dr. Michael J. Chandler observed that adolescents are apt to disregard or disobey messages from perceived authority figures. On this basis, he concluded that attributed warnings would be less effective in deterring adolescents from smoking. He stated, at p. 19:

> Adolescents are predisposed, as a function of their persistent cognitive immaturity, to view public disagreements between "experts" as evidence that everything is simply a matter of subjective opinion, and a licence to "do their own thing." A warning by Health and Welfare Canada on a publicly advertised product would provide them with just the sort of evidence they feel is required to justify doing whatever impulsive thing occurs to them at the moment.

[118] Thus, although the unattributed health warning requirement precludes large corporations from disseminating on their product packages the view that tobacco products are not harmful, I believe that any concern arising from this technical infringement of their rights is easily outweighed by the pressing health concerns raised by tobacco consumption. As noted by Dickson C.J. in *Edwards Books, supra,* at p. 759, the *Charter* does not require the elimination of "minuscule" constitutional burdens, and legislative action that increases the costs of exercising a right need not be prohibited if the burden is "trivial" or "insubstantial." In these cases, the only cost associated with the unattributed warning requirement is a potential reduction in profits. In my view, this is a cost that manufacturers of dangerous products can reasonably be expected to bear, given the health benefits of effective health warnings. As I stated in *Thomson Newspapers Ltd. v. Canada (Director of Investigation and Research, Restrictive Trade Practices Commission),* [1990] 1 S.C.R. 425, at pp. 506-7:

> In a modern industrial society, it is generally accepted that many activities in which individuals can engage must nevertheless to a greater or lesser extent be regulated by the state to ensure that the individual's pursuit of his or her self-interest is compatible with the community's interest in the realization of collective goals and aspirations. ...

The following is the judgment delivered by

[122] **McLACHLIN J.:** ...

[124] ... I agree with La Forest J. that the prohibition on advertising and promotion of tobacco products constitutes a violation of the right to free expression as the Attorney General conceded. Unlike La Forest J., I take the view that s. 9 of the Act, which requires tobacco manufacturers to place an unattributed health warning on tobacco packages, also infringes the right of free expression. As La Forest J. notes in para. 113, this Court has previously held that "freedom of expression necessarily entails the right to say nothing or the right not to say certain things": *Slaight Communications Inc. v. Davidson,* [1989] 1 S.C.R. 1038, at p. 1080, *per* Lamer J. (as he then was). Under s. 9(2), tobacco manufacturers are prohibited from displaying on their packages any writing other than the name, brand name, trade mark, and other information required by legislation. The combination of the unattributed health warnings and the prohibition against displaying any other information which would allow tobacco manufacturers to express their own views, constitutes an infringement of the right to free expression guaranteed by s. 2(*b*) of the *Charter*.

[125] The only remaining question is whether these infringements of the right of free expression are saved under s. 1 of the *Charter*, as being reasonable and "demonstrably justified in a free and democratic society." Acknowledging that

the evidence of justification is problematic, La Forest J. concludes that it nevertheless suffices to justify the infringement of the right of free expression, given the importance of the legislative goal, the context of the law and the need to defer to Parliament on such an important and difficult issue. With respect, I cannot agree....

[135] ... It is established that the deference accorded to Parliament or the legislatures may vary with the social context in which the limitation on rights is imposed. For example, it has been suggested that greater deference to Parliament or the Legislature may be appropriate if the law is concerned with the competing rights between different sectors of society than if it is a contest between the individual and the state: *Irwin Toy* [*Ltd. v. Quebec (Attorney General)*, [1989] 1 S.C.R. 927], at pp. 993-94; *Stoffman v. Vancouver General Hospital*, [1990] 3 S.C.R. 483, at p. 521. However, such distinctions may not always be easy to apply. For example, the criminal law is generally seen as involving a contest between the state and the accused, but it also involves an allocation of priorities between the accused and the victim, actual or potential. The cases at bar provide a cogent example. We are concerned with a criminal law, which pits the state against the offender. But the social values reflected in this criminal law lead La Forest J. to conclude that "the Act is the very type of legislation to which this Court has generally accorded a high degree of deference" (para. 70)....

[136] [H]owever, care must be taken not to extend the notion of deference too far. Deference must not be carried to the point of relieving the government of the burden which the *Charter* places upon it of demonstrating that the limits it has imposed on guaranteed rights are reasonable and justifiable.... To carry judicial deference to the point of accepting Parliament's view simply on the basis that the problem is serious and the solution difficult, would be to diminish the role of the courts in the constitutional process and to weaken the structure of rights upon which our constitution and our nation is founded....

[138] [W]hile I agree with La Forest J. that context, deference and a flexible and realistic standard of proof are essential aspects of the s. 1 analysis, these concepts ... must not be attenuated to the point that they relieve the state of the burden the *Charter* imposes of demonstrating that the limits imposed on our constitutional rights and freedoms are reasonable and justifiable in a free and democratic society....

[142] Against this background, I return to the cases at bar and the factors for s. 1 justification discussed in *Oakes.*

[143] The question at this stage is whether the objective of the infringing measure is sufficiently important to be capable in principle of justifying a limitation on the rights and freedoms guaranteed by the constitution. Given the importance of the *Charter* guarantees, this is not easily done. To meet the test, the objective must be one of pressing and substantial importance.

[144] Care must be taken not to overstate the objective. The objective relevant to the s. 1 analysis is *the objective of the infringing measure,* since it is the infringing measure and nothing else which is sought to be justified. If the objective is stated too broadly, its importance may be exaggerated and the analysis compromised. As my colleague has noted, the *Tobacco Products Control Act* is but one facet of a complex legislative and policy scheme to protect Canadians from the health risks of tobacco use. However, the objective of the impugned measures themselves is somewhat narrower than this. The objective of the advertising ban and trade mark usage restrictions must be to prevent people in Canada from being persuaded by advertising and promotion to use tobacco products. The objective of the mandatory package warning must be to discourage people who see the package from tobacco use. Both constitute important objectives, although the significance of the targeted decrease in consumption is reduced by the government's estimate that despite the ban, 65 percent of the Canadian magazine market will contain tobacco advertisements, given that the ban applies only to Canadian media and not to imported publications....

[146] While the limited objective of reducing tobacco-associated health risks by reducing advertising-related consumption and providing warnings of dangers is less significant than the broad objective of protecting Canadians generally from the risks associated with tobacco use, it nevertheless constitutes an objective of sufficient importance to justify overriding the right of free expression guaranteed by the *Charter.* Even a small reduction in tobacco use may work a significant benefit to the health of Canadians and justify a properly proportioned limitation of right of free expression....

[153] As a first step in the proportionality analysis, the government must demonstrate that the infringements of the right of free expression worked by the law are rationally connected to the legislative goal of reducing tobacco consumption. It must show a causal connection between the infringement and the benefit sought on the basis of reason or logic. To put it another way, the government must show that the restriction on rights serves the intended purpose. This must be demonstrated on a balance of probabilities.

[154] The causal relationship between the infringement of rights and the benefit sought may sometimes be proved by scientific evidence showing that as a matter of repeated observation, one affects the other. Where, however, legislation is directed at changing human behaviour, as in the case of the *Tobacco Products Control Act,* the causal relationship may not be scientifically measurable. In such cases, this Court has been

prepared to find a causal connection between the infringe-ment and benefit sought on the basis of reason or logic, with-out insisting on direct proof of a relationship between the infringing measure and the legislative objective . . . .

[155] . . . [In fact,] there was no direct evidence of a sci-entific nature showing a causal link between advertising bans and decrease in tobacco consumption.

[156] This leaves the question of whether there is less direct evidence that suggests as a matter of "reason" or "logic" that advertising bans and package warnings lead to a reduc-tion in tobacco use. The evidence relied upon by La Forest J. in support of rational connection falls into this category. . . .

[157] The question is whether this evidence establishes that it is reasonable or logical to conclude that there is a causal link between tobacco advertising and unattributed health warnings and tobacco use. To use the words of the Meese Commission on Pornography relied on in *Butler*, at p. 502, "would [it] be surprising . . . to find otherwise"? The govern-ment argues that it would be "surprising . . . to find otherwise." Why would tobacco companies spend great sums on advertis-ing if not to increase the consumption of tobacco, it asks?

[158] To this the tobacco companies reply that their advertising is directed not at increasing the size of the total market but at obtaining a larger share of the existing market. The evidence indicates that one of the thrusts of the advertis-ing programs of tobacco companies is securing a larger market share, but there is also evidence suggesting that advertising is used to increase the total market. For example, the Court was referred to an Imperial Tobacco Ltd. ("Imperial") document, *Project Viking*, vol. I: *A Behavioural Model of Smoking*, a mar-ket research study carried out to determine an advertising strategy for the company. The report suggests that advertising should be directed to "expanding the market, or at the very least, forestalling its decline" by proactively recruiting new smokers and reassuring present smokers who might otherwise quit in response to vigorous anti-smoking publicity. More-over, while purely informational advertising may not increase the total market, lifestyle advertising may, as a matter of com-mon sense, be seen as having a tendency to discourage those who might otherwise cease tobacco use from doing so. Con-versely, package warnings, attributed or not, may be seen as encouraging people to reduce or cease using tobacco. All this taken together with the admittedly inconclusive scientific evi-dence is sufficient to establish on a balance of probabilities a link based on reason between certain forms of advertising, warnings and tobacco consumption.

[159] On the other hand, there does not appear to be any causal connection between the objective of decreasing tobacco consumption and the absolute prohibition on the use of a tobacco trade mark on articles other than tobacco products

which is mandated by s. 8 of the Act. There is no causal con-nection based on direct evidence, nor is there, in my view, a causal connection based in logic or reason. It is hard to imagine how the presence of a tobacco logo on a cigarette lighter, for example, would increase consumption; yet, such use is banned. I find that s. 8 of the Act fails the rational connection test. . . .

[160] As the second step in the proportionality analysis, the government must show that the measures at issue impair the right of free expression as little as reasonably possible in order to achieve the legislative objective. The impairment must be "minimal," that is, the law must be carefully tailored so that rights are impaired no more than necessary. The tailoring pro-cess seldom admits of perfection and the courts must accord some leeway to the legislator. If the law falls within a range of reasonable alternatives, the courts will not find it overbroad merely because they can conceive of an alternative which might better tailor objective to infringement: see *Reference re ss. 193 and 195.1(1)(c) of the Criminal Code (Man.)*, [1990] 1 S.C.R. 1123, at pp. 1196-97; *R. v. Chaulk*, [1990] 3 S.C.R. 1303, at pp. 1340-41; *Ramsden v. Peterborough (City)*, [1993] 2 S.C.R. 1084, at pp. 1105-06. On the other hand, if the government fails to explain why a significantly less intrusive and equally effective measure was not chosen, the law may fail. . . .

[162] I turn first to the prohibition on advertising con-tained in s. 4 of the Act. It is, as has been observed, complete. It bans all forms of advertising of Canadian tobacco products while explicitly exempting all foreign advertising of non-Canadian products which are sold in Canada. It extends to advertising which arguably produces benefits to the consumer while having little or no conceivable impact on consumption. Purely informational advertising, simple reminders of pack-age appearance, advertising for new brands and advertising showing relative tar content of different brands—all these are included in the ban. Smoking is a legal activity yet consumers are deprived of an important means of learning about prod-uct availability to suit their preferences and to compare brand content with an aim to reducing the risk to their health.

[163] As this Court has observed before, it will be more difficult to justify a complete ban on a form of expression than a partial ban: *Ramsden v. Peterborough (City)*, *supra*, at pp. 1105-06; *Ford v. Quebec (Attorney General)*, *supra*, at pp. 772-73. The distinction between a total ban on expression, as in *Ford* where the legislation at issue required commercial signs to be exclusively in French, and a partial ban such as that at issue in *Irwin Toy*, *supra*, is relevant to the margin of apprecia-tion which may be allowed the government under the minimal impairment step of the analysis. In *Rocket*, *supra*, the law imposed a complete advertising ban on professionals seeking to advertise their services. I concluded that while the govern-ment had a pressing and substantial objective, and while that

objective was rationally connected to the means chosen, the minimal impairment requirement was not met since the government had exceeded a reasonable margin of appreciation given the need for consumers to obtain useful information about the services provided. A full prohibition will only be constitutionally acceptable under the minimal impairment stage of the analysis where the government can show that only a full prohibition will enable it to achieve its objective. Where, as here, no evidence is adduced to show that a partial ban would be less effective than a total ban, the justification required by s. 1 to save the violation of free speech is not established.

[164] As noted in my analysis of rational connection, while one may conclude as a matter of reason and logic that lifestyle advertising is designed to increase consumption, there is no indication that purely informational or brand preference advertising would have this effect. The government had before it a variety of less intrusive measures when it enacted the total ban on advertising, including: a partial ban which would allow information and brand preference advertising; a ban on lifestyle advertising only; measures such as those in Quebec's *Consumer Protection Act*, R.S.Q., c. P-40.1, to prohibit advertising aimed at children and adolescents; and labelling requirements only (which Health and Welfare believed would be preferable to an advertising ban: A.J. Liston's testimony). In my view, any of these alternatives would be a reasonable impairment of the right to free expression, given the important objective and the legislative context. . . .

[169] La Forest J. supports his conclusion that Parliament should be permitted to choose such measures as it sees fit by contrasting the importance of Parliament's objective with the low value of the expression at issue. This way of answering the minimal impairment requirement raises a number of concerns. First, to argue that the importance of the legislative objective justifies more deference to the government at the stage of evaluating minimal impairment, is to engage in the balancing between objective and deleterious effect contemplated by the third stage of the proportionality analysis in *Oakes*. While it may not be of great significance where this balancing takes place, care must be taken not to devalue the need for demonstration of minimum impairment by arguing the legislation is important and the infringement of no great moment.

[170] Second, just as care must be taken not to overvalue the legislative objective beyond its actual parameters, so care must be taken not to undervalue the expression at issue. Commercial speech, while arguably less important than some forms of speech, nevertheless should not be lightly dismissed. For example, in *Rocket, supra*, this Court struck down restrictions on dental advertising on the ground that the minimal impairment requirement had not been met. The *Health Disciplines Act*, R.S.O. 1980, c. 196, prohibited forms of advertising

which far from being unprofessional, might have benefited consumers and contributed to their health. The same may be said here. Tobacco consumption has not been banned in Canada. Yet the advertising ban deprives those who lawfully choose to smoke of information relating to price, quality and even health risks associated with different brands. It is no answer to suggest, as does my colleague, (para. 108) that the tobacco companies have failed to establish the true benefits of such information. Under s. 1 of the *Charter*, the onus rests on the government to show why restrictions on these forms of advertising are required.

[171] Third, in finding that the commercial speech here at issue is entitled "to a very low degree of protection under s. 1" (para. 75) and that "an attenuated level of s. 1 justification is appropriate in these cases" (para. 77), La Forest J. places a great deal of reliance on the fact that the appellants are motivated by profit. I note that the same may be said for many business persons or corporations that challenge a law as contrary to freedom of expression. While this Court has stated that restrictions on commercial speech may be easier to justify than other infringements, no link between the claimant's motivation and the degree of protection has been recognized. Book sellers, newspaper owners, toy sellers—all are linked by their shareholders' desire to profit from the corporation's business activity, whether the expression sought to be protected is closely linked to the core values of freedom of expression or not. In my view, motivation to profit is irrelevant to the determination of whether the government has established that the law is reasonable or justified as an infringement of freedom of expression.

[172] It remains to consider whether the requirement that the warning be unattributed pursuant to s. 9 of the Act fails to meet the minimum impairment requirement of proportionality. The appellant corporations contend that a warning similar to that used in the United States, which identifies the author as the Surgeon General, would be equally effective while avoiding the inference some may draw that it is the corporations themselves who are warning of the danger. They object not only to being forced to say what they do not wish to say, but also to being required to do so in a way that associates them with the opinion in question. This impairs their freedom of expression, they contend, more than required to achieve the legislative goal.

[173] The government is clearly justified in requiring the appellants to place warnings on tobacco packaging. The question is whether it was necessary to prohibit the appellants from attributing the message to the government and whether it was necessary to prevent the appellants from placing on their packaging any information other than that allowed by the regulations.

[174] As with the advertising ban, it was for the government to show that the unattributed warning, as opposed to an attributed warning, was required to achieve its objective of reducing tobacco consumption among those who might read the warning. Similarly, it was for the government to show why permitting tobacco companies to place additional information on tobacco packaging, such as a statement announcing lower tar levels, would defeat the government's objective. This it has failed to do. . . .

[175] Having found the requirement of minimum impairment is not satisfied for ss. 4 and 9 of the Act, it is unnecessary to proceed to the final stage of the proportionality analysis under s. 1—balancing the negative effects of the infringement of rights against the positive benefits associated with the legislative goal. A finding that the law impairs the right more than required contradicts the assertion that the infringement is proportionate. Neither the fact that commercial expression may be entitled to a lesser degree of protection than certain other forms of expression, nor the importance of reducing tobacco consumption, even to a small extent, negate this proposition. Freedom of expression, even commercial expression, is an important and fundamental tenet of a free and democratic society. If Parliament wishes to infringe this freedom, it must be prepared to offer good and sufficient justification for the infringement and its ambit. This it has not done. . . .

8 Multani v. Commission scolaire Marguerite-Bourgeoys, 2006

Section 2(*a*) of the *Charter* protects "freedom of conscience and religion." This obviously includes freedom of religious belief, but belief itself is rarely at issue in constitutional disputes. Rather, it is conduct emanating from religious belief that preoccupies lawmakers and courts. But belief is not unimportant, because conduct that by itself is prohibited may be permissible if it is linked to or based on religious belief.

In the case excerpted here, a young Sikh boy accidently dropped a kirpan he was wearing while playing in a Quebec schoolyard. A kirpan is a ceremonial dagger carrying religious significance for Sikhs. But weapons of all sorts are banned from school property. The question became: is a kirpan a knife or a religious object? School officials suggested that Multani seal the kirpan in his clothing so that it could neither fall out nor be easily removed. Multani's father was amenable to this "reasonable accommodation" of his son's religious beliefs, but higher school authorities rejected the compromise, insisting that kirpans are dangerous weapons. On appeal from the school commission's decision, the Quebec Superior Court restored the initial arrangement, but this decision was reversed on appeal to the Quebec Court of Appeal.

Multani's case is but one installment in a simmering drama in Quebec surrounding the limits of multiculturalism. Dependent on immigration to maintain its share of the Canadian population, Quebec has had to reconcile its commitment to cultural distinctness with the realities of an increasingly multicultural population. Quebec nationalism has largely been shorn of its ethnic character and has focused on maintaining the integrity of the French language. But tensions between the cultural practices of Sikh, Muslim, and Orthodox Jewish groups and the norms of the Quebec way of life flare up frequently in both local and provincial politics. The Quebec municipality of Hérouxville, in January 2007, published an inflammatory "*code de vie*" containing xenophobic overtones. Subsequently, the Quebec government appointed a commission of inquiry into the accommodation of cultural minorities.

The 2007 Quebec provincial election was fought in part on the issue of immigration and Quebec identity. The rural-based Action Démocratique du Québec polled surprisingly well, not least because ADQ leader Mario Dumont coyly played on Quebecers' fear of ethno-religious diversity among immigrants. "We can't defend the Québécois identity with one knee on the ground," he said during the campaign, referring to the "reasonable accommodation" of minority religious and cultural practices. Surveys consistently reveal more anxiety about immigration and cultural identity in Quebec than in the rest of Canada. The Supreme Court of Canada has generally been solicitous of the rights of Quebec minorities[1] and cannot be discounted as a contributing factor in recent controversies.

---

1   See, for example, *Syndicat Northcrest v. Amselem*, [2004] 2 S.C.R. 551 on the religious freedoms of Orthodox Jews.

A unanimous eight-justice panel of the Supreme Court reversed the Quebec Court of Appeal and declared null the decision banning the kirpan. (Multani had long since moved on from the school where the dispute arose.) In a judgment written by Justice Louise Charron, five members of the panel applied the *Charter* directly to the decision of the school's governing board, finding a violation of section 2(*a*) and concluding that the commission failed to justify the limitation of religious freedom under the terms of section 1. Charron's judgment incorporated the well-established law of reasonable accommodation into *Charter* section 1 analysis. That judgment is excerpted here.

Two other justices concurred in the result, but quarrelled with the direct application of the *Charter* to administrative bodies like the school commission. Writing for Justice Abella, Justice Marie Deschamps preferred to dispose of the case on the basis of administrative law principles according to which courts shall disturb decisions of administrative boards, agencies, and commissions only when those decisions are unreasonable on the facts. In other words, because administrative agencies were created throughout the 20th century precisely to relieve courts of the burden of adjudicating myriad claims of right, courts should generally defer to administrative decisions reasonably arrived at. In Deschamps's opinion, the Quebec Superior Court applied the administrative law principle properly and should not have been reversed on appeal.

For his part, Justice LeBel reopened an issue of *Charter* interpretation many Court watchers might have thought was closed. Early in the *Charter* era, Supreme Court justices toyed with a "definitional" approach to *Charter* rights according to which *Charter* claims would have to conform to strictly defined *Charter* rights in order to force governments to justify rights violations under section 1 analysis. A definitional approach would place a greater persuasive burden on *Charter* claimants and relieve governments of some of the work in justifying the constitutionality of laws.[2] The Court later repudiated this approach, arguing that rights should be broadly defined, making a violation easier to demonstrate and placing on the state the burden of justifying rights infringements.[3]

Not so fast, wrote LeBel in this case. "Case law developed over 20 years or more can no doubt be used to support any opinion or position. A variety of quotations can be taken from this Court's successive decisions. Attempts can be made to distinguish those decisions or to reconcile them. Doing this would probably not lead to the conclusion that the Court intended to create a straitjacket in which it would be confined when trying to resolve issues relating to the application of the *Canadian Charter* fairly and efficiently. The Court has not ruled out the possibility of reconciling or delimiting rights before applying section 1."[4] With this claim he sought to apply a definitional limit on freedom of religion. But he did so with a candour surprising all but the legal realist. ⌐

2　For an example of the definitional approach, see Justice Bertha Wilson's dissenting reasons in *R. v. Jones*, [1986] 2 S.C.R. 284.

3　*R. v. Oakes*, [1986] 1 S.C.R. 103.

4　*Multani* at para. 149, per LeBel J.

Discussion Questions

1. How does a *Charter* claimant establish that his or her religious freedom has been infringed?
2. The Court distinguished public school property from courtrooms and aircraft for the purposes of the lawful exercise of the right to wear a kirpan. How does context affect the exercise of this freedom? Is the Court's distinction persuasive?
3. Multani sought exemption from a rule of general application. "Reasonable accommodation" is the principle commonly used to describe this remedy for the adverse effect of a general rule or law. What limits should apply to such accommodations? How shall a court determine such limits?

MULTANI v. COMMISSION SCOLAIRE MARGUERITE-BOURGEOYS
2006 SCC 6, [2006] 1 S.C.R. 256

Hearing: April 12, 2005; Judgment: March 2, 2006.

Present: McLachlin C.J. and Major,* Bastarache, Binnie, LeBel, Deschamps, Fish, Abella, and Charron JJ.

Interveners: World Sikh Organization of Canada, Canadian Civil Liberties Association, Canadian Human Rights Commission, and Ontario Human Rights Commission.

* Major J. took no part in the judgment.

English version of the judgment of McLachlin C.J. and Bastarache, Binnie, Fish, and Charron JJ. delivered by

CHARRON J.:

1. Introduction

[1] This appeal requires us to determine whether the decision of a school board's council of commissioners prohibiting one of the students under its jurisdiction from wearing a kirpan to school as required by his religion infringes the student's freedom of religion. If we find that it does, we must determine whether that infringement is a reasonable limit that can be justified by the need to maintain a safe environment at the school.

[2] As I will explain below, I am of the view that an absolute prohibition against wearing a kirpan infringes the freedom of religion of the student in question under s. 2(*a*) of the *Canadian Charter of Rights and Freedoms* ("*Canadian Charter*"). The infringement cannot be justified under s. 1 of the *Canadian Charter*, since it has not been shown that such a prohibition minimally impairs the student's rights. The decision of the council of commissioners must therefore be declared a nullity.

2. Facts

[3] The appellant Balvir Singh Multani and his son Gurbaj Singh Multani are orthodox Sikhs. Gurbaj Singh, born in 1989, has been baptized and believes that his religion requires him to wear a kirpan at all times; a kirpan is a religious object that resembles a dagger and must be made of metal. On November 19, 2001, Gurbaj Singh accidentally dropped the kirpan he was wearing under his clothes in the yard of the school he was attending, École Sainte-Catherine-Labouré. On December 21, 2001, the school board, the Commission scolaire Marguerite-Bourgeoys ("CSMB"), through its legal counsel, sent Gurbaj Singh's parents a letter in which, as a

[TRANSLATION] "reasonable accommodation," it authorized their son to wear his kirpan to school provided that he complied with certain conditions to ensure that it was sealed inside his clothing. Gurbaj Singh and his parents agreed to this arrangement.

[4] In a resolution passed on February 12, 2002, the school's governing board refused to ratify the agreement on the basis that wearing a kirpan at the school violated art. 5 of the school's *Code de vie* (code of conduct), which prohibited the carrying of weapons and dangerous objects. For the purposes of this case, it is not in dispute that the governing board had, pursuant to the authority granted to it under s. 76 of the *Education Act*, R.S.Q., c. I-13.3, approved the *Code de vie*, which imposed certain rules of conduct.

[5] On March 19, 2002, based on a unanimous recommendation by a review committee to which a request by the Multanis to reconsider the governing board's decision had been referred, the CSMB's council of commissioners upheld that decision. The council of commissioners also notified the Multanis that a symbolic kirpan in the form of a pendant or one in another form made of a material rendering it harmless would be acceptable in the place of a real kirpan.

[6] On March 25, 2002, Balvir Singh Multani, personally and in his capacity as tutor to his son Gurbaj Singh, filed in the Superior Court, under art. 453 of the *Code of Civil Procedure*, R.S.Q., c. C-25, and s. 24(1) of the *Canadian Charter*, a motion for a declaratory judgment together with an application for an interlocutory injunction. In his motion, Mr. Multani asked the court to declare that the council of commissioners' decision was of no force or effect and that Gurbaj Singh had a right to wear his kirpan to school if it was sealed and sewn up inside his clothing. He submitted that this would represent a reasonable accommodation to the freedom of religion and right to equality guaranteed in ss. 3 and 10 of the *Charter of human rights and freedoms*, R.S.Q., c. C-12 ("*Quebec Charter*"), and ss. 2 and 15 of the *Canadian Charter*.

[7] On April 16, 2002, Tellier J. ordered an interlocutory injunction and authorized Gurbaj Singh to wear his kirpan, provided that he complied with the conditions initially proposed by the CSMB, until a final decision was rendered in the case. On May 17, 2002, Grenier J. of the Superior Court granted Mr. Multani's motion for a declaratory judgment, declared the council of commissioners' decision to be null and of no force or effect, and authorized Gurbaj Singh to wear his kirpan under certain conditions. The Quebec Court of Appeal allowed the appeal and dismissed the motion for a declaratory judgment on March 4, 2004. Balvir Singh Multani then appealed to this Court on behalf of himself and his son....

4. Issues

[13] Does the decision of the council of commissioners prohibiting Gurbaj Singh Multani from wearing his kirpan at Sainte-Catherine-Labouré school infringe his freedom of religion under s. 2(*a*) of the *Canadian Charter* or s. 3 of the *Quebec Charter*? Does the decision infringe his right to equality under s. 15 of the *Canadian Charter* or s. 10 of the *Quebec Charter*? If so, can the infringement be justified pursuant to s. 1 of the *Canadian Charter* or s. 9.1 of the *Quebec Charter*? . . .

[22] There is no question that the *Canadian Charter* applies to the decision of the council of commissioners, despite the decision's individual nature. The council is a creature of statute and derives all its powers from statute. Since the legislature cannot pass a statute that infringes the *Canadian Charter*, it cannot, through enabling legislation, do the same thing by delegating a power to act to an administrative decision maker: see *Slaight Communications* [*Inc. v. Davidson*, [1989] 1 S.C.R. 1038], at pp. 1077-78. As was explained in *Eldridge v. British Columbia (Attorney General)*, [1997] 3 S.C.R. 624, at para. 20, the *Canadian Charter* can apply in two ways:

> First, legislation may be found to be unconstitutional on its face because it violates a *Charter* right and is not saved by s. 1. In such cases, the legislation will be invalid and the Court compelled to declare it of no force or effect pursuant to s. 52(1) of the *Constitution Act, 1982*. Secondly, the *Charter* may be infringed, not by the legislation itself, but by the actions of a delegated decision-maker in applying it. In such cases, the legislation remains valid, but a remedy for the unconstitutional action may be sought pursuant to s. 24(1) of the *Charter*.

Deschamps and Abella JJ. take the view that the Court must apply s. 1 of the *Canadian Charter* only in the first case. I myself believe that the same analysis is necessary in the second case, where the decision maker has acted pursuant to an enabling statute, since any infringement of a guaranteed right that results from the decision maker's actions is also a limit "prescribed by law" within the meaning of s. 1. On the other hand . . . when the delegated power is not exercised in accordance with the enabling legislation, a decision not authorized by statute is not a limit "prescribed by law" and therefore cannot be justified under s. 1.

[23] In the case at bar, no one is suggesting that the council of commissioners failed to act in accordance with its enabling legislation. It is thus necessary to determine . . . whether the council of commissioners' decision infringes, as alleged, Gurbaj Singh's freedom of religion. . . . [W]here the legislation pursuant to which an administrative body has made a contested decision confers a discretion (in the instant case, the choice of means to keep schools safe) and does not

confer, either expressly or by implication, the power to limit the rights and freedoms guaranteed by the *Canadian Charter*, the decision should, if there is an infringement, be subjected to the test set out in s. 1 of the *Canadian Charter* to ascertain whether it constitutes a reasonable limit that can be demonstrably justified in a free and democratic society. If it is not justified, the administrative body has exceeded its authority in making the contested decision.

5.2 Internal Limits of Freedom of Religion, or Justification Within the Meaning of Section 1?

[24] The parties have been unable to agree on the most appropriate analytical approach. The appellant considers it clear that the council of commissioners' decision infringes his son's freedom of religion protected by s. 2(*a*) of the *Canadian Charter*. In response to the respondents' submissions, he maintains that only a limit that meets the test for the application of s. 1 of the *Canadian Charter* can be justified. The Attorney General of Quebec concedes that the prohibition against the appellant's son wearing his kirpan to school infringes the son's freedom of religion, but submits that, regardless of the conditions ordered by the Superior Court, the prohibition is a fair limit on freedom of religion, which is not an absolute right.

[25] According to the CSMB, freedom of religion has not been infringed, because it has internal limits. The CSMB considers that, in the instant case, the freedom of religion guaranteed by s. 2(*a*) must be limited by imperatives of public order, safety, and health, as well as by the rights and freedoms of others. In support of this contention, it relies primarily on *Trinity Western University v. British Columbia College of Teachers*, [2001] 1 S.C.R. 772, 2001 SCC 31, in which the Court defined the scope of the rights in issue (freedom of religion and the right to equality) in order to resolve any potential conflict. The CSMB is of the view that, in the case at bar, delineating the rights in issue in this way would preserve Gurbaj Singh's freedom of religion while, as in *Trinity Western University*, circumscribing his freedom to act in accordance with his beliefs. According to this line of reasoning, the outcome of this appeal would be decided at the stage of determining whether freedom of religion has been infringed rather than at the stage of reconciling the rights of the parties under s. 1 of the *Canadian Charter*.

[26] This Court has clearly recognized that freedom of religion can be limited when a person's freedom to act in accordance with his or her beliefs may cause harm to or interfere with the rights of others. . . . However, the Court has on numerous occasions stressed the advantages of reconciling competing rights by means of a s. 1 analysis. For example, in *B. (R.) v. Children's Aid Society of Metropolitan Toronto*, [1995]

1 S.C.R. 315, the claimants, who were Jehovah's Witnesses, contested an order that authorized the administration of a blood transfusion to their daughter. While acknowledging that freedom of religion could be limited in the best interests of the child, La Forest J., writing for the majority of the Court, stated the following, at paras. 109-10:

> This Court has consistently refrained from formulating internal limits to the scope of freedom of religion in cases where the constitutionality of a legislative scheme was raised; it rather opted to balance the competing rights under s. 1 of the *Charter*. . . .
>
> In my view, it appears sounder to leave to the state the burden of justifying the restrictions it has chosen. Any ambiguity or hesitation should be resolved in favour of individual rights. Not only is this consistent with the broad and liberal interpretation of rights favoured by this Court, but s. 1 is a much more flexible tool with which to balance competing rights than s. 2(*a*). . . .

[28] It is important to distinguish these decisions from the ones in which the Court did not conduct a s. 1 analysis because there was no conflict of fundamental rights. For example, in *Trinity Western University*, the Court, asked to resolve a potential conflict between religious freedoms and equality rights, concluded that a proper delineation of the rights involved would make it possible to avoid any conflict in that case. Likewise, in *Amselem*, a case concerning the *Quebec Charter*, the Court refused to pit freedom of religion against the right to peaceful enjoyment and free disposition of property, because the impact on the latter was considered "at best, minimal" (para. 64). Logically, where there is not an apparent infringement of more than one fundamental right, no reconciliation is necessary at the initial stage.

[29] In the case at bar, the Court does not at the outset have to reconcile two constitutional rights, as only freedom of religion is in issue here. Furthermore, since the decision genuinely affects both parties and was made by an administrative body exercising statutory powers, a contextual analysis under s. 1 will enable us to balance the relevant competing values in a more comprehensive manner.

[30] This Court has frequently stated, and rightly so, that freedom of religion is not absolute and that it can conflict with other constitutional rights. However, since the test governing limits on rights was developed in *Oakes*, the Court has never called into question the principle that rights are reconciled through the constitutional justification required by s. 1 of the *Canadian Charter*. . . .

[31] Thus, the central issue in the instant case is best suited to a s. 1 analysis. But before proceeding with this analysis, I will explain why the contested decision clearly infringes freedom of religion.

6. Infringement of Freedom of Religion

[32] This Court has on numerous occasions stressed the importance of freedom of religion. . . .

[34] In *Amselem*, the Court ruled that, in order to establish that his or her freedom of religion has been infringed, the claimant must demonstrate (1) that he or she sincerely believes in a practice or belief that has a nexus with religion, and (2) that the impugned conduct of a third party interferes, in a manner that is non-trivial or not insubstantial, with his or her ability to act in accordance with that practice or belief.

[35] The fact that different people practise the same religion in different ways does not affect the validity of the case of a person alleging that his or her freedom of religion has been infringed. What an individual must do is show that he or she sincerely believes that a certain belief or practice is required by his or her religion. The religious belief must be asserted in good faith and must not be fictitious, capricious or an artifice (*Amselem*, at para. 52). In assessing the sincerity of the belief, a court must take into account, *inter alia*, the credibility of the testimony of the person asserting the particular belief and the consistency of the belief with his or her other current religious practices (*Amselem*, at para. 53).

[36] In the case at bar, Gurbaj Singh must therefore show that he sincerely believes that his faith requires him at all times to wear a kirpan made of metal. Evidence to this effect was introduced and was not contradicted. No one contests the fact that the orthodox Sikh religion requires its adherents to wear a kirpan at all times. The affidavits of chaplain Manjit Singh and of Gurbaj Singh explain that orthodox Sikhs must comply with a strict dress code requiring them to wear religious symbols commonly known as the Five Ks: (1) the kesh (uncut hair); (2) the kangha (a wooden comb); (3) the kara (a steel bracelet worn on the wrist); (4) the kaccha (a special undergarment); and (5) the kirpan (a metal dagger or sword). Furthermore, Manjit Singh explains in his affidavit that the Sikh religion teaches pacifism and encourages respect for other religions, that the kirpan must be worn at all times, even in bed, that it must not be used as a weapon to hurt anyone, and that Gurbaj Singh's refusal to wear a symbolic kirpan made of a material other than metal is based on a reasonable religiously motivated interpretation.

[37] Much of the CSMB's argument is based on its submission that [TRANSLATION] "the kirpan is essentially a dagger, a weapon designed to kill, intimidate or threaten others." With respect, while the kirpan undeniably has characteristics of a bladed weapon capable of wounding or killing a person, this submission disregards the fact that, for orthodox Sikhs, the kirpan is above all a religious symbol. Chaplain Manjit Singh mentions in his affidavit that the word "kirpan" comes from "kirpa," meaning "mercy" and "kindness," and "aan,"

meaning "honour." There is no denying that this religious object could be used wrongly to wound or even kill someone, but the question at this stage of the analysis cannot be answered definitively by considering only the physical characteristics of the kirpan. Since the question of the physical makeup of the kirpan and the risks the kirpan could pose to the school board's students involves the reconciliation of conflicting values, I will return to it when I address justification under s. 1 of the *Canadian Charter*. In order to demonstrate an infringement of his freedom of religion, Gurbaj Singh does not have to establish that the kirpan is not a weapon. He need only show that his personal and subjective belief in the religious significance of the kirpan is sincere.

[38] Gurbaj Singh says that he sincerely believes he must adhere to this practice in order to comply with the requirements of his religion. . . .

[39] Furthermore, Gurbaj Singh's refusal to wear a replica made of a material other than metal is not capricious. He genuinely believes that he would not be complying with the requirements of his religion were he to wear a plastic or wooden kirpan. The fact that other Sikhs accept such a compromise is not relevant. . . .

[40] Finally, the interference with Gurbaj Singh's freedom of religion is neither trivial nor insignificant. Forced to choose between leaving his kirpan at home and leaving the public school system, Gurbaj Singh decided to follow his religious convictions and is now attending a private school. The prohibition against wearing his kirpan to school has therefore deprived him of his right to attend a public school.

[41] Thus, there can be no doubt that the council of commissioners' decision prohibiting Gurbaj Singh from wearing his kirpan to Sainte-Catherine-Labouré school infringes his freedom of religion. This limit must therefore be justified under s. 1 of the *Canadian Charter*.

7. Section 1 of the Canadian Charter
[42] . . .

7.1 Importance of the Objective
[44] As stated by the Court of Appeal, the council of commissioners' decision [TRANSLATION] "was motivated by [a pressing and substantial] objective, namely, to ensure an environment conducive to the development and learning of the students. This requires [the CSMB] to ensure the safety of the students and the staff. This duty is at the core of the mandate entrusted to educational institutions" (para. 77). The appellant concedes that this objective is laudable and that it passes the first stage of the test. The respondents also submitted fairly detailed evidence consisting of affidavits from various stakeholders in the educational community explaining the import-

ance of safety in schools and the upsurge in problems relating to weapons and violence in schools.

[45] Clearly, the objective of ensuring safety in schools is sufficiently important to warrant overriding a constitutionally protected right or freedom. It remains to be determined what level of safety the governing board was seeking to achieve by prohibiting the carrying of weapons and dangerous objects, and what degree of risk would accordingly be tolerated. . . . [T]he possibilities range from a desire to ensure absolute safety to a total lack of concern for safety. Between these two extremes lies a concern to ensure a reasonable level of safety.

[46] Although the parties did not present argument on the level of safety sought by the governing board, the issue was addressed by the intervener Canadian Human Rights Commission, which correctly stated that the standard that seems to be applied in schools is reasonable safety, not absolute safety. The application of a standard of absolute safety could result in the installation of metal detectors in schools, the prohibition of all potentially dangerous objects (such as scissors, compasses, baseball bats and table knives in the cafeteria) and permanent expulsion from the public school system of any student exhibiting violent behaviour. Apart from the fact that such a standard would be impossible to attain, it would compromise the objective of providing universal access to the public school system.

[47] On the other hand, when the governing board approved the article in question of the *Code de vie*, it was not seeking to establish a minimum standard of safety. As can be seen from the affidavits of certain stakeholders from the educational community, violence and weapons are not tolerated in schools, and students exhibiting violent or dangerous behaviour are punished. Such measures show that the objective is to attain a certain level of safety beyond a minimum threshold.

[48] I therefore conclude that the level of safety chosen by the governing council and confirmed by the council of commissioners was reasonable safety. The objective of ensuring a reasonable level of safety in schools is without question a pressing and substantial one.

7.2 Proportionality
7.2.1 Rational Connection
[Justice Charron holds that the Commission's decision to ban the kirpan is rationally connected to its policy against the carrying of weapons.]

7.2.2 Minimal Impairment
[50] The second stage of the proportionality analysis is often central to the debate as to whether the infringement of a right protected by the *Canadian Charter* can be justified.

The limit, which must minimally impair the right or freedom that has been infringed, need not necessarily be the least intrusive solution. In *RJR-MacDonald Inc. v. Canada (Attorney General)*, [1995] 3 S.C.R. 199, at para. 160, this Court defined the test as follows:

> The impairment must be "minimal," that is, the law must be carefully tailored so that rights are impaired no more than necessary. The tailoring process seldom admits of perfection and the courts must accord some leeway to the legislator. If the law falls within a range of reasonable alternatives, the courts will not find it overbroad merely because they can conceive of an alternative which might better tailor objective to infringement. . . .

[51] The approach to the question must be the same where what is in issue is not legislation, but a decision rendered pursuant to a statutory discretion. Thus, it must be determined whether the decision to establish an absolute prohibition against wearing a kirpan "falls within a range of reasonable alternatives."

[52] In considering this aspect of the proportionality analysis, Lemelin J. expressed the view that [TRANSLATION] "[t]he duty to accommodate this student is a corollary of the minimal impairment [test]" (para. 92). In other words, she could not conceive of the possibility of a justification being sufficient for the purposes of s. 1 if reasonable accommodation is possible (para. 75). This correspondence of the concept of reasonable accommodation with the proportionality analysis is not without precedent. In *Eldridge*, at para. 79, this Court stated that, in cases concerning s. 15(1) of the *Canadian Charter*, "reasonable accommodation" was equivalent to the concept of "reasonable limits" provided for in s. 1 of the *Canadian Charter*.

[53] In my view, this correspondence between the legal principles is logical. In relation to discrimination, the courts have held that there is a duty to make reasonable accommodation for individuals who are adversely affected by a policy or rule that is neutral on its face, and that this duty extends only to the point at which it causes undue hardship to the party who must perform it. Although it is not necessary to review all the cases on the subject, the analogy with the duty of reasonable accommodation seems to me to be helpful to explain the burden resulting from the minimal impairment test with respect to a particular individual, as in the case at bar. In my view, Professor José Woehrling correctly explained the relationship between the duty to accommodate or adapt and the *Oakes* analysis in the following passage:

> [TRANSLATION] Anyone seeking to disregard the duty to accommodate must show that it is necessary, in order to achieve a legitimate and important legislative objective, to apply the standard in its entirety, without the exceptions sought by the claimant. More specifically, in the context of s. 1 of the *Canadian Charter*, it is necessary, in applying the test from *R. v. Oakes*, to show, in succession, that applying the standard in its entirety constitutes a rational means of achieving the legislative objective, that no other means are available that would be less intrusive in relation to the rights in question (minimal impairment test), and that there is proportionality between the measure's salutary and limiting effects. At a conceptual level, the minimal impairment test, which is central to the section 1 analysis, corresponds in large part with the undue hardship defence against the duty of reasonable accommodation in the context of human rights legislation. This is clear from the Supreme Court's judgment in *Edwards Books*, in which the application of the minimal impairment test led the Court to ask whether the Ontario legislature, in prohibiting stores from opening on Sundays and allowing certain exceptions for stores that were closed on Saturdays, had done enough to accommodate merchants who, for religious reasons, had to observe a day of rest on a day other than Sunday.

(J. Woehrling, "L'obligation d'accommodement raisonnable et l'adaptation de la société à la diversité religieuse" (1998), 43 *McGill L.J.* 325, at p. 360)

[54] The council of commissioners' decision establishes an absolute prohibition against Gurbaj Singh wearing his kirpan to school. The respondents contend that this prohibition is necessary, because the presence of the kirpan at the school poses numerous risks for the school's pupils and staff. It is important to note that Gurbaj Singh has never claimed a right to wear his kirpan to school without restrictions. Rather, he says that he is prepared to wear his kirpan under the above-mentioned conditions imposed by Grenier J. of the Superior Court. Thus, the issue is whether the respondents have succeeded in demonstrating that an absolute prohibition is justified.

[55] According to the CSMB, to allow the kirpan to be worn to school entails the risks that it could be used for violent purposes by the person wearing it or by another student who takes it away from him, that it could lead to a proliferation of weapons at the school, and that its presence could have a negative impact on the school environment. In support of this last point, the CSMB submits that the kirpan is a symbol of violence and that it sends the message that the use of force is the way to assert rights and resolve conflicts, in addition to undermining the perception of safety and compromising the spirit of fairness that should prevail in schools, in that its presence suggests the existence of a double standard. Let us look at those arguments.

7.2.2.1 Safety in Schools

[56] According to the respondents, the presence of kirpans in schools, even under certain conditions, creates a risk that they will be used for violent purposes, either by those who wear them or by other students who might take hold of them by force.

[57] The evidence shows that Gurbaj Singh does not have behavioural problems and has never resorted to violence at school. The risk that this particular student would use his kirpan for violent purposes seems highly unlikely to me. In fact, the CSMB has never argued that there was a risk of his doing so.

[58] As for the risk of another student taking his kirpan away from him, it also seems to me to be quite low, especially if the kirpan is worn under conditions such as were imposed by Grenier J. of the Superior Court. In the instant case, if the kirpan were worn in accordance with those conditions, any student wanting to take it away from Gurbaj Singh would first have to physically restrain him, then search through his clothes, remove the sheath from his guthra, and try to unstitch or tear open the cloth enclosing the sheath in order to get to the kirpan. There is no question that a student who wanted to commit an act of violence could find another way to obtain a weapon, such as bringing one in from outside the school. Furthermore, there are many objects in schools that could be used to commit violent acts and that are much more easily obtained by students, such as scissors, pencils and baseball bats.

[59] In her brief reasons, Grenier J. explained that her decision was based in part on the fact that [TRANSLATION] "the evidence revealed no instances of violent incidents involving kirpans in schools in Quebec" and on "the state of Canadian and American law on this matter" (para. 6). In fact, the evidence in the record suggests that, over the 100 years since Sikhs have been attending schools in Canada, not a single violent incident related to the presence of kirpans in schools has been reported. . . .

[60] . . . Sikhs may wear kirpans in schools in Surrey, British Columbia. Although no other Ontario school board has expressly addressed the issue with the same depth as the Peel board, students may wear kirpans in the North York Board of Education and the Etobicoke Board of Education (which has a limit of six inches in size). No school boards in the Metropolitan Toronto area have a policy prohibiting or restricting kirpans. There is no evidence that kirpans have sparked a violent incident in any school, no evidence that any other school board in Canada bans kirpans, and no evidence of a student anywhere in Canada using a kirpan as a weapon. . . .

[62] The respondents maintain that freedom of religion can be limited even in the absence of evidence of a real risk of significant harm, since it is not necessary to wait for the harm to occur before correcting the situation. They submit that the same line of reasoning that was followed in *Hothi v. R.*, [1985] 3 W.W.R. 256 (Man. Q.B.) (aff'd [1986] 3 W.W.R. 671 (Man. C.A.)), and *Nijjar v. Canada 3000 Airlines Ltd.* (1999), 36 C.H.R.R. D/76 (Can. Trib.), in which the wearing of kirpans was prohibited in courts and on airplanes, should apply in this case. As was mentioned above, Lemelin J. of the Court of Appeal pointed out that safety concerns are no less serious in schools.

[63] There can be no doubt that safety is just as important in schools as it is on airplanes and in courts. However, it is important to remember that the specific context must always be borne in mind in resolving the issue. In *Nijjar*, Mr. Nijjar's complaint that he had been denied the right to wear his kirpan aboard a Canada 3000 Airlines aircraft was dismissed because, *inter alia*, he had failed to demonstrate that wearing a kirpan in a manner consistent with Canada 3000's policies would be contrary to his religious beliefs. It was apparent from Mr. Nijjar's testimony that wearing one particular type of kirpan rather than another was a matter of personal preference, not of religious belief. While it concluded that Mr. Nijjar had not been discriminated against on the basis of his religion, the Canadian Human Rights Tribunal did nevertheless consider the issue of reasonable accommodation. It made the following comment at para. 123 of its decision:

> In assessing whether or not the respondent's weapons policy can be modified so as to accommodate Sikhs detrimentally affected, consideration must be given to the environment in which the rule must be applied. In this regard, we are satisfied that aircraft present a unique environment. Groups of strangers are brought together and are required to stay together, in confined spaces, for prolonged periods of time. Emergency medical and police assistance are not readily accessible.

Then, at para. 125, the Tribunal distinguished the case before it from *Pandori*:

> Unlike the school environment in issue in the *Pandori* case, where there is an ongoing relationship between the student and the school and with that a meaningful opportunity to assess the circumstances of the individual seeking the accommodation, air travel involves a transitory population. Significant numbers of people are processed each day, with minimal opportunity for assessment. It will be recalled that Mr. Kinnear testified that Canada 3000 check-in personnel have between forty-five and ninety seconds of contact with each passenger.

[64] *Hothi* also involved special circumstances. The judge who prohibited the wearing of a kirpan in the courtroom was hearing the case of an accused charged with assault under

s. 245 of the *Criminal Code*, R.S.C. 1970, c. C-34. Dewar C.J. of the Manitoba Court of Queen's Bench considered (at p. 259) the special nature of courts and stated the following about the prohibition against wearing kirpans in courtrooms:

> [It] serves a transcending public interest that justice be administered in an environment free from any influence which may tend to thwart the process. Possession in the courtroom of weapons, or articles capable of use as such, by parties or others is one such influence.

[65] The facts in the case at bar are more similar to the facts in *Pandori* than to those in *Nijjar* and *Hothi*. The school environment is a unique one that permits relationships to develop among students and staff. These relationships make it possible to better control the different types of situations that arise in schools. The Ontario board of inquiry commented on the special nature of the school environment in *Pandori*, at para. 197:

> Courts and schools are not comparable institutions. One is a tightly circumscribed environment in which contending elements, adversarially aligned, strive to obtain justice as they see it, with judge and/or jury determining the final outcome. Schools on the other hand are living communities which, while subject to some controls, engage in the enterprise of education in which both teachers and students are partners. Also, a court appearance is temporary (a Khalsa Sikh could conceivably deal with the prohibition of the kirpan as he/she would on an airplane ride) and is therefore not comparable to the years a student spends in the school system.

[66] Although there is no need in the instant case for this Court to compare the desirable level of safety in a given environment with the desirable level in a school environment, these decisions show that each environment is a special case with its own unique characteristics that justify a different level of safety, depending on the circumstances.

[67] Returning to the respondents' argument, I agree that it is not necessary to wait for harm to be done before acting, but the existence of concerns relating to safety must be unequivocally established for the infringement of a constitutional right to be justified. Given the evidence in the record, it is my opinion that the respondents' argument in support of an absolute prohibition—namely that kirpans are inherently dangerous—must fail.

7.2.2.2 Proliferation of Weapons in Schools

[68] The respondents also contend that allowing Gurbaj Singh to wear his kirpan to school could have a ripple effect. They submit that other students who learn that orthodox Sikhs may wear their kirpans will feel the need to arm themselves so that they can defend themselves if attacked by a student wearing a kirpan.

[69] This argument is essentially based on the one discussed above, namely that kirpans in school pose a safety risk to other students, forcing them to arm themselves in turn in order to defend themselves. For the reasons given above, I am of the view that the evidence does not support this argument. It is purely speculative and cannot be accepted in the instant case: see *Eldridge*, at para. 89. Moreover, this argument merges with the next one, which relates more specifically to the risk of poisoning the school environment. I will therefore continue with the analysis.

7.2.2.3 Negative Impact on the School Environment

[70] The respondents submit that the presence of kirpans in schools will contribute to a poisoning of the school environment. They maintain that the kirpan is a symbol of violence and that it sends the message that using force is the way to assert rights and resolve conflict, compromises the perception of safety in schools and establishes a double standard.

[71] The argument that the wearing of kirpans should be prohibited because the kirpan is a symbol of violence and because it sends the message that using force is necessary to assert rights and resolve conflict must fail. Not only is this assertion contradicted by the evidence regarding the symbolic nature of the kirpan, it is also disrespectful to believers in the Sikh religion and does not take into account Canadian values based on multiculturalism.

[72] As for the submissions based on the other students' perception regarding safety and on feelings of unfairness that they might experience, these appear to stem from the affidavit of psychoeducator Denis Leclerc, who gave his opinion concerning a study in which he took part that involved, *inter alia*, questioning students and staff from 14 high schools belonging to the CSMB about the socio-educational environment in schools. The results of the study seem to show that there is a mixed or negative perception regarding safety in schools. It should be noted that this study did not directly address kirpans, but was instead a general examination of the situation in schools in terms of safety. Mr. Leclerc is of the opinion that the presence of kirpans in schools would heighten this impression that the schools are unsafe. He also believes that allowing Gurbaj Singh to wear a kirpan would engender a feeling of unfairness among the students, who would perceive this permission as special treatment. He mentions, for example, that some students still consider the right of Muslim women to wear the chador to be unfair, because they themselves are not allowed to wear caps or scarves.

[73] It should be noted that, in a letter submitted to counsel for the appellants, psychologist Mathieu Gattuso indicated

that, in light of the generally accepted principles concerning expert evidence, Denis Leclerc's affidavit does not constitute an expert opinion. It is clear from the examination of Mr. Leclerc that he did not study the situation in schools that authorize the wearing of kirpans and that, in his affidavit, he was merely giving a personal opinion.

[74] With respect for the view of the Court of Appeal, I cannot accept Denis Leclerc's position. Among other concerns, the example he presents concerning the chador is particularly revealing. To equate a religious obligation such as wearing the chador with the desire of certain students to wear caps is indicative of a simplistic view of freedom of religion that is incompatible with the *Canadian Charter*. Moreover, his opinion seems to be based on the firm belief that the kirpan is, by its true nature, a weapon. The CSMB itself vigorously defends this same position. For example, it states the following in its factum (at paras. 37-38):

> [TRANSLATION] Although kirpans were presented to the trial judge at the hearing, she failed to rule on the true nature of the kirpan. On the contrary, she seemed, in light of her comments, to accept the appellants' argument that in today's world, the kirpan has only symbolic value for Sikhs.
>
>   Yet whatever it may symbolize, the kirpan is still essentially a dagger, *a weapon designed to kill, intimidate or threaten others*. [Emphasis added.]

These assertions strip the kirpan of any religious significance and leave no room for accommodation. The CSMB also makes the following statement (at para. 51):

> [TRANSLATION] It is thus a paralogism … to liken a weapon to all objects whose purpose is not to kill or wound but that could potentially be used as weapons, such as compasses, paper cutters, baseball bats, sporting equipment, or cars. Does this mean that we should stop studying geometry or playing baseball?

[75] The appellants are perhaps right to state that the only possible explanation for the acceptance of these other potentially dangerous objects in schools is that the respondents consider the activities in which those objects are used to be important, while accommodating the religious beliefs of the appellant's son is not.

[76] Religious tolerance is a very important value of Canadian society. If some students consider it unfair that Gurbaj Singh may wear his kirpan to school while they are not allowed to have knives in their possession, it is incumbent on the schools to discharge their obligation to instil in their students this value that is, as I will explain in the next section, at the very foundation of our democracy.

[77] In my opinion, the respondents have failed to demonstrate that it would be reasonable to conclude that an absolute prohibition against wearing a kirpan minimally impairs Gurbaj Singh's rights.

7.2.3 Effects of the Measure

[78] Since we have found that the council of commissioners' decision is not a reasonable limit on religious freedom, it is not strictly necessary to weigh the deleterious effects of this measure against its salutary effects. I do believe, however, like the intervener Canadian Civil Liberties Association, that it is important to consider some effects that could result from an absolute prohibition. An absolute prohibition would stifle the promotion of values such as multiculturalism, diversity, and the development of an educational culture respectful of the rights of others. This Court has on numerous occasions reiterated the importance of these values. For example, in *Ross*, the Court stated the following, at para. 42:

> A school is a communication centre for a whole range of values and aspirations of a society. In large part, it defines the values that transcend society through the educational medium. The school is an arena for the exchange of ideas and must, therefore, be premised upon principles of tolerance and impartiality so that all persons within the school environment feel equally free to participate.

In *R. v. M. (M.R.)*, [1998] 3 S.C.R. 393, at para. 3, the Court made the following observation:

> [S]chools … have a duty to foster the respect of their students for the constitutional rights of all members of society. Learning respect for those rights is essential to our democratic society and should be part of the education of all students. These values are best taught by example and may be undermined if the students' rights are ignored by those in authority.

Then, in *Trinity Western University*, the Court stated the following, at para. 13:

> Our Court [has] accepted … that teachers are a medium for the transmission of values…. Schools are meant to develop civic virtue and responsible citizenship, to educate in an environment free of bias, prejudice and intolerance.

[79] A total prohibition against wearing a kirpan to school undermines the value of this religious symbol and sends students the message that some religious practices do not merit the same protection as others. On the other hand, accommodating Gurbaj Singh and allowing him to wear his kirpan under certain conditions demonstrates the importance

that our society attaches to protecting freedom of religion and to showing respect for its minorities. The deleterious effects of a total prohibition thus outweigh its salutary effects. . . .

9. Remedy

[81] Section 24(1) of the *Canadian Charter* reads as follows:

Anyone whose rights or freedoms, as guaranteed by this Charter, have been infringed or denied may apply to a court of competent jurisdiction to obtain such remedy as the court considers appropriate and just in the circumstances.

[82] Given that Gurbaj Singh no longer attends Sainte-Catherine-Labouré school, it would not be appropriate to restore the judgment of the Superior Court, as requested by the appellants. The Court accordingly considers that the appropriate and just remedy is to declare the decision prohibiting Gurbaj Singh from wearing his kirpan to be null.

10. Disposition

[83] I would allow the appeal, set aside the decision of the Court of Appeal, and declare the decision of the council of commissioners to be null, with costs throughout.

PART THREE

Labour Rights

Alberta Labour Reference, 1987

Alberta had enacted legislation that prohibited strikes and lockouts for three classes of public service employees: firefighters, police officers, and hospital workers. The government maintained that the no-strike laws were necessary to ensure the continued provision of essential services. The legislation provided for compulsory arbitration and also limited the matters that could be considered by an arbitration board. The Alberta Union of Provincial Employees had always opposed the legislation. In 1983, the Union announced that it was planning to challenge the constitutionality of the laws as a violation of the freedom of association provision of the recently adopted *Charter of Rights.* The Alberta government promptly pre-empted the Union by referring the legislation to the Alberta Court of Appeal.

The reference was unusual in that it was accompanied by public statements by the Attorney General of Alberta that the provincial government would not hesitate to use the section 33 "legislative override" power to protect the legislation if the court declared it invalid. The threatened use of section 33 provoked widespread criticism by the opposition and local newspaper editorials.[1] Alberta Premier Peter Lougheed, one of the original "gang of eight" provincial leaders who had opposed the *Charter* during 1980-81, responded by publicly defending his Attorney General's threatened use of section 33. The U.S. constitutional experience, which allows judges to make public policy, said Lougheed, "is not one that has a happy result or that we want to duplicate in Canada." Lougheed continued, "It is our view that . . . much more important is the question that elected legislators within provinces can make public policy."[2] The Alberta Court of Appeal upheld the legislation, and this decision was appealed to the Supreme Court of Canada by the Alberta Union of Provincial Employees.

The central question posed by the reference was whether the right to freedom of association declared in section 2(d) of the *Charter* included the right to strike. If it did, then Alberta's no-strike laws would be invalid, unless they could be saved by a section 1 "reasonable limits" defence. Seven other provinces and the government of Canada intervened before the Supreme Court of Canada to support Alberta's argument that the freedom of association provision did not extend the right to strike to labour unions. Three labour unions and the NDP government of Manitoba intervened on the opposing side.

In a 4-to-2 ruling, the Supreme Court upheld the legislation. Justice McIntyre's majority opinion held that the actions of an association do not enjoy any more constitutional protection than the sum of the rights enjoyed by its members individually. While individual workers have a right to quit work, this was not deemed analogous to the right of a union to strike. Justice McIntyre reinforced his interpretation of section 2(d) with an appeal to the intention of the framers of the *Charter* not to include the right to strike. He also cited social policy reasons as to why courts should resist invitations to become involved in labour law disputes. Last, but not least, McIntyre cited lack of institutional competence as militating

---

1   See "Opting out is overkill" *Calgary Herald* (21 November 1983) A5. See also "The weasel words have trapped us" *Calgary Herald* (24 November 1983) A6.

2   "Premier defends opting out" *Calgary Herald* (22 November 1983) A3.

against judicial involvement. "Judges do not have the expert knowledge," he concluded, and "specialized labour tribunals are better suited than courts for resolving labour problems." This concern with institutional competence—or the lack thereof—explains in part McIntyre's preference for giving a narrower interpretation to "freedom of association," thereby avoiding any resort to the section 1 "balancing" test.[3] All told, the McIntyre judgment presents a classic example of judicial self-restraint and the "interpretivist" approach to *Charter* interpretation.[4]

A very different approach with a different result was reached by Chief Justice Dickson, joined by Justice Wilson, dissenting. The Chief Justice chastised the majority for apparently taking the position that the *Charter* only protects rights already in place at the time of its adoption. He characterized this approach as "legalistic, ungenerous, [and] indeed vapid." The freedom of workers to associate and to bargain collectively as a union, Dickson declared, would be ineffective without a corresponding right to strike. Having found Alberta's legislation in violation of section 2(*d*), Dickson then applied the *Oakes* test. While some of the provisions met the section 1 "reasonable limitations" test, others did not, and should be declared invalid.

The key to understanding the Chief Justice's judgment may be his view that an important part of the purpose of the *Charter* in general and "freedom of association" in particular is to help social and economic "underdogs." This view of the *Charter* as a "progressive" document is found in his *obiter dicta* in *Edwards Books*,[5] and is repeated here. Freedom of association, Justice Dickson writes, "has enabled those who would otherwise be vulnerable and ineffective to meet on more equal terms the power and strength of those with whom their interests interact, and perhaps, conflict." Madame Justice Wilson appears to share the Chief Justice's "underdog" approach to *Charter* interpretation.

The *Alberta Labour Reference* provided an interesting preview of the Court's *Morgentaler* abortion decision, handed down nine months later.[6] In terms of issues, both cases represent invitations to the Court to "find" an implied right that is not explicitly enumerated in the text of the *Charter*. Justice McIntyre's caveat—that "the *Charter* should not be regarded as an empty vessel to be filled with whatever meaning we might wish from time to time"— turned out to be an accurate indicator of his similarly unreceptive response to Morgentaler's argument that the "liberty" and "security of the person" provisions of section 7 of the *Charter* contained a right to abortion. By contrast, Dickson and Wilson, the two dissenters in the *Alberta Labour Reference*, subsequently wrote the two most activist opinions for the majority in *Morgentaler*. Both cases illustrate how different theories of proper judicial role and different approaches to *Charter* interpretation can lead to very different results.

It merits notice that this case is just one of a string of *Charter* defeats for organized labour. In two similar decisions announced the same day as the *Alberta Labour Reference*, the Court rejected similar claims of a constitutionally protected "right to strike" (*PSAC v. Canada*,

---

3   For a discussion of section 1, see the introduction to this book.

4   For a discussion of the "interpretivist" approach to constitutional interpretation, see the introduction to this book.

5   *R. v. Edwards Books and Art Ltd.*, [1986] 2 S.C.R. 713.

6   See case 15.

[1987] 1 S.C.R. 424 and *RWDSU v. Saskatchewan*, [1987] 1 S.C.R. 460). A labour union also lost in the *Dolphin Delivery* case, when the Supreme Court refused to confer *Charter* protection (freedom of expression) on secondary picketing. This trend seemed to vindicate the fears of left-wing *Charter* opponents that the *Charter* would provide little benefit to organized labour. But trends can change, as case 10, *Health Services and Support*, shows. ⌐

Discussion Questions

1. The Court finds it important in this case to arrive at a precise definition of the right in question. What definitions are in contention and why was it important for the Court to define section 2(*d*)?
2. The majority and dissenting justices disagree on whether freedom of association includes the freedom to undertake activities in association with others and for which the association was formed. Explain.
3. What role in this decision is played by considerations of social policy and the institutional capacity of courts?
4. One reading of the majority judgment is that it forecloses any recognition of a *Charter* right to strike. Do you agree?

REFERENCE RE PUBLIC SERVICE EMPLOYEE RELATIONS ACT, LABOUR RELATIONS ACT, AND POLICE OFFICERS COLLECTIVE BARGAINING ACT OF ALBERTA
[1987] 1 S.C.R. 313

Hearing: June 27, 28, 1985; Judgment: April 9, 1987.

Present: Dickson C.J. and Beetz, McIntyre, Chouinard,* Wilson, Le Dain, and La Forest JJ.

Intervener (for the appellants): Attorney General of Manitoba; Interveners (for the respondent): Attorney General of Canada, Attorney General for Ontario, Attorney General of Quebec, Attorney General of Nova Scotia, Attorney General of British Columbia, Attorney General of Prince Edward Island, Attorney General for Saskatchewan, and Attorney General of Newfoundland.

* Chouinard J. took no part in the judgment.

The judgment of Beetz, Le Dain, and La Forest JJ. was delivered by

[141] **LE DAIN J.:** The background, the issues and the relevant authority and considerations in this appeal are fully set out in the reasons for judgment of the Chief Justice and Justice McIntyre. I agree with McIntyre J. that the constitutional guarantee of freedom of association in s. 2(*d*) of the *Canadian Charter of Rights and Freedoms* does not include, in the case of a trade union, a guarantee of the right to bargain collectively and the right to strike, and accordingly I would dismiss the appeal and answer the constitutional questions in the manner proposed by him. I wish to indicate, if only briefly, the general considerations that lead me to this conclusion.

[142] In considering the meaning that must be given to freedom of association in s. 2(*d*) of the *Charter* it is essential to keep in mind that this concept must be applied to a wide range of associations or organizations of a political, religious, social or economic nature, with a wide variety of objects, as well as activity by which the objects may be pursued. It is in this larger perspective, and not simply with regard to the perceived requirements of a trade union, however important they may be, that one must consider the implications of extending a constitutional guarantee, under the concept of freedom of association, to the right to engage in particular activity on the ground that the activity is essential to give an association meaningful existence.

[143] In considering whether it is reasonable to ascribe such a sweeping intention to the *Charter* I reject the premise that without such additional constitutional protection the guarantee of freedom of association would be a meaningless

and empty one. Freedom of association is particularly important for the exercise of other fundamental freedoms, such as freedom of expression and freedom of conscience and religion. These afford a wide scope for protected activity in association. Moreover, the freedom to work for the establishment of an association, to belong to an association, to maintain it, and to participate in its lawful activity without penalty or reprisal is not to be taken for granted. That is indicated by its express recognition and protection in labour relations legislation. It is a freedom that has been suppressed in varying degrees from time to time by totalitarian regimes.

[144] What is in issue here is not the importance of freedom of association in this sense, which is the one I ascribe to s. 2(*d*) of the *Charter*, but whether particular activity of an association in pursuit of its objects is to be constitutionally protected or left to be regulated by legislative policy. The rights for which constitutional protection are sought—the modern rights to bargain collectively and to strike, involving correlative duties or obligations resting on an employer—are not fundamental rights or freedoms. They are the creation of legislation, involving a balance of competing interests in a field which has been recognized by the courts as requiring a specialized expertise. It is surprising that in an area in which this Court has affirmed a principle of judicial restraint in the review of administrative action we should be considering the substitution of our judgment for that of the Legislature by constitutionalizing in general and abstract terms rights which the Legislature has found it necessary to define and qualify in various ways according to the particular field of labour relations involved. The resulting necessity of applying s. 1 of the *Charter* to a review of particular legislation in this field demonstrates in my respectful opinion the extent to which the Court becomes involved in a review of legislative policy for which it is really not fitted.

[146] **McINTYRE J.:** . . . The question raised in this appeal, stated in its simplest terms, is whether the *Canadian Charter of Rights and Freedoms* gives constitutional protection to the right of a trade union to strike as an incident to collective bargaining. The issue is not whether strike action is an important activity, nor whether it should be protected at law. The importance of strikes in our present system of labour relations is beyond question and each provincial legislature and the federal Parliament has enacted legislation which recognizes a general right to strike. The question for resolution in this appeal is whether such a right is guaranteed by the *Charter*. If this right is found in the *Charter*, a subsidiary question must be addressed: is the legislation in issue nevertheless "demonstrably justified" under s. 1 of the *Charter*? Since it is my conclusion that the *Charter* does not guarantee the right to strike, I need not consider this subsidiary question. . . .

Freedom of Association and Section 2(d) of the Charter

[148] Freedom of association is one of the most fundamental rights in a free society. The freedom to mingle, live and work with others gives meaning and value to the lives of individuals and makes organized society possible. The value of freedom of association as a unifying and liberating force can be seen in the fact that historically the conqueror, seeking to control foreign peoples, invariably strikes first at freedom of association in order to eliminate effective opposition. Meetings are forbidden, curfews are enforced, trade and commerce is suppressed, and rigid controls are imposed to isolate and thus debilitate the individual. Conversely, with the restoration of national sovereignty the democratic state moves at once to remove restrictions on freedom of association.

[149] It is clear that the importance of freedom of association was recognized by Canadian law prior to the *Charter*. It is equally clear that prior to the *Charter* a provincial Legislature or Parliament acting within its jurisdiction could regulate and control strikes and collective bargaining. The *Charter* has reaffirmed the historical importance of freedom of association and guaranteed it as an independent right. The courts must now define the range or scope of this right and its relation to other rights, both those grounded in the *Charter* and those existing at law without *Charter* protection.

[151] ... [W]hile a liberal and not overly legalistic approach should be taken to constitutional interpretation, the *Charter* should not be regarded as an empty vessel to be filled with whatever meaning we might wish from time to time. The interpretation of the *Charter*, as of all constitutional documents, is constrained by the language, structure, and history of the constitutional text, by constitutional tradition, and by the history, traditions, and underlying philosophies of our society.

The Value of Freedom of Association

[152] The starting point of the process of interpretation is an inquiry into the purpose or value of the right at issue. While freedom of association like most other fundamental rights has no single purpose or value, at its core rests a rather simple proposition: the attainment of individual goals, through the exercise of individual rights, is generally impossible without the aid and cooperation of others. "Man, as Aristotle observed, is a 'social animal, formed by nature for living with others,' associating with his fellows both to satisfy his desire for social intercourse and to realize common purposes." (L. J. MacFarlane, *The Theory and Practice of Human Rights* (1985), p. 82.) This thought was echoed in the familiar words of Alexis de Tocqueville:

The most natural privilege of man, next to the right of acting for himself, is that of combining his exertions with those of his fellow creatures and of acting in common with them. The right of association therefore appears to me almost as inalienable in its nature as the right of personal liberty. No legislator can attack it without impairing the foundations of society. (*Democracy in America* (1945), vol. l, at p. 196.)

[153] The increasing complexity of modern society, which has diminished the power of the individual to act alone, has greatly increased the importance of freedom of association. In the words of Professor T. I. Emerson in "Freedom of Association and Freedom of Expression" (1964), 74 *Yale L.J.* 1, at p. 1:

Freedom of association has always been a vital feature of American society. In modern times it has assumed even greater importance. More and more the individual, in order to realize his own capacities or to stand up to the institutionalized forces that surround him, has found it imperative to join with others of like mind in pursuit of common objectives.

... [154] Our society supports a multiplicity of organized groups, clubs and associations which further many different objectives, religious, political, educational, scientific, recreational, and charitable. This exercise of freedom of association serves more than the individual interest, advances more than the individual cause; it promotes general social goals. Of particular importance is the indispensable role played by freedom of association in the functioning of democracy. Paul Cavalluzzo said in "Freedom of Association and the Right to Bargain Collectively" in *Litigating the Values of a Nation: The Canadian Charter of Rights and Freedoms* (1986), at pp. 199-200:

Secondly, [freedom of association] is an effective check on state action and power. In many ways freedom of association is the most important fundamental freedom because it is the one human right which clearly distinguishes a totalitarian state from a democratic one. In a totalitarian system, the state cannot tolerate group activity because of the powerful check it might have on state power.

Associations serve to educate their members in the operation of democratic institutions. As de Tocqueville noted, *supra*, vol. II, at p. 116:

... [individuals] cannot belong to these associations for any length of time without finding out how order is maintained among a large number of men and by what contrivance they are made to advance, harmoniously and methodically, to the same object. Thus they learn to surrender their own will to that of all the rest and to make their own exertions subordinate to the common impulse, things which it is not less necessary to know in civil than in political associations. Political associations may therefore be considered as large free schools, where all the members of the community go to learn the general theory of association.

Associations also make possible the effective expression of political views and thus influence the formation of governmental and social policy.... Freedom of association then serves the interest of the individual, strengthens the general social order, and supports the healthy functioning of democratic government.

[155] In considering the constitutional position of freedom of association, it must be recognized that while it advances many group interests and, of course, cannot be exercised alone, it is nonetheless a freedom belonging to the individual and not to the group formed through its exercise. While some provisions in the Constitution involve groups, such as s. 93 of the *Constitution Act, 1867* protecting denominational schools, and s. 25 of the *Charter* referring to existing aboriginal rights, the remaining rights and freedoms are individual rights; they are not concerned with the group as distinct from its members. The group or organization is simply a device adopted by individuals to achieve a fuller realization of individual rights and aspirations. People, by merely combining together, cannot create an entity which has greater constitutional rights and freedoms than they, as individuals, possess. Freedom of association cannot therefore vest independent rights in the group....

[157] The recognition of this principle in the case at bar is of great significance. The only basis on which it is contended that the *Charter* enshrines a right to strike is that of freedom of association. Collective bargaining is a group concern, a group activity, but the group can exercise only the constitutional rights of its individual members on behalf of those members. If the right asserted is not found in the *Charter* for the individual, it cannot be implied for the group merely by the fact of association. It follows as well that the rights of the individual members of the group cannot be enlarged merely by the fact of association.

The Scope of Freedom of Association in Section 2(d)

[158] Various theories have been advanced to define freedom of association guaranteed by the Constitution. They range from the very restrictive to the virtually unlimited. To begin with, it has been said that freedom of association is limited to a right to associate with others in common pursuits

or for certain purposes. Neither the objects nor the actions of the group are protected by freedom of association....

[161] A second approach provides that freedom of association guarantees the collective exercise of constitutional rights or, in other words, the freedom to engage collectively in those activities which are constitutionally protected for each individual....

[162] It will be seen that this approach guarantees not only the right to associate but as well the right to pursue those objects of association which by their nature have constitutional protection.

[163] A third approach postulates that freedom of association stands for the principle that an individual is entitled to do in concert with others that which he may lawfully do alone, and conversely, that individuals and organizations have no right to do in concert what is unlawful when done individually....

[164] A fourth approach would constitutionally protect collective activities which may be said to be fundamental to our culture and traditions and which by common assent are deserving of protection....

[165] A fifth approach rests on the proposition that freedom of association, under s. 2(*d*) of the *Charter*, extends constitutional protection to all activities which are essential to the lawful goals of an association....

[166] The sixth and final approach so far isolated in the cases, and by far the most sweeping, would extend the protection of s. 2(*d*) of the *Charter* to all acts done in association, subject only to limitation under s. l of the *Charter*....

[170] Turning to the various approaches which have been briefly described above, I would conclude that both the fifth approach (which postulates that freedom of association constitutionally protects all activities which are essential to the lawful goals of an association) and the sixth (which postulates that freedom of association constitutionally protects all activities carried out in association, subject only to reasonable limitation under s. l of the *Charter*) are unacceptable definitions of freedom of association.

[171] The fifth approach rejects the individual nature of freedom of association. To accept it would be to accord an independent constitutional status to the aims, purposes, and activities of the association, and thereby confer greater constitutional rights upon members of the association than upon non-members. It would extend *Charter* protection to all the activities of an association which are essential to its lawful objects or goals, but, it would not extend an equivalent right to individuals. The *Charter* does not give, nor was it ever intended to give, constitutional protection to all the acts of an individual which are essential to his or her personal goals or objectives. If *Charter* protection is given to an association for

its lawful acts and objects, then the *Charter*-protected rights of the association would exceed those of the individual merely by virtue of the fact of association. The unacceptability of such an approach is clearly demonstrated by Peter Gall in "Freedom of Association and Trade Unions: A Double-Edged Constitutional Sword" in *Litigating the Values of a Nation: The Canadian Charter of Rights and Freedoms* (1986), at p. 247:

> A brief example illustrates this point. One of our levels of government may decide to ban the ownership of guns. This would not infringe any individual right under the *Charter*. But if some individuals have combined to form a gun club, does the *Charter*'s protection of freedom of association mean that the principal activity of the gun club, namely the ownership and use of guns, is now constitutionally protected? One is quickly forced to the conclusion that it does not. The *Charter* does not protect the right to bear arms, regardless of whether that activity is carried out by an individual or by an association. The mere fact that it is the principal activity of the gun club does not give it a constitutional status. I doubt whether there would be much, if any, disagreement on this point. Thus, by referring to this hypothetical situation we see that the principal activities of associations are not necessarily protected under the concept of freedom of association.

[172] The sixth approach, in my opinion, must be rejected as well, for the reasons expressed in respect of the fifth. It would in even more sweeping terms elevate activities to constitutional status merely because they were performed in association. For obvious reasons, the *Charter* does not give constitutional protection to all activities performed by individuals. There is, for instance, no *Charter* protection for the ownership of property, for general commercial activity, or for a host of other lawful activities. And yet, if the sixth approach were adopted, these same activities would receive protection if they were performed by a group rather than by an individual. In my view, such a proposition cannot be accepted. There is simply no justification for according *Charter* protection to an activity merely because it is performed by more than one person. . . .

[173] I am also of the view that the fourth approach, which postulates that freedom of association embraces those collective activities which have attained a fundamental status in our society because they are deeply rooted in our culture, traditions, and history, is an unacceptable definition. By focusing on the activity or the conduct itself, this fourth approach ignores the fundamental purpose of the right. The purpose of freedom of association is to ensure that various goals may be pursued in common as well as individually. Freedom of association is not concerned with the particular activities or goals themselves; it is concerned with how activities or goals may be pursued. While activities such as estab-

lishing a home, pursuing an education, or gaining a livelihood are important if not fundamental activities, their importance is not a consequence of their potential collective nature. Their importance flows from the structure and organization of our society and they are as important when pursued individually as they are when pursued collectively. Even institutions such as marriage and the family, which by their nature are collective, do not fall easily or completely under the rubric of freedom of association. For instance, freedom of association would have no bearing on the legal consequences of marriage, such as the control or ownership of matrimonial property. This is not to say that fundamental institutions, such as marriage, will never receive the protection of the *Charter*. The institution of marriage, for example, might well be protected by freedom of association in combination with other rights and freedoms. Freedom of association alone, however, is not concerned with conduct; its purpose is to guarantee that activities and goals may be pursued in common. When this purpose is considered, it is clear that s. 2(*d*) of the *Charter* cannot be interpreted as guaranteeing specific acts or goals, whether or not they are fundamental in our society.

[174] Of the remaining approaches, it must surely be accepted that the concept of freedom of association includes at least the right to join with others in lawful, common pursuits and to establish and maintain organizations and associations as set out in the first approach. This is essentially the freedom of association enjoyed prior to the adoption of the *Charter*. It is, I believe, equally clear that, in accordance with the second approach, freedom of association should guarantee the collective exercise of constitutional rights. Individual rights protected by the Constitution do not lose that protection when exercised in common with others. People must be free to engage collectively in those activities which are constitutionally protected for each individual. This second definition of freedom of association embraces the purposes and values of the freedoms which were identified earlier. For instance, the indispensable role played by freedom of association in the democratic process is fully protected by guaranteeing the collective exercise of freedom of expression. Group advocacy, which is at the heart of all political parties and special interest groups, would be protected under this definition. As well, group expression directed at educating or informing the public would be protected from *government interference* (see the judgment of this Court in *Dolphin Delivery* [*Ltd. v. Retail, Wholesale & Department Store Union, Local 580* (1984), 10 D.L.R. (4th) 198; aff'd on other grounds, [1986] 2 S.C.R. 573]). Indeed, virtually every group activity which is important to the functioning of democracy would be protected by guaranteeing that freedom of expression can be exercised in association with others. Furthermore, religious

groups would receive protection if their activities constituted the collective exercise of freedom of religion. Thus, the principal purposes or values of freedom of association would be realized by interpreting s. 2(*d*) as protecting the collective exercise of the rights enumerated in the *Charter*.

[175] One enters upon more controversial ground when considering the third approach which provides that whatever action an individual can *lawfully* pursue as an individual, freedom of association ensures he can pursue with others. Conversely, individuals and organizations have no constitutional right to do in concert what is unlawful when done alone. This approach is broader than the second, since constitutional protection attaches to all group acts which can be lawfully performed by an individual, whether or not the individual has a constitutional right to perform them. It is true, of course, that in this approach the range of *Charter*-protected activity could be reduced by legislation, because the Legislature has the power to declare what is and what is not lawful activity for the individual. The Legislature, however, would not be able to attack directly the associational character of the activity, since it would be constitutionally bound to treat groups and individuals alike. A simple example illustrates this point: golf is a lawful but not constitutionally protected activity. Under the third approach, the Legislature could prohibit golf entirely. However, the Legislature could not constitutionally provide that golf could be played in pairs but in no greater number, for this would infringe the *Charter* guarantee of freedom of association. This contrasts with the second approach, which would provide no protection against such legislation, because golf is not a constitutionally protected activity for the individual. Thus, the range of group activity protected by the third approach is greater than that of the second, but the greater range is to some extent illusory because of the power of the Legislature to say what is and what is not lawful activity for the individual. This approach, in my view, is an acceptable interpretation of freedom of association under the *Charter*. It is clear that, unlike the fifth and sixth approaches, this definition of freedom of association does not provide greater constitutional rights for groups than for individuals; it simply ensures that they are treated alike. If the state chooses to prohibit everyone from engaging in an activity and that activity is not protected under the Constitution, freedom of association will not afford any protection to groups engaging in the activity. Freedom of association as an independent right comes into play under this formulation when the state has permitted an individual to engage in an activity and yet forbidden the group from doing so. . . .

[176] It follows from this discussion that I interpret freedom of association in s. 2(*d*) of the *Charter* to mean that *Charter* protection will attach to the exercise in association of such rights as have *Charter* protection when exercised by the individual. Furthermore, freedom of association means the freedom to associate for the purposes of activities which are lawful when performed alone. But, since the fact of association will not by itself confer additional rights on individuals, the association does not acquire a constitutionally guaranteed freedom to do what is unlawful for the individual.

[177] When this definition of freedom of association is applied, it is clear that it does not guarantee the right to strike. Since the right to strike is not independently protected under the *Charter*, it can receive protection under freedom of association only if it is an activity which is permitted by law to an individual. Accepting this conclusion, the appellants argue that freedom of association must guarantee the right to strike because individuals may lawfully refuse to work. This position, however, is untenable for two reasons. First, it is not correct to say that it is lawful for an individual employee to cease work during the currency of his contract of employment. . . . The second reason is simply that there is no analogy whatever between the cessation of work by a single employee and a strike conducted in accordance with modern labour legislation. The individual has, by reason of the cessation of work, either breached or terminated his contract of employment. It is true that the law will not compel the specific performance of the contract by ordering him back to work as this would reduce "the employee to a state tantamount to slavery" (I. Christie, *Employment Law in Canada* (1980), p. 268). But, this is markedly different from a lawful strike. An employee who ceases work does not contemplate a return to work, while employees on strike always contemplate a return to work. In recognition of this fact, the law does not regard a strike as either a breach of contract or a termination of employment. Every province and the federal Parliament has enacted legislation which preserves the employer–employee relationship during a strike. . . .

[178] Modern labour relations legislation has so radically altered the legal relationship between employees and employers in unionized industries that no analogy may be drawn between the lawful actions of individual employees in ceasing to work and the lawful actions of union members in engaging in a strike. . . . It is apparent, in my view, that interpreting freedom of association to mean that every individual is free to do with others that which he is lawfully entitled to do alone would not entail guaranteeing the right to strike. I am supported in this conclusion by the Chief Justice, who states at p. 367 in his judgment, "There is no individual equivalent to a strike. The refusal to work by one individual does not parallel a collective refusal to work. The latter is *qualitatively* rather than quantitatively different." Restrictions on strikes are not aimed at and do not interfere with the collective or associa-

tional character of trade unions. It is therefore my conclusion that the concept of freedom of association does not extend to the constitutional guarantee of a right to strike. This conclusion is entirely consistent with the general approach of the *Charter* which accords rights and freedoms to the individual but, with a few exceptions noted earlier, does not confer group rights. It is also to be observed that the *Charter*, with the possible exception of s. 6(2)(*b*) (right to earn a livelihood in any province) and s. 6(4), does not concern itself with economic rights. Since trade unions are not one of the groups specifically mentioned by the *Charter*, and are overwhelmingly, though not exclusively, concerned with the economic interests of their members, it would run counter to the overall structure and approach of the *Charter* to accord by implication special constitutional rights to trade unions.

[179] Labour relations and the development of the body of law which has grown up around that subject have been for many years one of the major preoccupations of legislators, economic and social writers, and the general public. Strikes are commonplace in Canada and have been for many years. The framers of the Constitution must be presumed to have been aware of these facts. Indeed, questions of collective bargaining and a right to strike were discussed in the *Minutes of Proceedings and Evidence* of the Special Joint Committee of the Senate and of the House of Commons on the Constitution of Canada (Issue No. 43, pp. 68-79, January 22, 1981). It is apparent from the deliberations of the Committee that the right to strike was understood to be separate and distinct from the right to bargain collectively. And, while a resolution was proposed for the inclusion of a specific right to bargain collectively, no resolution was proposed for the inclusion of the right to strike. This affords strong support for the proposition that the inclusion of a right to strike was not intended.

[180] Specific reference to the right to strike appears in the constitutions of France (in the preamble of the Constitution of the Vth Republic of 1958) and Italy (Article 40). Further, in Japan (Article 28) the rights of trade unions are specifically guaranteed. The framers of the Constitution must be presumed to have been aware of these constitutional provisions. The omission of similar provisions in the *Charter*, taken with the fact that the overwhelming preoccupation of the *Charter* is with individual, political, and democratic rights with conspicuous inattention to economic and property rights, speaks strongly against any implication of a right to strike. Accordingly, if s. 2(*d*) is read in the context of the whole *Charter*, it cannot, in my opinion, support an interpretation of freedom of association which could include a right to strike.

[181] Furthermore, it must be recognized that the right to strike accorded by legislation throughout Canada is of relatively recent vintage. It is truly the product of this century and,

in its modern form, is in reality the product of the latter half of this century. It cannot be said that it has become so much a part of our social and historical traditions that it has acquired the status of an immutable, fundamental right, firmly embedded in our traditions, our political and social philosophy. There is then no basis, as suggested in the fourth approach to freedom of association, for implying a constitutional right to strike. It may well be said that labour relations have become a matter of fundamental importance in our society, but every incident of that general topic has not. The right to strike as an element of labour relations has always been the subject of legislative control. It has been abrogated from time to time in special circumstances and is the subject of legal regulation and control in all Canadian jurisdictions. In my view, it cannot be said that at this time it has achieved status as a fundamental right which should be implied in the absence of specific reference in the *Charter*.

[182] While I have reached a conclusion and expressed the view that the *Charter* upon its face cannot support an implication of a right to strike, there is as well, in my view, a sound reason grounded in social policy against any such implication. Labour law, as we have seen, is a fundamentally important as well as an extremely sensitive subject. It is based upon a political and economic compromise between organized labour—a very powerful socio-economic force—on the one hand, and the employers of labour—an equally powerful socio-economic force—on the other. The balance between the two forces is delicate and the public-at-large depends for its security and welfare upon the maintenance of that balance. One group concedes certain interests in exchange for concessions from the other. There is clearly no correct balance which may be struck giving permanent satisfaction to the two groups, as well as securing the public interest. The whole process is inherently dynamic and unstable. Care must be taken then in considering whether constitutional protection should be given to one aspect of this dynamic and evolving process while leaving the others subject to the social pressures of the day. Great changes—economic, social, and industrial—are afoot, not only in Canada and in North America, but as well in other parts of the world. Changes in the Canadian national economy, the decline in resource-based as well as heavy industries, the changing patterns of international trade and industry, have resulted in great pressure to reassess the traditional approaches to economic and industrial questions, including questions of labour law and policy. In such countries as Sweden (Prof. Dr. Axel Adlercreutz, *Sweden*, in *International Encyclopaedia for Labour Law and Industrial Relations* (1985), vol. 9, ed.-in-chief Prof. Dr. R. Blanpain) and West Germany (Prof. Dr. Th. Ramm, *Federal Republic of Germany* in *International Encyclopaedia for Labour Law and Industrial Relations* (1979),

vol. 5) different directions in labour relations have been taken. It has been said that these changes have led to increased efficiency and job satisfaction. Whatever the result of such steps, however, it is obvious that the immediate direction of labour policy is unclear. It is, however, clear that labour policy can only be developed step by step with, in this country, the Provinces playing their "classic federal role as laboratories for legal experimentation with our industrial relations ailments" (Paul Weiler, *Reconcilable Differences: New Directions in Canadian Labour Law* (1980), at p. 11). The fulfilment of this role in the past has resulted in the growth and development of the body of labour law which now prevails in Canada. The fluid and constantly changing conditions of modern society demand that it continue. To intervene in that dynamic process at this early stage of *Charter* development by implying constitutional protection for a right to strike would, in my view, give to one of the contending forces an economic weapon removed from and made immune, subject to s. 1, to legislative control which could go far towards freezing the development of labour relations and curtailing that process of evolution necessary to meet the changing circumstances of a modern society in a modern world. This, I repeat, is not to say that a right to strike does not exist at law or that it should be abolished. It merely means that at this stage of our *Charter* development such a right should not have constitutional status which would impair the process of future development in legislative hands. . . .

[183] To constitutionalize a particular feature of labour relations by entrenching a right to strike would have other adverse effects. Our experience with labour relations has shown that the courts, as a general rule, are not the best arbiters of disputes which arise from time to time. Labour legislation has recognized this fact and has created other procedures and other tribunals for the more expeditious and efficient settlement of labour problems. Problems arising in labour matters frequently involve more than legal questions. Political, social, and economic questions frequently dominate in labour disputes. The legislative creation of conciliation officers, conciliation boards, labour relations boards, and labour dispute-resolving tribunals, has gone far in meeting needs not attainable in the court system. The nature of labour disputes and grievances and the other problems arising in labour matters dictates that special procedures outside the ordinary court system must be employed in their resolution. Judges do not have the expert knowledge always helpful and sometimes necessary in the resolution of labour problems. The courts will generally not be furnished in labour cases, if past experience is to guide us, with an evidentiary base upon which full resolution of the dispute may be made. In my view, it is scarcely contested that specialized labour tribunals are better suited than courts for resolving labour problems, except

for the resolution of purely legal questions. If the right to strike is constitutionalized, then its application, its extent, and any questions of its legality, become matters of law. This would inevitably throw the courts back into the field of labour relations and much of the value of specialized labour tribunals would be lost. . . .

[184] A further problem will arise from constitutionalizing the right to strike. In every case where a strike occurs and relief is sought in the courts, the question of the application of s. 1 of the *Charter* may be raised to determine whether some attempt to control the right may be permitted. This has occurred in the case at bar. The section 1 inquiry involves the reconsideration by a court of the balance struck by the Legislature in the development of labour policy. The Court is called upon to determine, as a matter of constitutional law, which government services are essential and whether the alternative of arbitration is adequate compensation for the loss of a right to strike. In the *PSAC* case, the Court must decide whether mere postponement of collective bargaining is a reasonable limit, given the Government's substantial interest in reducing inflation and the growth in government expenses. In the *Dairy Workers* case, the Court is asked to decide whether the harm caused to dairy farmers through a closure of the dairies is of sufficient importance to justify prohibiting strike action and lockouts. None of these issues is amenable to principled resolution. There are no clearly correct answers to these questions. They are of a nature peculiarly apposite to the functions of the Legislature. However, if the right to strike is found in the *Charter*, it will be the courts which time and time again will have to resolve these questions, relying only on the evidence and arguments presented by the parties, despite the social implications of each decision. This is a legislative function into which the courts should not intrude. It has been said that the courts, because of the *Charter*, will have to enter the legislative sphere. Where rights are specifically guaranteed in the *Charter*, this may on occasion be true. But where no specific right is found in the *Charter* and the only support for its constitutional guarantee is an implication, the courts should refrain from intrusion into the field of legislation. That is the function of the freely-elected Legislatures and Parliament. . . .

The judgment of Dickson C.J. and Wilson J. was delivered by

[22] **DICKSON C.J.** (dissenting): . . . Freedom of association is the freedom to combine together for the pursuit of common purposes or the advancement of common causes. It is one of the fundamental freedoms guaranteed by the *Charter*, a *sine qua non* of any free and democratic society, protecting individuals from the vulnerability of isolation and ensuring the potential of effective participation in society. In every

area of human endeavour and throughout history individuals have formed associations for the pursuit of common interests and aspirations. Through association individuals are able to ensure that they have a voice in shaping the circumstances integral to their needs, rights and freedoms.

[23] Freedom of association is the cornerstone of modern labour relations. Historically, workers have combined to overcome the inherent inequalities of bargaining power in the employment relationship and to protect themselves from unfair, unsafe, or exploitative working conditions....

2. The Meaning of Section 2(d)

[73] At the outset, it should be noted that, contrary to submissions by the respondent and some of the interveners in support, the purpose of s. 2 of the *Charter* must extend beyond merely protecting rights which already existed at the time of the *Charter*'s entrenchment....

[74] Similarly, the scope of the *Charter*'s provisions is not to be confined by the fact of legislative regulation in a particular subject area. In argument, counsel for the respondent seemed to suggest that if freedom of association were interpreted to include strike activity, this would "constitutionalize" a statutory right. His argument appeared to be premised on the proposition that, because the "right to strike" was a subject of legislative regulation prior to the *Charter*'s entrenchment, it followed that strike activity could not be a matter for constitutional protection after entrenchment of the *Charter*. While it may be true that the *Charter* was not framed for the purpose of guaranteeing rights conferred by legislative enactment, the view that certain rights and freedoms cannot be protected by the *Charter*'s provisions because they are the subject of statutory regulation is premised on a fundamental misconception about the nature of judicial review under a written constitution.

[75] The Constitution is supreme law. Its provisions are not to be circumscribed by what the Legislature has done in the past, but, rather, the activities of the Legislature—past, present and future—must be consistent with the principles set down in the Constitution....

[76] This is not to say, however, that the legislative regulation of collective bargaining and strikes is entirely irrelevant to the manner in which a constitutional freedom to strike may be given effect in particular circumstances: see, on this point, my reasons in the *Dairy Workers* case, released concurrently. But the present case does not involve a challenge to the general labour law of Alberta which permits strike activity, subject to regulation. This appeal concerns the substitution of an entirely different mechanism for resolving labour disputes for particular employees, and one which does not merely regulate the freedom to strike but abrogates it entirely....

[78] A wide variety of alternative interpretations of freedom of association has been advanced in the jurisprudence summarized above and in argument before this Court.

[79] At one extreme is a purely constitutive definition whereby freedom of association entails only a freedom to belong to or form an association. On this view, the constitutional guarantee does not extend beyond protecting the individual's *status* as a member of an association. It would not protect his or her associational *actions*.

[80] In the trade union context, then, a constitutive definition would find a *prima facie* violation of s. 2(d) of the *Charter* in legislation such as s. 2(1) of the *Police Officers Act* which prohibits membership in any organization affiliated with a trade union. But it could find no violation of s. 2(d) in respect of legislation which prohibited a concerted refusal to work. Indeed, a wide variety of trade union activities, ranging from the organization of social activities for its members, to the establishment of union pension plans, to the discussion of collective bargaining strategy, could be prohibited by the state without infringing s. 2(d).

[81] The essentially formal nature of a constitutive approach to freedom of association is equally apparent when one considers other types of associational activity in our society. While the constitutive approach might find a possible violation of s. 2(d) in a legislative enactment which prohibited marriage for certain classes of people, it would hold inoffensive an enactment which precluded the same people from engaging in the activities integral to a marriage, such as cohabiting and raising children together. If freedom of association only protects the joining together of persons for common purposes, but not the pursuit of the very activities for which the association was formed, then the freedom is indeed legalistic, ungenerous, indeed vapid.

[82] In my view, while it is unquestionable that s. 2(d), at a minimum, guarantees the liberty of persons to *be* in association or belong to an organization, it must extend beyond a concern for associational status to give effective protection to the interests to which the constitutional guarantee is directed....

[83] A second approach, the derivative approach, prevalent in the United States, embodies a somewhat more generous definition of freedom of association than the formal, constitutive approach. In the Canadian context, it is suggested by some that associational action which relates specifically to one of the other freedoms enumerated in s. 2 is constitutionally protected, but other associational activity is not.

[84] I am unable, however, to accept that freedom of association should be interpreted so restrictively. Section 2(d) of the *Charter* provides an explicit and independent guarantee of freedom of association. In this respect it stands in marked

contrast to the First Amendment to the American Constitution. The derivative approach would, in my view, largely make surplusage of s. 2(*d*). The associational or collective dimensions of s. 2(*a*) and (*b*) have already been recognized by this Court in *R. v. Big M Drug Mart Ltd.* [[1985] 1 S.C.R. 295], without resort to s. 2(*d*). The associational aspect of s. 2(*c*) clearly finds adequate protection in the very expression of a freedom of peaceful assembly. What is to be learnt from the United States jurisprudence is not that freedom of association must be restricted to associational activities involving independent constitutional rights, but rather, that the express conferral of a freedom of association is unnecessary if all that is intended is to give effect to the collective enjoyment of other individual freedoms.

[85] I am also unimpressed with the argument that the inclusion of s. 2(*d*) with freedoms of a "political" nature requires a narrow or restrictive interpretation of freedom of association. I am unable to regard s. 2 as embodying purely political freedoms. Paragraph (*a*), which protects freedom of conscience and religion is quite clearly not exclusively political in nature. It would, moreover, be unsatisfactory to overlook our Constitution's history of giving special recognition to collectivities or communities of interest other than the government and political parties. Sections 93 and 133 of the *Constitution Act, 1867* and ss. 16-24, 25, 27 and 29 of the *Charter*, dealing variously with denominational schools, language rights, aboriginal rights, and our multicultural heritage implicitly embody an awareness of the importance of various collectivities in the pursuit of educational, linguistic, cultural and social as well as political ends. Just as the individual is incapable of resisting political domination without the support of persons with similar values, so too is he or she, in isolation, incapable of resisting domination, over the long term, in many other aspects of life.

[86] Freedom of association is protected in s. 2(*d*) under the rubric of "fundamental" freedoms. In my view, the "fundamental" nature of freedom of association relates to the central importance to the individual of his or her interaction with fellow human beings. The purpose of the constitutional guarantee of freedom of association is, I believe, to recognize the profoundly social nature of human endeavours and to protect the individual from state-enforced isolation in the pursuit of his or her ends. In the famous words of Alexis de Tocqueville in *Democracy in America* (1945), vol. 1, at p. 196:

> The most natural privilege of man, next to the right of acting for himself, is that of combining his exertions with those of his fellow creatures and of acting in common with them. The right of association therefore appears ... almost as inalienable in its nature as the right of personal

liberty. No legislator can attack it without impairing the foundations of society.

As social beings, our freedom to act with others is a primary condition of community life, human progress and civilized society. Through association, individuals have been able to participate in determining and controlling the immediate circumstances of their lives, and the rules, mores and principles which govern the communities in which they live. As John Stuart Mill stated, "if public spirit, generous sentiments, or true justice and equality are desired, association, not isolation, of interests, is the school in which these excellences are nurtured." (*Principles of Political Economy* (1893), vol. 2, at p. 352.)

[87] Freedom of association is most essential in those circumstances where the individual is liable to be prejudiced by the actions of some larger and more powerful entity, like the government or an employer. Association has always been the means through which political, cultural and racial minorities, religious groups and workers have sought to attain their purposes and fulfil their aspirations; it has enabled those who would otherwise be vulnerable and ineffective to meet on more equal terms the power and strength of those with whom their interests interact and, perhaps, conflict. T. I. Emerson, "Freedom of Association and Freedom of Expression" (1964), 74 *Yale L.J.* 1 at p. 1, states that:

> More and more the individual, in order to realize his own capacities or to stand up to the institutionalized forces that surround him, has found it imperative to join with others of like mind in pursuit of common objectives.

[88] What freedom of association seeks to protect is not associational activities *qua* particular activities, but the freedom of individuals to interact with, support, and be supported by, their fellow humans in the varied activities in which they choose to engage. But this is not an unlimited constitutional license for all group activity. The mere fact that an activity is capable of being carried out by several people together, as well as individually, does not mean that the activity acquires constitutional protection from legislative prohibition or regulation.

[89] I believe that ... s. 2(*d*) normally embraces the liberty to do collectively that which one is permitted to do as an individual. ... However, it is not in my view correct to regard this proposition as the exclusive touchstone for determining the presence or absence of a violation of s. 2(*d*). Certainly, if a legislature permits an individual to enjoy an activity which it forecloses to a collectivity, it may properly be inferred that the legislature intended to prohibit the collective activity because of its collective or associational aspect. Conversely, one may infer from a legislative proscription which applies

equally to individuals and groups that the purpose of the legislation was a *bona fide* prohibition of a particular activity because of detrimental qualities inhering in the activity (e.g., criminal conduct), and not merely because of the fact that the activity might sometimes be done in association.... There will, however, be occasions when no analogy involving individuals can be found for associational activity, or when a comparison between groups and individuals fails to capture the essence of a possible violation of associational rights. This is precisely the situation in this case. There is no individual equivalent to a strike. The refusal to work by one individual does not parallel a collective refusal to work. The latter is *qualitatively* rather than quantitatively different. The overarching consideration remains whether a legislative enactment or administrative action interferes with the freedom of persons to join and act with others in common pursuits. The legislative purpose which will render legislation invalid is the attempt to preclude associational conduct because of its concerted or associational nature.

[90] I wish to refer to one further concern. It has been suggested that associational activity for the pursuit of economic ends should not be accorded constitutional protection. If by this it is meant that something as fundamental as a person's livelihood or dignity in the workplace is beyond the scope of constitutional protection, I cannot agree. If, on the other hand, it is meant that concerns of an exclusively pecuniary nature are excluded from such protection, such an argument would merit careful consideration. In the present case, however, we are concerned with interests which go far beyond those of a merely pecuniary nature.

[91] Work is one of the most fundamental aspects in a person's life, providing the individual with a means of financial support and, as importantly, a contributory role in society. A person's employment is an essential component of his or her sense of identity, self-worth and emotional well-being. Accordingly, the conditions in which a person works are highly significant in shaping the whole compendium of psychological, emotional and physical elements of a person's dignity and self respect....

[92] The role of association has always been vital as a means of protecting the essential needs and interests of working people. Throughout history, workers have associated to overcome their vulnerability as individuals to the strength of their employers. The capacity to bargain collectively has long been recognized as one of the integral and primary functions of associations of working people. While trade unions also fulfil other important social, political and charitable functions, collective bargaining remains vital to the capacity of individual employees to participate in ensuring fair wages,

health and safety protections, and equitable and humane working conditions. As Professor Paul Weiler explains in *Reconcilable Differences: New Directions in Canadian Labour Law* (1980), at p. 31:

> An apt way of putting it is to say that good collective bargaining tries to subject the employment relationship and the work environment to the "rule of law." Many theorists of industrial relations believe that this function of protecting the employee from the abuse of managerial power, thereby enhancing the dignity of the worker as a person, is the primary value of collective bargaining, one which entitles the institution to positive encouragement from the law.

[93] Professor Weiler goes on to characterize collective bargaining as "intrinsically valuable as an experience in self-government" (p. 33), and writes at p. 32:

> ... [C]ollective bargaining is the most significant occasion upon which most of these workers ever participate in making social decisions about matters that are salient to their daily lives. That is the essence of collective bargaining.

A similar rationale for endorsing collective bargaining was advanced in the *Woods Task Force Report on Canadian Industrial Relations* (1968), at p. 96:

> 296. One of the most cherished hopes of those who originally championed the concept of collective bargaining was that it would introduce into the work place some of the basic features of the political democracy that was becoming the hallmark of most of the western world. Traditionally referred to as industrial democracy, it can be described as the substitution of the rule of law for the rule of men in the work place.

[94] Closely related to collective bargaining, at least in our existing industrial relations context, is the freedom to strike....

[97] I am satisfied, in sum, that whether or not freedom of association generally extends to protecting associational activity for the pursuit of exclusively pecuniary ends—a question on which I express no opinion—collective bargaining protects important employee interests which cannot be characterized as merely pecuniary in nature. Under our existing system of industrial relations, effective constitutional protection of the associational interests of employees in the collective bargaining process requires concomitant protection of their freedom to withdraw collectively their services, subject to s. 1 of the *Charter*....

Section 1

[101] The respondent submits that even if any of the legislative provisions at issue in this appeal violates freedom of association as guaranteed by s. 2(*d*) of the *Charter*, it can be upheld under s. 1 of the *Charter*. . . .

[102] . . . The onus of demonstrating that a limit on a right or freedom should be upheld under s. 1 is on the party seeking to uphold the limit. The standard of proof is the preponderance of probabilities and, as a general rule, evidence is required to meet this standard: see *R. v. Oakes*, [1986] 1 S.C.R. 103, and authorities therein.

[103] The constituent elements of any s. 1 inquiry are as follows. First, the legislative objective, in pursuit of which the measures in question are implemented, must be sufficiently significant to warrant overriding a constitutionally guaranteed right: it must be related to "concerns which are pressing and substantial in a free and democratic society." Second, the means chosen to advance such an objective must be reasonable and demonstrably justified in a free and democratic society. This requirement of proportionality of means to ends normally has three aspects: a) there must be a rational connection between the measures and the objective they are to serve; b) the measures should impair as little as possible the right or freedom in question; and, c) the deleterious effects of the measures must be justifiable in light of the objective which they are to serve. See *Oakes*, and authorities cited therein.

[104] As I understand the respondent's submissions, there are two objectives which the legislation in issue in this Reference is designed to achieve: 1) protection of essential services and 2) protection of government from political pressure through strike action. The question is whether either or both of these are "of sufficient importance to warrant overriding a constitutionally guaranteed right or freedom" (*Big M Drug Mart Ltd., supra,* at p. 352) or, in other words, whether they relate to "pressing and substantial concerns" (*Oakes,* at pp. 138-39). The proportionality of the measures in relation to the objectives must then be assessed.

[105] I observe at the outset that the analysis below is limited to assessing the justifications advanced by the province for its legislative action. It is the actual objectives of the Alberta Legislature and not some other legitimate but hypothetical objectives for passing the particular statutes in question that must be scrutinized. It may be that other rationales will be advanced in future cases. The Court has not been asked, in this case, to determine whether economic harm to third parties can justify the abrogation of the freedom to strike. Nor has it been asked to determine whether a universally applicable substitute for the confrontational strike/lockout paradigm of present-day industrial relations would be acceptable. It might be that some alternative scheme, be it a novel one of worker participation in employer decisions through ownership or otherwise, or a more familiar one, such as arbitration, would be acceptable. The Constitution does not freeze into place an existing formula of industrial relations.

1. The Protection of Essential Services

[106] The protection of services which are truly essential is in my view a legislative objective of sufficient importance for the purpose of s. 1 of the *Charter*. It is, however, necessary to define "essential services" in a manner consistent with the justificatory standards set out in s. 1. The logic of s. 1 in the present circumstances requires that an essential service be one the interruption of which would threaten serious harm to the general public or to a part of the population. In the context of an argument relating to harm of a non-economic nature I find the decisions of the Freedom of Association Committee of the I.L.O. to be helpful and persuasive. These decisions have consistently defined an essential service as a service "whose interruption would endanger the life, personal safety or health of the whole or part of the population" (*Freedom of Association: Digest of Decisions and Principles of the Freedom of Association Committee of the Governing Body of the I.L.O.* [3rd ed. (Geneva: International Labour Office, 1985)]). In my view, and without attempting an exhaustive list, persons essential to the maintenance and administration of the rule of law and national security would also be included within the ambit of essential services. Mere inconvenience to members of the public does not fall within the ambit of the essential services justification for abrogating the freedom to strike.

[107] Having decided that the protection of essential services is an objective of sufficient importance, it is necessary for the respondent to demonstrate proportionality between the measures adopted and the objective. Four classes of employees are covered by the Acts: public service employees (*Public Service Act*); firefighters and employees of employers who operate approved hospitals under the *Hospitals Act* (*Labour Relations Act*); and police officers (*Police Officers Act*). The government must, as a first step, prove, on a balance of probabilities, that these employees are "essential"; otherwise the abrogation of their freedom to strike would be over-inclusive and unjustified under s. 1.

[108] Counsel for the Attorney General for Alberta did not adduce any evidence on this point. He submitted only that essential services must not be interrupted and that, though some of the employees covered by the Acts are not essential, "they are so closely linked to those providing essential services as to make it reasonable that they should be treated in the same way." In *Oakes*, this Court acknowledged that the extent

of evidentiary submissions required under s. 1 would vary according to the nature of the case. . . .

[109] The essentiality of police officers and firefighters is, in my view, obvious and self-evident, and does not have to be proven by evidence. Interruption in police protection and firefighting would clearly endanger life, personal safety and health. Therefore, I believe the Legislature's decision to prevent such interruptions is rationally connected to the objective of protecting essential services.

[110] The situation with respect to employees of employers who operate approved hospitals under the *Hospitals Act* is quite different. Prohibiting the right to strike across the board in hospital employment is too drastic a measure for achieving the object of protecting essential services. It is neither obvious nor self-evident that *all* bargaining units in hospitals represent workers who provide essential services, or that those who do not provide essential services are "so closely linked" to those who do as to justify similar treatment. . . .

[111] Counsel for the Attorney General has not provided any evidence or information from which it can be concluded on a preponderance of probabilities that services will be interrupted whenever strike activity is undertaken by any of the bargaining units in a hospital. While it may be obvious or self-evident that strikes by certain hospital employees, such as nurses or doctors, would be inimical to the hospital's ability to dispense proper health care, the same cannot be said for all hospital workers without some evidentiary basis. For this reason, I do not believe it can be maintained that the employees covered by s. 117.1 of the *Labour Relations Act* are all "essential." The provision is too wide to be justified as relating to essential services for the purpose of s. 1.

[112] The *Public Service Act* is, in my opinion, a victim of the same defect. . . .

2. Protection of the Government from Political Pressure Argument

[113] As mentioned above, the respondent advances a second argument for justification under s. 1, namely, that the legislation is necessary to protect the government from the political pressure of strike action by its employees. In other words, even if public servants are not truly essential, the fact that they are employees of the government is sufficient reason for denying them the freedom to strike. I do not find this argument convincing. The respondent has not submitted any evidence from which it can be concluded that collective bargaining and strike activity in the public sector have or will cause undue political pressure on government. Indeed, all across Canada, collective bargaining and freedom to strike have played an important role in public sector labour relations. . . .

[115] In my opinion, the fact of government employment is not a sufficient reason for the purpose of s. 1 for limiting freedom of association through legislative prohibition of freedom to strike. It has not been shown that all public service employees have a substantial bargaining advantage on account of their employer's governmental status. Nor has it been shown that any political pressure exerted on the government during strikes is of an unusual or peculiarly detrimental nature.

3. Arbitration as a Substitute for Freedom to Strike

[116] As noted above, the provisions relating to police officers and firefighters meet the first test of proportionality: there is a rational connection between prohibiting freedom to strike in these services and the legislative objective of protecting essential services. It is helpful to consider, therefore, whether the measures adopted impair as little as possible the freedom of association of those affected. Clearly, if the freedom to strike were denied and no effective and fair means for resolving bargaining disputes were put in its place, employees would be denied any input at all in ensuring fair and decent working conditions, and labour relations law would be skewed entirely to the advantage of the employer. It is for this reason that legislative prohibition of freedom to strike must be accompanied by a mechanism for dispute resolution by a third party. I agree with the Alberta International Fire Fighters Association at p. 22 of its factum that "[i]t is generally accepted that employers and employees should be on an equal footing in terms of their positions in strike situations or at compulsory arbitration where the right to strike is withdrawn." The purpose of such a mechanism is to ensure that the loss in bargaining power through legislative prohibition of strikes is balanced by access to a system which is capable of resolving in a fair, effective and expeditious manner disputes which arise between employees and employers.

[117] As noted above, the purpose of the prohibitions of strike activity of police officers and firefighters is to prevent interruptions in essential services. If prohibition of strikes is to be the least drastic means of achieving this purpose it must, in my view, be accompanied by adequate guarantees for safeguarding workers' interests. Any system of conciliation or arbitration must be fair and effective or, in the words of the I.L.O. Committee on Freedom of Association "adequate, impartial and speedy . . . in which the parties can take part at every stage": Case No. 1247, *I.L.O. Official Bulletin, supra*, at p. 36.

[118] The contentious issues in respect to the legislative provisions concerning arbitration are as follows: (i) they require the arbitrator to consider certain items; (ii) they limit the arbitrability of certain items; and (iii) they place discretion in the hands of a minister or agency of the government

to decide whether or not a dispute will go to arbitration. I will deal with each of these in turn.

(i) The Arbitrator Must Consider Certain Items

[119] Under the *Public Service Act*, the *Labour Relations Act* and the *Police Officers Act* arbitrators are required to consider (i) the fiscal policies of the government as declared by the Provincial Treasurer in writing (s. 55(*a*)(iii) of the *Public Service Act*; s. 117.8(*a*)(iii) of the *Labour Relations Act*; s. 15(*a*)(iii) of the *Police Officers Act*); and (ii) wages and benefits in private and public unionized and non-unionized employment (s. 55(*a*)(i) of the *Public Service Act*; s. 117.8(*a*)(i) of the *Labour Relations Act*; s. 15(*a*)(i) of the *Police Officers Act*)....

[120] ... In my view the fiscal policy of the government is a measure of the employer's ability to pay, and there is nothing improper in requiring the arbitrator to consider it. The arbitrator is not bound by the statute to take the stated fiscal policy as the conclusive measure of the employer's ability to pay, and it would be open to the unions to make submissions requesting that the arbitrator depart from the fiscal policy.

[121] Turning to s. 55(*a*)(i) of the *Public Service Act*, s. 117.8(a)(i) of the *Labour Relations Act*, and s. 15(*a*)(i) of the *Police Officers Act*, which require that arbitrators consider the wages and benefits of private and public unionized and non-unionized employees, I do not believe these sections compromise the adequacy of the arbitration system. As Professor K. P. Swan has stated (in *The Search for Meaningful Criteria in Interest Arbitration*, Reprint Series No. 41, Industrial Relations Centre, Queen's University, 1978) at p. 11: "Fairness remains an essentially relative concept, and it therefore depends directly upon the identification of fair comparisons if it is to be meaningful." Under ss. 55(*a*)(i), 117.8(*a*)(i) and 15(*a*)(i) the arbitrator is required to consider, presumably for the sake of comparison, the wages of unionized, non-unionized, public sector and private sector employees. The appellant, Alberta International Fire Fighters Association, implies that ss. 55(*a*)(i), 117.8(*a*)(i) and 15(*a*)(i) mandate an unfair comparison; one that "is bound to result in lowering the wages of the unionized employees." I do not agree. A requirement to establish as broad a comparative base as possible does not, in my view, compromise the fairness of the arbitration, or disadvantage the employees concerned.

(ii) Limiting the Arbitrability of Certain Items

[122] Section 48(2) of the *Public Service Act* establishes that certain matters cannot be referred to arbitration or contained in an arbitral award. These matters are generally arbitrable in other labour relations contexts. ...

[123] As noted above, an arbitration system must be fair and effective if it is to be adequate in restoring to employees the bargaining power they are denied through prohibition of strike activity. In my opinion, the exclusion of these subjects from the arbitration process compromises the effectiveness of the process as a means of ensuring equal bargaining power in the absence of freedom to strike. Serious doubt is cast upon the fairness and effectiveness of an arbitration scheme where matters which would normally be bargainable are excluded from arbitration. "Given that without some binding mechanism for dispute resolution, meaningful collective bargaining is very unlikely, it seems more reasonable to ensure that the scope of arbitrability is as wide as the scope of bargainability if the bargaining process is to work at all": K. P. Swan, "Safety Belt or Strait-Jacket? Restrictions on the Scope of Public Sector Collective Bargaining," in *Essays in Collective Bargaining and Industrial Democracy* (1983), at p. 36.

[124] It may be necessary in some circumstances for a government employer to maintain absolute control over aspects of employment through exclusion of certain subjects from arbitration. The presumption, however, must be against such exclusion to ensure the effectiveness of an arbitration scheme as a substitute for freedom to strike is not compromised. In the present case, the government has not satisfied the onus upon it to demonstrate such necessity.

(iii) The Absence of a Right to go to Arbitration

[125] None of the arbitration schemes in the Acts in question in this Reference provides a right to refer a dispute to arbitration. Rather, a discretionary power is placed in a Minister or an administrative board to establish an arbitration board if deemed appropriate: see above, s. 50 of the *Public Service Act*, s. 117.3 of the *Labour Relations Act*, and s. 10 of the *Police Officers Act*. Under s. 50 of the *Public Service Act* the Public Service Employee Relations Board can direct the parties to continue collective bargaining or appoint a mediator instead of establishing an arbitration board. Under s. 117.3 of the *Labour Relations Act* and s. 10 of the *Police Officers Act* the Minister can direct the parties to continue collective bargaining and can prescribe the procedures or conditions under which it is to take place.

[126] The respondent makes no submissions in respect of these provisions. In the absence of argument or evidence demonstrative of why such government involvement is necessary in the arbitration process, I believe the legal capacity of a Minister or administrative board to determine when and under what circumstances a dispute is to reach arbitration compromises the fairness and effectiveness of compulsory arbitration as a substitute for the freedom to strike. In effect, under the

Labour Relations Act and *Police Officers Act* the employer—i.e., the executive branch of government—has absolute authority to determine at what point a dispute should go to arbitration. Such authority considerably undermines the balance of power between employer and employee which the arbitration scheme is designed to promote. Under previous legislation either party had an absolute right to remit the matter to an arbitra-tion board. In the present legislation they do not, and counsel for the respondent has not provided any reasons for this alteration. The discretionary power of a Minister or administrative board to determine whether or not a dispute goes to arbitration is, in my view, an unjustified compromise of the effectiveness of the arbitration procedure in promoting equality of bargaining power between the parties. . . .

Health Services and Support—Facilities Subsector Bargaining Assn. v. British Columbia, 2007

Health Services and Support—Facilities Subsector Bargaining Assn. v. British Columbia is the most explicit reversal of an earlier Supreme Court *Charter* ruling to date. The question for the Court was whether freedom of association in the *Charter* protects collective bargaining for unions. At issue was controversial legislation that granted health care employers absolute power to contract out of collective agreements, and to do so without consultation or giving notice as previously required. The legislation was motivated by governmental concerns about the increasing costs of the public health care system, which were said to have increased in the period from 1991 to 2001 at a rate three times that of the provincial economy. The B.C. government defended this legislation as necessary "to respond to growing demands on services, to reduce structural barriers to patient care, and to improve planning and accountability, so as to achieve long term sustainability."

In its first discussion on whether the *Charter* protects collective bargaining, the Supreme Court decisively rejected this possibility. This occurred in a 1987 ruling[1] in which the majority interpreted freedom of association narrowly, as merely a right to create associations without protection for the activities of the association. It also rejected the idea that freedom of association should be interpreted with consideration for the activities of labour unions, indicating that this right should not be interpreted any differently for organized labour than for any other organization of a political, religious, or social nature. An interesting part of the explanation for the Court's earlier refusal to recognize *Charter* protection for collective bargaining was concern about interfering with legislative responsibilities, particularly on matters for which the Court has no special expertise. In an opinion concurring with the majority ruling, Justice McIntyre explained that if the Court were to recognize a right to collective bargaining, it would then be required to assess any governmental decision to prohibit strikes or lockouts that involve issues that are not "amenable to principled resolution" and therefore permit "no clearly correct answers." He suggested the Court could and should avoid this problem. It could do so, he indicated, by refusing to recognize that a *Charter* right exists, which would ensure that issues of a nature "peculiarly apposite to the function of the Legislature" remain the responsibility of the legislature.[2]

This suggestion that the Court constrain its interpretation of rights to avoid having to render decisions for which no obviously correct answer exists has not generally characterized the Court's approach to the *Charter*. In fact, in *Health Services and Support*, the Court explicitly rejected the idea that it is appropriate to exercise deference to the legislature simply because the subject matter involves the complex issue of regulating labour relations. In this ruling, decided 20 years after the *Alberta Reference*, the Court suggested that its earlier denial

---

1 *Reference re Public Service Employee Relations Act (Alta.)*, [1987] 1 S.C.R. 313 ("*Alberta Labour Reference*").

2 *Ibid.* at para. 184.

of *Charter* protection for collective bargaining can "no longer stand" and that the Court's earlier handling of the relevant issues does not "withstand principled scrutiny." In explaining this clear reversal, the Court explicitly repudiated the following assumptions on which this earlier denial that the *Charter* protects collective bargaining was based: that the rights to strike and to bargain collectively are "modern rights" created by legislation, not "fundamental freedoms"; that recognition of a right to collective bargaining is inconsistent with the principle of judicial restraint in interfering with government regulation of labour relations; and that freedom of association protects only those activities performable by an individual.

Despite the Court's ruling that freedom of association protects collective bargaining, the Court made it clear in *Health Services and Support* that protection for collective bargaining is a limited right. It is a right to a process, not a guarantee of a certain substantive or economic outcome; it is a right to a general process of collective bargaining, not to a particular model of labour relations, nor to a specific bargaining method; and, more important, *Charter* protection is relevant only when interference with this right is so substantial that it undermines the very process that enables workers to pursue these objectives by engaging in meaningful negotiations with the employer.

The ruling came as a considerable surprise to many critics of the *Charter*, particularly those on the left who believed that jurisprudence on the *Charter* had become hostile to the interests of organized labour and who were doubtful that this would soon change. Nevertheless, six years before the *Health Services* decision, the Court had hinted that it was prepared to reassess its narrow interpretation of freedom of association. This occurred in the 2001 ruling, *Dunmore v. Ontario (Attorney General),*[3] where the Court rejected the earlier view that freedom of association applies only to activities capable of performance by individuals, and left room to recognize a right to collective bargaining in future cases. At issue in *Dunmore* was the exclusion of agricultural workers from Ontario's labour relations legislation, which the Court ruled was unconstitutional.

What remains unclear is whether the Court will also rule that the *Charter* protects the right of organized labour groups to strike and if so, what grounds might be considered a justification for limiting this right. ⌐

Discussion Questions

1. Is it appropriate for the Supreme Court to repudiate the basic assumptions of an earlier ruling on the interpretation and scope of a *Charter* right?
2. If the interpretation of rights is so fluid, what does this suggest for the philosophical question about whether judicial interpretations should be treated as the final word on the meaning of *Charter* rights?
3. Should economic concerns be considered a valid reason for a government to restrict a *Charter* right?

---

3   [2001] 3 S.C.R. 1016, 2001 SCC 94.

HEALTH SERVICES AND SUPPORT— FACILITIES SUBSECTOR BARGAINING ASSN. v. BRITISH COLUMBIA
2007 SCC 27

Hearing: February 8, 2006; Judgment: June 8, 2007.

Present: McLachlin C.J. and Bastarache, Binnie, LeBel, Deschamps, Fish, and Abella JJ.

Interveners: Attorney General of Ontario, Attorney General of New Brunswick, Attorney General of Alberta, Confederation of National Trade Unions, Canadian Labour Congress, Michael J. Fraser on his own behalf and on behalf of United Food and Commercial Workers Union Canada, and British Columbia Teachers' Federation.

The judgment of McLachlin C.J. and Bastarache, Binnie, LeBel, Fish, and Abella JJ. was delivered by

THE CHIEF JUSTICE AND LEBEL J.:

I. Introduction
A. Overview

[1] The appellants challenge the constitutional validity of Part 2 of the *Health and Social Services Delivery Improvement Act*, S.B.C. 2002, c. 2 ("Act"), as violative of the *Canadian Charter of Rights and Freedoms* guarantees of freedom of association (s. 2(*d*)) and equality (s. 15).

[2] We conclude that the s. 2(*d*) guarantee of freedom of association protects the capacity of members of labour unions to engage in collective bargaining on workplace issues. While some of the impugned provisions of the Act comply with this guarantee, ss. 6(2), 6(4) and 9 breach it and have not been shown to be justified under s. 1 of the *Charter*. We further conclude that the Act does not violate the right to equal treatment under s. 15 of the *Charter*....

B. The Background

[3] This case requires the Court to balance the need for governments to deliver essential social services effectively with the need to recognize the *Charter* rights of employees affected by such legislation, who were working for health and social service employers. The respondent government characterizes the impugned legislation as a crucial element of its response to a pressing health care crisis, necessary and important to the well-being of British Columbians. The appellants, unions and individual workers representing some of the subsectors of the health care sector affected by the legislation, by contrast, see the Act as an affront to the fundamental rights of employees and union members under the *Charter*, which they under-stand as including a collective right to pursue fundamental workplace goals through collective bargaining in respect of terms of employment.

C. The Act

[4] The Act was adopted as a response to challenges facing British Columbia's health care system. Demand for health care and the cost of providing needed health care services had been increasing significantly for years. For example, in the period from 1991 to 2001, the growth rate of health care costs in British Columbia was three times that of the provincial economy. As a result, the government of British Columbia found itself struggling to provide health care services to its citizens. The government characterized the state of affairs in 2001 as a "crisis of sustainability" in the health care system....

[5] The goals of the Act were to reduce costs and to facilitate the efficient management of the workforce in the health care sector. Not wishing to decrease employees' wages, the government attempted to achieve these goals in more sustainable ways. According to the government, the Act was designed in particular to focus on permitting health care employers to reorganize the administration of the labour force and on making operational changes to enhance management's ability to restructure service delivery (see British Columbia, *Debates of the Legislative Assembly*, 2nd Sess., 37th Parl., vol. 2, No. 28, January 25, 2002, at p. 865).

[6] The Act was quickly passed. It came into force three days after receiving a first reading as Bill 29 before the British Columbia legislature.

[7] There was no meaningful consultation with unions before it became law. The government was aware that some of the areas affected by Bill 29 were of great concern to the unions and had expressed a willingness to consult. However, in the end, consultation was minimal....

[8] In British Columbia, the collective bargaining structure in the health services is sectoral. Thus, the Act affects labour relations between "health sector employers" and their unionized employees. A "health sector employer," as defined under the Act, is a member of the Health Employers Association of British Columbia ("HEABC") established under s. 6 of the *Public Sector Employers Act*, R.S.B.C. 1996, c. 384, and whose employees are unionized (s. 3 of the Act). The HEABC is an employers' association accredited to act as the representative of its members in the bargaining process with health sector employees. Members of the HEABC are hospitals and other employers designated by regulation, including employers in the health sector receiving a substantial amount of funding from the Ministry of Health (A.R., at p. 212). Therefore, while the Act applies mainly to public sector employers, it also applies to some private sector employers.

[9] The appellants in the present case are unions and members of the unions representing the nurses, facilities or community subsectors—groups affected by the legislation. Although they were affected by the legislation, other groups like residents and paramedical professionals did not join the litigation.

[10] Only Part 2 of the Act is at issue in the current appeal (see Appendix). It introduced changes to transfers and multi-worksite assignment rights (ss. 4 and 5), contracting out (s. 6), the status of employees under contracting-out arrangements (s. 6), job security programs (ss. 7 and 8), and layoffs and bumping rights (s. 9).

[11] Part 2 gave health care employers greater flexibility to organize their relations with their employees as they see fit, and in some cases, to do so in ways that would not have been permissible under existing collective agreements and without adhering to requirements of consultation and notice that would otherwise obtain. It invalidated important provisions of collective agreements then in force, and effectively precluded meaningful collective bargaining on a number of specific issues. Section 10 invalidated any part of a collective agreement, past or future, which was inconsistent with Part 2, and any collective agreement purporting to modify these restrictions. In the words of the Act, s. 10: "Part [2] prevails over collective agreements." It is not open to the employees (or the employer) to contract out of Part 2 or to rely on a collective agreement inconsistent with Part 2.

[12] ... [W]hile some of the changes were relatively innocuous administrative changes, others had profound effects on the employees and their ability to negotiate workplace matters of great concern to them....

III. Analysis

A. Section 2(d) of the Charter

[19] At issue in the present appeal is whether the guarantee of freedom of association in s. 2(d) of the *Charter* protects collective bargaining rights. We conclude that s. 2(d) of the *Charter* protects the capacity of members of labour unions to engage, in association, in collective bargaining on fundamental workplace issues. This protection does not cover all aspects of "collective bargaining," as that term is understood in the statutory labour relations regimes that are in place across the country. Nor does it ensure a particular outcome in a labour dispute, or guarantee access to any particular statutory regime. What is protected is simply the right of employees to associate in a process of collective action to achieve workplace goals. If the government substantially interferes with that right, it violates s. 2(d) of the *Charter*: *Dunmore*. We note that the present case does not concern the right to strike, which was considered in earlier litigation on the scope of the guarantee of freedom of association.

[20] Our conclusion that s. 2(d) of the *Charter* protects a process of collective bargaining rests on four propositions. First, a review of the s. 2(d) jurisprudence of this Court reveals that the reasons evoked in the past for holding that the guarantee of freedom of association does not extend to collective bargaining can no longer stand. Second, an interpretation of s. 2(d) that precludes collective bargaining from its ambit is inconsistent with Canada's historic recognition of the importance of collective bargaining to freedom of association. Third, collective bargaining is an integral component of freedom of association in international law, which may inform the interpretation of *Charter* guarantees. Finally, interpreting s. 2(d) as including a right to collective bargaining is consistent with, and indeed, promotes, other *Charter* rights, freedoms and values....

[21] ... [I]n applying our analysis to the facts of the case, we find provisions of the Act to be in violation of s. 2(d) and not justified by s. 1 of the *Charter*.

(1) Reasons for Excluding Collective Bargaining from Section 2(d) in the Past Require Reconsideration

[22] In earlier decisions, the majority view in the Supreme Court of Canada was that the guarantee of freedom of association did not extend to collective bargaining. *Dunmore* opened the door to reconsideration of that view. We conclude that the grounds advanced in the earlier decisions for the exclusion of collective bargaining from the *Charter*'s protection of freedom of association do not withstand principled scrutiny and should be rejected.

[23] The first cases dealing squarely with the issue of whether collective bargaining is protected under s. 2(d) of the *Charter* were a group of three concurrently released appeals known as the labour "trilogy": *Reference re Public Service Employee Relations Act (Alta.)*, [1987] 1 S.C.R. 313 ("*Alberta Reference*"), *PSAC v. Canada*, [1987] 1 S.C.R. 424, and *RWDSU v. Saskatchewan*, [1987] 1 S.C.R. 460. The main reasons were delivered in the *Alberta Reference*, a case involving compulsory arbitration to resolve impasses in collective bargaining and a prohibition on strikes. Of the six justices participating in the case, three held that collective bargaining was not protected by s. 2(d); four held that strike activity was not protected. The next case to deal with the issue was *Professional Institute of the Public Service of Canada v. Northwest Territories (Commissioner)*, [1990] 2 S.C.R. 367 ("*PIPSC*"), in which the government of the Northwest Territories refused to enact legislation required in order for the PIPSC union to bargain collectively on behalf of nurses. A majority of four held that collective bargaining was not protected by s. 2(d).

[24] In these cases, different members of the majorities put forth five main reasons in support of the contention that collective bargaining does not fall within s. 2(d)'s protection.

[25] The first suggested reason was that the rights to strike and to bargain collectively are "modern rights" created by legislation, not "fundamental freedoms" (*Alberta Reference,* per Le Dain J., writing on behalf of himself, Beetz and La Forest JJ., at p. 391). The difficulty with this argument is that it fails to recognize the history of labour relations in Canada. . . . [T]he fundamental importance of collective bargaining to labour relations was the very reason for its incorporation into statute. Legislatures throughout Canada have historically viewed collective bargaining rights as sufficiently important to immunize them from potential interference. The statutes they passed did not create the right to bargain collectively. Rather, they afforded it protection. There is nothing in the statutory entrenchment of collective bargaining that detracts from its fundamental nature.

[26] The second suggested reason was that recognition of a right to collective bargaining would go against the principle of judicial restraint in interfering with government regulation of labour relations (*Alberta Reference,* at p. 391). The regulation of labour relations, it is suggested, involves policy decisions best left to government. This argument again fails to recognize the fact that worker organizations historically had the right to bargain collectively outside statutory regimes and takes an overbroad view of judicial deference. It may well be appropriate for judges to defer to legislatures on policy matters expressed in particular laws. But to declare a judicial "no go" zone for an entire right on the ground that it may involve the courts in policy matters is to push deference too far. Policy itself should reflect *Charter* rights and values.

[27] The third suggested reason for excluding collective bargaining from s. 2(*d*) of the *Charter* rested on the view that freedom of association protects only those activities performable by an individual (see *PIPSC,* per L'Heureux-Dubé and Sopinka JJ.). . . .

[28] This narrow focus on individual activities has been overtaken by *Dunmore,* where this Court rejected the notion that freedom of association applies only to activities capable of performance by individuals. . . .

[29] The fourth reason advanced for excluding collective bargaining rights from s. 2(*d*) was the suggestion of L'Heureux-Dubé J. that s. 2(*d*) was not intended to protect the "objects" or goals of an association (see *PIPSC,* at pp. 391-93). This argument overlooks the fact that it will always be possible to characterize the pursuit of a particular activity in concert with others as the "object" of that association. Recasting collective bargaining as an "object" begs the question of whether or not the activity is worthy of constitutional protection. L'Heureux-Dubé J.'s underlying concern—that the *Charter* not be used to protect the substantive outcomes of any and all associations—is a valid one. However, "collective bargaining" as a procedure has always been distinguishable from its final out-

comes (e.g., the results of the bargaining process, which may be reflected in a collective agreement). . . . In our view, it is entirely possible to protect the "procedure" known as collective bargaining without mandating constitutional protection for the fruits of that bargaining process. Thus, the characterization of collective bargaining as an association's "object" does not provide a principled reason to deny it constitutional protection.

[30] An overarching concern is that the majority judgments in the *Alberta Reference* and *PIPSC* adopted a decontextualized approach to defining the scope of freedom of association, in contrast to the purposive approach taken to other *Charter* guarantees. The result was to forestall inquiry into the purpose of that *Charter* guarantee. The generic approach of the earlier decisions to s. 2(*d*) ignored differences between organizations. Whatever the organization—be it trade union or book club—its freedoms were treated as identical. The unfortunate effect was to overlook the importance of collective bargaining—both historically and currently—to the exercise of freedom of association in labour relations.

[31] We conclude that the reasons provided by the majorities in the *Alberta Reference* and *PIPSC* should not bar reconsideration of the question of whether s. 2(*d*) applies to collective bargaining. This is manifestly the case since this Court's decision in *Dunmore,* which struck down a statute that effectively prohibited farm workers from engaging in collective bargaining by denying them access to the Province's labour relations regime, as violating of s. 2(*d*) of the *Charter. Dunmore* clarified three developing aspects of the law: what constitutes interference with the "associational aspect" of an activity; the need for a contextual approach to freedom of association; and the recognition that s. 2(*d*) can impose positive obligations on government. . . .

[36] In summary, a review of the jurisprudence leads to the conclusion that the holdings in the *Alberta Reference* and *PIPSC* excluding collective bargaining from the scope of s. 2(*d*) can no longer stand. None of the reasons provided by the majorities in those cases survive scrutiny, and the rationale for excluding inherently collective activities from s. 2(*d*)'s protection has been overtaken by *Dunmore.*

[37] Our rejection of the arguments previously used to exclude collective bargaining from s. 2(*d*) leads us to a reassessment of that issue, discussed below.

(2) Collective Bargaining Falls Within the Scope of Section 2(d) of the Charter

[38] The question is whether the s. 2(*d*) guarantee of freedom of association extends to the right of employees to join together in a union to negotiate with employers on workplace issues or terms of employment—a process described broadly as collective bargaining.

[39] The general purpose of the *Charter* guarantees and the language of s. 2(*d*) are consistent with at least a measure of protection for collective bargaining. The language of s. 2(*d*) is cast in broad terms and devoid of limitations. However, this is not conclusive. To answer the question before us, we must consider the history of collective bargaining in Canada, collective bargaining in relation to freedom of association in the larger international context, and whether *Charter* values favour an interpretation of s. 2(*d*) that protects a process of collective bargaining. ...

[41] The respondent argues that the right to collective bargaining is of recent origin and is merely a creature of statute. This assertion may be true if collective bargaining is equated solely to the framework of rights of representation and collective bargaining now recognized under federal and provincial labour codes. However, the origin of a right to collective bargaining in the sense given to it in the present case (i.e., a procedural right to bargain collectively on conditions of employment), precedes the adoption of the present system of labour relations in the 1940s. The history of collective bargaining in Canada reveals that long before the present statutory labour regimes were put in place, collective bargaining was recognized as a fundamental aspect of Canadian society. This is the context against which the scope of the s. 2(*d*) must be considered.

[42] Canadian labour history can be summarized by borrowing words from the 1968 *Report of the Task Force on Labour Relations*. As society entered into the industrialized era, "workers began to join unions and to engage in collective bargaining with their employers. Although employers resisted this development with all the resources at their command, it eventually became apparent that unions and collective bargaining were natural concomitants of a mixed enterprise economy. The state then assumed the task of establishing a framework of rights and responsibilities within which management and organized labour were to conduct their relations" (Task Force on Labour Relations, *Canadian Industrial Relations: The Report of Task Force on Labour Relations* (1968) ("Woods Report"), at p. 13).

[43] Canadian labour law traces its roots to various legal systems, most importantly to British and American law. Prior to the 1940s, British law had a significant influence on the development of our labour law. American law became an influential force when the United States passed the *Wagner Act* in 1935. ...

[44] The development of labour relations law in Canada may be divided into three major eras: repression, toleration and recognition. ...

[47] From the beginning, the law was used as a tool to limit workers' rights to unionize. ...

[51] A major shift in Canadian labour law took place in the aftermath of the Toronto Typographical Unions' strike that occurred in 1872. The strike by the Toronto typographers, inspired by the call for a nine-hour work day, led to numerous arrests and charges against the strikers for common law criminal conspiracy. At that time, Canada had not yet adopted legislation immunizing trade union members from criminal charges for conspiracy or restraint of trade. The criminal charges against the Toronto strikers raised public concern and revealed that Canada was behind the times—at least compared to Britain—on the issue of union protection and recognition.

[52] In consequence, Canada adopted its own legislation copied in part from the British *Trade Union Act* of 1871. The Canadian *Trade Unions Act* of 1872 "made it clear that no worker could be criminally prosecuted for conspiracy solely on the basis of attempting to influence the rate of wages, hours of labour, or other aspects of the work relation." ... Through this legislative action, the Canadian Parliament recognized the value for the individual of collective actions in the context of labour relations. ...

[53] By the beginning of the 1900s, the main criminal barriers to unionism in Canada had been brought down. Criminal law no longer prohibited employees from combining for the purposes of ameliorating their working conditions. ... However, courts continued to apply common law doctrines to restrain union activities. ... Moreover, nothing in the law required employers to recognize unions or to bargain collectively with them. Employers could simply ignore union demands and even refuse to hire union members. ...

[54] While employers could refuse to recognize and bargain with unions, workers had recourse to an economic weapon: the powerful tool of calling a strike to force an employer to recognize a union and bargain collectively with it. The law gave both parties the ability to use economic weapons to attain their ends. Before the adoption of the modern statutory model of labour relations, the majority of strikes were motivated by the workers' desire to have an employer recognize a union and bargain collectively with it. ...

[55] The first few decades of the 20th century saw Parliament's promotion of voluntary collective bargaining. The federal Parliament enacted a series of statutes to promote collective bargaining by conferring on the labour minister the power to impose conciliation on the parties in an attempt to bring them to compromise. ... This model failed, mainly because employers had no real incentive to participate in the process. ... In search of a better model, Canadian governments looked at what was happening in the United States.

[56] ... In 1914, the American Congress immunized unions from the application of antitrust law and adopted a non-interventionist attitude in order to let workers and

employers use their respective economic powers to manage their own labour relations. However, the Depression and resulting industrial tension of the 1930s rendered the old laissez-faire model inappropriate. The result was the *Wagner Act*, which explicitly recognized the right of employees to belong to a trade union of their choice, free of employer coercion or interference, and imposed a duty upon employers to bargain in good faith with their employees' unions....

[58] By the end of the 1930s, most Canadian provinces had passed legislation incorporating the main objectives of the *Wagner Act*.... However, it is Order in Council P.C. 1003, a regulation adopted by the federal government to rule labour relations in time of war, that firmly implemented the principles of the *Wagner Act* in Canada and triggered further development of provincial labour laws....

[60] P.C. 1003 was a compromise adopted to promote peaceful labour relations. On the one hand, it granted major protections to workers to organize without fear of unfair interference from the employers and guaranteed workers the right to bargain collectively in good faith with their employers without having to rely on strikes and other economic weapons. On the other hand, it provided employers with a measure of stability in their relations with their organized workers, without the spectre of intensive state intervention in the economy.... These elements of P.C. 1003 continue to guide our system of labour relations to this day....

[63] In summary, workers in Canada began forming collectives to bargain over working conditions with their employers as early as the 18th century. However, the common law cast a shadow over the rights of workers to act collectively. When Parliament first began recognizing workers' rights, trade unions had no express statutory right to negotiate collectively with employers. Employers could simply ignore them. However, workers used the powerful economic weapon of strikes to gradually force employers to recognize unions and to bargain collectively with them. By adopting the *Wagner Act* model, governments across Canada recognized the fundamental need for workers to participate in the regulation of their work environment. This legislation confirmed what the labour movement had been fighting for over centuries and what it had access to in the laissez-faire era through the use of strikes—the right to collective bargaining with employers....

[64] At the time the *Charter* was enacted in 1982, collective bargaining had a long tradition in Canada and was recognized as part of freedom of association in the labour context....

[66] Collective bargaining, despite early discouragement from the common law, has long been recognized in Canada. Indeed, historically, it emerges as the most significant collective activity through which freedom of association is expressed in the labour context. In our opinion, the concept of freedom of association under s. 2(*d*) of the *Charter* includes this notion of a procedural right to collective bargaining.

[67] This established Canadian right to collective bargaining was recognized in the Parliamentary hearings that took place before the adoption of the *Charter*. The acting Minister of Justice, Mr. Robert Kaplan, explained why he did not find necessary a proposed amendment to have the freedom to organize and bargain collectively expressly included under s. 2(*d*). These rights, he stated, were already implicitly recognized in the words "freedom of association."...

[68] The protection enshrined in s. 2(*d*) of the *Charter* may properly be seen as the culmination of a historical movement towards the recognition of a procedural right to collective bargaining....

[The Court discussed Canada's adherence to international documents recognizing a right to collective bargaining, which it indicated supports the recognition of this right being included in section 2(*d*) of the *Charter*.]

(c) Charter Values Support Protecting a Process of Collective Bargaining Under Section 2(d)

[80] Protection for a process of collective bargaining within s. 2(*d*) is consistent with the *Charter*'s underlying values. The *Charter*, including s. 2(*d*) itself, should be interpreted in a way that maintains its underlying values and its internal coherence....

[81] Human dignity, equality, liberty, respect for the autonomy of the person and the enhancement of democracy are among the values that underlie the *Charter*: *R. v. Zundel*, [1992] 2 S.C.R. 731; *Corbiere v. Canada (Minister of Indian and Northern Affairs)*, [1999] 2 S.C.R. 203, at para. 100; *R. v. Oakes*, [1986] 1 S.C.R. 103. All of these values are complemented and indeed, promoted, by the protection of collective bargaining in s. 2(*d*) of the *Charter*.

[82] The right to bargain collectively with an employer enhances the human dignity, liberty and autonomy of workers by giving them the opportunity to influence the establishment of workplace rules and thereby gain some control over a major aspect of their lives, namely their work....

[84] Collective bargaining also enhances the *Charter* value of equality. One of the fundamental achievements of collective bargaining is to palliate the historical inequality between employers and employees....

[85] Finally, a constitutional right to collective bargaining is supported by the *Charter* value of enhancing democracy. Collective bargaining permits workers to achieve a form of workplace democracy and to ensure the rule of law in the workplace. Workers gain a voice to influence the establishment of rules that control a major aspect of their lives....

[86] We conclude that the protection of collective bargaining under s. 2(*d*) of the *Charter* is consistent with and supportive of the values underlying the *Charter* and the purposes of the *Charter* as a whole. Recognizing that workers have the right to bargain collectively as part of their freedom to associate reaffirms the values of dignity, personal autonomy, equality and democracy that are inherent in the *Charter*.

(3) Section 2(d) of the Charter and the Right to Collective Bargaining

[87] The preceding discussion leads to the conclusion that s. 2(*d*) should be understood as protecting the right of employees to associate for the purpose of advancing workplace goals through a process of collective bargaining. The next question is what this right entails for employees, for government employers subject to the *Charter* under s. 32, and for Parliament and provincial legislatures which adopt labour laws....

[89] The scope of the right to bargain collectively ought to be defined bearing in mind the pronouncements of *Dunmore*, which stressed that s. 2(*d*) does not apply solely to individual action carried out in common, but also to associational activities themselves. The scope of the right properly reflects the history of collective bargaining and the international covenants entered into by Canada. Based on the principles developed in *Dunmore* and in this historical and international perspective, the constitutional right to collective bargaining concerns the protection of the ability of workers to engage in associational activities, and their capacity to act in common to reach shared goals related to workplace issues and terms of employment. In brief, the protected activity might be described as employees banding together to achieve particular work-related objectives. Section 2(*d*) does not guarantee the particular objectives sought through this associational activity. However, it guarantees the process through which those goals are pursued. It means that employees have the right to unite, to present demands to health sector employers collectively and to engage in discussions in an attempt to achieve workplace-related goals. Section 2(*d*) imposes corresponding duties on government employers to agree to meet and discuss with them. It also puts constraints on the exercise of legislative powers in respect of the right to collective bargaining, which we shall discuss below.

[90] Section 2(*d*) of the *Charter* does not protect all aspects of the associational activity of collective bargaining. It protects only against "substantial interference" with associational activity, in accordance with a test crafted in *Dunmore* by Bastarache J., which asked whether "excluding agricultural workers from a statutory labour relations regime, without expressly or intentionally prohibiting association, [can] constitute a substantial interference with freedom of association"

(para. 23).... It follows that the state must not substantially interfere with the ability of a union to exert meaningful influence over working conditions through a process of collective bargaining conducted in accordance with the duty to bargain in good faith. Thus the employees' right to collective bargaining imposes corresponding duties on the employer. It requires both employer and employees to meet and to bargain in good faith, in the pursuit of a common goal of peaceful and productive accommodation.

[91] The right to collective bargaining thus conceived is a limited right. First, as the right is to a process, it does not guarantee a certain substantive or economic outcome. Moreover, the right is to a general process of collective bargaining, not to a particular model of labour relations, nor to a specific bargaining method.... Finally, and most importantly, the interference, as *Dunmore* instructs, must be substantial—so substantial that it interferes not only with the attainment of the union members' objectives (which is not protected), but with the very process that enables them to pursue these objectives by engaging in meaningful negotiations with the employer.

[92] To constitute *substantial interference* with freedom of association, the intent or effect must seriously undercut or undermine the activity of workers joining together to pursue the common goals of negotiating workplace conditions and terms of employment with their employer that we call collective bargaining. Laws or actions that can be characterized as "union breaking" clearly meet this requirement. But less dramatic interference with the collective process may also suffice. In *Dunmore*, denying the union access to the labour laws of Ontario designed to support and give a voice to unions was enough. Acts of bad faith, or unilateral nullification of negotiated terms, without any process of meaningful discussion and consultation may also significantly undermine the process of collective bargaining. The inquiry in every case is contextual and fact-specific. The question in every case is whether the process of voluntary, good faith collective bargaining between employees and the employer has been, or is likely to be, significantly and adversely impacted.

[93] Generally speaking, determining whether a government measure affecting the protected process of collective bargaining amounts to substantial interference involves two inquiries. The first inquiry is into the importance of the matter affected to the process of collective bargaining, and more specifically, to the capacity of the union members to come together and pursue collective goals in concert. The second inquiry is into the manner in which the measure impacts on the collective right to good faith negotiation and consultation.

[94] Both inquiries are necessary. If the matters affected do not substantially impact on the process of collective bargaining,

the measure does not violate s. 2(*d*) and, indeed, the employer may be under no duty to discuss and consult. There will be no need to consider process issues. If, on the other hand, the changes substantially touch on collective bargaining, they will still not violate s. 2(*d*) if they preserve a process of consultation and good faith negotiation.

[95] Turning to the first inquiry, the essential question is whether the subject matter of a particular instance of collective bargaining is such that interfering with bargaining over that issue will affect the ability of unions to pursue common goals collectively.... The more important the matter, the more likely that there is substantial interference with the s. 2(*d*) right. Conversely, the less important the matter to the capacity of union members to pursue collective goals, the less likely that there is substantial interference with the s. 2(*d*) right to collective bargaining.

[96] ... Laws or state actions that prevent or deny meaningful discussion and consultation about working conditions between employees and their employer may substantially interfere with the activity of collective bargaining, as may laws that unilaterally nullify significant negotiated terms in existing collective agreements....

[97] Where it is established that the measure impacts on subject matter important to collective bargaining and the capacity of the union members to come together and pursue common goals, the need for the second inquiry arises: does the legislative measure or government conduct in issue respect the fundamental precept of collective bargaining—the duty to consult and negotiate in good faith? If it does, there will be no violation of s. 2(*d*), even if the content of the measures might be seen as being of substantial importance to collective bargaining concerns, since the process confirms the associational right of collective bargaining....

[99] Consistent with this, the *Canada Labour Code* and legislation from all provinces impose on employers and unions the right and duty to bargain in good faith.... The duty to bargain in good faith under labour codes is essentially procedural and does not dictate the content of any particular agreement achieved through collective bargaining....

[100] A basic element of the duty to bargain in good faith is the obligation to actually meet and to commit time to the process....

[101] The parties have a duty to engage in meaningful dialogue and they must be willing to exchange and explain their positions. They must make a reasonable effort to arrive at an acceptable contract....

[104] In principle, the duty to bargain in good faith does not inquire into the nature of the proposals made in the course of collective bargaining; the content is left to the bargaining forces of the parties.... However, when the examination of

the content of the bargaining shows hostility from one party toward the collective bargaining process, this will constitute a breach of the duty to bargain in good faith. In some circumstances, even though a party is participating in the bargaining, that party's proposals and positions may be "inflexible and intransigent to the point of endangering the very existence of collective bargaining" (*Royal Oak Mines*, at para. 46)....

[107] In considering whether the legislative provisions impinge on the collective right to good faith negotiations and consultation, regard must be had for the circumstances surrounding their adoption. Situations of exigency and urgency may affect the content and the modalities of the duty to bargain in good faith. Different situations may demand different processes and timelines. Moreover, failure to comply with the duty to consult and bargain in good faith should not be lightly found, and should be clearly supported on the record. Nevertheless, there subsists a requirement that the provisions of the Act preserve the process of good faith consultation fundamental to collective bargaining. That is the bottom line.

[108] Even where a s. 2(*d*) violation is established, that is not the end of the matter; limitations of s. 2(*d*) may be justified under s. 1 of the *Charter*, as reasonable limits demonstrably justified in a free and democratic society. This may permit interference with the collective bargaining process on an exceptional and typically temporary basis, in situations, for example, involving essential services, vital state administration, clear deadlocks and national crisis.

[109] In summary, s. 2(*d*) may be breached by government legislation or conduct that substantially interferes with the collective bargaining process. Substantial interference must be determined contextually, on the facts of the case, having regard to the importance of the matter affected to the collective activity, and to the manner in which the government measure is accomplished. Important changes effected through a process of good faith negotiation may not violate s. 2(*d*). Conversely, less central matters may be changed more summarily, without violating s. 2(*d*). Only where the matter is both important to the process of collective bargaining, and has been imposed in violation of the duty of good faith negotiation, will s. 2(*d*) be breached.

(4) Application of the Law to the Facts at Bar

[110] ... Ultimately, we conclude that ss. 6(2), 6(4) and 9 of the Act are unconstitutional because they infringe the right to collective bargaining protected under s. 2(*d*) and cannot be saved under s. 1. The remainder of Part 2 of the Act (consisting of ss. 3, 4, 5, 7, 8 and 10) does not violate the right to collective bargaining and withstands constitutional scrutiny under s. 2(*d*)....

(i) Does the Act Interfere with Collective Bargaining?

[113] Sections 4 to 10 of the Act have the potential to interfere with collective bargaining in two ways: first, by invalidating existing collective agreements and consequently undermining the past bargaining processes that formed the basis for these agreements; and second, by prohibiting provisions dealing with specified matters in future collective agreements and thereby undermining future collective bargaining over those matters. Future restrictions on the content of collective agreements constitute an interference with collective bargaining because there can be no real dialogue over terms and conditions that can never be enacted as part of the collective agreement.

[114] We pause to reiterate briefly that the right to bargain collectively protects not just the act of making representations, but also the right of employees to have their views heard in the context of a meaningful process of consultation and discussion. This rebuts arguments made by the respondent that the Act does not interfere with collective bargaining because it does not explicitly prohibit health care employees from making collective representations. While the language of the Act does not technically prohibit collective representations to an employer, the right to collective bargaining cannot be reduced to a mere right to make representations. The necessary implication of the Act is that prohibited matters cannot be adopted into a valid collective agreement, with the result that the process of collective bargaining becomes meaningless with respect to them. This constitutes interference with collective bargaining. . . .

[116] Sections 4 and 5 deal with transfer and reassignment of employees. Their effect was summarized by Garson J. at trial:

Sections 4 and 5 of [the Act] give health sector employers the right to reorganize the delivery of their services. Pursuant to these sections, employers have the right to transfer functions, services and employees to another health sector employer or within a worksite. The Regulation sets out employee transfer rights and obligations. For example employees must not be transferred outside of their geographic location without their consent. Employees who decline transfers in such circumstances are entitled to lay-off notice and the limited bumping rights available under the Act. Employees who decline transfers within their geographic region, however, will be deemed to have resigned 30 days after the refusal. [para. 38]

. . . [119] . . . [T]he effect of ss. 4 and 5, in conjunction with s. 10, is to render *future* collective bargaining over transfers and reassignments largely meaningless, since collective bargaining cannot alter the employer's right to make transfers and reassignments. Section 10 of the Act would render void any terms inconsistent with ss. 4 and 5. Because it is meaningless to bargain over an issue which cannot ever be included in a collective agreement, ss. 4 and 5, considered together with s. 10, interfere with future collective bargaining. . . .

[120] Section 6(2) gives the employer increased power to contract out non-clinical services. . . . The effect of s. 6(2), together with s. 10, is to invalidate these provisions in prior collective agreements. Further, s. 6(4), in conjunction with s. 10, invalidates any provision of a collective agreement that requires an employer to consult with a trade union prior to contracting outside the bargaining unit. For example, s. 17.12 of the Facilities Subsector Collective Agreement, which limits the ways in which the employer can contract out, is made void by ss. 6(4) and 10.

[121] The combined effect of ss. 6(2), 6(4) and 10 is to forbid the incorporation into future collective agreements of provisions protecting employees from contracting out, or the inclusion of a provision requiring the employer to consult with the union. . . . The prohibition both repudiates past collective bargaining relating to the issue of contracting out and makes future collective bargaining over this issue meaningless. It follows that ss. 6(2) and 6(4) have the effect of interfering with collective bargaining. . . .

[127] Section 9 made collective bargaining over specified aspects of layoff and bumping meaningless and also invalidated parts of collective agreements dealing with these issues, up to December 31, 2005. This constituted interference with both past and future collective bargaining, albeit an interference limited to the period between the enactment of the Act and December 31, 2005.

[128] We conclude that ss. 4, 5, 6(2), 6(4) and 9, in conjunction with s. 10, interfere with the process of collective bargaining, either by disregarding past processes of collective bargaining, by pre-emptively undermining future processes of collective bargaining, or both. This requires us to determine whether these changes substantially interfere with the associational right of the employees to engage in collective bargaining on workplace matters and terms of employment.

(ii) Was the Interference Substantial, so as to Constitute a Breach of Freedom of Association?

[129] To amount to a breach of the s. 2(*d*) freedom of association, the interference with collective bargaining must compromise the essential integrity of the process of collective bargaining protected by s. 2(*d*). Two inquiries are relevant here. First, substantial interference is more likely to be found in measures impacting matters central to the freedom of association of workers, and to the capacity of their associations (the unions) to achieve common goals by working in concert.

This suggests an inquiry into the nature of the affected right. Second, the manner in which the right is curtailed may affect its impact on the process of collective bargaining and ultimately freedom of association. To this end, we must inquire into the process by which the changes were made and how they impact on the voluntary good faith underpinning of collective bargaining. Even where a matter is of central importance to the associational right, if the change has been made through a process of good faith consultation it is unlikely to have adversely affected the employees' right to collective bargaining. Both inquiries, as discussed earlier, are essential.

1. The Importance of the Provisions

[130] The provisions dealing with contracting out (ss. 6(2) and 6(4)), layoffs (ss. 9(a), 9(b) and 9(c)) and bumping (s. 9(d)) deal with matters central to the freedom of association. Restrictions in collective agreements limiting the employer's discretion to lay off employees affect the employees' capacity to retain secure employment, one of the most essential protections provided to workers by their union. Similarly, limits in collective agreements on the management rights of employers to contract out allow workers to gain employment security. Finally, bumping rights are an integral part of the seniority system usually established under collective agreements, which is a protection of significant importance to the union.... Viewing the Act's interference with these essential rights in the context of the case as a whole, we conclude that its interference with collective bargaining over matters pertaining to contracting out, layoff conditions and bumping constitutes substantial interference with the s. 2(d) right of freedom of association.

[131] The same cannot be said of the transfers and reassignments covered under ss. 4 and 5 of the Act. These provisions, as discussed above, are concerned with relatively minor modifications to in-place schemes for transferring and reassigning employees. Significant protections remained in place. It is true that the Act took these issues off the collective bargaining table for the future. However, on balance ss. 4 and 5 cannot be said to amount to a substantial interference with the union's ability to engage in collective bargaining so as to attract the protection under s. 2(d) of the *Charter*.

2. The Process of Interference with Collective Bargaining Rights

[132] Having concluded that the subject matter of ss. 6(2), 6(4) and 9 of the Act is of central importance to the unions and their ability to carry on collective bargaining, we must now consider whether those provisions preserve the processes of collective bargaining. Together, these two inquiries will permit us to assess whether the law at issue here constitutes significant interference with the collective aspect of freedom of association, which *Dunmore* recognized....

[134] It is true that the government was facing a situation of exigency. It was determined to come to grips with the spiralling cost of health care in British Columbia. This determination was fuelled by the laudable desire to provide quality health services to the people of British Columbia. Concerns such as these must be taken into account in assessing whether the measures adopted disregard the fundamental s. 2(d) obligation to preserve the processes of good faith negotiation and consultation with unions.

[135] The difficulty, however, is that the measures adopted by the government constitute a virtual denial of the s. 2(d) right to a process of good faith bargaining and consultation. The absolute prohibition on contracting out in s. 6(2), as discussed, eliminates any possibility of consultation. Section 6(4) puts the nail in the coffin of consultation by making void any provisions in a collective agreement imposing a requirement to consult before contracting out. Section 9, in like fashion, effectively precludes consultation with the union prior to laying off or bumping.

[136] We conclude that ss. 6(2), 6(4) and 9 of the legislation constitute a significant interference with the right to bargain collectively and hence violate s. 2(d) of the *Charter*. The remaining issue is whether these infringements can be saved under s. 1 of the *Charter*, as limits that are reasonable and justifiable in a free and democratic society.

(b) Are the Violations of Section 2(d) Justified Under Section 1?

... [140] In this case, the infringement of the appellants' right to bargain collectively is unquestionably prescribed by law, since the interference with collective bargaining is set out in legislation. The question is whether the remaining elements of the *Oakes* test are made out, such that the law is a reasonable limit on the appellants' right to collective bargaining under s. 2(d).

[141] We find that the intrusions on collective bargaining represented by ss. 6(2), 6(4) and 9 are not minimally impairing, and therefore cannot be saved as a reasonable and justifiable limit in a free and democratic society....

[143] The government set out its objectives for enacting the Act as follows:

> The objective of the *Act* is to improve the delivery of health care services by enabling health authorities to focus resources on the delivery of clinical services, by enhancing the ability of health employers and authorities to respond quickly and effectively to changing circumstances, and by enhancing the accountability of decision-makers in public health care....

[144] These are pressing and substantial objectives. We agree with the respondent that the health care crisis in British Columbia is an important contextual factor in support of the conclusion that these objectives are pressing and substantial. . . .

[148] The second stage of the *Oakes* analysis requires the government to establish that there is a rational connection between the pressing and substantial objective and the means chosen by the government to achieve the objective. In other words, the government must establish, on the balance of probabilities, that the means adopted in the Act are rationally connected to achieving its pressing and substantial objectives. . . .

[149] . . . Although the evidence does not conclusively establish that the means adopted by the Act achieve the government's objectives, it is at least logical and reasonable to conclude so. We therefore move to the determinative inquiry of minimal impairment. . . .

[150] . . . The government need not pursue the least drastic means of achieving its objective. Rather, a law will meet the requirements of the third stage of the *Oakes* test so long as the legislation "falls within a range of reasonable alternatives" which could be used to pursue the pressing and substantial objective (*RJR-MacDonald Inc. v. Canada (Attorney General)*, [1995] 3 S.C.R. 199, at para. 160).

[151] We conclude that the requirement of minimal impairment is not made out in this case. The government provides no evidence to support a conclusion that the impairment was minimal. It contents itself with an assertion of its legislative goal—"to enhance management flexibility and accountability in order to make the health care system sustainable over the long term,"—adding that "the *Act* is a measured, reasonable, and effective response to this challenge, and . . . satisfies the minimal impairment requirement" (R.F., at para. 147). In the absence of supportive evidence, we are unable to conclude that the requirement of minimal impairment is made out in this case.

[152] The provisions at issue bear little evidence of a search for a minimally impairing solution to the problem the government sought to address.

[153] Section 6(2) forbids any provision "that in any manner restricts, limits or regulates the right of a health sector employer to contract outside of the collective agreement." It gives the employers absolute power to contract out of collective agreements. There is no need or incentive to consult with the union or the employees before sending the work they normally perform to an outside contractor. To forbid any contracting out clause completely and unconditionally strikes us as not minimally impairing. A more refined provision, for example, permitting contracting out after meaningful consultation with the union, might be envisaged.

[154] Section 6(4) makes void a provision in a collective agreement to consult before contracting out. The bite of s. 6(4) is arguably small; given the employer's absolute power to contract out under s. 6(2), there would appear to be no reason for an employer to agree to such a clause in any event. However, insofar as it hammers home the policy of no consultation under any circumstances, it can scarcely be described as suggesting a search for a solution that preserves collective bargaining rights as much as possible, given the legislature's goal.

[155] Section 9 evinces a similar disregard for the duty to consult the union, in this case before making changes to the collective agreement's layoff and bumping rules. It is true that s. 9 was temporally limited, being in force only to December 31, 2005. However, this is scant comfort to employees who may have been laid off or bumped before this date, without the benefit of a union to represent them on the issue.

[156] An examination of the record as to alternatives considered by the government reinforces the conclusion that the impairment in this case did not fall within the range of reasonable alternatives available to the government in achieving its pressing and substantial objective of improving health care delivery. The record discloses no consideration by the government of whether it could reach its goal by less intrusive measures, and virtually no consultation with unions on the matter.

[157] Legislators are not bound to consult with affected parties before passing legislation. On the other hand, it may be useful to consider, in the course of the s. 1 justification analysis, whether the government considered other options or engaged consultation with the affected parties, in choosing to adopt its preferred approach. The Court has looked at pre-legislative considerations in the past in the context of minimal impairment. This is simply evidence going to whether other options, in a range of possible options, were explored.

[158] In this case, the only evidence presented by the government, including the sealed evidence, confirmed that a range of options were on the table. One was chosen. The government presented no evidence as to why this particular solution was chosen and why there was no consultation with the unions about the range of options open to it. . . .

[160] This was an important and significant piece of labour legislation. It had the potential to affect the rights of employees dramatically and unusually. Yet it was adopted with full knowledge that the unions were strongly opposed to many of the provisions, and without consideration of alternative ways to achieve the government objective, and without explanation of the government's choices.

[161] We conclude that the government has not shown that the Act minimally impaired the employees' s. 2(*d*) right

of collective bargaining. It is unnecessary to consider the proportionality between the pressing and substantial government objectives and the means adopted by the law to achieve these objectives. We find that the offending provisions of the Act (ss. 6(2), 6(4) and 9) cannot be justified as reasonable limits under s. 1 of the *Charter* and are therefore unconstitutional.

[The majority concluded that the Act does not violate section 15 equality rights.]

The following are the reasons delivered by

DESCHAMPS J.:

[170] . . . I part company with my colleagues over their analysis relating to both the infringement of s. 2(*d*) and the justification of the infringement under s. 1 of the *Charter*.

[171] The interpretation that the Court is now giving to s. 2(*d*) of the *Charter* is a major step forward in the recognition of collective activities. However, the importance of this advance should not overshadow the justification analysis under s. 1 of the *Charter*. . . . I find that ss. 4, 5, 6(2), 6(4) and 9 of the Act infringe s. 2(*d*) of the *Charter*, but in my view only s. 6(4) of the Act is not demonstrably justified in a free and democratic society. . . .

[175] I have concerns with the majority's test for determining whether a government measure amounts to an infringement of s. 2(*d*). According to my colleagues, the test involves two inquiries, the first into the importance of the matter for the union and the employees, and the second into the impact of the measure on the collective right to good faith negotiation and consultation. . . .

[176] The majority focus on "substantial" interference with a collective bargaining process and purport to do so on the basis of this Court's decision in *Dunmore v. Ontario (Attorney General)*, [2001] 3 S.C.R. 1016, 2001 SCC 94 (majority reasons at paras. 19, 35 and 90). However, the "substantial interference" standard cannot be adopted in this case simply because it was mentioned in *Dunmore*. . . .

[177] Since the present appeal does not involve a claim of underinclusive legislation, but an obligation that the state not interfere in a collective bargaining process, I cannot agree with imposing a "substantial interference" standard.

[178] Moreover, the first inquiry of the majority's test ("the importance of the matter affected to the process of collective bargaining" (para. 93)) is focused on the substance of the workplace issue rather than on interference with the collective bargaining process, which is what the constitutionally guaranteed right protects against. Since there is no constitutional protection for the substantive outcome of a collective bargaining process, I consider that the matter affected is not the threshold issue when a claim is being evaluated under

s. 2(*d*) of the *Charter*. Rather, the primary focus of the inquiry should be whether the legislative measures infringe the ability of workers to act in common in relation to workplace issues. . . . I remain unconvinced that the importance of the workplace issue should "play a key role" in the infringement analysis.

[179] With respect to the second inquiry ("the manner in which the measure impacts on the collective right to good faith negotiation and consultation" (para. 93)), I am concerned with the way this test is restated and applied in the majority's reasons. For example, rather than focussing on the impact on the right, the majority refer to "the manner in which the government measure is accomplished" (para. 109), "the process by which the measure was implemented" (para. 112) and "the process by which the changes were made" (para. 129). With respect, these formulations imply a duty to consult that is inconsistent with the proposition that "[l]egislators are not bound to consult with affected parties before passing legislation" (para. 157), one with which I fully agree. Another concern is that the majority consider the "circumstances" surrounding the adoption of the legislative provisions, such as the spiralling health care costs faced by the government, at the stage of determining whether s. 2 (*d*) is infringed. In my view, those considerations are entirely relevant to the s. 1 justification analysis, but are irrelevant where the issue is whether freedom of association is infringed.

[180] Given these concerns, I find it more appropriate to rely on a somewhat different test than the one suggested by the majority, although the test I propose is built on the same foundation as theirs (see majority's reasons, para. 96). I am adjusting their test to take into consideration the fact that what is in issue is a positive infringement, not underinclusiveness, and that what is under scrutiny is legislation, not government action. My test can be stated as follows:

> Laws or state actions that prevent or deny meaningful discussion and consultation about significant workplace issues between employees and their employer may interfere with the activity of collective bargaining, as may laws that unilaterally nullify negotiated terms on significant workplace issues in existing collective agreements.

[181] This test still involves two inquiries. The first is into whether the process of negotiation between employers and employees or their representatives is interfered with in any way, and the second into whether the interference concerns a significant issue in the labour relations context. An approach under which interference with the process is considered first has the merit of focussing attention on the constitutionally protected right itself, rather than having the court indirectly protect the substance of clauses in collective agreements. Only

if the court determines that there has been interference with a process of negotiation should it turn to the second inquiry and consider whether the issues involved are significant, in order to ensure that the scope of s. 2(*d*) is not interpreted so as to exceed its purpose. In this way, not all workplace issues, but only significant ones, are relevant to s. 2(*d*). I agree with the majority that the "protection does not cover all aspects of 'collective bargaining,' as that term is understood in the statutory labour relations regimes that are in place across the country" (para. 19). There may be matters covered by collective agreements that do not warrant constitutional protection—it is not every workplace issue that triggers s. 2(*d*) protection, but only those of significance.

[182] Thus, legislation that alters terms of a collective agreement bearing on significant workplace issues, or that precludes negotiations on significant workplace issues that would normally be negotiable, will interfere with the collective bargaining process. Such legislative measures nullify negotiations that have already taken place or prevent future negotiations on the topics they cover.

[183] Even though I disagree with significant aspects of the majority's test for determining whether an infringement has occurred, I agree ... that certain provisions of the Act infringe s. 2(*d*) of the *Charter*. ...

C. Contextual Approach Required in the Section 1 Analysis

[190] Over the past decade, my colleague Bastarache J. has been at the forefront of articulating the basis for and operation of the contextual approach to s. 1 in a trilogy of judgments of this Court that have garnered majority support. This jurisprudence is a major contribution towards a full and proper understanding of the s. 1 analysis. Several consider-

ations are important to highlight in reviewing this case law. ...

[196] While the majority agree that a contextual approach to s. 1 is appropriate, they do not apply it in their justification analysis. In my view, the majority do not give context the importance it deserves. ...

[209] In my view, the vulnerability of health care users and their constitutionally protected rights are relevant contextual factors to be considered in determining whether the impugned legislative provisions are demonstrably justified under s. 1. ...

[251] In addressing the crisis of sustainability in health care, governments face a difficult public policy challenge with no end in sight in the immediate future. As alternatives are considered, competing rights and interests arise. Government must be accorded deference to enable them to navigate these difficult waters. At the same time, this Court must ensure that the path they take is respectful of the constitutional rights of those who are affected by it, and that any infringement of those rights is demonstrably justified.

[252] In the case at bar, the freedom of association of health care employees has been infringed in several instances, because provisions of the legislation enacted by the government interfere with their right to a process of collective bargaining with the employer. It is the collective bargaining process that is constitutionally protected, not the content of the actual provisions of the collective agreements. In my view, the government has established that four of the five infringements, namely those resulting from ss. 4, 5, 6(2) and 9 of the Act, are constitutionally justified. However, I find that s. 6(4) of the Act fails the minimal impairment and proportionate effects tests and thus is not saved under s. 1 of the *Charter*. ...

PART FOUR
Democratic Rights

11 Sauvé v. Canada (Chief Electoral Officer), 2002

S ection 3 of the *Charter* gives every Canadian citizen the right to vote. At the same time, section 1 permits such "reasonable limits" on this right as "can be demonstrably justified in a free and democratic society." A variety of historical disqualifications based on such criteria as sex, race, and wealth had already been found to be "unreasonable limits" on the franchise well before the *Charter* came into effect. Others—for example, the traditional disqualification of judges and the mentally disabled—have been abandoned since, and partly because of, the *Charter*'s advent.[1] We know that some reasonable limits remain, however, because age restrictions continue to enjoy almost universal support. Could the traditional disqualification of imprisoned criminals—another persistent holdout against the trend of franchise expansion—be similarly maintained? In *Sauvé* (2002),[2] a narrowly (and intensely) divided Court decided that it could not. The case also raised section 15 equality-rights issues,[3] but these occupied little of the Court's attention[4] and did not affect the outcome.

Several years earlier, the same litigant, Richard Sauvé, had already brought the issue to the Supreme Court. *Sauvé* (1993)[5] considered what was then a blanket prisoner disqualification, under which a petty offender who elected brief imprisonment in lieu of a fine might find himself disenfranchised on voting day while his accomplice paid the fine and voted. By the time *Sauvé* (1993) reached the Supreme Court, the law had been altered to disqualify only criminals imprisoned for terms of two years or more, but the judges preferred not to comment on this change, choosing instead to invalidate only the previous blanket disqualification. For Richard Sauvé this was a pyrrhic victory. As a convicted murderer he was imprisoned for more than two years and thus continued to be disenfranchised by the new law. Undaunted, Sauvé launched a new case.

Writing for the five-judge majority in *Sauvé* (2002), Justice McLachlin doubted that the prisoner disqualification met even the "pressing and substantial purpose" requirement of the *Oakes* test,[6] but she was likely prevented from deciding the case on this basis by the

---

1 See *Muldoon v. Canada*, [1988] 3 F.C. 628 (T.D.) and *Canadian Disability Rights Council v. Canada*, [1988] 3 F.C. 622 (T.D.).

2 *Sauvé v. Canada (Chief Electoral Officer)*, [2002] 3 S.C.R. 519.

3 This was either because prisoners deserved the status of an "analogous group" under section 15 or because the impact of the disqualification fell more heavily on Aboriginals, who are disproportionately represented in the prison population.

4 The majority, having found the disqualification unconstitutional under section 3, did not think it necessary to address section 15. In brief reasons, the minority denied that the disqualification infringed section 15.

5 *Sauvé v. Canada (Attorney General)*, [1993] 2 S.C.R. 438.

6 This is usually the easiest hurdle to clear in the *Oakes* test. See the introduction to *Oakes*, case 14.

precedent of *Sauvé* (1993). In that earlier case, the nine judges of the Supreme Court, including Justice McLachlin, unanimously invalidated the blanket disqualification in an unusually terse, one-paragraph opinion, the substance of which is contained in a single sentence:

> In our view, [the blanket disqualification] is drawn too broadly and fails to meet the proportionality test, particularly the minimal impairment component of the test, as expressed in the s. 1 jurisprudence of the Court.

In focusing entirely on the proportionality test, *Sauvé* (1993) clearly assumed that even a blanket disqualification of prisoners has the kind of compelling purpose required by the first part of the *Oakes* test. Having agreed to this in the earlier case, Justice McLachlin could not easily find that the less draconian disqualification at issue in *Sauvé* (2002) lacked a compelling purpose. However, grudgingly, she thus conceded a compelling purpose and moved on to the question of proportional means.

Writing for *Sauvé* (2002)'s four-judge minority, Justice Gonthier, who had also participated in *Sauvé* (1993), was happy to focus on proportional means. If the blanket disqualification in *Sauvé* (1993) "particularly" failed "the minimal impairment component" of the *Oakes* test, the government's task was to find more finely tuned means to its end. For Gonthier, this is precisely what the much vaunted concept of "dialogue" between courts and legislatures is all about. In his view, the appropriate legislative response in this particular dialogue was to disqualify only more serious criminals, as defined by the length of their incarceration. But what length, exactly? Just as those who agree in principle on an age-based voting restriction often disagree on what the cut-off age should be, so those who agree on a length-of-sentence criterion for prisoner disqualification can disagree on what the sentence cut-off should be. For example, while the government had chosen two years as the cut-off, the Royal Commission on Electoral Reform and Party Financing (the Lortie Commission) had previously suggested a 10-year sentence as the appropriate threshold for disqualification.[7] Gonthier was not inclined to micromanage this issue. The government's two-year threshold was good enough to meet the minimal impairment standard.

The two-year threshold wasn't good enough for Justice McLachlin. But neither would she agree to a longer sentence as more appropriate. In fact, she made it abundantly clear that no disqualification, no matter how finely tailored, would pass constitutional muster in her view. How is this possible, given that she had agreed to ground her conclusions on the issue of proportional means, as *Sauvé* (1993) requires? Had the cryptic judgment in *Sauvé* (1993) read simply that the disqualification "fails to meet the minimal impairment component" of the *Oakes* test, McLachlin would indeed have been reduced to debating the right length of sentence to use as a threshold for disqualification. But *Sauvé* (1993) speaks of the proportionality test as a whole; indeed, by "particularly" emphasizing its minimal impairment

---

7   Royal Commission on Electoral Reform and Party Financing, *Final Report* (Ottawa: Minister of Supply and Services, 1991) vol. I at 45.

component, it implicitly holds the door open to the possible involvement of the proportionality test's other components.[8]

Justice McLachlin walked through this door, especially with respect to the rational-connection component of proportionality. Rational connection requires that the challenged legislative means must actually achieve the compelling purpose to which they are directed. Only if they do, does it make sense to proceed to issues of minimal impairment. The judges unanimously agree that conclusive scientific proof is not required to establish such a rational connection between means and ends; the logic and common sense of a "reasonable person" will do. Because McLachlin's "reasonable person" could imagine no prisoner disqualification that achieves any plausible compelling purpose, none could meet the rational-connection test. Nor could there be any room for "dialogue" about "irrational" legislative means. Disagreeing with Gonthier's view that there had been appropriate dialogue about how best to achieve minimal impairment of the right to vote, McLachlin insisted that to apply the concept in this instance would debase it to a rule of "if at first you don't succeed, try, try again." It is not healthy dialogue to keep attempting what is fundamentally irrational.

Wherever McLachlin saw irrationality, Gonthier discerned plausible and defensible positions. Social contract theory, for example, which McLachlin saw as utterly hostile to a prisoner disqualification, was for Gonthier an important justification of the disqualification. In grounding the legitimacy of government on the foundational consent of its citizens (as institutionalized in democracies through public elections), contract theory establishes a "vital symbolic, theoretical and practical connection between having a voice in making the law and being obliged to obey it." Part of consenting to government, in other words, is agreeing to abide by its laws. For McLachlin, this meant that one cannot—as the government claimed to be doing—teach people to be law abiding by depriving them of the pedagogical tool best suited to teaching this lesson—the vote. In support of this position, she quoted John Stuart Mill's claim that "the possession and the exercise of political, and among others of electoral, rights, is one of the chief instruments both of moral and of intellectual training for the popular mind."[9] For Gonthier, by contrast, nothing could be more appropriate from the standpoint

---

8 Given the judicial preferences on display in *Sauvé* (2002), it is difficult to escape the conclusion that the key sentence of *Sauvé* (1993) was, in fact, the carefully crafted outcome of a strategic compromise between the contending factions. On the strategic dimensions of *Sauvé* and many other Canadian cases, see Rainer Knopff, Dennis Baker, and Sylvia LeRoy, "Courting Controversy: Strategic Judicial Decision Making" (forthcoming).

9 This quotation does not, of course, directly address the issue of prisoner voting. When he explicitly considers that question elsewhere, Mill admits that "[a]s far as the direct influence of [prisoners'] votes went, it would scarcely be worthwhile to exclude them," but that "[a]s an aid to the great object of giving a moral character to the exercise of the suffrage, it might be expedient that in the case of crimes evincing a high degree of insensibility to social obligation, the deprivation of this and other civic rights should form part of the sentence." *The Collected Works of John Stuart Mill* (Toronto: University of Toronto Press, 1977) 322n. Mill, moreover, was not a social contract theorist.

of the social contract than to temporarily deprive those who break the law of their law-making role. How else can one effectively teach the "connection between having a voice in making the law and being obliged to obey it"? To do otherwise is symbolically to demean the dignity of the vote. Just as McLachlin found support for her position in J.S. Mill, Gonthier could easily have invoked such contract theorists as Kant in support of his. "In my role as colegislator making the penal law," wrote Kant, "I cannot be the same person who, as a subject, is punished by the law; for, as a subject who is also a criminal, I cannot have a voice in legislation."[10]

This kind of vigorous point and counterpoint characterizes the extensive debate between the majority and dissenting opinions in *Sauvé* (2002); that debate repays careful investigation. ∼

Discussion Questions

1. Are all prisoner-voting disqualifications unjustified for the same reasons as previous racial and sexual disqualifications, or are some justified by relevant differences from these historical disqualifications?
2. The section 33 notwithstanding clause cannot be used to override judicial decisions based on section 3 of the *Charter*. What effect should this have on how activist or deferential judges should be in applying section 3?
3. The day the Supreme Court issued its judgment in *Sauvé* (2002) has been described as "the day the dialogue died"?[11] Do you agree?

---

10   Immanuel Kant, *The Metaphysical Elements of Justice*, Part 1 of *The Metaphysics of Morals*, trans. John Ladd (Indianapolis: Bobbs-Merrill, 1978) at 105. For a review of how the thought of many other philosophers bears on the question of prisoner voting, see Zdravko Planinc, "Should Imprisoned Criminals Have a Constitutional Right to Vote?" (1987) *Canadian Journal of Law and Society* 2.

11   Christopher Manfredi, "The Day the Dialogue Died: A Comment on Sauvé v. Canada" (2007) 45 *Osgoode Hall Law Journal* 105.

SAUVÉ v. CANADA (CHIEF ELECTORAL OFFICER)
2002 SCC 68, [2002] 3 S.C.R. 519

Hearing: December 10, 2001; Judgment: October 31, 2002.

Present: McLachlin C.J. and L'Heureux-Dubé, Gonthier, Iacobucci, Major, Bastarache, Binnie, Arbour, and LeBel JJ.

Interveners: The Attorney General for Alberta, the Attorney General of Manitoba, the Canadian Association of Elizabeth Fry Societies, the John Howard Society of Canada, the British Columbia Civil Liberties Association, the Aboriginal Legal Services of Toronto Inc., and the Canadian Bar Association.

The judgment of McLachlin C.J. and Iacobucci, Binnie, Arbour, and LeBel JJ. was delivered by

THE CHIEF JUSTICE:

[1] The right of every citizen to vote, guaranteed by s. 3 of the *Canadian Charter of Rights and Freedoms*, lies at the heart of Canadian democracy. The law at stake in this appeal denies the right to vote to a certain class of people—those serving sentences of two years or more in a correctional institution. The question is whether the government has established that this denial of the right to vote is allowed under s. 1 of the *Charter* as a "reasonable limit . . . demonstrably justified in a free and democratic society." I conclude that it is not. The right to vote, which lies at the heart of Canadian democracy, can only be trammeled for good reason. Here, the reasons offered do not suffice. . . .

[6] The respondents concede that the voting restriction at issue violates s. 3 of the *Charter*. The restriction is thus invalid unless demonstrably justified under s. 1. I shall therefore proceed directly to the s. 1 analysis. . . .

[8] My colleague Justice Gonthier . . . argues that in justifying limits on the right to vote under s. 1, we owe deference to Parliament because we are dealing with "philosophical, political and social considerations," because of the abstract and symbolic nature of the government's stated goals, and because the law at issue represents a step in a dialogue between Parliament and the courts.

[9] I must, with respect, demur. The right to vote is fundamental to our democracy and the rule of law and cannot be lightly set aside. Limits on it require not deference, but careful examination. This is not a matter of substituting the Court's philosophical preference for that of the legislature, but of ensuring that the legislature's proffered justification is supported by logic and common sense. . . .

[13] The core democratic rights of Canadians do not fall within a "range of acceptable alternatives" among which Parliament may pick and choose at its discretion. Deference may be appropriate on a decision involving competing social and political policies. It is not appropriate, however, on a decision to limit fundamental rights. This case is not merely a competition between competing social philosophies. It represents a conflict between the right of citizens to vote—one of the most fundamental rights guaranteed by the *Charter*—and Parliament's denial of that right. Public debate on an issue does not transform it into a matter of "social philosophy," shielding it from full judicial scrutiny. It is for the courts, unaffected by the shifting winds of public opinion and electoral interests, to safeguard the right to vote guaranteed by s. 3 of the *Charter*.

[14] *Charter* rights are not a matter of privilege or merit, but a function of membership in the Canadian polity that cannot lightly be cast aside. This is manifestly true of the right to vote, the cornerstone of democracy, exempt from the incursion permitted on other rights through s. 33 override.

[15] The *Charter* charges courts with upholding and maintaining an inclusive, participatory democratic framework within which citizens can explore and pursue different conceptions of the good. While a posture of judicial deference to legislative decisions about social policy may be appropriate in some cases, the legislation at issue does not fall into this category. To the contrary, it is precisely when legislative choices threaten to undermine the foundations of the participatory democracy guaranteed by the *Charter* that courts must be vigilant in fulfilling their constitutional duty to protect the integrity of this system.

[16] Nor can I concur in the argument that the philosophically-based or symbolic nature of the government's objectives in itself commands deference. . . . Parliament cannot use lofty objectives to shield legislation from *Charter* scrutiny. Section 1 requires valid objectives *and* proportionality.

[17] Finally, the fact that the challenged denial of the right to vote followed judicial rejection of an even more comprehensive denial, does not mean that the Court should defer to Parliament as part of a "dialogue." Parliament must ensure that whatever law it passes, at whatever stage of the process, conforms to the Constitution. The healthy and important promotion of a dialogue between the legislature and the courts should not be debased to a rule of "if at first you don't succeed, try, try again."

[18] While deference to the legislature is not appropriate in this case, legislative justification does not require empirical proof in a scientific sense. While some matters can be proved with empirical or mathematical precision, others, involving philosophical, political and social considerations, cannot. In this case, it is enough that the justification be convincing, in the sense that it is sufficient to satisfy the reasonable person looking at all the evidence and relevant considerations, that the state is justified in infringing the right at stake to the degree it has: see *RJR-MacDonald* [*Inc. v. The Attorney General*

of Canada, [1995] 3 S.C.R. 199], at para. 154, *per* McLachlin J.; *R. v. Butler*, [1992] 1 S.C.R. 452, at pp. 502-3, *per* Sopinka J. What is required is "rational, reasoned defensibility": *RJR-MacDonald*, at para. 127. Common sense and inferential reasoning may supplement the evidence: *R. v. Sharpe*, [2001] 1 S.C.R. 45, 2001 SCC 2, at para. 78, *per* McLachlin C.J. However, one must be wary of stereotypes cloaked as common sense, and of substituting deference for the reasoned demonstration required by s. 1.

[19] Keeping in mind these basic principles of *Charter* review, I approach the familiar stages of the *Oakes* test. I conclude that the government's stated objectives of promoting civic responsibility and respect for the law and imposing appropriate punishment, while problematically vague, are capable in principle of justifying limitations on *Charter* rights. However, the government fails to establish proportionality, principally for want of a rational connection between denying the vote to penitentiary inmates and its stated goals. . . .

[21] . . . [T]he government asserts two broad objectives as the reason for this denial of the right to vote: (1) to enhance civic responsibility and respect for the rule of law; and (2) to provide additional punishment, or "enhance the general purposes of the criminal sanction." The record leaves in doubt how much these goals actually motivated Parliament; the Parliamentary debates offer more fulmination than illumination. However, on the basis of "some glimmer of light," the trial judge at p. 878 concluded that they could be advanced as objectives of the denial. I am content to proceed on this basis. . . .

[22] . . . Vague and symbolic objectives such as these almost guarantee a positive answer to this question. Who can argue that respect for the law is not pressing? Who can argue that proper sentences are not important? Who can argue that either of these goals, taken at face value, contradict democratic principles? However, precisely because they leave so little room for argument, vague and symbolic objectives make the justification analysis more difficult. Their terms carry many meanings, yet tell us little about why the limitation on the right is necessary, and what it is expected to achieve in concrete terms. . . .

[23] . . . If Parliament can infringe a crucial right such as the right to vote simply by offering symbolic and abstract reasons, judicial review either becomes vacuously constrained or reduces to a contest of "our symbols are better than your symbols." Neither outcome is compatible with the vigorous justification analysis required by the *Charter*. . . .

[26] Quite simply, the government has failed to identify particular problems that require denying the right to vote, making it hard to say that the denial is directed at a pressing and substantial purpose. Nevertheless, despite the abstract nature of the government's objectives and the rather thin basis

upon which they rest, prudence suggests that we proceed to the proportionality analysis, rather than dismissing the government's objectives outright. . . .

[27] At this stage the government must show that the denial of the right to vote will promote the asserted objectives (the rational connection test); that the denial does not go further than reasonably necessary to achieve its objectives (the minimal impairment test); and that the overall benefits of the measure outweigh its negative impact (the proportionate effect test). . . .

[28] Will denying the right to vote to penitentiary inmates enhance respect for the law and impose legitimate punishment? The government must show that this is likely, either by evidence or in reason and logic: *RJR-MacDonald, supra*, at para. 153.

[29] The government advances three theories to demonstrate rational connection between its limitation and the objective of enhancing respect for law. First, it submits that depriving penitentiary inmates of the vote sends an "educative message" about the importance of respect for the law to inmates and to the citizenry at large. Second, it asserts that allowing penitentiary inmates to vote "demeans" the political system. Finally, it takes the position that disenfranchisement is a legitimate form of punishment, regardless of the specific nature of the offence or the circumstances of the individual offender. In my respectful view, none of these claims succeed.

[30] The first asserted connector with enhancing respect for the law is the "educative message" or "moral statement" theory. The problem here, quite simply, is that denying penitentiary inmates the right to vote is bad pedagogy. It misrepresents the nature of our rights and obligations under the law, and it communicates a message more likely to harm than to help respect for the law.

[31] Denying penitentiary inmates the right to vote misrepresents the nature of our rights and obligations under the law and consequently undermines them. In a democracy such as ours, the power of lawmakers flows from the voting citizens, and lawmakers act as the citizens' proxies. This delegation from voters to legislators gives the law its legitimacy or force. Correlatively, the obligation to obey the law flows from the fact that the law is made by and on behalf of the citizens. In sum, the legitimacy of the law and the obligation to obey the law flow directly from the right of every citizen to vote. As a practical matter, we require all within our country's boundaries to obey its laws, whether or not they vote. But this does not negate the vital symbolic, theoretical and practical connection between having a voice in making the law and being obliged to obey it. This connection, inherited from social contract theory and enshrined in the *Charter*, stands at the heart of our system of constitutional democracy.

[32] The government gets this connection exactly backwards when it attempts to argue that depriving people of a voice in government teaches them to obey the law. . . . [I]f we accept that governmental power in a democracy flows from the citizens, it is difficult to see how that power can legitimately be used to disenfranchise the very citizens from whom the government's power flows.

[33] Reflecting this truth, the history of democracy is the history of progressive enfranchisement. The universal franchise has become, at this point in time, an essential part of democracy. From the notion that only a few meritorious people could vote (expressed in terms like class, property and gender), there gradually evolved the modern precept that all citizens are entitled to vote as members of a self-governing citizenry. . . . Under s. 3 of the *Charter*, the final vestiges of the old policy of selective voting have fallen, including the exclusion of persons with a "mental disease" and federally appointed judges: see *Canadian Disability Rights Council v. Canada*, [1988] 3 F.C. 622 (T.D.); and *Muldoon v. Canada*, [1988] 3 F.C. 628 (T.D.). The disenfranchisement of inmates takes us backwards in time and retrenches our democratic entitlements. . . .

[35] More broadly, denying citizens the right to vote runs counter to our constitutional commitment to the inherent worth and dignity of every individual. As the South African Constitutional Court said in *August v. Electoral Commission*, 1999 (3) SALR 1, at para. 17, "[t]he vote of each and every citizen is a badge of dignity and of personhood. Quite literally, it says that everybody counts." . . .

[36] In recognition of the seminal importance of the right to vote in the constellation of rights, the framers of the *Charter* accorded it special protections. Unlike other rights, the right of every citizen to vote cannot be suspended under the "notwithstanding clause." . . .

[37] The government's vague appeal to "civic responsibility" is unhelpful, as is the attempt to lump inmate disenfranchisement together with legitimate voting regulations in support of the government's position. The analogy between youth voting restrictions and inmate disenfranchisement breaks down because the type of judgment Parliament is making in the two scenarios is very different. In the first case, Parliament is making a decision based on the experiential situation of all citizens when they are young. It is not saying that the excluded class is unworthy to vote, but regulating a modality of the universal franchise. In the second case, the government is making a decision that some people, whatever their abilities, are not morally worthy to vote—that they do not "deserve" to be considered members of the community and hence may be deprived of the most basic of their constitutional rights. But this is not the lawmakers' decision to make.

The *Charter* makes this decision for us by guaranteeing the right of "every citizen" to vote and by expressly placing prisoners under the protective umbrella of the *Charter* through constitutional limits on punishment. The *Charter* emphatically says that prisoners are protected citizens, and short of a constitutional amendment, lawmakers cannot change this.

[38] The theoretical and constitutional links between the right to vote and respect for the rule of law are reflected in the practical realities of the prison population and the need to bolster, rather than to undermine, the feeling of connection between prisoners and society as a whole. The government argues that disenfranchisement will "educate" and rehabilitate inmates. However, disenfranchisement is more likely to become a self-fulfilling prophecy than a spur to reintegration. Depriving at-risk individuals of their sense of collective identity and membership in the community is unlikely to instill a sense of responsibility and community identity, while the right to participate in voting helps teach democratic values and social responsibility (testimony of Professor Jackson, appellant's record at pp. 2001-2). As J. S. Mill wrote:

> To take an active interest in politics is, in modern times, the first thing which elevates the mind to large interests and contemplations; the first step out of the narrow bounds of individual and family selfishness, the first opening in the contracted round of daily occupations. . . . The possession and the exercise of political, and among others of electoral, rights, is one of the chief instruments both of moral and of intellectual training for the popular mind. . . .
>
> (J. S. Mill, "Thoughts on Parliamentary Reform" (1859), in J.M. Robson, ed., *Essays on Politics and Society*, Vol. XIX (1977), at pp. 322-23)

To deny prisoners the right to vote is to lose an important means of teaching them democratic values and social responsibility. . . .

[42] The government also argues that denying penitentiary inmates the vote will enhance respect for law because allowing people who flaunt the law to vote demeans the political system. . . . But . . . the argument that only those who respect the law should participate in the political process is a variant on the age-old unworthiness rationale for denying the vote. . . .

[43] . . . Until recently, large classes of people, prisoners among them, were excluded from the franchise [on] the assumption that they were not fit or "worthy" of voting—whether by reason of class, race, gender or conduct. . . . We should reject the retrograde notion that "worthiness" qualifications for voters may be logically viewed as enhancing the political process and respect for the rule of law. . . .

[45] This brings us to the government's final argument for rational connection—that disenfranchisement is a legitimate weapon in the state's punitive arsenal against the individual lawbreaker....

[46] The argument, stripped of rhetoric, proposes that it is open to Parliament to add a new tool to its arsenal of punitive implements—denial of constitutional rights. I find this notion problematic. I do not doubt that Parliament may limit constitutional rights in the name of punishment, provided that it can justify the limitation. But it is another thing to say that a particular class of people for a particular period of time will completely lose a particular constitutional right. This is tantamount to saying that the affected class is outside the full protection of the *Charter*. It is doubtful that such an unmodulated deprivation, particularly of a right as basic as the right to vote, is capable of justification under s. 1. Could Parliament justifiably pass a law removing the right of all penitentiary prisoners to be protected from cruel and unusual punishment? I think not. What of freedom of expression or religion? Why, one asks, is the right to vote different?

[47] The social compact requires the citizen to obey the laws created by the democratic process. But it does not follow that failure to do so nullifies the citizen's continued membership in the self-governing polity. Indeed, the remedy of imprisonment for a term rather than permanent exile implies our acceptance of continued membership in the social order. Certain rights are justifiably limited for penal reasons, including aspects of the right to liberty, security of the person, mobility, and security against search and seizure. But whether a right is justifiably limited cannot be determined by observing that an offender has, by his or her actions, withdrawn from the social compact. Indeed, the right of the state to punish and the obligation of the criminal to accept punishment is tied to society's acceptance of the criminal as a person with rights and responsibilities. Other *Charter* provisions make this clear. Thus s. 11 protects convicted offenders from unfair trials, and s. 12 from "cruel and unusual treatment or punishment."

[48] The second flaw in the argument that s. 51(*e*) furthers legitimate punishment is that it does not meet the dual requirements that punishment must not be arbitrary and must serve a valid criminal law purpose. Absence of arbitrariness requires that punishment be tailored to the acts and circumstances of the individual offender: *R. v. Smith*, [1987] 1 S.C.R. 1045, at p. 1073. In the immortal words of Gilbert and Sullivan, the punishment should fit the crime. Section 51(*e*) *qua* punishment bears little relation to the offender's particular crime. It makes no attempt to differentiate among inmates serving sentences of two years and those serving sentences of twenty. It is true that those serving shorter sentences will

be deprived of the right to vote for a shorter time. Yet the correlation of the denial with the crime remains weak. It is not only the violent felon who is told he is an unworthy outcast; a person imprisoned for a non-violent or negligent act, or an Aboriginal person suffering from social displacement receives the same message. They are not targeted, but they are caught all the same. For them the message is doubly invidious—not that they are cast out for their apparently voluntary rejection of society's norms, but that they are cast out arbitrarily, in ways that bear no necessary relation to their actual situation or attitude towards state authority.

[49] Punishment must also fulfill a legitimate penal purpose.... These include deterrence, rehabilitation, retribution, and denunciation.... Neither the record nor common sense supports the claim that disenfranchisement deters crime or rehabilitates criminals. On the contrary, as Mill recognized long ago, participation in the political process offers a valuable means of teaching democratic values and civic responsibility.

[50] This leaves retribution and denunciation. Parliament may denounce unlawful conduct. But it must do so in a way that closely reflects the moral culpability of the offender and his or her circumstances.... Denunciation as a symbolic expression of community values must be individually tailored in order to fulfill the legitimate penal purpose of condemning a *particular* offender's conduct (see *M. (C.A.)* [*R. v.*, [1996] 1 S.C.R. 500], at para. 81) and to send an appropriate "educative message" about the importance of law-abiding behavior.

[51] Section 51(*e*) imposes blanket punishment on all penitentiary inmates regardless of the particular crimes they committed, the harm they caused, or the normative character of their conduct. It is not individually tailored to the particular offender's act. It does not, in short, meet the requirements of denunciatory, retributive punishment. It follows that it is not rationally connected to the goal of imposing legitimate punishment....

[53] I conclude that the government has failed to establish a rational connection between s. 51(*e*)'s denial of the right to vote and the objectives of enhancing respect for the law and ensuring appropriate punishment.

[54] If the denial of a right is not rationally connected to the government's objectives, it makes little sense to go on to ask whether the law goes further than is necessary to achieve the objective. I simply observe that if it were established that denying the right to vote sends an educative message that society will not tolerate serious crime, the class denied the vote—all those serving sentences of two years or more—is too broad, catching many whose crimes are relatively minor and who cannot be said to have broken their ties to society. Similarly, if it were established that this denial somehow furthers legitimate

sentencing goals, it is plain that the marker of a sentence of two years or more catches many people who, on the government's own theory, should not be caught....

[57] If a connection could be shown between the denial of the right to vote and the government's objectives, the negative effects of denying citizens the right to vote would greatly outweigh the tenuous benefits that might ensue....

[60] The negative effects of s. 51(*e*) upon prisoners have a disproportionate impact on Canada's already disadvantaged Aboriginal population, whose over-representation in prisons reflects "a crisis in the Canadian criminal justice system": *R. v. Gladue*, [1999] 1 S.C.R. 688, at para. 64, *per* Cory and Iacobucci JJ. To the extent that the disproportionate number of Aboriginal people in penitentiaries reflects factors such as higher rates of poverty and institutionalized alienation from mainstream society, penitentiary imprisonment may not be a fair or appropriate marker of the degree of individual culpability....

The reasons of L'Heureux-Dubé, Gonthier, Major, and Bastarache JJ. were delivered by

GONTHIER J. (dissenting):

[68] ... The Chief Justice and I are in agreement that the right to vote is profoundly important, and ought not to be demeaned. Our differences lie principally in the fact that she subscribes to a philosophy whereby the temporary disenfranchising of criminals does injury to the rule of law, democracy and the right to vote, while I prefer deference to Parliament's reasonable view that it strengthens these same features of Canadian society.

[69] The reasons of the Chief Justice refer to the historical evolution of the franchise in Canada. This evolution has generally involved the weeding out of discriminatory exclusions. It is undeniable and, obviously, to be applauded, that, over time, Canada has been evolving towards the universalization of the franchise in such a manner. The provision in question in the case at bar, however, is strikingly and qualitatively different from these past discriminatory exclusions. It is a temporary suspension from voting based exclusively on the serious criminal *activity* of the offender. It is the length of the sentence, reflecting the nature of the offence and the criminal activity committed, that results in the temporary disenfranchisement during incarceration....

[70] ... While there is little logical correlation between maintaining a "decent and responsible citizenry" and any of the past discriminatory exclusions (such as land-ownership, religion, gender, ethnic background), there clearly is such a logical connection in the case of distinguishing persons who have committed serious criminal offences. "*Responsible* citizenship" does not relate to what gender, race, or religion a

person belongs to, but is logically related to whether or not a person engages in serious criminal activity....

[73] The reasons of the Chief Justice express the view that the temporary disenfranchisement of serious criminal offenders necessarily undermines their inherent "worth" or "dignity." I disagree. In fact, it could be said that the notion of punishment is predicated on the dignity of the individual: it recognizes serious criminals as rational, autonomous individuals who have made choices. When these citizens exercise their freedom in a criminal manner, society imposes a concomitant responsibility for that choice....

[74] If there is any negative connotation associated with this temporary disenfranchisement, it arises from the fact that a criminal act was perpetrated, an act for which the criminal offender is consequently being punished. This is not stereotyping. Criminal acts are rightly condemned by society. Serious criminals being punished and temporarily disenfranchised are not in any way of less "worth" or "dignity" because social condemnation is of the criminal acts and its purpose is not to diminish the individual prisoner as a person....

[92] ... [T]here seem generally to be two options available for dealing with the issue at hand. The first, that chosen by the Chief Justice, is to prefer an inclusive approach to democratic participation for serious criminal offenders incarcerated for two years or more. This view locates democratic participation as a central dimension of rehabilitation, insofar as the incarcerated offenders remain citizens with the fullest exercise of their democratic rights. By the same token, the unrestricted franchise enhances democratic legitimacy of government, and confirms or enhances the citizenship or standing of prisoners in society. To do otherwise, it is suggested, undermines the "dignity" or "worth" of prisoners. The alternative view, adopted by Parliament, considers that the temporary suspension of the prisoner's right to vote, in fact, enhances the general purposes of the criminal sanction, including rehabilitation. It does so by underlining the importance of civic responsibility and the rule of law. This approach sees the temporary removal of the vote as a deterrent to offending or re-offending and the return of the vote as an inducement to reject further criminal conduct. In withdrawing for a time one expression of political participation concurrently with personal freedom, the significance of both are enhanced. Rather than undermine the dignity or worth of prisoners, the removal of their vote takes seriously the notion that they are free actors and attaches consequences to actions that violate certain core values as expressed in the *Criminal Code*.

[93] Both of these approaches, however, entail accepting logically prior political or social philosophies about the nature and content of the right to vote. The former approach, that accepted by the reasons of the Chief Justice, entails accepting a

philosophy that preventing criminals from voting does damage to both society and the individual, and undermines prisoners' inherent worth and dignity. The latter approach also entails accepting a philosophy, that not permitting serious incarcerated criminals to vote is a social rejection of serious crime which reflects a moral line which safeguards the social contract and the rule of law and bolsters the importance of the nexus between individuals and the community. Both of these social or political philosophies, however, are *aimed at the same goal*: that of supporting the fundamental importance of the right to vote itself. Further, both of these social or political philosophies are supported by the practices of the various Canadian provinces, the practices of other liberal democracies, and academic writings. Finally, neither position can be proven empirically—rather, the selection of one over the other is largely a matter of philosophical preference. What is *key* to my approach is that the acceptance of one or the other of these social or political philosophies dictates much of the constitutional analysis which ensues, since the reasonableness of any limitation upon the right to vote and the appropriateness of particular penal theories and their relation to the right to vote will logically be related to whether or not the justification for that limitation is based upon an "acceptable" social or political philosophy.

[94] The reasons of the Chief Justice hold . . . that the challenge of the Government is to present a justification that is "convincing, in the sense that it is sufficient to satisfy the reasonable person looking at all the evidence and relevant considerations, that the state is justified in infringing the right at stake to the degree it has." . . .

[95] The reasons of the Chief Justice apply something seemingly more onerous than the "justification" standard referred to just above. She describes the right to vote as a "core democratic right" and suggests that its exemption from the s. 33 override somehow raises the bar for the government in attempting to justify its restriction (paras. 13 and 14). This altering of the justification standard is problematic in that it seems to be based upon the view that there is only one plausible social or political philosophy upon which to ground a justification for or against the limitation of the right. This approach, however, is incorrect on a basic reading of s. 1 of the *Charter*, which clearly does not constrain Parliament or authorize this Court to prioritize one reasonable social or political philosophy over reasonable others, but only empowers this Court to strike down those limitations which are not reasonable and which cannot be justified in a free and democratic society.

[96] . . . It does not follow from the fact that Parliament is denied the authority to remove or qualify the right to vote in its sole discretion under s. 33 that limitations on that right may not be justified under s. 1, or that a more onerous s. 1

analysis must necessarily apply . . . . It does not behoove the Court to read s. 33 into s. 3 by finding in s. 3, when divorced from s. 1, the statement of a political philosophy which pre-empts another political philosophy which is reasonable and justified under the latter section. The *Charter* was not intended to monopolize the ideological space. . . .

[100] In her reasons, the Chief Justice claims . . . that Parliament is relying on "lofty objectives," and suggests at para. 23 that the presence of "symbolic and abstract" objectives is problematic. However, the reasons of the Chief Justice have the very same objective—to protect the value of the right to vote and the rule of law—and rely on equally vague concepts. Breaking down the meaning and value of the right to vote, one is unavoidably led to abstract and symbolic concepts such as the rule of law, the legitimacy of law and government, and the meaning of democracy. The Chief Justice discusses these concepts at length, along with theories of individual motivation. For instance, relying on the philosopher J.S. Mill, she suggests at para. 38 that "[t]o deny prisoners the right to vote is to lose an important means of teaching them democratic values and social responsibility." This type of statement is as symbolic, abstract and philosophical as the government's claim that denying serious incarcerated criminals the right to vote will strengthen democratic values and social responsibility. . . .

[104] Linden J.A., in the Federal Court of Appeal below, stressed the importance of deference to Parliament. In para. 56 of his reasons, he stated:

> This case is another episode in the continuing dialogue between courts and legislatures on the issue of prisoner voting. In 1992 and 1993, two appeal courts and the Supreme Court of Canada held that a blanket disqualification of prisoners from voting, contained in earlier legislation which was challenged, violated section 3 of the Charter and could not be saved by section 1 of the Charter. Parliament responded to this judicial advice by enacting legislation aimed at accomplishing part of its objectives while complying with the Charter. That legislation, which is being challenged in this case, disqualifies from voting only prisoners who are serving sentences of two years or more. [Footnotes omitted.]

This Court has stressed the importance of "dialogue" in *Vriend v. Alberta*, [1998] 1 S.C.R. 493, at paras. 138-39 and in *Mills* [*R. v.*, [1999] 3 S.C.R. 668], at paras. 20, 57 and 125. (See also P.W. Hogg and A.A. Bushell, "The Charter Dialogue Between Courts and Legislatures" (1997), 35 *Osgoode Hall L.J.* 75.) I am of the view that since this case is about evaluating choices regarding social or political philosophies and about shaping, giving expression, and giving practical application to values, especially values that may lie outside the *Charter* but are of fundamental importance to Canadians, "dialogue" is of particular importance. In my view, especially in the context of the case at bar, the heart of the dialogue metaphor is that neither the courts nor Parliament hold a monopoly on the determination of values. Importantly, the dialogue metaphor *does not signal a lowering of the s. 1 justification standard.* It simply suggests that when, after a full and rigorous s. 1 analysis, Parliament has satisfied the court that it has established a reasonable limit to a right that is demonstrably justified in a free and democratic society, the dialogue ends; the court lets Parliament have the last word and does not substitute Parliament's reasonable choices with its own. . . .

[109] What social or political philosophy has motivated Parliament to insist on the temporary disenfranchisement of prisoners? Is it reasonable and rational? I suggest that, in enacting s. 51(*e*) of the Act and in providing a justification of that provision before the courts, Parliament has indicated that it has drawn a line. This line reflects a moral statement about serious crime, and about its significance to and within the community. The core of this moral statement is the denunciation of serious crime, serious antisocial acts. Parliament has indicated that criminal conduct of such severity that it warrants imprisonment for a sentence of two years or more also carries with it the disenfranchisement of the offender for the duration of his or her incarceration. . . .

[115] The denunciation of crime and its effects on society is often explained by reference to the notion of the social contract. The social contract is the theoretical basis upon which the exercise of rights and participation in the democratic process rests. In my view, the social contract necessarily relies upon the acceptance of the rule of law and civic responsibility and on society's need to promote the same. The preamble to the *Charter* establishes that ". . . Canada is founded upon principles that recognize the supremacy of God and the rule of law. . . ." In *Reference re Manitoba Language Rights*, [1985] 1 S.C.R. 721, at p. 750, this Court cited with approval a passage from *The Authority of Law* (1979) by Professor Raz, wherein he states that " 'The rule of law' means literally what it says. . . . It has two aspects: (1) that people should be ruled by the law and obey it, and (2) that the law should be such that people will be able to be guided by it." The important point arising from that passage is the corollary that promoting law-abiding behaviour can be thought to be a dimension of the rule of law as well. Further, the rule of law, as was said in the *Reference re Secession of Quebec*, [1998] 2 S.C.R. 217, at p. 257, "vouchsafes to the citizens and residents of the country a stable, predictable and ordered society in which to conduct their affairs." Given its fundamental importance in our society, it is not surprising that Parliament occasionally insists to take some

action to promote it, to safeguard it. As was stated by Wilson J. in *Operation Dismantle v. The Queen*, [1985] 1 S.C.R. 441, at p. 489: "There is no liberty without law and there is no law without some restriction of liberty: see Dworkin, *Taking Rights Seriously* (1977), p. 267."

[116] Permitting the exercise of the franchise by offenders incarcerated for serious offences undermines the rule of law and civic responsibility because such persons have demonstrated a great disrespect for the community in their committing serious crimes: such persons have attacked the stability and order within our community. Society therefore may choose to curtail temporarily the availability of the vote to serious criminals both to punish those criminals and to insist that civic responsibility and respect for the rule of law, as goals worthy of pursuit, are prerequisites to democratic participation. I say "goals worthy of pursuit" because it is clear that not all those who are otherwise eligible to vote are guaranteed to exercise civic responsibility, since, for example, there may be serious criminal offenders who may have avoided being apprehended and therefore still vote. This does not, however, detract from the laudability of the goal.

[117] Related to the notion of the social contract is the importance of reinforcing the significance of the relationship between individuals and their community when it comes to voting. This special relationship is inherent in the fact that it is only "citizens" who are guaranteed the right to vote within s. 3 of the *Charter*. This limitation of the scope of s. 3 of the *Charter* stands in stark contrast to the protections offered by the fundamental freedoms, legal rights, and equality rights in the *Charter*, which are available to "everyone" or to "every individual." I am of the view that this limitation reflects the special relationship, characterized by entitlements and responsibilities, between citizens and their community. It is this special relationship and its responsibilities which serious criminal offenders have assaulted. . . .

[120] From the perspective of the person whose criminal activity has resulted in their temporary disenfranchisement, their benefiting from society brought with it the responsibility to be subjected to the sanctions which the state decides will be attached to serious criminal activity such as they have chosen to undertake. This understanding is complemented by the rehabilitative view that those who are in jail will hope and expect to regain the exercise of the vote on their release from incarceration, just like they hope and expect to regain the exercise of the fullest expressions of their liberty. Once released from prison, they are on the road to reintegration into the community. Obtaining the vote once released or paroled is a recognition of regaining the nexus with the community that was temporarily suspended during the incarceration. . . .

[135] I now turn to the application of the *Oakes* test. . . .

[139] Parliament's two principal objectives in s. 51(*e*) of the Act, accepted by both the trial judge and the Federal Court of Appeal below, are: the enhancement of civic responsibility and respect for the rule of law, and the enhancement of the general purposes of the criminal sanction. Above, I developed the view that these objectives are based upon a reasonable and rational social or political philosophy. Thus, I am of the view that any provision which seeks to advance such objectives clearly has a pressing and substantial purpose. . . .

[150] This Court has unanimously agreed that "[r]ational connection is to be established, upon a civil standard, through reason, logic or simply common sense": *RJR-MacDonald, supra, per* La Forest J., at para. 86, McLachlin J., at paras. 156-58, and Iacobucci J., at para. 184; referred to in *Thomson Newspapers* [*Co. v. Canada (Attorney General)*, [1998] 1 S.C.R. 877], at para. 39. The existence of scientific proof is simply of probative value in supporting this reason, logic or common sense. In the case at bar, as discussed above, a causal relationship between disenfranchising prisoners and the objectives approved of above is not empirically demonstrable. However, this Court has clearly stated that Parliament must be afforded a margin of appreciation in regard to legitimate objectives which may, nonetheless, be based upon somewhat inconclusive social science evidence: Sopinka J. in *Butler, supra*, at pp. 502-3. . . . Thus, it is clear that this Court's approach to this dimension of the test demands not the strongest connection, the most convincing rational connection, but a logical or rational connection.

[157] . . . [R]eason, logic and common sense, as well as extensive expert evidence support a conclusion that there is a rational connection between disenfranchising offenders incarcerated for serious crimes and the objectives of promoting civic responsibility and the rule of law and the enhancement of the general objectives of the penal sanction. The rational connection between the disenfranchisement and the first objective is explained above, in my discussion of dignity and the fact that removing the right to vote from serious incarcerated criminals does no injury to, but rather recognizes their dignity. It is also explained . . . below in my discussion of the salutary effects of the measure [where] I discuss the legislation's expression of societal values and its signalling effect. The Chief Justice prefers a different line of reasoning. Citing J.S. Mill as her authority, she states that "denying penitentiary inmates the right to vote is more likely to send messages that undermine respect for the law and democracy than messages that enhance those values" (para. 41). However, apart from one philosopher, she provides no support for this contention; she simply replaces one reasonable position with another, dismissing the government's position as "unhelpful" (para. 37 of the Chief Justice's reasons).

[158] The rational connection between the legislation and the enhancement of the criminal sanction is also elaborated on elsewhere. Below, . . . on minimal impairment, I explain at length that the disenfranchisement is carefully tailored to apply to perpetrators of serious crimes. I therefore disagree with the Chief Justice's statement that denial of the right to vote is insufficiently tailored and therefore not rationally connected to legitimate punishment. . . .

[160] The Crown must demonstrate that the impairment of rights is minimal, i.e. that the law was carefully tailored so that *Charter* rights are impaired no more than is necessary to meet the legislative provision's objectives. . . . This analysis does not, notably, require the Crown to have adopted the absolutely least intrusive means for promoting the purpose, although it does require that the Crown prefer a significantly less intrusive means if it is of *equal effectiveness*. . . .

[161] I emphasize that it was "particularly" on the ground of minimal impairment that this Court, in the first *Sauvé* case, established that the previous s. 51(*e*) of the Act, which disenfranchised all prisoners regardless of the duration of their incarceration, was contrary to the *Charter* and incapable of being justified under s. 1. Our decision was, at pp. 439-40:

> We are all of the view that these appeals should be dismissed.
>
> The Attorney General of Canada has properly conceded that s. 51(*e*) of the *Canada Elections Act*, R.S.C., 1985, c. E-2, contravenes s. 3 of the *Canadian Charter of Rights and Freedoms* but submits that s. 51(*e*) is saved under s. 1 of the *Charter*. We do not agree. In our view, s. 51(*e*) is drawn too broadly and fails to meet the proportionality test, particularly the minimal impairment component of the test, as expressed in the s. 1 jurisprudence of the Court.

The language of Iacobucci J.'s reasons seem to imply that, while Parliament's complete ban of prisoner voting in the old provision was unconstitutional, Parliament was free to investigate where an appropriate line could be drawn. This is exactly what it was in the process of doing at the time the first *Sauvé* case was heard. It has drawn a line in the form of s. 51(*e*) of the Act.

[162] The appellants and their experts have argued that there are less intrusive means for the Crown to pursue its objectives: disenfranchisement could be left to the discretion of the sentencing judge; as *per* the Lortie Commission, only those convicted of the most serious offences (those punishable by a maximum of life) and the most serious sentences (those punishable by 10 years in jail or more) could lose the vote; an offence-oriented approach could define specific types of crimes which could be seen as bearing a rational connection

to the franchise; or the measure could allow for the vote to be restored if the offender demonstrated good behaviour while incarcerated. To these I add that it is obvious that any higher cutoff line, i.e. 5, 10, or 25 years of incarceration, would also, technically, be less intrusive.

[163] I am of the view that no less intrusive measure would be equally effective. Since Parliament has drawn a line which identifies which incarcerated offenders have committed serious enough crimes to warrant being deprived of the vote, any alternative line will not be of equal effectiveness. Equal effectiveness is a dimension of the analysis that should not be underemphasized, as it relates directly to Parliament's ability to pursue its legitimate objectives effectively. Any other line insisted upon amounts to *second-guessing* Parliament as to what amounts to "serious" crime. . . .

[174] In my view, it is particularly inappropriate, in the case at bar, to find the justification of the limitation of the right to be unconvincing at this phase of the *Oakes* test. First, as was noted above, there is a need for deference to Parliament in its drawing of a line, especially since this Court gave the impression that it was up to Parliament to do exactly that after the first *Sauvé* case was heard in 1993. Second, also as developed above, the analysis of social and political philosophies and the accommodation of values in the context of the *Charter* must be sensitive to the fact that there may be many possible reasonable and rational balances. Developing this point, it is important to note that, given the theoretical nature of the arguments raised by both parties in the case at bar, they do not gain proportionally in strength as the bar is moved higher. Symbolic and theoretical justifications such as employed in this case do not get stronger as the line changes. The fundamental premises underlying the line chosen would be the same if the cutoff was 10 years, or even 25 years. See, for example, *Driskell* [*v. Manitoba (Attorney General)*, [1999] 11 W.W.R. 615], in which similar analytical problems to those in the case at bar arose and resulted in a line of five years being held unconstitutional. Line drawing, amongst a range of acceptable alternatives, is for Parliament. . . .

[175] The final prong of the *Oakes* test demands that the effects of the limiting measure (the impugned provision) must not so severely trench on *Charter* rights that the legislative objective, albeit important, is outweighed by the infringement of the rights. . . .

[178] It is my view that the arguments in this dimension of the analysis are basically either persuasive or not. If the objectives are taken to reflect a moral choice by Parliament which has great symbolic importance and effect and which are based on a reasonable social or political philosophy, then their resulting weight is great indeed. Over all, while the temporary disenfranchisement is clear, the salutary effects and objectives are, in my view, of greater countervailing weight. Generally, I agree with the analysis of Linden J.A. at the Federal Court of Appeal below to this effect. . . .

[181] Linden J.A. found that the primary salutary effect was that the legislation, *intrinsically*, expresses societal values in relation to serious criminal behaviour and the right to vote in our society. He thus concluded . . . that it has more than symbolic effect:

> This legislation sends a message signalling Canadian values, to the effect that those people who are found guilty of the most serious crimes will, while separated from society, lose access to one of the levers of electoral power. This is an extremely important message, one which is not sent by incarceration alone. Incarceration is essentially separation from the community. Incarceration alone signals a denunciation of the offender's anti-societal behaviour and indicates society's hope for rehabilitation through separation from the community. Incarceration by itself, however, leaves those convicted of serious crimes free to exercise all the levers of electoral power open to all law-abiding citizens. This maintains a political parity between those convicted of society's worst crimes and their victims. Disqualification from voting, however, signals a denunciation of the criminal's anti-societal behaviour *and* sends the message that those people convicted of causing the worst forms of indignity to others will be deprived of one aspect of the political equality of citizens—the right to vote. It can be said that, in this context, "kindness toward the criminal can be an act of cruelty toward his victims, and the larger community." [Footnotes omitted; emphasis in original.]

Linden J.A. suggested that value emerges from the signal or message that those who commit serious crimes will temporarily lose one aspect of the political equality of citizens. Therefore, "the enactment of the measure is itself a salutary effect." I agree. . . .

[188] When the objectives and the salutary effects are viewed in the totality of the context, they outweigh the temporary disenfranchisement of the serious criminal offender which mirrors the fact of his or her incarceration. In my view, Parliament has enacted a law which is reasonable, and which is justified in a free and democratic society. . . .

[204] The reasons of the Chief Justice, at para. 60, refer to the fact that this Court, in *R. v. Gladue*, [1999] 1 S.C.R. 688, noted that the over-representation of Aboriginal persons in the criminal justice system and the prison population reflects a "crisis in the Canadian criminal justice system." I agree that a sad and pressing social problem exists, but suggest that it is quite a leap to then say that Parliament is incapable of enacting a provision which disenfranchises serious criminal offenders

who have been sentenced to two or more years of incarceration. As noted above, it is not plausible to say that the temporary disenfranchisement is in some way targeted at Aboriginal people: it hinges only upon the commission of serious criminal offences. If there is a problem with the over-representation of Aboriginal people in our criminal justice system and prisons, then that issue must continue to be addressed, by not only continuing to pay attention to the sentencing considerations pursuant to s. 718.2(*e*) of the *Criminal Code*, which are specifically aimed at such a reduction, but also by addressing some of the root causes of the over-representation identified by this Court in *Gladue, supra*, including poverty, substance abuse, lack of education, lack of employment opportunities, and bias against Aboriginal people. The continuing need to address these factors does not, however, preclude the ability of Parliament to address other pressing social problems, including denouncing serious crime, enhancing the meaning of the criminal sanction and promoting civic responsibility and the rule of law, which s. 51(*e*) of the Act is directed to. Also in *Gladue*, at para. 78, this Court stated that it is unreasonable to assume that Aboriginal people do not believe in goals of punishment such as denunciation, deterrence and separation, to which I add, obviously, the principle of rehabilitation. These goals of punishment, as discussed above, are related to the temporary disenfranchisement of serious criminal offenders and are ultimately aimed at the reintegration of offenders, Aboriginal or otherwise, back into the community....

Harper v. Canada (Attorney General), 2004

Before he became Prime Minister of Canada, Stephen Harper served for a time as presi... of the National Citizens Coalition (NCC), a conservative public interest group. Harper enthusiastically continued the NCC's lengthy campaign, begun under his predecessor, against legal restrictions on "third party" spending in election campaigns. The case below, bearing Harper's name, culminates the litigation component of the NCC campaign.

"Third parties," as the term is used in this context, are political interests other than the registered parties and candidates who officially compete for electoral office. They include individuals and interest groups such as the NCC. Laws that impose election spending limits on political parties, as Canada's have since 1974, can be circumvented if non-electoral interests may spend freely in ways that might benefit or harm official candidates and parties. Thus election spending limits typically target both official and third parties. At the same time, the high value of freedom of expression in liberal democracies weighs against restricting all election spending to official parties; citizens, both individually and in groups, are typically left some freedom to make their political views known outside political parties. How much money can they spend in exercising this freedom, and in what ways can they spend it, without making a mockery of the very idea of election spending limits? That question divided the Supreme Court in *Harper*.

The NCC began its litigation campaign against what it called "gag laws" in the 1980s. Between 1984 and 2003, it successfully persuaded an unbroken succession of trial and appeal courts in Alberta and Ontario to strike down the third-party spending limits.[1] Until *Harper*, these judgments were not appealed to the Supreme Court and thus technically prevailed only in the jurisdiction of the court deciding them. Nevertheless, the difficulty and confusion of applying third-party spending limits differentially across the country meant that they were not applied anywhere in the federal elections of 1984, 1988, 1993, and 2000.

In the meantime, a slightly different political spending issue had come out of Quebec and was making its way to the Supreme Court. Seeking to equalize the two sides in a referendum campaign, Quebec's referendum law allowed only those affiliated with the official "Oui" and "Non" committees to make significant campaign expenditures. During the 1992 referendum on the Charlottetown Accord, Quebec's Equality Party, led by Robert Libman, encouraged abstention from the vote. Because his party could not reasonably promote this position in affiliation with either official committee, Libman challenged the spending restrictions in court. Although *Libman* concerned referenda rather than elections, it raised essentially the same freedom-of-expression issues that the NCC had so successfully pursued.

---

1   *National Citizens' Coalition v. Canada (Attorney General)*, [1984] 5 W.W.R. 436 (Alta. Q.B.); *Somerville v. Canada (Attorney General)* (25 June 1993), Calgary, oral judgment (Alta. Q.B.) (unreported); *Somerville v. Canada (Attorney General)* (1996), 39 Alta. L.R. (3d) 326 (Alta. C.A.); *Harper v. Canada (Attorney General)* (2001), 93 Alta. L.R. (3d) 281 (Q.B.); *Harper v. Canada (Attorney General)* (2002), 14 Alta. L.R. (4th) 4 (C.A.); and *Canada (Commissioner of Canada Elections) v. National Citizens' Coalition*, 2003 CarswellOnt 3947 (Ct. J.).

Reaching the Supreme Court in 1997, *Libman* (and by implication the NCC) met with mixed results. On the one hand, the Court's unanimous, unsigned opinion struck down Quebec's third-party spending rules as infringing freedom of expression in a manner too restrictive to meet the "minimal impairment" requirement of the *Oakes* test.[2] On the other hand, and more important, the Court enthusiastically embraced the principle of spending limits on third parties. The purpose of such limits—to ensure democratic fairness by equalizing the persuasive power and resources of the political contenders—was "pressing and substantial" and third-party spending limits were a "rational" way of achieving this purpose. Quebec simply had to tailor its restrictions more carefully in order to satisfy the minimal-impairment requirement. Strikingly, the Court suggested that Quebec would find a laudable example in the $1,000 federal third-party spending limit struck down by the Alberta Court of Appeal in 1996. In doing so, the judges tipped their hand on how they were likely to treat the NCC's litigation campaign when it reached them. The NCC, under Stephen Harper's leadership, would soon give them the opportunity.

Harper launched his challenge before an Alberta court in 2000 in response to revised federal third-party spending limits of $150,000, not more than $3,000 of which could be spent to promote or oppose particular candidates within any electoral district. Included within the spending limits was the promotion of any position "associated" with a registered party or candidate. Harper argued that the law violated both the *Charter*'s section 2 right to freedom of expression and its section 3 right to vote. In its 2004 judgment, the Supreme Court unanimously rejected the section 3 challenge, but disagreed on section 2. We reproduce only the section 2 disagreement below.

Given how praiseworthy the *Libman* judgment had found the previous, less liberal, federal third-party spending limits, it comes as no surprise to find the Court upholding the revised law. What may seem surprising is Chief Justice McLachlin's dissenting judgment (joined by Justices Major and Binnie), which found the new limits too "draconian" to pass constitutional muster. After all, Justices McLachlin and Major had both been part of the unanimous *Libman* Court. The preferences they make evident in *Harper* are certainly consistent with the bottom-line outcome of *Libman*, which struck down even more "draconian" provincial spending limits, but they sit uneasily with *Libman*'s praise of the existing $1,000 federal limit on third-party spending, which must have appeared equally unjustifiable to Justices McLachlin and Major. A plausible speculation is that they considered *Libman*'s support of the earlier federal limits as non-binding *obiter dictum*, and thus something they could live with in order to gain the advantages of unsigned unanimity when undertaking something as controversial as striking down Quebec's referendum law. The sensitivity of Quebec to *Charter*-based intrusions of the Supreme Court is well known and likely to be particularly acute regarding matters as entangled with autonomist sentiments as referendum laws. When turning to federal legislation, Justices McLachlin and Major obviously felt freer to express their disagreement.

---

2 According to the Court, the limits were "so restrictive that they come close to being a total ban."

Chief Justice McLachlin's dissent emphasized that "[p]olitical speech, the type of speech here at issue, is the single most important and protected type of expression. It lies at the core of the guarantee of free expression." This meant that a higher or more searching degree of scrutiny should be applied at the stage of section 1 analysis than when the expression fell further from the core. In fact, Justice McLachlin is often inclined to apply a high standard of justification even in cases involving expression much more distant from the "core" of free expression, such as the commercial advertising at stake in *RJR-MacDonald* (case 7). Indeed, Justice McLachlin arguably applied an even higher degree of scrutiny to the restrictions on tobacco advertising in *RJR-MacDonald* than she did to the political expression at issue in *Harper*. In *RJR-MacDonald*, she found the advertising ban to fail both the rational connection and minimal impairment components of proportionality analysis, while in *Harper* she found a "rational connection"[3] and focused on the law's failure to meet the "minimal impairment" criterion. In short, she saw the tobacco advertising ban as more problematic from a section 1 perspective than the limit on third-party political expression.

Chief Justice McLachlin, of course, was at least consistently libertarian in voting to strike down both the *RJR-MacDonald* advertising ban and the *Harper* political spending limits. But although her view prevailed in *RJR-MacDonald*, it lost in *Harper*. This poses another anomaly—namely, that "the political speech at issue in *Harper* fared no better than obscene pornography [*Butler*, case 6] . . . and rather worse than tobacco advertising."[4] ∼

Discussion Questions

1. Why does each side in this judicial dispute think it is supported by the *Libman* precedent?
2. The "minimal impairment" criterion of the *Oakes* test is central to the disagreement between the majority and dissenting opinions. Why do the judges disagree on this issue and who do you think gets the better of the debate?
3. Can the law at issue in *Harper* be seen as part of the interinstitutional "dialogue" between courts and legislatures? If so, is it legitimate dialogue?

3　She appeared to do so because of the *Libman* precedent, which had also found a rational connection. This part of the *Libman* judgment could not as easily be treated as *obiter dictum* as the praise of the federal $1,000 spending limit on third parties.

4　Robert E. Charney and S. Zachary Green, "It's My Party and I'll Run If I Want To: Figueroa, Harper, and the Animal Alliance Environment Voters Party" (2006) 21 *National Journal of Constitutional Law* 257 at 268.

HARPER v. CANADA (ATTORNEY GENERAL)
2004 SCC 33; [2004] 1 S.C.R. 827

Hearing: February 10, 2004; Judgment: May 18, 2004.

Present: McLachlin C.J. and Iacobucci, Major, Bastarache, Binnie, Arbour, LeBel, Deschamps, and Fish JJ.

Interveners: Attorney General of Ontario, Attorney General of Quebec, Attorney General of Manitoba, Democracy Watch and National Anti-Poverty Organization, Environment Voters, a division of Animal Alliance of Canada, and John Herbert Bryden.

The reasons of McLachlin C.J. and Major and Binnie JJ. were delivered by

[1] **THE CHIEF JUSTICE AND MAJOR J.** (dissenting in part): This Court has repeatedly held that liberal democracy demands the free expression of political opinion, and affirmed that political speech lies at the core of the *Canadian Charter of Rights and Freedoms'* guarantee of free expression. It has held that the freedom of expression includes the right to attempt to persuade through peaceful interchange. And it has observed that the electoral process is the primary means by which the average citizen participates in the public discourse that shapes our polity. The question now before us is whether these high aspirations are fulfilled by a law that effectively denies the right of an ordinary citizen to give meaningful and effective expression to her political views during a federal election campaign.

[2] The law at issue sets advertising spending limits for citizens—called third parties—at such low levels that they cannot effectively communicate with their fellow citizens on election issues during an election campaign. The practical effect is that effective communication during the writ period is confined to registered political parties and their candidates. Both enjoy much higher spending limits. This denial of effective communication to citizens violates free expression where it warrants the greatest protection—the sphere of political discourse. As in *Libman v. Quebec (Attorney General)*, [1997] 3 S.C.R. 569, the incursion essentially denies effective free expression and far surpasses what is required to meet the perceived threat that citizen speech will drown out other political discourse. It follows that the law is inconsistent with the guarantees of the *Charter* and, hence, invalid. . . .

[3] The *Canada Elections Act*, S.C. 2000, c. 9, sets limits for spending on advertising for individuals and groups. It limits citizens to spending a maximum of $3,000 in each electoral district up to a total of $150,000 nationally. Section 350 provides:

350. (1) A third party shall not incur election advertising expenses of a total amount of more than $150,000 during an election period in relation to a general election.

(2) Not more than $3,000 of the total amount referred to in subsection (1) shall be incurred to promote or oppose the election of one or more candidates in a given electoral district, including by

    (*a*) naming them;

    (*b*) showing their likenesses;

    (*c*) identifying them by their respective political affiliations; or

    (*d*) taking a position on an issue with which they are particularly associated.

Section 350(2)(*d*) is particularly restrictive. It prohibits individuals from spending more than the allowed amounts on any issue with which a candidate is "particularly associated." The candidates in an election are typically associated with a wide range of views on a wide range of issues. The evidence shows that the effect of the limits is to prevent citizens from effectively communicating their views on issues during an election campaign.

[4] The limits do not permit citizens to effectively communicate through the national media. The Chief Electoral Officer testified that it costs approximately $425,000 for a one-time full-page advertisement in major Canadian newspapers. The Chief Electoral Officer knows from personal experience that this is the cost of such communication with Canadians, because he used this very method to inform Canadians of the changes to the *Canada Elections Act* prior to the last federal election. It is telling that the Chief Electoral Officer would have been unable to communicate this important change in the law to Canadians were he subject—as are other Canadians—to the national expenditure limit of $150,000 imposed by the law.

[5] Nor do the limits permit citizens to communicate through the mail. The Canada Post bulk mailing rate for some ridings amounts to more than $7,500, effectively prohibiting citizens from launching a mail campaign in these ridings without exceeding the $3,000 limit.

[6] The $3,000 riding limits are further reduced by the national limit of $150,000, which precludes citizens from spending the maximum amount in each of the 308 ridings in Canada. This effectively diminishes the $3,000 riding maximum. Quite simply, it puts effective radio and television communication within constituencies or throughout the country beyond the reach of "third party" citizens.

[7] Under the limits, a citizen may place advertisements in a local paper within her constituency. She may print some

flyers and distribute them by hand or post them in conspicuous places. She may write letters to the editor of regional and national newspapers and hope they will be published. In these and other ways, she may be able to reach a limited number of people on the local level. But she cannot effectively communicate her position to her fellow citizens throughout the country in the ways those intent on communicating such messages typically do—through mail-outs and advertising in the regional and national media. The citizen's message is thus confined to minor local dissemination with the result that effective local, regional and national expression of ideas becomes the exclusive right of registered political parties and their candidates.

[8] Comparative statistics underline the meagerness of the limits. The national advertising spending limits for citizens represent 1.3 percent of the national advertising limits for political parties. In Britain, a much more geographically compact country, the comparable ratio is about 5 percent. It is argued that the British limits apply to different categories of advertising over a greater period, but the discrepancy nevertheless remains significant.

[9] It is therefore clear that the *Canada Elections Act's* advertising limits prevent citizens from effectively communicating their views on election issues to their fellow citizens, restricting them instead to minor local communication. As such, they represent a serious incursion on free expression in the political realm. The Attorney General raises three reasons why this restriction is justified as a reasonable limit in a free and democratic society under s. 1 of the *Charter*: to ensure the equality of each citizen in elections; to prevent the voices of the wealthy from drowning out those of others; and to preserve confidence in the electoral system. Whether that is so is the question in this appeal....

[10] One cannot determine whether an infringement of a right is justified without examining the seriousness of the infringement. Our jurisprudence on the guarantee of the freedom of expression establishes that some types of expression are more important and hence more deserving of protection than others. To put it another way, some restrictions on freedom of expression are easier to justify than others.

[11] Political speech, the type of speech here at issue, is the single most important and protected type of expression. It lies at the core of the guarantee of free expression....

[16] The ability to engage in effective speech in the public square means nothing if it does not include the ability to attempt to persuade one's fellow citizens through debate and discussion. This is the kernel from which reasoned political discourse emerges. Freedom of expression must allow a citizen to give voice to her vision for her community and nation, to advocate change through the art of persuasion in the hope

of improving her life and indeed the larger social, political and economic landscape....

[17] Freedom of expression protects not only the individual who speaks the message, but also the recipient. Members of the public—as viewers, listeners and readers—have a right to information on public governance, absent which they cannot cast an informed vote; see *Edmonton Journal* [*v. Alberta (Attorney General)*, [1989] 2 S.C.R. 1326], at pp. 1339-40. Thus the *Charter* protects listeners as well as speakers; see *Ford v. Quebec (Attorney General)*, [1988] 2 S.C.R. 712 , at pp. 766-67....

[19] The *Canada Elections Act* undercuts the right to listen by withholding from voters an ingredient that is critical to their individual and collective deliberation: substantive analysis and commentary on political issues of the day. The spending limits impede the ability of citizens to communicate with one another through public fora and media during elections and curtail the diversity of perspectives heard and assessed by the electorate. Because citizens cannot mount effective national television, radio and print campaigns, the only sustained messages voters see and hear during the course of an election campaign are from political parties.

[20] It is clear that the right here at issue is of vital importance to Canadian democracy. In the democracy of ancient Athens, all citizens were able to meet and discuss the issues of the day in person. In our modern democracy, we cannot speak personally with each of our fellow citizens. We can convey our message only through methods of mass communication. Advertising through mail-outs and the media is one of the most effective means of communication on a large scale. We need only look at the reliance of political parties on advertising to realize how important it is to actually reaching citizens—in a word, to effective participation. The ability to speak in one's own home or on a remote street corner does not fulfill the objective of the guarantee of freedom of expression, which is that each citizen be afforded the opportunity to present her views for public consumption and attempt to persuade her fellow citizens. Pell J.'s observation could not be more apt: "[s]peech without effective communication is not speech but an idle monologue in the wilderness"; see *United States v. Dellinger*, 472 F.2d 340 (7th Cir. 1972), at p. 415.

[21] This is the perspective from which we must approach the question whether the limitation on citizen spending is justified. It is no answer to say that the citizen can speak through a registered political party. The citizen may hold views not espoused by a registered party. The citizen has a right to communicate those views. The right to do so is essential to the effective debate upon which our democracy rests, and lies at the core of the free expression guarantee. That does not mean that the right cannot be limited. But it does mean

that limits on it must be supported by a clear and convincing demonstration that they are necessary, do not go too far, and enhance more than harm the democratic process. . . .

[22] . . . The Attorney General states that the objective of the legislation is to promote fair elections.

[23] In more concrete terms, the limits are purported to further three objectives: first, to favour equality, by preventing those with greater means from dominating electoral debate; second, to foster informed citizenship, by ensuring that some positions are not drowned out by others (this is related to the right to participate in the political process by casting an informed vote); third, to enhance public confidence by ensuring equality, a better informed citizenship and fostering the appearance and reality of fairness in the democratic process.

[24] These are worthy social purposes, endorsed as pressing and substantial by this Court in *Libman*. . . .

[29] The Attorney General has offered no evidence to support a connection between the limits on citizen spending and electoral fairness. However, reason or logic may establish the requisite causal link; see *Sharpe* [*R. v.*, [2001] 1 S.C.R. 45, 2001 SCC 2]; *R. v. Butler*, [1992] 1 S.C.R. 452 . In *Thomson Newspapers* [*Co. v. Canada (Attorney General)*, [1998] 1 S.C.R. 877], the Court accepted as reasonable the conclusion that polls exert significant influence on the electoral process and individual electoral choice. More to the point, in *Libman*, *supra*, the Court concluded that electoral spending limits are rationally connected to the objective of fair elections. While some of the evidence on which this conclusion was based has since been discredited, the conclusion that limits may in theory further electoral fairness is difficult to gainsay.

[30] Nevertheless, the supposition that uncontrolled spending could favour the messages of wealthier citizens or adversely affect the ability of less wealthy citizens to become informed on electoral issues is not irrational, particularly in a regime where party spending is limited. It follows that spending limits may, at least in principle, promote electoral fairness. . . .

[32] . . . "The impairment must be 'minimal,' that is, the law must be carefully tailored so that rights are impaired no more than necessary": *RJR-MacDonald Inc. v. Canada (Attorney General)*, [1995] 3 S.C.R. 199, at para. 160. . . .

[34] . . . The Attorney General presented no evidence that wealthier Canadians—alone or in concert—will dominate political debate during the electoral period absent limits. It offered only the hypothetical possibility that, without limits on citizen spending, problems could arise. . . . This minimizes the Attorney General's assertions of necessity and lends credence to the argument that the legislation is an overreaction to a non-existent problem.

[35] On the other side of the equation, the infringement on the right is severe. We earlier reviewed the stringency of the limits. They prevent citizens from effectively communicating with their fellow citizens on election issues during a campaign. Any communication beyond the local level is effectively rendered impossible, and even at that level is seriously curtailed. The spending limits do not allow citizens to express themselves through mail-outs within certain ridings, radio and television media, nor the national press. Citizens are limited to 1.3 percent of the expenditures of registered political parties. This is significantly lower than other countries that have also imposed citizen spending limits. It is not an exaggeration to say that the limits imposed on citizens amount to a virtual ban on their participation in political debate during the election period. In actuality, the only space left in the marketplace of ideas is for political parties and their candidates. The right of each citizen to have her voice heard, so vaunted in *Figueroa* [*v. Canada (Attorney General)*, [2003] 1 S.C.R. 912, 2003 SCC 37], is effectively negated unless the citizen is able or willing to speak through a political party.

[36] On this point, this case is indistinguishable from *Libman*, *supra*, where the Court held that the spending limits imposed on citizens in the course of a referendum campaign did not satisfy the requirement of minimal impairment. . . .

[37] In *Libman*, *supra*, at para. 63, the Court stated that "[i]t can be seen from the evidence that the legislature went to considerable lengths, in good faith, in order to adopt means that would be as non-intrusive as possible while at the same time respecting the objective it had set." Here, too, Parliament's good faith is advanced, said to be evidenced by the ongoing *dialogue* with the courts as to where the limits should be set. But as in *Libman*, good faith cannot remedy an impairment of the right to freedom of expression.

[38] There is no demonstration that limits this draconian are required to meet the perceived dangers of inequality, an uninformed electorate and the public perception that the system is unfair. On the contrary, the measures may themselves exacerbate these dangers. Citizens who cannot effectively communicate with others on electoral issues may feel they are being treated unequally compared to citizens who speak through political parties. The absence of their messages may result in the public being less well informed than it would otherwise be. And a process that bans citizens from effective participation in the electoral debate during an election campaign may well be perceived as unfair. These fears may be hypothetical, but no more so than the fears conjured by the Attorney General in support of the infringement.

[39] This is not to suggest that election spending limits are never permissible. On the contrary, this Court in *Libman*

has recognized that they are an acceptable, even desirable, tool to ensure fairness and faith in the electoral process. Limits that permit citizens to conduct effective and persuasive communication with their fellow citizens might well meet the minimum impairment test. The problem here is that the draconian nature of the infringement—to effectively deprive all those who do not or cannot speak through political parties of their voice during an election period—overshoots the perceived danger. Even recognizing that "[t]he tailoring process seldom admits of perfection" (*RJR-MacDonald, supra,* at para. 160), and according Parliament a healthy measure of deference, we are left with the fact that nothing in the evidence suggests that a virtual ban on citizen communication through effective advertising is required to avoid the hypothetical evils of inequality, a misinformed public and loss of public confidence in the system....

[40] The same logic that leads to the conclusion that the Attorney General has not established that the infringement minimally impairs the citizen's right of free speech applies equally to the final stage of the proportionality analysis, which asks us to weigh the benefits conferred by the infringement against the harm it may occasion.

[41] Given the unproven and speculative nature of the danger the limits are said to address, the possible benefits conferred by the law are illusory....

[42] Having had the advantage of reviewing the reasons of Bastarache J., we believe it is important to make three observations. First, whether or not citizens dispose of sufficient funds to meet or exceed the existing spending limits is irrelevant. What is important is that citizens have the capacity, should they so choose, to exercise their right to free political speech. The spending limits as they currently stand do not allow this. Instead, they have a chilling effect on political speech, forcing citizens into a Hobson's choice between not expressing themselves at all or having their voice reduced to a mere whisper. Faced with such options, citizens could not be faulted for choosing the former.

[43] Second, it is important to recognize that the spending limits do not constrain the right of only a few citizens to speak. They constrain the political speech of all Canadians, be they of superior or modest means. Whether it is a citizen incurring expenditures of $3001 for leafleting in her riding or a group of citizens pooling 1501 individual contributions of $100 to run a national advertising campaign, the *Charter* protects the right to free political speech.

[44] Finally, even it *were* true that spending limits constrained the political speech rights of only a few citizens, it would be no answer to say, as suggests Bastarache J., at para. 112, that few citizens can afford to spend more than the limits anyway. This amounts to saying that even if the breach of

s. 2(*b*) is not justified, it does not matter because it affects only a few people. *Charter* breaches cannot be justified on this basis. Moreover, one may question the premise that only a few people are affected by the spending limits. Indeed, if so few can afford to spend more than the existing limits, why, one may ask, are they needed? ...

The judgment of Iacobucci, Bastarache, Arbour, LeBel, Deschamps, and Fish JJ. was delivered by

BASTARACHE J.: . . .

[75] The central issue at this stage of the analysis is the nature and sufficiency of the evidence required for the Attorney General to demonstrate that the limits imposed on freedom of expression are reasonable and justifiable in a free and democratic society. The Attorney General of Canada alleges that the lower courts erred in requiring scientific proof that harm had actually occurred and, specifically, by requiring conclusive proof that third party advertising influences voters and election outcomes, rendering them unfair....

[77] The legislature is not required to provide scientific proof based on concrete evidence of the problem it seeks to address in every case. Where the court is faced with inconclusive or competing social science evidence relating the harm to the legislature's measures, the court may rely on a reasoned apprehension of that harm....

[86] The Attorney General of Canada argues that although the impugned provisions limit the political expression of some, the provisions enhance the political expression of others. This Court explored this dichotomy in *Libman, supra,* at para. 61:

> ... the legislature's objective, namely to enhance the exercise of the right to vote, must be borne in mind. Thus, while the impugned provisions do in a way restrict one of the most basic forms of expression, namely political expression, *the legislature must be accorded a certain deference to enable it to arbitrate between the democratic values of freedom of expression and referendum fairness.* The latter is related to the very values the Canadian *Charter* seeks to protect, in particular the political equality of citizens that is at the heart of a free and democratic society. *The impugned provisions impose a balance between the financial resources available to the proponents of each option* in order to ensure that the vote by the people will be free and informed and that the discourse of each option can be heard. *To attain this objective, the legislature had to try to strike a balance between absolute freedom of individual expression and equality among the different expressions for the benefit of all. From this point of view, the impugned provisions are therefore not purely restrictive of freedom of expression. Their primary purpose is to promote political*

expression by ensuring an equal dissemination of points of view and thereby truly respecting democratic traditions. [Emphasis added.]

Further, by limiting political expression, the spending limits bring greater balance to the political discourse and allow for more meaningful participation in the electoral process. Thus, the provisions also enhance a second *Charter* right, the right to vote.

[87] Under the egalitarian model of elections, Parliament must balance the rights and privileges of the participants in the electoral process: candidates, political parties, third parties and voters. Advertising expense limits may restrict free expression to ensure that participants are able to meaningfully participate in the electoral process. For candidates, political parties and third parties, meaningful participation means the ability to inform voters of their position. For voters, meaningful participation means the ability to hear and weigh many points of view. The difficulties of striking this balance are evident. Given the right of Parliament to choose Canada's electoral model and the nuances inherent in implementing this model, the Court must approach the justification analysis with deference. The lower courts erred in failing to do so (Paperny J.A., at para. 135). In the end, the electoral system, which regulates many aspects of an election, including its duration and the control and reimbursement of expenses, reflects a political choice, the details of which are better left to Parliament.

[88] On balance, the contextual factors favour a deferential approach to Parliament in determining whether the third party advertising expense limits are demonstrably justified in a free and democratic society. Given the difficulties in measuring this harm, a reasoned apprehension that the absence of third party election advertising limits will lead to electoral unfairness is sufficient....

[91] The overarching objective of the third party election advertising limits is electoral fairness. Equality in the political discourse promotes electoral fairness and is achieved, in part, by restricting the participation of those who have access to significant financial resources. The more voices that have access to the political discourse, the more voters will be empowered to exercise their right in a meaningful and informed manner. Canadians understandably have greater confidence in an electoral system which ultimately encourages increased participation.

[92] For the purpose of the s. 1 analysis, however, "it is desirable to state the purpose of the limiting provision as precisely and specifically as possible so as to provide a clear framework for evaluating its importance, and the precision with which the means have been crafted to fulfil that objec-

tive"; see *Thomson Newspapers*, at para. 98. More narrowly characterized, the objectives of the third party election advertising scheme are threefold: first, to promote equality in the political discourse; second, to protect the integrity of the financing regime applicable to candidates and parties; and third, to ensure that voters have confidence in the electoral process....

[Keeping in mind that it is not necessary "to provide evidence of actual harm to demonstrate that each objective is pressing and substantial," Justice Bastarache concluded that all three objectives do indeed fulfill this requirement.]

[104] At this stage of the analysis, the Attorney General "must show a causal connection between the infringement and the benefit sought on the basis of reason or logic"; see *RJR-MacDonald, supra*, at para. 153. The lower courts erred by demanding too stringent a level of proof, in essence, by requiring the Attorney General to establish an empirical connection between third party spending limits and the objectives of s. 350. There is sufficient evidence establishing a rational connection between third party advertising expense limits and promoting equality in the political discourse, protecting the integrity of the financing regime applicable to candidates and parties, and maintaining confidence in the electoral process.

[105] To establish that third party advertising expense limits promote equality in the political discourse, the Attorney General must establish, first, that political advertising influences voters, and second, that in the absence of regulation some voices could dominate and, in effect, drown others out....

[106] ... That political advertising influences voters accords with logic and reason. Surely, political parties, candidates, interest groups and corporations for that matter would not spend a significant amount of money on advertising if it was ineffective. Indeed, advertising is the primary expenditure of candidates and political parties.

[107] Where advertising influences the electorate, and those who have access to significant financial resources are able to purchase an unlimited amount of advertising, it follows that they will be able to dominate the electoral discourse to the detriment of others, both speakers and listeners. An upper limit on the amount that third parties can dedicate to political advertising curtails their ability to dominate the electoral debate. Thus, third party advertising expense limits are rationally connected to promoting equality in the political discourse....

[108] Third party advertising can directly support a particular candidate or political party. Third party advertising can also indirectly support a candidate or political party by

taking a position on an issue associated with that candidate or political party. In effect, third party advertising can create an imbalance between the financial resources of each candidate or political party; see *Libman, supra,* at para. 44. For candidate and political party spending limits to be truly effective, the advertising expenses of third parties must also be limited. Indeed, the Lortie Commission concluded that the electoral financing regime would be destroyed if third party advertising was not limited concomitantly with candidate and political party spending (Berger J.A., dissenting, at para. 261). The Commission explained, at p. 327 of the Lortie Report:

> If individuals or groups were permitted to run parallel campaigns augmenting the spending of certain candidates or parties, those candidates or parties would have an unfair advantage over others not similarly supported. At the same time, candidates or parties who were the target of spending by individuals or groups opposed to their election would be put at a disadvantage compared with those who were not targeted. Should such activity become widespread, the purpose of the legislation would be destroyed, the reasonably equal opportunity the legislation seeks to establish would vanish, and the overall goal of restricting the role of money in unfairly influencing election outcomes would be defeated.

Thus, limiting third party advertising expenses is rationally connected with preserving the integrity of the financing regime set for candidates and parties.

[109] Limits on third party advertising expenses foster confidence in the electoral process in three ways. The limits address the perception that candidates and political parties can circumvent their spending limits through the creation of *special interest groups.* The limits also prevent the possibility that the wealthy can dominate the electoral discourse and dictate the outcome of elections. Finally, the limits assist in preventing overall advertising expenses from escalating. Thus, third party advertising expense limits advance the perception that access to the electoral discourse does not require wealth to be competitive with other electoral participants. Canadians, in turn, perceive the electoral process as substantively fair as it provides for a reasonable degree of equality between citizens who wish to participate in that process....

[110] To be reasonable and demonstrably justified, the impugned measures must impair the infringed right or freedom as little as possible. The oft-cited quote from *RJR-MacDonald, supra,* at para. 160, sets out the appropriate standard:

> The impairment must be "minimal," that is, the law must be carefully tailored so that rights are impaired no more than necessary. The tailoring process seldom admits of

perfection and the courts must accord some leeway to the legislator. If the law falls within a range of reasonable alternatives, the courts will not find it overbroad merely because they can conceive of an alternative which might better tailor objective to infringement.

Thus, the impugned measures need not be the least impairing option. ...

[112] The Chief Justice and Major J. assert that short of spending well over $150,000 nationally and $3,000 in a given electoral district, citizens cannot effectively communicate their views on election issues to their fellow citizens (para. 9). Respectfully, this ignores the fact that third party advertising is not restricted prior to the commencement of the election period. Outside this time, the limits on third party intervention in political life do not exist. Any group or individual may freely spend money or advertise to make its views known or to persuade others. In fact, many of these groups are not formed for the purpose of an election but are already organized and have a continued presence, mandate and political view which they promote. Many groups and individuals will reinforce their message during an electoral campaign.

[113] The nature of Canada's political system must be considered when deciding whether individuals and groups who engage in election advertising will be affected unduly by the limits set out in s. 350. First, as the Court discussed in *Figueroa,* there are few obstacles for individuals to join existing political parties or to create their own parties to facilitate individual participation in elections. Still, some will participate outside the party affiliations; this explains why the existence of multiple organizations and parties of varying sizes requires Parliament to balance their participation during the election period. Further, the reality in Canada is that regardless of the spending limits in the Act, the vast majority of Canadian citizens simply cannot spend $150,000 nationally or $3,000 in a given electoral district. What prevents most citizens from effectively exercising their right of political free speech as defined by the Chief Justice and Major J. is a lack of means, not legislative restrictions. Contrary to what the Chief Justice and Major J. say at para. 44, I do not suggest that since the breach of s. 2(*b*) only affects a few people, it is therefore justifiable. As discussed, the objective is to ensure the political discourse is not dominated by those who have greater resources. The proper focus is on protecting the right to meaningful participation of the entire electorate. Let me now examine in more detail how this is achieved.

[114] Section 350 minimally impairs the right to free expression. The definition of "election advertising" in s. 319 only applies to advertising that is associated with a candidate or party. Where an issue is not associated with a candidate or

political party, third parties may partake in an unlimited advertising campaign.

[115] The $3,000 limit per electoral district and $150,000 national limit allow for meaningful participation in the electoral process while respecting the right to free expression. Why? First, because the limits established in s. 350 allow third parties to advertise in a limited way in some expensive forms of media such as television, newspaper and radio. But, more importantly, the limits are high enough to allow third parties to engage in a significant amount of low cost forms of advertising such as computer generated posters or leaflets or the creation of a 1-800 number. In addition, the definition of "election advertising" in s. 319 does not apply to many forms of communication such as editorials, debates, speeches, interviews, columns, letters, commentary, the news and the Internet which constitute highly effective means of conveying information. Thus, as the trial judge concluded, at para. 78, the limits allow for "modest, national, informational campaigns and reasonable electoral district informational campaigns."

[116] Second, the limits set out in s. 350 are justifiably lower than the candidate and political party advertising limits, as recommended by the Lortie Commission. As this Court explained in *Libman, supra*, at paras. 49-50, the third party limit must be low enough to ensure that a particular candidate who is targeted by a third party has sufficient resources to respond. It cannot be forgotten that small political parties, who play an equally important role in the electoral process, may be easily overwhelmed by a third party having access to significant financial resources. The limits must also account for the fact that third parties generally have lower overall expenses than candidates and political parties. The limits must also appreciate that third parties tend to focus on one issue and may therefore achieve their objective less expensively. Thus, the limits seek to preserve a balance between the resources available to candidates and parties taking part in an election and those resources that might be available to third parties during this period. Professor Fletcher confirmed (in evidence) that the limits set out in s. 350 achieve this goal.

[117] The Chief Justice and Major J. rely on the higher ratio of advertising spending limits for citizens to political parties in Britain as compared to Canada as evidence that the Canadian spending limits are too low (para. 8). In my view, this comparison is inappropriate. The British provisions apply to different categories of advertising and apply over different time periods.

[118] Certainly, one can conceive of less impairing limits. Indeed, any limit greater than $150,000 would be less impairing. Nevertheless, s. 350 satisfies this stage of the *Oakes* analysis. The limits allow third parties to inform the electorate of their message in a manner that will not overwhelm candidates, political parties or other third parties. The limits preclude the voices of the wealthy from dominating the political discourse, thereby allowing more voices to be heard. The limits allow for meaningful participation in the electoral process and encourage informed voting. The limits promote a free and democratic society. . . .

[119] The final stage of the *Oakes* analysis requires the Court to weigh the deleterious effects against the salutary effects.

[120] Section 350 has several salutary effects. It enhances equality in the political discourse. By ensuring that affluent groups or individuals do not dominate the political discourse, s. 350 promotes the political expression of those who are less affluent or less capable of obtaining access to significant financial resources and ensures that candidates and political parties who are subject to spending limits are not overwhelmed by third party advertising. Section 350 also protects the integrity of the candidate and political party spending limits by ensuring that these limits are not circumvented through the creation of phony third parties. Finally, s. 350 promotes fairness and accessibility in the electoral system and consequently increases Canadians' confidence in it. The deleterious effect of s. 350 is that the spending limits do not allow third parties to engage in unlimited political expression. That is, third parties are permitted to engage in informational but not necessarily persuasive campaigns, especially when acting alone. When weighed against the salutary effects of the legislation, the limits must be upheld. As the Court explained in *Libman, supra*, at para. 84:

> [P]rotecting the fairness of referendum campaigns is a laudable objective that will *necessarily* involve certain restrictions on freedom of expression. *Freedom of political expression, so dear to our democratic tradition, would lose much value if it could only be exercised in a context in which the economic power of the most affluent members of society constituted the ultimate guidepost of our political choices.* Nor would it be much better served by a system that undermined the confidence of citizens in the referendum process. [First emphasis in original; second emphasis added.]

Accordingly, s. 350 should be upheld as a demonstrably justified limit in a free and democratic society. . . .

PART FIVE

Legal Rights

Re B.C. Motor Vehicle Act, 1985

The *B.C. Motor Vehicle Reference* is an example of a case that is relatively unimportant with respect to the policy issue at stake, but very significant in terms of its impact on constitutional interpretation and development. While the fate of section 94(2) of B.C.'s *Motor Vehicle Act* was quickly forgotten, the Supreme Court's decision in this case has gone on to be one of the Court's most frequently cited judgments.

Section 94(1) of B.C.'s *Motor Vehicle Act* made it an offence for a person to drive if his licence had been revoked or he had been legally prohibited from driving. Section 94(2) made it an absolute liability offence—that is, guilt was established by proof of driving, whether or not the driver knew of the prohibition or suspension. The offence was punishable by a fine and a minimum term of imprisonment. Shortly after the adoption of the *Charter*, the B.C. government had doubts about the compatibility of section 94(2) with the *Charter*, and so referred the question to the provincial Court of Appeal. The latter found that the provision violated the *Charter*, and there was an automatic appeal to the Supreme Court of Canada.

At issue was whether the absolute liability provision violated the "principles of fundamental justice" set forth in section 7 of the *Charter*. The Attorney-General of British Columbia argued that the meaning of section 7 was limited to "procedural fairness" alone, and that section 7 did not authorize judges to pass judgment on the fairness of the "substance" of impugned legislation.

The notion of "substantive due process" had a long and checkered history in American constitutional law. Between 1900 and 1937, the American Supreme Court had used the due-process clause of the American Constitution to strike down numerous progressive laws that imposed new social and economic regulations on American business. In effect, the American Court had used substantive due process to protect the laissez-faire economic system and conservative economic interests from the emerging welfare state. This culminated in the New Deal "court crisis" of 1937, after which the substantive-due-process precedents were abandoned and discredited. However, substantive due process re-emerged in American jurisprudence in the 1970s, most notably in the abortion decision.[1] As the *Charter* was being drafted, the term "fundamental justice" replaced "due process" in order to avoid the substantive connotations the latter term had acquired in American law.

Speaking for a unanimous court, Justice Lamer rejected a strict dichotomy between "substantive" and "procedural" interpretations of section 7. The two could not be so easily separated. The entire array of procedural safeguards enumerated in sections 8 through 14 of the *Charter* constitute the substance of principles of fundamental justice articulated in section 7. More to the point, Justice Lamer wrote: "A law that has the potential to convict a person who has not really done anything wrong offends the principles of fundamental justice. . . . In other words, absolute liability and imprisonment cannot be combined."

Justice Lamer was well aware that attributing substantive meaning to the concept of principles of fundamental justice could unduly widen the scope of judicial review under

---

1 *Roe v. Wade*, 410 U.S. 113 (1973). See the introduction to *Morgentaler v. The Queen*, case 15.

section 7, resulting in what he called a "super judicial legislature." To discourage this, he stressed that a substantive interpretation of section 7 was limited to the field of criminal law and legal rights, "the inherent domain of the judiciary," and would not be applied "in the realm of general public policy." However, several subsequent decisions by lower courts extended this doctrine to areas of economic and social policy. The closest the Supreme Court of Canada has come to applying a substantive interpretation of section 7 outside the criminal law area was its decision in *Chaoulli*, where it split, 3 to 3, on whether a ban on private medical insurance for services covered by medicare is "arbitrary" and therefore a violation of section 7.[2] If the Supreme Court were to use section 7 to review the reasonableness of social and economic policy, the scope of the *Charter* and thus the power of the judges would expand considerably.

Of equal significance was Justice Lamer's handling of the historical evidence of the "framers' intent" to limit section 7 to a narrow procedural meaning. While conceding the admissibility of the framers' intent as relevant to determining the proper interpretation of *Charter* rights, Justice Lamer cautioned against granting such extrinsic evidence anything more than "minimal weight." To attach any more significance to the "original understanding" of *Charter* rights, he cautioned, "would in effect be assuming a fact which is nearly impossible of proof, i.e., the intention of the legislative bodies which adopted the *Charter*." Moreover, it would reintroduce the much criticized "frozen concepts" doctrine, as opposed to a "large and liberal" interpretation of the *Charter* mandated by the frequently cited "living tree" approach.[3]

By freeing constitutional law from the drafters' intentions, the Court has granted itself and all other Canadian judges the discretion to read new meaning into the *Charter* sections other than what the framers' understood and intended those sections to mean. Future litigants can now invoke the symbol of the *Charter* as a living tree and argue that, even if the meaning they attribute to a *Charter* right was not part of its original meaning, the judge is still free to add the new meaning.[4]

This aspect of the *B.C. Motor Vehicle Reference* is best illustrated by an anecdote from the *Borowski* anti-abortion case.[5] The very day the Supreme Court handed down its decision in the *Motor Vehicle Reference*—December 17, 1985—pro-life crusader Joe Borowski began his hearing before the Court of Appeal of Saskatchewan. Borowski's lawyer, Morris Schumiatcher, argued that the sections of the *Criminal Code* allowing therapeutic abortions violate the "right to life" of the unborn child/foetus as protected by section 7 of the *Charter*. The history of the drafting of the *Charter* clearly indicates that the government rejected requests to include either a right to abortion for women or a right to life for the unborn. The Crown attorney had effectively used this evidence of the framers' intent to rebut Schumiatcher's arguments. The court would be unjustified, the Crown argued, to give a meaning to the *Charter* that had been explicitly rejected by the people who wrote it.

---

2   See case 22.

3   See the introduction to this book.

4   See *Henrietta Muir Edwards v. Attorney-General for Canada (Persons Case)*, [1930] A.C. 124 (P.C.).

5   Transcript of Appeal Proceedings on October 3 and 4, 1988, *Borowski v. Canada (Attorney General)*, [1989] 1 S.C.R. 342.

On the third and last day of the hearing, Schumiatcher was making his closing statement when one of his assistants hurriedly arrived clutching a document. After a brief huddle, Schumiatcher excitedly announced to the Court that he had just received a copy of a Supreme Court decision handed down in Ottawa the previous day. The case was the *B.C. Motor Vehicle Reference*. Schumiatcher triumphantly quoted Justice Lamer's comments about the non-binding character of the "original intent." The three judges were now free, Schumiatcher exhorted them, to adopt the living-tree approach and to expand the meaning of section 7 to include the unborn. Ironically, but not surprisingly, Dr. Henry Morgentaler, Borowski's counterpart in the legal battle over Canada's abortion law, subsequently made extensive use of the *B.C. Motor Vehicle* precedent, but for the opposite purpose—to urge the Supreme Court to find a right to abortion in section 7 of the *Charter*.[6]

Note that the Supreme Court has not been consistent on this matter. In other cases it has relied heavily on the use of the original understanding of *Charter* text to bolster the authority of its decisions. The most important judicial use of original understanding was the *Quebec Association of Protestant School Boards* decision[7] striking down the education provisions of Bill 101. Referring to the "Canada clause" of section 23 of the *Charter*, the Court declared:

> This set of constitutional provisions was not enacted by the legislator in a vacuum.... the legislator knew, and clearly had in mind the regimes governing Anglophone and Francophone linguistic minorities in various provinces in Canada ... and their intention was to remedy the perceived defects of these regimes by uniform corrective measures, namely those contained in s. 23 of the *Charter*. ⌐

Discussion Questions

1. What is the difference between a procedural and a substantive interpretation of section 7 of the *Charter*?
2. How does the Court define the principles of fundamental justice?
3. According to the Court, what is the relationship between section 7 and section 1?
4. To which types of legal disputes does this reference opinion appear to confine the application of section 7?

---

6   See case 15.

7   *A.G. Quebec v. Quebec Association of Protestant School Boards*, [1984] 2 S.C.R. 66.

RE B.C. MOTOR VEHICLE ACT
[1985] 2 S.C.R. 486

Hearing: November 15, 1984; Judgment: December 17, 1985.

Present: Dickson C.J. and Beetz, McIntyre, Chouinard, Lamer, Wilson, and Le Dain JJ.

Interveners: the Attorney General of Canada, the Attorney General for Ontario, the Attorney General for Saskatchewan, the Attorney General for Alberta, the British Columbia Branch of the Canadian Bar Association.

The judgment of Dickson, Beetz, Chouinard, Le Dain, and Lamer JJ. was delivered by

[1] **LAMER J.:**

Introduction

[2] A law that has the potential to convict a person who has not really done anything wrong offends the principles of fundamental justice and, if imprisonment is available as a penalty, such a law then violates a person's right to liberty under s. 7 of the *Charter of Rights and Freedoms* (*Constitution Act, 1982*, as enacted by the *Canada Act 1982*, 1982 (U.K.), c. 11).

[3] In other words, absolute liability and imprisonment cannot be combined.

The Facts

[4] On August 16, 1982, the Lieutenant-Governor in Council of British Columbia referred the following question to the Court of Appeal of that province, by virtue of s. 1 of the *Constitutional Question Act*, R.S.B.C. 1979, c. 63:

Is s. 94(2) of the *Motor Vehicle Act*, R.S.B.C. 1979, as amended by the *Motor Vehicle Amendment Act, 1982*, consistent with the *Canadian Charter of Rights and Freedoms?*

[5] On February 3, 1983, the Court of Appeal handed down reasons in answer to the question in which it stated that s. 94(2) of the *Act* is inconsistent with the *Canadian Charter of Rights and Freedoms*...

The Legislation

[6] *Motor Vehicle Act*, R.S.B.C. 1979, c. 288, s. 94, as amended by the *Motor Vehicle Amendment Act, 1982*, 1982 (B.C.), c. 36, s. 19:

94.(1) A person who drives a motor vehicle on a highway or industrial road while
  (a) he is prohibited from driving a motor vehicle under sections 90, 91, 92 or 92.1, or
  (b) his driver's licence or his right to apply for or obtain a driver's licence is suspended under section 82 or 92 as it was before its repeal and replacement came

into force pursuant to the *Motor Vehicle Amendment Act, 1982*,
commits an offence and is liable,
  (c) on a first conviction, to a fine of not less than $300 and not more than $2 000 and to imprisonment for not less than 7 days and not more than 6 months, and
  (d) on a subsequent conviction, regardless of when the contravention occurred, to a fine of not less than $300 and not more than $2 000 and to imprisonment for not less than 14 days and not more than one year.
(2) Subsection (1) creates an absolute liability offence in which guilt is established by proof of driving, whether or not the defendant knew of the prohibition or suspension....

Section 7

1. Introduction

[10] The issue in this case raises fundamental questions of constitutional theory, including the nature and the very legitimacy of constitutional adjudication under the *Charter* as well as the appropriateness of various techniques of constitutional interpretation....

[12] The novel feature of the *Constitution Act*... is not that it has suddenly empowered courts to consider the content of legislation. This the courts have done for a good many years when adjudicating upon the *vires* of legislation....

[13] The truly novel features of the *Constitution Act, 1982* are that it has sanctioned the process of constitutional adjudication and has extended its scope so as to encompass a broader range of values. Content of legislation has always been considered in constitutional adjudication. Content is now to be equally considered as regards new constitutional issues. Indeed, the values subject to constitutional adjudication now pertain to the rights of individuals as well as the distribution of governmental powers. In short, it is the scope of constitutional adjudication which has been altered rather than its nature, at least, as regards the right to consider the content of legislation.

[14] In neither case, be it before or after the *Charter*, have the courts been enabled to decide upon the appropriateness of policies underlying legislative enactments. In both instances, however, the courts are empowered, indeed required, to measure the content of legislation against the guarantees of the Constitution....

[15] In this respect, s. 7 is no different than other *Charter* provisions. As the Attorney General for Ontario has noted in his factum:

Section 7, like most of the other sections in the *Charter*, limits the bounds of legislative action. It is the function of the Court to determine whether the challenged legislation has honoured those boundaries. This process necessitates judicial review of the content of the legislation.

Yet, in the context of s. 7, and in particular, of the interpretation of "principles of fundamental justice," there has prevailed in certain quarters an assumption that all but a narrow construction of s. 7 will inexorably lead the courts to "question the wisdom of enactments," to adjudicate upon the merits of public policy.

[16] From this have sprung warnings of the dangers of a judicial "super-legislature" beyond the reach of Parliament, the provincial legislatures and the electorate. The Attorney General for Ontario, in his written argument, stated that,

> ... the judiciary is neither representative of, nor responsive to the electorate on whose behalf, and under whose authority policies are selected and given effect in the laws of the land.

This is an argument which was heard countless times prior to the entrenchment of the *Charter* but which has in truth, for better or for worse, been settled by the very coming into force of the *Constitution Act, 1982*. It ought not to be forgotten that the historic decision to entrench the *Charter* in our Constitution was taken not by the courts but by the elected representatives of the people of Canada. It was those representatives who extended the scope of constitutional adjudication and entrusted the courts with this new and onerous responsibility. Adjudication under the *Charter* must be approached free of any lingering doubts as to its legitimacy.

[17] The concerns with the bounds of constitutional adjudication explain the characterization of the issue in a narrow and restrictive fashion, *i.e.*, whether the term "principles of fundamental justice" has a substantive or merely procedural content. In my view, the characterization of the issue in such fashion preempts an open-minded approach to determining the meaning of "principles of fundamental justice."

[18] The substantive/procedural dichotomy narrows the issue almost to an all-or-nothing proposition. Moreover, it is largely bound up in the American experience with substantive and procedural due process. It imports into the Canadian context American concepts, terminology and jurisprudence, all of which are inextricably linked to problems concerning the nature and legitimacy of adjudication under the U.S. Constitution. That Constitution, it must be remembered, has no s. 52 nor has it the internal checks and balances of ss. 1 and 33. We would, in my view, do our own Constitution a disservice to simply allow the American debate to define the issue for us, all the while ignoring the truly fundamental structural differences between the two constitutions. Finally, the dichotomy creates its own set of difficulties by the attempt to distinguish between two concepts whose outer boundaries are not always clear and often tend to overlap. Such difficulties can and should, when possible, be avoided.

[19] The overriding and legitimate concern that courts ought not to question the wisdom of enactments, and the presumption that the legislator could not have intended same, have to some extent distorted the discussion surrounding the meaning of "principles of fundamental justice." This has led to the spectre of a judicial "super-legislature" without a full consideration of the process of constitutional adjudication and the significance of ss. 1 and 33 of the *Charter* and s. 52 of the *Constitution Act, 1982*. This in turn has also led to a narrow characterization of the issue and to the assumption that only a procedural content to "principles of fundamental justice" can prevent the courts from adjudicating upon the merits or wisdom of enactments. If this assumption is accepted, the inevitable corollary, with which I would have to then agree, is that the legislator intended that the words "principles of fundamental justice" refer to procedure only.

[20] But I do not share that assumption. Since way back in time and even recently the courts have developed the common law beyond procedural safeguards without interfering with the "merits or wisdom" of enactments. ...

[21] The task of the Court is not to choose between substantive or procedural content *per se* but to secure for persons "the full benefit of the *Charter*'s protection" (Dickson J. (as he then was) in *R. v. Big M Drug Mart Ltd.*, [1985] 1 S.C.R. 295, at p. 344), under s. 7, while avoiding adjudication of the merits of public policy. This can only be accomplished by a purposive analysis. ...

[22] I propose therefore to approach the interpretation of s. 7 in the manner set forth by Dickson J. in *Hunter v. Southam Inc.*, [1984] 2 S.C.R. 145, and *R. v. Big M Drug Mart Ltd.*, *supra*, and by Le Dain J. in *R. v. Therens*, [1985] 1 S.C.R. 613. In *R. v. Big M Drug Mart Ltd.*, Dickson J. wrote at p. 344:

> In *Hunter v. Southam Inc.*, [1984] 2 S.C.R. 145, this Court expressed the view that the proper approach to the definition of the rights and freedoms guaranteed by the *Charter* was a purposive one. The meaning of a right or freedom guaranteed by the *Charter* was to be ascertained by an analysis of the *purpose* of such a guarantee; it was to be understood, in other words, in the light of the interests it was meant to protect. ...

[23] ... [Section 7] states "and the right not to be deprived thereof except in accordance with the principles of fundamental justice." On the facts of this case it is not necessary to decide whether the section gives any greater protection, such as deciding whether, absent a breach of the principles of fundamental justice, there still can be, given the way the section is structured, a violation of one's rights to life, liberty and security

of the person under s. 7. Furthermore, because of the fact that only deprivation of liberty was considered in these proceedings and that no one took issue with the fact that imprisonment is a deprivation of liberty, my analysis of s. 7 will be limited, as was the course taken by all, below and in this Court, to determining the scope of the words "principles of fundamental justice." I will not attempt to give any further content to liberty nor address that of the words life or security of the person.

[24] In the framework of a purposive analysis, designed to ascertain the purpose of the s. 7 guarantee and "the interests it was meant to protect" (*R. v. Big M Drug Mart Ltd., supra*), it is clear to me that the interests which are meant to be protected by the words "and the right not to be deprived thereof except in accordance with the principles of fundamental justice" of s. 7 are the life, liberty and security of the person. The principles of fundamental justice, on the other hand, are not a protected interest, but rather a qualifier of the right not to be deprived of life, liberty and security of the person. . . .

[26] . . . As a qualifier, the phrase serves to establish the parameters of the interests but it cannot be interpreted so narrowly as to frustrate or stultify them. For the narrower the meaning given to "principles of fundamental justice" the greater will be the possibility that individuals may be deprived of these most basic rights. . . .

[26] For these reasons, I am of the view that it would be wrong to interpret the term "fundamental justice" as being synonymous with natural justice as the Attorney General of British Columbia and others have suggested. To do so would strip the protected interests of much, if not most, of their content and leave the "right" to life, liberty and security of the person in a sorely emaciated state. . . .

[28] Sections 8 to 14 . . . address specific deprivations of the "right" to life, liberty and security of the person in breach of the principles of fundamental justice, and as such, violations of s. 7. They are designed to protect, in a specific manner and setting, the right to life, liberty and security of the person set forth in s. 7. It would be incongruous to interpret s. 7 more narrowly than the rights in ss. 8 to 14. . . .

[29] . . . Clearly, some of those sections embody principles that are beyond what could be characterized as "procedural."

[30] Thus, ss. 8 to 14 provide an invaluable key to the meaning of "principles of fundamental justice." Many have been developed over time as presumptions of the common law, others have found expression in the international conventions on human rights. All have been recognized as essential elements of a system for the administration of justice which is founded upon a belief in "the dignity and worth of the human person" (preamble to the *Canadian Bill of Rights*, R.S.C. 1970, App. III) and on "the rule of law" (preamble to the *Canadian Charter of Rights and Freedoms*).

[31] It is this common thread which, in my view, must guide us in determining the scope and content of "principles of fundamental justice." In other words, the principles of fundamental justice are to be found in the basic tenets of our legal system. They do not lie in the realm of general public policy but in the inherent domain of the judiciary as guardian of the justice system. . . .

[32] Thus, it seems to me that to replace "fundamental justice" with the term "natural justice" misses the mark entirely. It was, after all, clearly open to the legislator to use the term natural justice, a known term of art, but such was not done. We must, as a general rule, be loath to exchange the terms actually used with terms so obviously avoided.

[33] Whatever may have been the degree of synonymy between the two expressions in the past . . . as of the last few decades this country has given a precise meaning to the words natural justice for the purpose of delineating the responsibility of adjudicators (in the wide sense of the word) in the field of administrative law.

[34] It is, in my view, that precise and somewhat narrow meaning that the legislator avoided, clearly indicating thereby a will to give greater content to the words "principles of fundamental justice." . . .

[35] A number of courts have placed emphasis upon the Minutes of the Proceedings and Evidence of the Special Joint Committee of the Senate and of the House of Commons on the Constitution in the interpretation of "principles of fundamental justice." . . .

[36] In particular, the following passages dealing with the testimony of federal civil servants from the Department of Justice, have been relied upon:

> Mr. Strayer (Assistant Deputy Minister, Public Law):
>
> Mr. Chairman, it was our belief that the words "fundamental justice" would cover the same thing as what is called procedural due process, that is the meaning of due process in relation to requiring fair procedure. However, it in our view does not cover the concept of what is called substantive due process, which would impose substantive requirements as to policy of the law in question.
>
> This has been most clearly demonstrated in the United States in the area of property, but also in other areas such as the right to life. The term due process has been given the broader concept of meaning both the procedure and substance. Natural justice or fundamental justice in our view does not go beyond the procedural requirements of fairness. . . .
>
> The term "fundamental justice" appears to us to be essentially the same thing as natural justice.

Mr. Tassé (Deputy Minister) also said of the phrase "principles of fundamental justice" in testimony before the Committee:

We assume that the Court would look at that much like a Court would look at the requirements of natural justice....

[37] The Honourable Jean Chrétien, then federal Minister of Justice, also indicated to the Committee that, while he thought "fundamental justice marginally more appropriate than natural justice" in s. 7, either term was acceptable to the Government....

[38] The first issue which arises is whether the Minutes of the Proceedings and Evidence of the Special Joint Committee may even be considered admissible as extrinsic aids to the interpretation of *Charter* provisions. Such extrinsic materials were traditionally excluded from consideration in constitutional adjudication....

[39] In *Reference re Upper Churchill Water Rights Reversion Act,* [1984] 1 S.C.R. 297, at p. 317, however, McIntyre J. stated that,

The general exclusionary rule formerly considered to be applicable in dealing with the admissibility of extrinsic evidence in constitutional cases has been set aside or at least greatly modified and relaxed.

[40] Indeed, in the reference *Re: Anti-Inflation Act,* [1976] 2 S.C.R. 373, Laskin C.J. stated, at p. 389:

... [N]o general principle of admissibility or inadmissibility can or ought to be propounded by this Court, and ... the questions of resort to extrinsic evidence and what kind of extrinsic evidence may be admitted must depend on the constitutional issues on which it is sought adduce such evidence.

[41] This approach was adopted by Dickson J. in the reference *Re Residential Tenancies Act, 1979* [[1981] 1 S.C.R. 714]....

[42] It is to be noted, however, that McIntyre J.'s remarks are in relation to the interpretation of the challenged statutory enactment rather than the interpretation of the Constitution itself. The same is true of the remarks of Laskin C.J. and Dickson J.

[43] With respect to the interpretation of the Constitution, however, such extrinsic materials were considered, in at least two cases, by this Court.

[44] In *Re: Authority of Parliament in relation to the Upper House,* [1980] 1 S.C.R. 54, the Court stated, at p. 66:

It is, we think, proper to consider the historical background which led to the provision which was made in the *Act* for the creation of the Senate as a part of the apparatus for the enactment of federal legislation. In the debates which occurred at the Quebec Conference in 1864, considerable time was occupied in discussing the provisions

respecting the Senate. Its important purpose is stated in the following passages in speeches delivered in the debates on Confederation in the parliament of the province of Canada....

[45] The other case is *Attorney General of Canada v. Canadian National Transportation, Ltd.,* [1983] 2 S.C.R. 206. Laskin C.J., in that case, referred to the pre-Confederation debates in the course of interpreting ss. 91(27) and 92(14) of the *Constitution Act, 1867* (at p. 225).

[46] I would adopt this approach when interpreting the *Charter.* Consequently, the Minutes of the Proceedings and Evidence of the Special Joint Committee on the Constitution should, in my view, be considered....

[47] Having said that, however, I nonetheless believe that the logic underlying the reluctance to allow the use of materials such as speeches in Parliament carries considerable force with respect to the Minutes of the Committee as well.

[48] In *Reference re Upper Churchill Water Rights Reversion Act, supra,* McIntyre J. wrote at p. 319:

... I would say that the speeches and public declarations by prominent figures in the public and political life of Newfoundland on this question should not be received as evidence. They represent, no doubt, the considered views of the speakers at the time they were made, but cannot be said to be expressions of the intent of the Legislative Assembly.

[50] If speeches and declarations by prominent figures are inherently unreliable (*per* McIntyre J. in *Reference re Upper Churchill Water Rights Reversion Act, supra,* at p. 319) and "speeches made in the legislature at the time of enactment of the measure are inadmissible as having little evidential weight" (*per* Dickson J. in the reference *Re: Residential Tenancies Act 1979, supra,* at p. 721), the Minutes of the Proceedings of the Special Joint Committee, though admissible, and granted somewhat more weight than speeches should not be given too much weight. The inherent unreliability of such statements and speeches is not altered by the mere fact that they pertain to the *Charter* rather than a statute.

[51] Moreover, the simple fact remains that the *Charter* is not the product of a few individual public servants, however distinguished, but of a multiplicity of individuals who played major roles in the negotiating, drafting and adoption of the *Charter.* How can one say with any confidence that within this enormous multiplicity of actors, without forgetting the role of the provinces, the comments of a few federal civil servants can in any way be determinative?

[52] Were this Court to accord any significant weight to this testimony, it would in effect be assuming a fact which is nearly impossible of proof, *i.e.,* the intention of the legislative

bodies which adopted the *Charter*. In view of the indeterminate nature of the data, it would in my view be erroneous to give these materials anything but minimal weight.

[53] Another danger with casting the interpretation of s. 7 in terms of the comments made by those heard at the Special Joint Committee Proceedings is that, in so doing, the rights, freedoms and values embodied in the *Charter* in effect become frozen in time to the moment of adoption with little or no possibility of growth, development and adjustment to changing societal needs. . . . If the newly planted "living tree" which is the *Charter* is to have the possibility of growth and adjustment over time, care must be taken to ensure that historical materials, such as the Minutes of Proceedings and Evidence of the Special Joint Committee, do not stunt its growth. . . .

[54] The appellant states that s. 7 "is a blend of s. 1(*a*) and s. 2(*e*) of the *Canadian Bill of Rights*." Considerable emphasis is then placed upon the case of *Duke v. The Queen*, [1972] S.C.R. 917, in which this Court interpreted the words "principles of fundamental justice" in s. 2(*e*) of the *Canadian Bill of Rights*. Fauteux C.J. noted, at p. 923:

> Without attempting to formulate any final definition of those words, I would take them to mean, generally, that the tribunal which adjudicates upon his rights must act fairly, in good faith, without bias, and in a judicial temper, and must give to him the opportunity adequately to state his case.

[55] However, as Le Dain J. has written in *R. v. Therens, supra*, with the implicit support of the majority . . .

> In considering the relationship of a decision under the *Canadian Bill of Rights* to an issue arising under the *Charter*, a court cannot, in my respectful opinion, avoid bearing in mind an evident fact of Canadian judicial history, which must be squarely and frankly faced: that on the whole, with some notable exceptions, the courts have felt some uncertainty or ambivalence in the application of the *Canadian Bill of Rights* because it did not reflect a clear constitutional mandate to make judicial decisions having the effect of limiting or qualifying the traditional sovereignty of Parliament. . . .

[58] In section 2(*e*) of the *Canadian Bill of Rights*, the words "principles of fundamental justice" were placed explicitly in the context of, and qualify a "right to a fair hearing." Section 7 of the *Charter* does not create the same context. In section 7, the words "principles of fundamental justice" are placed in the context of, and qualify much more fundamental rights, the "right to life, liberty and security of the person." The distinction is important. . . .

[66] Whether any given principle may be said to be a principle of fundamental justice within the meaning of s. 7 will rest upon an analysis of the nature, sources, *rationale* and essential role of that principle within the judicial process and in our legal system, as it evolves.

[67] Consequently, those words cannot be given any exhaustive content or simple enumerative definition, but will take on concrete meaning as the courts address alleged violations of s. 7.

[68] I now turn to such an analysis of the principle of *mens rea* and absolute liability offences in order to determine the question which has been put to the Court in the present Reference.

Absolute Liability and Fundamental Justice in Penal Law

[69] It has from time immemorial been part of our system of laws that the innocent not be punished. This principle has long been recognized as an essential element of a system for the administration of justice which is founded upon a belief in the dignity and worth of the human person and on the rule of law. It is so old that its first enunciation was in Latin *actus non facit reum nisi mens sit rea*.

[70] As Glanville Williams said:

> There is no need here to go into the remote history of *mens rea*; suffice it to say that the requirement of a guilty state of mind (at least for the more serious crimes) had been developed by the time of Coke, which is as far back as the modern lawyer needs to go. "If one shoot at any wild fowl upon a tree, and the arrow killeth any reasonable creature afar off, without any evil intent in him, this is *per infortunium*." . . .

[72] This view has been adopted by this Court in unmistakable terms in many cases, amongst which the better known are *Beaver v. The Queen*, [1957] S.C.R. 531, and the most recent and often quoted judgment of Dickson J. writing for the Court in *R. v. City of Sault Ste. Marie, supra*.

[73] This Court's decision in the latter case is predicated upon a certain number of postulates one of which, given the nature of the rules it elaborates, has to be to the effect that absolute liability in penal law offends the principles of fundamental justice. Those principles are, to use the words of Dickson J., to the effect that "there is a generally held revulsion against punishment of the morally innocent." He also stated that the argument that absolute liability "violates fundamental principles of penal liability" was the most telling argument against absolute liability and one of greater force than those advanced in support thereof. . . .

[75] A law enacting an absolute liability offence will violate s. 7 of the *Charter* only if and to the extent that it has the potential of depriving of life, liberty, or security of the person.

[76] Obviously, imprisonment (including probation orders) deprives persons of their liberty. An offence has that potential as of the moment it is open to the judge to impose imprisonment. There is no need that imprisonment, as in s. 94(2), be made mandatory.

[77] I am therefore of the view that the combination of imprisonment and of absolute liability violates s. 7 of the *Charter* and can only be salvaged if the authorities demonstrate under s. 1 that such a deprivation of liberty in breach of those principles of fundamental justice is, in a free and democratic society, under the circumstances, a justified reasonable limit to one's rights under s. 7....

[79] ... I would not want us to be taken by this conclusion as having inferentially decided that absolute liability may not offend s. 7 as long as imprisonment or probation orders are not available as a sentence. The answer to that question is dependant upon the content given to the words "security of the person." That issue was and is a live one....

[83] ... In penal law, absolute liability always offends the principles of fundamental justice irrespective of the nature of the offence; it offends s. 7 of the *Charter* if as a result, anyone is deprived of his life, liberty or security of the person, irrespective of the requirement of public interest. In such cases it might only be salvaged for reasons of public interest under s. 1.

[84] In this latter regard, something might be added.

[85] Administrative expediency, absolute liability's main supportive argument, will undoubtedly under s. 1 be invoked and occasionally succeed. Indeed, administrative expediency certainly has its place in administrative law. But when administrative law chooses to call in aid imprisonment through penal law, indeed sometimes criminal law and the added stigma attached to a conviction, exceptional, in my view, will be the case where the liberty or even the security of the person guaranteed under s. 7 should be sacrificed to administrative expediency. Section 1 may, for reasons of administrative expediency, successfully come to the rescue of an otherwise violation of s. 7, but only in cases arising out of exceptional conditions, such as natural disasters, the outbreak of war, epidemics, and the like.

[86] Of course I understand the concern of many as regards corporate offences, specially, as was mentioned by the Court of Appeal, in certain sensitive areas such as the preservation of our vital environment and our natural resources. This concern might well be dispelled were it to be decided, given the proper case, that s. 7 affords protection to human persons only and does not extend to corporations.

[87] Even if it be decided that s. 7 does extend to corporations, I think the balancing under s. 1 of the public interest against the financial interests of a corporation would give very different results from that of balancing public interest and the liberty or security of the person of a human being.

[88] Indeed, the public interest as regards "air and water pollution offences" requires that the guilty be dealt with firmly, but the seriousness of the offence does not in my respectful view support the proposition that the innocent *human* person be open to conviction, quite the contrary....

Section 1

[94] Having found that s. 94(2) offends s. 7 of the *Charter* there remains the question as to whether the appellants have demonstrated that the section is salvaged by the operation of s. 1 of the *Charter*. No evidence was adduced in the Court of Appeal or in this Court....

[95] I do not take issue with the fact that it is highly desirable that "bad drivers" be kept off the road. I do not take issue either with the desirability of punishing severely bad drivers who are in contempt of prohibitions against driving. The bottom line of the question to be addressed here is: whether the Government of British Columbia has demonstrated as justifiable that the risk of imprisonment of a few innocent is, given the desirability of ridding the roads of British Columbia of bad drivers, a reasonable limit in a free and democratic society. That result is to be measured against the offence being one of strict liability open to a defence of due diligence, the success of which does nothing more than let those few who did nothing wrong remain free.

[96] As did the Court of Appeal, I find that this demonstration has not been satisfied, indeed, not in the least.

[97] In the result, I would dismiss the appeal and answer the question in the negative, as did the Court of Appeal, albeit for somewhat different reasons, and declare s. 94(2) of the *Motor Vehicle Act*, R.S.B.C. 1979, as amended by the *Motor Vehicle Amendment Act, 1982*, inconsistent with s. 7 of the *Canadian Charter of Rights and Freedoms*.

[98] Having come to this conclusion, I choose, as did the Court of Appeal, not to address whether the section violates the rights guaranteed under ss. 11(*d*) and 12 of the *Charter*.

[Justice McIntyre wrote a short concurring opinion.]

[101] **WILSON J.** (concurring): I agree with my colleague, Mr. Justice Lamer, that s. 94(2) of the *Motor Vehicle Act* violates s. 7 of the *Charter* and is not saved by s. 1. I reach that result, however, by a somewhat different route.

[102] I start with a consideration of statutory "offences." These are divisible into offences for which *mens rea* is required

and those for which it is not. Statutory offences are subject to a presumption in favour of a *mens rea* requirement as a matter of interpretation, but the courts have increasingly come to accept the proposition that legislatures may create non *mens rea* offences provided they make it clear that the *actus reus* itself is prohibited. This is typically so in the case of the so-called "regulatory" or "public welfare" offences. There is no moral delinquency involved in these offences. They are simply designed to regulate conduct in the public interest.

[103] Two questions, therefore, have to be answered on this appeal. The first is do absolute liability offences created by statute *per se* offend the *Charter*? The second is, assuming they do not, can they be attended by mandatory imprisonment or can such a sanction only be attached to true *mens rea* offences? Certainly, in the absence of the *Charter*, legislatures are free to create absolute liability offences and to attach to them any sanctions they please. Does s. 7 of the *Charter* circumscribe their power in this regard?

Absolute Liability Offenses

[104] Section 7 affirms the right to life, liberty and security of the person while at the same time indicating that a person may be deprived of such a right if the deprivation is effected "in accordance with the principles of fundamental justice." I do not view the latter part of the section as a qualification on the right to life, liberty and security of the person in the sense that it limits or modifies that right or defines its parameters. Its purpose seems to me to be the very opposite, namely to protect the right against deprivation or impairment unless such deprivation or impairment is effected in accordance with the principles of fundamental justice.

[105] Section 7 does not, however, affirm a right to the principles of fundamental justice *per se*. There must first be found an impairment of the right to life, liberty or security of the person. It must then be determined whether that impairment has been effected in accordance with the principles of fundamental justice. If it has, it passes the threshold test in s. 7 itself but the Court must go on to consider whether it can be sustained under s. 1 as a limit prescribed by law on the s. 7 right which is both reasonable and justified in a free and democratic society. If, however, the limit on the s. 7 right has been effected through a violation of the principles of fundamental justice, the enquiry, in my view, ends there and the limit cannot be sustained under s. 1. I say this because I do not believe that a limit on the s. 7 right which has been imposed in violation of the principles of fundamental justice can be either "reasonable" or "demonstrably justified in a free and democratic society." . . .

[106] Assuming that I am correct in my analysis of s. 7 and its relationship to s. 1, an absolute liability offence cannot violate s. 7 unless it impairs the right to life, liberty or security of the person. It cannot violate s. 7 because it offends the principles of fundamental justice because they are not protected by s. 7 absent an impairment of the s. 7 right. Leaving aside for the moment the mandatory imprisonment sanction, I cannot find an interference with life, liberty or security of the person in s. 94 of the *Motor Vehicle Act*. It is true that the section prevents citizens from driving their vehicles when their licences are suspended. Citizens are also prevented from driving on the wrong side of the road. Indeed, all regulatory offences impose some restriction on liberty broadly construed. But I think it would trivialize the *Charter* to sweep all those offences into s. 7 as violations of the right to life, liberty and security of the person even if they can be sustained under s. 1. It would be my view, therefore, that absolute liability offences of this type do not *per se* offend s. 7 of the *Charter*.

2. Absolute Liability Plus Mandatory Imprisonment

[107] The real question, as I see it, is whether s. 7 of the *Charter* is violated by the attachment of a mandatory imprisonment sanction to an absolute liability offence. Clearly a s. 7 right is interfered with here in that a person convicted of such an offence automatically loses his liberty. . . . Given that we can have statutory non *mens rea* offences, what is repugnant to fundamental justice in imprisoning someone for their commission? . . . I believe we must turn to the theory of punishment for the answer.

3. Punishment and Fundamental Justice

[126] It is now generally accepted among penologists that there are five main objectives of a penal system: see Nigel Walker, *Sentencing in a Rational Society*, 1969. They are:

(1) to protect offenders and suspected offenders against unofficial retaliation;
(2) to reduce the incidence of crime;
(3) to ensure that offenders atone for their offences;
(4) to keep punishment to the minimum necessary to achieve the objectives of the system; and
(5) to express society's abhorrence of crime.

Apart from death, imprisonment is the most severe sentence imposed by the law and is generally viewed as a last resort i.e., *as appropriate only when it can be shown that no other sanction can achieve the objectives of the system.*

[127] The Law Reform Commission of Canada in its Working Paper 11, "Imprisonment and Release," in *Studies on Imprisonment* (1976), states at p. 10:

Justice requires that the sanction of imprisonment not be disproportionate to the offence, and humanity dictates that it must not be heavier than necessary to achieve its objective.

[128] Because of the absolute liability nature of the offence created by s. 94(2) of the *Motor Vehicle Act* a person can be convicted under the section even although he was unaware at the time he was driving that his licence was suspended and was unable to find this out despite the exercise of due diligence. While the legislature may as a matter of government policy make this an offence, and we cannot question its wisdom in this regard, the question is whether it can make it mandatory for the courts to deprive a person convicted of it of his liberty without violating s. 7. This, in turn, depends on whether attaching a mandatory term of imprisonment to an absolute liability offence such as this violates the principles of fundamental justice. I believe that it does. I think the conscience of the court would be shocked and the administration of justice brought into disrepute by such an unreasonable and extravagant penalty. It is totally disproportionate to the offence and quite incompatible with the objective of a penal system referred to in paragraph (4) above.

[129] It is basic to any theory of punishment that the sentence imposed bear some relationship to the offence; it must be a "fit" sentence proportionate to the seriousness of the offence. Only if this is so can the public be satisfied that the offender "deserved" the punishment he received and feel a confidence in the fairness and rationality of the system. This is not to say that there is an inherently appropriate relationship between a particular offence and its punishment but rather that there is a scale of offences and punishments into which the particular offence and punishment must fit. Obviously this cannot be done with mathematical precision and many different factors will go into the assessment of the seriousness of a particular offence for purposes of determining the appropriate punishment but it does provide a workable conventional framework for sentencing. Indeed, judges in the exercise of their sentencing discretion have been employing such a scale for over a hundred years.

[130] I believe that a mandatory term of imprisonment for an offence committed unknowingly and unwittingly and after the exercise of due diligence is grossly excessive and inhumane. It is not required to reduce the incidence of the offence. It is beyond anything required to satisfy the need for "atonement." And society, in my opinion, would not be abhorred by an unintentional and unknowing violation of the section. I believe, therefore, that such a sanction offends the principles of fundamental justice embodied in our penal system. Section 94(2) is accordingly inconsistent with s. 7 of the *Charter* and must, to the extent of the inconsistency, be declared of no force and effect under s. 52. . . .

The Queen v. Oakes, 1986

The Charter has "judicialized politics and politicized the judiciary" in part because interpretive controversies over the meaning of vaguely formulated rights are political as well as legal controversies, with policy consequences extending well beyond the confines of the particular case. Giving concrete meaning to broad constitutional standards, however, does not exhaust the political aspects of the judicial task. If a right, having been defined, is found to be violated, the court must ask whether the violation is saved by section 1 of the *Charter*, which permits such "reasonable limits prescribed by law as are demonstrably justified in a free and democratic society." This question makes the political nature of *Charter* jurisprudence even more transparent; it is clearly not a traditionally legal question, as the Supreme Court has itself admitted. Despite the ritual judicial denial of the claim that constitutional review involves second-guessing the wisdom of legislative choices, many observers think that this is precisely what section 1 requires.

In the *Oakes* case, the Supreme Court attempted a comprehensive articulation of the standards it would use in addressing the section 1 question. The case involved a "reverse onus" provision in the *Narcotic Control Act*, under which someone found guilty of "possession" was deemed also to be guilty of "trafficking" unless he could prove otherwise. Having been found guilty of the first charge, Oakes claimed that the reverse onus violated his section 11(*d*) right to be presumed innocent (of trafficking) until proven guilty. The Court agreed, and thereby set aside the established interpretation of a similar guarantee of the presumption of innocence in the *Canadian Bill of Rights*. The fact that there might be a "rational connection" between the "basic fact" (possession) and the "presumed fact" (trafficking) was considered irrelevant to establishing the violation because "a basic fact may rationally tend to prove a presumed fact, but not prove its existence beyond a reasonable doubt," as required in criminal cases. Justice Dickson was careful to add, however, that such a rational connection could be used as part of a section 1 defence.

To establish a section 1 defence, the onus is on the state to demonstrate to a "very high degree of probability" that the *Charter* violation is justified by a "pressing and substantial" objective, and that the means used are "proportional" to that objective. Proportional means have three characteristics: (1) they are not arbitrary and thus actually achieve the objective—that is, they are "rationally connected" to the objective; (2) they impair the right as little as possible; and (3) their costs are proportional to their benefits—that is, "the more severe the deleterious effects, the more [pressing and substantial] the objective must be."

The Court readily conceded that controlling drug trafficking was a sufficiently compelling purpose to justify a violation of *Charter* rights. The means, however, were not proportional to this end because the reverse onus applied to all cases of possession and there was no "rational connection" between trafficking and possession of small quantities of illegal drugs.

The Court's deference regarding the objective of the policy characterizes most, though not all, forays by the Court into section 1 analysis. This is perhaps not surprising. Challenging the very purpose of a policy would most obviously place the Court in a naked political confrontation with the legislature. On the other hand, if the Court accepts the purpose of the law, and limits its scrutiny to the means chosen to achieve that purpose, it might be easier to sustain the claim that it is not second-guessing the wisdom of legislative policy.[1] In *Oakes*, for example, the Court's judgment may be read as saying no more than that the legislature had been somewhat insensitive or careless in determining how to achieve its legitimate end. Indeed, having conceded the legitimacy of some violation of *Charter* rights to control trafficking, the Court implied that more carefully tailored and hence less intrusive means were possible—perhaps a reverse onus that applied only to possession of sufficiently "large" quantities.

As subsequent cases show,[2] however, the Court cannot consistently hide the political nature of section 1 jurisprudence by concentrating on the question of means. To reject legislative means, the Court must compare them, more or less explicitly, to "better" alternatives. But political controversy is as often about means as it is about ends, and the legislative choice of means may be carefully, rather than carelessly, deliberated. In such cases, some will consider the judicial evaluation of alternative means to be no less a matter of second-guessing policy wisdom than is the evaluation of objectives. ∼

Discussion Questions

1. Why did the Court decide the same issue differently under the *Bill of Rights*? Why did it overrule the *Bill of Rights* precedent?

2. Suppose section 11(*d*) of the *Charter* simply protected the right of an accused to be tried "according to law in a fair and public hearing by an independent and impartial tribunal," without any explicit reference to the presumption of innocence. What difference, if any, would (should) this have made to the Court's ruling?

3. Assess Chief Justice Dickson's reasons for concluding that the purpose of the challenged law was sufficiently pressing and substantial "to warrant overriding a constitutionally protected right or freedom in certain cases."

---

1   See Patrick Monahan, *Politics and the Constitution: The Charter, Federalism, and the Supreme Court of Canada* (Toronto: Carswell/Methuen, 1987) 67-68.

2   See, for example, the discussion of *Edwards Books* in case 3.

THE QUEEN v. DAVID EDWIN OAKES
[1986] 1 S.C.R. 103

Hearing: March 12, 1985; Judgment: February 28, 1986.

Present: Dickson C.J. and Estey, McIntyre, Chouinard, Lamer, Wilson, and Le Dain JJ.

The judgment of Dickson C.J., Chouinard, Lamer, Wilson, and Le Dain JJ. was delivered by

[1] **DICKSON C.J.:** This appeal concerns the constitutionality of s. 8 of the *Narcotic Control Act*, R.S.C. 1970, c. N-1. The section provides, in brief, that if the Court finds the accused in possession of a narcotic, he is presumed to be in possession for the purpose of trafficking. Unless the accused can establish the contrary, he must be convicted of trafficking. The Ontario Court of Appeal held that this provision constitutes a "reverse onus" clause and is unconstitutional because it violates one of the core values of our criminal justice system, the presumption of innocence, now entrenched in s. 11(*d*) of the *Canadian Charter of Rights and Freedoms*. The Crown has appealed. . . .

[3] The respondent, David Edwin Oakes, was charged with unlawful possession of a narcotic for the purpose of trafficking, contrary to s. 4(2) of the *Narcotic Control Act*. He elected trial by magistrate without a jury. At trial, the Crown adduced evidence to establish that Mr. Oakes was found in possession of eight one gram vials of *cannabis* resin in the form of hashish oil. Upon a further search conducted at the police station, $619.45 was located. Mr. Oakes told the police that he had bought ten vials of hashish oil for $150 for his own use, and that the $619.45 was from a workers' compensation cheque. He elected not to call evidence as to possession of the narcotic. Pursuant to the procedural provisions of s. 8 of the *Narcotic Control Act*, the trial judge proceeded to make a finding that it was beyond a reasonable doubt that Mr. Oakes was in possession of the narcotic.

[4] Following this finding, Mr. Oakes brought a motion to challenge the constitutional validity of s. 8 of the *Narcotic Control Act*, which he maintained imposes a burden on an accused to prove that he or she was not in possession for the purpose of trafficking. He argued that s. 8 violates the presumption of innocence contained in s. 11(*d*) of the *Charter*. . . .

[15] Before examining the presumption of innocence contained in s. 11(*d*) of the *Charter*, it is necessary to clarify the meaning of s. 8 of the *Narcotic Control Act*. The procedural steps contemplated by s. 8 were clearly outlined by Branca J.A. in *R. v. Babcock and Auld*.

[Justice Branca observed that the trial of an accused charged with trafficking was divided into two parts. First, the trial "proceeds as if it was a prosecution . . . on a simple charge of possession," with the burden of proof resting on the Crown. Second, if simple possession is proven, the onus shifts to the accused to prove that he was not in possession for the purposes of trafficking.]

[26] I conclude that s. 8 of the *Narcotic Control Act* contains a reverse onus provision imposing a legal burden on an accused to prove on a balance of probabilities that he or she was not in possession of a narcotic for the purpose of trafficking. It is therefore necessary to determine whether s. 8 of the *Narcotic Control Act* offends the right to be "presumed innocent until proven guilty" as guaranteed by s. 11(*d*) of the *Charter*. . . .

[28] To interpret the meaning of s. 11(*d*), it is important to adopt a purposive approach. . . . To identify the underlying purpose of the *Charter* right in question . . . it is important to begin by understanding the cardinal values it embodies.

[29] The presumption of innocence is a hallowed principle lying at the very heart of criminal law. Although protected expressly in s. 11(*d*) of the *Charter*, the presumption of innocence is referable and integral to the general protection of life, liberty and security of the person contained in s. 7 of the *Charter* (see *Re B.C. Motor Vehicle Act* . . .). The presumption of innocence protects the fundamental liberty and human dignity of any and every person accused by the State of criminal conduct. An individual charged with a criminal offence faces grave social and personal consequences, including potential loss of physical liberty, subjection to social stigma and ostracism from the community, as well as other social, psychological and economic harms. In light of the gravity of these consequences, the presumption of innocence is crucial. It ensures that until the State proves an accused's guilt beyond all reasonable doubt, he or she is innocent. This is essential in a society committed to fairness and social justice. The presumption of innocence confirms our faith in humankind; it reflects our belief that individuals are decent and law-abiding members of the community until proven otherwise.

[30] The presumption of innocence has enjoyed long-standing recognition at common law. In the leading case, *Woolmington v. Director of Public Prosecutions*, [1935] A.C. 462 (H.L.), Viscount Sankey wrote at pp. 481-82:

Throughout the web of the English Criminal Law one golden thread is always to be seen, that it is the duty of the prosecution to prove the prisoner's guilt subject to what I have already said as to the defence of insanity and subject also to any statutory exception. If, at the end of and on the whole of the case, there is a reasonable doubt, created by the evidence given by either the prosecution or the prisoner, as to whether the prisoner killed the deceased with a malicious intention, the prosecution has not made out the case and the prisoner is entitled to an acquittal. No matter what the charge or where the trial, the principle that the prosecution must prove the guilt of the prisoner is part of the common law of England and no attempt to whittle it down can be entertained. . . .

[32] In light of the above, the right to be presumed innocent until proven guilty requires that s. 11(*d*) have, at a minimum, the following content. First, an individual must be proven guilty beyond a reasonable doubt. Second, it is the State which must bear the burden of proof. . . . Third, criminal prosecutions must be carried out in accordance with lawful procedures and fairness. The latter part of s. 11(*d*), which requires the proof of guilt "according to law in a fair and public hearing by an independent and impartial tribunal," underlines the importance of this procedural requirement. . . .

[33] Having considered the general meaning of the presumption of innocence, it is now, I think, desirable to review briefly the authorities on reverse onus clauses in Canada and other jurisdictions. . . .

[34] Section 2(*f*) of the *Canadian Bill of Rights*, which safeguards the presumption of innocence, provides:

> . . . no law of Canada shall be construed or applied so as to . . .
> (f) deprive a person charged with a criminal offence of the right to be presumed innocent until proved guilty according to law in a fair and public hearing by an independent and impartial tribunal. . . .

The wording of this section closely parallels that of s. 11(*d*). For this reason, one of the Crown's primary contentions is that the *Canadian Bill of Rights* jurisprudence should be determinative of the outcome of the present appeal.

[35] The leading case decided under s. 2(*f*) of the *Canadian Bill of Rights* and relied on by the Crown, is *R. v. Appleby* [[1972] S.C.R. 303], *supra*. In that case, the accused had challenged s. 224A(1)(*a*) (now s. 237(1)(*a*)) of the *Criminal Code*, R.S.C. 1970, c. C-34, which imposes a burden upon an accused to prove that he or she, though occupying the driver's seat, did not enter the vehicle for the purpose of setting it in motion and did not, therefore, have care and control. This Court rejected the arguments of the accused that s. 2(*f*) had been violated; it relied on the *Woolmington* case which held that the presumption of innocence was subject to "statutory exceptions." As Ritchie J. stated in his judgment for the majority at pp. 315-16:

> It seems to me, therefore, that if Woolmington's case is to be accepted, the words "presumed innocent until proved guilty according to law . . ." as they appear in s. 2(*f*) of the *Bill of Rights*, must be taken to envisage a law which rec-

ognizes the existence of statutory exceptions reversing the onus of proof with respect to one or more ingredients of an offence in cases where certain specific facts have been proved by the Crown in relation to such ingredients. . . .

[38] Although there are important lessons to be learned from the *Canadian Bill of Rights* jurisprudence, it does not constitute binding authority in relation to the constitutional interpretation of the *Charter*. As this Court held in *R. v. Big M Drug Mart Ltd.* [[1985] 1 S.C.R. 295], *supra*, the *Charter*, as a constitutional document, is fundamentally different from the statutory *Canadian Bill of Rights*, which was interpreted as simply recognizing and declaring existing rights. (See also *Singh v. Minister of Employment and Immigration*, [1985] 1 S.C.R. 177 *per* Wilson J.; *R. v. Therens*, [1985] 1 S.C.R. 613, *per* Le Dain J.). . . .

[39] With this in mind, one cannot but question the appropriateness of reading into the phrase "according to law" in s. 11(*d*) of the *Charter* the statutory exceptions acknowledged in *Woolmington* and in *Appleby*. The *Woolmington* case was decided in the context of a legal system with no constitutionally entrenched human rights document. In Canada, we have tempered parliamentary supremacy by entrenching important rights and freedoms in the Constitution. Viscount Sankey's statutory exception proviso is clearly not applicable in this context and would subvert the very purpose of the entrenchment of the presumption of innocence in the *Charter*. I do not, therefore, feel constrained in this case by the interpretation of s. 2(*f*) of the *Canadian Bill of Rights* presented in the majority judgment in *Appleby*. Section 8 of the *Narcotic Control Act* is not rendered constitutionally valid simply by virtue of the fact that it is a statutory provision. . . .

[59] As we have seen, the potential for a rational connection between the basic fact and the presumed fact to justify a reverse onus provision has been elaborated in some of the cases discussed above and is now known as the "rational connection test." In the context of s. 11(*d*), however, the following question arises: if we apply the rational connection test to the consideration of whether s. 11(*d*) has been violated, are we adequately protecting the constitutional principle of the presumption of innocence? . . . A basic fact may rationally tend to prove a presumed fact, but not prove its existence beyond a reasonable doubt. An accused person could thereby be convicted despite the presence of a reasonable doubt. This would violate the presumption of innocence.

[60] I should add that this questioning of the constitutionality of the "rational connection test" as a guide to interpreting s. 11(*d*) does not minimize its importance. The appropriate stage for invoking the rational connection test, however, is under s. 1 of the *Charter*. This consideration did not arise

under the *Canadian Bill of Rights* because of the absence of an equivalent to s. 1. At the Court of Appeal level in the present case, Martin J.A. sought to combine the analysis of s. 11(*d*) and s. 1 to overcome the limitations of the *Canadian Bill of Rights* jurisprudence. To my mind, it is highly desirable to keep s. 1 and s. 11(*d*) analytically distinct. Separating the analysis into two components is consistent with the approach this Court has taken to the *Charter* to date. . . .

[61] To return to s. 8 of the *Narcotic Control Act*, I am in no doubt whatsoever that it violates s. 11(*d*) of the *Charter* by requiring the accused to prove on a balance of probabilities that he was not in possession of the narcotic for the purpose of trafficking. Mr. Oakes is compelled by s. 8 to prove he is *not* guilty of the offence of trafficking. He is thus denied his right to be presumed innocent and subjected to the potential penalty of life imprisonment unless he can rebut the presumption. This is radically and fundamentally inconsistent with the societal values of human dignity and liberty which we espouse, and is directly contrary to the presumption of innocence enshrined in s. 11(*d*). Let us turn now to s. 1 of the *Charter*. . . .

[63] It is important to observe at the outset that s. 1 has two functions: first, it constitutionally guarantees the rights and freedoms set out in the provisions which follow; and, second, it states explicitly the exclusive justificatory criteria (outside of s. 33 of the *Constitution Act, 1982*) against which limitations on those rights and freedoms must be measured. Accordingly, any s. 1 inquiry must be premised on an understanding that the impugned limit violates constitutional rights and freedoms—rights and freedoms which are part of the supreme law of Canada. . . .

[64] A second contextual element of interpretation of s. 1 is provided by the words "free and democratic society." Inclusion of these words as the final standard of justification for limits on rights and freedoms refers the Court to the very purpose for which the *Charter* was originally entrenched in the Constitution: Canadian society is to be free and democratic. The Court must be guided by the values and principles essential to a free and democratic society which I believe embody, to name but a few, respect for the inherent dignity of the human person, commitment to social justice and equality, accommodation of a wide variety of beliefs, respect for cultural and group identity, and faith in social and political institutions which enhance the participation of individuals and groups in society. The underlying values and principles of a free and democratic society are the genesis of the rights and freedoms guaranteed by the *Charter* and the ultimate standard against which a limit on a right or freedom must be shown, despite its effect, to be reasonable and demonstrably justified.

[65] The rights and freedoms guaranteed by the *Charter* are not, however, absolute. It may become necessary to limit rights and freedoms in circumstances where their exercise would be inimical to the realization of collective goals of fundamental importance. For this reason, s. 1 provides criteria of justification for limits on the rights and freedoms guaranteed by the *Charter*. These criteria impose a stringent standard of justification, especially when understood in terms of the two contextual considerations discussed above, namely, the violation of a constitutionally guaranteed right or freedom and the fundamental principles of a free and democratic society.

[66] The onus of proving that a limit on a right or freedom guaranteed by the *Charter* is reasonable and demonstrably justified in a free and democratic society rests upon the party seeking to uphold the limitation. It is clear from the text of s. 1 that limits on the rights and freedoms enumerated in the *Charter* are exceptions to their general guarantee. The presumption is that the rights and freedoms are guaranteed unless the party invoking s. 1 can bring itself within the exceptional criteria which justify their being limited. This is further substantiated by the use of the word "demonstrably" which clearly indicates that the onus of justification is on the party seeking to limit. . . .

[67] The standard of proof under s. 1 is the civil standard, namely, proof by a preponderance of probability. The alternative criminal standard, proof beyond a reasonable doubt, would, in my view, be unduly onerous on the party seeking to limit. Concepts such as "reasonableness," "justifiability" and "free and democratic society" are simply not amenable to such a standard. Nevertheless, the preponderance of probability test must be applied rigorously. Indeed, the phrase "demonstrably justified" in s. 1 of the *Charter* supports this conclusion. Within the broad category of the civil standard, there exist different degrees of probability depending on the nature of the case. . . .

[68] Having regard to the fact that s. 1 is being invoked for the purpose of justifying a violation of the constitutional rights and freedoms the *Charter* was designed to protect, a very high degree of probability will be, in the words of Lord Denning, "commensurate with the occasion." Where evidence is required in order to prove the constituent elements of a s. 1 inquiry, and this will generally be the case, it should be cogent and persuasive and make clear to the Court the consequences of imposing or not imposing the limit. . . . A court will also need to know what alternative measures for implementing the objective were available to the legislators when they made their decisions. I should add, however, that there may be cases where certain elements of the s. 1 analysis are obvious or self-evident.

[69] To establish that a limit is reasonable and demonstrably justified in a free and democratic society, two central criteria must be satisfied. First, the objective, which the measures responsible for a limit on a *Charter* right or freedom are

designed to serve, must be "of sufficient importance to warrant overriding a constitutionally protected right or freedom": *R. v. Big M Drug Mart Ltd., supra,* at p. 352. The standard must be high in order to ensure that objectives which are trivial or discordant with the principles integral to a free and democratic society do not gain s. 1 protection. It is necessary, at a minimum, that an objective relate to concerns which are pressing and substantial in a free and democratic society before it can be characterized as sufficiently important.

[70] Second, once a sufficiently significant objective is recognized, then the party invoking s. 1 must show that the means chosen are reasonable and demonstrably justified. This involves "a form of proportionality test": *R. v. Big M Drug Mart Ltd., supra,* at p. 352. Although the nature of the proportionality test will vary depending on the circumstances, in each case courts will be required to balance the interests of society with those of individuals and groups. There are, in my view, three important components of a proportionality test. First, the measures adopted must be carefully designed to achieve the objective in question. They must not be arbitrary, unfair or based on irrational considerations. In short, they must be rationally connected to the objective. Second, the means, even if rationally connected to the objective in this first sense, should impair "as little as possible" the right or freedom in question: *R. v. Big M Drug Mart Ltd., supra,* at p. 352. Third, there must be a proportionality between the *effects* of the measures which are responsible for limiting the *Charter* right or freedom, and the objective which has been identified as of "sufficient importance."

[71] With respect to the third component, it is clear that the general effect of any measure impugned under s. 1 will be the infringement of a right or freedom guaranteed by the *Charter*; this is the reason why resort to s. 1 is necessary. The inquiry into effects must, however, go further. A wide range of rights and freedoms are guaranteed by the *Charter*, and an almost infinite number of factual situations may arise in respect of these. Some limits on rights and freedoms protected by the *Charter* will be more serious than others in terms of the nature of the right or freedom violated, the extent of the violation, and the degree to which the measures which impose the limit trench upon the integral principles of a free and democratic society. Even if an objective is of sufficient importance, and the first two elements of the proportionality test are satisfied, it is still possible that, because of the severity of the deleterious effects of a measure on individuals or groups, the measure will not be justified by the purposes it is intended to serve. The more severe the deleterious effects of a measure, the more important the objective must be if the measure is to be reasonable and demonstrably justified in a free and democratic society.

[72] Having outlined the general principles of a s. 1 inquiry, we must apply them to s. 8 of the *Narcotic Control Act*. Is the reverse onus provision in s. 8 a reasonable limit on the right to be presumed innocent until proven guilty beyond a reasonable doubt as can be demonstrably justified in a free and democratic society?

[73] The starting point for formulating a response to this question is, as stated above, the nature of Parliament's interest or objective which accounts for the passage of s. 8 of the *Narcotic Control Act*. According to the Crown, s. 8 of the *Narcotic Control Act* is aimed at curbing drug trafficking by facilitating the conviction of drug traffickers. In my opinion, Parliament's concern that drug trafficking be decreased can be characterized as substantial and pressing. The problem of drug trafficking has been increasing since the 1950s at which time there was already considerable concern. . . . Throughout this period, numerous measures were adopted by free and democratic societies, at both the international and national levels. . . .

[76] The objective of protecting our society from the grave ills associated with drug trafficking, is, in my view, one of sufficient importance to warrant overriding a constitutionally protected right or freedom in certain cases. Moreover, the degree of seriousness of drug trafficking makes its acknowledgement as a sufficiently important objective for the purposes of s. 1, to a large extent, self-evident. The first criterion of a s. 1 inquiry, therefore, has been satisfied by the Crown.

[77] The next stage of inquiry is a consideration of the means chosen by Parliament to achieve its objective. The means must be reasonable and demonstrably justified in a free and democratic society. As outlined above, this proportionality test should begin with a consideration of the rationality of the provision: is the reverse onus clause in s. 8 rationally related to the objective of curbing drug trafficking? At a minimum, this requires that s. 8 be internally rational; there must be a rational connection between the basic fact of possession and the presumed fact of possession for the purpose of trafficking. Otherwise, the reverse onus clause could give rise to unjustified and erroneous convictions for drug trafficking of persons guilty only of possession of narcotics.

[78] In my view, s. 8 does not survive this rational connection test. As Martin J.A. of the Ontario Court of Appeal concluded, possession of a small or negligible quantity of narcotics does not support the inference of trafficking. In other words, it would be irrational to infer that a person had an intent to traffic on the basis of his or her possession of a very small quantity of narcotics. The presumption required under s. 8 of the *Narcotic Control Act* is overinclusive and could lead to results in certain cases which would defy both rationality and fairness. In light of the seriousness of the offence in question, which carries with it the possibility of

imprisonment for life, I am further convinced that the first component of the proportionality test has not been satisfied by the Crown.

[79] Having concluded that s. 8 does not satisfy this first component of proportionality, it is unnecessary to consider the other two components. . . .

[Justices Estey and McIntyre concurred in the reasons of Chief Justice Dickson with respect to the relationship of section 11(*d*) and section 1 of the *Charter*, but adopted the reasons of Justice Martin in the court below for the disposition of all other issues.]

Morgentaler v. The Queen, 1988

The *Morgentaler* decision is one of the most publicized and controversial *Charter* decisions to date, due in part to the emotional and divisive character of its subject matter—abortion. *Morgentaler* also reflects the flamboyant personality of its appellant. Pro-choice crusader Dr. Henry Morgentaler's victory culminated almost 20 years of civil disobedience in protest of Canada's abortion law. In the early 1970s, Morgentaler openly defied the abortion law by performing unauthorized abortions in his Montreal clinic. In three successive trials, juries refused to convict him. However, in 1974, the Quebec Court of Appeal overturned his first jury acquittal and took the unprecedented step of directly convicting him rather than returning the case for retrial. In 1975, the Supreme Court of Canada rejected Morgentaler's appeal, and he was sentenced to 18 months in prison.

Ironically, Morgentaler's legal defeat laid the basis for a subsequent political victory. In response to protests, Parliament amended the *Criminal Code* to withdraw the power to convict from appeal courts. In the light of what was immediately dubbed "the Morgentaler amendment," the federal Attorney General granted Morgentaler a new trial. After his third jury acquittal, Morgentaler was released from prison. The newly elected Parti Québécois government of René Lévesque dropped outstanding charges against Morgentaler, and announced that it would no longer enforce section 251 (the abortion section) of the *Criminal Code* in Quebec. The Lévesque government subsequently supported the creation of community health clinics that included abortion services. By 1980, Morgentaler had achieved his objective of easy and inexpensive access to abortion services in Quebec. In the rest of Canada, however, the section 251 regime was still in effect.

In 1983, Morgentaler renewed his campaign of civil disobedience. With financial backing from the Canadian Abortion Rights Action League (CARAL), he opened abortion clinics in Toronto and Winnipeg. Once again he was brought to trial and acquitted by a jury, and once again he saw his acquittal overturned by a court of appeal. This time, however, armed with the new *Charter of Rights*, Morgentaler prevailed in the Supreme Court of Canada.

The contrast between the Supreme Court's handling of the first *Morgentaler* appeal and its 1988 decision reveals just how much the *Charter* changed the Court's willingness to use the power of judicial review. In his 1975 appeal, Morgentaler used the 1960 *Bill of Rights* to challenge the validity of section 251 of the *Criminal Code*. At oral argument before the Supreme Court, Morgentaler's lawyers argued that section 251 violated women's right to liberty and also "equality before the law." After hearing these arguments, the Court recessed briefly and then announced that section 251 did not violate the *Bill of Rights*. The Crown was told it need not even argue the *Bill of Rights* issues.

In its written judgment six months later, the six-judge majority did not even address the *Bill of Rights* issues. Chief Justice Laskin dissented for other reasons, but explained why the Court was unwilling to accept Morgentaler's *Bill of Rights* arguments. In distinguishing the *Morgentaler* case from the then recently decided American abortion decision, *Roe v. Wade* (1973), the Chief Justice observed, "how foreign to our constitutional traditions, to our constitutional law and to our conceptions of judicial review was any interference by a Court with the substantive content of legislation." This difference, Laskin explained, stemmed from the fact that the *Canadian Bill of Rights* was not constitutionally entrenched:[1]

> It cannot be forgotten that it is a statutory instrument, illustrative of Parliament's primacy within the limits of its assigned legislative authority, and this is a relevant consideration in determining how far the language of the *Canadian Bill of Rights* should be taken in assessing the quality of federal enactments which are challenged under s. 1(a).

The constitutional status of the *Charter* appears to have erased whatever doubts the Court had about the legitimacy of its power to review and nullify Parliament's laws. However, the *Morgentaler* decision was much narrower than was generally reported. The Supreme Court did not declare a constitutional right to abortion or "freedom of choice." Only Justice Wilson took this position, and even she acknowledged a legitimate state interest in protecting the life of the foetus/unborn child at some point in the second trimester of a pregnancy. The other six carefully and explicitly avoided this "substantive" policy issue.

The two dissenters, McIntyre and La Forest, looked behind the text of the *Charter* to the framers' understanding of its meaning. They found that the legislative history of the *Charter* in 1980-81 indicated that it was intentionally neutral on the abortion issue. They concluded that when the *Charter* is purposely silent on an issue, so too must be the judges.

The other four judges who ruled against the abortion law did so because they said that it violated the "procedural fairness" required by section 7, not because there is any independent right to abortion. These four further disagreed among themselves on just how serious even the procedural violations were. Two, Dickson and Lamer, suggested that certain elements of the current law—such as removal of the decision-making power for the abortion decision from the pregnant woman—violated the "security of the person." The other two judges— Beetz and Estey—defined the procedural problems more narrowly and thus as remediable. While certain requirements as currently written—such as approval by a therapeutic abortion committee (TAC)—created unfair delays and burdens, a revised version of the TAC might be acceptable. Unlike Dickson and Lamer, Beetz and Estey ruled that in principle there was no legal problem with the requirement of the current law that abortions be permitted only when the continuation of a pregnancy "would threaten the life or health of the mother," or with the requirement that an independent and impartial third party be the judge of this issue.

A significant aspect of the three plurality opinions was their extensive reliance on "social facts" or "extrinsic evidence." In 1975, Chief Justice Laskin rejected similar evidence that indicated unequal access to abortion services across the country. "This is a reach for equality by judicially unmanageable standards," declared Laskin. "It would mean that the Court would have to come to . . . decide how large or small an area must be within which an acceptable distribution of physicians and hospitals must be found."[2] Thirteen years later, in the second *Morgentaler* appeal, the dissenters, McIntyre and La Forest, were still skeptical about the use of extrinsic evidence to support the "unequal access" argument. McIntyre declared that he would prefer to rely on "evidence given under oath in my consideration of factual matters." He also noted that there had been no first-hand testimony by doctors or patients that supported the lack-of-access argument.

---

1   *Morgentaler v. The Queen*, [1976] 1 S.C.R. 616 at 632.

2   *Ibid.* at 653.

Justices Wilson, Dickson, and Beetz had no such qualms. They cited at length from the Badgley Report to support the lack-of-access claim. The Badgley Report had been commissioned in 1976 by the Trudeau government in response to the first *Morgentaler* case. It was intended to serve as the basis for possible legislative reform of the abortion law, but Parliament had never acted on it. Now, 10 years later, the Badgley Report was being used by judges to strike down the same abortion law. This extensive use of and reliance on extrinsic evidence is a clear indicator of the greater policy-making role the Court has accepted under the *Charter*.

Despite similarities, the *Morgentaler* decision differs significantly from the 1973 American abortion decision. In *Roe v. Wade*, the American Supreme Court declared that there was an implied "right to privacy" in the American Constitution and that it included a woman's right to determine for herself whether to continue or terminate a pregnancy. The Court effectively precluded any legislative response to protect the interests of the unborn or the father except in the last trimester of a pregnancy. By contrast, in the *Morgentaler* decision, by limiting their ruling to procedural requirements of the criminal law, the majority left the door open for Parliament to respond with an amended abortion law.

Six months later, in July 1988, the Mulroney government introduced a motion in the House of Commons for a reformed abortion law. The motion proposed easy access to abortions during the "early stages" of a pregnancy, but in "subsequent stages" an abortion would be permitted only if two doctors found that continuation of the pregnancy would "endanger the woman's life or seriously endanger her health." After two days of almost around-the-clock debate, the government motion was defeated in a "free vote" (147 to 76). Both "pro-life" and "pro-choice" MPs voted against the compromise measure. Both sides offered their own amendments that would have greatly restricted or eased access to abortion, but these too were defeated. The "pro-life" amendment came closest to adoption, losing 118 to 105.

After the 1988 election, the Mulroney government introduced Bill C-43, yet another attempt to retain some criminal sanction against abortion. Bill C-43 would have made abortion at any time an offence, punishable by up to two years in jail, unless performed by a doctor who was of the opinion that without an abortion the life or health of the pregnant woman would be threatened. The vote on Bill C-43 was not a free vote. It passed the House of Commons by a vote of 140 to 131. But in the Senate, for the first time ever, there was a tied vote, so the Bill died. The Mulroney government had no appetite for reviving it. Indeed, no federal government since has touched this highly divisive issue.[3]

The *Morgentaler* decision pulled the legal rug out from under a parallel challenge to Canada's abortion law brought by Joe Borowski, a former Manitoba Cabinet minister and prominent pro-life activist. Borowski was to Canada's pro-life movement what Morgentaler was to the pro-choice camp—a hero, a symbol, and an opportunity to win in the courts what they could not win in Parliament. Whereas Morgentaler's challenge had emphasized the rights of women to "liberty" and "security of the person" under section 7 of the *Charter*, Borowski's challenge argued that the human foetus was included in the "everyone" entitled to the section 7 "right to life." While Morgentaler claimed section 251 placed too many restrictions on abortions, Borowski maintained that it too easily permitted them.

---

3   Thomas Flanagan, "The Staying Power of the Status Quo: Collective Choice in Canada's Parliament after Morgentaler" (1999) 30 *Canadian Journal of Political Science* 31.

Like Morgentaler, Borowski had been travelling the long route to an ultimate Supreme Court decision for many years.[4] When the Supreme Court heard his case in October 1988, however, it had already declared section 251 unconstitutional in *Morgentaler*, creating a serious problem for Borowski. How could he challenge the constitutionality of a law that no longer existed? In legal parlance, Borowski's case had become moot—no longer a live controversy—with the death of section 251. The Court dismissed his case for precisely this reason on March 9, 1989. Although the Court had agreed to hear Borowski's substantive arguments, it did not address them. To do so, wrote Justice Sopinka for a unanimous Court, would be to create a new kind of "private reference," a procedure that would intrude on the prerogative of the executive and possibly pre-empt Parliament's policy options on the abortion issue.

Similar compunctions about mootness did not trouble the Court in its consideration of another abortion case that burst onto the scene in the summer of 1989, close on the heels of the *Borowski* decision. When Chantal Daigle broke up with her boyfriend, Jean-Guy Tremblay, she decided to abort the foetus she had conceived with him. Tremblay persuaded a Quebec Superior Court judge to issue an injunction preventing the abortion because the foetus was a "human being" protected under the Quebec *Charter of Human Rights*. After this decision was hurriedly confirmed by the Quebec Court of Appeal, the Supreme Court agreed to interrupt its summer vacation to hear an expedited final appeal in August 1989. Before the Court could hear Daigle's appeal, however, she slipped across the border to have an abortion in the United States, making her case as moot as Borowski's had been. Nevertheless, the Court heard the substantive issues and decided that if the Quebec legislature had intended to include the foetus in the category of "human beings" guaranteed the right to life under the Quebec *Charter*, it would have done so more explicitly. *Daigle* was based on the Quebec rather than the Canadian *Charter of Rights*, but it had obvious implications for the latter and was widely portrayed as a major legal victory for the pro-choice side in the abortion controversy. ⁓

Discussion Questions

1. How important was social fact evidence to the majority's analysis of the section 7 violation?
2. Arrange the four opinions in *Morgentaler* on a spectrum with judicial restraint at one end and judicial activism at the other. Justify your placement of each opinion on the spectrum.
3. Should the Court have heard Morgentaler's appeal in the first place? Why or why not?

---

4   For a full account of both sagas, see F.L. Morton, *Morgentaler v. Borowski: Abortion, the Charter, and the Courts* (Toronto: McClelland & Stewart, 1992).

DR. HENRY MORGENTALER, ET AL. v. THE QUEEN
[1988] 1 S.C.R. 30

Hearing: October 7, 8, 9, 10, 1986; Judgment: January 28, 1988.

Present: Dickson C.J. and Beetz, Estey, McIntyre, Lamer, Wilson, and La Forest JJ.

Intervener: The Attorney General of Canada.

The judgment of Dickson C.J. and Lamer J. was delivered by

DICKSON C.J.: The principal issue raised by this appeal is whether the abortion provisions of the *Criminal Code*, R.S.C. 1970, c. C-34, infringe the "right to life, liberty and security of the person and the right not to be deprived thereof except in accordance with the principles of fundamental justice" as formulated in s. 7 of the *Canadian Charter of Rights and Freedoms*. The appellants, Dr. Henry Morgentaler, Dr. Leslie Frank Smoling and Dr. Robert Scott, have raised thirteen distinct grounds of appeal. During oral submissions, however, it became apparent that the primary focus of the case was upon the s. 7 argument. It is submitted by the appellants that s. 251 of the *Criminal Code* contravenes s. 7 of the *Canadian Charter of Rights and Freedoms* and that s. 251 should be struck down. Counsel for the Crown admitted during the course of her submissions that s. 7 of the *Charter* was indeed "the key" to the entire appeal. . . . In view of my resolution of the s. 7 issue, it will not be necessary for me to address the appellants' other *Charter* arguments and I expressly refrain from commenting upon their merits.

During argument before this Court, counsel for the Crown emphasized repeatedly that it is not the role of the judiciary in Canada to evaluate the wisdom of legislation enacted by our democratically elected representatives, or to second-guess difficult policy choices that confront all governments. In *Morgentaler v. The Queen*, [1976] 1 S.C.R. 616, at p. 671, [hereinafter "*Morgentaler (1975)*"] I stressed that the Court had "not been called upon to decide, or even to enter, the loud and continuous public debate on abortion." Eleven years later, the controversy persists, and it remains true that this Court cannot presume to resolve all of the competing claims advanced in vigorous and healthy public debate. Courts and legislators in other democratic societies have reached completely contradictory decisions when asked to weigh the competing values relevant to the abortion question. . . .

But since 1975, and the first *Morgentaler* decision, the Court has been given added responsibilities. I stated in *Morgentaler (1975)*, at p. 671, that:

> The values we must accept for the purposes of this appeal are those expressed by Parliament which holds the view

that the desire of a woman to be relieved of her pregnancy is not, of itself, justification for performing an abortion.

Although no doubt it is still fair to say that courts are not the appropriate forum for articulating complex and controversial programmes of public policy, Canadian courts are now charged with the crucial obligation of ensuring that the legislative initiatives pursued by our Parliament and legislatures conform to the democratic values expressed in the *Canadian Charter of Rights and Freedoms*. As Justice McIntyre states in his reasons for judgment, at p. 138, "the task of the Court in this case is not to solve nor seek to solve what might be called the abortion issue, but simply to measure the content of s. 251 against the *Charter*." It is in this latter sense that the current *Morgentaler* appeal differs from the one we heard a decade ago. . . .

The Criminal Code

251. (1) Every one who, with intent to procure the miscarriage of a female person, whether or not she is pregnant, uses any means for the purpose of carrying out his intention is guilty of an indictable offence and is liable to imprisonment for life.

(2) Every female person who, being pregnant, with intent to procure her own miscarriage, uses any means or permits any means to be used for the purpose of carrying out her intention is guilty of an indictable offence and is liable to imprisonment for two years.

(3) In this section, "means" includes

(*a*) the administration of a drug or other noxious thing,

(*b*) the use of an instrument, and

(*c*) manipulation of any kind.

(4) Subsections (1) and (2) do not apply to

(*a*) a qualified medical practitioner, other than a member of a therapeutic abortion committee for any hospital, who in good faith uses in an accredited or approved hospital any means for the purpose of carrying out his intention to procure the miscarriage of a female person, or

(*b*) a female person who, being pregnant, permits a qualified medical practitioner to use in an accredited or approved hospital any means described in paragraph (*a*) for the purpose of carrying out her intention to procure her own miscarriage, if, before the use of those means, the therapeutic abortion committee for that accredited or approved hospital, by a majority of the members of the committee and at a meeting of the committee at which the case of such female person has been reviewed,

(*c*) has by certificate in writing stated that in its opinion the continuation of the pregnancy of such female person would or would be likely to endanger her life or health, and

(*d*) has caused a copy of such certificate to be given to the qualified medical practitioner. . . .

Section 7 of the Charter

In his submissions, counsel for the appellants argued that the Court should recognize a very wide ambit for the rights protected under s. 7 of the *Charter*. Basing his argument largely on American constitutional theories and authorities, Mr. Manning submitted that the right to "life, liberty and security of the person" is a wide-ranging right to control one's own life and to promote one's individual autonomy. The right would therefore include a right to privacy and a right to make unfettered decisions about one's own life.

In my opinion, it is neither necessary nor wise in this appeal to explore the broadest implications of s. 7 as counsel would wish us to do. I prefer to rest my conclusions on a narrower analysis than that put forward on behalf of the appellants. I do not think it would be appropriate to attempt an all-encompassing explication of so important a provision as s. 7 so early in the history of *Charter* interpretation. The Court should be presented with a wide variety of claims and factual situations before articulating the full range of s. 7 rights. I will therefore limit my comments to some interpretive principles already set down by the Court and to an analysis of only two aspects of s. 7, the right to "security of the person" and "the principles of fundamental justice."

The goal of *Charter* interpretation is to secure for all people "the full benefit of the *Charter's* protection": *R. v. Big M Drug Mart Ltd.*, [1985] 1 S.C.R. 295, at p. 344. To attain that goal, this Court has held consistently that the proper technique for the interpretation of *Charter* provisions is to pursue a "purposive" analysis of the right guaranteed. A right recognized in the *Charter* is "to be understood, in other words, in the light of the interests it was meant to protect": *R. v. Big M Drug Mart Ltd.*, at p. 344. (See also *Hunter v. Southam Inc.*, [1984] 2 S.C.R. 145; and *R. v. Therens*, [1985] 1 S.C.R. 613.)

In *Singh v. Minister of Employment and Immigration*, [1985] 1 S.C.R. 177, at p. 204, Justice Wilson emphasized that there are three distinct elements to the s. 7 right, that "life, liberty, and security of the person" are independent interests, each of which must be given independent significance by the Court (p. 205). This interpretation was adopted by a majority of the Court, *per* Justice Lamer, in *Re B.C. Motor Vehicle Act*, [1985] 2 S.C.R. 486, at p. 500. It is therefore possible to treat only one aspect of the first part of s. 7 before determining whether any infringement of that interest accords with the principles of fundamental justice. (See *Singh*, *Re B.C. Motor Vehicle Act*, and *R. v. Jones*, [1986] 2 S.C.R. 284.)

With respect to the second part of s. 7, in early academic commentary one of the principal concerns was whether the reference to "principles of fundamental justice" enables the courts to review the substance of legislation. . . . In *Re B.C. Motor Vehicle Act*, Lamer J. noted at p. 497 that any attempt to draw a sharp line between procedure and substance would be ill-conceived. He suggested further that it would not be beneficial in Canada to allow a debate which is rooted in United States constitutional dilemmas to shape our interpretation of s. 7. . . .

Lamer J. went on to hold that the principles of fundamental justice referred to in s. 7 can relate both to procedure and to substance, depending upon the circumstances presented before the Court.

I have no doubt that s. 7 does impose upon courts the duty to review the substance of legislation once it has been determined that the legislation infringes an individual's right to "life, liberty and security of the person." The section states clearly that those interests may only be impaired if the principles of fundamental justice are respected. Lamer J. emphasized, however, that the courts should avoid "adjudication of the merits of public policy" (p. 499). In the present case, I do not believe that it is necessary for the Court to tread the fine line between substantive review and the adjudication of public policy. As in the *Singh* case, it will be sufficient to investigate whether or not the impugned legislative provisions meet the procedural standards of fundamental justice. First it is necessary to determine whether s. 251 of the *Criminal Code* impairs the security of the person.

The law has long recognized that the human body ought to be protected from interference by others. At common law, for example, any medical procedure carried out on a person without that person's consent is an assault. Only in emergency circumstances does the law allow others to make decisions of this nature. Similarly, art. 19 of the *Civil Code of Lower Canada* provides that "[t]he human person is inviolable" and that "[n]o person may cause harm to the person of another without his consent or without being authorized by law to do so." "Security of the person," in other words, is not a value alien to our legal landscape. With the advent of the *Charter*, security of the person has been elevated to the status of a constitutional norm. This is not to say that the various forms of protection accorded to the human body by the common and civil law occupy a similar status. "Security of the person" must be given content in a manner sensitive to its constitutional position. The above examples are simply illustrative of our respect for individual physical integrity. . . .

The case law leads me to the conclusion that state interference with bodily integrity and serious state-imposed psychological stress, at least in the criminal law context, constitute a breach of security of the person. It is not necessary in this case to determine whether the right extends further, to protect either interests central to personal autonomy, such as a right to privacy, or interests unrelated to criminal justice....

At the most basic, physical and emotional level, every pregnant woman is told by the section that she cannot submit to a generally safe medical procedure that might be of clear benefit to her unless she meets criteria entirely unrelated to her own priorities and aspirations. Not only does the removal of decision-making power threaten women in a physical sense; the indecision of knowing whether an abortion will be granted inflicts emotional stress. Section 251 clearly interferes with a woman's bodily integrity in both a physical and emotional sense. Forcing a woman, by threat of criminal sanction, to carry a foetus to term unless she meets certain criteria unrelated to her own priorities and aspirations, is a profound interference with a woman's body and thus a violation of security of the person. Section 251, therefore, is required by the *Charter* to comport with the principles of fundamental justice.

Although this interference with physical and emotional integrity is sufficient in itself to trigger a review of s. 251 against the principles of fundamental justice, the operation of the decision-making mechanism set out in s. 251 creates additional glaring breaches of security of the person. The evidence indicates that s. 251 causes a certain amount of delay for women who are successful in meeting its criteria. In the context of abortion, any unnecessary delay can have profound consequences on the woman's physical and emotional well-being....

[Chief Justice Dickson here quotes relevant findings of the 1977 Badgley Report. The Badgley Report was commissioned by the federal government in the wake of the first *Morgentaler* case (1973-75). It found uneven access to and delays in access to abortion since the 1969 reforms. The delays were linked to increased threat to the health of the mother in later-stage abortions.]

The above physical interference caused by the delays created by s. 251, involving a clear risk of damage to the physical well-being of a woman, is sufficient, in my view, to warrant inquiring whether s. 251 comports with the principles of fundamental justice. However, there is yet another infringement of security of the person. It is clear from the evidence that s. 251 harms the psychological integrity of women seeking abortions. A 1985 report of the Canadian Medical Association, discussed in the Powell Report, at p. 15, emphasized that the procedure involved in s. 251, with the concomitant delays, greatly increases the stress levels of patients and that this can lead to more physical complications associated with abortion....

In its supplementary factum and in oral submissions, the Crown argued that evidence of what could be termed "administrative inefficiency" is not relevant to the evaluation of legislation for the purposes of s. 7 of the *Charter*. The Crown argued that only evidence regarding the purpose of legislation is relevant. The assumption, of course, is that any impairment to the physical or psychological interests of individuals caused by s. 251 of the *Criminal Code* does not amount to an infringement of security of the person because the injury is caused by practical difficulties and is not intended by the legislator.

The submission is faulty on two counts. First, as a practical matter it is not possible in the case of s. 251 to erect a rigid barrier between the purposes of the section and the administrative procedures established to carry those purposes into effect....

Secondly, were it nevertheless possible in this case to dissociate purpose and administration, this Court has already held as a matter of law that purpose is not the only appropriate criterion in evaluating the constitutionality of legislation under the *Charter*....

Even if the purpose of legislation is unobjectionable, the administrative procedures *created by law* to bring that purpose into operation may produce unconstitutional effects, and the legislation should then be struck down....

In summary, s. 251 is a law which forces women to carry a foetus to term contrary to their own priorities and aspirations and which imposes serious delay causing increased physical and psychological trauma to those women who meet its criteria. It must, therefore, be determined whether that infringement is accomplished in accordance with the principles of fundamental justice, thereby saving s. 251 under the second part of s. 7....

My discussion will ... be limited to various aspects of the administrative structure and procedure set down in s. 251 for access to therapeutic abortions....

The procedure surrounding the defence is rather complex. A pregnant woman who desires to have an abortion must apply to the "therapeutic abortion committee" of an "accredited or approved hospital." Such a committee is empowered to issue a certificate in writing stating that in the opinion of a majority of the committee, the continuation of the pregnancy would be likely to endanger the pregnant woman's life or health. Once a copy of the certificate is given to a qualified medical practitioner who is not a member of the therapeutic abortion committee, he or she is permitted to perform an abortion on the pregnant woman and both the doctor and the woman are freed from any criminal liability....

As is so often the case in matters of interpretation, however, the straightforward reading of this statutory scheme is not fully revealing. In order to understand the true nature and scope of s. 251, it is necessary to investigate the practical operation of the provisions. The Court has been provided with a myriad of factual submissions in this area. One of the most useful sources of information is the Badgley Report....

The Badgley Report contains a wealth of detailed information which demonstrates, however, that many of the most serious problems with the functioning of s. 251 are created by procedural and administrative requirements established in the law.... [For example], the seemingly neutral requirement of s. 251(4) that at least four physicians be available to authorize and to perform an abortion meant in practice that abortions would be absolutely unavailable in almost one quarter of all hospitals in Canada.

Other administrative and procedural requirements of s. 251(4) reduce the availability of therapeutic abortions even further. For the purposes of s. 251, therapeutic abortions can only be performed in "accredited" or "approved" hospitals. As noted above, an "approved" hospital is one which a provincial minister of health has designated as such for the purpose of performing therapeutic abortions. The minister is under no obligation to grant any such approval. Furthermore, an "accredited" hospital must not only be accredited by the Canadian Council on Hospital Accreditation, it must also provide specified services. Many Canadian hospitals do not provide all of the required services, thereby being automatically disqualified from undertaking therapeutic abortions. The Badgley Report stressed the remarkable limitations created by these requirements, especially when linked with the four-physician rule discussed above (p. 105):

> Of the total of 1,348 non-military hospitals in Canada in 1976, 789 hospitals, or 58.5 percent, were ineligible in terms of their major treatment functions, the size of their medical staff, or their type of facility to establish therapeutic abortion committees.

Moreover, even if a hospital is eligible to create a therapeutic abortion committee, there is no requirement in s. 251 that the hospital need do so. The Badgley Committee discovered that in 1976, of the 559 general hospitals which met the procedural requirements of s. 251, only 271 hospitals in Canada, or only 20.1 per cent of the total, had actually established a therapeutic abortion committee (p. 105).

Even though the Badgley Report was issued ten years ago, the relevant statistics do not appear to be out of date. Indeed, Statistics Canada reported that in 1982 the number of hospitals with therapeutic abortion committees had actually fallen to 261....

A further flaw with the administrative system established in s. 251(4) is the failure to provide an adequate standard for therapeutic abortion committees which must determine when a therapeutic abortion should, as a matter of law, be granted.

Subsection (4) states simply that a therapeutic abortion committee may grant a certificate when it determines that a continuation of a pregnancy would be likely to endanger the "life or health" of the pregnant woman. It was noted above that "health" is not defined for the purposes of the section....

Various expert doctors testified at trial that therapeutic abortion committees apply widely differing definitions of health. For some committees, psychological health is a justification for therapeutic abortion; for others it is not. Some committees routinely refuse abortions to married women unless they are in physical danger, while for other committees it is possible for a married woman to show that she would suffer psychological harm if she continued with a pregnancy, thereby justifying an abortion. It is not typically possible for women to know in advance what standard of health will be applied by any given committee....

It is no answer to say that "health" is a medical term and that doctors who sit on therapeutic abortion committees must simply exercise their professional judgment. A therapeutic abortion committee is a strange hybrid, part medical committee and part legal committee [in the words of Parker A.C.J.H.C.]....

When the decision of the therapeutic abortion committee is so directly laden with legal consequences, the absence of any clear legal standard to be applied by the committee in reaching its decision is a serious procedural flaw.

The combined effect of all of these problems with the procedure stipulated in s. 251 for access to therapeutic abortions is a failure to comply with the principles of fundamental justice. In *Re B.C. Motor Vehicle Act*, Lamer J. held, at p. 503, that "the principles of fundamental justice are to be found in the basic tenets of our legal system." One of the basic tenets of our system of criminal justice is that when Parliament creates a defence to a criminal charge, the defence should not be illusory or so difficult to attain as to be practically illusory. The criminal law is a very special form of governmental regulation, for it seeks to express our society's collective disapprobation of certain acts and omissions. When a defence is provided, especially a specifically-tailored defence to a particular charge, it is because the legislator has determined that the disapprobation of society is not warranted when the conditions of the defence are met.

Consider then the case of a pregnant married woman who wishes to apply for a therapeutic abortion certificate because she fears that her psychological health would be impaired seriously if she carried the foetus to term. The uncontroverted evidence reveals that there are many areas in Canada where such a woman would simply not have access to a therapeutic abortion....

The Crown argues in its supplementary factum that women who face difficulties in obtaining abortions at home can simply travel elsewhere in Canada to procure a therapeutic abortion. That submission would not be especially troubling if the difficulties facing women were not in large measure created by the procedural requirements of s. 251 itself. If women were seeking anonymity outside their home town or were simply confronting the reality that it is often difficult to obtain medical services in rural areas, it might be appropriate to say "let them travel." But the evidence establishes convincingly that it is the law itself which in many ways *prevents* access to local therapeutic abortion facilities. . . . Parliament must be given room to design an appropriate administrative and procedural structure for bringing into operation a particular defence to criminal liability. But if that structure is "so manifestly unfair, having regard to the decisions it is called upon to make, as to violate the principles of *fundamental* justice," that structure must be struck down. In the present case, the structure—the system regulating access to therapeutic abortions—is manifestly unfair. It contains so many potential barriers to its own operation that the defence it creates will in many circumstances be practically unavailable to women who would *prima facie* qualify for the defence, or at least would force such women to travel great distances at substantial expense and inconvenience in order to benefit from a defence that is held out to be generally available.

I conclude that the procedures created in s. 251 of the *Criminal Code* for obtaining a therapeutic abortion do not comport with the principles of fundamental justice. It is not necessary to determine whether s. 7 also contains a substantive content leading to the conclusion that, in some circumstances at least, the deprivation of a pregnant woman's right to security of the person can never comport with fundamental justice. Simply put, assuming Parliament can act, it must do so properly. . . .

V. Section 1 Analysis

Section 1 of the *Charter* can potentially be used to "salvage" a legislative provision which breaches s. 7. . . . A statutory provision which infringes any section of the *Charter* can only be saved under s. 1 if the party seeking to uphold the provision can demonstrate first, that the objective of the provision is "of sufficient importance to warrant overriding a constitutionally protected right or freedom" (*R. v. Big M Drug Mart Ltd.*, at p. 352) and second, that the means chosen in overriding the right or freedom are reasonable and demonstrably justified in a free and democratic society. This second aspect ensures that the legislative means are proportional to the legislative ends (*Oakes*, at pp. 139-40). In *Oakes*, at p. 139, the Court referred to three considerations which are typically useful in assessing the proportionality of means to ends. First, the means chosen to achieve an important objective should be rational, fair and

not arbitrary. Second, the legislative means should impair as little as possible the right or freedom under consideration. Third, the effects of the limitation upon the relevant right or freedom should not be out of proportion to the objective sought to be achieved.

The appellants contended that the sole purpose of s. 251 of the *Criminal Code* is to protect the life and health of pregnant women. The respondent Crown submitted that s. 251 seeks to protect not only the life and health of pregnant women, but also the interests of the foetus. On the other hand, the Crown conceded that the Court is not called upon in this appeal to evaluate any claim to "foetal rights" or to assess the meaning of "the right to life." I expressly refrain from so doing. In my view, it is unnecessary for the purpose of deciding this appeal to evaluate or assess "foetal rights" as an independent constitutional value. Nor are we required to measure the full extent of the state's interest in establishing criteria unrelated to the pregnant woman's own priorities and aspirations. What we must do is evaluate the particular balance struck by Parliament in s. 251, as it relates to the priorities and aspirations of pregnant women and the government's interests in the protection of the foetus.

Section 251 provides that foetal interests are not to be protected where the "life or health" of the woman is threatened. Thus, Parliament itself has expressly stated in s. 251 that the "life or health" of pregnant women is paramount. The procedures of s. 251(4) are clearly related to the pregnant woman's "life or health" for that is the very phrase used by the subsection. As McIntyre J. states in his reasons (at p. 155), the aim of s. 251(4) is "to restrict abortion to cases where the continuation of the pregnancy would, or would likely, be injurious to the life or health of the woman concerned, not to provide unrestricted access to abortion." I have no difficulty in concluding that the objective of s. 251 as a whole, namely, to balance the competing interests identified by Parliament, is sufficiently important to meet the requirements of the first step in the *Oakes* inquiry under s. 1. I think the protection of the interests of pregnant women is a valid governmental objective, where life and health can be jeopardized by criminal sanctions. Like Beetz and Wilson JJ., I agree that protection of foetal interests by Parliament is also a valid governmental objective. It follows that balancing these interests, with the lives and health of women a major factor, is clearly an important governmental objective. As the Court of Appeal stated at p. 366, "the contemporary view [is] that abortion is not always socially undesirable behavior."

I am equally convinced, however, that the means chosen to advance the legislative objectives of s. 251 do not satisfy any of the three elements of the proportionality component of *R. v. Oakes*. The evidence has led me to conclude that the infringement of the security of the person of pregnant women caused by s. 251 is not accomplished in accordance with the principles of fundamental justice. It has been demonstrated that the procedures and administrative structures created by s. 251 are often arbitrary and unfair. The procedures established to implement the policy of s. 251 impair s. 7 rights far more than is necessary because they hold out an illusory defence to many women who would *prima facie* qualify under the exculpatory provisions of s. 251(4). In other words, many women whom Parliament professes not to wish to subject to criminal liability will nevertheless be forced by the practical unavailability of the supposed defence to risk liability or to suffer other harm such as a traumatic late abortion caused by the delay inherent in the s. 251 system. Finally, the effects of the limitation upon the s. 7 rights of many pregnant women are out of proportion to the objective sought to be achieved. Indeed, to the extent that s. 251(4) is designed to protect the life and health of women, the procedures it establishes may actually defeat that objective. The administrative structures of s. 251(4) are so cumbersome that women whose health is endangered by pregnancy may not be able to gain a therapeutic abortion, at least without great trauma, expense and inconvenience.

I conclude, therefore, that the cumbersome structure of subs. (4) not only unduly subordinates the s. 7 rights of pregnant women but may also defeat the value Parliament itself has established as paramount, namely, the life and health of the pregnant woman. As I have noted, counsel for the Crown did contend that one purpose of the procedures required by subs. (4) is to protect the interests of the foetus. State protection of foetal interests may well be deserving of constitutional recognition under s. 1. Still, there can be no escape from the fact that Parliament has failed to establish either a standard or a procedure whereby any such interests might prevail over those of the woman in a fair and non-arbitrary fashion.

Section 251 of the *Criminal Code* cannot be saved, therefore, under s. 1 of the *Charter*. . . .

The judgment of Estey and Beetz JJ. was delivered by

BEETZ J.: . . . Access to abortion without risk of criminal penalty under the *Criminal Code* is expressed by Parliament in subss. (4), (5), (6) and (7) of s. 251 as relieving provisions in respect of the indictable offences defined at s. 251(1) and (2). According to Laskin C.J. (dissenting) in *Morgentaler v. The Queen*, [1976] . . . these relieving provisions "simply permit a person to make conduct lawful which would otherwise be unlawful" (at p. 631). In the same case, Pigeon J. said that in 1969 "an explicit and specific definition was made of the circumstances under which an abortion could lawfully be performed" (at p. 660). . . .

Given that it appears in a criminal law statute, s. 251(4) cannot be said to create a "right," much less a constitutional right, but it does represent an exception decreed by Parliament pursuant to what the Court of Appeal aptly called "the contemporary view that abortion is not always socially undesirable behaviour." Examining the content of the rule by which Parliament decriminalizes abortion is the most appropriate first step in considering the validity of s. 251 as against the constitutional right to abortion alleged by the appellants in argument. . . .

That abortions are recognized as lawful by Parliament based on a specific standard under its ordinary laws is important, I think, to a proper understanding of the existence of a right of access to abortion founded on rights guaranteed by s. 7 of the *Charter*. The constitutional right does not have its source in the *Criminal Code*, but, in my view, the content of the standard in s. 251(4) that Parliament recognized in the *Criminal Law Amendment Act, 1968-69* was for all intents and purposes entrenched at least as a minimum in 1982 when a distinct right in s. 7 became part of Canadian constitutional law.

The Right to Security of the Person in Section 7

. . . A pregnant woman's person cannot be said to be secure if, when her life or health is in danger, she is faced with a rule of criminal law which precludes her from obtaining effective and timely medical treatment. . . .

If a rule of criminal law precludes a person from obtaining appropriate medical treatment when his or her life or health is in danger, then the state has intervened and this intervention constitutes a violation of that man's or that woman's security of the person. "Security of the person" must include a right of access to medical treatment for a condition representing a danger to life or health without fear of criminal sanction. If an act of Parliament forces a person whose life or health is in danger to choose between, on the one hand, the commission of a crime to obtain effective and timely medical treatment and, on the other hand, inadequate treatment or no treatment at all, the right to security of the person has been violated.

This interpretation of s. 7 of the *Charter* is sufficient to measure the content of s. 251 of the *Criminal Code* against that of the *Charter* in order to dispose of this appeal. While I agree with McIntyre J. that a breach of a right to security must be "based upon an infringement of some interest which would be of such nature and such importance as to warrant constitutional protection," I am of the view that the protection of life or health is an interest of sufficient importance in this regard. Under the *Criminal Code*, the only way in which a pregnant woman can legally secure an abortion when the continuation of the pregnancy would or would be likely to endanger her life or health is to comply with the procedure set forth in s. 251(4). Where the continued pregnancy does constitute a danger to life or health, the pregnant woman faces a choice: (1) she can endeavour to follow the s. 251(4) procedure, which, as we shall see, creates an additional medical risk given its inherent delays and the possibility that the danger will not be recognized by the state-imposed therapeutic abortion committee; or (2) she can secure medical treatment without respecting s. 251(4) and subject herself to criminal sanction under s. 251(2).

Delays Caused by Section 251 Procedure

[Justice Beetz's treatment of the causes of delay is similar to that of Chief Justice Dickson. He then goes on to consider whether the delays violate the section 7 right to security of the person.]

The delays which a pregnant woman may have to suffer as a result of the requirements of s. 251(4) must undermine the security of her person in order that there be a violation of this element of s. 7 of the *Charter*. As I said earlier, s. 7 cannot be invoked simply because a woman's pregnancy amounts to a medically dangerous condition. If, however, the delays occasioned by s. 251(4) of the *Criminal Code* result in an additional danger to the pregnant woman's health, then the state has intervened and this intervention constitutes a violation of that woman's security of the person. By creating this additional risk, s. 251 prevents access to effective and timely medical treatment for the continued pregnancy which would or would be likely to endanger her life or health. If an effective and timely therapeutic abortion may only be obtained by committing a crime, then s. 251 violates the pregnant woman's right to security of the person.

The evidence reveals that the delays caused by s. 251(4) result in at least three broad types of additional medical risks. The risk of post-operative complications increases with delay. Secondly, there is a risk that the pregnant woman require a more dangerous means of procuring a miscarriage because of the delay. Finally, since a pregnant woman knows her life or health is in danger, the delay created by the s. 251(4) procedure may result in an additional psychological trauma. . . .

The delays mean therefore that the state has intervened in such a manner as to create an additional risk to health, and consequently this intervention constitutes a violation of the woman's security of the person.

The Principles of Fundamental Justice

I turn now to a consideration of the manner in which pregnant women are deprived of their right to security of the person by s. 251. Section 7 of the *Charter* states that everyone has the right not to be deprived of security of the person

except in accordance with the principles of fundamental justice. As I will endeavour to demonstrate, s. 251(4) does not accord with the principles of fundamental justice.

I am of the view, however, that certain elements of the procedure for obtaining a therapeutic abortion which counsel for the appellants argued could not be saved by the second part of s. 7 are in fact in accordance with the principles of fundamental justice. The expression of the standard in s. 251(4)(*c*), and the requirement for some independent medical opinion to ascertain that the standard has been met as well as the consequential necessity of some period of delay to ascertain the standard are not in breach of s. 7 of the *Charter*.

Counsel for the appellants argued that the expression of the standard in s. 251(4)(*c*) is so imprecise that it offends the principles of fundamental justice. He submits that pregnant women are arbitrarily deprived of their s. 7 right by reason of the different meanings that can be given to the word "health" in s. 251(4)(*c*) by therapeutic abortion committees.

I agree with McIntyre J. and the Ontario Court of Appeal that the expression "the continuation of the pregnancy of such female person would or would be likely to endanger her life or health" found in s. 251(4)(*c*) does provide, as a matter of law, a sufficiently precise standard by which therapeutic abortion committees can determine when therapeutic abortions should be granted. . . .

Laskin C.J. held in *Morgentaler (1975)*, at p. 634, that s. 251(4)(*c*) was not so vague so as to constitute a violation of "security of the person" without due process of law under s. 1(*a*) of the *Canadian Bill of Rights*. . . .

I agree with Laskin C.J. that the standard is manageable because it is addressed to a panel of doctors exercising medical judgment on a medical question. This being the case, the standard must necessarily be flexible. Flexibility and vagueness are not synonymous. Parliament has set a medical standard to be determined over a limited range of circumstances. With the greatest of respect, I cannot agree with the view that the therapeutic abortion committee is a "strange hybrid, part medical committee and part legal committee" as the Chief Justice characterizes it (at p. 69). In section 251(4) Parliament has only given the committee the authority to make a medical determination regarding the pregnant woman's life or health. The committee is not called upon to evaluate the sufficiency of the state interest in the foetus as against the woman's health. This evaluation of the state interest is a question of law already decided by Parliament in its formulation of s. 251(4). Evidence has been submitted that many committees fail to apply the standard set by Parliament by requiring the consent of the pregnant woman's spouse, by refusing to authorize second abortions or by refusing all abortions to married women. In so far as these and other requirements fall outside s. 251(4)(*c*), they constitute an unfounded interpretation of the plain terms of the *Criminal Code*. These patent excesses of authority do not, however, mean that the standard of s. 251 is vague. . . .

Just as the expression of the standard in s. 251(4)(*c*) does not offend the principles of fundamental justice, the requirement that an independent medical opinion be obtained for a therapeutic abortion to be lawful also cannot be said to constitute a violation of these principles when considered in the context of pregnant women's right to security of the person. . . .

As I noted in my analysis of s. 251(4), by requiring that a committee state that the medical standard has been met for the criminal sanction to be lifted, Parliament seeks to assure that there is a reliable, independent and medically sound opinion that the continuation of the pregnancy would or would be likely to endanger the woman's life or health. Whatever the failings of the current system, I believe that the purpose pursuant to which it was adopted does not offend the principles of fundamental justice. As I shall endeavour to explain, the current mechanism in the *Criminal Code* does not accord with the principles of fundamental justice. This does not preclude, in my view, Parliament from adopting another system, free of the failings of s. 251(4), in order to ascertain that the life or health of the pregnant woman is in danger, by way of a reliable, independent and medically sound opinion.

Parliament is justified in requiring a reliable, independent and medically sound opinion in order to protect the state interest in the foetus. This is undoubtedly the objective of a rule which requires an independent verification of the practising physician's opinion that the life or health of the pregnant woman is in danger. It cannot be said to be simply a mechanism designed to protect the health of the pregnant woman. While this latter objective clearly explains the requirement that the practising physician be a "qualified medical practitioner" and that the abortion take place in a safe place, it cannot explain the necessary intercession of an in-hospital committee of three physicians from which is excluded the practising physician.

While a second medical opinion is very often seen as necessary in medical circles when difficult questions as to a patient's life or health are at issue, the independent opinion called for by the *Criminal Code* has a different purpose. Parliament requires this independent opinion because it is not only the woman's interest that is at stake in a decision to authorize an abortion. The Ontario Court of Appeal alluded to this at p. 378 when it stated that "One cannot overlook the fact that the situation respecting a woman's right to control her own person becomes more complex when she becomes pregnant, and that some statutory control may be appropriate." The presence of the foetus accounts for this complexity. By requiring an independent medical opinion that the pregnant woman's life or health is in fact endangered, Parliament seeks to ensure that, in any given case, only therapeutic reasons will justify the decision to abort. The amendments to the *Criminal Code* in 1969 amounted to a recognition by Parliament, as I have said, that the interest in the life or health of the pregnant woman takes precedence over the interest of the state in the protection of the foetus when the continuation of the pregnancy would or would be likely to endanger the pregnant woman's life or health. Parliament decided that it was necessary to ascertain this from a medical point of view before the law would allow the interest of the pregnant woman to indeed take precedence over that of the foetus and permit an abortion to be performed without criminal sanction.

I do not believe it to be unreasonable to seek independent medical confirmation of the threat to the woman's life or health when such an important and distinct interest hangs in the balance. I note with interest that in a number of foreign jurisdictions, laws which decriminalize abortions require an opinion as to the state of health of the woman independent from the opinion of her own physician. . . .

This said, the practising physician must, according to s. 251(4)(*a*), be in "good faith" and, consequently, have no reason to believe that the standard in s. 251(4)(*c*) has not been met. The practising physician is, however, properly excluded from the body giving the independent opinion. I believe that Parliament is justified in requiring what is no doubt an extraordinary medical practice in its regulation of the criminal law of abortion in accordance with the various interests at stake.

The assertion that an independent medical opinion, distinct from that of the pregnant woman and her practising physician, does not offend the principles of fundamental justice would need to be reevaluated if a right of access to abortion is founded upon the right to "liberty" in s. 7 of the *Charter*. I am of the view that there would still be circumstances in which the state interest in the protection of the foetus would require an independent medical opinion as to the danger to the life or health of the pregnant woman. Assuming without deciding that a right of access to abortion can be founded upon the right to "liberty," there would be a point in time at which the state interest in the foetus would become compelling. From this point in time, Parliament would be entitled to limit abortions to those required for therapeutic reasons and therefore require an independent opinion as to the health exception. The case law reveals a substantial difference of opinion as to the state interest in the protection of the foetus as against the pregnant woman's right to liberty. Wilson J., for example, in her discussion of s. 1 of the *Charter* in the case at bar, notes the following, at p. 183:

The precise point in the development of the foetus at which the state's interest in its protection becomes "compelling" I leave to the informed judgment of the legislature which is in a position to receive guidance on the subject from all the relevant disciplines. It seems to me, however, that it might fall somewhere in the second trimester.

This view as to when the state interest becomes compelling may be compared with that of O'Connor J. of the United States Supreme Court in her dissenting opinion in *City of Akron v. Akron Center for Reproductive Health, Inc.*, 462 U.S. 416 (1983), at pp. 460-61:

In *Roe* [*Roe v. Wade*, 410 U.S. 113 (1973)], the Court held that although the State had an important and legitimate interest in protecting potential life, that interest could not become compelling until the point at which the fetus was viable. The difficulty with this analysis is clear: potential life is no less potential in the first weeks of pregnancy than it is at viability or afterward. At any stage in pregnancy, there is the potential for human life. Although the Court refused to "resolve the difficult question of when life begins," *id.*, at 159, the Court chose the point of viability—when the foetus is capable of life independent of its mother—to permit the complete proscription of abortion. The choice of viability as the point at which state interest in potential life becomes compelling is no less arbitrary than choosing any point before viability or any point afterward. Accordingly, I believe that the State's interest in protecting potential human life exists throughout the pregnancy.

As I indicated at the outset of my reasons, it is nevertheless possible to resolve this appeal without attempting to delineate the right to "liberty" in s. 7 of the *Charter*. The violation of the right to "security of the person" and the relevant principles of fundamental justice are sufficient to invalidate s. 251 of the *Criminal Code*.

Some delay is inevitable in connection with any system which purports to limit to therapeutic reasons the grounds upon which an abortion can be performed lawfully....

One ... example of a rule which is unnecessary is the requirement in s. 251(4) that therapeutic abortions must take place in an eligible hospital to be lawful. I have observed that s. 251(4) directs that therapeutic abortions take place in accredited or approved hospitals, with at least four physicians, and that, because of the lack of such hospitals in many parts of Canada, this often causes delay for women seeking treatment....

Experts testified at trial that the principal justification for the in-hospital rule is the problem of post-operative complications. There are of course instances in which the danger to life or health observed by the therapeutic abortion committee will constitute sufficient grounds for the procedure to take place in a hospital. There are other instances in which the circumstances of the procedure itself requires that it be performed in hospital, such as certain abortions performed at an advanced gestational age or cases in which the patient is particularly vulnerable to what might otherwise be a simple procedure.

In many cases, however, there is no medical justification that the therapeutic abortion take place in a hospital. Experts testified at trial, that many first trimester therapeutic abortions may be safely performed in specialized clinics outside of hospitals because the possible complications can be handled, and in some cases better handled, by the facilities of a specialized clinic....

The substantial increase in the percentage of abortions performed on an out-patient basis since 1975 underscores the view that the in-hospital requirement, which may have been justified when it was first adopted, has become exorbitant....

... Although the protection of health of the woman is the objective which the in-hospital rule is intended to serve, the requirement that all therapeutic abortions be performed in eligible hospitals is unnecessary to meet that objective in all cases. In this sense, the rule is manifestly unfair and offends the principles of fundamental justice. I appreciate that the precise nature of the administrative solution may be complicated by the constitutional division of powers between Parliament and the provinces. There is no doubt that Parliament could allow the criminal law exception to operate in all hospitals, for example, though the provinces retain the power to establish these hospitals under s. 92(7) of the *Constitution Act, 1867*. On the other hand, if Parliament decided to allow therapeutic abortions to be performed in provincially licensed clinics, it is possible that both Parliament and the provinces would be called upon to collaborate in the implementation of the plan.

An objection can also be raised in respect of the requirement that the committee come from the accredited or approved hospital in which the abortion is to be performed. It is difficult to see a connection between this requirement and any of the practical purposes for which s. 251(4) was enacted. It cannot be said to have been adopted in order to promote the safety of therapeutic abortions or the safety of the pregnant woman. Nor is the rule designed to preserve the state interest in the foetus. The integrity of the independent medical opinion is no better served by a committee within the hospital than a committee from outside the hospital as long as the practising physician remains excluded in both circumstances as part of a proper state participation in the choice of the procedure necessary to secure an independent opinion....

... [I]t is plain that the requirement that the therapeutic abortion committee come from the hospital in which the abortion will be performed serves no real purpose. The risk resulting from the delay caused by s. 251(4) in this respect is unnecessary. Consequently, this requirement violates the principles of fundamental justice.

Other aspects of the committee requirement in s. 251(4) add to the manifest unfairness of the administrative structure. These include requirements which are at best only tenuously connected to the purpose of obtaining independent confirmation that the standard in s. 251(4)(*c*) has been met and which do not usefully contribute to the realization of that purpose. Hospital boards are entitled to appoint committees made up of three or more qualified medical practitioners. As I observed earlier, if more than three members are appointed, precious time can be lost when quorum cannot be established because members are absent....

Similarly, the exclusion of all physicians who practise therapeutic abortions from the committees is exorbitant. This rule was no doubt included in s. 251(4) to promote the independence of the therapeutic abortion committees' appreciation of the standard. As I have said, the exclusion of the practising physician, although it diverges from usual medical practice, is appropriate in the criminal context to ensure the independent opinion with respect to the life or health of that physician's patient. The exclusion of all physicians who perform therapeutic abortions from committees, even when they have no connection with the patient in question, is not only unnecessary but potentially counterproductive. There are no reasonable grounds to suspect bias from a physician who has no connection with the patient simply because, in the course of his or her medical practice, he or she performs *lawful* abortions. Furthermore, physicians who perform therapeutic abortions have useful expertise which would add to the precision and the integrity of the independent opinion itself. Some state control is appropriate to ensure the independence of the opinion. However, this rule as it now stands is excessive and can increase the risk of delay because fewer physicians are qualified to serve on the committees.

The foregoing analysis of the administrative structure of s. 251(4) is by no means a complete catalogue of all the current systems' strengths and failings. It demonstrates, however, that the administrative structure put in place by Parliament has enough shortcomings so that s. 251(4), when considered as a whole, violates the principles of fundamental justice. These shortcomings stem from rules which are not necessary to the purposes for which s. 251(4) was established. These unnecessary rules, because they impose delays which result in an additional risk to women's health, are manifestly unfair.

Section 1 of the Charter

I agree with Wilson J.'s characterization of s. 251, explained in the following terms, at p. 181:

> In my view, the primary objective of the impugned legislation must be seen as the protection of the foetus. It undoubtedly has other ancillary objectives, such as the protection of the life and health of pregnant women, but I believe that the main objective advanced to justify a restriction on the pregnant woman's s. 7 right is the protection of the foetus.

The primary objective of the protection of the foetus is the main objective relevant to the analysis of s. 251 under the first test of *Oakes*. With the greatest respect, I believe the Chief Justice incorrectly identifies (at p. 75) the objective of *balancing* foetal interests and those of pregnant women, "with the lives and health of women a major factor," as "sufficiently important to meet the requirements of the first step in the *Oakes* inquiry under s. 1."

The focus in *Oakes* is the objective "which the measures responsible for a limit on a *Charter* right or freedom are designed to serve" (*supra*, at p. 138). In the context of the criminal law of abortion, the objective, which the measures in s. 251 responsible for a limit on the s. 7 *Charter* right are designed to serve, is the protection of the foetus. The narrow aim of s. 251(4) should not be confused with the primary objective of s. 251 as a whole....

Does the objective of protecting the foetus in s. 251 relate to concerns which are pressing and substantial in a free and democratic society? The answer to the first step of the *Oakes* test is yes. I am of the view that the protection of the foetus is and, as the Court of Appeal observed, always has been, a valid objective in Canadian criminal law. I have already elaborated on this objective in my discussion of the principles of fundamental justice. I think s. 1 of the *Charter* authorizes reasonable limits to be put on a woman's right having regard to the state interest in the protection of the foetus.

I turn now to the second test in *Oakes*. The Crown must show that the means chosen in s. 251 are reasonable and demonstrably justified. In *Oakes, supra,* at p. 139, the Chief Justice outlined three components of the proportionality test....

For the purposes of the first component of proportionality, I observe that it was necessary, in my discussion of s. 251(4) and the principles of fundamental justice, to explain my view that certain of the rules governing access to therapeutic abortions free from criminal sanction are unnecessary in respect of the objectives which s. 251 is designed to serve. A rule which is unnecessary in respect of Parliament's objectives cannot be said to be "rationally connected" thereto or to be "carefully designed to achieve the objective in question." Furthermore, not only are some of the rules in s. 251 unnecessary to the primary objective of the protection of the foetus and the ancillary objective of the protection of the pregnant woman's life or health, but their practical effect is to undermine the health of the woman which Parliament purports to consider so important. Consequently, s. 251 does not meet the proportionality test in *Oakes*.

There is no saving s. 251 by simply severing the offending portions of s. 251(4). The current rule expressed in s. 251, which articulates both Parliament's principal and ancillary objectives, cannot stand without the exception in s. 251(4). The violation of pregnant women's security of the person would be greater, not lesser, if s. 251(4) was severed leaving the remaining subsections of s. 251 as they are in the *Criminal Code*.

Given my conclusion in respect of the first component of the proportionality test, it is not necessary to address the questions as to whether the means in s. 251 "impair as little as possible" the s. 7 *Charter* right and whether there is a proportionality between the effects of s. 251 and the objective of protecting the foetus. Thus, I am not required to answer the difficult question concerning the circumstances in which there is a proportionality between the effects of s. 251 which limit the right of pregnant women to security of the person and the objective of the protection of the foetus. I do feel bound, however, to comment upon the balance which Parliament sought to achieve between the interest in the protection of the foetus and the interest in the life or health of the pregnant woman in adopting the amendments to the *Criminal Code* in 1969....

The gist of s. 251(4) is, as I have said, that the objective of protecting the foetus is not of sufficient importance to defeat the interest in protecting pregnant women from pregnancies which represent a danger to life or health. I take this parliamentary enactment in 1969 as an indication that, in a free and democratic society, it would be unreasonable to limit the pregnant woman's right to security of the person by a rule prohibiting abortions in all circumstances when her life or health would or would likely be in danger. This decision of the Canadian Parliament to the effect that the life or health of the pregnant woman takes precedence over the state interest in the foetus is also reflected in legislation in other free and democratic societies....

I note that the laws in some of these foreign jurisdictions, unlike s. 251 of the *Criminal Code*, require a higher standard of danger to health in the latter months of pregnancy, as opposed to the early months, for an abortion to be lawful. Would such a rule, if it was adopted in Canada, constitute a reasonable limit on the right to security of the person under

s. 1 of the *Charter*? As I have said, given the actual wording of s. 251, pursuant to which the standard necessary for a lawful abortion does not vary according to the stage of pregnancy, this Court is not required to consider this question under s. 1 of the *Charter*. It is possible that a future enactment by Parliament along the lines of the laws adopted in these jurisdictions could achieve a proportionality which is acceptable under s. 1. As I·have stated, however, I am of the view that the objective of protecting the foetus would not justify the *complete* removal of the exculpatory provisions from the *Criminal Code*.

Finally, I wish to stress that we have not been asked to decide nor is it necessary, given my own conclusion that s. 251 contains rules unnecessary to the protection of the foetus, to decide whether a foetus is included in the word "everyone" in s. 7 so as to have a right to "life, liberty and security of the person" under the *Charter*.

WILSON J.: ... My colleagues, the Chief Justice and Justice Beetz, have attacked [the law's procedural] requirements in reasons which I have had the privilege of reading. They have found that the requirements do not comport with the principles of fundamental justice in the procedural sense and have concluded that, since they cannot be severed from the provisions creating the substantive offence, the whole of s. 251 must fall.

With all due respect, I think that the Court must tackle the primary issue first. A consideration as to whether or not the procedural requirements for obtaining or performing an abortion comport with fundamental justice is purely academic if such requirements cannot as a constitutional matter be imposed at all.... Moreover, it would, in my opinion, be an exercise in futility for the legislature to expend its time and energy in attempting to remedy the defects in the procedural requirements unless it has some assurance that this process will, at the end of the day, result in the creation of a valid criminal offence. I turn, therefore, to what I believe is the central issue that must be addressed....

It seems to me ... that to commence the analysis with the premise that the s. 7 right encompasses only a right to physical and psychological security and to fail to deal with the right to liberty in the context of "life, liberty and security of the person" begs the central issue in the case. If either the right to liberty or the right to security of the person or a combination of both confers on the pregnant woman the right to decide for herself (with the guidance of her physician) whether or not to have an abortion, then we have to examine the legislative scheme not only from the point of view of fundamental justice in the procedural sense but in the substantive sense as well. I think, therefore, that we must answer the question: what is meant by the right to liberty in the context of the abortion issue? Does it, as Mr. Manning suggests, give the pregnant woman control over decisions affecting her own body? . . .

In order to ascertain the content of the right to liberty we must, as Dickson C.J. stated in *R. v. Big M Drug Mart Ltd.*, [1985] 1 S.C.R. 295, commence with an analysis of the purpose of the right. . . .

The *Charter* is predicated on a particular conception of the place of the individual in society. An individual is not a totally independent entity disconnected from the society in which he or she lives. Neither, however, is the individual a mere cog in an impersonal machine in which his or her values, goals and aspirations are subordinated to those of the collectivity. The individual is a bit of both. The *Charter* reflects this reality by leaving a wide range of activities and decisions open to legitimate government control while at the same time placing limits on the proper scope of that control. Thus, the rights guaranteed in the *Charter* erect around each individual, metaphorically speaking, an invisible fence over which the state will not be allowed to trespass. The role of the courts is to map out, piece by piece, the parameters of the fence.

The *Charter* and the right to individual liberty guaranteed under it are inextricably tied to the concept of human dignity.

The idea of human dignity finds expression in almost every right and freedom guaranteed in the *Charter*. Individuals are afforded the right to choose their own religion and their own philosophy of life, the right to choose with whom they will associate and how they will express themselves, the right to choose where they will live and what occupation they will pursue. These are all examples of the basic theory underlying the *Charter*, namely that the state will respect choices made by individuals and, to the greatest extent possible, will avoid subordinating these choices to any one conception of the good life.

Thus, an aspect of the respect for human dignity on which the *Charter* is founded is the right to make fundamental personal decisions without interference from the state. This right is a critical component of the right to liberty. Liberty, as was noted in *Singh*, is a phrase capable of a broad range of meaning. In my view, this right, properly construed, grants the individual a degree of autonomy in making decisions of fundamental personal importance.

This view is consistent with the position I took in the case of *R. v. Jones*, [1986] 2 S.C.R. 284. One issue raised in that case was whether the right to liberty in s. 7 of the *Charter* included a parent's right to bring up his children in accordance with his conscientious beliefs. In concluding that it did I stated at pp. 318-19:

I believe that the framers of the Constitution in guaranteeing "liberty" as a fundamental value in a free and

democratic society had in mind the freedom of the individual to develop and realize his potential to the full, to plan his own life to suit his own character, to make his own choices for good or ill, to be non-conformist, idiosyncratic and even eccentric—to be, in to-day's parlance, "his own person" and accountable as such. John Stuart Mill described it as "pursuing our own good in our own way." This, he believed, we should be free to do "so long as we do not attempt to deprive others of theirs or impede their efforts to obtain it." He added: "Each is the proper guardian of his own health, whether bodily or mental and spiritual. Mankind are greater gainers by suffering each other to live as seems good to themselves than by compelling each to live as seems good to the rest."

Liberty in a free and democratic society does not require the state to approve the personal decisions made by its citizens; it does, however, require the state to respect them.

This conception of the proper ambit of the right to liberty under our *Charter* is consistent with the American jurisprudence on the subject. . . .

For our purposes the most interesting development in this area of American law are the decisions of the Supreme Court in *Roe v. Wade*, 410 U.S. 113 (1973), and its sister case *Doe v. Bolton*, 410 U.S. 179 (1973). In *Roe v. Wade* the Court held that a pregnant woman has the right to decide whether or not to terminate her pregnancy. This conclusion, the majority stated, was mandated by the body of existing law ensuring that the state would not be allowed to interfere with certain fundamental personal decisions such as education, child-rearing, procreation, marriage and contraception. The Court concluded that the right to privacy found in the Fourteenth Amendment guarantee of liberty ". . . is broad enough to encompass a woman's decision whether or not to terminate her pregnancy." . . .

This right was not, however, to be taken as absolute. At some point the legitimate state interests in the protection of health, proper medical standards, and pre-natal life would justify its qualification. Lawrence H. Tribe, Professor of Law at Harvard University, in his work entitled *American Constitutional Law* (1978), conveniently summarizes the limits the Court found to be inherent in the woman's right. I quote from pp. 924-25:

Specifically, the Court held that, because the woman's right to decide whether or not to end a pregnancy is fundamental, only a compelling interest can justify state regulation impinging in any way upon that right. During the first trimester of pregnancy, when abortion is less hazardous in terms of the woman's life than carrying the child to term would be, the state may require only that the abortion be performed by a licensed physician; no further regulations peculiar to abortion as such are compellingly justified in that period.

After the first trimester, the compelling state interest in the mother's health permits it to adopt reasonable regulations in order to promote safe abortions—but requiring abortions to be performed in hospitals, or only after approval of another doctor or committee in addition to the woman's physician, is impermissible, as is requiring that the abortion procedure employ a technique that, however preferable from a medical perspective, is not widely available.

Once the fetus is viable, in the sense that it is capable of survival outside the uterus with artificial aid, the state interest in preserving the fetus becomes compelling, and the state may thus proscribe its premature removal (i.e., its abortion) except to preserve the mother's life or health.

... In my opinion, the respect for individual decision-making in matters of fundamental personal importance reflected in the American jurisprudence also informs the Canadian *Charter*. Indeed, as the Chief Justice pointed out in *R. v. Big M Drug Mart Ltd.*, beliefs about human worth and dignity "are the *sine qua non* of the political tradition underlying the *Charter*." I would conclude, therefore, that the right to liberty contained in s. 7 guarantees to every individual a degree of personal autonomy over important decisions intimately affecting their private lives.

The question then becomes whether the decision of a woman to terminate her pregnancy falls within this class of protected decisions. I have no doubt that it does. This decision is one that will have profound psychological, economic and social consequences for the pregnant woman. The circumstances giving rise to it can be complex and varied and there may be, and usually are, powerful considerations militating in opposite directions. It is a decision that deeply reflects the way the woman thinks about herself and her relationship to others and to society at large. It is not just a medical decision; it is a profound social and ethical one as well. Her response to it will be the response of the whole person. ...

Given then that the right to liberty guaranteed by s. 7 of the *Charter* gives a woman the right to decide for herself whether or not to terminate her pregnancy, does s. 251 of the *Criminal Code* violate this right? Clearly it does. The purpose of the section is to take the decision away from the woman and give it to a committee. Furthermore, as the Chief Justice correctly points out, at p. 56, the committee bases its decision on "criteria entirely unrelated to [the pregnant woman's] own priorities and aspirations." The fact that the decision whether a woman will be allowed to terminate her pregnancy is in the hands of a committee is just as great a violation of the woman's right to personal autonomy in decisions of an intimate and private nature as it would be if a committee were established to decide whether a woman should be allowed to continue her pregnancy. Both these arrangements violate the woman's right to liberty by deciding for her something that she has the right to decide for herself.

Section 7 of the *Charter* also guarantees everyone the right to security of the person. Does this, as Mr. Manning suggests, extend to the right of control over one's own body?

I agree with the Chief Justice and with Beetz J. that the right to "security of the person" under s. 7 of the *Charter* protects both the physical and psychological integrity of the individual. ... I agree with my colleague and I think that his comments are very germane to the instant case because, as the Chief Justice and Beetz J. point out, the present legislative scheme for the obtaining of an abortion clearly subjects pregnant women to considerable emotional stress as well as to unnecessary physical risk. I believe, however, that the flaw in the present legislative scheme goes much deeper than that. In essence, what it does is assert that the woman's capacity to reproduce is not to be subject to her own control. It is to be subject to the control of the state. She may not choose whether to exercise her existing capacity or not to exercise it. This is not, in my view, just a matter of interfering with her right to liberty in the sense (already discussed) of her right to personal autonomy in decision-making, it is a direct interference with her physical "person" as well. She is truly being treated as a means—a means to an end which she does not desire but over which she has no control. She is the passive recipient of a decision made by others as to whether her body is to be used to nurture a new life. Can there be anything that comports less with human dignity and self-respect? How can a woman in this position have any sense of security with respect to her person? I believe that s. 251 of the *Criminal Code* deprives the pregnant woman of her right to security of the person as well as her right to liberty.

2. The Scope of Rights Under Section 7

I turn now to a consideration of the degree of personal autonomy the pregnant woman has under s. 7 of the *Charter* when faced with a decision whether or not to have an abortion or, to put it into the legislative context, the degree to which the legislature can deny the pregnant woman access to abortion without violating her s. 7 right. This involves a consideration of the extent to which the legislature can "deprive" her of it under the second part of s. 7 and the extent to which it can put "limits" on it under s. 1. ...

(a) The Principles of Fundamental Justice

... I believe ... that a deprivation of the s. 7 right which has the effect of infringing a right guaranteed elsewhere in the

Charter cannot be in accordance with the principles of fundamental justice.

In my view, the deprivation of the s. 7 right with which we are concerned in this case offends s. 2(*a*) of the *Charter*. I say this because I believe that the decision whether or not to terminate a pregnancy is essentially a moral decision, a matter of conscience. I do not think there is or can be any dispute about that. The question is: whose conscience? Is the conscience of the woman to be paramount or the conscience of the state? I believe, for the reasons I gave in discussing the right to liberty, that in a free and democratic society it must be the conscience of the individual. Indeed, s. 2(*a*) makes it clear that this freedom belongs to "everyone," i.e., to each of us individually. . . .

In *R. v. Big M Drug Mart Ltd.*, *supra*, Dickson C.J. made some very insightful comments about the nature of the right enshrined in s. 2(*a*) of the *Charter* at pp. 345-47:

> It should also be noted, however, that an emphasis on individual conscience and individual judgment also lies at the heart of our democratic political tradition. *The ability of each citizen to make free and informed decisions is the absolute prerequisite for the legitimacy, acceptability, and efficacy of our system of self-government.* It is because of the centrality of the rights associated with freedom of individual conscience both to basic beliefs about human worth and dignity and to a free and democratic political system that American jurisprudence has emphasized the primacy or "firstness" of the First Amendment. It is this same centrality that in my view underlies their designation in the *Canadian Charter of Rights and Freedoms* as "fundamental." They are the *sine qua non* of the political tradition underlying the *Charter*. . . .
>
> Viewed in this context, the purpose of freedom of conscience and religion becomes clear. *The values that underlie our political and philosophic traditions demand that every individual be free to hold and to manifest whatever beliefs and opinions his or her conscience dictates, provided inter alia only that such manifestations do not injure his or her neighbours or their parallel rights to hold and manifest beliefs and opinions of their own.* . . .

The Chief Justice sees religious belief and practice as the paradigmatic example of conscientiously-held beliefs and manifestations and as such protected by the *Charter*. But I do not think he is saying that a personal morality which is not founded in religion is outside the protection of s. 2(*a*). Certainly, it would be my view that conscientious beliefs which are not religiously motivated are equally protected by freedom of conscience in s. 2(*a*). In so saying I am not unmindful of the fact that the *Charter* opens with an affirmation that "Canada is founded upon principles that recognize the supremacy of God . . . ." But I am also mindful that the values entrenched

in the *Charter* are those which characterize a free and democratic society. . . .

It seems to me, therefore, that in a free and democratic society "freedom of conscience and religion" should be broadly construed to extend to conscientiously-held beliefs, whether grounded in religion or in a secular morality. Indeed, as a matter of statutory interpretation, "conscience" and "religion" should not be treated as tautologous if capable of independent, although related, meaning. Accordingly, for the state to take sides on the issue of abortion, as it does in the impugned legislation by making it a criminal offence for the pregnant woman to exercise one of her options, is not only to endorse but also to enforce, on pain of a further loss of liberty through actual imprisonment, one conscientiously-held view at the expense of another. It is to deny freedom of conscience to some, to treat them as means to an end, to deprive them, as Professor MacCormick puts it, of their "essential humanity." . . .

Legislation which violates freedom of conscience in this manner cannot, in my view, be in accordance with the principles of fundamental justice within the meaning of s. 7.

(b) Section 1 of the Charter

. . . In my view, the primary objective of the impugned legislation must be seen as the protection of the foetus. It undoubtedly has other ancillary objectives, such as the protection of the life and health of pregnant women, but I believe that the main objective advanced to justify a restriction on the pregnant woman's s. 7 right is the protection of the foetus. I think this is a perfectly valid legislative objective.

Miss Wein submitted on behalf of the Crown that the Court of Appeal was correct in concluding at p. 378 that "the situation respecting a woman's right to control her own person becomes more complex when she becomes pregnant, and that some statutory control may be appropriate." I agree. I think s. 1 of the *Charter* authorizes reasonable limits to be put upon the woman's right having regard to the fact of the developing foetus within her body. The question is: at what point in the pregnancy does the protection of the foetus become such a pressing and substantial concern as to outweigh the fundamental right of the woman to decide whether or not to carry the foetus to term? At what point does the state's interest in the protection of the foetus become "compelling" and justify state intervention in what is otherwise a matter of purely personal and private concern? . . .

It would be my view, and I think it is consistent with the position taken by the United States Supreme Court in *Roe v. Wade*, that the value to be placed on the foetus as potential life is directly related to the stage of its development during gestation. The undeveloped foetus starts out as a newly fertilized ovum; the fully developed foetus emerges ultimately as an infant. A developmental progression takes place in between these two extremes and, in my opinion, this progression has a direct bearing on the value of the foetus as potential life. It is a fact of human experience that a miscarriage or spontaneous abortion of the foetus at six months is attended by far greater sorrow and sense of loss than a miscarriage or spontaneous abortion at six days or even six weeks. This is not, of course, to deny that the foetus is potential life from the moment of conception. Indeed, I agree with the observation of O'Connor J., dissenting in *City of Akron v. Akron Center for Reproductive Health, Inc., supra*, at p. 461, . . . that the foetus is potential life from the moment of conception. It is simply to say that in balancing the state's interest in the protection of the foetus as potential life under s. 1 of the *Charter* against the right of the pregnant woman under s. 7 greater weight should be given to the state's interest in the later stages of pregnancy than in the earlier. The foetus should accordingly, for purposes of s. 1, be viewed in differential and developmental terms. . . .

. . . A developmental view of the foetus, on the other hand, supports a permissive approach to abortion in the early stages of pregnancy and a restrictive approach in the later stages. In the early stages the woman's autonomy would be absolute; her decision, reached in consultation with her physician, not to carry the foetus to term would be conclusive. The state would have no business inquiring into her reasons. Her reasons for having an abortion would, however, be the proper subject of inquiry at the later stages of her pregnancy when the state's compelling interest in the protection of the foetus would justify it in prescribing conditions. The precise point in the development of the foetus at which the state's interest in its protection becomes "compelling" I leave to the informed judgment of the legislature which is in a position to receive guidance on the subject from all the relevant disciplines. It seems to me, however, that it might fall somewhere in the second trimester. Indeed, . . . a differential abortion policy with a time limit in the second trimester is already in operation in the United States, Great Britain, France, Italy, Sweden, the Soviet Union, China, India, Japan and most of the countries of Eastern Europe although the time limits vary in these countries from the beginning to the end of the second trimester. . . .

The judgment of McIntyre and La Forest JJ. was delivered by

McINTYRE J. (dissenting): . . . I would say at the outset that it may be thought that this case does not raise the *Charter* issues which were argued and which have been addressed in the reasons of my colleagues. The charge here is one of conspiracy to breach the provisions of s. 251 of the *Criminal Code*. There is no doubt, and it has never been questioned, that the appellants adopted a course which was clearly in defiance of the

provisions of the *Code* and it is difficult to see where any infringement of their rights, under s. 7 of the *Charter*, could have occurred. There is no female person involved in the case who has been denied a therapeutic abortion and, as a result, the whole argument on the right to security of the person, under s. 7 of the *Charter*, has been on a hypothetical basis. The case, however, was addressed by all the parties on that basis and the Court has accepted that position.

Section 251(1) and (2) of the *Criminal Code* make it an indictable offence for a person to use any means to procure the miscarriage of a female person. . . . Subsection (4) provides that subss. (1) and (2) shall not apply where an abortion is performed in accordance with paras. (*a*), (*b*), (*c*) and (*d*). . . . It is clear from the foregoing that abortion is prohibited and that subs. (4) provides relieving provisions allowing an abortion in certain limited circumstances. It cannot be said that s. 251 of the *Criminal Code* confers any general right to have or to procure an abortion. On the contrary, the provision is aimed at protecting the interests of the unborn child and only lifts the criminal sanction where an abortion is necessary to protect the life or health of the mother.

In considering the constitutionality of s. 251 of the *Criminal Code*, it is first necessary to understand the background of this litigation and some of the problems which it raises. Section 251 of the *Code* has been denounced as ill-conceived and inadequate by those at one extreme of the abortion debate and as immoral and unacceptable by those at the opposite extreme. There are those, like the appellants, who assert that on moral and ethical grounds there is a simple solution to the problem: the inherent "right of women to control their own bodies" requires the repeal of s. 251 in favour of the principle of "abortion on demand." Opposing this view are those who contend with equal vigour, and also on moral and ethical grounds, for a clear and simple solution: the inherent "right to life of the unborn child" requires the repeal of s. 251(4), (5), (6) and (7) in order to leave an absolute ban on abortions. The battle lines so drawn are firmly held and the attitudes of the opposing parties admit of no compromise. From the submission of the Attorney General of Canada (set out in his factum at paragraph 6), however, it may appear that a majority in Canada do not see the issue in such black and white terms. Paragraph 6 is in these words:

> The evidence of opinion surveys indicates that there is a surprising consistency over the years and in different survey groups in the spectrum of opinions on the issue of abortion. Roughly 21 to 23% of people at one end of the spectrum are of the view, on the one hand, that abortion is a matter solely for the decision of the pregnant woman and that any legislation on this subject is an unwarranted interference with a woman's right to deal with her own

body, while about 19 to 20% are of the view, on the other hand, that destruction of the living fetus is the killing of human life and tantamount to murder. The remainder of the population (about 60%) are of the view that abortion should be prohibited in some circumstances.

Parliament has heeded neither extreme. Instead, an attempt has been made to balance the competing interests of the unborn child and the pregnant woman. Where the provisions of s. 251(4) are met, the abortion may be performed without legal sanction. Where they are not, abortion is deemed to be socially undesirable and is punished as a crime. In *Morgentaler v. The Queen*, [1976] 1 S.C.R. 616 [hereinafter *Morgentaler (1975)*], Laskin C.J. said (in dissent, but not on this point), at p. 627:

> What is patent on the face of the prohibitory portion of s. 251 is that Parliament has in its judgment decreed that interference by another, or even by the pregnant woman herself, with the ordinary course of conception is socially undesirable conduct subject to punishment. That was a judgment open to Parliament in the exercise of its plenary criminal law power, and the fact that there may be safe ways of terminating a pregnancy or that any woman or women claim a personal privilege to that end, becomes immaterial. I need cite no authority for the proposition that Parliament may determine what is not criminal as well as what is, and may hence introduce dispensations or exemptions in its criminal legislation.

Parliament's view that abortion is, in its nature, "socially undesirable conduct" is not new. Parliament's policy, as expressed by s. 251 of the *Code*, is consistent with that which has governed Canadian criminal law since Confederation and before....

Scope of Judicial Review Under the Charter

Before the adoption of the *Charter*, there was little question of the limits of judicial review of the criminal law. For all practical purposes it was limited to a determination of whether the impugned enactment dealt with a subject which could fall within the criminal law power in s. 91(27) of the *Constitution Act, 1867*. There was no doubt of the power of Parliament to say what was and what was not criminal and to prohibit criminal conduct with penal sanctions, although from 1960 onwards legislation was subject to review under the *Canadian Bill of Rights*: see *Morgentaler (1975)*, *supra*. The adoption of the *Charter* brought a significant change. The power of judicial review of legislation acquired greater scope but, in my view, that scope is not unlimited and should be carefully confined to that which is ordained by the *Charter*. I am well aware that there will be disagreement about what was ordained by the *Charter* and, of course, a measure of interpretation of the

Charter will be required in order to give substance and reality to its provisions. But the courts must not, in the guise of interpretation, postulate rights and freedoms which do not have a firm and a reasonably identifiable base in the *Charter*....

While I differ with the Chief Justice in the disposition of this appeal, I would accept his words, referred to above, which describe the role of the Court, but I would suggest that in "ensuring that the legislative initiatives pursued by our Parliament and legislatures conform to the democratic values expressed in the *Canadian Charter of Rights and Freedoms*" the courts must confine themselves to such democratic values as are clearly found and expressed in the *Charter* and refrain from imposing or creating other values not so based.

It follows, then, in my view, that the task of the Court in this case is not to solve nor seek to solve what might be called the abortion issue, but simply to measure the content of s. 251 against the *Charter*. While this may appear to be self-evident, the distinction is of vital importance. If a particular interpretation enjoys no support, express or reasonably implied, from the *Charter*, then the Court is without power to clothe such an interpretation with constitutional status. It is not for the Court to substitute its own views on the merits of a given question for those of Parliament. The Court must consider not what is, in its view, the best solution to the problems posed; its role is confined to deciding whether the solution enacted by Parliament offends the *Charter*. If it does, the provision must be struck down or declared inoperative, and Parliament may then enact such different provisions as it may decide. I adopt the words of Holmes J., which were referred to in *Ferguson v. Skrupka*, 372 U.S. 726 (1963), at pp. 729-30:

> There was a time when the Due Process Clause was used by this Court to strike down laws which were thought unreasonable, that is, unwise or incompatible with some particular economic or social philosophy. In this manner the Due Process Clause was used, for example, to nullify laws prescribing maximum hours for work in bakeries, *Lochner v. New York*, ... outlawing "yellow dog" contracts, *Coppage v. Kansas*, ... setting minimum wages for women, *Adkins v. Children's Hospital*, ... and fixing the weight of loaves of bread, *Jay Burns Baking Co. v. Bryan* ....

This intrusion by the judiciary into the realm of legislative value judgments was strongly objected to at the time, particularly by Mr. Justice Holmes and Mr. Justice Brandeis. Dissenting from the Court's invalidating a state statute which regulated the resale price of theatre and other tickets, Mr. Justice Holmes said: "I think the proper course is to recognize that a state legislature can do whatever it sees fit to do unless it is restrained by some express prohibition in the Constitution of the United States or of the State, and that Courts should be careful not to extend such prohibitions beyond their obvious meaning by reading into them conceptions of public policy that the particular Court may happen to entertain."

And in an earlier case he had emphasized that, "The criterion of constitutionality is not whether we believe the law to be for the public good."

The doctrine that prevailed in *Lochner, Coppage, Adkins, Burns,* and like cases—that due process authorizes courts to hold laws unconstitutional when they believe the legislature has acted unwisely—has long since been discarded. We have returned to the original constitutional proposition that courts do not substitute their social and economic beliefs for the judgment of legislative bodies, who are elected to pass laws.

Holmes J. wrote in 1927, but his words have retained their force in American jurisprudence.... In my view, although written in the American context, the principle stated is equally applicable in Canada.

It is essential that this principle be maintained in a constitutional democracy. The Court must not resolve an issue such as that of abortion on the basis of how many judges may favour "pro-choice" or "pro-life." To do so would be contrary to sound principle and the rule of law affirmed in the preamble to the *Charter* which must mean that no discretion, including a judicial discretion, can be unlimited. But there is a problem, for the Court must clothe the general expression of rights and freedoms contained in the *Charter* with real substance and vitality. How can the courts go about this task without imposing at least some of their views and predilections upon the law? This question has been the subject of much discussion and comment. Many theories have been postulated but few have had direct reference to the problem in the Canadian context. In my view, this Court has offered guidance in this matter. In such cases as *Hunter v. Southam Inc.,* [1984] 2 S.C.R. 145, at pp. 155-56, and *R. v. Big M Drug Mart Ltd.,* [1985] 1 S.C.R. 295, at p. 344, it has enjoined what has been termed a "purposive approach" in applying the *Charter* and its provisions. I take this to mean that the Courts should interpret the *Charter* in a manner calculated to give effect to its provisions, not to the idiosyncratic view of the judge who is writing. This approach marks out the limits of appropriate *Charter* adjudication. It confines the content of *Charter* guaranteed rights and freedoms to the purposes given expression in the *Charter.* Consequently, while the courts must continue to give a fair, large and liberal construction to the *Charter* provisions, this approach prevents the Court from abandoning its traditional adjudicatory function in order to formulate its own conclusions on questions of public policy, a step which this Court has said on numerous occasions it must not take. That *Charter* interpretation is to be purposive necessarily implies the converse: it is not to be "non-purposive." A court is not entitled to define a right in a manner unrelated to the interest which the right in question was meant to protect. I endeavoured to formulate an approach to the problem in *Reference Re Public Service Employee Relations Act,* [1987] 1 S.C.R. 313, in these words, at p. 394:

> It follows that while a liberal and not overly legalistic approach should be taken to constitutional interpretation, the *Charter* should not be regarded as an empty vessel to be filled with whatever meaning we might wish from time to time. The interpretation of the *Charter,* as of all constitutional documents, is constrained by the language, structure and history of the constitutional text, by constitutional tradition, and by the history, traditions, and underlying philosophies of our society.

The approach, as I understand it, does not mean that judges may not make some policy choices when confronted with competing conceptions of the extent of rights or freedoms. Difficult choices must be made and the personal views of judges will unavoidably be engaged from time to time. The decisions made by judges, however, and the interpretations that they advance or accept must be plausibly inferable from something in the *Charter.* It is not for the courts to manufacture a constitutional right out of whole cloth. I conclude on this question by citing and adopting the following words, although spoken in dissent, from the judgment of Harlan J. in *Reynolds v. Sims,* 377 U.S. 533 (1964), which, in my view, while stemming from the American experience, are equally applicable in a consideration of the Canadian position. Harlan J. commented, at pp. 624-25, on the

> ... current mistaken view of the Constitution and the constitutional function of this Court. This view, in a nutshell, is that every major social ill in this country can find its cure in some constitutional "principle," and that this Court should "take the lead" in promoting reform when other branches of government fail to act. The Constitution is not a panacea for every blot upon the public welfare, nor should this Court, ordained as a judicial body, be thought of as a general haven for reform movements. The Constitution is an instrument of government, fundamental to which is the premise that in a diffusion of governmental authority lies the greatest promise that this Nation will realize liberty for all its citizens. This Court, limited in function in accordance with that premise, does not serve its high purpose when it exceeds its authority, even to satisfy justified impatience with the slow workings of the political process. For when, in the name of constitutional interpretation, the Court adds something to the Constitution that was deliberately excluded from it, the Court in reality substitutes its view of what should be so for the amending process.

The Right to Abortion and Section 7 of the Charter

The judgment of my colleague, Wilson J., is based upon the proposition that a pregnant woman has a right, under s. 7 of the *Charter*, to have an abortion. The same concept underlies the judgment of the Chief Justice. . . .

All laws, it must be noted, have the potential for interference with individual priorities and aspirations. In fact, the very purpose of most legislation is to cause such interference. It is only when such legislation goes beyond interfering with priorities and aspirations, and abridges rights, that courts may intervene. If a law prohibited membership in a lawful association it would be unconstitutional, not because it would interfere with priorities and aspirations, but because of its interference with the guaranteed right of freedom of association under s. 2(*d*) of the *Charter*. Compliance with the *Income Tax Act* has, no doubt, frequently interfered with priorities and aspirations. The taxing provisions are not, however, on that basis unconstitutional, because the ordinary taxpayer enjoys no right to be tax free. Other illustrations may be found. In my view, it is clear that before it could be concluded that any enactment infringed the concept of security of the person, it would have to infringe some underlying right included in or protected by the concept. For the appellants to succeed here, then, they must show more than an interference with priorities and aspirations; they must show the infringement of a right which is included in the concept of security of the person.

The proposition that women enjoy a constitutional right to have an abortion is devoid of support in the language of s. 7 of the *Charter* or any other section. While some human rights documents . . . expressly address the question of abortion, the *Charter* is entirely silent on the point. It may be of some significance that the *Charter* uses specific language in dealing with other topics, such as voting rights, religion, expression and such controversial matters as mobility rights, language rights and minority rights, but remains silent on the question of abortion which, at the time the *Charter* was under consideration, was as much a subject of public controversy as it is today. Furthermore, it would appear that the history of the constitutional text of the *Charter* affords no support for the appellants' proposition. A reference to the Minutes of the Special Joint Committee of Senate and House of Commons on the Constitution of Canada (Proceedings 32nd. Parl., Sess. 1 (1981), vol. 46, p. 43) reveals the following exchange:

> **Mr. Crombie:** . . . And I ask you then finally, what effect will the inclusion of the due process clause have on the question of marriage, procreation, or the parental care of children? . . .
>
> **Mr. Chrétien:** The point, Mr. Crombie, that it is important to understand the difference is that we pass legislation

here on abortion, criminal code, and we pass legislation on capital punishment; parliament [*sic*] has the authority to do that, and the court at this moment, because we do not have the due process of law written there, cannot go and see whether we made the right decision or the wrong decision in Parliament.

> If you write down the words, "due process of law" here, the advice I am receiving is the court could go behind our decision and say that their decision on abortion was not the right one, their decision on capital punishment was not the right one, and it is a danger, according to legal advice I am receiving, that it will very much limit the scope of the power of legislation by the Parliament and we do not want that; and it is why we do not want the words "due process of law." These are the two main examples that we should keep in mind.
>
> You can keep speculating on all the things that have never been touched, but these are two very sensitive areas that we have to cope with as legislators and my view is that Parliament has decided a certain law on abortion and a certain law on capital punishment, and it should prevail and we do not want the courts to say that the judgment of Parliament was wrong in using the constitution.

This passage, of course, revolves around the second and not the first limb of s. 7, but it offers no support for the suggestion that it was intended to bring the question of abortion into the *Charter*.

It cannot be said that the history, traditions and underlying philosophies of our society would support the proposition that a right to abortion could be implied in the *Charter*. . . .

History of the Law of Abortion

[At English common law, abortion before quickening was not a criminal offence. Quickening occurred when the pregnant woman could feel the foetus in her womb—usually around four months. In 1803, the law of criminal abortion was codified in England. In 1861, the distinction between pre- and post-quickening was abolished. All abortions were treated as felony offences. In *R. v. Bournei* (1939), the crime of abortion was held to be subject to the defence of necessity—viz. saving the mother's life. In Canada, abortion was first made a statutory crime in 1869, and has continued to be so under the various revisions of the *Criminal Code*. In 1969, Parliament significantly reformed the abortion law by adding the exculpatory provisions of section 251(4).]

The historical review of the legal approach in Canada taken from the judgment of the Court of Appeal serves, as well, to cast light on the underlying philosophies of our society and establishes that there has never been a general right to abortion in Canada. There has always been clear recognition of a public interest in the protection of the unborn and there has been no evidence or indication of any general acceptance of the concept of abortion at will in our society. It is to be observed as well that at the time of adoption of the *Charter* the sole provision for an abortion in Canadian law was that to be found in s. 251 of the *Criminal Code*. It follows then, in my view, that the interpretive approach to the *Charter*, which has been accepted in this Court, affords no support for the entrenchment of a constitutional right of abortion.

As to an asserted right to be free from any state interference with bodily integrity and serious state-imposed psychological stress, I would say that to be accepted, as a constitutional right, it would have to be based on something more than the mere imposition, by the State, of such stress and anxiety. It must, surely, be evident that many forms of government action deemed to be reasonable, and even necessary in our society, will cause stress and anxiety to many, while at the same time being acceptable exercises of government power in pursuit of socially desirable goals. The very facts of life in a modern society would preclude the entrenchment of such a constitutional right. . . .

To invade the s. 7 right of security of the person, there would have to be more than state-imposed stress or strain. A breach of the right would have to be based upon an infringement of some interest which would be of such nature and such importance as to warrant constitutional protection. This, it would seem to me, would be limited to cases where the state-action complained of, in addition to imposing stress and strain, also infringed another right, freedom or interest which was deserving of protection under the concept of security of the person. For the reasons outlined above, the right to have an abortion—given the language, structure and history of the *Charter* and given the history, traditions and underlying philosophies of our society—is not such an interest. . . .

It is for these reasons I would conclude, that save for the provisions of the *Criminal Code*, which permit abortion where the life or health of the woman is at risk, no right of abortion can be found in Canadian law, custom or tradition, and that the *Charter*, including s. 7, creates no further right. Accordingly, it is my view that s. 251 of the *Code* does not in its terms violate s. 7 of the *Charter*. Even accepting the assumption that the concept of security of the person would extend to vitiating a law which would require a woman to carry a child to the completion of her pregnancy at the risk of her life or health, it must be observed that this is not our case. As has been pointed out, s. 251 of the *Code* already provides for abortion in such circumstances.

Procedural Fairness

I now turn to the appellant's argument regarding the procedural fairness of s. 251 of the *Criminal Code*. . . . Because abortions are not generally available to all women who seek them, the argument goes, the defence is illusory, or practically so, and the section therefore fails to comport with the principles of fundamental justice.

Precise evidence on the questions raised is, of course, difficult to obtain and subject to subjective interpretation depending upon the views of those adducing it. Much evidence was led at trial based largely on the Ontario experience. Additional material in the form of articles, reports and studies was adduced, from which the Court was invited to conclude that access to abortion is not evenly provided across the country and that this could be the source of much dissatisfaction. While I recognize that in constitutional cases a greater latitude has been allowed concerning the reception of such material, I would prefer to place principal reliance upon the evidence given under oath in court in my considerations of the factual matters. Evidence was adduced from the chairman of a therapeutic abortion committee at a hospital in Hamilton, where in 1982 eleven hundred and eighty-seven abortions were performed, who testified that of all applications received by his committee in that year less than a dozen were ultimately refused. Refusal in each case was based upon the fact that a majority of the committee was not convinced that "the continuation of the pregnancy would be detrimental to the woman's health." All physicians who performed abortions under the *Criminal Code* provisions admitted in cross-examination that they had never had an application for a therapeutic abortion on behalf of the patient ultimately refused by an abortion committee. No woman testified that she personally had applied for an abortion anywhere in Canada and had been refused, and no physician testified to his participation in such an application. . . . In all, the extent to which the statutory procedure contributes to the problems connected with procuring an abortion is anything but clear. Accordingly, even if one accepts that it would be contrary to the principles of fundamental justice for Parliament to make available a defence which, by reason of its terms, is illusory or practically so, it cannot, in my view, be said that s. 251 of the *Code* has had that effect.

It would seem to me that a defence created by Parliament could only be said to be illusory or practically so when the *defence is not available in the circumstances in which it is held out as being available.* The very nature of the test assumes, of course, that it is for Parliament to define the defence and, in so doing, to designate the terms and conditions upon which it may be available. . . .

... I would suggest it is apparent that the Court's role is not to second-guess Parliament's policy choice as to how broad or how narrow the defence should be. The determination of when "the disapprobation of society is not warranted" is in Parliament's hands. . . .

It was further argued that the defence in s. 251(4) is procedurally unfair in that it fails to provide an adequate standard of "health" to guide the abortion committees which are charged with the responsibility for approving or disapproving applications for abortions. It is argued that the meaning of the word "health" in s. 251(4) is so vague as to render the sub-section unconstitutional. This argument was . . . dealt with fully and effectively in the Court of Appeal . . . :

> . . . In this case, however, from a reading of s. 251 with its exception, there is no difficulty in determining what is proscribed and what is permitted. It cannot be said that no sensible meaning can be given to the words of the section. Thus, it is for the courts to say what meaning the statute will bear. Counsel was unable to give the Court any authority for holding a statute void for uncertainty. In any event, there is no doubt the respondents knew that the acts they proposed and carried out were in breach of the section. The fact that they did not approve of the law in this regard does not make it "uncertain." . . .

Finally, this Court has dealt with the matter. Dickson J. (as he then was), speaking for the majority in *Morgentaler (1975)*, *supra*, in concluding a discussion of s. 251(4) of the *Criminal Code*, said, at p. 675:

> Whether one agrees with the Canadian legislation or not is quite beside the point. Parliament has spoken unmistakably in clear and unambiguous language.

In the same case, Laskin C.J., while dissenting on other grounds, said at p. 634:

> The contention under point 2 is equally untenable as an attempt to limit the substance of legislation in a situation which does not admit of it. In submitting that the standard upon which therapeutic abortion committees must act is uncertain and subjective, counsel who make the submission cannot find nourishment for it even in *Doe v.*

Bolton. There it was held that the prohibition of abortion by a physician except when "based upon his best clinical judgment that an abortion is necessary" did not prescribe a standard so vague as to be constitutionally vulnerable. *A fortiori*, under the approach taken here to substantive due process, the argument of uncertainty and subjectivity fails. It is enough to say that Parliament has fixed a manageable standard because it is addressed to a professional panel, the members of which would be expected to bring a practised judgment to the question whether "the continuation of the pregnancy . . . would or would be likely to endanger . . . life or health."

In my opinion, then, the contention that the defence provided in s. 251(4) of the *Criminal Code* is illusory cannot be supported

Conclusion

Before leaving this case, I wish to make it clear that I express no opinion on the question of whether, or upon what conditions, there should be a right for a pregnant woman to have an abortion free of legal sanction. No valid constitutional objection to s. 251 of the *Criminal Code* has, in my view, been raised and, consequently, if there is to be a change in the law concerning this question it will be for Parliament to make. Questions of public policy touching on this controversial and divisive matter must be resolved by the elected Parliament. It does not fall within the proper jurisdiction of the courts. Parliamentary action on this matter is subject to judicial review but, in my view, nothing in the *Canadian Charter of Rights and Freedoms* gives the Court the power or duty to displace Parliament in this matter involving, as it does, general matters of public policy. . . .

. . . The solution to this question in this country must be left to Parliament. It is for Parliament to pronounce on and to direct social policy. This is not because Parliament can claim all wisdom and knowledge but simply because Parliament is elected for that purpose in a free democracy and, in addition, has the facilities—the exposure to public opinion and information—as well as the political power to make effective its decisions. . . .

For all of these reasons, I would dismiss the appeal.

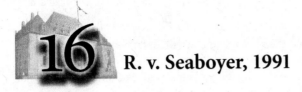

R. v. Seaboyer, 1991

Few *Charter* decisions have provoked as much opposition as the *Seaboyer* ruling. A 7-to-2 majority ruled unconstitutional what is commonly referred to as rape-shield legislation. The legislation represented Parliament's second attempt to address what it considered to be prejudicial assumptions in how the common law has historically dealt with sexual assaults, which, overwhelmingly, are committed against women. Before the legislation, the common law permitted questioning about the prior sexual conduct of a complainant without proof of how this information was relevant to a specific issue in the trial. This form of questioning would often undermine the credibility of the woman who alleged she had been sexually assaulted, by allowing inferences to be drawn that she was not to be believed and had likely consented to the alleged sexual assault. This legal tactic also had the effect of discouraging many women from pressing or pursuing claims that they had been sexually assaulted.

The legislation subject to the *Charter* challenge in *Seaboyer* was introduced in 1982. It prevented defence lawyers from cross-examining and leading evidence about a complainant's sexual conduct with three exceptions: rebuttal evidence, evidence going to identity, and evidence relating to consent to sexual activity on the same occasion as the trial incident. The Court was seriously divided about whether the excluded information undermines the *Charter* right to make a full answer and defence to the charge of sexual assault. The majority concluded that the impugned legislation had the potential to exclude otherwise admissible evidence that might be highly relevant to the defence. The dissenting judges did not accept that a *Charter* right had been violated because they believed the legislation excluded only irrelevant or prejudicial evidence. Justice L'Heureux-Dubé, who wrote the dissenting judgment, indicated that even if a case could be made that the legislation excludes relevant evidence, this evidence would be so prejudicial that its exclusion would be justified.

The Court's ruling provoked widespread criticism, particularly from women's groups who worried that the ruling would preserve inappropriate stereotypes about women and sexual assault and that it would also discourage the reporting of sexual assault. The decision also generated broad public discussion about when, if ever, a woman's sexual history is relevant in the context of sexual assault trials. Initially, the federal government indicated it would try to address the majority's concerns about the exclusionary rule. But after extensive lobbying by and consultation with women's groups, Kim Campbell, then Minister of Justice, interpreted the situation as an opportunity to fundamentally change the way the law deals with sexual assault, by addressing and defining consent in sexual relations.

The proposed legislation was subject to extensive review by a parliamentary committee created for that specific purpose, in a rare example where *Charter* considerations assumed a prominent part of parliamentary review and debate. The new legislation amended the *Criminal Code* to define consent in sexual relations, and to make it clear that consent cannot be presumed to have been given based on a woman's conduct or her previous sexual history. The legislation now requires that all reasonable steps be taken to ascertain that consent has been given and explicitly states that mistaken belief about consent is not a valid consideration at trial if it arises from situations of intoxication, recklessness, or wilful blindness. Thus, while the earlier law had allowed an accused to be acquitted if able to convince the judge or jury of an honest belief that the victim had consented, the new legislation makes this defence much more difficult to establish.

Despite all-party support for the legislation, the measures were extremely controversial. Many of the critics were defence lawyers, who argued that the legislation would undermine a fair trial, while other critics mocked the new rape-shield provisions as being more consistent with contract law than criminal law, suggesting that the legislation did not reflect a realistic portrayal of sexual relationships between men and women. Many women's groups rejected the claim that innocent men would be convicted under these measures and argued that if a man is uncertain after taking reasonable steps to ensure that his partner has consented to a sexual act, he should simply abstain.

An interesting aspect of the parliamentary response was the extent to which the legislation appears as a conversation initiated by Parliament to the Court (well before the metaphor of dialogue would become a popular way of characterizing the institutional relationship between Parliament and the judiciary). The legislation was presented as Parliament's efforts to balance conflicting *Charter* rights, and not simply as the protection of the right to a fair trial as the majority had framed the issue, and included a preamble that expressed Parliament's assumptions about how the *Charter* appropriately resolves the relevant issues. In the preamble, Parliament expressed its "grave" concerns about sexual violence, its belief that the right to a fair trial coexists with a woman's right to equality and security, and its view (in contradiction to the majority's ruling) that "evidence of the complainant's sexual history is rarely relevant and that its admission should be subject to particular scrutiny, bearing in mind the inherently prejudicial character of such evidence."

The legislation was subsequently challenged, and upheld by a unanimous Supreme Court as consistent with the *Charter* in *R. v. Darrach*.[1] ~

Discussion Questions

1. Which judicial position is the most persuasive—the majority's or the minority's?
2. Is the use of a legislative preamble an appropriate way for Parliament to clarify its position on how *Charter* considerations appropriately guide legislation?
3. Is the metaphor of dialogue a useful one to assess the legislative response to this ruling?

---

1   [2000] 2 S.C.R. 443.

R. v. SEABOYER; R. v. GAYME
[1991] 2 S.C.R. 577

Hearing: March 26, 27, 1991; Judgment: August 22, 1991.

Present: Lamer C.J. and La Forest, L'Heureux-Dubé, Sopinka, Gonthier, Cory, McLachlin, Stevenson, and Iacobucci JJ.

Interveners: The Attorney General of Canada, the Attorney General of Quebec, the Attorney General for Saskatchewan, the Canadian Civil Liberties Association, and Women's Legal Education and Action Fund et al.

The judgment of Lamer C.J. and La Forest, Sopinka, Cory, McLachlin, Stevenson, and Iacobucci JJ. was delivered by

McLACHLIN J.: These cases raise the issue of the constitutionality of ss. 276 and 277 of the *Criminal Code*, R.S.C., 1985, c. C-46 (formerly ss. 246.6 and 246.7), commonly known as the "rape-shield" provisions. The provisions restrict the right of the defence on a trial for a sexual offence to cross-examine and lead evidence of a complainant's sexual conduct on other occasions. The question is whether these restrictions offend the guarantees accorded to an accused person by the *Canadian Charter of Rights and Freedoms*.

My conclusion is that one of the sections in issue, s. 276, offends the *Charter*. While its purpose—the abolition of outmoded, sexist-based use of sexual conduct evidence—is laudable, its effect goes beyond what is required or justified by that purpose. At the same time, striking down s. 276 does not imply reversion to the old common law rules, which permitted evidence of the complainant's sexual conduct even though it might have no probative value to the issues on the case and, on the contrary, might mislead the jury. Instead, relying on the basic principles that actuate our law of evidence, the courts must seek a middle way that offers the maximum protection to the complainant compatible with the maintenance of the accused's fundamental right to a fair trial.

A second issue arises as to the procedure to be followed where a constitutional question is raised on a preliminary inquiry to determine if there is sufficient evidence to commit the accused for trial. On this issue I conclude that the preliminary inquiry judges correctly declined to consider the constitutionality of the legislation and that the cases should be remitted for trial in accordance with the principles of evidence as canvassed in these reasons.

The Background

I deal first with *Seaboyer*. The accused was charged with sexual assault of a woman with whom he had been drinking in a bar. On the preliminary inquiry the judge refused to allow the accused to cross-examine the complainant on her sexual conduct on other occasions. The appellant contends that he should have been permitted to cross-examine as to other acts of sexual intercourse which may have caused bruises and other aspects of the complainant's condition which the Crown had put in evidence. While the theory of the defence has not been detailed at this early stage, such evidence might arguably be relevant to consent, since it might provide other explanations for the physical evidence tendered by the Crown in support of the use of force against the complainant.

The *Gayme* case arose in different circumstances. The complainant was 15, the appellant 18. They were friends. The Crown alleges that the appellant sexually assaulted her at his school. The defence, relying on the defences of consent and honest belief in consent, contends that there was no assault and that the complainant was the sexual aggressor. In pursuance of this defence, the appellant at the preliminary inquiry sought to cross-examine and present evidence on prior and subsequent sexual conduct of the complainant. Accordingly, he brought a motion for an order declaring that ss. 276 and 277 of the *Code* were unconstitutional. The judge rejected the motion, on the ground that he lacked jurisdiction to hear it, and committed the appellant for trial.

In neither *Seaboyer* nor *Gayme* did the preliminary inquiry judge consider the questions individually; they ruled that the blanket exclusion in the *Criminal Code* prevented them from considering whether the questions were otherwise relevant and admissible....

Relevant Legislation

Criminal Code, s. 276:

> **276.** (1) In proceedings in respect of an offence under section 271, 272 or 273, no evidence shall be adduced by or on behalf of the accused concerning the sexual activity of the complainant with any person other than the accused unless
>
> (*a*) it is evidence that rebuts evidence of the complainant's sexual activity or absence thereof that was previously adduced by the prosecution;
>
> (*b*) it is evidence of specific instances of the complainant's sexual activity tending to establish the identity of the person who had sexual contact with the complainant on the occasion set out in the charge; or
>
> (*c*) it is evidence of sexual activity that took place on the same occasion as the sexual activity that forms the subject-matter of the charge, where that evidence relates to the consent that the accused alleges he believed was given by the complainant.
>
> (2) No evidence is admissible under paragraph (1)(*c*) unless
>
> (*a*) reasonable notice in writing has been given to the prosecutor by or on behalf of the accused of his

intention to adduce the evidence together with particulars of the evidence sought to be adduced; and

(*b*) a copy of the notice has been filed with the
clerk of the court.

(3) No evidence is admissible under subsection (1)
unless the judge, provincial court judge or justice, after
holding a hearing in which the jury and the members of
the public are excluded and in which the complainant is
not a compellable witness, is satisfied that the requirements of this section are met.

Criminal Code, s. 277:

277. In proceedings in respect of an offence under
section 271, 272 or 273, evidence of sexual reputation,
whether general or specific, is not admissible for the purpose of challenging or supporting the credibility of the
complainant....

Discussion

1. Do ss. 276 and 277 of the Criminal Code Infringe Sections 7 and 11(d) of the Charter?

(a) The Approach to ss. 7 and 11(d) of the Charter

Everyone, under s. 7 of the *Charter*, has the right to life, liberty
and security of person and the right not to be deprived thereof
except in accordance with the principles of fundamental
justice.

The first branch of s. 7 need not detain us. It is not disputed that ss. 276 and 277 of the *Criminal Code* have the
capacity to deprive a person of his or her liberty. A person
convicted of sexual assault may be sentenced to life imprisonment. In so far as ss. 276 and 277 may affect conviction, they
may deprive a person of his or her liberty.

The real issue under s. 7 is whether the potential for deprivation of liberty flowing from ss. 276 and 277 takes place in
a manner that conforms to the principles of fundamental
justice. The principles of fundamental justice are the fundamental tenets upon which our legal system is based. We find
them in the legal principles which have historically been
reflected in the law of this and other similar states: *R. v. Beare*,
[1988] 2 S.C.R. 387. The sections which follow s. 7, like the
right to a fair trial enshrined in s. 11(d), reflect particular
principles of fundamental justice: *Re B.C. Motor Vehicle Act*,
[1985] 2 S.C.R. 486. Thus the discussion of s. 7 and s. 11(d)
is inextricably intertwined.

The principles of fundamental justice reflect a spectrum
of interests, from the rights of the accused to broader societal
concerns. Section 7 must be construed having regard to those
interests and "against the applicable principles and policies
that have animated legislative and judicial practice in the
field" (*Beare, supra*, at pp. 402-3 *per* La Forest J.). The ultimate

question is whether the legislation, viewed in a purposive way,
conforms to the fundamental precepts which underlie our
system of justice....

(b) The Positions of the Parties

(i) The Arguments in Favour of the Legislation

The supporters of the legislation submit that it conforms to,
and indeed furthers, the principles of fundamental justice,
both in purpose and effect.

The main purpose of the legislation is to abolish the old
common law rules which permitted evidence of the complainant's sexual conduct which was of little probative value and
calculated to mislead the jury. The common law permitted
questioning on the prior sexual conduct of a complainant without proof of relevance to a specific issue in the trial. Evidence
that the complainant had relations with the accused and others
was routinely presented (and accepted by judges and juries)
as tending to make it more likely that the complainant had
consented to the alleged assault and as undermining her credibility generally. These inferences were based not on facts, but
on the myths that unchaste women were more likely to consent to intercourse and in any event, were less worthy of belief.
These twin myths are now discredited. The fact that a woman
has had intercourse on other occasions does not in itself
increase the logical probability that she consented to intercourse with the accused. Nor does it make her a liar. In an
effort to rid the criminal law of these outmoded and illegitimate notions, legislatures throughout the United States and
in England, Australia and Canada passed "rape-shield" laws.
(I note that the term "rape shield" is less than fortunate; the
legislation offers protection not against rape, but against the
questioning of complainants in trials for sexual offences.)

Three subsidiary purposes of such legislation may be discerned. The first, and the one most pressed before us, was the
preservation of the integrity of the trial by eliminating evidence which has little or no probative force but which unduly
prejudices the judge or jury against the complainant. If we
accept, as we must, that the purpose of the criminal trial is to
get at the truth in order to convict the guilty and acquit the
innocent, then it follows that irrelevant evidence which may
mislead the jury should be eliminated in so far as possible.
There is no doubt that evidence of the complainant's sexual
activities has often had this effect. Empirical studies in the
United States suggest that juries often misused evidence of
unchastity and improperly considered "victim-precipitating"
conduct, such as going to a bar or getting into a car with the
defendant, to "penalize" those complainants who did not fit
the stereotype of the "good woman" either by convicting the
defendant of a lesser charge or by acquitting the defendant ....

The second rationale cited in support of rape-shield legislation is that it encourages the reporting of crime. Despite the fact that the statistics do not demonstrate with any certainty that reporting of sexual offences has increased in Canada as a consequence of rape-shield provisions, I accept that it is a legitimate legislative goal to attempt to encourage such reporting by eliminating to the greatest extent possible those elements of the trial which cause embarrassment or discomfort to the complainant. As time passes and the existence of such provisions becomes better known, they may well have some effect in promoting reporting. Certainly failure to consider the position of the complainant in the trial process may have the opposite effect.

A third and related reason sometimes offered for rape-shield legislation is protection of the witness's privacy. This is really the private aspect upon which the social interest in encouraging the reporting of sexual offences is based. In addition to furthering reporting, our system of justice has an interest in preventing unnecessary invasion of witnesses' privacy.

The goals of the legislation—the avoidance of unprobative and misleading evidence, the encouraging of reporting and the protection of the security and privacy of the witnesses—conform to our fundamental conceptions of justice. The concern with the legislation is not as to its purpose, which is laudable, but with its effect. The reasons for these concerns emerge from a consideration of the appellants' position, to which I now turn.

(ii) The Arguments Against the Legislation

The appellants contend that the legislation, however laudable its goals, in fact infringes their right to present evidence relevant to their defence and hence violates their right to a fair trial, one of the most important of the principles of fundamental justice.

The precept that the innocent must not be convicted is basic to our concept of justice. One has only to think of the public revulsion felt at the improper conviction of Donald Marshall in this country or the Birmingham Six in the United Kingdom to appreciate how deeply held is this tenet of justice. Lamer J. (as he then was) put it this way in *Re B.C. Motor Vehicle Act, supra*, at p. 513:

> It has from time immemorial been part of our system of laws that the innocent not be punished. This principle has long been recognized as an essential element of a system for the administration of justice which is founded upon a belief in the dignity and worth of the human person and on the rule of law....

It is this fundamental principle—that the innocent not be punished—that is urged in support of the contention that

ss. 276 and 277 violate the *Charter*. The interest is both individual, in that it affects the accused, and societal, for no just society can tolerate the conviction and punishment of the innocent.

The right of the innocent not to be convicted is reflected in our society's fundamental commitment to a fair trial, a commitment expressly embodied in s. 11(d) of the *Charter*. It has long been recognized that an essential facet of a fair hearing is the "opportunity adequately to state [one's] case."... This applies with particular force to the accused, who may not have the resources of the state at his or her disposal. Thus our courts have traditionally been reluctant to exclude even tenuous defence evidence....

The right of the innocent not to be convicted is dependent on the right to present full answer and defence. This, in turn, depends on being able to call the evidence necessary to establish a defence and to challenge the evidence called by the prosecution....

In short, the denial of the right to call and challenge evidence is tantamount to the denial of the right to rely on a defence to which the law says one is entitled. The defence which the law gives with one hand, may be taken away with the other. Procedural limitations make possible the conviction of persons who the criminal law says are innocent.

(iii) The Issue Between the Parties

All the parties agree that the right to a fair trial—one which permits the trier of fact to get at the truth and properly and fairly dispose of the case—is a principle of fundamental justice. Nor is there any dispute that encouraging reporting of sexual offences and protection of the complainant's privacy are legitimate goals provided they do not interfere with the primary objective of a fair trial. Where the parties part company is on the issue of whether ss. 276 and 277 of the *Criminal Code* in fact infringe the right to a fair trial. The supporters of the legislation urge that it furthers the right to a fair trial by eliminating evidence of little or no worth and considerable prejudice. The appellants, on the other hand, say that the legislation goes too far and in fact eliminates relevant evidence which should be admitted notwithstanding the possibility of prejudice.

This raises two questions. First, what are the fundamental principles governing the right to introduce relevant defence evidence which may also be prejudicial? Second, does the legislation infringe these principles?

(c) The Principles Governing the Right to Call Defence Evidence

It is fundamental to our system of justice that the rules of evidence should permit the judge and jury to get at the truth and properly determine the issues....

The problem which arises is that a trial is a complex affair, raising many different issues. Relevance must be determined not in a vacuum, but in relation to some issue in the trial. Evidence which may be relevant to one issue may be irrelevant to another issue. What is worse, it may actually mislead the trier of fact on the second issue. Thus the same piece of evidence may have value to the trial process but bring with it the danger that it may prejudice the fact-finding process on another issue.

The law of evidence deals with this problem by giving the trial judge the task of balancing the value of the evidence against its potential prejudice. Virtually all common law jurisdictions recognize a power in the trial judge to exclude evidence on the basis that its probative value is outweighed by the prejudice which may flow from it. . . .

Canadian courts, like courts in most common law jurisdictions, have been extremely cautious in restricting the power of the accused to call evidence in his or her defence, a reluctance founded in the fundamental tenet of our judicial system that an innocent person must not be convicted. It follows from this that the prejudice must substantially outweigh the value of the evidence before a judge can exclude evidence relevant to a defence allowed by law.

These principles and procedures are familiar to all who practise in our criminal courts. They are common sense rules based on basic notions of fairness, and as such properly lie at the heart of our trial process. In short, they form part of the principles of fundamental justice enshrined in s. 7 of the *Charter*. They may be circumscribed in some cases by other rules of evidence, but as will be discussed in more detail below, the circumstances where truly relevant and reliable evidence is excluded are few, particularly where the evidence goes to the defence. In most cases, the exclusion of relevant evidence can be justified on the ground that the potential prejudice to the trial process of admitting the evidence clearly outweighs its value.

This then is the yardstick by which ss. 276 and 277 of the *Code* are to be measured. Do they exclude evidence the probative value of which is not substantially outweighed by its potential prejudice? If so, they violate the fundamental principles upon which our justice system is predicated and infringe s. 7 of the *Charter*.

The parties, as I understand their positions, agree on this view of the principles of fundamental justice. The Attorney General for Ontario, for the respondent, does not assert that the *Charter* permits exclusion of evidence of real value to an accused's defence. Rather, he contends that any evidence which might be excluded by ss. 276 and 277 of the *Code* would be of such trifling value in relation to the prejudice that might flow from its reception that its exclusion would enhance

rather than detract from the fairness of the trial. Others who defend the legislation, do so on the ground that it does not exclude evidence relevant to the defence, that the exceptions contained in the provisions "encompass *all* potential situations where evidence of a complainant's sexual history with men other than the accused would be *relevant* to support a legitimate defence" (emphasis in original): see Grant, [Yola Althea Grant, "The Penetration of the Rape Shield: R. v. Seaboyer and R. v. Gayme in the Ontario Court of Appeal" (1989-1990) 3 C.J.W.L. 592], at p. 601. It is to this issue, which I see as the crux of the case, which I now turn.

(d) The Effect of the Legislation: What Evidence Is Excluded?

Section 277 excludes evidence of sexual reputation for the purpose of challenging or supporting the credibility of the plaintiff. The idea that a complainant's credibility might be affected by whether she has had other sexual experience is today universally discredited. There is no logical or practical link between a woman's sexual reputation and whether she is a truthful witness. It follows that the evidence excluded by s. 277 can serve no legitimate purpose in the trial. Section 277, by limiting the exclusion to a purpose which is clearly illegitimate, does not touch evidence which may be tendered for valid purposes, and hence does not infringe the right to a fair trial.

I turn then to s. 276. Section 276, unlike s. 277, does not condition exclusion on use of the evidence for an illegitimate purpose. Rather, it constitutes a blanket exclusion, subject to three exceptions—rebuttal evidence, evidence going to identity, and evidence relating to consent to sexual activity on the same occasion as the trial incident. The question is whether this may exclude evidence which is relevant to the defence and the probative value of which is not substantially outweighed by the potential prejudice to the trial process. To put the matter another way, can it be said *a priori*, as the Attorney General for Ontario contends, that any and all evidence excluded by s. 276 will necessarily be of such trifling weight in relation to the prejudicial effect of the evidence that it may fairly be excluded?

In my view, the answer to this question must be negative. The Canadian and American jurisprudence affords numerous examples of evidence of sexual conduct which would be excluded by s. 276 but which clearly should be received in the interests of a fair trial, notwithstanding the possibility that it may divert a jury by tempting it to improperly infer consent or lack of credibility in the complainant.

Consider the defence of honest belief. It rests on the concept that the accused may honestly but mistakenly (and not necessarily reasonably) have believed that the complainant was consenting to the sexual act. If the accused can raise a reasonable doubt as to his intention on the basis that he honestly held such a belief, he is not guilty under our law and is entitled to an acquittal. The basis of the accused's honest belief in the complainant's consent may be sexual acts performed by the complainant at some other time or place. Yet section 276 would preclude the accused leading such evidence.

Another category of evidence eliminated by s. 276 relates to the right of the defence to attack the credibility of the complainant on the ground that the complainant was biased or had motive to fabricate the evidence. . . .

. . . Evidence of sexual activity excluded by s. 276 may be relevant to explain the physical conditions on which the Crown relies to establish intercourse or the use of force, such as semen, pregnancy, injury or disease—evidence which may go to consent. . . . In the case of young complainants where there may be a tendency to believe their story on the ground that the detail of their account must have come from the alleged encounter, it may be relevant to show other activity which provides an explanation for the knowledge. . . .

Even evidence as to pattern of conduct may on occasion be relevant. Since this use of evidence of prior sexual conduct draws upon the inference that prior conduct infers similar subsequent conduct, it closely resembles the prohibited use of the evidence and must be carefully scrutinized. . . . Yet such evidence might be admissible in non-sexual cases under the similar fact rule. Is it fair then to deny it to an accused, merely because the trial relates to a sexual offence? . . .

[Section] 276 has the potential to exclude evidence of critical relevance to the defence. Can it honestly be said, as the Attorney General for Ontario contends, that the value of such evidence will always be trifling when compared with its potential to mislead the jury? I think not. The examples show that the evidence may well be of great importance to getting at the truth and determining whether the accused is guilty or innocent under the law—the ultimate aim of the trial process. They demonstrate that s. 276, enacted for the purpose of helping judges and juries arrive at the proper and just verdict in the particular case, overshoots the mark, with the result that it may have the opposite effect of impeding them in discovering the truth.

The conclusion that s. 276 overreaches is supported by consideration of how it impacts on the justifications for s. 276 set out above. The first and most important justification for s. 276 is that it prevents the judge or jury from being diverted by irrelevant evidence of other sexual conduct of the complainant which will unfairly prejudice them against the complainant and thus lead to an improper verdict. Accepting that evidence that diverts the trier of fact from the real issue and prejudices the chance of a true verdict can properly be excluded even if it possesses some relevance, the fact remains that a provision

which categorically excludes evidence without permitting the trial judge to engage in the exercise of whether the possible prejudicial effect of the evidence outweighs its value to the truth-finding process runs the risk of overbreadth. . . .

The argument based on the reporting of sexual offences similarly fails to justify the wide reach of s. 276. . . . [I]t is counterproductive to encourage reporting by a rule which impairs the ability of the trier of fact to arrive at a just result and determine the truth of the report. Reporting is but the first step in the judicial process, not an end in itself. But even if it is assumed that increased reporting will result in increased convictions, the argument is unpersuasive. . . .

[T]he justification of maintaining the privacy of the witness fails to support the rigid exclusionary rule embodied in s. 276 of the *Code*. First, it can be argued that important as it is to take all measures possible to ease the plight of the witness, the constitutional right to a fair trial must take precedence in case of conflict. . . .

Secondly, s. 276 goes further than required to protect privacy because it fails to permit an assessment of the effect on the witness of the evidence—an effect which may be great in some cases and small in others—in relation to the cogency of the evidence.

The failings of s. 276 are inherent in its concept. Commentators have identified two fundamental flaws in rape-shield provisions similar to s. 276. The first is that such provisions fail to distinguish between the different purposes for which evidence may be tendered. The legislation may misdefine the evil to be addressed as evidence of sexual activity, when in fact the evil to be addressed is the narrower evil of the *misuse* of evidence of sexual activity for irrelevant and misleading purposes, namely the inference that the complainant consented to the act or that she is an unreliable witness. The result of this misdefinition of the problem is a blanket prohibition of evidence of sexual activity, regardless of whether the evidence is tendered for an illegitimate purpose or for a valid one. . . .

A second and related criticism of provisions such as s. 276 is that they adopt a "pigeon-hole" approach which is incapable of dealing adequately with the fundamental evidentiary problem at stake, that of determining whether or not the evidence is truly relevant, and not merely irrelevant and misleading. This amounts, in effect, to predicting relevancy on the basis of a series of categories. . . .

Scholars have criticized rape-shield legislation adopting the format of a blanket exclusion supplemented by exceptions on the ground that this approach is inherently incapable of permitting the Court sufficient latitude to properly determine relevance in the individual case. . . .

In short, the problem with legislation like s. 276 . . . is its failure to rely on the governing concept of whether the evidence is being tendered for an irrelevant, illegitimate purpose, and its reliance instead on categories of admissible evidence which can never anticipate the multitude of circumstances which may arise in trials for sexual offences. The failing is summed up succinctly by Doherty . . . where he characterizes s. 276 as calling for "a mechanical 'pigeon-holing' approach to the question of admissibility based on criteria which may in a given case have little to do with the potential value of the evidence."

To summarize, s. 276 has the potential to exclude otherwise admissible evidence which may in certain cases be relevant to the defence. Such evidence is excluded absolutely, without any means of evaluating whether in the circumstances of the case the integrity of the trial process would be better served by receiving it than by excluding it. Accepting that the rejection of relevant evidence may sometimes be justified for policy reasons, the fact remains that s. 276 may operate to exclude evidence where the very policy which imbues the section—finding the truth and arriving at the correct verdict—suggests the evidence should be received. Given the primacy in our system of justice of the principle that the innocent should not be convicted, the right to present one's case should not be curtailed in the absence of an assurance that the curtailment is clearly justified by even stronger contrary considerations. What is required is a law which protects the fundamental right to a fair trial while avoiding the illegitimate inferences from other sexual conduct that the complainant is more likely to have consented to the act or less likely to be telling the truth. . . .

(f) Other Jurisdictions

In support of the contention that s. 276 of the *Code* does not infringe the principles of fundamental justice or the right to a fair trial, it is argued that provisions similar to s. 276 have been upheld in other jurisdictions.

The first point to note is that s. 276 is among the most draconian approaches to the problem of eradicating improper inferences as to consent and credibility from the evidence of the sexual activities of the complainant. . . . Provisions in England, Australia and many of the United States generally allow for some measure of judicial discretion to deal with the impossibility of foreseeing all eventualities and avoiding the unfairness of excluding evidence which may be highly relevant to the defence. . . .

(g) Summary

I conclude that the operation of s. 276 of the *Criminal Code* permits the infringement of the rights enshrined in ss. 7 and 11(*d*) of the *Charter*. In achieving its purpose—the abolition of the outmoded, sexist-based use of sexual conduct evidence —it overshoots the mark and renders inadmissible evidence which may be essential to the presentation of legitimate defences and hence to a fair trial. In exchange for the elimination of the possibility that the judge and jury may draw illegitimate inferences from the evidence, it exacts as a price the real risk that an innocent person may be convicted. The price is too great in relation to the benefit secured, and cannot be tolerated in a society that does not countenance in any form the conviction of the innocent. Support for this conclusion is found in other rules of evidence which have adapted to meet the dangers of arbitrarily excluding valuable evidence, as well as the law in other jurisdictions, which by one means or another rejects the idea that rape-shield legislation, however legitimate its aims, should be cast so widely as to deprive the accused of the tools with which to build a legitimate defence.

Section 277 does not, by contrast, offend the Charter.

2. Is Section 276 Saved by Section 1 of the Charter?

Is s. 276 of the *Criminal Code* justified in a free and democratic society, notwithstanding the fact that it may lead to infringements of the *Charter*?

The first step under s. 1 is to consider whether the legislation addresses a pressing and substantial objective: *R. v. Oakes*, [1986] 1 S.C.R. 103. As already discussed, it does.

The second requirement under s. 1 is that the infringement of rights be proportionate to the pressing objective. This inquiry involves three considerations. The first—whether there exists a rational connection between the legislative measure and the objective—is arguably met; s. 276 does help to exclude unhelpful and potentially misleading evidence of the complainant's prior sexual conduct. The second consideration under proportionality is whether the legislation impairs the right as little as possible. It has been suggested that legislatures must be given some room to manoeuvre, particularly where the legislation is attempting to fix a balance between competing groups in society: *Irwin Toy Ltd. v. Quebec (Attorney General)*, [1989] 1 S.C.R. 927. Assuming that this case, although criminal and as such a contest between the state and the accused, might fall into this class, it still cannot be said that the degree of impairment effected by s. 276 is appropriately restrained. In creating exceptions to the exclusion of evidence of the sexual activity of the complainant on other occasions, Parliament correctly recognized that justice requires a measured approach, one which admits evidence which is truly relevant to the defence notwithstanding potential prejudicial effect. Yet Parliament at the same time excluded other evidence of sexual conduct which might be equally relevant to a legitimate defence and which appears to pose no greater danger of prejudice than the exceptions it recognizes. To the extent the section excludes relevant defence evidence whose value is not clearly outweighed by the danger it presents, the section is overbroad.

I turn finally to the third aspect of the proportionality requirement—the balance between the importance of the objective and the injurious effect of the legislation. The objective of the legislation, as discussed above, is to eradicate the erroneous inferences from evidence of other sexual encounters that the complainant is more likely to have consented to the sexual act in issue or less likely to be telling the truth. The subsidiary aims are to promote fairer trials and increased reporting of sexual offences and to minimize the invasion of the complainant's privacy. In this way the personal security of women and their right to equal benefit and protection of the law are enhanced. The effect of the legislation, on the other hand, is to exclude relevant defence evidence, the value of which outweighs its potential prejudice. As indicated in the discussion of s. 7, all parties agree that a provision which rules out probative defence evidence which is not clearly outweighed by the prejudice it may cause to the trial strikes the wrong balance between the rights of complainants and the rights of the accused. The line must be drawn short of the point where it results in an unfair trial and the possible conviction of an innocent person. Section 276 fails this test.

I conclude that s. 276 is not saved by s. 1 of the Charter....

[The majority addressed whether the legislation could be saved by applying the doctrine of constitutional exemption, allowing judges to decline to apply section 276 in cases where a constitutional violation would occur, and ruled this would not be appropriate in this case.]

4. What Follows from Striking Down Section 276?

The first question is whether the striking down of s. 276 revives the old common law rules of evidence permitting liberal and often inappropriate reception of evidence of the complainant's sexual conduct....

The answer to this question is no. The rules in question are common law rules. Like other common law rules of evidence, they must be adapted to conform to current reality. As all counsel on these appeals accepted, the reality in 1991 is that evidence of sexual conduct and reputation in itself cannot be regarded as logically probative of either the complainant's credibility or consent. Although they still may inform the thinking of many, the twin myths which s. 276 sought to eradicate are just that—myths—and have no place in a rational and just system of law. It follows that the old rules which permitted evidence of sexual conduct and condoned invalid inferences from it solely for these purposes have no place in our law....

In the absence of legislation, it is open to this Court to suggest guidelines for the reception and use of sexual conduct evidence. Such guidelines should be seen for what they are—an attempt to describe the consequences of the application of the general rules of evidence governing relevance and the reception of evidence—and not as judicial legislation cast in stone.

In my view the trial judge under this new regime shoulders a dual responsibility. First, the judge must assess with a high degree of sensitivity whether the evidence proffered by the defence meets the test of demonstrating a degree of relevance which outweighs the damages and disadvantages presented by the admission of such evidence.... The trial judge must ensure that evidence is tendered for a legitimate purpose, and that it logically supports a defence. The fishing expeditions which unfortunately did occur in the past should not be permitted. The trial judge's discretion must be exercised to ensure that neither the *in camera* procedure nor the trial become forums for demeaning and abusive conduct by defence counsel.

The trial judge's second responsibility will be to take special care to ensure that, in the exceptional case where circumstances demand that such evidence be permitted, the jury is fully and properly instructed as to its appropriate use. The jurors must be cautioned that they should not draw impermissible inferences from evidence of previous sexual activity. While such evidence may be tendered for a purpose logically probative of the defence to be presented, it may be important to remind jurors that they not allow the allegations of past sexual activity to lead them to the view that the complainant is less worthy of belief, or was more likely to have consented for that reason. It is hoped that a sensitive and responsive exercise of discretion by the judiciary will reduce and even eliminate the concerns which provoked legislation such as s. 276, while at the same time preserving the right of an accused to a fair trial.

I would summarize the applicable principles as follows:

1. On a trial for a sexual offence, evidence that the complainant has engaged in consensual sexual conduct on other occasions (including past sexual conduct with the accused) is not admissible solely to support the inference that the complainant is by reason of such conduct:
   (a) more likely to have consented to the sexual conduct at issue in the trial;
   (b) less worthy of belief as a witness.
2. Evidence of consensual sexual conduct on the part of the complainant may be admissible for purposes other than an inference relating to the consent or credibility of the complainant where it possesses probative value on an issue in the trial and where that

probative value is not substantially outweighed by the danger of unfair prejudice flowing from the evidence.

By way of illustration only, and not by way of limitation, the following are examples of admissible evidence:

(A) Evidence of specific instances of sexual conduct tending to prove that a person other than the accused caused the physical consequences of the rape alleged by the prosecution;

(B) Evidence of sexual conduct tending to prove bias or motive to fabricate on the part of the complainant;

(C) Evidence of prior sexual conduct, known to the accused at the time of the act charged, tending to prove that the accused believed that the complainant was consenting to the act charged (without laying down absolute rules, normally one would expect some proximity in time between the conduct that is alleged to have given rise to an honest belief and the conduct charged);

(D) Evidence of prior sexual conduct which meets the requirements for the reception of similar act evidence, bearing in mind that such evidence cannot be used illegitimately merely to show that the complainant consented or is an unreliable witness;

(E) Evidence tending to rebut proof introduced by the prosecution regarding the complainant's sexual conduct.

3. Before evidence of consensual sexual conduct on the part of a victim is received, it must be established on a *voir dire* (which may be held *in camera*) by affidavit or the testimony of the accused or third parties, that the proposed use of the evidence of other sexual conduct is legitimate.

4. Where evidence that the complainant has engaged in sexual conduct on other occasions is admitted on a jury trial, the judge should warn the jury against inferring from the evidence of the conduct itself, either that the complainant might have consented to the act alleged, or that the complainant is less worthy of credit. . . .

Conclusion

I would dismiss the appeals and affirm the order of the Court of Appeal that these cases proceed to trial. I would answer the constitutional questions as follows:

1. Whether s. 246.6 [now 276] or 246.7 [now 277] of the *Criminal Code* is inconsistent with s. 7 or s. 11(d) of the *Canadian Charter of Rights and Freedoms*?

   Yes, s. 276 is inconsistent with s. 7 and s. 11(d). Section 277 is not.

2. If s. 246.6 or 246.7 of the *Criminal Code* is inconsistent with either s. 7 or s. 11(d) of the *Canadian Charter of Rights and Freedoms*, whether that inconsistency is justified on the basis of s. 1 thereof. No.

The reasons of L'Heureux-Dubé and Gonthier JJ. were delivered by

L'HEUREUX-DUBÉ J. (dissenting in part):

Introduction

These two appeals are about relevance, myths and stereotypes in the context of sexual assaults. More particularly, is the prior sexual history of a complainant, in the trial of an accused charged with sexual assault, relevant and/or admissible? . . .

Analysis

Of tantamount importance in answering the constitutional questions in this case is a consideration of the prevalence and impact of discriminatory beliefs on trials of sexual offences. These beliefs affect the processing of complaints, the law applied when and if the case proceeds to trial, the trial itself and the ultimate verdict. It is my view that the constitutional questions must be examined in their broader political, social and historical context in order to attempt any kind of meaningful constitutional analysis. . . .

[T]he provisions that are the subject of the constitutional challenge in the present case are commonly referred to as "rape shield" provisions. Implicit in this description is a presumption as to their purpose: that it is solely to shield a complainant from the rigours of cross-examination at trial. As I hope to make clear through the course of my reasons, although protecting the complainant may be one of the purposes of the provisions, it is neither the only one, nor necessarily the most important. As a result, I will not use this inaccurate shorthand in referring to these provisions.

Sexual Assault

Sexual assault is not like any other crime. In the vast majority of cases the target is a woman and the perpetrator is a man (98.7 percent of those charged with sexual assault are men: *Crime Statistics 1986* . . . .

Conservative estimates inform us that, in Canada, at least one woman in five will be sexually assaulted during her lifetime. . . . While social scientists agree that the incidence of sexual assault is great, they also agree that it is impossible, for a variety of reasons, to measure accurately the actual rate of victimization. . . . While there is a large gap between reported incidents and actual victimization, there is a further gap between what researchers tell us are the actual numbers and what the actual numbers are.

There are a number of reasons why women may not report their victimization: fear of reprisal, fear of a continuation of their trauma at the hands of the police and the criminal justice system, fear of a perceived loss of status and lack of desire to report due to the typical effects of sexual assault such as depression, self-blame or loss of self-esteem. Although all of the reasons for failing to report are significant and important, more relevant to the present inquiry are the numbers of victims who choose not to bring their victimization to the attention of the authorities due to their perception that the institutions with which they would have to become involved will view their victimization in a stereotypical and biased fashion. . . .

The woman who comes to the attention of the authorities has her victimization measured against the current rape mythologies, i.e. who she should be in order to be recognized as having been, in the eyes of the law, raped; who her attacker must be in order to be recognized, in the eyes of the law, as a potential rapist; and how injured she must be in order to be believed. If her victimization does not fit the myths, it is unlikely that an arrest will be made or a conviction obtained. . . .

[P]olice rely in large measure upon popular conceptions of sexual assault in order to classify incoming cases as "founded" or "unfounded." It would appear as though most forces have developed a convenient shorthand regarding their decisions to proceed in any given case. This shorthand is composed of popular myth regarding rapists (distinguishing them from men as a whole), and stereotype about women's character and sexuality. . . . [T]he most common of these myths and stereotypes [are]:

1. *Struggle and Force: Woman As Defender of Her Honor.* There is a myth that a woman cannot be raped against her will, that if she really wants to prevent a rape she can.

The prosecution attempts to show that she did struggle, or had no opportunity to do so, while the defence attempts to show that she did not. . . .

2. *Knowing the Defendant: The Rapist As a Stranger.* There is a myth that rapists are strangers who leap out of bushes to attack their victims. . . . [T]he view that interaction between friends or between relatives does not result in rape is prevalent. . . .

3. *Sexual Reputation: The Madonna–Whore Complex.* . . . [W]omen . . . are categorized into one-dimensional types. They are maternal or they are sexy. They are good or they are bad. They are madonnas or they are whores.

The legal rules use these distinctions.

4. *General Character: Anything Not 100 Percent Proper and Respectable.* . . . Being on welfare or drinking or drug use could be used to discredit anyone, but where women are involved, these issues are used to imply that the woman consented to sex with the defendant or that she contracted to have sex for money.

5. *Emotionality of Females.* Females are assumed to be "more emotional" than males. The expectation is that if a woman is raped, she will get hysterical during the event and she will be visibly upset afterward. If she is able to "retain her cool," then people assume that "nothing happened." . . .

6. *Reporting Rape.* Two conflicting expectations exist concerning the reporting of rape. One is that if a woman is raped she will be too upset and ashamed to report it, and hence most of the time this crime goes unreported. The other is that if a woman is raped she will be so upset that she will report it. Both expectations exist simultaneously.

7. *Woman as Fickle and Full of Spite.* Another stereotype is that the feminine character is especially filled with malice. Woman is seen as fickle and as seeking revenge on past lovers.

8. *The Female Under Surveillance: Is the Victim Trying to Escape Punishment?* . . . It is assumed that the female's sexual behavior, depending on her age, is under the surveillance of her parents or her husband, and also more generally of the community. Thus, the defense argues, if a woman says she was raped it must be because she consented to sex that she was not supposed to have. She got caught, and now she wants to get back in the good graces of whomever's surveillance she is under.

9. *Disputing That Sex Occurred.* That females fantasize rape is another common stereotype. Females are assumed to make up stories that sex occurred when in fact nothing happened. . . . Similarly, women are thought

to fabricate the sexual activity not as part of a fantasy life, but out of spite.

10. *Stereotype of the Rapist.* One stereotype of the rapist is that of a stranger who leaps out of the bushes to attack his victim and later abruptly leaves her....
[S]tereotypes of the rapist can be used to blame the victim. She tells what he did. And because it often does not match what jurors think rapists do, his behavior is held against her.

A corollary of this myth is the belief that rapists are not "normal" and are "mentally ill."

...This list of stereotypical conceptions about women and sexual assault is by no means exhaustive. Like most stereotypes, they operate as a way, however flawed, of understanding the world and, like most such constructs, operate at a level of consciousness that makes it difficult to root them out and confront them directly. This mythology finds its way into the decisions of the police regarding their "founded"/"unfounded" categorization, operates in the mind of the Crown when deciding whether or not to prosecute, influences a judge's or juror's perception of guilt or innocence of the accused and the "goodness" or "badness" of the victim, and finally, has carved out a niche in both the evidentiary and substantive law governing the trial of the matter....

Absolutely pivotal to an understanding of the nature and purpose of the provisions and constitutional questions at issue in this case is the realization of how widespread the stereotypes and myths about rape are, notwithstanding their inaccuracy.

The appellants argue that we, as a society, have become more enlightened, that prosecutors, police, judges and jurors can be trusted to perform their tasks without recourse to discriminatory views about women manifested through rape myth. Unfortunately, social science evidence suggests otherwise. Rape myths still present formidable obstacles for complainants in their dealings with the very system charged with discovering the truth....

The Larger Legal Context

...The common law has always viewed victims of sexual assault with suspicion and distrust. As a result, unique evidentiary rules were developed. The complainant in a sexual assault trial was treated unlike any other. In the case of sexual offences, the common law "enshrined" prevailing mythology and stereotype by formulating rules that made it extremely difficult for the complainant to establish her credibility and fend off inquiry and speculation regarding her "morality" or "character."...

Under the guise of a principled application of the legal concept of relevance, the common law allowed the accused to delve at great length into the moral character of the complainant by adducing "relevant" sexual history. The prejudicial impact of such an inquiry has already been discussed at length. The true nature and purpose of the inquiry into sexual history is revealed by the resulting prejudice and by the fact that these concepts were only applicable in respect of sexual offences and, in addition, were not deemed relevant to the credibility of the male accused.

Application of the relevance concept was not the only way in which the common law integrated stereotype and myth into trials of sexual offences. Also part of the unique body of evidentiary law surrounding sexual offences were, among other things, the doctrine of recent complaint and corroboration rules. These evidentiary concepts were also based upon stereotypes of the female complainant requiring independent evidence to support her evidence and, in addition, evidence that she raised a "hue and cry" after her assault. It is noteworthy that both recent complaint and corroboration rules formed exceptions to general rules of evidence....

Parliament intervened on two notable occasions, both relevant to the inquiry here. In 1976, Parliament repealed the existing s. 142 of the *Criminal Code*, R.S.C. 1970, c. C-34, and enacted a provision designed to alleviate some of the problems caused by the virtually unrestricted inquiry into a complainant's previous sexual history allowed at common law (*Criminal Law Amendment Act, 1975*, S.C. 1974-75-76, c. 93, s. 8)....

Though the motives of Parliament were commendable, judicial interpretation of the section thwarted any benefit that may have accrued to the complainant. In fact, the provision, as judicially interpreted, provided less protection to the complainant than that offered at common law, surely a surprising result considering the obvious mischief Parliament intended to cure in enacting it....

It may be argued that, not only did the Court feel a somewhat misplaced need to "balance" the "protection" of the complainant against "restrictions" placed upon the accused, it tipped the balance further in favour of the accused. This is obviously a curious result given the fact that the infirmities of the common law led Parliament to intervene. That the complainant should walk away with less than she already had is lamentable....

The failure of the courts, as was indicated earlier, both to take cognizance of and to implement the objectives of Parliament in this earlier legislation, combined with further criticism of the manner in which complainants of sexual offences were treated, generated a sweeping set of reforms in 1982. The Honourable Jean Chrétien, then Minister of Justice and Attorney General of Canada, articulated the principles underlying this second, larger reform package in this manner:

The inequality of the present law has placed an unfair burden on female victims of sexual assault. It has added to the trauma, stigma and embarrassment of being sexually assaulted, and has deterred many victims from reporting these serious crimes to the police.... Bill C-53 would alleviate the legal impediment which allows this to occur....

[Justice L'Heureux-Dubé proceeded with a lengthy discussion of Parliament's intentions with respect to reforming how the law deals with sexual assault complaints.]

The literature and case law in this area abound with examples of the supposed relevant evidence that is excluded by s. 276. For the most part, however, the "relevant" evidence provided in these examples is, on a principled inquiry, irrelevant; any semblance of relevance depends in large measure upon acceptance of stereotype about women and rape. Much of the remainder is admissible under the provision. One hesitates, however, to construct an argument around the speculative scenarios offered. Many of the scenarios are pure fantasy and have absolutely no grounding in life or experience....

Many argue that the most convincing support for the argument that the provision is drawn too narrowly is provided by so-called "similar fact evidence," or "pattern of conduct evidence," i.e. that the complainant has had consensual sexual relations in circumstances that look an awful lot like those supporting the assault allegation and, hence, such evidence is probative of consent. I am of the firm opinion that such evidence is almost invariably irrelevant and, in any event, is nothing more than a prohibited propensity argument, besides being highly prejudicial to the integrity and fairness of the trial process....

A second category of so-called relevant evidence is also widely set up as conclusively demonstrating the infirmity of the provision, namely evidence of mistaken belief in consent. Again, I am of the firm opinion that no relevant evidence regarding the defence of honest but mistaken belief in consent is excluded by the provision under attack here....

It is my view that, assuming that both the trier of fact and the trier of law are operating in an intellectual environment that is free of rape myth and stereotype about women, any evidence excluded by this subsection would not satisfy the "air of reality" that must accompany this defence nor would it provide reasonable grounds for the jury to consider in assessing whether the belief was honestly held. The structure of the exception provided for in s. 276(1)(c) is thus not offensive to such a defence.

Evidence of prior acts of prostitution or allegations of prostitution are properly excluded by the provision. In my opinion, this evidence is never relevant and, besides its irrelevance, is hugely prejudicial. I vehemently disagree with the assertion of the appellant Seaboyer that "a prostitute is generally more willing to consent to sexual intercourse and is less credible as a witness because of that mode of life."...

Many also argue that the provision does not allow evidence going to show motive to fabricate or bias. Clearly, most such alleged motives or bias will not be grounded in the complainant's past sexual history. Moreover, much of this evidence depends for its relevance on certain stereotypical visions of women; that they lie about sexual assault, and that women who allege sexual assault often do so in order to get back in the good graces of those who may have her sexual conduct under scrutiny. Thus, again, refutation of stereotype strikes at the heart of the argument. As to evidence that a complainant has made prior false allegations of sexual assault, such evidence is admissible under the existing provision since this evidence does not involve the admission of her previous sexual history.

As I stated at the outset, the evidence which is excluded by the provision is simply irrelevant. It is based upon discriminatory beliefs about women and sexual assault. In addition, the impugned provision provides wide avenues for the introduction of sexual history evidence that is relevant. Paradoxically, some of the exceptions may be cast overly broadly with the unfortunate result that a large body of evidence may still be improperly admitted on the basis of specious relevancy claims.

If I am wrong in concluding that no relevant sexual history evidence is excluded by the contested provision, I am of the view that such exclusion is proper due to its extremely prejudicial effect on the trial of the legal issues....

The Constitutional Questions

... It is my view that neither "fairness" nor "the principles of fundamental justice" mandate the constitutional invalidity of s. 276. Rather, in order to achieve fairness and to conduct trials in accordance with fundamental tenets of criminal law, this provision must be upheld in all of its vigour....

The constitutional question posed by the present case is whether, notwithstanding the already established irrelevance and/or prejudicial nature of the evidence excluded by the impugned provision, an accused, nevertheless, has a constitutional right to adduce such evidence. On my view of the scope of these constitutional guarantees, this question must be answered with a resounding and compelling no.

It is noncontroversial to state that an accused does not have a constitutional right to adduce irrelevant evidence. To the extent that much, if not all, of the evidence excluded by the provision at issue here is irrelevant, there is no constitutional issue. Nor, in my view, does an accused have the right under the *Charter*, whether under the rubric of a right to a fair trial or the right to make full answer and defence, to adduce evidence that prejudices and distorts the fact-finding process at trial. As a corollary, neither do notions of a "fair trial" or "full answer and defence" recognize a right in the accused to adduce any evidence that may lead to an acquittal. Such propositions cast ss. 7 and 11(*d*) in an extremely narrow fashion and deny meaningful content to notions of "fairness" and "principles of fundamental justice." . . .

[Although not necessary for her findings, Justice L'Heureux-Dubé considered the section 1 question.]

. . . In the face of a previous legislative provision that was emasculated by the courts and on the heels of this, the continued application of stereotype, Parliament's measured and considered response was to codify those situations wherein sexual history evidence may be both relevant and sufficiently probative such that its admission was warranted. Parliament exhibited a marked, and justifiedly so, distrust of the ability of the courts to promote and achieve a non-discriminatory application of the law in this area. In view of the history of government attempts, the harm done when discretion is posited in trial judges and the demonstrated inability of the judiciary to change its discriminatory ways, Parliament was justified in so choosing. My attempt to illustrate the tenacity of these discriminatory beliefs and their acceptance at all levels of society clearly demonstrates that discretion in judges is antithetical to the goals of Parliament.

While some degree of latitude must be accorded to the legislative choice of Parliament due to the troubled history that informed its choice, the fact that Parliament had to choose between the interests of competing groups also requires such an approach. This is not a typical situation where the government and accused persons have squared off or where the government is "best characterized as the singular antagonist of the individual whose right has been infringed" (*Irwin Toy Ltd. v. Quebec (Attorney General)*) [[1989] 1 S.C.R. 927]. Rather it is plain that Parliament, in coming to its legislative decision, weighed the claims of different groups and attempted to do that which best balanced their concerns. These circumstances of the legislative decision require that the impugned provisions be accorded a special place in the s. 1 analysis: . . .

Due to the concerns underlying the passage of this legislation and the extensive efforts of Parliament to assess the viability of a number of means, this is not a situation where the courts are better situated than or even as well situated as

Parliament to determine whether the "least drastic means" has been chosen. The appropriate standard of review at this stage of the proportionality inquiry is thus one of reasonableness, i.e. whether the government had a reasonable basis for concluding that the legislative solution they chose impaired the right as little as possible given the government's pressing and substantial objective. It is clear from my reasons to this point that the legislative choice is, at a minimum, in the realm of the reasonable.

. . . [T]he nature of the problem facing Parliament did not admit of a solution through the exercise of discretion of trial judges. History demonstrates that it was discretion in trial judges that saturated the law in this area with stereotype. My earlier discussion shows that we are not, all of a sudden, a society rid of such beliefs, and hence, discretionary decision making in this realm is absolutely antithetical to the achievement of government's pressing and substantial objective. . . .

Parliament was faced with a historical record which demonstrated that this discretion was abused and exercised in a discriminatory fashion by trial judges and with overwhelming social science research that says things have not changed. In this context, the notion that Parliament could have, in the name of minimal impairment, awarded a discretion to trial judges, loses sight altogether of the objective that has been found to be pressing and substantial. . . .

In summary, sexual history evidence excluded by s. 276 of the *Criminal Code* is mostly irrelevant and, moreover, so prejudicial that its exclusion both at common law and under the *Canadian Charter of Rights and Freedoms* is mandated. Neither s. 7 nor s. 11(*d*), upon a principled inquiry, directs a different conclusion. However, even assuming that s. 276 is unconstitutional in its effect, it is easily justified under s. 1. In my view, once the constitutional questions are viewed within their larger context, the conclusions reached in these reasons are absolutely uncontentious.

Although for me the questions pertaining to the constitutional exemption and the effect of striking down s. 276 do not arise, I will nevertheless, before disposing of these appeals, make some brief remarks in respect of them.

My colleague, McLachlin J., articulates three reasons for her rejection of the "doctrine of constitutional exemption" in this case: namely, (1) it would not substantially uphold the law and the will of the legislature would become increasingly obscured; (2) applying the doctrine would be indistinguishable in result from striking down the legislation; and (3) applying the doctrine in this case would be difficult. It seems to me, however, that the same rationales highlight the infirmity of the guidelines suggested by the majority with respect to the admission of evidence of prior sexual history. More particularly, the objectives of Parliament in enacting the legislation, identified earlier in these reasons, are ill served by the guidelines. The view that the objectives of Parliament and the values of the *Charter* are better served in this fashion ignores the larger context within which the guidelines will be applied. Furthermore, as a full discussion of this context shows, any optimism that the guidelines will be effectively and consis-

tently applied in a manner that is cognizant of both the objectives of Parliament and the infirmities of the common law is badly misplaced. My final objection to the guidelines, as my previous discussion indicates, is that they are entirely too broad and support the very stereotype and myth that they are meant to eradicate. . . .

R. v. Daviault, 1994

Does drunkenness reduce criminal responsibility in sexual assault prosecutions? A fundamental principle of the criminal law is that the morally innocent shall not be punished. This principle is protected by sections 7 and 11(*d*) of the *Charter*. In practical terms, this means that the Crown must prove beyond a reasonable doubt in court that the accused voluntarily committed the criminal act—the *actus reus*—and that he or she did so with *mens rea*—a guilty mind.

What effect does the consumption of alcohol have on voluntariness of one's conduct? What effect should it have on criminal liability for wrongful acts? A man could get very drunk in a bar, drive to a friend's house, and then sexually assault the occupant. Is it possible that the offender was so drunk as to lose all control over his conduct, akin to the sufferer of an epileptic seizure? Further, should it matter? On the one hand, if a person is charged with a criminal offence, it seems proper that the person's mental state at the time of the offence is what should govern the determination of the accused's responsibility for that offence. *How* the accused arrived at a state of involuntariness is logically beside the point. On the other hand, if the accused's intoxication is self-induced, should not the accused assume responsibility for criminal conduct committed after voluntarily becoming intoxicated?

Canadian legal principles in this area have been in turmoil for some time. Prior to the *Charter*, the common-law rule, while controversial, was relatively clear. Criminal offences were divided by courts into two categories: general intent and specific intent. A general intent offence is one in which the offender musters the intent simply to commit the criminal act. In a specific intent offence, the offender forms the general intent to commit a criminal act and also intends to do so for a specific, ulterior purpose. For example, assault is a general intent offence. Assault with the intent to inflict bodily harm is a specific intent offence. Given this analytic distinction, courts must then classify offences as either general or specific intent.[1]

A specific intent offence requires a higher, more sophisticated intellectual process. Accordingly, specific intent offences are more serious and more heavily punished. However, the mental acuity required for the commission of a specific intent offence is vulnerable to factors that impair mental functioning. Courts have held that evidence of self-induced intoxication can be considered in cases involving specific intent offences—for example, if someone is very drunk, it is possible that he or she is either not acting voluntarily or with the criminal intent required for conviction of the offence. But in general intent cases, a Supreme Court majority held in *Leary v. The Queen*[2] that self-induced intoxication cannot be considered evidence of diminished criminal intent. The intent to get drunk, in other words, is "substituted" for the intent to commit a general intent offence while drunk. The "*Leary* rule" is that, in general intent cases, evidence of self-induced intoxication cannot be considered by a trier of fact as evidence casting doubt on the *mens rea* element.

---

1   *The Queen v. George*, [1960] S.C.R. 871.

2   [1978] 1 S.C.R. 29.

In the *Charter* era, such a "policy-oriented" departure from the strict principle that only the morally guilty shall be punished was certain to become vulnerable. Two justices in *R. v. Bernard* edged away from the *Leary* rule by distinguishing between two degrees of drunkenness. Writing for one other justice in a 5-to-2 decision, Justice Bertha Wilson refused to use the *Charter* to overturn the *Leary* rule. However, she would have allowed "evidence of intoxication to go to the trier of fact in general intent offences only if it is evidence of extreme intoxication involving an absence of awareness akin to a state of insanity or automatism."[3] Wilson's view did not attract a majority of the Court in support, but it provided the germ of change that was to come.

The change came in *R. v. Daviault*. Henri Daviault was charged with sexual assault, a general intent offence; he led evidence at trial that he was so drunk as to have no idea what he was doing at the time of the offence. He was acquitted. The Quebec Court of Appeal applied the pre-*Charter Leary* rule, granted the Crown's appeal, and entered a conviction. Daviault appealed. The Supreme Court, by a 6-to-3 majority, adopted Justice Wilson's approach in *Bernard*, allowing evidence of intoxication to be considered in general intent cases, but limiting the new rule to instances of extreme intoxication akin to automatism. In effect, drunkenness could serve as a defence to a charge of sexual assault. Daviault was committed to a new trial and later acquitted for other evidentiary reasons.

The decision produced outrage. Feminists and social conservatives, not normally considered political allies, united in opposition to the ruling. When general knowledge of the abhorrent facts in *Daviault* was compounded by news that a few lower courts subsequently acquitted accused persons who were drunk while committing sexual assaults, political pressure was brought to bear on the federal government to act. In 1995, Parliament passed an amendment to the *Criminal Code* depriving accused persons of the defence of self-induced intoxication in cases involving the violation of the bodily integrity of others. The new law reflected the assumptions of the dissenting judgment in *Daviault*, not the majority holding. Parliament's response is an example of robust "dialogue"—a legislative response that takes issue with the Court ruling rather than merely parroting it. Some observers considered this to be an "in your face" response to the Court. Others found it refreshingly consonant with the widespread opposition to the Court's ruling.[4] ∽

Discussion Questions

1. How does the *Charter*'s application to the common law compare to its application to statutes?
2. One way to describe the difference between the majority and minority judgments in *Daviault* is to say that the majority was preoccupied with logic while the minority was preoccupied with policy considerations. Explain.
3. Was the *Daviault* decision a good or bad candidate for Parliament's use of the section 33 override?

---

3 *R. v. Bernard*, [1988] 2 S.C.R. 833 at para. 90.

4 For a discussion of the response to *Daviault*, see Janet Hiebert, *Charter Conflicts: What Is Parliament's Role?* (Montreal and Kingston: McGill-Queen's University Press, 2002) 96-107.

R. v. DAVIAULT
[1994] 3 S.C.R. 63

Hearing: February 4, 1994; Judgment: September 30, 1994.

Present: Lamer C.J. and La Forest, L'Heureux-Dubé, Sopinka, Gonthier, Cory, McLachlin, Iacobucci, and Major JJ.

[Reasons concurring in the majority judgment by Chief Justice Lamer and Justice La Forest are omitted.]

The judgment of L'Heureux-Dubé, Cory, McLachlin, and Iacobucci JJ. was delivered by

CORY J.:

Issue

Can a state of drunkenness which is so extreme that an accused is in a condition that closely resembles automatism or a disease of the mind as defined in s. 16 of the *Criminal Code*, R.S.C., 1985, c. C-46, constitute a basis for defending a crime which requires not a specific but only a general intent? That is the troubling question that is raised on this appeal. . . .

Originally a crime was considered to be the commission of a physical act which was specifically prohibited by law. It was the act itself which was the sole element of the crime. If it was established that the act was committed by the accused then a finding of guilt would ensue. However, as early as the twelfth century, in large part through the influence of the canon law, it was established that there must also be a mental element combined with the prohibited act to constitute a crime. That is to say that the accused must have *meant* or intended to commit the prohibited act. The physical act and the mental element which together constitute a crime came to be known as the *actus reus* denoting the act, and the *mens rea* for the mental element. Like so many maxims they are imprecise and in many instances misleading.

For my purposes it is sufficient to say that for a great many years it has been understood that, unless the legislator provides otherwise, a crime must consist of the following elements. First, a physical element which consists of committing a prohibited act, creating a prohibited state of affairs, or omitting to do that which is required by the law. Second, the conduct in question must be willed; this is usually referred to as voluntariness. Some writers classify this element as part of the *actus reus*, others prefer to associate it with *mens rea*; however, all seem to agree that it is required. (See, generally, J. C. Smith and B. Hogan, *Criminal Law* (7th ed. 1992), at pp. 37 ff.) If persons other than lawyers were asked what constituted willed or voluntary conduct they would respond that such an act or conduct must involve a mental element. It is the mental element, that is the act of will, which makes the act or conduct willed or voluntary. . . .

A review of the history of the defence of intoxication shows that, originally, intoxication was never a defence to any crime. However, with the evolution of criminal law, this rule came to be progressively relaxed and the defence of intoxication was admitted for crimes of specific intent. Although one of the justifications for this was the courts' preoccupation with the harshness of criminal liability and criminal sanctions, clearly this development was also influenced by the development of the requirements for mental elements in crimes. The defence of intoxication was based on the recognition and belief that alcohol affected mental processes and the formulation of intention (see, for example, D. McCord, "The English and American History of Voluntary Intoxication to Negate *Mens Rea*" (1990), 11 *J. Legal Hist.* 372, at p. 378). I would agree with the authors who feel that the progressive expansion of the intoxication defence has paralleled the progressive expansion of theories of the mental elements of crimes. (See, for example, T. Quigley, "A Shorn Beard" (1987), 10:3 *Dalhousie L.J.* 167.) In my view, the need for this historical expansion is justified and emphasized by the increased concern for the protection of fundamental rights enshrined in the *Charter*.

It can thus be seen that with the development of principles recognizing constituent elements of crimes, particularly the need for a mental element, there came the realization that persons who lack the requisite mental element for a crime should not be found guilty of committing that crime. For centuries it has been recognized that both the physical and the mental elements are an integral part of a criminal act. It has long been a fundamental concept of our criminal law.

This appeal is concerned with situations of intoxication that are so extreme that they are akin to automatism. Such a state would render an accused incapable of either performing a willed act or of forming the minimal intent required for a general intent offence. I will approach the issue primarily on the basis that the extreme intoxication renders an accused incapable of forming the requisite minimum intent. I have taken the reasons of Sopinka J. to have dealt with the issue on the basis of *mens rea*.

Categorization of Crimes as Requiring Either a Specific Intent or a General Intent

The distinction between crimes of specific and general intent has been acknowledged and approved by this Court on numerous occasions. . . . On this issue, I am in general agreement with Sopinka J.'s presentation. The categorization of crimes as being either specific or general intent offences and the consequences that flow from that categorization are now well established in this Court. However, as he observes, we are not dealing here with ordinary cases of intoxication but with the limited situation of very extreme intoxication and the need, under the *Charter*, to create an exception in situations where intoxication is such that the mental element is negated. Sopinka J. sees no need for such an exception. This is where I must disagree with my colleague.

It may now be convenient to review the approach that courts have taken with regard to drunkenness as a factor in considering the mental element in crimes of general intent.

Drunkenness as a Factor in the Consideration of Criminal Liability

This issue has been the subject of many judicial decisions in Commonwealth countries. It is useful here to contrast the two opposite positions which have emerged in the absence of *Charter* considerations. The first position is illustrated by the decision of this Court in *Leary* [[1978] 1 S.C.R. 29], and also corresponds to the English position. The second position is that which prevails in Australia and New Zealand. It is best illustrated by the *O'Connor* decision, (1980), 4 A. Crim. R. 348. . . .

The Alternative Options

What options are available with regard to the admissibility and significance of evidence of drunkenness as it may pertain to the mental element in general intent offences? One choice would be to continue to apply the *Leary* rule. Yet, as I will attempt to demonstrate in the next section, the rule violates the *Charter* and cannot be justified. Thus this choice is unacceptable.

Another route would be to follow the [Australian] *O'Connor* decision. Evidence relating to drunkenness would then go to the jury along with all other relevant evidence in determining whether the mental element requirement had been met. It is this path that is enthusiastically recommended by the majority of writers in the field. Yet it cannot be followed. It is now well established by this Court that there are two categories of offences. Those requiring a specific intent and others which call for nothing more than a general intent. To follow *O'Connor* would mean that all evidence of intoxication of any degree would always go to the jury in general intent offences. This, in my view, is unnecessary. Further, in *Bernard* [[1988] 2 S.C.R. 833], the majority of this Court rejected this approach.

A third alternative, which I find compelling, is that proposed by Wilson J. in *Bernard*. I will examine the justifications for adopting this position in more detail shortly, but before doing that it may be helpful to review the nature of the *Charter* violations occasioned by a rigid application of the *Leary* rule.

How the Leary Rule Violates Sections 7 and 11(d) of the Charter

What then is the rule of law established by the decision in *Leary*? The conclusion of the majority in that case establishes that, even in a situation where the level of intoxication reached by the accused is sufficient to raise a reasonable doubt as to his capacity to form the minimal mental element required for a general intent offence for which he is being tried, he still cannot be acquitted. In such a situation, self-induced intoxication is substituted for the mental element of the crime. The result of the decision in *Leary*, applied to this case, is that the intentional act of the accused to voluntarily become intoxicated is substituted for the intention to commit the sexual assault or for the recklessness of the accused with regard to the assault. This is a true substitution of *mens rea*. First, it would be rare that the events transpiring from the consumption of alcohol through to the commission of the crime could be seen as one continuous series of events or as a single transaction. Secondly, the requisite mental element or *mens rea* cannot necessarily be inferred from the physical act or *actus reus* when the very voluntariness or consciousness of that act may be put in question by the extreme intoxication of the accused.

It has not been established that there is such a connection between the consumption of alcohol and the crime of assault that it can be said that drinking leads inevitably to the assault. Experience may suggest that alcohol makes it easier for violence to occur by diminishing the sense of what is acceptable behaviour. However, studies indicate that it is not in itself a cause of violence. . . .

In my view, the strict application of the *Leary* rule offends both ss. 7 and 11(*d*) of the *Charter* for a number of reasons. The mental aspect of an offence, or *mens rea*, has long been recognized as an integral part of crime. The concept is fundamental to our criminal law. That element may be minimal in general intent offences; nonetheless, it exists. In this case, the requisite mental element is simply an intention to commit the sexual assault or recklessness as to whether the actions will constitute an assault. The necessary mental element can ordinarily be inferred from the proof that the assault was committed by the accused. However, the substituted *mens rea* of an intention to become drunk cannot establish the *mens rea* to commit the assault.

R. v. Whyte, [1988] 2 S.C.R. 3, dealt with the substitution of proof of one element for proof of an essential element of an offence and emphasized the strict limitations that must be imposed on such substitutions. The position is put in this way, at pp. 18-19:

> In the passage from *Vaillancourt* quoted earlier, Lamer J. recognized that in some cases substituting proof of one

element for proof of an essential element will not infringe the presumption of innocence if, upon proof of the substituted element, it would be unreasonable for the trier of fact not to be satisfied beyond a reasonable doubt of the existence of the essential element. This is another way of saying that a statutory presumption infringes the presumption of innocence if it requires the trier of fact to convict in spite of a reasonable doubt. *Only if the existence of the substituted fact leads inexorably to the conclusion that the essential element exists, with no other reasonable possibilities, will the statutory presumption be constitutionally valid.* [Emphasis added.]

The substituted *mens rea* set out in *Leary* does not meet this test. The consumption of alcohol simply cannot lead inexorably to the conclusion that the accused possessed the requisite mental element to commit a sexual assault, or any other crime. Rather, the substituted *mens rea* rule has the effect of eliminating the minimal mental element required for sexual assault. Furthermore, *mens rea* for a crime is so well recognized that to eliminate that mental element, an integral part of the crime, would be to deprive an accused of fundamental justice. See *R. v. Vaillancourt*, [1987] 2 S.C.R. 636.

In that same case it was found that s. 11(*d*) would be infringed in those situations where an accused could be convicted despite the existence of reasonable doubt pertaining to one of the essential elements of the offence; see *Vaillancourt, supra*, at pp. 654-56. That would be the result if the *Leary* rule was to be strictly applied. For example, an accused in an extreme state of intoxication akin to automatism or mental illness would have to be found guilty although there was reasonable doubt as to the voluntary nature of the act committed by the accused. This would clearly infringe both ss. 7 and 11(*d*) of the *Charter*. In my view, the mental element of voluntariness is a fundamental aspect of the crime which cannot be taken away by a judicially developed policy. It simply cannot be automatically inferred that there would be an objective foresight that the consequences of voluntary intoxication would lead to the commission of the offence. It follows that it cannot be said that a reasonable person, let alone an accused who might be a young person inexperienced with alcohol, would expect that such intoxication would lead to either a state akin to automatism, or to the commission of a sexual assault. Nor is it likely that someone can really intend to get so intoxicated that they would reach a state of insanity or automatism.

Sopinka J. refers to the common law rules of automatism in order to support his position that voluntariness is not a requirement of fundamental justice. With respect I cannot agree. The decision of this Court in *Revelle v. The Queen*, [1981] 1 S.C.R. 576, predates the *Charter*. The rule that self-induced automatism cannot be a defence has never been subjected to a *Charter* analysis. In my view, automatism raises the same concerns as those presented in this case. Thus, to state that the rule in *Leary*, which precludes the accused from negating the mental element of voluntariness on the basis of an extreme state of intoxication, does not violate the *Charter* because the same principle has been developed in the context of the defence of automatism begs the very question which is now before this Court. The presumption of innocence requires that the Crown bear the burden of establishing all elements of a crime. These elements include the mental element of voluntariness. That element cannot be eliminated without violating s. 11(*d*) and s. 7 of the *Charter*.

It was argued by the respondent that the "blameworthy" nature of voluntary intoxication is such that it should be determined that there can be no violation of the *Charter* if the *Leary* approach is adopted. I cannot accept that contention. Voluntary intoxication is not yet a crime. Further, it is difficult to conclude that such behaviour should always constitute a fault to which criminal sanctions should apply. However, assuming that voluntary intoxication is reprehensible, it does not follow that its consequences in any given situation are either voluntary or predictable. Studies demonstrate that the consumption of alcohol is not the cause of the crime. A person intending to drink cannot be said to be intending to commit a sexual assault.

Further, self-induced intoxication cannot supply the necessary link between the minimal mental element or *mens rea* required for the offence and the *actus reus*. . . . Here, the question is not whether there is some symmetry between the physical act and the mental element but whether the necessary link exists between the minimal mental element and the prohibited act; that is to say that the mental element is one of intention with respect to the *actus reus* of the crime charged. As well, as Sopinka J. observes, the minimum *mens rea* for an offence should reflect the particular nature of the crime. See *R. v. Creighton*, [1993] 3 S.C.R. 3. I doubt that self-induced intoxication can, in all circumstances, meet this requirement for all crimes of general intent.

In summary, I am of the view that to deny that even a very minimal mental element is required for sexual assault offends the *Charter* in a manner that is so drastic and so contrary to the principles of fundamental justice that it cannot be justified under s. 1 of the *Charter*. The experience of other jurisdictions which have completely abandoned the *Leary* rule, coupled with the fact that under the proposed approach, the defence would be available only in the rarest of cases, demonstrate that there is no urgent policy or pressing objective which needs to be addressed. Studies on the relationship between intoxication and crime do not establish any rational link. Finally, as the *Leary* rule applies to all crimes of general intent, it cannot be said to be well tailored to address a particular objective and it would not meet either the proportionality or the minimum impairment requirements.

What then should be the fate of the *Leary* rule?

Approach That Should Be Taken When a Common Law Principle Is Found to Infringe the Provisions of the Charter

In *R. v. Swain*, [1991] 1 S.C.R. 933, Lamer C.J. (concurred in by Sopinka J. and myself) wrote on this issue. At page 978 he stated:

Before turning to s. 1, however, I wish to point out that because this appeal involves a *Charter* challenge to a common law, judge-made rule, the *Charter* analysis involves somewhat different considerations than would apply to a challenge to a legislative provision. For example, having found that the existing common law rule limits an accused's rights under s. 7 of the *Charter*, it may not be strictly necessary to go on to consider the application of s. 1. Having come to the conclusion that the common law rule enunciated by the Ontario Court of Appeal limits an accused's right to liberty in a manner which does not accord with the principles of fundamental justice, it could, in my view, be appropriate to consider at this stage whether an alternative common law rule could be fashioned which would not be contrary to the principles of fundamental justice.

If a new common law rule could be enunciated which would not interfere with an accused person's right to have control over the conduct of his or her defence, I can see no conceptual problem with the Court's simply enunciating such a rule to take the place of the old rule, without considering whether the old rule could nonetheless be upheld under s. 1 of the *Charter*. Given that the common law rule was fashioned by judges and not by Parliament or a legislature, judicial deference to elected bodies is not an issue. If it is possible to reformulate a common law rule so that it will not conflict with the principles of fundamental justice, such a reformulation should be undertaken.

This then is the approach that should be adopted when a common law principle is found to infringe the *Charter*. This, again, militates in favour of the adoption of a flexible application of the *Leary* rule, as was suggested by Wilson J.

Justifications for the Adoption of the Flexible Approach Suggested by Wilson J.

As I have said, the position adopted by Wilson J. in *Bernard* has much to commend it and should be adopted. Indeed, the original case which is the basis for much of our jurisprudence pertaining to intoxication seems to confirm this position. In *Director of Public Prosecutions v. Beard*, [1920] A.C. 479, Lord Birkenhead set out the three propositions which have been so frequently referred to in cases involving intoxication and criminal behaviour, at pp. 500-502:

1. That insanity, whether produced by drunkenness or otherwise, is a defence to the crime charged. The distinction between the defence of insanity in the true sense caused by excessive drinking, and the defence of drunkenness which produces a condition such that the drunken man's mind becomes incapable of forming a specific intention, has been preserved throughout the cases. The insane person cannot be convicted of a crime: ... but, upon a verdict of insanity, is ordered to be detained during His Majesty's pleasure. The law takes no note of the cause of the insanity. If actual insanity in fact supervenes, as the result of alcoholic excess, it furnishes as complete an answer to a criminal charge as insanity induced by any other cause....
2. That evidence of drunkenness which renders the accused incapable of forming the specific intent essential to constitute the crime should be taken into consideration with the other facts proved in order to determine whether or not he had this intent.
3. *That evidence of drunkenness falling short of a proved incapacity in the accused to form the intent necessary to constitute the crime, and merely establishing that his mind was affected by drink so that he more readily gave way to some violent passion, does not rebut the presumption that a man intends the natural consequences of his acts.* [Emphasis added.]

It does not appear to me that the decision was meant to create a complete bar to the defence of intoxication in the context of crimes of general intent....

Far more writers have supported the approach advocated by Dickson J. in *Leary*, and adopted in *O'Connor*. In my view, the most vehement and cogent criticism of [the *Leary* rule is that it substitutes] proof of drunkenness for proof of the requisite mental element. The authors deplore the division of crimes into those requiring a specific intent and those which mandate no more than a general intent. They are also critical of the resulting presumption of recklessness, and of the loss of a requirement of a true *mens rea* for the offence. They would prefer an approach that would permit evidence of drunkenness to go to the jury together with all the other relevant evidence in determining whether the requisite *mens rea* had been established....

I find further support for adopting the approach suggested by Wilson J. in studies pertaining to the effect of the *O'Connor* and *Kamipeli* decisions which have been undertaken in Australia and New Zealand. (Reference to these studies can be found in the English Law Commission's *Intoxication and Criminal Liability* [Law Commission, Great Britain, Consultation Paper No. 127 (1993)], at pp. 60-63.) One of these studies was conducted in New South Wales, by means of a survey of approximately 510 trials (see Judge G. Smith, "Footnote to O'Connor's Case" [(1981), 5 Crim. L.J. 270]). The author, Judge George Smith, concluded, at p. 277, that:

> Those figures disclose that a "defence" of intoxication which could not have been relied upon pre-*O'Connor* was raised in eleven cases or 2.16 per cent of the total. Acquittals followed in three cases or 0.59 per cent of the total, but only in one case or 0.2 per cent of the total could it be said with any certainty that the issue of intoxication was the factor which brought about the acquittal....
>
> It seems to me that no one with any experience of the criminal courts should be greatly surprised at this result for the simple practical reason that any "defence" of drunkenness poses enormous difficulties in the conduct of a case. To name but one, if the accused has sufficient recollection to describe relevant events, juries will be reluctant to believe that he acted involuntarily or without intent whereas, if he claims to have no recollection, he will be unable to make any effective denial of facts alleged by the Crown....
>
> Certainly my inquiries would indicate that the decision in *O'Connor's* case, far from opening any floodgates has at most permitted an occasional drip to escape from the tap.

That study clearly indicates that the *O'Connor* decision has not had an effect of any significance on trials or on the numbers of acquittals arising from evidence of severe intoxication.

There are some who argue that Wilson J.'s suggestion favours the extremely drunk while ignoring those who are less inebriated. (See, for example, T. Quigley, in "*Bernard* on Intoxication: Principle, Policy and Points In Between—Two Comments" [(1989), 67 C.R. (3d) 168, 173], at pp. 171-73.) I cannot agree with that contention. It must be remembered that those who are a "little" drunk can readily form the requisite mental element to commit the offence. The alcohol-induced relaxation of both inhibitions and socially acceptable behaviour has never been accepted as a factor or excuse in determining whether the accused possessed the requisite *mens rea*. Given the minimal nature of the mental element required for crimes of general intent, even those who are significantly drunk will usually be able to form the requisite *mens rea* and will be found to have acted voluntarily. In reality it is only those who can demonstrate that they were in such an extreme degree of intoxication that they were in a state akin to automatism or insanity that might expect to raise a reasonable doubt as to their ability to form the minimal mental element required

for a general intent offence. Neither an insane person nor one in a state of automatism is capable of forming the minimum intent required for a general intent offence. Similarly, as the words themselves imply, "drunkenness akin to insanity or automatism" describes a person so severely intoxicated that he is incapable of forming even the minimal intent required of a general intent offence. The phrase refers to a person so drunk that he is an automaton. As such he may be capable of voluntary acts such as moving his arms and legs but is quite incapable of forming the most basic or simple intent required to perform the act prohibited by a general intent offence. I believe that Wilson J.'s modification of the *Leary* rule is a judge-fashioned remedy that can be adopted to remedy a judge-made law which, by eliminating the mental element of a crime, offends the *Charter*.

It is obvious that it will only be on rare occasions that evidence of such an extreme state of intoxication can be advanced and perhaps only on still rarer occasions is it likely to be successful. Nonetheless, the adoption of this alternative would avoid infringement of the *Charter*.

I would add that it is always open to Parliament to fashion a remedy which would make it a crime to commit a prohibited act while drunk.

The appellant in this case is an elderly alcoholic. It is difficult if not impossible to present him in a sympathetic light. Yet any rule on intoxication must apply to all accused, including the young and inexperienced drinker. The strict rule in *Leary* is not a minor or technical infringement but a substantial breach of the *Charter* eliminating the mental elements of crimes of general intent in situations where the accused is in an extreme state of intoxication. I would think that this judge-made rule should be applied flexibly, as suggested by Wilson J., so as to comply with the *Charter*. Such an approach would mean that except in those rare situations where the degree of intoxication is so severe it is akin to automatism, drunkenness will not be a defence to crimes of general intent.

It should not be forgotten that if the flexible "Wilson" approach is taken, the defence will only be put forward in those rare circumstances of extreme intoxication. Since that state must be shown to be akin to automatism or insanity, I would suggest that the accused should be called upon to establish it on the balance of probabilities. This Court has recognized, in *R. v. Chaulk*, [1990] 3 S.C.R. 1303, that although it constituted a violation of the accused's rights under s. 11(*d*) of the *Charter*, such a burden could be justified under s. 1. In this case, I feel that the burden can be justified. Drunkenness of the extreme degree required in order for it to become relevant will only occur on rare occasions. It is only the accused who can give evidence as to the amount of alcohol consumed and its effect upon him. Expert evidence would be required to confirm that the accused was probably in a state akin to automatism or insanity as a result of his drinking. . . .

Disposition

In the result, I would allow the appeal, set aside the order of the Court of Appeal and direct a new trial.

The reasons of Sopinka, Gonthier, and Major JJ. were delivered by

SOPINKA J. (dissenting): This appeal raises a single question of law: can evidence of extreme intoxication tantamount to a state of automatism negative the intent required for sexual assault, an offence which has been classified as an offence of general intent? The appellant challenges the correctness of this Court's decision in *Leary v. The Queen*, [1978] 1 S.C.R. 29, which held that voluntary intoxication can never negate the *mens rea* for an offence of general intent.

Facts

The facts which give rise to this appeal are not in dispute. The complainant is a 65-year old woman who is partially paralysed and thus confined to a wheelchair. She knew the appellant through his wife, who was the complainant's dressmaker and ran errands for her. The complainant testified that at approximately 6:00 p.m. on May 30, 1989, at her request, the appellant arrived at her home carrying a 40-ounce bottle of brandy. The complainant drank part of a glass of brandy and then fell asleep in her wheelchair. When she awoke during the night to go to the bathroom, the appellant appeared, grabbed her chair, wheeled her into the bedroom, threw her on the bed and sexually assaulted her. The appellant left the apartment at about 4:00 a.m. The complainant subsequently discovered that the bottle of brandy was empty. The trial judge found as a fact that the appellant had drunk the rest of the bottle between 6:00 p.m. and 3:00 a.m.

The appellant was a chronic alcoholic. He testified that he had spent the day at a bar where he had consumed seven or eight bottles of beer. He recalled having a glass of brandy upon his arrival at the complainant's residence but had no recollection of what occurred between then and when he awoke nude in the complainant's bed. He denied sexually assaulting her.

The defence called a pharmacologist, Louis Léonard, to testify as an expert witness. Mr. Léonard testified that the appellant's alcoholic history made him less susceptible to the effects of alcohol. He hypothesized that, if the appellant had consumed seven or eight beers during the day and then 35 ounces of brandy on the evening in question, his blood-alcohol content would have been between 400 and 600 milligrams per 100 millilitres of blood. That blood-alcohol ratio would cause death or a coma in an ordinary person. Mr. Léonard

testified that an individual with this level of alcohol in his blood might suffer an episode of "l'amnésie-automatisme," also known as a "blackout." In such a state the individual loses contact with reality and the brain is temporarily dissociated from normal functioning. The individual has no awareness of his actions when he is in such a state and will likely have no memory of them the next day.

Mr. Léonard further testified that it is difficult to distinguish between a person in a blackout and someone who is simply acting under the influence of alcohol. He stated that if a person acting under the influence of alcohol behaves in a manner which requires higher cognitive functions or reflection, it is unlikely that the person is in a blackout. On the other hand, if the person departs from his normal behaviour to act in a gratuitous or violent manner, it is more likely that he is in a blackout.

The appellant was charged with one count of sexual assault. The trial judge found as a fact that the appellant had committed the offence as described by the complainant. However, he acquitted the appellant because he had a reasonable doubt about whether the appellant, by virtue of his extreme intoxication, had possessed the minimal intent necessary to commit the offence of sexual assault: [1991] R.J.Q. 1794. The Quebec Court of Appeal overturned this ruling: [1993] R.J.Q. 692, 80 C.C.C. (3d) 175, 19 C.R. (4th) 291, 54 Q.A.C. 27. The appellant now appeals to this Court as of right, pursuant to s. 691(2)(*a*) of the *Criminal Code*, R.S.C., 1985, c. C-46. . . .

Sexual assault is a crime of general intent. In *Leary v. The Queen, supra*, a majority of this Court held that drunkenness is not a defence to a crime of general intent. While some of the judges of this Court have sought to overrule *Leary*, it has not happened. Accordingly, I agree with the Court of Appeal's decision that the trial judge was bound by the decision in *Leary*. Furthermore, I reject the appellant's submission that *Leary* ought to be overruled. In the remainder of these reasons I propose to trace the development of the law governing the defence of intoxication and identify the policy considerations which support the rule espoused in *Leary*. Then I will respond to the various criticisms of the *Leary* rule and in particular whether it contravenes either s. 7 or s. 11(*d*) of the *Canadian Charter of Rights and Freedoms*. Finally, I will explain why, in my view, the alternatives which have been put forward are unsatisfactory. . . .

B. Criticisms of the Leary Rule

The *Leary* rule has been roundly criticized in the academic literature as well as in the dissenting judgments of Dickson C.J. in *Leary* itself and in *R. v. Bernard*. The main grounds upon which the *Leary* rule has been attacked are as follows:

1. The *Leary* rule violates ss. 7 and 11(*d*) of the *Charter* since it permits an accused to be convicted despite the existence of a reasonable doubt as to whether he has the *mens rea* of the offence charged.
2. The distinction between offences of specific and general intent is illogical.
3. The *Leary* rule is inconsistent with the defence of honest but mistaken belief in consent.

I will respond to each of these criticisms in turn.

1. The Leary Rule Violates Sections 7 and 11(d) of the Charter

The appellant's main objection to the *Leary* rule is that it allows an individual to be convicted even where the Crown has failed to prove beyond a reasonable doubt the requisite *mens rea* for the offence. This in the appellant's submission constitutes a violation of ss. 7 and 11(*d*) of the *Charter*. This objection is based upon the assumption that a particular *mens rea*, namely the intent to perform the *actus reus*, is a constitutionally required element of the offence of sexual assault. This assumption is not warranted. In my view the *Leary* rule does not relieve the Crown of the responsibility of proving the existence of a *mens rea* or any of the other elements of the offence of sexual assault which are required by the principles of fundamental justice.

As McIntyre J. pointed out in *R. v. Bernard*, only in rare cases will accused persons be able to establish that they were so intoxicated that they were unable to form the minimal intent required to commit the offence of sexual assault. Thus, in the vast majority of cases there can be no question of the *Leary* rule violating ss. 7 and 11(*d*) of the *Charter*. However, according to the findings of the trial judge, the present case is one of the rare cases in which the accused was sufficiently intoxicated to raise a reasonable doubt as to whether he intended to commit the offence of sexual assault. Application of the *Leary* rule in circumstances such as those of the case at bar obviously permits the accused to be convicted despite the existence of a reasonable doubt as to whether he intended to perform the *actus reus* of the offence of sexual assault. In my view this does not violate either s. 7 or s. 11(*d*) of the *Charter*. None of the relevant principles of fundamental justice require that the intent to perform the *actus reus* of an offence of general intent be an element of the offence. In my opinion the requirements of the principles of fundamental justice are satisfied by proof that the accused became voluntarily intoxicated.

The premise upon which the alleged breach of fundamental justice is based is that symmetry between the *actus reus*, or some aspect of it, and the *mens rea* is constitutionally required.

This, it is said, is a principle of fundamental justice which is of universal application. This issue has been recently thrashed out in relation to whether consequences forming part of the *actus reus* must be foreseen on an objective or subjective basis or some variation thereof. . . .

The majority of the Court has . . . authoritatively determined [in *R. v. Creighton*, [1993] 3 S.C.R. 3] that the general rule that the mental fault element of a crime must extend to the *actus reus*, including consequences forming part thereof, is subject to exceptions. It does not have universal application as a principle of fundamental justice. The principles of fundamental justice can exceptionally be satisfied provided the definition of the offence requires that a blameworthy mental element be proved and that the level of blameworthiness not be disproportionate to the seriousness of the offence. In my opinion, for the reasons that follow, these requirements are satisfied in this case and, given the history of the *Leary* rule and its underlying social utility, an exception should be made to accommodate it.

The first requirement of the principles of fundamental justice is that a blameworthy or culpable state of mind be an essential element of every criminal offence that is punishable by imprisonment. This principle reflects the fact that our criminal justice system refuses to condone the punishment of the morally innocent. As both McIntyre and Wilson JJ. pointed out in *R. v. Bernard*, individuals who render themselves incapable of knowing what they are doing through the voluntary consumption of alcohol or drugs can hardly be said to fall within the category of the morally innocent. Such individuals possess a sufficiently blameworthy state of mind that their imprisonment does not offend the principle of fundamental justice which prohibits imprisonment of the innocent. . . .

The *Charter* calls for a similar response. Central to its values are the integrity and dignity of the human person. These serve to define the principles of fundamental justice. They encompass as an essential attribute and are predicated upon the moral responsibility of every person of sound mind for his or her acts. The requirement of *mens rea* is an application of this principle. To allow generally an accused who is not afflicted by a disease of the mind to plead absence of *mens rea* where he has voluntarily caused himself to be incapable of *mens rea* would be to undermine, indeed negate, that very principle of moral responsibility which the requirement of *mens rea* is intended to give effect to.

The second requirement of the principles of fundamental justice is that punishment must be proportionate to the moral blameworthiness of the offender. This was held to be a principle of fundamental justice in *R. v. Martineau*, [1990] 2 S.C.R. 633, and *R. v. Creighton, supra*. There are a few crimes in respect of which a special level of *mens rea* is constitutionally required by reason of the stigma attaching to a conviction and by reason of the severity of the penalty imposed by law. Accordingly, murder and attempted murder require a *mens rea* based on a subjective standard. No exception from the principle of fundamental justice should be made with respect to these offences and, as specific intent offences, drunkenness is a defence.

By contrast, sexual assault does not fall into the category of offences for which either the stigma or the available penalties demand as a constitutional requirement subjective intent to commit the *actus reus*. Sexual assault is a heinous crime of violence. Those found guilty of committing the offence are rightfully submitted to a significant degree of moral opprobrium. That opprobrium is not misplaced in the case of the intoxicated offender. Such individuals deserve to be stigmatized. Their moral blameworthiness is similar to that of anyone else who commits the offence of sexual assault and the effects of their conduct upon both their victims and society as a whole are the same as in any other case of sexual assault. Furthermore, the sentence for sexual assault is not fixed. To the extent that it bears upon his or her level of moral blameworthiness, an offender's degree of intoxication at the time of the offence may be considered during sentencing. Taking all of these factors into account, I cannot see how the stigma and punishment associated with the offence of sexual assault are disproportionate to the moral blameworthiness of a person like the appellant who commits the offence after voluntarily becoming so intoxicated as to be incapable of knowing what he was doing. The fact that the *Leary* rule permits an individual to be convicted despite the absence of symmetry between the *actus reus* and the mental element of blameworthiness does not violate a principle of fundamental justice.

It is further contended that the *Leary* rule violates the presumption of innocence because it permits an individual to be convicted despite the existence of a reasonable doubt as to whether or not that individual performed the *actus reus* of his or her own volition. This argument is premised upon the assumption that voluntariness is a constitutionally required element of the *actus reus* of an offence of universal application. Again, I do not think that this assumption is warranted.

It is true that as a general rule, an act must be the voluntary act of an accused in order for the *actus reus* to exist. See *R. v. Parks*, [1992] 2 S.C.R. 871, at p. 896, *per* La Forest J., and *R. v. Théroux*, [1993] 2 S.C.R. 5, at p. 17, *per* McLachlin J. This, as in the case of *mens rea*, is a general rule of the criminal law, but when elevated to a principle of fundamental justice it too, exceptionally, is not absolute. One well-recognized exception is made relating to the defence of non-insane automatism. As I explain below, automatism does not apply to excuse an offence if the accused's state is brought on by his or her own fault. The condition of automatism deprives the accused of volition to commit the offence but the general rule gives way to the policy that, in the circumstances, the perpetrator who by his or her own fault brings about the condition should not escape punishment. An accused person who voluntarily drinks alcohol or ingests a drug to the extent that he or she becomes an automaton is in the same position. The rules of fundamental justice are satisfied by a showing that the drunken state was attained through the accused's own blameworthy conduct.

2. The Distinction Between Offences of Specific and General Intent Is Irrational

Another criticism of the current rules governing the availability of the intoxication defence is that the distinction between offences of specific and general intent is illogical. Critics of the rule contend that there is no principled basis for distinguishing between offences of general and specific intent and thus there is no logical reason why intoxication should be a defence to offences of specific intent but not to offences of general intent.

The appellant does not, however, take issue with the proposition that in general the distinction between offences of specific and general intent is a valid one. His submission is that when drunkenness reaches the stage of automatism, the distinction should no longer apply. This essentially was the tentative view of Wilson J. as expressed in her *obiter* statement in *R. v. Bernard* to which I referred above.

Notwithstanding the position of the appellant, I propose to briefly address the criticism of the rule that it is illogical. In my view, the concept has strong policy underpinnings which, despite the fact that its definition and application may have produced some illogical results, have permitted it to survive for over 150 years in England and to be adopted in Canada and most states of the United States. . . .

By reason of the fact that the mental element for various crimes varies from crime to crime and must frequently be implied from the nature of the offence and the wording of the statute, classification of specific and general intent offences has occurred on a case-by-case basis. This approach is bound to result in some illogical results which are exacerbated by applying the terms "specific" and "general" without regard to their policy underpinnings. In my opinion the terms "specific" and "general" in themselves do not fully spell out the policy that lies behind their use and should not be applied as if they were rigid statutory standards. Regard must be had for the policy behind them as outlined above.

The principles that emerge from the cases which serve as guidelines in classifying offences as specific or general intent offences are as follows. General intent offences as a rule are those which require the minimal intent to do the act which constitutes the *actus reus*. Proof of intent is usually inferred from the commission of the act on the basis of the principle that a person intends the natural consequences of his or her act. Without attempting to exhaust the policy reasons for excluding the defence of drunkenness from this category of offences, I would observe that it is seldom, even in cases of extreme drunkenness, that a person will lack this minimal degree of consciousness. Moreover, these are generally offences that persons who are drunk are apt to commit and it would defeat the policy behind them to make drunkenness a defence.

Specific intent offences are as a rule those that require a mental element beyond that of general intent offences and include "those generally more serious offences where the *mens rea* must involve not only the intentional performance of the *actus reus* but, as well, the formation of further ulterior motives and purposes" (*per* McIntyre J. in *R. v. Bernard, supra*, at p. 880). These are often referred to as "ulterior intent" offences. See *Majewski* [*Director of Public Prosecutions v.*, [1977] A.C. 443]. Professor Colvin, in "A Theory of the Intoxication Defence" (1981), 59 *Can. Bar Rev.* 750, correctly points out that it is the further intent in addition to the basic intent that is the hallmark of ulterior intent offences. The policy behind this classification is in part the importance of the mental element over and above the minimal intent required for general intent offences. This distinction demands that the accused not be convicted if the added important mental state is negated by the drunken condition of the accused. Failure to prove the added element will often result in conviction of a lesser offence for which the added element is not required. One example is the offence of assault to resist or prevent arrest which is a specific intent offence. Absent the intent to resist arrest, the accused would be convicted of assault *simpliciter*, a general intent offence.

In addition to the ulterior intent offences there are certain offences which by reason of their serious nature and the importance of the mental element are classed as specific intent offences notwithstanding that they do not fit the criteria usually associated with ulterior intent offences. The outstanding example is murder. This is the most serious of criminal offences which carries a fixed penalty. By reason of the importance of the required mental element and the fixed penalty, this offence is classified as a specific intent offence. The defence of drunkenness is allowed so as to reduce the crime to manslaughter tempering the harshness of the law which precludes drunkenness as a consideration as to sentence. The classification of murder as a specific intent offence illustrates the proper application of policy in a case in which the application of the normal criteria might lead to a different result.

I accept that the application of the terms "specific" and "general" may lead to some illogical results. This is not surprising in light of the circumstances outlined above. Moreover, even the clearest unifying principle will in its application not produce perfect harmony. I am, however, convinced that the underlying policy of the *Leary* rule is sound. I am of the opinion that the criticism of the rule on the grounds of illogicality has been overdone. Applying criteria similar to the above, Professor Colvin has been able to explain "the broad pattern of the decisions emanating from the courts." See Colvin, *supra*, at p. 768.

With respect to the fact that some illogicality exists, I would refer to the statement of Lord Salmon in *Majewski, supra*, at pp. 483-84:

> . . . I accept that there is a degree of illogicality in the rule that intoxication may excuse or expunge one type of intention and not another. This illogicality is, however, acceptable to me because the benevolent part of the rule removes undue harshness without imperilling safety and the stricter part of the rule works without imperilling justice. It would be just as ridiculous to remove the benevolent part of the rule (which no one suggests) as it would be to adopt the alternative of removing the stricter part of the rule for the sake of preserving absolute logic. Absolute logic in human affairs is an uncertain guide and a very dangerous master.

McIntyre J. expressed a similar view in *R. v. Bernard* stating, at p. 878, that "any logical weakness in this position is justified on the basis of sound social policy."

Rather than jettison a rule that has stood for over 150 years, I would prefer to clarify the distinction in terms of its underlying roots. This requires that the mental element of offences be clearly identified and defined. This will assist in establishing the importance of the mental element as well as the purpose to be served in criminalizing the conduct. In applying the criteria for the identification of offences of specific and general intent, it can then be determined whether their application in a particular case serves the public interest in punishing the offender notwithstanding the absence of the *mens rea* associated with the offence.

This approach is particularly apt when application of the normal criteria relating to general and specific intent offences does not lead to a clear conclusion. A case in the Supreme Court of California, *People v. Hood*, 462 P.2d 370 (1969), provides a good illustration. The defendant was convicted of the offences of assault with a deadly weapon upon a peace officer and assault with intent to murder a police officer. On appeal Traynor C.J. considered whether evidence of the appellant's intoxication should be considered with respect to the offence of assault with a deadly weapon upon a peace officer or the included offences of simple assault or assault with a deadly weapon. Applying the criteria relating to specific and general intent he found that the offences could be placed in either class. It was therefore necessary to rely "on other considerations" (p. 378). After considering the nature of the offence, the mental requirement and the effect of alcohol on human behaviour he concluded as follows, at p. 379:

> It would therefore be anomalous to allow evidence of intoxication to relieve a man of responsibility for the crimes of assault with a deadly weapon or simple assault, which are so frequently committed in just such a manner.

Applying the relevant criteria in this way, I see no reason to disagree with the traditional classification of sexual assault as an offence of general intent. Accordingly, the Court of Appeal was right in holding that the *Leary* rule applies and drunkenness cannot be relied on to negative the requisite intent.

3. Leary is Inconsistent with the Defence of Honest but Mistaken Belief in Consent

In *R. v. Bernard*, Dickson C.J. contended that the decision in *Leary* is inconsistent with the decisions in *Pappajohn v. The Queen*, [1980] 2 S.C.R. 120; *Sansregret v. The Queen*, [1985] 1 S.C.R. 570; *R. v. Bulmer*, [1987] 1 S.C.R. 782; and *R. v. Robertson*, [1987] 1 S.C.R. 918, which established that an honest but mistaken belief in consent will negate the *mens rea* required for rape, indecent assault or sexual assault (a proposition affirmed in this Court's recent decision in *R. v. Osolin*, [1993] 4 S.C.R. 595). Whether or not self-induced intoxication may be considered a factor capable of inducing an honest but mistaken belief in consent is not presently before the Court and therefore I do not wish to express an opinion on this issue. However, I note that it is possible to reconcile the policy underlying the decision in *Leary* with the decisions in *Pappajohn* etc. This is illustrated by *R. v. Moreau* (1986), 26 C.C.C. (3d) 359 (Ont. C.A.), in which Martin J.A. held that as a result of *Leary* an accused cannot rely on self-induced intoxication as the basis for his belief that the complainant consented, but this does not preclude an accused from relying upon other grounds for such a belief. The test is whether the accused would have made the same mistake if he had been sober. See also *R. v. Murray* (1986), 31 C.C.C. (3d) 323 (N.S.S.C.A.D.). Whether the drunkenness can be relied on to advance a defence of honest belief may involve policy considerations other than those that I have canvassed in this case and I prefer to leave that matter for another day. A conclusion in the affirmative would not necessarily be inconsistent with the application of *Leary* to offences of general intent.

C. Alternatives to the Leary Rule

A number of alternatives to the *Leary* rule were put forward. First, it was suggested that an extreme case of intoxication could be treated as akin to automatism. Second, it was suggested that it be treated as insanity. Finally, it was suggested that a third category be developed which would be a state equivalent to automatism but without the fault exception. This would be required to be proved on a balance of probabilities and perhaps would require the accused to continue in custody as in the case of insanity. In my view the alternatives are equally unsatisfactory.

In *R. v. Revelle* (1979), 48 C.C.C. (2d) 267 (Ont. C.A.), aff'd [1981] 1 S.C.R. 576, Martin J.A. stated at p. 272:

> It is well established that if automatism is produced solely by drunkenness only the defence of drunkenness, which is limited to crimes of specific intent, need be left to the jury.

See also *R. v. Hartridge*, [1967] 1 C.C.C. 346 (Sask. C.A.); *Rabey v. The Queen*, [1980] 2 S.C.R. 513, at p. 552, *per* Dickson J. (dissenting), and *Bratty v. Attorney-General for Northern Ireland* [[1963] A.C. 386 (H.L.)].

This proposition is only one manifestation of the more general rule that the defence of automatism is not available to a person whose automatous state is caused by his or her own fault or negligence. This rule recognizes that an individual who through his own fault or negligence renders himself intoxicated and subsequently commits a criminal offence is not entitled to the acquittal which would follow if the defence of automatism were made out. Such an individual is far from blameless. I see no reason to reject the authorities cited above and make the defence of automatism available to such an individual.

A second alternative to the *Leary* rule which has been suggested was that extreme cases of intoxication might be treated as insanity. I should note that both at trial and on appeal counsel for the appellant conceded that there was no evidence to suggest that the appellant was insane. In my view this point was properly conceded because as the law currently stands the evidence did not support the conclusion that the appellant was insane.

In order to support the defence of insanity an accused must show that he was suffering from a disease of the mind. Consumption of alcohol or drugs may give rise to conditions such as *delerium tremens* and certain other psychoses which qualify as diseases of the mind. This is made clear by Lord Birkenhead's first proposition in *Beard, supra*, as well as by the decisions in cases such as *R. v. Malcolm* (1989), 50 C.C.C. (3d) 172 (Man. C.A.); *R. v. Mailloux* (1985), 25 C.C.C. (3d) 171 (Ont. C.A.), aff'd [1988] 2 S.C.R. 1029, and *R. v. Hilton* (1977), 34 C.C.C. (2d) 206 (Ont. C.A.). However, as a general rule the term "disease of the mind" does not include self-induced states caused by alcohol or drugs: *Cooper v. The Queen*, [1980] 1 S.C.R. 1149, at p. 1159, *per* Dickson J. (as he then was).

This aspect of Dickson J.'s reasons in *Cooper* was *obiter dicta* but I do not doubt its correctness. Since that decision was rendered this Court has acknowledged that the question of whether a condition should be treated as a disease of the mind has a substantial policy component. In *Rabey v. The Queen, supra*, the majority endorsed the reasons of Martin J.A. in the Court of Appeal, reported at (1977), 37 C.C.C. (2d) 461. At pages 472-73 of those reasons Martin J.A. stated:

> Although the term "disease of the mind" is not capable of precise definition, certain propositions may, I think, be asserted with respect to it. "Disease of the mind" is a legal term, not a medical term of art; although a legal concept, it contains a substantial medical component as well as a legal or policy component.
>
> The legal or policy component relates to (a) the scope of the exemption from criminal responsibility to be afforded by mental disorder or disturbance, and (b) the protection of the public by the control and treatment of persons who have caused serious harms while in a mentally disordered or disturbed state. The medical component of the term, generally, is medical opinion as to how the mental condition in question is viewed or characterized medically. Since the medical component of the term reflects or should reflect the state of medical knowledge at a given time, the concept of "disease of the mind" is capable of evolving with increased medical knowledge with respect to mental disorder or disturbance.

This passage was quoted with approval by La Forest J. in *R. v. Parks, supra*, at pp. 898-99. Also pertinent are Dickson J.'s comments from *Cooper, supra*, at p. 1159. There, in discussing the definition of disease of the mind, Dickson J. said:

> Underlying all of this discussion is the concept of responsibility and the notion that an accused is not legally responsible for acts resulting from mental disease or mental defect.

Policy considerations support Dickson J.'s dictum that self-induced states caused by alcohol or drugs normally should not be considered diseases of the mind. Individuals who through their own fault or negligence place themselves in an automatous state by consuming alcohol or drugs deserve to be held legally responsible for their actions. Unlike those whose conditions are not self-induced, such individuals have the opportunity to avoid entering an automatous state. Such individuals deserve to be punished for their crimes rather than dealt with under the provisions of the *Criminal Code* designed for individuals who are found not to be criminally responsible on account of a mental disorder. Those latter provisions embody concerns about protection of the public and treatment of the offender but, unlike the offence-creating provisions of the *Criminal Code*, are not concerned with deterrence, punishment or retribution. For these reasons I do not consider that there is any reason to overrule *Cooper* and hold that extreme intoxication should be treated as a disease of the mind.

The final alternative to the *Leary* rule is to create a new defence of automatism caused by voluntary intoxication which would have to be proved by the defence on the balance of probabilities. The argument in favour of this approach is presumably that individuals who can raise this defence are entitled to an acquittal because they will have shown that they lacked the requisite *mens rea*. It should be clear from the foregoing that I do not favour this course of action. Permitting an accused to raise such a defence would ignore the fact that those who commit criminal offences after voluntarily becoming intoxicated are not blameless. In my view such individuals possess a culpable state of mind which deserves to be considered a form of *mens rea*. It is not inconsistent with the principles of fundamental justice to punish such individuals for the crimes which they commit.

Conclusion

For all of these reasons, in my opinion the best course is for the Court to reaffirm the traditional rule that voluntary intoxication does not constitute a defence to an offence of general intent, subject to the comments I have made with respect to improvements in the definition and application of the distinction between offences of specific and general intent. If a different approach is considered desirable because the *Leary* approach does not comport with social policy, Parliament is free to intervene. I note that this observation was made by McIntyre J. in *R. v. Bernard* but Parliament has not intervened. It has been suggested that Parliament should create a new offence of dangerous intoxication. Such a recommendation was made by the Butler Committee in England and by the Law Reform Commission in Canada. (See Butler Committee Report on Mentally Abnormal Offenders (1975) (Cmnd. 6244, paras. 18.51-18.59) and Law Reform Commission of Canada, *Recodifying Criminal Law*, Report 30, vol. 1 (1986), at pp. 27-28.) Such legislation could be coupled with amendments to the *Criminal Code* to extend the defence of drunkenness to some or all offences to which it does not apply. Such changes, however, are for Parliament and not for this Court to make.

In *Majewski*, Lord Elwyn-Jones L.C. summed up the situation in words with which I fully agree. He stated, at p. 475:

> It may well be that Parliament will at some future time consider, as I think it should, the recommendation in the Butler Committee Report on Mentally Abnormal Offenders (Cmnd. 6244, 1975) that a new offence of "dangerous intoxication" should be created. But in the meantime it would be irresponsible to abandon the common law rule, as "mercifully relaxed," which the courts have followed for a century and a half.

Disposition

The trial judge stated that but for his opinion that the appellant's extreme state of drunkenness constituted a defence, he would have convicted the appellant. I agree with the Court of Appeal that the trial judge erred in law in this regard. The Court of Appeal was right, therefore, to substitute a conviction. I would dismiss the appeal.

18 R. v. Mills, 1999

The legislation subject to this *Charter* challenge has been interpreted by some as an example of Parliament's contribution to constitutional dialogue. This metaphor has become a popular way some scholars and judges characterize parliamentary and judicial interactions when interpreting the *Charter*.[1]

After Parliament legislated strict new rules to define consent in sexual assault cases in response to the Supreme Court's ruling in *Seaboyer*,[2] which struck down earlier rape shield legislation, some who worked in rape crisis centres began observing a new trend in sexual assault cases: defence lawyers trying to obtain confidential records of sexual assault complainants to show inconsistencies in their statements, with the hope of undermining their credibility or to discourage them from proceeding with sexual assault charges.[3] The issue whether courts should grant access to these records was before the Court in *R. v. O'Connor*.[4] At the time, there was no legislation addressing this issue. In *O'Connor*, the Court interpreted the common law as allowing defence lawyers to obtain a judicial order that would compel counsellors or others working at sexual assault centres to provide confidential records of alleged victims of sexual assault for lawyers to use in court to defend their clients. The Court split 5 to 4 on what the rules should be for governing access to and release of these materials. The majority ruled that access to these therapeutic records should be relatively easy to obtain because these records could be relevant and necessary for the accused to have a fair trial. The minority disagreed, and would have established a considerably higher threshold for demonstrating that these records were necessary and admissible. Unlike the majority, which viewed the issue of relevance only from the perspective of whether the records were necessary for a fair trial, the minority took a different approach, arguing that equality and privacy rights were also at stake.

The federal government was not prepared to accept the majority's reformulated common-law rule and introduced new legislation that established a higher threshold for demonstrating the relevance of these records and using them for trial purposes. It is this legislation that was challenged in *Mills*. What was interesting about the legislative response was that it drew heavily from the minority decision, and instructed trial judges to consider not only the extent to which the materials are necessary for the accused to make a full answer and defence of the charge of sexual assault, but also the effects of granting access to these records on the privacy and equality rights of the alleged victim. Clearly aware that the legislation had serious *Charter* implications, the government attached a legislative preamble to indicate Parliament's view of how the *Charter* should guide the resolution of this issue. The preamble

---

1 See the discussion and criticism of use of this metaphor in (2007) 45 *Osgoode Hall Law Journal* 1.

2 *R. v. Seaboyer*, [1991] 2 S.C.R. 577.

3 *House of Commons Debates* (4 February 1997) 7650.

4 [1995] 4 S.C.R. 411.

stated that judicial orders for access to these therapeutic records should be considered not only in terms of their relevance for a fair trial but also in terms of how they affect equality and privacy rights. This willingness to pass legislation that clearly differed from the majority view, and its inclusion of a legislative preamble suggesting Parliament's preferred interpretation of the *Charter*, are considered by some as why this legislative response can be understood as *Charter* dialogue.

The legislation provoked varied responses from *Charter* commentators. Although women's groups and others critical of the Supreme Court's *O'Connor* decision welcomed the parliamentary response, others disputed the legitimacy of Parliament's decision to pass legislation that clearly differed from the interpretation of a majority of the Court, particularly because the notwithstanding clause was not invoked to support the legislation.

Soon after the legislation was passed, it was subject to a *Charter* challenge in *R. v. Mills*. The trial courts found themselves in a difficult position in the two-and-a-half-year period between passage of the legislation and the Supreme Court's disposition in *Mills*. The issue was whose interpretation they should adhere to—the reformulation of a common-law rule by the majority of the Supreme Court in *O'Connor*, or Parliament's legislative response, which clearly reflected the minority Supreme Court position.

The survival of this legislation was not a sure thing because of the extent to which it contradicted the majority position in *O'Connor*. Nevertheless, the Supreme Court upheld the constitutionality of the legislation by an 8-to-1 margin. Two factors help explain why the Court was willing to uphold the legislation. First, the earlier *O'Connor* ruling had been based on the common law, and therefore lacked Parliament's input into the issue. Thus, in *Mills*, the Court acknowledged that in its earlier ruling it had been operating in a "legislative vacuum" and therefore had developed what it considered the "preferred common law rule," without being aware of Parliament's views on the subject. The implication of this explanation is that the Court might have broached the issue differently had it known Parliament's view on the subject. Second, the Court indicated its acceptance for the idea of constitutional dialogue, in that Parliament's view on how to balance conflicting *Charter* rights could reasonably influence the Court. In a rare admission that the Court does not have exclusive responsibility to interpret the *Charter*, the Court stated that the judiciary "does not hold a monopoly" on protecting rights and freedoms, and that Parliament plays an important role, particularly when acting to protect sexual assault complainants. But while the Court indicated that Parliament has a valid role to play in this regard, it is a role that continues to be subject to judicial oversight. ⁓

Discussion Questions

1. Some critics argue that Bill C-46 was so inconsistent with the majority's ruling in *O'Connor* that the government should have enacted the notwithstanding clause. Is this position persuasive?
2. Was the Supreme Court too deferential to Parliament in the *Mills* ruling?
3. Is use of the dialogue metaphor appropriate when assessing Bill C-46 or the judicial decision in *Mills*?

R. v. MILLS
[1999] 3 S.C.R. 668

Hearing: January 19, 1999; Judgment: November 25, 1999.

Present: Lamer C.J. and L'Heureux-Dubé, Gonthier, Cory,*
McLachlin, Iacobucci, Major, Bastarache, and Binnie JJ.

Interveners: The Attorney General of Canada, the Attorney
General for Ontario, the Attorney General of Quebec, the
Attorney General of Nova Scotia, the Attorney General of
Manitoba, the Attorney General of British Columbia, the
Attorney General of Prince Edward Island, the Attorney
General for Saskatchewan, the Canadian Mental Health
Association, the Canadian Psychiatric Association, the Child
and Adolescent Services Association, the Criminal Lawyers'
Association (Ontario), the Association québécoise des avocats
et avocates de la défense, the Women's Legal Education and
Action Fund, the Canadian Civil Liberties Association, the
Canadian Council of Criminal Defence Lawyers, the Alberta
Association of Sexual Assault Centres, and the Sexual Assault
Centre of Edmonton.

* Cory J. took no part in the judgment.

[1] **THE CHIEF JUSTICE** (dissenting in part): The issue in
this appeal is whether Bill C-46 (now S.C. 1997, c. 30) strikes
the appropriate constitutional balance between protecting the
accused's right to a fair trial and the privacy and equality
rights of complainants and witnesses when an accused seeks
access to their confidential records in sexual assault proceedings. While I agree with McLachlin and Iacobucci JJ.'s finding
that Bill C-46 complies with ss. 7 and 11(*d*) of the *Canadian
Charter of Rights and Freedoms* as it applies to the production
of records in the possession of third parties, I take a different
view of the legislative regime's approach to records in the
hands of the Crown. In my opinion, Bill C-46's treatment of
records that form part of the case to meet tips the balance too
heavily in favour of privacy to the detriment of the accused's
right to make full answer and defence.

[2] As my colleagues have explained, s. 278.2(2) of the
Criminal Code, R.S.C., 1985, c. C-46, extends the application
of the legislative scheme for the production of therapeutic
records to documents in the Crown's possession or control. If
the complainant or witness expressly waives the protection of
the legislation, then the records may be produced to the
accused as at common law according to the principles in *R. v.
Stinchcombe*, [1991] 3 S.C.R. 326.

[3] Absent waiver, however, Bill C-46 requires the accused
to submit to the same two-stage procedure for production
applicable to records held by third parties: disclosure to the
trial judge and production to the accused. The first stage
obliges the accused to establish that the record in the Crown's
possession is "likely relevant to an issue at trial or to the competence of a witness to testify" (ss. 278.3(3)(*b*) and 278.5(1)(*b*)).
The trial judge must also decide whether disclosure to the
court is "necessary in the interests of justice" and consider the
salutary and deleterious effects of production on the accused's
right to make full answer and defence, and on the complainant's or witness's right to privacy and equality (s. 278.5(1)(*c*)
and 278.5(2)). If the first step is satisfied, the second stage
involves judicial inspection of the documents to determine
whether and to what extent they should be produced to the
accused (ss. 278.6 to 278.91).

[4] My colleagues observe that the majority in *R. v.
O'Connor*, [1995] 4 S.C.R. 411, did not comment on the procedure applicable to the production of records which the
Crown possesses in the absence of an express waiver. Parliament was unquestionably free to fashion a legislative scheme
to address this issue. I agree . . . that the courts' creation of a
common law procedure for production does not curtail Parliament's jurisdiction to modify that scheme, particularly after
having the benefit of evaluating its impact. However, I cannot
agree with my colleagues that the legislative means chosen are
impeccably consistent with ss. 7 and 11(*d*) of the *Charter*.

[5] As this Court maintained in *Stinchcombe, supra*, at
p. 336, the right of an accused to make full answer and defence
is a pillar of criminal justice on which we rely heavily to prevent
the conviction of the innocent. It is a principle of fundamental
justice protected by ss. 7 and 11(*d*) of the *Charter*. Flowing
from the right to make full answer and defence is the Crown's
constitutional and ethical duty to disclose all information in
its possession reasonably capable of affecting the accused's
ability to raise a reasonable doubt concerning his innocence:
R. v. Egger, [1993] 2 S.C.R. 451, at p. 466. This obligation is
subject only to the Crown's discretion to withhold disclosure
on the basis that the material is irrelevant or privileged.

[6] The duty of disclosure is premised on the presumption that material in the Crown's possession has probative
value. The *O'Connor* majority endorsed this presumption at
para. 12, where we surmised that "[g]enerally speaking, the
Crown would not obtain possession or control of therapeutic
records unless the information the records contained was
somehow relevant to the case against the accused." This reasoning applies with even greater force, in my view, when the
Crown seeks access to documents without the complainant's
cooperation, such as by way of a search warrant.

[7] McLachlin and Iacobucci JJ. emphasize in their reasons that the Crown's duty of disclosure is not absolute. The
Charter entrenches the right to a fair trial, they maintain, not
the best trial. The principles of fundamental justice do not
guarantee the most favourable procedures conceivable. All of

this is true. However, in my respectful view my colleagues understate the importance of Crown disclosure to trial fairness. Disclosure of records in the Crown's hands furthers the search for truth as it enables the defence to challenge the accuracy and cogency of the prosecution's case. The accused's ability to access relevant information that may ultimately deprive him of his liberty strikes at the very core of the principles of fundamental justice.

[8] The requirement in Bill C-46 that the accused must prove the relevance of records that form part of the case to meet is a serious incursion on the meaningful exercise of the right to make full answer and defence. Not only does the legislative scheme supplant the presumption of relevance, but it also raises the relevance bar. The standard of relevance which the accused must satisfy according to ss. 278.3(3)(*b*) and 278.5(1)(*b*)—likely relevance to an issue at trial or to the competence of a witness to testify—is higher than that required for disclosure under a *Stinchcombe* application, which is whether the information "may be useful to the defence": *O'Connor*, *supra*, at para. 22, and *Stinchcombe*, *supra*, at p. 345.

[9] Moreover, I do not agree with McLachlin and Iacobucci JJ.'s assertion that the notification requirement in s. 278.2(3) provides the accused with much assistance in establishing the likely relevance of a document in the Crown's possession. I reiterate the concerns which the majority expressed in *O'Connor*, *supra*, at paras. 25-26, about placing an accused in the position of having to persuade the trial judge that documents are relevant without any knowledge of their contents. It will be difficult indeed for an accused to establish the likely relevance of a record which he knows to exist, but which he has never seen. By displacing the presumption of relevance and increasing the relevance threshold, ss. 278.3(3)(*b*) and 278.5(1)(*b*) give the Crown a distinct advantage over the defence, as it holds information that the accused must surmount a significant obstacle to obtain. These provisions therefore infringe the accused's right to a fair trial.

[10] Having found that ss. 278.3(3)(*b*) and 278.5(1)(*b*) violate ss. 7 and 11(*d*) of the *Charter* as they apply to records in the Crown's possession, I must consider whether the infringement is a reasonable limit prescribed by law that is demonstrably justified in a free and democratic society. I am mindful that violations of s. 7 are rarely saved by s. 1: *New Brunswick (Minister of Health and Community Services) v. G. (J.)*, [1999] 3 S.C.R. 46, at para. 99. . . . Iacobucci J. summarized the analytical framework applicable to s. 1 as follows in *Egan v. Canada*, [1995] 2 S.C.R. 513, at para. 182:

A limitation to a constitutional guarantee will be sustained once two conditions are met. First, the objective of the legislation must be pressing and substantial. Second,

the means chosen to attain this legislative end must be reasonable and demonstrably justifiable in a free and democratic society. In order to satisfy the second requirement, three criteria must be satisfied: (1) the rights violation must be rationally connected to the aim of the legislation; (2) the impugned provision must minimally impair the *Charter* guarantee; and (3) there must be a proportionality between the effect of the measure and its objective so that the attainment of the legislative goal is not outweighed by the abridgement of the right.

[11] Without a doubt, Bill C-46 was adopted to address a pressing and substantial objective, which is the protection of the privacy and equality rights of complainants and witnesses in the context of sexual assault trials. The legislative scheme also rationally advances this important aim. In my opinion, however, ss. 278.3(3)(*b*) and 278.5(1)(*b*) fail to protect those rights in a manner that minimally impairs the right of an accused to make full answer and defence. The requirement that the accused must demonstrate the likely relevance of records held by the Crown is more intrusive than reasonably necessary to achieve the legislative goals: see *M. v. H.*, [1999] 2 S.C.R. 3, at para. 118. In addition, the risk of suppressing relevant evidence and of convicting an innocent person outweighs the salutary effects of the impugned provisions on privacy and equality rights. I accordingly conclude that the violations are not justified by s. 1.

[12] While in my view ss. 278.3(3)(*b*) and 278.5(1)(*b*) are unconstitutional as they apply to records in the Crown's hands, I remain sensitive that the production of therapeutic records to the defence is injurious to a complainant's privacy rights. Indeed, disclosure may be all the more invasive to a complainant's dignity and psychological integrity when they are obtained by the Crown without her consent.

[13] In this regard, I emphasize that records which the Crown procures absent waiver would still be subject to the principles in *Stinchcombe*. The prosecution would be free to rebut the presumption that the documents are relevant. I remark in passing that this may be difficult for the Crown to accomplish in respect of documents obtained pursuant to a search warrant, as in most cases the evidentiary basis upon which the warrant was secured will itself be disclosed. As with any *Stinchcombe* application, the Crown may likewise attempt to resist disclosure by demonstrating that the records are privileged.

[14] If the Crown is unable to discharge this burden, then the records should be disclosed to the trial judge rather than the accused (as they normally would under a *Stinchcombe* application), because of the privacy rights at stake, if the trial judge is satisfied that the other requirements in s. 278.5(1)

and (2) are met. The second stage of the legislative regime—judicial examination of the documents to determine whether and to what extent they should be produced to the accused—would then proceed according to the criteria in ss. 278.6 to 278.91, as explained by my colleagues. In my view, relieving the accused of the burden of showing relevance strikes a more appropriate balance between the various rights at stake. It removes a significant barrier to the accused's ability to raise a reasonable doubt concerning his innocence while preserving a large measure of protection for the privacy and equality rights of complainants and witnesses.

[15] I turn last to a consideration of the appropriate remedy under s. 52(1) of the *Constitution Act, 1982*. My finding of unconstitutionality is limited to two provisions of an otherwise complex legislative scheme. I believe that a combination of reading down the sections and reading in new language is the most appropriate way to vindicate the *Charter* rights at play "while refraining from intrusion into the legislative sphere beyond what is necessary": *R. v. Laba*, [1994] 3 S.C.R. 965, at p. 1012, *per* Sopinka J. Sections 278.3(3)(*b*) and 278.5(1)(*b*) of the *Criminal Code* should therefore be interpreted such that they no longer apply to an application for the production of records in the Crown's possession. Language along the following lines should be read into both ss. 278.3(3)(*b*) and 278.5(1)(*b*): "unless the record is in the possession or control of the prosecutor in the proceedings, in which case this paragraph does not apply." The principles for Crown disclosure enunciated in *Stinchcombe* and *O'Connor* would partially apply instead of those paragraphs, such that the Crown would have the opportunity to show the trial judge that the documents are irrelevant or privileged. . . .

The judgment of L'Heureux-Dubé, Gonthier, McLachlin, Iacobucci, Major, Bastarache, and Binnie JJ. was delivered by

McLACHLIN AND IACOBUCCI JJ.:

I. Introduction

[17] The question of when accused persons should have access to private records of complainants and witnesses in sexual assault trials is a vexed one. This Court addressed this issue in *R. v. O'Connor*, [1995] 4 S.C.R. 411. Following this decision, and a lengthy consultation process, Parliament reviewed the issue and drafted Bill C-46, (now S.C. 1997, c. 30) which came into force on May 12, 1997 and amended the *Criminal Code*, R.S.C., 1985, c. C-46. The issue in the present appeal is whether Bill C-46 is constitutional. The resolution of this appeal requires understanding how to define competing rights, avoiding the hierarchical approach rejected by this Court in *Dagenais v. Canadian Broadcasting Corp.*, [1994] 3 S.C.R. 835, at p. 877. On the one hand stands the accused's

right to make full answer and defence. On the other hand stands the complainant's and witness's right to privacy. Neither right may be defined in such a way as to negate the other and both sets of rights are informed by the equality rights at play in this context. Underlying this question is the relationship between the courts and Parliament when Parliament alters a judicially created common law procedure that already embodies *Charter* standards.

II. Summary

[18] This appeal presents an apparent conflict among the rights to full answer and defence, privacy, and equality, all of which are protected by the *Canadian Charter of Rights and Freedoms* (ss. 7 and 11(*d*), s. 8, and s. 15, respectively). The underlying issue is what is required by the "principles of fundamental justice" protected by s. 7. Bill C-46 reflects Parliament's effort at balancing these rights. Our task is to decide whether Parliament's balance is a constitutional one. . . .

[20] As noted above, this Court has previously addressed the issue of disclosure of third party records in sexual assault proceedings: see *O'Connor, supra*. However, it is important to keep in mind that the decision in *O'Connor* is not necessarily the last word on the subject. The law develops through dialogue between courts and legislatures: see *Vriend v. Alberta*, [1998] 1 S.C.R. 493. Against the backdrop of *O'Connor*, Parliament was free to craft its own solution to the problem consistent with the *Charter*.

[21] As this Court's decision in *Dagenais, supra*, makes clear, *Charter* rights must be examined in a contextual manner to resolve conflicts between them. Therefore, unlike s. 1 balancing, where societal interests are sometimes allowed to override *Charter* rights, under s. 7 rights must be defined so that they do not conflict with each other. The rights of full answer and defence, and privacy, must be defined in light of each other, and both must be defined in light of the equality provisions of s. 15.

[22] Turning to the legislation at issue in this appeal, we find it constitutional. It is undisputed that there are several important respects in which Bill C-46 differs from the regime set out in *O'Connor*. However, these differences are not fatal because Bill C-46 provides sufficient protection for all relevant *Charter* rights. There are, admittedly, several provisions in the Bill that are subject to differing interpretations. However, in such situations we will interpret the legislation in a constitutional manner where possible: see *Slaight Communications Inc. v. Davidson*, [1989] 1 S.C.R. 1038, at p. 1078. By so doing, we conclude that Bill C-46 is a constitutional response to the problem of production of records of complainants or witnesses in sexual assault proceedings. . . .

(1) The O'Connor Regime and Bill C-46

[43] The respondent in this appeal and several interveners argued that the provisions of Bill C-46 are unconstitutional to the extent that they are inconsistent with the reasons of the majority of this Court in *O'Connor, supra* . . . .

[44] This Court's decision in *O'Connor* concerned the common law procedure to be followed by an accused seeking production of therapeutic records in the hands of third parties. As a preliminary matter, Lamer C.J. and Sopinka J., for the majority on the issue of production, also discussed the issue of disclosure of therapeutic records in the hands of the Crown. In their opinion, the Crown's obligation to disclose records in its possession or control, as established in *Stinchcombe, supra*, is unaltered by the confidential nature of therapeutic records where the records have been shared with the Crown or "confidentiality has been waived for the purpose of proceeding against the accused" (para. 9). Even if privileged, these records must be disclosed to the accused where "clearly relevant and important to the ability of the accused to raise a defence" (para. 11).

[45] In the context of ordering production of records that are in the hands of third parties, Lamer C.J. and Sopinka J. outlined a two-stage process. At the first stage, the issue is whether the document sought by the accused ought to be produced to the judge; at the second stage, the trial judge must balance the competing interests to decide whether to order production to the accused. At the first stage, the onus is on the accused to establish that the information in question is "*likely to be relevant*" (para. 19 (emphasis in original)). Unlike in the Crown disclosure context, where relevance is understood to mean "may be useful to the defence," the threshold of *likely relevance* in this context requires that the presiding judge be satisfied "that there is a reasonable possibility that the information is logically probative to *an issue at trial or the competence of a witness to testify*" (para. 22 (emphasis in original)). This shift in onus and the higher threshold, as compared to when records are in the possession of the Crown, was necessitated by the fact that the information in question is not part of the state's "case to meet," the state has not been given access to it, and third parties are under no obligation to assist the defence.

[46] Lamer C.J. and Sopinka J. held that the threshold of likely relevance at this first stage is not a significant or onerous burden. It is meant to prevent requests for production that are "speculative, fanciful, disruptive, unmeritorious, obstructive and time-consuming" (para. 24). Although Lamer C.J. and Sopinka J. disagreed with L'Heureux-Dubé J. that therapeutic records are rarely relevant to the accused, they declined to set out "categories of relevance" (para. 27).

[47] If the first stage is passed, the record is disclosed to the court and the application for production moves onto the second stage where the judge determines whether the record should be produced to the accused. At this second stage, Lamer C.J. and Sopinka J. require the trial judge to balance the competing interests in order to determine whether a non-production order would be a reasonable limit on the accused's ability to make full answer and defence. They list a series of factors that trial judges should consider in making this determination (at para. 31):

> (1) [T]he extent to which the record is necessary for the accused to make full answer and defence; (2) the probative value of the record in question; (3) the nature and extent of the reasonable expectation of privacy vested in that record; (4) whether production of the record would be premised upon any discriminatory belief or bias; and (5) the potential prejudice to the complainant's dignity, privacy or security of the person that would be occasioned by production of the record in question.

Although L'Heureux-Dubé J., for the minority on this issue, outlined the same five factors as the majority, she also included two additional factors: the integrity of the trial process and the societal interest in reporting sexual crimes. Lamer C.J. and Sopinka J. held that the former is better dealt with when determining admissibility of the evidence and that the latter, while a relevant factor, was "not a paramount consideration" as there are many other avenues open to the trial judge to protect this interest than declining production (at paras. 32 and 33).

(b) Bill C-46

[48] On May 12, 1997, approximately 17 months after this Court released its decision in *O'Connor*, Bill C-46 came into force. Bill C-46 sets out a process to govern the production of the private records of complainants and witnesses in sexual assault trials in place of the common law regime this Court established in *O'Connor*. The preamble to the Bill indicates that Parliament was concerned about the incidence of sexual violence and abuse in Canadian society, its prevalence against women and children, and its "particularly disadvantageous impact on the equal participation of women and children in society and on the rights of women and children to security of the person, privacy and equal benefit of the law as guaranteed by sections 7, 8, 15 and 28 of the [*Charter*]." The preamble expressly declares that Parliament seeks to provide a framework of laws that are fair to and protect the rights of both accused persons and complainants.

[49] While the Bill retains the two-stage structure set out in *O'Connor*, there are significant differences between the two regimes. . . .

[50] Bill C-46 begins by defining the records to which it applies: "any form of record that contains personal information for which there is a reasonable expectation of privacy,"

excluding investigatory or prosecutorial records: s. 278.1. It goes on to define the types of offences that will trigger its application: s. 278.2(1). Generally, these are sexual assault and similar sexual offences. Section 278.2(1) states that an accused person charged with these offences cannot obtain the records relating to complainants or witnesses covered by s. 278.1, except in accordance with the process set out by the Bill.

[51] A third preliminary section, s. 278.2(2), states that the Bill applies to records in the possession or control of any person, including the Crown prosecutor, unless the complainant or witness "has expressly waived the application of [the Bill]." Absent waiver, documents in the possession of the prosecution are treated in the same manner as documents in the hands of a private individual or organization and therefore are subject to disclosure pursuant to the Bill's procedures.

[52] Yet another preliminary provision sets out "assertions" that are "not sufficient on their own" on an application for production to establish that a record is "likely relevant to an issue at trial or to the competence of a witness to testify": s. 278.3(4).

[53] This brings us to the heart of the Bill—the process established to govern the production of private records to an accused person in sexual offence proceedings. Like *O'Connor*, Parliament has set up a two-stage process: (1) disclosure to the judge; and (2) production to the accused. At the first stage, the accused must establish that the record sought is "likely relevant to an issue at trial or to the competence of a witness to testify" and that "the production of the record is necessary in the interests of justice" (s. 278.5(1)). Bill C-46 diverges from *O'Connor* by directing the trial judge to consider the salutary and deleterious effects of production to the court on the accused's right to full answer and defence and the complainant's or witness's right to privacy and equality. A series of factors is listed that the trial judge is directed to take into account in deciding whether the document should be produced to the court (s. 278.5(2)):

(*a*) the extent to which the record is necessary for the accused to make a full answer and defence;

(*b*) the probative value of the record;

(*c*) the nature and extent of the reasonable expectation of privacy with respect to the record;

(*d*) whether production of the record is based on a discriminatory belief or bias;

(*e*) the potential prejudice to the personal dignity and right to privacy of any person to whom the record relates;

(*f*) society's interest in encouraging the reporting of sexual offences;

(*g*) society's interest in encouraging the obtaining of treatment by complainants of sexual offences; and

(*h*) the effect of the determination on the integrity of the trial process.

[54] If the requirements of this first stage are met, the record will be ordered produced to the trial judge. At the second stage, the judge looks at the record in the absence of the parties (s. 278.6(1)), holds a hearing if necessary (s. 278.6(2)), and determines whether the record should be produced on the basis that it is "likely relevant to an issue at trial or to the competence of a witness to testify" and that its production is "necessary in the interests of justice" (s. 278.7). Again at this stage, the judge must consider the salutary and deleterious effects on the accused's right to make full answer and defence and on the right to privacy and equality of the complainant or witness, and is directed to "take into account" the factors set out at s. 278.5(2): s. 278.7(2). When ordering production, the judge may impose conditions on production: s. 278.7(3).

[55] The respondent and several supporting interveners argue that Bill C-46 is unconstitutional to the extent that it establishes a regime for production that differs from or is inconsistent with that established by the majority in *O'Connor*. However, it does not follow from the fact that a law passed by Parliament differs from a regime envisaged by the Court in the absence of a statutory scheme, that Parliament's law is unconstitutional. Parliament may build on the Court's decision, and develop a different scheme as long as it remains constitutional. Just as Parliament must respect the Court's rulings, so the Court must respect Parliament's determination that the judicial scheme can be improved. To insist on slavish conformity would belie the mutual respect that underpins the relationship between the courts and legislature that is so essential to our constitutional democracy: *Vriend, supra*. We turn now to a brief discussion of that relationship.

(2) Relationship Between the Courts and the Legislature Generally

[56] A posture of respect towards Parliament was endorsed by this Court in *Slaight Communications, supra*, at p. 1078, where we held that if legislation is amenable to two interpretations, a court should choose the interpretation that upholds the legislation as constitutional. Thus courts must presume that Parliament intended to enact constitutional legislation and strive, where possible, to give effect to this intention.

[57] This Court has also discussed the relationship between the courts and the legislature in terms of a dialogue, and emphasized its importance to the democratic process. In *Vriend, supra*, at para. 139, Iacobucci J. stated:

> To my mind, a great value of judicial review and this dialogue among the branches is that each of the branches is

made somewhat accountable to the other. The work of the legislature is reviewed by the courts and the work of the court in its decisions can be reacted to by the legislature in the passing of new legislation (or even overarching laws under s. 33 of the *Charter*). This dialogue between and accountability of each of the branches have the effect of enhancing the democratic process, not denying it.

... If the common law were to be taken as establishing the only possible constitutional regime, then we could not speak of a dialogue with the legislature. Such a situation could only undermine rather than enhance democracy. Legislative change and the development of the common law are different. As this Court noted in *R. v. Salituro*, [1991] 3 S.C.R. 654, at p. 666, the common law changes incrementally, "while complex changes to the law with uncertain ramifications should be left to the legislature." While this dialogue obviously is of a somewhat different nature when the common law rule involves interpretation of the *Charter*, as in *O'Connor*, it remains a dialogue nonetheless.

[58] Moreover, in this Court's recent decision *Reference re Secession of Quebec*, [1998] 2 S.C.R. 217, we affirmed the proposition that constitutionalism can facilitate democracy rather than undermine it, and that one way in which it does this is by ensuring that fundamental human rights and individual freedoms are given due regard and protection (at paras. 74-78). Courts do not hold a monopoly on the protection and promotion of rights and freedoms; Parliament also plays a role in this regard and is often able to act as a significant ally for vulnerable groups. This is especially important to recognize in the context of sexual violence. The history of the treatment of sexual assault complainants by our society and our legal system is an unfortunate one. Important change has occurred through legislation aimed at both recognizing the rights and interests of complainants in criminal proceedings, and debunking the stereotypes that have been so damaging to women and children, but the treatment of sexual assault complainants remains an ongoing problem. If constitutional democracy is meant to ensure that due regard is given to the voices of those vulnerable to being overlooked by the majority, then this court has an obligation to consider respectfully Parliament's attempt to respond to such voices.

[59] Parliament has enacted this legislation after a long consultation process that included a consideration of the constitutional standards outlined by this Court in *O'Connor*. While it is the role of the courts to specify such standards, there may be a range of permissible regimes that can meet these standards. It goes without saying that this range is not confined to the specific rule adopted by the Court pursuant to its competence in the common law. In the present case,

Parliament decided that legislation was necessary in order to address the issue of third party records more comprehensively. As is evident from the language of the preamble to Bill C-46, Parliament also sought to recognize the prevalence of sexual violence against women and children and its disadvantageous impact on their rights, to encourage the reporting of incidents of sexual violence, to recognize the impact of the production of personal information on the efficacy of treatment, and to reconcile fairness to complainants with the rights of the accused. Many of these concerns involve policy decisions regarding criminal procedure and its relationship to the community at large. Parliament may also be understood to be recognizing "horizontal" equality concerns, where women's inequality results from the acts of other individuals and groups rather than the state, but which nonetheless may have many consequences for the criminal justice system. It is perfectly reasonable that these many concerns may lead to a procedure that is different from the common law position but that nonetheless meets the required constitutional standards.

[60] We cannot presume that the legislation is unconstitutional simply because it is different from the common law position. The question before us is not whether Parliament can amend the common law; it clearly can. The question before us is whether in doing so Parliament has nonetheless outlined a constitutionally acceptable procedure for the production of private records of complainants in sexual assault trials. This question is considered at length below, following the discussion of the constitutional rights at stake in this appeal....

[The majority discussed tensions between the requirements for a full answer and defence, privacy, and equality, and why no single principle should be considered to trump another, but instead should be defined in light of competing principles.]

[94] In summary, the following broad considerations apply to the definition of the rights at stake in this appeal. The right of the accused to make full answer and defence is a core principle of fundamental justice, but it does not automatically entitle the accused to gain access to information contained in the private records of complainants and witnesses. Rather, the scope of the right to make full answer and defence must be determined in light of privacy and equality rights of complainants and witnesses. It is clear that the right to full answer and defence is not engaged where the accused seeks information that will only serve to distort the truth-seeking purpose of a trial, and in such a situation, privacy and equality rights are paramount. On the other hand, where the information contained in a record directly bears on the right to make full answer and defence, privacy rights must yield to the need to avoid convicting the innocent. Most cases, however, will not

be so clear, and in assessing applications for production, courts must determine the weight to be granted to the interests protected by privacy and full answer and defence in the particular circumstances of each case. Full answer and defence will be more centrally implicated where the information contained in a record is part of the case to meet or where its potential probative value is high. A complainant's privacy interest is very high where the confidential information contained in a record concerns the complainant's personal identity or where the confidentiality of the record is vital to protect a therapeutic relationship. . . .

D. Analysis of Sections 278.1 to 278.91 of Bill C-46

[96] In enacting Bill C-46, Parliament was concerned with preserving an accused's access to private records that may be relevant to an issue on trial, while protecting the right to privacy of complainants and witnesses to the greatest extent possible. Notwithstanding Parliament's good intentions, the respondent suggests that Bill C-46 violates the constitutional right of the accused to a fair trial and full defence on a number of grounds. We will consider each in turn.

(1) The Definition of Documents Subject to the Legislation: Sections 278.1 and 278.2(1)

[97] . . . [T]he Bill applies to all records of complainants and witnesses in sexual offence proceedings containing "personal information for which there is a reasonable expectation of privacy," including "medical, psychiatric, therapeutic, counselling, education, employment, child welfare, adoption and social services records, personal journals and diaries, and records containing personal information the production or disclosure of which is protected by any other Act of Parliament or a provincial legislature." . . .

[99] [T]he legislation applies only to records "for which there is a *reasonable* expectation of privacy" (s. 278.1 (emphasis added)). Only documents that truly raise a legally recognized privacy interest are caught and protected: see *R. v. Regan* (1998), 174 N.S.R. (2d) 230 (S.C.). The Bill is therefore carefully tailored to reflect the problem Parliament was addressing—how to preserve an accused's access to private records that may be relevant to an issue on trial while protecting, to the greatest extent possible, the privacy rights of the subjects of such records, including both complainants and witnesses. By limiting its coverage to records in which there is a reasonable expectation of privacy, the Bill is consistent with the definition of s. 8 privacy rights discussed above. Moreover, as will be discussed below, the mere fact that records are within the ambit of Bill C-46 will not, in itself, prevent the accused from obtaining access to them. Applied in this way, ss. 278.1 and 278.2(1) will not catch more records than they should, and are not overly broad.

[100] It must also be remembered that the definition of records in ss. 278.1 and 278.2(1) simply establishes the starting point for the analysis proposed by the Bill. Documents falling within the ambit of these provisions, after being subject to the legislative regime, may or may not be ordered to be disclosed to the accused. It is therefore the procedures established by the Bill and not the spectrum of records subject to these procedures that will determine the fairness or constitutionality of the legislation. If the legislative regime fairly provides access to all constitutionally required documents, then the spectrum of records brought under the Bill, if in keeping with the Bill's objectives, cannot be challenged.

[101] The broad scope of Bill C-46 has also been challenged as imposing an excessive burden on judicial resources. However, the Bill safeguards the efficiency and resources of the judicial system while furthering its objective of protecting, to the greatest extent possible, the rights of all those involved in sexual offence proceedings, by mandating that judges can only review the records in question once these records have been established as likely relevant and their production to the court has been established as necessary in the interests of justice. The balancing process required at the first stage ensures that records are not needlessly or casually produced to the court for review: see *O'Connor*, *supra*, at para. 152, *per* L'Heureux-Dubé J. Moreover, as many interveners have pointed out, production of records to the court had become almost routine in sexual assault cases. It is unlikely that Bill C-46's procedures will be substantially more onerous on judicial resources. Finally, Parliament, with the benefit of a full legislative inquiry, has ruled on such questions of administrative convenience. We see no reason to disturb its conclusion. If the system proves unworkable in practice, then Parliament, not this Court, is better positioned to fix it.

(2) Third Party Records in the Possession of the Crown: Sections 278.2(2) and (3)

[102] The next provision at issue extends the application of the legislative regime for the production of private records to records "in the possession or control of any person," including the Crown: s. 278.2(2). . . .

[104] The respondent objects to the fact that this provision prevents the automatic disclosure of all relevant and non-privileged information in the possession of the Crown. He submits that this is contrary to the constitutional obligation upon the Crown set out in *Stinchcombe*, and is inconsistent with this Court's conclusion in *O'Connor* that "the Crown's disclosure obligations established in the *Stinchcombe* decision are unaffected by the confidential nature of therapeutic records" (para. 13, *per* Lamer C.J. and Sopinka J.). The respondent also argues that s. 278.2(2) gives the Crown an

unfair advantage in that only the accused is subject to the legislative regime. The Crown can obtain private records through the complainant directly or through the power of a search warrant. The Bill not only exempts the Crown from the obligation to comply with the legislation regime when seeking private records, but also allows the Crown to possess information that the defence does not have.

[105] The first response to the respondent's argument is that it is premature. Section 278.2 simply defines the scope of the legislation. It does not by itself deny access to documents to which the defence is constitutionally entitled. If the procedures set out in the sections that follow fairly provide access to all constitutionally required documents, then the accused has no constitutional complaint.

[106] Second, the argument that this provision contradicts *Stinchcombe* and *O'Connor* rests on an overstatement of the Crown obligation to disclose that was affirmed in those cases. It is true that *Stinchcombe* spoke of a duty on the Crown to disclose to the defence all relevant documents in the Crown's possession, subject to privilege. Privacy interests, however, were not at issue in *Stinchcombe*. In *O'Connor*, the Court considered the Crown's obligation to disclose private records in the context of sexual offence proceedings where the complainant has made an informed waiver of her privacy rights. The majority in *O'Connor* concluded that "the Crown's well-established duty to disclose all information in its possession is not affected by the confidential nature of therapeutic records": *O'Connor, supra*, at para. 7. This conclusion, however, was premised upon the assumption that the records in the Crown's possession have been freely and voluntarily surrendered by the complainant or witness: "where the documents in question have been shared with an agent of the state (namely, the Crown), it is apparent that the complainant's privacy interest in those records has disappeared" (*O'Connor, supra*, at para. 8). Lamer C.J. and Sopinka J. further found that "fairness must require that if the complainant is *willing to release* this information in order to further the criminal prosecution, then the accused should be entitled to use the information in the preparation of his or her defence" (*O'Connor, supra*, at para. 9 (emphasis added)). Bill C-46 imposes the same waiver rule. Where a fully informed complainant expressly waives the protection of the legislation, by declaration or by voluntarily providing her records to the Crown, the Bill C-46 procedure does not apply and the records are producible as at common law: s. 278.2(2). Bill C-46 thus conforms to the constitutional standard of *O'Connor*.

[107] The respondent argues, however, that *O'Connor* should not be read as requiring the disclosure of confidential records pursuant to *Stinchcombe* only in cases of an express waiver and that s. 278.2(2) is unconstitutional. He asserts that any reasonable expectation of privacy is lost once the records are in the possession of the Crown, regardless of how the records came into the Crown's possession. Once in the Crown's hands, the records become "the property of the public" to be used to ensure that justice is done and must be disclosed pursuant to the common law.

[108] This argument erroneously equates Crown possession or control with a total loss of any reasonable expectation of privacy. Privacy is not an all or nothing right. It does not follow from the fact that the Crown has possession of the records that any reasonable expectation of privacy disappears. Privacy interests in modern society include the reasonable expectation that private information will remain confidential to the persons to whom and restricted to the purposes for which it was divulged, *Dyment* [*R. v.*, [1988] 2 S.C.R. 417], at p. 429. Where private information is disclosed to individuals outside of those to whom, or for purposes other than for which, it was originally divulged, the person to whom the information pertains may still hold a reasonable expectation of privacy in this information, *R. v. Boudreau*, [1998] O.J. No. 3526 (QL) (Gen. Div.), at para. 18. Third party records may fall into the possession of the Crown without the knowledge, consent, or assistance of the complainant or witness. Where the complainant or witness has not expressly waived her privacy right, Parliament can legitimately take steps to protect those privacy rights. Such protection is to be found in the procedures for production set out in ss. 278.5 and 278.7 of the Bill.

[109] The *O'Connor* majority did not address what procedure was to be followed where third party records were in the possession of the Crown without the existence of an express waiver. It was therefore open to Parliament to fill this void legislatively. Viewed in this context, s. 278.2(2) ensures that the range of interests triggered by production will be balanced pursuant to the procedure set out in ss. 278.5 and 278.7. The mere fact that this procedure differs from that set out in *Stinchcombe* does not, without more, establish a constitutional violation. As noted, *Stinchcombe* and *O'Connor* did not address the situation at issue here, namely, records in the Crown's possession in which a complainant or witness has a reasonable, and non-waived, expectation of privacy. We are thus returned to our starting point—that s. 278.2 in itself violates no rights and any violation can be determined only by examining its impact in conjunction with ss. 278.5 through 278.8.

[110] When the arguments that s. 278.2 is inconsistent with *Stinchcombe* and *O'Connor* are cleared away, the respondent's fundamental objection to the section emerges—it unfairly favours the Crown. The Crown can obtain the complainant's private records through a search warrant or subpoena. Where the complainant or witness does not expressly waive the protection of the legislation, the accused can get

these documents only by applying under the Bill C-46 regime. If the accused does not succeed, the Crown may possess documents that the accused does not have. This, it is argued, puts the Crown at an advantage.

[111] All this is true. But it begs the real question—is the Crown's advantage unconstitutional? In other words, does it deprive the accused of his right to make full answer and defence? That will be so only if the legislation prevents the accused from getting access to all constitutionally required documents. There is no principle of fundamental justice that the Crown and defence must enjoy precisely the same privileges and procedures.... The real question is whether the procedures that Parliament has enacted prevent the accused from making full answer and defence. This is the true meaning of the passage from *O'Connor, supra,* at para. 34, which states that "[f]airness requires that the accused be treated on an equal footing" with the Crown, which has access to search warrants. Obviously, the search warrant procedure involves a different array of factors from those that are relevant to production of third party records to the accused. All that was meant by this passage is that the accused must have a procedure for obtaining evidence that respects all the relevant constitutional rights at stake, just as the prosecution does through the warrant process. As we will explain below, Bill C-46 is just such a procedure.

[112] In *Stinchcombe,* this Court acknowledged that the Crown, by virtue of its unique role as agent of the state, has greater access to certain types of information than the accused. The Court therefore imposed a duty on the Crown to disclose all relevant information to the defence. The goal behind imposing this duty upon the Crown was not, however, to ensure equivalency of treatment between the accused and the Crown. Rather, the duty to disclose was imposed to advance the overall fairness, justice, efficacy, and truth finding elements of criminal proceedings. Since the right to full answer and defence must be defined in light of other principles of fundamental justice, that right is not an absolute one. Thus, while acknowledging the disparity in access to certain types of information, Sopinka J. conditioned the Crown's duty to disclose by investing in the Crown a discretion to withhold information where necessary to respect the rules of privilege, to protect persons from harassment or injury, or where this information is clearly irrelevant, at pp. 336 and 339. Similarly, in *O'Connor, supra,* at para. 16, Lamer C.J. and Sopinka J. held:

> ... *Stinchcombe* recognized that, even in the context of disclosure, there are limits on the right of an accused to access information. For example, when the Crown asserts that the information is privileged, the trial judge must then balance the competing claims at issue. In such cases, the information will only be disclosed where the trial

judge concludes that the asserted privilege "does not constitute a reasonable limit on the constitutional right to make full answer and defence" (*Stinchcombe,* at p. 340).

Stinchcombe and *O'Connor* accept that it is constitutionally permissible for the Crown to be subject to different treatment, to different procedures, or even to end up with documents that the accused has not seen, as long as the accused can make full answer and defence and the trial is fundamentally fair.

[113] ... [W]hen addressing the disparity of treatment between defence counsel and the Crown, we must remember the specific problem Bill C-46 was enacted to address. Through Bill C-46, Parliament sought to preserve an accused's access to private records that may be relevant to the defence in a sexual offence proceeding while protecting, to the greatest extent possible, the privacy rights of complainants and witnesses. The context of the Bill is one in which defence counsel were routinely seeking access to the private records of complainants or witnesses in sexual offence proceedings.... The greater procedural burden placed on the accused under Bill C-46 reflects the fact that unlike the Crown, the accused bears no responsibility to protect the rights of others. To protect such rights, when they are threatened by the acts of the accused, greater procedural protections are required....

[116] We conclude that the fact that s. 278.2 may result in the Crown holding documents that the accused does not possess does not of itself deprive the accused of the right to make full answer and defence. Parliament has balanced the inevitably advantageous documentary position the prosecution enjoys with safeguards to protect the accused's interest in getting those documents that may be relevant to the defence. Provided the remainder of Bill C-46 permits the accused to obtain the documents to which the defence is entitled, the fact that the Crown may possess documents that the accused does not, does not vitiate the process. Section 278.2 is constitutional in that it does not violate ss. 7 or 11(*d*) of the *Charter.*

(3) The "Insufficient Grounds" Section: Section 278.3(4)

[117] Section 278.3(4) lists a series of "assertions" that cannot "on their own" establish that a record is likely relevant. The respondent submits that on a plain reading, this provision prevents the accused from relying on the listed factors when attempting to establish the likely relevance of the records. This, he argues, interferes with the right to make full answer and defence by restricting what the judge can consider in determining whether the records must be produced to the defence. The legislation raises the bar for production, he asserts, making it difficult if not impossible for the accused to meet the likely relevance test of ss. 278.5 and 278.7. The

Respondent contends that it is unconstitutional to exclude the assertions listed in s. 278.3(4) as irrelevant.

[118] This submission forgets that when legislation is susceptible to more than one interpretation, we must always choose the constitutional reading. See *Slaight, supra*, at p. 1078. This mistake leads the respondent to overstate the purpose and effect of s. 278.3(4).... It does not entirely prevent an accused from relying on the factors listed, but simply prevents reliance on bare *"assertions"* of the listed matters, where there is no other evidence and they stand "on their own."

[119] As has frequently been noted, speculative myths, stereotypes, and generalized assumptions about sexual assault victims and classes of records have too often in the past hindered the search for truth and imposed harsh and irrelevant burdens on complainants in prosecutions of sexual offences. See *Seaboyer* [*R. v.*, [1991] 2 S.C.R. 577], at p. 634. The myths that a woman's testimony is unreliable unless she made a complaint shortly after the event (recent complaint), or if she has had previous sexual relations, are but two of the more notorious examples of the speculation that in the past has passed for truth in this difficult area of human behaviour and the law. The notion that consultation with a psychiatrist is, by itself, an indication of untrustworthiness is a more recent, but equally invidious, example of such a myth. The purpose of s. 278.3(4) is to prevent these and other myths from forming the entire basis of an otherwise unsubstantiated order for production of private records....

[121] We conclude that s. 278.3(4) does not violate ss. 7 or 11(*d*) of the *Charter*.

(4) The First Stage: Production to the Judge—Sections 278.4 and 278.5

[122] Bill C-46, as noted, contemplates a two-stage procedure for gaining access to documents. At the first stage, the issue is whether the document should be produced to the judge. If that stage is passed, the judge looks at the document to determine whether it should be produced to the accused. Section 278.5 establishes the procedure for production to the judge at the first stage....

[125] Parliament, after studying the issue, concluded that the rights of both the complainant and the accused should be considered when deciding whether to order production to the judge. In coming to this conclusion, Parliament must be taken to have determined, as a result of lengthy consultations, and years of Parliamentary study and debate, that trial judges have sufficient evidence to engage in an informed balancing process at this stage. Parliament began consultations on the production of complainants' private records in sexual assault cases in June 1994. The *O'Connor* decision became a part of that discussion when it was released December 14, 1995, and

was subsequently addressed in the consultations which continued until March 1997. In developing the Bill C-46 production regime, we must therefore remember that Parliament had the benefit of information not available to the Court when it penned *O'Connor*. Specifically, Parliament had the advantage of being able to assess how the *O'Connor* regime was operating. The record indicates that Parliament received many submissions that under the *O'Connor* regime, private records were routinely being produced to the court at the first stage, leading to the recurring violation of the privacy interests of complainants and witnesses. While it is true that little statistical data existed at the time of the drafting of Bill C-46 on the application of *O'Connor*, it was open to Parliament to give what weight it saw fit to the evidence presented at the consultations. As a result of the consultation process, Parliament decided to supplement the "likely relevant" standard for production to the judge proposed in *O'Connor* with the further requirement that production be "necessary in the interests of justice." The result was s. 278.5. This process is a notable example of the dialogue between the judicial and legislative branches discussed above. This Court acted in *O'Connor*, and the legislature responded with Bill C-46. As already mentioned, the mere fact that Bill C-46 does not mirror *O'Connor* does not render it unconstitutional.

[126] Section 278.5(1) requires the accused at the stage of production to a judge to demonstrate not only that the information is "likely relevant" but, in addition, that the production of the record "is necessary in the interests of justice." The first requirement takes up the unanimous view in *O'Connor* that the accused, to get production to the judge, must show that the record is "likely relevant." The additional requirement that production to the judge be "necessary in the interests of justice" encompasses (but is not confined to) the concern of the minority in *O'Connor* that even where likely relevance is shown, there should be room for the court to consider the rights and interests of all those affected by disclosure before documents are ordered disclosed to the court.

[127] Section 278.5(1) is followed by s. 278.5(2) which gives substance to the requirement that trial judges consider the broad range of rights and interests affected before ordering disclosure to the court. Under this section, a trial judge is required to consider the salutary and deleterious effects of production to the court on the accused's right to make full answer and defence and on the rights to privacy and equality of the complainant or witness and any other person to whom the record relates. The section directs the trial judge to "take into account" a series of factors in deciding whether the document should be produced to the court: (a) the extent to which the record is necessary for the accused to make full answer and defence; (b) the probative value of the record; (c) the

nature and extent of the reasonable expectation of privacy with respect to the record; (d) whether production of the record is based on a discriminatory belief or bias; (e) the potential prejudice to the personal dignity and right to privacy of any person to whom the record relates; (f) society's interest in encouraging the reporting of sexual offences; (g) society's interest in encouraging the obtaining of treatment by complainants of sexual offences; and (h) the effect of the determination on the integrity of the trial process.

[128] ... [The respondent's] objection is that the accused must ... show that disclosure to the judge is "necessary in the interests of justice." He argues that this requires a weighing and balancing of interests that cannot properly be done without reviewing the documents in question. To this end, s. 278.5 calls upon the trial judge to do the impossible—to weigh competing rights in a vacuum. The respondent contends that likely relevance should be the only requirement at the stage of deciding whether the judge can see the document. In imposing the additional requirement that production be established as "necessary in the interests of justice," s. 278.5 risks depriving the accused of documents relevant to his defence and hence is unconstitutional.

[129] The question comes down to this: once likely relevance is established, is it necessarily unconstitutional that a consideration of the rights and interests of those affected by production to the court might result in production not being ordered? The answer to this question depends on whether a consideration of the range of rights and interests affected, in addition to a finding of likely relevance, will ultimately prevent the accused from seeing documents that are necessary to enable him to defend himself—to raise all the defences that might be open to him at trial. The non-disclosure of third party records with a high privacy interest that may contain relevant evidence will not compromise trial fairness where such non-disclosure would not prejudice the accused's right to full answer and defence. ...

[133] The criterion in s. 278.5 that production must be "necessary in the interests of justice" invests trial judges with the discretion to consider the full range of rights and interests at issue before ordering production, in a manner scrupulously respectful of the requirements of the *Charter*; see: *Baron* [*v. Canada*, [1993] 1 S.C.R. 416], at p. 442, *per* Sopinka J. The fact that the approach set out in s. 278.5 does not accord with *O'Connor*'s pronouncement, at para. 24, that at the stage of production to the Court, "considerations of privacy should not enter into the analysis," does not render it unconstitutional. In *O'Connor*, the Court was operating in a legislative

vacuum, and fashioned what it considered to be the preferred common law rule. While the rule from that case was of course informed by the *Charter*, it should not be read as a rigid constitutional template. As discussed above, the relationship between the courts and legislatures allows a range of constitutional options. While this Court may have considered it preferable not to consider privacy rights at the production stage, that does not preclude Parliament from coming to a different conclusion, so long as its conclusion is consistent with the *Charter* in its own right. As we have explained, the Bill's directive to consider what is "necessary in the interests of justice," read correctly, does include appropriate respect for the right to full answer and defence.

[134] This leaves the argument that the judge cannot consider the factors listed in s. 278.5(2) without looking at the documents. However, s. 278.5(2) does not require that the judge engage in a conclusive and in-depth evaluation of each of the factors. It rather requires the judge to "take them into account"—to the extent possible at this early stage of proceedings—in deciding whether to order a particular record produced to himself or herself for inspection. Section 278.5(2) serves as a check-list of the various factors that may come into play in making the decision regarding production to the judge. Therefore, while the s. 278.5(2) factors are relevant, in the final analysis the judge is free to make whatever order is "necessary in the interests of justice"—a mandate that includes all of the applicable "principles of fundamental justice" at stake. ...

[138] We conclude that s. 278.5 is constitutional. The respondent's argument depends on reading the requirement in s. 278.5(1)(*c*), that production can only be ordered where "necessary in the interests of justice," as capable of blocking production even where the accused might constitutionally require access to the documents in question. A finding of unconstitutionality also hinges on reading s. 278.5(2) as consisting of a check-list of factors and rights to be conclusively assessed and weighed-off against one other. Such readings, however, cannot stand. It can never be in the interests of justice for an accused to be denied the right to make full answer and defence and, pursuant to s. 278.5(2) the trial judge is merely directed to "consider" and "take into account" the factors and rights listed. Where the record sought can be established as "likely relevant," the judge must consider the rights and interests of all those affected by production and decide whether it is necessary in the interests of justice that he or she take the next step of viewing the documents. If in doubt, the interests of justice require that the judge take that step.

(5) Stage Two: Production to the Accused, Section 278.7—
The Consideration of Societal Interests, Sections 278.5(2)(f)
and (g), and the Integrity of the Trial Process,
Section 278.5(2)(h)

[139] Once the first hurdle is passed and the records are produced to the judge, the judge must determine whether it is in the interests of justice that they be produced to the defence. Again the judge must be satisfied that the records are "likely relevant" and that production, this time to the accused, is necessary in the interests of justice. In making this decision, the judge must once again consider the factors set out in s. 278.5(2).

[140] The respondent accepts that weighing competing interests is appropriate at this second stage of the analysis. However, the respondent contends that the requirement under s. 278.7(2), that the trial judge take the factors specified in s. 278.5(2)(a) to (h) into account, inappropriately alters the constitutional balance established in *O'Connor*. Specifically, the respondent contends that ss. 278.5(2)(f) and (g) elevate the societal interest in encouraging the reporting of sexual offences and encouraging of treatment of complainants of sexual offences, to a status equal to the accused's right to make full answer and defence. This, he suggests, alters the constitutional balance established in *O'Connor*, where the majority specifically determined these factors to be of secondary importance to defence interests in any balancing of competing interests and better taken into account through other avenues. The respondent also contends that s. 278.5(2)(h) unfairly requires trial judges to consider the effect of disclosure on the integrity of the trial process. The respondent submits that this is a question going to admissibility.

[141] ... Trial judges are not required to rule conclusively on each of the factors nor are they required to determine whether factors relating to the privacy and equality of the complainant or witness "outweigh" factors relating to the accused's right to full answer and defence. To repeat, trial judges are only asked to "take into account" the factors listed in s. 278.5(2) when determining whether production of part or all of the impugned record to the accused is necessary in the interest of justice (s. 278.7(1)). ...

[143] This leaves the argument that s. 278.5(2)(h) goes to admissibility and that any consideration of it at the stage of production distorts the fairness of the trial. While the *O'Connor* majority held that this factor was "more appropriately dealt with at the admissibility stage," this conclusion does not amount to a finding that a consideration of this factor at the stage of production would result in unfairness to the accused: see *O'Connor*, at para. 32. As noted above, when preparing Bill C-46 Parliament had the advantage of being able to assess how the *O'Connor* regime was operating. From the information available to Parliament and the submissions it received during the consultation process, Parliament concluded that the effect of production on the integrity of the trial was a factor that should be included in the list of factors for trial judges to "take into account" at both stages of an application for production. Several interveners have interpreted this factor as requiring courts to consider, along with the other enumerated factors, whether the search for truth would be advanced by the production of the records in question; that is, the question is whether the material in question would introduce discriminatory biases and beliefs into the fact-finding process. We agree with this interpretation of the inquiry required by s. 278.5(2)(h) and believe it to be in keeping with the purposes set out in the preamble of the legislation.

[144] By giving judges wide discretion to consider a variety of factors and requiring them to make whatever order is necessary in the interest of justice at both stages of an application for production, Parliament has created a scheme that permits judges not only to preserve the complainant's privacy and equality rights to the maximum extent possible, but also to ensure that the accused has access to the documents required to make full answer and defence. ...

VII. Conclusion and Disposition

[146] ... We answer the constitutional questions as follows:

1. Do ss. 278.1 to 278.91 of the *Criminal Code*, R.S.C., 1985, c. C-46, infringe s. 7 of the *Canadian Charter of Rights and Freedoms*?

   Answer: No.

2. If so, is the infringement demonstrably justified in a free and democratic society?

   Answer: Given the answer to question 1, it is not necessary to answer this question.

3. Do ss. 278.1 to 278.91 of the *Criminal Code*, R.S.C., 1985, c. C-46, infringe s. 11(d) of the *Canadian Charter of Rights and Freedoms*?

   Answer: No.

4. If so, is the infringement demonstrably justified in a free and democratic society?

   Answer: Given the answer to question 3, it is not necessary to answer this question.

 **United States v. Burns, 2001**

The *Canadian Charter* binds Canadian governments, not foreign ones. Nonetheless, the *Charter* affects Canada's relations with other countries. In extradition matters, for example, if a person accused of a crime in the United States flees to Canada, Canadian authorities may undertake to return that person to the United States for trial; however, they cannot do so in a manner that infringes the *Charter*. This much is settled law. The specific *Charter* standards that bind Canadian authorities are a matter of greater controversy.

In 1991, a majority of the Supreme Court ruled in *Kindler*[1] that the minister of justice may surrender a fugitive to the United States without first having to seek assurances that the death penalty will not be imposed on that fugitive upon his return. Joseph Kindler was convicted of murder in Pennsylvania and sentenced to death, but escaped to Canada thereafter. Justice La Forest, on behalf of the majority, wrote that it would be contrary to the principles of international comity to require that the receiving country's justice system be like Canada's in order for Canada to extradite fugitives to that country. While Canada and the United States differ on the merits and use of capital punishment, the two countries do have reciprocal extradition arrangements, and the American policy does not "shock the conscience" of Canadians. Only a criminal justice policy in a foreign country that would shock the Canadian conscience would impede the extradition of a fugitive from Canada to that country.

Kindler was decided on the basis of section 7 of the *Charter*, not section 12, which applies to Canadian authorities. No punishment in this case is meted out by Canadian authorities. Canada's role in Kindler's punishment was simply to extradite him to the United States where he faced punishment. The Supreme Court noted, however, that section 7 does apply to Canadian authorities, and that the principles of fundamental justice binding Canadian authorities—in this case the minister of justice—include those principles reflected in sections 8 to 14 of the *Charter*.[2] If conduct by a Canadian official occurs in a causal chain ending potentially in the administration of cruel and unusual treatment or punishment by foreign authorities, then that conduct must conform to the *Charter*.

In 2001, the Supreme Court considered the case of Glen Burns and Atif Rafay, two young men from British Columbia accused of the brutal murder of Rafay's parents and sister in Washington State. The two fled to Canada and were apprehended in an RCMP undercover operation. If convicted in the United States, they faced the death penalty. They argued that extradition to the United States would violate their *Charter* rights because it would shock

---

1   *Kindler v. Canada (Minister of Justice)*, [1991] 2 S.C.R. 779. See also the companion case of *Reference re Ng Extradition (Can.)*, [1991] 2 S.C.R. 858. Both Kindler and Ng were extradited to the United States and subsequently executed.

2   The relationship between section 7 and sections 8 to 14 of the *Charter* was first addressed by the Court in *Re B.C. Motor Vehicle Act*, case 13.

the Canadian conscience to have two young Canadian citizens extradited to face the death penalty. The Minister of Justice moved to extradite them without seeking assurances from the Americans. On appeal, the BC Court of Appeal held 2 to 1 that the Minister was required under section 6 of the *Charter* and under principles of administrative law to seek assurance that the death penalty would not be imposed if, upon surrender, the two were tried and convicted of murder.

The Supreme Court, in a unanimous, unsigned decision, upheld the decision of the BC Court of Appeal. The rule enunciated in this decision is that in all but exceptional circumstances (on which the Court did not elaborate), before extradition can proceed, the minister must seek assurances that the death penalty will not be imposed. To do otherwise would violate section 7 of the *Charter*.

Within 10 years, the Court changed its mind on the status of the death penalty in a requesting country for the purpose of determining the constitutionality of Canada's extradition policy. What caused the change? The Court argued that the *Kindler* and *Ng* decisions required a balancing of international and domestic factors militating both against and in favour of extradition without assurances. Some of the factors to be balanced "will evolve over time." And some of these concern the "practical and philosophic difficulties" that have come increasingly to the attention of courts in Canada, as well as those at the state and federal levels south of the border. The Court indicated that the death penalty's finality would aggravate gross injustices committed against the wrongfully convicted, of whom there have been many in Canada and abroad. In abolitionist countries, injustices can at least be remedied.

These difficulties tip the balance against extradition without assurances. Factors militating in favour of extradition without assurances have been found to be without foundation. For example, the safe-haven argument, according to which Canada must extradite without assurances to prevent this country from attracting murderers seeking to escape justice in their own countries, was found to lack empirical support.

The Court in *Burns* did not strike down provisions of Canadian law or the Canada–U.S. extradition treaty. Article 6 of that treaty declares that in circumstances like those of Kindler and Burns, extradition "may" be refused if Canadian law on the death penalty differs from that of a U.S. jurisdiction. Now, in the light of *Burns*, that provision is to be read to mean that extradition *shall* be refused unless assurances are obtained (except in exceptional circumstances). Legal provisions can technically be upheld, but *Charter*-inspired interpretation can alter their meanings dramatically.

Burns is also emblematic of the role that international law and legal precedent increasingly play in *Charter* interpretation. While the Court at times relied on American legal precedent early in the *Charter*'s life,[3] in this case, the Court marshalled international legal thinking to distance itself from American constitutional and legal doctrine. ∿

---

3   Christopher Manfredi, "The Use of United States Decisions by the Supreme Court of Canada Under the Charter of Rights and Freedoms" (1990) 23 *Canadian Journal of Political Science* 499.

Discussion Questions

1. The Court held that section 12 does not apply to this dispute but that section 7 does. Why?
2. The Court's view of the death penalty has changed since 1991. What factors influenced the Court's new understanding?
3. Human rights are, in principle, universal. They are instantiated in particular documents for particular jurisdictions. Does the *Canadian Charter of Rights and Freedoms* represent a *Canadian* standard of rights or a Canadian statement of *(universal) rights*? How does *Burns* assist in answering this question?

UNITED STATES v. BURNS
2001 SCC 7, [2001] 1 S.C.R. 283

Hearing: March 22, 1999; Rehearing: May 23, 2000; Judgment: February 15, 2001.

Present: McLachlin C.J. and L'Heureux-Dubé, Gonthier, Iacobucci, Major, Bastarache, Binnie, Arbour, and LeBel JJ.

Interveners: Amnesty International, the International Centre for Criminal Law & Human Rights, the Criminal Lawyers' Association (Ontario), the Washington Association of Criminal Defence Lawyers, and the Senate of the Republic of Italy.

THE COURT:

[1] Legal systems have to live with the possibility of error. The unique feature of capital punishment is that it puts beyond recall the possibility of correction. In recent years, aided by the advances in the forensic sciences, including DNA testing, the courts and governments in this country and elsewhere have come to acknowledge a number of instances of wrongful convictions for murder despite all of the careful safeguards put in place for the protection of the innocent. The instances in Canada are few, but if capital punishment had been carried out, the result could have been the killing by the government of innocent individuals. The names of Marshall, Milgaard, Morin, Sophonow and Parsons signal prudence and caution in a murder case. Other countries have also experienced revelations of wrongful convictions, including states of the United States where the death penalty is still imposed and carried into execution.

[2] The possibility of a miscarriage of justice is but one of many factors in the balancing process which governs the decision by the Minister of Justice to extradite two Canadian citizens, Glen Sebastian Burns and Atif Ahmad Rafay, to the United States. A competing principle of fundamental justice is that Canadians who are accused of crimes in the United States can ordinarily expect to be dealt with under the law which the citizens of that jurisdiction have collectively determined to apply to offences committed within their territory, including the set punishment.

[3] Awareness of the potential for miscarriages of justice, together with broader public concerns about the taking of life by the state, as well as doubts about the effectiveness of the death penalty as a deterrent to murder in comparison with life in prison without parole for 25 years, led Canada to abolish the death penalty for all but a handful of military offences in 1976, and subsequently to abolish the death penalty for all offences in 1998.

[4] The abolitionist view is shared by some, but not a majority, of the United States. . . .

I. Facts

[The Court recounts the facts of the case. Burns and Rafay, young adults at the time of the incident in which they were implicated, are Canadian citizens. Both are alleged to have participated in the brutal slaying of Rafay's parents and sister in their Washington State home in order to reap a life insurance settlement. The suspects returned to Canada after the incident. RCMP undercover agents, in cooperation with Washington police, obtained information from the suspects suggesting they were the murderers. U.S. authorities requested extradition of the two and the Minister of Justice was prepared to surrender them without first obtaining assurances that the two would not be subject to the death penalty upon conviction. This decision was based on a 1991 Supreme Court decision in *Kindler v. Canada (Minister of Justice)* in which the constitutionality of ministerial discretion to extradite to the death penalty was affirmed. Burns and Rafay successfully challenged the Minister's decision in the British Columbia Court of Appeal. That decision was appealed to the Supreme Court by the Canadian Minister of Justice.]

IV. Relevant Constitutional and Statutory Provisions

. . . *Extradition Act*, R.S.C. 1985, c. E-23 (as am. by S.C. 1992, c. 13)

> **25.** (1) Subject to this Part, the Minister of Justice, on the requisition of a foreign state, may, within a period of ninety days after the date of a fugitive's committal for surrender, under the hand and seal of the Minister, order the fugitive to be surrendered to the person or persons who are, in the Minister's opinion, duly authorized to receive the fugitive in the name and on behalf of the foreign state, and the fugitive shall be so surrendered accordingly.

V. Relevant Provisions from International Documents

[26] *Extradition Treaty between Canada and the United States of America* (amended by an Exchange of Notes), Can. T.S. 1976 No. 3, in force March 22, 1976

Article 6

When the offense for which extradition is requested is punishable by death under the laws of the requesting State and the laws of the requested State do not permit such punishment for that offense, extradition may be refused unless the requesting State provides such assurances as the requested State considers sufficient that the death penalty shall not be imposed, or, if imposed, shall not be executed.

. . . [27] . . .

VII. Analysis

[28] The evidence amply justifies the extradition of the respondents to Washington State to stand trial on charges of aggravated first degree murder. . . .

[29] The respondents' position is that the death penalty is so horrific, the chances of error are so high, the death row phenomenon is so repugnant, and the impossibility of correction is so draconian, that it is simply unacceptable that Canada should participate, however indirectly, in its imposition. While the government of Canada would not itself administer the lethal injection or erect the gallows, no executions can or will occur without the act of extradition by the Canadian government. The Minister's decision is a prior and essential step in a process that may lead to death by execution.

[30] The root questions here are whether the Constitution supports the Minister's position that assurances need only be sought in exceptional cases, or whether the Constitution supports the respondents' position that assurances must *always* be sought barring exceptional circumstances, and if so, whether such exceptional circumstances are present in this case. . . .

1. The Extradition Act Confers a Broad Statutory Discretion on the Minister

[32] The appeal reaches this Court by way of a judicial review of the exercise by the Minister of his discretion under s. 25(1) of the *Extradition Act*. . . :

> 25. (1) Subject to this Part, the Minister of Justice, on the requisition of a foreign state, may, within a period of ninety days after the date of a fugitive's committal for surrender, under the hand and seal of the Minister, order the fugitive to be surrendered to the person or persons who are, in the Minister's opinion, duly authorized to receive the fugitive in the name and on behalf of the foreign state, and the fugitive shall be so surrendered accordingly.

Section 25 creates a broad discretion which the Minister must exercise in accordance with the dictates of the *Charter*. . . . None of the parties to this litigation has attacked the constitutional validity of this discretion which has previously been found by a majority of this Court to pass *Charter* scrutiny: see *Kindler, supra*. In that case, the Court recognized that the Minister's discretion was limited by the *Charter*, and that the *Charter* required a balancing on the facts of each case of the applicable principles of fundamental justice. We affirm the correctness of the balancing test, and for reasons which will become apparent, we conclude that in the circumstances of this case the application of the balancing test and the ultimate requirement of adherence to "the basic tenets of our legal system" (*Re B.C. Motor Vehicle Act*, [1985] 2 S.C.R. 486, at p. 503) require the Minister to seek assurances.

[33] The authority of the Minister under s. 25 is predicated on the existence of an extradition treaty (s. 3). The extradition treaty in question here was concluded by Canada and the United States in 1971 at a time when Canada still retained the death penalty, although no executions had been carried out since 1962. In the United States executions, which had occurred at the rate of about 50 per year in the late 1950s, "slowed to a trickle and then stopped" in the 1960s (W. S. White, "Capital Punishment's Future" (1993), 91 *Mich. L. Rev.* 1429, at p. 1429). A *de facto* moratorium occurred commencing June 2, 1967. This was reinforced five years later when the Supreme Court of the United States, in *Furman v. Georgia*, 408 U.S. 238 (1972), declared the death penalty regime of the State of Georgia to be unconstitutional. By 1976, the year in which the extradition treaty was ratified and came into force, there had been a realignment of positions. Canada had abolished the death penalty for all but a few military crimes (*Criminal Law Amendment Act (No. 2), 1976*, S.C. 1974-75-76, c. 105). In the same year the United States Supreme Court declared that the death penalty *could* be constitutional if appropriate procedural safeguards are put in place: *Gregg v. Georgia*, 428 U.S. 153 (1976). Executions resumed on January 17, 1977 when Gary Gilmore was shot by a firing squad in Utah (H. H. Haines, *Against Capital Punishment: The Anti-Death Penalty Movement in America, 1972-1994* (1996), at p. 211). In recognition, perhaps, of this fluid state of affairs the parties agreed that the extradition treaty should include Article 6 in respect of seeking assurances. As set out above, Article 6 provides as follows:

> When the offense for which extradition is requested is punishable by death under the laws of the requesting State and the laws of the requested State do not permit such punishment for that offense, extradition may be refused unless the requesting State provides such assurances as the requested State considers sufficient that the death penalty shall not be imposed, or, if imposed, shall not be executed.

[34] In his decision, the then Minister said that where a committal judge under the Act is satisfied that the requesting state has made out a *prima facie* case against the fugitive, he will approach the issue

> from the premise that assurances should be sought only in circumstances where the particular facts of the case warrant that special exercise of discretion. Such assurances are not to be sought routinely in every case in which the death penalty is applicable.

As stated, the Minister saw nothing in the circumstances here to warrant asking for such assurances.

[35] The question is not whether we agree with the Minister's decision. The only issue under the *Charter* is whether,

as a matter of constitutional law, the Minister had the power to decide as he did. The *Charter* does not give the Court a general mandate to set Canada's foreign policy on extradition. Yet the Court is the guardian of the Constitution and death penalty cases are uniquely bound up with basic constitutional values. While the death penalty arises as a possibility only in a small fraction of the extradition cases dealt with by the Minister and departmental officials, it raises issues of fundamental importance to Canadian society.

2. The Minister Is Responsible for the Performance of Canada's International Law Enforcement Obligations

... [38] We affirm that it is generally for the Minister, not the Court, to assess the weight of competing considerations in extradition policy, but the availability of the death penalty, like death itself, opens up a different dimension. The difficulties and occasional miscarriages of the criminal law are located in an area of human experience that falls squarely within "the inherent domain of the judiciary as guardian of the justice system": *Re B.C. Motor Vehicle Act, supra,* at p. 503. It is from this perspective, recognizing the unique finality and irreversibility of the death penalty, that the constitutionality of the Minister's decision falls to be decided....

5. The Outcome of This Appeal Is Governed by Section 7 of the Charter ("Fundamental Justice")

... [59] It is evident that the respondents are deprived of their liberty and security of the person by the extradition order: *Kindler, supra,* at p. 831. Their lives are potentially at risk. The issue is whether the threatened deprivation is in accordance with the principles of fundamental justice.

[60] This Court has recognized from the outset that the punishment or treatment reasonably anticipated in the requesting country is clearly relevant. Section 7 is concerned not only with the act of extraditing, but also the *potential* consequences of the act of extradition....

[61] In their submissions on whether extradition without assurances is contrary to the principles of fundamental justice, the parties drew heavily on the decisions in *Kindler* and *Ng.* It may be helpful to recall the facts of those cases. Kindler was an American citizen who had escaped to Canada after being convicted in Pennsylvania for the brutal murder of an 18-year-old who was scheduled to testify against him in a burglary case. The jury which convicted Kindler had recommended that he face the death penalty. Prior to being sentenced, he escaped to Canada. After seven months as a fugitive in Quebec, Kindler was captured and escaped again. After remaining at large for nearly two years, Kindler was recaptured. Judicial review of Kindler's surrender order was dismissed by this Court even though (unlike this case) the

death penalty was no longer simply a possibility. It had already been recommended by the jury. Nevertheless, we held that the Minister was entitled to extradite without assurances.

[62] In the companion appeal, the respondent Ng was a British subject born in Hong Kong and subsequently resident in the United States. He had been arrested in Calgary after shooting at two department store security guards who tried to apprehend him for shoplifting. Once his identity was established, he was extradited to the State of California to face numerous charges of murder. He has since been convicted and sentenced to death for murdering 11 people—six men, three women and two baby boys—during what one newspaper described as a "spree of sexual torture and murder in rural California." In that case, as well, the Minister was held to have the power, though not the duty, to extradite without assurances.

[63] The respondents submit that even if the analytical framework developed in *Kindler* and *Ng* is accepted (i.e., balancing "the conflicting considerations" or "factors": *Kindler,* at p. 850), the result of those cases should not determine the outcome here. *Kindler* and *Ng* should either be distinguished on the facts or revisited on the weight to be given to the "factor" of capital punishment because of changed circumstances in the 10 years since those cases were decided.

6. The Proper Analytical Approach (the "Balancing Process") Was Set Out by this Court in Its Decisions in Kindler and Ng

[64] It is important to recognize that neither *Kindler* nor *Ng* provides a blanket approval to extraditions to face the death penalty. In *Kindler,* La Forest J., at p. 833, referred to a s. 7 "balancing process" in which "the global context must be kept squarely in mind." At p. 835, he acknowledged the possible existence of circumstances that "may constitutionally vitiate an order for surrender."

[65] It is inherent in the *Kindler* and *Ng* balancing process that the outcome may well vary from case to case depending on the mix of contextual factors put into the balance. Some of these factors will be very specific, such as the mental condition of a particular fugitive. Other factors will be more general, such as the difficulties, both practical and philosophic, associated with the death penalty. Some of these factors will be unchanging; others will evolve over time. The outcome of this appeal turns more on the practical and philosophic difficulties associated with the death penalty that have increasingly preoccupied the courts and legislators in Canada, the United States and elsewhere rather than on the specific circumstances of the respondents in this case. Our analysis will lead to the conclusion that in the absence of exceptional circumstances, which we refrain from trying to anticipate, assurances in death penalty cases are always constitutionally required.

[66] The Minister approached this extradition decision on the basis of the law laid down in *Kindler* and *Ng* and related cases. Having regard to some of the expressions used in the case law, he concluded that the *possibility* of the death penalty does not pose a situation that is "simply unacceptable" (*Allard* [*United States v.*, [1987] 1 S.C.R. 564], at p. 572), nor would surrender of the respondents without assurances "shoc[k] the conscience" of Canadians (*Schmidt* [*Canada v.*, [1987] 1 S.C.R. 500], at p. 522; *Kindler, supra*, and *Ng, supra*) or violate "the Canadian sense of what is fair and right" (*per* McLachlin J. in *Kindler*, at p. 850). A similar pre-*Charter* formulation was applied in a death penalty case under the *Canadian Bill of Rights*, S.C. 1960, c. 44, where Laskin C.J. asked "whether the punishment prescribed is so excessive as to outrage standards of decency" in *Miller v. The Queen*, [1977] 2 S.C.R. 680, at p. 688.

[67] While we affirm that the "balancing process" set out in *Kindler* and *Ng* is the correct approach, the phrase "shocks the conscience" and equivalent expressions are not to be taken out of context or equated to opinion polls. The words were intended to underline the very exceptional nature of circumstances that would constitutionally limit the Minister's decision in extradition cases. The words were not intended to signal an abdication by judges of their constitutional responsibilities in matters involving fundamental principles of justice....

[68] Use of the "shocks the conscience" terminology was intended to convey the exceptional weight of a factor such as the youth, insanity, mental retardation or pregnancy of a fugitive which, because of its paramount importance, may control the outcome of the *Kindler* balancing test on the facts of a particular case. The terminology should not be allowed to obscure the ultimate assessment that is required: namely whether or not the extradition is in accordance with the principles of fundamental justice. The rule is *not* that departures from fundamental justice are to be tolerated unless in a particular case it shocks the conscience. An extradition that violates the principles of fundamental justice will *always* shock the conscience. The important inquiry is to determine what constitutes the applicable principles of fundamental justice in the extradition context.

[69] The "shocks the conscience" language signals the possibility that even though the rights of the fugitive are to be considered in the context of other applicable principles of fundamental justice, which are normally of sufficient importance to uphold the extradition, a particular treatment or punishment may sufficiently violate our sense of fundamental justice as to tilt the balance against extradition. Examples might include stoning to death individuals taken in adultery, or lopping off the hands of a thief. The punishment is so extreme that it becomes the controlling issue in the extradition and overwhelms the rest of the analysis. The respondents

contend that now, unlike perhaps in 1991 when *Kindler* and *Ng* were decided, capital punishment is *the* issue....

8. Factors That Arguably Favour Extradition Without Assurances

[72] Within this overall approach, a number of the "basic tenets of our legal system" relevant to this appeal may be found in previous extradition cases:

- that individuals accused of a crime should be brought to trial to determine the truth of the charges (see *Cotroni* [*United States of America v.*, [1989] 1 S.C.R. 1469], at pp. 1487 and 1495), the concern in this case being that if assurances are sought and refused, the Canadian government could face the possibility that the respondents might avoid a trial altogether;

- that justice is best served by a trial in the jurisdiction where the crime was allegedly committed and the harmful impact felt (*Mellino* [*Argentina v.*, [1987] 1 S.C.R. 536], at pp. 555 and 558; *Idziak* [*v. Canada (Minister of Justice)*, [1992] 3 S.C.R. 631], at p. 662; and see *Cotroni, supra*, at p. 1488);

- that individuals who choose to leave Canada leave behind Canadian law and procedures and must generally accept the local law, procedure and punishments which the foreign state applies to its own residents. As Wilson J., dissenting in the result in *Cotroni* ... stated ...: "A Canadian citizen who leaves Canada for another state must expect that he will be answerable to the justice system of that state in respect of his conduct there." ...

- that extradition is based on the principles of comity and fairness to other cooperating states in rendering mutual assistance in bringing fugitives to justice (*Mellino, supra*, at p. 551; and see *Idziak, supra*, at p. 663); subject to the principle that the fugitive must be able to receive a fair trial in the requesting state (*Mellino, supra*, at p. 558; *Allard, supra*, at p. 571).

[73] A state seeking Canadian cooperation today may be asked to yield up a fugitive tomorrow. The extradition treaty is part of an international network of mutual assistance that enables states to deal both with crimes in their own jurisdiction and transnational crimes with elements that occur in more than one jurisdiction. Given the ease of movement of people and things from state to state, Canada needs the help of the international community to fight serious crime within our own borders. Some of the states from whom we seek cooperation may not share our constitutional values. Their cooperation is nevertheless important. The Minister points out that Canada satisfies itself that certain minimum stan-

dards of criminal justice exist in the foreign state before it makes an extradition treaty in the first place.

[74] The Minister argues, very fairly, that expressions of judicial deference to ministerial extradition decisions extend in an unbroken line from *Schmidt* to *Kindler*. Such deference, taken together with the proposition that an individual (including a Canadian) who commits crimes in another state "must expect [to be] answerable to the justice system of that state in respect of his conduct there" (*Cotroni, supra*, at p. 1510), provides a sufficient basis, the Minister says, for upholding the extradition without assurances.

9. Countervailing Factors That Arguably Favour Extradition Only with Assurances

[75] We now turn to the factors that appear to weigh against extradition without assurances that the death penalty will not be imposed.

(a) Principles of Criminal Justice as Applied in Canada

[76] The death penalty has been rejected as an acceptable element of criminal justice by the Canadian people, speaking through their elected federal representatives, after years of protracted debate. Canada has not executed anyone since 1962. Parliament abolished the last legal vestiges of the death penalty in 1998 (*An Act to amend the National Defence Act and to make consequential amendments to other Acts*, S.C. 1998, c. 35) some seven years after the decisions of this Court in *Kindler* and *Ng*. In his letter to the respondents, the Minister of Justice emphasized that "in Canada, Parliament has decided that capital punishment is not an appropriate penalty for crimes committed here, and I am firmly committed to that position."

[77] While government policy at any particular moment may or may not be consistent with principles of fundamental justice, the fact that successive governments and Parliaments over a period of almost 40 years have refused to inflict the death penalty reflects, we believe, a fundamental Canadian principle about the appropriate limits of the criminal justice system.

[78] We are not called upon in this appeal to determine whether capital punishment would, if authorized by the Canadian Parliament, violate s. 12 of the *Charter* ("cruel and unusual treatment or punishment"), and if so in what circumstances. It is, however, incontestable that capital punishment, whether or not it violates s. 12 of the *Charter*, and whether or not it could be upheld under s. 1, engages the underlying values of the prohibition against cruel and unusual punishment. It is final. It is irreversible. Its imposition has been described as arbitrary. Its deterrent value has been doubted. Its implementation necessarily causes psychological and physical suffering. It has been rejected by the Canadian Parliament for offences committed within Canada. Its potential

imposition in this case is thus a factor that weighs against extradition without assurances.

(b) The Abolition of the Death Penalty Has Emerged as a Major Canadian Initiative at the International Level, and Reflects a Concern Increasingly Shared by Most of the World's Democracies

... [80] ... [I]n *Reference re Public Service Employee Relations Act (Alta.)*, [1987] 1 S.C.R. 313, at p. 348, Dickson C.J. stated:

> [D]eclarations, covenants, conventions, judicial and quasi-judicial decisions of international tribunals, customary norms—must, in my opinion, be relevant and persuasive sources for interpretation of the *Charter*'s provisions.

... [81] Although this particular appeal arises in the context of Canada's bilateral extradition arrangements with the United States, it is properly considered in the broader context of international relations generally, including Canada's multilateral efforts to bring about change in extradition arrangements where fugitives may face the death penalty, and Canada's advocacy at the international level of the abolition of the death penalty itself.

(i) International Initiatives Opposing Extradition Without Assurances

[82] A provision for assurances is found in the extradition arrangements of countries other than Canada and the United States. Article 11 of the Council of Europe's *European Convention on Extradition*, Eur. T.S. No. 24, signed December 13, 1957, is virtually identical to Article 6 of the Canada–U.S. treaty. To the same effect is Article 4(*d*) of the *Model Treaty on Extradition* passed by the General Assembly of the United Nations in December 1990 which states that extradition may be refused:

> (*d*) If the offence for which extradition is requested carries the death penalty under the law of the requesting State, unless that State gives such assurance as the requested State considers sufficient that the death penalty will not be imposed or, if imposed, will not be carried out;

[83] We are told that from 1991 onwards Article 4(*d*) has gained increasing acceptance in state practice. Amnesty International submitted that Canada currently is the only country in the world, to its knowledge, that has abolished the death penalty at home but continues to extradite without assurances to face the death penalty abroad. Counsel for the Minister, while not conceding the point, did not refer us to any evidence of state practice to contradict this assertion.

[84] The United Nations Commission on Human Rights Resolutions 1999/61 (adopted April 28, 1999) and 2000/65 (adopted April 27, 2000) call for the abolition of the death penalty, and in terms of extradition state that the Commission

> [r]equests States that have received a request for extradition on a capital charge to reserve explicitly the right to refuse extradition in the absence of effective assurances from relevant authorities of the requesting State that capital punishment will not be carried out;

Canada supported these initiatives. When they are combined with other examples of Canada's international advocacy of the abolition of the death penalty itself, as described below, it is difficult to avoid the conclusion that in the Canadian view of fundamental justice, capital punishment is unjust and it should be stopped.

(ii) International Initiatives to Abolish the
Death Penalty

[85] As stated, there have been important initiatives within the international community denouncing the death penalty, with the government of Canada often in the forefront.... [The Court cites a variety of international legal instruments, supported by Canada, which limit or proscribe the death penalty.]

[89] This evidence does not establish an international law norm against the death penalty, or against extradition to face the death penalty. It does show, however, significant movement towards acceptance internationally of a principle of fundamental justice that Canada has already adopted internally, namely the abolition of capital punishment.

(iii) State Practice Increasingly Favours Abolition of the
Death Penalty

[90] State practice is frequently taken as reflecting underlying legal principles. To the extent this is true in the criminal justice field, it must be noted that since *Kindler* and *Ng* were decided in 1991, a greater number of countries have become abolitionist....

[92] The existence of an international trend against the death penalty is useful in testing our values against those of comparable jurisdictions. This trend against the death penalty supports some relevant conclusions. First, criminal justice, according to international standards, is moving in the direction of abolition of the death penalty. Second, the trend is more pronounced among democratic states with systems of criminal justice comparable to our own. The United States (or those parts of it that have retained the death penalty) is

the exception, although of course it is an important exception. Third, the trend to abolition in the democracies, particularly the Western democracies, mirrors and perhaps corroborates the principles of fundamental justice that led to the rejection of the death penalty in Canada.

*(c) Almost All Jurisdictions Treat Some Personal
Characteristics of the Fugitive as Mitigating Factors in
Death Penalty Cases*

[93] Examples of potential mitigating factors include youth, insanity, mental retardation and pregnancy. In this case, the respondents rely on the fact that at the time of the crime they were 18.... The respondents, at 18 years of age, had just passed the borderline from ineligibility to eligibility for the death penalty in Washington State. It is worth noting that only 16 of the 38 retentionist states of the United States have an age limitation of 18 years, another 5 have chosen 17, while the others use 16 by law or judicial interpretation. It is correct that Canada would hold the respondents fully responsible for their actions under the *Criminal Code*, but Canada is an abolitionist country. The relative youth of the respondents at the time of the offence does constitute a mitigating circumstance in this case, although it must be said, a factor of limited weight.

(d) Other Factors

[94] Other factors that weigh against extradition without assurances include the growing awareness of the rate of wrongful convictions in murder cases, and concerns about the "death row phenomenon"....

10. An Accelerating Concern About Potential Wrongful Convictions Is a Factor of Increased Weight Since Kindler and Ng Were Decided

[95] The avoidance of conviction and punishment of the innocent has long been in the forefront of "the basic tenets of our legal system." It is reflected in the presumption of innocence under s. 11(*d*) of the *Charter* and in the elaborate rules governing the collection and presentation of evidence, fair trial procedures, and the availability of appeals. The possibility of miscarriages of justice in murder cases has long been recognized as a legitimate objection to the death penalty, but our state of knowledge of the scope of this potential problem has grown to unanticipated and unprecedented proportions in the years since *Kindler* and *Ng* were decided. This expanding awareness compels increased recognition of the fact that the extradition decision of a Canadian Minister could pave the way, however unintentionally, to sending an innocent individual to his or her death in a foreign jurisdiction.

(a) The Canadian Experience

[96] Our concern begins at home. There have been well-publicized recent instances of miscarriages of justice in murder cases in Canada. Fortunately, because of the abolition of the death penalty, meaningful remedies for wrongful conviction are still possible in this country. . . . [The Court cites several notorious cases of wrongful convictions in Canada and refers to similar debates in the United States and Great Britain.]

(d) Conclusion

[117] The recent and continuing disclosures of wrongful convictions for murder in Canada, the United States and the United Kingdom provide tragic testimony to the fallibility of the legal system, despite its elaborate safeguards for the protection of the innocent. When fugitives are sought to be tried for murder by a retentionist state, however similar in other respects to our own legal system, this history weighs powerfully in the balance against extradition without assurances.

11. The "Death Row Phenomenon" Is of Increasing Concern Even to Retentionists

[The Court cites evidence from various jurisdictions on the considerable length of time inmates spend on death row.]

[121] The role of the death row phenomenon in extradition proceedings was not conclusively determined by this Court in *Kindler*. Cory J., with whom Lamer C.J. concurred, was of the view that it would be wrong to extradite someone who would face the death row phenomenon: see pp. 822-24. Sopinka J. did not deal with the question while McLachlin J. (at p. 856) alluded to "the complexity of the issue." La Forest J. was critical of the concept. He said (at p. 838):

> While the psychological stress inherent in the death row phenomenon cannot be dismissed lightly, it ultimately pales in comparison to the death penalty. Besides, the fact remains that a defendant is never forced to undergo the full appeal procedure, but the vast majority choose to do so. It would be ironic if delay caused by the appellant's taking advantage of the full and generous avenue of the appeals available to him should be viewed as a violation of fundamental justice; . . .

[122] There is now, however, as is shown in the report of Chief Justice Guy of Washington State [Status Report on the Death Penalty (March 2000)], a widening acceptance amongst those closely associated with the administration of justice in retentionist states that the finality of the death penalty, combined with the determination of the criminal justice system to satisfy itself fully that the conviction is not wrongful, seems inevitably to provide lengthy delays, and the associated psychological trauma. . . .

[123] The death row phenomenon is not a controlling factor in the s. 7 balance, but even many of those who regard its horrors as self-inflicted concede that it is a relevant consideration. To that extent, it is a factor that weighs in the balance against extradition without assurances.

12. The Balance of Factors in This Case Renders Extradition of the Respondents Without Assurances a Prima Facie Infringement of Their Section 7 Rights

[124] Reviewing the factors for and against unconditional extradition, we conclude that to order extradition of the respondents without obtaining assurances that the death penalty will not be imposed would violate the principles of fundamental justice.

[125] The Minister has not pointed to any public purpose that would be served by extradition *without* assurances that is not substantially served by extradition *with* assurances, carrying as it does in this case the prospect on conviction of life imprisonment without release or parole. With assurances, the respondents will be extradited and be made answerable to the legal system where the murders took place. The evidence shows that on previous occasions when assurances have been requested of foreign states they have been forthcoming without exception. . . . There is no basis in the record to support the hypothesis, and counsel for the Minister did not advance it, that the United States would prefer no extradition at all to extradition with assurances. Under Washington State law it by no means follows that the prosecutor will seek the death penalty if the respondents are extradited to face charges of aggravated first degree murder.

[126] It is true that if assurances are requested, the respondents will not face the same punishment regime that is generally applicable to crimes committed in Washington State, but the reality is that Washington requires the assistance of Canada to bring the respondents to justice. Assurances are not sought out of regard for the respondents, but out of regard for the principles that have historically guided this country's criminal justice system and are presently reflected in its international stance on capital punishment.

[127] International experience, particularly in the past decade, has shown the death penalty to raise many complex problems of both a philosophic and pragmatic nature. While there remains the fundamental issue of whether the state can ever be justified in taking the life of a human being within its power, the present debate goes beyond arguments over the effectiveness of deterrence and the appropriateness of vengeance and retribution. It strikes at the very ability of the

criminal justice system to obtain a uniformly correct result even where death hangs in the balance.

[128] International experience thus confirms the validity of concerns expressed in the Canadian Parliament about capital punishment. It also shows that a rule requiring that assurances be obtained prior to extradition in death penalty cases not only accords with Canada's principled advocacy on the international level, but is also consistent with the practice of other countries with whom Canada generally invites comparison, apart from the retentionist jurisdictions in the United States.

[129] The "balancing process" mandated by *Kindler* and *Ng* remains a flexible instrument. The difficulty in this case is that the Minister proposes to send the respondents without assurances into the death penalty controversy at a time when the legal system of the requesting country is under such sustained and authoritative *internal* attack. Although rumblings of this controversy in Canada, the United States and the United Kingdom pre-dated *Kindler* and *Ng*, the concern has grown greatly in depth and detailed proof in the intervening years. The imposition of a moratorium (*de facto* or otherwise) in some of the retentionist states of the United States attests to this concern, but a moratorium itself is not conclusive, any more than the lifting of a moratorium would be. What is important is the recognition that despite the best efforts of all concerned, the judicial system is and will remain fallible and reversible whereas the death penalty will forever remain final and irreversible.

[130] The arguments in favour of extradition without assurances would be as well served by extradition with assurances. There was no convincing argument that exposure of the respondents to death in prison by execution advances Canada's public interest in a way that the alternative, eventual death in prison by natural causes, would not. This is perhaps corroborated by the fact that other abolitionist countries do not, in general, extradite without assurances.

[131] The arguments against extradition without assurances have grown stronger since this Court decided *Kindler* and *Ng* in 1991. Canada is now abolitionist for all crimes, even those in the military field. The international trend against the death penalty has become clearer. The death penalty controversies in the requesting State—the United States—are based on pragmatic, hard-headed concerns about wrongful convictions. None of these factors is conclusive, but taken together they tilt the s. 7 balance against extradition without assurances.

[132] Accordingly, we find that the Minister's decision to decline to request the assurances of the State of Washington that the death penalty will not be imposed on the respondents as a condition of their extradition, violates their rights under s. 7 of the *Charter*.

13. Extradition of the Respondents Without Assurances Cannot Be Justified Under Section 1 of the Charter

[133] The final issue is whether the Minister has shown that the violation of the respondents' s. 7 rights that would occur if they were extradited to face the death penalty can be upheld under s. 1 of the *Charter* as reasonable and demonstrably justifiable in a free and democratic society. The Court has previously noted that it would be rare for a violation of the fundamental principles of justice to be justifiable under s. 1: *Re B.C. Motor Vehicle Act, supra*, at p. 518. Nevertheless, we do not foreclose the possibility that there may be situations where the Minister's objectives are so pressing, and where there is no other way to achieve those objectives other than through extradition without assurances, that a violation might be justified. In this case, we find no such justification. . . .

20 Charkaoui v. Canada (Citizenship and Immigration), 2007

Like other Western countries, Canada responded to the 9/11 terrorist attacks with sympathy for the United States and concern about its own security against terrorism. In addition, concerns circulated about Canada's large immigrant population serving as a base from which incursions into the United States could be launched and as a fund-raising network for financing terrorism abroad. For liberal democracies, responding to terrorism is bedevilling. On the one hand, liberal democracies are founded on individual rights whose importance only increases when pressure mounts for their abridgment. Clamping down on rights in the face of threats to national security seems like razing a village in order to save it. On the other hand, as Michael Ignatieff argues, liberal democracies are not suicide pacts. They are vulnerable to attack because of their very openness and are entitled to protect themselves from those who exploit liberal freedoms for terrorist causes.[1]

This difficult balance between security and rights is directly engaged in the following decision. Adil Charkaoui and two others, Hassan Almrei and Mohamed Harkat, were subjects of "security certificates" issued by the Minister of Citizenship and Immigration and the Minister of Public Safety and Emergency Preparedness. Such certificates are issued in respect to persons considered by the government to be threats to Canada's national security. Under the *Immigration and Refugee Protection Act* (*IRPA*) (proclaimed in November 2001, but debated in the House of Commons before 9/11), permanent residents and foreign nationals in Canada named in security certificates are rendered "inadmissible" in Canada—and subject to deportation—if the government considers that there is sufficient evidence that their presence constitutes a threat to national security, and if a Federal Court judge confirms the reasonableness of the certificate. The judicial hearing is mandatory, but the government can request that the hearing be held *in camera*, without the named person present.

Information on the basis of which a judicial determination is made may be considered harmful to national security if disclosed to the named individual and to the public, more generally. Accordingly, the *Act* provided that in such cases the relevant information could be kept from the named individual, his or her counsel, and from the public. In reviewing the reasonableness of the security certificate's issue, the judge would have access only to the government's information, not to the named individual's reaction to it or to the named person's evidence raised in reaction to the government's information.

In *Charkaoui*, the Court examined whether the security certificate process ran afoul of principles of procedural fairness guaranteed by the *Charter*. In a unanimous decision written by Chief Justice Beverley McLachlin, the Court found two *Charter* breaches in the security certificate system. First, the Court held that the rules limiting the appellants' access to the information forming the basis for the government's position intruded too onerously on their right to a fair hearing protected by section 7 of the *Charter*. Someone in jeopardy at the hands of the state has a right to know the case against him or her and to be able to

1   Michael Ignatieff, *The Lesser Evil: Political Ethics in an Age of Terror* (Toronto: Penguin, 2004).

respond to that case. "Here the principle has not merely been limited; it has been effectively gutted," McLachlin wrote. "How can one meet a case one does not know?" Second, the *Act* made a distinction between permanent residents and foreign nationals in Canada. Permanent residents, if detained, were entitled to a mandatory review within 48 hours of their detention. Foreign nationals were subject to mandatory detention and their detention could not be reviewed until 120 days had elapsed from the judicial determination of the reasonableness of the certificate. The Court considered the more onerous treatment of foreign nationals to be arbitrary and thus contrary to the section 9 protection against arbitrary detention and against the section 10(*c*) right to have the validity of one's detention confirmed by way of *habeas corpus*.

Both breaches were found to be unjustifiable under section 1 analysis. While section 1, as a matter of course, applies to breaches of sections 9 and 10(*c*), it has been somewhat more controversial in respect to section 7 violations. In a sense, section 7 contains its own limiting clause. The provision guarantees the right to life, liberty, and security of the person and these can only be limited in accordance with the principles of fundamental justice. Can a limit on a section 7 right be contrary to the principles of fundamental justice as set out in section 7 and yet justified as a reasonable limitation under the terms of section 1? In *Re B.C. Motor Vehicle Act* (case 13), the Court was divided on the question. Justice Wilson, writing on her own behalf, suggested that if a limit on a section 7 right has been effected "through a violation of the principles of fundamental justice, the enquiry, in my opinion, ends there and the limit cannot be sustained under s. 1." Writing for the majority, Justice Lamer averred that section 1 "may, for reasons of administrative expediency, successfully come to the rescue of an otherwise violation of section 7, but only in cases arising out of exceptional conditions, such as natural disasters, the outbreak of war, epidemics, and the like." While the Court routinely undertakes a section 1 analysis following a finding that government action has violated section 7, a majority has not yet used section 1 to save such a violation.[2]

So it was here. In its application of the minimal-impairment branch of the *Oakes* test to the judicial hearing provisions of the *Immigration and Refugee Protection Act*, the Court referred to several other examples, both domestic and foreign, of procedures that have combined the safeguarding of national security with fair-hearing rights of persons alleged to have threatened it. The harsh *IRPA* regime was found not to constitute a minimal impairment of *Charter* rights. While the Court gave the government one year to devise a more *Charter*-friendly security certificate process, its section 1 analysis substantially set out the terms of such a process. The government, in October 2007, introduced legislation in Parliament that adopts the special advocate system used in the United Kingdom and suggested in this case by the Chief Justice as a possible way of meeting the minimal impairment requirement.

The Court was mindful of a public inquiry unfolding as the appellants' cases were winding through the judicial system. In 2002, while changing planes in the United States en route to Canada, Canadian citizen Maher Arar was detained and deported to Syria by American authorities, on the strength of RCMP information linking him to terrorist groups. Arar was tortured while in Syria and gave a false confession. Upon Arar's return to Canada in 2003, a commission of inquiry was created, which later found that RCMP information shared

---

2   Peter Hogg, *Constitutional Law of Canada*, 5th ed., vol. 2 (Toronto: Carswell, 2007) 156.

with American authorities, and likely forming the basis for Arar's deportation to
erroneous. In January 2007, Arar was offered an apology and compensation of
million by the Canadian government.

Arar's ordeal garnered special attention by the Court in *Charkaoui*. It appeared to influence the Court's decision. Would the Court have decided this case differently if timing and
political events were different? For example, what if a terrorist incident occurred in Canada
a short time before the hearing or the decision itself? The Court's authority depends on
continuing public confidence in its processes and its decision making. Decisions wildly out
of step with the public temper may reduce public confidence in the institution. That having
been said, the judicial function is premised on its insulation from intemperate public opinion.
It is instructive in this regard that in the wake of the 9/11 attacks, the Court was deliberating
on a case it heard earlier in 2001 concerning the constitutionality of the impending deportation of an alleged Tamil Tiger fundraiser and member. The appellant argued that he was
going to be deported to torture in Sri Lanka and that he had no access to the information
on the basis of which the government claimed the contrary. In circumstances similar to those
of the appellants in *Charkaoui*, he did not have the opportunity to respond to the government's case. The Court, in January 2002, ordered a new deportation hearing, giving little
hint of sensitivity to heightened public concern about terrorism and national security.[3] ～

Discussion Questions

1. What influence does the experience of other countries in implementing national
   security policy exert on the Supreme Court of Canada in *Charkaoui*?
2. In *Re B.C. Motor Vehicle Act* (1985), the Court considered the relationship between
   section 7 and section 1. How does that treatment compare to the Court's consideration of the same issue in this case?
3. Heightened national security concerns are either legitimate or not. Should the
   legitimacy of such concerns influence the courts' assessment of the constitutionality
   of policies limiting the rights of persons suspected of threatening national security?

---

3 *Suresh v. Canada (Minister of Citizenship and Immigration)*, [2002] 1 S.C.R. 3.

CHARKAOUI v. CANADA
(CITIZENSHIP AND IMMIGRATION)
2007 SCC 9, [2007] 1 S.C.R. 350

Hearing: June 13, 14, 15, 2006; Judgment: February 23, 2007.

Present: McLachlin C.J. and Bastarache, Binnie, LeBel, Deschamps, Fish, Abella, Charron, and Rothstein JJ.

Interveners: Attorney General of Ontario, Amnesty International, British Columbia Civil Liberties Association, Canadian Bar Association, Canadian Civil Liberties Association, Canadian Council for Refugees, African Canadian Legal Clinic, International Civil Liberties Monitoring Group, National Anti-Racism Council of Canada, Canadian Arab Federation, Canadian Council on American-Islamic Relations, Canadian Muslim Civil Liberties Association, Criminal Lawyers' Association (Ontario), Federation of Law Societies of Canada, University of Toronto, Faculty of Law—International Human Rights Clinic, Human Rights Watch.

The judgment of the Court was delivered by

THE CHIEF JUSTICE:

I. Introduction

[1] One of the most fundamental responsibilities of a government is to ensure the security of its citizens. This may require it to act on information that it cannot disclose and to detain people who threaten national security. Yet in a constitutional democracy, governments must act accountably and in conformity with the Constitution and the rights and liberties it guarantees. These two propositions describe a tension that lies at the heart of modern democratic governance. It is a tension that must be resolved in a way that respects the imperatives both of security and of accountable constitutional governance.

[2] In this case, we are confronted with a statute, the *Immigration and Refugee Protection Act*, S.C. 2001, c. 27 ("*IRPA*"), that attempts to resolve this tension in the immigration context by allowing the Minister of Citizenship and Immigration (the "Minister"), and the Minister of Public Safety and Emergency Preparedness (collectively "the ministers") to issue a certificate of inadmissibility leading to the detention of a permanent resident or foreign national deemed to be a threat to national security. The certificate and the detention are both subject to review by a judge, in a process that may deprive the person named in the certificate of some or all of the information on the basis of which the certificate was issued or the detention ordered. The question is whether the solution that Parliament has enacted conforms to the Constitution, and in particular the guarantees in the *Canadian Charter of Rights and Freedoms* that protect against unjus-

tifiable intrusions on liberty, equality and the freedom from arbitrary detention and from cruel and unusual treatment.

[3] I conclude that the *IRPA* unjustifiably violates s. 7 of the *Charter* by allowing the issuance of a certificate of inadmissibility based on secret material without providing for an independent agent at the stage of judicial review to better protect the named person's interests. I also conclude that some of the time limits in the provisions for continuing detention of a foreign national violate ss. 9 and 10(*c*) because they are arbitrary. I find that s. 12 has not been shown to be violated since a meaningful detention review process offers relief against the possibility of indefinite detention. Finally, I find that there is no breach of the s. 15 equality right.

II. Background

[4] The provisions of the *IRPA* at issue in this case, reproduced in the Appendix, are part of Canada's immigration law. Their purpose is to permit the removal of non-citizens living in Canada—permanent residents and foreign nationals—on various grounds, including connection with terrorist activities. The scheme permits deportation on the basis of confidential information that is not to be disclosed to the person named in the certificate or anyone acting on the person's behalf or in his or her interest. The scheme was meant to "facilitat[e] the early removal of persons who are inadmissible on serious grounds, including persons posing a threat to the security of Canada" (*Clause by Clause Analysis* (2001), at p. 72). In reality, however, it may also lead to long periods of incarceration.

[5] The *IRPA* requires the ministers to sign a certificate declaring that a foreign national or permanent resident is inadmissible to enter or remain in Canada on grounds of security, among others: s. 77. A judge of the Federal Court then reviews the certificate to determine whether it is reasonable: s. 80. If the state so requests, the review is conducted *in camera* and *ex parte*. The person named in the certificate has no right to see the material on the basis of which the certificate was issued. Non-sensitive material may be disclosed; sensitive or confidential material must not be disclosed if the government objects. The named person and his or her lawyer cannot see undisclosed material, although the ministers and the reviewing judge may rely on it. At the end of the day, the judge must provide the person with a summary of the case against him or her—a summary that does not disclose material that might compromise national security. If the judge determines that the certificate is reasonable, there is no appeal and no way to have the decision judicially reviewed: s. 80(3).

[6] The consequences of the issuance and confirmation of a certificate of inadmissibility vary, depending on whether the person is a permanent resident of Canada or a foreign national whose right to remain in Canada has not yet been

confirmed. Permanent residents who the ministers have reasonable grounds to believe are a danger to national security *may* be held in detention. In order to detain them, the ministers must issue a warrant stating that the person is a threat to national security or to another person, or is unlikely to appear at a proceeding or for removal. Foreign nationals, meanwhile, *must* be detained once a certificate is issued: under s. 82(2), the detention is automatic. While the detention of a permanent resident must be reviewed within 48 hours, a foreign national, on the other hand, must apply for review, but may not do so until 120 days after a judge of the Federal Court determines the certificate to be reasonable. In both cases, if the judge finds the certificate to be reasonable, it becomes a removal order. Such an order deprives permanent residents of their status; their detention is then subject to review on the same basis as that of other foreign nationals.

[7] The removal order cannot be appealed and may be immediately enforced, thus eliminating the requirement of holding or continuing an examination or an admissibility hearing: s. 81(*b*). The detainee, whether a permanent resident or a foreign national, may no longer apply for protection: s. 81(*c*). Additionally, a refugee or a protected person determined to be inadmissible on any of the grounds for a certificate loses the protection of the principle of non-refoulement under s. 115(1) if, in the opinion of the Minister, the person should not be allowed to remain in Canada on the basis of the nature and severity of acts committed or of danger to the security of Canada: s. 115(2). This means that he or she may, at least in theory, be deported to torture.

[8] A permanent resident detained under a certificate is entitled to a review of his or her detention every six months. Under s. 83(3), a judge must order the detention of a permanent resident to be continued if the judge is satisfied that the person continues to pose a danger to security or to the safety of another, or is unlikely to appear at a proceeding or for removal.

[9] The detention of foreign nationals, on the other hand, is mandatory. If a foreign national has not been removed within 120 days of the certificate being found reasonable by a judge, however, the judge may order the person released on appropriate conditions if "satisfied that the foreign national will not be removed from Canada within a reasonable time and that the release will not pose a danger to national security or to the safety of any person": s. 84(2). Even if released, the foreign national may be deported.

[10] Mr. Charkaoui is a permanent resident, while Messrs. Harkat and Almrei are foreign nationals who had been recognized as Convention refugees. All were living in Canada when they were arrested and detained. At the time of the decisions on appeal, all had been detained for some time—

since 2003, 2002 and 2001 respectively. In 2001, a judge of the Federal Court determined Mr. Almrei's certificate to be reasonable; another determined Mr. Harkat's certificate to be reasonable in 2005. The reasonableness of Mr. Charkaoui's certificate has yet to be determined. Messrs. Charkaoui and Harkat were released on conditions in 2005 and 2006 respectively, but Mr. Harkat has been advised that he will be deported to Algeria, which he is contesting in other proceedings. Mr. Almrei remains in detention. In all these cases, the detentions were based on allegations that the individuals constituted a threat to the security of Canada by reason of involvement in terrorist activities. In the course of their detentions, all three appellants challenged, unsuccessfully, the constitutionality of the *IRPA*'s certificate scheme and detention review process.

III. Issues

[11] The appellants argue that the *IRPA*'s certificate scheme under which their detentions were ordered is unconstitutional. They argue that it violates five provisions of the *Charter*: the s. 7 guarantee of life, liberty and security of the person; the s. 9 guarantee against arbitrary detention; the s. 10(*c*) guarantee of a prompt review of detention; the s. 12 guarantee against cruel and unusual treatment; and the s. 15 guarantee of equal protection and equal benefit of the law. . . .

A. Does the Procedure Under the IRPA for Determining the Reasonableness of the Certificate Infringe Section 7 of the Charter, and If So, Is the Infringement Justified Under Section 1 of the Charter?

1. *Is Section 7 of the Charter Engaged?*

. . . [18] In determining whether s. 7 applies, we must look at the interests at stake rather than the legal label attached to the impugned legislation. As Professor Hamish Stewart writes:

> Many of the principles of fundamental justice were developed in criminal cases, but their application is not restricted to criminal cases: they apply whenever one of the three protected interests is engaged. Put another way, the principles of fundamental justice apply in *criminal* proceedings, not because they are criminal proceedings, but because the liberty interest is always engaged in criminal proceedings. [Emphasis in original.]

> ("Is Indefinite Detention of Terrorist Suspects Really Constitutional?" (2005), 54 *U.N.B.L.J.* 235, at p. 242)

I conclude that the appellants' challenges to the fairness of the process leading to possible deportation and the loss of liberty associated with detention raise important issues of liberty and security, and that s. 7 of the *Charter* is engaged.

2. How Do Security Considerations Affect the Section 7 Analysis?

[19] Section 7 of the *Charter* requires that laws that interfere with life, liberty and security of the person conform to the principles of fundamental justice—the basic principles that underlie our notions of justice and fair process. These principles include a guarantee of procedural fairness, having regard to the circumstances and consequences of the intrusion on life, liberty or security....

[22] The question at the s. 7 stage is whether the principles of fundamental justice relevant to the case have been observed in substance, having regard to the context and the seriousness of the violation. The issue is whether the process is fundamentally unfair to the affected person. If so, the deprivation of life, liberty or security of the person simply does not conform to the requirements of s. 7. The inquiry then shifts to s. 1 of the *Charter*, at which point the government has an opportunity to establish that the flawed process is nevertheless justified having regard, notably, to the public interest.

[23] It follows that while administrative constraints associated with the context of national security may inform the analysis on whether a particular process is fundamentally unfair, security concerns cannot be used to excuse procedures that do not conform to fundamental justice at the s. 7 stage of the analysis. If the context makes it impossible to adhere to the principles of fundamental justice in their usual form, adequate substitutes may be found. But the principles must be respected to pass the hurdle of s. 7. That is the bottom line.

[24] In the instant case, the context is the detention, incidental to their removal or an attempt to remove them from the country, of permanent residents and foreign nationals who the ministers conclude pose a threat to national security. This context may impose certain administrative constraints that may be properly considered at the s. 7 stage. Full disclosure of the information relied on may not be possible. The executive branch of government may be required to act quickly, without recourse, at least in the first instance, to the judicial procedures normally required for the deprivation of liberty or security of the person.

[25] At the same time, it is a context that may have important, indeed chilling, consequences for the detainee. The seriousness of the individual interests at stake forms part of the contextual analysis. As this Court stated in *Suresh*, "[t]he greater the effect on the life of the individual by the decision, the greater the need for procedural protections to meet the common law duty of fairness and the requirements of fundamental justice under s. 7 of the *Charter*" (para. 118). Thus, "factual situations which are closer or analogous to criminal proceedings will merit greater vigilance by the courts": *Dehghani v. Canada (Minister of Employment and Immigration)*, [1993] 1 S.C.R. 1053, at p. 1077, *per* Iacobucci J.

[26] The potential consequences of deportation combined with allegations of terrorism have been under a harsh spotlight due to the recent report of the Commission of Inquiry into the Actions of Canadian Officials in Relation to Maher Arar. Mr. Arar, a Canadian citizen born in Syria, was detained by American officials and deported to Syria. The report concludes that it is "very likely that, in making the decisions to detain and remove Mr. Arar to Syria, the U.S. authorities relied on information about Mr. Arar provided by the RCMP," including unfounded suspicions linking Mr. Arar to terrorist groups: *Report of the Events Relating to Maher Arar: Analysis and Recommendations* (2006) ("Arar Inquiry"), at p. 30. In Syria, Mr. Arar was tortured and detained under inhumane conditions for over 11 months. In his report, Commissioner O'Connor recommends enhanced review and accountability mechanisms for agencies dealing with national security, including not only the Royal Canadian Mounted Police, but also Citizenship and Immigration Canada and the Canada Border Services Agency. He notes that these immigration-related institutions can have an important impact on individual rights but that there is a lack of transparency surrounding their activities because their activities often involve sensitive national security information that cannot be disclosed to the public: *A New Review Mechanism for the RCMP's National Security Activities* (2006), at pp. 562-65. Moreover, the sensitive nature of security information means that investigations lead to fewer prosecutions. This, in turn, restricts the ability of courts to guarantee individual rights: "Unless charges are laid, ... the choice of investigative targets, methods of information collection and exchange, and means of investigation generally will not be subject to judicial scrutiny, media coverage or public debate" (p. 439).

[27] The procedures required to conform to the principles of fundamental justice must reflect the exigencies of the security context. Yet they cannot be permitted to erode the essence of s. 7. The principles of fundamental justice cannot be reduced to the point where they cease to provide the protection of due process that lies at the heart of s. 7 of the *Charter*. The protection may not be as complete as in a case where national security constraints do not operate. But to satisfy s. 7, meaningful and substantial protection there must be.

3. Relevant Principles of Fundamental Justice

[28] The overarching principle of fundamental justice that applies here is this: before the state can detain people for significant periods of time, it must accord them a fair judicial process....

[29] This basic principle has a number of facets. It comprises the right to a *hearing*. It requires that the hearing be *before an independent and impartial magistrate*. It demands a *decision by the magistrate on the facts and the law*. And it entails

the *right to know the case put against one,* and the *right to answer that case.* Precisely how these requirements are met will vary with the context. But for s. 7 to be satisfied, each of them must be met in substance.

[30] The *IRPA* process includes a hearing. The process consists of two phases, one executive and one judicial. There is no hearing at the executive phase that results in issuance of the certificate. However, this is followed by a review before a judge, where the named person is afforded a hearing. Thus, the first requirement, that of a hearing, is met.

[31] Questions arise, however, on the other requirements, namely: that the judge be independent and impartial; that the judge make a judicial decision based on the facts and the law; and finally, that the named person be afforded an opportunity to meet the case put against him or her by being informed of that case and being allowed to question or counter it. I conclude that the *IRPA* scheme meets the first requirement of independence and impartiality, but fails to satisfy the second and third requirements, which are interrelated here.

4. Is the Judge Independent and Impartial?

[32] Although the scope of the required hearing can vary according to context (*Baker v. Canada (Minister of Citizenship and Immigration),* [1999] 2 S.C.R. 817), a hearing must include "[a]n independent judicial phase and an impartial judge" (*Ferras,* at para. 25). This requirement is also consistent with the unwritten constitutional principle of judicial independence: *Reference re Remuneration of Judges of the Provincial Court of Prince Edward Island,* [1997] 3 S.C.R. 3. It has also been called "the cornerstone of the common law duty of procedural fairness" (*Application under s. 83.28 of the Criminal Code (Re),* [2004] 2 S.C.R. 248, 2004 SCC 42 (*"Re Bagri"*), at para. 81), and is necessary in order to ensure judicial impartiality: *R. v. Lippé,* [1991] 2 S.C.R. 114, at p. 139. It is not enough that the judge in fact be independent and impartial; fundamental justice requires that the judge also appear to be independent and impartial. This flows from the fact that judicial independence has two facets: actual independence and perceived independence (*Valente v. The Queen,* [1985] 2 S.C.R. 673, at p. 689).

[33] The *IRPA* scheme provides for the certificate issued by the ministers to be reviewed by a "designated judge," a judge of the Federal Court of Canada. The question here is whether, from an institutional perspective, the role assigned to designated judges under the *IRPA* leads to a perception that independence and impartiality are compromised.

[34] The designated judge has been aptly described as the "cornerstone of the procedure established by Parliament" in the *IRPA* (*Charkaoui (Re),* [2004] 3 F.C.R. 32, 2003 FC 1419, at para. 120, *per* Noël J.). The judge is the sole avenue of review

for the named person and the only person capable of providing the essential judicial component of the process.

[35] When reviewing the certificate, the judge sees all the material relied on by the government. But if the government claims confidentiality for certain material, the judge cannot share this material with the named person. The judge must make his or her decision without hearing any objections the named person might be able to make, were he or she granted access to the whole of the record. Part of the hearing may be held *in camera,* with only the judge and the government lawyers in the room. The named person is not there. His or her lawyer is not there. There is no one to speak for the person or to test the evidence put against him or her.

[36] These circumstances may give rise to a perception that the designated judge under the *IRPA* may not be entirely independent and impartial as between the state and the person named in the certificate....

[37] Three related concerns arise with respect to independence and impartiality. First is the concern that the *IRPA* may be perceived to deprive the judge of his or her independent judicial role and co-opt the judge as an agent of the executive branch of government. Second is the concern that the designated judge functions as an investigative officer rather than a judge. Third is the concern that the judge, whose role includes compensating for the fact that the named person may not have access to material and may not be present at the hearing, will become associated with this person's case.

[38] The first concern is linked to the degree of deference that the judge accords to the ministers' conclusion that the facts supported the issuance of a certificate and the detention of the named person. Judges working under the process have eschewed an overly deferential approach, insisting instead on a searching examination of the reasonableness of the certificate on the material placed before them....

[42] I conclude that a non-deferential role for the designated judge goes some distance toward alleviating the first concern, that the judge will be perceived to be in the camp of the government.

[43] The second concern is that the judge may be seen to function more as an investigator than as an independent and impartial adjudicator. The law is clear that the principles of fundamental justice are breached if a judge is reduced to an executive, investigative function. At the same time, the mere fact that a judge is required to assist in an investigative activity does not deprive the judge of the requisite independence....

[44] The *IRPA* provisions before the Court ... preserve the essential elements of the judicial role....

[45] The third concern is that the judge's role as sole protector of the named person's interest may associate the judge, in fact or perception, with that interest. A judge who is obliged

to take on a "defence" role in the absence of counsel may unconsciously become associated with that camp: *R. v. Taubler* (1987), 20 O.A.C. 64, at p. 71; *R. v. Turlon* (1989), 49 C.C.C. (3d) 186 (Ont. C.A.), at p. 191. This concern must be balanced against the opposite concern that the judge may appear to be part of the government scheme and hence in the government's camp. The critical consideration, however, is that the *IRPA* permits—indeed requires—the judge to conduct the review in an independent and judicial fashion. Provided the judge does so, the scheme cannot be condemned on the ground that he or she is, in fact or perception, in the named person's camp.

[46] I conclude that, on its face, the *IRPA* process is designed to preserve the independence and impartiality of the designated judge, as required by s. 7. Properly followed by judges committed to a searching review, it cannot be said to compromise the perceived independence and impartiality of the designated judge.

[47] I note that this conclusion conclusively rebuts the appellant Charkaoui's contention that the *IRPA* breaches the unwritten constitutional principle of judicial independence affirmed in *Provincial Court Judges' Assn. of New Brunswick v. New Brunswick (Minister of Justice)*, [2005] 2 S.C.R. 286, 2005 SCC 44.

5. Is the Decision Based on the Facts and the Law?

[48] To comply with s. 7 of the *Charter*, the magistrate must make a decision based on the facts and the law. In the extradition context, the principles of fundamental justice have been held to require, "at a minimum, a meaningful judicial assessment of the case on the basis of the evidence and the law. A judge considers the respective rights of the litigants or parties and makes findings of fact on the basis of evidence and applies the law to those findings. Both facts and law must be considered for a true adjudication. Since *Bonham's Case* [(1610), 8 Co. Rep. 113b, 77 E.R. 646], the essence of a judicial hearing has been the treatment of facts revealed by the evidence in consideration of the substantive rights of the parties as set down by law" (*Ferras*, at para. 25). The individual and societal interests at stake in the certificate of inadmissibility context suggest similar requirements.

[49] The *IRPA* process at issue seeks to meet this requirement by placing material before the judge for evaluation. As a practical matter, most if not all of the material that the judge considers is produced by the government and can be vetted for reliability and sufficiency only by the judge. The normal standards used to ensure the reliability of evidence in court do not apply: s. 78(*j*). The named person may be shown little or none of the material relied on by the ministers and the judge, and may thus not be in a position to know or challenge the case against him or her. It follows that the judge's decision,

while based on the evidence before him or her, may not be based on all of the evidence available.

[50] There are two types of judicial systems, and they ensure that the full case is placed before the judge in two different ways. In inquisitorial systems, as in Continental Europe, the judge takes charge of the gathering of evidence in an independent and impartial way. By contrast, an adversarial system, which is the norm in Canada, relies on the parties—who are entitled to disclosure of the case to meet, and to full participation in open proceedings—to produce the relevant evidence. The designated judge under the *IRPA* does not possess the full and independent powers to gather evidence that exist in the inquisitorial process. At the same time, the named person is not given the disclosure and the right to participate in the proceedings that characterize the adversarial process. The result is a concern that the designated judge, despite his or her best efforts to get all the relevant evidence, may be obliged—perhaps unknowingly—to make the required decision based on only part of the relevant evidence. . . .

[51] Judges of the Federal Court have worked assiduously to overcome the difficulties inherent in the role the *IRPA* has assigned to them. To their credit, they have adopted a pseudo-inquisitorial role and sought to seriously test the protected documentation and information. But the role remains *pseudo-inquisitorial*. The judge is not afforded the power to independently investigate all relevant facts that true inquisitorial judges enjoy. At the same time, since the named person is not given a full picture of the case to meet, the judge cannot rely on the parties to present missing evidence. The result is that, at the end of the day, one cannot be sure that the judge has been exposed to the whole factual picture.

[52] Similar concerns arise with respect to the requirement that the decision be based on the law. Without knowledge of the information put against him or her, the named person may not be in a position to raise legal objections relating to the evidence, or to develop legal arguments based on the evidence. The named person is, to be sure, permitted to make legal representations. But without disclosure and full participation throughout the process, he or she may not be in a position to put forward a full legal argument.

6. Is the "Case to Meet" Principle Satisfied?

[53] Last but not least, a fair hearing requires that the affected person be informed of the case against him or her, and be permitted to respond to that case. This right is well established in immigration law. . . .

[54] Under the *IRPA*'s certificate scheme, the named person may be deprived of access to some or all of the information put against him or her, which would deny the person the ability to know the case to meet. Without this information,

the named person may not be in a position to contradict errors, identify omissions, challenge the credibility of informants or refute false allegations. This problem is serious in itself. It also underlies the concerns, discussed above, about the independence and impartiality of the designated judge, and the ability of the judge to make a decision based on the facts and law.

[55] Confidentiality is a constant preoccupation of the certificate scheme. The judge "shall ensure" the confidentiality of the information on which the certificate is based and of any other evidence if, in the opinion of the judge, disclosure would be injurious to national security or to the safety of any person: s. 78(*b*). At the request of either minister "at any time during the proceedings," the judge "shall hear" information or evidence in the absence of the named person and his or her counsel if, in the opinion of the judge, its disclosure would be injurious to national security or to the safety of any person: s. 78(*e*). The judge "shall provide" the named person with a summary of information that enables him or her to be reasonably informed of the circumstances giving rise to the certificate, but the summary cannot include anything that would, in the opinion of the judge, be injurious to national security or to the safety of any person: s. 78(*h*). Ultimately, the judge may have to consider information that is not included in the summary: s. 78(*g*). In the result, the judge may be required to decide the case, wholly or in part, on the basis of information that the named person and his or her counsel never see. The named person may know nothing of the case to meet, and although technically afforded an opportunity to be heard, may be left in a position of having no idea as to what needs to be said.

[56] The same concerns arise with respect to the detention review process under ss. 83 and 84 of the *IRPA*. Section 78 applies to detention reviews under s. 83, and it has been found to apply to detention reviews under s. 84(2): *Almrei v. Canada (Minister of Citizenship and Immigration)*, [2005] 3 F.C.R. 142, 2005 FCA 54, at paras. 71-72.

[57] The right to know the case to be met is not absolute. Canadian statutes sometimes provide for *ex parte* or *in camera* hearings, in which judges must decide important issues after hearing from only one side. In *Rodgers*, the majority of this Court declined to recognize notice and participation as invariable constitutional norms, emphasizing a context-sensitive approach to procedural fairness. . . .

[58] More particularly, the Court has repeatedly recognized that national security considerations can limit the extent of disclosure of information to the affected individual. In *Chiarelli*, this Court found that the Security Intelligence Review Committee could, in investigating certificates under the former *Immigration Act, 1976*, S.C. 1976-77, c. 52 (later R.S.C. 1985, c. I-2), refuse to disclose details of investigation techniques and police sources. The context for elucidating the principles of fundamental justice in that case included the state's "interest in effectively conducting national security and criminal intelligence investigations and in protecting police sources" (p. 744). In *Suresh*, this Court held that a refugee facing the possibility of deportation to torture was entitled to disclosure of all the information on which the Minister was basing his or her decision, "[s]ubject to privilege or similar valid reasons for reduced disclosure, such as safeguarding confidential public security documents" (para. 122). And, in *Ruby v. Canada (Solicitor General)*, [2002] 4 S.C.R. 3, 2002 SCC 75, the Court upheld the section of the *Privacy Act*, R.S.C. 1985, c. P-21, that mandates *in camera* and *ex parte* proceedings where the government claims an exemption from disclosure on grounds of national security or maintenance of foreign confidences. The Court made clear that these societal concerns formed part of the relevant context for determining the scope of the applicable principles of fundamental justice (paras. 38-44). . . .

[61] In the context of national security, non-disclosure, which may be extensive, coupled with the grave intrusions on liberty imposed on a detainee, makes it difficult, if not impossible, to find substitute procedures that will satisfy s. 7. Fundamental justice requires substantial compliance with the venerated principle that a person whose liberty is in jeopardy must be given an opportunity to know the case to meet, and an opportunity to meet the case. Yet the imperative of the protection of society may preclude this. Information may be obtained from other countries or from informers on condition that it not be disclosed. Or it may simply be so critical that it cannot be disclosed without risking public security. This is a reality of our modern world. If s. 7 is to be satisfied, either the person must be given the necessary information, or a substantial substitute for that information must be found. Neither is the case here.

[62] The only protection the *IRPA* accords the named person is a review by a designated judge to determine whether the certificate is reasonable. The ministers argue that this is adequate in that it maintains a "delicate balance" between the right to a fair hearing and the need to protect confidential security intelligence information. The appellants, on the other hand, argue that the judge's efforts, however conscientious, cannot provide an effective substitute for informed participation.

[63] I agree with the appellants. The issue at the s. 7 stage, as discussed above, is not whether the government has struck the right balance between the need for security and individual liberties; that is the issue at the stage of s. 1 justification of an established limitation on a *Charter* right. The question at the s. 7 stage is whether the basic requirements of procedural

justice have been met, either in the usual way or in an alternative fashion appropriate to the context, having regard to the government's objective and the interests of the person affected. The fairness of the *IRPA* procedure rests entirely on the shoulders of the designated judge. Those shoulders cannot by themselves bear the heavy burden of assuring, in fact and appearance, that the decision on the reasonableness of the certificate is impartial, is based on a full view of the facts and law, and reflects the named person's knowledge of the case to meet. The judge, working under the constraints imposed by the *IRPA*, simply cannot fill the vacuum left by the removal of the traditional guarantees of a fair hearing. The judge sees only what the ministers put before him or her. The judge, knowing nothing else about the case, is not in a position to identify errors, find omissions or assess the credibility and truthfulness of the information in the way the named person would be. Although the judge may ask questions of the named person when the hearing is reopened, the judge is prevented from asking questions that might disclose the protected information. Likewise, since the named person does not know what has been put against him or her, he or she does not know what the designated judge needs to hear. If the judge cannot provide the named person with a summary of the information that is sufficient to enable the person to know the case to meet, then the judge cannot be satisfied that the information before him or her is sufficient or reliable. Despite the judge's best efforts to question the government's witnesses and scrutinize the documentary evidence, he or she is placed in the situation of asking questions and ultimately deciding the issues on the basis of incomplete and potentially unreliable information.

[64] The judge is not helpless; he or she can note contradictions between documents, insist that there be at least some evidence on the critical points, and make limited inferences on the value and credibility of the information from its source. Nevertheless, the judge's activity on behalf of the named person is confined to what is presented by the ministers. The judge is therefore not in a position to compensate for the lack of informed scrutiny, challenge and counter-evidence that a person familiar with the case could bring. Such scrutiny is the whole point of the principle that a person whose liberty is in jeopardy must know the case to meet. Here that principle has not merely been limited; it has been effectively gutted. How can one meet a case one does not know? ...

8. Is the Limit Justified Under Section 1 of the Charter?

... [68] The protection of Canada's national security and related intelligence sources undoubtedly constitutes a pressing and substantial objective. Moreover, the *IRPA*'s provisions regarding the non-disclosure of evidence at certificate hearings are rationally connected to this objective. ...

[69] The realities that confront modern governments faced with the challenge of terrorism are stark. In the interest of security, it may be necessary to detain persons deemed to pose a threat. At the same time, security concerns may preclude disclosure of the evidence on which the detention is based. But these tensions are not new. As we shall see, Canada has already devised processes that go further in preserving s. 7 rights while protecting sensitive information; until recently, one of these solutions was applicable in the security certificate context. Nor are these tensions unique to Canada: in the specific context of anti-terrorism legislation, the United Kingdom uses special counsel to provide a measure of protection to the detained person's interests, while preserving the confidentiality of information that must be kept secret. These alternatives suggest that the *IRPA* regime, which places on the judge the entire burden of protecting the person's interest, does not minimally impair the rights of non-citizens, and hence cannot be saved under s. 1 of the *Charter*.

(a) Less Intrusive Alternatives

[70] This is not the first time Canada has had to reconcile the demands of national security with the procedural rights guaranteed by the *Charter*. In a number of legal contexts, Canadian government institutions have found ways to protect sensitive information while treating individuals fairly. In some situations, the solution has involved the use of special counsel, in a manner closely approximating an adversarial process.

[71] The Security Intelligence Review Committee ("SIRC") is an independent review body that monitors the activities of the Canadian Security Intelligence Service ("CSIS"). Established in 1984 under the *Canadian Security Intelligence Service Act*, S.C. 1984, c. 21 (now R.S.C. 1985, c. C-23), SIRC is composed of three to five members of the Privy Council who are not currently serving in Parliament. Under the former *Immigration Act*, SIRC had the power to vet findings of inadmissibility based on alleged threats to national security; a ministerial certificate could not be issued without a SIRC investigation. If the Minister of Employment and Immigration and the Solicitor General were of the opinion that a non-citizen was inadmissible due to involvement in organized crime, espionage, subversion, acts of violence, etc., they were first obliged to make a report to SIRC: *Immigration Act*, s. 39(2). SIRC would then investigate the grounds for the report, providing the affected person with "a statement summarizing such information available to it as will enable the person to be as fully informed as possible of the circumstances giving rise to the report": s. 39(6). After completing its investigation, SIRC would send a report to the Governor in Council containing its recommendation as to whether a security certificate should be issued: s. 39(9). A copy of the same report

would be provided to the non-citizen: s. 39(10). If the Governor in Council was satisfied that the non-citizen was inadmissible on appropriate grounds, he or she could then direct the Minister of Employment and Immigration to issue a security certificate: s. 40(1).

[72] Empowered to develop its own investigative procedures, SIRC established a formal adversarial process, with "a court-like hearing room" and "procedures that mirrored judicial proceedings as much as possible." The process also included an independent panel of lawyers with security clearances to act as counsel to SIRC (M. Rankin, "The Security Intelligence Review Committee: Reconciling National Security with Procedural Fairness" (1990), 3 *C.J.A.L.P.* 173, at p. 179).

[73] A SIRC member presiding at a hearing had the discretion to balance national security against procedural fairness in determining how much information could be disclosed to the affected person. The non-citizen and his or her counsel would normally be present in the hearing room, except when sensitive national security evidence was tendered. (The presiding SIRC member would decide whether to exclude the non-citizen during certain testimony.) At such a juncture, independent, security-cleared SIRC counsel would act on behalf of the non-citizen. The SIRC counsel were instructed to cross-examine witnesses for CSIS "with as much vigour as one would expect from the complainant's counsel" (Rankin, at p. 184; SIRC *Annual Report 1988-1989* (1989) ("SIRC *Annual Report*"), at p. 64). At the end of this *ex parte* portion of the hearing, the excluded person would be brought back into the room and provided with a summary, which would include "the gist of the evidence, without disclosing the national security information" (SIRC *Annual Report*, at p. 64). The SIRC counsel would negotiate the contents of the summary with CSIS, under the supervision of the presiding SIRC member (*ibid.*). The affected person and his or her counsel would then be allowed to ask their own questions, and to cross-examine on the basis of the summary (Rankin, at p. 184).

[74] In the words of Professor Rankin, SIRC's procedures represented "an attempt to preserve the best features of the adversarial process with its insistence on vigorous cross-examination, but not to run afoul of the requirements of national security" (p. 185). These procedures illustrate how special counsel can provide not only an effective substitute for informed participation, but can also help bolster actual informed participation by the affected person. Since the special counsel had a role in determining how much information would be included in the summary, disclosure was presumably more complete than would otherwise have been the case. Sensitive national security information was still protected, but the executive was required to justify the breadth of this protection.

[75] In 1988 Parliament added s. 40.1 to the *Immigration Act* to empower the Minister and the Solicitor General to issue security certificates in respect of foreign nationals. Section 40.1 effectively bypassed the SIRC investigation process where foreign nationals were concerned, instead referring the certificate to a designated judge of the Federal Court for subsequent review. Security certificates in respect of permanent residents remained subject to SIRC scrutiny until 2002, when Parliament repealed the *Immigration Act* and replaced it with the *IRPA*.

[76] Certain elements of SIRC process may be inappropriate to the context of terrorism. Where there is a risk of catastrophic acts of violence, it would be foolhardy to require a lengthy review process *before* a certificate could be issued. But it was not suggested before this Court that SIRC's special counsel system had not functioned well in connection with the review of certificates under the *Immigration Act*, nor was any explanation given for why, under the new system for vetting certificates and reviewing detentions, a special counsel process had not been retained.

[77] The SIRC process is not the only example of the Canadian legal system striking a better balance between the protection of sensitive information and the procedural rights of individuals. A current example is found in the *Canada Evidence Act*, R.S.C. 1985, c. C-5 ("*CEA*"), which permits the government to object to the disclosure of information on grounds of public interest, in proceedings to which the Act applies: ss. 37 to 39. Under the recent amendments to the *CEA* set out in the *Anti-terrorism Act*, S.C. 2001, c. 41, a participant in a proceeding who is required to disclose or expects to disclose potentially injurious or sensitive information, or who believes that such information might be disclosed, must notify the Attorney General about the potential disclosure, and the Attorney General may then apply to the Federal Court for an order prohibiting the disclosure of the information: ss. 38.01, 38.02, 38.04. The judge enjoys considerable discretion in deciding whether the information should be disclosed. If the judge concludes that disclosure of the information would be injurious to international relations, national defence or national security, but that the public interest in disclosure outweighs in importance the public interest in non-disclosure, the judge may order the disclosure of all or part of the information, on such conditions as he or she sees fit. No similar residual discretion exists under the *IRPA*, which requires judges not to disclose information the disclosure of which would be injurious to national security or to the safety of any person. Moreover, the *CEA* makes no provision for the use of information that has not been disclosed. While the *CEA* does not address the same problems as the *IRPA*, and hence is of limited assistance here, it illustrates Parliament's concern under other legislation for striking a sensitive balance between

the need for protection of confidential information and the rights of the individual.

[78] Crown and defence counsel in the recent Air India trial (*R. v. Malik*, [2005] B.C.J. No. 521 (QL), 2005 BCSC 350) were faced with the task of managing security and intelligence information and attempting to protect procedural fairness. The Crown was in possession of the fruits of a 17-year-long investigation into the terrorist bombing of a passenger aircraft and a related explosion in Narita, Japan. It withheld material on the basis of relevance, national security privilege and litigation privilege. Crown and defence counsel came to an agreement under which defence counsel obtained consents from their clients to conduct a preliminary review of the withheld material, on written undertakings not to disclose the material to anyone, including the client. Disclosure in a specific trial, to a select group of counsel on undertakings, may not provide a working model for general deportation legislation that must deal with a wide variety of counsel in a host of cases. Nevertheless, the procedures adopted in the Air India trial suggest that a search should be made for a less intrusive solution than the one found in the *IRPA*.

[79] The Arar Inquiry provides another example of the use of special counsel in Canada. The Commission had to examine confidential information related to the investigation of terrorism plots while preserving Mr. Arar's and the public's interest in disclosure. The Commission was governed by the *CEA*. To help assess claims for confidentiality, the Commissioner was assisted by independent security-cleared legal counsel with a background in security and intelligence, whose role was to act as *amicus curiae* on confidentiality applications. The scheme's aim was to ensure that only information that was rightly subject to national security confidentiality was kept from public view. There is no indication that these procedures increased the risk of disclosure of protected information.

[80] Finally, I note the special advocate system employed by the Special Immigration Appeals Commission ("SIAC") in the United Kingdom. SIAC and the special advocate system were created in response to *Chahal v. United Kingdom*, 15 November 1996, *Reports of Judgments and Decisions* 1996-V, p. 1831, in which the European Court of Human Rights had held that the procedure then in place was inadequate. The court in *Chahal* commented favourably on the idea of security-cleared counsel instructed by the court, identifying it as being Canadian in origin (perhaps referring to the procedure developed by SIRC).

[81] The U.K.'s special advocate system resembles the Canadian SIRC model. Section 6(1) of the *Special Immigration Appeals Commission Act 1997* (U.K.), 1997, c. 68, states that the special advocate is appointed to "represent the interests of an appellant" in any proceedings before SIAC from

which the appellant and his or her legal representatives are excluded. Section 6(4), however, specifies that the special advocate "shall not be responsible to the person whose interests he is appointed to represent." Rule 35 of the *Special Immigration Appeals Commission (Procedure) Rules 2003*, S.I. 2003/1034, sets out the special advocate's three main functions: (1) to make submissions to the Commission at any hearings from which the appellant and the appellant's representatives are excluded; (2) to cross-examine witnesses at any such hearings; and (3) to make written submissions to the Commission. After seeing the protected information, the special advocate may not communicate with the appellant or the appellant's representative without authorization from the Commission: rule 36. If the special advocate requests such authorization, the Commission gives the Secretary of State an opportunity to object to the proposed communication before deciding whether to authorize it: rule 38.

[82] The use of special advocates has received widespread support in Canadian academic commentary. Professor Roach, for example, criticizes the Court of Appeal's conclusion in *Charkaoui (Re)*, 2004 FCA 421, that such a measure is not constitutionally required:

> In my view, this approach was in error because *in camera* and *ex parte* hearings offend basic notions of a fair hearing and *special advocates constitute one example of an approach that is a more proportionate response to reconciling the need to keep some information secret and the need to ensure as much fairness and adversarial challenge as possible.* [Emphasis added.]

(K. Roach, "Ten Ways to Improve Canadian Anti-Terrorism Law" (2006), 51 *Crim. L.Q.* 102, at p. 120)

[83] This said, the U.K.'s special advocate system has also been criticized for not going far enough. In April 2005, the House of Commons Constitutional Affairs Committee published a report on the operation of SIAC and the use of special advocates (*The operation of the Special Immigration Appeals Commission (SIAC) and the use of Special Advocates*). The Committee listed three important disadvantages faced by special advocates: (1) once they have seen the confidential material, they cannot, subject to narrow exceptions, take instructions from the appellant or the appellant's counsel; (2) they lack the resources of an ordinary legal team, for the purpose of conducting in secret a full defence; and (3) they have no power to call witnesses (para. 52).

[84] Despite these difficulties, SIAC itself has commented favourably on the assistance provided by special advocates, stating that as a result of the "rigorous cross-examination" of the government's evidence by the special advocate, it was satisfied that the government's assertions were unsupported by the

evidence (*M. v. Secretary of State for the Home Department*, [2004] UKSIAC 17/2002 (BAILII), March 8, 2004, at para. 10). The England and Wales Court of Appeal upheld SIAC's decision: [2004] 2 All E.R. 863, [2004] EWCA Civ 324.

(b) The IRPA Scheme Does Not Minimally Impair the Named Person's Rights

[85] Parliament is not required to use the *perfect*, or least restrictive, alternative to achieve its objective: *R. v. Chaulk*, [1990] 3 S.C.R. 1303. However, bearing in mind the deference that is owed to Parliament in its legislative choices, the alternatives discussed demonstrate that the *IRPA* does not minimally impair the named person's rights.

[86] Under the *IRPA*, the government effectively decides what can be disclosed to the named person. Not only is the named person not shown the information and not permitted to participate in proceedings involving it, but no one but the judge may look at the information with a view to protecting the named person's interests. Why the drafters of the legislation did not provide for special counsel to objectively review the material with a view to protecting the named person's interest, as was formerly done for the review of security certificates by SIRC and is presently done in the United Kingdom, has not been explained. The special counsel system may not be perfect from the named person's perspective, given that special counsel cannot reveal confidential material. But, without compromising security, it better protects the named person's s. 7 interests.

[87] I conclude that the *IRPA*'s procedures for determining whether a certificate is reasonable and for detention review cannot be justified as minimal impairments of the individual's right to a judicial determination on the facts and the law and right to know and meet the case. Mechanisms developed in Canada and abroad illustrate that the government can do more to protect the individual while keeping critical information confidential than it has done in the *IRPA*. Precisely what more should be done is a matter for Parliament to decide. But it is clear that more must be done to meet the requirements of a free and democratic society.

B. Does the Detention of Permanent Residents or Foreign Nationals Under the IRPA Infringe Sections 7, 9, 10(c) or 12 of the Charter, and If So, Are the Infringements Justified Under Section 1 of the Charter?

1. Time Constraints on Review for Foreign Nationals: Breach of Section 9 or Section 10(c)?

[88] Section 9 of the *Charter* guarantees freedom from arbitrary detention. This guarantee expresses one of the most fundamental norms of the rule of law. The state may not detain arbitrarily, but only in accordance with the law. The appellant Mr. Almrei argues that detention under the *IRPA* is arbitrary with respect to foreign nationals, first because it permits their detention without warrant and without regard to their personal circumstances, and second because it prevents review until 120 days after the certificate is confirmed. In both respects, foreign nationals are treated differently than permanent residents. . . .

[The Court rejected the first argument.]

[91] The lack of review for foreign nationals until 120 days after the reasonableness of the certificate has been judicially determined violates the guarantee against arbitrary detention in s. 9 of the *Charter*, a guarantee which encompasses the right to prompt review of detention under s. 10(*c*) of the *Charter*. Permanent residents named in certificates are entitled to an automatic review within 48 hours. The same time frame for review of detention applies to both permanent residents and foreign nationals under s. 57 of the *IRPA*. And under the *Criminal Code*, a person who is arrested with or without a warrant is to be brought before a judge within 24 hours, or as soon as possible: s. 503(1). These provisions indicate the seriousness with which the deprivation of liberty is viewed, and offer guidance as to acceptable delays before this deprivation is reviewed.

[92] The government submits that the detention provisions, and more specifically the absence of review for foreign nationals until 120 days after the certificate has been determined to be reasonable, reflect its objective of creating a timely removal process for individuals thought to constitute a danger to national security, and asserts that when the provisions were drafted, it was thought that the removal process would be so fast that there would be no need for review. This is more an admission of the excessiveness of the 120-day period than a justification.

[93] It is clear that there may be a need for some flexibility regarding the period for which a suspected terrorist may be detained. Confronted with a terrorist threat, state officials may need to act immediately, in the absence of a fully documented case. It may take some time to verify and document the threat. Where state officials act expeditiously, the failure to meet an arbitrary target of a fixed number of hours should not mean the automatic release of the person, who may well be dangerous. However, this cannot justify the complete denial of a timely detention review. Permanent residents who pose a danger to national security are also meant to be removed expeditiously. If this objective can be pursued while providing permanent residents with a mandatory detention review within 48 hours, then how can a denial of review for foreign nationals for 120 days after the certificate is confirmed be considered a minimal impairment?

[94] I conclude that the lack of timely review of the detention of foreign nationals violates s. 9 and s. 10(*c*) and cannot be saved by s. 1.

2. Do Extended Periods of Detention Under the Scheme Violate Section 7 or the Section 12 Guarantee Against Cruel and Unusual Treatment?

[The appellants argued that the *IRPA*'s provisions governing detention fall afoul of the *Charter* right not to be subjected to cruel and unusual treatment or punishment. The Court rejected their argument, noting, first, that the section 12 bar is quite high. If a legislative scheme permits detainees to challenge their detention and have a realistic prospect of release upon satisfaction of reasonable conditions, detention is neither cruel nor unusual. Such is the case here. Second, the Court held that the *IRPA*, properly interpreted, provides sufficient safeguards against indefinite detention.]

[123] [T]he *IRPA*, interpreted in conformity with the *Charter*, permits robust ongoing judicial review of the continued need for and justice of the detainee's detention pending deportation. On this basis, I conclude that extended periods of detention pending deportation under the certificate provisions of the *IRPA* do not violate s. 7 or s. 12 of the *Charter*, provided that reviewing courts adhere to the guidelines set out above. Thus, the *IRPA* procedure itself is not unconstitutional on this ground. However, this does not preclude the possibility of a judge concluding at a certain point that a particular detention constitutes cruel and unusual treatment or is inconsistent with the principles of fundamental justice, and therefore infringes the *Charter* in a manner that is remediable under s. 24(1) of the *Charter*.

[124] These conclusions are consistent with English and American authority. Canada, it goes without saying, is not alone in facing the problem of detention in the immigration context in situations where deportation is difficult or impossible. Courts in the United Kingdom and the United States have suggested that detention in this context can be used only during the period where it is reasonably necessary for deportation purposes. . . .

[125] A case raising similar issues is the decision of the House of Lords in *A. v. Secretary of State for the Home Department*, [2005] 3 All E.R. 169, [2004] UKHL 56 ("*Re A*"). This was an appeal brought by nine foreign nationals who were suspected of involvement in terrorism, but were not charged with any crime. The United Kingdom government sought to deport them, but in most cases this was impossible due to a risk of torture. So most of the individuals were detained at Belmarsh Prison under s. 23 of the *Anti-terrorism, Crime and Security Act 2001* (U.K.), 2001, c. 24. This provision empowered the government to detain suspected international terrorists under the provisions governing detention pending deportation, despite the fact that removal from the United Kingdom was temporarily or indefinitely prevented, in derogation from art. 5 of the *European Convention on Human Rights*: see *Chahal*.

[126] The government claimed that this derogation was necessary to combat the national security threat posed by Al-Qaeda terrorists. The House of Lords, by a majority of 8 to 1, accepted that Al-Qaeda terrorism represented a serious threat to the life of the nation, but seven of the eight Lords who accepted this premise nevertheless concluded that s. 23 was not strictly required by the exigencies of the situation. These same seven Lords also concluded that s. 23 was incompatible with art. 14 of the *European Convention on Human Rights*, because of the way it discriminated between nationals and non-nationals. The derogation permitting permanent detention of non-nationals treated them more harshly than nationals. Absent the possibility of deportation, it lost its character as an immigration provision, and hence constituted unlawful discrimination.

[127] The finding in *Re A* of breach of the detention norms under the European Convention on Human Rights was predicated on the U.K. Act's authorization of permanent detention. The *IRPA*, unlike the U.K. legislation under consideration in *Re A*, does not authorize indefinite detention and, interpreted as suggested above, provides an effective review process that meets the requirements of Canadian law.

[128] The fairness of the detention review procedure arises as an independent issue. I concluded above that this procedure, like the certificate determination procedure, denies the right to a fair hearing and does so in a way that does not minimally impair the detainee's rights. For the reasons given earlier, Parliament must therefore revisit the provisions for detention review in order to meaningfully protect the procedural rights of detainees.

C. Do the Certificate and Detention Review Procedures Discriminate Between Citizens and Non-Citizens, Contrary to Section 15 of the Charter, and If So, Is the Discrimination Justified Under Section 1 of the Charter?

[The Court found that no breach of section 15 was established. There was no evidence that the appellants were detained for purposes unrelated to the goals of deportation undergirding the *IRPA*.]

D. Are the IRPA Certificate Provisions Inconsistent with the Constitutional Principle of the Rule of Law?

[The appellants argued that the *IRPA* bars an appeal from a judge's determination of the reasonableness of a security certificate, and that the law allows for a warrant for arrest issued by a member of the political executive or for arrest without a warrant. They argued that these provisions violate the constitutional principle of the rule of law. The Court dismissed the argument.]

IV. Conclusion

[138] The scheme set up under Division 9 of Part 1 of the *IRPA* suffers from two defects that are inconsistent with the *Charter*.

[139] The first is that s. 78(g) allows for the use of evidence that is never disclosed to the named person without providing adequate measures to compensate for this non-disclosure and the constitutional problems it causes. It is clear from approaches adopted in other democracies, and in Canada itself in other security situations, that solutions can be devised that protect confidential security information and at the same time are less intrusive on the person's rights. It follows that the *IRPA*'s procedure for the judicial confirmation of certificates and review of detention violates s. 7 of the *Charter* and has not been shown to be justified under s. 1 of the *Charter*. I would declare the procedure to be inconsistent with the *Charter*, and hence of no force or effect.

[140] However, in order to give Parliament time to amend the law, I would suspend this declaration for one year from the date of this judgment. If the government chooses to go forward with the proceedings to have the reasonableness of Mr. Charkaoui's certificate determined during the one-year suspension period, the existing process under the *IRPA* will apply. After one year, the certificates of Mr. Harkat and Mr. Almrei (and of any other individuals whose certificates have been deemed reasonable) will lose the "reasonable" status that has been conferred on them, and it will be open to them to apply to have the certificates quashed. If the government intends to employ a certificate after the one-year delay, it will need to seek a fresh determination of reasonableness under the new process devised by Parliament. Likewise, any detention review occurring after the delay will be subject to the new process.

[141] The second defect is found in s. 84(2) of the *IRPA*, which denies a prompt hearing to foreign nationals by imposing a 120-day embargo, after confirmation of the certificate, on applications for release. Counsel for the ministers submitted in oral argument that if this Court were to find that s. 84(2) violates the *Charter*, the appropriate remedy would be to strike s. 84(2) and read foreign nationals into s. 83. This is a good first step, but it does not provide a complete solution, since s. 83 deals with detention review only *until the certificate has been determined to be reasonable*, whereas s. 84(2) deals with detention review *after it has been determined to be reasonable*. Striking s. 84(2) would therefore leave no provision for review of detention of foreign nationals once the certificate has been deemed reasonable.

[142] Accordingly, I conclude that the appropriate remedy is to strike s. 84(2) as well as to read foreign nationals into s. 83 and to strike the words "until a determination is made under subsection 80(1)" from s. 83(2). . . .

PART SIX

Social and Economic Rights

21 Gosselin v. Quebec (Attorney General), 2002

Many who are skeptical about the benefits of the *Charter* question its relevance for facilitating greater social justice, such as improving the conditions of those who are most in need—the poor who lack adequate housing, food, and other basic necessities. Their skepticism arises from the rights tradition on which the *Charter* is based—one that allows individuals to invoke rights to constrain the state from interfering with their liberty, but does not generally recognize claims of rights that would compel the state to provide the conditions or resources necessary for those who are economically marginalized in society.

Gosselin v. Quebec (Attorney General) was the first decision where the Supreme Court was required to address the question whether government has a positive obligation under the *Charter* to ensure that individuals have adequate financial assistance for food, clothing, and housing. At issue was whether judicial review should consider if the level of social assistance provided by a province violates sections 7 and 15 of the *Charter*. The majority of the Court did not accept the argument that *Charter* rights are violated by the failure of government to provide adequate levels of social assistance. But the Court did not rule out the possibility that one day it might interpret the *Charter* in this manner.

In 1984, Quebec passed legislation that changed entitlements in its social assistance scheme in a manner that provided young people under 30 substantially lower benefits than those given to others, unless they agreed to participate in either a designated work activity or education program. Initially, the legislation was insulated from *Charter* review because it was subject to the notwithstanding clause. But this lapsed in 1987. The *Charter* claim was that, after the expiration of the notwithstanding clause in 1987, the legislation should be declared an unjustifiable restriction of the right to security of the person, since it had the effect of leaving those subject to the reduced levels of assistance in a position of abject poverty that threatened both their physical and psychological integrity. The requested remedy for this violation was reimbursement of all affected welfare recipients for the difference between what they actually received and what they would have received had they been 30 years of age or over for the period after the notwithstanding clause had lapsed, for a total of roughly $389 million plus interest.

The majority and minority disagreed sharply on how to interpret age-based distinctions in the *Charter*. The majority ruled that the objectives of the legislation are relevant when determining if an age-based distinction constitutes discrimination, whereas the minority indicated that, since age itself is an explicitly prohibited ground of discrimination, any consideration for legislative intent is more appropriately addressed within the context of section 1. But the more interesting issue was how the Court responded to the claim that the social assistance scheme violates section 7.

As will be remembered from the *B.C. Motor Vehicle Reference*,[1] the Court rejected the argument that section 7 should be interpreted with deference for the framers' intentions,

---

1   *Re B.C. Motor Vehicle Act*, [1985] 2 SCR 486.

which clearly supported the view that section 7 should have a procedural dimension only and should not authorize judges to evaluate the fairness or substance of legislation. Yet, at the same time, Justice Lamer (as he then was) suggested that the Court's decision to engage in a substantive interpretation of section 7 would be limited to the field of criminal law and legal rights, which were, as he stated, "the inherent domain of the judiciary." But it appears that the Court no longer feels bound by this earlier self-imposed constraint on how to interpret section 7. Although the majority of the Court in *Gosselin* concluded that there was "insufficient evidence" to support what it recognized as a "novel" interpretation of the *Charter*, it left open the possibility "that a positive obligation to sustain life, liberty, or security of the person may be made out in special circumstances," which it did not define. But two justices thought the case for a positive interpretation of section 7 had been made in this case. Justices Arbour and L'Heureux-Dubé found that the Quebec legislation violated section 7 in a manner not justified under section 1.

The Court was also seriously divided on how to characterize the benefits and effects of the workfare scheme in the legislation. The majority thought the legislative objective had been motivated by a genuine intent to improve the conditions of poor, young Quebecers, because it would provide them the remedial education and skills training they lacked, but which were necessary to eventually integrate into the workforce and become self-sufficient. As the majority opined: "[s]imply handing over a bigger welfare cheque would have done nothing to help welfare recipients under 30 escape from unemployment and its potentially devastating social and psychological consequences above and beyond the short-term loss of income." Thus, the legislative scheme "constituted an affirmation of young people's potential rather than a denial of their dignity." But the minority thought the objective of the legislation was seriously flawed. Justice Arbour held that "[t]he right to a minimum level of social assistance is intimately intertwined with considerations of one's basic health and . . . even one's survival." Thus, "[w]ithout the ability to secure the immediate needs of the present, the future is little more than a far-off possibility, remote both in perception and in reality." ∼

Discussion Questions

1. Are *Charter* skeptics persuasive in their argument that the *Charter* is of little assistance to those most in need?

2. What are the implications of the Court's apparent rejection of Justice Lamer's suggestion, in the *B.C. Motor Vehicle Reference*, that a substantive interpretation of section 7 would be limited to the field of criminal law and legal rights?

3. Is it appropriate for the Court to interpret the *Charter* in a manner that compels the state to provide the conditions or resources necessary for those who are economically marginalized in society?

GOSSELIN v. QUEBEC
(ATTORNEY GENERAL)
2002 SCC 84, [2002] 4 S.C.R. 429

Hearing: October 29, 2001; Judgment: December 19, 2002.

Present: McLachlin C.J. and L'Heureux-Dubé, Gonthier, Iacobucci, Major, Bastarache, Binnie, Arbour, and LeBel JJ.

Interveners: The Attorney General for Ontario, the Attorney General for New Brunswick, the Attorney General of British Columbia, the Attorney General for Alberta, Rights and Democracy (also known as International Centre for Human Rights and Democratic Development), Commission des droits de la personne et des droits de la jeunesse, the National Association of Women and the Law (NAWL), the Charter Committee on Poverty Issues (CCPI), and the Canadian Association of Statutory Human Rights Agencies (CASHRA).

[The Court divided on several issues. A 5-to-4 majority ruled no violation of equality had occurred, with the dissenting judges concluding that equality had been restricted in a manner not justified under section 1; a 7-to-2 majority ruled there was no violation of section 7, with the dissenting judges ruling that section 7 had been restricted and the violation could not be justified under section 1; and a 6-to-1 majority ruled that there was no violation of the *Quebec Charter*, with two judges indicating there was no need to determine the issue.]

The judgment of McLachlin C.J. and Gonthier, Iacobucci, Major, and Binnie JJ. was delivered by

THE CHIEF JUSTICE:

I. Introduction

[1] Louise Gosselin was born in 1959. She has led a difficult life, complicated by a struggle with psychological problems and drug and alcohol addictions. From time to time she has tried to work, attempting jobs such as cook, waitress, salesperson, and nurse's assistant, among many. But work would wear her down or cause her stress, and she would quit. For most of her adult life, Ms. Gosselin has received social assistance.

[2] In 1984, the Quebec government altered its existing social assistance scheme in an effort to encourage young people to get job training and join the labour force. Under the scheme, which has since been repealed, the base amount payable to welfare recipients under 30 was lower than the base amount payable to those 30 and over. The new feature was that, to receive an amount comparable to that received by older people, recipients under 30 had to participate in a designated work activity or education program.

[3] Ms. Gosselin contends that the lower base amount payable to people under 30 violates: (1) s. 15(1) of the *Canad-*

ian Charter of Rights and Freedoms ("*Canadian Charter*"), which guarantees equal treatment without discrimination based on grounds including age; (2) s. 7 of the *Canadian Charter*, which prevents the government from depriving individuals of liberty and security except in accordance with the principles of fundamental justice; and (3) s. 45 of the *Quebec Charter of Human Rights and Freedoms*, R.S.Q., c. C-12 ("*Quebec Charter*"). She further argues that neither of the alleged *Canadian Charter* violations can be demonstrably justified under s. 1.

[4] On this basis, Ms. Gosselin asks this Court to order the Quebec government to pay the difference between the lower and the higher base amounts to all the people who: (1) lived in Quebec and were between the ages of 18 and 30 at any time from 1985 to 1989; (2) received the lower base amount payable to those under 30; and (3) did not participate in the government programs, for whatever reason. On her submissions, this would mean ordering the government to pay almost $389 million in benefits *plus* the interest accrued since 1985. Ms. Gosselin claims this remedy on behalf of over 75 000 unnamed class members, none of whom came forward in support of her claim.

[5] In my view, the evidence fails to support Ms. Gosselin's claim on any of the asserted grounds. Accordingly, I would dismiss the appeal.

II. Facts and Decisions

[6] In 1984, in the face of alarming and growing unemployment among young adults, the Quebec legislature made substantial amendments to the *Social Aid Act*, R.S.Q., c. A-16, creating a new scheme—the scheme at issue in this litigation. Section 29(*a*) of the *Regulation respecting social aid*, R.R.Q. 1981, c. A-16, r. 1, made under the Act continued to cap the base amount of welfare payable to those under 30 at roughly one third of the base amount payable to those 30 and over. However, the 1984 scheme for the first time made it possible for people under 30 to increase their welfare payments, over and above the basic entitlement, to the same (or nearly the same) level as those in the 30-and-over group.

[7] The new scheme was based on the philosophy that the most effective way to encourage and enable young people to join the workforce was to make increased benefits conditional on participation in one of three programs: On-the-job Training, Community Work, or Remedial Education. Participating in either On-the-job Training or Community Work boosted the welfare payment to a person under 30 up to the base amount for those 30 and over; participating in Remedial Education brought an under-30 within $100 of the 30-and-over base amount. The 30-and-over base amount still represented only 55 percent of the poverty level for a single person. For example, in 1987, non-participating under-30s were entitled

to $170 per month, compared to $466 per month for welfare recipients 30 and over. According to Statistics Canada, the poverty level for a single person living in a large metropolitan area was $914 per month in 1987. Long-term dependence on welfare was neither socially desirable nor, realistically speaking, economically feasible. The Quebec scheme was designed to encourage under-30s to get training or basic education, helping them to find permanent employment and avoid developing a habit of relying on social assistance during these formative years.

[8] The government initially made available 30 000 places in the three training programs. The record indicates that the percentage of eligible under-30s who actually participated in the programs averaged around one-third, but it does not explain this participation rate. Although Ms. Gosselin filed a class action on behalf of over 75 000 individuals, she provided no direct evidence of any other young person's experience with the government programs. She alone provided first-hand evidence and testimony as a class member in this case, and she in fact participated in each of the Community Work, Remedial Education and On-the-job Training Programs at various times. She ended up dropping out of virtually every program she started, apparently because of her own personal problems and personality traits. The testimony from one social worker, particularly as his clinic was attached to a psychiatric hospital and therefore received a disproportionate number of welfare recipients who also had serious psychological problems, does not give us a better or more accurate picture of the situation of the other class members, or of the relationship between Ms. Gosselin's personal difficulties and the structure of the welfare program. . . .

III. Issues

[12] This case raises the important question of how to determine when the differential provision of government benefits crosses the line that divides appropriate tailoring in light of different groups' circumstances, and discrimination. To what extent does the *Canadian Charter* restrict a government's discretion to extend different kinds of help, and different levels of financial assistance, to different groups of welfare recipients? How much evidence is required to compel a government to retroactively reimburse tens of thousands of people for alleged shortfalls in their welfare payments, arising from a conditional benefits scheme? These issues have implications for the range of options available to governments throughout Canada in tailoring welfare programs to address the particular needs and circumstances of individuals requiring social assistance.

[13] The specific legal issues are found in the stated constitutional questions:

1. Did s. 29(*a*) of the *Regulation respecting social aid*, R.R.Q. 1981, c. A-16, r. 1, adopted under the *Social Aid Act*, R.S.Q., c. A-16, infringe s. 15(1) of the *Canadian Charter of Rights and Freedoms* on the ground that it established a discriminatory distinction based on age with respect to individuals, capable of working, aged 18 to 30 years?
2. If so, is the infringement justified in a free and democratic society under s. 1 of the *Canadian Charter of Rights and Freedoms*?
3. Did s. 29(*a*) of the *Regulation respecting social aid*, R.R.Q. 1981, c. A-16, r. 1, adopted under the *Social Aid Act*, R.S.Q., c. A-16, infringe s. 7 of the *Canadian Charter of Rights and Freedoms* on the ground that it deprived those to whom it applied of their right to security of the person contrary to the principles of fundamental justice?
4. If so, is the infringement justified in a free and democratic society under s. 1 of the *Canadian Charter of Rights and Freedoms*?

[14] A further issue is whether s. 29(*a*) of the Regulation violates s. 45 of the *Quebec Charter*, and if so, whether a remedy is available.

[15] A preliminary issue arises in connection with s. 33 of the *Canadian Charter*—the "notwithstanding clause." By virtue of *An Act respecting the Constitution Act, 1982*, R.S.Q., c. L-4.2, the Quebec legislature withdrew all Quebec laws from the *Canadian Charter* regime for five years from their inception. This means that the Act is immune from *Canadian Charter* scrutiny from June 23, 1982 to June 23, 1987, and the programs part of the scheme is immune from April 4, 1984 to April 4, 1989 (see *An Act to amend the Social Aid Act*, S.Q. 1984, c. 5, ss. 4 and 5). It could be argued, therefore, that the scheme is protected from *Canadian Charter* scrutiny on s. 7 or s. 15(1) grounds for the whole period *except* for the four months from April 4, 1989 to August 1, 1989. This raises the further question of whether evidence on the legislation's impact *outside* the four-month period subject to *Canadian Charter* scrutiny can be used to generate conclusions about compliance with the *Canadian Charter within* the four-month period. In view of my conclusion that the program is constitutional in any event, I need not resolve these issues.

IV. Analysis

. . . [28] The Regulation at issue made a distinction on the basis of an enumerated ground, age. People under 30 were subject to a different welfare regime than people 30 and over. The question is whether this distinction in purpose or effect resulted in substantive inequality contrary to s. 15(1)'s purpose of ensuring that governments treat all individuals as equally worthy of concern, respect, and consideration. More precisely, the question is whether a reasonable person in Ms. Gosselin's position would, having regard to all the circumstances and the context of the legislation, conclude that the Regulation in purpose or effect treated welfare recipients under 30 as less worthy of respect than those 30 and over, marginalizing them on the basis of their youth.

[29] To answer this question, we must consider the four factors set out in *Law* [*v. Canada (Minister of Employment and Immigration)*, [1999] 1 S.C.R. 497]. None of these factors is a prerequisite for finding discrimination, and not all factors will apply in every case. The list of factors is neither absolute nor exhaustive. In addition, the factors may overlap, since they are all designed to illuminate the relevant contextual considerations surrounding a challenged distinction. Nonetheless, the four factors provide a useful guide to evaluating an allegation of discrimination, and I will examine each of them in turn.

(a) Pre-existing Disadvantage

[30] A key marker of discrimination and denial of human dignity under s. 15(1) is whether the affected individual or group has suffered from "pre-existing disadvantage, vulnerability, stereotyping, or prejudice": *Law*, at para. 63.... The contextual factor of pre-existing disadvantage invites us to scrutinize group-based distinctions carefully to ensure that they are not based, either intentionally or unconsciously, on these kinds of unfounded generalizations and stereotypes.

[31] Many of the enumerated grounds correspond to historically disadvantaged groups. For example, it is clear that members of particular racial or religious groups should not be excluded from receiving public benefits on account of their race or religion. However, unlike race, religion, or gender, age is not strongly associated with discrimination and arbitrary denial of privilege. This does not mean that examples of age discrimination do not exist. But age-based distinctions are a common and necessary way of ordering our society. They do not automatically evoke a context of pre-existing disadvantage suggesting discrimination and marginalization under this first contextual factor, in the way that other enumerated or analogous grounds might.

[32] ... Concerns about age-based discrimination typically relate to discrimination against people of advanced age who are presumed to lack abilities that they may in fact possess....

[33] Both as a general matter, and based on the evidence and our understanding of society, young adults as a class simply do not seem especially vulnerable or undervalued. There is no reason to believe that individuals between ages 18 and 30 in Quebec are or were particularly susceptible to negative preconceptions. No evidence was adduced to this effect,

and I am unable to take judicial notice of such a counter-intuitive proposition....

[35] Given the lack of pre-existing disadvantage experienced by young adults, Ms. Gosselin attempts to shift the focus from age to welfare, arguing that *all* welfare recipients suffer from stereotyping and vulnerability. However, this argument does not assist her claim. The ground of discrimination upon which she founds her claim is *age*.... Re-defining the group as welfare recipients aged 18 to 30 does not help us answer that question, in particular because the 30-and-over group that Ms. Gosselin asks us to use as a basis of comparison also consists entirely of welfare recipients.

[36] I conclude that the appellant has not established that people aged 18 to 30 have suffered historical disadvantage on the basis of their age. There is nothing to suggest that people in this age group have historically been marginalized and treated as less worthy than older people.

(b) Relationship Between Grounds and the Claimant Group's Characteristics or Circumstances

[37] The second contextual factor we must consider in determining whether the distinction is discriminatory in the sense of denying human dignity and equal worth is the relationship between the ground of distinction (age) and the actual characteristics and circumstances of the claimant's group: *Law*, at para. 70. A law that is closely tailored to the reality of the affected group is unlikely to discriminate within the meaning of s. 15(1). By contrast, a law that imposes restrictions or denies benefits on account of presumed or unjustly attributed characteristics is likely to deny essential human worth and to be discriminatory. Both purpose and effect are relevant here, insofar as they would affect the perception of a reasonable person in the claimant's position: see *Law*, at para. 96.

[38] ... The evidence indicates that the purpose of the challenged distinction, far from being stereotypical or arbitrary, corresponded to the actual needs and circumstances of individuals under 30.... North America experienced a deep recession in the early 1980s, which hit Quebec hard and drove unemployment from a traditional rate hovering around 8 percent to a peak of 14.4 percent of the active population in 1982, and among the young from 6 percent (1966) to 23 percent. At the same time, the federal government tightened eligibility requirements for federal unemployment insurance benefits, and the number of young people entering the job market for the first time surged. These three events caused an unprecedented increase in the number of people capable of working who nevertheless ended up on the welfare rolls.

[39] The situation of young adults was particularly dire. The unemployment rate among young adults was far higher

than among the general population. People under 30, capable of working and without any dependants, made up a greater proportion of welfare recipients than ever before. Moreover, this group accounted for the largest—and steadily growing—proportion of *new entrants* into the welfare system: by 1983 fully two-thirds of new welfare recipients were under 30, and half were under the age of 23. In addition to coming onto the welfare rolls in ever greater numbers, younger individuals did so for increasingly lengthy periods of time. In 1975, 60 percent of welfare recipients under 30 not incapable of working left the welfare rolls within six months. By 1983, only 30 percent did so.

[40] Behind these statistics lay a complex picture. The "new economy" emerging in the 1980s offered diminishing prospects for unskilled or under-educated workers. At the same time, a disturbing trend persisted of young Quebecers dropping out of school and trying to join the workforce. The majority of unemployed youths in the early 1980s were school drop-outs. Unemployed youths were, on average, significantly less educated than the general population, and the unemployment rate among young people with fewer than eight years of education stood at 40 percent to 60 percent. Lack of skills and basic education were among the chief causes of youth unemployment.

[41] The government's short-term purpose in the scheme at issue was to get recipients under 30 into work and training programs that would make up for the lower base amount they received while teaching them valuable skills. The differential regime of welfare payments was tailored to help the burgeoning ranks of unemployed youths obtain the skills and basic education they needed to get permanent jobs. The mechanism was straightforward. In order to increase their welfare benefits, people under 30 would be required to participate in On-the-job Training, Community Work or Remedial Education Programs. Participating in the training and community service programs would bring welfare benefits up to the basic level payable to the 30-and-over group, and in the education program to about $100 less.

[42] The government's longer-term purpose was to provide young welfare recipients with precisely the kind of remedial education and skills training they lacked and needed in order eventually to integrate into the workforce and become self-sufficient. This policy reflects the practical wisdom of the old Chinese proverb: "Give a man a fish and you feed him for a day. Teach him how to fish and you feed him for a lifetime." This was not a denial of young people's dignity; it was an affirmation of their potential.

[43] Simply handing over a bigger welfare cheque would have done nothing to help welfare recipients under 30 escape from unemployment and its potentially devastating social and psychological consequences above and beyond the short-term loss of income. Moreover, opposition to the incentive program entirely overlooks the cost to young people of being on welfare during the formative years of their working lives. For young people without significant educational qualifications, skills, or experience, entering into the labour market presents considerable difficulties. A young person who relies on welfare during this crucial initial period is denied those formative experiences which, for those who successfully undertake the transition into the productive workforce, lay the foundation for economic self-sufficiency and autonomy, not to mention self-esteem. The longer a young person stays on welfare, the more difficult it becomes to integrate into the workforce at a later time. In this way, reliance on welfare can contribute to a vicious circle of inability to find work, despair, and increasingly dismal prospects.

[44] Instead of turning a blind eye to these problems, the government sought to tackle them at their roots, designing social assistance measures that might help welfare recipients achieve long-term autonomy. Because federal rules in effect at the time prohibited making participation in the programs mandatory, the province's only real leverage in promoting these programs lay in making participation a prerequisite for increases in welfare. Even if one does not agree with the reasoning of the legislature or with its priorities, one cannot argue based on this record that the legislature's purpose lacked sufficient foundation in reality and common sense to fall within the bounds of permissible discretion in establishing and fine-tuning a complex social assistance scheme. Logic and common sense support the legislature's decision to structure its social assistance programs to give young people, who have a greater potential for long-term insertion into the workforce than older people, the incentive to participate in programs specifically designed to provide them with training and experience. . . . In this case, far from ignoring the actual circumstances of under-30s, the scheme at issue was designed to address their needs and abilities. A reasonable person in the claimant's circumstances would have taken this into account.

[45] Turning to effect, Ms. Gosselin argues that . . . notwithstanding the legislature's intentions, the practical consequence of the Regulation was to abandon young welfare recipients, leaving them to survive on a grossly inadequate sum of money. In this way the program did not correspond to their actual needs, she argues, and amounted to discriminatory marginalization of the affected group. . . .

[47] . . . There is no indication in the record that any welfare recipient under 30 wanting to participate in one of the programs was refused enrollment. . . . As the trial judge emphasized, the record contains no first-hand evidence supporting

Ms. Gosselin's claim about the difficulties with the programs, and no indication that Ms. Gosselin can be considered representative of the under-30 class. It is, in my respectful opinion, utterly implausible to ask this Court to find the Quebec government guilty of discrimination under the *Canadian Charter* and order it to pay hundreds of millions of taxpayer dollars to tens of thousands of unidentified people, based on the testimony of a single affected individual. Nor does Ms. Gosselin present sufficient evidence that her own situation was a result of discrimination in violation of s. 15(1). The trial judge did not find evidence indicating a violation, and my review of the record does not reveal any error in this regard. . . .

[54] It may well be that some under-30s fell through the cracks of the system and suffered poverty. However, absent concrete evidence, it is difficult to infer from this that the program failed to correspond to the actual needs of under-30s. I find no basis to interfere with the trial judge's conclusion that the record here simply does not support the contention of adverse effect on younger welfare recipients. This makes it difficult to conclude that the effect of the program did not correspond to the actual situation of welfare recipients under 30.

[55] I add two comments. Perfect correspondence between a benefit program and the actual needs and circumstances of the claimant group is not required to find that a challenged provision does not violate the *Canadian Charter*. The situation of those who, for whatever reason, may have been incapable of participating in the programs attracts sympathy. Yet the inability of a given social program to meet the needs of each and every individual does not permit us to conclude that the program failed to correspond to the actual needs and circumstances of the affected group. As Iacobucci J. noted in *Law, supra*, at para. 105, we should not demand "that legislation must always correspond perfectly with social reality in order to comply with s. 15(1) of the *Charter*." Crafting a social assistance plan to meet the needs of young adults is a complex problem, for which there is no perfect solution. No matter what measures the government adopts, there will always be some individuals for whom a different set of measures might have been preferable. The fact that some people may fall through a program's cracks does not show that the law fails to consider the overall needs and circumstances of the group of individuals affected, or that distinctions contained in the law amount to discrimination in the substantive sense intended by s. 15(1).

[56] Second, we cannot infer disparity between the purpose and effect of the scheme and the situation of those affected, from the mere failure of the government to prove that the assumptions upon which it proceeded were correct. . . .

[57] A final objection is that the selection of 30 years of age as a cut-off failed to correspond to the actual situation of young adults requiring social assistance. However, all age-based legislative distinctions have an element of this literal kind of "arbitrariness." That does not invalidate them. Provided that the age chosen is reasonably related to the legislative goal, the fact that some might prefer a different age—perhaps 29 for some, 31 for others—does not indicate a lack of sufficient correlation between the distinction and actual needs and circumstances. Here, moreover, there is no evidence that a different cut-off age would have been preferable to the one selected.

[58] I conclude that the record in this case does not establish lack of correlation in purpose or effect between the ground of age and the needs and circumstances of welfare recipients under 30 in Quebec.

(c) The Ameliorative Purpose or Effect of the Impugned Law upon a More Disadvantaged Person or Group in Society

[59] A third factor to be considered in determining whether the group-based devaluation of human worth targeted by s. 15 is established, is whether the challenged distinction was designed to improve the situation of a more disadvantaged group. . . .

[62] . . . [T]he Regulation was aimed at ameliorating the situation of welfare recipients under 30. A reasonable person in Ms. Gosselin's position would take this into account in determining whether the scheme treated under-30s as less worthy of respect and consideration than those 30 and over.

(d) Nature and Scope of the Interests Affected by the Impugned Law

[63] This factor directs us to consider the impact of the impugned law—how "severe and localized the . . . consequences [are] on the affected group": *Egan v. Canada*, [1995] 2 S.C.R. 513, at para. 63, quoted in *Law, supra*, at para. 74. . . .

[66] We must decide this case on the evidence before us, not on hypotheticals, or on what we think the evidence ought to show. My assessment of the evidence leads me to conclude that, notwithstanding its possible short-term negative impact on the economic circumstances of some welfare recipients under 30 as compared to those 30 and over, the thrust of the program was to improve the situation of people in this group, and to enhance their dignity and capacity for long-term self-reliance. The nature and scope of the interests affected point not to discrimination but to concern for the situation of welfare recipients under 30. Absent more persuasive evidence to

the contrary, I cannot conclude that a reasonable person in the claimant's position would have experienced this scheme as discriminatory, based on the contextual factors and the concern for dignity emphasized in *Law*.

(e) Summary of Contextual Factors Analysis

[67] The question is whether a reasonable welfare recipient under age 30 who takes into account the contextual factors relevant to the claim would conclude that the lower base amount provided to people under 30 treated her, in purpose or effect, as less worthy and less deserving of respect, consideration and opportunity than people 30 and over. On the evidence before us, the answer to this question must be no.

[68] Looking at the four contextual factors set out in *Law*, I cannot conclude that the denial of human dignity fundamental to a finding of discrimination is established. This is not a case where the complainant group suffered from pre-existing disadvantage and stigmatization. Lack of correspondence between the program and the actual circumstances of recipients under 30 is not established, in either purpose or effect. The "ameliorative purpose" factor is neutral with respect to discrimination. Finally, the findings of the trial judge and the evidence do not support the view that the overall impact on the affected individuals undermined their human dignity and their right to be recognized as fully participating members of society, notwithstanding their membership in the class affected by the distinction.

[69] A reasonable welfare recipient under 30 might have concluded that the program was harsh, perhaps even misguided. . . . But she would not reasonably have concluded that it treated younger people as less worthy or less deserving of respect in a way that had the purpose or effect of marginalizing or denigrating younger people in our society. If anything, she would have concluded that the program treated young people as more able than older people to benefit from training and education, more able to get and retain a job, and more able to adapt to their situations and become fully participating and contributing members of society.

[70] Far from relying on false stereotypes, the program was calibrated to address the particular needs and circumstances of young adults requiring social assistance, considered from both short-term and long-term perspectives. I do not suggest that stereotypical thinking must always be present for a finding that s. 15 is breached. However, its absence is a factor to be considered. The age-based distinction was made for an ameliorative, non-discriminatory purpose, and its social and economic thrust and impact were directed to enhancing the position of young people in society by placing them in a better position to find employment and live fuller, more independent lives. Nor, on the findings of the trial judge, is it established

that the program's effect was to undermine the worth of its members in comparison with older people.

[71] The most compelling way to put the claimant's case is this. We are asked to infer from the apparent lack of widespread participation in programs that some recipients under 30 must at some time have been reduced to utter poverty. From this we are further asked to infer that at least some of these people's human dignity and ability to participate as fully equal members of society were compromised.

[72] The inferences that this argument asks us to draw are problematic. The trial judge, as discussed, was unable to find evidence of actual adverse impact on under-30s as a group. Moreover, the argument rests on a standard of perfection in social programs. As this Court noted in *Law*, that is not the standard to be applied. Some people will always fall through the cracks of social programs. That does not establish denial of human dignity and breach of s. 15. What is required is demonstration that the program as a whole and in the context of *Law*'s four factors in purpose or effect denied human dignity to the affected class, penalizing or marginalizing them simply for being who they were. In this case, that has not been shown. . . .

[74] I conclude that the impugned law did not violate the essential human dignity of welfare recipients under 30. We must base our decision on the record before us, not on personal beliefs or hypotheticals. On the facts before us, the law did not discriminate against Ms. Gosselin, either individually or as a member of the group of 18- to 30-year-olds in Quebec. The differential welfare scheme did not breach s. 15(1) of the *Canadian Charter*.

B. Does the Social Assistance Scheme Violate Section 7 of the Canadian Charter?

. . . [79] In my view, it is both unnecessary and undesirable to attempt to state an exhaustive definition of the administration of justice at this stage, delimiting all circumstances in which the administration of justice might conceivably be implicated. The meaning of the administration of justice, and more broadly the meaning of s. .7, should be allowed to develop incrementally, as heretofore unforeseen issues arise for consideration. The issue here is not whether the administration of justice is implicated—plainly it is not—but whether the Court ought to apply s. 7 despite this fact.

[80] Can s. 7 apply to protect rights or interests wholly unconnected to the administration of justice? The question remains unanswered. . . .

[81] Even if s. 7 could be read to encompass economic rights, a further hurdle emerges. Section 7 speaks of the right *not to be deprived* of life, liberty and security of the person, except in accordance with the principles of fundamental justice.

Nothing in the jurisprudence thus far suggests that s. 7 places a positive obligation on the state to ensure that each person enjoys life, liberty or security of the person. Rather, s. 7 has been interpreted as restricting the state's ability to *deprive* people of these. Such a deprivation does not exist in the case at bar.

[82] One day s. 7 may be interpreted to include positive obligations. To evoke Lord Sankey's celebrated phrase in *Edwards v. Attorney-General for Canada*, [1930] A.C. 124 (P.C.), at p. 136, the *Canadian Charter* must be viewed as "a living tree capable of growth and expansion within its natural limits" .... The question therefore is not whether s. 7 has ever been—or will ever be—recognized as creating positive rights. Rather, the question is whether the present circumstances warrant a novel application of s. 7 as the basis for a positive state obligation to guarantee adequate living standards.

[83] I conclude that they do not. With due respect for the views of my colleague Arbour J., I do not believe that there is sufficient evidence in this case to support the proposed interpretation of s. 7. I leave open the possibility that a positive obligation to sustain life, liberty, or security of the person may be made out in special circumstances. However, this is not such a case. The impugned program contained compensatory "workfare" provisions and the evidence of actual hardship is wanting. The frail platform provided by the facts of this case cannot support the weight of a positive state obligation of citizen support.

[84] In view of my conclusions under s. 15(1) and s. 7 of the *Canadian Charter*, the issue of justification under s. 1 does not arise. Nor does the issue of *Canadian Charter* remedies arise. ...

[Chief Justice McLachlin indicated she did not accept the view that section 45 of the *Quebec Charter* invites courts to review the adequacy of Quebec's social assistance regime.]

[Justice L'Heureux-Dubé wrote a dissenting opinion in which she agreed with Justices Arbour, Bastarache, and LeBel that the legislation violated section 15 and could not be upheld under section 1, agreed with Justice Arbour that section 7 had been violated and could not be upheld under section 1, and indicated that the legislation violated section 45 of the *Quebec Charter*.]

The following are the reasons delivered by

BASTARACHE J. (dissenting):
... [150] ...

(1) Section 7

... [205] The appellant in this case argues that the statutory framework that reduced benefits for those under 30 infringed her right to security of the person, since it had the effect of leaving her and the members of her class in a position of abject poverty that threatened both their physical and psychological integrity. In order to establish a s. 7 breach, the claimant must first show that she was deprived of her right to life, liberty or security of the person, and then must establish that the state caused such deprivation in a manner that was not in accordance with the principles of fundamental justice.

[206] The protection provided for by s. 7's right to life, liberty and security of the person is reflective of our country's traditional and long-held concern that persons should, in general, be free from the constraints of the state and be treated with dignity and respect. ...

[208] In this case, the appellant has gone to great lengths to demonstrate that the negative effects of living on the reduced level of support were seriously harmful to the physical and psychological well-being of those affected. Certainly, those who, like the appellant, were living on a reduced benefit were not in a very "secure" position. The remaining question at this first stage of the s. 7 analysis is, however, whether this position of insecurity was brought about by the state.

[209] The requirement that the violation of a person's rights under s. 7 must emanate from a particular state action can be found in the wording of the section itself. Section 7 does not grant a right to security of the person, full stop. Rather, the right is protected only insofar as the claimant is deprived of the right to security of the person by the state, in a manner that is contrary to the principles of fundamental justice. The nature of the required nexus between the right and a particular state action has evolved over time.

[210] In *Reference re ss. 193 and 195.1(1)(c) of the Criminal Code (Man.)*, [1990] 1 S.C.R. 1123 ("*Prostitution Reference*"), Lamer J., as he then was, held that s. 7 was not necessarily limited to purely criminal or penal matters (p. 1175). Nonetheless, he did maintain that, given the context of the surrounding rights and the heading "Legal Rights" under which s. 7 is found, it was proper to conclude that "the restrictions on liberty and security of the person that s. 7 is concerned with are those that occur as a result of an individual's interaction with the justice system, and its administration" (p. 1173). ...

[213] [I]n certain exceptional circumstances, this Court has found that s. 7 rights may include situations outside of the traditional criminal context—extending to other areas of judicial competence. In this case, however, there is no link between the harm to the appellant's security of the person and the judicial system or its administration. The appellant was not implicated in any judicial or administrative proceedings, or even in an investigation that would at some point lead to such a proceeding. At the very least, a s. 7 claim must arise as a result

of a determinative state action that in and of itself deprives the claimant of the right to life, liberty or security of the person.

[214] Some may find this threshold requirement to be overly formalistic. The appellant, for instance, argues that this Court has found that respect for human dignity underlies most if not all of the rights protected under the *Charter*. Undoubtedly, I agree that respect for the dignity of all human beings is an important, if not foundational, value in this or any society, and that the interpretation of the *Charter* may be aided by taking such values into account. However, this does not mean that the language of the *Charter* can be totally avoided by proceeding to a general examination of such values or that the court can through the process of judicial interpretation change the nature of the right. As held in *Blencoe* [*v. British Columbia (Human Rights Commission)*, [2000] 2 S.C.R. 307, 2000 SCC 44], "[w]hile notions of dignity and reputation underlie many *Charter* rights, they are not stand-alone rights that trigger s. 7 in and of themselves" (para. 97). A purposive approach to *Charter* interpretation, while coloured by an overarching concern with human dignity, democracy and other such "*Charter* values," must first and foremost look to the purpose of the section in question. Without some link to the language of the *Charter*, the legitimacy of the entire process of *Charter* adjudication is brought into question.

[215] In the *Charter*, s. 7 is grouped, along with ss. 8 to 14, under the heading "Legal Rights," in French, "*Garanties juridiques.*" Given the wording of this heading, as well as the subject matter of ss. 8 to 14, it is apparent that s. 7 has, as its primary goal, the protection of one's right to life, liberty and security of the person against the coercive power of the state (P. W. Hogg, *Constitutional Law of Canada* (loose-leaf ed.), vol. 2, at p. 44-9; *Prostitution Reference, supra, per* Lamer J.). The judicial nature of the s. 7 rights is also evident from the fact that people may only be deprived of those rights in accordance with the principles of fundamental justice. As Lamer J. held in *Re B.C. Motor Vehicle Act*, [1985] 2 S.C.R. 486, such principles are to be found "in the basic tenets of our legal system. They do not lie in the realm of general public policy but in the inherent domain of the judiciary as guardian of the justice system" (p. 503). It is this strong relationship between the right and the role of the judiciary that leads me to the conclusion that some relationship to the judicial system or its administration must be engaged before s. 7 may be applied.

[216] ... [A]t the very least, in order for one to be deprived of a s. 7 right, some determinative state action, analogous to a judicial or administrative process, must be shown to exist. Only then may the process of interpreting the principles of fundamental justice or the analysis of government action be undertaken.

[217] In this case, there has been no engagement with the judicial system or its administration, and thus, the protections of s. 7 are not available. As will be discussed below, I have concluded that s. 29(*a*) of the Regulation, by treating individuals differently on the basis of their age, constitutes an infringement of the appellant's equality rights. However, s. 7 does not have the same comparative characteristics as the s. 15 right. The appellant's situation must be viewed in more absolute terms. In this case, the threat to the appellant's right to security of the person was brought upon her by the vagaries of a weak economy, not by the legislature's decision not to accord her more financial assistance or to require her to participate in several programs in order for her to receive more assistance.

[218] The appellant and several of the interveners made forceful arguments regarding the distinction that is sometimes drawn between negative and positive rights, as well as that which is made between economic and civil rights, arguing that security of the person often requires the positive involvement of government in order for it to be realized. This is true. The right to be tried within a reasonable time, for instance, may require governments to spend more money in order to establish efficient judicial institutions. However, in order for s. 7 to be engaged, the threat to the person's right itself must emanate from the state. ...

[220] The appellant also directed our attention to the dissenting statements of Dickson C.J. in *Reference re Public Service Employee Relations Act (Alta.)*, [1987] 1 S.C.R. 313, in which he noted that a conceptual approach in which freedoms are said to involve simply an absence of interference or constraint "may be too narrow since it fails to acknowledge situations where the absence of government intervention may in effect substantially impede the enjoyment of fundamental freedoms" (p. 361). The question of whether a fundamental freedom can be infringed through the lack of government action was canvassed most recently in the case of *Dunmore* [*v. Ontario (Attorney General)*], [2001] 3 S.C.R. 1016, 2001 SCC 94. In that case, I held that legislation that is underinclusive may, in unique circumstances, substantially impact the exercise of a constitutional freedom (para. 22). I explained that in order to meet the requirement that there be some form of government action as prescribed by s. 32 of the *Canadian Charter*, the legislation must have been specifically designed to safeguard the exercise of the fundamental freedom in question. The affected group was required to show that it was substantially incapable of exercising the freedom sought without the protection of the legislation, and that its exclusion from the legislation substantially reinforced the inherent difficulty to exercise the freedom in question. While the existence of the *Social Aid Act* might constitute sufficient government

action to engage s. 32, none of the other factors enumerated in *Dunmore* are present in this case.

[221] In *Dunmore*, I found that the Ontario *Labour Relations Act, 1995*, S.O. 1995, c. 1, Sched. A, instantiated the freedom to organize and that without its protection agricultural workers were substantially incapable of exercising their freedom to associate. The legislation reinforced the already precarious position of agricultural workers in the world of labour relations. In undertaking the underinclusiveness analysis, a complainant must demonstrate that he or she is being deprived of the right itself and not simply the statutory benefit that is being provided to other groups. Here, the *Social Aid Act* seeks to remedy the situation of those persons who find themselves without work or other assistance by providing them with financial support and job training so that they can integrate to the active workforce. As in *Delisle v. Canada (Deputy Attorney General)*, [1999] 2 S.C.R. 989, and *Haig v. Canada*, [1993] 2 S.C.R. 995, the exclusion of people under 30 from the full, unconditional benefit package does not render them substantially incapable of exercising their right to security of the person without government intervention. Leaving aside the possibilities that might exist on the open market, training programs are offered to assist in finding work and to provide additional benefits.

[222] The appellant has failed to demonstrate that there exists an inherent difficulty for young people under 30 to protect their right to security of the person without government intervention. Nor has the existence of a higher base benefit for recipients 30 years of age and over been shown to reduce, on its own, or substantially, the potential of young people to exercise their right to security of the person. The fact that the remedial programs instituted by the reforms of 1984 might not have been designed in a manner that was overly favourable to the appellant does not help the appellant in meeting her burden. My concern here is with the ability of the appellant's group to access the right itself, not to benefit better from the statutory scheme. The appellant has failed to show a substantial incapability of protecting her right to security. She has not demonstrated that the legislation, by excluding her, has reduced her security any more than it would have already been, given market conditions.

[223] For these reasons, I would hold that s. 29(*a*) of the Regulation does not infringe s. 7 of the *Canadian Charter*. The threat to the appellant's security of the person was not related to the administration of justice, nor was it caused by any state action, nor did the underinclusive nature of the Regulation substantially prevent or inhibit the appellant from protecting her own security. Such a result should not be unexpected. As I noted in *Dunmore*, *supra*, total exclusion of a group from a statutory scheme protecting a certain right may in some limited circumstances engage that right to such an extent that it is in essence the substantive right that has been infringed as opposed to the equality right protected under s. 15(1) of the *Charter*. However, the underinclusiveness of legislation will normally be the province of s. 15(1), and so it is to the equality analysis that we must now turn.

(2) Section 15

...[225] Among the grounds of prohibited discrimination enumerated under s. 15(1), age is the one that tends to cause the most theoretical confusion. The source of such confusion in implementing the s. 15(1) guarantee of age equality is rooted in our understanding of substantive equality. In protecting substantive equality, this Court has recognized that like people should be treated alike and, reciprocally, different people must often be treated differently. Most of the grounds enumerated under s. 15(1) tend to be characteristics that our society has deemed to be "irrelevant" to one's abilities. The problem with age is that because we all, as human beings trapped in the continuum of time, experience the process of aging, it is sometimes difficult to assess discriminative behaviour....

[226] Moreover, whereas distinctions based on most other enumerated or analogous grounds may often be said to be using the characteristic as an illegitimate proxy for merit, distinctions based on age as a proxy for merit or ability are often made and viewed as legitimate. This acceptance of distinctions based on age is due to the fact that at different ages people *are* capable of different things. Ten-year-olds, in general, do not make good drivers. The same might be said for the majority of centenarians. It is in recognition of these developmental differences that several laws draw distinctions on the basis of age.

[227] However, despite this apparent recognition that age is of a different sort than the other grounds enumerated in s. 15(1), the fact of the matter is that it was included as a prohibited ground of discrimination in the *Canadian Charter*.... Legislation that draws a distinction based on such a ground is suspect because it often leads to discrimination and denial of substantive equality. This is the case whether the distinction is based on race, gender or age. While distinctions based on age may often be justified, they are nonetheless equally suspect. While age is a ground that is experienced by all people, it is not necessarily experienced in the same way by all people at all times. Large cohorts may use age to discriminate against smaller, more vulnerable cohorts. A change in economic, historical or political circumstances may mean that presumptions and stereotypes about a certain age group no longer hold true. Moreover, the fact remains that, while one's age is constantly changing, it is a personal characteristic that at any given moment one can do nothing to alter. Accord-

ingly, age falls squarely within the concern of the equality provision that people not be penalized for characteristics they either cannot change or should not be asked to change.

[228] The fact that the Regulation here makes a distinction based on a personal characteristic that is specifically enumerated under s. 15 should therefore raise serious concerns when considering whether such a distinction is in fact discriminatory. While not creating a presumption of discrimination, a distinction based on an enumerated ground reveals a strong suggestion that the provision in question is discriminatory for the purposes of s. 15. . . .

[242] In my view, the treatment of legislative purpose at this stage of the s. 15(1) analysis must not undermine or replace that which will be undertaken when applying s. 1. . . .

[244] [G]iving too much weight here to what the government says was its objective in designing the scheme would amount to accepting a s. 1 justification before it is required. . . .

[245] . . . [T]he legislature's intention is much less important at this stage of the *Law* analysis than the real effects on the claimant. The fundamental question, then, in this case, is not how the legislature viewed the scheme, nor how members of the majority would have viewed it in relation to the claimant group. The approach set out for us by *Law* is to ask how any member of the majority, reasonably informed, would feel in the shoes of the claimant, experiencing the effects of the legislation. This approach is essential: if people whom the legislature views as different are not demonstrably different at all, the measure should not be acceptable. . . .

[259] It can be argued that the government could not design a perfect program, and that in a program such as this, some people are bound to fall through the cracks. Indeed, the Chief Justice accepts this argument, noting that a government need not achieve a perfect correspondence between a benefit program and the actual needs and circumstances of the claimant group. But in light of the importance of the interest affected, this should not provide a bar to a finding that Ms. Gosselin's dignity was adversely affected. The severe harm suffered by the appellant as a result of the age-based distinction far exceeds the margin of imperfection Iacobucci J. contemplated in *Law, supra,* at para. 105. . . . The Chief Justice appears to believe that the appellant has the onus, under s. 15(1), to demonstrate not only that *she* is harmed, but also that the government program allows more than an acceptable number of *other* individuals to fall through the cracks. Given the government's resources, it is much more appropriate to require it to adduce proof of the importance and purpose of the program and its minimal impairment of equality rights in discharging its burden under s. 1. . . .

[276] In assessing whether the legislation in place was minimally impairing to the right, the first fact that comes to light is that only 11 percent of social assistance recipients under the age of 30 were in fact enrolled in the employment programs that allowed them to receive the base amount allocated to beneficiaries 30 years of age and over. This in and of itself is not determinative of the fact that the legislation was not minimally impairing, but it does bring to our attention the real possibility that the programs were not designed in a manner that would infringe upon the appellant's rights as little as is reasonably possible. . . .

[290] . . . I find that s. 29(*a*) of the Regulation's *Charter* breach should not be upheld as a justified and reasonable limit under s. 1. In the legislative and social context of the legislation, which provided a safety net for those without means to support themselves, a rights-infringing limitation must be carefully crafted. In this case, the programs left too many opportunities for young people to fall through the seams of the legislation. This is borne out to some degree by the low participation rate among beneficiaries under the age of 30 and the fact that there was no basis for the assumption that beneficiaries under 30 were living with their parents and had lesser needs. While the respondent argues that no evidence was presented to show that most if any of the 73 percent of recipients under 30 were not participating in the programs for anything more than personal reasons, I would point out that at the s. 1 stage of analysis, it is the government's responsibility to show that the legislation limits the right as little as reasonably possible. . . .

[292] In determining the appropriate remedy in the case of legislation that is found to violate a *Charter* right, courts must walk a fine line between fulfilling their judicial role of protecting rights and intruding on the legislature's role. . . .

[299] I would deny the appellant's request for an order for damages pursuant to s. 24(1) of the *Charter.* . . .

[Justice Bastarache held that the Court has no power to declare any portion of a law invalid due to a conflict with s. 45 of the *Quebec Charter.*]

The following are the reasons delivered by

ARBOUR J. (dissenting):

. . . [308] I would allow this appeal on the basis of the appellant's s. 7 *Charter* claim. In doing so, I conclude that the s. 7 rights to "life, liberty and security of the person" include a positive dimension. Few would dispute that an advanced modern welfare state like Canada has a positive moral obligation to protect the life, liberty and security of its citizens.

There is considerably less agreement, however, as to whether this positive moral obligation translates into a legal one. Some will argue that there are interpretive barriers to the conclusion that s. 7 imposes a positive obligation on the state to offer such basic protection.

[309] In my view these barriers are all less real and substantial than one might assume. This Court has never ruled, nor does the language of the *Charter* itself require, that we must reject any positive claim against the state—as in this case—for the most basic positive protection of life and security. This Court has consistently chosen instead to leave open the possibility of finding certain positive rights to the basic means of subsistence within s. 7. In my view, far from resisting this conclusion, the language and structure of the *Charter*— and of s. 7 in particular—actually *compel* it. Before demonstrating all of this it will be necessary to deconstruct the various firewalls that are said to exist around s. 7, precluding this Court from reaching in this case what I believe to be an inevitable and just outcome....

[311] There was some discussion in the courts below concerning whether s. 7 extends its protection to the class of so-called "economic rights." That discussion gets its impetus from certain dicta of Dickson C.J. in *Irwin Toy Ltd. v. Quebec (Attorney General)*, [1989] 1 S.C.R. 927. In *Irwin Toy*, Dickson C.J. compared the wording of s. 7 to similar provisions in the American *Bill of Rights* and noted the following, at p. 1003:

> The intentional exclusion of property from s. 7, and the substitution therefore of "security of the person"...leads to a general inference that economic rights as generally encompassed by the term "property" are not within the perimeters of the s. 7 guarantee.

...[312] [T]he rights at issue in this case are so connected to the sorts of interests that fall under s. 7 that it is a gross mischaracterization to attach to them the label of "economic rights." Their only kinship to the economic "property" rights that are *ipso facto* excluded from s. 7 is that they involve some economic value. But if this is sufficient to attract the label "economic right," there are few rights that would not be economic rights. It is in the very nature of rights that they crystallize certain benefits, which can often be quantified in economic terms. What is truly significant, from the standpoint of inclusion under the rubric of s. 7 rights, is not therefore whether a right can be expressed in terms of its economic value, but as Dickson C.J. suggests, whether it "fall[s] within 'security of the person'" or one of the other enumerated rights in that section. It is principally because corporate-commercial "property" rights fail to do so, and not because they contain an economic component *per se*, that they are excluded from

s. 7. Conversely, it is because the right to a minimum level of social assistance is clearly connected to "security of the person" and "life" that it distinguishes itself from corporate-commercial rights in being a candidate for s. 7 inclusion.

[313] In my view, this tells decisively against any argument that relies upon a supposed economic rights prohibition within s. 7 of the *Charter*. ...

C. Negative Versus Positive Rights and the Requirement of State Action

[319] There is a suggestion that s. 7 contains only negative rights of non-interference and therefore cannot be implicated absent any positive state action. This is a view that is commonly expressed but rarely examined. It is of course true that in virtually all past s. 7 cases it was possible to identify some definitive act on the part of the state which could be said to constitute an interference with life, liberty or security of the person and consequently ground the claim of a s. 7 violation. It may also be the case that no such definitive state action can be located in the instant appeal, though this will largely depend on how one chooses to define one's terms and, in particular, the phrase "state action." One should first ask, however, whether there is in fact any requirement, in order to ground a s. 7 claim, that there be some affirmative state action interfering with life, liberty or security of the person, or whether s. 7 can impose on the state a duty to act where it has not done so. (I use the terms "affirmative," "definitive" or "positive" to mean an identifiable action in contrast to mere inaction.) No doubt if s. 7 contemplates the existence only of negative rights, which are best described as rights of "non-interference," then active state interference with one's life, liberty or security of the person by way of some definitive act will be necessary in order to engage the protection of that section. But if, instead, s. 7 rights include a positive dimension, such that they are not merely rights of non-interference but also what might be described as rights of "performance," then they may be violable by mere inaction or failure by the state to actively provide the conditions necessary for their fulfilment. We must not sidestep a determination of this issue by assuming from the start that s. 7 includes a requirement of affirmative state action. That would be to beg the very question that needs answering.

[320] It is not often clear whether the theory of negative rights underlying the view that s. 7 can only be invoked in response to a definitive state action is intended to be one of general application, extending to the *Charter* as a whole, or one that applies strictly to s. 7. As a theory of the *Charter* as a whole, any claim that only negative rights are constitutionally recognized is of course patently defective. The rights to

vote (s. 3), to trial within a reasonable time (s. 11(*b*)), to be presumed innocent (s. 11(*d*)), to trial by jury in certain cases (s. 11(*f*)), to an interpreter in penal proceedings (s. 14), and minority language education rights (s. 23) to name but some, all impose positive obligations of performance on the state and are therefore best viewed as positive rights (at least in part). By finding that the state has a positive obligation in certain cases to ensure that its labour legislation is properly inclusive, this Court has also found there to be a positive dimension to the s. 2(*d*) right to associate (*Dunmore v. Ontario (Attorney General)*, [2001] 3 S.C.R. 1016, 2001 SCC 94). Finally, decisions like *Schachter v. Canada*, [1992] 2 S.C.R. 679, and *Vriend* [*v. Alberta*, [1998] 1 S.C.R. 493], confirm that "[i]n some contexts it will be proper to characterize s. 15 as providing positive rights" (*Schachter, supra*, at p. 721). This list is illustrative rather than exhaustive.

[321]   Moreover, there is no sense in which the actual language of s. 7 limits its application to circumstances where there has been positive state interference. It is sometimes suggested that the requirement is implicit in the use of the concept of "deprivation" within s. 7. This is highly implausible....

[329]   The finding that s. 7 may impose positive obligations on the state brings us directly to a frequently expressed objection in the context of claims like the ones at issue in the present case that courts cannot enforce positive rights of an individual to the basic means of basic subsistence. The suggestion is that they cannot do so without being drawn outside their proper judicial role and into the realm of deciding complex matters of social policy better left to legislatures. I turn now to this concern.

D. Justiciability

... [331] ... Questions of resource allocation typically involve delicate matters of policy. Legislatures are better suited than courts to addressing such matters, given that they have the express mandate of the taxpayers as well as the benefits of extensive debate and consultation.

[332]   It does not follow, however, that courts are precluded from entertaining a claim such as the present one. While it may be true that courts are ill-equipped to decide policy matters concerning resource allocation—questions of how much the state should spend, and in what manner—this does not support the conclusion that justiciability is a threshold issue barring the consideration of the substantive claim in this case. As indicated above, this case raises altogether a different question: namely, whether the state is under a positive obligation to provide basic means of subsistence to those who cannot provide for themselves. In contrast to the sorts of policy matters expressed in the justiciability concern, this

is a question about what kinds of claims individuals can assert against the state. The role of courts as interpreters of the *Charter* and guardians of its fundamental freedoms against legislative or administrative infringements by the state requires them to adjudicate such rights-based claims. One can in principle answer the question of whether a *Charter* right exists—in this case, to a level of welfare sufficient to meet one's basic needs—without addressing how much expenditure by the state is necessary in order to secure that right. It is only the latter question that is, properly speaking, non-justiciable.

[333]   Of course, in practice it will often be the case that merely knowing whether the right exists is of little assistance to the claimant. For, unless we also know what is required, or how much expenditure is needed, in order to safeguard the right, it will usually be difficult to know whether the right has been violated. This difficulty does not arise in the present case. Once a right to a level of welfare sufficient to meet one's basic needs is established, there is no question on the facts of this case that the right has been violated. This Court need not enter into the arena of determining what would satisfy such a "basic" level of welfare because that determination has already been made by the legislature, which is itself the competent authority to make it.

[334]   Indeed, the very welfare scheme that is challenged here includes provisions that set out the basic amount. Section 23 of the *Regulation respecting social aid*, R.R.Q. 1981, c. A-16, r. 1, provides that the amount receivable is established according to the "ordinary needs" ("*besoins ordinaires*") of the recipients. The bare minimum a single adult aged 30 or over can receive is $466. This is the amount that was deemed by the legislature itself to be sufficient to meet the "ordinary needs" of a single adult. The present case comes before us on the basis that the government failed to provide a level of assistance that, according to its own standards, was necessary to meet the ordinary needs of adults aged 18 to 29. The only outstanding questions are whether this is in fact established and, if so, whether the claimants had a right to the provision of their ordinary needs.

[335]   Thus any concern over the justiciability of positive claims against the state has little bearing on this case. At any rate, these issues, to some extent, obscure the real question. At this stage we are less concerned with what, if anything, the state must do in order to bring itself under a positive obligation than with whether s. 7 can support such positive obligations to begin with. I have already indicated several reasons for thinking that it can. I now want to supplement these reasons by means of an interpretive analysis of s. 7. As it turns out, any acceptable approach to *Charter* interpretation—be it textual, contextual, or purposive—quickly makes apparent that

interpreting the rights contained in s. 7 as including a positive component is not only possible, but also necessary....

[350] Clearly, positive rights are not at odds with the purpose of the *Charter*. Indeed, the *Charter* compels the state to act positively to ensure the protection of a significant number of rights.... Positive rights are not an exception to the usual application of the *Charter*, but an inherent part of its structure. The *Charter* as a whole can be said to have a positive purpose in that at least some of its constituent parts do....

[357] ... In my view, the results are unequivocal: every suitable approach to *Charter* interpretation, including textual analysis, purposive analysis, and contextual analysis, mandates the conclusion that the s. 7 rights of life, liberty and security of the person include a positive dimension....

[385] ... Legislative intervention aimed at providing for essential needs touching on the personal security and survival of indigent members of society is sufficient to satisfy whatever "minimum state action" requirement might be necessary in order to engage s. 32 of the *Charter*. By enacting the *Social Aid Act*, the Quebec government triggered a state obligation to ensure that any differential treatment or underinclusion in the provision of these essential needs did not run afoul of the fundamental rights guaranteed by the *Charter*, and in particular by s. 7. It failed to discharge this obligation. The evidence shows that the underinclusion of welfare recipients aged 18 to 29 under the *Social Aid Act* substantially impeded their ability to exercise their right to personal security (and potentially even their right to life). In the circumstances, I must conclude that this effective lack of government intervention constituted a violation of their s. 7 rights.

IV. The Principles of Fundamental Justice

[386] Under most circumstances, it would now be necessary to determine whether this *prima facie* violation of the appellant's s. 7 rights was "in accordance with the principles of fundamental justice." Such an inquiry appears to have no application to this case for two reasons. First, my analysis indicates that the protection of positive rights is most naturally grounded in the first clause of s. 7, which provides a free-standing right to life, liberty and security of the person and makes no mention of the principles of fundamental justice. Moreover, as Lamer J. observed in *Re B.C. Motor Vehicle Act*, *supra*, at p. 503 "the principles of fundamental justice are to be found in the basic tenets of our legal system. They do not lie in the realm of general public policy but in the inherent domain of the judiciary as guardian of the justice system." But positive rights, by nature violable by mere inaction on the part of the state, do not bring the justice system into motion by empowering agents of the state to actively curtail the life, liberty and security of the person of individuals. The source of

a positive rights violation is in the legislative process, which is of course itself quite distinct from the "inherent domain of the judiciary" and "the justice system" as it has been traditionally conceived. Indeed, the kinds of considerations that would serve to justify the decision to enact one form of protective legislation over another "lie in the realm of ... public policy," which this Court has specifically divorced from the principles of fundamental justice. The principles of fundamental justice therefore have little relevance in the present circumstances, which invoke the inherent domain of the legislature and not that of the justice system.

[387] In view of this, any limitation that might be placed on the s. 7 right asserted in this case—if not in all cases where it is a positive right that is asserted—must be found, not in the principles of fundamental justice, but in the reasonable limits prescribed by law that can be justified in a free and democratic society. Accordingly, it is to s. 1 that we must turn....

[391] In this case, the legislated differential treatment, or underinclusion, is purportedly directed at: (1) preventing the attraction of young adults to social assistance; and (2) facilitating their integration into the workforce by encouraging participation in the employment programs. Insofar as either of these "double objectives" is understood as being principally driven by cost considerations, it would fail (barring cases of prohibitive cost) to be pressing and substantial. However, it is possible to frame these objectives in such a way as to ensure that they are properly adapted to the justificatory analysis under s. 1 by focusing instead on their long-term tendency to promote the liberty and inherent dignity of young people. Thus framed, they might indeed satisfy the "pressing and substantial objective" requirement under *Oakes*.

[392] The problem, in my view, is that subsequent stages of the *Oakes* analysis raise doubts concerning the appropriateness of framing the objectives in this manner. For example, it is difficult to accept that denial of the basic means of subsistence is rationally connected to values of promoting the long-term liberty and inherent dignity of young adults. Indeed, the long-term importance of continuing education and integration into the workforce is undermined where those at whom such "help" is directed cannot meet their basic short-term subsistence requirements. Without the ability to secure the immediate needs of the present, the future is little more than a far-off possibility, remote both in perception and in reality. We have already seen, for example, how the inability to afford a telephone, suitable clothes and transportation makes job hunting difficult if not impossible. More drastically, inadequate food and shelter interfere with the capacity both for learning as well as for work itself. There appears, therefore, to be little rational connection between the objectives, as tentatively framed, and the means adopted in pursuit of those objectives....

[394] This is sufficient, in my view, to establish that the government has not in this case discharged the always heavy burden of justifying a *prima facie* violation of s. 7 under s. 1. I note in passing that it will be a rare case indeed in which the government can successfully claim that the deleterious effects of denying welfare recipients their most basic requirements are proportional to the salutary effects of doing so in contemplation of long-term benefits, for reasons that are largely encompassed by my discussion of rational connection. This is not that rare case. For this reason among others, I find that the violation of the claimants' right to life, liberty and security of the person is not saved by s. 1. . . .

[The dissenting reasons of Justice LeBel are omitted.]

Chaoulli v. Quebec (Attorney General), 2005

The *Chaoulli* case involved judicial intervention in a major public policy issue concerning Canada's system of publicly insured health care: did Quebec legislation banning private insurance for services covered by the public health care plan violate the *Canadian Charter of Rights and Freedoms* or the Quebec *Charter of Human Rights and Freedoms*?

The litigation was initiated by George Zeliotis, who had experienced long waiting lists for heart surgery and a hip operation and Jacques Chaoulli, a Montreal physician who had been trying to operate a private hospital. The crux of their case was that the long waiting lists resulting from the public health plan's monopoly of insured medical services violated the right to security of the person under the *Canadian Charter* and to the inviolability of the person under the *Quebec Charter*.

The public policy stakes in this case were large. The *Canada Health Act*, which sets out the conditions under which provinces receive federal funding for health services, does not prohibit private insurance for services available through the public plan. However, there is a widespread perception that Canada's system of comprehensive and universal, publicly administered medicare would be jeopardized if private medical insurance became widely available in the country. In addition to Quebec, five other provinces—Alberta, British Columbia, Manitoba, Ontario, and Prince Edward Island—prohibit private insurance for services offered by the public plan. A sixth province, Nova Scotia, has no such ban, but, like Manitoba and Ontario, prohibits physicians operating in the private sector from charging more than physicians receive from the public plan. Only three provinces—New Brunswick, Newfoundland and Labrador, and Saskatchewan—set no limits on what physicians operating outside the public system can charge and have no ban on private medical insurance. But these are smaller provinces with relatively few physicians operating in the private sector. If the *Canadian Charter* challenge to Quebec's prohibition on private medical insurance were to succeed, similar legislation in provinces containing over 90 percent of Canada's population would be invalid, tipping Canada's health care decisively in the direction of a two-tier system.

Were you to judge the outcome of this case by the media response to the Supreme Court's decision, you would conclude that the challenge had been completely successful and that Quebec's legislation had been found to violate the *Canadian Charter of Rights and Freedoms*, invalidating the ban on private medical insurance all across the country. According to a front page headline in the *Toronto Star*, "The Supreme Court has delivered a hammer-blow to medicare." "The new face of medicare," trumpeted *The Globe and Mail*.[1] But, in fact, the Court did not find that the legislation violated the *Canadian Charter*. The justices split 3 to 3 on that question. The decisive opinion was written by Justice Deschamps, who found that

---

1   Quoted in Peter H. Russell, "Chaoulli: The Political Versus the Legal Life of a Judicial Decision" in Colleen M. Flood, Kent Roach, and Lorne Sossin, eds., *Access to Care, Access to Justice: The Legal Debate over Private Health Insurance in Canada* (Toronto: University of Toronto Press, 2005).

the legislation violated the *Quebec Charter*. Deschamps did not find it necessary to make a ruling on the *Canadian Charter*. The three justices—Bastarache, Major, and McLachlin—who did find that the legislation violated the *Canadian Charter* also found that it violated the *Quebec Charter*. This means that the common denominator of the Court's majority decision was that Quebec's prohibition of private health insurance contravened Quebec's *Charter of Human Rights and Freedoms*. There was no ruling that applied to the rest of Canada. The ban on private health insurance, despite newspaper headlines suggesting the contrary, remained intact elsewhere in the country.

In confining her judgment to the *Quebec Charter*, Justice Deschamps followed a jurisprudential strategy set down by Justice Jean Beetz in the early years of the *Charter* when he suggested that it is best, when possible, to decide cases on the basis of rights-protecting laws that do not have the full constitutional weight of the *Canadian Charter*.[2] Such a strategy Beetz argued will ensure that these statutory, quasi-constitutional instruments continue to play a role in developing the protection of rights and freedoms.

Justice Deschamps accepted the trial judge's finding that the ban on private health care insurance infringed the right to life and security of the person protected in section 7 of the *Canadian Charter*, and since the right to inviolability of the person in the *Quebec Charter* is even wider than the right to security of the person, the ban on private insurance must also violate that right. However, Justice Deschamps rejected the trial judge's finding that the Quebec government's rationale for the ban on private insurance satisfies the standard of justification in the *Quebec Charter* for limiting rights. Justice Deschamps equated that standard of justification with section 1 of the *Canadian Charter*—except that in her view the burden of proof for meeting the standard is on the government. After reviewing the government's reasons for believing that private health insurance would weaken public medicare, she concluded that the government had failed to prove that its ban on private insurance meets the minimal impairment test—that is, that there are not other ways of protecting public medicare which are less intrusive on the inviolability of the person. Thus, she concludes that the Quebec legislation violates a right guaranteed by the *Quebec Charter* and is not a reasonable limit on that right.

The real fireworks in this case were set off by a sharp division among the other six justices who focused their opinions on section 7 of the *Canadian Charter*. Chief Justice McLachlin, Justice Major, and Justice Bastarache found that the ban on private health care violates section 7 and cannot be justified as a reasonable limit under section 1. The other three justices, Binnie, LeBel, and Fish, disagreed. The crux of their disagreement is the interpretation of "principles of fundamental justice" in section 7. All six justices agreed with the trial judge's conclusion that waiting-list delays in the public health system infringe the right to life and security of the person—although the Binnie group underlined that it is some Quebec residents, not all Quebecers, who experience this deprivation. It is on the second part of section 7 that

---

2   In *Singh v. Minister of Employment and Immigration*, [1985] 1 S.C.R. 177, Justice Beetz and two other justices based their decision that refugee applicants were entitled to a hearing on the statutory *Canadian Bill of Rights*. Three other justices based a similar finding on the *Canadian Charter of Rights and Freedoms*.

the judges divided: has the deprivation of the rights been done in a way that breaches "principles of fundamental justice"? The judges agreed that these words require that laws which encroach on the right to life and security must not be "arbitrary," but they differed over what "arbitrary" means. For the Chief Justice's group, if a law encroaching on a section 7 right cannot be shown to be necessary, it breaches principles of fundamental justice. For the Binnie group, the test is whether the law is related to the objective that lies behind it and does not contradict that objective. The Binnie trio's understanding of "principles of fundamental justice" clearly sets a much lower standard for government to meet than the Chief Justice trio's test of necessity.

It is evident that much more lies behind this split in the Court than a technical point of jurisprudence. The two groups of justices appeared to have profoundly different views on the extent to which *Charter*-based judicial review should second-guess the policy decisions of democratic governments. The Chief Justice's group regarded the arguments of government as well as those of the Romanow Commission of Inquiry as unproven assertions of belief. They had confidence in their own assessment of health policy in other jurisdictions, which led them to the observation that public medicare systems can function without prohibitions on private insurance. On that basis they concluded that such a prohibition is unnecessary and therefore arbitrary. The Binnie group was clearly upset by this judicial foray into the field of policy analysis. They were satisfied that the ban on public health insurance is well connected to the government's aim to sustain a high quality, needs-based, public medicare system. They contended that a facts-based debate about the merits of one-tier versus two-tier health systems "does not fit easily within the institutional competence of courts of law."

Echoes of the right-versus-left political debate over medicare can be heard in these conflicting judicial opinions. Justice Deschamps talked somewhat scathingly about the "iconic status" of Canada's medicare program and the emotional way in which its supporters, including her colleagues, Justices Binnie and LeBel, defend it. The Chief Justice's group talked about the medicare program giving the public plan "a virtual monopoly" that effectively limits access to private medicine to the very rich. The opinion of the Binnie group resonates with an opposing ideology. These justices contended that the beneficiaries of removing the ban on private health insurance would be "the more advantaged members of society" and they recalled the admonition of an earlier Chief Justice, Brian Dickson, that the *Canadian Charter* should not become an instrument to be used by the wealthy to "roll back" the benefits of a legislative scheme that helps the poorer members of society.

It would not have been difficult for the Quebec government to bring in legislation overriding this decision. Indeed, this is what the opposition Parti Québécois urged should be done. The Charest Liberal government decided to implement the Court's decision—but in a very limited way. It brought in legislation allowing private health insurance for cataract surgery and knee and hip replacements, but imposing strict restrictions on the expansion of private care.[3]

---

3   Rheal Seguin, "Quebec tables bill to expand private health coverage: 'Rigid' checks are to oversee clinic care" *The Globe and Mail* (16 June 2006).

As for Canada in general, the future of *Charter*-based judicial review of medicare and other legislation encroaching on "the right to life, liberty and security of the person" depends on new appointments to the Court. Shortly before the *Chaoulli* decision was rendered, Justices Abella and Charron filled Ontario vacancies on the Court. In 2006, the Harper government's first Supreme Court appointee, Justice Marshall Rothstein, filled the Prairie-province vacancy created by Justice Major's retirement from the Court. How these three new members of the Court align themselves with the two opposing interpretations of "the principle of fundamental justice" in section 7, articulated in *Chaoulli*, will have a major bearing on whether we will witness under the McLachlin court a major increase in judicial activism and the expansion of judicial power. A test is likely to come soon, as *Charter*-based challenges to the prohibition of private health insurance are under way in several provinces. ⁓

Discussion Questions

1. In what way did media coverage of this decision distort its real legal significance?
2. How and why did McLachlin, Major, and Bastarache differ from Binnie, LeBel, and Fish in their appraisal of the Report of the Romanow Commission?
3. If the McLachlin, Major, and Bastarache approach to section 7 became the Court's majority position, how would this affect *Charter*-based judicial review?

CHAOULLI v. QUEBEC (ATTORNEY GENERAL)
2005 SCC 35, [2005] 1 S.C.R. 791

Hearing: June 8, 2004; Judgment: June 9, 2005.*

Present: McLachlin C.J. and Major, Bastarache, Binnie, LeBel, Deschamps, and Fish JJ.

Interveners: Attorney General of Ontario, Attorney General of New Brunswick, Attorney General for Saskatchewan, Augustin Roy, Senator Michael Kirby, Senator Marjory Lebreton, Senator Catherine Callbeck, Senator Joan Cook, Senator Jane Cordy, Senator Joyce Fairbairn, Senator Wilbert Keon, Senator Lucie Pépin, Senator Brenda Robertson and Senator Douglas Roche, Canadian Medical Association and Canadian Orthopaedic Association, Canadian Labour Congress, Charter Committee on Poverty Issues and Canadian Health Coalition, Cambie Surgeries Corp., False Creek Surgical Centre Inc., Delbrook Surgical Centre Inc., Okanagan Plastic Surgery Centre Inc., Specialty MRI Clinics Inc., Fraser Valley MRI Ltd., Image One MRI Clinic Inc., McCallum Surgical Centre Ltd., 4111044 Canada Inc., South Fraser Surgical Centre Inc., Victoria Surgery Ltd., Kamloops Surgery Centre Ltd., Valley Cosmetic Surgery Associates Inc., Surgical Centres Inc., British Columbia Orthopaedic Association, and British Columbia Anesthesiologists Society.

* On August 4, 2005, the Court stayed the judgment for a period of 12 months from the date of the judgment.

English version of the reasons delivered by

[1] **DESCHAMPS J.:** Quebeckers are prohibited from taking out insurance to obtain in the private sector services that are available under Quebec's public health care plan. Is this prohibition justified by the need to preserve the integrity of the plan?

[2] As we enter the 21st century, health care is a constant concern. The public health care system, once a source of national pride, has become the subject of frequent and sometimes bitter criticism. This appeal does not question the appropriateness of the state making health care available to all Quebeckers. On the contrary, all the parties stated that they support this kind of role for the government. Only the state can make available to all Quebeckers the social safety net consisting of universal and accessible health care. The demand for health care is constantly increasing, and one of the tools used by governments to control this increase has been the management of waiting lists. The choice of waiting lists as a management tool falls within the authority of the state and not of the courts. The appellants do not claim to have a solution that will eliminate waiting lists. Rather, they submit that the delays resulting from waiting lists violate their rights

under the *Charter of Human Rights and Freedoms*, R.S.Q., c. C-12 ("*Quebec Charter*"), and the *Canadian Charter of Rights and Freedoms* ("*Canadian Charter*"). They contest the validity of the prohibition in Quebec, as provided for in s. 15 of the *Health Insurance Act*, R.S.Q., c. A-29 ("*HEIA*"), and s. 11 of the *Hospital Insurance Act*, R.S.Q., c. A-28 ("*HOIA*"), on private insurance for health care services that are available in the public system. The appellants contend that the prohibition deprives them of access to health care services that do not come with the wait they face in the public system.

[3] The two sections in issue read as follows:

15. No person shall make or renew a contract of insurance or make a payment under a contract of insurance under which an insured service is furnished or under which all or part of the cost of such a service is paid to a resident or a deemed resident of Québec or to another person on his behalf.

11. (1) No one shall make or renew, or make a payment under a contract under which

   (*a*) a resident is to be provided with or to be reimbursed for the cost of any hospital service that is one of the insured services;

   (*b*) payment is conditional upon the hospitalization of a resident; or

   (*c*) payment is dependent upon the length of time the resident is a patient in a facility maintained by an institution contemplated in section 2.

[4] In essence, the question is whether Quebeckers who are prepared to spend money to get access to health care that is, in practice, not accessible in the public sector because of waiting lists may be validly prevented from doing so by the state. For the reasons that follow, I find that the prohibition infringes the right to personal inviolability and that it is not justified by a proper regard for democratic values, public order and the general well-being of the citizens of Quebec.

[5] The validity of the prohibition is contested by the appellants, George Zeliotis and Jacques Chaoulli. Over the years, Mr. Zeliotis has experienced a number of health problems and has used medical services that were available in the public system, including heart surgery and a number of operations on his hip. The difficulties he encountered prompted him to speak out against waiting times in the public health care system. Mr. Chaoulli is a physician who has tried unsuccessfully to have his home-delivered medical activities recognized and to obtain a licence to operate an independent private hospital. Mr. Zeliotis and Mr. Chaoulli joined forces to apply to the court by way of motion for a declaration that s. 15 *HEIA* and s. 11 *HOIA* are unconstitutional and invalid....

I. Legislative Context

[16] Although the federal government has express jurisdiction over certain matters relating to health, such as quarantine, and the establishment and maintenance of marine hospitals (s. 91(11) of the *Constitution Act, 1867*), it is in practice that it imposes its views on the provincial governments in the health care sphere by means of its spending power.... In order to receive federal funds, a provincial plan must conform to the principles set out in the *Canada Health Act*, R.S.C. 1985, c. C-6: it must be administered publicly, it must be comprehensive and universal, it must provide for portability from one province to another and it must be accessible to everyone. These broad principles have become the hallmarks of Canadian identity. Any measure that might be perceived as compromising them has a polarizing effect on public opinion. The debate about the effectiveness of public health care has become an emotional one. The Romanow Report stated that the *Canada Health Act* has achieved an iconic status that makes it untouchable by politicians.... The tone adopted by my colleagues Binnie and LeBel JJ. is indicative of this type of emotional reaction. It leads them to characterize the debate as pitting rich against poor when the case is really about determining whether a specific measure is justified under either the *Quebec Charter* or the *Canadian Charter*. I believe that it is essential to take a step back and consider these various reactions objectively. The *Canada Health Act* does not prohibit private health care services, nor does it provide benchmarks for the length of waiting times that might be regarded as consistent with the principles it lays down, and in particular with the principle of real accessibility.

[17] In reality, a large proportion of health care is delivered by the private sector. First, there are health care services in respect of which the private sector acts, in a sense, as a subcontractor and is paid by the state. There are also many services that are not delivered by the state, such as home care or care provided by professionals other than physicians. In 2001, private sector services not paid for by the state accounted for nearly 30 percent of total health care spending (Canadian Institute for Health Information, *National Health Expenditure Trends, 1975–2003* (2003), at p. 16, Figure 13, "Public and Private Shares of Total Health Expenditure, by Use of Funds, Canada, 2001"). In the case of private sector services that are not covered by the public plan, Quebeckers may take out private insurance without the spectre of the two-tier system being evoked. The *Canada Health Act* is therefore only a general framework that leaves considerable latitude to the provinces. In analysing the justification for the prohibition, I will have occasion to briefly review some of the provisions of Canada's provincial plans. The range of measures shows that there are many ways to deal with the public sector/private sector dynamic without resorting to a ban....

III. Priority Given to Arguments Based on the Quebec Charter

[25] The *Canadian Charter* is neither an ordinary statute nor an extraordinary statute like the *Canadian Bill of Rights*, R.S.C. 1985, App. III. It is a part of the Constitution: *Law Society of Upper Canada v. Skapinker*, [1984] 1 S.C.R. 357, at p. 365. As a result, the *Canadian Charter* is different from the *Quebec Charter* in that the *Quebec Charter* is the product of the legislative will of Quebec's National Assembly. In addition, while the *Quebec Charter* has no constitutional dimension, it is also different from ordinary statutes by virtue of its considerably broader purpose: to guarantee respect for human beings (see A. Morel, "La coexistence des Chartes canadienne et québécoise: problèmes d'interaction" (1986), 17 R.D.U.S. 49). The *Quebec Charter* protects not only the fundamental rights and freedoms, but also certain civil, political, economic and social rights. By virtue of s. 52, Quebec courts have the power to review legislation to determine whether it is consistent with the rules set out in the *Quebec Charter*. The *Quebec Charter* has an identity that is independent of the statutes of Quebec.

[26] In the case of a challenge to a Quebec statute, it is appropriate to look first to the rules that apply specifically in Quebec before turning to the *Canadian Charter*, especially where the provisions of the two charters are susceptible of producing cumulative effects, but where the rules are not identical. This is the approach suggested by Beetz J. in *Singh v. Minister of Employment and Immigration*, [1985] 1 S.C.R. 177, at p. 224:

> Thus, the *Canadian Bill of Rights* retains all its force and effect, together with the various provincial charters of rights. Because these constitutional or quasi-constitutional instruments are drafted differently, they are susceptible of producing cumulative effects for the better protection of rights and freedoms. But this beneficial result will be lost if these instruments fall into neglect.

[27] In the instant case, s. 7 of the *Canadian Charter* and s. 1 of the *Quebec Charter* have numerous points in common:

Canadian Charter

> **7.** Everyone has the right to life, liberty and security of the person and the right not to be deprived thereof except in accordance with the principles of fundamental justice.

Quebec Charter

> **1.** Every human being has a right to life, and to personal security, inviolability and freedom.

[28] The similarities between these two provisions probably explain in part why the Superior Court and the Court of Appeal considered only the *Canadian Charter* in their decisions. With regard to certain aspects of the two charters, the law is the same. For example, the wording of the right to life and liberty is identical. It is thus appropriate to consider the two together. Distinctions must be made, however, and I believe that it is important to begin by considering the specific protection afforded by the *Quebec Charter* for the reason that it is not identical to the protection afforded by the *Canadian Charter*.

[29] The most obvious distinction is the absence of any reference to the principles of fundamental justice in s. 1 of the *Quebec Charter*. The analysis dictated by s. 7 of the *Canadian Charter* is twofold. Under the approach that is generally taken, the claimant must prove, first, that a deprivation of the right to life, liberty and security of the person has occurred and, second, that the deprivation is not in accordance with the principles of fundamental justice....

[30] According to established principles, the onus is on the claimant to prove a violation of constitutional rights: *R. v. Collins*, [1987] 1 S.C.R. 265, and *Rio Hotel Ltd. v. New Brunswick (Liquor Licensing Board)*, [1987] 2 S.C.R. 59; see also Hogg, at p. 44-3. Under s. 7 of the *Canadian Charter*, the claimant would thus have a dual burden. The effect of placing this burden of proof on the claimant is that it makes his or her task more onerous. There is no such dual burden of proof under the *Quebec Charter* because the principles of fundamental justice are not incorporated into s. 1 of the *Quebec Charter*. For this reason, the *Quebec Charter* has a scope that is potentially broader. This characteristic should not be disregarded.

[31] Ruling on the points in issue by applying the *Quebec Charter* enhances an instrument that is specific to Quebec; this approach is also justified by the rules of Canadian constitutional law....

V. Infringement of the Rights Protected by Section 1 of the Quebec Charter

[37] The appellant Zeliotis argues that the prohibition infringes Quebeckers' right to life. Some patients die as a result of long waits for treatment in the public system when they could have gained prompt access to care in the private sector. Were it not for s. 11 *HOIA* and s. 15 *HEIA*, they could buy private insurance and receive care in the private sector.

[38] The Superior Court judge stated [TRANSLATION] "that there [are] serious problems in certain sectors of the health care system" (p. 823). The evidence supports that assertion. After meticulously analysing the evidence, she found that the right to life and liberty protected by s. 7 of the *Canadian Charter* had been infringed. As I mentioned above, the right

to life and liberty protected by the *Quebec Charter* is the same as the right protected by the *Canadian Charter*. Quebec society is no different from Canadian society when it comes to respect for these two fundamental rights. Accordingly, the trial judge's findings of fact concerning the infringement of the right to life and liberty protected by s. 7 of the *Canadian Charter* apply to the right protected by s. 1 of the *Quebec Charter*.

[39] Not only is it common knowledge that health care in Quebec is subject to waiting times, but a number of witnesses acknowledged that the demand for health care is potentially unlimited and that waiting lists are a more or less implicit form of rationing....

[41] The *Quebec Charter* also protects the right to personal inviolability. This is a very broad right. The meaning of "inviolability" is broader than the meaning of the word "security" used in s. 7 of the *Canadian Charter*. In civil liability cases, it has long been recognized in Quebec that personal inviolability includes both physical inviolability and mental or psychological inviolability....

[42] In the instant case, Dr. Eric Lenczner, an orthopaedic surgeon, testified that the usual waiting time of one year for patients who require orthopaedic surgery increases the risk that their injuries will become irreparable. Clearly, not everyone on a waiting list is in danger of dying before being treated. According to Dr. Edwin Coffey, people may face a wide variety of problems while waiting. For example, a person with chronic arthritis who is waiting for a hip replacement may experience considerable pain. Dr. Lenczner also stated that many patients on non-urgent waiting lists for orthopaedic surgery are in pain and cannot walk or enjoy any real quality of life.

[43] Canadian jurisprudence shows support for interpreting the right to security of the person generously in relation to delays. In *R. v. Morgentaler*, [1988] 1 S.C.R. 30, at p. 59, Dickson C.J. found, based on the consequences of delays, that the procedure then provided for in s. 251 of the *Criminal Code*, R.S.C. 1970, c. C-34, jeopardized the right to security of the person. Beetz J., at pp. 105-6, with Estey J. concurring, was of the opinion that the delay created an additional risk to health and constituted a violation of the right to security of the person.... If the evidence establishes that the right to security of the person has been infringed, it supports, *a fortiori*, the finding that the right to the inviolability of the person has been infringed.

[44] In the opinion of my colleagues Binnie and LeBel JJ., there is an internal mechanism that safeguards the public health system. According to them, Quebeckers may go outside the province for treatment where services are not available in Quebec. This possibility is clearly not a solution for the system's deficiencies. The evidence did not bring to light any administrative mechanism that would permit Quebeckers

suffering as a result of waiting times to obtain care outside the province. The possibility of obtaining care outside Quebec is case-specific and is limited to crisis situation.

[45] I find that the trial judge did not err in finding that the prohibition on insurance for health care already insured by the state constitutes an infringement of the right to life and security. This finding is no less true in the context of s. 1 of the *Quebec Charter*. Quebeckers are denied a solution that would permit them to avoid waiting lists, which are used as a tool to manage the public plan. I will now consider the justification advanced under s. 9.1 of the *Quebec Charter*.

VI. Justification for the Prohibition

[46] Section 9.1 of the *Quebec Charter* sets out the standard for justification. It reads as follows:

> **9.1.** In exercising his fundamental freedoms and rights, a person shall maintain a proper regard for democratic values, public order and the general well-being of the citizens of Québec.

In this respect, the scope of the freedoms and rights, and limits to their exercise, may be fixed by law.

[47] The Court had occasion to consider the scope of this provision in *Ford v. Quebec (Attorney General)*, [1988] 2 S.C.R. 712. In its view, in the context of the relationship between citizens and the state, the provision is of the same nature as s. 1 of the *Canadian Charter*. . . .

[48] The interpretation adopted by the Court in that decision still applies today, and the analytical approach developed in *R. v. Oakes*, [1986] 1 S.C.R. 103, must be followed. This approach is well known. First, the court must determine whether the objective of the legislation is pressing and substantial. Next, it must determine whether the means chosen to attain this legislative end are reasonable and demonstrably justifiable in a free and democratic society. For this second part of the analysis, three tests must be met: (1) the existence of a rational connection between the measure and the aim of the legislation; (2) minimal impairment of the protected right by the measure; and (3) proportionality between the effect of the measure and its objective (*Egan v. Canada*, [1995] 2 S.C.R. 513, at para. 182). It is the minimal impairment analysis that has proven to be the most delicate stage in the instant case. The other stages cannot, however, be bypassed.

A. Purpose of the Statute

[49] The prohibitions are set out in the *HOIA* and the *HEIA*. The general objective of these statutes is to promote health care of the highest possible quality for all Quebeckers regardless of their ability to pay. . . .

B. Proportionality
(1) Rational Connection

[57] The next question is whether the prohibition on private insurance has a rational connection with the objective of preserving the public plan. Does this measure assist the state in implementing a public plan that provides high-quality health care services that are accessible to all residents of Quebec?

[58] According to the trial judge, the effect of the measure adopted by the state is to "significantly" limit private health care. Although the effect of a measure is not always indicative of a rational connection between the measure and its objective, in the instant case the consequences show an undeniable connection between the objective and the measure. The public plan is preserved because it has a quasi-monopoly.

(2) Minimal Impairment

[59] The trial judge made certain assertions that suggest she found that the measure met the minimal impairment test. However, her approach was not appropriate to s. 9.1 of the *Quebec Charter*. Her comments must therefore be considered in their context, not only because she failed to address the *Quebec Charter*, but also because she appears to have placed the onus on the appellants to prove that private insurance would provide a solution to the problem of waiting lists. . . .

[60] The burden of proof does not rest on the appellants. Under s. 9.1 of the *Quebec Charter*, the onus was on the Attorney General of Quebec to prove that the prohibition is justified. He had to show that the measure met the minimal impairment test. The trial judge did not consider the evidence on the basis that there was a burden on the Attorney General of Quebec.

[61] To determine whether the Attorney General of Quebec has discharged this burden, I will begin by analysing the expert evidence submitted to the Superior Court. I will then examine the situations in the other provinces of Canada and in certain countries of the Organization for Economic Cooperation and Development ("OECD"). Finally, I will address the deference the Court must show where the government has chosen among a number of measures that may impair protected rights.

(a) The Experts Who Testified at Trial and Whose Evidence Was Accepted by the Superior Court Judge

[62] As can be seen from the evidence, the arguments made in support of the position that the integrity of the public system could be jeopardized by abolishing the prohibition can be divided into two groups. The first group of arguments relates to human reactions of the various people affected by the public plan, while the second group relates to the consequences for the plan itself.

(i) Human Reactions

[63]

1. Some witnesses asserted that the emergence of the private sector would lead to a reduction in popular support in the long term because the people who had private insurance would no longer see any utility for the public plan. . . .

2. Some witnesses were of the opinion that the quality of care in the public plan would decline because the most influential people would no longer have any incentive to bring pressure for improvements to the plan. Dr. Bergman cited a study by the World Bank in support of his expert report. Dr. Marmor relied on this argument but confirmed that there is no direct evidence to support this view.

3. There would be a reduction in human resources in the public plan because many physicians and other health care professionals would leave the plan out of a motive for profit: Dr. Charles J. Wright cited a study done in the United Kingdom, but admitted that he had read only a summary and not the study itself. Although Dr. Marmor supported the assertion, he testified that there is really no way to confirm it empirically. In his opinion, it is simply a matter of common sense.

4. An increase in the use of private health care would contribute to an increase in the supply of care for profit and lead to a decline in the professionalism and ethics of physicians working in hospitals. No study was cited in support of this opinion that seems to be based only on the witnesses' common sense.

[64] It is apparent from this summary that for each threat mentioned, no study was produced or discussed in the Superior Court. . . . The evidence that the existence of the health care system would be jeopardized by human reactions to the emergence of a private system carries little weight.

(ii) Impact on the Public Plan

[65]

1. There would be an increase in overall health expenditures: the alleged increase would come primarily from the additional expenditures incurred by individuals who decide to take out private insurance; the rest of the increase in costs would be attributable to the cost of management of the private system by the state.

2. Insurers would reject the most acute patients, leaving the most serious cases to be covered by the public plan.

3. In a private system, physicians would tend to lengthen waiting times in the public sector in order to direct patients to the private sector from which they would derive a profit.

[66] Once again, I am of the opinion that the reaction some witnesses described is highly unlikely in the Quebec context. First, if the increase in overall costs is primarily attributable to the individual cost of insurance, it would be difficult for the state to prevent individuals who wished to pay such costs from choosing how to manage their own finances. Furthermore, because the public plan already handles all the serious cases, I do not see how the situation could be exacerbated if that plan were relieved of the clientele with less serious health problems. . . .

[69] There is other evidence in the record that might be of assistance in the justification analysis. In this regard, it is useful to observe the approaches of the other Canadian provinces because they also operate within the financial framework established by the *Canada Health Act.*

(b) Overview of Other Provincial Plans

[70] The approach to the role of the private sector taken by the other nine provinces of Canada is by no means uniform. In addition to Quebec, six other provinces have adopted measures to discourage people from turning to the private sector. The other three, in practice, give their residents free access to the private sector.

[71] Ontario (*Health Care Accessibility Act*, R.S.O. 1990, c. H.3, s. 2), Nova Scotia (*Health Services and Insurance Act*, R.S.N.S. 1989, c. 197, s. 29(2)) and Manitoba (*Health Services Insurance Act*, R.S.M. 1987, c. H35, s. 95(1)) prohibit non-participating physicians from charging their patients more than what physicians receive from the public plan. In practice, there is no financial incentive to opt for the private sector. It is worth noting that Nova Scotia does not prohibit insurance contracts to cover health care obtained in the private sector. Ontario and Manitoba prohibit insurance contracts but refund amounts paid by patients to non-participating physicians.

[72] Alberta (*Alberta Health Care Insurance Act*, R.S.A. 2000, c. A-20, s. 9(1)), British Columbia (*Medicare Protection Act*, R.S.B.C. 1996, c. 286, s. 18(2)) and Prince Edward Island (*Health Services Payment Act*, R.S.P.E.I. 1988, c. H-2, ss. 10, 10.1 and 14.1) have adopted a very different approach. In those provinces, non-participating physicians are free to set the amount of their fees, but the cost of the services is not refunded and contracts for insurance to cover services offered by the public plan are prohibited. This is the same policy as has been adopted by Quebec.

[73] Saskatchewan (*Saskatchewan Medical Care Insurance Act*, R.S.S. 1978, c. S-29, s. 18(1.1)), New Brunswick (*Medical Services Payment Act*, R.S.N.B. 1973, c. M-7, s. 2.01(a), and *General Regulation—Medical Services Payment Act*, N.B. Reg. 84-20, Sch. 2, para. (n.1)), and Newfoundland and Labrador (*Medical Care Insurance Act*, 1999, S.N.L. 1999, c. M-5.1, s. 10(5), and *Medical Care Insurance Insured Services Regulations*, C.N.L.R. 21/96, s. 3) are open to the private sector. New Brunswick allows physicians to set their own fees. In Saskatchewan, this right is limited to non-participating physicians. The cost is not refunded by the public plan, but patients may purchase insurance to cover those costs. Newfoundland and Labrador agrees to reimburse patients, up to the amount covered by the public plan, for fees paid to non-participating physicians. In Newfoundland and Labrador, patients may subscribe to private insurance to cover the difference.

[74] Even if it were assumed that the prohibition on private insurance could contribute to preserving the integrity of the system, the variety of measures implemented by different provinces shows that prohibiting insurance contracts is by no means the only measure a state can adopt to protect the system's integrity....

[75] In the context of s. 9.1 of the *Quebec Charter*, I must conclude that a comparison with the plans of the other Canadian provinces does not support the position of the Attorney General of Quebec.

[76] There are also many reports in the record on which to base an overview of current practices in several OECD countries.

(c)   Overview of Practices in Certain OECD Countries

[77] Mr. Chaoulli, echoed by at least one of the witnesses (Dr. Coffey), argued that Canada is the only OECD country to prohibit insurance for health care provided by non-participating physicians. This assertion must be clarified as it relates to Canada: it is true of only six provinces. It must also be qualified in the international context: while no such prohibition is found in any other OECD country, it should nonetheless be mentioned that measures to protect the public plan have been implemented in a number of countries, even some of the countries whose health care plans have been provided as models. There is no single model; the approach in Europe is no more uniform than in Canada.

[78] In a number of European countries, there is no insurance paid for directly out of public funds. In Austria, services are funded through decentralized agencies that collect the necessary funds from salaries. People who want to obtain health care in the private sector in addition to the services covered by the mandatory social insurance are free to do so, but private insurance may cover no more than 80 percent of the cost billed by professionals practising in the public sector. The same type of plan exists in Germany and the Netherlands, but people who opt for private insurance are not required to pay for the public plan. Only nine percent of Germans opt for private insurance.

[79] Australia's public system is funded in a manner similar to the Quebec system. However, Australia's system is different in that the private and public sectors coexist, and insurance covering private sector health care is not prohibited. The government attempts to balance access to the two sectors by allowing taxpayers to deduct 30 percent of the cost of private insurance. Insurance rates are regulated to prevent insurers from charging higher premiums for higher-risk individuals (C.H. Tuohy, C.M. Flood and M. Stabile, "How Does Private Finance Affect Public Health Care Systems? Marshaling the Evidence from OECD Nations" (2004), 29 *J. Health Pol.* 359)

[80] The United Kingdom does not restrict access to private insurance for health care (*The Health of Canadians—The Federal Role*, vol. 3, *Health Care Systems in Other Countries*, Interim Report (2002), at p. 38). Nor does the United Kingdom limit a physician's ability to withdraw from the public plan. However, physicians working full-time in public hospitals are limited in the amounts that they may bill in the private sector to supplement income earned in the public sector (p. 40). Only 11.5 percent of Britons had taken out private insurance in 1998 (Tuohy, Flood and Stabile, at p. 374), and only 8 percent of hospital beds in the United Kingdom are private (Quebec and France, *Health Indicators: International Comparisons: 15 years of Evolution: Canada, France, Germany, Québec, United Kingdom, United States* (1998), at p. 55). New Zealand has a plan similar to that of the United Kingdom with the difference that 40 percent of New Zealanders have private insurance (Tuohy, Flood and Stabile, at p. 363).

[81] Sweden does not prohibit private insurance, and the state does not refund the cost of health care paid for in the private sector. Private insurance accounts for only two percent of total health care expenditures and there are only nine private hospitals....

[82] It can be seen from the systems in these various OECD countries that a number of governments have taken measures to protect their public plans from abuse. The measures vary from country to country depending on the nature of their specific systems. For example, in the United Kingdom, there are limits on the amounts physicians may earn in the private sector in addition to what they receive from the public plan. Australia has opted to regulate insurance premiums, but it is alone in this respect....

[84] It cannot therefore be concluded from the evidence relating to the Quebec plan or the plans of the other provinces of Canada, or from the evolution of the systems in place in

various OECD countries, that the Attorney General of Quebec has discharged his burden of proof under s. 9.1 of the *Quebec Charter*. A number of measures are available to him to protect the integrity of Quebec's health care plan. The choice of prohibiting private insurance contracts is not justified by the evidence. However, is this a case in which the Court should show deference?

(d) Level of Deference Required

... [86] Under the charters, the government is responsible for justifying measures it imposes that impair rights. The courts can consider evidence concerning the historical, social and economic aspects, or any other evidence that may be material.

[87] It cannot be said that the government lacks the necessary resources to show that its legislative action is motivated by a reasonable objective connected with the problem it has undertaken to remedy. The courts are an appropriate forum for a serious and complete debate. As G. Davidov said in "The Paradox of Judicial Deference" (2000-2001), 12 *N.J.C.L.* 133, at p. 143, "[c]ourts do not have to define goals, choose means or come up with ideas. They do not have to create social policies; they just have to understand what the other branches have created. No special expertise is required for such an understanding." In fact, if a court is satisfied that all the evidence has been presented, there is nothing that would justify it in refusing to perform its role on the ground that it should merely defer to the government's position. When the courts are given the tools they need to make a decision, they should not hesitate to assume their responsibilities. Deference cannot lead the judicial branch to abdicate its role in favour of the legislative branch or the executive branch. ...

[89] The courts have a duty to rise above political debate. They leave it to the legislatures to develop social policy. But when such social policies infringe rights that are protected by the charters, the courts cannot shy away from considering them. The judicial branch plays a role that is not played by the legislative branch. ...

[90] From this perspective, it is through the combined action of legislatures and courts that democratic objectives can be achieved. ...

[91] The court's reasons for showing deference must always reflect the two guiding principles of justification: the measure must be consistent with democratic values and it must be necessary in order to maintain public order and the general well-being of citizens. The variety of circumstances that may be presented to a court is not conducive to the rigidity of an exhaustive list. ...

[97] For many years, the government has failed to act; the situation continues to deteriorate. This is not a case in which

missing scientific data would allow for a more informed decision to be made. The principle of prudence that is so popular in matters relating to the environment and to medical research cannot be transposed to this case. Under the Quebec plan, the government can control its human resources in various ways, whether by using the time of professionals who have already reached the maximum for payment by the state, by applying the provision that authorizes it to compel even non-participating physicians to provide services (s. 30 *HEIA*) or by implementing less restrictive measures, like those adopted in the four Canadian provinces that do not prohibit private insurance or in the other OECD countries. While the government has the power to decide what measures to adopt, it cannot choose to do nothing in the face of the violation of Quebeckers' right to security. The government has not given reasons for its failure to act. Inertia cannot be used as an argument to justify deference.

[98] In the instant case, the effectiveness of the prohibition has by no means been established. The government has not proved, by the evidence in the record, that the measure minimally impairs the protected rights. Moreover, the evidence shows that a wide variety of measures are available to governments, as can be seen from the plans of other provinces and other countries.

(3) Proportionality

[99] Having found that s. 15 *HEIA* and s. 11 *HOIA* do not meet the minimal impairment test, I do not need to consider proportionality. If the prohibition is not minimally impairing, it obviously cannot be regarded as a measure that sufficiently addresses the effect of the measure on the protected rights.

VII. Conclusion

[100] The relief sought by the appellants does not necessarily provide a complete response to the complex problem of waiting lists. However, it was not up to the appellants to find a way to remedy a problem that has persisted for a number of years and for which the solution must come from the state itself. Their only burden was to prove that their right to life and to personal inviolability had been infringed. They have succeeded in proving this. The Attorney General of Quebec, on the other hand, has not proved that the impugned measure, the prohibition on private insurance, was justified under s. 9.1 of the *Quebec Charter*. Given that this finding is sufficient to dispose of the appeal, it is not necessary to answer the other constitutional questions.

[101] For these reasons, I would allow the appeal with costs throughout and would answer the questions relating to the *Quebec Charter* as follows:

Question 1:   Does s. 11 of the *Hospital Insurance Act*, R.S.Q., c. A-28, infringe the rights guaranteed by s. 1 of the *Quebec Charter*?

Answer: Yes.

Question 2:   If so, is the infringement a reasonable limit prescribed by law as can be demonstrably justified in a free and democratic society under s. 9.1 of the *Quebec Charter*?

Answer: No.

Question 3:   Does s. 15 of the *Health Insurance Act*, R.S.Q., c. A-29, infringe the rights guaranteed by s. 1 of the *Quebec Charter*?

Answer: Yes.

Question 4:   If so, is the infringement a reasonable limit prescribed by law as can be demonstrably justified in a free and democratic society under s. 9.1 of the *Quebec Charter*?

Answer: No.

The reasons of McLachlin C.J. and Major and Bastarache JJ. were delivered by

[102] **THE CHIEF JUSTICE AND MAJOR J.:** We concur in the conclusion of our colleague Deschamps J. that the prohibition against contracting for private health insurance violates s. 1 of the *Quebec Charter of Human Rights and Freedoms*, R.S.Q., c. C-12, and is not justifiable under s. 9.1. On the argument that the anti-insurance provision also violates s. 7 of the *Canadian Charter of Rights and Freedoms* ("*Charter*"), we conclude that the provision impermissibly limits the right to life, liberty and security of the person protected by s. 7 of the *Charter* and has not been shown to be justified as a reasonable limit under s. 1 of the *Charter*.

[103] The appellants do not seek an order that the government spend more money on health care, nor do they seek an order that waiting times for treatment under the public health care scheme be reduced. They only seek a ruling that because delays in the public system place their health and security at risk, they should be allowed to take out insurance to permit them to access private services.

[104] The *Charter* does not confer a freestanding constitutional right to health care. However, where the government puts in place a scheme to provide health care, that scheme must comply with the *Charter*. We are of the view that the prohibition on medical insurance in s. 15 of the *Health Insurance Act*, R.S.Q., c. A-29, and s. 11 of the *Hospital Insurance Act*, R.S.Q., c. A-28 (see Appendix), violates s. 7 of the *Charter* because it impinges on the right to life, liberty and security of the person in an arbitrary fashion that fails to conform to the principles of fundamental justice.

[105] The primary objective of the *Canada Health Act*, R.S.C. 1985, c. C-6, is "to protect, promote and restore the physical and mental well-being of residents of Canada and *to facilitate reasonable access* to health services without financial or other barriers" (s. 3). By imposing exclusivity and then failing to provide public health care of a reasonable standard within a reasonable time, the government creates circumstances that trigger the application of s. 7 of the *Charter*.

[106] The *Canada Health Act*, the *Health Insurance Act*, and the *Hospital Insurance Act* do not expressly prohibit private health services. However, they limit access to private health services by removing the ability to contract for private health care insurance to cover the same services covered by public insurance. The result is a virtual monopoly for the public health scheme. The state has effectively limited access to private health care except for the very rich, who can afford private care without need of insurance. This virtual monopoly, on the evidence, results in delays in treatment that adversely affect the citizen's security of the person. Where a law adversely affects life, liberty or security of the person, it must conform to the principles of fundamental justice. This law, in our view, fails to do so. . . .

I. Section 7 of the Charter

[109] Section 7 of the *Charter* guarantees that "[e]veryone has the right to life, liberty and security of the person and the right not to be deprived thereof except in accordance with the principles of fundamental justice." The disposition of this appeal therefore requires us to consider (1) whether the impugned provisions deprive individuals of their life, liberty or security of the person; and (2) if so, whether this deprivation is in accordance with the principles of fundamental justice: see, e.g., *R. v. Malmo-Levine*, [2003] 3 S.C.R. 571, 2003 SCC 74, at para. 83.

A. Deprivation of Life, Liberty, or Security of the Person

[110] The issue at this stage is whether the prohibition on insurance for private medical care deprives individuals of their life, liberty or security of the person protected by s. 7 of the *Charter*.

[111] The appellants have established that many Quebec residents face delays in treatment that adversely affect their security of the person and that they would not sustain but for the prohibition on medical insurance. It is common ground that the effect of the prohibition on insurance is to allow only the very rich, who do not need insurance, to secure private

health care in order to avoid the delays in the public system. Given the ban on insurance, most Quebeckers have no choice but to accept delays in the medical system and their adverse physical and psychological consequences.

[112] Delays in the public system are widespread and have serious, sometimes grave, consequences. There was no dispute that there is a waiting list for cardiovascular surgery for life-threatening problems. Dr. Daniel Doyle, a cardiovascular surgeon who teaches and practises in Quebec City, testified that a person with coronary disease is [TRANSLATION] "sitting on a bomb" and can die at any moment. He confirmed, without challenge, that patients die while on waiting lists: A.R., at p. 461. Inevitably, where patients have life-threatening conditions, some will die because of undue delay in awaiting surgery....

[116] In addition to threatening the life and the physical security of the person, waiting for critical care may have significant adverse psychological effects. Serious psychological effects may engage s. 7 protection for security of the person. These "need not rise to the level of nervous shock or psychiatric illness, but must be greater than ordinary stress or anxiety": *New Brunswick (Minister of Health and Community Services) v. G.(J.)*, [1999] 3 S.C.R. 46, at para. 60. ...

[124] We conclude, based on the evidence, that prohibiting health insurance that would permit ordinary Canadians to access health care, in circumstances where the government is failing to deliver health care in a reasonable manner, thereby increasing the risk of complications and death, interferes with life and security of the person as protected by s. 7 of the *Charter*.

[125] The remaining question is whether this inference is in accordance with the principles of fundamental justice. "[I]f the state [interferes] with security of the person, the *Charter* requires such interference to conform with the principles of fundamental justice": *Morgentaler*, at p. 54, per Dickson C.J.

B. Deprivation in Accordance with the Principles of Fundamental Justice

[126] Having concluded that the ban on private medical insurance constitutes a deprivation of life and security of the person, we now consider whether that deprivation is in accordance with the principles of fundamental justice. Our colleagues Binnie and LeBel JJ. argue that the record here provides no ground for finding that the deprivation violates the principles of fundamental justice. With respect, we cannot agree. ...

[128] The principle of fundamental justice implicated in this case is that laws that affect the life, liberty or security of the person shall not be arbitrary. We are of the opinion that the evidence before the trial judge supports a finding that the impugned provisions are arbitrary and that the deprivation

of life and security of the person that flows from them cannot therefore be said to accord with the principles of fundamental justice.

(1) Laws Shall Not Be Arbitrary: A Principle of Fundamental Justice

[129] It is a well-recognized principle of fundamental justice that laws should not be arbitrary: see, e.g., *Malmo-Levine*, at para. 135; *Rodriguez*, at p. 594. The state is not entitled to arbitrarily limit its citizens' rights to life, liberty and security of the person.

[130] A law is arbitrary where "it bears no relation to, or is inconsistent with, the objective that lies behind [it]." To determine whether this is the case, it is necessary to consider the state interest and societal concerns that the provision is meant to reflect: *Rodriguez*, at pp. 594-95.

[131] In order not to be arbitrary, the limit on life, liberty and security requires not only a theoretical connection between the limit and the legislative goal, but a real connection on the facts. The onus of showing lack of connection in this sense rests with the claimant. The question in every case is whether the measure is arbitrary in the sense of bearing no real relation to the goal and hence being manifestly unfair. The more serious the impingement on the person's liberty and security, the more clear must be the connection. Where the individual's very life may be at stake, the reasonable person would expect a clear connection, in theory and in fact, between the measure that puts life at risk and the legislative goals.

(2) Whether the Prohibition on Private Medical Insurance Is Arbitrary

... [135] The government argues that the interference with security of the person caused by denying people the right to purchase private health insurance is necessary to providing effective health care under the public health system. It argues that if people can purchase private health insurance, they will seek treatment from private doctors and hospitals, which are not banned under the Act. According to the government's argument, this will divert resources from the public health system into private health facilities, ultimately reducing the quality of public care.

[136] In support of this contention, the government called experts in health administration and policy. Their conclusions were based on the "common sense" proposition that the improvement of health services depends on exclusivity (R.R., at p. 591). They did not profess expertise in waiting times for treatment. Nor did they present economic studies or rely on the experience of other countries. They simply assumed, as a matter of apparent logic, that insurance would make private

health services more accessible and that this in turn would undermine the quality of services provided by the public health care system.

[137] The appellants, relying on other health experts, disagreed and offered their own conflicting "common sense" argument for the proposition that prohibiting private health insurance is neither necessary nor related to maintaining high quality in the public health care system. Quality public care, they argue, depends not on a monopoly, but on money and management. They testified that permitting people to buy private insurance would make alternative medical care more accessible and reduce the burden on the public system. The result, they assert, would be better care for all. The appellants reinforce this argument by pointing out that disallowing private insurance precludes the vast majority of Canadians (middle-income and low-income earners) from accessing additional care, while permitting it for the wealthy who can afford to travel abroad or pay for private care in Canada.

[138] To this point, we are confronted with competing but unproven "common sense" arguments, amounting to little more than assertions of belief. We are in the realm of theory. But as discussed above, a theoretically defensible limitation may be arbitrary if in fact the limit lacks a connection to the goal.

[139] This brings us to the evidence called by the appellants at trial on the experience of other developed countries with public health care systems which permit access to private health care. The experience of these countries suggests that there is no real connection in fact between prohibition of health insurance and the goal of a quality public health system.

[140] The evidence adduced at trial establishes that many western democracies that do not impose a monopoly on the delivery of health care have successfully delivered to their citizens medical services that are superior to and more affordable than the services that are presently available in Canada. This demonstrates that a monopoly is not necessary or even related to the provision of quality public health care.

[141] In its report *The Health of Canadians—The Federal Role*, the Standing Senate Committee on Social Affairs, Science and Technology discussed in detail the situations in several countries, including Sweden, Germany and the United Kingdom. The following discussion of the health care systems in these three countries is drawn directly from the findings in volume 3 of that report (*The Health of Canadians—The Federal Role*, vol. 3, *Health Care Systems in Other Countries*, Interim Report (2002) ("Kirby Report")).

[142] In Sweden, as in Canada, access to public health care is universal. The public health care system is financed predominantly by the public sector through a combination of general taxation and social insurance (i.e., employer/employee contributions) and employs a user fee mechanism.

Unlike in Canada, private health care insurance that covers the same benefits as public insurance is "legal" in Sweden. However, only a small minority of the population purchase private insurance. The result is a system of public health care coverage that provides quality care on a broader basis than in Canada and encompasses physicians, hospital services, drugs and dental care: Kirby Report, vol. 3, at pp. 29-36. In Sweden, the availability of private health care insurance appears not to have harmed the public health care system.

[143] In Germany, public health care insurance is administered by 453 Sickness Funds—private non-profit organizations structured on a regional task or occupational basis. Sickness Fund membership is compulsory for employees with gross incomes lower than approximately $63,000 Canadian, and voluntary for those with gross incomes above that level. Although all Sickness Funds are regulated at the federal level through what is known as the "Social Code Book," they are essentially run by representatives of employees and employers. As in Sweden, public health care coverage is broader in Germany than in Canada, including physician services, hospitals, prescription drugs, diagnostic services, dental care, rehabilitative care, medical devices, psychotherapists, nursing care at home, medical services by non-physicians (physiotherapists, speech therapists, occupational therapists, etc.) and income support during sick leave: Kirby Report, vol. 3, at p. 14.

[144] In Germany, as in Sweden, private health insurance is available to individuals at a certain income level who may voluntarily opt out of the Sickness Funds. Private coverage is currently offered by 52 private insurance companies that are obliged to offer an insurance policy with the same benefits as the Sickness Funds at a premium that is no higher than the average maximum contribution to the Sickness Funds. . . .

[145] Despite the availability of alternatives, 88 percent of the German population are covered by the public Sickness Funds: this includes 14 percent to whom private insurance is available. Of the remaining 12 percent, only 9 percent are covered by private insurance and less than 1 percent have no health insurance at all. The remaining 2 percent are covered by government insurance for military and other personnel: Kirby Report, vol. 3, at p. 15.

[146] The United Kingdom offers a comprehensive public health care system—the National Health Service (NHS)— while also allowing for private insurance. Unlike Canada, the United Kingdom allows people to purchase private health care insurance that covers the same benefits as the NHS if these services are supplied by providers working outside of the NHS. Despite the existence of private insurance, only 11.5 percent of the population have purchased it: Kirby Report, vol. 3, at pp. 37-44. Again, it appears that the public system has not suffered as a result of the existence of private alternatives.

[147] After reviewing a number of public health care systems, the Standing Senate Committee on Social Affairs, Science and Technology concluded in the Kirby Report that far from undermining public health care, private contributions and insurance improve the breadth and quality of health care for all citizens. . . .

[149] In summary, the evidence on the experience of other western democracies refutes the government's theoretical contention that a prohibition on private insurance is linked to maintaining quality public health care.

[150] Binnie and LeBel JJ. suggest that the experience of other countries is of little assistance. With respect, we cannot agree. This evidence was properly placed before the trial judge and, unless discredited, stands as the best guide with respect to the question of whether a ban on private insurance is necessary and relevant to the goal of providing quality public health care.

[151] Binnie and LeBel JJ. also suggest that the government's continued commitment to a monopoly on the provision of health insurance cannot be arbitrary because it is rooted in reliance on "a series of authoritative reports [that analysed] health care in this country and in other countries." . . . But the conclusions of other bodies on other material cannot be determinative of this litigation. They cannot relieve the courts of their obligation to review government action for consistency with the *Charter* on the evidence before them.

[152] When we look to the evidence rather than to assumptions, the connection between prohibiting private insurance and maintaining quality public health care vanishes. The evidence before us establishes that where the public system fails to deliver adequate care, the denial of private insurance subjects people to long waiting lists and negatively affects their health and security of the person. The government contends that this is necessary in order to preserve the public health system. The evidence, however, belies that contention.

[153] We conclude that on the evidence adduced in this case, the appellants have established that in the face of delays in treatment that cause psychological and physical suffering, the prohibition on private insurance jeopardizes the right to life, liberty and security of the person of Canadians in an arbitrary manner, and is therefore not in accordance with the principles of fundamental justice.

II. Section 1 of the Charter

[154] Having concluded that the prohibition on private health insurance constitutes a breach of s. 7, we must now consider whether that breach can be justified under s. 1 of the *Charter* as a reasonable limit demonstrably justified in a free and democratic society. The evidence called in this case falls short of demonstrating such justification.

[155] The government undeniably has an interest in protecting the public health regime. However, given the absence of evidence that the prohibition on the purchase and sale of private health insurance protects the health care system, the rational connection between the prohibition and the objective is not made out. Indeed, we question whether an arbitrary provision, which by reason of its arbitrariness cannot further its stated objective, will ever meet the rational connection test under *R. v. Oakes*, [1986] 1 S.C.R. 103.

[156] In addition, the resulting denial of access to timely and effective medical care to those who need it is not proportionate to the beneficial effects of the prohibition on private insurance to the health system as a whole. On the evidence here and for the reasons discussed above, the prohibition goes further than necessary to protect the public system: it is not minimally impairing.

[157] Finally, the benefits of the prohibition do not outweigh the deleterious effects. Prohibiting citizens from obtaining private health care insurance may, as discussed, leave people no choice but to accept excessive delays in the public health system. The physical and psychological suffering and risk of death that may result outweigh whatever benefit (and none has been demonstrated to us here) there may be to the system as a whole.

[158] In sum, the prohibition on obtaining private health insurance, while it might be constitutional in circumstances where health care services are reasonable as to both quality and timeliness, is not constitutional where the public system fails to deliver reasonable services. Life, liberty and security of the person must prevail. To paraphrase Dickson C.J. in *Morgentaler*, at p. 73, if the government chooses to act, it must do so properly.

[159] We agree with Deschamps J.'s conclusion that the prohibition against contracting for private health insurance violates s. 1 of the *Quebec Charter of Human Rights and Freedoms* and is not justifiable under s. 9.1. We also conclude that this prohibition violates s. 7 of the *Canadian Charter of Rights and Freedoms* and cannot be saved under s. 1.

[160] We would allow the appeal, with costs to the appellants throughout.

The reasons of Binnie, LeBel, and Fish JJ. were delivered by

BINNIE AND LEBEL JJ. (dissenting):

I. Introduction

[161] The question in this appeal is whether the province of Quebec not only has the constitutional authority to establish a comprehensive single-tier health plan, but to discourage a second (private) tier health sector by prohibiting the purchase and sale of private health insurance. The appellants argue that timely access to needed medical service is not being provided

in the publicly funded system and that the province cannot therefore deny to those Quebeckers (who can qualify) the right to purchase private insurance to pay for medical services whenever and wherever such services can be obtained for a fee, i.e., in the private sector. This issue has been the subject of protracted debate across Canada through several provincial and federal elections. We are unable to agree with our four colleagues who would allow the appeal that such a debate can or should be resolved as a matter of law by judges. We find that, on the *legal* issues raised, the appeal should be dismissed.

[162] Our colleagues the Chief Justice and Major J. state at para. 105:

> By imposing exclusivity and then failing to provide *public health care of a reasonable standard within a reasonable time*, the government creates circumstances that trigger the application of s. 7 of the [*Canadian*] *Charter*. [Emphasis added.]

[163] The Court recently held in *Auton (Guardian ad litem of) v. British Columbia (Attorney General)*, [2004] 3 S.C.R. 657, 2004 SCC 78, that the government was not required to fund the treatment of autistic children. It did not on that occasion address in constitutional terms the scope and nature of "reasonable" health services. Courts will now have to make that determination. What, then, are constitutionally required "reasonable health services"? What is treatment "within a reasonable time"? What are the benchmarks? How short a waiting list is short enough? How many MRIs does the Constitution require? The majority does not tell us. The majority lays down no manageable constitutional standard. The public cannot know, nor can judges or governments know, how much health care is "reasonable" enough to satisfy s. 7 of the *Canadian Charter of Rights and Freedoms* ("*Canadian Charter*") and s. 1 of the *Charter of Human Rights and Freedoms*, R.S.Q. c. C-12 ("*Quebec Charter*"). It is to be hoped that we will know it when we see it.

[164] The policy of the *Canada Health Act*, R.S.C. 1985, c. C-6, and its provincial counterparts is to provide health care based on need rather than on wealth or status. The evidence certainly established that the public health care system put in place to implement this policy has serious and persistent problems. This does not mean that the courts are well placed to perform the required surgery. The resolution of such a complex fact-laden policy debate does not fit easily within the institutional competence or procedures of courts of law. The courts can use s. 7 of the *Canadian Charter* to pre-empt the ongoing public debate only if the current health plan violates an established "principle of fundamental justice." Our colleagues McLachlin C.J. and Major J. argue that Quebec's enforcement of a single-tier health plan meets this legal test

because it is "arbitrary." In our view, with respect, the prohibition against private health insurance is a rational consequence of Quebec's commitment to the goals and objectives of the *Canada Health Act....*

[166] The Quebec government views the prohibition against private insurance as essential to preventing the current single-tier health system from disintegrating into a *de facto* two-tier system. The trial judge found, and the evidence demonstrated, that there is good reason for this fear. The trial judge concluded that a private health sector fuelled by private insurance would frustrate achievement of the objectives of the *Canada Health Act*. She thus found no *legal* basis to intervene, and declined to do so. This raises the issue of *who* it is that *should* resolve these important and contentious issues. Commissioner Roy Romanow makes the following observation in his Report:

> Some have described it as a perversion of Canadian values that they cannot use their money to purchase faster treatment from a private provider for their loved ones. I believe it is a far greater perversion of Canadian values to accept a system where money, rather than need, determines who gets access to care.
>
> (*Building on Values: The Future of Health Care in Canada: Final Report* (2002) ("Romanow Report"), at p. xx)

Whether or not one endorses this assessment, his premise is that the debate is about *social* values. It is not about constitutional law. We agree.

[167] We believe our colleagues the Chief Justice and Major J. have extended too far the strands of interpretation under the *Canadian Charter* laid down in some of the earlier cases, in particular the ruling on abortion in *R. v. Morgentaler*, [1988] 1 S.C.R. 30 (which involved criminal liability, not public health policy). We cannot find in the constitutional law of Canada a "principle of fundamental justice" dispositive of the problems of waiting lists in the Quebec health system. In our view, the appellants' case does not rest on constitutional law but on their disagreement with the Quebec government on aspects of its social policy. The proper forum to determine the social policy of Quebec in this matter is the National Assembly....

II. Analysis

[177] The appellants' principal argument is that the existence of waiting lists in Quebec and the concurrent prohibition on private health insurance violate s. 7 of the *Canadian Charter*, which guarantees everyone the right to life, liberty and security of the person, and the right not to be deprived thereof except in accordance with the principles of fundamental justice.

[178] The legal question raised by our colleagues the Chief Justice and Major J. under the *Canadian Charter* is

whether or not the Quebec health plan violates a principle of fundamental justice and, if so, whether the plan can nevertheless be saved under s. 1.

[179] The reasons of our colleague Deschamps J., on the other hand, are limited to s. 1 of the *Quebec Charter* which protects the right of every human being to life and to personal security, inviolability and freedom. The *Quebec Charter* does not talk explicitly about "principles of fundamental justice." Nevertheless, in our view, the legislative limits fixed by the *Quebec Charter* are no more favourable to the appellants' case than are those fixed by the *Canadian Charter*. Rights under the *Quebec Charter* are to be exercised with "proper" regard to "democratic" values (including those of the electorate) "public order and the general well-being of the citizens of Québec" (including those who cannot afford, or may not qualify for, private health insurance coverage)....

[180] Our colleagues the Chief Justice and Major J. agree with the appellants that there is a violation of s. 7 of the *Canadian Charter*. As mentioned earlier, their opinion rests in substantial part on observations made by various members of this Court in *Morgentaler*. At issue in that case was the criminal liability of doctors and their patients under s. 251 of the *Criminal Code*, R.S.C. 1970, c. C-34, for performing abortions. The nub of the legal challenge was that in creating the abortion offence Parliament had qualified the charge with a "therapeutic abortion" defence, but the defence was not working. The factual and legal issues raised in that criminal law problem are, we think, far removed from the debate over a two-tier health system. *Morgentaler* applied a "manifest unfairness" test which has never been adopted by the Court outside the criminal law, and certainly not in the context of the design of social programs. The *Morgentaler* judgment fastened on *internal* inconsistencies in s. 251 of the Code, which find no counterpart here. In our view, with respect, *Morgentaler* provides no support for the appellants in this case, as we discuss commencing at para. 259....

B. Canadian Charter of Rights and Freedoms

[190] ...

(1) The Application of Section 7 to Matters Not Falling Within the Administration of Justice

...[193] Section 7 gives rise to some of the most difficult issues in *Canadian Charter* litigation. Because s. 7 protects the most basic interests of human beings—life, liberty and security—claimants call on the courts to adjudicate many difficult moral and ethical issues. It is therefore prudent, in our view, to proceed cautiously and incrementally in applying s. 7, particularly in distilling those principles that are so vital to our society's conception of "principles of fundamental justice" as to be constitutionally entrenched....

[196] It will likely be a rare case where s. 7 will apply in circumstances entirely unrelated to adjudicative or administrative proceedings. That said, the Court has consistently left open the possibility that s. 7 may apply outside the context of the administration of justice: *Gosselin v. Quebec (Attorney General)*, [2002] 4 S.C.R. 429, 2002 SCC 84, at paras. 78-80 and 414.

[197] The Court has been moving away from a narrow approach to s. 7, which restricted the scope of the section to legal rights to be interpreted in light of the rights enumerated in ss. 8 to 14. ... In *Blencoe v. British Columbia (Human Rights Commission)*, [2000] 2 S.C.R. 307, 2000 SCC 44, the majority held that s. 7 can apply outside of the criminal context. Further, in *Winnipeg Child and Family Services v. K.L.W.*, [2000] 2 S.C.R. 519, 2000 SCC 48, the Court noted that it had held in *B.(R.) v. Children's Aid Society of Metropolitan Toronto*, [1995] 1 S.C.R. 315, that the wardship provisions of the *Child Welfare Act*, R.S.O. 1980, c. 66, denying parents the ability to choose medical treatment for their infants, implicated the s. 7 liberty interests of parents.

[198] Placing s. 7 under the heading "Legal Rights" in the *Canadian Charter* does not narrow or control its scope. Such a result would be unduly formalistic and inconsistent with the large, liberal and purposive interpretation of s. 7 that has been the hallmark of this Court's approach since *Re B.C. Motor Vehicle Act*, [1985] 2 S.C.R. 486. This is evidenced by the refusal of the majority in that case to restrict "principles of fundamental justice" solely to procedural guarantees. Lamer J. observed that "the principles of fundamental justice are to be found in the basic tenets and principles, *not only of our judicial process*, but also of the other components of our legal system" (p. 512 (emphasis added)).

[199] Claimants whose life, liberty or security of the person is put at risk are entitled to relief only to the extent that their complaint arises from a breach of an identifiable principle of fundamental justice. *The real control over the scope and operation of s. 7 is to be found in the requirement that the applicant identify a violation of a principle of fundamental justice.* The further a challenged state action lies from the traditional adjudicative context, the more difficult it will be for a claimant to make that essential link. As will become clear, that is precisely the difficulty encountered by the claimants here: they are unable to demonstrate that any principle of fundamental justice has been contravened.

(2) Which Section 7 Interests Are Engaged?

[200] Section 7 interests are enumerated as life, liberty and security of the person. As stated, we accept the trial judge's finding that the current state of the Quebec health system, linked to the prohibition against health insurance for insured services,

is capable, at least in the cases of *some* individuals on *some* occasions, of putting at risk their life or security of the person.

[201] We do not agree with the appellants, however, that the Quebec Health Plan puts the "liberty" of Quebeckers at risk. The argument that "liberty" includes freedom of contract (in this case to contract for private medical insurance) is novel in Canada, where economic rights are not included in the *Canadian Charter* and discredited in the United States. In that country, the liberty of individuals (mainly employers) to contract out of social and economic programs was endorsed by the Supreme Court in the early decades of the 20th century on the theory that laws that prohibited employers from entering into oppressive contracts with employees violated their "liberty" of contract; see, e.g., *Lochner v. New York*, 198 U.S. 45 (1905), at p. 62:

> ... a prohibition to enter into any contract of labor in a bakery for more than a certain number of hours a week, is, in our judgment, so wholly beside the matter of a proper, reasonable and fair provision, as to run counter to that liberty of person and of free contract provided for in the Federal Constitution.

Of this line of cases, which was not brought to an end until *West Coast Hotel Co. v. Parrish*, 300 U.S. 379 (1937), Professor L.H. Tribe has written that the Supreme Court of the United States:

> ... relied on the Fourteenth Amendment's Due Process Clause to strike down economic legislation that the Court saw as improperly *infringing on contractual liberty*, but in which the Court was widely (even if not always correctly) perceived to be substituting its own judgment, in the absence of any actual constitutional mandate, for that of the legislature. [Emphasis added.]

(*American Constitutional Law* (3rd ed. 2000), vol. 1, at p. 1318)

... [207] As stated, the principal legal hurdle to the appellants' *Canadian Charter* challenge is not the preliminary step of identifying a s. 7 interest potentially affected in the case of *some* Quebeckers in *some* circumstances. The hurdle lies in their failure to find a fundamental principle of justice that is violated by the Quebec health plan so as to justify the Court in striking down the prohibition against private insurance for what the government has identified as "insured services."

C. Principles of Fundamental Justice

[208] For a principle to be one of fundamental justice, it must count among the basic tenets of our *legal* system: *Re B.C. Motor Vehicle Act*, at p. 503. It must generally be accepted as such among reasonable people. As explained by the majority in *Malmo-Levine*, at para. 113:

> The requirement of "general acceptance among reasonable people" enhances the legitimacy of judicial review of state action, and ensures that the values against which state action is measured are not just fundamental "in the eye of the beholder *only*": *Rodriguez*, at pp. 607 and 590. ...

[209] Thus, the formal requirements for a principle of fundamental justice are threefold. First, it must be a *legal* principle. Second, the reasonable person must regard it as vital to our societal notion of justice, which implies a significant *societal consensus*. Third, it must be capable of being *identified with precision* and applied in a manner that yields *predictable results*. These requirements present insurmountable hurdles to the appellants. The aim of "health care of a reasonable standard within a reasonable time" is not a *legal* principle. There is no "societal consensus" about what it means or how to achieve it. It cannot be "identified with precision." As the testimony in this case showed, a level of care that is considered perfectly reasonable by some doctors is denounced by others. ...

[210] Much of the argument pursued by the Chief Justice and Major J., as well as by Deschamps J. in her reasons relating to the *Quebec Charter*, revolves around the vexing issue of waiting lists, which have notoriously fuelled major public debates and controversies.

[211] The case history of the appellant Zeliotis illustrates why rationing of health services is necessary and how it works. The trial judge, having heard all the evidence, concluded that the delays Mr. Zeliotis experienced in obtaining hip surgery were caused not by excessive waiting lists but by a number of other factors, including his pre-existing depression and his indecision and unfounded medical complaints. ...

(a) There Is No Consensus About What Constitutes "Reasonable" Waiting Times

[212] A review of the expert evidence and the medical literature suggests that there is no consensus regarding guidelines for timely medical treatment. Dr. Wright remarked:

> So the issue of defining what is a reasonable waiting list is a very difficult one because if you have a hundred (100) surgeons, you have a hundred (100) opinions, it's very difficult to come to a consensus on these questions. [A.R., at p. 1186] ...

(b) The Experts Accepted by the Trial Judge Relied on More Than Just "Common Sense"

[214] Our colleagues the Chief Justice and Major J. dismiss the experts accepted by the trial judge as relying on little more than "common sense" (para. 137). Although we agree that the experts offered "common sense," they offered a good deal more. The experts heard by the trial court included

Mr. Claude Castonguay, who was Quebec's Minister of Health in 1970 (the [TRANSLATION] "father of Quebec health insurance") and who chaired the Commission of Inquiry on Health and Social Welfare, as well as a number of other public health experts, including Dr. Fernand Turcotte, a professor of medicine at Laval University, who holds degrees from the University of Montreal and Harvard and has been certified by the Royal College of Physicians and Surgeons of Canada as a specialist in community medicine; Dr. Howard Bergman, Chief of the Division of Geriatric Medicine at Montreal's Jewish General Hospital, Director of the Division of Geriatric Medicine and a professor in the departments of Internal Medicine and Family Medicine at McGill University, a fellow of the American Geriatrics Society and an associate professor at the University of Montreal in the department of health administration; Dr. Charles J. Wright, a physician specialized in surgery, Director of the Centre for Clinical Epidemiology & Evaluation at the Vancouver Hospital & Health Sciences Centre, and a faculty member of the University of British Columbia and of the British Columbia Office of Health Technology Assessment; Professor Jean-Louis Denis, a community health doctor of the University of Montreal's [TRANSLATION] "health services organization"; Professor Theodore R. Marmor, a professor of public policy and management and of political science at Yale University, who holds a PhD from Harvard University in politics and history and is a graduate research fellow at Oxford; and Dr. J. Edwin Coffey, a graduate of McGill University in medicine who specializes in obstetrics and gynecology, a fellow of the Royal College of Physicians and Surgeons of Canada and of the American College of Obstetricians and Gynecologists, and a former associate professor in the McGill University Faculty of Medicine. The respondent's experts testified and were cross-examined. The trial judge found them to be credible and reliable. We owe deference to her findings in this respect.

[215] The trial judge, having heard the evidence, concluded as follows:

> [TRANSLATION] ... although some of these specialists indicated a desire to be free to obtain private insurance, none of them gave their full and absolute support to the applicants' proposals, as they explained *that it was neither clear nor obvious that a reorganization of the health system with a parallel private system would solve all the existing problems of delays and access.* On the contrary, the specialists who testified remained quite circumspect about this complex and difficult question. [Emphasis added; p. 796.]

The exception to the consensus was the appellants' expert, Dr. Coffey, who stated that in his opinion the development of a private insurance scheme would not affect the public health scheme. This is the argument accepted by our colleagues the Chief Justice and Major J. However on this point the trial judge observed, as on others, [TRANSLATION] "*that Dr. Coffey stood alone in both his expert evaluation and the conclusions he reached*" (p. 808 (emphasis in original)). ...

(c) The Lack of Accurate Data

[217] How serious is the waiting-list problem? No doubt it is serious; but how serious? The first major evidentiary difficulty for the appellants is the lack of accurate data. The major studies concluded that the real picture concerning waiting lists in Canada is subject to contradictory evidence and conflicting claims (Romanow Report, at p. 139, and the Kirby Report, vol. 4, at p. 41, and vol. 6, at pp. 109-10). This can also be seen from the evidence of the experts who testified at trial in the present case....

[226] We have similar concerns about the use made by the appellants of various reports in connection with other OECD countries. These "country" reports were included in an *Interim* Kirby Report but not in its final version. The Final Kirby Report's recommendation was to stick with a single-tier system. We think the Court is sufficiently burdened with conflicting evidence about our own health system without attempting a detailed investigation of the merits of trade-offs made in other countries, for their own purposes....

[229] We are not to be taken as disputing the undoubted fact that there are serious problems with the single-tier health plan in Canada. Our point is simply that bits of evidence must be put in context. With respect, it is particularly dangerous to venture selectively into aspects of foreign health care systems with which we, as Canadians, have little familiarity. At the very least such information should be filtered and analysed at trial through an expert witness.

[230] Taking the good with the bad, the Final Kirby Report recommended continuation of a single-tier health system (as did the Romanow Report). The authors of the Kirby Report were fully aware of the extracts from their interim report relied upon by our colleagues the Chief Justice and Major J., yet they specifically rejected two-tier health care....

(2) Arbitrariness

[231] Our colleagues the Chief Justice and Major J. take the view that a law which arbitrarily violates life or security of the person is unconstitutional. We agree that this is a principle of fundamental justice. We do not agree that it applies to the facts of this case.

[232] A deprivation of a right will be arbitrary and will thus infringe s. 7 if it bears no relation to, or is inconsistent with, the state interest that lies behind the legislation....

[233] We agree with our colleagues the Chief Justice and Major J. that a law is arbitrary if "it bears no relation to, or is

inconsistent with, the objective that lies behind [the legislation]" (para. 130). We do not agree with the Chief Justice and Major J. that the prohibition against private health insurance "bears no relation to, or is inconsistent with" the preservation of access to a health system based on need rather than wealth in accordance with the *Canada Health Act*. We also do not agree with our colleagues' expansion of the *Morgentaler* principle to invalidate a prohibition simply because a court believes it to be "unnecessary" for the government's purpose. There must be more than that to sustain a valid objection.

[234] The accepted definition in *Rodriguez* states that a law is arbitrary only where "it bears no relation to, or is inconsistent with, the objective that lies behind the legislation." To substitute the term "unnecessary" for "inconsistent" is to substantively alter the meaning of the term "arbitrary." "Inconsistent" means that the law logically contradicts its objectives, whereas "unnecessary" simply means that the objective could be met by other means. It is quite apparent that the latter is a much broader term that involves a policy choice. If a court were to declare unconstitutional every law impacting "security of the person" that the court considers unnecessary, there would be much greater scope for intervention under s. 7 than has previously been considered by this Court to be acceptable. . . .

[235] Rejecting the findings in the courts below based on their own reading of the evidence, our colleagues the Chief Justice and Major J. state (at para. 128):

> We are of the opinion that the evidence before the trial judge supports a finding that the impugned provisions are arbitrary and that the deprivation of life and security of the person that flows from them cannot therefore be said to accord with the principles of fundamental justice.

We note that our colleagues refer to the evidence *before* the trial judge rather than the view taken of that evidence *by* the trial judge. The trial judge reached a contrary conclusion on the facts, and deference is due to her view of that evidence; see *Housen v. Nikolaisen*, [2002] 2 S.C.R. 235, 2002 SCC 33. In any event, with respect, we accept the contrary conclusions of the trial judge and the Quebec Court of Appeal. We approach the issue of arbitrariness in three steps:

(i)   What is the "state interest" sought to be protected?
(ii) What is the relationship between the "state interest" thus identified and the prohibition against private health insurance?
(iii) Have the appellants established that the prohibition bears no relation to, or is inconsistent with, the state interest?

We will address each question in turn.

(a) What Is the "State Interest" Sought to Be Protected?

[236] Quebec's legislative objective is to provide high quality health care, at a reasonable cost, for as many people as possible in a manner that is consistent with principles of efficiency, equity and fiscal responsibility. Quebec (along with the other provinces and territories) subscribes to the policy objectives of the *Canada Health Act*, which include (i) the equal provision of medical services to all residents, regardless of status, wealth or personal insurability, and (ii) fiscal responsibility. An overbuilt health system is seen as no more in the larger public interest than a system that on occasion falls short. The legislative task is to strike a balance among competing interests. . . .

(b) What Is the Relationship Between the "State Interest" Thus Identified and the Prohibition Against Private Health Insurance?

. . . [239] In *principle*, Quebec wants a health system where access is governed by need rather than wealth or status. Quebec does not want people who are uninsurable to be left behind. To accomplish this objective endorsed by the *Canada Health Act*, Quebec seeks to discourage the growth of private-sector delivery of "insured" services based on wealth and insurability. We believe the prohibition is rationally connected to Quebec's objective and is not inconsistent with it.

[240] In *practical terms*, Quebec bases the prohibition on the view that private insurance, and a consequent major expansion of private health services, would have a harmful effect on the public system. . . .

[242] The trial judge considered all the evidence and concluded that the expansion of private health care would undoubtedly have a negative impact on the public health system (at p. 827):

> [TRANSLATION] The evidence has shown that the right of access to a parallel private health care system claimed by the applicants *would have repercussions on the rights of the population as a whole. We cannot bury our heads in the sand. The effect of establishing a parallel private health care system would be to threaten the integrity, proper functioning and viability of the public system.* . . .

(vi) Conclusion on "Arbitrariness"

[256] For all these reasons, we agree with the conclusion of the trial judge and the Quebec Court of Appeal that in light of the legislative objectives of the *Canada Health Act* it is not "arbitrary" for Quebec to discourage the growth of private sector health care. Prohibition of private health insurance is directly related to Quebec's interest in promoting a need-based system and in ensuring its viability and efficiency. Prohibition

of private insurance is not "inconsistent" with the state interest; still less is it "unrelated" to it.

[257] In short, it cannot be said that the prohibition against private health insurance "bears no relation to, or is inconsistent with" preservation of a health system predominantly based on need rather than wealth or status, as required by the *Rodriguez* test, at pp. 594-95.

[258] As to our colleagues' dismissal of the factual basis for Quebec's legislative choice, the public has invested very large sums of money in a series of authoritative reports to analyse health care in this country and in other countries. The reports uniformly recommend the retention of single-tier medicine. People are free to challenge (as do the appellants) the government's reliance on those reports but such reliance cannot be dismissed as "arbitrary." . . .

(4) Conclusion Under Section 7 of the Canadian Charter

[265] For the foregoing reasons, even accepting (as we do) the trial judge's conclusion that the claimants have established a deprivation of the life and security of *some* Quebec residents occasioned in *some* circumstances by waiting list delays, the deprivation would not violate any *legal* principle of fundamental justice within the meaning of s. 7 of the *Canadian Charter*. On that point, too, we share the opinion of the trial judge and the Quebec Court of Appeal, as previously mentioned.

D. The Appellants' Challenge Under the Quebec Charter

[266] The *Quebec Charter* is a major quasi-constitutional instrument. Our colleague Deschamps J. finds a violation of s. 1. . . .

[272] Under s. 1 of the *Quebec Charter*, as at the first stage of a s. 7 analysis, the claimant bears the burden of establishing, on a balance of probabilities, that the impugned law infringes his or her protected rights and interests. If such a claim is made out, the focus of the analysis may shift to s. 9.1 of the *Quebec Charter* in order to determine whether the claimed exercise of the right is made with due regard for "democratic values, public order and the general well-being of the citizens of Québec."

[273] In our view, on the evidence, the exercise by the appellants of their claimed *Quebec Charter* rights to defeat the prohibition against private insurance would not have "proper regard for democratic values" or "public order," as the future of a publicly supported and financed single-tier health plan should be in the hands of elected representatives. Nor would it have proper regard for the "general well-being of the

citizens of Québec," who are the designated beneficiaries of the health plan, and in particular for the well-being of the less advantaged Quebeckers.

[274] Those who seek private health insurance are those who can afford it and can qualify for it. They will be the more advantaged members of society. They are differentiated from the general population, not by their health problems, which are found in every group in society, but by their income status. We share the view of Dickson C.J. that the *Canadian Charter* should not become an instrument to be used by the wealthy to "roll back" the benefits of a legislative scheme that helps the poorer members of society. He observed in *Edwards Books*, at p. 779:

> In interpreting and applying the *Charter* I believe that the courts must be cautious to ensure that it does not simply become an instrument of better situated individuals to roll back legislation which has as its object the improvement of the condition of less advantaged persons.

The concern, of course, is that once the health needs of the wealthier members of society are looked after in the "upper tier," they will have less incentive to continue to pressure the government for improvements to the public system as a whole.

[275] The comments of Dickson C.J. are even more relevant to the *Quebec Charter* given its broad scope and its potential application to a wide range of private relationships.

[276] This is not a case, in our view, where the onus of proof determines the outcome. The evidence amply supports the validity of the prohibition of private insurance under the *Quebec Charter*. The objectives are compelling. A rational connection is demonstrated. The decision boils down to an application of the minimal impairment test. In respect of questions of social and economic policy, this test leaves a substantial margin of appreciation to the Quebec legislature. Designing, financing and operating the public health system of a modern democratic society like Quebec remains a challenging task. It calls for difficult choices. In the end, we find that the choice made a generation ago by the National Assembly of Quebec remains within the range of options that are justifiable under s. 9.1. Shifting the design of the health system to the courts is not a wise choice. . . .

[278] The evidence reviewed above establishes that the impugned provisions were part of a system which is mindful and protective of the interests of all, not only of some.

[279] We would dismiss the appeal.

PART SEVEN

Remedies

R. v. Collins, 1987

A centuries-old legal maxim holds that where there is a right, there is also a remedy. Rights without remedies are mere words for the person whose right has been violated. With some narrow exceptions, this is as true in constitutional law as it is in common law.

The *Canadian Charter*'s remedial provisions are contained in section 24.[1] Section 24(1), the general remedial provision, instructs courts to grant such remedies "as the court considers appropriate and just in the circumstances." Courts have interpreted this provision as broadly as it is set out, relying on it to make declarations of right, leaving the detailed implementation of the right to expert officials;[2] strike down laws in whole or in part;[3] alter the interpretation of laws to bring them into conformity with *Charter* principles;[4] add or "read in" words to a law to remedy an underinclusive list of beneficiaries of state action;[5] and temporarily suspend a declaration of invalidity to allow governments time to fashion new legislation without creating a legal vacuum in the meantime.[6] More controversially, section 24(1) might support a "constitutional exemption," a declaration that though a legislative provision is constitutionally valid, its application in a particular case would be unconstitutional.[7]

Section 24(2) sets a new Canadian standard governing the exclusion of illegally obtained evidence in legal proceedings. When evidence is collected in a manner that infringes someone's rights, "the evidence shall be excluded if it is established that, having regard to all the circumstances, the admission of it in the proceedings would bring the administration of justice into disrepute." This provision was drafted to avoid two extreme possibilities. The first possibility is to exclude all evidence illegally obtained, raising the prospect that factually guilty criminals would be acquitted due to the exclusion of evidence obtained as a result of even trivial breaches of rights. The second possibility is to admit all relevant evidence, regardless of the manner in which it was obtained. This was roughly the state of Canadian

---

1   Note also that section 52 of the *Constitution Act, 1982* also has a remedial component in that it declares "of no force or effect" laws found by courts to be unconstitutional.

2   *Mahe v. Alberta*, [1990] 1 S.C.R. 342.

3   *R. v. Hess*, [1990] 2 S.C.R. 906.

4   *R. v. Butler*, [1992] 1 S.C.R. 452.

5   *Vriend v. Alberta*, [1998] 1 S.C.R. 493.

6   *Dunmore v. Ontario (Attorney General)*, [2001] 3 S.C.R. 1016.

7   The signal case concerns Robert Latimer, who was found guilty of second-degree murder for killing his severely disabled daughter. The trial court held that, in the circumstances of the case, eligibility for parole after a statutory minimum of 10 years would violate Latimer's right not to be subject to cruel and unusual punishment. It granted a constitutional exemption from the law and imposed one year of prison followed by one year of probation. The Saskatchewan Court of Appeal disagreed and imposed the statutory 10-year imprisonment. The Supreme Court did not pronounce on the constitutional exemption because it did not find a section 12 violation: *R. v. Latimer*, [2001] 1 S.C.R. 3.

law prior to 1982. In *The Queen v. Wray*,[8] the accused in a murder investigation was interrogated in an abusive and duplicitous manner and finally produced a confession, including a statement about where in a swamp a gun might be found. The murder weapon was indeed found in that area. At trial the prosecution sought to link the accused to the murder weapon—and the murder—by admitting that part of the confession in which the accused told police about the location of the gun. However, the confession was excluded because of the disrepute into which the administration of justice would be brought were the evidence admitted. The Court of Appeal affirmed, but the Supreme Court of Canada ordered a new trial, declaring that all evidence having probative value, regardless of the manner of its collection, is admissible.

The section 24(2) test, by avoiding these extremes, is a partial exclusionary rule, instructing the courts to consider the effect of admission or exclusion of illegally obtained evidence on public confidence in the justice system. Courts must, in a sense, become judges of public opinion. The interesting problem is that the integrity of the administration of justice depends on courts being insulated from public opinion; they are to decide cases on the basis of the facts and law, not on the basis of public reactions to their decisions. Yet it remains true that no independent court can function at all in the absence of continued public confidence. Section 24 requires judges to assess public confidence—not unreflective, visceral public reaction, but a public opinion that would be formed on the basis of a full and rational deliberation on the circumstances of a case.

The Supreme Court first considered section 24(2) in *R. v. Therens*, which involved the exclusion of breathalyzer evidence obtained one week after the *Charter*'s entrenchment in April 1982. Following a car accident, the accused was asked to provide a breath sample and was not informed of his right to counsel pursuant to section 10 of the *Charter*. Police officers were apparently operating under the pre-*Charter* understanding that a request to provide a breath sample is not "detention" and so would not trigger the detainee's right to be informed of his right to instruct counsel. The Supreme Court ruled otherwise and then considered whether the evidence of alcohol consumption should be excluded pursuant to section 24(2). Lower courts had interpreted section 24(2) in pre-*Charter* terms—to require exclusion if admission of the evidence would shock the community. But the Court held that section 24(2) imposes a standard much more solicitous of the rights of the accused. The majority in *Therens* considered the breach of Therens's rights to be flagrant. A message had to be sent that, in the age of the *Charter*, rights could not be disregarded by police with impunity. But two dissenting justices would have admitted the evidence, arguing that the police officer acted in good faith, not in flagrant and wilful denial of Therens's rights. According to the minority, police officers could be forgiven for failing to anticipate how courts would interpret the new *Charter* standard within one week of its entrenchment.

In *R. v. Collins*, Ruby Collins, sitting at a restaurant table, was the recipient of a flying chokehold by a police officer who suspected her of heroin trafficking. The police did not have a judicial warrant for the search. Was Collins's section 8 right not to be subject to unreasonable search and seizure breached? If so, should the heroin evidence obtained as a

---

8   [1971] S.C.R. 272.

result of that illegal search be admitted against her at trial? For the majority, Justice Lamer wrote that for warrantless police searches to be reasonable, the search must be according to law, the law itself must be reasonable, and the manner of the search must be reasonable.

No one contested the constitutionality of the law governing searches. The next question was whether the search complied with the law, and the law in this case required that the officers have reasonable grounds to believe that drugs would be found on her person. Accepting the defence argument that hearsay evidence of Collins's heroin addiction on which the police relied did not constitute reasonable grounds, the trial judge found that the search was unreasonable. Nonetheless, he admitted the heroin evidence, citing pre-*Charter* evidentiary rules. In the Supreme Court, Justice Lamer and four colleagues considered the defence objection groundless and ordered a new trial based on the admissibility of that evidence.

But *Collins* established much more than this. Regardless of grounds the police had for searching Collins, a large quantity of heroin was found in her possession. This was real evidence tending to a finding of guilt. Was it therefore admissible? Should the courts, in other words, follow pre-*Charter* rules governing the admissibility of evidence, or does section 24(2) set a new standard? The Court set out a list of factors to be considered in applying section 24(2) that has largely stood the test of time. ⁓

Discussion Questions

1. What test did the Court develop for the section 8 protection against unreasonable search and seizure?
2. What factors are to be considered when courts weigh the admissibility of illegally obtained evidence?
3. Section 24(2) requires courts to consider the reputation of the administration of justice. To what extent does this involve a consideration of public opinion regarding a basic matter of criminal procedure?

R. v. COLLINS
[1987] 1 S.C.R. 265

Hearing: May 27, 1986; Judgment: April 9, 1987.

Present: Dickson C.J. and McIntyre, Chouinard,* Lamer, Wilson, Le Dain, and La Forest JJ.

* Chouinard J. took no part in the judgment.

The judgment of Dickson C.J. and Lamer, Wilson, and La Forest JJ. was delivered by

[1] **LAMER J.:** The appellant, Ruby Collins, was seated in a pub in the town of Gibsons when she was suddenly seized by the throat and pulled down to the floor by a man who said to her "police officer." The police officer, then noticing that she had her hand clenched around an object, instructed her to let go of the object. As it turned out, she had a green balloon containing heroin.

[2] It is common knowledge that drug traffickers often keep their drugs in balloons or condoms in their mouths so that they may, when approached by the Narcotics Control Agent, swallow the drugs without harm and recoup them subsequently. The "throat hold" is used to prevent them from swallowing the drugs.

[3] The issue is whether the evidence obtained under these circumstances is to be excluded under s. 24(2) of the *Charter*.

The Facts

[4] Constables Rodine and Woods of the RCMP Drug Squad at Vancouver attended at Gibsons to assist the Gibsons Detachment in dealing with a "heroin problem." They commenced a surveillance at 11:00 a.m. at the Ritz Motel. Ruby Collins and her husband Richard were observed moving their belongings from one room to another and going to and from a car parked in front of their room. The officers ceased their surveillance at noon.

[5] At 2:50 p.m., the officers entered the Cedars Pub, where they observed Ruby Collins seated at a table with two other people. Richard Collins and another person joined the first group at 3:35 p.m. At 3:50 p.m., Richard Collins and one of the others left the pub, and the officers followed them. They arrested Richard Collins and the other man at a nearby trailer court. Richard Collins was searched and was found to be in possession of heroin.

[6] The officers returned to the pub at 4:15 p.m. They observed Ruby Collins sitting with another woman at a different table. Constable Woods went directly to Ruby Collins [where he applied the throat hold and noticed the balloon in her hand]. . . .

Legislation

[7] The search of Ruby Collins was purportedly authorized by s. 10(1) of the *Narcotic Control Act*, R.S.C. 1970, c. N-1, as amended, as that section read prior to the amendments of December 1985:

> **10.** (1) A peace officer may, at any time,
> (*a*) without a warrant enter and search any place other than a dwelling-house, and under the authority of a writ of assistance or a warrant issued under this section, enter and search any dwelling-house in which he reasonably believes there is a narcotic by means of or in respect of which an offence under this Act has been committed;
> (*b*) search any person found in such place; and
> (*c*) seize and take away any narcotic found in such place, any thing in such place in which he reasonably suspects a narcotic is contained or concealed, or any other thing by means of or in respect of which he reasonably believes an offence under this Act has been committed or that may be evidence of the commission of such an offence.

[8] The relevant provisions of the *Canadian Charter of Rights and Freedoms* are ss. 8 and 24:

> **8.** Everyone has the right to be secure against unreasonable search or seizure. . . .
> **24.** (1) Anyone whose rights or freedoms, as guaranteed by this Charter, have been infringed or denied may apply to a court of competent jurisdiction to obtain such remedy as the court considers appropriate and just in the circumstances.
> (2) Where, in proceedings under subsection (1), a court concludes that evidence was obtained in a manner that infringed or denied any rights or freedoms guaranteed by this Charter, the evidence shall be excluded if it is established that, having regard to all the circumstances, the admission of it in the proceedings would bring the administration of justice into disrepute.

. . . [9] . . .

The Law

[19] The appellant seeks the exclusion of evidence that she was in possession of heroin, alleging that the heroin was discovered pursuant to a search which was unreasonable under s. 8 of the *Charter*. This Court in *Therens* [*R. v.*, [1985] 1 S.C.R. 613], held that evidence cannot be excluded as a remedy under s. 24(1) of the *Charter*, but must meet the test of exclusion under s. 24(2). . . .

[20] . . . On the facts of this case . . . there are only two issues to be addressed:

(1) was the search conducted by the police officer unreasonable?

(2) if so, having regard to all the circumstances, would the admission of the evidence bring the administration of justice into disrepute?

The Reasonableness of the Search

[21] The appellant, in my view, bears the burden of persuading the court that her *Charter* rights or freedoms have been infringed or denied. That appears from the wording of s. 24(1) and (2), and most courts which have considered the issue have come to that conclusion (see *R. v. Lundrigan* (1985), 19 C.C.C. (3d) 499 (Man. C.A.), and the cases cited therein and Gibson, *The Law of the Charter: General Principles* (1986), p. 278). The appellant also bears the initial burden of presenting evidence. The standard of persuasion required is only the civil standard of the balance of probabilities and, because of this, the allocation of the burden of persuasion means only that, in a case where the evidence does not establish whether or not the appellant's rights were infringed, the court must conclude that they were not.

[22] The courts have also developed certain presumptions. In particular, this Court held in *Hunter v. Southam Inc.*, [1984] 2 S.C.R. 145, at p. 161:

> In *United States v. Rabinowitz*, 339 U.S. 56 (1950), the Supreme Court of the United States had held that a search without warrant was not *ipso facto* unreasonable. Seventeen years later, however, in *Katz*, Stewart J. concluded that a warrantless search was *prima facie* "unreasonable" under the Fourth Amendment. The terms of the Fourth Amendment are not identical to those of s. 8 and American decisions can be transplanted to the Canadian context only with the greatest caution. Nevertheless, I would in the present instance respectfully adopt Stewart J.'s formulation as equally applicable to the concept of "unreasonableness" under s. 8, and would require the party seeking to justify a warrantless search to rebut this presumption of unreasonableness.

This shifts the burden of persuasion from the appellant to the Crown. As a result, once the appellant has demonstrated that the search was a warrantless one, the Crown has the burden of showing that the search was, on a balance of probabilities, reasonable.

[23] A search will be reasonable if it is authorized by law, if the law itself is reasonable and if the manner in which the search was carried out is reasonable. In this case, the Crown argued that the search was carried out under s. 10(1) of the *Narcotic Control Act, supra*. As the appellant has not challenged the constitutionality of s. 10(1) of the Act, the issues that remain to be decided here are whether the search was unreasonable because the officer did not come within s. 10 of the Act, or whether, while being within s. 10, he carried out the search in a manner that made the search unreasonable.

[24] For the search to be lawful under s. 10, the Crown must establish that the officer believed on reasonable grounds that there was a narcotic in the place where the person searched was found. The nature of the belief will also determine whether the manner in which the search was carried out was reasonable. For example, if a police officer is told by a reliable source that there are persons in possession of drugs in a certain place, the officer may, depending on the circumstances and the nature and precision of the information given by that source, search persons found in that place under s. 10, but surely, without very specific information, a seizure by the throat, as in this case, would be unreasonable. Of course, if he is lawfully searching a person whom he believes on reasonable grounds to be a "drug handler," then the "throat hold" would not be unreasonable.

[25] Because of the presumption of unreasonableness, the Crown in this case had to present evidence of the officer's belief and the reasonable grounds for that belief. It may be surmised that there were reasonable grounds based on information received from the local police. However, the Crown failed to establish such reasonable grounds in the examination-in-chief of Constable Woods, and, as set out earlier, when it attempted to do so on its re-examination, the appellant's counsel objected. As a result, the Crown never did establish the constable's reasonable grounds. Without such evidence, it is clear that the trial judge was correct in concluding that the search was unreasonable because unlawful and carried out with unnecessary violence.

[26] However, the problem is that the objection raised by the appellant's counsel was groundless: this Court has held that reasonable grounds can be based on information received from third parties without infringing the hearsay rule (*Eccles v. Bourque* [[1975] 2 S.C.R. 739]), and the question put to the constable in this case was not outside the ambit of the ground covered in cross-examination. A further problem is that the record does not disclose why the question was not answered: it is not clear whether the trial judge maintained the objection or whether the Crown had reacted to the objection by withdrawing the question. It is worthy of mention that, because a conviction was entered, the Crown could not in any event appeal against the decision.

[27] This Court has two options. We could resolve the doubt against the Crown, which had the burden of persuasion, and simply proceed on the basis that there was no such evidence. Alternatively, we could order a new trial. I would order a new trial on the basis that the trial judge either made an incorrect ruling or failed to make a ruling, and, in any

event, the appellant should not, in the particular circumstances of this case, be allowed to benefit from her counsel's unfounded objection.

[28] However, before ordering a new trial, we must decide whether we agree with the trial judge and the Court of Appeal that the evidence of the heroin would be admissible regardless of the constable's grounds for the search, for there then would be no point in a new trial and we should dismiss the appeal. As a result, I must determine whether I would exclude the evidence under s. 24(2) on the assumption that Constable Woods testifies that he had not received any further information, thereby leaving matters in that regard as they stand at present on the record.

Bringing the Administration of Justice into Disrepute

[29] On the record as it now stands, the appellant has established that the search was unreasonable and violated her rights under s. 8 of the *Charter*. As Seaton J.A. pointed out in the Court of Appeal, s. 24(2) has adopted an intermediate position with respect to the exclusion of evidence obtained in violation of the *Charter*. It rejected the American rule excluding all evidence obtained in violation of the Bill of Rights and the common law rule that all relevant evidence was admissible regardless of the means by which it was obtained. Section 24(2) requires the exclusion of the evidence "if it is established that, having regard to all the circumstances, the admission of it in the proceedings would bring the administration of justice into disrepute."

[30] At the outset, it should be noted that the use of the phrase "if it is established that" places the burden of persuasion on the applicant, for it is the position which he maintains which must be established. Again, the standard of persuasion required can only be the civil standard of the balance of probabilities. Thus, the applicant must make it more probable than not that the admission of the evidence would bring the administration of justice into disrepute.

[31] It is whether *the admission of the evidence* would bring the administration of justice into disrepute that is the applicable test. Misconduct by the police in the investigatory process often has some effect on the repute of the administration of justice, but s. 24(2) is not a remedy for police misconduct, requiring the exclusion of the evidence if, because of this misconduct, the administration of justice was brought into disrepute. Section 24(2) could well have been drafted in that way, but it was not. Rather, the drafters of the *Charter* decided to focus on the admission of the evidence in the proceedings, and the purpose of s. 24(2) is to prevent having the administration of justice brought into *further disrepute* by the admission of the evidence in the proceedings. This further disrepute will result from the admission of evidence that would deprive the accused of a fair hearing, or from judicial condonation of unacceptable conduct by the investigatory and prosecutorial agencies. It will also be necessary to consider any disrepute that may result from the exclusion of the evidence. It would be inconsistent with the purpose of s. 24(2) to exclude evidence if its exclusion would bring the administration of justice into greater disrepute than would its admission. Finally, it must be emphasized that even though the inquiry under s. 24(2) will necessarily focus on the specific prosecution, it is the long-term consequences of regular admission or exclusion of this type of evidence on the repute of the administration of justice which must be considered (see on this point Gibson, *supra*, p. 245).

[32] The concept of disrepute necessarily involves some element of community views, and the determination of disrepute thus requires the judge to refer to what he conceives to be the views of the community at large. This does not mean that evidence of the public's perception of the repute of the administration of justice, which Professor Gibson suggested could be presented in the form of public opinion polls (*supra*, pp. 236-47), will be determinative of the issue (see *Therens*, *supra*, pp. 653-54). The position is different with respect to obscenity, for example, where the court must assess the level of tolerance of the community, whether or not it is reasonable, and may consider public opinion polls (*R. v. Prairie Schooner News Ltd. and Powers* (1970), 1 C.C.C. (2d) 251 (Man. C.A.), at p. 266, cited in *Towne Cinema Theatres Ltd. v. The Queen*, [1985] 1 S.C.R. 494, at p. 513). It would be unwise, in my respectful view, to adopt a similar attitude with respect to the *Charter*. Members of the public generally become conscious of the importance of protecting the rights and freedoms of accused only when they are in some way brought closer to the system either personally or through the experience of friends or family. Professor Gibson recognized the danger of leaving the exclusion of evidence to uninformed members of the public when he stated at p. 246:

> The ultimate determination must be with the courts, because they provide what is often the only effective shelter for individuals and unpopular minorities from the shifting winds of public passion.

The *Charter* is designed to protect the accused from the majority, so the enforcement of the *Charter* must not be left to that majority.

[33] The approach I adopt may be put figuratively in terms of the reasonable person test proposed by Professor Yves-Marie Morissette in his article "The Exclusion of Evidence under the Canadian Charter of Rights and Freedoms: What To Do and What Not To Do" (1984), 29 *McGill L.J.* 521, at p. 538. In applying s. 24(2), he suggested that the relevant

question is: "Would the admission of the evidence bring the administration of justice into disrepute in the eyes of the reasonable man, dispassionate and fully apprised of the circumstances of the case?" The reasonable person is usually the average person in the community, but only when that community's current mood is reasonable.

[34] The decision is thus not left to the untrammelled discretion of the judge. In practice, as Professor Morissette wrote, the reasonable person test is there to require of judges that they "concentrate on what they do best: finding within themselves, with cautiousness and impartiality, a basis for their own decisions, articulating their reasons carefully and accepting review by a higher court where it occurs." It serves as a reminder to each individual judge that his discretion is grounded in community values, and, in particular, long term community values. He should not render a decision that would be unacceptable to the community when that community is not being wrought with passion or otherwise under passing stress due to current events. In effect, the judge will have met this test if the judges of the Court of Appeal will decline to interfere with his decision, even though they might have decided the matter differently, using the well-known statement that they are of the view that the decision was not unreasonable.

[35] In determining whether the admission of evidence would bring the administration of justice into disrepute, the judge is directed by s. 24(2) to consider "all the circumstances." ...

[36] As a matter of personal preference, I find it useful to group the factors according to the way in which they affect the repute of the administration of justice. Certain ... factors ... are relevant in determining the effect of the admission of the evidence on the fairness of the trial. The trial is a key part of the administration of justice, and the fairness of Canadian trials is a major source of the repute of the system and is now a right guaranteed by s. 11(*d*) of the *Charter*. If the admission of the evidence in some way affects the fairness of the trial, then the admission of the evidence would *tend* to bring the administration of justice into disrepute and, subject to a consideration of the other factors, the evidence generally should be excluded.

[37] It is clear to me that the factors relevant to this determination will include the nature of the evidence obtained as a result of the violation and the nature of the right violated and not so much the manner in which the right was violated. Real evidence that was obtained in a manner that violated the *Charter* will rarely operate unfairly for that reason alone. The real evidence existed irrespective of the violation of the *Charter* and its use does not render the trial unfair. However, the situation is very different with respect to cases where, after a

violation of the *Charter*, the accused is conscripted against himself through a confession or other evidence emanating from him. The use of such evidence would render the trial unfair, for it did not exist prior to the violation and it strikes at one of the fundamental tenets of a fair trial, the right against self-incrimination. Such evidence will generally arise in the context of an infringement of the right to counsel. Our decisions in *Therens, supra*, and *Clarkson v. The Queen*, [1986] 1 S.C.R. 383, are illustrative of this. The use of self-incriminating evidence obtained following a denial of the right to counsel will generally go to the very fairness of the trial and should generally be excluded. ...

[38] There are other factors which are relevant to the seriousness of the *Charter* violation and thus to the disrepute that will result from judicial acceptance of evidence obtained through that violation. As Le Dain J. wrote in *Therens, supra*, at p. 652:

> The relative seriousness of the constitutional violation has been assessed in the light of whether it was committed in good faith, or was inadvertent or of a merely technical nature, or whether it was deliberate, wilful or flagrant. Another relevant consideration is whether the action which constituted the constitutional violation was motivated by urgency or necessity to prevent the loss or destruction of the evidence.

I should add that the availability of other investigatory techniques and the fact that the evidence could have been obtained without the violation of the *Charter* tend to render the *Charter* violation more serious. We are considering the actual conduct of the authorities and the evidence must not be admitted on the basis that they could have proceeded otherwise and obtained the evidence properly. In fact, their failure to proceed properly when that option was open to them tends to indicate a blatant disregard for the *Charter*, which is a factor supporting the exclusion of the evidence.

[39] The final relevant group of factors consists of those that relate to the effect of excluding the evidence. The question under s. 24(2) is whether the system's repute will be better served by the admission or the exclusion of the evidence, and it is thus necessary to consider any disrepute that may result from the exclusion of the evidence. In my view, the administration of justice would be brought into disrepute by the exclusion of evidence essential to substantiate the charge, and thus the acquittal of the accused, because of a trivial breach of the *Charter*. Such disrepute would be greater if the offence was more serious. I would thus agree with Professor Morissette that evidence is more likely to be excluded if the offence is less serious (*supra*, pp. 529-31). I hasten to add, however, that if the admission of the evidence would result in an unfair trial,

the seriousness of the offence could not render that evidence admissible. If any relevance is to be given to the seriousness of the offence in the context of the fairness of the trial, it operates in the opposite sense: the more serious the offence, the more damaging to the system's repute would be an unfair trial.

[40] Finally, a factor which, in my view, is irrelevant is the availability of other remedies. Once it has been decided that the administration of justice would be brought into disrepute by the admission of the evidence, the disrepute will not be lessened by the existence of some ancillary remedy (see Gibson, *supra*, at p. 261).

[41] I would agree with Howland C.J.O. in *Simmons* [*R. v.* (1984), 11 C.C.C. (3d) 193 (Ont. C.A.)], that we should not gloss over the words of s. 24(2) or attempt to substitute any other test for s. 24(2). At least at this early stage of the *Charter's* development, the guidelines set out are sufficient and the actual decision to admit or exclude is as important as the statement of any test. Indeed, the test will only take on concrete meaning through our disposition of cases. However, I should at this point add some comparative comment as regards the test I enunciated in *Rothman* [*v. The Queen*, [1981] 1 S.C.R. 640], a pre-*Charter* confession case dealing with the resort to "tricks," which was coined in the profession as the "community shock test." That test has been applied to s. 24(2) by many courts, including the lower courts in this case. I still am of the view that the resort to tricks that are not in the least unlawful let alone in violation of the *Charter* to obtain a statement should not result in the exclusion of a free and voluntary statement unless the trick resorted to is a dirty trick, one that shocks the community. That is a very high threshold, higher, in my view, than that to be attained to bring the administration of justice into disrepute in the context of a violation of the *Charter*.

[42] There are two reasons why the threshold for exclusion under s. 24(2) is lower. The first, an obvious one, is that, under s. 24(2), there will have been a violation of the most important law in the land, as opposed to the absence of any unlawful behaviour as a result of the resort to tricks in *Rothman*.

[43] The second reason is based on the language of s. 24(2). Indeed, while both the English text of s. 24(2) and *Rothman* use the words "*would* bring the administration of justice into disrepute," the French versions are very different. The French text of s. 24(2) provides "*est susceptible de déconsidérer l'administration de la justice*," which I would translate as "*could* bring the administration of justice into disrepute." This is suppportive of a somewhat lower threshold than the English text. As Dickson J. (as he then was) wrote in *Hunter v. Southam Inc., supra,* at p. 157:

> Since the proper approach to the interpretation of the *Charter of Rights and Freedoms* is a purposive one, before it is possible to assess the reasonableness or unreasonable-

ness of the impact of a search or of a statute authorizing a search, it is first necessary to specify the purpose underlying s. 8: in other words, to delineate the nature of the interests it is meant to protect.

As one of the purposes of s. 24(2) is to protect the right to a fair trial, I would favour the interpretation of s. 24(2) which better protects that right, the less onerous French text. . . . Section 24(2) should thus be read as "the evidence shall be excluded if it is established that, having regard to all the circumstances, the admission of it in the proceedings *could* bring the administration of justice into disrepute." . . .

Conclusion

[44] As discussed above, we must determine in this case whether the evidence should be excluded on the record as it stands at present.

[45] The evidence obtained as a result of the search was real evidence, and, while prejudicial to the accused as evidence tendered by the Crown usually is, there is nothing to suggest that its use at the trial would render the trial unfair. In addition, it is true that the cost of excluding the evidence would be high: someone who was found guilty at trial of a relatively serious offence will evade conviction. Such a result could bring the administration of justice into disrepute. However, the administration of justice would be brought into greater disrepute, at least in my respectful view, if this Court did not exclude the evidence and dissociate itself from the conduct of the police in this case which, always on the assumption that the officer merely had suspicions, was a flagrant and serious violation of the rights of an individual. Indeed, we cannot accept that police officers take flying tackles at people and seize them by the throat when they do not have reasonable and probable grounds to believe that those people are either dangerous or handlers of drugs. Of course, matters might well be clarified in this case if and when the police officer is offered at a new trial an opportunity to explain the grounds, if any, that he had for doing what he did. But if the police officer does not then disclose additional grounds for his behaviour, the evidence must be excluded.

[46] I would allow the appeal and order a new trial.

The following are the reasons delivered by

[45] **McINTYRE J.** (dissenting): . . .

[48] . . . I am content to adopt the judgment of Seaton J.A. in the Court of Appeal in the case at bar, now reported in (1983), 5 C.C.C. (3d) 141. In my view, he has correctly stated the principles upon which this issue must be decided. I would, accordingly, adopt his result and dismiss the appeal.

[49] With the exception of his conclusion, there is little, if anything, inconsistent in the judgment of Seaton J.A. with

what my colleague, Lamer J., has said up to the point where he discusses his approach to the question of how a court should determine, in accordance with s. 24(2) of the *Charter*, whether the admission of evidence would bring the administration of justice into disrepute. It is with respect to that aspect of my colleague's judgment that a divergence in our views appears. With the very greatest deference to my colleague, I would not approve of a test so formulated. I would prefer the less formulated approach of Seaton J.A., who said at p. 151:

> Disrepute in whose eyes? That which would bring the administration of justice into disrepute in the eyes of a policeman might be the precise action that would be highly regarded in the eyes of a law teacher. I do not think that we are to look at this matter through the eyes of a policeman or a law teacher, or a judge for that matter. I think that it is the community at large, including the policeman and the law teacher and the judge, through whose eyes we are to see this question. It follows, and I do not think this is a disadvantage of the suggestion, that there will be a gradual shifting. I expect that there will be a trend away from admission of improperly obtained evidence.
>
> I do not suggest that the courts should respond to public clamour or opinion polls. I do suggest that the views of the community at large, developed by concerned and thinking citizens, ought to guide the courts when they are questioning whether or not the admission of evidence would bring the administration of justice into disrepute.

In this, I take it that Seaton J.A. in deciding the question has adopted an approach similar to that of the reasonable man, so well known in the law of torts. This is by no means a perfect test, but one which has served well and which has, by its application over the generations, led to the development of a serviceable body of jurisprudence from which has emerged a set of rules generally consistent with what might be termed social attitudes. I would suggest that such an approach, developing rules and principles on a case-by-case basis, will produce an acceptable standard for the application of s. 24(2) of the *Charter*.

[50] This view has judicial support in the words of Seaton J.A., referred to above, and in the words of Esson J.A. in the British Columbia Court of Appeal in *R. v. Strachan* (1986), 24 C.C.C. (3d) 205. Speaking for the Court, he said, at p. 236:

> It may be, as some have contended, that the so-called "community shock" test for applying s. 24(2) is not a completely satisfactory basis for deciding whether the admission of evidence will bring the administration of justice into disrepute. But it surely cannot be right to

decide that issue without consideration for the concerns of and prevailing views in the community. Some commentators have expressed the view that this will put the decision in the hands of "red necks," which . . . in this context seems to mean those who have not studied the subject at a graduate level. By that logic, we should not leave to juries the most serious issues in criminal cases. But we do and the Charter requires that to be done. One of the virtues of the jury system is to require community values to be reflected in the decision-making process. As that ideal way of reflecting community values is not available in relation to the question whether to exclude, it may be appropriate to have regard to such legendary devices as "the reasonable man" or "right thinking people generally." If due regard is had to community values, the remedy of exclusion will likely be confined to those relatively rare cases where there is some real reason for describing a denial as flagrant, and in which exclusion would not unduly prejudice the public interest in law enforcement.

Further support from the academic world may be found in the words of Yves-Marie Morissette, "The Exclusion of Evidence under the Canadian Charter of Rights and Freedoms: What To Do and What Not To Do" (1984), 29 *McGill L.J.* 521, at p. 538:

> Instead of reiterating unconvincing appeals to evanescent community views, Canadian judges should concentrate on what they do best: finding within themselves, with cautiousness and impartiality, a basis for their own decisions, articulating their reasons carefully and accepting review by a higher court where it occurs. A convenient and longstanding legal fiction exists for the purposes of judicial dialectics: the reasonable man, whether it be the man on the Clapham omnibus or, perhaps today in Canada, the career-woman on the Voyageur bus. One commendable feature of this concept is its coherence. Judges may disagree among themselves on what the reasonable man would do in any given case, but in the end the courts never disagree *with* the reasonable man. They are, in reality, the reasonable man. The question should be: "*Would the admission of the evidence bring the administration of justice into disrepute in the eyes of a reasonable man, dispassionate and fully apprised of the circumstances of the case?*" If in due course the reasonable man takes into account the findings of opinion polls, so be it, but for the time being section 24(2) should remain entirely within the control of the courts. [Emphasis added.]

[51] I do not suggest that we should adopt the "community shock" test or that we should have recourse to public opinion polls and other devices for the sampling of public opinion. I do not suggest that we should seek to discover some

theoretical concept of community views or standards on this question. I do suggest that we should adopt a method long employed in the common law courts and, by whatever name it may be called, apply the standard of the reasonable man. The question should be as stated by Yves-Marie Morissette, *supra*, "Would the admission of the evidence bring the administration of justice into disrepute in the eyes of a reasonable man, dispassionate and fully apprised of the circumstances of the case?" I am aware that the trial judge appeared to apply the community shock test. However, it is clear from the passage quoted above that Seaton J.A., in expressing his approval and dismissing the appeal, was in essence adopting the test of the reasonable man. I would observe as well that Esson J.A. in *Strachan, supra*, in accepting the need for a consideration of community values brought in the reasonable man.

[52] Applying this test to the case at bar, I am led to the conclusion that the administration of justice would not fall into disrepute by the admission of this evidence. This is not a case where the search revealed a concealed capsule or two of heroin, such as one might have for personal use. Here, the appellant, with heroin in her hand contained in a balloon, was found in a public bar among other people. In my view, the admission of this evidence on a trial for possession of narcotics for the purpose of trafficking would not—in the eyes of a reasonable man, dispassionate and fully apprised of the circumstances of the case—bring the administration of justice into disrepute. The circumstances of the case include the events described by Nemetz C.J.B.C., at p. 143:

> The facts are not in dispute. Constables Rodine and Woods of the drug section of the R.C.M.P. were on duty at Gibsons, a small community near Vancouver. They took up a surveillance-post near a pub in the village. There they saw the appellant and another woman seated at a table. A short time later the pair were joined by Richard Collins and another man. About 15 minutes later, Collins and the stranger left the pub and drove in a car to a trailer-park a short distance from the pub. The police followed them. They searched the car and there found heroin, some multicoloured balloons and other parapher-

nalia. Richard Collins was arrested. At 4:15 p.m., Constables Rodine and Woods returned to the pub. The appellant and her companion were still there.

The police then entered the bar and found heroin in the possession of the appellant, not concealed but in her hand in a public place. I express no view as to the cogency or weight of this evidence but, in my view, a reasonable man would not be offended at the thought that on the issue of possession for the purpose of trafficking the trier of fact should be permitted to consider it. I would dismiss the appeal.

The following are the reasons delivered by

[53] **Le DAIN J.:** I agree with Justice Lamer that the appeal should be allowed and a new trial ordered. Assuming, as we must on the present record, that the police officer did not have grounds for a reasonable belief that the accused was in possession of a narcotic, I am in agreement with the conclusion that, having regard to all the circumstances, and in particular the relative seriousness of the violation of the right guaranteed by s. 8 of the *Charter* to be secure against unreasonable search, the admission of the evidence would bring the administration of justice into disrepute. I am also in general agreement with what Lamer J. says concerning the nature of the test under s. 24(2) of the *Charter* and the factors to be weighed, but I do not wish to be understood as necessarily subscribing to what is said concerning the nature and relative importance under s. 24(2) of the factor which he refers to as the effect of the admission of the evidence on the fairness of the trial. Since, as Lamer J. indicates, it is not necessary to consider this factor in the present case, I prefer to reserve my opinion with respect to it. I am concerned about the possible implications for such matters as self-incrimination and confession, aspects of fairness to which Lamer J. refers and which are the subject of special provision in the *Charter* or in well established rules of law. I am also concerned as to whether there is a basis in s. 24(2) for the view that, to the extent this factor is relevant, it should generally lead to the exclusion of the evidence.

24 R. v. Askov, 1990

Section 11(*b*) of the *Charter* gives any person charged with a criminal offence the right "to be tried within a reasonable time." This right embodies the fundamental precept that "justice delayed is justice denied." Fundamental as this right is to the criminal justice system, it requires some authority to define the length of time that is reasonable to allow in bringing an accused person to trial. If elected legislators decline to set standards of reasonableness, by default the responsibility for doing so ends up entirely in the hands of the judiciary. That is what has happened in giving guidance on the practical meaning of section 11(*b*) of the *Charter*. In taking on this responsibility, the courts in effect developed judicial legislation to guide those who administer the justice system. The Supreme Court's decision in *Askov* was a milestone in the Supreme Court of Canada's struggle to establish a coherent set of rules and principles on the right to be tried within a reasonable time.

On November 5, 1983, a police surveillance team apprehended Elijah Anton Askov and three other men who were brandishing a sawed-off shotgun and a knife at Peter Belmont, the operator of an "exotic" dancers service, in an attempt to extort money from him. The four men were charged with conspiracy to commit extortion. Askov and two of the men were held in custody until bail was granted on May 7, 1984. Their preliminary hearing took place on September 21, 1984. It took two more years for their trial to begin, and when it did, on September 2, 1986, their lawyer asked for a stay of proceedings on the ground that the trial had been unreasonably delayed. The trial judge granted the stay, but her order was set aside by the Ontario Court of Appeal. That is the decision the Supreme Court reviewed and reversed in *Askov*.

In *Mills*,[1] the Court's first decision on section 11(*b*), rendered in 1986, Chief Justice Dickson and Justice Lamer wrote a lengthy opinion on how courts should interpret the right. But their opinion did not win the support of other justices. In a series of section 11(*b*) cases following *Mills*, the Court dealt with various factors to be taken into account in interpreting section 11(*b*). There was general agreement on the need for a flexible approach to the reasonable time requirement. The different degrees of complexity in criminal cases rule out a standard time for all cases. In each case, the cause of delay must be considered—did the delay result from actions or lack of action by the prosecutors, or from delaying tactics of the accused? There was agreement that an accused could waive the right to a speedy trial but that such a waiver cannot be simply inferred from a failure to complain about delay. But there was a lack of consensus on several other issues. In interpreting the right, what weight should be given to society's interest in seeing accused persons brought to justice quickly and having fair trials that are not jeopardized by witnesses' fading memories? What weight should be given to how much the delay has caused prejudice and hardship to the accused? And—a key issue in *Askov*—how should the institutional resources of the court system be taken into account?

---

1 *Mills v. The Queen*, [1986] 1 S.C.R. 863.

Justice Cory's opinion in *Askov*, concurred in by Chief Justice Dickson, Justices La Forest, L'Heureux-Dubé, and Gonthier, and on most of its main points by Justices Lamer, Wilson, Sopinka, and McLachlin, brought the Court much closer to a consensus on the interpretation of section 11(*b*). The justices were in agreement that the cause of the two-year delay between the preliminary hearing and the trial was institutional—a lack of adequate court resources, and that two years was an unreasonable length of time for a delay of this kind. In reaching this conclusion the Court relied on the research of Professor Carl Baar, a leading scholar in the field of judicial studies, showing that in Brampton, in Ontario's Peel District where the Askov trial was to be heard, time spent awaiting trial was significantly longer for similar types of cases than in other Canadian and U.S. jurisdictions. Baar described the *Askov* case as representing one of the worst delays in the worst district, not only in Canada but "anywhere north of the Rio Grande." Sifting through the comparative data on time spent awaiting trial, Justice Cory went on to conclude "that a period of delay in a range of some six to eight months between committal and trial might be deemed to be the outside limit of what is reasonable." This conclusion was supported by all nine justices. The Court was unanimous in finding that Askov's and his co-accused's right to a trial within a reasonable time had been violated, and that there was no basis on which such a violation could be justified.

The justices were also unanimous in their choice of remedy—they directed a stay of proceedings. This meant that Askov and his co-accused would walk. Justice Cory acknowledged that the charges against the accused were very serious and threatening to the community. But the infringement of the accused persons' rights in this case was also serious. In the Court's view, any other remedy, such as moving the trial to another venue or recognizing a transitional period to provide time to bolster the system's resources, would render the right to a trial in a reasonable time meaningless.

The *Askov* decision broke like a bombshell on the Ontario government. The government responded on two fronts. It moved rapidly to appoint judges to the Provincial Court. Fortunately, Ontario had a pool of well-qualified candidates selected by its Judicial Appointments Advisory Committee ready for appointment. The decision had the effect of enabling the province's Attorney General to secure more funds for the court system.[2] That was the good news. But on the prosecutorial side, the news was shocking. The Attorney General announced that thousands of cases in the province's criminal justice system had no chance of meeting the *Askov* time requirement, and would therefore have to be terminated, allowing the accused, many of whom were charged with serious crimes, to go free. Between October 22, 1990 and September 6, 1991, 47,000 charges were stayed. When account is taken of cases in which there were multiple charges, this amounts to the termination of approximately 25,000 criminal cases.[3]

The *Askov* ruling caused considerable consternation for trial judges faced with the challenge of applying it. The ruling indicated that six to eight months was the outside limit for the period from "committal" to trial. Committal in this context means the finding of the

---

2   Peter H. Russell, "Canadian Constraints on Judicialization From Without" (1993) *International Political Science Review* 170. Russell also chaired Ontario's Judicial Appointments Advisory Committee at this time.

3   For an account of the public reaction to *Askov*, see Kent Roach, *The Supreme Court on Trial: Judicial Activism or Democratic Dialogue* (Toronto: Irwin Law, 2001) 180-82.

preliminary inquiry judge that the prosecution has enough evidence to justify committing the accused to trial. But what about summary conviction cases, where there is no preliminary hearing? And how should the ruling in *Askov* be related to previous cases, which had considered that the relevant period for assessing reasonable time was from the laying of charges to trial? When Justice Cory, at a conference of judges and lawyers in the United Kingdom in August 1991, expressed shock at the rigidity with which the *Askov* rule was being interpreted and surprise at the extent of the decision's impact, Ontario's Attorney General Howard Hampton called for a review of the decision.[4]

Ontario's Attorney General did not have to wait long for the review. In March 1992, the Supreme Court released its decision in *Morin*,[5] an Ontario case involving a delay of 14½ months in bringing a person charged with driving while impaired to trial. In *Morin*, while the Court did not repudiate its decision in *Askov*, it considerably softened its approach to section 11(*b*). Justice Sopinka, who wrote the main opinion for the Court, said that the provincial courts could take 8 to 10 months from committal to trial as an "administrative guideline" for not unreasonable institutional delay between committal and trial. He emphasized that this was a guideline, not a rigid rule, and acknowledged that, in addition to the time from committal to trial, there would have to be allowance for time between laying the charge and committal. The Court now gave more weight to the need for the accused to demonstrate prejudice caused by the delay. In upholding the Ontario Court of Appeal's decision that 14½ months was not an unreasonable time for Morin to wait after she was charged to be brought to trial, Justice Sopinka took into account the burgeoning population and increase in criminal caseloads in the district where the trial was to take place.

The Supreme Court's performance in *Askov* was not one of its shining hours in the *Charter* era. After the decision, Professor Baar revealed how the Court had taken mistaken inferences from his comparative data.[6] When social science evidence is used in determining factual matters that are relevant to constitutional rights, it is best submitted in the lower courts where it can be subject to thorough examination. The decision also had a tone of moral outrage that indicated a lack of sufficient sensitivity to its practical consequences. Moreover, Canadians may well continue to ask why the Supreme Court regards the termination of proceedings as the only possible remedy for a breach of section 11(*b*). When an accused is held in custody for a long time while waiting for trial, a judicial order to speed up the trial date seems to be a remedy that is both sensible and just.[7]

Askov also raises questions about the performance of the political branches. The case exposed shameful conditions in the administration of justice that the Ontario government had allowed to develop in the Peel District of the province. A more alert and responsible government could have done much more to reduce delays in Peel by pushing Crown prosecutors to screen charges more carefully, to disclose more of their case to defence lawyers, and to be more open to negotiating pleas—defence lawyers referred to the district as "no

---

4   "Hampton calls for review of ruling in Askov" *The Globe and Mail* (17 July 1991) A5.

5   *R. v. Morin*, [1992] 1 S.C.R. 771.

6   Carl Baar, "Criminal Court Delay and the Charter" (1993) 72 *Canadian Bar Review* 305.

7   For a discussion of these options, see Anthony G. Amsterdam, "Speedy Criminal Trial: Rights and Remedies" (1975) 27 *Stanford Law Review* 525.

deal Peel."[8] And it should not have needed the shock of *Askov* to wake up the government to the need to appoint more judges. In the United States, a number of states have enacted legislation setting standards for speedy trials. In Canada, where the federal Parliament has exclusive jurisdiction over criminal law and procedure, this option was considered by federal legislators in the early 1980s, but then dropped.

In the *Charter* era, legislative responsibilities that elected legislators decline to accept are apt to be taken up by the judiciary. Although the legislative effort of the Supreme Court in *Askov* was clumsy, at least the justices recognized its inadequacies and began the process of correcting their work in *Morin*. The process of refining time standards for bringing accused persons to trial continues. James Kelly reports that in the 12 years following *Askov*, the Supreme Court considered trial delay in 22 cases, and that the average time accepted as reasonable in these cases was 16 months.[9] ∼

Discussion Questions

1. What can we learn from this case about the use of statistical data in judicial decisions interpreting the constitution?
2. How was the Court's interpretation of section 11(*b*) modified in subsequent judicial decisions?
3. How would you assess the impact of judicial decisions on section 11(*b*) on the administration of criminal justice in Canada?

---

8   Kent Roach, *supra* note 3 at 181.

9   James Kelly, *Governing with the Charter: Legislative and Judicial Activism and Framers' Intent* (Vancouver: University of British Columbia Press, 2005) 130.

R. v. ASKOV
[1990] 2 S.C.R. 1199

Hearing: March 23, 1990; Judgment: October 18, 1990.

Present: Dickson C.J.* and Lamer C.J.** and Wilson,
La Forest, L'Heureux-Dubé, Sopinka, Gonthier, Cory, and
McLachlin JJ.

* Chief Justice at the time of hearing.

** Chief Justice at the time of judgment.

[This is the most important case the Court has rendered on
section 11(*b*) of the *Charter*, guaranteeing the right to a trial
within a reasonable time. Justice Cory's opinion provides for
the first time a clear majority position on the factors to be
taken into account in determining whether this right has been
violated. The Court found that the accused's rights were violated primarily because Ontario had failed to provide adequate court resources in the Peel area. Within three months,
more than 12,000 cases in Ontario had been either stayed by
judges or had charges withdrawn by the Crown for failing to
meet the standard established in the *Askov* case, which has
generally been interpreted to require a trial between six to
eight months after a charge has been laid.]

The judgment of Dickson C.J. and La Forest, L'Heureux-
Dubé, Gonthier, and Cory JJ. was delivered by

CORY J.: Section 11(*b*) of the *Canadian Charter of Rights and
Freedoms* provides that any person charged with an offence has
the right to be tried within a reasonable time. What constitutes an unreasonable delay of a trial must be determined on
this appeal. In order to reach a conclusion it will be necessary
to consider and apply criteria or factors which should be used
to ascertain if a delay is unreasonable and in particular, to
consider the consequences of so-called institutional delays.

Factual Background

All the appellants, Askov, Hussey, Melo and Gugliotta, were
charged with conspiracy to commit extortion against Peter
Belmont. As well, Askov, Hussey and Melo were jointly
charged with the offences of possession of a prohibited
weapon, possession of a weapon for a purpose dangerous to
the public peace, pointing a firearm and assault with a weapon.
Hussey was also charged with criminal negligence in the operation of a motor vehicle....

[Askov and Melo were arrested on November 12, 1983, Hussey
on November 14, and Gugliotta on November 30.]

It is necessary to set out the proceedings following the
arrest in some detail. The appellants Melo, Askov and Hussey
were initially denied bail. They were detained in custody for
almost six months. On May 7, 1984, they were each ordered
to be released on a recognizance of $50,000. Gugliotta was
released on December 2, 1983 shortly after his arrest on a
recognizance of $20,000. The terms of release for all the appel-
lants involved reporting to the police and abstention from
communicating with their co-accused. These conditions were
varied from time to time to permit more freedom of movement for the appellants. All the applications which were made
for more lenient bail conditions were granted. Nonetheless,
the appellants remained under considerable restraint.

Askov was re-arrested on an unrelated charge on October
1, 1984.

With three of the accused in custody, the Crown, in a
commendable manner, was prepared as soon as December
1983 to set an early date for the preliminary hearing. However,
at the request of the appellants the matter was put over to
February 14, 1984 when all counsel agreed on a date in the
first week of July for the preliminary hearing to be held. At
this time it was specifically indicated that an earlier date could
be arranged if a request was made by the appellants, but none
was forthcoming. When the preliminary hearing commenced
on July 4, 1984, it could not be completed because another
preliminary had been set for a later day in the same week. As
a result, the preliminary hearing could not be completed until
September 21, 1984, some ten months after the arrests.

On October 1, 1984, the appellants appeared before Judge
Keenan presiding in the assignment court. A trial date was set
for the first available date which was October 15, 1985, more
than a year away and nearly two years from the date of the
initial arrests. Despite what seems far too lengthy a delay, an
earlier date could not be set due to other cases which had
priority either because the accused was in custody or because
the offence date was earlier than that of the case at bar. On
October 25, 1985, when it was apparent that the case simply
could not be heard during that session, counsel for all the
appellants and the Crown appeared and the case was put over
for trial to September 2, 1986. When the trial finally began on
that date, counsel for the appellants moved to stay the proceedings on the grounds that the trial had been unreasonably
delayed. The stay was granted by order of Judge Bolan, the
senior judge of the District Court of the Judicial District of
Peel. The Crown appealed the order of Bolan Dist. Ct. J. to the
Court of Appeal, which set aside the stay and directed that the
trial proceed....

The United States

In the United States the Sixth Amendment ensures that "[i]n
all criminal prosecutions, the accused shall enjoy the right to
a speedy and public trial." The United States Supreme Court

considered the issue in *Barker v. Wingo*, 407 U.S. 514 (1972). In that case Barker, who was charged with murder, was brought to trial five years after the murder was committed. The delay was caused by the necessity of trying an accomplice beforehand. This prerequisite trial was extremely complicated; the accomplice was tried no less than six times. During this ongoing process, Barker initially had agreed to continuances or adjournments. He only began to assert his right to a speedy trial three and one-half years after the charges were laid.

The court held that a flexible approach should be taken to cases involving delay and that the multiple purposes or aims of the Sixth Amendment must be appreciated. Powell J., giving the reasons for the court, recognized the general concern that all persons accused with crimes should be treated according to fair and decent procedures. He particularly noted that there were three individual interests which the right was designed to protect. They were:

(i)   to prevent oppressive pre-trial incarceration;
(ii) to minimize the anxiety and concern of the accused; and
(iii) to limit the possibility that the defence will be impaired or prejudiced.

However, Powell J. went on to observe that unlike other constitutional rights which only have an individual interest, the right to a speedy trial involved the added dimension of a societal interest. He found that a delay could result in increased financial cost to society and as well, could have a negative effect upon the credibility of the justice system. Further, it was noted that a delay could work to the advantage of the accused....

In order to balance the individual right and the communal aspect of the Sixth Amendment, the U.S. Supreme Court adopted an approach of *ad hoc* balancing "in which the conduct of both the prosecution and the defendant are weighed" (p. 530). The balancing is undertaken by reference to four factors identified by Powell J. as the test for infringement of the right to a "speedy trial." They are as follows:

(i)   the length of the delay;
(ii) the reason for the delay;
(ii) the accused's assertion of the right; and
(iv) prejudice to the accused.

The first factor is the triggering mechanism or threshold determination of the excessiveness of the delay. If that delay appears *prima facie* excessive, the Court must then consider the three remaining factors to determine whether the accused has been deprived of the Sixth Amendment right.

Position in Canada Subsequent to the Passing of the Charter

Immediately following the passage of the *Charter*, the approach taken by the U.S. Supreme Court in *Barker v. Wingo, supra*, was widely approved and adopted....

The issue was first considered by this Court in *Mills v. The Queen, supra*. Lamer J. in his dissenting reasons called into question the appropriateness of adopting the American approach in the Canadian setting.... Although he favoured a flexible balancing test, he rejected the approach taken in *Barker v. Wingo, supra*. His difference with the reasoning in that case was grounded on the proposition that in the context of the Canadian *Charter*, the s. 11(*b*) right was by its very nature an individual right and that the provision did not have a collective or societal dimension....

Since there was no need to balance any interest of society, the test did not need to take into account the conduct of the parties, particularly that of the accused. As well, actual prejudice to the accused did not need to be considered, as actual prejudice is also a component of society's interest in a fair trial....

The Court next examined the application of s. 11(*b*) in *R. v. Rahey* [[1987] 1 S.C.R. 588]. Rahey was charged with six counts of making false returns in his income tax forms and one count of wilful income tax evasion. His trial before a provincial court judge began six months after he was charged. In the eleven-month period which followed the closing of the Crown's case there were no fewer than nineteen adjournments, all initiated by the trial judge. For nine of these adjournments, Rahey made no objection. When the judge ordered further adjournments, he contended that they constituted a violation of his s. 11(*b*) *Charter* rights. He brought an application to stay before the Supreme Court of Nova Scotia and later an appeal to this Court where a stay of proceedings was granted.

Four judges delivered written reasons. Lamer J., with Dickson C.J. concurring, restated his position in *Mills*, but extended the "transitional period" to include the period up to the issuance of the reasons in *Rahey*. Wilson J., with Estey J. concurring, maintained her position set forth in *Mills* and referred again to the necessity of focussing on the prejudice resulting from the unreasonable delay and not upon the prejudice flowing from the charge. Le Dain J., with Beetz J. concurring, supported the approach taken by the U.S. Supreme Court in *Barker v. Wingo*....

In *R. v. Conway*, [1989] 1 S.C.R. 1659, Conway sought to obtain from this Court a stay of proceedings to prevent a third trial which would take place more than five years after the initial charge of murder had been laid.

Conway was charged with first degree murder in connection with the stabbing death. Some sixteen months after he was charged, the accused was tried and convicted of the included offence of second degree murder. An appeal was taken and one year later a new trial was directed by the Court of Appeal. It was agreed that there was no time lost during the period from the launching of the appeal until the order was given by the Court of Appeal directing a new trial. Conway then had difficulty finding a counsel to represent him at the second trial. It was conceded that the problem arose in no small part from Conway's own actions. . . .

L'Heureux-Dubé J., writing for the majority of a panel of five judges, which included Dickson C.J. and La Forest J., dismissed the appeal and rejected the stay. She held that the overall delay did not prevent the accused from obtaining a fair trial. . . . The critical factor in the decision was the conduct of the accused Conway who was responsible for much of the delay. It was held that the rest of the delay was justified by the inherent time requirements of the case. Further, it was noted that it was impossible to conclude that the accused had been prejudiced. . . .

The facts in *R. v. Smith*, [1989] 2 S.C.R. 1120, are relatively straightforward. Smith was charged with theft. The preliminary inquiry could not be scheduled until over a year had passed from the time he was charged. The institutional reasons which caused this delay arose from the scheduling of the preliminary hearing for four days in August, at a time when the provincial court judges were on holiday. The preliminary hearing could not be rescheduled until late in December because the investigating officer was unavailable before that date. Once again the scheduled December date came within a holiday period for provincial court judges and a further adjournment was required. When the case finally came to trial, an application was brought for a stay which was granted.

In this Court, Sopinka J., writing for all members of the Court, upheld the stay. He recognized that there was still a considerable disagreement as to the factors that should be taken into account on the balancing process and also with regard to the composition of the constituent components of the prejudice issue. However, he was of the view that the problem did not have to be dealt with in light of the facts of the case. . . .

On the facts of *Smith*, Sopinka J. determined that the length of time was longer than could be justified particularly in light of the cause of the delays. . . .

Purpose of Section 11(b)

I agree with the position taken by Lamer J. that s. 11(*b*) explicitly focusses upon the individual interest of liberty and security of the person. Like other specific guarantees provided by s. 11, this paragraph is primarily concerned with an aspect of fundamental justice guaranteed by s. 7 of the *Charter*. There could be no greater frustration imaginable for innocent persons charged with an offence than to be denied the opportunity of demonstrating their innocence for an unconscionable time as a result of unreasonable delays in their trial. The time awaiting trial must be exquisite agony for accused persons and their immediate family. It is a fundamental precept of our criminal law that every individual is presumed to be innocent until proven guilty. It follows that on the same fundamental level of importance, all accused persons, each one of whom is presumed to be innocent, should be given the opportunity to defend themselves against the charges they face and to have their name cleared and reputation re-established at the earliest possible time.

Although the primary aim of s. 11(*b*) is the protection of the individual's rights and the provision of fundamental justice for the accused, nonetheless there is, in my view, at least by inference, a community or societal interest implicit in s. 11(*b*). That community interest has a dual dimension. First, there is a collective interest in ensuring that those who transgress the law are brought to trial and dealt with according to the law. Second, those individuals on trial must be treated fairly and justly. Speedy trials strengthen both those aspects of the community interest. A trial held within a reasonable time must benefit the individual accused as the prejudice which results from criminal proceedings is bound to be minimized. If the accused is in custody, the custodial time awaiting trial will be kept to a minimum. If the accused is at liberty on bail and subject to conditions, then the curtailments on the liberty of the accused will be kept to a minimum. From the point of view of the community interest, in those cases where the accused is detained in custody awaiting trial, society will benefit by the quick resolution of the case either by reintegrating into society the accused found to be innocent or if found guilty by dealing with the accused according to the law. . . .

There are as well important practical benefits which flow from a quick resolution of the charges. There can be no doubt that memories fade with time. Witnesses are likely to be more reliable testifying to events in the immediate past as opposed to events that transpired many months or even years before the trial. Not only is there an erosion of the witnesses' memory with the passage of time, but there is bound to be an erosion of the witnesses themselves. Witnesses are people; they are moved out of the country by their employer; or for reasons related to family or work they move from the east coast to the west coast; they become sick and unable to testify in court; they are involved in debilitating accidents; they die and their testimony is forever lost. Witnesses too are concerned that their evidence be taken as quickly as possible. Testifying is often thought to be an ordeal. It is something that weighs on the minds of witnesses and is a source of worry and frustration for them until they have given their testimony.

It can never be forgotten that the victims may be devastated by criminal acts. They have a special interest and good reason to expect that criminal trials take place within a reasonable time. From a wider point of view, it is fair to say that all crime disturbs the community and that serious crime alarms the community. All members of the community are thus entitled to see that the justice system works fairly, efficiently and with reasonable dispatch. The very reasonable concern and alarm of the community which naturally arises from acts of crime cannot be assuaged until the trial has taken place. The trial not only resolves the guilt or innocence of the individual, but acts as a reassurance to the community that serious crimes are investigated and that those implicated are brought to trial and dealt with according to the law.

The failure of the justice system to deal fairly, quickly and efficiently with criminal trials inevitably leads to the community's frustration with the judicial system and eventually to a feeling of contempt for court procedures. When a trial takes place without unreasonable delay, with all witnesses available and memories fresh, it is far more certain that the guilty parties who committed the crimes will be convicted and punished and those that did not, will be acquitted and vindicated. It is no exaggeration to say that a fair and balanced criminal justice system simply cannot exist without the support of the community. Continued community support for our system will not endure in the face of lengthy and unreasonable delays.

Further, implicit support for the concept that there is a societal aspect to s. 11(*b*) can be derived from the observation that the last thing that some wish for is a speedy trial. There is no doubt that many accused earnestly hope that the memory of a witness will fail and that other witnesses will become unavailable. . . .

I believe the inferred societal interest should be considered in conjunction with the main and primary concept of the protection of the individual's right to fundamental justice. This is closer to the views expressed by Wilson J. in *Mills*, *supra*. At some level, the conduct of and prejudice to the accused must be examined. Although it must be recognized that the primary goal of s. 11(*b*) is the protection of the individual's interest in fundamental justice, nevertheless that same section contains a secondary and inferred societal interest that should not be ignored. If the recognition of both the primary individual interest and the inferred society interest is accepted as the true aim of s. 11(*b*), then I think the various factors which should be taken into consideration in determining whether there has been an unreasonable delay can be clarified and set forth in a consistent test.

Factors to Be Taken into Account in Determining Whether or Not There Has Been an Infringement of Section 11(b)

(i) The Length of the Delay

It is clear that the longer the delay, the more difficult it should be for a court to excuse it. This is not a threshold requirement as in the United States, but rather is a factor to be balanced along with the others. However, very lengthy delays may be such that they cannot be justified for any reason.

(ii) Explanation for the Delay

This category referred to by Sopinka J. in *Smith, supra*, may be usefully subdivided with the aspects of systemic delay and conduct of the accused amplified.

(a) The Conduct of the Crown (or Delay Attributable to the Crown)

Generally speaking, this category will comprise all of the potential factors causing delay which flow from the nature of the case, the conduct of the Crown, including officers of the state, and the inherent time requirements of the case. Delays attributable to the actions of the Crown or its officers will weigh in favour of the accused. For example, the nineteen adjournments initiated by the trial judge in *Rahey* or the unavailability of judges because of holidays in *Smith* are examples where the actions or the lack of actions of Crown officers weighed against the state in the assessment of the reasonableness of the delay.

It is under this heading that the complexity of the case should be taken into account. Complex cases which require longer time for preparation, a greater expenditure of resources by Crown officers and the longer use of institutional facilities will justify delays longer than those that would be acceptable in simple cases.

(b) Systemic or Institutional Delays

On a more specific level, the question of delays caused by systemic or institutional limitations should also be discussed under the heading of delays attributable to the Crown. This factor will often be the most difficult to assess. A careful and sensitive balancing will be required in order to properly assess the significance of this aspect of delay. First, let us consider the problem from the point of view of society. Section 11(*b*) applies to all Canadians in every part of our land. In a country as vast and diverse as ours, the institutional problems are bound to differ greatly from province to province and from district to district within each province. Differences of climate, terrain, population and financial resources will require different solutions for the problem of providing adequate facilities and personnel. Lack of financial resources may require imaginative answers to difficult problems, including the provision of temporary facilities. The problems presented and the solutions required will vary between heavily populated centres such as Toronto and Montréal and the sparsely populated districts bordering on Hudson Bay.

Wise political decisions will be required with regard to the allocation of scarce funds. Due deference will have to be given to those political decisions as the provisions of courtroom facilities and Crown Attorneys must, for example, be balanced against the provision of health care and highways. Yet solutions must be found as indeed they have been in many jurisdictions outside Ontario. Similarly situated communities can provide a rough comparison and some guidance as to what time period constitutes an unreasonable delay of the trial of an accused person. That comparison should always be made with the more efficient of the comparable jurisdictions.

The right guaranteed by s. 11(*b*) is of such fundamental importance to the individual and of such significance to the community as a whole that the lack of institutional resources cannot be employed to justify a continuing unreasonable postponement of trials. . . .

Where inordinate delays do occur, it is those who are responsible for the lack of facilities who should bear the public criticism that is bound to arise as a result of the staying of proceedings which must be the inevitable consequence of unreasonable delays. Members of the community will not and should not condone or accept a situation where those alleged to have committed serious crimes are never brought to trial solely as a result of unduly long delays. It is a serious consequence with potentially dangerous overtones for the community. It is right and proper that there be criticism of the situation when it occurs.

The response to the question of "how long is too long" as it applies to institutional delay will always be difficult to fashion in our country. The question must be answered in light of the particular facts of each case. There can be no certain standard of a fixed time which will be applicable in every region of the country. Nonetheless, an inquiry into what is reasonable in any region should not be taken in isolation and must, of necessity, involve a comparison with other jurisdictions. Consideration must be given to the geography, the population and the material resources of the province and district. The comparison of similar and thus comparable districts must always be made with the better districts and not with the worst. . . .

To summarize, when considering delays occasioned by inadequate institutional resources, the question of how long a delay is too long may be resolved by comparing the questioned jurisdiction to the standard maintained by the best comparable jurisdiction in the country. The comparison need

not be too precise or exact. Rather, it should look to the appropriate ranges of delay to determine what is a reasonable limit. In all cases it will be incumbent upon the Crown to show that the institutional delay in question is justifiable.

(c) The Conduct of the Accused (or Delay Attributable to the Accused)

As Lamer J. so cogently observed in *Mills*, it is a fundamental precept of our criminal justice system that it is the responsibility of the Crown to bring the accused to trial. Further, the right to be tried within a reasonable time is an aspect of fundamental justice protected by s. 7 of the *Charter*. It follows that any inquiry into the conduct of the accused should in no way absolve the Crown from its responsibility to bring the accused to trial. Nonetheless, there is a societal interest in preventing an accused from using the guarantee as a means of escaping trial. It should be emphasized that an inquiry into the actions of the accused should be restricted to discovering those situations where the accused's acts either directly caused the delay (as in *Conway*), or the acts of the accused are shown to be a deliberate and calculated tactic employed to delay the trial. . . .

In addition, since the protection of the right of the individual is the primary aim of s. 11(*b*), the burden of proving that the direct acts of the accused caused the delay must fall upon the Crown. This would be true except in those cases where the effects of the accused's action are so clear and readily apparent that the intent of the accused to cause a delay is the inference that must be drawn from the record of his or her actions.

(iii) Waiver

While the question of waiver could be discussed under factor (ii)(c) above (Delay Attributable to the Accused), for reasons of clarity, I prefer to examine the issue separately.

The accused should not be required to assert the explicitly protected individual right to trial within a reasonable time. It is now well established that any waiver of a *Charter* right must be "clear and unequivocal . . . with full knowledge of the rights the procedure was enacted to protect and of the effect the waiver will have on those rights in the process." See *Korponay v. Attorney General of Canada*, [1982] 1 S.C.R. 41, at p. 49. The failure of an accused to assert the right does not give the Crown licence to proceed with an unfair trial. Failure to assert the right would be insufficient in itself to impugn the motives of the accused as might be the case with regard to other s. 11 rights. Rather there must be something in the conduct of the accused that is sufficient to give rise to an inference that the accused has understood that he or she had a s. 11(*b*) guarantee, understood its nature and has waived the right provided by that guarantee. Although no particular magical incantation of words is required to waive a right, nevertheless the waiver must be expressed in some manner. Silence or lack of objection cannot constitute a lawful waiver. . . .

In sum, the burden always rests with the Crown to bring the case to trial. Further, the mere silence of the accused is not sufficient to indicate a waiver of a *Charter* right; rather, the accused must undertake some direct action from which a consent to delay can be properly inferred. The onus rests upon the Crown to establish on a balance of probabilities that the actions of the accused constitute a waiver of his or her rights.

(iv) Prejudice to the Accused

The different positions taken by Members of the Court with regard to the prejudice suffered by an accused as a result of a delayed trial are set forth in *Mills* and *Rahey*. Perhaps the differences can be resolved in this manner. It should be inferred that a very long and unreasonable delay has prejudiced the accused. . . . Nevertheless, it will be open to the Crown to attempt to demonstrate that the accused has not been prejudiced. This would preserve the societal interest by providing that a trial would proceed in those cases where despite a long delay no resulting damage had been suffered by the accused. . . .

Application of the Principles to the Case at Bar

As the disposition of this case will ultimately turn on the factors headed (ii) Explanation for the Delay, particularly (b) Systemic or Institutional Delay and (c) Delays Attributable to the Accused; and (iii) Waiver, I need but briefly deal with the factors titled (i) The Length of the Delay and (iv) Prejudice to the Accused.

(i) The Length of the Delay

No matter what standard of measure is used or what test is applied, the trial in this case has been inordinately delayed. . . . The experienced trial judge who has presided for many years in Peel District described the delay as "clearly excessive and unreasonable." It is interesting to note that the delay at issue in *Mills* was nineteen months, in *Rahey* eleven months, and in *Smith* one year. Although the period of delay in *Conway* is comparable to that of this case, it must be remembered that in that case the delay was directly attributable to the actions of Conway.

The period of delay in the case at bar is so lengthy that unless there is some very strong basis for justifying the delay, which becomes clear from an examination of the other factors, then it would be impossible for a court to tolerate such a delay.

(ii) Prejudice to the Accused

The trial judge found that the appellants had been prejudiced by the delay. In support, he noted the lengthy period of incarceration for three of the appellants and the restrictions contained in the bail terms. Those conditions of bail included curfews, a direction not to associate with the co-accused and a system of regular reporting to the police. There has been no attack on these findings. Consequently, it is impossible to say that the Crown discharged the burden that rested upon it to show that the delay caused no prejudice to the appellants. As a result, the prejudice suffered by the appellants weighs against the Crown and cannot be used to excuse the length of delay.

(iii) Explanation for the Delay

(a) Delays Attributable to the Crown

It is clear that delays cannot be attributable to any action of the Crown. At no time did the Crown make any requests for adjournments or take any step that delayed the trial of the action in any way.

There is nothing in the case that is so complex or inherently difficult that it would justify a lengthy delay. . . .

(b) Systemic or Institutional Delay

This trial was to be heard in Brampton, in the District of Peel in Ontario. This district has long been notorious for the inordinate length of time required to obtain a trial date. The delays are said to be caused by lack of facilities. The evidence submitted contains a study done by Prof. Carl Baar, Director of the Judicial Administration Program at Brock University. From the research and comparative studies that he has undertaken, Professor Baar has concluded that the Peel District (referred to as Brampton by Professor Baar) experiences extremely long delays that are out of the ordinary compared to the rest of Ontario, the rest of Canada or the United States. He notes that the situation has arisen partly as a result of rapid urban growth and the presence of a very large international airport which generates a great many drug-related offences. He also finds that a shortage of court space and judges are significant factors which contribute to the lengthy delays. His research indicates that comparatively speaking it is without doubt one of the worst districts in Canada, if not the worst, in terms of delays between committal and trial. Ontario can take no pride in this situation and must indeed bear the responsibility for it. . . .

It is apparent that the situation in Peel District has been in a deplorable state for many years. Something is terribly wrong. As Justice Zuber noted the situation is "enormously complex" and there is no "magic solution" or "quick fix." Nonetheless, something must be done. Urgent attention to the situation is required. The response of the Government of Ontario has been neither overwhelming nor particularly successful. A program known as the Delay Reduction Initiative instituted by the Government is summarized in the Chaloner affidavit. . . .

The most recent statistics set forth in the Chaloner affidavit for the period from October 1988 to December 1989 clearly indicate that in four of the six target areas, including Peel District, there is no visible long-term trend towards improvement of the mean average time of case delays. . . .

The only conclusion which can be drawn from an analysis of the material filed is that the problem of systemic delay in Peel has not and cannot be resolved simply by introducing a more efficient caseflow management system. More resources must be supplied to this district perhaps by way of additional Crown Attorneys and courtrooms. This conclusion cannot come as a surprise. The problem has existed for many years, back at least as far as 1981. . . .

The extent and gravity of the problem in Peel is brought home by reference to the comparative study done in 1987 by Professor Baar. The study illustrated that in Canada, New Brunswick and Quebec were best able to bring their cases to trial within the thirty to ninety-day range. In terms of the time taken to completely dispose of a case from committal to disposition, the median total time in New Brunswick's lower courts (provincial courts) was 152 days. The median total time in upper courts (s. 96 courts) was 72 days. By comparison, in Ontario the best district was London with a median total time of 239 days and the median upper court time of 105 days. Toronto, Ottawa and St. Catherines were all close together with median total times of between 315 and 349 days, and upper court times between 133 and 144 days.

Professor Baar wrote that "[b]y all measures used in the study, Brampton District Court was significantly slower than any other location studied: median total time was 607 days and median upper court time was 423 days." Nor can any comfort be drawn by comparison to the United States. Professor Baar concluded that the Peel District is generally substantially slower than the slowest United States jurisdictions. Further, he noted that the delay in the present case was longer than ninety per cent of all cases in terms of median total time among those heard even in Peel District. This case therefore represents one of the worst from the point of view of delay in the worst district not only in Canada, but so far as the studies indicate, anywhere north of the Rio Grande.

If it should be argued that the statistics from New Brunswick cannot represent a basis for comparison, then surely those from Quebec can and do provide a guide for comparison. A review of the recent statistics kept by the courts in Montréal, Longueuil and Terrebonne by comparison reveals how very unsatisfactory and intolerable is the state of affairs in Peel.

At Montréal, for the 5½ month period beginning January 8, 1990, the delay between the date of remitting a case for trial at the next assize and the date of trial is 82½ days. This figure includes the time for all trials save one which was remitted by the Court of Appeal for a second trial. If from this figure are deducted those cases where the defence either requested an adjournment or brought a motion such as *certiorari*, the time was 60 days.

In the District of Terrebonne, taking into account all the cases before the Superior Court, the delay between remission for trial and trial is 91.5 days. If one case with exceptional circumstances is deleted, the waiting period drops to 86 days.

In the District of Longueuil, the waiting period for trial is 90.5 days. Once again, if the exceptional cases are deleted, the waiting period drops to 66.75 days.

The average time in the three districts to commence a trial is 84.3 days and if from the total there is deducted those cases where a second trial was directed or the defence requested an adjournment, the waiting period is only 63.5 days.

Making a very rough comparison and more than doubling the longest waiting period to make every allowance for the special circumstances in Peel would indicate that a period of delay in a range of some six to eight months between committal and trial might be deemed to be the outside limit of what is reasonable. The usual delays in Peel are more than four times as long as those of busy metropolitan districts in the province of Quebec and the delay in this case is more than eight times as long. The figures from the comparable districts demonstrate that the Peel District situation is unreasonable and intolerable.

The delay in this case is such that it is impossible to come to any other conclusion than that the s. 11(*b*) *Charter* rights guaranteed to the individual accused have been infringed. As well, the societal interest in ensuring that these accused be brought to trial within a reasonable time has been grossly offended and denigrated. Indeed the delay is of such an inordinate length that public confidence in the administration of justice must be shaken. . . . Yet, that trial can only be undertaken if the *Charter* right to trial within a reasonable time has not been infringed. In this case that right has been grievously infringed and the sad result is that a stay of proceedings must be entered. To conclude otherwise would render meaningless a right enshrined in the *Charter* as the supreme law of the land. . . .

This conclusion should not be taken as a direction to build an expensive courthouse at a time of fiscal restraint. Rather, it is a recognition that this situation is unacceptable and can no longer be tolerated. Surely an imaginative solution could be found that would rectify the problem. For example, courtroom space might be found in other nearby government buildings. Or perhaps an interim solution could be achieved by the installation of portable structures similar to those used in the school system. If the children who represent the most precious resource of the nation can be taught in portable classrooms, then as a temporary solution trials can take place in similar accommodation.

Arguments can always be raised as to why interim solutions should not be used. Yet, imaginative cooperation can surely resolve these problems. If temporary structures cannot be used for criminal cases for reasons of security, then the criminal trials might proceed in the courthouse while the civil cases are heard in the nearby government buildings or portable buildings.

Another temporary solution might be to encourage changes of venue. . . .

These tentative suggestions may very well be unworkable. But some solution must be found to eradicate this malignant growth of unreasonable trial delay that constitutes such an unacceptable blight upon the administration of justice in Peel District.

(c) Delay Attributable to the Accused

In order to consider this factor, it is necessary to examine the conduct of the accused in order to ascertain whether it was such that it excused the delay by in effect bringing it about. At the outset, I would repeat that in this case it is clear that there was no direct action on the part of the appellants which resulted in any delay apart from that which occurred prior to the preliminary hearing. . . .

The complete transcript also reveals that there was no evidence to even support a finding that the appellants had a concealed plan to wait until the delay was unreasonable before complaining or bringing a motion. . . .

(iv) Waiver

. . . On the facts of this case there was no explicit waiver of their rights by the appellants. . . .

The silence of the appellants or their failure to raise an objection to a long delay is certainly not enough in the circumstances to infer waiver. Rather, the onus rests upon the Crown to demonstrate that the actions of the accused amounted to an agreement to the delay or waiver of their right.

In summary, the appellants did not specifically waive their s. 11(b) rights. Neither can it be inferred from their actions that they waived those rights.

The foregoing review indicates that there is no basis upon which this delay can be justified and as a result, a stay of proceedings must be directed. Courts may frequently be requested to take such a step. Fortunately, Professor Baar's work indicates that most regions of this country are operating within reasonable and acceptable time limits with the result that such relief will be infrequently granted. However, in situations such

as this where the delay is extensive and beyond justification there is no alternative but to direct a stay of proceedings.

The following are the reasons delivered by

LAMER C.J.: I agree with Justice Cory's resolution of this appeal and with most of his reasons. However, with respect, I am unable to accept his position that one of the objectives of s. 11(b) of the *Canadian Charter of Rights and Freedoms* is the protection of a societal interest in speedy trials. I also respectfully disagree that prejudice suffered by the accused resulting from the delay is a factor to be considered when determining the "reasonableness" of the delay.

Societal Interest

As I stated in my reasons in *Mills v. The Queen*, [1986] 1 S.C.R. 863, at pp. 917-18, reasons in which Dickson C.J. and Wilson J. concurred, and in which I still firmly believe, while society may have an interest in the efficient functioning of the criminal justice system, this interest is not what s. 11(b) is designed to protect. . . .

Prejudice

Cory J. adopts the consideration of "prejudice" from Wilson J.'s position in *Mills*, at p. 967:

> There may, indeed, be an irrebuttable presumption in favour of prejudice flowing from the fact of an accused's being charged with a criminal offence but that is not protected by s. 11(b) of the *Charter*. The prejudice arising from anxiety, stress and stigmatization by family and friends also exists where the accused is tried within a reasonable time. What the accused has to demonstrate under s. 11(b), in my opinion, is that he has suffered an impairment of his liberty and security interests as a result of the Crown's failure to bring him to trial within a reasonable time, not as a result of the Crown's having charged him.

In *Mills*, I took the position that because of the very nature of our criminal justice system, a certain degree of prejudice, including, at p. 920, "stigmatization of the accused, loss of privacy, stress and anxiety resulting from a multitude of factors, including possible disruption of family, social life and work, legal costs, uncertainty as to the outcome and sanction," will inevitably be imposed upon an individual charged with a criminal offence and will thereby infringe the rights of liberty and security of the person. Therefore, there exists an irrebuttable presumption of prejudice from the moment the charge is laid. . . .

Making prejudice affecting the fairness of the trial a relevant consideration for s. 11(b) sets a precedent which could have dangerous consequences for the scope of other *Charter* rights. For example, s. 10(*b*) of the *Charter* guarantees the right, upon arrest or detention, to be informed of the right to retain and instruct counsel without delay. Suppose an individual is arrested and there is considerable delay in advising him or her of the right to retain counsel. Even if the individual later states that had he or she been promptly informed of the right to retain and instruct counsel, he or she would not have done so because of financial considerations, the rights guaranteed under s. 10(*b*) have still been restricted. This person may not have suffered any prejudice, but surely his or her rights have been infringed. Of course, lack of prejudice would be a consideration when fashioning a remedy under s. 24(1) or when applying s. 24(2). But the absence or presence of prejudice is not, in my respectful view, in any way relevant to the initial issue of *Charter* breach.

The following are the reasons delivered by

WILSON J.: ...

[Justice Wilson concurred with Chief Justice Lamer on whether section 11(*b*) protects a societal as well as an individual interest. On the issue of the relevance of prejudice to the accused, she sided with the Cory majority—an accused should bear the onus of proving that the delay harmed his or her interests.]

The following are the reasons delivered by

SOPINKA J.: I have had the benefit of reading the reasons for judgment prepared in this appeal by Chief Justice Lamer and Justice Cory. I am of the view that this appeal must be allowed for the reasons given by Cory J., with the exception of his reference to a societal interest. In this respect, I agree with Lamer C.J.'s comments concerning the purported societal interest in s. 11(*b*) of the *Canadian Charter of Rights and Freedoms*.

The following are the reasons delivered by

McLACHLIN J.: I agree in substance and result with the reasons of Justice Cory. I wish to add only the following comments relevant to the process of determining whether a trial has unreasonably been delayed.

Like Cory J., I see s. 11(*b*) of the *Canadian Charter of Rights and Freedoms* as designed to serve both the interests of the accused and the interests of the prosecution, as well as the interests of society generally. This requires adoption of a balancing approach such as that which has prevailed in the United States, "in which the conduct of both the prosecution and the defendant are weighed": *Barker v. Wingo*, 407 U.S. 514 (1972), *per* Powell J., at p. 530.

Two elements must be assessed under s. 11(*b*). The first is the length of the delay. The second is its reasonableness.

The length of the delay is to be determined by the norms usually prevailing in similar jurisdictions, as Cory J. suggests. The question at this stage is whether the delay is *prima facie* excessive. If it is not, it is unnecessary to pursue the analysis further. If it is, it is necessary to go on to consider whether the delay is reasonable, notwithstanding its length.

The reasonableness of the delay may depend on a variety of factors.... The ultimate question in each case is whether, after considering all relevant factors, the *prima facie* excessive delay can be justified as reasonable.

The factors to be considered will often pull in opposite directions. Thus, it is impossible to dictate in advance how the balancing is to be done in each case. Yet certain parameters can be suggested. The accused will rarely be entitled to the benefit of s. 11(*b*) where the Crown can show that the accused caused the delay or has suffered no prejudice as a consequence of the delay. On the other hand, lengthy and avoidable delay caused entirely by the Crown's sloppiness or inattention, or by unjustified delays in the legal system, will frequently entitle an accused to the benefit of s. 11(*b*).

In this case, the delay is *prima facie* excessive; indeed it is grossly excessive. We must therefore proceed to the second stage of the analysis to ask whether it is reasonable. The trial judge found that the accused had been prejudiced by the delay. As for the cause of the delay, the defence neither caused the delay nor agreed to it; I agree with Cory J. that failure to protest the delay should not be determinative against the accused in this case. Here the prosecution caused the delay. That delay was not due to inherent difficulties in the case but to systemic or institutional causes. Notwithstanding ample time since the advent of the *Charter* to increase the ability of the courts in Peel County to process their heavy trial lists within a reasonable time, this has not been done. Taking these factors together, the result is clear. The delay cannot be justified; it is unreasonable.

I would allow the appeal and direct a stay of proceedings.

PART EIGHT

Equality Rights

25 Andrews v. Law Society of British Columbia, 1989

*A*ndrews was the first case based exclusively on section 15 to be decided by the Supreme Court. The case arose out of circumstances identical to those of Skapinker, who took the first major *Charter* case to the Supreme Court, but who had to rely on section 6 "mobility rights" because section 15 had not yet come into effect.[1] Like *Skapinker, Andrews* will be remembered not so much for the precise legal issue it settled as for the interpretive orientation it established. Just as *Skapinker* provided the Court with the opportunity to indicate the general approach it would take to the *Charter*, so *Andrews* gave it the opportunity to establish the principles of section 15 jurisprudence. The Court's discussion of such terms as "equality" and "discrimination," and of the overall structure of section 15 and its relationship to other parts of the *Charter*, has become the point of departure for subsequent debate (both in and out of court) about section 15's "equality rights." The pathbreaking importance of this case was recognized by several interest groups who, while not much concerned with the particulars of Andrews's claim, sought and received intervener status in order to persuade the Court to lay a foundation for section 15 jurisprudence that was compatible with their section 15 litigation strategies.[2]

Andrews wished to practise law in British Columbia and had met all the standards for admission to the bar except for the requirement of Canadian citizenship contained in section 42(*a*) of the *Barristers and Solicitors Act*. He argued that this legislative discrimination against non-citizens infringed section 15 of the *Charter*. Because "citizenship" is not one of the prohibited grounds of discrimination explicitly enumerated by section 15, the case raised questions about the reach of that section's open-ended wording. The Court unanimously agreed that the citizenship requirement violated section 15 but divided on the question whether it could be saved as a "reasonable limit" under section 1: five members of the six-judge panel[3] concluded that it could not be so defended; Justice McIntyre, who wrote the controlling opinion on most other issues, dissented on this section 1 question.

The Court was obviously concerned about the potential for the open-ended wording of section 15 to force the judicial evaluation of almost all legislation. This would occur especially if the term "discrimination" were interpreted in a neutral fashion as meaning simply "distinction," and if the open-ended phraseology were taken literally to cover all distinctions. Most laws make distinctions and would, under such an interpretation, violate section 15;[4]

---

1 See *Law Society of Upper Canada v. Skapinker*, [1984] 1 S.C.R. 357.

2 Intervening on the side of Andrews were the Women's Legal Education and Action Fund (LEAF), the Coalition of Provincial Organizations of the Handicapped, the Canadian Association of University Teachers, and the Ontario Confederation of University Faculty Associations. The Federation of Law Societies of Canada and several provincial Attorneys General intervened on the other side.

3 Justice Le Dain was on the panel but took no part in the judgment.

4 Justice McIntyre, following the court below, uses the example of laws forbidding children or drunk persons from driving.

they could thus be sustained only as "reasonable limits" under section 1. Although such an interpretation had been suggested by leading commentators, it was too daunting for the Court. Justice La Forest, for example, could not "accept that all legislative classifications must be rationally supportable before the courts" because this would involve the judicial assessment of "much economic and social policy-making [that] is simply beyond the institutional competence of the courts." The proper judicial role, he said, "is to protect against incursions on fundamental values, not to second guess policy decisions."

Writing for a unanimous court on this point, Justice McIntyre reduced the potential for violating section 15 by placing two limitations on its scope. First, he held that "discrimination" did not mean merely "distinction," but required the showing of some harm or prejudice. Second, he restricted the reach of the open-ended wording to grounds "analogous" to the enumerated grounds. Both qualifications on the scope of section 15 were designed to ensure that many legislative distinctions will not violate the *Charter*'s equality rights and will thus not have to defend themselves under section 1 as "reasonable limits . . . demonstrably justified in a free and democratic society."

Neither qualification applied in this case, however. Justice McIntyre found that non-citizens were harmed by the legislation and that citizenship was an analogous ground because non-citizens "are a good example of a 'discrete and insular minority' who come within the protection of s. 15." Justice Wilson added that discrete and insular minorities were groups "lacking in political power and as such vulnerable to having their interests overlooked and their rights to equal concern and respect violated. They are among 'those groups in society to whose needs and wishes elected officials have no apparent interest in attending.'" This emphasis on section 15's role in protecting groups that lack power and influence is consistent with Chief Justice Dickson's theory, enunciated in both *Edwards Books* and the *Alberta Labour Reference*, that an important purpose of the *Charter* is to help social and economic "underdogs."[5]

While the Court clearly intended to limit the scope of section 15 challenges, the limits are not terribly clear and are likely to generate considerable controversy. For example, the question whether an unlisted group is an "underdog" deserving constitutional protection will not be easy to determine.[6] Nor is the question whether a legislative distinction causes harm likely to be free of difficulty. A further source of ambiguity is introduced by the way in which the Court chose to define the term "discrimination." It does not mean just direct, intentional discrimination against the enumerated or analogous groups, but also the "disparate impact" on these groups of otherwise neutral policies. This means that classifications not based on an analogous ground will nevertheless be subject to section 15 challenge if they have an unintentional negative "effect" on a group defined by an enumerated or analogous group. For example, war veterans are overwhelmingly male. Does this mean that a "veterans preference," which does not appear to be based on an "analogous ground," is nevertheless open to challenge because its indirect effect is to deny "equal benefit of the law"

---

5   See *Edwards Books and Art Ltd.*, [1986] 2 S.C.R. 713 and *Reference re Public Service Employee Relations Act (Alta.)*, [1987] 1 S.C.R. 313.

6   Consider, for example, the disagreement between Justices Dickson and McIntyre about the power of the labour movement in the *Alberta Labour Reference*, case 9.

to women? Justice McIntyre insists that "[a] complainant under s. 15(1) must show not only that he or she is not receiving equal treatment before and under the law or that the law has a differential impact on him or her in the protection or benefit accorded by law but, in addition, must show that the legislative impact of the law is discriminatory [that is, harmful]." He intends this to be a formula for limiting the scope of section 15. In fact, it opens as many interpretive doors as it closes, and the precise scope of section 15 will remain an open question for some time to come. ⌒

Discussion Questions

1. How does the approach to equality rights adopted by the Court in this case differ from the theory of formal equality?
2. How would you say the Court defined unconstitutional discrimination in this case?
3. What alternative approach to equality rights, if any, would you have preferred the Court to have taken?

ANDREWS v. LAW SOCIETY OF BRITISH COLUMBIA
[1989] 1 S.C.R. 143

Hearing: October 5, 6, 1987; Judgment: February 2, 1989.

Present: Dickson C.J. and McIntyre, Lamer, Wilson, Le Dain,* La Forest, and L'Heureux-Dubé JJ.

Interveners: The Attorney General for Ontario, the Attorney General of Quebec, the Attorney General of Nova Scotia, the Attorney General for Saskatchewan, the Attorney General for Alberta, the Federation of Law Societies of Canada (for the appellants); the Women's Legal Education and Action Fund, the Coalition of Provincial Organizations of the Handicapped, the Canadian Association of University Teachers, and the Ontario Confederation of University Faculty Associations (for the respondents).

* Le Dain J. took no part in the judgment.

The judgment of Dickson C.J.C. and Wilson and L'Heureux-Dubé JJ. was delivered by

WILSON J.: I have had the benefit of the reasons of my colleague, Justice McIntyre, and I am in complete agreement with him as to the way in which s. 15(1) of the *Canadian Charter of Rights and Freedoms* should be interpreted and applied. I also agree with my colleague as to the way in which s. 15(1) and s. 1 of the *Charter* interact. I differ from him, however, on the application of s. 1 to this particular case....

I agree with my colleague that a rule which bars an entire class of persons from certain forms of employment solely on the ground that they are not Canadian citizens violates the equality rights of that class. I agree with him also that it discriminates against them on the ground of their personal characteristics, i.e., their non-citizen status. I believe, therefore, that they are entitled to the protection of s. 15.

Before turning to s. 1, I would like to add a brief comment to what my colleague has said concerning non-citizens permanently resident in Canada forming the kind of "discrete and insular minority" to which the Supreme Court of the United States referred in *United States v. Carolene Products Co.,* 304 U.S. 144 (1938), at pp. 152-53, n. 4.

Relative to citizens, non-citizens are a group lacking in political power and as such vulnerable to having their interests overlooked and their rights to equal concern and respect violated. They are among "those groups in society to whose needs and wishes elected officials have no apparent interest in attending": see J. H. Ely, Democracy and Distrust (1980), at p. 151. Non-citizens, to take only the most obvious example, do not have the right to vote. Their vulnerability to becoming a disadvantaged group in our society is captured by John

Stuart Mill's observation in Book III of Considerations on Representative Government that "in the absence of its natural defenders, the interests of the excluded is always in danger of being overlooked...." I would conclude therefore that non-citizens fall into an analogous category to those specifically enumerated in s. 15. I emphasize, moreover, that this is a determination which is not to be made only in the context of the law which is subject to challenge but rather in the context of the place of the group in the entire social, political and legal fabric of our society. While legislatures must inevitably draw distinctions among the governed, such distinctions should not bring about or reinforce the disadvantage of certain groups and individuals by denying them the rights freely accorded to others.

I believe also that it is important to note that the range of discrete and insular minorities has changed and will continue to change with changing political and social circumstances. For example, Stone J., writing in 1938, was concerned with religious, national and racial minorities. In enumerating the specific grounds in s. 15, the framers of the *Charter* embraced these concerns in 1982 but also addressed themselves to the difficulties experienced by the disadvantaged on the grounds of ethnic origin, colour, sex, age and physical and mental disability. It can be anticipated that the discrete and insular minorities of tomorrow will include groups not recognized as such today. It is consistent with the constitutional status of s. 15 that it be interpreted with sufficient flexibility to ensure the "unremitting protection" of equality rights in the years to come.

While I have emphasized that non-citizens are, in my view, an analogous group to those specifically enumerated in s. 15 and, as such, are entitled to the protection of the section, I agree with my colleague that it is not necessary in this case to determine what limit, if any, there is on the grounds covered by s. 15 and I do not do so....

Having found an infringement of s. 15 of the *Charter,* I turn now to the question whether the citizenship requirement for entry into the legal profession in British Columbia constitutes a reasonable limit which can be "demonstrably justified in a free and democratic society" under s. 1.

As my colleague has pointed out, the onus of justifying the infringement rests upon those seeking to uphold the legislation, in this case the Attorney General of British Columbia and the Law Society of British Columbia, and the analysis to be conducted is that set forth by Chief Justice Dickson in *R. v. Oakes,* [1986] 1 S.C.R. 103.

The first hurdle to be crossed in order to override a right guaranteed in the *Charter* is that the objective sought to be achieved by the impugned law must relate to concerns which are "pressing and substantial" in a free and democratic society.... This, in my view, remains an appropriate standard when it is recognized that not every distinction between individuals and groups will violate s. 15. If every distinction between individuals and groups gave rise to a violation of s. 15, then this standard might well be too stringent for application in all cases and might deny the community at large the benefits associated with sound and desirable social and economic legislation. This is not a concern, however, once the position that every distinction drawn by law constitutes discrimination is rejected as indeed it is in the judgment of my colleague, McIntyre J. Given that s. 15 is designed to protect those groups who suffer social, political and legal disadvantage in our society, the burden resting on government to justify the type of discrimination against such groups is appropriately an onerous one.

The second step in a s. 1 inquiry involves the application of a proportionality test which requires the Court to balance a number of factors. . . .

I appreciate the desirability of lawyers being familiar with Canadian institutions and customs but I agree with McLachlin J.A. that the requirement of citizenship is not carefully tailored to achieve that objective and may not even be rationally connected to it. McDonald J. pointed out in *Re Dickenson and Law Society of Alberta* (1978), 84 D.L.R. (3d) 189, at p. 195 that such a requirement affords no assurance that citizens who want to become lawyers are sufficiently familiar with Canadian institutions and "it could be better achieved by an examination of the particular qualifications of the applicant, whether he is a Canadian citizen, a British subject, or something else."

The second justification advanced by the appellants in support of the citizenship requirement is that citizenship evidences a real attachment to Canada. Once again I find myself in agreement with the following observations of McLachlin J.A., at pp. 612-13:

> The second reason for the distinction—that citizenship implies a commitment to Canadian society—fares little better upon close examination. Only those citizens who are not natural-born Canadians can be said to have made a conscious choice to establish themselves here permanently and to opt for full participation in the Canadian social process, including the right to vote and run for public office. While no doubt most citizens, natural-born or otherwise, are committed to Canadian society, citizenship does not ensure that that is the case. Conversely, non-citizens may be deeply committed to our country.

The third ground advanced to justify the requirement relates to the role lawyers are said to play in the governance of our country. McLachlin J.A. disputed the extent to which the practice of law involves the performance of a governmental function. She stated at p. 614:

> While lawyers clearly play an important role in our society, it cannot be contended that the practice of law involves performing a state or government function. In this respect, the role of lawyers may be distinguished from that of legislators, judges, civil servants and policemen. The practice of law is first and foremost a private profession. Some lawyers work in the courts, some do not. Those who work in the courts may represent the Crown or act against it. It is true that all lawyers are officers of the court. That term, in my mind, implies allegiance and certain responsibilities to the institution of the court. But it does not mean that lawyers are part of the process of government.

Although I am in general agreement with her characterization of the role of lawyers *qua* lawyers in our society, my problem with this basis of justification is more fundamental. To my mind, even if lawyers do perform a governmental function, I do not think the requirement that they be citizens provides any guarantee that they will honourably and conscientiously carry out their public duties. They will carry them out, I believe, because they are good lawyers and not because they are Canadian citizens.

In my view, the reasoning advanced in support of the citizenship requirement simply does not meet the tests in *Oakes* for overriding a constitutional right particularly, as in this case, a right designed to protect "discrete and insular minorities" in our society. I would respectfully concur in the view expressed by McLachlin J.A. at p. 617 that the citizenship requirement does not "appear to relate closely to those ends, much less to have been carefully designed to achieve them with minimum impairment of individual rights." . . .

LA FOREST J.: . . . My colleague, Justice McIntyre, has set forth the facts and the judicial history of this appeal and it is unnecessary for me to repeat them. Nor need I enter into an extensive examination of the law regarding the meaning of s. 15(1), because in so far as it is relevant to this appeal I am in substantial agreement with the views of my colleague. I hasten to add that the relevant question as I see it is restricted to whether the impugned provision amounts to discrimination in the sense in which my colleague has defined it, i.e., on the basis of "irrelevant personal differences" such as those listed in s. 15 and, traditionally, in human rights legislation.

I am not prepared to accept at this point that the only significance to be attached to the opening words that refer more generally to equality is that the protection afforded by the section is restricted to discrimination through the application of law. It is possible to read s. 15 in this way and I have no doubt that on any view redress against that kind of discrimination will constitute the bulk of the courts' work under the provision. Moreover, from the manner in which it was drafted, I also have no doubt that it was so intended. However, it can reasonably be argued that the opening words, which take up half the section, seem somewhat excessive to accomplish the modest role attributed to them, particularly having regard to the fact that s. 32 already limits the application of the *Charter* to legislation and governmental activity. It may also be thought to be out of keeping with the broad and generous approach given to other *Charter* rights, not the least of which is s. 7, which like s. 15 is of a generalized character. In the case of s. 7, it will be remembered, the Court has been at pains to give real meaning to each word of the section so as to ensure that the rights to life, liberty and security of the person are separate, if closely related rights. That having been said, I am convinced that it was never intended in enacting s. 15 that it become a tool for the wholesale subjection to judicial scrutiny of variegated legislative choices in no way infringing on values fundamental to a free and democratic society. Like my colleague, I am not prepared to accept that *all* legislative classifications must be rationally supportable before the courts. Much economic and social policy-making is simply beyond the institutional competence of the courts: their role is to protect against incursions on fundamental values, not to second guess policy decisions.

I realize that it is no easy task to distinguish between what is fundamental and what is not and that in this context this may demand consideration of abstruse theories of equality. For example, there may well be legislative or governmental differentiation between individuals or groups that is so grossly unfair to an individual or group and so devoid of any rational relationship to a legitimate state purpose as to offend against the principle of equality before and under the law as to merit intervention pursuant to s. 15. For these reasons I would think it better at this stage of *Charter* development to leave the question open. I am aware that in the United States, where Holmes J. has referred to the equal protection clause there as the "last resort of constitutional arguments" (*Buck v. Bell*, 274 U.S. 200 (1927), at p. 208), the courts have been extremely reluctant to interfere with legislative judgment. Still, as I stated, there may be cases where it is indeed the last constitutional resort to protect the individual from fundamental unfairness. Assuming there is room under s. 15 for judicial intervention beyond the traditionally established and analogous policies against discrimination discussed by my colleague, it bears repeating that considerations of institutional functions and resources should make courts extremely wary about questioning legislative and governmental choices in such areas. As I have indicated, however, this issue does not arise here. For we are concerned in this case with whether or not the legislation amounts to discrimination of a kind similar to those enumerated in s. 15. It was conceded that the impugned legislation does distinguish the respondents from

other persons on the basis of a personal characteristic which shares many similarities with those enumerated in s. 15. The characteristic of citizenship is one typically not within the control of the individual and, in this sense, is immutable. Citizenship is, at least temporarily, a characteristic of personhood not alterable by conscious action and in some cases not alterable except on the basis of unacceptable costs.

Moreover, non-citizens are an example without parallel of a group of persons who are relatively powerless politically, and whose interests are likely to be compromised by legislative decisions. History reveals that Canada did not for many years resist the temptation of enacting legislation the animating rationale of which was to limit the number of persons entering into certain employment. Discrimination on the basis of nationality has from early times been an inseparable companion of discrimination on the basis of race and national or ethnic origin, which are listed in s. 15. . . .

There is no question that citizenship may, in some circumstances, be properly used as a defining characteristic for certain types of legitimate governmental objectives. I am sensitive to the fact that citizenship is a very special status that not only incorporates rights and duties but serves a highly important symbolic function as a badge identifying people as members of the Canadian polity. Nonetheless, it is, in general, irrelevant to the legitimate work of government in all but a limited number of areas. By and large, the use in legislation of citizenship as a basis for distinguishing between persons, here for the purpose of conditioning access to the practice of a profession, harbours the potential for undermining the essential or underlying values of a free and democratic society that are embodied in s. 15. Our nation has throughout its history drawn strength from the flow of people to our shores. Decisions unfairly premised on citizenship would be likely to "inhibit the sense of those who are discriminated against that Canadian society is not free or democratic as far as they are concerned and . . . such persons are likely not to have faith in social and political institutions which enhance the participation of individuals and groups in society, or to have confidence that they can freely and without obstruction by the state pursue their and their families' hopes and expectations of vocational and personal development" (*Kask v. Shimizu*, [1986] 4 W.W.R. 154, at p. 161, per McDonald J. (Alta. Q.B.)).

While it cannot be said that citizenship is a characteristic which "bears no relation to the individual's ability to perform or contribute to society" (*Fontiero v. Richardson*, 411 U.S. 677 (1973), at p. 686), it certainly typically bears an attenuated sense of relevance to these. That is not to say that no legislative conditioning of benefits (for example) on the basis of citizenship is acceptable in the free and democratic society that is Canada, merely that legislation purporting to do so ought to be measured against the touchstone of our Constitution. It requires justification.

I turn then to a consideration of the justifiability, fairness or proportionality of the scheme. I agree with McIntyre J. that any such justification must be found under s. 1 of the *Charter*, essentially because, in matters involving infringements of fundamental rights, it is entirely appropriate that government sustain the constitutionality of its conduct. I am in general agreement with what he has to say about the manner in which legislation must be approached under the latter provision, in particular the need for a proportionality test involving a sensitive balancing of many factors in weighing the legislative objective. If I have any qualifications to make, it is that I prefer to think in terms of a single test for s. 1, but one that is to be applied to vastly differing situations with the flexibility and realism inherent in the word "reasonable" mandated by the Constitution.

The degree to which a free and democratic society such as Canada should tolerate differentiation based on personal characteristics cannot be ascertained by an easy calculus. There will rarely, if ever, be a perfect congruence between means and ends, save where legislation has discriminatory purposes. The matter must, as earlier cases have held, involve a test of proportionality. In cases of this kind, the test must be approached in a flexible manner. The analysis should be functional, focussing on the character of the classification in question, the constitutional and societal importance of the interests adversely affected, the relative importance to the individuals affected of the benefit of which they are deprived, and the importance of the state interest.

With deference, however, I am unable to agree with McIntyre J.'s application of these principles to the present case. I therefore turn to the task of balancing the objectives sought to be accomplished by the legislation against the means sought to achieve that objective....

While there is no evidence on this point, the Attorney General offers three purposes sought to be attained by the legislation. These are:

1. Citizenship ensures a familiarity with Canadian institutions and customs;
2. Citizenship implies a commitment to Canadian society;
3. Lawyers play a fundamental role in the Canadian system of democratic government and as such should be citizens....

[Like Justice Wilson, Justice La Forest essentially followed the reasoning of McLachlin J.A. in the Court of Appeal on these points.]

The third objective advanced by the Attorney General has more substance. It is that certain state activities should for both symbolic and practical reasons be confined to those who are full members of our political society. The Attorney General reduced his arguments regarding this objective to the following syllogism:

(a) persons who are involved in the processes or structure of government, broadly defined, should be citizens;
(b) lawyers are involved in the processes or structure of government;
(c) lawyers, therefore, should be citizens.

I do not quarrel with the first assertion as a general proposition. The Court of Appeal accepted it, noting that this rationale underlies the common requirement that legislators, voters, judges, police and senior public servants be citizens. However, it rejected the second proposition that lawyers play a vital role in the administration of law and justice and are themselves as much a part of the government processes as are judges, legislators and so on. It rejected the notion that the practice of law itself involved performing a state or government function....

I agree....It is only in the most unreal sense that it can be said that a lawyer working for a private client plays a role in the administration of justice that would require him or her to be a citizen in order to be allowed to participate therein. Obviously lawyers occupy a position of trust and responsibility in our society, but that is true of all professions, and the members of some of these, like that of chartered accountants, for instance, are privy to matters of the most serious import.

On a more mundane level, the essential purpose behind occupational licensing is to protect the public from unqualified practitioners. But as Lenoir points out ([Robert L., "Citizenship as a Requirement for the Practice of Law in Ontario" (1981), 13 *Ottawa Law Rev.* 527], at p. 547), "Citizenship has not been shown to bear any correlation to one's professional or vocational competency or qualification." Like him, I see no sufficient additional dimension to the lawyer's function to insist on citizenship as a qualification for admission to this profession.

It is not without significance that a requirement of citizenship has not been found to be necessary to the practice of law in either the United States (see *In re Griffiths*, 413 U.S. 717 (1973)), or England (see *Solicitors (Amendment) Act 1974 (U.K.)*, 1974, c. 26, s. 1); see also *Re Howard* [[1976] 1 N. S.W.L.R. 641], at p. 647. The doctrine of privileged communications was pressed into service, but that doctrine exists for the protection of the client. I fail to see what this has to do with the requirement of citizenship.

A requirement of citizenship would be acceptable if limited to Crown Attorneys or lawyers directly employed by government and, therefore, involved in policy-making or administration, so that it could be said that the lawyer was an architect or instrumentality of government policy; see *Reyners v. The Belgian State*, [1974] 2 Common Market Law R. 305. But ordinary lawyers are not privy to government information any more than, say, accountants, and there are rules to restrict lawyers from obtaining confidential governmental information.

I would conclude that although the governmental objectives, as stated, may be defensible, it is simply misplaced *vis-à-vis* the legal profession as a whole. However, even accepting the legitimacy and importance of the legislative objectives, the legislation exacts too high a price on persons wishing to practice law in that it may deprive them, albeit perhaps temporarily, of the "right" to pursue their calling. . . .

The judgment of McIntyre and Lamer JJ. was delivered by

McINTYRE J. (dissenting in part): This appeal raises only one question. Does the citizenship requirement for entry into the legal profession contained in s. 42 of the *Barristers and Solicitors Act*, R.S.B.C. 1979, c. 26, (the "*Act*") contravene s. 15(1) of the *Canadian Charter of Rights and Freedoms*? Section 42 provides:

> 42. The benchers may call to the Bar of the Province and admit as a solicitor of the Supreme Court
>> (a) a Canadian citizen with respect to whom they are satisfied that he . . .

and s. 15 of the *Charter* states:

> 15. (1) Every individual is equal before and under the law and has the right to the equal protection and equal benefit of the law without discrimination and, in particular, without discrimination based on race, national or ethnic origin, colour, religion, sex, age or mental or physical disability.
>
> (2) Subsection (1) does not preclude any law, program or activity that has as its object the amelioration of conditions of disadvantaged individuals or groups including those that are disadvantaged because of race, national or ethnic origin, colour, religion, sex, age or mental or physical disability.

The respondent, Andrews, was a British subject permanently resident in Canada at the time these proceedings were commenced. He had taken law degrees at Oxford and had fulfilled all the requirements for admission to the practice of law in British Columbia, except that of Canadian citizenship. He commenced proceedings for a declaration that s. 42 of the *Act* violates the *Charter*. He also sought an order in the nature of mandamus requiring the benchers of the Law Society of British Columbia to consider his application for call to the Bar and admission as a solicitor. His action was dismissed at

trial before Taylor J. in the Supreme Court of British Columbia in a judgment reported at (1985), 22 D.L.R. (4th) 9. An appeal was allowed in the Court of Appeal (Hinkson, Craig and McLachlin JJ.A., at (1986), 27 D.L.R. (4th) 600), and this appeal is taken by the Law Society of British Columbia, by leave granted November 27, 1986. Pursuant to an order of this Court on January 28, 1987, Gorel Elizabeth Kinersly, an American citizen who was at the time a permanent resident of Canada articling in the Province of British Columbia, was added as a co-respondent in this appeal. . . .

Following the judgment in his favour, the respondent Andrews was called to the Bar and admitted as a solicitor in the Province of British Columbia and is now a Canadian citizen. The co-respondent, Kinersly, who had expressed an intention to become a Canadian citizen, became eligible to do so on March 15, 1988. . . .

The Concept of Equality

Section 15(1) of the *Charter* provides for every individual a guarantee of equality before and under the law, as well as the equal protection and equal benefit of the law without discrimination. This is not a general guarantee of equality; it does not provide for equality between individuals or groups within society in a general or abstract sense, nor does it impose on individuals or groups an obligation to accord equal treatment to others. It is concerned with the application of the law. No problem regarding the scope of the word "law," as employed in s. 15(1), can arise in this case because it is an Act of the Legislature which is under attack. Whether other governmental or quasi-governmental regulations, rules, or requirements may be termed laws under s. 15(1) should be left for cases in which the issue arises.

The concept of equality has long been a feature of Western thought. As embodied in s. 15(1) of the *Charter*, it is an elusive concept and, more than any of the other rights and freedoms guaranteed in the *Charter*, it lacks precise definition. As has been stated by John H. Schaar, "Equality of Opportunity and Beyond," in *Nomos IX: Equality*, ed. J. Roland Pennock and John W. Chapman (1967), at p. 228:

> Equality is a protean word. It is one of those political symbols—liberty and fraternity are others—into which men have poured the deepest urgings of their heart. Every strongly held theory or conception of equality is at once a psychology, an ethic, a theory of social relations, and a vision of the good society.

It is a comparative concept, the condition of which may only be attained or discerned by comparison with the condition of others in the social and political setting in which the question arises. It must be recognized at once, however, that every difference in treatment between individuals under the law will not necessarily result in inequality and, as well, that identical treatment may frequently produce serious inequality. . . . The same thought has been expressed in this Court in the context of s. 2(*b*) of the *Charter* in *R. v. Big M Drug Mart Ltd.*, [1985] 1 S.C.R. 295, where Dickson C.J. said at p. 347:

> The equality necessary to support religious freedom does not require identical treatment of all religions. In fact, the interests of true equality may well require differentiation in treatment.

In simple terms, then, it may be said that a law which treats all identically and which provides equality of treatment between "A" and "B" might well cause inequality for "C," depending on differences in personal characteristics and situations. To approach the ideal of full equality before and under the law—and in human affairs an approach is all that can be expected—the main consideration must be the impact of the law on the individual or the group concerned. Recognizing that there will always be an infinite variety of personal characteristics, capacities, entitlements and merits among those subject to a law, there must be accorded, as nearly as may be possible, an equality of benefit and protection and no more of the restrictions, penalties or burdens imposed upon one than another. In other words, the admittedly unattainable ideal should be that a law expressed to bind all should not because of irrelevant personal differences have a more burdensome or less beneficial impact on one than another.

McLachlin J.A. in the Court of Appeal expressed the view, at p. 605, that:

> . . . [T]he essential meaning of the constitutional requirement of equal protection and equal benefit is that persons who are "similarly situated be similarly treated" and conversely, that persons who are "differently situated be differently treated." . . .

In this, she was adopting and applying as a test a proposition which seems to have been widely accepted with some modifications in both trial and appeal court decisions throughout the country on s. 15(1) of the *Charter*. See, for example, *Reference Re Family Benefits Act* (1986), 75 N.S.R. (2d) 338 (N.S.S.C.A.D.), at p. 351; *Reference Re Use of French in Criminal Proceedings in Saskatchewan* (1987), 44 D.L.R. (4th) 16 (Sask. C.A.), at p. 46; *Smith, Kline & French Laboratories Ltd. v. Canada (Attorney General)*, [1987] 2 F.C. 359, at p. 366; *R. v. Ertel* (1987), 35 C.C.C. (3d) 398, at p. 419. The reliance on this concept appears to have derived, at least in recent times, from J. T. Tussman and J. tenBroek, "The Equal Protection of Laws" (1949), 37 *Calif. L. Rev.* 341. The similarly situated test is a restatement of the Aristotelian principle of formal equal-

ity—that "things that are alike should be treated alike, while things that are unalike should be treated unalike in proportion to their unalikeness" (*Ethica Nichomacea*, trans. W. Ross, Book V3, at p. 1131a-6 (1925)).

The test as stated, however, is seriously deficient in that it excludes any consideration of the nature of the law. If it were to be applied literally, it could be used to justify the Nuremberg laws of Adolf Hitler. Similar treatment was contemplated for all Jews. The similarly situated test would have justified the formalistic separate but equal doctrine of *Plessy v. Ferguson*, 163 U.S. 637 (1896), a doctrine that incidentally was still the law in the United States at the time that Professor Tussman and J. tenBroek wrote their much cited article: see M. David Lepofsky and H. Schwartz "Case Note" (1988), 67 *Can. Bar Rev.* 115, at pp. 119-20. The test, somewhat differently phrased, was applied in the British Columbia Court of Appeal in *R. v. Gonzales* (1962), 132 C.C.C. 237. The Court upheld, under s. 1(*b*) of the *Canadian Bill of Rights*, R.S.C. 1970, App. III, a section of the *Indian Act*, R.S.C. 1970, c. I-6, which made it an offence for an Indian to have intoxicants in his possession off a reserve. In his locality there were no reserves. Tysoe J.A. said that equality before the law could not mean "the same laws for all persons," and defined the right in these words, at p. 243:

> . . . [I]n its context s. 1(b) means in a general sense that there has existed and there shall continue to exist in Canada a right in every person to whom a particular law relates or extends no matter what may be a person's race, national origin, colour, religion or sex to stand on an equal footing with every other person to whom that particular law relates or extends and a right to the protection of the law.

This approach was rejected in this Court by Ritchie J. in *R. v. Drybones*, [1970] S.C.R. 282, in a similar case involving a provision of the *Indian Act* making it an offence for an Indian to be intoxicated off a reserve. He said, at p. 297:

> . . . I cannot agree with this interpretation pursuant to which it seems to me that the most glaring discriminatory legislation against a racial group would have to be construed as recognizing the right of each of its individual members "to equality before the law," so long as all the other members are being discriminated against in the same way.

Thus, mere equality of application to similarly situated groups or individuals does not afford a realistic test for a violation of equality rights. For, as has been said, a bad law will not be saved merely because it operates equally upon those to whom it has application. Nor will a law necessarily be bad because it makes distinctions.

A similarly situated test focussing on the equal application of the law to those to whom it has application could lead to results akin to those in *Bliss v. Attorney General of Canada*, [1979] 1 S.C.R. 183. In *Bliss*, a pregnant woman was denied unemployment benefits to which she would have been entitled had she not been pregnant. She claimed that the *Unemployment Insurance Act, 1971*, violated the equality guarantees of the *Canadian Bill of Rights* because it discriminated against her on the basis of her sex. Her claim was dismissed by this Court on the grounds that there was no discrimination on the basis of sex, since the class into which she fell under the *Act* was that of pregnant persons, and within that class, all persons were treated equally. This case, of course, was decided before the advent of the *Charter.* . . .

For the reasons outlined above, the test cannot be accepted as a fixed rule or formula for the resolution of equality questions arising under the *Charter*. Consideration must be given to the content of the law, to its purpose, and its impact upon those to whom it applies, and also upon those whom it excludes from its application. The issues which will arise from case to case are such that it would be wrong to attempt to confine these considerations within such a fixed and limited formula.

It is not every distinction or differentiation in treatment at law which will transgress the equality guarantees of s. 15 of the *Charter*. It is, of course, obvious that legislatures may—and to govern effectively—must treat different individuals and groups in different ways. Indeed, such distinctions are one of the main preoccupations of legislatures. The classifying of individuals and groups, the making of different provisions respecting such groups, the application of different rules, regulations, requirements and qualifications to different persons is necessary for the governance of modern society. As noted above, for the accommodation of differences, which is the essence of true equality, it will frequently be necessary to make distinctions. What kinds of distinctions will be acceptable under s. 15(1) and what kinds will violate its provisions?

In seeking an answer to these questions, the provisions of the *Charter* must have their full effect. In *R. v. Big M Drug Mart Ltd.*, this Court emphasized this point at p. 344, where Dickson C.J. stated:

This Court has already, in some measure, set out the basic approach to be taken in interpreting the *Charter*. In *Hunter v. Southam Inc.*, [1984] 2 S.C.R. 145, this Court expressed the view that the proper approach to the definition of the rights and freedoms guaranteed by the *Charter* was a purposive one. The meaning of a right or freedom guaranteed by the *Charter* was to be ascertained by an analysis of the *purpose* of such a guarantee; it was to be understood, in other words, in the light of the interests it was meant to protect.

In my view this analysis is to be undertaken, and the purpose of the right or freedom in question is to be sought by reference to the character and the larger objects of the *Charter* itself, to the language chosen to articulate the specific right or freedom, to the historical origins of the concepts enshrined, and where applicable, to the meaning and purpose of the other specific rights and freedoms with which it is associated within the text of the *Charter*. The interpretation should be, as the judgment in Southam emphasizes, a generous rather than a legalistic one, aimed at fulfilling the purpose of the guarantee and securing for individuals the full benefit of the *Charter*'s protection. At the same time it is important not to overshoot the actual purpose of the right or freedom in question, but to recall that the *Charter* was not enacted in a vacuum, and must therefore, as this Court's decision in *Law Society of Upper Canada v. Skapinker*, [1984] 1 S.C.R. 357, illustrates, be placed in its proper linguistic, philosophic and historical contexts. [Emphasis in original.]

These words are not inconsistent with the view I expressed in *Reference re Public Service Employee Relations Act (Alta.)*, [1987] 1 S.C.R. 313.

The principle of equality before the law has long been recognized as a feature of our constitutional tradition and it found statutory recognition in the *Canadian Bill of Rights*. However, unlike the *Canadian Bill of Rights*, which spoke only of equality before the law, s. 15(1) of the *Charter* provides a much broader protection. Section 15 spells out four basic rights: (1) the right to equality before the law; (2) the right to equality under the law; (3) the right to equal protection of the law; and (4) the right to equal benefit of the law. The inclusion of these last three additional rights in s. 15 of the *Charter* was an attempt to remedy some of the shortcomings of the right to equality in the *Canadian Bill of Rights*. It also reflected the expanded concept of discrimination being developed under the various Human Rights Codes since the enactment of the *Canadian Bill of Rights*. The shortcomings of the *Canadian Bill of Rights* as far as the right to equality is concerned are well known. In *Attorney General of Canada v. Lavell*, [1974] S.C.R. 1349, for example, this Court upheld s. 12(1)(*b*) of the *Indian Act* which deprived women, but not men, of their membership in Indian Bands if they married non-Indians. The provision was held not to violate equality *before* the law although it might, the Court said, violate equality *under* the law if such were protected. In *Bliss, supra*, this Court held that the denial of unemployment insurance benefits to women because they were pregnant did not violate the guarantee of equality before the law, because any inequality in the protection and benefit of the law was "not created by legislation but by nature" (p. 190). The case was distinguished from the

Court's earlier decision in *Drybones, supra,* as not involving (pp. 191-92) the imposition of a penalty on a racial group to which other citizens are not subjected, but as involving rather "a definition of the qualifications required for entitlement to benefits." It is readily apparent that the language of s. 15 was deliberately chosen in order to remedy some of the perceived defects under the *Canadian Bill of Rights.* The antecedent statute is part of the "linguistic, philosophic and historical context" of s. 15 of the *Charter.*

It is clear that the purpose of s. 15 is to ensure equality in the formulation and application of the law. The promotion of equality entails the promotion of a society in which all are secure in the knowledge that they are recognized at law as human beings equally deserving of concern, respect and consideration. It has a large remedial component. Howland C.J. and Robins J.A. (dissenting in the result but not with respect to this comment) in *Reference re an Act to Amend the Education Act (1986),* 53 O.R. (2d) 513, attempt to articulate the broad range of values embraced by s. 15. They state at p. 554:

> In our view, s. 15(1) read as a whole constitutes a compendious expression of a positive right to equality in both the substance and the administration of the law. It is an all-encompassing right governing all legislative action. Like the ideals of "equal justice" and "equal access to the law," the right to equal protection and equal benefit of the law now enshrined in the *Charter* rests on the moral and ethical principle fundamental to a truly free and democratic society that all persons should be treated by the law on a footing of equality with equal concern and respect.

It must be recognized, however, as well that the promotion of equality under s. 15 has a much more specific goal than the mere elimination of distinctions. If the *Charter* was intended to eliminate all distinctions, then there would be no place for sections such as 27 (multicultural heritage); 2(*a*) (freedom of conscience and religion); 25 (aboriginal rights and freedoms); and other such provisions designed to safeguard certain distinctions. Moreover, the fact that identical treatment may frequently produce serious inequality is recognized in s. 15(2), which states that the equality rights in s. 15(1) do "not preclude any law, program or activity that has as its object the amelioration of conditions of disadvantaged individuals or groups...."

Discrimination

The right to equality before and under the law, and the rights to the equal protection and benefit of the law contained in s. 15, are granted with the direction contained in s. 15 itself that they be without discrimination. Discrimination is unacceptable in a democratic society because it epitomizes the worst effects of the denial of equality, and discrimination reinforced by law is particularly repugnant. The worst oppression will result from discriminatory measures having the force of law. It is against this evil that s. 15 provides a guarantee.

Discrimination as referred to in s. 15 of the *Charter* must be understood in the context of pre-*Charter* history. Prior to the enactment of s. 15(1), the Legislatures of the various provinces and the federal Parliament had passed during the previous fifty years what may be generally referred to as Human Rights Acts....

What does discrimination mean? The question has arisen most commonly in a consideration of the Human Rights Acts and the general concept of discrimination under those enactments has been fairly well settled. There is little difficulty, drawing upon the cases in this Court, in isolating an acceptable definition. In *Ontario Human Rights Commission and O'Malley v. Simpsons-Sears Ltd.,* [1985] 2 S.C.R. 536, at p. 551, discrimination (in that case adverse effect discrimination) was described in these terms: "It arises where an employer ... adopts a rule or standard ... which has a discriminatory effect upon a prohibited ground on one employee or group of employees in that it imposes, because of some special characteristic of the employee or group, obligations, penalties, or restrictive conditions not imposed on other members of the work force." It was held in that case, as well, that no intent was required as an element of discrimination, for it is in essence the impact of the discriminatory act or provision upon the person affected which is decisive in considering any complaint. At page 547, this proposition was expressed in these terms:

> The Code aims at the removal of discrimination. This is to state the obvious. Its main approach, however, is not to punish the discriminator, but rather to provide relief for the victims of discrimination. It is the result or the effect of the action complained of which is significant. If it does, in fact, cause discrimination; if its effect is to impose on one person or group of persons obligations, penalties, or restrictive conditions not imposed on other members of the community, it is discriminatory.

In *Canadian National Railway Co. v. Canada (Canadian Human Rights Commission),* [1987] 1 S.C.R. 1114, better known as the *Action Travail des Femmes* case, where it was alleged that the Canadian National Railway was guilty of discriminatory hiring and promotion practices contrary to s. 10 of the *Canadian Human Rights Act,* S.C. 1976-77, c. 33, in denying employment to women in certain unskilled positions, Dickson C.J. in giving the judgment of the Court said, at pp. 1138-39:

> A thorough study of "systemic discrimination" in Canada is to be found in the Abella Report on equality in employment. The terms of reference of the Royal Commission

instructed it "to inquire into the most efficient, effective and equitable means of promoting employment opportunities, eliminating systemic discrimination and assisting individuals to compete for employment opportunities on an equal basis." (Order in Council P.C. 1983-1924 of 24 June 1983). Although Judge Abella chose not to offer a precise definition of systemic discrimination, the essentials may be gleaned from the following comments, found at p. 2 of the Abella Report.

Discrimination . . . means practices or attitudes that have, whether by design or impact, the effect of limiting an individual's or a group's right to the opportunities generally available because of attributed rather than actual characteristics. . . .

It is not a question of whether this discrimination is motivated by an intentional desire to obstruct someone's potential, or whether it is the accidental by-product of innocently motivated practices or systems. If the barrier is affecting certain groups in a disproportionately negative way, it is a signal that the practices that lead to this adverse impact may be discriminatory.

There are many other statements which have aimed at a short definition of the term discrimination. In general, they are in accord with the statements referred to above. I would say then that discrimination may be described as a distinction, whether intentional or not but based on grounds relating to personal characteristics of the individual or group, which has the effect of imposing burdens, obligations, or disadvantages on such individual or group not imposed upon others, or which withholds or limits access to opportunities, benefits, and advantages available to other members of society. Distinctions based on personal characteristics attributed to an individual solely on the basis of association with a group will rarely escape the charge of discrimination, while those based on an individual's merits and capacities will rarely be so classed.

The Court in the case at bar must address the issue of discrimination as the term is used in s. 15(1) of the *Charter*. In general, it may be said that the principles which have been applied under the Human Rights Acts are equally applicable in considering questions of discrimination under s. 15(1). Certain differences arising from the difference between the *Charter* and the Human Rights Acts must, however, be considered. To begin with, discrimination in s. 15(1) is limited to discrimination caused by the application or operation of law, whereas the Human Rights Acts apply also to private activities. Furthermore, and this is a distinction of more importance, all the Human Rights Acts passed in Canada specifically designate a certain limited number of grounds upon which discrimination is forbidden. Section 15(1) of the *Charter* is not so limited. The enumerated grounds in s. 15(1) are not exclu-

sive and the limits, if any, on grounds for discrimination which may be established in future cases await definition. The enumerated grounds do, however, reflect the most common and probably the most socially destructive and historically practised bases of discrimination and must, in the words of s. 15(1), receive particular attention. Both the enumerated grounds themselves and other possible grounds of discrimination recognized under s. 15(1) must be interpreted in a broad and generous manner, reflecting the fact that they are constitutional provisions not easily repealed or amended but intended to provide a "continuing framework for the legitimate exercise of governmental power" and, at the same time, for "the unremitting protection" of equality rights: see *Hunter v. Southam Inc.*, [1984] 2 S.C.R. 145, at p. 155.

It should be noted as well that when the Human Rights Acts create exemptions or defences, such as a *bona fide* occupational requirement, an exemption for religious and political organizations, or definitional limits on age discrimination, these generally have the effect of completely removing the conduct complained of from the reach of the *Act*. See, for example, exemptions for special interest organizations contained in the *Human Rights Code*, R.S.B.C. 1979, c. 186, as am., s. 22; The *Human Rights Act*, S.M. 1974, c. 65, as am., s. 6(7); and the *Human Rights Code*, 1981, S.O. 1981, c. 53, s. 17. "Age" is often restrictively defined in the Human Rights Acts; in British Columbia, it is defined in s. 1 of the *Code* to mean an age between 45 and 65; in s. 38 of the *Individual's Rights Protection Act*, R.S.A. 1980, c. I-2, it is defined as eighteen and over. For an example of the application of a *bona fide* occupational requirement, see *Bhinder v. Canadian National Railway Co.*, [1985] 2 S.C.R. 561. Where discrimination is forbidden in the Human Rights Acts it is done in absolute terms, and where a defence or exception is allowed it, too, speaks in absolute terms and the discrimination is excused. There is, in this sense, no middle ground. In the *Charter*, however, while s. 15(1), subject always to subs. (2), expresses its prohibition of discrimination in absolute terms, s. 1 makes allowance for a reasonable limit upon the operation of s. 15(1). A different approach under s. 15(1) is therefore required. While discrimination under s. 15(1) will be of the same nature and in descriptive terms will fit the concept of discrimination developed under the Human Rights Acts, a further step will be required in order to decide whether discriminatory laws can be justified under s. 1. The onus will be on the state to establish this. This is a distinct step called for under the *Charter* which is not found in most Human Rights Acts, because in those Acts justification for or defence to discrimination is generally found in specific exceptions to the substantive rights.

Relationship Between Section 15(1) and Section 1 of the Charter

In determining the extent of the guarantee of equality in s. 15(1) of the *Charter*, special consideration must be given to the relationship between s. 15(1) and s. 1. It is indeed the presence of s. 1 in the *Charter* and the interaction between these sections which has led to the differing approaches to a definition of the s. 15(1) right, and which has made necessary a judicial approach differing from that employed under the *Canadian Bill of Rights*. Under the *Canadian Bill of Rights*, a test was developed to distinguish between justified and unjustified legislative distinctions within the concept of equality before the law itself in the absence of anything equivalent to the s. 1 limit: see *MacKay v. The Queen*, [1980] 2 S.C.R. 370, where it was said, at p. 407:

> ... and whether it is a necessary departure from the general principle of universal application of the law for the attainment of some necessary and desirable social objective. Inequalities created for such purposes may well be acceptable under the *Canadian Bill of Rights*.

It may be noted as well that the 14th Amendment to the American Constitution, which provides that no State shall deny to any person within its jurisdiction the "equal protection of the laws," contains no limiting provisions similar to s. 1 of the *Charter*. As a result, judicial consideration has led to the development of varying standards of scrutiny of alleged violations of the equal protection provision which restrict or limit the equality guarantee within the concept of equal protection itself. Again, article 14 of the *European Convention on Human Rights*, 23 U.N.T.S. 222, which secures the rights guaranteed therein without discrimination, lacks a s. 1 or its equivalent and has also developed a limit within the concept itself. In the *Belgian Linguistic Case (No. 2)* (1968), 1 E.H.R.R. 252, at p. 284, the court enunciated the following test:

> ... [T]he principle of equality of treatment is violated if the distinction has no objective and reasonable justification. The existence of such a justification must be assessed in relation to the aim and effects of the measure under consideration, regard being had to principles which normally prevail in democratic societies. A difference in treatment in the exercise of a right laid down in the Convention must not only pursue a legitimate aim: Article 14 is likewise violated when it is clearly established that there is no reasonable relationship of proportionality between the means employed and the aim sought to be realised.

The distinguishing feature of the *Charter*, unlike the other enactments, is that consideration of such limiting factors is made under s. 1. This Court has described the analytical approach to the *Charter* in *R. v. Oakes*, [1986] 1 S.C.R. 103; *R. v. Edwards Books and Art Ltd.*, [1986] 2 S.C.R. 713, and other cases, the essential feature of which is that the right guaranteeing sections be kept analytically separate from s. 1. In other words, when confronted with a problem under the *Charter*, the first question which must be answered will be whether or not an infringement of a guaranteed right has occurred. Any justification of an infringement which is found to have occurred must be made, if at all, under the broad provisions of s. 1. It must be admitted at once that the relationship between these two sections may well be difficult to determine on a wholly satisfactory basis. It is, however, important to keep them analytically distinct if for no other reason than the different attribution of the burden of proof. It is for the citizen to establish that his or her *Charter* right has been infringed and for the state to justify the infringement.

Approaches to Section 15(1)

Three main approaches have been adopted in determining the role of s. 15(1), the meaning of discrimination set out in that section, and the relationship of s. 15(1) and s. 1. The first one, which was advanced by Professor Peter Hogg in *Constitutional Law of Canada* (2nd ed. 1985) would treat every distinction drawn by law as discrimination under s. 15(1). There would then follow a consideration of the distinction under the provisions of s. 1 of the *Charter*. He said, at pp. 800-801:

> I conclude that s. 15 should be interpreted as providing for the universal application of every law. When a law draws a distinction between individuals, on any ground, that distinction is sufficient to constitute a breach of s. 15, and to move the constitutional issue to s. 1. The test of validity is that stipulated by s. 1, namely, whether the law comes within the phrase "such reasonable limits prescribed by law as can be demonstrably justified in a free and democratic society."

He reached this conclusion on the basis that, where the *Charter* right is expressed in unqualified terms, s. 1 supplies the standard of justification for any abridgment of the right. He argued that the word "discrimination" in s. 15(1) could be read as introducing a qualification in the section itself, but he preferred to read the word in a neutral sense because this reading would immediately send the matter to s. 1, which was included in the *Charter* for this purpose.

The second approach put forward by McLachlin J.A. in the Court of Appeal involved a consideration of the reasonableness and fairness of the impugned legislation under s. 15(1). She stated, as has been noted above, at p. 610:

> The ultimate question is whether a fair-minded person, weighing the purposes of legislation against its effects on

the individuals adversely affected, and giving due weight to the right of the Legislature to pass laws for the good of all, would conclude that the legislative means adopted are unreasonable or unfair.

She assigned a very minor role to s. 1 which would, it appears, be limited to allowing in times of emergency, war, or other crises the passage of discriminatory legislation which would normally be impermissible.

A third approach, sometimes described as an "enumerated or analogous grounds" approach, adopts the concept that discrimination is generally expressed by the enumerated grounds. Section 15(1) is designed to prevent discrimination based on these and analogous grounds. The approach is similar to that found in human rights and civil rights statutes which have been enacted throughout Canada in recent times.... The analysis of discrimination in this approach must take place within the context of the enumerated grounds and those analogous to them. The words "without discrimination" require more than a mere finding of distinction between the treatment of groups or individuals. Those words are a form of qualifier built into s. 15 itself and limit those distinctions which are forbidden by the section to those which involve prejudice or disadvantage.

I would accept the criticisms of the first approach made by McLachlin J.A. in the Court of Appeal. She noted that the labelling of every legislative distinction as an infringement of s. 15(1) trivializes the fundamental rights guaranteed by the *Charter* and, secondly, that to interpret "without discrimination" as "without distinction" deprives the notion of discrimination of content. She continued, at p. 607:

> Third, it cannot have been the intention of Parliament that the government be put to the requirement of establishing under s. 1 that all laws which draw distinction between people are "demonstrably justified in a free and democratic society." If weighing of the justifiability of unequal treatment is neither required or permitted under s. 15, the result will be that such universally accepted and manifestly desirable legal distinctions as those prohibiting children or drunk persons from driving motor vehicles will be viewed as violations of fundamental rights and be required to run the gauntlet of s. 1.
>
> Finally, it may further be contended that to define discrimination under s. 15 as synonymous with unequal treatment on the basis of personal classification will be to elevate s. 15 to the position of subsuming the other rights and freedoms defined by the *Charter*.

In rejecting the Hogg approach, I would say that it draws a straight line from the finding of a distinction to a determination of its validity under s. 1, but my objection would be that it virtually denies any role for s. 15(1).

I would reject, as well, the approach adopted by McLachlin J.A. She seeks to define discrimination under s. 15(1) as an unjustifiable or unreasonable distinction. In so doing she avoids the mere distinction test but also makes a radical departure from the analytical approach to the *Charter* which has been approved by this Court. In the result, the determination would be made under s. 15(1) and virtually no role would be left for s. 1.

The third or "enumerated and analogous grounds" approach most closely accords with the purposes of s. 15 and the definition of discrimination outlined above and leaves questions of justification to s. 1. However, in assessing whether a complainant's rights have been infringed under s. 15(1), it is not enough to focus only on the alleged ground of discrimination and decide whether or not it is an enumerated or analogous ground. The effect of the impugned distinction or classification on the complainant must be considered. Once it is accepted that not all distinctions and differentiations created by law are discriminatory, then a role must be assigned to s. 15(1) which goes beyond the mere recognition of a legal distinction. A complainant under s. 15(1) must show not only that he or she is not receiving equal treatment before and under the law or that the law has a differential impact on him or her in the protection or benefit accorded by law but, in addition, must show that the legislative impact of the law is discriminatory.

Where discrimination is found a breach of s. 15(1) has occurred and—where s. 15(2) is not applicable—any justification, any consideration of the reasonableness of the enactment; indeed, any consideration of factors which could justify the discrimination and support the constitutionality of the impugned enactment would take place under s. 1. This approach would conform with the directions of this Court in earlier decisions concerning the application of s. 1 and at the same time would allow for the screening out of the obviously trivial and vexatious claim. In this, it would provide a workable approach to the problem.

It would seem to me apparent that a legislative distinction has been made by s. 42 of the *Barristers and Solicitors Act* between citizens and non-citizens with respect to the practice of law. The distinction would deny admission to the practice of law to non-citizens who in all other respects are qualified. Have the respondents, because of s. 42 of the *Act*, been denied equality before and under the law or the equal protection of the law? In practical terms it should be noted that the citizenship requirement affects only those non-citizens who are permanent residents. The permanent resident must wait for a minimum of three years from the date of establishing permanent residence status before citizenship may be acquired. The distinction therefore imposes a burden in the form of some delay on permanent residents who have acquired all or some of their legal training abroad and is, therefore, discriminatory.

The rights guaranteed in s. 15(1) apply to all persons whether citizens or not. A rule which bars an entire class of persons from certain forms of employment, solely on the grounds of a lack of citizenship status and without consideration of educational and professional qualifications or the other attributes or merits of individuals in the group, would, in my view, infringe s. 15 equality rights. Non-citizens, lawfully permanent residents of Canada, are—in the words of the U.S. Supreme Court in *United States v. Carolene Products Co.*, 304 U.S. 144 (1938), at pp. 152-53, n. 4, subsequently affirmed in *Graham v. Richardson*, 403 U.S. 365 (1971), at p. 372—a good example of a "discrete and insular minority" who come within the protection of s. 15.

Section 1

Having accepted the proposition that s. 42 has infringed the right to equality guaranteed in s. 15, it remains to consider whether, under the provisions of s. 1 of the *Charter*, the citizenship requirement which is clearly prescribed by law is a reasonable limit which can be "demonstrably justified in a free and democratic society."

The onus of justifying the infringement of a guaranteed *Charter* right must, of course, rest upon the parties seeking to uphold the limitation, in this case, the Attorney General of British Columbia and the Law Society of British Columbia. As is evident from the decisions of this Court, there are two steps involved in the s. 1 inquiry. First, the importance of the objective underlying the impugned law must be assessed. In *Oakes*, it was held that to override a *Charter* guaranteed right the objective must relate to concerns which are "pressing and substantial" in a free and democratic society. However, given the broad ambit of legislation which must be enacted to cover various aspects of the civil law dealing largely with administrative and regulatory matters and the necessity for the Legislature to make many distinctions between individuals and groups for such purposes, the standard of "pressing and substantial" may be too stringent for application in all cases. To hold otherwise would frequently deny the community-at-large the benefits associated with sound social and economic legislation. In my opinion, in approaching a case such as the one before us, the first question the Court should ask must relate to the nature and the purpose of the enactment, with a view to deciding whether the limitation represents a legitimate exercise of the legislative power for the attainment of a desirable social objective which would warrant overriding constitutionally protected rights. The second step in a s. 1 inquiry involves a proportionality test whereby the Court must attempt to balance a number of factors. The Court must examine the nature of the right, the extent of its infringement, and the degree to which the limitation furthers the attainment of the desirable goal embodied in the legislation. Also involved in the inquiry will be the importance of the right to the individual or group concerned, and the broader social impact of both the impugned law and its alternatives. As the Chief Justice has stated in *R. v. Edwards Books and Art Ltd.*, *supra*, at pp. 768-69:

> Both in articulating the standard of proof and in describing the criteria comprising the proportionality requirement the Court has been careful to avoid rigid and inflexible standards.

I agree with this statement. There is no single test under s. 1; rather, the Court must carefully engage in the balancing of many factors in determining whether an infringement is reasonable and demonstrably justified.

The section 15(1) guarantee is the broadest of all guarantees. It applies to and supports all other rights guaranteed by the *Charter*. However, it must be recognized that Parliament and the Legislatures have a right and a duty to make laws for the whole community: in this process, they must make innumerable legislative distinctions and categorizations in the pursuit of the role of government. When making distinctions between groups and individuals to achieve desirable social goals, it will rarely be possible to say of any legislative distinction that it is clearly the right legislative choice or that it is clearly a wrong one. As stated by the Chief Justice in *R. v. Edwards Books and Art Ltd.*, at pp. 781-82:

> A "reasonable limit" is one which, having regard to the principles enunciated in *Oakes*, it was reasonable for the legislature to impose. The courts are not called upon to substitute judicial opinions for legislative ones as to the place at which to draw a precise line.

In dealing with the many problems that arise legislatures must not be held to the standard of perfection, for in such matters perfection is unattainable. I would repeat the words of my colleague, La Forest J., in *R. v. Edwards Books and Art Ltd.*, at p. 795:

> By the foregoing, I do not mean to suggest that this Court should, as a general rule, defer to legislative judgments when those judgments trench upon rights considered fundamental in a free and democratic society. Quite the contrary, I would have thought the *Charter* established the opposite regime. On the other hand, having accepted the importance of the legislative objective, one must in the present context recognize that if the legislative goal is to be achieved, it will inevitably be achieved to the detriment

of some. Moreover, attempts to protect the rights of one group will also inevitably impose burdens on the rights of other groups. There is no perfect scenario in which the rights of all can be equally protected.

In seeking to achieve a goal that is demonstrably justified in a free and democratic society, therefore, a legislature must be given reasonable room to manoeuvre to meet these conflicting pressures.

Disposition

... There is no difficulty in determining that in general terms the *Barristers and Solicitors Act* of British Columbia is a statute enacted for a valid and desirable social purpose, the creation and regulation of the legal profession and the practice of law. The narrower question, however, is whether the requirement that only citizens be admitted to the practice of law in British Columbia serves a desirable social purpose of sufficient importance to warrant overriding the equality guarantee. It is incontestable that the legal profession plays a very significant—in fact, a fundamentally important—role in the administration of justice, both in the criminal and the civil law. I would not attempt to answer the question arising from the judgments below as to whether the function of the profession may be termed judicial or quasi-judicial, but I would observe that in the absence of an independent legal profession, skilled and qualified to play its part in the administration of justice and the judicial process, the whole legal system would be in a parlous state. In the performance of what may be called his private function, that is, in advising on legal matters and in representing clients before the courts and other tribunals, the lawyer is accorded great powers not permitted to other professionals. As pointed out by Taylor J. at first instance, by the use of the subpoena which he alone can procure on behalf of another, he can compel attendance upon examinations before trial and at trial upon pain of legal sanction for refusal. He may, as well, require the production of documents and records for examination and use in the proceedings. He may in some cases require the summoning of jurors, the sittings of courts and, in addition, he may make the fullest inquiry into the matters before the court with a full privilege against actions for slander arising out of his conduct in the court. The solicitor is also bound by the solicitor and client privilege against the disclosure of communications with his client concerning legal matters. This is said to be the only absolute privilege known to the law. Not only may the solicitor decline to disclose solicitor and client communications, the courts will not permit him to do so. This is a privilege against all comers, including the Crown, save where the disclosure of a crime would be involved. The responsibilities involved in its maintenance and in its breach where crimes are concerned are such that citizenship

with its commitment to the welfare of the whole community is not an unreasonable requirement for the practice of law. While it may be arguable whether the lawyer exercises a judicial, quasi-judicial, or governmental role, it is clear that at his own discretion he can invoke the full force and authority of the State in procuring and enforcing judgments or other remedial measures which may be obtained. It is equally true that in defending an action he has the burden of protecting his client from the imposition of such state authority and power. By any standard, these powers and duties are vital to the maintenance of order in our society and the due administration of the law in the interest of the whole community.

The lawyer has, as well, what may be termed a public function. Governments at all levels, federal, provincial and municipal, rely extensively upon lawyers, both in technical and policy matters. In the drafting of legislation, regulations, treaties, agreements and other governmental documents and papers lawyers play a major role. In various aspects of this work they are called upon to advise upon legal and constitutional questions which frequently go to the very heart of the governmental role. To discharge these duties, familiarity is required with Canadian history, constitutional law, regional differences and concerns within the country and, in fact, with the whole Canadian governmental and political process. It is entirely reasonable, then, that legislators consider and adopt measures designed to maintain within the legal profession a body of qualified professionals with a commitment to the country and to the fulfilment of the important tasks which fall to it.

McLachlin J.A. was of the view that the citizenship requirement would not ensure familiarity with Canadian institutions and customs, nor would it ensure a commitment to Canada going beyond one involved in the concept of allegiance, as recognized by the taking of an oath of allegiance. I would agree with her that the desired results would not be insured by the citizenship requirement but I would observe, at the same time, that no law will ever ensure anything. To abolish the requirement of citizenship on the basis that it would fail to insure the attainment of its objectives would, in my view, be akin to abolishing the law against theft, for it has certainly not insured the elimination of that crime. Citizenship, however, which requires the taking on of obligations and commitments to the community, difficult sometimes to describe but felt and understood by most citizens, as well as the rejection of past loyalties may reasonably be said to conduce to the desired result.

I would observe, as well, that the comment of McLachlin J. A. that the citizenship requirement was first adopted in British Columbia in 1971 requires some explanation. I do not think that the historical argument should be pushed too far: things need not always remain as once they were although, as noted in *R. v. Big M Drug Mart Ltd.* and *Reference re Public Service Employee Relations Act (Alta.)*, *supra*, *Charter* construction should be consistent with the history, traditions and social philosophies of our society. The concept of citizenship has been a requirement for entry into the legal profession in British Columbia from its earliest days. When the Law Society was formed in 1874 the profession was open to British subjects. At that time, the idea of a separate Canadian citizenship, as distinct from the general classification of British subject which included Canadians, was scarcely known—though as early as 1910, *Immigration Act*, S.C. 1910, c. 27, the term "Canadian citizen" was defined for the purposes of the *Immigration Act* as a "British subject who has Canadian domicile." The concept of citizenship in those early days was embodied in the expression, British Subject, and thus it was recognized as a requirement for entry into the legal profession in British Columbia. As Canada moved away from its colonial past, a separate identity for Canadians emerged and in 1946 with the passage of *The Canadian Citizenship Act*, S.C. 1946, c. 15, the term, Canadian citizen, was formally recognized, giving effect to what had long been felt and accepted by most Canadians. In adopting the term as a qualification for entry into the legal profession in British Columbia, the Legislature was merely continuing its earlier requirement that the concept of citizenship, as then recognized in the term "British subject," be necessary for entry into the profession.

Public policy, of which the citizenship requirement in the *Barristers and Solicitors Act* is an element, is for the Legislature to establish. The role of the *Charter*, as applied by the courts, is to ensure that in applying public policy the Legislature does not adopt measures which are not sustainable under the *Charter*. It is not, however, for the courts to legislate or to substitute their views on public policy for those of the Legislature. I would repeat for ease of reference the words of the Chief Justice in *R. v. Edwards Books and Art Ltd.*, *supra*, at pp. 781–82:

> A "reasonable limit" is one which having regard to the principles enunciated in *Oakes*, it was reasonable for the legislature to impose. The courts are not called upon to substitute judicial opinions for legislative ones as to the place at which to draw a precise line.

The function of the Court is to measure the legislative enactment against the requirements of the *Charter* and where the enactment infringes the *Charter*, in this case the provisions of s. 15(1), and is not sustainable under s. 1, the remedial power of the Court is set out in s. 52 of the *Constitution Act, 1982*: "any law that is inconsistent with the provisions of the Constitution is, to the extent of the inconsistency, of no force or effect."

The essence of s. 1 is found in the expression "reasonable" and it is for the Court to decide if s. 42 of the *Barristers and Solicitors Act* of British Columbia is a reasonable limit. In reaching the conclusion that it is, I would say that the legislative choice in this regard is not one between an answer that is clearly right and one that is clearly wrong. Either position may well be sustainable and, as noted by the Chief Justice, *supra*, the Court is not called upon to substitute its opinion as to where to draw the line. The Legislature in fixing public policy has chosen the citizenship requirement and, unless the Court can find that choice unreasonable, it has no power under the *Charter* to strike it down or, as has been said, no power to invade the legislative field and substitute its views for that of the Legislature. In my view, the citizenship requirement is reasonable and sustainable under s. 1. It is chosen for the achievement of a desirable social goal: one aspect of the due regulation and qualification of the legal profession. This is an objective of importance and the measure is not disproportionate to the object to be attained. The maximum delay imposed upon the non-citizen from the date of acquisition of permanent resident status is three years. It will frequently be less. No impediment is put in the way of obtaining citizenship. In fact, the policy of the Canadian government is to encourage the newcomer to become a citizen. It is reasonable, in my view, to expect that the newcomer who seeks to gain the privileges and status within the land and the right to exercise the great powers that admission to the practice of law will give should accept citizenship and its obligations as well as its advantages and benefits. I would therefore allow the appeal and restore the judgment at trial. . . .

26   Law v. Canada, 1999

In *Law v. Canada*, the Supreme Court consolidated the various strands of its equality-rights jurisprudence that had been articulated in the numerous equality-rights cases it had decided since handing down its first major decision on section 15, 10 years earlier in *Andrews*.[1] Justice Iacobucci wrote the opinion for the full Court of nine judges. Most of the opinion was devoted to setting out the various considerations that guide the Court's judgment in determining whether a claim should be upheld under section 15(1) of the *Charter*. At the end of the decision, Justice Iacobucci applied these guidelines to the section 15 claim brought before the Court by Nancy Law.

Mrs. Law, whose husband had died at the age of 50, claimed survivor's benefits under the Canada Pension Plan (CPP). The CPP denies regular survivor's benefits to surviving spouses under the age of 45 if they are able-bodied and without children. At the time she was widowed, Nancy Law was 30 years old, had no children, and was not disabled. Accordingly, she was denied the benefits that an over-45 surviving spouse would receive immediately. She would be eligible for a survivor's benefit at age 65, but at a reduced rate. Law claimed that these CPP provisions discriminated against her on the basis of age and therefore violated section 15 of the *Charter*. Her claim was rejected by the Pension Appeals Board and the Federal Court of Appeal, and was rejected again here in the first application of the Supreme Court's consolidation of its section 15 jurisprudence.

The thread running throughout Justice Iacobucci's discourse on section 15 is the justices' understanding of section 15's underlying purpose. The justices believe that the *Charter*'s equality-rights clause was intended to have a reforming, "ameliorative" effect on Canadian society. Its purpose, as Justice McIntyre stated in *Andrews*, was to promote "a society in which all are secure in the knowledge that they are recognized as human beings equally deserving of concern, respect and consideration." Thus, section 15 is always to be seen as an instrument of social reform aimed at making society more inclusive, combating demeaning stereotypes, and overcoming hurtful and humiliating discrimination. The other general consideration, more methodological than substantive, is the importance of context. In ascertaining whether differential treatment is unconstitutional discrimination, courts must consider such things as whether the differential treatment that is the subject of the *Charter* challenge is associated with a long historical struggle against unequal treatment or whether failure to take into account the special circumstances of a group will result in severe hardship. The Court's section 15 jurisprudence calls for a lot of empirical fact-finding.

The Court's opinion in *Law* was not intended to serve as a set of rules that provide an easily applied litmus test for violations of section 15. However, toward the end of the judgment, Iacobucci set out "guidelines" to the three steps to be taken in deciding whether a challenged law or governmental practice amounts to unconstitutional discrimination. First, there must be a finding of a differential treatment based on some personal characteristic. Second, that differential treatment must be based on one of the grounds enumerated in

---

1   *Andrews v. Law Society of British Columbia*, case 25.

section 15 or analogous grounds. Third, the differential treatment must result in placing an extra burden or denying a benefit in a way that has the effect of perpetuating or promoting the view that the person is less worthy of respect than others in society. What courts should be looking for in this third step is what amounts to a denial of the claimant's "human dignity." Several formulations are advanced of what is involved in respecting human dignity, including such things as unfair treatment that does not relate to a person's capacities or needs or that amounts to social marginalization.

It is at the third step—the denial of human dignity—that Nancy Law's claim failed. The challenged section of the CPP certainly involves differential treatment on the basis of age, one of the enumerated grounds in section 15. But the Court did not think the legislation in either purpose or effect violates the human dignity of Nancy Law or others in similar circumstances. It simply reflects the practical reality that people in her situation are more able to replace the income lost from a spouse's death. In a concluding comment, Justice Iacobucci remarked that this is one of the rare cases where differential treatment based on an enumerated ground is not discrimination under section 15(1).

In this case, the Supreme Court was unanimous in supporting the general approach to section 15(1) that Justice Iacobucci elucidated. However, as equality-rights cases continued to come before the Court, it soon became clear that the Court would not be unanimous in applying the generalities of Iacobucci's equality-rights doctrine. In particular, it is the third and crucial stage of his approach, and the notion of human dignity it turns on, that is the key to divisions within the Court, and perhaps also to the difficulties of lower court judges and lawyers as they struggle to apply the Iacobucci doctrine. ⌒

Discussion Questions

1. Why did the Court in this case reject an equality rights claim based on one of the explicitly prohibited grounds of discrimination in section 15?
2. How does Justice Iacobucci identify a denial of human dignity?
3. Assess the Court's interpretation of section 15 in this case as a guide to courts, lawyers, and citizens as to what constitutes unconstitutional discrimination.

LAW v. CANADA (MINISTER OF EMPLOYMENT AND IMMIGRATION)
[1999] 1 S.C.R. 497

Hearing: January 20, 1998; Rehearing: December 3, 1998; Judgment: March 25, 1999.

Present: Lamer C.J. and L'Heureux-Dubé, Gonthier, Cory, McLachlin, Iacobucci, Major, Bastarache, and Binnie JJ.

The judgment of the Court was delivered by

IACOBUCCI J.:

I. Introduction and Overview

[1] This appeal concerns the constitutionality of ss. 44(1)(*d*) and 58 of the *Canada Pension Plan*, R.S.C., 1985, c. C-8, which draw distinctions on the basis of age with regard to entitlement to survivor's pensions. The issue is whether the provisions infringe s. 15(1) of the *Canadian Charter of Rights and Freedoms* on the ground that they discriminate against persons under the age of 45 on the basis of age and, if so, whether the infringement is justified under s. 1 of the *Charter*. In my view, a purposive reading and application of s. 15(1) results in the conclusion that the appellant has not established discrimination within the meaning of the *Charter*.

[2] Section 15 of the *Charter* guarantees to every individual the right to equal treatment by the state without discrimination. It is perhaps the *Charter*'s most conceptually difficult provision. In this Court's first s. 15 case, *Andrews v. Law Society of British Columbia*, [1989] 1 S.C.R 143, at p. 164, McIntyre J. noted that, as embodied in s. 15(1) of the *Charter*, the concept of equality is "an elusive concept," and that "more than any of the other rights and freedoms guaranteed in the *Charter*, it lacks precise definition." Part of the difficulty in defining the concept of equality stems from its exalted status. The quest for equality expresses some of humanity's highest ideals and aspirations, which are by their nature abstract and subject to differing articulations. The challenge for the judiciary in interpreting and applying s. 15(1) of the *Charter* is to transform these ideals and aspirations into practice in a manner which is meaningful to Canadians and which accords with the purpose of the provision.

[3] In *Andrews*, McIntyre J., who delivered the unanimous reasons of the Court on the issue of the proper approach to s. 15(1), cautioned at p. 168 that it would be inappropriate to attempt to confine analysis under s. 15(1) to a "fixed and limited formula." This sentiment has been echoed in subsequent decisions....

[4] Indeed, in the brief history of this Court's interpretation of s. 15(1) of the *Charter*, there have been several important substantive developments in equality law, relating to, among other things, the meaning of adverse effects discrimination, the role of context in identifying discrimination more generally, and the *indicia* of an analogous ground. All of these developments have been guided by the Court's evolving understanding of the purpose of equality protection under s. 15(1). All have augmented and enriched anti-discrimination jurisprudence under the *Charter*.

[5] Throughout these developments, although there have been differences of opinion among the members of this Court as to the appropriate interpretation of s. 15(1), I believe it is fair to say that there has been and continues to be general consensus regarding the basic principles relating to the purpose of s. 15(1) and the proper approach to equality analysis. In my view, the present case is a useful juncture at which to summarize and comment upon these basic principles, in order to provide a set of guidelines for courts that are called upon to analyze a discrimination claim under the *Charter*.

[6] In accordance with McIntyre J.'s caution in *Andrews*, *supra*, I think it is sensible to articulate the basic principles under s. 15(1) as guidelines for analysis, and not as a rigid test which might risk being mechanically applied. Equality analysis under the *Charter* must be purposive and contextual. The guidelines which I review below are just that—points of reference which are designed to assist a court in identifying the relevant contextual factors in a particular discrimination claim, and in evaluating the effect of those factors in light of the purpose of s. 15(1).

[7] The analysis in these reasons proceeds from the general to the more specific. I begin, after describing the background of the case, with a review of general principles regarding the proper approach to be followed in analyzing a discrimination claim. This portion of the reasons is concerned with outlining elements or stages of analysis, whose content and application I then develop. The second portion of my analysis is a discussion of the basic principles which this Court has articulated in past jurisprudence regarding the purpose of s. 15(1), and the fundamentally purposive nature of each stage of analysis under the provision. Next, on the basis of previous cases, I review some of the contextual factors which may assist a court in determining whether the purpose of s. 15(1) has been engaged within the context of a particular case. A summary of the elements of a discrimination claim, the purpose of s. 15(1), and the contextual factors then follows. Finally, I apply the principles articulated in this analysis to the case at bar.

II. Background

A. The Legislation

...[8] The Canada Pension Plan (the "CPP") is a compulsory social insurance scheme which was enacted in 1965 in order to provide contributors and their families with reasonable minimum levels of income upon the retirement, disability or death of the wage earner: see *House of Commons Debates*, vol. VI, 2nd Sess., 26th Parl., August 10, 1964, at p. 6636. Among the benefits available under the CPP is the survivor's pension. This monthly benefit is paid to a surviving spouse whose deceased partner has made sufficient contributions to the CPP, and who meets the eligibility criteria specified in s. 44(1)(*d*), namely, an age threshold, responsibility for dependent children or disability.

[9] A claimant who is over the age of 45 at the time of the contributor's death, or is maintaining dependent children of the deceased contributor, or is (or becomes) disabled, is entitled to receive the survivor's pension at the full rate. However, s. 58 gradually reduces that pension for able-bodied surviving spouses without dependent children who are between the ages of 35 and 45 by 1/120th of the full rate for each month that the claimant's age is less than 45 years at the time of the contributor's death. Pursuant to s. 44(1)(*d*), unless they should become disabled, able-bodied surviving spouses without dependent children who are under 35 at the time of the death of the contributor are precluded from receiving a survivor's pension until they reach the age of 65.

B. Facts

[10] The appellant, Nancy Law, married Jason Law in 1980. Mr. Law died in 1991, at the age of 50, having contributed to the CPP for 22 years. At the time of his death, the appellant was 30 years old. Prior to Mr. Law's death, the couple had co-owned a small business. The appellant was responsible for business operations and her husband had the requisite technical knowledge and expertise. The business failed soon after Mr. Law's death.

[11] The appellant applied to receive survivor's benefits under the CPP. Her husband had made sufficient contributions under the CPP such that she would qualify for survivor benefits if she came within the class of persons entitled to receive them. However, her application was refused because she was under 35 years of age at the time of her husband's death, she was not disabled, and she did not have dependent children.

[12] The appellant appealed this decision to the Minister of National Health and Welfare, who rejected the appeal in May, 1992. She then appealed to the Pension Plan Review Tribunal, arguing that the age distinctions in ss. 44(1)(*d*) and 58 of the CPP discriminate against her on the basis of age

contrary to s. 15(1) of the *Charter*. The tribunal found that the legislation discriminates against those who, at the time of the contributor's death, have not reached age 35, have no dependent children and are not disabled. However, the tribunal was unable to reach a consensus regarding s. 1 of the *Charter*. The majority concluded that the discrimination was justified under s. 1 and, although a more precise test of need could have been crafted, the measures adopted were a reasonable attempt by Parliament to achieve the objective of the CPP. The dissenting member of the tribunal found that the age distinctions in the impugned provisions were arbitrary and that Parliament could have targeted needy dependents without discrimination by legislating a test to determine need.

[13] The appellant then appealed to the Pension Appeals Board, which, in a trial *de novo*, concluded that the impugned age distinctions do not violate the appellant's equality rights. The majority of the board also found that, even if the distinctions did infringe s. 15(1) of the *Charter*, they would be justified under s. 1. A subsequent appeal to the Federal Court of Appeal was dismissed largely for the reasons of the Pension Appeals Board....

VI. Analysis

A. Approach to Section 15(1)

[21] ...

(1) Andrews Revisited

[23] McIntyre J. in *Andrews* adopted an approach to s. 15(1) which focuses upon three central elements: (1) whether a law imposes differential treatment between the claimant and others; (2) whether an enumerated or analogous ground of discrimination is the basis for the differential treatment; and (3) whether the law in question has a "discriminatory" purpose or effect....

[24] McIntyre J. began his discussion of the requirement of differential treatment by noting, at p. 164, that equality is a comparative concept, "the condition of which may only be attained or discerned by comparison with the condition of others in the social and political setting in which the question arises." It is impossible to evaluate a s. 15(1) claim without identifying specific personal characteristics or circumstances of the individual or group bringing the claim, and comparing the treatment of that person or group to the treatment accorded to a relevant comparator. This comparison determines whether the s. 15(1) claimant may be said to experience differential treatment, which is the first step in determining whether there is discriminatory inequality for the purpose of s. 15(1).

[25] At the same time, McIntyre J. emphasized that true equality does not necessarily result from identical treatment. Formal distinctions in treatment will be necessary in some

contexts in order to accommodate the differences between individuals and thus to produce equal treatment in a substantive sense: see pp. 164-69. Correspondingly, a law which applies uniformly to all may still violate a claimant's equality rights. The main consideration, McIntyre J. stated, at p. 165, must be the *impact* of the law upon the individual or group to whom it applies, as well as upon those whom it excludes from its application. He explained that the determination of the impact of legislation, by its nature, must be undertaken in a contextual manner, taking into account the content of the law, its purpose, and the characteristics and circumstances of the claimant, among other things. Hence, equality in s. 15 must be viewed as a substantive concept. Differential treatment, in a substantive sense, can be brought about either by a formal legislative distinction, or by a failure to take into account the underlying differences between individuals in society.

[26] Moving on to discuss the requirement that a s. 15(1) claimant show that differential treatment is discriminatory in order to establish a *Charter* violation, McIntyre J. defined "discrimination" in the following terms, at pp. 174-75:

> ... [D]iscrimination may be described as a distinction, whether intentional or not but based on grounds relating to personal characteristics of the individual or group, which has the effect of imposing burdens, obligations, or disadvantages on such individual or group not imposed upon others, or which withholds or limits access to opportunities, benefits, and advantages available to other members of society. Distinctions based on personal characteristics attributed to an individual solely on the basis of association with a group will rarely escape the charge of discrimination, while those based on an individual's merits and capacities will rarely be so classed.

[27] Importantly, McIntyre J. explained that the determination of whether a distinction in treatment imposes a burden or withholds a benefit so as to constitute "discrimination" within the meaning of s. 15(1) is to be undertaken in a purposive way. As he stated, at pp. 180-81, "[t]he words 'without discrimination' require more than a mere finding of distinction between the treatment of groups or individuals." ... The protection of equality rights is concerned with distinctions which are truly discriminatory. A discriminatory burden or denial of a benefit, McIntyre J. stated, is to be understood in a substantive sense and in the context of the historical development of Canadian anti-discrimination law, notably the human rights codes: "The words 'without discrimination' ... are a form of qualifier built into s. 15 itself and limit those distinctions which are forbidden by the section to those which involve prejudice or disadvantage" (pp. 180-81). ...

[29] Finally, regarding the role of the various grounds of discrimination expressly listed in s. 15(1), McIntyre J. stated,

at p. 175, that they "reflect the most common and probably the most socially destructive and historically practised bases of discrimination," but noted that a s. 15(1) claim may also be brought on an analogous ground, in accordance with the provision's wording and with a proper interpretation of its remedial purpose. In her majority reasons elaborating on the specific issue of analogous grounds, Wilson J. explained, at p. 152, that a ground may qualify as analogous to those listed in s. 15(1) if persons characterized by the trait in question are, among other things, "lacking in political power," "vulnerable to having their interests overlooked and their rights to equal concern and respect violated," and "vulnerab[le] to becoming a disadvantaged group" on the basis of the trait. Just as for the other two elements of the s. 15(1) analysis outlined by McIntyre J., Wilson J. emphasized at p. 152 that the determination of whether a ground qualifies as analogous under s. 15(1) is to be undertaken in a contextual manner:

> ... [T]his is a determination which is not to be made only in the context of the law which is subject to challenge but rather in the context of the place of the group in the entire social, political and legal fabric of our society. While legislatures must inevitably draw distinctions among the governed, such distinctions should not bring about or reinforce the disadvantage of certain groups and individuals by denying them the rights freely accorded to others.

[30] In summary, then, the *Andrews* decision established that there are three key elements to a discrimination claim under s. 15(1) of the *Charter*: differential treatment, an enumerated or analogous ground, and discrimination in a substantive sense involving factors such as prejudice, stereotyping, and disadvantage. Of fundamental importance, as stressed repeatedly by all of the judges who wrote, the determination of whether each of these elements exists in a particular case is always to be undertaken in a purposive manner, taking into account the full social, political, and legal context of the claim.

(2) Post-Andrews Jurisprudence

[31] The general approach adopted in *Andrews* was regularly applied in subsequent decisions of the Court: see, e.g., *Turpin* [[1989] 1 S.C.R. 1296]; *R. v. Hess; R. v. Nguyen,* [1990] 2 S.C.R. 906; *McKinney* [*v. University of Guelph,* [1990] 3 S.C.R. 229]; *Tétreault-Gadoury v. Canada (Employment and Immigration Commission),* [1991] 2 S.C.R. 22; *Swain* [[1991] 1 S.C.R. 933]; *Symes v. Canada,* [1993] 4 S.C.R. 695; *Egan v. Canada,* [1995] 2 S.C.R. 513; *Miron v. Trudel,* [1995] 2 S.C.R. 418; *Thibaudeau v. Canada,* [1995] 2 S.C.R. 627; *Benner v. Canada (Secretary of State),* [1997] 1 S.C.R. 358; *Eaton v. Brant County Board of Education,* [1997] 1 S.C.R. 241; *Eldridge v.*

British Columbia (Attorney General), [1997] 3 S.C.R. 624; Vriend v. Alberta, [1998] 1 S.C.R. 493....

[39] In my view, the proper approach to analyzing a claim of discrimination under s. 15(1) of the *Charter* involves a synthesis of these various articulations. Following upon the analysis in *Andrews, supra*, and the two-step framework set out in *Egan, supra*, and *Miron, supra*, among other cases, a court that is called upon to determine a discrimination claim under s. 15(1) should make the following three broad inquiries. First, does the impugned law (a) draw a formal distinction between the claimant and others on the basis of one or more personal characteristics, or (b) fail to take into account the claimant's already disadvantaged position within Canadian society resulting in substantively differential treatment between the claimant and others on the basis of one or more personal characteristics? If so, there is differential treatment for the purpose of s. 15(1). Second, was the claimant subject to differential treatment on the basis of one or more of the enumerated and analogous grounds? And third, does the differential treatment discriminate in a substantive sense, bringing into play the *purpose* of s. 15(1) of the *Charter* in remedying such ills as prejudice, stereotyping, and historical disadvantage? The second and third inquiries are concerned with whether the differential treatment constitutes discrimination in the substantive sense intended by s. 15(1).

B. The Purpose of Section 15(1)

...[42] What is the purpose of the s. 15(1) equality guarantee? There is great continuity in the jurisprudence of this Court on this issue. In *Andrews, supra*, all judges who wrote advanced largely the same view. McIntyre J. stated, at p. 171, that the purpose of s. 15 is to promote "a society in which all are secure in the knowledge that they are recognized at law as human beings equally deserving of concern, respect and consideration." The provision is a guarantee against the evil of oppression, he explained at pp. 180-81, designed to remedy the imposition of unfair limitations upon opportunities, particularly for those persons or groups who have been subject to historical disadvantage, prejudice, and stereotyping.

[43] Similarly, La Forest J., concurring with respect to the proper approach to s. 15(1), stated that the equality guarantee was designed to prevent the imposition of differential treatment that was likely to "inhibit the sense of those who are discriminated against that Canadian society is not free or democratic as far as they are concerned," and that was likely to decrease their "confidence that they can freely and without obstruction by the state pursue their and their families' hopes and expectations of vocational and personal development."...

[51] All of these statements share several key elements. It may be said that the purpose of s. 15(1) is to prevent the

violation of essential human dignity and freedom through the imposition of disadvantage, stereotyping, or political or social prejudice, and to promote a society in which all persons enjoy equal recognition at law as human beings or as members of Canadian society, equally capable and equally deserving of concern, respect and consideration. Legislation which effects differential treatment between individuals or groups will violate this fundamental purpose where those who are subject to differential treatment fall within one or more enumerated or analogous grounds, and where the differential treatment reflects the stereotypical application of presumed group or personal characteristics, or otherwise has the effect of perpetuating or promoting the view that the individual is less capable, or less worthy of recognition or value as a human being or as a member of Canadian society....

[53] What is human dignity? There can be different conceptions of what human dignity means. For the purpose of analysis under s. 15(1) of the *Charter*, however, the jurisprudence of this Court reflects a specific, albeit non-exhaustive, definition. As noted by Lamer C.J. in *Rodriguez v. British Columbia (Attorney General)*, [1993] 3 S.C.R. 519, at p. 554, the equality guarantee in s. 15(1) is concerned with the realization of personal autonomy and self-determination. Human dignity means that an individual or group feels self-respect and self-worth. It is concerned with physical and psychological integrity and empowerment. Human dignity is harmed by unfair treatment premised upon personal traits or circumstances which do not relate to individual needs, capacities, or merits. It is enhanced by laws which are sensitive to the needs, capacities, and merits of different individuals, taking into account the context underlying their differences. Human dignity is harmed when individuals and groups are marginalized, ignored, or devalued, and is enhanced when laws recognize the full place of all individuals and groups within Canadian society. Human dignity within the meaning of the equality guarantee does not relate to the status or position of an individual in society *per se*, but rather concerns the manner in which a person legitimately feels when confronted with a particular law. Does the law treat him or her unfairly, taking into account all of the circumstances regarding the individuals affected and excluded by the law?

[54] The equality guarantee in s. 15(1) of the *Charter* must be understood and applied in light of the above understanding of its purpose. The overriding concern with protecting and promoting human dignity in the sense just described infuses all elements of the discrimination analysis.

[55] In order to determine whether the fundamental purpose of s. 15(1) is brought into play in a particular claim, it is essential to engage in a comparative analysis which takes into consideration the surrounding context of the claim and the

claimant. I now propose to comment briefly on the nature of the comparative approach, and then to examine some of the contextual factors that a court should consider in determining whether s. 15(1) has been infringed. Each factor may be more or less relevant depending upon the circumstances of the case.

C. The Comparative Approach

[56] As discussed above, McIntyre J. emphasized in *Andrews, supra,* that the equality guarantee is a comparative concept. Ultimately, a court must identify differential treatment *as compared* to one or more other persons or groups. Locating the appropriate comparator is necessary in identifying differential treatment and the grounds of the distinction. Identifying the appropriate comparator will be relevant when considering many of the contextual factors in the discrimination analysis....

[58] When identifying the relevant comparator, the natural starting point is to consider the claimant's view. It is the claimant who generally chooses the person, group, or groups with whom he or she wishes to be compared for the purpose of the discrimination inquiry, thus setting the parameters of the alleged differential treatment that he or she wishes to challenge. However, the claimant's characterization of the comparison may not always be sufficient. It may be that the differential treatment is not between the groups identified by the claimant, but rather between other groups. Clearly a court cannot, *ex proprio motu,* evaluate a ground of discrimination not pleaded by the parties and in relation to which no evidence has been adduced: see *Symes, supra,* at p. 762. However, within the scope of the ground or grounds pleaded, I would not close the door on the power of a court to refine the comparison presented by the claimant where warranted.

D. Establishing Discrimination in a Purposive Sense: Contextual Factors

... [59] ...

(2) Contextual Factors

[62] ...

(a) Pre-existing Disadvantage

[63] As has been consistently recognized throughout this Court's jurisprudence, probably the most compelling factor favouring a conclusion that differential treatment imposed by legislation is truly discriminatory will be, where it exists, pre-existing disadvantage, vulnerability, stereotyping, or prejudice experienced by the individual or group: see, e.g., *Andrews, supra,* at pp. 151-53, *per* Wilson J., p. 183, *per* McIntyre J., pp. 195-97, *per* La Forest J.; *Turpin, supra,* at pp. 1331-33; *Swain, supra,* at p. 992, *per* Lamer C.J.; *Miron, supra,* at paras. 147-48,

per McLachlin J.; *Eaton, supra,* at para. 66. These factors are relevant because, to the extent that the claimant is already subject to unfair circumstances or treatment in society by virtue of personal characteristics or circumstances, persons like him or her have often not been given equal concern, respect, and consideration. It is logical to conclude that, in most cases, further differential treatment will contribute to the perpetuation or promotion of their unfair social characterization, and will have a more severe impact upon them, since they are already vulnerable.

[64] One consideration which the Court has frequently referred to with respect to the issue of pre-existing disadvantage is the role of stereotypes. A stereotype may be described as a misconception whereby a person or, more often, a group is unfairly portrayed as possessing undesirable traits, or traits which the group, or at least some of its members, do not possess. In my view, probably the most prevalent reason that a given legislative provision may be found to infringe s. 15(1) is that it reflects and reinforces existing inaccurate understandings of the merits, capabilities and worth of a particular person or group within Canadian society, resulting in further stigmatization of that person or the members of the group or otherwise in their unfair treatment. This view accords with the emphasis placed by this Court ever since *Andrews, supra,* upon the role of s. 15(1) in overcoming prejudicial stereotypes in society....

[65] It should be stressed that, while it is helpful to demonstrate the existence of historic disadvantage, it is of course not *necessary* to show such disadvantage in order to establish a s. 15(1) violation, for at least two distinct reasons. On the one hand, this Court has stated several times that, although a distinction drawn on such a basis is an important *indicium* of discrimination, it is not determinative....

[66] On the other hand, it may be misleading or inappropriate in some cases to speak about "membership" within a group for the purpose of a s. 15(1) claim. The *Charter* guarantees equality rights to individuals. In this respect, it must be made clear that the s. 15(1) claimant is not required to establish membership in a sociologically recognized group in order to be successful. It will always be helpful to the claimant to be able to identify a pattern of discrimination against a class of persons with traits similar to the claimant, i.e., a group, of which the claimant may consider herself or himself a member. Nonetheless, an infringement of s. 15(1) may be established by other means, and may exist even if there is no one similar to the claimant who is experiencing the same unfair treatment.

[67] At the same time, I also do not wish to suggest that the claimant's association with a group which has historically been more disadvantaged will be conclusive of a violation under s. 15(1), where differential treatment has been estab-

lished. This *may* be the result, but whether or not it is the result will depend upon the circumstances of the case and, in particular, upon whether or not the distinction truly affects the dignity of the claimant....

(b) Relationship Between Grounds and the Claimant's Characteristics or Circumstances

[69] What are some factors other than an individual's or a group's pre-existing disadvantage which may be referred to by a s. 15(1) claimant in order to demonstrate a negative effect upon the claimant's dignity? One factor in some circumstances may be the relationship between the ground upon which the claim is based and the nature of the differential treatment. Some of the enumerated and analogous grounds have the potential to correspond with need, capacity, or circumstances....

[71] Examples are prevalent in the jurisprudence of this Court of legislation or other state action which either failed to take into account the actual situation of a claimant, or alternatively quite properly treated a claimant differently on the basis of actual personal differences between individuals. In *Eldridge, supra,* for example, a provincial government's failure to provide limited funding for sign language interpreters for deaf persons when receiving medical services was found to violate s. 15(1), in part on the basis that the government's failure to take into account the actual needs of deaf persons infringed their human dignity. Conversely, in *Weatherall* [*v. Canada (Attorney General)*, [1993] 2 S.C.R. 872], it was stated that the decision to permit cross-gender prison searches of male prisoners but not of female prisoners likely did not violate s. 15(1), because such a difference in treatment was appropriate in light of the historical, biological and sociological differences between men and women.

(c) Ameliorative Purpose or Effects

[72] Another possibly important factor will be the ameliorative purpose or effects of impugned legislation or other state action upon a more disadvantaged person or group in society. As stated by Sopinka J. in *Eaton, supra,* at para. 66: "the purpose of s. 15(1) of the *Charter* is not only to prevent discrimination by the attribution of stereotypical characteristics to individuals, but also to ameliorate the position of groups within Canadian society who have suffered disadvantage by exclusion from mainstream society." An ameliorative purpose or effect which accords with the purpose of s. 15(1) of the *Charter* will likely not violate the human dignity of more advantaged individuals where the exclusion of these more advantaged individuals largely corresponds to the greater need or the different circumstances experienced by the disadvantaged group being targeted by the legislation. I emphasize

that this factor will likely only be relevant where the person or group that is excluded from the scope of ameliorative legislation or other state action is more advantaged in a relative sense. Underinclusive ameliorative legislation that excludes from its scope the members of a historically disadvantaged group will rarely escape the charge of discrimination: see *Vriend, supra,* at paras. 94-104, *per* Cory J.

(d) Nature of the Interest Affected

[74] A further contextual factor which may be relevant in appropriate cases in determining whether the claimant's dignity has been violated will be the nature and scope of the interest affected by the legislation. This point was well explained by L'Heureux-Dubé J. in *Egan, supra,* at paras. 63-64. As she noted, at para. 63, "[i]f all other things are equal, the more severe and localized the ... consequences on the affected group, the more likely that the distinction responsible for these consequences is discriminatory within the meaning of s. 15 of the *Charter.*" L'Heureux-Dubé J. explained, at para. 64, that the discriminatory calibre of differential treatment cannot be fully appreciated without evaluating not only the economic but also the constitutional and societal significance attributed to the interest or interests adversely affected by the legislation in question. Moreover, it is relevant to consider whether the distinction restricts access to a fundamental social institution, or affects "a basic aspect of full membership in Canadian society," or "constitute[s] a complete non-recognition of a particular group." ...

(3) The Nature and Extent of the Claimant's Burden Under Section 15(1)

[76] Having emphasized the importance of a claimant demonstrating that impugned legislation infringes s. 15(1) in a purposive sense, it will be useful at this point to review the nature of the claimant's burden as a practical matter. There are three points which should be addressed.

[77] First, I should underline that none of the foregoing discussion implies that the claimant must adduce data, or other social science evidence not generally available, in order to show a violation of the claimant's dignity or freedom. Such materials may be adduced by the parties, and may be of great assistance to a court in determining whether a claimant has demonstrated that the legislation in question is discriminatory. However, they are not required. A court may often, where appropriate, determine on the basis of judicial notice and logical reasoning alone whether the impugned legislation infringes s. 15(1). It is well established that a court may take judicial notice of notorious and undisputed facts....

[80] Second, it is equally important to emphasize that the requirement that a claimant establish a s. 15(1) infringement

in this purposive sense does not entail a requirement that the claimant prove any matters which cannot reasonably be expected to be within his or her knowledge. As this Court has previously stated, the s. 15(1) claimant is not required to establish that the *intent* of the legislature in enacting the impugned legislation was discriminatory. . . .

[82] Third, it should be stressed that in some cases it may not be necessary as a practical matter for a claimant to focus the purposive analysis upon more than one element of the discrimination claim. . . .

E. Summary of Guidelines

[88] Before moving on to apply the principles that I have just discussed to the facts of this case, I believe it would be useful to summarize some of the main guidelines for analysis under s. 15(1) to be derived from the jurisprudence of this Court, as reviewed in these reasons. As I stated above, these guidelines should not be seen as a strict test, but rather should be understood as points of reference for a court that is called upon to decide whether a claimant's right to equality without discrimination under the *Charter* has been infringed. Inevitably, the guidelines summarized here will need to be supplemented in practice by the explanation of these guidelines in these reasons and those of previous cases, and by a full appreciation of the context surrounding the specific s. 15(1) claim at issue. It goes without saying that as our s. 15 jurisprudence evolves it may well be that further elaborations and modifications will emerge.

General Approach

(1) It is inappropriate to attempt to confine analysis under s. 15(1) of the *Charter* to a fixed and limited formula. A purposive and contextual approach to discrimination analysis is to be preferred, in order to permit the realization of the strong remedial purpose of the equality guarantee, and to avoid the pitfalls of a formalistic or mechanical approach.

(2) The approach adopted and regularly applied by this Court to the interpretation of s. 15(1) focuses upon three central issues:

(A) whether a law imposes differential treatment between the claimant and others, in purpose or effect;

(B) whether one or more enumerated or analogous grounds of discrimination are the basis for the differential treatment; and

(C) whether the law in question has a purpose or effect that is discriminatory within the meaning of the equality guarantee.

(3) Accordingly, a court that is called upon to determine a discrimination claim under s. 15(1) should make the following three broad inquiries:

(A) Does the impugned law (a) draw a formal distinction between the claimant and others on the basis of one or more personal characteristics, or (b) fail to take into account the claimant's already disadvantaged position within Canadian society resulting in substantively differential treatment between the claimant and others on the basis of one or more personal characteristics?

(B) Is the claimant subject to differential treatment based on one or more enumerated and analogous grounds?
and

(C) Does the differential treatment discriminate, by imposing a burden upon or withholding a benefit from the claimant in a manner which reflects the stereotypical application of presumed group or personal characteristics, or which otherwise has the effect of perpetuating or promoting the view that the individual is less capable or worthy of recognition or value as a human being or as a member of Canadian society, equally deserving of concern, respect, and consideration? . . .

F. Application to the Case at Bar

(1) Differential Treatment

. . . [90] The CPP grants benefits to surviving spouses over the age of 35 immediately following the death of the contributor. However, these benefits are not available to able-bodied spouses without dependent children who are less than 35 years of age at the time of the death of the contributor, until they reach age 65 or unless they should become disabled in the interim. In addition, while those over age 45 are entitled to receive benefits at the full rate, those between the ages of 35 and 45 receive a reduced sum. Thus, as a result of the ages specified under the CPP, a clear distinction is drawn between claimants over and under age 35, and also between claimants who are over age 45 and those between the ages of 35 and 45. In my view, both the delay in the receipt of benefits and the reduced entitlement to benefits constitute a denial of equal benefit of the law under the first step of the equality analysis.

(2) Distinction on the Basis of Enumerated or Analogous Grounds

[91] Age is one of the enumerated grounds of discrimination in s. 15(1) of the *Charter*. The appellant alleges that she was rendered ineligible for survivor's benefits by virtue of her age and that its use as a distinguishing criterion was

discriminatory. The appellant does not base her discrimination claim upon any ground other than that of age. In answer, the respondent contends that, although age is a factor in determining eligibility, it cannot be said that the appellant was ineligible solely because of this factor. Rather, the respondent argues that entitlement under s. 44(1)(d) of the CPP depends on the interplay of the three factors included therein, namely, age, disability and responsibility for dependent children. This was the position adopted by the Pension Appeals Board. With respect, I cannot accept this view. In my opinion, it does not follow from the fact that any one of several criteria, including age, might determine entitlement to a survivor's pension, that the legislation does not draw a distinction on the basis of age. . . .

[92] As an able-bodied woman without children, the appellant does not suggest that the CPP discriminates by denying her equal benefits as compared to surviving spouses who have disabilities or dependent children. The appellant submits that the issue in dispute is whether age is properly included among the factors which determine eligibility for survivor's benefits and the amount that is provided. Had the appellant been able-bodied, without dependent children, and over age 45 at the time of her spouse's death, she would have been immediately entitled to receive full benefits. However, as an able-bodied, childless woman who was 30 years of age at the time of her spouse's death, she is denied any benefits until she reaches age 65, provided she does not subsequently become disabled. Similarly, for surviving spouses age 35 to 45, it is their age alone that serves to reduce the amount of benefits they receive as compared to those over age 45. In my view, the survivor's pension provisions of the CPP clearly draw distinctions on the basis of the enumerated ground of age. . . .

(3) Discrimination

[95] The central question in the present case is whether the age discrimination drawn by ss. 44(1)(d) and 58 of the CPP impose a disadvantage upon the appellant as a younger adult in a manner which constitutes discrimination under s. 15(1) of the *Charter*. The appellant is asserting her claim solely on the basis of age—specifically, on the basis of being an adult under the age of 45. Relatively speaking, adults under the age of 45 have not been consistently and routinely subjected to the sorts of discrimination faced by some of Canada's discrete and insular minorities. For this reason it will be more difficult as a practical matter for this Court to reason, from facts of which the Court may appropriately take judicial notice, that the legislative distinction at issue violated the human dignity of the appellant.

[96] The appellant argues that the impugned CPP provisions infringe s. 15(1) of the *Charter* in both their purpose

and their effect. She submits that the original intent underlying the distinctions created by ss. 44(1)(d) and 58 was to provide benefits to those surviving spouses most in need, based on an assumed correlation between, among other things, increased age and one's ability to enter or re-enter the workforce following the death of one's spouse. The appellant argues that this assumed correlation is faulty because, in fact, young people generally, and the appellant in particular, have difficulty in obtaining employment, and the legislation's assumptions to the contrary are based on false stereotypes regarding the advantages of youth. . . .

[99] The questions, to take up the dignity-related concerns discussed above, may be put in the following terms. Do the impugned CPP provisions, in purpose or effect, violate essential human dignity and freedom through the imposition of disadvantage, stereotyping, or political or social prejudice? Does the law, in purpose or effect, conform to a society in which all persons enjoy equal recognition as human beings or as members of Canadian society, equally capable and equally deserving of concern, respect, and consideration? Does the law, in purpose or effect, perpetuate the view that people under 45 are less capable or less worthy of recognition or value as human beings or as members of Canadian society?

[100] Before answering these questions, it is useful to note that, although the appellant has referred this Court to government reports and other sources which favour extending survivor's pensions to younger spouses on the basis that they suffer immediate financial need, she has not demonstrated that either the purpose or the effect of the impugned legislative provisions violates her human dignity in the sense discussed above so as to constitute discrimination. I agree with the appellant that surviving spouses of all ages are vulnerable, economically and otherwise, immediately following the death of a spouse. However, as both the appellant and respondent acknowledged in their submissions before this Court, the purpose and function of the impugned CPP provisions is not to remedy the *immediate* financial need experienced by widows and widowers, but rather to enable older widows and widowers to meet their basic needs *during the longer term*. . . .

[102] The answers to the questions which I posed above with respect to human dignity thus lie, in part, in the aim and effects of the legislation in providing *long-term* financial security for Canadians who lose a spouse, coupled with the greater flexibility and opportunity of younger people without dependent children or disabilities to achieve long-term security absent their spouse. Yes, the law imposes a disadvantage on younger spouses in this class. But it is unlikely to be a substantive disadvantage, viewed in the long term. The law on its face treats such younger people differently, but the differential treatment does not reflect or promote the notion that they are

less capable or less deserving of concern, respect, and consideration, when the dual perspectives of long-term security and the greater opportunity of youth are considered. Nor does the differential treatment perpetuate the view that people in this class are less capable or less worthy of recognition or value as human beings or as members of Canadian society....

[104] The challenged legislation simply reflects the fact that people in the appellant's position are more able to overcome long-term need because of the nature of a human being's life cycle. Those who are younger when they lose a spouse are more able to replace the income lost from the death of a spouse....

[108] In these circumstances, recalling the purposes of s. 15(1), I am at a loss to locate any violation of human dignity. The impugned distinctions in the present case do not stigmatize young persons, nor can they be said to perpetuate the view that surviving spouses under age 45 are less deserving of concern, respect or consideration than any others. Nor do they withhold a government benefit on the basis of stereotypical assumptions about the demographic group of which the appellant happens to be a member. I must conclude that, when considered in the social, political, and legal context of the claim, the age distinctions in ss. 44(1)(*d*) and 58 of the CPP are not discriminatory.

[109] In finding that the impugned legislative provisions do not infringe s. 15(1) of the *Charter*, I do not wish in any way to minimize the emotional and economic upset which affects surviving dependents when a spouse dies. My analysis herein is not meant to suggest that young people do not suffer following the death of a loved one, but only that the impugned CPP provisions are not discriminatory between younger and older adults within the purpose and meaning of s. 15(1) of the *Charter*.

[110] I conclude, then, that this is one of the rare cases contemplated in *Andrews, supra*, in which differential treatment based on one or more of the enumerated or analogous grounds in s. 15(1) is not discriminatory. It is important to identify such cases through a purposive analysis of s. 15(1), in order to ensure that analysis under s. 15(1) does not become mechanistic, but rather addresses the true social, political and legal context underlying each and every equality claim.

G. Section 1 of the Charter

[111] As I have found no violation of s. 15(1) of the *Charter*, it is not necessary to turn to s. 1.

27   M. v. H., 1999

The 1999 *M. v. H.* decision represented a significant turning point in terms of state recognition of same-sex partners and their relationships in Canada. The decision had enormous implications for provincial and federal governments because it conveyed the following message: social policies oriented toward spouses that deny recognition or benefits to same-sex partners lack constitutional validity. This decision would have been extremely difficult to anticipate at the time of the *Charter*'s adoption.

When the *Charter* was debated, lesbian and gay activists had little reason to assume that it would be a useful resource in their efforts to pressure politicians to undertake substantial social policy changes to redress discrimination on the basis of sexual orientation. At the time, both federal and provincial legislation relied heavily on a heterosexual definition of "spouse" that had the effect of denying entitlements or recognition to same-sex partners and their relationships. But legislatures were not the only obstacle in overcoming this form of discrimination. Courts routinely accepted the validity of these legislative distinctions either by using a heterosexual definition of "spouse" or "marriage" or by ruling that, in the absence of a statutory basis for recognizing same-sex spouses, judges were powerless to disagree with legislation. During the entrenchment debate, Jean Chrétien, who was then the federal Justice Minister, indicated that the federal Liberal government was not prepared to include sexual orientation as a prohibited category of discrimination in the *Charter*. But he did suggest that, in time, courts might interpret equality in a more expansive manner.

A decade after the equality rights came into force (their application was delayed for three years after the *Charter* was adopted to allow legislatures to identify and revise legislation that might be inconsistent with equality), the Supreme Court ruled in *Egan v. Canada*[1] that the *Charter*'s equality rights do indeed protect individuals from discrimination on the basis of sexual orientation. However, because the Court's ruling was heavily qualified, this decision was not immediately helpful to those hoping for swift legislative changes to redress discrimination against gay men or lesbians. Although the Court was unanimous in its conclusion that section 15 equality rights prohibit discrimination on the basis of sexual orientation, it split on the question whether the legislation at issue, the federal *Old Age Security Act* and the allowance it provided for some qualifying spouses of pensioners, actually violated the *Charter*. Five judges ruled that the heterosexual definition of "spouse" in the *Act* violated equality, while four judges ruled it did not. But Justice Sopinka, one of the five who ruled that equality was violated, concluded that the legislation imposed a reasonable limit under section 1. He argued that legislatures needed more time to recognize new social relationships because the idea of interpreting "spouse" to include same-sex partners represented a "novel concept" and the legislative changes would have significant fiscal implications. The result of this section 1 ruling was that a narrow majority upheld the validity of the *Act*, relieving federal or provincial legislatures of the immediate pressure of having to redress this form of discrimination.

---

1 [1995] 2 S.C.R. 513.

However, it was not long before the Court expressed impatience with what it perceived to be inappropriate delays in introducing the necessary social policy reforms. Three years later, the Court indicated judicial fatigue with legislative inaction in addressing discrimination on the basis of sexual orientation. In *Vriend v. Alberta*,[2] the Court categorically rejected the Alberta government's argument for deference to its explicit decision not to include sexual orientation as a protected ground against discrimination in its provincial human rights code. In *Vriend*, lawyers for the Alberta government argued, unsuccessfully, that the omission of sexual orientation as a prohibited ground of discrimination was justified under section 1, reminding the Court that Justice Sopinka had only a few years earlier suggested that legislatures should be given time to develop an incremental approach to reform legislation affecting spouses and families.

M. v. H. was handed down the following year, and this time the Court clearly was not prepared to accept legislative inaction on this issue. At issue was the failure in Ontario's *Family Law Act* to recognize same-sex relationships in its processes for resolving property and other issues that arise when family relationships are dissolved. Government lawyers had argued that same-sex partners had options other than statutory ones, such as contract law, and that the differential treatment was therefore acceptable. The Court rejected this argument, concluding that the denial of access to the court-enforced and court-protected support system available to others whose relationships have dissolved was not justified under section 1. But it was not simply the lack of equal benefit of the law that troubled the Court. The Court also ruled that the legislation violated equality because it promoted a view that those in same-sex relationships are less worthy of state recognition and protection than those in heterosexual unions and that this message perpetuates the disadvantages incurred by those in same-sex relationships because of the continued social prejudices they encounter.

Although the legislation had immediate implications for Ontario, it also had important consequences for the federal and other provincial governments because they similarly based legislative entitlements and obligations on a heterosexual definition of "spouse." In Ontario, the Progressive Conservative government of Mike Harris indicated that, although the Court's view of family did not correspond with his definition, his government would comply with the Court's decision, suggesting that he did not believe that use of the notwithstanding clause was a valid political response to a judicial ruling. But the government's lack of enthusiasm for the legislative changes it introduced was conveyed in the title of its legislation, which suggested grudging acceptance for the ruling: *Amendments Because of the Supreme Court of Canada Decision in M. v. H. Act, 1999*. This legislation amended more than 67 legislative acts by recognizing "same-sex partners" for inclusion in most social policy entitlements. The federal government responded to this ruling in 2000 by introducing the *Modernization of Benefits and Obligations Act*, which introduced a new term, "common-law partner," and expanded the common-law definition of "non-married relationships" to include same-sex partners. The legislation was extremely controversial, as critics argued that it would affect the definition of "marriage." In response to pressure from the Canadian Alliance, the Liberal government agreed to include a preamble in the legislation, stating that the amendments did not affect the definition of "marriage," which remained "the lawful union of one man and one woman to the exclusion of all others." ∼

---

2   [1998] 1 S.C.R. 493.

Discussion Questions

1. What consequences for social policy flow from the Supreme Court's indication that equality requires not only equal benefit of the law, but also that the law treat same-sex partners with the same degree of respect and recognition given to opposite-sex couples?
2. Was the Court justified in its decision that deference is not appropriate when legislatures have failed to redress discrimination in the benefits given to same-sex partners?
3. Was it appropriate for the Court to suspend the effects of its ruling? What other remedies were available?

M. v. H.
[1999] 2 S.C.R. 3

Hearing: March 18, 1998; Judgment: May 20, 1999.

Present: Lamer C.J. and L'Heureux-Dubé, Gonthier, Cory, McLachlin, Iacobucci, Major, Bastarache, and Binnie JJ.

Interveners: The Foundation for Equal Families, the Women's Legal Education and Action Fund (LEAF), Equality for Gays and Lesbians Everywhere (EGALE), the Ontario Human Rights Commission, the United Church of Canada, the Evangelical Fellowship of Canada, the Ontario Council of Sikhs, the Islamic Society of North America, Focus on the Family, and REAL Women of Canada.

The judgment of Lamer C.J. and L'Heureux-Dubé, Cory, McLachlin, Iacobucci, and Binnie JJ. was delivered by

CORY AND IACOBUCCI JJ.:

I. Introduction and Overview

[1] The principal issue raised in this appeal is whether the definition of "spouse" in s. 29 of the *Family Law Act*, R.S.O. 1990, c. F.3 ("*FLA*") infringes s. 15(1) of the *Canadian Charter of Rights and Freedoms*, and, if so, whether the legislation is nevertheless saved by s. 1 of the *Charter*. In addition, M. was granted leave to cross-appeal on the issue of the appropriate remedy to be granted and also as to costs.

[2] Our view on this principal issue may be summarized as follows. Section 15(1) of the *Charter* is infringed by the definition of "spouse" in s. 29 of the *FLA*. This definition, which only applies to Part III of the *FLA*, draws a distinction between individuals in conjugal, opposite-sex relationships of a specific degree of duration and individuals in conjugal, same-sex relationships of a specific degree of duration.... Essentially, the definition of "spouse" in s. 29 of the *FLA* extends the obligation to provide spousal support, found in Part III of the *FLA*, beyond married persons to include individuals in conjugal opposite-sex relationships of some permanence. Same-sex relationships are capable of being both conjugal and lengthy, but individuals in such relationships are nonetheless denied access to the court-enforced system of support provided by the *FLA*. This differential treatment is on the basis of a personal characteristic, namely sexual orientation, that, in previous jurisprudence, has been found to be analogous to those characteristics specifically enumerated in s. 15(1).

[3] The crux of the issue is that this differential treatment discriminates in a substantive sense by violating the human dignity of individuals in same-sex relationships. As *Law v. Canada (Minister of Employment and Immigration)*, [1999] 1 S.C.R. 497, established, the inquiry into substantive discrimi-

nation is to be undertaken in a purposive and contextual manner. In the present appeal, several factors are important to consider. First, individuals in same-sex relationships face significant pre-existing disadvantage and vulnerability, which is exacerbated by the impugned legislation. Second, the legislation at issue fails to take into account the claimant's actual situation. Third, there is no compelling argument that the ameliorative purpose of the legislation does anything to lessen the charge of discrimination in this case. Fourth, the nature of the interest affected is fundamental, namely the ability to meet basic financial needs following the breakdown of a relationship characterized by intimacy and economic dependence. The exclusion of same-sex partners from the benefits of the spousal support scheme implies that they are judged to be incapable of forming intimate relationships of economic interdependence, without regard to their actual circumstances. Taking these factors into account, it is clear that the human dignity of individuals in same-sex relationships is violated by the definition of "spouse" in s. 29 of the *FLA*.

[4] This infringement is not justified under s.1 of the *Charter* because there is no rational connection between the objectives of the spousal support provisions and the means chosen to further this objective. The objectives were accurately identified by Charron J.A., in the court below, as providing for the equitable resolution of economic disputes when intimate relationships between financially interdependent individuals break down, and alleviating the burden on the public purse to provide for dependent spouses. Neither of these objectives is furthered by the exclusion of individuals in same-sex couples from the spousal support regime. If anything, these goals are undermined by this exclusion.

[5] In this case, the remedy of reading in is inappropriate, as it would unduly recast the legislation, and striking down the *FLA* as a whole is excessive. Therefore the appropriate remedy is to declare s. 29 of no force and effect and to suspend the application of the declaration for a period of six months.

[6] In our elaboration of this position in these joint reasons, Cory J. has addressed the issues of mootness and the breach of s. 15(1) of the *Charter*. Iacobucci J. has addressed s. 1 of the *Charter*, the appropriate remedy, costs and the disposition.

CORY J.:

[7] At the outset, it must be stressed that the questions to be answered are narrow and precise in their scope. The *FLA* provides a means whereby designated persons may apply to the court for support from a spouse or, if unmarried, from a man or woman with whom they lived in an opposite-sex conjugal relationship. The Act specifically extends the obligation for support beyond married persons who, as a result of their married status, have additional rights under the Act.

[8] The question to be resolved is whether the extension of the right to seek support to members of unmarried opposite-sex couples infringes s. 15(1) of the *Charter* by failing to provide the same rights to members of same-sex couples.

II. Factual Background

[9] M. and H. are women who met while on vacation in 1980. It is agreed that in 1982 they started living together in a same-sex relationship that continued for at least five years. . . .

[13] By September of 1992, M. and H.'s relationship had deteriorated. . . .

[14] The parties did not divide the personal property or household contents. M. alleged that she encountered serious financial problems after the separation. In October 1992, M. sought an order for partition and sale of the house; a declaration that she was the beneficial owner of certain lands and premises owned by H. and by the companies M. named as defendants; and an accounting of the transactions carried out by the companies. By Notice of Cross-Application, H. and the corporate defendants sought damages for slander of title, partition and sale of property, the repayment of certain loans, and other relief. M. then amended her application to include a claim for support pursuant to the provisions of the *FLA*, and served Notice of a Constitutional Question challenging the validity of the definition of "spouse" in s. 29 of the Act. . . .

B. Does Section 29 of the FLA Infringe Section 15(1) of the Charter?

[45] The Attorney General for Ontario, displaying great candour, very fairly conceded that s. 29 of the *FLA* contravenes the provisions of s. 15 of the *Charter*. His entire argument was directed at demonstrating that the section was nonetheless justifiable and saved by s. 1 of the *Charter*. The Court is certainly not bound by this concession. Although, in my view, he was correct in taking this position, it would not be appropriate in this appeal to undertake only a s. 1 analysis without considering whether s. 15 has in fact been violated. The s. 15(1) issue in this case is important not only to the parties but also to many Canadians. It was the subject of extensive submissions by the respondent H. and many of the interveners.

1. Approach to Section 15(1)

[46] In the recent decision of this Court in *Law, supra*, Iacobucci J. summarized some of the main guidelines for analysis under s. 15(1) to be derived from the jurisprudence of this Court. He emphasized that these guidelines do not represent a strict test, but rather should be understood as points of reference for a court that is called upon to decide whether a claimant's right to equality without discrimination under the *Charter* has been infringed: see para. 88.

[47] Iacobucci J. explained that the s. 15(1) equality guarantee is to be interpreted and applied in a purposive and contextual manner, in order to permit the realization of the provision's strong remedial purpose, and to avoid the pitfalls of a formalistic or mechanical approach. Following a review of this Court's jurisprudence regarding the fundamental purpose of s. 15(1), he stated this purpose in the following terms, at para. 88:

> In general terms, the purpose of s. 15(1) is to prevent the violation of essential human dignity and freedom through the imposition of disadvantage, stereotyping, or political or social prejudice, and to promote a society in which all persons enjoy equal recognition at law as human beings or as members of Canadian society, equally capable and equally deserving of concern, respect and consideration.

Iacobucci J. stated that the existence of a conflict between the purpose or effect of an impugned law, on the one hand, and this fundamental purpose of the equality guarantee, on the other, is essential in order to found a discrimination claim.

[48] In *Law*, Iacobucci J. reviewed various articulations of the proper approach to be taken in analyzing a s. 15(1) claim, as expressed in the jurisprudence of this Court. At para. 39, he summarized the basic elements of this Court's approach as involving three broad inquiries, in the following terms:

> In my view, the proper approach to analyzing a claim of discrimination under s. 15(1) of the *Charter* involves a synthesis of these various articulations. Following upon the analysis in *Andrews* [*v. Law Society of British Columbia*], [1989] 1 S.C.R. 143, and the two-step framework set out in *Egan, supra*, and *Miron* [*v. Trudel*, [1995] 2 S.C.R. 418], among other cases, a court that is called upon to determine a discrimination claim under s. 15(1) should make the following three broad inquiries. First, does the impugned law (a) draw a formal distinction between the claimant and others on the basis of one or more personal characteristics, or (b) fail to take into account the claimant's already disadvantaged position within Canadian society resulting in substantively differential treatment between the claimant and others on the basis of one or more personal characteristics? If so, there is differential treatment for the purpose of s. 15(1). Second, was the claimant subject to differential treatment on the basis of one or more of the enumerated and analogous grounds? And third, does the differential treatment discriminate in a substantive sense, bringing into play the *purpose* of s. 15(1) of the *Charter* in remedying such ills as prejudice, stereotyping, and historical disadvantage? [Emphasis in original.]

2. The Structure of the Family Law Act

[49] To begin, it may be useful to review briefly the structure of the *FLA* and the rights and obligations it establishes. First and foremost, it is of critical importance to recognize that the *FLA* contains more than one definition of "spouse." The first definition is set out in s. 1(1) and includes only persons who are actually married, or who have entered into a void or voidable marriage in good faith. This definition applies to *all* parts of the Act.

[50] The second definition is found in s. 29, and extends the meaning of "spouse," but only for certain purposes. Specifically, unmarried opposite-sex couples who have cohabited for at least three years, or who are the natural or adoptive parents of a child and have also cohabited in a relationship of "some permanence," bear a mutual obligation of support under Part III of the *FLA*. They also have the right to enter into cohabitation agreements to regulate their relationship under Part IV, and may bring a claim for dependants' relief in tort under Part V.

[51] All these rights and obligations are obviously available to married persons as well. However, married persons have additional rights under the *FLA* that are denied common law cohabitants, even those who meet the requirements of s. 29. Under Part I, a husband or wife may apply for an equal share of the wealth generated during the marriage, and of the matrimonial home. Under Part II, both married spouses have a right to possession of the matrimonial home, regardless of who owns the property. Moreover, the ability of the owner of the matrimonial home to sell or encumber the property without the consent of the other spouse is severely restricted. These mutual rights and obligations are denied *all* unmarried opposite-sex cohabitants.

[52] These observations on the structure of the *FLA* serve to emphasize that this appeal has nothing to do with marriage *per se*. Much of the *FLA* is devoted solely to regulating the relationship that exists between married persons, or persons who intend to be married. They alone are guaranteed certain property rights that are not extended to any unmarried persons. In some specific instances—such as Part III dealing with support obligations—the legislature has seen fit to extend the rights and obligations that arise under the *FLA beyond* married persons to include certain *unmarried* persons as well.

[53] In other words, the *FLA* draws a distinction by specifically according rights to individual members of unmarried cohabiting opposite-sex couples, which by omission it fails to accord to individual members of same-sex couples who are living together. It is this distinction that lies at the heart of the s. 15 analysis. The rights and obligations that exist between married persons play no part in this analysis. The legislature did not extend full marital status, for the purposes of all the rights and obligations under the *FLA*, to those unmarried cohabitants included in s. 29 of the Act. Rather, the definition of "spouse" in s. 29 only applies for certain purposes. Specifically, it allows persons who became financially dependent in the course of a lengthy intimate relationship some relief from financial hardship resulting from the breakdown of that relationship. It follows that this provision was designed to reduce the demands on the public welfare system. This will be discussed more fully in the s. 1 analysis below.

[54] . . . [T]he legislature drafted s. 29 to allow either a man *or* a woman to apply for support, thereby recognizing that financial dependence can arise in an intimate relationship in a context entirely unrelated either to child rearing or to any gender-based discrimination existing in our society. . . .

[55] [I]n this appeal there is no need to consider whether same-sex couples can marry, or whether same-sex couples must, for all purposes, be treated in the same manner as unmarried opposite-sex couples. The only determination that must be made is whether, in extending the spousal support obligations set out in Part III of the *FLA* to include unmarried men or women in certain opposite-sex relationships, the legislature infringed the equality rights of men or women in similar same-sex relationships, and if so, whether that infringement may be saved by s. 1 of the *Charter*. . . .

[57] The definition [of "spouse" in section 29 of the *FLA*] clearly indicates that the legislature decided to extend the obligation to provide spousal support *beyond* married persons. Obligations to provide support were no longer dependent upon marriage. The obligation was extended to include those relationships which:

(i)   exist between a man and a woman;

(ii) have a specific degree of permanence;

(iii) are conjugal.

Only individuals in relationships which meet these minimum criteria may apply for a support order under Part III of the *FLA*.

[58] Same-sex relationships are capable of meeting the last two requirements. Certainly same-sex couples will often form long, lasting, loving and intimate relationships. The choices they make in the context of those relationships may give rise to the financial dependence of one partner on the other. Though it might be argued that same-sex couples do not live together in "conjugal" relationships, in the sense that they cannot "hold themselves out" as husband and wife, on this issue I am in agreement with the reasoning and conclusions of the majority of the Court of Appeal. . . .

[60] Certainly an opposite-sex couple may, after many years together, be considered to be in a conjugal relationship although they have neither children nor sexual relations.

Obviously the weight to be accorded the various elements or factors to be considered in determining whether an opposite-sex couple is in a conjugal relationship will vary widely and almost infinitely. The same must hold true of same-sex couples. Courts have wisely determined that the approach to determining whether a relationship is conjugal must be flexible. This must be so, for the relationships of all couples will vary widely. . . .

[61] Since gay and lesbian individuals are capable of being involved in conjugal relationships, and since their relationships are capable of meeting the *FLA*'s temporal requirements, the distinction of relevance to this appeal is between persons in an opposite-sex, conjugal relationship of some permanence and persons in a same-sex, conjugal relationship of some permanence. In this regard, I must disagree with the dissenting opinion in the court below, which characterized the distinction arising in s. 29 as being between opposite-sex and same-sex *couples*. This conclusion would require that the section be scrutinized for any discriminatory impact it may have on same-sex couples, and not on the individual members of that couple. Section 29 defines "spouse" as "*either* of a man and woman" who meet the other requirements of the section. It follows that the definition could not have been meant to define a couple. Rather it explicitly refers to the *individual* members of the couple. Thus the distinction of relevance must be between individual persons in a same-sex, conjugal relationship of some permanence and individual persons in an opposite-sex, conjugal relationship of some permanence.

[62] Thus it is apparent that the legislation has drawn a formal distinction between the claimant and others, based on personal characteristics. As stated in *Law, supra*, the first broad inquiry in the s. 15(1) analysis determines whether there is differential treatment imposed by the impugned legislation between the claimant and others. It is clear that there is differential treatment here. Under s. 29 of the *FLA*, members of opposite-sex couples who can meet the requirements of the statute are able to gain access to the court-enforced system of support provided by the *FLA*. It is this system that ensures the provision of support to a dependent spouse. Members of same-sex couples are denied access to this system entirely on the basis of their sexual orientation.

4. Sexual Orientation Is an Analogous Ground

[63] Not every legislative distinction is discriminatory. Before it can be found that it gives rise to discrimination, it must be shown that an equality right was denied on the basis of an enumerated or analogous ground, and that this differential treatment discriminates "in a substantive sense, bringing into play the *purpose* of s. 15(1) of the *Charter*": *Law, supra*, at para. 39 (emphasis in original).

[64] In *Egan, supra*, this Court unanimously affirmed that sexual orientation is an analogous ground to those enumerated in s. 15(1). Sexual orientation is "a deeply personal characteristic that is either unchangeable or changeable only at unacceptable personal costs" (para. 5). In addition, a majority of this Court explicitly recognized that gays, lesbians and bisexuals, "whether as individuals or couples, form an identifiable minority who have suffered and continue to suffer serious social, political and economic disadvantage" (para. 175, *per* Cory J.; see also para. 89, *per* L'Heureux-Dubé J.).

5. The Existence of Discrimination in a Purposive Sense

[65] The determination of whether differential treatment imposed by legislation on an enumerated or analogous ground is discriminatory within the meaning of s. 15(1) of the *Charter* is to be undertaken in a purposive and contextual manner. The relevant inquiry is whether the differential treatment imposes a burden upon or withholds a benefit from the claimant in a manner that reflects the stereotypical application of presumed group or personal characteristics, or which otherwise has the effect of perpetuating or promoting the view that the individual is less capable or worthy of recognition or value as a human being or as a member of Canadian society, equally deserving of concern, respect, and consideration: *Law, supra*, at para. 88.

[66] The respondent H. has argued that the differential treatment imposed by s. 29 of the *FLA* does not deny the respondent M. the equal benefit of the law since same-sex spouses are not being denied an economic benefit, but simply the opportunity to gain access to a court-enforced process. Such an analysis takes too narrow a view of "benefit" under the law. It is a view this Court should not adopt. The type of benefit salient to the s. 15(1) analysis cannot encompass only the conferral of an economic benefit. It must also include access to a process that could confer an economic or other benefit: *Egan, supra*, at paras. 158-59; *Vriend v. Alberta*, [1998] 1 S.C.R. 493, at para. 87. Further, the spousal support provisions of the *FLA* help protect the economic interests of individuals in intimate relationships. When a relationship breaks down, the support provisions help to ensure that a member of a couple who has contributed to the couple's welfare in intangible ways will not find himself or herself utterly abandoned. This protective aspect of the spousal support provisions is properly considered in relation to s. 15(1). Thus it is appropriate to conclude that s. 29 of the *FLA* creates a distinction that withholds a benefit from the respondent M. The question is whether this denial of a benefit violates the purpose of s. 15(1).

[67] In *Law*, Iacobucci J. explained that there are a variety of contextual factors that may be referred to by a s. 15(1) claimant in order to demonstrate that legislation demeans

his or her dignity. The list of factors is not closed, and there is no specific formula that must be considered in every case. In *Law* itself, Iacobucci J. listed four important contextual factors in particular which may influence the determination of whether s. 15(1) has been infringed. He emphasized, at paras. 59-61, that in examining these contextual factors, a court must adopt the point of view of a reasonable person, in circumstances similar to those of the claimant, who takes into account the contextual factors relevant to the claim.

[68] One factor which may demonstrate that legislation that treats the claimant differently has the effect of demeaning the claimant's dignity is the existence of pre-existing disadvantage, stereotyping, prejudice, or vulnerability experienced by the individual or group at issue....

[69] In this case, there is significant pre-existing disadvantage and vulnerability, and these circumstances are exacerbated by the impugned legislation. The legislative provision in question draws a distinction that prevents persons in a same-sex relationship from gaining access to the court-enforced and protected support system. This system clearly provides a benefit to unmarried heterosexual persons who come within the definition set out in s. 29, and thereby provides a measure of protection for their economic interests. This protection is denied to persons in a same-sex relationship who would otherwise meet the statute's requirements, and as a result, a person in the position of the claimant is denied a benefit regarding an important aspect of life in today's society. Neither common law nor equity provides the remedy of maintenance that is made available by the *FLA*. The denial of that potential benefit, which may impose a financial burden on persons in the position of the claimant, contributes to the general vulnerability experienced by individuals in same-sex relationships.

[70] A second contextual factor that was discussed in *Law* as being potentially relevant to the s. 15(1) inquiry is the correspondence, or the lack of it, between the ground on which a claim is based and the actual need, capacity, or circumstances of the claimant or others: para. 70. Iacobucci J. nonetheless cautioned that the mere fact that the impugned legislation takes into account the claimant's actual situation will not necessarily defeat a s. 15(1) claim, as the focus of the inquiry must always remain upon the central question of whether, viewed from the perspective of the claimant, the differential treatment imposed by the legislation has the effect of violating human dignity. However, the legislation at issue in the current appeal fails to take into account the claimant's actual situation. As I have already discussed, access to the court-enforced spousal support regime provided in the *FLA* is given to individuals in conjugal relationships of a specific degree of permanence. Being in a same-sex relationship does not mean that it is an impermanent or a non-conjugal relationship.

[71] A third contextual factor referred to by Iacobucci J. in *Law, supra,* at para. 72, is the question of whether the impugned legislation has an ameliorative purpose or effect for a group historically disadvantaged in the context of the legislation:

> An ameliorative purpose or effect which accords with the purpose of s. 15(1) of the *Charter* will likely not violate the human dignity of more advantaged individuals where the exclusion of these more advantaged individuals largely corresponds to the greater need or the different circumstances experienced by the disadvantaged group being targeted by the legislation. I emphasize that this factor will likely only be relevant where the person or group that is excluded from the scope of ameliorative legislation or other state action is more advantaged in a relative sense. Underinclusive ameliorative legislation that excludes from its scope the members of an historically disadvantaged group will rarely escape the charge of discrimination: see *Vriend, supra,* at paras. 94-104, *per* Cory J.

In other words, the existence of an ameliorative purpose or effect may help to establish that human dignity is not violated where the person or group that is excluded is more advantaged with respect to the circumstances addressed by the legislation. Gonthier J. argues that the legislation under scrutiny in the present appeal is just such ameliorative legislation—that it is meant to target women in married or opposite-sex relationships. He proceeds to argue that in this legal context, women in same-sex relationships are not similarly disadvantaged. For the reasons expressed elsewhere, we disagree with this characterization of the legislation. Accordingly, we reject the idea that the allegedly ameliorative purpose of this legislation does anything to lessen the charge of discrimination in this case.

[72] A fourth contextual factor specifically adverted to by Iacobucci J. in *Law,* at para. 74, was the nature of the interest affected by the impugned legislation. Drawing upon the reasons of L'Heureux-Dubé J. in *Egan, supra,* Iacobucci J. stated that the discriminatory calibre of differential treatment cannot be fully appreciated without considering whether the distinction in question restricts access to a fundamental social institution, or affects a basic aspect of full membership in Canadian society, or constitutes a complete non-recognition of a particular group. In the present case, the interest protected by s. 29 of the *FLA* is fundamental, namely the ability to meet basic financial needs following the breakdown of a relationship characterized by intimacy and economic dependence. Members of same-sex couples are entirely ignored by the statute, notwithstanding the undeniable importance to them of the benefits accorded by the statute.

[73] The societal significance of the benefit conferred by the statute cannot be overemphasized. The exclusion of

same-sex partners from the benefits of s. 29 of the *FLA* promotes the view that M., and individuals in same-sex relationships generally, are less worthy of recognition and protection. It implies that they are judged to be incapable of forming intimate relationships of economic interdependence as compared to opposite-sex couples, without regard to their actual circumstances. As the intervener EGALE submitted, such exclusion perpetuates the disadvantages suffered by individuals in same-sex relationships and contributes to the erasure of their existence.

[74] Therefore I conclude that an examination of the four factors outlined above, in the context of the present appeal, indicate that the human dignity of individuals in same-sex relationships is violated by the impugned legislation. In light of this, I conclude that the definition of "spouse" in s. 29 of the *FLA* violates s. 15(1).

IACOBUCCI J.:

C. Is Section 29 of the FLA Justified Under Section 1 of the Charter?

1. Stare Decisis and Egan

[75] At the outset, I wish to address the appellant's submission that an independent examination of the s. 1 issues is unnecessary in the present case. The appellant asserts that the principle of *stare decisis* binds this Court to the decision in *Egan, supra,* and that the s. 1 analysis in that case ought to apply with equal force to the case at bar. Although I recognize the fundamental role of precedent in legal analysis, I cannot accept this submission. Granted, *Egan,* like the case now before this Court, was also concerned with the opposite-sex definition of "spouse" in provincial legislation. However, the similar focus of the two cases is not sufficient to bind the Court to the *Egan* decision. The instant case is based on entirely different legislation with its own unique objectives and legislative context. As a result, it must be evaluated on its own merits.

2. Approach to Section 1

[76] The analytical framework for determining whether a law constitutes a "reasonable" limit that can be "demonstrably justified in a free and democratic society" under s. 1 of the *Charter* was first set out by Dickson C.J. in *R. v. Oakes,* [1986] 1 S.C.R. 103....

[77] However, it is important not to lose sight of the underlying principles animating this general approach....

[78] As noted by this Court in *Vriend, supra,* at para. 134, the introduction of the *Charter* brought about "a redefinition of our democracy." Central to this democratic vision is a dialogue of mutual respect between the courts and the legislatures, which includes the idea that [*Vriend,* at para. 136]:

In carrying out their duties, courts are not to second-guess legislatures and the executives; they are not to make value judgments on what they regard as the proper policy choice; this is for the other branches. Rather, the courts are to uphold the Constitution and have been expressly invited to perform that role by the Constitution itself. But respect by the courts for the legislature and executive role is as important as ensuring that the other branches respect each others' role and the role of the courts.

This Court has often stressed the importance of deference to the policy choices of the legislature in the context of determining whether the legislature has discharged its burden of proof under s. 1 of the *Charter....* However, it is important to note that deference is not a kind of threshold inquiry under s. 1. As a general matter, the role of the legislature demands deference from the courts to those types of policy decisions that the legislature is best placed to make. The simple or general claim that the infringement of a right is justified under s. 1 is not such a decision. As Cory J. stated in *Vriend, supra,* at para. 54: "The notion of judicial deference to legislative choices should not ... be used to completely immunize certain kinds of legislative decisions from *Charter* scrutiny."

[79] Under s. 1, the burden is on the legislature to prove that the infringement of a right is justified. In attempting to discharge this burden, the legislature will have to provide the court with evidence and arguments to support its general claim of justification. Sometimes this will involve demonstrating why the legislature had to make certain policy choices and why it considered these choices to be reasonable in the circumstances. These policy choices may be of the type that the legislature is in a better position than the court to make, as in the case of difficult policy judgments regarding the claims of competing groups or the evaluation of complex and conflicting social science research: *Irwin Toy, supra,* at p. 993, *per* Dickson C.J. and Lamer and Wilson JJ. Courts must be cautious not to overstep the bounds of their institutional competence in reviewing such decisions. The question of deference, therefore, is intimately tied up with the nature of the particular claim or evidence at issue and not in the general application of the s. 1 test; it can only be discussed in relation to such specific claims or evidence and not at the outset of the analysis.

[80] I therefore agree with my colleague, Bastarache J., that an examination of *context* is essential in determining whether deference is appropriate. It may also be the case that a discussion of context is appropriate at the outset of a s. 1 analysis, depending on the nature of the evidence at issue, for ease of reference when later applying the various steps of s. 1: see, for example, *Thomson Newspapers Co. v. Canada (Attorney General),* [1998] 1 S.C.R. 877, at para. 88, *per* Bastarache J.

However, with respect to his reasons in the present appeal, I am concerned that Bastarache J. implies that the question of *deference* in a general sense should also be determined at the outset of the inquiry. For example, Bastarache J. states that the question to ask in this case is whether the Court can "rewrite the boundary in order to include that smaller number of individuals [in same-sex relationships] who are in such a position [of dependency], or must it defer to legislative determination of the issue?" (para. 304). The question of rewriting boundaries is, to my mind, at most a question of the appropriate remedy should the rights infringement be unjustified. The question of deference to the role of the legislature certainly enters into any discussion of remedy, as discussed in *Vriend, supra,* and can enter into the discussion of whether the legislature has discharged its burden under any of the steps of the s. 1 test. However, the question of deference is not an issue that can be determined prior to engaging in any of these specific inquiries. Nor should it be determined at the outset of the inquiry, given the court's important role in applying s. 1 of the *Charter* to determine whether the infringement of a guaranteed right can be justified in a free and democratic society.

[81] I will therefore not deal with the question of deference at the outset and will instead discuss it, where appropriate, under the various steps of the s. 1 test.

3. Pressing and Substantial Objective

[82] Section 29 of the *FLA* defines "spouse" as being either of a man and woman who are married to each other or cohabiting within the meaning of the Act. Same-sex couples are necessarily excluded from this definition, thereby giving rise to the charge that the legislation is underinclusive. In *Vriend, supra,* at paras. 109-11, this Court found that where a law violates the *Charter* owing to under-inclusion, the first stage of the s. 1 analysis is properly concerned with the object of the legislation as a whole, the impugned provisions of the Act, and the omission itself. . . .

[86] . . . There is considerable disagreement between the parties as to the underlying purpose of [the *FLA*]. . . .

[93] As I see the matter, the objectives of the impugned spousal support provisions were accurately identified by Charron J.A. in the court below . . . [who] identified the objectives of the Part III provisions as both a means to provide "for the equitable resolution of economic disputes that arise when intimate relationships between individuals who have been financially interdependent break down" and to "alleviate the burden on the public purse by shifting the obligation to provide support for needy persons to those parents and spouses who have the capacity to provide support to these individuals" (p. 450). I find support for this position in the legislative

debates, the terms of the provisions, as well as the jurisprudence of this Court. . . .

[100] . . . I turn to the objective of the omission. As I have already stated, when dealing with underinclusive legislation it is important also to consider the impugned omission when construing the objective. Often legislation does not simply further one goal but rather strikes a balance among several goals, some of which may be in tension. This balancing exercise may only become apparent after asking whether, in the case of underinclusive legislation, there is any objective being furthered by the impugned omission. A consideration of what is omitted from legislation may also lead a court to refine its interpretation of the objectives of the impugned legislation, perhaps reducing its scope. I agree with my colleague, Bastarache J., at para. 329, that if the omission is not taken into account in construing the objective then it is more likely that the omission will cause the impugned legislation to fail the rational connection step of the proportionality analysis.

[101] However, the concerns just outlined do not imply that the court must find that there is a separate objective being furthered by the omission. Even if there is no such objective the omission must still be evaluated as part of the means chosen to further the objective of the specific provision in question, under the proportionality analysis. Otherwise the court risks collapsing the two stages of the *Oakes* test (pressing and substantial objective and proportionality) into a general question regarding the reasonableness of the omission. There may be exceptions to this general approach, such as when there is evidence of a deliberate omission by the legislature that is "on its face the very antithesis of the principles embodied in the legislation as a whole": *Vriend, supra,* at para. 116.

[102] With these concerns in mind, I turn to the present appeal. The appellant does not argue that a separate objective is furthered by the impugned omission. Rather, the argument is that a proper consideration of the exclusion of same-sex couples from the definition of "spouse" in s. 29 of the *FLA* reduces the apparent scope of the objective furthered by that provision. The appellant made two arguments in this regard. First, the appellant argued that the *FLA* is a remedial statute designed to address the power imbalance that continues to exist in many opposite-sex relationships. Thus, it was submitted that the inclusion of same-sex couples in a scheme established to deal with problems that are not typical of their relationships is inappropriate. Further, the appellant asserted that where persons fall outside the rationale for which a benefit was established, the legislature is justified in withholding it from those persons.

[103] With respect, I disagree with these submissions. As I stated above, I do not believe that the purpose of the *FLA* in

general, nor Part III in particular, is to remedy the disadvantages suffered by women in opposite-sex relationships.

[104] The second objective for the omission advanced by the appellant is the promotion of opposite-sex relationships to ensure the protection of children. Having found that neither the *FLA* as a whole nor the spousal support provisions in Part III of the Act are primarily concerned with the protection of children, I must also reject the submission that this is part of the objective of s. 29 of the *FLA*.

[105] Finally, I note that Bastarache J. accepts that the rejection of the *Equality Rights Statute Law Amendment Act, 1994* by the Ontario legislature can provide evidence regarding the objective of s. 29 of the *FLA*. In particular, he argues, at para. 349: "It can therefore be inferred that the legislature's purpose was also to exclude all types of relationships not typically characterized by the state of economic dependency apparent in traditional family relationships." With respect, I cannot agree that a failed amendment can provide evidence as to the objective of the legislation that was to have been amended. Section 17 of the *Interpretation Act*, R.S.O. 1990, c. I.11, provides: "The repeal or amendment of an Act shall be deemed not to be or to involve any declaration as to the previous state of the law." If the amendment of an Act may not be used to interpret the meaning of the Act prior to the amendment, then I do not see how a *failed* amendment may be used in this manner.

[106] Therefore I endorse the description of the objectives of the impugned provisions provided by Charron J.A. in the court below. These objectives are consonant with the overall scheme of the *FLA* and are not plausibly reinterpreted through examining the omission of same-sex spouses. Providing for the equitable resolution of economic disputes when intimate relationships between financially interdependent individuals break down, and alleviating the burden on the public purse to provide for dependent spouses, are to my mind pressing and substantial objectives. These objectives promote both social justice and the dignity of individuals— values Dickson C.J. identified in *Oakes, supra*, at p. 136, as values underlying a free and democratic society.

[107] In saying this, I wish to note my disagreement with my colleague, Bastarache J., who argues, at para. 354, that s. 29 of the *FLA* "must be respectful of the equality of status and opportunity of all persons" in order to be consistent with *Charter* values and therefore pass this stage of the s. 1 analysis. While I agree that an objective must be consistent with the principles underlying the *Charter* in order to pass the first stage of the s. 1 analysis, I find Bastarache J.'s approach unnecessarily narrow. It may be that a violation of s. 15(1) can be justified because, although not designed to promote equality, it is designed to promote *other* values and principles of a free

and democratic society. This possibility must be left open, as the inquiry into *Charter* values under s. 1 is a broad inquiry into the values and principles that, as Dickson C.J. stated in *Oakes, supra*, at p. 136, "are the *genesis* of the rights and freedoms guaranteed by the *Charter*" (emphasis added).

4. *Proportionality Analysis*

(a) Rational Connection

... [109] ... In my view, it defies logic to suggest that a gender-neutral support system is rationally connected to the goal of improving the economic circumstances of heterosexual women upon relationship breakdown. In addition, I can find no evidence to demonstrate that the exclusion of same-sex couples from the spousal support regime of the *FLA* in any way furthers the objective of assisting heterosexual women....

[112] The second of the objectives put forth by the appellant, namely, the protection of children, also fails the rational connection test. The appellant submits that the exclusion of same-sex partners from Part III of the *FLA* is rationally connected to this objective as such couples are far less likely to engage in parenting than opposite-sex couples....

[116] If anything, the goals of the legislation are undermined by the impugned exclusion. Indeed, the *inclusion* of same-sex couples in s. 29 of the *FLA* would better achieve the objectives of the legislation while respecting the *Charter* rights of individuals in same-sex relationships. In these circumstances, I conclude that the exclusion of same-sex couples from s. 29 of the Act is simply not rationally connected to the dual objectives of the spousal support provisions of the legislation.

[117] Given this lack of a rational connection, s. 29 of the *FLA* is not saved by s. 1 of the *Charter*. Although it is therefore not strictly necessary to consider the other two branches of the second stage of the *Oakes* test, I will discuss them briefly in order to clarify some fundamental misunderstandings advanced in this appeal.

(b) Minimal Impairment

[118] ... The appellant suggests that the exclusion of same-sex couples from s. 29 of the *FLA* minimally impairs the respondent's s. 15 rights since reasonable alternative remedies are available where economic dependence does occur in such relationships. I cannot accept these submissions.

[119] The appellant's arguments on this point are based on the remedies available under the equitable doctrine of unjust enrichment (e.g. constructive trust) and the law of contract. Turning first to the equitable remedies, the doctrine of unjust enrichment allows claimants to found an action on indirect or non-financial contributions to the acquisition, maintenance, or preservation of an asset held by the other spouse. However, to be successful, the applicant must demonstrate his

or her spouse's enrichment, a corresponding personal deprivation and the absence of any juristic reason for the enrichment. . . .

[120] Moreover, . . . equitable common law remedies such as a constructive trust are proprietary in nature and . . . not all relationships will give rise to property claims. Indeed, as submitted by LEAF, the *FLA* expressly recognizes that entitlement to the division of property is in addition to, and not in lieu of entitlement to support. Thus, it seems to me that compared to awards of spousal support, the equitable remedies are less flexible, impose more onerous requirements on claimants, and are available under far narrower circumstances. I do not accept that they provide an adequate alternative to spousal support under the *FLA*.

[121] In my view, the law of contract is an equally unacceptable alternative to the spousal support scheme under the *FLA*. The appellant emphasizes that the impugned provisions of the Act do not preclude same-sex partners from contracting for mutual support obligations. However, the voluntary assumption of such obligations is not equivalent to a statutory entitlement to apply for a support order. . . .

[124] In sum, neither the common law equitable remedies nor the law of contract are adequate substitutes for the *FLA*'s spousal support regime. Indeed, if these remedies were considered satisfactory there would have been no need for the spousal support regime, or its extension to unmarried, opposite-sex couples. It must also be remembered that the exclusion of same-sex partners from this support regime does not simply deny them a certain benefit, but does so in a manner that violates their right to be given equal concern and respect by the government. The alternative regimes just outlined do not address the fact that exclusion from the statutory scheme has moral and societal implications beyond economic ones. . . . Therefore the existence of these remedies fails to minimize sufficiently the denial of same-sex partners' constitutionally guaranteed equality rights.

[125] However, the appellant asserts that the circumstances of this case call for a measure of deference to the decision of the Ontario legislature. In this context, it is argued that it was reasonable for the government to conclude that it had impaired the rights of same-sex partners as little as possible.

[126] As I see the matter, the deferential approach advocated by the appellant is inappropriate in the case at bar. This Court has resorted to such an approach where the impugned legislation involves the balancing of claims of competing groups (see, e.g., *Irwin Toy, supra*, at pp. 999-1000; *McKinney v. University of Guelph*, [1990] 3 S.C.R. 229, at pp. 317-19, *per* La Forest J.; and *Egan, supra*, at para. 29, *per* La Forest J. and at paras. 105-8, *per* Sopinka J.). . . . This is not such a case. As no group will be disadvantaged by granting members of

same-sex couples access to the spousal support scheme under the *FLA*, the notion of deference to legislative choices in the sense of balancing claims of competing groups has no application to this case. . . .

[128] In addition, the deferential approach is not warranted, as submitted by the appellant, on the basis that Part III of the *FLA* and s. 29 thereof are steps in an incremental process of reform of spousal support. As this Court noted in *Vriend, supra*, government incrementalism, or the notion that government ought to be accorded time to amend discriminatory legislation, is generally an inappropriate justification for *Charter* violations. However, even if I were to accept that such a justification might be suitable in the present case, it seems to me that its application to the facts of the case at bar cannot legitimize the continued exclusion of same-sex couples from the *FLA*'s spousal support regime.

[129] . . . [T]here is no evidence of any progress with respect to this group since the inception of the spousal support regime. If the legislature refuses to act so as to evolve towards *Charter* compliance then deference as to the timing of reforms loses its *raison d'être*.

[130] Moreover, in contrast to *Egan, supra*, where Sopinka J. relied in part on incrementalism in upholding the impugned legislation under s. 1 of the *Charter*, there is no concern regarding the financial implications of extending benefits to gay men and lesbians in the case at bar. As already pointed out, rather than increasing the strain on the public coffers, the extension will likely go some way toward alleviating those concerns because same-sex couples as a group will be less reliant on government welfare if the support scheme is available to them. Thus, I conclude that government incrementalism cannot constitute a reason to show deference to the legislature in the present case.

[131] Finally, as this Court has emphasized on other occasions, "[d]eference must not be carried to the point of relieving the government of the burden which the *Charter* places upon it of demonstrating that the limits it has imposed on guaranteed rights are reasonable and justifiable": *RJR-MacDonald, supra*, at para. 136, *per* McLachlin J. See also *Eldridge* [*v. British Columbia (Attorney General)*, [1997] 3 S.C.R. 624]; *Tétreault-Gadoury v. Canada (Employment and Immigration Commission)*, [1991] 2 S.C.R. 22; and *Vriend, supra*.

[132] In the present case, the government has failed to show that it had a reasonable basis for concluding that the rights of same-sex couples were impaired no more than was reasonably necessary to achieve its goals. The exclusion from the s. 29 definition of "spouse," and consequently from the *FLA* spousal support regime, is absolute. No effort has been made to tailor the limiting measure. I conclude that the appellant's case also fails at the minimal impairment stage of the s. 1 analysis.

(c) Proportionality Between the Effect
of the Measure and the Objective

[133] ... The damaging effects engendered by the exclusion of same-sex couples from s. 29 of the *FLA*, as noted by Cory J., are numerous and severe. Such harms cannot be justified where the statute has not achieved what it set out to do. Where, as here, the impugned measures actually undermine the objectives of the legislation it cannot be said that the deleterious effects of the measures are outweighed by the promotion of any laudable legislative goals, nor by the salutary effects of those measures.

[134] I therefore conclude that the exclusion of same-sex couples from s. 29 of the *FLA* cannot be justified as a reasonable limit on constitutional rights under s. 1 of the *Charter*. Before turning to a discussion of the appropriate remedy, I wish to emphasize, like Cory J., that the sole issue presented by this case is whether the *Charter* mandates that same-sex couples be accorded the right to apply for spousal support under the *FLA*. This appeal does not challenge traditional conceptions of marriage, as s. 29 of the Act expressly applies to *unmarried* opposite-sex couples. That being said, I do not wish to be understood as making any comment on marriage or indeed on related issues....

VI. Remedy

[136] ... In the court below, the words "a man and woman" were read out of the definition of "spouse" in s. 29 of the *FLA* and replaced with the words "two persons." The application of the order was suspended for a period of one year. With respect, I am not convinced that that is a suitable remedy in the circumstances of the present case....

[141] If the remedy adopted by the court below is allowed to stand, s. 29 of the *FLA* will entitle members of same-sex couples who otherwise qualify under the definition of "spouse" to apply for spousal support. However, any attempt to opt out of this regime by means of a cohabitation agreement provided for in s. 53 or a separation agreement set out in s. 54 would not be recognized under the Act. Both ss. 53 and 54 extend to common-law cohabitants but apply only to agreements entered into between "a man and woman." Any extension of s. 29 of the Act would have no effect upon these Part IV domestic contract provisions of the *FLA*, which do not rely upon the Part III definition of "spouse." Thus, same-sex partners would find themselves in the anomalous position of having no means of opting out of the default system of support rights. As this option is available to opposite-sex couples, and protects the ability of couples to choose to order their own affairs in a manner reflecting their own expectations, reading in would in effect remedy one constitutional wrong only to create another, and thereby fail to ensure the validity of the legislation.

[142] In addition, reading into the definition of "spouse" in s. 29 of the Act will have the effect of including same-sex couples in Part V of the *FLA* (Dependants' Claim for Damages), as that part of the Act relies upon the definition of "spouse" as it is defined in Part III. In my opinion, where reading in to one part of a statute will have significant repercussions for a separate and distinct scheme under that Act, it is not safe to assume that the legislature would have enacted the statute in its altered form. In such cases, reading in amounts to the making of *ad hoc* choices, which Lamer C.J. in *Schachter* [*v. Canada*, [1992] 2 S.C.R. 679], at p. 707, warned is properly the task of the legislatures, not the courts.

[143] In cases where reading in is inappropriate, the court must choose between striking down the legislation in its entirety and severing only the offending portions of the statute. As noted by Lamer C.J. in *Schachter*, at p. 697, "[w]here the offending portion of a statute can be defined in a limited manner it is consistent with legal principles to declare inoperative only that limited portion. In that way, as much of the legislative purpose as possible may be realized."

[144] In the case at bar, striking down the whole of the *FLA* would be excessive as only the definition of "spouse" in Part III of the Act has been found to violate the *Charter*. This is not a case where the parts of the legislative scheme which do offend the *Charter* are so inextricably bound up with the non-offending portions of the statute that what remains cannot independently survive. As a result, it would be safe to assume that the legislature would have passed the constitutionally sound parts of the statute without the unsound parts. See *Attorney-General for Alberta v. Attorney-General for Canada*, [1947] A.C. 503, at p. 518; *Schachter, supra*, at p. 697.

[145] On the basis of the foregoing, I conclude that severing s. 29 of the Act such that it alone is declared of no force or effect is the most appropriate remedy in the present case. This remedy should be temporarily suspended for a period of six months....

[147] ... I note that declaring s. 29 of the *FLA* to be of no force or effect may well affect numerous other statutes that rely upon a similar definition of the term "spouse." The legislature may wish to address the validity of these statutes in light of the unconstitutionality of s. 29 of the *FLA*. On this point, I agree with the majority of the Court of Appeal which noted that if left up to the courts, these issues could only be resolved on a case-by-case basis at great cost to private litigants and the public purse. Thus, I believe the legislature ought to be given some latitude in order to address these issues in a more comprehensive fashion....

GONTHIER J. (dissenting): . . .

[268] The *Charter* cannot possibly require the Legislative Assembly to revise the *FLA* to exclude non-procreative opposite-sex couples from its scope. As La Forest J. indicated, the legislative and administrative scheme necessary to do so would be highly intrusive and would likely violate *Charter* privacy guarantees. By contrast, exclusion of same-sex couples, who are inherently, rather than situationally, non-procreative, from the *FLA* support regime raises none of these concerns. . . .

[270] The entire issue in this appeal is whether the distinction drawn by the Legislative Assembly between cohabiting opposite-sex couples and all other relationships is maintainable. My colleagues' implicit suggestion is that the simplest way to render s. 29 constitutionally viable would be to restrict its application to married couples alone. I see no reason to conclude that the *Charter* operates so restrictively. Here, the Legislative Assembly has made a distinction on the basis of a fundamental biological and social reality to address a unique form of disadvantage specific to opposite-sex couples. On the other hand, if the Legislative Assembly is obliged to address all of the manifestations of economic interdependence between individuals, it is difficult to see how drawing the line to include same-sex couples, but to exclude those relationships which are not conjugal (and which can be similarly distinguished on enumerated or analogous grounds), can itself withstand constitutional challenge.

[271] It may be, of course, that extending the definition of "spouse" to include same-sex couples or other relationships or otherwise providing for support obligations based on dependency would be a prudent or reasonable policy decision. My colleague Iacobucci J.'s view, for example, is that to make this extension would advance what he sees as the purpose of the legislation. However, the wisdom or desirability of such an extension is not itself a matter properly within the consideration of this Court. The legislature itself considered the desirability of extending the scope of s. 29 to same-sex couples, but in the end, decided to the contrary. We must take seriously the contention that the legislation violates the *Charter*. Yet we must be careful not to jump from the assertion that a legislative change would be prudent to the contention that such a change is constitutionally mandated. In my view, my colleagues make that jump. For this reason, I respectfully disagree. . . .

[273] One of the fundamental principles in Canadian society is that individuals enjoy freedom and are expected to provide for their own needs. This rule is obviously not absolute. Canadians take pride in our social programs which lend a hand to those who, for differing reasons, cannot provide for themselves. At the same time, these social programs have specific policy goals, and in pursuit of those goals, they target specific groups of people. When the State provides assistance, only those who need the assistance should receive it. In this appeal, the impugned legislation sought to redress a historical fact that individuals in opposite-sex relationships suffer a *systemic* dynamic of dependence, which manifests in a support obligation that exists not only while the two individuals are in the relationship, but also after the relationship breaks down. Usually, it is the female partner who suffers the greatest burden upon marriage or common-law relationship breakdown: *Moge* [*v. Moge*, [1992] 3 S.C.R. 813]. The legislature has, since 1859, used a variety of legislative tools to alleviate this systemic suffering, which is unique to opposite-sex relationships. The statutory language, the preamble, and the legislative debates reveal that this legislation is one of those tools.

[274] In my view, the s. 15(1) claim in this case fails because s. 29 of the *FLA* seeks to ameliorate a historical and structural disadvantage specific to individuals in certain types of opposite-sex relationships, and in so doing, accurately corresponds with the needs, capacity, and circumstances of the claimant and these opposite-sex couples. Although individuals in same-sex relationships suffer pre-existing disadvantage in many areas of life, it has not been shown that this is one of them. In fact, the contrary has been shown: individuals in same-sex relationships generally exhibit less dependency in the relationship; they do not have a structural wage differential between the partners in the relationship; and they do not exhibit the same gendered division of domestic and child-care responsibilities. Although any of these elements may be present in a same-sex relationship, none will have been created by the structural dynamic of dependence which the legislature has seen fit to address, but rather will be attributable to the individual idiosyncrasies of the claimant.

[275] . . . The right to equality in s. 15(1) does not guarantee equality in the abstract; it rests on a comparison with others. This requires us to examine whether the claimant group suffers pre-existing disadvantage, stereotyping, prejudice or vulnerability *as compared with* the selected comparison group, and as related to the subject-matter of the legislation. In this case, individuals in same-sex relationships are not disadvantaged in relation to the dynamic of dependence which the legislation seeks to address. As such, the ameliorative purpose of the *FLA* is not underinclusive of a group which is disadvantaged in relation to that purpose. Moreover, although the claimant is affected by her exclusion from the mandatory support regime, this regime both confers a benefit *and* imposes a burden. Mandatory support restricts personal choice and reduces the concomitant financial advantages. The legislation does not render individuals in same-sex relationships "invisible." They are fully entitled to impose support obligations upon themselves, if they so choose. However, the circumstances unique to individuals in opposite-sex relationships

which warrant the reduction of that group's autonomy do not similarly exist in same-sex relationships.

[276] By analysing all of the contextual factors, it is apparent that the claimant's human dignity is not violated by s. 29 of the *FLA*. A reasonable person in the position of the claimant, having taken into account all of the contextual factors relevant to the claim, would not find their human dignity violated by a provision which appropriately takes into account their actual needs, capacity, and circumstances as compared to those of opposite-sex couples subject to the legislation. For these reasons, it is my view that the s. 15(1) claim must fail. . . .

[Justices Major and Bastarache wrote separate reasons that concurred with the majority's decision. Justice Major reached the result on a more narrow basis than the majority. Justice Bastarache differed with how the majority interpreted the purpose of the legislation.]

28 Auton v. British Columbia (Attorney General), 2004

An essential purpose of a bill of rights is to protect individuals from legislation, or the conduct of those acting on behalf of the state, where decisions or actions interfere with protected rights. In this sense, the protection offered by bills of rights is most often construed in a negative sense as providing *freedom from* state actions that interfere with rights. But the claim made in *Auton* represented a different view of rights. It rested on a more positive interpretation in the sense that the *Charter* confers the *right to* receive a social policy entitlement that the legislature had not intended to provide.

The question whether the *Charter* should protect positive rights is sharply contested. Critics of the idea of interpreting *Charter* rights in positive terms argue that reasonable, rights-respecting people will disagree about the meaning or scope of these rights or the extent of the state's obligation to provide publicly funded programs or services to facilitate positive rights. For this reason, they believe there is little justification in asking judges to define positive rights, which require value-laden decisions that ultimately have little to do with the legal training or interpretive duties normally associated with judicial review. Moreover, since the recognition of social rights ultimately implicates the full range of a legislature's decisions about how best to allocate limited resources, judgments about allocating social benefits should be made by Parliament so that they can be reviewed and revised to correspond to changes in the nation's circumstances and priorities. In contrast, supporters of justiciable social and economic rights argue that a negative approach to rights is too restrictive and will not provide the necessary conditions for realizing equality. They also suggest that the distinction between negative and positive rights is not as clear as critics of positive rights would suggest. Negative interpretations of rights often have financial implications for the state, particularly if a government incurs substantial costs in order to comply with a judicially authorized remedy. For example, following the Supreme Court's ruling that equality was violated in *M. v. H.*[1] (the equality claim was based on the differential treatment resulting from the interpretation of "spouse" in the Ontario *Family Law Act*), provincial and federal governments incurred financial costs to overhaul hundreds of laws to include same-sex partners in recognition and benefit schemes.

The Supreme Court has been reluctant to recognize social rights under the *Charter*. Although on several occasions the Court has ruled that existing legislation must be modified to address discrimination or other *Charter* violations, the Court has not been prepared to rule that *Charter* rights are implicated because Parliament or a provincial legislature has failed to introduce legislation that would create new benefits. This reluctance was obvious in this case. The overarching issue in *Auton* was whether a province's public health plan under the *Canada Health Act* is required to provide a particular health treatment beyond what is considered a "core" service administered by doctors and hospitals. More specifically, the question was whether the B.C. government's refusal to fund a particular form of therapy for preschool-aged autistic children violates equality. The provincial health plan makes a distinction between "core" services, as required by the *Canada Health Act*, and non-core

---

1   [1999] 2 S.C.R. 3.

services, which the government provides at its discretion. Some non-core services that are entitled for partial public funding are those provided by chiropractors, dentists, optometrists, podiatrists, physical therapists, massage therapists, and naturopathic doctors. The treatment in question was designated as a non-core service. This is a controversial and expensive form of behavioural therapy for young autistic children (applied behavioural analysis [ABA] or intensive behavioural intervention [IBI]). Although some limited forms of this treatment were funded, there was no funding for intensive, universal treatment for all autistic children between the ages of three and six.

Those arguing that the province's public health plan discriminates against autistic children believed that an earlier Supreme Court ruling supported their position. This earlier decision was *Eldridge v. British Columbia (Attorney General)*,[2] where the Court ruled that the province was required to provide translators for deaf people attempting to access hospital services, even though legislation did not explicitly authorize this. But the Court disagreed that *Eldridge* supports the *Charter* claim made in *Auton*. It characterized the *Eldridge* case as being concerned with unequal access to a benefit that the legislation had conferred, whereas the *Auton* case was said to involve access to a benefit that the legislation had not granted. The Court suggested that despite its sympathy for the petitioners it was not for the Court to decide "what the public health system should provide," which was a matter for Parliament or the legislature. As the Court stated, the health plan "does not promise that any Canadian will receive funding for all medically required treatment. All that is conferred is core funding for services provided by medical practitioners." Funding for non-core services is at the government's discretion and thus the "benefit here claimed—funding for all medically required services—was not provided for by the law." But this explanation did not address an important dimension of the *Charter* claim made in *Auton*: that discrimination arises from the discretionary legislative decision to provide some non-core services for non-disabled children or adults with mental illness while deciding not to fund ABA/IBI therapy to autistic children. In addressing the argument that the denial of this therapy constitutes a *Charter* violation, the Court advanced a narrow, technical view of how to determine whether discrimination has occurred. Lawyers arguing on behalf of autistic children had argued that the Court should compare the services provided to autistic children with those services provided to non-disabled children or to adults with mental illness. But the Court disagreed, ruling that the decision about whether discrimination has occurred concerns whether the legislation treats autistic children differently than it does a "non-disabled person or a person suffering a disability other than a mental disability (here autism) seeking or receiving funding for a non-core therapy important for his or her present and future health, which is emergent and only recently becoming recognized as medically required."

The federal and seven provincial Attorneys General intervened in the case, no doubt aware of the implications a positive ruling in this case could have had for provincial health budgets. Reaction to the Supreme Court's decision in *Auton* was mixed. While some commentators approved of the decision, because of apprehension about the fiscal implications this decision would have should the Court recognize *Charter* claims for services under the public health system, others believed the court's approach to what constitutes discrimination in this case was overly restrictive. ∼

2 [1997] 3 S.C.R. 624.

Discussion Questions

1. Was the Supreme Court persuasive when explaining why its ruling in *Eldridge* did not support the rights claim made in *Auton*?

2. Should the *Charter* be interpreted as protecting positive rights? How would interpreting the *Charter* to recognize positive rights change the judicial role?

3. Is the government justified in its decision to fund some non-core services and yet not fund therapy for autistic children? Whose role is it to decide?

AUTON (GUARDIAN AD LITEM OF) v. BRITISH COLUMBIA (ATTORNEY GENERAL)
2004 SCC 78, [2004] 3 S.C.R. 657

Hearing: June 9, 2004; Judgment: November 19, 2004.

Present: McLachlin C.J. and Major, Bastarache, Binnie, LeBel, Deschamps, and Fish JJ.

Interveners: Attorney General of Canada, Attorney General of Ontario, Attorney General of Quebec, Attorney General of Nova Scotia, Attorney General of New Brunswick, Attorney General of Prince Edward Island, Attorney General of Alberta, Attorney General of Newfoundland and Labrador, Canadian Association for Community Living and Council of Canadians with Disabilities, Women's Legal Education and Action Fund and DisAbled Women's Network Canada, Autism Society Canada, Michelle Dawson, Families for Effective Autism Treatment of Alberta Foundation, Friends of Children with Autism, and Families for Early Autism Treatment of Ontario.

The judgment of the Court was delivered by

THE CHIEF JUSTICE:

I. Introduction

[1] This case raises the issue of whether the Province of British Columbia's refusal to fund a particular treatment for preschool-aged autistic children violates the right to equality under the *Canadian Charter of Rights and Freedoms*. The petitioners are autistic children and their parents. They argue that the government's failure to fund applied behavioral therapy for autism unjustifiably discriminated against them. In the background lies the larger issue of when, if ever, a province's public health plan under the *Canada Health Act*, R.S.C. 1985, c. C-6 ("*CHA*"), is required to provide a particular health treatment outside the "core" services administered by doctors and hospitals.

[2] One sympathizes with the petitioners, and with the decisions below ordering the public health system to pay for their therapy. However, the issue before us is not what the public health system should provide, which is a matter for Parliament and the legislature. The issue is rather whether the British Columbia Government's failure to fund these services under the health plan amounted to an unequal and discriminatory denial of benefits under that plan, contrary to s. 15 of the *Charter*. Despite their forceful argument, the petitioners fail to establish that the denial of benefits violated the *Charter*.

[3] The government must provide the services authorized by law in a non-discriminatory manner. Here, however, discrimination has not been established. First, the claim for discrimination is based on the erroneous assumption that the

CHA and the relevant British Columbia legislation provided the benefit claimed. Second, on the facts here and applying the appropriate comparator, it is not established that the government excluded autistic children on the basis of disability. For these reasons, the claim fails and the appeal is allowed.

II. History of the Case

[4] The four infant petitioners suffer from autism, a neuro-behavioural syndrome caused by a dysfunction of the central nervous system that impairs social interaction, hinders communication and results in repetitive, stereotyped behaviour. The symptoms and effects of autism vary from mild to severe. Over 90 percent of untreated autistic children end up in group homes or other residential facilities.

[5] The cause and cure of autism remain unknown. However, a 1987 study published by a Texas researcher, Dr. O. Ivar Lovaas, suggested that applied behavioural therapy based on the repetitive use of stimuli and emphasized cues might help some autistic children between ages three and six. The therapy is intensive and therefore expensive—between $45,000 and $60,000 per year. It is not always successful; the trial judge found only that in "some cases" it may produce "significant results" ((2000), 78 B.C.L.R. (3d) 55, 2000 BCSC 1142, at para. 51). While increasingly accepted, Applied Behavioural Analysis ("ABA") or Intensive Behavioural Intervention ("IBI") therapy is not uncontroversial. Objections range from its reliance in its early years on crude and arguably painful stimuli, to its goal of changing the child's mind and personality. Indeed one of the interveners in this appeal, herself an autistic person, argues against the therapy.

[6] The infant petitioners received Lovaas therapy. Their parents, the adult petitioners, funded the treatment, although Connor Auton's mother ultimately became unable to continue for financial reasons. Until the government forbade it on the ground that new options were being evaluated, some families used funds for support services from the Ministry of Children and Families to help finance Lovaas therapy for their children with the tacit support of Ministry workers in some regions. Over a period of years, the petitioners and others lobbied the Ministers of Health, of Education, and of Children and Families for funding for Lovaas therapy, without success. In 1995, the petitioners commenced this action.

[7] In the years leading up to the trial in 2000, the government funded a number of programs for autistic children and their families. This was done through the Ministry of Children and Families, which in 1997 had been given responsibility for child and youth mental health. The programs included infant development, supported child care, at-home respite, respite relief, contracted respite, occupational therapy, physical therapy, speech and language therapy, homemaker and home support

services, hearing services, child care workers and specific behavioural support. Under the latter category, some programs attempted to positively treat autism. The Ministry provided services to autistic children through contracted agencies, some of which employed some behavioural analysis techniques. However, the focus was on teaching families the techniques to enable them to work themselves with the children.

[8] An early intervention ABA/IBI program called LEAP had been established in Ladner but it was underfunded and equipped to serve only six children. Other centres and groups provided some ABA/IBI but the Crown's expert, Dr. Glen Davies, testified that these programs were not intensive, not delivered early enough in the child's development, and were rarely of sufficient duration to maximize the child's development. Finally, in May 1999, the Ministry announced an Autism Action Plan and an Autism Action Implementation Plan, which acknowledged the importance of early intervention, diagnosis and assessment, but stated that services for autistic children had to be balanced with services to children with other special needs. Moreover, the plan did not specifically target ABA/IBI therapy. As of the date of trial a year or so later, the Ministry had not produced much. No new funding had been provided and a concrete plan for intensive early treatment remained to be developed.

[9] In a nutshell, at the time of trial the government funded a number of programs for young autistic children, and appeared to be moving toward funding some form of early intervention therapy. However, it had not established funding for intensive, universal ABA/IBI therapy available to all autistic children between the ages of three and six.

[10] This delay appears to have been due to a number of factors. The first was the 1997 decision to transfer child and youth mental health from the Ministry of Health to the Ministry of Children and Families, which put a non-medical slant on treatment. The second was financial constraint: in 1998, the deputy ministers of the ministries of Health, Education, and Children and Families informed families that the government was not "in a resource position" to fund ABA/IBI therapy.

[11] A final factor may have been the emergent and somewhat controversial nature of ABA/IBI therapy, although by the time of the trial the evidence was sufficient to convince the trial judge that it was "medically necessary." . . .

III. Analysis

. . . [20] This case engages s. 15's guarantee of "equal benefit of the law without discrimination . . . based on . . . mental . . . disability."

[21] Different cases have formulated the requirements for a successful s. 15(1) claim in different ways. Nevertheless, there is "broad agreement on the general analytic framework":

Eldridge v. British Columbia (Attorney General), [1997] 3 S.C.R. 624, at para. 58. In *Andrews v. Law Society of British Columbia*, [1989] 1 S.C.R. 143, at pp. 168 *et seq.*—this Court's seminal statement on the interpretation of s. 15(1)—the s. 15 analysis was described in two steps: first, whether there is unequal treatment under the law; and, second, whether the treatment is discriminatory. . . .

[22] The dual requirements of *Andrews*, *supra*, and *Eldridge*, *supra*, were broken into three requirements in *Law v. Canada (Minister of Employment and Immigration)*, [1999] 1 S.C.R. 497, at para. 88: (1) differential treatment under the law; (2) on the basis of an enumerated or analogous ground; (3) which constitutes discrimination.

[23] There is no magic in a particular statement of the elements that must be established to prove a claim under s. 15(1). It is the words of the provision that must guide. Different cases will raise different issues. In this case, as will be discussed, an issue arises as to whether the benefit claimed is one provided by the law. The important thing is to ensure that all the requirements of s. 15(1), as they apply to the case at hand, are met.

[24] A complicating factor is that however one states the requirements for s. 15(1), they inevitably overlap. For example, the nature of the benefit, the enumerated or analogous ground at issue, and the choice of a correct comparator play a role in all three steps: see *Hodge v. Canada (Minister of Human Resources Development)*, [2004] 3 S.C.R. 357, 2004 SCC 65. Frameworks thus do not describe discreet linear steps; rather, they serve as a guide to ensure that the language and purpose of s. 15(1) are respected.

[25] Whatever framework is used, an overly technical approach to s. 15(1) is to be avoided. In *Andrews*, *supra*, at pp. 168-69, McIntyre J. warned against adopting a narrow, formalistic analytical approach, and stressed the need to look at equality issues substantively and contextually. The Court must look at the reality of the situation and assess whether there has been discriminatory treatment having regard to the purpose of s. 15(1), which is to prevent the perpetuation of pre-existing disadvantage through unequal treatment.

[26] In this case, the following issues arise from an application of the language of s. 15(1) to the facts:

(1) Is the claim for a benefit *provided by law*? If not, what relevant benefit is provided by law?

(2) Was the relevant benefit denied to the claimants while being granted to a comparator group alike in all ways relevant to benefit, except for the personal characteristic associated with an enumerated or analogous ground?

(3) If the claimants succeed on the first two issues, is discrimination established by showing that the

distinction denied their equal human worth and human dignity?

(1) Is the Claim for a Benefit Provided by Law?

[27] In order to succeed, the claimants must show unequal treatment under the law—more specifically that they failed to receive a benefit that the law provided, or was saddled with a burden the law did not impose on someone else. The primary and oft-stated goal of s. 15(1) is to combat discrimination and ameliorate the position of disadvantaged groups within society. Its specific promise, however, is confined to benefits and burdens "of the law." Combatting discrimination and ameliorating the position of members of disadvantaged groups is a formidable task and demands a multi-pronged response. Section 15(1) is part of that response. Section 15(2)'s exemption for affirmative action programs is another prong of the response. Beyond these lie a host of initiatives that governments, organizations and individuals can undertake to ameliorate the position of members of disadvantaged groups.

[28] The specific role of s. 15(1) in achieving this objective is to ensure that when governments choose to enact benefits or burdens, they do so on a non-discriminatory basis. This confines s. 15(1) claims to benefits and burdens imposed by law....

[29] Most s. 15(1) claims relate to a clear statutory benefit or burden. Consequently, the need for the benefit claimed or burden imposed to emanate from law has not been much discussed. Nevertheless, the language of s. 15(1) as well as the jurisprudence demand that it be met before a s. 15(1) claim can succeed.

[30] In this case, the issue of whether the benefit claimed is one conferred by law does arise, and must be carefully considered. The claim, as discussed, is for funding for a "medically necessary" treatment. The unequal treatment is said to lie in funding medically required treatments for non-disabled Canadian children or adults with mental illness, while refusing to fund medically required ABA/IBI therapy to autistic children. The decisions under appeal proceeded on this basis. The trial judge, affirmed by the Court of Appeal, ruled that the discrimination lay in denying a "medically necessary" service to a disadvantaged group while providing "medically necessary" services for others. Thus the benefit claimed, in essence, is funding for all medically required treatment.

[31] This raises the question of whether the legislative scheme in fact provides anyone with all medically required treatment. An examination of the scheme shows that it does not....

[32] The scheme designates two distinct categories of funded treatment based on service. First, the scheme provides complete funding for services delivered by medical practitioners, referred to as "core" services. This is required by the *CHA*. Many medically necessary or required services, including ABA/IBI therapy for autistic children, fall outside this core.

[33] Secondly, the *CHA* permits the provinces at their discretion to fund non-core medical services—services that are not delivered by physicians. British Columbia does this by naming classes of "health care practitioners" whose services may be partially funded. It then falls to the Medical Services Commission, an administrative body, to designate particular practitioners and procedures within these categories for funding.

[34] It was suggested that the reference by the *Medicare Protection Act*, R.S.B.C. 1996, c. 286 ("*MPA*"), to "medically required" services is an indication that all medically required or necessary non-core services must be funded. However, the Act does not say this. Section 1 uses the phrase "medically required services" in conjunction with the services of doctors or "medical practitioners" or an "approved diagnostic facility" (s. 1 "benefits," paras. (a) and (c)). Only these services are funded on the basis of being "medically required." "Medically required" in the *MPA* does not touch the services of "health care practitioners" which are funded only if the Province chooses to place a class of health care practitioner on an "enrolled" list by legislation or regulation....

[35] In summary, the legislative scheme does not promise that any Canadian will receive funding for all medically required treatment. All that is conferred is core funding for services provided by medical practitioners, with funding for non-core services left to the Province's discretion. Thus, the benefit here claimed—funding for all medically required services—was not provided for by the law.

[36] More specifically, the law did not provide funding for ABA/IBI therapy for autistic children. The British Columbia *MPA* authorized partial funding for the services of the following health care practitioners: chiropractors, dentists, optometrists, podiatrists, physical therapists, massage therapists and naturopathic doctors. In addition, provincial regulations authorized funding for the services of physical therapists, massage therapists and nurses. At the time of trial, the Province had not named providers of ABA/IBI therapy as "health care practitioners," whose services could be funded under the plan.

[37] It followed that the Medical Services Commission, charged with administration of the *MPA*, had no power to order funding for ABA/IBI therapy. The Commission, as an administrative body, had no authority to enlarge the class of "health care practitioners." That could be done only by the government. Since the government had not designated ABA/IBI therapists as "health care practitioners," the Commission was not permitted to list their services for funding. This is how things stood at the time of trial. British Columbia's law

governing non-core benefits did not provide the benefit that the petitioners were seeking.

[38] The petitioners rely on *Eldridge* in arguing for equal provision of medical benefits. In *Eldridge*, this Court held that the Province was obliged to provide translators to the deaf so that they could have equal access to core benefits accorded to everyone under the British Columbia medicare scheme. The decision proceeded on the basis that the law provided the benefits at issue—physician-delivered consultation and maternity care. However, by failing to provide translation services for the deaf, the Province effectively denied to one group of disabled people the benefit it had granted by law. *Eldridge* was concerned with unequal access to a benefit that the law conferred and with *applying* a benefit-granting law in a non-discriminatory fashion. By contrast, this case is concerned with access to a benefit that the law has not conferred. For this reason, *Eldridge* does not assist the petitioners.

[39] However, this does not end the inquiry. Courts should look to the reality of the situation to see whether the claimants have been denied benefits of the legislative scheme other than those they have raised. This brings up the broader issue of whether the legislative scheme is discriminatory, since it provides non-core services to some groups while denying funding for ABA/IBI therapy to autistic children. The allegation is that the scheme is itself discriminatory, by funding some non-core therapies while denying equally necessary ABA/IBI therapy.

[40] . . . We must look behind the words and ask whether the statutory definition is itself a means of perpetuating inequality rather than alleviating it. Section 15(1) requires not merely formal equality, but substantive equality: *Andrews, supra*, at p. 166.

[41] It is not open to Parliament or a legislature to enact a law whose policy objectives and provisions single out a disadvantaged group for inferior treatment: *Corbiere v. Canada (Minister of Indian and Northern Affairs)*, [1999] 2 S.C.R. 203. On the other hand, a legislative choice not to accord a particular benefit absent demonstration of discriminatory purpose, policy or effect does not offend this principle and does not give rise to s. 15(1) review. This Court has repeatedly held that the legislature is under no obligation to create a particular benefit. It is free to target the social programs it wishes to fund as a matter of public policy, provided the benefit itself is not conferred in a discriminatory manner: *Granovsky v. Canada (Minister of Employment and Immigration)*, [2000] 1 S.C.R. 703, 2000 SCC 28, at para. 61; *Nova Scotia (Attorney General) v. Walsh*, [2002] 4 S.C.R. 325, 2002 SCC 83, at para. 55; *Hodge, supra*, at para. 16.

[42] A statutory scheme may discriminate either directly, by adopting a discriminatory policy or purpose, or indirectly, by effect. Direct discrimination on the face of a statute or in its policy is readily identifiable and poses little difficulty. Discrimination by effect is more difficult to identify. Where stereotyping of persons belonging to a group is at issue, assessing whether a statutory definition that excludes a group is discriminatory, as opposed to being the legitimate exercise of legislative power in defining a benefit, involves consideration of the purpose of the legislative scheme which confers the benefit and the overall needs it seeks to meet. If a benefit program excludes a particular group in a way that undercuts the overall purpose of the program, then it is likely to be discriminatory: it amounts to an arbitrary exclusion of a particular group. If, on the other hand, the exclusion is consistent with the overarching purpose and scheme of the legislation, it is unlikely to be discriminatory. Thus, the question is whether the excluded benefit is one that falls within the general scheme of benefits and needs which the legislative scheme is intended to address.

[43] The legislative scheme in the case at bar, namely the *CHA* and the *MPA*, does not have as its purpose the meeting of all medical needs. As discussed, its only promise is to provide full funding for core services, defined as physician-delivered services. Beyond this, the provinces may, within their discretion, offer specified non-core services. It is, by its very terms, a partial health plan. It follows that exclusion of particular non-core services cannot, without more, be viewed as an adverse distinction based on an enumerated ground. Rather, it is an anticipated feature of the legislative scheme. It follows that one cannot infer from the fact of exclusion of ABA/IBI therapy for autistic children from non-core benefits that this amounts to discrimination. There is no discrimination by effect.

[44] The correctness of this conclusion may be tested by considering the consequences to the legislative scheme of obliging provinces to provide non-core medical services required by disabled persons and people associated with other enumerated and analogous grounds, like gender and age. Subject to a finding of no discrimination at the third step, a class of people legally entitled to non-core benefits would be created. This would effectively amend the medicare scheme and extend benefits beyond what it envisions—core physician-provided benefits plus non-core benefits at the discretion of the Province.

[45] Had the situation been different, the petitioners might have attempted to frame their legal action as a claim to the benefit of equal application of the law by the Medical Services Commission. This would not have been a substantive claim for funding for particular medical services, but a procedural claim anchored in the assertion that benefits provided by the law were not distributed in an equal fashion. Such a

claim, if made out, would be supported by *Eldridge, supra.* The argument would be that the Medical Services Commission violated s. 15(1) by approving non-core services for non-disabled people, while denying equivalent services to autistic children and their families.

[46] Such a claim depends on a prior showing that there is a benefit provided by law. There can be no administrative duty to distribute non-existent benefits equally. Had the legislature designated ABA/IBI therapists (or a broader group of therapists which included them) as "health care practitioners" under the *MPA* at the time of trial, this would have amounted to a legislated benefit, which the Commission would be charged with implementing. The Commission would then have been obliged to implement that benefit in a non-discriminatory fashion. However, this is not the case. Here, the legislature had not legislated funding for the benefit in question, and the Commission had no power to deal with it.

[47] I conclude that the benefit claimed, no matter how it is viewed, is not a benefit provided by law. This is sufficient to end the inquiry. However, since this is the first case of this type to reach this Court, it is appropriate to consider whether the petitioners would have succeeded had they established that ABA/IBI therapy was a benefit provided by law, by being designated as a non-core benefit.

(2) Denial of a Benefit Granted to a Comparator Group, on an Enumerated or Analogous Ground

[48] This question first requires us to determine the appropriate comparator group, and then to ask whether, as compared with people in that group, the petitioners have been denied a benefit.

[49] The first task is to determine the appropriate comparator group. The petitioners suggested that they should be compared with non-disabled children and their parents, as well as adult persons with mental illness. A closer look reveals problems with both suggested comparators.

[50] The law pertaining to the choice of comparators . . . establishes the following propositions.

[51] First, the choice of the correct comparator is crucial, since the comparison between the claimants and this group permeates every stage of the analysis. "[M]isidentification of the proper comparator group at the outset can doom the outcome of the whole s. 15(1) analysis": *Hodge, supra,* at para. 18.

[52] Second, while the starting point is the comparator chosen by the claimants, the Court must ensure that the comparator is appropriate and should substitute an appropriate comparator if the one chosen by the claimants is not appropriate: *Hodge, supra,* at para. 20.

[53] Third, the comparator group should mirror the characteristics of the claimant or claimant group relevant to

the benefit or advantage sought, except for the personal characteristic related to the enumerated or analogous ground raised as the basis for the discrimination: *Hodge, supra,* at para. 23. The comparator must align with both the benefit and the "universe of people potentially entitled" to it and the alleged ground of discrimination: *Hodge,* at paras. 25 and 31.

[54] Fourth, a claimant relying on a personal characteristic related to the enumerated ground of disability may invite comparison with the treatment of those suffering a different type of disability, or a disability of greater severity: *Hodge, supra,* at paras. 28 and 32. Examples of the former include the differential treatment of those suffering mental disability from those suffering physical disability in *Battlefords and District Co-operative Ltd. v. Gibbs,* [1996] 3 S.C.R. 566, and the differential treatment of those suffering chronic pain from those suffering other workplace injuries in *Nova Scotia (Workers' Compensation Board) v. Martin,* [2003] 2 S.C.R. 504, 2003 SCC 54. An example of the latter is the treatment of persons with temporary disabilities compared with those suffering permanent disabilities in *Granovsky, supra.*

[55] Applying these criteria, I conclude that the appropriate comparator for the petitioners is a non-disabled person or a person suffering a disability other than a mental disability (here autism) seeking or receiving funding for a non-core therapy important for his or her present and future health, which is emergent and only recently becoming recognized as medically required. It will be recalled that in many jurisdictions ABA/IBI therapy remained unfunded at the time of trial. Indeed, it was only in the year preceding the trial that two Canadian provinces had authorized funding for ABA/IBI therapy to autistic children. The comparators, as noted, must be like the claimants in all ways save for characteristics relating to the alleged ground of discrimination. People receiving well-established non-core therapies are not in the same position as people claiming relatively new non-core benefits. Funding may be legitimately denied or delayed because of uncertainty about a program and administrative difficulties related to its recognition and implementation. This has nothing to do with the alleged ground of discrimination. It follows that comparison with those receiving established therapies is inapt.

[56] The petitioners' comparators were deficient in that they focussed on the non-existent medical benefit of medically required care, as discussed above. However, even if I were to assume that the benefit is one provided by law—more particularly, that the B.C. legislation had listed ABA/IBI therapists as "health care practitioners" whose services could be considered funded benefits—the petitioners' comparators would still be deficient, because they have left the recent and emergent nature of ABA/IBI therapy out of the equation. This error was replicated in the decisions below.

[57] The remaining question is whether, applying the appropriate comparator, the claimant or claimant group was denied a benefit made available to the comparator group. Differential treatment having regard to the appropriate comparator may be established either by showing an explicit distinction (direct discrimination) or by showing that the effect of the government action amounted to singling the claimant out for less advantageous treatment on the basis of the alleged ground of discrimination (indirect discrimination). In indirect discrimination, the terms on which the claimants are denied the benefit operate as a proxy for their group status. For example, in *British Columbia (Public Service Employee Relations Commission) v. BCGSEU*, [1999] 3 S.C.R. 3, facially neutral physical requirements for firefighters were set at aerobic levels not generally attainable by female firefighters—levels, moreover, which were not required for performance of the job. The specified aerobic levels made no mention of gender. On their face, they did not discriminate. Yet, in effect, they excluded women, not on the basis of ability to do the job, but on the basis of gender. The aerobic levels served as a proxy for gender. Hence, they were held to discriminate on the basis of gender.

[58] As discussed, the appropriate comparator in this case is a member of a non-disabled group or a person suffering a disability other than a mental disability that requests or receives funding for non-core therapy important to present and future health, but which is emergent and only recently becoming recognized as medically required. On the evidence adduced here, differential treatment either directly or by effect is not established. There was no evidence of how the Province had responded to requests for new therapies or treatments by non-disabled or otherwise disabled people. We know that it was slow in responding to the demands for ABA/IBI funding for autistic children. But we do not know whether it acted in a similar manner with respect to other new therapies.

[59] Indeed, the conduct of the government considered in the context of the emergent nature of ABA/IBI therapy for autistic children raises doubts about whether there was a real denial or differential treatment of autistic children. The government put in place a number of programs, albeit not intensive ABA/IBI therapy, directed to helping autistic children and their families. In the year before the trial, the government had announced an Autism Action Plan and an Autism Action Implementation Plan which acknowledged the importance of early intervention, diagnosis and assessment. The government's failing was to delay putting in place what was emerging in the late-1990s as the most, indeed the only known, effective therapy for autism, while continuing to fund increasingly discredited treatments.

[60] As discussed earlier, the delay in providing funding for ABA/IBI therapy seems to have been related to three factors. The first was the inauspicious decision to transfer child and youth mental health from the Ministry of Health to the Ministry of Children and Families, which meant that the decision makers lacked medical and psychiatric expertise and viewed autism from a social rather than medical perspective. The second was financial concerns and competing claims on insufficient resources. The third was the emergent nature of the recognition that ABA/IBI therapy was appropriate and medically required.

[61] With hindsight, it is possible to say that the government should have moved more quickly. But on the evidence before us, it is difficult to say that the government in purpose or effect put autistic children and their families "on the back burner" when compared to non-disabled or otherwise disabled groups seeking emergent therapies. Rather, to use the trial judge's phrase, the government's failing was that its actions to that point did not meet the "gold standard of scientific methodology" ((2000), 78 B.C.L.R. (3d) 55, at para. 66).

[62] The issue, however, is not whether the government met the gold standard of scientific methodology, but whether it denied autistic people benefits it accorded to others in the same situation, save for mental disability. There is no evidence suggesting that the government's approach to ABA/IBI therapy was different than its approach to other comparable, novel therapies for non-disabled persons or persons with a different type of disability. In the absence of such evidence, a finding of discrimination cannot be sustained.

(3) Discrimination

[63] If differential denial of a benefit provided by law on a ground enumerated in s. 15(1) or analogous thereto were established, it would still be necessary to examine whether the distinction was discriminatory in the sense of treating autistic children as second-class citizens and denying their fundamental human dignity. The failure to establish the basis for a claim for discrimination deprives us of the necessary foundation for this final inquiry.

B. Did the Government's Conduct Infringe the Petitioners' Rights Under Section 7 of the Charter?

[64] Section 7 of the *Charter* provides:

> Everyone has the right to life, liberty and security of the person and the right not to be deprived thereof except in accordance with the principles of fundamental justice.

... [67] [T]he limited submissions before us do not permit us to conclude that the government's conduct in the case at bar infringed the petitioners' s. 7 rights.

IV. Conclusion

... [69] I would answer the constitutional questions as follows:

1. Do the definitions of "benefits" and "health care practitioner" in s. 1 of the *Medicare Protection Act*, R.S.B.C. 1996, c. 286, and ss. 17-29 of the *Medical and Health Care Services Regulation*, B.C. Reg. 426/97, infringe s. 15(1) of the *Canadian Charter of Rights and Freedoms* by failing to include services for autistic children based on applied behavioural analysis?

No.

2. If so, is the infringement a reasonable limit prescribed by law as can be demonstrably justified in a free and democratic society under s. 1 of the *Canadian Charter of Rights and Freedoms*?

It is unnecessary to answer this question.

3. Do the definitions of "benefits" and "health care practitioner" in s. 1 of the *Medicare Protection Act*, R.S.B.C. 1996, c. 286, and ss. 17-29 of the *Medical and Health Care Services Regulation*, B.C. Reg. 426/97, infringe s. 7 of the *Canadian Charter of Rights and Freedoms* by failing to include services for autistic children based on applied behavioural analysis?

No.

4. If so, is the infringement a reasonable limit prescribed by law as can be demonstrably justified in a free and democratic society under s. 1 of the *Canadian Charter of Rights and Freedoms*?

It is unnecessary to answer this question. . . . .

29 Newfoundland (Treasury Board) v. N.A.P.E., 2004

It is often argued that the essence of constitutional law is the idea of justification, the notion that government action must be justified on the basis of principles commanding broad and rational consent. In this understanding, constitutions do not so much limit state power as provide for its legitimate exercise.

In Canada, this principle is embodied in section 1 of the *Charter*, which declares that *Charter* rights are "subject only to such reasonable limits prescribed by law as can be demonstrably justified in a free and democratic society." Two important questions are raised by the principle of justification. First, what standard of justification shall govern? Second, to whom is government responsible for justifying infringements of rights?

As for the standard of justification, the Supreme Court in *R. v. Oakes* made it clear that governments would have a relatively onerous standard to meet. While the civil standard of proof (proof on a balance or preponderance of probabilities, to be contrasted with the criminal standard, which is proof beyond a reasonable doubt) would apply and, while "there exist different degrees of probability depending on the nature of the case," nonetheless, "the preponderance of probability test must be applied rigorously," recognizing that the impugned limit "violates constitutional rights and freedoms—rights and freedoms which are part of the supreme law of Canada."[1] One step in the "*Oakes* test," the minimal-impairment test, provides that the legislative limit on a right must impair the right "as little as possible" while still advancing the government's legitimate objective.

This was a high bar for a government to meet, and almost as soon as the test was enunciated, the Court introduced subtle glosses. In *Edwards Books*, the minimal-impairment test was downgraded to a requirement that governments must impair rights "as little as reasonably possible."[2] In *Irwin Toy*, the Court introduced a distinction between legislation in which the state is arrayed as a "singular antagonist" against the individual rights bearer and legislation in which the state "mediates between the competing claims of different groups in the community."[3] In latter instances, a more deferential judicial approach to the government's justificatory burden is appropriate. In former cases—prototypically criminal cases—a stringent section 1 standard is imposed on government. In *Keegstra*, involving the constitutionality of anti-hate speech provisions of the *Criminal Code*, the Court went further by drawing distinctions between different types of criminal provisions and relaxing the burden on the state regarding criminal provisions that advance multicultural tolerance and the status of different vulnerable groups (like the anti-hate provisions of the *Criminal Code*), but maintaining a stringent *Oakes* standard in cases involving legal rights of accused persons.[4]

---

1 *R. v. Oakes*, case 14.

2 *R. v. Edwards Books and Art Ltd.*, [1986] 2 S.C.R. 713 at 772.

3 *Irwin Toy Ltd v. Quebec (Attorney General)*, [1989] 1 S.C.R. 927 at 990.

4 *R. v. Keegstra*, case 5.

But in *RJR-MacDonald*, involving the constitutionality of federal legislation banning most tobacco advertising, a majority of the Court cautioned against carrying the idea of deference to the legislature too far. "While remaining sensitive to the social and political context of the impugned law and allowing for difficulties of proof inherent in that context," wrote Justice McLachlin, "the courts must nevertheless insist that before the state can override constitutional rights, there be a reasoned demonstration of the good which the law may achieve in relation to the seriousness of the infringement. It is the task of the courts to maintain this bottom line if the rights conferred by our constitution are to have force and meaning."[5]

This brief survey indicates that the standard of section 1 justification has varied with the circumstances of *Charter* cases and with particular judges. For instance, Justice La Forest generally applied section 1 deferentially, while Chief Justice McLachlin has often imposed a stringent justificatory standard on the state.

The second question concerns lines of accountability in a constitutional democracy. On the one hand, judicial review exists to ensure governments do not trample people's *Charter* rights, even when pursuing legitimate policy objectives. Democratic governments, after all, are capable of intemperate, excessive responses to policy problems. On the other hand, governments are democratically elected and accountable to electors for their conduct while in office. Further, public policies rarely infringe rights flagrantly and obviously; usually, they limit rights (as all rights must be limited) to advance other worthy state objectives. It is not clear that courts are better equipped than other institutions of government to evaluate the constitutional merits of such complex policies. In such cases, judicial deference to the legislature would seem appropriate.

The following decision brings these two questions together by raising once again the prospect that certain "political questions" warrant judicial deference. Early in the *Charter* era, the Supreme Court dismissed the American political-questions doctrine, according to which certain kinds of state action—mainly relating to foreign policy—are the preserve of non-judicial branches.[6] But the Court, as we have seen, has at times adopted a more deferential posture to the legislature on questions falling outside the courts' traditional fields of expertise.

At issue in *N.A.P.E.* was the legislative termination of a Newfoundland government commitment to implement a schedule of pay increases to female government workers. The government admitted that female workers had for years been paid less than men in jobs of "equal value." The "pay equity" program was to redress this systemic discrimination. But the provincial government fell into financial difficulty in 1991 and had to postpone its commitment, it alleged, in order to maintain other essential services. The employees' union challenged the legislation reneging on the commitment as a violation of section 15 equality rights.

A unanimous Court had no difficulty finding a section 15 violation, but, as in so many cases, the rub was in section 1 analysis. The Court had also to deal with a novel approach to section 1 analysis applied by the Newfoundland Court of Appeal. Distinguishing between questions of policy and law, the Court of Appeal argued that under the "separation of powers

---

5   *RJR-MacDonald v. Canada (Attorney General)*, case 7.

6   *Operation Dismantle v. The Queen*, [1985] 1 S.C.R. 441.

doctrine" embedded in the Canadian Constitution, courts should only incidentally decide matters of policy as they dispose of legal issues. "In light of the controversy that has reigned for years over judicial incursions into the policy field of the elected branches of government," the Newfoundland court argued, "it is inconceivable that the *Charter* would be framed without intent to hold s. 1 justifications of policy choices within tolerable limits under the Separation of Powers Doctrine. That intent is confirmed on a perusal of s. 1. . . . [Section] 1 of the *Charter* is harmonized with the Separation of Powers Doctrine by foreclosing the potential for the judiciary to assume the role of final arbitrator of the correctness of policy initiatives within the purview of the political branches of government."[7] The Court of Appeal proposed to "oil [the] hinges [of proportionality analysis in the *Oakes* test] to assure they swing in harmony with the Separation of Powers."[8] This meant that a consistently deferential standard of reasonableness should be applied by courts in undertaking section 1 analysis.

The Supreme Court declined the invitation to alter the *Oakes* test, but it did affirm the lower court's disposition of the appeal by applying a highly relaxed version of the *Oakes* test to the Newfoundland law. In doing so, it enraged equality rights advocates. The Women's Legal Education and Action Fund, an intervener in the case on the side of N.A.P.E., took particular exception to the Court's section 1 analysis. "LEAF is extremely disturbed by the Court's further ruling that this oppressive treatment of women was justifiable. [The Newfoundland government won on section 1 of the *Charter*.] The Court held that the Newfoundland government's *discrimination against women was justified* in a free and democratic society because a severe fiscal deficit could override the government's obligation to remedy wage discrimination. Over 5,000 women in Newfoundland were denied justice. The decision in *N.A.P.E.* shows how much work LEAF has yet to do in the area of equality rights and social justice."[9] ～

Discussion Questions

1. If a government grants legislative benefits to a group, should it assume a constitutional obligation to maintain these benefits in the face of other priorities and circumstances?
2. The Court relaxed the evidentiary burden on the Newfoundland government when it examined whether the section 15 violation was justified under section 1. What were its reasons for doing so?
3. The Court grappled with the Newfoundland Court of Appeal argument that the *Oakes* test misrepresents section 1. How so?
4. *N.A.P.E.* represents a new chapter in the ongoing clash between constitutional supremacy and judicial supremacy. Elaborate.

---

7   *Newfoundland Assn. of Public Employees v. R.* (2002), 221 D.L.R. (4th) 513 at 642-43 (Nfld. CA).

8   *Ibid.* at 649.

9   LEAF, "Legal Work: Significant Cases," online at <http://www.leaf.ca/legal/briefs/2004-newfoundland.html> (emphasis in original).

NEWFOUNDLAND (TREASURY BOARD) v. N.A.P.E.
2004 SCC 66, [2004] 3 S.C.R. 381

Hearing: May 12, 2004; Judgment: October 28, 2004.

Present: McLachlin C.J. and Major, Bastarache, Binnie, LeBel, Deschamps, and Fish JJ.

Interveners: Attorney General of Quebec, Attorney General of New Brunswick, Attorney General of British Columbia, Attorney General of Alberta, Canadian Association for Community Living, Canadian Hearing Society, Council of Canadians with Disabilities, Hospital Employees' Union, British Columbia Government and Service Employees' Union, Health Sciences Association, Women's Legal Education and Action Fund, and Canadian Labour Congress.

The judgment of the Court was delivered by

[1] **BINNIE J.:** In this appeal, the Court is required to consider what sort of government fiscal crisis is sufficient (if any) to justify limiting a right or freedom guaranteed by the *Canadian Charter of Rights and Freedoms*. The appellant union says cost considerations can never amount to such a justification. Therefore, scheduled progress towards pay equity should not have been sacrificed as it was in the Province's fiscal crisis that arose in the spring of 1991. The respondent government replies that the Court should not second-guess budgetary allocations made by the House of Assembly in the severe and unanticipated financial emergency occurring at that time. Marshall J.A. of the Court of Appeal of Newfoundland and Labrador was not only persuaded by the government's position on the facts but went on to argue that the jurisprudence under s. 1 of the *Charter* should be rewritten to explicitly require compliance with the doctrine of the separation of powers at every step of the way. Thus rewritten, he concluded, the even greater measure of judicial deference to legislative and executive choices that he advocates would allow the law at issue in this case to be justified....

I. Facts

[4] The collective agreements that had been in force between the government and the public sector unions for a number of years included a prohibition against discrimination on the ground of sex (art. 4.01). Despite this provision, the parties had negotiated collective agreements from year to year which, they eventually acknowledged, paid female-dominated work classifications less than was paid to male-dominated classifications for work of equal value. There had been in existence, the government agreed on June 24, 1988, systemic discrimination. The resulting Pay Equity Agreement between the government and the major public sector unions, including the

appellant, did not itself achieve pay equity, but laid out a process and methodology for its implementation. The intention was to begin the pay equity process in the hospital sector and in Newfoundland Hydro, but eventually to "bring in pay equity in all segments" of the provincial public service (Newfoundland Preliminary Report (*Hansard*), Vol. XLI, No. 11, March 19, 1991, at p. 363).

[5] Under the scheme of the Pay Equity Agreement, the first wage adjustment was to be made effective April 1, 1988, and thereafter the adjustments would come in increments over a period of four years at a rate per year not exceeding 1 percent of the 1987 payroll for each job "grouping" as defined therein. The full balance to achieve pay equity was to be paid out in the fifth year, on April 1, 1992. The agreement established a Pay Equity Steering Committee for the hospital sector with a membership that included equal representation from the unions and government.

[6] The complex task of evaluating work of equal value across different job classifications, and working out the wage adjustments necessary to achieve equity, took longer than anticipated. Eventually, on March 20, 1991, the financial analysis was complete. The government estimated the immediate cost at that date of implementation of the initial stages of pay equity in the health care sector at $24 million.

[7] At the time these cost estimates were received, the provincial government was experiencing what the President of the Treasury Board said was a financial crisis unprecedented in the Province's history. Existing and projected budgetary deficits had risen to the point where the Province's credit rating in financial markets was seriously at risk. He told the House of Assembly:

> For the first time in our history we are faced with the prospect of having a limitation on what we can borrow.... We could not take the chance that our credit rating would drop one more notch....
>
> We were facing a horrendous problem that had to be dealt with for the sake of the people of the Province.

(*Hansard, supra*, at pp. 359 and 361)

[8] The House of Assembly responded on April 18, 1991 with passage of the *Public Sector Restraint Act*, that was made retroactive by about three weeks to the Province's fiscal year end, being March 31, 1991.

[9] Section 5 of the Act purported to freeze the wage scales of *all* public sector employees, from cabinet ministers to hospital workers, for one year, later extended to March 31, 1993. (An exception was made for increases to individual wages on account of step progression within a job classification or reclassification.) Pay equity was in part exempted from

the freeze. It would still be implemented but the first adjustment was delayed to March 31, 1991 instead of April 1, 1988. It was provided that nothing would be paid on account of the three-year period from April 1, 1988 through to March 31, 1991. The effect of the Act, according to the President of the Treasury Board, was that "it *erases* an obligation we had there of approximately $24 million" (*Hansard, supra*, at pp. 362-3 (emphasis added)).

[10] Eventually the government and the union (without prejudice to the union's position in this litigation) agreed that instead of the contemplated five-year payout the pay equity objective would be implemented by a series of adjustments not exceeding 2 percent of individual salaries each year until pay equity as between male and female employees was achieved.

[11] In April 1991, grievances were filed on behalf of some affected employees in respect of matters including non-payment of the pay equity wage adjustments. The parties subsequently agreed to proceed only with the grievances concerning pay equity. . . .

IV. Constitutional Questions

[29] On October 29, 2003, the Chief Justice stated the following constitutional questions:

1. Does s. 9 of the *Public Sector Restraint Act*, S.N. 1991, c. 3, infringe s. 15(1) of the *Canadian Charter of Rights and Freedoms*?
2. If so, is the infringement a reasonable limit prescribed by law as can be demonstrably justified in a free and democratic society under s. 1 of the *Canadian Charter of Rights and Freedoms*?

To which the appellant adds a supplementary question:

3. Did the Court of Appeal err in adding a further step to the section 1 analysis, namely a requirement for the Court to determine explicitly at each stage whether the separation of powers doctrine has been offended?

V. Analysis

[30] Pay equity has been one of the most difficult and controversial workplace issues of our times. There is no doubt that in the 1980s women hospital workers in Newfoundland and Labrador (and elsewhere) were being paid less than men for work of equal value. By 1988, it had become a significant collective bargaining issue between the provincial government and the public sector unions.

[31] The Pay Equity Agreement signed on June 24, 1988 was a major achievement. No doubt it was bought by the public sector unions with concessions on other fronts. Progress on such an important issue, once achieved, should not be lightly set aside. Yet, the effect of the *Public Sector Restraint Act* was not only to shift the start of the provincial government's pay equity adjustments from 1988 to 1991, but to eliminate any liability for amounts otherwise payable to the underpaid female hospital workers in respect of the three fiscal years ending March 31, 1991. For those workers who retired prior to 1991, the Act meant they derived no benefit at all from the agreement their union had achieved. Nevertheless the provincial government argues that the *Public Sector Restraint Act* is entirely valid on the basis that: (1) there being nothing in the *Charter* (the government says) imposing pay equity as a constitutional obligation, there can be no constitutional impediment to its repeal, let alone a "deferral" of its effective date; (2) in any event, there is nothing in the *Public Sector Restraint Act* that creates a distinction that qualifies as discrimination within s. 15(1) of the *Charter*; and (3) if any such discrimination is found to exist it is justified under s. 1 of the *Charter*.

[32] I do not believe there is much substance in the first two points. The battleground in this case is the s. 1 justification. Nevertheless, I propose to deal with the points in the order presented.

A. Absence of a Constitutional Obligation

[33] The respondent says that female workers have no right under s. 15(1) of the *Charter* to equal pay for work of equal value. What the government gave in 1988, the government could take away in 1991. It is true that in the ordinary course, legislative adoption of a remedial measure does not "constitutionalize" it so as to fetter its repeal: *Reference re Canada Assistance Plan (B.C.)*, [1991] 2 S.C.R. 525, at p. 563. Here, however, the provincial government signed a Pay Equity Agreement on June 24, 1988 which changed the legal landscape by creating enforceable contractual rights to end pay discrimination by a procedure contractually binding on all of the parties. . . .

[37] . . . For present purposes, it is sufficient to hold that the question whether the targeting of acquired rights of women hospital workers in this case was discriminatory is clearly within the ambit of s. 15(1) scrutiny.

B. Does Section 9 of the Public Sector Restraint Act Breach Section 15(1) of the Charter?

[38] Counsel for the appellant concisely summarized her s. 15(1) argument against the *Public Service Restraint Act*:

It repudiates recognition by the state of the undervaluation of work done by women, it identifies pay inequity for women as acceptable and it repudiates state responsibility [as employer] for redressing systemic discrimination for women.

While this description necessarily sacrifices nuance in the interest of brevity, it certainly captures the essence of the debate.

[39] The provincial government has an uphill battle contesting an infringement of s. 15(1) in light of the opening clauses of the Pay Equity Agreement it signed on June 24, 1988:

PURPOSE

1.1 *To achieve pay equity by redressing systemic gender discrimination in compensation for work performed by employees in female dominated classes* within the bargaining units represented by AAHP, IBEW, CUPE, NAPE and NLNU, and whose members are employees covered by *The Public Service (Collective Bargaining) Act, 1973.* [Emphasis added.]

[40] The value placed on a person's work is more than just a matter of dollars and cents. The female hospital workers were being told that they did not deserve equal pay despite making a contribution of equal value. . . .

[41] This case thus fits easily within the framework established in *Law v. Canada (Minister of Employment and Immigration)*, [1999] 1 S.C.R. 497, which identified the affirmation of human dignity and self-worth as a central purpose of s. 15(1) of the *Charter*.

[42] The effect of the *Public Sector Restraint Act* in 1991 was to affirm a policy of gender discrimination which the provincial government had itself denounced three years previously. The Act draws a clear formal distinction between those who were entitled to benefit from pay equity, and everyone else. The appropriate comparator group consists of men in male-dominated classifications performing work of equal value. That group was not similarly targeted. They were paid according to their contractual entitlement. The adverse impact of the legislation therefore fell disproportionately on women, who were already at a disadvantage relative to male-dominated jobs as they earned less money. It is true that the Act targeted an advantage secured to "female *dominated* classes," and thus presumably included some males, but such inclusion does not change the result. The category of "female dominated classes" was established in the original Pay Equity Agreement, wherein the government formally acknowledged that in relation to workers thus defined the pay differential constituted "systemic gender discrimination." . . .

C. Is Section 9 of the Public Sector Restraint Act Saved by Section 1?

[52] It should be stated at the outset that legislation aimed at perpetuating pay inequity is a very serious matter. Counsel for the respondent acknowledged at the hearing that this is so, but argued that this is one of those "exceedingly rare cases" where the issue is not about "administrative convenience or cost *simpliciter* or majorit[arian] [p]reference." It is, he says, about "the province's ability to deliver on some of its most basic social programs, such as education, health and welfare." . . .

[54] Marshall J.A. [of the Nfld. Court of Appeal] advocated adding a further question "at the end of each stage of the appraisal of compliance with the *Oakes* criteria," namely

> . . . whether the exercise of the judicial power in coming to those findings was in consonance with the Separation of Powers Doctrine. [para. 372]

(1) The Section 1 Record

[55] As with any matter that must be approached with close attention to context, the evidence led in support of a s. 1 justification is very important to the outcome. The only evidence before the Board consisted of an extract from *Hansard* and some budget documents. The government witnesses were not employed in the relevant policy group at the time.

[56] Ordinarily such a casually introduced s. 1 record would be a matter of serious concern. However the essential subject matter of the s. 1 justification in this case consists of the public accounts of the Province that are filed with the House of Assembly, and comments by the Minister of Finance and the President of the Treasury Board as to what they thought the accounts disclosed and what they proposed to do about it, which are reported in *Hansard*. This is all material of which courts may take judicial notice. . . .

[58] The [labour arbitration] Board was critical of the government in failing to call witnesses who could describe at first hand what alternatives were examined to secure cost reductions that might, if adopted, have avoided a deferral of pay equity. I agree with the Board that the government ought to have called witnesses who were better placed to explain the government accounts and ministerial observations. However, in the context of this particular subject matter, I do not agree that failure to do so was fatal to the government's s. 1 case. There are serious limits to how far the courts can penetrate Cabinet privilege in order to require information about the deliberations of the Executive Council: *Canada (Auditor General) v. Canada (Minister of Energy, Mines and Resources)*, [1989] 2 S.C.R. 49, at p. 89. What transpires in the budgetary process, of course, lies at the high end of Cabinet confidences, and here there was no need to precipitate a confrontation between the courts and the government. In my view, the material brought to the Board's attention, and of which we may take judicial notice, is sufficient for the purposes of disposing of this appeal.

(2) Was There a Pressing and Substantial Legislative Objective?

[59] It cannot reasonably be disputed that the provincial government faced a severe fiscal crisis in the spring of 1991. In part, this was due to a reduction of anticipated federal transfer payments by $130 million. Over 45 percent of Newfoundland government spending is financed either through federal equalization payments or federally established program financing, "money that is transferred down here," as it was explained by the President of the Treasury Board (*Hansard, supra*, at p. 364).

[60] The Minister of Finance advised the House of Assembly that instead of a modest surplus of $10 million for the fiscal year ending March 31, 1991, there would be a deficit of $120 million. The prospective deficit for 1991-92, unless serious expenditure cuts were made, would be "in the vicinity of $200 million" (*Hansard, supra*, at p. 359). Deficits of this magnitude could have serious consequences for the Province, not only in borrowing to meet the current account deficit but in refinancing existing provincial debt as it fell due....

[61] The government's s. 1 evidence includes its expenditure reduction program. In addition to the freeze of wage scales for public sector employees including members of the House of Assembly, Cabinet Ministers, executives, managers and non-unionized employees, the budgetary measures froze or cut budgets for government-funded agencies; closed 360 acute care hospital beds; froze per capita student grants and equalization grants to school boards; made government-wide reductions in operating budgets; reduced or eliminated a range of programs; imposed a 10 percent reduction in executive and management positions; laid off 1,300 permanent, 350 part-time and 350 seasonal employees and eliminated a further 500 vacant positions in government departments; and terminated medicare coverage for items such as routine dental surgery in hospitals and basic vision assessment under the optometry and medicare programs.

[62] It seems to me the severity of these measures, including the cut to pay equity, corroborates the government's statement that it believed itself, on reasonable grounds, to be in the middle of a fiscal crisis.

[63] The appellant union says that these cost savings should not be recognized as sufficiently important to justify the limitation of *Charter* rights. It relies on the statement of Lamer C.J. in *Reference re Remuneration of Judges of the Provincial Court of Prince Edward Island*, [1997] 3 S.C.R. 3 ("*PEI Provincial Court Judges Reference*"), at para. 284:

Three main principles emerge from this discussion. First, *a measure whose sole purpose is financial, and which infringes Charter rights, can never be justified under s. 1*

(*Singh* and *Schachter*). Second, financial considerations are relevant to tailoring the standard of review under minimal impairment (*Irwin Toy, McKinney* and *Egan*). Third, financial considerations are relevant to the exercise of the court's remedial discretion, when s. 52 is engaged (*Schachter*). [Emphasis added.]

[64] It seems to me that these and other similar statements have to be read in context. It is true, as the Court recently affirmed in *Nova Scotia (Workers' Compensation Board) v. Martin*, [2003] 2 S.C.R. 504, 2003 SCC 54, that "[b]udgetary considerations in and of themselves cannot *normally* be invoked as a free-standing pressing and substantial objective for the purposes of s. 1 of the *Charter*" (para. 109 (emphasis added)). The spring of 1991 was not a "normal" time in the finances of the provincial government. At some point, a financial crisis can attain a dimension that elected governments must be accorded significant scope to take remedial measures, even if the measures taken have an adverse effect on a *Charter* right, subject, of course, to the measures being proportional both to the fiscal crisis and to their impact on the affected *Charter* interests. In this case, the fiscal crisis was severe and the cost of putting into effect pay equity according to the original timetable was a large expenditure ($24 million) relative even to the size of the fiscal crisis....

[69] It was ... clear from an early date that financial considerations wrapped up with other public policy considerations *could* qualify as sufficiently important objectives under s. 1....

[72] ... [C]ourts will continue to look with strong scepticism at attempts to justify infringements of *Charter* rights on the basis of budgetary constraints. To do otherwise would devalue the *Charter* because there are *always* budgetary constraints and there are *always* other pressing government priorities. Nevertheless, the courts cannot close their eyes to the periodic occurrence of financial emergencies when measures must be taken to juggle priorities to see a government through the crisis. It cannot be said that in weighing a delay in the timetable for implementing pay equity against the closing of hundreds of hospital beds, as here, a government is engaged in an exercise "whose sole purpose is financial." The weighing exercise has as much to do with social values as it has to do with dollars. In the present case, the "potential impact" is $24 million, amounting to more than 10 percent of the projected budgetary deficit for 1991-92. The delayed implementation of pay equity is an extremely serious matter, but so too (for example) is the layoff of 1,300 permanent, 350 part-time and 350 seasonal employees, and the deprivation to the public of the services they provided....

[74] In my view, the union's argument that budgetary issues should effectively be given no weight in these circum-

stances goes too far. With respect, the need to address a fiscal crisis such as that described by the President of the Treasury Board was a pressing and substantial legislative objective.

[75] Loss of credit rating, and its impact on the government's ability to borrow, and the added cost of borrowing to finance the provincial debt which, in the case of Newfoundland, requires "[h]undreds of millions of dollars every year in interest" (*Hansard, supra*, at p. 362), are matters of high importance. The President of the Treasury Board told the House of Assembly that "the financial health of the Province was at stake" (*Hansard, supra*, at p. 359). The Newfoundland Government had already experienced a period of trusteeship in the 1930s, a fact glumly referred to by the President of the Treasury Board in his speech. The financial health of the Province is the golden goose on which all else relies. The government in 1991 was not just debating rights versus dollars but rights versus hospital beds, rights versus layoffs, rights versus jobs, rights versus education and rights versus social welfare. The requirement to reduce expenditures, and the allocation of the necessary cuts, *was* undertaken to promote other values of a free and democratic society: *Oakes, supra*, at p. 136; *M. v. H.*, [1999] 2 S.C.R. 3, at para. 107. And, as Sopinka J. pointed out in *Egan v. Canada*, [1995] 2 S.C.R. 513, at para. 104, "[I]t is not realistic for the Court to assume that there are unlimited funds to address the needs of all." . . .

(3) Was There a Rational Connection Between the Legislative Measure and the Pressing and Substantial Objective?

[77] As the pay equity payout represented a significant portion of the budget, its postponement was rationally connected to averting a serious fiscal crisis in Newfoundland and Labrador.

(4) Minimal Impairment

[78] Were the *Charter* rights of the female hospital workers impaired no more than was reasonably necessary to achieve the pressing and substantial legislative objective of fiscal viability?

[79] In the *PEI Provincial Court Judges Reference, supra*, a decision much relied on by the appellant to oppose the relevance of budgetary constraints, Lamer C.J. stated, at para. 283:

> While purely financial considerations are not sufficient to justify the infringement of *Charter* rights, they are relevant to determining *the standard of deference for the test of minimal impairment* when reviewing legislation which is enacted for a purpose which is not financial. [Emphasis added; emphasis in original deleted.]

[80] A few preliminary points should be emphasized. Marshall J.A. noted that the s. 1 case is essentially about budgets and that the making of a budget is a quintessentially political activity. However, these facts do not immunize the budget choices from *Charter* review. The notion that there are inherently "political" questions beyond the courts' jurisdiction was emphatically rejected in *Operation Dismantle Inc. v. The Queen*, [1985] 1 S.C.R. 441. . . .

[81] If an individual's *Charter* right or freedom is violated by the state, it is no answer to say the violation was driven or is justified for political reasons. Indeed forms of state discrimination that are undertaken for political reasons are among the most odious, as the recent history of parts of the world from South Africa to the Balkans can attest.

[82] The second preliminary point is that in framing the *Charter*, Canadian legislators chose to identify certain rights and freedoms as having special constitutional status and these were placed for protection in a legal strongbox. As such they have a privileged status, and the appellant is right to call attention to that fact. However, of course, *Charter* rights must yield when the requisites of s. 1 are satisfied.

[83] Thirdly, the *Oakes* test recognizes that in certain types of decisions there may be no obviously correct or obviously wrong solution, but a range of options each with its advantages and disadvantages. Governments act as they think proper within a range of reasonable alternatives, and the Court acknowledged in *M. v. H., supra*, at para. 78, that "the role of the legislature demands deference from the courts to those types of policy decisions that the legislature is best placed to make." . . .

[84] It is therefore recognized that in such cases governments have a large "margin of appreciation" within which to make choices. It seems evident that the scope of that "margin" will be influenced, amongst other things, by the scale of the financial challenge confronting a government and the size of the expenditure required to avoid a *Charter* infringement in relation to that financial challenge. . . .

[The Court here mentions that the proportionality of the government's conduct in this case is supported by the scale of the province's fiscal crisis, by the relatively significant cost of the pay equity plan were it to be implemented on schedule, and by the government's commitment to implement the pay equity plan on a new timetable.]

(d) The Appellant Union Was Invited to Participate in a Government Process Examining Alternatives

[89] The Board majority condemned the government's s. 1 case because of the government's failure to give adequate consideration to "alternative means" to combat the deficit.

The only "alternative" mentioned to the House by the President of the Treasury Board was an additional 900 layoffs:

> Twenty-four million dollars would have meant another 900 laid off in the hospital sector—900 jobs. So we had a choice to make, and we chose to remove the retroactivity from the pay equity agreement.

> (*Hansard, supra*, at p. 362)

[90] The documentary evidence, however, demonstrates that other options were also considered and rejected including a hiring freeze, layoffs and cuts to other programs such as social assistance as well as tax increases. In fact, to avoid additional cuts the government also borrowed approximately $50 million to finance its current expenses.

[91] The criticism of the Board majority that the government failed adequately to consider alternative measures overlooks the more telling point that the appellant union, on behalf of the female hospital workers, had been invited by the government to participate in a process to identify just such alternative measures. . . .

(5) Proportionality of Means to Objective

[98] The salutary effects of the legislation were far reaching. Maintaining the credit rating had a positive effect on interest rates and lender confidence. The government was better able to finance the provincial debt and continue to provide essential programs to its residents. The effect of the Act on the *Charter* rights of female employees who continued to work after March 1991, in purely financial terms, was to defer pay equity and leave the women hospital workers with their traditionally lower wage scales for a further three years. In light of the exceptional circumstances already recited, I accept on a balance of probabilities that the detrimental impact of a delay in achieving pay equity, deeply unfortunate as it was, did not outweigh the importance of preserving the fiscal health of a provincial government through a temporary but serious financial crisis. The seriousness of that crisis, combined with the relative size of the $24 million required to bring pay equity in line with the original schedule, are the compelling factors in that respect.

(6) Proportionality of Salutary Effects of the Act to Deleterious Effects of the Act

[99] For the reasons already stated, the evidence shows that taken as a whole the fiscal measures adopted by the Province did more good than harm, despite the adverse effects on the women hospital workers, serious and deeply regrettable though such adverse effects were.

(7) Should Conformity with the Separation of Powers Doctrine Be Added as an Element of the Section 1 Analysis?

[100] As stated, Marshall J.A. proposed that a court should ask itself at each stage of the s. 1 analysis whether the judicial response to the questions posed conform to the separation of powers doctrine. He wrote, at para. 362:

> . . . [I]t cannot be said that s. 1 endows the judiciary with licence to stand in the shoes of the other branches of government as ultimate arbitrator of which policy choices were in the best interests of the governed. For the foregoing reasons, it would appear that the *Oakes* proportionality requirements court such a risk. Accordingly, it seems that some revisitation of them is in order.

[101] The essential propositions advanced by Marshall J.A. were that the *Oakes* test does not sufficiently respect the actual wording of s. 1 of the *Charter* (para. 262) and that in the result inadequate deference is paid to legislative and executive choices at each and every stage of the s. 1 justification. It is thus out of step with the doctrine of the separation of powers. While I respect the care and detail with which Marshall J.A. set out his concerns in the course of a 231-page judgment, I do not agree with his analysis.

(a) Fidelity to the Text of Section 1

[102] The *Oakes* test, of course, is itself based on the text of s. 1. Thus in *Oakes* itself, Dickson C.J. observed at p. 137:

> It is clear from the text of s. 1 that limits on the rights and freedoms enumerated in the *Charter* are exceptions to their general guarantee. The presumption is that the rights and freedoms are guaranteed unless the party invoking s. 1 can bring itself within the exceptional criteria which justify their being limited. This is further substantiated by the use of the word "demonstrably" which clearly indicates that the onus of justification is on the party seeking to limit: *Hunter v. Southam Inc.* . . .

[103] The textual analysis was carried forward by McLachlin J. in *RJR-MacDonald Inc. v. Canada (Attorney General)*, [1995] 3 S.C.R. 199. Referring to the words "reasonable limits prescribed by law as can be demonstrably justified in a free and democratic society," she wrote at paras. 128 and 136:

> The process is not one of mere intuition, nor is it one of deference to Parliament's choice. *It is a process of demonstration.* This reinforces the notion inherent in the word *"reasonable"* of rational inference from evidence or established truths. . . .

No doubt Parliament and the legislatures, generally speaking, *do* enact measures that they, representing the majority view, consider to be reasonable limits that have been demonstrated to *their* satisfaction as justifiable. Deference to the legislative choice to the degree proposed by Marshall J.A. would largely circumscribe and render superfluous the independent second look imposed on the courts by s. 1 of the *Charter*. Deference to the majority view on that scale would leave little protection to minorities. Marshall J.A.'s proposal, with respect, is not based on fidelity to the text of s. 1 but to dilution of the requirement of "demonstrable" justification.

(b) The Separation of Powers

[104] No one doubts that the courts and the legislatures have different roles to play, and that our system works best when constitutional actors respect the role and mandate of other constitutional actors, including an "appreciation by the judiciary of its own position in the constitutional scheme" (*Auditor General, supra,* at p. 91, *per* Dickson C.J.). While the separation of powers is a defining feature of our constitutional order (*PEI Provincial Court Judges Reference, supra*), the separation of powers cannot be invoked to undermine the operation of a specific written provision of the Constitution like s. 1 of the *Charter*. Section 1 itself expresses an important aspect of the separation of powers by defining, within its terms, limits on legislative sovereignty.

[105] Judicial review of governmental action long predates the adoption of the *Charter*. Since Confederation, courts have been required *by* the Constitution to ensure that state action complies with the Constitution. The *Charter* has placed new limits on government power in the area of human rights, but judicial review of those limits involves the courts in the same *role* in relation to the separation of powers as they have occupied from the beginning, that of the constitutionally mandated referee. As the Court affirmed in *Vriend v. Alberta*, [1998] 1 S.C.R. 493, at para. 56, ". . . it is not the courts which limit the legislatures. Rather, it is the Constitution, which must be interpreted by the courts, that limits the legislatures. This is necessarily true of all constitutional democracies." . . .

[107] Marshall J.A. makes a number of suggestions as to how this redefinition of Parliamentary sovereignty can be squared with his view of the Separation of Powers.

[108] Firstly, Marshall J.A. would seemingly impose on a rights claimant not only the onus of establishing entitlement to the right but also of showing that its exercise "in the specific circumstances" of the case is reasonable. He writes at para. 244:

The new constitutional mechanism for enforcing fundamental rights rather addressed individual impotence in the face of encroachments upon them by providing a means of their protection through the courts *to the extent that their exercise in the specific circumstances obtaining could be shown reasonable* in a free and democratic society. [Emphasis added.]

[109] To the extent Marshall J.A. is advocating a removal of the onus on government to justify infringement of a *Charter* right, and to substitute an onus under s. 1 on the complainant to show that his or her exercise of the right is reasonable, it would again contradict the text of s. 1 in which the word "reasonable" modifies "limits" not "rights." Nowhere in the *Charter* is it suggested that the exercise of fundamental rights and freedoms should be presumed unreasonable unless and until a claimant proves the contrary "in the specific circumstances."

[110] Secondly, Marshall J.A. would seemingly remove from judicial scrutiny "policy initiatives within the purview of the political branches of government." He writes, at paras. 362 and 351:

It is true that s. 1 effectively invests it [the judiciary] with responsibility to pass upon the justifiability of policy choices behind *Charter* infringements. However, that power is exercisable in the context of judicial deference to the other branches of government, and in harmony with the Separation of Powers Doctrine. . . .

In the result, s. 1 of the *Charter* is harmonized with the Separation of Powers Doctrine by foreclosing the potential for the judiciary to assume the role of final arbitrator of the correctness of policy initiatives within the purview of the political branches of government.

[111] The "political branches" of government are the legislature and the executive. Everything that they do by way of legislation and executive action could properly be called "policy initiatives." If the "political branches" are to be the "final arbitrator" of compliance with the *Charter* of their "policy initiatives," it would seem the enactment of the *Charter* affords no real protection at all to the rightsholders the *Charter*, according to its text, was intended to benefit. *Charter* rights and freedoms, on this reading, would offer rights without a remedy.

[112] Thirdly, Marshall J.A. would preclude the courts from looking at alternative measures the "political branches" might have adopted to achieve their legitimate objectives with minimal impairment to *Charter* rights and freedoms. Thus he writes, at para. 424:

A perusal of s. 1's wording reflects intent that the judicial justification power be rationalized through deference to the adopted policy choice *without inquiry into other options* which the judiciary might consider to have been available. [Emphasis added.]

[113] With respect, it is difficult to understand how a court could satisfy itself that a particular legislative limit is "reasonable" if it is blinkered from considering whether other less limiting measures were available.

[114] Marshall J.A.'s concerns lead back to his fundamental point that in appropriate cases, courts should defer to legislative and executive choices. Yet it is not at all necessary to rewrite the Court's jurisprudence to reflect this concern. While I do not agree with Marshall J.A. that the courts should "oil th[e] hinges" of the *Oakes* test to ensure that it "swing[s] in harmony with the Separation of Powers" (because in my view such an approach would contradict the explicit wording of s. 1), it is nevertheless clear that there is built into the *Oakes* test a healthy respect for legislative choice in areas of economic and social policy....

[116] In summary, whenever there are boundaries to the legal exercise of state power such boundaries have to be refereed. Canadian courts have undertaken this role in relation to the division of powers between Parliament and the provincial legislatures since Confederation. The boundary between an individual's protected right or freedom and state power must also be refereed. The framers of the *Charter* identified the courts as the referee. While I recognize that the separation of powers is an important constitutional principle, I believe that the s. 1 test set out in *Oakes* and the rest of our voluminous s. 1 jurisprudence already provides the proper framework in which to consider what the doctrine of separation of powers requires in particular situations, as indeed was the case here. To the extent Marshall J.A. invites a greater level of deference to the will of the legislature, I believe acceptance of such an invitation would simply be inconsistent with the clear words of s. 1 and undermine the delicate balance the *Charter* was intended to achieve. I would therefore not do as he suggests.

Reference re Same-Sex Marriage, 2004

If *Charter* commentators were to identify the most significant social policy change that can be attributed to the *Charter* in its first quarter century, the definition of marriage would certainly be a leading contender. As of 2005, Canada became one of only a handful of nations that recognizes marriages between same-sex partners.

The federal Parliament has jurisdiction over marriage, but, until 2005, had never actually defined marriage. Instead, Canada relied on a common-law definition of marriage dating back to 1866, which defined marriage "as understood in Christendom" as "the voluntary union for life of one man and one woman, to the exclusion of all others."[1]

The transformation in the definition of marriage has been contentious. In the aftermath of the Supreme Court's ruling in *M. v. H.* (case 27), which declared unconstitutional social policy distinctions that discriminated against same-sex partners, many politicians and religious groups expressed concern that the *Charter* might be interpreted in a manner that alters this traditional definition of marriage. Pressure from the opposition Reform/Alliance parties, as well as criticism within the Liberal caucus, were sufficiently powerful to convince the Liberal government to twice accede to political pressure (in 1999 and, again, in 2000) to declare that the traditional definition of marriage would not be altered by legislative changes being introduced to redress the denial of social policy benefits for same-sex partners.

Despite this attempt to preserve an opposite-sex definition of marriage, many within and outside government believed that Parliament would soon have to change the definition of marriage to include same-sex unions or risk having the courts change the common-law definition. The logic of the Court's approach to equality in *M. v. H.*—that equality requires not only equal benefits in law but also that the state treat same-sex partners with the same degree of respect and recognition given to those in heterosexual relationships—provided strong indication that the Supreme Court might not accept the constitutional validity of a definition of marriage that denies same-sex partners the opportunity to marry. A few years after the *M. v. H.* ruling, provincial courts of appeal in British Columbia, Ontario, and Quebec ruled that the common-law definition of marriage violates equality. In 2003, the Liberal government decided not to appeal one of these rulings, the Ontario Court of Appeal decision in *Halpern v. Canada (Attorney General)*,[2] which not only held that the common-law prohibition on same-sex marriage was unconstitutional, but issued a new definition of marriage to replace the old common-law definition, allowing same-sex partners to marry. Soon after, the government developed draft legislation that changed the definition of marriage to read: "Marriage, for civil purposes, is the lawful union of two persons to the exclusion of all others." However, faced with strong opposition from the Alliance party, as well as substantial opposition from within its own ranks, the government decided to delay the introduction

1 *Hyde v. Hyde and Woodmansee* (1866), L.R. 1 P. & D. 130 at 133.

2 (2003), 65 O.R. (3d) 161 (C.A.).

of the legislation until it had asked the Supreme Court to review the draft bill and address several constitutional questions.

These questions addressed whether Ottawa has jurisdictional capacity to define marriage; whether the recognition of same-sex partners' ability to marry is consistent with the *Charter*; and whether the *Charter*'s safeguarding of religious freedom protects religious officials from having to marry same-sex partners, contrary to their beliefs. Omitted from the reference were two related questions central to the ongoing political debate: (1) is the opposite-sex definition of marriage contrary to the *Charter*, and (2) would the creation of a new category of relationship, a civil union for same-sex partners, be acceptable under the *Charter* as an alternative to same-sex marriage?

At the time of the reference, the Liberal government was incurring serious internal strife, as leader Jean Chrétien was under strong pressure from within his own caucus to resign. His likely successor, Paul Martin, indicated his discomfort with the draft legislation and suggested he supported use of the notwithstanding clause should courts force churches to perform same-sex marriages. Martin was chosen as leader of the party soon after the reference case was initiated and, shortly thereafter, his government added a fourth question for the Court to address: is the opposite-sex requirement for civil marriage in the common law consistent with the *Charter*?

The Court's ruling was unanimous and succinct by recent standards. The Court answered the first three questions in the affirmative, which did not surprise most commentators. But it declined to answer the fourth question, which went to the heart of the debate taking place at the time: is same-sex marriage constitutionally required? The Court's refusal suggests reluctance to be drawn into this political debate, particularly as the use of the reference device was broadly seen as a political strategy intended to weaken opposition to the proposed legislation. The Court characterized the circumstances for the reference as "unique," in part because no precedent exists for answering a reference question that "mirrors issues already disposed of in lower courts where an appeal was available but not pursued." The Court further indicated that since the government had stated its intention to address the issue regardless of the Court's opinion, the "hypothetical benefit" Parliament would derive from its advisory opinion on this question did not warrant the Court's answer.

In February 2005, Martin's government introduced a bill defining marriage in a manner inclusive of both heterosexual and same-sex unions. Despite his earlier expressed reluctance about recognizing same-sex marriage, Martin presented the issue as involving fundamental rights, and suggested that any position short of marriage would require use of the notwithstanding clause, a position for which he now indicated his disapproval. In opposing the legislation, Conservative opposition leader Stephen Harper argued against conceiving same-sex marriage as a fundamental human right and recommended amendments to preserve the traditional definition of marriage while allowing provinces to offer civil unions. The legislation passed the House of Commons in June 2005, by a vote of 158 to 133, in which one Cabinet minister resigned for refusing to support the bill.

But the controversy over same-sex marriage did not end. Harper reopened the issue in the 2005 federal election campaign, promising that, if elected, he would hold a free vote on marriage. Upon the election of his government with minority status, Harper carried through with his promise to revisit the marriage issue, but, in December 2006, a motion calling on the government to introduce legislation to restore the traditional definition of marriage was defeated by a vote of 175 to 123. ⌇

Discussion Questions

1. Why do you think the Supreme Court was reluctant to address the fourth question submitted by the government about whether the traditional, opposite-sex requirement for marriage is constitutional?
2. Was the Court justified in its decision not to answer this fourth question?
3. Should the government have asked the Supreme Court to rule on the constitutionality of its draft legislation, particularly when it made clear its unequivocal intention to introduce legislation allowing for same-sex marriage regardless of how the Court answered the *Charter* questions?

REFERENCE RE SAME-SEX MARRIAGE
2004 SCC 79, [2004] 3 S.C.R. 698

Hearing: October 6, 7, 2004; Judgment: December 9, 2004.

Present: McLachlin C.J. and Major, Bastarache, Binnie, LeBel, Deschamps, Fish, Abella, and Charron JJ.

Interveners: The Attorney General of Quebec, the Attorney General of Alberta, the Canadian Human Rights Commission, the Ontario Human Rights Commission, the Manitoba Human Rights Commission, the Canadian Civil Liberties Association, the British Columbia Civil Liberties Association, the Canadian Bar Association, the Canadian Conference of Catholic Bishops, the Ontario Conference of Catholic Bishops, the Seventh-Day Adventist Church in Canada, the United Church of Canada, the Canadian Unitarian Council, the Church of Jesus Christ of Latter-Day Saints, the Metropolitan Community Church of Toronto, Egale Canada Inc. and Egale Couples, the B.C. Couples, the Ontario Couples and the Quebec Couple, the Working Group on Civil Unions, the Association for Marriage and the Family in Ontario, the Canadian Coalition of Liberal Rabbis for same-sex marriage and Rabbi Debra Landsberg, as its nominee, the Foundation for Equal Families, Mouvement laïque québécois, Coalition pour le mariage civil des couples de même sexe, the Interfaith Coalition on Marriage and Family, and the Honourable Anne Cools, Member of the Senate, and Roger Gallaway, Member of the House of Commons.

The following is the opinion delivered by

THE COURT:

I. Introduction

[1] On July 16, 2003, the Governor in Council issued Order in Council P.C. 2003-1055 asking this Court to hear a reference on the federal government's *Proposal for an Act respecting certain aspects of legal capacity for marriage for civil purposes* ("*Proposed Act*"). The operative sections of the *Proposed Act* read as follows:

> 1. Marriage, for civil purposes, is the lawful union of two persons to the exclusion of all others.
> 2. Nothing in this Act affects the freedom of officials of religious groups to refuse to perform marriages that are not in accordance with their religious beliefs.

It will be noted that s. 1 of the *Proposed Act* deals only with civil marriage, not religious marriage.

[2] The Order in Council sets out the following questions:

1. Is the annexed *Proposal for an Act respecting certain aspects of legal capacity for marriage for civil purposes* within the exclusive legislative authority of the Parliament of Canada? If not, in what particular or particulars, and to what extent?
2. If the answer to question 1 is yes, is section 1 of the proposal, which extends capacity to marry to persons of the same sex, consistent with the *Canadian Charter of Rights and Freedoms*? If not, in what particular or particulars, and to what extent?
3. Does the freedom of religion guaranteed by paragraph 2(*a*) of the *Canadian Charter of Rights and Freedoms* protect religious officials from being compelled to perform a marriage between two persons of the same sex that is contrary to their religious beliefs?

[3] On January 26, 2004, the Governor in Council issued Order in Council P.C. 2004-28 asking a fourth question, namely:

4. Is the opposite-sex requirement for marriage for civil purposes, as established by the common law and set out for Quebec in section 5 of the *Federal Law–Civil Law Harmonization Act, No. 1*, consistent with the *Canadian Charter of Rights and Freedoms*? If not, in what particular or particulars and to what extent?

[4] With respect to Question 1, we conclude that s. 1 of the *Proposed Act* is within the exclusive legislative competence of Parliament, while s. 2 is not.

[5] With respect to Question 2, we conclude that s. 1 of the *Proposed Act*, which defines marriage as the union of two persons, is consistent with the *Canadian Charter of Rights and Freedoms*.

[6] With respect to Question 3, we conclude that the guarantee of freedom of religion in the *Charter* affords religious officials protection against being compelled by the state to perform marriages between two persons of the same sex contrary to their religious beliefs.

[7] For reasons to be explained, the Court declines to answer Question 4.

II. The Reference Questions

[8] Certain interveners suggest that the Court should decline to answer any of the questions posed on this Reference on the ground that they are not justiciable. They argue that the questions are essentially political, should be dealt with in Parliament and lack sufficient precision with respect to the *Proposed Act*'s purpose to permit of *Charter* analysis.

[9] The reference provisions of the *Supreme Court Act*, R.S.C. 1985, c. S-26, are broad. In particular, s. 53(1) provides:

> **53.** (1) The Governor in Council may refer to the Court for hearing and consideration important questions of law or fact concerning ...
>
> (*d*) the powers of the Parliament of Canada, or of the legislatures of the provinces, or of the respective governments thereof, whether or not the particular power in question has been or is proposed to be exercised.

[10] The Court has recognized that it possesses a residual discretion not to answer reference questions where it would be inappropriate to do so because, for example, the question lacks sufficient legal content, or where the nature of the question or the information provided does not permit the Court to give a complete or accurate answer: see, e.g., *Reference re Canada Assistance Plan (B.C.)*, [1991] 2 S.C.R. 525, at p. 545; *Reference re Objection by Quebec to a Resolution to Amend the Constitution*, [1982] 2 S.C.R. 793, at p. 806; and *Reference re Secession of Quebec*, [1998] 2 S.C.R. 217 ("*Secession Reference*"), at paras. 26-30.

[11] We conclude that none of the questions posed here lack the requisite legal content for consideration on a reference. The political underpinnings of the instant reference are indisputable. However, much as in the *Secession Reference*, these political considerations provide the context for, rather than the substance of, the questions before the Court. Moreover, any lack of precision with respect to the *Proposed Act*'s purpose can be addressed in the course of answering the questions.

[12] Question 4 raises other concerns. While it possesses the requisite legal content to be justiciable, it raises considerations that render a response on this reference inappropriate, as discussed more fully below.

A. Question 1: Is the Proposed Act Within the Exclusive Legislative Authority of the Parliament of Canada?

[13] It is trite law that legislative authority under the *Constitution Act, 1867* is assessed by way of a two-step process: (1) characterization of the "pith and substance" or dominant characteristic of the law; and (2) concomitant assignment to one of the heads of power enumerated in ss. 91 and 92 of that Act: see, e.g., *R. v. Hydro-Québec*, [1997] 3 S.C.R. 213, at para. 23, *per* Lamer C.J. and Iacobucci J. (dissenting, but not on this point).

[14] An answer to Question 1 requires that we engage in this process with respect to both operative sections of the *Proposed Act*.

(1) Section 1 of the Proposed Act

[15] Section 1 of the *Proposed Act* provides:

> **1.** Marriage, for civil purposes, is the lawful union of two persons to the exclusion of all others.

(a) Determination of Legislative Competence

[16] The dominant characteristic of s. 1 of the *Proposed Act* is apparent from its plain text: marriage as a civil institution. In saying that marriage for civil purposes is "the lawful union of two persons to the exclusion of all others," this section stipulates the threshold requirements of that institution: "two persons," regardless of gender, are legally capable of being married. In pith and substance, therefore, the section pertains to the capacity for marriage.

[17] Turning to the assignment of this matter to an enumerated head of power, we note that legislative authority in respect of marriage is divided between the federal Parliament and the provincial legislatures. Section 91(26) of the *Constitution Act, 1867* confers on Parliament competence in respect of "Marriage and Divorce" whereas s. 92(12) of that Act confers on the provinces competence in respect of "[t]he Solemnization of Marriage in the Province."

[18] As early as 1912, this Court recognized that s. 91(26) confers on Parliament legislative competence in respect of the capacity to marry, whereas s. 92(12) confers authority on the provinces in respect of the performance of marriage once that capacity has been recognized: see *In Re Marriage Laws* (1912), 46 S.C.R. 132. Subsequent decisions have upheld this interpretation. Thus, the capacity to marry in instances of consanguinity (*Teagle v. Teagle*, [1952] 3 D.L.R. 843 (B.C.S.C.)) or in view of prior marital relationships (*Hellens v. Densmore*, [1957] S.C.R. 768) falls within the exclusive legislative competence of Parliament.

[19] We have already concluded that, in pith and substance, s. 1 of the *Proposed Act* pertains to legal capacity for civil marriage. *Prima facie*, therefore, it falls within a subject matter allocated exclusively to Parliament (s. 91(26)).

(b) Objections: The Purported Scope of Section 91(26)

[20] Some interveners nevertheless suggested that s. 91(26) cannot be interpreted as granting legislative competence over same-sex marriage to Parliament. Any law allowing same-sex marriage is alleged to exceed the bounds of s. 91(26) in two key respects: (i) the meaning of "marriage" is constitutionally fixed, necessarily incorporating an opposite-sex requirement; and (ii) any such law would trench upon subject matters clearly allocated to the provincial legislatures.

(i) The Meaning of Marriage Is Not Constitutionally Fixed

[21] Several interveners say that the *Constitution Act, 1867* effectively entrenches the common law definition of "marriage" as it stood in 1867. That definition was most notably articulated in *Hyde v. Hyde* (1866), L.R. 1 P. & D. 130, at p. 133:

> What, then, is the nature of this institution as understood in Christendom? Its incidents may vary in different countries, but what are its essential elements and invariable features? If it be of common acceptance and existence, it must needs (however varied in different countries in its minor incidents) have some pervading identity and universal basis. I conceive that marriage, as understood in Christendom, may for this purpose be defined as the voluntary union for life of one man and one woman, to the exclusion of all others.

[22] The reference to "Christendom" is telling. *Hyde* spoke to a society of shared social values where marriage and religion were thought to be inseparable. This is no longer the case. Canada is a pluralistic society. Marriage, from the perspective of the state, is a civil institution. The "frozen concepts" reasoning runs contrary to one of the most fundamental principles of Canadian constitutional interpretation: that our Constitution is a living tree which, by way of progressive interpretation, accommodates and addresses the realities of modern life. In the 1920s, for example, a controversy arose as to whether women as well as men were capable of being considered "qualified persons" eligible for appointment to the Senate of Canada. Legal precedent stretching back to Roman Law was cited for the proposition that women had always been considered "unqualified" for public office, and it was argued that this common understanding in 1867 was incorporated in s. 24 of the *Constitution Act, 1867* and should continue to govern Canadians in succeeding ages. Speaking for the Privy Council in *Edwards v. Attorney-General for Canada*, [1930] A.C. 124 (P.C.) (the "*Persons*" case), Lord Sankey L.C. said at p. 136:

> Their Lordships do not conceive it to be the duty of this Board—it is certainly not their desire—to cut down the provisions of the [*B.N.A.*] *Act* by a narrow and technical construction, but rather to give it a *large and liberal interpretation* so that the Dominion to a great extent, but within certain fixed limits, may be mistress in her own house, as the Provinces to a great extent, but within certain fixed limits, are mistresses in theirs. [Emphasis added.]

This approach applies to the construction of the powers enumerated in ss. 91 and 92 of the *Constitution Act, 1867*.

[23] A large and liberal, or progressive, interpretation ensures the continued relevance and, indeed, legitimacy of Canada's constituting document. By way of progressive interpretation our Constitution succeeds in its ambitious enterprise, that of structuring the exercise of power by the organs of the state in times vastly different from those in which it was crafted. For instance, Parliament's legislative competence in respect of telephones was recognized on the basis of its authority over interprovincial "undertakings" in s. 92(10)(*a*) even though the telephone had yet to be invented in 1867: *Toronto Corporation v. Bell Telephone Co. of Canada*, [1905] A.C. 52 (P.C.). Likewise, Parliament is not limited to the range of criminal offences recognized by the law of England in 1867 in the exercise of its criminal law power in s. 91(27): *Proprietary Articles Trade Association v. Attorney-General for Canada*, [1931] A.C. 310 (P.C.), at p. 324. Lord Sankey L.C. noted in the *Persons* case, at p. 135, that early English decisions are not a "secure foundation on which to build the interpretation" of our Constitution. We agree.

[24] The arguments presented to this Court in favour of a departure from the "living tree" principle fall into three broad categories: (1) marriage is a pre-legal institution and thus cannot be fundamentally modified by law; (2) even a progressive interpretation of s. 91(26) cannot accommodate same-sex marriage since it falls outside the "natural limits" of that head of power, a corollary to this point being the objection that s. 15 of the *Charter* is being used to "amend" s. 91(26); and (3) in this instance, the intention of the framers of our Constitution should be determinative. As we shall see, none of these arguments persuade.

[25] First, it is argued, the institution of marriage escapes legislative redefinition. Existing in its present basic form since time immemorial, it is not a legal construct, but rather a supra-legal construct subject to legal incidents. In the *Persons* case, Lord Sankey L.C., writing for the Privy Council, dealt with this very type of argument, though in a different context. In addressing whether the fact that women never had occupied public office was relevant to whether they could be considered "persons" for the purposes of being eligible for appointment to the Senate, he said at p. 134:

> The fact that no woman had served or has claimed to serve such an office is not of great weight when it is remembered that custom would have prevented the claim being made or the point being contested.
>
> Customs are apt to develop into traditions which are stronger than law and remain unchallenged long after the reason for them has disappeared.
>
> The appeal to history therefore in this particular matter is not conclusive.

Lord Sankey L.C. acknowledged, at p. 134, that "several centuries ago" it would have been understood that "persons" should refer only to men. Several centuries ago it would have been understood that marriage should be available only to opposite-sex couples. The recognition of same-sex marriage in several Canadian jurisdictions as well as two European countries belies the assertion that the same is true today.

[26] Second, some interveners emphasize that while Lord Sankey L.C. envisioned our Constitution as a "living tree" in the *Persons* case, he specified that it was "capable of growth and expansion within its natural limits" (p. 136). These natural limits, they submit, preclude same-sex marriage. As a corollary, some suggest that s. 1 of the *Proposed Act* would effectively amount to an amendment to the *Constitution Act, 1867* by interpretation based on the values underlying s. 15(1) of the *Charter*.

[27] The natural limits argument can succeed only if its proponents can identify an objective core of meaning which defines what is "natural" in relation to marriage. Absent this, the argument is merely tautological. The only objective core which the interveners before us agree is "natural" to marriage is that it is the voluntary union of two people to the exclusion of all others. Beyond this, views diverge. We are faced with competing opinions on what the natural limits of marriage may be.

[28] Lord Sankey L.C.'s reference to "natural limits" did not impose an obligation to determine, in the abstract and absolutely, the core meaning of constitutional terms. Consequently, it is not for the Court to determine, in the abstract, what the natural limits of marriage must be. Rather, the Court's role is to determine whether marriage as defined in the *Proposed Act* falls within the subject matter of s. 91(26).

[29] In determining whether legislation falls within a particular head of power, a progressive interpretation of the head of power must be adopted. The competing submissions before us do not permit us to conclude that "marriage" in s. 91(26) of the *Constitution Act, 1867*, read expansively, excludes same-sex marriage.

[30] Third, it is submitted that the intention of the framers should be determinative in interpreting the scope of the heads of power enumerated in ss. 91 and 92 given the decision in *R. v. Blais*, [2003] 2 S.C.R. 236, 2003 SCC 44. That case considered the interpretive question in relation to a particular constitutional agreement, as opposed to a head of power which must continually adapt to cover new realities. It is therefore distinguishable and does not apply here.

(ii) The Scope Accorded to Section 91(26) Does Not Trench on Provincial Competence

[31] The potential impact on provincial powers of a federal law on same-sex marriage does not undermine the constitutionality of s. 1 of the *Proposed Act*. Arguments to the effect that it does can be met: (1) they ignore the incidental nature of

any effect upon provincial legislative competence; and (2) they conflate same-sex relationships with same-sex marriage.

[32] Clearly, federal recognition of same-sex marriage would have an impact in the provincial sphere. For instance, provincial competence over the solemnization of marriage provided for in s. 92(12) would be affected by requiring the issuance of marriage licences, the registration of marriages, and the provision of civil solemnization services to same-sex couples. Further, provincial competence in relation to property and civil rights provided for in s. 92(13) would be affected in that a host of legal incidents attendant upon marital status would attach to same-sex couples: e.g., division of property upon dissolution of marriage. These effects, however, are incidental and do not relate to the core of the powers over solemnization and property and civil rights. Incidental effects of federal legislation in the provincial sphere are permissible so long as they do not relate, in pith and substance, to a provincial head of power (*Attorney-General of Saskatchewan v. Attorney-General of Canada*, [1949] 2 D.L.R. 145 (P.C.), at p. 152).

[33] Our law has always recognized that some conjugal relationships are based on marital status, while others are not. The provinces are vested with competence in respect of non-marital same-sex relationships, just as they are vested with competence in respect of non-marital opposite-sex relationships (via the power in respect of property and civil rights under s. 92(13)). For instance, the province of Quebec has established a civil union regime as a means for individuals in committed conjugal relationships to assume a host of rights and responsibilities: see the *Act instituting civil unions and establishing new rules of filiation*, S.Q. 2002, c. 6. Marriage and civil unions are two distinct ways in which couples can express their commitment and structure their legal obligations. Civil unions are a relationship short of marriage and are, therefore, provincially regulated. The authority to legislate in respect of such conjugal relationships cannot, however, extend to marriage. If we accept that provincial competence in respect of same-sex relationships includes same-sex marriage, then we must also accept that provincial competence in respect of opposite-sex relationships includes opposite-sex marriage. This is clearly not the case. Likewise, the scope of the provincial power in respect of solemnization cannot reasonably be extended so as to grant jurisdiction over same-sex marriage to the provincial legislatures. Issues relating to solemnization arise only upon conferral of the right to marry. Just as an opposite-sex couple's ability to marry is not governed by s. 92(12), so a same-sex couple's ability to marry cannot be governed by s. 92(12).

[34] The principle of exhaustiveness, an essential characteristic of the federal distribution of powers, ensures that the whole of legislative power, whether exercised or merely potential, is

distributed as between Parliament and the legislatures.... In essence, there is no topic that cannot be legislated upon, though the particulars of such legislation may be limited by, for instance, the *Charter*. A jurisdictional challenge in respect of any law is therefore limited to determining to which head of power the law relates. Legislative competence over same-sex marriage must be vested in either Parliament or the legislatures. Neither s. 92(12) nor s. 92(13) can accommodate this matter. Given that a legislative void is precluded, s. 91(26) most aptly subsumes it.

(2) Section 2 of the Proposed Act

[35]   Section 2 of the *Proposed Act* provides:

> **2.** Nothing in this Act affects the freedom of officials of religious groups to refuse to perform marriages that are not in accordance with their religious beliefs.

[36]   Section 2 of the *Proposed Act* relates to those who may (or must) perform marriages. Legislative competence over the performance or solemnization of marriage is exclusively allocated to the provinces under s. 92(12) of the *Constitution Act, 1867*.

[37]   The Attorney General of Canada suggests that s. 2 of the *Proposed Act* is declaratory, merely making clear Parliament's intention that other provisions of the *Proposed Act* not be read in a manner that trenches on the provinces' jurisdiction over the solemnization of marriage. The provision might be seen as an attempt to reassure the provinces and to assuage the concerns of religious officials who perform marriages. However worthy of attention these concerns are, only the provinces may legislate exemptions to existing solemnization requirements, as any such exemption necessarily relates to the "solemnization of marriage" under s. 92(12). Section 2 of the *Proposed Act* is therefore *ultra vires* Parliament.

[38]   While it is true that Parliament has exclusive jurisdiction to enact declaratory legislation relating to the interpretation of its own statutes, such declaratory provisions can have no bearing on the constitutional division of legislative authority. That is a matter to be determined, should the need arise, by the courts. It follows that a federal provision seeking to ensure that the Act within which it is situated is not interpreted so as to trench on provincial powers can have no effect and is superfluous.

[39]   The Court is asked in Question 1 whether s. 2 of the *Proposed Act* is within the *exclusive* legislative competence of Parliament. Because s. 2 of the *Proposed Act* relates to a subject matter allocated to the provinces, it follows that it does not fall within the *exclusive* legislative competence of Parliament. The answer to the second part of the first question must therefore be "no."

B. Question 2: Is Section 1 of the Proposed Act, Which Extends Capacity to Marry to Persons of the Same Sex, Consistent with the Charter?

[40]   To determine whether a provision is consistent with the *Charter*, it is first necessary to ascertain whether its purpose or effect is to curtail a *Charter* right: *R. v. Big M Drug Mart Ltd.*, [1985] 1 S.C.R. 295, at p. 331. If so, the further question arises of whether the curtailment is justified under s. 1 of the *Charter*.

(1) Purpose of Section 1 of the Proposed Act

[41]   The purpose of s. 1 of the *Proposed Act* is to extend the right to civil marriage to same-sex couples. The course of events outlined below in relation to Question 4 suggests that the provision is a direct legislative response to the findings of several courts that the opposite-sex requirement for civil marriage violates the equality guarantee enshrined in s. 15(1) of the *Charter*: see *EGALE Canada Inc. v. Canada (Attorney General)* (2003), 225 D.L.R. (4th) 472, 2003 BCCA 251; *Halpern v. Canada (Attorney General)* (2003), 65 O.R. (3d) 161 (C.A.); and *Hendricks v. Québec (Procureur général)*, [2002] R.J.Q. 2506 (Sup. Ct.).

[42]   The preamble to the *Proposed Act* is also instructive. The Act's stated purpose is to ensure that civil marriage as a legal institution is consistent with the *Charter*:

> WHEREAS, in order to reflect values of tolerance, respect and equality consistent with the *Canadian Charter of Rights and Freedoms*, access to marriage for civil purposes should be extended to couples of the same sex;
>
> AND WHEREAS everyone has the freedom of conscience and religion under the *Canadian Charter of Rights and Freedoms* and officials of religious groups are free to refuse to perform marriages that are not in accordance with their religious beliefs;

[43]   Turning to the substance of the provision itself, we note that s. 1 embodies the government's policy stance in relation to the s. 15(1) equality concerns of same-sex couples. This, combined with the circumstances giving rise to the *Proposed Act* and with the preamble thereto, points unequivocally to a purpose which, far from violating the *Charter*, flows from it.

(2) Effect of Section 1 of the Proposed Act

[44]   Section 1 of the *Proposed Act* was impugned before this Court on the basis that, in its effect, it violates ss. 15(1) and 2(*a*) of the *Charter*.

(a) Section 15(1): Equality

[45]   Some interveners submit that the mere legislative recognition of the right of same-sex couples to marry would have the effect of discriminating against (1) religious groups who do not recognize the right of same-sex couples to marry

(religiously) and/or (2) opposite-sex married couples. No submissions have been made as to how the *Proposed Act*, in its effect, might be seen to draw a distinction for the purposes of s. 15, nor can the Court surmise how it might be seen to do so. It withholds no benefits, nor does it impose burdens on a differential basis. It therefore fails to meet the threshold requirement of the s. 15(1) analysis laid down in *Law v. Canada (Minister of Employment and Immigration)*, [1999] 1 S.C.R. 497.

[46] The mere recognition of the equality rights of one group cannot, in itself, constitute a violation of the rights of another. The promotion of *Charter* rights and values enriches our society as a whole and the furtherance of those rights cannot undermine the very principles the *Charter* was meant to foster.

(b) Section 2(a): Religion

[47] The question at this stage is whether s. 1 of the proposed legislation, considered in terms of its effects, is consistent with the guarantee of freedom of religion under s. 2(*a*) of the *Charter*. It is argued that the effect of the *Proposed Act* may violate freedom of religion in three ways: (1) the *Proposed Act* will have the effect of imposing a dominant social ethos and will thus limit the freedom to hold religious beliefs to the contrary; (2) the *Proposed Act* will have the effect of forcing religious officials to perform same-sex marriages; and (3) the *Proposed Act* will create a "collision of rights" in spheres other than that of the solemnization of marriages by religious officials.

[48] The first allegation of infringement says in essence that equality of access to a civil institution like marriage may not only conflict with the views of those who are in disagreement, but may also violate their legal rights. This amounts to saying that the mere conferral of rights upon one group can constitute a violation of the rights of another. This argument was discussed above in relation to s. 15(1) and was rejected.

[49] The second allegation of infringement, namely the allegation that religious officials would be compelled to perform same-sex marriages contrary to their religious beliefs, will be addressed below in relation to Question 3.

[50] This leaves the issue of whether the *Proposed Act* will create an impermissible collision of rights. The potential for a collision of rights does not necessarily imply unconstitutionality. The collision between rights must be approached on the contextual facts of actual conflicts. The first question is whether the rights alleged to conflict can be reconciled: *Trinity Western University v. British Columbia College of Teachers*, [2001] 1 S.C.R. 772, 2001 SCC 31, at para. 29. Where the rights cannot be reconciled, a true conflict of rights is made out. In such cases, the Court will find a limit on religious freedom

and go on to balance the interests at stake under s. 1 of the *Charter*: *Ross v. New Brunswick School District No. 15*, [1996] 1 S.C.R. 825, at paras. 73-74. In both steps, the Court must proceed on the basis that the *Charter* does not create a hierarchy of rights (*Dagenais v. Canadian Broadcasting Corp.*, [1994] 3 S.C.R. 835, at p. 877) and that the right to religious freedom enshrined in s. 2(*a*) of the *Charter* is expansive.

[51] Here, we encounter difficulty at the first stage. The *Proposed Act* has not been passed, much less implemented. Therefore, the alleged collision of rights is purely abstract. There is no factual context. In such circumstances, it would be improper to assess whether the *Proposed Act*, if adopted, would create an impermissible collision of rights in as yet undefined spheres. . . .

[52] The right to same-sex marriage conferred by the *Proposed Act* may conflict with the right to freedom of religion if the Act becomes law, as suggested by the hypothetical scenarios presented by several interveners. However, the jurisprudence confirms that many if not all such conflicts will be resolved *within* the *Charter*, by the delineation of rights prescribed by the cases relating to s. 2(*a*). Conflicts of rights do not imply conflict with the *Charter*; rather the resolution of such conflicts generally occurs within the ambit of the *Charter* itself by way of internal balancing and delineation.

[53] The protection of freedom of religion afforded by s. 2(*a*) of the *Charter* is broad and jealously guarded in our *Charter* jurisprudence. We note that should impermissible conflicts occur, the provision at issue will by definition fail the justification test under s. 1 of the *Charter* and will be of no force or effect under s. 52 of the *Constitution Act, 1982*. In this case the conflict will cease to exist.

[54] In summary, the potential for collision of rights raised by s. 1 of the *Proposed Act* has not been shown on this reference to violate the *Charter*. It has not been shown that impermissible conflicts—conflicts incapable of resolution under s. 2(*a*)—will arise.

C. Question 3: Does the Freedom of Religion Guaranteed by Section 2(a) of the Charter Protect Religious Officials from Being Compelled to Perform Same-Sex Marriages Contrary to Their Religious Beliefs?

[55] The *Proposed Act* is limited in its effect to marriage for civil purposes: see s. 1. It cannot be interpreted as affecting religious marriage or its solemnization. However, Question 3 is formulated broadly and without reference to the *Proposed Act*. We therefore consider this question as it applies to the performance, by religious officials, of both religious and civil marriages. We also must consider the question to mean "compelled by the *state*" to perform, since s. 2(*a*) relates only to

state action; the protection of freedom of religion against private actions is not within the ambit of this question. We note that it would be for the Provinces, in the exercise of their power over the solemnization of marriage, to legislate in a way that protects the rights of religious officials while providing for solemnization of same-sex marriage. It should also be noted that human rights codes must be interpreted and applied in a manner that respects the broad protection granted to religious freedom under the *Charter*.

[56] Against this background, we return to the question. The concern here is that if the *Proposed Act* were adopted, religious officials could be required to perform same-sex marriages contrary to their religious beliefs. Absent state compulsion on religious officials, this conjecture does not engage the *Charter*. If a promulgated statute were to enact compulsion, we conclude that such compulsion would almost certainly run afoul of the *Charter* guarantee of freedom of religion, given the expansive protection afforded to religion by s. 2(*a*) of the *Charter*.

[57] The right to freedom of religion enshrined in s. 2(*a*) of the *Charter* encompasses the right to believe and entertain the religious beliefs of one's choice, the right to declare one's religious beliefs openly and the right to manifest religious belief by worship, teaching, dissemination and religious practice: *Big M Drug Mart, supra*, at pp. 336-37. The performance of religious rites is a fundamental aspect of religious practice.

[58] It therefore seems clear that state compulsion on religious officials to perform same-sex marriages contrary to their religious beliefs would violate the guarantee of freedom of religion under s. 2(*a*) of the *Charter*. It also seems apparent that, absent exceptional circumstances which we cannot at present foresee, such a violation could not be justified under s. 1 of the *Charter*.

[59] The question we are asked to answer is confined to the performance of same-sex marriages by religious officials. However, concerns were raised about the compulsory use of sacred places for the celebration of such marriages and about being compelled to otherwise assist in the celebration of same-sex marriages. The reasoning that leads us to conclude that the guarantee of freedom of religion protects against the compulsory celebration of same-sex marriages, suggests that the same would hold for these concerns.

[60] Returning to the question before us, the Court is of the opinion that, absent unique circumstances with respect to which we will not speculate, the guarantee of religious freedom in s. 2(*a*) of the *Charter* is broad enough to protect religious officials from being compelled by the state to perform civil or religious same-sex marriages that are contrary to their religious beliefs.

D. Question 4: Is the Opposite-Sex Requirement for Marriage for Civil Purposes, as Established by the Common Law and Set Out for Quebec in Section 5 of the Federal Law–Civil Law Harmonization Act, No. 1, Consistent with the Charter?

(1) Threshold Issue: Whether the Court Should Answer Question 4

[61] The first issue is whether this Court should answer the fourth question, in the unique circumstances of this reference. This issue must be approached on the basis that the answer to Question 4 may be positive or negative; the preliminary analysis of the discretion not to answer a reference question cannot be predicated on a presumed outcome. The reference jurisdiction vested in this Court by s. 53 of the *Supreme Court Act* is broad and has been interpreted liberally: see, e.g., *Secession Reference, supra*. The Court has rarely exercised its discretion not to answer a reference question reflecting its perception of the seriousness of its advisory role.

[62] Despite this, the Court may decline to answer reference questions where to do so would be inappropriate, either because the question lacks sufficient legal content (which is not the case here) or because attempting to answer it would for other reasons be problematic.

[63] In the *Secession Reference, supra*, at para. 30, we noted that instances where the Court has refused to answer reference questions on grounds other than lack of legal content tend to fall into two broad categories: (1) where the question is too ambiguous or imprecise to allow an accurate answer: see, e.g., *Reference re Goods and Services Tax*, [1992] 2 S.C.R. 445, at p. 485; and *Reference re Remuneration of Judges of the Provincial Court of Prince Edward Island*, [1997] 3 S.C.R. 3, at para. 256; and (2) where the parties have not provided the Court with sufficient information to provide a complete answer: see, e.g., *Reference re Authority of Parliament in relation to the Upper House*, [1980] 1 S.C.R. 54, at pp. 75-77; and *Reference re Remuneration of Judges of the Provincial Court of Prince Edward Island*, at para. 257. These categories highlight two important considerations, but are not exhaustive.

[64] A unique set of circumstances is raised by Question 4, the combined effect of which persuades the Court that it would be unwise and inappropriate to answer the question.

[65] The first consideration on the issue of whether this Court should answer the fourth question is the government's stated position that it will proceed by way of legislative enactment, regardless of what answer we give to this question. In oral argument, counsel reiterated the government's unequivocal intention to introduce legislation in relation to same-sex marriage, regardless of the answer to Question 4. The government has clearly accepted the rulings of lower courts on this

question and has adopted their position as its own. The common law definition of marriage in five provinces and one territory no longer imports an opposite-sex requirement. In addition, s. 5 of the *Federal Law–Civil Law Harmonization Act, No. 1*, S.C. 2001, c. 4, no longer imports an opposite-sex requirement. Given the government's stated commitment to this course of action, an opinion on the constitutionality of an opposite-sex requirement for marriage serves no legal purpose. On the other hand, answering this question may have serious deleterious effects, which brings us to our next point.

[66] The second consideration is that the parties to previous litigation have now relied upon the finality of the judgments they obtained through the court process. In the circumstances, their vested rights outweigh any benefit accruing from an answer to Question 4. Moreover, other same-sex couples acted on the finality of *EGALE*, *Halpern* and *Hendricks* to marry, relying on the Attorney General of Canada's adoption of the result in those cases. While the effects of the *EGALE* and *Hendricks* decisions were initially suspended, the suspensions were lifted with the consent of the Attorney General. As a result of these developments, same-sex marriages have generally come to be viewed as legal and have been regularly taking place in British Columbia, Ontario and Quebec. Since this reference was initiated, the opposite-sex requirement for marriage has also been struck down in the Yukon, Manitoba, Nova Scotia and Saskatchewan: *Dunbar v. Yukon*, [2004] Y.J. No. 61 (QL), 2004 YKSC 54; *Vogel v. Canada (Attorney General)*, [2004] M.J. No. 418 (QL) (Q.B.); *Boutilier v. Nova Scotia (Attorney General)*, [2004] N.S.J. No. 357 (QL) (S.C.); and *N.W. v. Canada (Attorney General)*, [2004] S.J. No. 669 (QL), 2004 SKQB 434. In each of those instances, the Attorney General of Canada conceded that the common law definition of marriage was inconsistent with s. 15(1) of the *Charter* and was not justifiable under s. 1, and publicly adopted the position that the opposite-sex requirement for marriage was unconstitutional.

[67] As noted by this Court in *Nova Scotia (Attorney General) v. Walsh*, [2002] 4 S.C.R. 325, 2002 SCC 83, at para. 43:

> The decision to marry or not is intensely personal and engages a complex interplay of social, political, religious, and financial considerations by the individual.

The parties in *EGALE*, *Halpern* and *Hendricks* have made this intensely personal decision. They have done so relying upon the finality of the judgments concerning them. We are told that thousands of couples have now followed suit. There is no compelling basis for jeopardizing acquired rights, which would be a potential outcome of answering Question 4.

[68] There is no precedent for answering a reference question which mirrors issues already disposed of in lower courts where an appeal was available but not pursued. Reference questions may, on occasion, pertain to already adjudicated disputes: see, e.g., *Reference re Truscott*, [1967] S.C.R. 309; *Reference re Regina v. Coffin*, [1956] S.C.R. 191; *Reference re Minimum Wage Act of Saskatchewan*, [1948] S.C.R. 248; and *Reference re Milgaard (Can.)*, [1992] 1 S.C.R. 866. In those cases, however, no appeal to the Supreme Court was possible, either because leave to appeal had been denied (*Truscott* and *Milgaard*) or because no right of appeal existed (*Coffin* and *Minimum Wage Act of Saskatchewan*). The only instance that we are aware of where a reference was pursued in lieu of appeal is *Reference re Newfoundland Continental Shelf*, [1984] 1 S.C.R. 86. That reference is also distinguishable: unlike the instant reference, it was not a direct response to the findings of a lower appellate court and the parties involved in the prior proceedings had consented to the use of the reference procedure.

[69] The final consideration is that answering this question has the potential to undermine the government's stated goal of achieving uniformity in respect of civil marriage across Canada. There is no question that uniformity of the law is essential. This is the very reason that Parliament was accorded legislative competence in respect of marriage under s. 91(26) of the *Constitution Act, 1867*. However, as discussed, the government has already chosen to address the question of uniformity by means of the *Proposed Act*, which we have found to be within Parliament's legislative competence and consistent with the *Charter*. Answering the fourth question will not assist further. Given that uniformity is to be addressed legislatively, this rationale for answering Question 4 fails to compel.

[70] On the other hand, consideration of the fourth question has the potential to undermine the uniformity that would be achieved by the adoption of the proposed legislation. The uniformity argument succeeds only if the answer to Question 4 is "no." By contrast, a "yes" answer would throw the law into confusion. The decisions of the lower courts in the matters giving rise to this reference are binding in their respective provinces. They would be cast into doubt by an advisory opinion which expressed a contrary view, even though it could not overturn them. The result would be confusion, not uniformity.

[71] In sum, a unique combination of factors is at play in Question 4. The government has stated its intention to address the issue of same-sex marriage by introducing legislation regardless of our opinion on this question. The parties to previous litigation have relied upon the finality of their judgments and have acquired rights which in our view are entitled to protection. Finally, an answer to Question 4 would not only fail to ensure uniformity of the law, but might undermine it. These circumstances, weighed against the hypothetical benefit Parliament might derive from an answer, convince the Court that it should exercise its discretion not to answer Question 4.

(2) The Substance of Question 4

[72] For the reasons set out above, the Court exercises its discretion not to answer this question.

III. Conclusion

[73] The Court answers the reference questions as follows:

1. Is the annexed *Proposal for an Act respecting certain aspects of legal capacity for marriage for civil purposes* within the exclusive legislative authority of the Parliament of Canada? If not, in what particular or particulars, and to what extent?

    Answer: With respect to s. 1: Yes. With respect to s. 2: No.

2. If the answer to question 1 is yes, is section 1 of the proposal, which extends capacity to marry to persons of the same sex, consistent with the *Canadian Charter of Rights and Freedoms*? If not, in what particular or particulars, and to what extent?

    Answer: Yes.

3. Does the freedom of religion guaranteed by paragraph 2(*a*) of the *Canadian Charter of Rights and Freedoms* protect religious officials from being compelled to perform a marriage between two persons of the same sex that is contrary to their religious beliefs?

    Answer: Yes.

4. Is the opposite-sex requirement for marriage for civil purposes, as established by the common law and set out for Quebec in section 5 of the *Federal Law–Civil Law Harmonization Act, No. 1*, consistent with the *Canadian Charter of Rights and Freedoms*? If not, in what particular or particulars and to what extent?

    Answer: The Court exercises its discretion not to answer this question. . . .

PART NINE

Language Rights

Mahe v. Alberta, 1990

The *Constitution Act, 1867* contains only two sections explicitly recognizing rights. These sections confer rights on groups rather than individuals. These are section 93, which sets out school rights for the Protestant minority in Quebec and the Roman Catholic minority in other provinces, and section 133, which sets out rights to use French in the federal Parliament and courts and reciprocal rights to use English in the Quebec legislature and courts. When Manitoba became a province of Canada, a similar provision enshrined the right to use English and French in its legislature and courts. These rights sections in Canada's founding Constitution are specific to the Canadian historical experience. They reflect the accommodation of European cultures upon which Confederation was based.

Section 93 guaranteed that Quebec Protestants would have the same rights to separate schools that Catholics enjoyed in Ontario. It protected not only any school rights enjoyed by Protestant and Catholic minorities in any province at the time of Confederation but any rights that might be established thereafter. This guarantee of denominational schools was varied slightly for the prairie provinces when they became part of Canada and a more extensive guarantee was included in Newfoundland's terms of union in 1949.

The provisions of section 93 show how little the Fathers of Confederation looked to the courts to enforce constitutional rights. Appeals against provinces for denying section 93 rights were to go to the federal Cabinet, and if a province failed to comply with the federal government's instructions, the federal Parliament could pass remedial legislation. The first and only time a federal government threatened to use these remedial powers was when Charles Tupper introduced a Remedial Bill in response to an appeal by Manitoba Catholics in 1895. The proposed Remedial Bill was a major reason for defeat of Tupper's Conservative government by Wilfrid Laurier's Liberals in the 1896 federal election. Laurier favoured provincial rights over the rights of Manitoba's Catholic minority. Since then, appeals against denials of section 93 rights have been dealt with in the courts.

In the years when the most important section 93 cases were heard, Canada's highest court was the Judicial Committee of the Privy Council, and it was remarkably restrained in interpreting section 93. In 1892, it reversed the Supreme Court of Canada and upheld Manitoba legislation establishing a secular school system and withdrawing public funding for Roman Catholic separate schools.[1] In 1917, it upheld an Ontario regulation prohibiting the use of French in all schools, including Roman Catholic separate schools, even though in some parts of the province most of the separate school students at that time were French-speaking.[2] These JCPC decisions were a major factor in preventing Canada west of Quebec from developing along bicultural lines.

---

1 *Barrett v. The City of Winnipeg* (1892), A.C. 445.

2 *Ottawa Roman Catholic Separate School v. Mackell* (1917), A.C. 62.

Section 29 of the *Charter* stipulates that nothing in the *Charter* can abrogate the historic section 93 denominational school rights. In 1984, the Supreme Court rejected a section 15 *Charter* challenge to Ontario legislation extending public funding to the full secondary-school program of the province's Roman Catholic Separate Schools.[3] The Court based its decision not so much on section 29 of the *Charter* as on the plenary authority section 93 gives provinces to develop a system of denominational schools.

Section 93 came up in a peripheral way in *Mahe*. The central issues in the case were whether the right to minority-language education facilities included the minority's right to manage and control its educational facilities, and whether that right to management and control could be met in Edmonton by including minority-language trustees on the city's Roman Catholic Separate School Board. This raised the side issue whether the denominational school rights would be violated by this arrangement. The Court ruled that because the Separate School Board would lose no power over religious aspects of its schools there was no abrogation of denominational school rights.

Although the Supreme Court has made it clear that the "new Constitution" is not to invalidate fundamental provisions of the "old Constitution," the rights sections of the old Constitution have been changing, reflecting the secularization of Canadian society and an emphasis on minority language rights over minority faith-based rights. In 1997, in response to a unanimous resolution of Quebec's National Assembly, the federal Parliament supported a constitutional amendment making the section 93 guarantee of denominational school rights inapplicable in Quebec. This amendment reflects the desire of English-speaking and French-speaking Quebecers to organize their schools around language communities rather than religious communities. The following year, Newfoundlanders voted by a 73 percent majority to scrap their faith-based school system.[4]

Fundamental to Pierre Trudeau and his government in pressing for a *Charter of Rights* was a vision of Canada in which French-speaking Canadians would feel at home in all parts of the country and English-speaking Canadians would feel secure in Quebec. This vision is reflected in sections 16 to 23 of the *Charter*. The fact that the *Charter*'s legislative override clause does not apply to these sections is indicative of their importance to the *Charter*'s framers. These sections of the *Charter* extend the language rights in section 133 of the Constitution in four ways. First, section 16 states, for the first time, that English and French are "the official languages of Canada." Second, the right to use English or French is extended to communications with all federal head offices and all other offices "where there is significant demand." Third, New Brunswick becomes Canada's first province in which English and French are official languages, and the right to use both languages is extended to its legislature, provincial courts, and governmental services. Fourth, section 23 establishes a complex set of minority-language education rights. This section gives citizens who are members of the English-speaking minority in Quebec or the French-speaking minority in the other provinces the right to have their children receive their primary- and secondary-school instruction in the minority language in that province. The minority-language instruction

---

3   *Reference Re Bill 30, An Act to Amend the Education Act (Ont.),* [1987] 1 S.C.R. 1148.

4   For details, see Peter H. Russell, *Constitutional Odyssey: Can Canadians Become a Sovereign People?*, 3d ed. (Toronto: University of Toronto Press, 2004) at 249.

is to be supported by public funds where numbers warrant. A similar numbers-warrant qualification applies to the right to have the instruction provided through "minority language educational facilities."

In interpreting constitutional language rights, the Supreme Court's performance has been virtually the polar opposite of the Judicial Committee's treatment of denominational school rights. With one notable exception, it has given these rights, both the old rights in the *Constitution Act, 1867* and the new rights in the *Charter*, a broad and liberal interpretation. This trend was evident before the *Charter* in 1979 when, after decades in which there was virtually no litigation based on the historic language rights, two cases came before the Court. *Blaikie*[5] involved a collision between Bill 101, Quebec's *Charter of the French Language*, the most important legislative initiative of Quebec's recently elected Parti Québécois government, and section 133 in the *Constitution Act, 1867*. The other case, *Forest*,[6] involved a challenge, based on Manitoba's equivalent of section 133, to that province's *Official Language Act*, which had been enacted nearly a century earlier, and that had made English the official language of Manitoba.

The Supreme Court vigorously applied the constitutional guarantees in both the 1979 cases. In *Blaikie*, the Court held that the provision in section 133 that the Acts of Quebec's legislature "shall be printed and published in both English and French" required more than providing an English translation of Quebec's laws. It required that the legislation be actually enacted in both languages so that, contrary to Bill 101, the English version had the same legal status as the French version. Moreover, the Court required that not just Acts, but all regulations and subordinate legislation be available in English as well as French, and that the right to use both languages in the courts of Quebec apply to all administrative agencies exercising adjudicative responsibilities. The Court applied similar guarantees of bilingualism just as vigorously in *Forest*—except that here it was applying them to a regime that had been much more extreme in its unilingualism than Quebec has ever been. The 1890 Manitoba *Act* actually forbade the use of French in the records and journals of the legislature and in court proceedings and provided that Acts of the legislature be printed and published in English only. This legislation had remained in force since its enactment—despite several *successful* challenges at the lower-court level. Now it was found to be unconstitutional by Canada's highest court and in an era when judicial decisions, no matter how challenging and counter-majoritarian they may be, cannot simply be ignored.

There was a remarkable sequel to *Forest*. Even with a brigade of translators, 90 years of legislation cannot be translated overnight. Are statutes and regulations that have not been translated into French unconstitutional? In 1985, this question was referred to the Supreme Court in a highly charged political context. In 1983, a referendum in the city of Winnipeg, where over half of Manitoba's population live, resulted in a 4-to-1 majority against proceeding with a constitutional amendment that would give the province time to translate its laws. In the 1985 reference case, the Supreme Court seemed to be between a rock and a hard place.[7] If it ruled that Manitoba's English-only laws were valid, it would make a mockery of

---

5   *Attorney General of Quebec v. Blaikie*, [1979] 2 S.C.R. 1016.

6   *Attorney General of Manitoba v. Forest*, [1979] 2 S.C.R. 1032.

7   *Reference re Manitoba Language Rights*, [1985] 2 S.C.R. 347.

its decision in *Forest*. If it made the opposite ruling and rendered nearly the entire provincial statute book null and void, it would plunge the province into the dark sea of legal anarchy. The Court's solution was to draw on international experience in upholding the laws of unconstitutional regimes and in order to safeguard the rule of law give temporary validity to the English-only laws while they were being translated into French. "The Constitution," said the Court, "will not suffer a province without laws." It gave Manitoba five years to get the job done, and it gave the world a new contribution to constitutional theory.

One of the Supreme Court's very first *Charter* decisions was the Association of Quebec Protestant School Boards' *Charter*-based challenge to Quebec's Bill 101.[8] In effect, the case pitted the "Quebec Clause" in Bill 101 against the *Charter*'s "Canada Clause." Sections 72-73 of Bill 101 restricted access to publicly funded English-language schools to the children of Anglophone parents already living in Quebec. It was called the "Quebec Clause" because it was designed to stem the growth of English-speaking Quebec. Section 23(1)(*b*) of the *Charter* gave the right to instruction in English to children of parents who had received their primary education in English outside Quebec and at any time in the future moved to Quebec.[9] It applied in a reciprocal way to French-speaking Quebecers who moved to other provinces. It was called the "Canada Clause" because it was designed to enable English-speaking and French-speaking Canadians to move anywhere in Canada with assurance that their children could be educated in their parents' mother tongue. In a unanimous unsigned *per curiam* decision, the Court struck down sections 72-73 of Bill 101. It refused to consider the section 1 arguments advanced by Quebec showing demographic data about the decline in the percentage of French speakers in the province. Because the "Quebec Clause," in the judges' view, was a complete denial of the *Charter* right, it could not be considered as a reasonable limit. In no subsequent case has the Court made this distinction between a denial of a right and a limit on a right. Coming on the heels of Quebec's loss in the *Quebec Veto* case,[10] this decision contributed to Quebec's sense of alienation from the rest of Canada and fueled its agitation for constitutional change.

In a trio of cases decided in 1986, the Supreme Court seemed to be applying the breaks to its language-rights express. Two of the cases, one from Quebec[11] and the other from Manitoba,[12] involved challenges to unilingual summonses issued for traffic violations. In both cases, the Court's majority rejected the challenge on the ground that section 133 states that English or French "may be used" in any process issuing from a court in these provinces so that in this context the minority language is optional, not mandatory. The third case was initiated by New Brunswick Acadians who sought a ruling that their right to use French in

---

8   *Attorney General of Quebec v. Association of Quebec Protestant School Boards*, [1984] 2 S.C.R. 66.

9   Section 23(1)(*a*) confers the right to minority-language education to new Canadians whose first language is English or French. As a last minute concession to Quebec, section 59 was added to the *Constitution Act, 1982*, suspending the enforcement of section 23(1)(*a*) until such time as the legislative assembly or government of Quebec brings it into force.

10   See *Re: Objection to a Resolution to Amend the Constitution (Quebec Veto Reference)*, [1982] 2 S.C.R. 793.

11   *MacDonald v. City of Montreal*, [1986] 1 S.C.R. 460.

12   *Bilodeau v. Attorney General of Manitoba*, [1986] 1 S.C.R. 449.

New Brunswick's courts implied a right to be understood in French. Again, the Court's majority, which included all of the Court's Francophone justices, rejected the language-rights claim. Justice Beetz's majority opinion recognized that there is a common law right to be heard and understood in court, which, as one aspect of a universal right to a fair hearing, should be interpreted in a broad and liberal way. But, he argued, the language rights in Canada's Constitution are founded on political compromise and should be interpreted narrowly. The development of such a right should be left primarily to legislatures and the political process. Justice Wilson took the opposite view, contending that there was a "principle of growth" in the language-rights provisions of the Constitution and that, if these rights are to be developed to their full potential, courts must go beyond the literal words of these provisions.

The Court's decision in *Mahe* indicates that, for now, Justice Wilson's approach appears to have won out over Justice Beetz's. The case was the culmination of a struggle by French-speaking minority communities across Canada, in the words of Michael Behiels, to "infuse s. 23 (of the *Charter*) with real power."[13] On the other side of the struggle were provincial governments (five of them were interveners in the case) concerned that their control over education might be diluted by judicial interpretation of the *Charter*'s section 23. The key issue in the case was whether the right to receive instruction in "minority language education facilities" includes the right to control and manage such facilities. The Court, in a unanimous opinion written by Chief Justice Dickson, answered this question in the affirmative. Early in his analysis, the Chief Justice backed the Court away from Justice Beetz's position, stating that "it must be open to the Court to breathe new life into a compromise that is clearly expressed."

While the case was certainly seen as a victory for the various associations of Francophone parents that brought it on, the Court did not give them all that they were after. In their submissions, these groups argued that the management and control of minority education facilities required that the direction of such facilities be exercised by an independent Francophone school board. Dickson did not think that the number of students likely to attend Francophone schools in Edmonton was sufficient to justify such an independent board. It would suffice to guarantee Francophone representation on the Separate School Board and give these representatives full control over all aspects of French-language instruction. He put forward the idea of a sliding scale of entitlement based on the number of children who qualify for minority-language education as the methodology for applying section 23(3). One additional point that he granted to the Francophone parents was to hold that an Alberta education regulation requiring no less than 300 minutes per week of instruction in the English language in all schools, including Francophone schools, infringed section 23 and was invalid until and unless such a limitation was justified under section 1 of the *Charter*.

Three years later, in *Re Public School Act (Man.)* (1993),[14] the Court struck down Manitoba legislation respecting French-language schools because it made no provision for Francophone parents to control and manage French-language education. In a 2000 case, the Court

---

13 Michael D. Behiels, *Canada's Francophone Minority Communities: Constitutional Renewal and the Winning of School Governance* (Montreal and Kingston: McGill-Queen's University Press, 2004) at 169.

14 [1993] 1 S.C.R. 839.

ruled that Prince Edward Island must provide a school in the community of Summerside for the 49 students enrolled there for French-language education, rather than bus those students to a French-language school 28 kilometres away.[15] The Court's liberal and vigorous treatment of the *Charter*'s language of education rights has certainly qualified the province's exclusive jurisdiction over education much more than the denominational education rights in section 93 ever did. Indeed, this may be the *Charter*'s most significant impact on the federal division of powers. ⌐

Discussion Questions

1 Do you agree that "it must be open to the Court to breathe new life into a compromise that is clearly expressed"?
2. Of the judges who participated in Justice Beetz's majority in *Société des Acadiens v. Association of Parents* in 1986, only Justice Lamer was still on the Supreme Court when *Mahe* was heard and decided by a seven-judge panel. Do you think it would have made a difference in *Mahe* if Justice Lamer had been on the panel?
3. Are judges well suited to determine "where numbers warrant"?

---

15   *Arsenault-Cameron v. Prince Edward Island*, [2000] 1 S.C.R. 3.

MAHE v. ALBERTA
[1990] 1 S.C.R. 342

Hearing: June 14, 1989; Judgment: March 15, 1990.

Present: Dickson C.J. and Wilson, La Forest, L'Heureux-Dubé, Sopinka, Gonthier, and Cory JJ.

Interveners: The Attorney General of Canada, the Attorney General for Ontario, the Attorney General of Quebec, the Attorney General for New Brunswick, the Attorney General of Manitoba, the Attorney General of Manitoba, the Attorney General for Saskatchewan, the Association canadienne-française de l'Alberta, the Commissioner of Official Languages for Canada, Alliance Quebec, Alliance for Languages Communities in Quebec, the Association canadienne-française de l'Ontario, the Association française des conseils scolaires de l'Ontario, the Association des enseignantes et des enseignantes franco-ontariens, the Quebec Association of Protestant School Boards, the Edmonton Roman Catholic Separate School District No. 7, and the Alberta School Trustees' Association.

The judgment of the Court was delivered by

THE CHIEF JUSTICE: In this appeal the Court is asked to determine whether the educational system in the city of Edmonton satisfies the demands of s. 23 of the *Canadian Charter of Rights and Freedoms*. ...

Section 23 is one component in Canada's constitutional protection of the official languages. The section is especially important in this regard, however, because of the vital role of education in preserving and encouraging linguistic and cultural vitality. It thus represents a linchpin in this nation's commitment to the values of bilingualism and biculturalism.

The appellants claim that their rights under s. 23 are not satisfied by the existing educational system in Edmonton nor by the legislation under which it operates, resulting in an erosion of their cultural heritage, contrary to the spirit and intent of the *Charter*. In particular, the appellants argue that s. 23 guarantees the right, in Edmonton, to the "management and control" of a minority-language school—that is, to a Francophone school run by a Francophone school board. Our task then is to determine the meaning of s. 23 of the *Charter*.

Constitutional Questions

The following constitutional questions, stated by order of the Court, indicate the range of the issues which this appeal raises:

1. Have the rights of the linguistic minority population in metropolitan Edmonton to minority language educational facilities pursuant to s. 23(3)(*b*) of the *Canadian Charter of Rights and Freedoms* been infringed or denied?

2. Does the right to minority language instruction and educational facilities pursuant to s. 23(3)(*a*) and s. 23(3)(*b*) of the *Charter* include management and control by the minority of:
   (a) the instruction?
   (b) the educational facilities?
   If so, what is the nature and extent of such management and control?

3. (a) Are the *School Act*, R.S.A. 1980, c. S-3, and the regulations passed thereunder inconsistent with or in contravention of s. 23 of the *Charter*?
   (b) If so, is such inconsistency or contravention justified under s. 1 of the *Charter*?

4. Are the rights guaranteed by s. 23 of the *Charter* affected by the provisions of s. 93 of the *Constitution Act, 1867*, s. 29 of the *Charter* and s. 17 of the *Alberta Act*? If so, how?

The Parties and Interveners

The appellants Jean-Claude Mahe and Paul Dubé are parents whose first language learned and still understood is French. The appellant Angeline Martel is a parent who received her primary school instruction in French. All three have school age children, and thus qualify under s. 23(1) of the *Charter* as persons who, subject to certain limitations, "have the right to have their children receive primary and secondary school instruction" in the language of the linguistic minority population of the province—in this case, the French language. They may therefore conveniently be called "s. 23 parents," and their children "s. 23 students." The fourth appellant, the Association de l'école Georges et Julia Bugnet, is an incorporated society whose prime objective is the encouragement of French language education in the province of Alberta.

A number of interveners were granted status in this appeal: the Attorneys General of Canada, Ontario, Québec, New Brunswick, Manitoba, and Saskatchewan; Alliance Quebec; the Edmonton Roman Catholic Separate School District No. 7; the Alberta School Trustees' Association; the Association canadienne-française de l'Alberta; the Quebec Association of Protestant School Boards; the Association canadienne-française de l'Ontario; the Association française des conseils scolaires de l'Ontario; the Association des enseignantes et des enseignants franco-ontariens; and, the Commissioner of Official Languages for Canada.

Facts

The appellants were and still are dissatisfied with the provision of French language education in Alberta, particularly in

Edmonton. In 1982 they forwarded a proposal to the Minister of Education of Alberta for a new French-language public elementary school in Edmonton, which would have the following features: (1) it would instruct Francophone children exclusively in the French language and in a totally "French" environment; (2) it would be administered by a Committee of Parents under the structure of an autonomous French School Board; and (3) it would have a programme reflecting the French linguistic culture.

The appellants were advised that it was a policy of the Province, acting through the Department of Education, to *not* create any French school jurisdictions. The appellants were encouraged to take their proposal to either the Edmonton Roman Catholic Separate School Board or to the Edmonton Public School Board. The appellants did this, but both Boards rejected their proposal. The Roman Catholic Separate School Board did decide to conduct a study with respect to whether the needs of Francophone students in Edmonton were being met. As a result of that study, in June of 1983 the Roman Catholic Separate School Board directed that a Francophone school, École Maurice Lavallée, be established in September of 1984 under the direction of the Edmonton Roman Catholic Separate School District No. 7.

The evidence relating to the chronology of the development of École Maurice Lavallée is somewhat sketchy. It appears that prior to September 1984, École Maurice Lavallée had been a French immersion school. After that date it continued to offer an immersion programme in grades 7 and 8, but from kindergarten to grade 6 it became a "French only" school, with admission restricted to students of parents who qualified under s. 23 of the *Charter*. Evidence was presented that as of September 1985, the Roman Catholic Separate School Board District No. 7 intended to commence a Junior High programme at the school and to move its immersion course out of Maurice Lavallée over a two-year period. After this transition period the school would be comprised entirely of "s. 23 students." At about the same time, the Roman Catholic Board also adopted a motion that they would promote and pursue the establishment of a grade 9 to 12 Francophone programme at a school named École J.H. Picard. It appears that as of the date of the hearing before the Court of Appeal, the Roman Catholic Board had in fact established a Francophone high school at École J.H. Picard, although details of the operation of this school have not been provided to us.

At École Maurice Lavallée, French is the language of instruction and administration, the personnel are all Francophone, and the stated aim of the school is "to primarily reflect the cultural heritage of the French linguistic minority in Alberta." The government emphasized in its argument that the school is not a French immersion school. The respondent also pointed out that non-residents are granted admission to the school if they qualify under s. 23 of the *Charter* and that the school has a Parent Advisory Committee which is incorporated pursuant to the *Societies Act*, R.S.A. 1980, c. S-18, and which acts as an advisory body to the Board of Trustees.

As a result of the failure of the government to accede to all of their requests, the appellants commenced the action which has culminated in the present appeal. . . .

At the heart of this appeal is the claim of the appellants that the term "minority language educational facilities" referred to in s. 23(3)(*b*) includes administration by distinct school boards. The respondent takes the position that the word "facilities" means a school building. The respondent submits that the rights of the Francophone minority in metropolitan Edmonton have not been denied because those rights are being met with current Francophone educational facilities. . . .

Analysis

The primary issue raised by this appeal is the degree, if any, of "management and control" of a French language school which should be accorded to s. 23 parents in Edmonton. (The phrase "management and control," it should be noted, is not a term of art: it appears to have been introduced in earlier s. 23 cases and has now gained such currency that it was utilized by all the groups in this appeal.) The appellants appear to accept that, with a few exceptions, the government has provided whatever other services or rights might be mandated in Edmonton under s. 23: their fundamental complaint is that they do not have the exclusive management and control of the existing Francophone schools. The other issues raised by the appellants in their statement of claim are either consequent upon or secondary to this primary issue. . . .

(1) The Purpose of Section 23

The general purpose of s. 23 is clear: it is to preserve and promote the two official languages of Canada, and their respective cultures, by ensuring that each language flourishes, as far as possible, in provinces where it is not spoken by the majority of the population. The section aims at achieving this goal by granting minority language educational rights to minority language parents throughout Canada.

My reference to cultures is significant: it is based on the fact that any broad guarantee of language rights, especially in the context of education, cannot be separated from a concern for the culture associated with the language. Language is more than a mere means of communication, it is part and parcel of the identity and culture of the people speaking it. It is the means by which individuals understand themselves and the world around them. . . .

In my view the appellants are fully justified in submitting that "history reveals that s. 23 was designed to correct, on a national scale, the progressive erosion of minority official language groups and to give effect to the concept of the 'equal partnership' of the two official language groups in the context of education."

The remedial aspect of s. 23 was indirectly questioned by the respondent and several of the interveners in an argument which they put forward for a "narrow construction" of s. 23. The following statements by Beetz J. in a case dealing with s. 16 of the *Charter, Société des Acadiens du Nouveau-Brunswick Inc. v. Association of Parents for Fairness in Education,* [1986] 1 S.C.R. 549, at p. 578, were relied upon in support of this argument:

> Unlike language rights which are based on political compromise, legal rights tend to be seminal in nature because they are rooted in principle. Some of them, such as the one expressed in s. 7 of the *Charter*, are so broad as to call for frequent judicial determination.
>
> Language rights, on the other hand, although some of them have been enlarged and incorporated into the *Charter*, remain nonetheless founded on political compromise.
>
> This essential difference between the two types of rights dictates a distinct judicial approach with respect to each. More particularly, the courts should pause before they decide to act as instruments of change with respect to language rights. This is not to say that language rights provisions are cast in stone and should remain immune altogether from judicial interpretation. But, in my opinion, the courts should approach them with more restraint than they would in construing legal rights.

I do not believe that these words support the proposition that s. 23 should be given a particularly narrow construction, or that its remedial purpose should be ignored. Beetz J. makes it clear in this quotation that language rights are not cast in stone nor immune from judicial interpretation. In *Reference Re Bill 30, An Act to amend the Education Act (Ont.),* [1987] 1 S.C.R. 1148, at p. 1176, Wilson J. made the following comments in respect of the above quotation:

> While due regard must be paid not to give a provision which reflects a political compromise too wide an interpretation, it must still be open to the Court to breathe life into a compromise that is clearly expressed.

I agree. Beetz J.'s warning that courts should be careful in interpreting language rights is a sound one. Section 23 provides a perfect example of why such caution is advisable. The provision provides for a novel form of legal right, quite different from the type of legal rights which courts have traditionally dealt with. Both its genesis and its form are evidence of the unusual nature of s. 23. Section 23 confers upon a group a right which places positive obligations on government to alter or develop major institutional structures. Careful interpretation of such a section is wise: however, this does not mean that courts should not "breathe life" into the expressed purpose of the section, or avoid implementing the possibly novel remedies needed to achieve that purpose.

(2) The Context of Section 23(3)(b): An Overview of Section 23

The proper way of interpreting s. 23, in my opinion, is to view the section as providing a general right to minority language instruction. Paragraphs (*a*) and (*b*) of subs. (3) qualify this general right: para. (*a*) adds that the right to instruction is only guaranteed where the "number of children" warrants, while para. (*b*) further qualifies the general right to instruction by adding that where numbers warrant it includes a right to "minority language educational facilities." In my view, subs. (3)(*b*) is included in order to indicate the upper range of possible institutional requirements which may be mandated by s. 23 (the government may, of course, provide more than the minimum required by s. 23).

Another way of expressing the above interpretation of s. 23 is to say that s. 23 should be viewed as encompassing a "sliding scale" of requirement, with subs. (3)(*b*) indicating the upper level of this range and the term "instruction" in subs. (3)(*a*) indicating the lower level. . . .

The sliding scale approach can be contrasted with that which views s. 23 as only encompassing two rights—one with respect to instruction and one with respect to facilities—each providing a certain level of services appropriate for one of two numerical thresholds. On this interpretation of s. 23, which could be called the "separate rights" approach, a specified number of s. 23 students would trigger a particular level of instruction, while a greater, specified number of students would require, in addition, a particular level of minority language educational facilities. Where the number of students fell between the two threshold numbers, only the lower level of instruction would be required.

The sliding scale approach is preferable to the separate rights approach, not only because it accords with the text of s. 23, but also because it is consistent with the purpose of s. 23. The sliding scale approach ensures that the minority group receives the full amount of protection that its numbers warrant. Under the separate rights approach, if it were accepted, for example, that "X" number of students ensured a right to full management and control, then presumably "X − 1" students would not bring about any rights to management and control or even to a school building. Given the variety of possible means of fulfilling the purpose of s. 23, such a result is unacceptable. Moreover, the separate rights approach places parties like the appellants in the paradoxical position of forwarding an argument which, if accepted, might ultimately harm the overall position of minority language students in Canada. If, for instance, the appellants succeeded in persuading this Court that s. 23 mandates a completely separate school board—as opposed to some sort of representation on an existing board— then other groups of s. 23 parents with slightly fewer numbers might find themselves without a right to *any* degree of management and control—even though their numbers might justify granting them some degree of management and control.

(3) Management and Control Under Section 23(3)(b): Introduction

Both the trial judge and the Court of Appeal found that s. 23(3)(*b*) allows for the possibility of securing to minority language parents a measure of management and control. Purvis J. held that s. 23 bestows "a degree of exclusive management and control over provision and administration of minority language schools" while, as mentioned earlier, Kerans J.A. stated (at p. 539) that:

> ... s. 23(3)(*b*) offers the minority-language group the right, where numbers warrant, to establish and control an independent school system, but that a province shall select the institutional means by which that right will be implemented.

Courts in Ontario, Saskatchewan, Nova Scotia and Prince Edward Island have reached similar conclusions (*Reference Re Education Act of Ontario, supra; Commission des Écoles Fransaskoises v. Saskatchewan* (1988), 48 D.L.R. (4th) 315 (Sask. Q.B.); *Lavoie v. Nova Scotia (Attorney General), supra;* and *Reference Re Minority Language Educational Rights (P.E.I.)* (1988), 69 Nfld. & P.E.I.R. 236 (P.E.I.S.C., App. Div.)). ...

(4) Management and Control: The Text of Section 23(3)(b)

In my view, the words of s. 23(3)(*b*) are consistent with and supportive of the conclusion that s. 23 mandates, where the numbers warrant, a measure of management and control. Consider, first, the words of subs. (3)(*b*) in the context of the entire section. Instruction must take place somewhere and accordingly the right to "instruction" includes an implicit right to be instructed in facilities. If the term "minority language educational facilities" is not viewed as encompassing a degree of management and control, then there would not appear to be any purpose in including it in s. 23. This common sense conclusion militates against interpreting "facilities" as a reference to physical structures. Indeed, once the sliding scale approach is accepted it becomes unnecessary to focus too intently upon the word "facilities." Rather, the text of s. 23 supports viewing the entire term "minority language educational facilities" as setting out an upper level of management and control. ...

(5) Management and Control: The Purpose of Section 23

The foregoing textual analysis of s. 23(3)(*b*) is strongly supported by a consideration of the overall purpose of s. 23. That purpose, as discussed earlier, is to preserve and promote minority language and culture throughout Canada. In my view, it is essential, in order to further this purpose, that, where the numbers warrant, minority language parents possess a measure of management and control over the educational facilities in which their children are taught. Such management and control is vital to ensure that their language and culture flourish. It is necessary because a variety of management issues in education, e.g., curricula, hiring, expenditures, can affect linguistic and cultural concerns. I think it incontrovertible that the health and survival of the minority language and culture can be affected in subtle but important ways by decisions relating to these issues. To give but one example, most decisions pertaining to curricula clearly have an influence on the language and culture of the minority students.

(6) The Meaning of the Phrase "Management and Control"

Section 23 clearly encompasses a right to management and control. On its own, however, the phrase "management and control" is imprecise and requires further specification. This can be accomplished by considering what type of management and control is needed in order to fulfill the purpose of s. 23.

The appellants argue for a completely independent Francophone school board. Much is to be said in support of this position and indeed it may be said to reflect the ideal. ...

Historically, separate or denominational boards have been the principal bulwarks of minority language education in the absence of any provision for minority representation and authority within public or common school boards. Such independent boards constitute, for the minority, institutions which it can consider its own with all this entails in terms of opportunity of working in its own language and of sharing a common culture, interests and understanding and being afforded the fullest measure of representation and control. These are particularly important in setting overall priorities and responding to the special educational needs of the minority.

In some circumstances an independent Francophone school board is necessary to meet the purpose of s. 23. However, where the number of students enrolled in minority schools is relatively small, the ability of an independent board to fulfill this purpose may be reduced and other approaches may be appropriate whereby the minority is able to identify with the school but has the benefit of participating in a larger organization through representation and a certain exclusive authority within the majority school board. Under these circumstances, such an arrangement avoids the isolation of an independent school district from the physical resources which the majority school district enjoys and facilitates the sharing of resources with the majority board, something which can be crucial for smaller minority schools. By virtue of having a larger student population, it can be expected that the majority board would have greater access to new educational developments and resources. Where the number of s. 23 students is not sufficiently large, a complete isolation of the minority schools would tend to frustrate the purpose of s. 23 because, in the long run, it would contribute to a decline in the status of the minority language group and its educational facilities. Graduates of the minority schools would be less well-prepared (thus hindering career opportunities for the minority) and potential students would be disinclined to enter minority language schools....

In my view, the measure of management and control required by s. 23 of the *Charter* may, depending on the numbers of students to be served, warrant an independent school board. Where numbers do not warrant granting this maximum level of management and control, however, they may nonetheless be sufficient to require linguistic minority representation on an existing school board. In this latter case:

(1) The representation of the linguistic minority on local boards or other public authorities which administer minority language instruction or facilities should be guaranteed;

(2) The number of minority language representatives on the board should be, at a minimum, proportional to the number of minority language students in the school district, i.e., the number of minority language students for whom the board is responsible;

(3) The minority language representatives should have exclusive authority to make decisions relating to the minority language instruction and facilities, including:

    (a) expenditures of funds provided for such instruction and facilities;

    (b) appointment and direction of those responsible for the administration of such instruction and facilities;

    (c) establishment of programs of instruction;

    (d) recruitment and assignment of teachers and other personnel; and

    (e) making of agreements for education and services for minority language pupils.

I do not doubt that in future cases courts will have occasion to expand upon or refine these words. It is impossible at this stage in the development of s. 23 to foresee all of the circumstances relevant to its implementation.

There are a few general comments I wish to add in respect of the above description. First, the matter of the quality of education to be provided to the minority students was not dealt with above because, strictly speaking, it does not pertain to the issue of management and control. It is, of course, an important issue and one which was raised in this appeal. I think it should be self-evident that in situations where the above degree of management and control is warranted the quality of education provided to the minority should in principle be on a basis of equality with the majority. This proposition follows directly from the purpose of s. 23. However, the specific form of educational system provided to the minority need not be identical to that provided to the majority. The different circumstances under which various schools find themselves, as well as the demands of a minority language education itself, make such a requirement impractical and undesirable. It should be stressed that the funds allocated for the minority language schools must be at least equivalent on a per student basis to the funds allocated to the majority schools. Special circumstances may warrant an allocation for minority language schools that exceeds the per capita allocation for majority schools. I am confident that this will be taken into account not only in the enabling legislation, but in budgetary discussions of the board....

Having canvassed the degrees of management and control which s. 23 *might* require, the next step is to determine what degree the numbers in Edmonton warrant granting. Before I approach this task, however, it will be convenient at this point to consider the issue of denominational rights.

(7) Denominational Schools' Rights

Under the terms of s. 29 of the *Charter* any interpretation of s. 23 must be consistent with the rights and privileges of denominational schools. Section 29 reads:

> **29.** Nothing in this *Charter* abrogates or derogates from any rights or privileges guaranteed by or under the Constitution of Canada in respect of denominational, separate or dissentient schools.

The rights of denominational, separate or dissentient schools referred to in s. 29 are generally provided for in s. 93(1) of the *Constitution Act, 1867*:

> **93.** In and for each Province the Legislature may exclusively make Laws in relation to Education, subject and according to the following Provisions:
>
> (1) Nothing in any such Law shall prejudicially affect any Right or Privilege with respect to Denominational Schools which any Class of Persons have by Law in the Province at the Union:

The province of Alberta is governed by a slightly different provision. When Alberta became a province in 1905, it adopted s. 93 of the *British North America Act, 1867* (later renamed the *Constitution Act, 1867*), but with an amendment to s. 93(1). The amendment is set out in s. 17 of the *Alberta Act*:

> Section 93 of the *Constitution Act, 1867*, shall apply to the said province, with the substitution for paragraph (1) of the said section 93, of the following paragraph:
>
> "(1) Nothing in any such law shall prejudicially affect any right or privilege with respect to separate schools which any class of persons have at the date of the passing of this *Act*, under the terms of chapters 29 and 30 of the Ordinances of the North-west Territories, passed in the year 1901, or with respect to religious instruction in any public or separate school as provided for in the said ordinances." ...

... [T]he powers of management and control which s. 23 would accord to minority language groups under the interpretation proposed would not affect any rights in respect of the denominational aspects of education or related non-denominational aspects. The minority language trustees on a denominational school board who are to be given powers over management and control will be, at the same time, denominational trustees: in such instances, the denominational board is not required to cede powers to a non-denominational group of persons, it is only required to give certain of its members authority over minority language education. The proposed regulation would not remove a denominational board's power to manage and control, or alter its denominational character.

The transfer of the powers in respect of management and control thus amounts to the *regulation* of a non-denominational aspect of education, namely, the language of instruction, a form of regulation which the courts have long held to be valid. ...

(8) The "Numbers Warrant" Provision

What is being considered when a court addresses the "numbers warrant" question—existing demand, potential demand, or something else? The appellants' position was that the *existing* demand for Francophone services is not a reliable indicator of demand because the demand for any service will to some extent follow the provision of that service. The respondent, on the other hand, argued that the courts cannot simply use the total number of *potential* s. 23 students as a gauge, since it is highly unlikely that all of these students will take advantage of a proposed service. There is some force to both of these arguments; accordingly, the approach I have taken mediates between the concerns which they raise. In my view, the relevant figure for s. 23 purposes is the number of persons who will eventually take advantage of the contemplated programme or facility. It will normally be impossible to know this figure

exactly, yet it can be roughly estimated by considering the parameters within which it must fall—the known demand for the service and the total number of persons who potentially could take advantage of the service.

The numbers warrant provision requires, in general, that two factors be taken into account in determining what s. 23 demands: (1) the services appropriate, in pedagogical terms, for the numbers of students involved; and (2) the cost of the contemplated services. The first, pedagogical requirements, recognizes that a threshold number of students is required before certain programmes or facilities can operate effectively. There is no point, for example, in having a school for only ten students in an urban centre. The students would be deprived of the numerous benefits which can only be achieved through studying and interacting with larger numbers of students. The welfare of the students, and thus indirectly the purposes of s. 23, demands that programmes and facilities which are inappropriate for the numbers of students involved should not be required.

Cost, the second factor, is not usually explicitly taken into account in determining whether or not an individual is to be accorded a right under the *Charter*. In the case of s. 23, however, such a consideration is mandated. Section 23 does not, like some other provisions, create an absolute right. Rather, it grants a right which must be subject to financial constraints, for it is financially impractical to accord to every group of minority language students, no matter how small, the same services which a large group of s. 23 students are accorded. I note, however, that in most cases pedagogical requirements will prevent the imposition of unrealistic financial demands upon the state. Moreover, the remedial nature of s. 23 suggests that pedagogical considerations will have more weight than financial requirements in determining whether numbers warrant.

In my view, the phrase "where numbers warrant" does not provide an explicit standard which courts can use to determine the appropriate instruction and facilities (in light of the aforementioned considerations) in every given situation. The standard will have to be worked out over time by examining the particular facts of each situation which comes before the courts, but, in general, the inquiry must be guided by the purpose of s. 23. In particular, the fact that s. 23 is a remedial section is significant, indicating that the section does not aim at merely guaranteeing the status quo.

Thus, a number of complex and subtle factors must be taken into account beyond simply counting the number of students. For example, what is appropriate may differ between rural and urban areas. Another factor to consider is that s. 23 speaks of "wherever in the province" the "numbers warrant." This means that the calculation of the relevant numbers is not restricted to existing school boundaries (although the redrawing of school boundaries will often involve a certain cost which must be taken into account). . . .

(9) The Situation in Edmonton

We can now examine the facts underlying this appeal to determine whether s. 23 parents in Edmonton should be accorded a measure of management and control as contemplated by s. 23.

At the time of the trial, there were approximately 2,948 citizens in Edmonton whose first language learned and still understood was French and who, therefore, qualified under s. 23 of the *Charter*. These citizens had approximately 4,127 children from birth to age 19, of whom 3,750 were between five and 19 years of age. The vast majority of these parents were separate school supporters. The enrollment at the existing Francophone school, École Maurice Lavallée was 242 students from kindergarten to grade 6, with room for more. No one has been turned away for lack of space. The capacity of the school is 720 students. At the time of trial there were 315 in attendance, of whom 73 were in grades 7 and 8 immersion programme.

It does not appear that any financial or pedagogical problems have accompanied the operation of the existing Francophone school, École Maurice Lavallée. In view of the substantial numbers of students involved I do not think that such problems would be likely. It is, no doubt, slightly more expensive on a per student basis to operate a school with 242 students as compared to a school with 1,000 students. However, the remedial nature of s. 23 means that such differences in cost, if not unreasonable, must be accepted. It seems clear that even at the present level of demand, there are sufficient students to justify in both pedagogical and financial terms the creation of an independent school, such as the one presently existing as well as providing for a continuing course of primary and secondary schooling. A recognition of this fact appeared to be common ground between all of the parties involved in this appeal, as well as by both of the Alberta courts.

Having established that the existing Francophone school in Edmonton is required in order to comply with s. 23, I believe it is reasonable to require, in addition, that the minority language parents enjoy the right to representation on the separate school board and the degree of management and control that this entails (as specified above). In general, wherever the numbers of students justify creating a minority language school, these numbers would also justify granting the minority language parents a measure of management and control. Because a Francophone school already exists in Edmonton, the pedagogical and financial effects of granting management and control in the case at hand are not likely to be great. Reorganization of the relevant school board to provide for a

degree of management and control would not significantly change the pedagogical structure, nor would it be very expensive. At the time of the trial there were approximately 424,622 students enrolled in the public or separate school systems in Alberta in some 146 different jurisdictions. These jurisdictions are administered by Boards of Trustees elected by eligible voters within the boundaries of the districts. Forty-seven of these jurisdictions had fewer than 500 students; of these 25 had fewer than 250 students; of these 8 had fewer than 100 students; and of these 4 had 50 students or less. Of these same 47 districts: 35 were separate school districts whose formation was guaranteed by constitutional guarantees under s. 93 of the *Constitution Act, 1867*, s. 17 of the *Alberta Act*, and s. 29 of the *Charter*; three were in National Parks and subject to federal–provincial agreements; two were consolidated school districts formed under now defunct legislation; one was a regional district formed pursuant to an agreement of three other school jurisdictions; and of the remaining six, four were formed in 1937 and the other two in 1966.

In Edmonton there were approximately 116,788 students enrolled in the public and separate school systems in some nine school jurisdictions. Five of these districts had less than 5,000 students (specifically, the numbers of students in these districts were 4,187, 3,043, 2,600, 758, and 381).

. . . Overall, I think it clear that the numbers described above show that requiring a Francophone school, together with a degree of management and control to the parents, is, in respect of a group of students who, at a minimum, number at least 242, a reasonable requirement. At the same time, I am not satisfied on the basis of present evidence that it has been established that numbers of students likely to attend Francophone schools in Edmonton are sufficient to mandate under s. 23 the establishment of an independent Francophone school board. In reaching this conclusion, I have considered the likely demand upon a Francophone school, and have also allowed for additional numbers of students that will come from an extension of the programme to include secondary school grades. If actual experience reveals a larger than anticipated demand, however, it may be necessary to reconsider whether the appropriate degree of management and control mandates the establishment of an independent minority language school board.

To conclude: the numbers of minority language students in Edmonton warrant as a minimum the provision of s. 23 rights by way of minority language representation on school boards administering minority language schools in the manner and with the authority above described. These rights are not provided at the present time. The Province must enact legislation (and regulations, if necessary) that are in all respects consistent with the provisions of s. 23 of the *Charter*.

Remedies

The appellants' statement of claim, as I have indicated, includes requests for a number of declarations. These declarations fall into two general groups: (1) in respect of the alleged invalidity of certain provisions of the *School Act* of Alberta; and (2) in respect of the rights which must be accorded to s. 23 parents in Edmonton.

The appellants did not specify in their statement of claim which provisions of the Alberta legislation they desired to have struck down, but it appears from their arguments that their main concern was with provisions 13, 158, and 159 of the *School Act*, and Regulation 490/82 passed thereunder:

13(1) The Minister may establish any portion of Alberta as a public school district.

158 Subject to section 159, all pupils in school shall be taught in the English language.

159(1) A board may authorize

(a) that French be used as a language of instruction, or

(b) that any other language be used as a language of instruction in addition to the English language, in all or any of its schools....

Regulation 490/82:

2 Where, pursuant to section 159 of the School Act, a board authorizes a program that uses French as a language of instruction,

(a) if the program commences in grade 1, then with respect to grades 1 and 2,

(i) the amount of time French is used as the language of instruction,

(ii) the nature and extent of English language instruction, if any, and

(iii) the point at which the English language arts program, if any, is initiated

is in the discretion of the board;

(b) regardless of when the program commences, after grade 2,

(i) not less than 300 minutes per week of instruction in English language arts shall be provided for each pupil in each of grades 3, 4, 5, and 6,

(ii) not less than 150 hours per year of instruction in English language arts shall be provided for each pupil in each of grades 7, 8 and 9, and

(iii) not less than 125 hours per year or the equivalent of 5 credits per year of instruction in English language arts shall be provided for each pupil in each of grades 10, 11 and 12....

Regulation 490/82, which mandates that a minimum of approximately 20 per cent of class time be spent on English language education, is not "permissive" legislation and is, therefore, on a different footing from the other impugned provisions. In their statement of claim the appellants asked for a declaration to the effect that 100 per cent of their children's instruction should be in French. The appellants' position is that the regulation directly contradicts s. 23. I agree that Regulation 490/82 may impede the achievement of the purpose of s. 23. The appellants' rights under s. 23 include a general right for their children to be instructed entirely in the French language. However, by virtue of s. 1 of the *Charter*, "reasonable" limitations of *Charter* rights are permitted. Both of the Alberta courts held that if Regulation 490/82 does in fact infringe s. 23, it could nevertheless be upheld as a reasonable limitation on s. 23 rights. In support of this finding they referred to evidence that a knowledge of English is required for any student in Alberta.

I am prepared to agree with the Alberta courts that a certain amount of mandatory English language instruction is a reasonable limitation on s. 23. It seems indisputable that some English language education is important for all students in Alberta. It is not self-evident, however, that a full 300 minutes a week of English instruction is necessary in Francophone schools. It is for the respondent to prove that this limit infringes the s. 23 right no more than is necessary, and in the absence of such a demonstration I conclude that the Regulation is not saved by s. 1. This conclusion does not, of course, preclude the respondent from attempting in the future to prove that some mandatory English instruction, perhaps even 300 minutes per week, is a reasonable limit under s. 1....

APPENDIX
The Constitution Act, 1982

Schedule B
Constitution Act, 1982

Enacted as Schedule B to the *Canada Act 1982*, (U.K.) 1982,
c. 11, which came into force on April 17, 1982

PART I

Canadian Charter of Rights and Freedoms

Whereas Canada is founded upon principles that recognize the supremacy of God and the rule of law:

Guarantee of Rights and Freedoms

1. The *Canadian Charter of Rights and Freedoms* guarantees the rights and freedoms set out in it subject only to such reasonable limits prescribed by law as can be demonstrably justified in a free and democratic society.

Rights and freedoms in Canada

Fundamental Freedoms

2. Everyone has the following fundamental freedoms:
    (*a*) freedom of conscience and religion;
    (*b*) freedom of thought, belief, opinion and expression, including freedom of the press and other media of communication;
    (*c*) freedom of peaceful assembly; and
    (*d*) freedom of association.

Fundamental freedoms

Democratic Rights

3. Every citizen of Canada has the right to vote in an election of members of the House of Commons or of a legislative assembly and to be qualified for membership therein.

Democratic rights of citizens

4. (1) No House of Commons and no legislative assembly shall continue for longer than five years from the date fixed for the return of the writs of a general election of its members.

Maximum duration of legislative bodies

(2) In time of real or apprehended war, invasion or insurrection, a House of Commons may be continued by Parliament and a legislative assembly may be continued by the legislature beyond five years if such continuation is not opposed by the votes of more than one-third of the members of the House of Commons or the legislative assembly, as the case may be.

Continuation in special circumstances

Annual sitting of legislative bodies

5. There shall be a sitting of Parliament and of each legislature at least once every twelve months.

Mobility Rights

Mobility of citizens

6. (1) Every citizen of Canada has the right to enter, remain in and leave Canada.

Rights to move and gain livelihood

(2) Every citizen of Canada and every person who has the status of a permanent resident of Canada has the right

(*a*) to move to and take up residence in any province; and

(*b*) to pursue the gaining of a livelihood in any province.

Limitation

(3) The rights specified in subsection (2) are subject to

(*a*) any laws or practices of general application in force in a province other than those that discriminate among persons primarily on the basis of province of present or previous residence; and

(*b*) any laws providing for reasonable residency requirements as a qualification for the receipt of publicly provided social services.

Affirmative action programs

(4) Subsections (2) and (3) do not preclude any law, program or activity that has as its object the amelioration in a province of conditions of individuals in that province who are socially or economically disadvantaged if the rate of employment in that province is below the rate of employment in Canada.

Legal Rights

Life, liberty and security of person

7. Everyone has the right to life, liberty and security of the person and the right not to be deprived thereof except in accordance with the principles of fundamental justice.

Search or seizure

8. Everyone has the right to be secure against unreasonable search or seizure.

Detention or imprisonment

9. Everyone has the right not to be arbitrarily detained or imprisoned.

Arrest or detention

10. Everyone has the right on arrest or detention

(*a*) to be informed promptly of the reasons therefor;

(*b*) to retain and instruct counsel without delay and to be informed of that right; and

(*c*) to have the validity of the detention determined by way of *habeas corpus* and to be released if the detention is not lawful.

Proceedings in criminal and penal matters

11. Any person charged with an offence has the right

(*a*) to be informed without unreasonable delay of the specific offence;

(*b*) to be tried within a reasonable time;

(*c*) not to be compelled to be a witness in proceedings against that person in respect of the offence;

(*d*) to be presumed innocent until proven guilty according to law in a fair and public hearing by an independent and impartial tribunal;

(*e*) not to be denied reasonable bail without just cause;

(*f*) except in the case of an offence under military law tried before a military tribunal, to the benefit of trial by jury where the maximum punishment for the offence is imprisonment for five years or a more severe punishment;

(*g*) not to be found guilty on account of any act or omission unless, at the time of the act or omission, it constituted an offence under Canadian or international law or was criminal according to the general principles of law recognized by the community of nations;

(*h*) if finally acquitted of the offence, not to be tried for it again and, if finally found guilty and punished for the offence, not to be tried or punished for it again; and

(*i*) if found guilty of the offence and if the punishment for the offence has been varied between the time of commission and the time of sentencing, to the benefit of the lesser punishment.

12. Everyone has the right not to be subjected to any cruel and unusual treatment or punishment.

Treatment or punishment

13. A witness who testifies in any proceedings has the right not to have any incriminating evidence so given used to incriminate that witness in any other proceedings, except in a prosecution for perjury or for the giving of contradictory evidence.

Self-crimination

14. A party or witness in any proceedings who does not understand or speak the language in which the proceedings are conducted or who is deaf has the right to the assistance of an interpreter.

Interpreter

Equality Rights

15. (1) Every individual is equal before and under the law and has the right to the equal protection and equal benefit of the law without discrimination and, in particular, without discrimination based on race, national or ethnic origin, colour, religion, sex, age or mental or physical disability.

Equality before and under law and equal protection and benefit of law

(2) Subsection (1) does not preclude any law, program or activity that has as its object the amelioration of conditions of disadvantaged individuals or groups including those that are disadvantaged because of race, national or ethnic origin, colour, religion, sex, age or mental or physical disability.

Affirmative action programs

Official Languages of Canada

16. (1) English and French are the official languages of Canada and have equality of status and equal rights and privileges as to their use in all institutions of the Parliament and government of Canada.

Official languages of Canada

(2) English and French are the official languages of New Brunswick and have equality of status and equal rights and privileges as to their use in all institutions of the legislature and government of New Brunswick.

Official languages of New Brunswick

(3) Nothing in this Charter limits the authority of Parliament or a legislature to advance the equality of status or use of English and French.

Advancement of status and use

16.1. (1) The English linguistic community and the French linguistic community in New Brunswick have equality of status and equal rights and privileges, including the right to distinct educational institutions and such distinct cultural institutions as are necessary for the preservation and promotion of those communities.

English and French linguistic communities in New Brunswick

(2) The role of the legislature and government of New Brunswick to preserve and promote the status, rights and privileges referred to in subsection (1) is affirmed.

Role of the legislature and government of New Brunswick

Proceedings of Parliament

17. (1) Everyone has the right to use English or French in any debates and other proceedings of Parliament.

Proceedings of New Brunswick legislature

(2) Everyone has the right to use English or French in any debates and other proceedings of the legislature of New Brunswick.

Parliamentary statutes and records

18. (1) The statutes, records and journals of Parliament shall be printed and published in English and French and both language versions are equally authoritative.

New Brunswick statutes and records

(2) The statutes, records and journals of the legislature of New Brunswick shall be printed and published in English and French and both language versions are equally authoritative.

Proceedings in courts established by Parliament

19. (1) Either English or French may be used by any person in, or in any pleading in or process issuing from, any court established by Parliament.

Proceedings in New Brunswick courts

(2) Either English or French may be used by any person in, or in any pleading in or process issuing from, any court of New Brunswick.

Communications by public with federal institutions

20. (1) Any member of the public in Canada has the right to communicate with, and to receive available services from, any head or central office of an institution of the Parliament or government of Canada in English or French, and has the same right with respect to any other office of any such institution where

(*a*) there is a significant demand for communications with and services from that office in such language; or

(*b*) due to the nature of the office, it is reasonable that communications with and services from that office be available in both English and French.

Communications by public with New Brunswick institutions

(2) Any member of the public in New Brunswick has the right to communicate with, and to receive available services from, any office of an institution of the legislature or government of New Brunswick in English or French.

Continuation of existing constitutional provisions

21. Nothing in sections 16 to 20 abrogates or derogates from any right, privilege or obligation with respect to the English and French languages, or either of them, that exists or is continued by virtue of any other provision of the Constitution of Canada.

Rights and privileges preserved

22. Nothing in sections 16 to 20 abrogates or derogates from any legal or customary right or privilege acquired or enjoyed either before or after the coming into force of this Charter with respect to any language that is not English or French.

Minority Language Educational Rights

Language of instruction

23. (1) Citizens of Canada

(*a*) whose first language learned and still understood is that of the English or French linguistic minority population of the province in which they reside, or

(*b*) who have received their primary school instruction in Canada in English or French and reside in a province where the language in which they received that instruction is the language of the English or French linguistic minority population of the province,

have the right to have their children receive primary and secondary school instruction in that language in that province.

Continuity of language instruction

(2) Citizens of Canada of whom any child has received or is receiving primary or secondary school instruction in English or French in Canada, have the right to have all their children receive primary and secondary school instruction in the same language.

(3) The right of citizens of Canada under subsections (1) and (2) to have their children receive primary and secondary school instruction in the language of the English or French linguistic minority population of a province

    (*a*) applies wherever in the province the number of children of citizens who have such a right is sufficient to warrant the provision to them out of public funds of minority language instruction; and

    (*b*) includes, where the number of those children so warrants, the right to have them receive that instruction in minority language educational facilities provided out of public funds.

Application where numbers warrant

Enforcement

24. (1) Anyone whose rights or freedoms, as guaranteed by this Charter, have been infringed or denied may apply to a court of competent jurisdiction to obtain such remedy as the court considers appropriate and just in the circumstances.

Enforcement of guaranteed rights and freedoms

(2) Where, in proceedings under subsection (1), a court concludes that evidence was obtained in a manner that infringed or denied any rights or freedoms guaranteed by this Charter, the evidence shall be excluded if it is established that, having regard to all the circumstances, the admission of it in the proceedings would bring the administration of justice into disrepute.

Exclusion of evidence bringing administration of justice into disrepute

General

25. The guarantee in this Charter of certain rights and freedoms shall not be construed so as to abrogate or derogate from any aboriginal, treaty or other rights or freedoms that pertain to the aboriginal peoples of Canada including

    (*a*) any rights or freedoms that have been recognized by the Royal Proclamation of October 7, 1763; and

    (*b*) any rights or freedoms that now exist by way of land claims agreements or may be so acquired.

Aboriginal rights and freedoms not affected by Charter

26. The guarantee in this Charter of certain rights and freedoms shall not be construed as denying the existence of any other rights or freedoms that exist in Canada.

Other rights and freedoms not affected by Charter

27. This Charter shall be interpreted in a manner consistent with the preservation and enhancement of the multicultural heritage of Canadians.

Multicultural heritage

28. Notwithstanding anything in this Charter, the rights and freedoms referred to in it are guaranteed equally to male and female persons.

Rights guaranteed equally to both sexes

29. Nothing in this Charter abrogates or derogates from any rights or privileges guaranteed by or under the Constitution of Canada in respect of denominational, separate or dissentient schools.

Rights respecting certain schools preserved

30. A reference in this Charter to a Province or to the legislative assembly or legislature of a province shall be deemed to include a reference to the Yukon Territory and the Northwest Territories, or to the appropriate legislative authority thereof, as the case may be.

Application to territories and territorial authorities

31. Nothing in this Charter extends the legislative powers of any body or authority.

Legislative powers not extended

Application of Charter

Application of Charter

32. (1) This Charter applies

(*a*) to the Parliament and government of Canada in respect of all matters within the authority of Parliament including all matters relating to the Yukon Territory and Northwest Territories; and

(*b*) to the legislature and government of each province in respect of all matters within the authority of the legislature of each province.

Exception

(2) Notwithstanding subsection (1), section 15 shall not have effect until three years after this section comes into force.

Exception where express declaration

33. (1) Parliament or the legislature of a province may expressly declare in an Act of Parliament or of the legislature, as the case may be, that the Act or a provision thereof shall operate notwithstanding a provision included in section 2 or sections 7 to 15 of this Charter.

Operation of exception

(2) An Act or a provision of an Act in respect of which a declaration made under this section is in effect shall have such operation as it would have but for the provision of this Charter referred to in the declaration.

Five year limitation

(3) A declaration made under subsection (1) shall cease to have effect five years after it comes into force or on such earlier date as may be specified in the declaration.

Re-enactment

(4) Parliament or the legislature of a province may re-enact a declaration made under subsection (1).

Five year limitation

(5) Subsection (3) applies in respect of a re-enactment made under subsection (4).

Citation

Citation

34. This Part may be cited as the *Canadian Charter of Rights and Freedoms.*

Suggestions for Further Reading

Baker, Dennis, and Rainer Knopff. "Charter Checks and Parliamentary Balances" (2007) 16 *Constitutional Forum* 71.

Baker, Dennis, and Rainer Knopff. "Minority Retort: A Parliamentary Power to Resolve Judicial Disagreement in Close Cases" (2002) 21 *Windsor Yearbook of Access to Justice* 348.

Bayefsky, Anne F., and Mary Eberts, eds. *Equality Rights and the Canadian Charter of Rights and Freedoms* (Toronto: Carswell, 1985).

Beckton, Clare F., and A. Wayne Mackay. *The Courts and the Charter* (Toronto: University of Toronto Press, 1985).

Brodie, Ian. *Friends of the Court: The Privileging of Interest Group Litigants in Canada* (Albany, NY: State University of New York Press, 2002).

Cairns, Alan C. *Charter versus Federalism: The Dilemmas of Constitutional Reform* (Montreal and Kingston: McGill-Queen's University Press, 1992).

Cavalluzzo, Paul. "Judicial Review and the Bill of Rights: Drybones and Its Aftermath" (1971) 9 *Osgoode Hall Law Journal* 511.

Choudhry, Sujit, and Claire E. Hunter. "Measuring Judicial Activism on the Supreme Court of Canada: A Comment on Newfoundland (Treasury Board) v. NAPE" (2003) 48 *McGill Law Journal* 525.

Choudhry, Sujit. "So What Is the Real Legacy of Oakes? Two Decades of Proportionality Analysis Under the Canadian Charter's Section 1" (2006) 34 *Supreme Court Law Review* (2d) 501.

Clarke, Jeremy. "Beyond the Democratic Dialogue, and Towards a Federalist One: Provincial Arguments and Supreme Court Responses in Charter Litigation" (2006) 39 *Canadian Journal of Political Science* 293.

Epp, Charles R. *The Rights Revolution* (Chicago: University of Chicago Press, 1998).

Fudge, Judy. "Legally Speaking: Courts, Democracy, and the Market" (2003) 19 *Supreme Court Law Review* (2d) 111.

Gaudreault-Desbiens, Jean-François. "La Charte canadienne des droits et libertés et le fédéralisme: quelques remarques sur les vingt premières années d'une relation amigugé" (2003) *Revue du Barreau* 271.

Hennigar, Mathew. "Expanding the 'Dialogue' Debate: Canadian Federal Government Responses to Lower Court Charter Decisions" (2004) 37 *Canadian Journal of Political Science* 3.

Hiebert, Janet L. *Charter Conflicts: What Is Parliament's Role?* (Montreal and Kingston: McGill-Queen's University Press, 2002).

———. *Limiting Rights: The Dilemma of Judicial Review* (Montreal and Kingston: McGill-Queen's University Press, 1996).

Hirschl, Ran. *Towards Juristocracy: The Origins and Consequences of the New Constitutionalism* (Cambridge, MA: Harvard University Press, 2004).

Hogg, Peter W., and A.A. Bushell. "The Charter Dialogue Between Courts and Legislatures (Or Perhaps the Charter of Rights Isn't Such a Bad Thing After All)" (1997) 35 *Osgoode Hall Law Journal* 75.

Howe, Paul, and Peter H. Russell, eds. *Judicial Power and Canadian Democracy* (Montreal and Kingston: McGill-Queen's University Press, 2001).

Huscroft, Grant A. "'Thank God We're Here': Judicial Exclusivity in Charter Interpretation and Its Consequences" (2004) 25 *Supreme Court Law Review* (2d) 239.

Hutchinson, Allan, and Andrew Petter. "Private Rights/Public Wrongs: The Liberal Lie of the Charter" (1988) 38 *University of Toronto Law Journal* 278.

James, Patrick, Donald E. Abelson, and Michael Lusztig, eds. *The Myth of the Sacred: The Charter, the Courts, and the Politics of the Constitution in Canada* (Montreal and Kingston: McGill-Queen's University Press, 2002).

Kahana, Tsvi. "The Notwithstanding Mechanism and Public Discussion: Lessons from the Ignored Practice of Section 33 of the Charter" (2001) 44 *Canadian Public Administration* 255.

Kelly, James B. "Bureaucratic Activism and the Charter of Rights and Freedoms: The Department of Justice and Its Entry into the Centre of Government" (1999) 42 *Canadian Public Administration* 476.

———. *Governing with the Charter: Legislative and Judicial Activism and Framers' Intent* (Vancouver: University of British Columbia Press, 2005).

Knopff, Rainer. "How Democratic Is the Charter? And Does It Matter?" (2003) 19 *Supreme Court Law Review* (2d) 199.

———. "Populism and the Politics of Rights: The Dual Attack on Representative Democracy" (1998) 31 *Canadian Journal of Political Science* 683.

———. "What Do Constitutional Equality Rights Protect Canadians Against?" (1987) 20 *Canadian Journal of Political Science* 265.

Knopff, Rainer, and F.L. Morton. *Charter Politics* (Scarborough, ON: Nelson Canada, 1992).

LaSelva, Samuel V. *The Moral Foundations of Canadian Federalism* (Montreal and Kingston: McGill-Queen's University Press, 1996).

Laskin, Bora. "Our Civil Liberties—The Role of the Supreme Court" (1955) 41 *Queen's Quarterly* 445.

Leeson, Howard. "Section 33, The Notwithstanding Clause: A Paper Tiger?" in Paul Howe and Peter H. Russell, eds., *Judicial Power and Canadian Democracy* (Montreal and Kingston: McGill-Queen's University Press, 2001).

MacIvor, Heather. *Canadian Politics and Government in the Charter Era* (Toronto: Thomson-Nelson, 2006).

———. "The Charter of Rights and Party Politics" (2004) 10 *Choices* 1.

MacLennan, Christopher. *Toward the Charter: Canadians and the Demand for a National Bill of Rights, 1929-1960* (Montreal and Kingston: McGill-Queen's University Press, 2003).

Manfredi, Christopher P. "The Day the Dialogue Died: A Comment on Sauvé v. Canada" (2007) 45 *Osgoode Hall Law Journal* 105.

———. *Feminist Activism in the Supreme Court* (Vancouver: University of British Columbia Press, 2004).

———. *Judicial Power and the Charter: Canada and the Paradox of Liberal Constitutionalism*, 2d ed. (Don Mills, ON: Oxford University Press, 2001).

Manfredi, Christopher, and Mark Rush. *Judging Democracy* (Peterborough, ON: Broadview Press, 2008).

Morton, F.L. "Dialogue or Monologue" in Paul Howe and Peter H. Russell, eds., *Judicial Power and Canadian Democracy* (Montreal and Kingston: McGill-Queen's University Press, 2001).

———. "The Political Impact of the Canadian Charter of Rights and Freedoms" (1987) 20 *Canadian Journal of Political Science* 31.

———. "The Politics of Rights: What Canadians Should Know About the American Bill of Rights" (1988) 1 *Windsor Review of Legal and Social Issues* 61.

Morton, F.L., and Rainer Knopff. *The Charter Revolution and the Court Party* (Peterborough, ON: Broadview Press, 2000).

Morton, F.L., Peter H. Russell, and Troy Riddell. "The Canadian Charter of Rights and Freedoms: A Descriptive Analysis of the First Decade, 1982-1992" (1995) 5 *National Journal of Constitutional Law* 1.

Petter, Andrew. "The Politics of the Charter" (1986) 8 *Supreme Court Law Review* 473.

———. "Taking Dialogue Theory Much Too Seriously (Or Perhaps Charter Dialogue Isn't Such a Good Thing After All" (2007) 45 *Osgoode Hall Law Journal* 147.

Pinard, Danielle. "Une Malheureuse celebration de la Charte des droits et libertés de la personne par la Cour suprême du Canada: l'arrête Chaoulli" in *La Charter Québécoise: origines, enjeux et perspectives* (Montreal: Revue du Barreau du Québec, 2006).

Roach, Kent. *The Supreme Court on Trial: Judicial Activism or Democratic Dialogue?* (Toronto: Irwin Law, 2001).

Russell, Peter H. "The Political Purposes of the Canadian Charter of Rights and Freedoms" (1983) 61 *Canadian Bar Review* 30.

———. "Standing Up for Notwithstanding" (1991) 29 *Alberta Law Review* 293.

Schmeiser, D.A. *Civil Liberties in Canada* (Toronto: Oxford University Press, 1964).

Scott, F.R. *Civil Liberties and Canadian Federalism* (Toronto: University of Toronto Press, 1959).

———. "The Privy Council and Minority Rights" (1930) *Queen's Quarterly* 668.

Sharpe, Robert J. *Charter Litigation* (Toronto: Butterworths, 1987).

Smith, Miriam. *Lesbian and Gay Rights in Canada: Social Movements and Equality-Seeking, 1971-1995* (Toronto: University of Toronto Press, 1999).

———. *Political Institutions and Lesbian and Gay Rights in the United States and Canada* (New York: Routledge, 2008).

Sniderman, Paul M., Joseph F. Fletcher, Peter H. Russell, and Philip E. Tetlock. *The Clash of Rights: Liberty, Equality and Legitimacy in Pluralist Democracy* (New Haven, CT: Yale University Press, 1997).

Strayer, Barry. "Life Under the Charter: Adjusting the Balance Between Legislatures and Courts" (1988) *Public Law* 347.

Stuart, Don. *Charter Justice in Canadian Criminal Law*, 4th ed. (Toronto: Thomson Carswell, 2005).

Tarnopolsky, W.S. *The Canadian Bill of Rights* (Toronto: McClelland & Stewart, 1975).

Weiler, Paul. "Rights and Judges in a Democracy: A New Canadian Version" (1984) 18 *University of Michigan Journal of Law Reform* 51.

Whyte, John D. "On Not Standing for Notwithstanding" (1990) 28 *Alberta Law Review* 347.

Wilson, Bertha. "The Making of a Constitution: Approaches to Judicial Interpretation" (1988) *Public Law* 370.